Jane Austin Shopped Here

Being a Compendium of Buildings, Businesses, Houses, Locales, Sites, Streets, and British or Regency Terms

with

a Special Emphasis on the Regency Era (1811-1820)

as compiled by

Teresa DesJardien

Regency Author

Jane Austin Shopped Here / Teresa DesJardien. - 1st ed.
ISBN 978-1-9454582-1-7

For: Matt and Jenny,
and Abby and Steve,
and Harper, Julia, Lyla, Aileen, and Isadora.

Know that I love you, always.

Book Design: Adam Russell
Cover Art Design: Melissa Russell
Author photo by: Matthew DesJardien

Table of Contents

Special notes - See Numbers 1 - 10 1

Key Code - See Number 11 2

Using/the origin of this Guide 3

List of Historical Eras 5

British Kings & Queens and their Reigns 6

List of Teresa DesJardien's Regency Romances titles 37

Map of London 39

Alphabetical Listings 41

-A- 43

-B- 72

-C- 131

-D- 215

-E- 243

-F- 256

-G- 310

-H- 343

-I- 400

-J- 424

-K- 429

-M- 492

-N- 539

-O- 555

-P- 569

-Q- 619

-R- 624

-S- 664

-T- ... 744

-U- ... 788

-V- ... 796

-W- ... 802

-X- ... 848

-Y- ... 848

-Z- ... 851

Special Sections: ... 853

BRIDGES: ... 855

BRITISH COUNTIES (and areas outside London): ... 863

CHURCHES (and CHAPELS): ... 876

CLUBS: ... 925

INNS and PUBS (and COACHING INNS): ... 940

THEATRES: ... 954

BIBLIOGRAPHY: ... 966

ABOUT THE AUTHOR ... 973

Special notes:

1. UNLESS OTHERWISE INDICATED BY DATE OR EXPLANATION, THE PRESENCE OF A STREET NAME IN THIS LISTING MEANS I HAVE EVERY REASON TO BELIEVE THE STREET EXISTED DURING THE TIME OF THE 19TH CENTURY ENGLISH REGENCY.

2. The City (capital "C") refers to a specific area of London - not the larger, sprawling confines we think of as the greater city of London today. Also called the Square Mile and Old London, the City refers to the area once contained within the ancient Roman walls.
   - Absolutely do see: City, the, under C.
   - See: gates.
   - See: London Wall.

3. Most listings are for houses, streets, cities, or boroughs within London.
   I only provide distances to listings that are outside larger London. For instance: Oxford College (which is 56 miles/90 km from London.)

4. Usually immediately following any location's name I list what part of the city it is in.
   (Names were invented for the following example):
   Timmon Place - Junction Road, Barbridge.

This is to help you locate the area on a *modern* map. "Barbridge" being the modern name for the area - which may have been known in Tudor times as Barrye, in Georgian days as Barrige, in Regency times as Bar-by-the-bridge, etc. I usually use its most modern name to aid the modern reader in locating the site.

Whenever you're in doubt, check the references to be sure you use an era-appropriate name for the district.

5. I use the American spelling for many words (color instead of colour, defense instead of defence, dueling instead of duelling, etc.,) except where it is part of an actual name or a quoted reference. But "theatre" is so abundant and so much a part of place names, I have used the English spelling throughout this work (instead of the American "theater.")

6. You will find a mix of how the possessive "s" is used in this work. This mix was unavoidable, due to how any one place has chosen to spell its name. To make the usage uniform would have been to ignore basic facts. (Where the choice was mine, I used s'.)

Examples of the s' use: Fishmongers', Pilgrims', Skinners'.

Examples of s's use: Brooks's, St. James's, St. Thomas's.

I beg your indulgence of any other irregularities of form; I admit my main interest was in compiling information clearly, but not necessarily always by the book.

7. Dates: I use the American style: Month/Day/Year. 7/2/1810 means July 2nd. I have not added "AD" to many listed dates in this work, as virtually every date in this listing is AD (Anno Domini.) I only added it where it helped with clarity.

8. In the lists, place names are **bolded**. Other things (such as terms, or inventions, or events) are *not* - in order to make them different in appearance in the listings, that they not be mistaken for the name of a place. For an example, see: *abbey*, under A in the Alpha section.

9. Where I mention a person, I try to give a quick definition of who they are/were - with a few exceptions, primarily:
    1. Christopher Wren. After the Great Fire of 1666, when so much of London burned to the ground, Wren was the architect who designed and oversaw much of the rebuilding, particularly with the City's churches. His name is so ubiquitous, that I have shortened mention of him to merely: Wren.
    2. The same holds true for the author William Shakespeare, because his surname is clue enough for identification.
    3. Also: the author Charles Dickens.
    4. In the CHURCHES section (and others) there are many references to architects, whose occupation in context is clear without further elucidation.

10. Just to get you started, you may care to leap ahead to see: London, under L in the Alpha section. This is a *quick look* list of where to find areas (throughout this entire work) such as "financial London," "marriage-minded London," "rough/dark London," etc.

11. Code Key:

    AKA = also known as

    b. = born (year of birth)

    C. = century

    ca. = circa

    d. = died (year of death)

    km = kilometers

MP = Member of Parliament

£ = pound, British monetary unit

PM = Prime Minister

Prinny = Nickname for the Prince Regent from 1811-1820; became George IV 1820-1830. (See: Prinny, under P in the Alpha section.)

RAF = Royal Air Force

St. = Saint. Not "street." Street is always spelled out. St. is always alphabetical as if it were spelled out, s-a-i-n-t.)

UK = United Kingdom

U.S./USA = United States of America

WWI = World War I

WWII = World War II

Some notes on using/the origin of this guide:

The information on these pages has been garnered from many sources, some of which conflict. I have indicated these conflicts wherever I was aware of their existence.

Early on, I intended this guide purely for my own use. I was weary of constantly pausing to look up a street or building to be certain it existed during the Regency, (and whether it was burned down - as happened. A lot.) My initial goal was very simple: to have an alphabetical list of streets and places, that I might be able to glance at one source to know if a place existed and in what architectural phase of its existence it stood during the time of the 19th century surrounding the English Regency (1811-1820.)

Regrettably, because I hadn't at first intended this work for anyone other than myself, I didn't take the scholarly approach in terms of annotation; I didn't keep a line-by-line notation of source data. *Please note, however, that all sources have been recorded in the Bibliography, and direct quotes have been duly attributed.* When it became obvious that such an item-by-item annotation would have enhanced this work...well, the opportunity had irretrievably passed. The good news is that the preponderance of entries have all been second-sourced (if not much more,) greatly increasing my confidence in the data herein.

Also, as mentioned above, not every listing is actually a street or building. For instance: "fencing." I included such a listing to make it easy to refer to sites that had something to do with the sport of fencing. I've done the same for booksellers, drapers, food, hospitals, prisons, etc. Too, when I've stumbled across an unusual or uncommon term, they've gone into the alphabetical listing as well. For instance: ha-ha (a ditch used for animal control, which when observed from a distance "disappears" visually, allowing the land to appear uninterrupted, and perhaps causing the passing rider to call out, "Ha ha!" in surprise.)

I have found the longer I study the 19th century Regency, the more I understand that we cannot grasp all there is to know of the past. My wish is that whatever information there is in these pages will grant you not only a helpful resource, but also a solid jumping-off point from which to pursue your own specific research needs.

Happy researching -

Teresa DesJardien

Historical Eras:

- Roman Britain: 43AD through the start of the 5th century (also the Iron Age.)
- Dark Ages: Roughly 450-1450AD. The Dark Ages are also called:
    1. Medieval Times ("medieval" is the Latin word for: middle ages,) and,
    2. The Middle Ages.
        - The Saxons: Ca. the 440s.
        - The Anglo-Saxons: 5-11th centuries; from the end of Roman Britain to the Norman Conquest in 1066.
        - Norman period: 1066-1154.
        - Plantagenet period: 1154-1399.
        - Lancastrian period: 1399-1461.
- Renaissance, the: Ca. the 14-17th centuries.
- Yorkist period: 1461-1485.
- Tudor period: 1485-1603.
- Reformation, the: 1529-1536. In other words, born of Henry VIII's desire to divorce his barren first wife/his subsequent break from Rome/Catholicism - but which went on for several decades thereafter, into Elizabeth I's time.

    It includes the Protestant Reformation. (Some state it started with Martin Luther's Ninety-five Theses in 1517.) Although I gave an ending date of 1536 here, that date is debated - including that it includes the Dissolution (see, immediately below) - along with the claim that the Reformation never did end because Protestantism yet exists.
- The Dissolution. Also called the Dissolution of the Monasteries. Was a part of the Reformation. 1536-1541. Henry VIII had himself declared as the leader of the church in England, at which time he dissolved (and raided) all the until-then Catholic monasteries and churches throughout much of Britain. Some were demolished, some converted to Church of England.
- Jacobean period: 1567-1625. When James VI of Scotland becomes slightly renamed as he becomes James I of England, (thereby confusing schoolchildren for generations.)
- Stuart period: (The Stuarts had held the position of High Steward of Scotland since ca. 1150.) Mary I of Scotland (Mary Queen of Scots) reigned Scotland Dec/1542-Jul/1567. She was raised in France; she changed from Stewart, adopting the spelling as: Stuart. Period lasted 1603-1714.
- Cromwellian era: (Also: the era of the Commonwealth. Also: the Interregnum.) Refers to the time when Oliver Cromwell was the Lord Protector of England, 1649-1658, after Charles I was beheaded and the monarchy was abolished. Oliver Cromwell died in 1658, his son Richard replaced him. The monarchy was restored in 1660, with Charles II resuming Stuart rule.
- Restoration era: That is, the restoration of the monarchy (with Charles II.) Also sometimes called: the Stuarts restored. 1660-1689.
- William and Mary's co-rule: Came to the throne in 1689, a co-regency offered by Parliament (to William III and Queen Mary II.) Mary died in 1694, whereupon William ruled alone until 1702. Childless, they were succeeded by Mary's sister, Anne. William & Mary's reigns were

distinguished by their signing the English Bill of Rights.

- Georgian period: 1714-1811. Is sometimes lumped in with the Regency era, and it is all referred to as the Hanoverian era, which technically still exists today (as Queen Elizabeth II descended from the House of Saxe-Gotha-Coburg.) The royal family name was changed to Windsor in 1917. (See the note under: House of Windsor, below.)
- Enlightenment, the: Mid 18th to mid 19th centuries; a belief in the power of reason. George III's reign helped spread those notions. Too, the Enlightenment influenced the French revolutionary wars, 1792-1802.
- Regency period: 1811-1820. The period of time in the English monarchy wherein George III's oldest son, George Augustus Frederick, served as regent due to George III's incapacity. The latter was called mad, but may have suffered from porphyria. The king died in 1820, at which time (and until his own death in 1830) George Augustus was king as George IV. (See: Prinny, under P in the Alpha section.)
- Industrial Revolution, the: Ca. 1750-1860s (it is often closely associated with when railways opened up commerce/travel, starting in the 1840s.) Britain moved from being mostly rural to largely urban; shifting from farms, to cottage industries, and then to factories.
- William IV: 1830-1837 (Part of the Hanoverian period as well.)
- Victorian period: 1837-1901.
- Edwardian period: 1901-1919.
- Windsor period: 1917-present.

HOUSE OF WINDSOR:

The present Queen Elizabeth II descended from the House of Saxe-Coburg-Gotha. In 1917 her father (George V) arguably (but probably) due to anti-German/WWI sentiments, proclaimed their family name would now be Windsor. When Elizabeth II married Prince Philip in 1952 she reconfirmed by proclamation that she and her children "shall be styled and known as the House and Family of Windsor."

BRITISH KINGS & QUEENS AND THEIR REIGNS:

For brevity's sake, I have *not* provided details of reigns (but just names,) until starting at the year 1042AD, with Edward the Confessor.

With apologies to Ireland, Scotland, and Wales, (and the greater British Empire,) I have included here primarily *English* monarchs, those most often mentioned in this work.

Special note: Since 1254, England and Ireland had the same monarch (until 1936, when the Republic of Ireland broke from the monarchy, although Northern Ireland remains united with

England.) Since 1327, this union included Wales. Since 1603, it included Scotland.

The descriptions of these reigns are brief and simplified.

Inheritance note: Until the law was changed in 2011 (by adoption within 16 British Commonwealth countries, including England,) the royal line of succession had been limited to males only. True, females did become queen in their own right sometimes (Queen Elizabeth I, Queen Victoria, Queen Elizabeth II, etc.) but this was always in cases where no male had a claim to the throne. And, true, sometimes (especially in the further past) some of those males who seized the throne had a very thin claim to it - let's just say that "might makes right" enhanced their cause at the time. Being of the male gender served them as well, as England had long supported the rule of primogeniture (that only the eldest male inherited from the father - unlike in, say, Germany, where all sons inherited.)

So, from 2011 on, the succession of British monarchs will be determined by order of birth without regard to gender.

Anglo-Saxon kings:

Egbert - 827-839.
Aethelwulf - 839-856.
Aethelbald - 856-860.
Aethelbert - 860-866.
Aethelred - 866-871.
Alfred the Great - 871-899.
Edward the Elder - 899-924.
Athelstan - 924-9349.
Edmund - 939-946.
Eadred - 946-955.
Eadwig - 955-959.
Edgar - 959-975.
Edward the Martyr - 975-978.
Aethelred II the Unready - 978-1016.
Edmund II Ironside - 1016-1016.
Canute (Cnut the Great) the Dane - 1016-1035.
Harold I - 1035-1040.
Harthacanute - 1040-1042.

The Last Two of the Anglo-Saxon Kings:

Edward the Confessor: House of Wessex.

Born 1002 or 1003 or 1004.
Died 1/4/1066.
Reigned 1042-1066.

Edward the Confessor ordered the 11th century rebuild of Westminster Abbey. (See:

Henry III, below - For the 13th century rebuild of Westminster Abbey.)

Edward died childless; this led to the Norman Conquest.

Harold II: (AKA: Harold Godwinson, or Harold Godwin.) House of Wessex.

Born ca. 1020 or 22.

Died 10/14/1066.

Reigned from 1/6/1066-10/14/1066, only nine months.

Harold had no royal bloodline. He was elected by the Witan, a council of ranking nobles and religious leaders. He claimed Edward the Confessor had granted him the throne on the dying king's deathbed. (Harold's sister, Edith, had been married to King Edward the Confessor.) September/1066, the Norman Invasion began. Harold II's short reign was ended when he was killed in the Battle of Hastings, as an arrow hit in or near his eye, and led to his being slain by sword or ax by William of Normandy (William the Conqueror.)

House of Normandy:

William I: (AKA: William the Conqueror. AKA: William the Bastard - but never to his face; he was the illegitimate son of Robert the Devil, of Normandy.)

Born ca. 1027 or 1028, in Normandy.

Died 9/9/1087.

Reigned 1066-1087.

Like Harold II, William claimed Edward the Confessor had promised him the throne.

Having killed Harold II on the field of battle, on 12/10/1066, William, Duke of Normandy since 1035, marched on London. English nobles realized he was going to succeed, so they submitted to him; William I was crowned on 12/25/1066. He was the first ever to be crowned in Westminster Abbey (as have been all kings/queens since.) His wife, Matilda of Flanders, was the first Queen of England to be crowned formally (May/1068.)

In 1085 William I commissioned Domesday Book, in order to know the extent of his lands and how much he could tax it. It is the medieval period's most important (two) documents. (See: Domesday Book, under D in the Alpha section.)

He was purportedly severe with his English populace.

He died several months after he fell from this horse at the siege of Mantes, Normandy; although other sources say the corpulent king was knocked hard into his pommel, or else fell ill from the heat and exhaustion. His eldest, Robert (Curthose, a nickname that meant "short stockings") then ruled *Normandy*; second son Richard, had died somewhere between 12-18 years earlier, so third son William inherited the *English* throne.

William II: (AKA: William Rufus.)

Born sometime in 1056 or 1057, in Normandy.

Died 8/2/1100.

Reigned 1087-1100.

He was William I's third son; on their father's death, older brothers Robert

Curthose (with whom William II always had a contentious relationship) had become the ruler in Normandy; second son Richard was dead; so William inherited the English throne. It is said he was cruel and extravagant.

William II did not marry; he was childless. Killed by an arrow while hunting in the New Forest; it is not clear if this was an accident or something more sinister supposedly ordered by his younger brother, Henry. That brother, Henry, became the new English king.

Henry I: (AKA: Henry Beauclerc.)

Born in the summer of 1068, probably in Selby, Yorkshire.
Died 12/1/1135.
Reigned 1100-1135.

Henry was the fourth son of William the Conqueror.

On hearing of his brother, William II's, death, Henry hurried to Westminster, emphasizing his native birth over that of his older (Normandy-born) brother, Robert Curthose (who was the King of Normandy, and was at that time away on Crusade); Henry I was crowned on 8/5/1100.

In November/1100 Henry I married Edith, a descendant of the last Saxon kings, thereby uniting Saxony and Normandy lines through their union. Edith changed her name to Matilda, in order to please Norman barons who might not be fond of a Saxon queen.

Through the death of his wife, then his heir, then trying to persuade political leaders to give the succession to his daughter (also called Matilda, and whose husband, the Emperor Henry V of Germany, died in 1125; she remarried, Geoffrey of Anjou; she and Geoffrey were not popular in England,) and Henry I's own remarriage, it came down to Henry dying of food poisoning in France and being succeeded by his nephew, Stephen of Blois.

Stephen:

Born sometime in 1097, in Blois, France.
Died 10/25/1154.
Reigned 1135-1154.

Stephen was the son of Stephen-Henry, Count of Blois/France and his wife, Adela, daughter of William I and Matilda of Flanders.

Stephen had been sent to the English court of King Henry I ca. 1107, the latter of whom knighted him.

When he heard Henry I had died, Stephen hurried to Winchester and took control of the Treasury. Was made king over the former Empress Matilda (not his own wife, Matilda of Boulogne, nor his own mother, Matilda of Flanders,) a fact which led to civil war.

Stephen was a weak king. During his reign England was struck almost constantly by Scots and Welsh raids, to great deficit. Too, a series of events in which allies switched sides; changes were not capitalized on; Stephen being captured and released; and people being weary of civil war - it all led to everyone agreeing that (the one-time Empress) Matilda's son, Henry, should be crowned when Stephen died of stomach disease.

House of Plantagenet:

Henry II: (AKA: Henry Plantagenet. AKA: Henry of Anjou.)

Born 3/5/1133, in LeMans, France.

Died 7/6/1189.

Reigned 1154-1189.

Unlike King Stephen, Henry II was a strong king; a fine soldier, he claimed much of French land.

He married Eleanor of Aquitaine in 1152.

Henry II's Chancellor of England, Thomas á Becket, went on to become the Archbishop of Canterbury. (You may care to see: St. Thomas, under S in the Alpha section.)

He laid down the fundamentals for the English jury system.

Henry II's five year old son, also Henry, was married to 3 year old Margaret of France, daughter of Louis VII, in 1160. (Margaret, at age 20, and the Young King had one premature son, William, in 1177, who only lived three days.)

Concerned about succession, Henry II had this eldest son, Henry, crowned in 1170 (age 15,) despite himself not being dead; Prince Henry was then called the Young King. (While the Young King was in title co-ruler with his father, Henry II gave him no meaningful or autonomous powers.)

Henry II's and Thomas á Becket's relationship worsened over this curious crowning, the only of its kind in English history (and also over Henry II's attempt to limit church power.) Becket was murdered at his own Canterbury Cathedral by four of Henry's knights, who may have taken an angry comment of the king's too literally.

Henry II's sons rose against him; but then they more or less made peace. The eldest (the Young King) died of dysentery in 1183, age 28. The second eldest died, trampled by a horse, in 1186. The third (of four) sons, Richard, rose to rule following Henry II's death of a perforated ulcer in 1189.

Richard I: (AKA: Richard the Lionheart, or the Lionhearted. Also: Richard Coeur de Lion.)

Born 9/8/1157, in Oxford, England.

Died 3/26/1199.

Reigned 1189-1199.

His nickname came from being brave/a good military leader.

Richard I married Berengaria of Navarre; they had no children (although Richard did have two illegitimate sons.)

The king used treasury money to go on Crusade in Jerusalem. He only spent 6 months of his reign in England. While Richard I was crusading, his remaining (and often discontented) brother, John, was attempting to seize the throne. (Richard's nephew, Arthur, had been dubbed Richard's heir, an act that had angered John.)

Back from the Crusades, Richard went to Limoges to suppress a riot; while there he was shot during a siege by a bolt from a crossbowman, dying from the gangrenous wound 11 days later. John, who'd been ruling while Richard was abroad, finally received the throne in his own right.

John: (AKA: John Lackland, because his father, Henry II, hadn't granted him any land as a young man, unlike his three older brothers.)

Born 12/24/1166, in Oxford, England.

Died 10/18/1216.

Reigned 1199-1216. (He was the acting king from 1189-99, for his brother, Richard, who was mostly abroad during those years.)

Short and fat, nonetheless John had been his father's favorite (until they were estranged.)

He came to rule because a rattled Richard I, on his deathbed, called for John to be ruler, rather than his actual heir, nephew Arthur.

John was crowned, but his wife (Isabella of Gloucester) was not made queen; he divorced her and made her his ward (to retain her inheritance.) John then married 12 year old Isabella of Angouleme.

Fighting with the Archbishop of Canterbury led to an interdict on England (banning all church services); John confiscated church property in response; he was excommunicated by Pope Innocent III. This excommunication was lifted in 1213, and the interdict in 1214.

John was cruel, greedy, and self-indulgent. Rebelling barons seized London. At Runnymede, in 1215, King John was forced to sign the Magna Carta (AKA: the Great Charter,) granting many legal rights to the people and limiting the king's power.

John died of dysentery at Newark Castle, Lincolnshire, leaving his young son to rule.

Henry III:

Born 10/1/1207, at Winchester, England.

Died 11/16/1272.

Reigned 1216-1272.

Henry III became king at almost ten years of age. Since Henry III was young, William Marshal (soldier and statesman) was named as his regent; Marshal died in 1219. Hubert de Burgh (Justiciar of England and Ireland) then became the regent. He was brought up by priests, devoted to art and the church, and proved to be a weak leader led by others.

Henry III came of age in 1228, with de Burgh remaining influential. The king married Eleanor of Provence in 1236. Henry III is known for rebuilding a then-11th C. version of Westminster Abbey, now in the Gothic style. (See: Westminster Abbey, under W in the Alpha section.)

In 1264 Henry III was captured by rebels/barons, and made to establish a "Parliament" at Westminster; this was the beginning of the House of Commons. (See: House of Commons, under H in the Alpha section.)

Despite growing senile, he knew he was dying, and so called for his son, Prince Edward, to come back from the Crusades to assume the throne. Henry III was buried in the rebuilt Westminster Abbey.

Edward I: (AKA: Edward Longshanks, because he was tall. AKA: Hammer of the Scots, due to battle wins.)

Born 6/18/1239, at Westminster.
Died 7/7/1307.
Reigned 1272-1307.

Prince Edward was a lawyer, soldier, and a statesman.

In Dec/1272 he was in Sicily; he learned that (since November/his father's death) he'd become king. He returned to England in 1274; his chief minister had governed while he was away. Edward I was crowned in Aug/1274.

He and his wife (Eleanor of Castile, married in 1254) went on Crusade in the Holy Land; they were known to be a close couple.

Edward I was not popular in Scotland; rebels were led against him by the Scotsman William Wallace. The Longbow had been invented, and Edward's troops used this new weapon, defeating the Scottish army. This was when the Stone of Scone was seized from Scone and moved to the Coronation chair in Westminster Abbey. (See: Westminster Abbey/Stone of Scone.) Scottish forces/William Wallace continued to challenge the king.

Queen Eleanor died in 1290; this led to the construction of 12 crosses in her honor. (See: Charing Cross, under C in the Alpha section.)

Edward I married anew in 1299, to Margaret Of France, Philip IV of France's sister. (Between the two wives, Edward I had six sons and twelve daughters.)

In 1305 William Wallace was captured, found guilty of treason, and put to a gruesome death. Battles continued, with Edward I dying of dysentery at Burgh-on-Sands, Northumberland, in 1307, while on his way to fight Robert Bruce, King of Scots.

Edward II: (AKA: Edward of Caernarvon.)

Born 4/25/1284, at Caernarvon, Wales.
Died 9/21/1327.
Reigned 1307-1327.

His three older brothers had all died, making Prince Edward heir to Edward I (even though as a child he mostly lived with his mother, who would become estranged from Edward I.)

Became king on 7/8/1307.

In 1308, Edward II (age 23) married 12 year old Isabella, daughter of Philip IV of France.

Edward II is described as inept and frivolous, with many "favorites." He had a rocky relationship with his English barons - and by 1314 there was a very poor harvest. It all led to Civil War in 1321.

Summoned to France in 1323 to pay homage to Charles IV, when he returned to England his disenchanted wife, Isabella, remained in France with her lover, Roger Mortimer (and her son, the heir, Prince Edward.)

In 1326, Mortimer, Isabella, and Prince Edward were warmly greeted by the populace when they came to England. This forced Edward II to flee to Gloucester, and then to Wales. Isabella took the Tower of London, and called a council; the realized plan was that Edward II must abdicate and allow his young son to rule (with Isabella and Mortimer as regents.)

Edward III was crowned in 1327 at age 15.

The deposed king died in captivity at Berkeley Castle, Gloucestershire, in a supposed particularly brutal manner, 9/21/1327, although some believe he escaped and lived in obscurity.

Edward III:

Born 11/13/1312, at Windsor Castle.

Died 6/21/1377.

Reigned 1327-1377.

Before he was made king (1327,) in 1326 Prince Edward, at age 14, was betrothed to Philippa of Hainault (age 12.) They married in 1328. That same year, Edward threw off his mother and Mortimer's regency (despite not yet coming of age at 21.)

Scottish problems continued. Too, The Hundred Years War began in 1337, because Edward III believed he had a right to the French throne. There were many battles with France. Despite improving the status of the monarchy after his father's chaotic reign, the cost of the war created a whole new reason for a discontented populace for Edward III.

His oldest son was yet another Edward, the Black Prince, nicknamed for the color of his armor.

In 1348 Edward III created the Order of the Garter. (See: Order of the Garter, under O in the Alpha section.) In that same year, the disease called the Black Death (bubonic plague) killed 1/3 of the English population. Due to the lack of laborers, wages soared, and food was scarce. Battles and treaties abounded. The Black Prince died in 1376; the Black Prince's son (Edward III's young grandson,) Richard, then became heir.

Edward III's 50 year reign ended when he died in 1377 after suffering a stroke.

Richard II:

Born 1/6/1367, in Bordeaux, France.

Died 2/14/1400.

Reigned 1377-1399.

The son of the Black Prince, Richard became king at the age of 10. With his father and grandfather dead, Richard's uncle became his regent (John of Gaunt.) Gaunt continued the war with France. To pay for the war, a new tax, the Poll Tax, was instituted, at a shocking one shilling per person. This led to the Peasant's Revolt in 1381, under rebel Wat Tyler. The rebellion was put down with severe harshness.

Later, when many of Richard's supporters were found guilty of treason by Parliament, Richard dissolved that body; he said he would rule without advisors. The king's wife, Anne of Bohemia, died in 1394. He married again in 1396, to Isabella, daughter of the French king, Charles VI.

Richard II, due to his disregard of inheritance rules, and his perversion of justice, was unpopular. In 1399 his cousin, Henry of Bolingbroke (who was John of Gaunt's son, and who had previously fully supported Richard II, until Richard was seen to have a tyrannical rule) seized the throne while Richard was in Ireland. Richard was forced to abdicate, making his Bolingbroke cousin the new king, Henry IV.

Richard II was imprisoned at Pontefract Castle, Yorkshire, where he died in 1400, possibly from starvation.

House of Lancaster:

Henry IV: (AKA: Henry Bolingbroke. AKA: Henry of Lancaster.)

Born 4/3/1367, at Bolingbroke Castle, Lincolnshire.

Died 3/20/1413.

Reigned 1399-1413.

His first wife, Mary de Bohun, had been kidnapped on his orders because Henry desired a marriage with the 12 year old heiress (1380); Mary gave birth for the first time in 1386 (to the later Henry V.) She died in childbirth in 1394, before Henry IV was crowned but not before having six children with him.

The old king (Richard II) had gotten angry with Cousin Henry, and had him banished in 1398; Henry had countered by seizing the throne in 1399 while Richard II was in Ireland. As noted above, Richard II was forced to abdicate; his usurper was made Henry IV in 1399.

The new king founded the Order of the Bath in 1399. (See: Order of the Bath, under O in the Alpha section.)

Henry IV married Joan of Navarre in 1403 (but this marriage resulted in no children.)

He spent much of his reign fighting against assassination attempts, rebellions, and schemes.

Henry IV died in 1413, age 45, after long suffering from a disfiguring skin problem and an unnamed "grave" illness (possibly leprosy; other sources say he was simply worn out by revolts and a lack of money.) He died in the Jerusalem Chamber, Westminster Abbey (a 14th C. abbot's retiring room.)

Henry V:

Born either on 9/16/1386 or 8/9/1387, records are unclear; at Monmouth Castle, Wales.

Died 8/31/1422.

Reigned 1413-1422.

Eldest son of Henry IV. He was knighted at the mere age of 12, already having battle experience. While he was yet Prince Henry, in 1403, he took an arrow to the face at the Battle of Shrewsbury. It was safely removed, but left a scar. He was a good soldier, and said to be pious and stern.

Once crowned, Henry V resumed plans to take back France, continuing the Hundred Years War (which had started four generations earlier, during Edward III's time.) After many losses, the French sued for peace; Henry took the city of Rouen, and was recognized because of it (and previous battle wins) as the next King of France (once

Charles VI of France, who was insane, was to die.) Henry V married Charles VI's daughter, Catherine of Valois, in 1420. These acts disinherited the Dauphin (Charles VI's prior heir,) making (the already English king) Henry V heir to the French throne.

On 8/31/1422 Henry V died from dysentery/a wound from battle while in France. (Charles VI of France also died shortly thereafter, in Oct/1422.) Henry V's infant son inherited the crowns of both England and France.

Henry VI:

Born 12/6/1421, at Windsor Castle.

Died 5/21/1471.

Reigned 1422-1461, and again in 1470-71. Disputed King of France from 1422-53.

Henry VI was not quite nine months old when his father died and left him king. His regents were his uncles (John, Duke of Bedford, and Humphrey, Duke of Gloucester,) and Henry Beaufort (Duke of Somerset.) Henry VI was said to be gentle and retiring.

In Oct/1422 Charles VI of France died, and under the peace that had been achieved by Henry V, Henry VI became the King of France (as well as already being the King of England.) The French were highly resistant; Joan of Arc was part of the French armies that battled and retrieved lands from the English (1429-1430.) Henry VI's claim on the French throne was (temporarily) put aside, and the Dauphin of France was crowned as Charles VII.

Though he'd "ruled" since 1422, at age of seven Henry was finally *crowned* King of *England* (1429.)

Joan of Arc was burned at the stake in 1431.

Henry VI was crowned King of *France* at Notre Dame in Dec/1431, (so there were two claimants to the French throne, Henry VI and Charles VII.)

Henry took on ruling without regents in 1437 (almost age 16.) French forces kept reclaiming French land. To make peace between England and France, the Treaty of Tours led to Henry VI marrying Margaret of Anjou in 1445.

Henry VI, at age 18, founded two colleges: Eton College (near Windsor,) and King's College (Cambridge.)

In 1453 the Battle of Castillon marked the end of the Hundred Years War; this same year Henry VI had a breakdown in August. His son, Prince Edward, was born in October. In 1454, Henry's mental health was restored.

The Wars of the Roses began in 1455 (civil war, wherein the English barons objected to how the Lancasters had risen to the throne in Henry IV's time, 1399; claiming not only was his father and grandfather invalid, but also the present Henry VI as king.)

He was captured in battle. Richard Plantagenet, the ambitious Duke of York, became Protector of the realm while Henry was a captive.

Under the Oct/1460 Act of Accord, Richard, Duke of York, was named heir to the throne (not Henry VI's young son, Prince Edward) - but York was killed in battle in Dec/1460. Henry VI was released that month, but due to another bout of mental illness could not rule. More battles, and Henry VI being captured again led to, in 1461, Henry being deposed by York's son, Edward, who was now the Duke of York (his father having died.)

Henry VI was briefly restored to the throne in 1470.

Deposed again, Henry VI died in 1471 in the Tower of London. Some claim he died of a broken heart upon learning of his son, Edward's, death the day before*, others suspect his murder (stabbed to death) was ordered by Edward IV. (*Son Edward, age 17, died in battle at the Battle of Tewkesbury. Some sources, including Shakespeare, give the young prince a different death - but all contemporary sources state Edward died in battle.)

House of York:

Edward IV: (Edward Plantagenet.)

Born 4/28/1442, at Rouen, France.

Died 4/9/1483.

Reigned 1461-1483.

Edward was the son of Richard Plantagenet, Duke of York, and noblewoman Cecily Neville.

At age 17, in 1460 Edward fought against the Lancastrian forces at the Battle of Northampton, where Henry VI was captured.

In that same year Edward IV's father (Richard Plantagenet, Duke of York) was named Henry VI's heir (over King Henry VI's own son.)

In 1461, however, the Duke of York died, so the new heir to the throne was Edward Plantagenet, now the Duke of York. Battles ensued, leading to Edward IV being crowned at Westminster Abbey in 1461 with Richard Neville, Earl of Warwick, being the real power behind the 19 year old's new throne.

He was not a popular ruler, said to lack morals.

In 1464 Edward secretly married Elizabeth Woodville, which angered Warwick, whose fortunes ebbed and flowed, leading to Warwick trying to install George, Edward IV's younger brother, to the throne. Fortunes turned and turned again, with Edward IV fleeing to Burgundy.

In 1470, Warwick restored Henry VI briefly to the throne. Henry's brother, an often rebellious Prince George, joined with Henry, turning against Warwick, at the Battle of Barnet, 1471; Warwick fell from his horse and was killed. Edward IV resumed the throne in May/1471.

Alas, Edward had a final falling out with brother George, who was executed for treason in 1478, supposedly drowned in a butt of malmsey wine.

Edward IV died suddenly in 1483; it is not known what struck him down, but pneumonia, typhoid, and poison have all been suggested. He was succeeded by his 12 year old son, another Edward (and with Edward IV's brother, Richard of Gloucester, as young Edward V's named regent.)

Edward V:

Born 11/2/1470, in Westminster Abbey. His mother, Elizabeth Woodville, had sought sanctuary during the Wars of the Roses (from the Lancastrians) there.

Died (presumed) 1483.

Reigned 1483: For two months, although he was never coronated.

At age 12, named king when his father died in Apr/1483. Edward V learned he was the new king five days after Edward IV's death. While traveling to London to claim the throne, Prince Edward, his mother (Elizabeth Woodville,) and the entire Woodville party were seized by Richard, Duke of Gloucester, (Edward IV's brother/Edward V's official regent.)

Edward V was the uncrowned king...but in May/1483 Richard of Gloucester took the official title Lord High Protector - and put Edward V in the Tower of London. Edward's brother, Richard (age 9,) joined him there.

Parliament declared the old king Edward IV's marriage to Elizabeth Woodville as invalid; the young would-be king and his brother were declared illegitimate. In 1483, Richard of Gloucester took the throne, becoming Richard III. The two young princes (Edward V and Richard) went missing, and were soon presumed dead - and their uncle Richard III has, right or wrong, long been suspected in their deaths.

Richard III:

Born 10/2/1452, at Fotheringhay Castle, Northamptonshire.

Died 8/22/1485.

Reigned 1483-1485.

Was another son of Richard, Duke of York, and Cecily Neville (as had been his brother, Edward IV.)

Richard's wife since 1472, Anne Neville, was crowned as Queen consort when he took the throne in 1483; she died in Mar/1485.

Shakespeare's *Richard III* portrays Richard as being a hunchback, but when his remains were unearthed in 2012, it was discovered he suffered rather from severe scoliosis (curvature of the spine); contemporary sources confirm this by saying Richard III had "one shoulder higher than the right," and that he was "crook-backed" (rather than hunchbacked.)

Despite Richard III proving to be a capable ruler, he wasn't much liked. Henry Tudor challenged Richard's right to the throne. They met in battle at Bosworth Field. Richard was killed, Aug/1485, the last English king to be killed on the field of battle; Henry Tudor, right there on that same field, had Richard III's crown placed on his head and was proclaimed as Henry VII.

House of Tudor:

Henry VII: (AKA: Henry Tudor. AKA: Henry Richmond.)

Born 1/28/1457, Pembroke Castle, Wales.

Died 4/21/1509.

Reigned 1485-1509.

Son of Margaret Beaufort and Edmund Tudor, the latter having died before Henry was born. His mother remarried in 1458, to Henry Stafford, who died in 1471. Henry's mother married a third time, in 1472, to Thomas Stanley.

At Richard III's death (under Henry's sword,) Henry was crowned Henry VII in

1485.

He married Elizabeth of York in 1486 (eldest daughter of Edward IV.) This united the House of Lancaster and the House of York.

Henry VII was greedy, but proved to be a skilled politician. Pretenders to the throne rose and fell; trades and treaties between many European countries were made and sometimes denied; taxes were set and annoyed the populace; but the country's wealth rose.

Playing cards were invented during his reign; his wife Elizabeth's face has appeared in many a deck since. (You may care to see: playing cards, under P in the Alpha section.)

In 1497 the explorer John Cabot discovered a new, uninhabited land: he called it New-Found-Land (in what would become Canada.)

Prince Arthur (Henry VII's firstborn) and Catherine of Aragon (later married to Henry VIII) were married by proxy in 1499, but Catherine remained in Aragon until 1501; another marriage ceremony was held two weeks later, at St. Paul's Cathedral, this time with teenaged Arthur and Catherine present. Arthur died of a viral infection five months later, in 1502; his younger brother, Prince Henry, became the heir.

By 1503 Prince Henry and his brother's widow, Catherine of Aragon, were betrothed. Many clerics doubted that the Pope had the right to allow a prince to marry his brother's widow - and Henry VII wasn't so sure he liked this arrangement for his now-heir either...but the young Prince Henry was spending time with Catherine. Despite doubts, the realm's nobles were worried about the succession and so urged the union be made.

Henry VII died from tuberculosis in 1509.

Henry VIII:

Born 6/28/1491, at Greenwich Palace.
Died 1/28/1547.
Reigned 1509-1547.

Henry was born the second son, but his older brother, Arthur, had died in 1502.

Henry was betrothed to Arthur's widow, Catherine of Aragon, in 1503, with Papal dispensation to allow it.

With Henry VII dead in 1509, the very nearly eighteen year old prince became Henry VIII, and married 23 year old Catherine of Aragon.

Of course, Henry VIII is famous for his six wives, as the chant goes regarding their fates:

Divorced. Beheaded. Died.
Divorced. Beheaded. Survived.

DIVORCED: *Catherine of Aragon* - Was queen 1509-1531, when Henry returned her Christmas gift, saying it wasn't proper to receive since they were "no longer married." After 23 years of marriage, and no sons being born, Henry desired to secure the succession; he was openly living with Anne Boleyn by then.

Anne and Henry secretly married in 1533, because she was pregnant and he wanted the child to be legitimate. In that year, Thomas Cranmer (Archbishop of Canterbury) declared the Henry-Catherine marriage null and void, and the one to Anne Boleyn legal.

Catherine of Aragon died in 1536, amid rumors that Anne Boleyn had slowly poisoned her (but Catherine probably died from cancer.)

BEHEADED: *Anne Boleyn* - Was queen 1533-1536. Anne was accused of adultery. Ironically, Henry's marriage to Anne was declared by Cranmer to be null and void because Henry had had an earlier affair with Anne's sister, Mary. Anne was beheaded on 5/19/1536.

DIED: *Jane Seymour* - Was queen 5/30/1536-10/24/1537. She died of childbirth fever eight days after giving birth to Prince Edward (later to be the doomed Edward VI.)

DIVORCED: *Anne of Cleves* - Was queen 1/3/1540-7/8/1540. From the moment he met her in person, Henry did not like the look of his new bride; from that (or the king's lack of health) the marriage was unconsummated.

By late June, Henry's eye had been caught by Kathryn Howard, who had been moved into Lambeth Palace/visited by the king.

Anne of Cleves, understandably worried about her fate, agreed to a divorce based on a prior contract of Anne to the Duke of Lorraine, and "inadequate consent" (Anne is said to have been a bit naïve, only belatedly realizing her marriage wasn't going well,) and on the grounds of nonconsummation. The divorce was granted.

BEHEADED: *Kathryn Howard* - Was queen 7/28/1540-11/28/1541, when a proclamation was issued that said she was no longer queen and must now be again called Kathryn Howard. She had been accused of adultery. She was beheaded on 6/28/1542.

SURVIVED: *Katherine Parr* - Was queen 7/12/1543-1547. It's said that Katherine was perhaps more a companion than a true wife to the now obese Henry VIII. He liked her religious-oriented chatter and playing cards with her. Katherine was kind to Henry's three (legitimate) children, making sure they had places at court.

Henry died in 1547. Katherine outlived him, dying in 1548. She is still the most-married English queen, having had two marriages before Henry VIII, and one brief one after, the same year she died of childbirth fever (while in her final marriage, to Thomas Seymour.)

In addition to marrying six times, Henry VIII (in dogged pursuit of a living male heir,) is equally known for breaking from the Catholic Church/the Pope, and founding the Anglican Church, of which he styled himself the head.

- See: Church of England, under C in the Alpha section.
- See: Dissolution of the Monasteries, under D in the Alpha section.

Henry VIII had been well-educated. He didn't want to be seen as punitive as his father. (Alas, by the time he died, he'd been called a tyrant.) He was more interested in hunting and sport than in government.

In 1517 Martin Luther published his 95 theses against practices in the Catholic church (the beginning of the Reformation.)

Henry VIII's reign is also known for involving Thomas Wolsey, Archbishop of York, and cardinal in the Catholic Church, Lord Chancellor of England (in which position he wielded a great deal of power, 1515-1529,) opposed to Henry's divorce from Catherine, and statesman. Wolsey was accused of treason (for failing to get the Pope's agreement to Henry's divorce from Catherine of Aragon); on the way to London to answer charges he died from illness.

Henry VIII's reign also included: Thomas More, humanist, lawyer, opposed to the Protestant Reformation; social philosopher, and statesman. He was Lord High Chancellor of England 1529-1532. Too, he opposed Henry VIII's separation from the Catholic Church. Henry had him executed/beheaded for exercising ecclesiastical jurisdiction without the king's permission, in 1535. Thomas More was made a saint, honored by the Catholic and Anglican churches.

The Act of Union between Wales and England went forward, 1536. The Reformation reached Scotland, under John Knox (founder of the Presbyterian Church of Scotland,) in 1541.

CHILDREN: Henry fathered Mary Tudor in 1516 (later to be Mary I,) with his first wife, Catherine of Aragon.

He fathered Elizabeth in 1533 (later to be Elizabeth I,) with his second wife, Anne Boleyn.

He fathered three sons with Catherine of Aragon, all of whom died: Henry, d.1511, not quite two months old. An unnamed son, d.1513, either stillborn or died shortly after birth. Another unnamed son, d.1515, stillborn.

He fathered two sons with Anne Boleyn, both of whom died: an unnamed son, d.1534, through miscarriage. An unnamed probable son, d.1524, miscarriage at four months' development.

He fathered one son with Jane Seymour, Edward (who became Edward VI, reigned for six years, and died at the young age of 15.)

Henry VIII's health was declining (he is now believed to have been suffering from cirrhosis and syphilis) by the time of his sixth and final marriage (to Katherine Parr); by 1546 he could no longer walk and must be carried or got about in a wheeled chair. He died, age 55, in 1547, leaving his young son as king, with Edward Seymour as Edward VI's regent.

Edward VI:

Born 10/12/1537, at Hampton Court.

Died 7/6/1553.

Reigned 1547-1553.

Became king at age nine. The young king's regent (styled as the Protector) for two years was Edward Seymour, 1st Duke of Somerset/Edward VI's uncle, and eldest brother of Edward VI's mother (Jane Seymour, who had died eight days after giving birth to Edward VI.) But the Duke of Somerset was unpopular with the gentry and he was overthrown in 1549.

Edward VI was a sickly child, perhaps afflicted by tuberculosis.

During Edward VI's brief six year time as king, the Book of Common Prayer was introduced in 1549, rewritten/clarified by Thomas Cranmer in 1552. (See: Book of Common Prayer, under B in the Alpha section.)

A weakening Edward VI opposed his two stepsisters (Mary and Elizabeth) being heir(s) to the throne, due to their declared illegitimacy and Mary's Catholicism; he declared for his Protestant cousin Lady Jane Grey instead (granddaughter of Henry VIII's sister, Mary.)

Edward VI died at age 15, from either tuberculosis or a lung infection, having been weakened a year earlier by smallpox.

Lady Jane Grey:

Born October/1537, at Bradgate, Leicestershire.

Died 1554.

Reigned: 7/10/1553-7/19/1553. Only 15 years old, she ruled for just nine days, declared Queen of England on 7/10/1553, but deposed on 7/19/1553.

Jane was well educated, intended to be the gracious lady of some worthy gentleman. She was introduced to the royal court in 1551. In a triple wedding with two of her sisters also marrying, Jane married Lord Guildford Dudley in 1553.

Once raised to the throne, she declared her husband would not be king, but instead the Duke of Clarence; Dudley was furious.

Mary Tudor, Henry VIII's eldest daughter, declared to the Council that under the Act of Succession of 1544, *she* was queen. She had popular support. Mary was declared queen on 7/19/1553, ending Jane's nine day reign. Jane and Dudley were imprisoned in the Tower of London, and seven months later, in Feb/1554, Jane and her husband were beheaded.

Mary I:

Born 2/18/1516, at Greenwich Palace.

Died 11/17/1558.

Reigned 1553-1558.

Born to Henry VIII and his first wife, Catherine of Aragon. Henry divorced Catherine, making Mary illegitimate - although Henry remained affectionate toward her (and her half-sister Princess Elizabeth, daughter of Anne Boleyn, as well.)

Mary's health wavered over the years. In 1533 her household was disbanded, she was reduced from Princess Mary to Lady Mary, and she was sent to serve as a maid of honour in Princess Elizabeth's household. Mary protested her illegitimacy, refused to accept any marriage nor enter a convent unless her mother (from whom she was kept separated) said she could.

She was forced to sign the Oath of Supremacy in June/1536 (after her mother had died in January,) and was accepted back at court.

In 1537, her half-brother Edward (later Edward VI, in 1547,) son of Henry VIII and Jane Seymour, was born, putting Mary in second place as heir, a state worsened by the young Edward's resistance to his stepsisters inheriting (and leading to Lady Jane Grey's 9-day reign.)

The day Lady Jane was made queen, Mary wrote to the Council, claiming inheritance of the crown, was supported, and became queen.

She introduced a proclamation that her mother's marriage to Henry VIII was legal and that she herself was legitimate. She planned to marry Philip of Spain; her English subjects feared an even more Catholic-leaning monarchy. Nonetheless, she married King Philip in 1554 (thereby making her also the Queen Consort of Spain, when he ascended to his throne in 1556.) She had her sister Elizabeth put in the Tower of London, fearing the public would back the Protestant Elizabeth.

Mary declared she was pregnant in 1555 - but no child was forthcoming. In that year, Protestants were arrested as heretics; if they didn't renounce Protestantism they were burned at the stake. In 1556, Thomas Cranmer (Archbishop of Canterbury/supporter of the English Protestant Reformation) was burned. From these severities, Mary got her nickname: Bloody Mary (although note that the nickname was granted some 100 years later.) Battles with France made Mary even less popular.

Once again, in 1558, there was a phantom pregnancy. With no children, and in poor health, Mary was forced to declare her half-sister, Elizabeth, should succeed her. Mary I died of a reproductive disease (possibly cysts or uterine cancer) on 11/17/1558.

Elizabeth I:

Born 9/7/1533, at Greenwich Palace.

Died 3/24/1603.

Reigned 1558-1603.

Over the years, Elizabeth I kept many suitors dangling, but "the Virgin Queen" never married in her 45 years as ruler.

Some highlights of her reign: in 1559 the Act of Uniformity (re)declared the official faith of England to be Protestantism (turning back from the Catholicism revived by her half-sister, Mary I of England.)

In 1563, smallpox left Elizabeth with facial scars she covered with makeup, and hair loss she covered with wigs.

She had many political run-ins with her 1st cousin, once removed (related through their mutual grandparent, Henry VII,) Mary Queen of Scots, (AKA: Mary Stuart, AKA: Mary I of Scotland,) mother of infant James VI of Scotland. Here it's important to note that Mary I of Scotland was forced to abdicate to her infant son, James VI, in 1567.

(Mary I of Scotland is not to be confused with Bloody Mary/Mary Tudor, who was Elizabeth's half-sister, the latter of whose death had made Elizabeth queen.)

Cousin Mary I of Scotland went on to be part of rebellions against Elizabeth's reign.

Elizabeth also funded Francis Drake's world exploration. Virginia (in what would become America) was named for the queen, in 1584.

She was noted for her learning, wisdom, and wit. She also chose well when it came to advisors. England, under her, became feared and respected. During her reign, Shakespeare was at his zenith.

Cousin Mary I of Scotland was found guilty of trying to overthrow Elizabeth, but while Mary was sentenced to death, Elizabeth held off, not wanting to have reprisals from other European leaders and reluctant to harm her cousin; yet the execution went forward on 2/8/1587.

English troops triumphed over the Spanish Armada in 1588.

Elizabeth died in 1603, leaving her Scottish nephew (perhaps in a touch of irony,) James VI, son of Cousin Mary, as her heir.

House of Stuart: (See: Historical Era/Stuart era, above - For explanation of why Stewart changed to Stuart.)

James I: (AKA: James Stewart, or James Stuart. AKA: James VI of Scotland.)

Born 6/19/1566, at Edinburgh Castle, Scotland.

Died 3/27/1625.

Reigned 1603-1625.

He was crowned as an infant as: King James VI of Scotland (in 1567, when his mother, Mary, was forced to abdicate the throne of Scotland); AND as King James I of England, Ireland and Wales (in 1603, when he was 37 years old.) He was the first king to rule over Scotland and England.

In 1604 he declared himself King of Great Britain, despite neither the English nor the Scottish governments approving the sound/implications of the new title. (See: Great Britain, under G in the Alpha section.) Note: the term United Kingdom was not used until 1801.

James was the son of Henry Stuart/Lord Darnley, and Mary Queen of Scots. James's father was murdered (an act possibly involving his wife, who had been desiring a divorce.) The last time Mary I Queen of Scots saw her son was when he wasn't even a year old, in 1567; she was kidnapped or went willingly at that time; her second marriage was to the man behind her husband's murder: James Hepburn, the Earl of Bothwell.

Mary I's half-brother, James Stewart, Earl of Moray, was infant James VI's Scottish regent, until Moray was murdered in 1570. Matthew Stewart, Earl of Lennox, then became his regent, but within a year or so Lennox succumbed to battle wounds. Next regent: James Douglas, Earl of Morton - who was executed in 1581, when James VI was age 15.

In 1582, James VI was imprisoned in Ruthven Castle, but was released in 1583. In 1584, James began to take over rule in Scotland.

His mother was beheaded in 1587 in Fotheringhay Castle, Northamptonshire, for her part in a plot against the English Queen Elizabeth I.

A scholarly man, James VI married Anne of Denmark in 1589. Following time spent in Denmark, in 1590 James became obsessed with witchcraft. He published "Daemonologie" in 1597, and "The True Law of Free Monarchies" in 1598, the latter declaring the divine right of kings to answer only to God.

Once he became King James I (of England, Ireland and Wales; had already been King James VI of Scotland for 36 years) in 1603, he kept the same privy council Elizabeth I had had, as had been agreed.

Some marks of his reign: In 1605, James survived the Gunpowder Plot, which Guy

Fawkes and Catholic supporters had intended to kill him and members of parliament.

The King James Authorised version of the Bible was published in 1611; it is the best-selling book in history; considered important not least because of its scholarly translation by 47 men. Though, the new work displeased Puritans.

Under his reign, many were accused/tortured/died under accusations of witchcraft.

His heir, Prince Henry, died of typhoid in 1612; his second son, Prince Charles, became the heir.

In 1618 the Thirty Years' War began, a religious and European power struggle.

Pilgrims, in The Mayflower, sailed for the new land (what would become America) in 1620.

Suffering a stroke in early Mar/1625, James I died from dysentery on 3/27/1625.

Charles I:

Born 11/19/1600, Dunfermline Palace, Scotland.
Died 1/30/1649.
Reigned 1625-1649.

Charles, son of James I, became king on 3/27/1625; he married Henrietta Maria of France (by proxy) on 5/1/1625. He married her in person in Canterbury, on 6/13/1625. She could remain Catholic, but the children were to be raised Protestant.

In 1626 Charles I had Dudley Digges (diplomat/sat in the House of Commons) arrested; this infuriated parliament, as there was supposed to be freedom of speech in the House of Commons. Charles dismissed Parliament. He went on to become increasingly unpopular, raising taxes, and repeatedly dismissing Parliament. He imprisoned more members of the Commons.

There were Scottish riots, resisting the king's insistence that the Book of Common Prayers be used in Scotland; Charles I expelled Scottish bishops; war between Scotland and England resulted.

Oliver Cromwell (who would go on to depose the king) was elected as a member of Parliament in 1628.

Almost bankrupt, Charles I seized silver from the Tower of London, calling it "a loan." He tried to enforce treason charges against a peer and members of Parliament, who refused the charges; Charles was forced to flee to Hampton Court in Jan/1642. Parliament took control of the Militia. Charles I was forced to York.

Parliament presented Nineteen Propositions, trying to reach a settlement with Charles I, who rejected them. He began the English Civil War in 1642; Royalists and Parliamentarians battled until 1646, when in May, Charles I surrendered to the Scots at Newark. He escaped imprisonment in 1647. Oliver Cromwell's troops had their share of battle wins. Charles I was recaptured.

Parliament indicted him with a charge of treason against England in 1649, although many parliament members stayed away, objecting to the trial. Still, on 1/30/1649, Charles I was publicly beheaded outside the Banqueting House in Whitehall.

Interregnum: Literally, "between reigns." That is, when normal government (in this case, the monarchy,) is suspended. (AKA: the Commonwealth.)

Oliver Cromwell:

Born 4/25/1599, in Huntingdonshire (Cambridgeshire,) England.

Died 9/3/1658.

Protector: Was Lord Protector of the Commonwealth 1649-1658. The British monarchy had been abolished.

Before the time of the Commonwealth, in early 1628, Oliver Cromwell became a Member of Parliament; two months later Charles I dismissed Parliament, a controlling practice he exercised multiple times.

After inheriting property in Ely, Oliver Cromwell moved there and became tithe collector for Ely Cathedral. He was a staunch Puritan.

The Civil War between Charles I and the Puritans broke out, and Cromwell became a captain in the Parliamentarian army, and had successes. His New Model Army (where low born soldiers could advance) was established in 1645. The Parliamentarians had triumphs. Charles I surrendered to the Scots in 1646; the Civil War ended.

A Puritan Parliament declared Christmas carols and feasting would no longer be allowed. All MPs who did not support Cromwell and the army were forcibly removed from Parliament. Charles I was tried for treason. He was publicly beheaded on 1/30/1649, and Parliament declared England was now a republic. Those who believed Charles I's son (also Charles) was now king fled to Ireland; Cromwell was sent there by Parliament to seize control.

When Prince Charles (later to be Charles II) made it to Scotland, Cromwell took troops there, too. Prince Charles was crowned the King of Scotland at Scone in 1651. (Not to be mistaken for Bonnie Prince Charlie, a later Stuart claimant to the British throne in the 18th century.)

Oliver Cromwell dissolved Parliament (with a troop of musketeers behind him,) and tried to form a nascent and stable government. In 1653, he was named Lord Protector of England for life; he was offered the crown, but refused it in 1657. Charles I had believed he was special to God and above the law; Cromwell thought every man must answer to the law. Note, though, that like Charles I, Cromwell became hated, arguably for these reasons among others: he was excessively anti-Irish and anti-Catholic; he had enemy troops slaughtered rather than captured; Irish civilians were also slaughtered and were forced into indentured servitude (essentially slavery); and largely because Cromwell became what he had meant to get rid of, a dictator who made poor and even cruel choices.

Oliver Cromwell had a fever in 1658, and died of it at the Palace of Whitehall. (He and a few supporters were exhumed in 1661, and posthumously given "executions.") Oliver's son, Richard, took his place.

Richard Cromwell:

Born: 10/4/1626, in Huntingdonshire (Cambridgeshire,) England.

Died 7/12/1712.

Protector: Lord Protector of the Commonwealth 1658-1660.

Oliver Cromwell's third son, Richard trained as a lawyer; became an MP in 1656.

He was made a member of the Council of State, under his father, Oliver, in 1657. The senior Cromwell died in 1658; Richard was declared the new Lord Protector the same day.

England was £2 million in debt. No one was happy, not least because Richard Cromwell had no military experience, had had nothing to do with removing Charles I (which made him suspect in some eyes,) and had an uneasy relationship with the struggling Parliament. Parliament removed Richard/forced a resignation in 1660, just nine months later. Richard fled to France. Little is known of him until he died at Cheshunt, Hertfordshire, England in 1712.

House of Stuart (restored):

Charles II: (Nicknamed the Merry Monarch.)

Born 5/29/1630, at St. James's Palace.

Died 2/6/1685.

Reigned 1660-1685.

Son of Charles I, he had been declared by the Scots as King Charles II of Scotland in 1649 (following his father's beheading.) The Scots wanted Charles II to make Presbyterianism the faith in England; he was forced to agree to the term, but he remained in exile from the British throne, until after many battles he was proclaimed Charles II by the English Parliament in 1660. Thus began the Restoration.

Charles II was popular, but was a weak king, with inept foreign policy.

The Indemnity and Oblivion Act of 1660 pardoned many for the deeds done during the Interregnum. Charles II married Catherine of Braganza in 1662 for political purposes (and was indifferent to her.) Despite his earlier agreement to make the English faith Presbyterianism, in 1661 the Corporation Act required holders of public positions to be Church of England members.

Plague came again to London. (See: Great Plague of 1665, under G, in the Alpha section.) The devastation of the Great Plague was followed the next year by the Great Fire of London. (See: Great Fire of 1666, under G, in the Alpha section.) The brilliant St. Paul's Cathedral was rebuilt following the Great Fire, in 1675-1710, by Christopher Wren. (See: St. Paul's Cathedral, under the CHURCHES section.)

Charles began his affair with Nell Gwynn (actress) in 1668, his favorite mistress (out of 13 during his life.) Charles II had no legitimate children (but 14 illegitimate ones,) and the lack of a legal heir (except for his Catholic brother, James) created tension between the king and Parliament.

Charles II had a seizure in 1685; he converted to Catholicism and died four days after the seizure. His brother, James, succeeded him after all.

James II: (AKA: James VII of Scotland, at the same time he became James II of England and Ireland, upon his brother's death, 1685.)

Born 10/14/1633, at St. James's Palace.

Died 9/16/1701.

Reigned 1685-1688.

Brother of Charles II. James, at age 26, was made Lord High Admiral and Warden of the Cinque Ports. He married a very pregnant Anne Hyde in that same year, 1660. He was named Duke of Albany, Scotland, in late 1660.

He was the head of the firefighting operations during the Great Fire. (See: Great Fire of 1666, under G, in the Alpha section.)

James had secretly converted to Catholicism around 1668.

His wife died of breast cancer, and James remarried in 1673 to Mary of Modena, a Catholic ceremony that made his religious leanings clear; he had to resign as Lord Admiral.

During 1680 James was made Lord High Commissioner of Scotland, moving to Edinburgh.

In 1685, Charles II died and James was crowned as James II.

James persecuted Protestant clergy, and was mostly hated by his English populace. Rebellions were attempted; Catholic appointments by James II vexed Parliament; James's son/new heir (over the Duke of York) was born in 1688 - but Prince James Francis Edward was being raised by Mary, his *Catholic* mother. It all led to a Protestant Parliament chasing James II to France, and a 1689 declaration by them that James II had abdicated the throne.

William, son of William of Orange and husband to Mary (she was James II's Protestant daughter,) were suggested as becoming the new king or queen (over James II's infant son, Prince James Francis Edward) and James II's other (also raised Protestant) daughter, Anne. Anne, along with her sister Mary, refused to rule over Mary's husband William - so it was determined that William and Mary would jointly rule.

James II strove to regain the crown, to no avail. The Bill of Rights (citizens' basic civil rights) was drawn up at the end of 1689, and settled the succession on William and Mary.

The exiled James II had a stroke in 1701 and was partially paralyzed for six months, before dying of a brain hemorrhage at Saint-Germain-en-Laye, France.

William III and Mary II: Husband and wife, co-reigned.

William III: (AKA: William Henry Stuart.) House of Orange.
Born 11/4/1650, at William, The Hague, Netherlands.
Died 3/8/1702.
Co-reigned 1689-1702 (until his death in 1702.)

Mary II:
Born 4/30/1662, at St, James's Palace.
Died 12/28/1694.
Co-reigned 1689-1694 (until her death in 1694.)

William III was the son of William II, Prince of Orange (the Netherlands,) and of Mary Stuart, daughter of Charles I. William II had died of smallpox before William III was born. His mother, Mary, died also of smallpox, but not until 1660, when William was ten years old.

Mary II, William III's wife, was the daughter of James II and Anne Hyde (who was the daughter of Charles II's chief minister.)

William was 12 years older than Mary.

The Netherlands did not have a good relationship with England. There were invasions, support from the Holy Roman Emperor, England and France sued for peace. And then came the marriage to Mary in 1677 at St. James's Palace, London. This result was born of lingering concerns that Charles II's brother (Catholic James, Duke of York) would inherit the crown - so William and Mary, despite being often in the Netherlands, were put forward as heirs to the English throne.

As noted under the James II section, above, Mary's father (James II) did not go quietly after Parliament claimed that his fleeing in 1689 constituted an abdication. Battles were waged. But William III and Mary II sat on their co-thrones, until Mary died in 1694 of smallpox. She'd had three miscarriages; she and William produced no heirs. William III ruled on alone, until he fell from his horse in 1702, which led to pneumonia and killed him a month later. Anne, his sister-in-law (Mary's sister) then became the monarch.

Queen Anne: (AKA: Anne Stuart.)

Born 2/6/1665, St. James's Palace.

Died 8/1/1714.

Reigned 1702-1714.

Some 19 years before she took the crown, Anne married Prince George of Denmark (son of Frederick III of Denmark) at the Chapel Royal in St. James's Palace in 1683.

Anne had 17 pregnancies, and her only surviving child, William Henry, died of smallpox at age 11 in 1700.

During her reign, the Statute of Anne passed in 1710, essentially establishing copyright law. (See: Stationers' Hall, under S in the Alpha section.)

Anne suffered from gout, and pains in the arms, legs, and stomach. By 1713 she had to be got about in a sedan chair or a litter. In 1714 she suffered a stroke, and died two days later. Through her husband Prince George (d.1708) and the Act of Settlement 1701, the crown passed to the Hanoverians: George I, great-grandson of James I.

<u>House of Hanover:</u>

George I: (AKA: George Ludwig, born to Ernest Augustus, Duke of Brunswick-Luneburg, and Sophia of the Palatinate; she was granddaughter to King James I.)

Born 5/28/1660 - Born in Osnabruck, Hanover, Germany.

Died 5/28/1727.

Reigned 1714-1727.

George married Sophia Dorothea of Celle, Germany, in 1682; he divorced her in 1694 on grounds of desertion (she refused to live with him, after they'd both had lovers.)

George, before he became king, disagreed with his brothers' contention that they should accept the concept of primogeniture (where the eldest male inherits all, practiced in England, but not in Germany.) In 1701 the Act of Settlement decided the succession would go to the heirs of George's mother, Sophia of the Palatinate, because she was the Protestant granddaughter of James I (this was shortly before Queen Anne's reign.) Prince

George, Anne's husband, and his children were made British subjects in 1705.

George, not yet king, married a second time: Caroline of Ansbach, 1705.

His mother (Sophia of the Palatinate) died in 1714, making George heir to the throne; in August of that same year Queen Anne died; George I reached Britain in September, and was crowned in October. Coming to the throne at age 54, George I is said not to have spoken all but a few words of English, but documents from his later days show he wrote well enough in this tongue. (He was known to speak in Dutch, French, German, Italian, and Latin.) At any rate, history still says his lack of English led to national policy being left to the government/Robert Walpole. (George lived a large part of his reign in Hanover, Germany.)

There was a Jacobite rebellion, but it fizzled. The South Sea Bubble burst. (See: South Sea Company, under S in the Alpha section.) Robert Walpole became the first Prime Minister of Britain in 1721, although the PM term was not yet used. (See: Prime Ministers, under P in the Alpha section.)

George I had a stroke and died in 1727, leaving his son, George Augustus to inherit the crown.

George II: (AKA: George Augustus.)

Born 10/30/1683 - Born in Herrenhausen, Hanover, Germany.

Died 10/25/1760.

Reigned 1727-1760.

Unlike the rumors of his father's inability to speak English, George II spoke English (and German, and Italian,) but did have an accent. He was George I's only son.

Twenty-two year old George married Wilhelmina Charlotte Caroline of Brandenburg (better known as Caroline of Ansbach) in 1705.

At George II's coronation, music (*Zadok the Priest*, by Handel) was first used, and is still used at British coronations.

George II, more English in style than his father, nonetheless went on depending on Robert Walpole to run the country.

Those who would come to be known as the first Prime Ministers came and went. There were Jacobite rebellions; Bonnie Prince Charlie of Scotland tried to put a Stuart back on the throne, but the effort was crushed at Culloden Moor. George II was the last English king to lead an army into battle. His son and heir (Frederick Louis) died from a pulmonary embolism in 1751; George II's grandson, George William, became the heir. The Seven Years War began in 1756, over French lands in North America.

George II died of an aortic aneurysm in 1760, leaving his grandson to become George III.

George III: (AKA: George William Frederick.)

Born 6/4/1738 - First of the Hanoverian monarchs born in London, England, at Norfolk House, St. James Square. Even so, he was known to have a gently Germanic accent.

Died 1/29/1820.

Reigned 1760-1820.

George III's father (Prince Frederick Louis) died when George was 12 years old, making Prince George the heir of his grandfather, George II. George II died in 1760, and Prince George became George III at age 22.

The Civil List Act of 1760 had George III surrender control of Crown estates to the Treasury, and in return he had an annual income from the Civil List. (See: Civil List, under C in the Alpha section.)

In 1761 he married Charlotte of Mecklenburg-Strelitz at St. James's Palace. She had 16 pregnancies, although there was one miscarriage, and two of her children died young (Octavius and Alfred); 13 survived to adulthood. George III bought and moved into Buckingham House in 1762. (See: Buckingham House, under B in the Alpha section, later to become Buckingham Palace.)

George III was generally liked by his populace, who gave him the nickname "Farmer George," because he liked simple, straightforward things such as agriculture. He was known for saying, "What? What?" rather frequently.

The Enlightenment began, resulting in great statesmen, architecture, improvements in the rights of man, and artists, including such famous authors as Austen, Bryon, Keats, Wollstonecroft, and Wordsworth.

George III's first episode of mental instability was in 1765; at the time it was called "madness," but may have been symptoms caused by porphyria (a genetic disease with various symptoms, among them feelings of anxiety, confusion, or depression.)

Besides his recurring bouts of mental decline, George III is also known for: sharp disapproval of his heir (See: Prinny, under P in the Alpha section); losing the American Colonies to revolution in 1776, the fact of which it is said he never quite got over; he made it illegal for someone in the royal family to marry without the monarch's permission; and being horrified by France's bloody Revolution. In 1801 the Act of Union made the Kingdom of Ireland united with England, and together (with the already incorporated Scotland, 1707,) they became the United Kingdom of Great Britain and Ireland. (See: Act of Union, under A in the Alpha section.)

In 1810, under the Regency Act, Prinny was made regent over his by then blind and deeply unstable father. George III, age 81, died on 1/29/1820 of complications of his condition.

George IV: (AKA: George Augustus Frederick.)

Born 8/12/1762, at St. James's Palace.

Died 6/26/1830.

Regent for George III 1810-1820.

Reigned 1820-1830.

Unlike the three prior Georges, Prince George did not have a Germanic accent, having been born and raised in England.

He married in 1795, to Caroline of Brunswick, to whom he had taken an instant dislike. He had had a prior, secret marriage in 1785 to Maria Anne FitzHerbert, but it contravened the Royal Marriages Act, because Prince George had not gotten his father's permission and because Mrs. FitzHerbert was a Catholic (this latter also forbidden by law for royal marriages.) The marriage was deemed invalid, and Prinny was forced to deny the marriage - but he quietly continued the relationship.

Of his 1795 dictated marriage to Caroline of Brunswick: the relationship was doomed. The prince and Caroline lived less than a year together, had one daughter (Princess Charlotte,) then permanently lived apart (although Caroline continued to ever fight for her right to be called queen.)

When younger, Prince George was called “the First Gentleman of Europe,” and was seen to be a lover of architecture and art. As he aged, his reputation lost its luster, from overspending and from having a messy personal life.

Prinny* had more mistresses. (*Note: To use the disfavored nickname “Prinny” in front of George or to use it in print, was to risk his severe disfavor or even imprisonment.) He liked to dine; by 1797 he weighed 17-1/2 stones (245 lbs.) He began proceedings to discredit his wife, Caroline; he also restricted access to their daughter, Princess Charlotte.

In 1810 Prince George was made regent over his father, George III, who was yet again suffering from a deep bout of mental instability. Prinny’s continuing moves against Caroline were seen with less and less approval from the populace; regardless of her general support, in 1814 Caroline felt the need to remove from Britain to Italy.

In 1815 British and German troops defeated Napoleon at the Battle of Waterloo.

Prinny’s only child, Charlotte, married in 1816 to Leopold of Saxe-Coburg-Saalfeld. A year and a half later, Charlotte died giving birth to a stillborn son. Prinny was devastated. Then his mother (also a Charlotte) died just a year later; Prinny became depressed. He became even more determined to divorce his wife, Caroline.

In 1820 George III died, and Prinny became George IV. Caroline returned to Britain amid population acclaim; but when she tried (uninvited) to be admitted at Westminster Abbey/George IV’s coronation, she lost a lot of popular support; she died a month later, from either a bowel obstruction or cancer (although in her agony she claimed she was poisoned.)

By 1830 George IV weighed 20 stone (280 lbs.) and suffered from cataracts, and had developed a dependency on laudanum. When he died of a heart attack on 6/26/1830, his only child was gone; his brother, Prince William, was made king.

(See: Prinny, under P in the Alpha section.)

William IV: (AKA: William Henry. Nicknamed: the Sailor King.)

Born 8/21/1765, at Buckingham House (later Buckingham Palace.)

Died 6/20/1837.

Reigned 1830-1837.

Third born of George III, brother to George IV. (The second brother, Frederick Augustus, had died in 1827 of dropsy and cardiovascular disease.)

In 1778, William joined the Royal Navy, a midshipman; a lieutenant by 1785; a captain by 1786; a rear admiral by 1789. He left active service in 1790. (He was made an admiral in 1798, but not given a ship.)

William took a mistress in 1791, actress Dorothea Bland (called Mrs. Jordan,) with whom he had 10 illegitimate children; their relationship ended in 1811. That same year

William was named honorary Admiral of the Fleet.

With his niece, Princess Charlotte, dead, William needed to secure the succession. He married Adelaide of Saxe-Meningen in 1818. All of their five children (including one set of twin boys) were stillborn or died shortly after birth.

William became heir to the throne when his (second born) brother Prince Frederick died in 1827. When the oldest brother, George IV, died in 1830, William Henry became William IV.

He was loved by the populace, having a lack of pretension and disliking pomp (unlike his flamboyant brother, George IV.) He is known for supporting the Catholic Relief Act, which gave long-denied rights to Catholics; and the abolition of slavery in Britain. (See: slaves, under S in the Alpha section.) Also, that the old Houses of Parliament burned down in 1830; rebuilt in 1834, standing and serving as the home of the Commons and the Lords yet today.

- See: Lower House, under L in the Alpha section.
- See: Parliament, under P in the Alpha section.
- See: Upper House, under U in the Alpha section.

Because William IV had no living children, the daughter of deceased younger brother Edward became William IV's heir. Called Alexandrina Victoria, she became Queen Victoria at the tender age of 18 when her uncle William IV died of heart failure in 1837.

Victoria: (AKA: Birth name - Alexandrina Victoria. Named for Alexander, Tsar of Russia. Called "Drina" when younger. AKA: Princess Victoria of Kent.)

Born 5/24/1819, at Kensington Palace.

Died 1/22/1901.

Reigned 1837-1901.

Victoria's mother was Victoria Mary Louisa of Saxe-Saalfeld-Coburg. Her father, 4th-born son of George III, Prince Edward, died when Victoria was only eight months old.

She first met her cousin, Albert (of Saxe-Coburg-Gotha,) in 1836 (at not quite 17 years old.)

When she became queen in 1837, Victoria had turned 18 a month earlier, and so did not require a regent. She inherited a crown that had become disrespected/treated with irreverence during the run of George I-George IV.

She proposed to Albert in October/1839; they married in December/1840. Albert has been described as a "pillar of respectability," was bright and interested in inventions, and a bit of an (unofficial) co-ruler with Victoria. The crown returned to a state of esteem.

Victoria is known for: her long reign (63 years); the Great Exhibition of 1851 (a celebration of art, industry, science, and more); purchasing Balmoral Castle in Scotland in 1852; the Crimean War (1854-56); bringing interior Christmas trees into vogue; Prince Albert's early death at age 42 in 1861 of typhoid fever, and Victoria's life-long mourning for him.

The British Empire doubled during her lifetime. Victoria was declared the Empress of India in 1877. Her Golden Jubilee was celebrated in 1887 (50 years reign); her Diamond Jubilee in 1897 (60 years reign.)

When Victoria died of a hemorrhagic stroke at age 81 in 1901, her son (Albert) Edward succeeded her, (as his older sister, Victoria Adelaide, could not inherit the crown over a male.)

House of Saxe-Coburg-Gotha: Prince Albert was the source of the house of Saxe-Coburg-Gotha coming into the British royals. (See: Victoria, above.) The House name changed to Windsor in 1917. (See: Historical Eras/House of Windsor, above in this section.)

Edward VII: (AKA: Albert Edward. AKA to the family: Bertie.)

Born 11/9/1841, Buckingham Palace.

Died 5/6/1910.

Reigned 1901-1910.

Bertie, although not a brilliant scholar, studied at Oxford in 1859, and Cambridge in 1861. He also made several international tours.

He met Princess Alexandra of Denmark in 1861, and proposed to her in 1862, marrying her in 1863. Bertie had six children with his wife. He continued to travel, making affiliations with places such as France, Russia, and Scandinavia.

His mother, Queen Victoria, died in 1901, and Bertie took the throne and the name of Edward VII. He inherited from his mother the title of Emperor of India.

Two months before he was crowned, he underwent an emergency appendectomy. (See: appendicitis, under A in the Alpha section.)

He was much admired by the populace. He enjoyed watching horse-racing, yachting, liked to gamble, and had his share of affairs.

The "Edwardian period" is named for him.

In 1910 Edward VII had a fatal heart attack. His oldest son, Albert Victor, had died at age 28 in 1892. So his second son, George Frederick, took the throne as George V.

House of Windsor:

George V: (AKA: George Frederick Ernest Albert.)

Born 6/3/1865, at Marlborough House, London.

Died 1/20/1936.

Reigned 1910-1936.

At age 12, George (and his older brother, Albert Edward, called Bertie) joined the naval training ship, HMS Britannia, where they had lessons, (bringing along their tutor.) In 1880 they were both made midshipmen in the Royal Navy; George became a sub-Lieutenant in 1884; and a Lieutenant in 1885. Older brother Bertie (Albert Victor) died in 1892 of pneumonia, which caused George to leave the Royal Navy in order to take up his new duties as heir.

In 1893 he married Princess Victoria Mary of Teck (known as May; she had been betrothed to Bertie/Albert Victor, but he died before they could marry.) Like his father, George Frederick was a frequent traveler, along with his wife; he loved the sea.

He ascended to the British throne in 1910, also named Emperor of India. During his reign: WWI played out; an independent Irish parliament formed in 1916-22 (southern

Ireland became the Republic of Ireland; northern Ireland remained part of the UK); George V (aware of strong anti-German sentiments) changed the family name from Saxe-Coburg-Gotha to: Windsor (1917); George's Silver Jubilee (25 year reign) was celebrated in 1935.

George V died in 1936 of pleurisy; his eldest son was crowned as Edward VIII.

Edward VIII: (AKA: Edward Albert Christian George Andrew Patrick David. AKA to the family: David.)

Born 6/23/1894, at White Lodge, Richmond, Surrey.

Died 5/28/1972.

Reigned 1936 (for 11 months.) Abdicated on 12/11/1936. (He was never crowned.)

Edward joined the Osborne Naval College in 1907, and the Royal Naval College, Dartmouth, in 1909. He was taken from the Royal Naval College in 1910, and put on the ship *Hindustan* as a midshipman. He went to Magdalen College, Oxford, in 1910, but left in 1913 without gaining any qualifications.

WWI came, and David was forbidden to serve on the front lines, but did often visit troops on battlefields.

His younger brother, Albert*, married Elizabeth Bowes-Lyon (later known fondly to the country as "the Queen Mum," Elizabeth II's mother) in 1923; Albert and Elizabeth had their first-born child, Elizabeth Alexandra Mary, in 1926 - later to be Queen Elizabeth II. (*Albert, like his grandfather, Edward VII, was known to the family as: Bertie.)

David was seen as being quite a bit of a playboy. He met Wallis Simpson in 1931. She was objectionable as a consort for a king, due to being a divorcee (later to be twice divorced,) and a commoner, and an American. Despite his playboy ways, most of the country was quite fond of Edward/David, being largely unaware of his relationship with Mrs. Wallis until Dec/1936.

Earlier, in Jan/1936, George V died, and David was made king as Edward VIII. That same year, Wallis Simpson filed for divorce from her second husband. Edward VIII's open affection for her was yet opposed by his family, his government, and the Church of England.

On 12/10/1936, Edward VIII signed abdication papers, giving up the British throne in order to marry his lady; the two were officially to live abroad, and could only return to the UK by invitation of the sovereign (which happened a few times following familial deaths.) Some say Edward VIII gave up his reign for love. Some say he was highly encouraged to abdicate because of his playboy ways and because of beliefs he held (it is said he had pro-Hitler leanings.) Regardless if it was his choice or that of others, Edward VIII left the throne behind on 12/11/1936.

He married Wallis Simpson on 6/3/1937 in France; none of the royal family were allowed to attend. He and Wallis were granted the style of Duke and Duchess of Windsor for the remainder of their lives.

Edward died of throat cancer in 1972, and was buried at Frogmore (Windsor Great Park, Berkshire) in the royal burial ground. Wallis Simpson was buried there as well, in 1986. They died childless.

George VI: (AKA: Albert Frederick Arthur George. AKA to his family, like his grandfather, Edward VII, as: Bertie.) He chose the royal name of "George" in order to create a semblance of continuity with his father, George V's, time as monarch.)

Born 12/14/1895, at Sandringham, Norfolk.

Died 2/6/1952.

Reigned 1936-1952.

Albert had a stutter; it (and the fact he hadn't been raised to the expectation of being the heir) made him reluctant to assume the crown. But he was also known as having bravery and a strong sense of duty.

At age 14 he became a Royal Naval College, Osborne cadet, where he finished at the bottom of his class in 1911. Still, he was allowed into the Royal Navy Academy, Dartmouth, that same year. He was a midshipman in 1913, on the *HMS Collingwood.* In 1918, when the Royal Airforce separated from the Royal Navy, he transferred to the former, qualifying as an RAF pilot in 1919.

By 1920 he'd started to take on more royal duties.

He married Elizabeth Bowes-Lyon in 1923 (after she'd turned him down twice before, not wanting to become a royal.) She became beloved to the nation. She, along with her mother-in-law, Queen Mary, were highly supportive of George VI. In 1926 their first daughter was born, called Lilibet by her family, (and who became Queen Elizabeth II in 1952.)

Besides fathering the longest reigning monarch, George VI is known for: being the monarch who no longer ruled over southern Ireland (which had become the Republic of Ireland in 1936); providing comfort and continuity during WWII (they remained at Buckingham Palace for the whole of the war); instituting in 1940 the George Cross and the George Medal, awarded to civilians for acts of bravery; and the Festival of Britain in 1951, a great uplift to the nation following the war.

George VI was the last British monarch to be called the Emperor (or Empress) of India, 1948.

A heavy smoker, he died of lung cancer in 1952.

Elizabeth II: (AKA: Elizabeth Alexandra Mary. AKA to close family: Lilibet.)

Born 4/21/1926, at 17 Bruton Street, London.

Reigned 1952-Present.

Princess Elizabeth was age 9 when her grandfather, George V, died, and her Uncle David (Edward VIII) became king. She had turned 10 by the time Uncle David abdicated in 1936, and her own father (George VI) reluctantly took the throne. The world waited to see if George VI and his queen would go on to have a son. They did not. (Elizabeth has one younger sister, Margaret.)

Elizabeth met Capt. Philip of Greece (her second cousin, once removed) when she was 13 years old, in 1939.

She and her family stayed in London throughout WWII, to show solidarity with the people (although Elizabeth and Margaret spent much of that time at Windsor Castle.) Elizabeth served in the British Army, in a branch called the Auxiliary Territorial Service, as a mechanic.

Philip of Greece renounced his Greek nationality in 1947. He became a British citizen, taking the surname Mountbatten. Formally engaged to Elizabeth, in 1947 Philip was made the Duke of Edinburgh, Earl of Merioneth, and Baron Greenwich. They married on 11/20/1947 at Westminster Abbey. It was the first coronation to be televised.

Prince Charles was born in 1948. Princess Anne in 1950.

Elizabeth learned her father had died while she and Philip were in Kenya in February/1952. Elizabeth was crowned in June/1953, the first televised royal coronation.

Prince Andrew was born in 1960. Prince Edward in 1964.

Elizabeth II's Silver Jubilee (25 year reign) was in 1977.

Lady Diana Spencer (formerly Princess Diana, divorced from Prince Charles on 8/28/1996,) died in a car crash on 8/31/1997.

The Queen Mother (or Queen Mum, Elizabeth Bowes-Lyon,) died on 3/30/2002, at age 101.

Elizabeth's Golden Jubilee (50 year reign) was celebrated in 2002 throughout the Commonwealth. Her diamond wedding anniversary (60 years married) was in 2007. The Diamond Jubilee (60 year reign) was in 2012. In 2015, Elizabeth II became the longest reigning UK monarch, surpassing even Queen Victoria's 63 years; Elizabeth II's Sapphire Jubilee in 2017 marked her reign at then 65 years.

Teresa DesJardien is the author of these Regency Romances, available through Amazon.com:

e-book = Electronic delivery (read on device.)
POD = Print on Demand (paperback book.)

A June Bride –
In a marriage of convenience, love isn't part of the plan.

eBook ISBN: 9780986212659
POD ISBN: 9780986212604

The Marriage Mart –
Love is a nuisance for a lady in the market for a husband.

eBook ISBN: 9780986212666
POD ISBN: 9780986212611

Haunted Hearts –
Even love wears a disguise on All Hallow's Eve.

eBook ISBN: 9780986212673
POD ISBN: 9780986212628

A Heart's Treasure –
It was a delightful treasure hunt, an adventure that could only lead to mischief...and love.

eBook ISBN: 9780986212680
POD ISBN: 9780986212635

A Scandalous Proposal – *She'd found just the right man. Now if only she weren't so attracted to the wrong one.*

eBook ISBN: 9780986212697
POD ISBN: 9780986212642

A Winsome Widow – *It began as a simple wager, but all bets are off when it comes to gambling on love.*

eBook ISBN: 9781945458002
POD ISBN: 9781945458019

Love's Magic – *Can ancient magic and the healing power of love work their wonders on a wary heart?*

eBook ISBN: 9781945458026
POD ISBN: 9781945458033

Borrowed Kisses – *No lady had ever caught Nathaniel's heart...not until he borrowed one special kiss.*

eBook ISBN: 9781945458040
POD ISBN: 9781945458057

London Map

the Highway
Enfield
Ponders End
Irelands Gr.
Chingford
Winchmore Hill
Southgate
Edmonton
Tottenham
Woodford
Claybury
Tanners End
Bruce Castle
Higham Hill
Snaresbrook
Valentines
Colney Hatch
Hornsey
Mill Hill
Page Street
Hendon
Hanson Bridge
Crouch End
Laytonstone
Lea Bridge
Ilford
Barking
Kingsbury
Willesden
Willesden Green
Kilborn Abbey
Primrose Hill
Kentish Town
Kingsland
Grove Street
Old Ford
Bow
New Road
Plaistow Level
the Marshes
Abbey Wood
Plumstead
Woolwich
Black Heath
Charlton
Shooters Hill
Wickham
Welling
Deptford
Runnets Wood
Eltham
Rush Gr.
Mottingham
South End
Southend
Plaistow
Postern Wood
Masons Hill
Langley
Norbury Farm
Stocks Farm
Mitcham
Mitcham Common
Croydon
Broad Green
Merton
Morden
Wimbledon
Robin Hood
Richmond Park
Streatham
Knights Hill
Sydenham
Perry Street
Dulwich
Dulwich College
Brixton
Goose Green
Camberwell
Barnes
Chiswick
Acton
Ealing
Drayton
Twyford
Apperton
Canal from Uxbridge to Paddington
Kensington Gravel Pits
Shepherds Bush

Alphabetical Listings

Alphabetical listing of:

STREETS, BUSINESSES, HOUSES, LOCALES, SITES (and some terms) IN LONDON AND ITS ENVIRONS:

Note: London addresses were not given numbers until the end of the 18th century. Before then (and in large part because most people couldn't read) the ancient practice of signs (hanging or standing) was used. For instance, the famous red-and-white striped pole would be found in front of a barber's place of business, the golden ball for mercers, etc. (See: signs, hanging, for more.)

PLEASE BE SURE TO READ "City, the" (under C) and "gates" (under G.) This will help you understand the difference between "city" (small c) and "City" (capitalized.) It is *AN IMPORTANT DISTINCTION.*

-A-

999 - Emergency phone number, equivalent to America's "911." A telephone was first used in London in 1896. (See: nine-nine-nine, under N.)

abbey - Under the rule of an abbot (or abbess) rather than a prior. (See: priory.) Note: There are homes in Britain that retained the title Abbey (as in the fictional Downton Abbey) following the Dissolution. Even though the mansion/property came under Crown or private ownership, such houses might retain Abbey in their names even though they were no longer affiliated with religion.

Abbey Garden - (See: Westminster Palace/Abbey Garden.)

Abbey Lodge - At Regent's Park's west gate. Designed by John Nash in 1822. A little lodge with niches for statues on the outside. On an 1827 map it was called "West Gate." (See: Hanover Gate.)

Abbey Road - Westminster. Dates from 1829, developed from a prior farming track called Abbey

Lane. The villas came in in the 1840s. This is the road made famous by the Beatles' album cover.

Abchurch Lane - The City. Dates from at least 1291. Known for one Mother Wells' cakes that she baked here in the early 17th century. Later in that century and into the 18th, there was an "eating house" here called Pontack's, although the exact location is unknown. This lane was cut in two when the new King William Street came through in the 1830s.

- St. Mary Abchurch: 1198. (See under the CHURCHES section.)

Abingdon Street - Westminster. A long terrace of Georgian houses, "a magnificent specimen of real English ugliness," as described by Harold P. Clunn in THE FACE OF LONDON.

Accession Council - (See: St. James's Palace/Accession Council.)

Ackermann's Repository of Arts - Sold prints that depicted elegant living. (See: Strand/96.)

acre - A measure of land. It originally meant any kind of field of any size, but Edward I set an acre as the amount of land a team of oxen could plow in a day: 4,840 square yards. (You may care to see: hectare.)

Act of Union - The union of England and Scotland: 1707, thereby forming Great Britain. (The Union with Scotland Act was in 1706, by the Parliament of England; the Union with England Act in 1707, by the Parliament of Scotland.)

The union of Great Britain and Ireland: 1800, adopted by both the Parliament of England, and the Parliament of Ireland in 1801.

(Before then, in simple terms, the Anglo-Saxon kingdoms had been united to become the Kingdom of England ca. the year 800. Wales was conquered in the 13th century.)

- See: flag, British.
- See: Canada.
- See: India.

activities/entertainments/sports - The following is a list of leisure events for Regency era persons, primarily the privileged class. (It is not all-inclusive):

- amateur theatrics - Held by both the lowly and the grand, but probably more by the latter, who would have the resources for staging and costuming.
- angling - (See: fishing, below.)
- archery - (See at its own listing.)
- art - (See: painting, below.)
- auctions - There were auctions for cattle, art, carriages, and (not unlike today) all manner of things.
  - See: Christie's.
  - See: Sotheby's.
- badminton - (See under B.)

- balls - (As in dances.) Some were public, but often a ball was held in a private home. Mainly made up of dancing and conversation. Were held both in town and in the country. Ranged from humble to very grand. Could be a masquerade (fancy dress/costume) ball.
    - See: dances, below.
    - See: parties, below.
- billiards - (See under B.)
- birds of prey - Used for hunting small game. (See: mews.)
- bird hunting
- board games - They had some for children. Also, backgammon, chess, draughts.
    - See: games, children's, under G.
    - See: parlor games, below.
- boating:
    - See: regattas, under R.
    - See: river races, below.
    - See under B.
- book clubs - Readers who gathered to share and discuss titles. For either males or females; less often, both. (See: booksellers/bookshops.)
- bowling; ninepins; skittles - Games with a ball rolled at pins. (See at B, N, and S.)
- boxing; fisticuffs (this latter was more like a fistfight); pugilism. (See at B, F, and P.) Boxing would not have been attended by ladies.
- card-playing -
    - See: bridge.
    - See: Crockford's, under the CLUBS section.
    - See: gaming, below.
    - See: Hazard, under H.
    - See: playing cards.
- chess, and other board games - (See: parlor games, below.)
- church/chapel attendance -
    - See: Church of England, under C.
    - See: definition of church and chapel, under the CHURCHES section - Near the top.
- circuses - (See under C.)
- clubs - Primarily gentlemen's clubs, to which women were not allowed during the Regency. (See the CLUBS section.)

- cockpits - By the time of the Regency, was largely frowned upon, existing as a bit of an underground activity.
    - See: cockfighting.
    - See: cockpits.
- coffee-houses - Were on the wane by the time of the Regency. (See: coffee-houses.)
- confectionaries - Sweets shops.
    - See: confectioner.
    - See: Gunter's.
- coursing - Greyhounds chasing after hares. (See under C.) Hares had long since been "coursed" (chased, either on foot or horseback. Greyhounds chased (sight hounds,) rather than the scent hounds used in foxhunting. Hare coursing took the place of deer hunting (there weren't enough deer left to hunt); foxhunting took the place of hare coursing, although the latter lived on via the greyhounds racing at ovals.
- cricket - The game. (See under C.)
- croquet - More Victorian than Regency, not becoming popular until ca. the 1850s. (See under C.)
- dances - Like a ball, but perhaps less formal, and perhaps far less grand. Even servants, given permission by the master, could host a dance. (See: parties, below.)
- dining - Either at home, or at the home of a friend/ acquaintance.
    - See: picnic.
    - See: restaurant.
    - See: the INNS/PUBS section - The notes at the start of.
- drawing rooms - (See under D.)
- drinking - Going down to the local pub is quintessentially British. Sharing a bottle or two at home is an ancient pastime as well. (See the INNS/PUBS section.)
- fairs -
    - See: fairs.
    - See: frost fairs.
    - See: harvest frolic, below.
- fencing - Men only. (See under F.)
- fireworks - Viewed at venues, such as: Vauxhall Gardens. (See: pleasure gardens, under P.)

- fishing -
  - See: fish.
  - See: fishing.
- football - People have played with balls from antiquity. There was certainly by the 19th C. some form of a game (or games) where the ball was kicked, but it was not anything formal until "football" (soccer) came along midway in that century. (See: soccer.)
- foxhunting - An exclusive sport for those who owned land and could afford to keep hounds.
  - See: foxhunting, under F.
  - See: Mason's Yard, Maxwell, Henry - For the red coats called hunting pinks.
- gaming - Sometimes also called gambling. Both men and women gamed (with money stakes) at cards, dice, other games of chance. Alcohol and/or conviviality sometimes led to wild wagers on any manner of thing. Fortunes were won and lost, all in a night.
  - See: the CLUBS section - Which were male-only. Specifically see: White's, under CLUBS.
  - See: gaming, under G.
- gardening - By and large, the upper class didn't tend their own gardens, except perhaps to clip flowers for a bouquet or such. Though, there were serious amateur Botanists; alas, history almost exclusively tells us only about *men* of such interests. Bringing botanicals from far afield was an active pursuit in the 18-19th centuries. (See: gardens, under G.)
- golf - (See.)
- hare-coursing - Sometimes happened spontaneously, when a hare happened to be spotted, but could also be a planned event.
- harvest frolics - Often servants and laborers were included. Could also be called a: Harvest Home.
- holiday, taking a - Often a traveling trip, even if only by taking a day's walking tour.
- home arts such as lacemaking, tatting, etc. (See: knitting, below.)
- horse-racing - Note: Men often rode their own horses, not necessarily hiring a jockey, especially in casual races among associates. The horse races were a fashionable place for women to be seen, although they usually remained in the carriages, for safety's sake and because no seating was provided.

  - ➢ See: horse-racing, under H.
  - ➢ See: jockeys.
  - ➢ See: races.
- hunting/shooting parties - Not done from February to August, as those were the animal/bird mating and birth seasons.
  - ➢ See: Manton's - For guns.
  - ➢ See: Maxwell/Henry, under M - For hunting clothes.
  - ➢ See: pheasant-shooting.
- knitting - Many people knew how to knit, rich and poor. It was a common source for gift-giving. Indeed, any of the home arts such as: CROCHETING, HAND-STITCHING/SEWING (there were no mechanical sewing machines,) LACEMAKING, TATTING, etc. (see individually in their Alpha sections) were practiced by the general populace, women almost exclusively (if such was not their employment, such as for tailors or leatherworkers.) Among the lower classes such skills were simply practical (mending stockings, for instance); the upper classes had more time for decorative pieces, and might display them to demonstrate their womanly attributes.
- leaping - Literally jumping for distance. Usually an event at a fair or public event. Servants were far more likely to be the participants, striving to win a pair of gloves or the like, with their longest leap.
- lectures - Often for men only, but not exclusively. (See under L.)
- letters - (See: writing letters, below.)
- libraries - (See.)
- lotteries - (See.)
- markets - (See.)
- masquerades - (See: balls, above.)
- maypoles
- menageries - (See: zoos, below.)
- Morris dancers - (See.)
- Mummers - (See.)
- museums - One must pay to enter.
  - ➢ See: individual listings - Such as: Bloomsbury/British Museum/Montagu House.
  - ➢ See: museums, under M.
- music, listening to - People provided instrumental and sung music in their homes/assemblies; it was part of being a good host, as well as a way to display

your own musical charms, if you had them. Of course, you could also hire musicians. There were also the theatres, which frequently provided music sets, even at "straight" (spoken) plays. (See the THEATRES section.) Group singing, such as Christmas wassailing, was quite acceptable, as was performing duets, etc.

- nutting - Going out in autumn in order to harvest ripened nuts. This was a family kind of event (although workers would no doubt harvest the preponderance of nuts available.) Aprons, hats, and shawls might be pressed into service as containers.
- painting - Done by both men and women. (However, due to sexism it was rare for a woman artist to actually sell her work until well into the Victorian era and beyond.)
- panoramas - (See.)
- parks - Strolling through, or riding in one's carriage. (See by name, such as: Green Park; Hyde Park; Regent Park, etc.)
- parlor games - Such as: Authors. Blindman's Bluff (some resources claim it is more correctly: Blindman's Buff.) Chess. Draughts (is checkers in America.) Nine Man's Morris, and many more. While not strictly "parlor games," don't forget card-playing. (See, above.)
- parties - It could be called a party, an assembly, a ball, a soiree, a masquerade, a dinner, etc. Depending on which you mean, some parties were more about dancing, or conversation, or dining, or gaming, etc.
- playing cards - (See: card-playing, above.)
- playing instruments - (See: music, above.)
- pleasure gardens - (See.)
- polo - (Rare during the Regency. See under P.)
- pool - (See: snooker.)
- prostitution - (See.)
- pubs - (See: drinking, above.)
- quilting - (See under Q.)
- races -
    - boat races: (See: regattas, under R.)
    - foot races: Servants (usually women) might enter a foot race at a fair or public event, striving to be first and thereby win a garment or a bit of new fabric.
    - horse races: (See: under H. Also see, above.)
- reading - If you knew how. A humble but literate household would consider itself

fortunate in owning a handful of books (one of which would inevitably be a Bible.)

- reading aloud - To one's family, or guests, or children. Magazines and periodicals might be read in addition to books. Was a very common and much appreciated entertainment for someone to read aloud to a group. Might occur in book clubs as well. (See: book clubs, above.)
- river racing
- rowing -
    - See: boating, above.
    - See: river racing, above.
- sewing - Many women did at least some form of sewing. There were many handcrafts: crocheting, hand-stitching, knitting, lacemaking, tatting.
    - See: knitting, above.
    - See: quilting, under Q.
    - See: sewing, under S.
- shooting parties - (See: hunting, above.)
- shopping - Enjoyed by everyone (who could afford it.)
    - See: markets, under M.
    - See: shopping, under S.
- singing - (See: music, above.)
- skittles - (See: bowling, above.)
- snooker - Later 19th century. (See under S.)
- societies - (See under S, many listings.) Example: Society of Arts. Could range from a humble gathering of a few like minds, to a large, formal organization.
- spas - (See.)
- steeplechase - An often spontaneous horse race, over obstacles (although some were registered matches.) Men only. They would challenge each other (or more than two) to race by horse from one location to another, the first to arrive there being the winner. The term "steeplechase" came from the fact they often chose (because they were both visible or easy to spot) to race from the site of one church steeple to another. Not strictly legal, but happened anyway. The first Steeplechase purpose-built course was built in Bedford in 1810.
- still-room - Where one made one's own cordials, medicines, remedies, etc. (See still-room, under S.)
- stitchery - Practiced by rich and poor. There were no ready-made clothes.
    - See: knitting, above.

    - You may care to see: sewing machines - A post-Regency invention.
- swimming - (Was usually more like "wading," because the bathing costumes were rather heavy when wet, especially for women. One was often accompanied by an attendant paid for the service.)
- swinging - (See: swing, under S.)
- table tennis - Began in the 1880s.
- taverns -
    - See: drinking, above.
    - See: taverns, under T.
    - See listings under the INNS/PUBS section.
- tea-gardens - (See.)
- tennis - (See.)
- theatre-going - (See the THEATRES section.)
- touring - Either by walking or by carriage. Could last a day or a month. (See: holiday, above.)
- wagering -
    - See: gaming, under G.
    - See under W.
- walking - Jane Austen (and some of her characters) were very fond of going for a walk. This could include wandering about the countryside, or strolling through a park, around one's locale, etc. A woman *could* walk alone with a man if he was someone whose acquaintance she'd formally already made.
    - See: formal acquaintance, under F.
    - See: holiday, above.
- weaving - Many women did some weaving at home, mostly as a source of income, but sometimes as an activity for ladies of leisure.
    - See: fabrics/cotton.
    - See: fabrics/silk.
- wrestling - Competitions were often at public events; men only.
- writing letters - A common pastime, for those who could read. (See: Post, the.)
- zoos - Would have been called menageries. One paid to enter. (See under Z.)

Acton - Ealing. Elizabeth I visited its three medieval springs, known as Acton Wells. Fashionable as a spa into the 18th century. Horse races were held here in the second half of the 18th century. During the Regency this area was farmland.

- Acton Cemetery: 1895. Park Royal Road.

- Goldsmiths' Almshouses: East Churchfield Road. By Charles Beazley, 1811. Described as resembling a birthday cake.
- North Acton: Generally considered part of the Park Royal area. In the 1930s known for its industrial sprawl.
- St. Mary: Parish church. On the corner of High Street and King Street. Red brick. The square tower was rebuilt in 1865.
- South Acton: Was farmland until 1859 (after which it developed rapidly.)
- Wells House Road: Site of the Acton Wells assembly rooms. Later became a school, then a farmhouse.
- West Acton: (See under W.)

Adam Street - The Strand. (See: Adelphi/4.)

- 7: Still standing. Decorated with honeysuckle reliefs. (See: John Adam Street, under J.)

Addington - Croydon. Henry VIII had a hunting lodge here.

- Addington Palace: 1780. A 19th C. home to the Archbishops of Canterbury. Described as a "rather plain mansion." Grounds by Capability Brown. In the 20th C. was a country club.
- New Addington: (See: Addington Temple.)
- St. Mary the Blessed Virgin: (See under the CHURCHES section.)

Addington Temple - Croydon. The old name for the area generally covered by the modern name of New Addington. Was farmland well into the 20th century.

Addison Bridge Place - Samuel Taylor Coleridge (poet, d. 1834) lived here at one time.

address - During the Regency era, one was unlikely to ask for a person's "address," but rather instead their "direction." (Example: "I will need your direction in order to call upon you tomorrow.")

Adelaide House - Built over the ancient London Bridge site, in 1921-24.

Adelphi Buildings - (See: Adelphi, the.)

Adelphi Terrace - (Not to be confused with the Adelphi Theatre.) Is part of the Adelphi compound, whereas the entire thing was referred to as: Adelphi. (See, immediately below.)

Adelphi, the - (AKA: Adelphi Buildings.) Beside the Thames, just off the Strand; it was built on the site of Durham House (where the Bishops of Durham had lived; on a quay built on the Thames specifically for this compound.) The land was purchased, ca. 1760, from the Earl of Pembroke, by the four Adam brothers. AN ENCYCLOPAEDIA OF LONDON states: "Robert and James Adam obtained a 99-year lease from the Duke of St. Albans, who then possessed the land, in 1768." Construction took place 1772-4 (two other sources said 1768-72) with Robert, James, and William Adam in charge, and with John Adam as an adviser.

LONDON by Knopf Guides describes it as: "...composed of houses in a relatively plain classical style, with beautifully fashioned interiors, in a long terrace overlooking the Thames. The houses were much sought after by artists at the end of the 18th and beginning of the 19th centuries."

The entire Adelphi consisted of four streets:

- Adelphi Terrace: It faced the river. 1760s. George Bernard Shaw (playwright) lived at 10 Adelphi Terrace from 1896 to 1927. Adelphi Terrace was demolished in 1936; rebuilt as the new Adelphi building (a building of far less stature and size) in 1938-9, 12 floors, 323,550 square feet.
- Adam Street. 1760s. (See at its own listing.)
- John Street: 1760s. Is now known as John Adam Street. (See under J.)
- Robert Street: 1760s.

Mostly gone now, each of these four streets had eleven four-story brick house terraces. Adelphi had a wharf, and basement rooms for storing and handling goods.

Although the Art Society (Royal Society of Arts,) still remains at this old location, again most of the Adelphi is now gone. (See: Royal Society of Arts.) The Society's exterior is almost as it was erected and survived the 1936 demolition (which had to be done due to extensive vandalism.)

The only original rooms surviving from the first building are:

Adam Street: (Note: 7, 8, and 9 were described as tall, plain, dark brick houses.)

- 5 Adam Street.
- 7 Adam Street.
- 8 Adam Street: Is presently a modernized private members' club (simply called: Adam Street,) but it is open to non-members for lunch. The kind of place not easily spotted except for the "8" on one of the double doors.
- 9 Adam Street.
- 10 Adam Street.
- 18 Adam Street.

John Adam Street:

- 2 John Adam Street.
- 4 John Adam Street.
- 6-8 John Adam Street: (See: Royal Society of Arts.)

Lower Robert Street:

- An underground tunnel that was part of the Adelphi's original sub-structure. Still exists; runs from York Buildings down to the Embankment.

Robert Street:

- 1-3 Robert Street: Still standing. Robert Adam lived here for a while.

Royal Terrace: Demolished in 1936. Below are the known Regency addresses there:

- 4 Royal Terrace: Robert Adam's house. Lived here from 1772-1786. Another source said Robert and his brother, James, lived at 3 Robert Street from 1778. Behind the terrace street, connecting it to the Strand, were Adam Street and Robert Street.
- 5 Royal Terrace: The actor Garrick died here in 1779. His widow died here in 1822.
- 6 Royal Terrace: Existed during the Regency.
- 7 Royal Terrace: Savage Club, founded 1857.
- 8 Royal Terrace: Society for the Encouragement of Arts, Manufactures & Commerce. (See under: Royal Society of Arts.)

Adelphi Theatre - 1806. Not to be confused with the Adelphi residence. (See under the THEATRES section.)

Adeney - A tailor. (See: Sackville Street/16.)

Admiral's House - (See: Hampstead Heath/Admiral House.)

Admiralty - (See: Admiralty, the.)

Admiralty Arch - 1910. Separates the Mall from Trafalgar Square. Originally designed to be offices and residences for Royal Navy personnel, and to be a ceremonial passage from Trafalgar Square to Buckingham Palace. Now it houses governmental offices. Three arches, on either side of which is a large wing. The central arch is only opened for ceremonial purposes. It is on one end of the Mall, the other end of the Mall hosting the Victoria Memorial, 1916, designed in memory of Queen Victoria, by Sir Aston Webb. (See: Mall, the, under M.)

Admiralty House - Was added on the south side of the Admiralty in 1786-88, by Samuel Pepys Cockerell, to provide more working room and enlarge the First Lord of the Admiralty's home. (As noted under "Admiralty," above, some of the highest ranking Naval officers lived and worked here.) Entered via the Old Admiralty's courtyard. Red brick.

Admiralty Screen - (See: Admiralty, the.)

Admiralty, the - (Also called: Old Admiralty Building.) Whitehall Street, Spring Gardens, the

Mall, Westminster. By Thomas Ripley, 1722-26, replacing the first 1695-1723 Admiralty here.

Built as a residential building (it looks much more like a private home than a government building) for the Lords of the Admiralty, with but one boardroom designed for the purpose of running the Royal Navy. (It was "normal business" for statesmen to work out of their homes still at this time, a practice that survived from the Middle Ages into the early decades of the 19th century.)

Entrance has two flying horses.

Admiral Horatio Nelson (naval hero) gave orders from here.

Smoking was never allowed within.

The new Admiralty was built in 1895.

"The Admiralty" is also another way of referring to the Royal Navy in general.

- Admiralty Screen: Elegant stone screen, an early commission by Robert Adam, 1759-61.
- Ministry of Defence: Created in 1964; this building is now occupied by a branch thereof.

  - See: Admiralty House - At its own listing.
  - See: Marines.
  - See: Royal Navy - Administrative office of.
  - See: Silver Cross, under the INNS/PUBS section.
  - See: Whitehall/Admiralty.

advocate - (See: lawyer/advocate.)

Agar Street - Covent Garden, Westminster. (Pronounced: aye-gar.) Existed by at least 1824-5, when, as a boy, Charles Dickens had employment on this street. (See: Charing Cross Hospital.)

Agar Town - In 1815 this area was meadow land. By ca. 1840 was a shanty town. In about 1850 it became St. Pancras Station.

age, of - (See: of age.)

age of consent - (For sexual activity.) In England in 1275, it was set at age 12. In 1885 it was changed to age 16, although for those minding children from a position of trust (a doctor, teacher, etc.) the age of consent rose to 18.

- See: marriage - Note regarding minimum ages.
- You may care to see: of age. (Re: turning 21.)

Agnew - (AKA: Thomas Agnew & Sons. Also commonly called: Agnew's.) London art dealer/auction house. Established in Manchester in 1817. Established in London in 1860 by

Agnew's sons; prominent in the London art scene in the late 19th century.

Air Pilots and Air Navigators, Guild of - Founded in 1929. Has no hall.

Air Street - Spoiled the continuity of the Quadrant. (See: Regent Street/Quadrant.) The facing buildings, to compensate, were connected on the first floor (in America, this would be the second floor) via small bridges; the newer Quadrant, ca. 1920s, was built over Air Street, eliminating this need.

ait - Denotes small islands in the Thames. Also seen as "eyot" (and pronounced identically.) Used as part of a place name (as in: Platt's Eyot.)

Albany - Bachelor gentleman's quarters. (See: Piccadilly/Albany - Much more at.)

Albany Cottage - (See: Regent's Park/North Villa.)

Albany Street - Just east of Regent's Park. 1820-5, by Nash.

Albemarle Street - Early 18th C., Mayfair, near Green Park.

- 7: Grillon's Hotel. In 1812-13 a gentlemen's dining club (simply referred to as Grillon's) was founded here as a dining club, intended to be free of political debates. Meetings held in the hotel, weekly, during the sitting of Parliament. The dining club would later meet at the Hotel Cecil; existed into the 20th century; Grillon's was not at 7 Albemarle Street in the Regency; the site then was instead a White Hart Inn. Louis XVIII stayed at this inn for two days in 1814, on his way back to his newly restored throne in France. (See under G.)
- 13: One of Robert Adam's homes, where he died of a burst blood vessel in his stomach, 1792.
- 21: Royal Institution, since 1799. Established to further the teaching of the practical application of science. Chemical lectures were given here. Michael Farraday (scientist/inventor) started here in 1813 (and stayed until his death); the Davy-Farraday Research laboratory was founded and located here in 1890. Number 21 is now known as Farraday Museum.
- 30-34: Brown's Hotel (see under B.)
- 50: John Murray, publisher. Established in London in 1768 by John Murray I. His son (John Murray II, who also lived at this address) made the publishing house well known, and published Jane Austen and Lord Byron, among other greats. (Byron's autobiography was burned here in 1824 following his death, as friends had found its contents too shocking.) The 7th John Murray ran the establishment until it was taken over in 2002 by Hodder Headline, which was acquired in 2004 by Lagardère, an imprint under Hachette UK.
- Garrard's: Jeweler. (See under G.)
- Grillon's Hotel: (See: 7, above.)

Albert Gate - Near Hyde Park Corner.

Albert Hall - 1867. Concert Hall. Named for Queen Victoria's consort, Albert (d. 1861.)

Albert Memorial - 1863-72. Statue of Queen Victoria's much grieved-for husband, Albert.

Albion Street - Known as Grub Street until the early 19th century. Narrow alleys and courts, hosting the lower end of literary types (hack writers and undistinguished publishers; the term "Grub Street" came to mean any work of low literary worth.) Ca. 1830 its name was changed to Milton Street.

- See: Grub Street.
- See: Milton Street.

Albion Terrace - Along Wandsworth Road, south of the Thames. Was a small row consisting of seventeen households. Victorian era (prior to 1848.) Between 1859-62 its name was changed to Milton Terrace.

Albion, the - 10 Thornhill Road, Islington. A former coaching inn, Georgian. Now a pub.

Albury Street - Deptford. (See: Deptford/Albury Street.)

Aldermanbury Square - City. Laid out in 1962, following severe WWII damage to the area.

Aldermen - Leading citizens elected by the City's wards.

- See: Court of Aldermen.
- See: Court of Common Council.
- See: wards.

Aldersgate - One of the City's medieval gates. (See: gates.) Dates from at least the 10th century. Perhaps named for alders that grew there...although some think the name was almost certainly derived from the personal name Ealdred or Aldred. In 1335 the gate was covered with lead and had a small house for the gatekeeper made under it. Demolished in 1617 and rebuilt. Damaged in 1666's Great Fire, but repaired and "beautified." In 1739, repaired again. Removed in 1761. Thomas More House in the Barbican stands near this gate's site.

Not to be confused with Aldgate.

(Also see: Aldersgate Street/62.)

Aldersgate Street - Connected the City and Islington (as did City Road.)

- 61: A pub called the Lord Raglan (Crimean War commander,) stands where a pub has stood since Shakespeare's time; rebuilt in the mid 19th century.
- 62: Aldersgate. Taken down in 1761 (when all of London's gates were demolished.) All that remains now is a commemorating City Corporation plate at its site at the house number: 62.

Aldford House - Park Lane, Westminster. 1897.

Aldgate - The City. Not to be confused with Aldersgate.

- See: Aldgate High Street.

- See: gates.

May be the Æstagate mentioned in a 1052 chronicle; certainly was Alegate by 1108, with Aldgate being seen in 1486. One of the six ancient gates leading from the east into the city in Roman times, this locale is sometimes referred to as "where the East End meets London."

Rebuilt 1108-1147. Repaired in 1215. Chaucer lived in the room above the gate in 1374-85. Rebuilt again in 1607-9. Pulled down in 1761. The street covering the site goes by the same name. From the 17th to the early 20th century, was a home to dressmakers and tailors. There have been glasshouses near Aldgate since 1567, (in 1696 there were 24.) Three of the glassmakers' houses survived into the 20th century.

- Hoop and Grapes: Tavern. (See: Aldgate High Street/47.)
- Sir John Cass's Foundation School: On the corner of Houndsditch. 1710. Moved in 1869 to Duke's Place.

Aldgate High Street - City.

- 47: Hoop & Grapes. May date back to the 1200s. One of the oldest London pubs, surviving from shortly after the Great Fire of 1666. Described as having a long, low, dark interior.
- Three Nuns Hotel: Rebuilt in 1880, but there at least by author Daniel Defoe's time (17th century.)

Aldgate Pump - There since King John's time. Was called St. Michael's Well in the 15th C. owing to a nearby chapel (and well) of that name. A pump was built over the well sometime around the end of the 16th century. The well was moved several feet west ca. 1860-70 so the road could be broadened. Filled in, in 1876. A cistern below the ground was connected to the New River supply, so the Pump still exists after a fashion, a bronze spout shaped as a dog's head.

Aldridge's Horse and Carriage Repository - (See: Horse and Carriage Repository.)

Aldwych - Westminster. Early 20th century. Is a one-way crescent, (eastbound, and both ends connect to the Strand,) and the area surrounding it. AN ENCYCLOPAEDIA OF LONDON states: "This therefore was the village that clustered round their church...and the high road, connecting it with the Hospital of St. Giles, was known up to the beginning of the 17th century as the 'Via de Aldwych,' and is now represented by Drury Lane. The village seems to have faded away, somewhat resurrected in the form of Aldwych Street." Aldwych translates as: old town (or settlement.)

Alexandra Palace - Muswell Hill. 1873. Burned down within days of its opening. Rebuilt. Described as a bit of a white elephant.

Alexander Square - South Kensington, 1827-30.

All-England Club, the Lawn Tennis Championships of the -

- See: tennis.
- See: Wimbledon.

Almack's Assembly Rooms - (Also known simply as: Almack's. Also as: Willis's Rooms, the following proprietor.) Not to be confused with Almack's Club. (See: Almack's Club, at its own listing.)

At 26-28 King's Street, St. James's. This suite of assembly rooms was built specifically for Almack (a Scotsman,) by Robert Mylne. (There are indications Almack's name may actually have been William McCall, or MacCall, and "Almack" was used by him as a fractured anagram.) Opened on 2/20/1765. Three elegant rooms. A club enjoyed by both sexes, a great novelty for the time, for dancing, gaming, gossip, and searching for mates.

No strong drink was allowed.

In ca. 1770 it was described as having: a chaste decoration, gilt columns, pilasters, classic medallions, mirrors, etc. According to THE FACE OF LONDON: "It contained a supper room with a spacious gallery and a ballroom 100 feet long by 40 feet wide, in which as many as 1,700 persons were present upon one occasion."

The only way to attend was to secure vouchers from one of the seven patronesses (or by personal introduction, a rarity.)

VOUCHERS were delivered to a person's home after they were approved by at least one of the patronesses. The voucher was used to purchase tickets to the ball and supper held on Wednesday nights (although the rooms could be rented out for private affairs at any other time); Almack's Wednesday assemblies ran for twelve weeks. The tickets were presented to the doorman (Mr. Willis, for some years) before you were allowed to enter. You could bring a guest, but only one who had already passed the scrutiny of the patronesses. The subscription cost (in essence, the ticket cost, once you'd received your voucher) was ten guineas.

THE WALTZ AT ALMACK'S: The waltz, introduced to London in 1811, took the city by storm in 1812. However, it was not allowed at Almack's as it was deemed scandalous. Tsar Alexander I came to Almack's, unaware of the waltz's ban, in 1814. He called for the waltz, and the patronesses felt they could not deny him, so the waltz was finally permitted at Almack's.

ALMACK'S ONLY RAN FOR 12 WEEKS, starting after Easter.

Very exclusive. No more than two ladies from any one family were to be on the Ladies List at a given time. Ladies' tickets could only be transferred from mother to daughter or between two unmarried sisters; men could not transfer tickets. No lady or gentleman was allowed to obtain more than six tickets from any one patroness. If you came late or dressed inappropriately, you might very well be turned away, even if you were the Duke of Wellington (who really was once turned away for wearing pantaloons instead of the required breeches.) The Patronesses absolutely insisted that gentlemen would appear at their assemblies wearing knee-breeches, a white cravat, and a *chapeau bras* (a kind of flattish, not-high crowned hat.) Only Members of Parliament could break the cardinal rule of 11:00pm (that is, all attendees MUST arrive prior to 11:00pm; no one was admitted so little as one minute late,) but even the Members of Parliament could only arrive late if they had been delayed by business in the House.

The food consisted of lemonade, tea, bread and butter, and stale cake (sources from the time do not write fondly of the offerings.)

During at least part of the Regency, the seven Patronesses often referred to were*:

- Lady Castlereagh
- Lady Cowper (who remarried and became Viscountess Palmerston);
- Lady Jersey (born Sarah Sophia Fane; described by Captain Gronow as "a theatrical tragedy queen: and whilst attempting the sublime, she frequently made herself ridiculous, being inconceivably rude, and in her manner often ill-bred." Not to be confused with her mother, also Lady Jersey/Sarah Anne Child.)
- Lady Sefton ("kind and amiable");
- Madame de Lieven ("haughty and exclusive"; a Russian princess who married Prince Khristofor Andreyevich Lieven);
- Miss Burrell (a Scotswoman; married Sir Peter Burrell in 1807; the family, by royal license, took the name of Drummond-Burrell that same year, possibly at Sir Peter's father's request. Mrs. Drummond-Burrell, along with Princess Esterhazy and Lady Castlereagh, Capt. Gronow described as: *"de très grandes dames.")*
- Princess Esterhazy ("a *bon enfant.*")

*Contemporary sources annually discussed who were to be the patronesses the following year; their members were not set in stone.

The dances in 1814 were listed as Scotch reels and old English country-dances. In 1815 Lady Jersey introduced (from Paris) the quadrille. The waltz was introduced "about this time" (1813 is likely.)

In 1843 it became the Willis Sales Rooms, remaining thus until 1944.

(See: St. James's/King Street/26-28.)

Almack's Club - (Not to be confused with Almack's Assembly Rooms. For the latter, see above at its own listing.) Founded in 1764; opened in 1765, (in the site that became the British Institution in 1805, in Pall Mall.) Twenty-seven noblemen founded it. Rule Number 30 of the original Rules of the Club states: "Any member of this Society that shall become a candidate for any other Club, (Old White's excepted,) shall be ipso facto excluded, and his name struck out of the book." The gambling ran "very deep" here.

In 1780, the place took on the name of: Goosetree's. William Pitt was a member at this time, one of about 25.

Almonry, the - Westminster. Known as a vice district. It was pulled down to make way for Victoria Street.

- Caxton's House: (AKA: Caxton Hall.) William Caxton (printer) was allowed by the Abbey of Westminster to set up business here in 1476 or 77. It was pulled down in 1838. (Not to be confused with a more modern block of buildings known as Caxton House.)

almshouses - These were charity homes for the poor. Historically meager places to reside. "Alms" are, under ancient Christian tradition, donated monies or services in support of the indigent, poor, or sick.

- See: Dulwich.
- See: East Acton.
- See: Hopton Street - Same as at: Southwark/Hopton's Almshouses. (See under S.)
- See: Lady Mico's Almshouses.
- See: Leathersellers' Hall.
- See: Lewisham.
- See: Merchant-Taylors' Hall.
- See: Pest Houses.
- See: Sion College.
- See: Southwark/Hopton Almshouses.
- See: Trinity Almshouses.

Alperton - Brent. In the 18-19th centuries was a typical country village. The Grand Junction Canal came in in 1801, which change brought pleasure-boaters and anglers to the area.

Alsatia - Dangerous, rough district. Land that had at one time been sanctified continued as a place to escape arrest. Every sort of criminal might spend at least some time here. Sir Walter Scott (novelist) described the low area in "The Fortunes of Nigel," 1822 (set in the early 17th century.) Flooded sometimes by the River Fleet.

Amen Corner - (See: Amen Court.)

Amen Court - Late 17th C. houses for the canons of nearby St. Paul's Cathedral. *Amen Corner* is a short "stubby" street that leads to Amen Court. It is said that as the monks walked from St. Paul's reciting the Lord's Prayer, they reached this area as they concluded with "Amen."

- 1-3: Late 17th century buildings.

America - (AKA: The United States of America. Also, prior to 1776: some people referred to America as one of "the Colonies" (Britain had many colonies at the time) after the American Declaration of Independence, and even after the War of 1812; King George III never did entirely make peace with the idea of America's secession.

In quick and limited terms, America came into being when:

The Mayflower arrived at what would be Cape Cod, Massachusetts, on 11/21/1620, where English religious pilgrims founded the Massachusetts Bay Colony (when more colonists arrived in 1630.)

The subsequent 13 colonies remained under British control, but by the 1760s and after the 1773 Boston Tea Party grumbles toward separation from England turned angry.

The American War of Independence ran from 1775-1783.

After Britain had to withdraw from America, the Treaty of Paris was signed in 1783, recognizing the independence of the United States.

In simple terms, the subsequent War of 1812 was fought because Britain was yet seizing American ships and their sailors, claiming they had the right to do so. (See: impressment.) The end of the war finally brought an end to the practice (1815.) The War of 1812 was called by the British (at the time it was happening): "the American War."

Note: While yet a colony, America was one of the places to which transported (British) criminals were banished. (See: transportation.) This practice ended once America declared independence in 1776.

American Embassy, the - AKA: United States Embassy. (See: United States Embassy.)

amphibians - (See: animals, various listings at.)

Ancaster House - Off Curzon Street. 1873, built by the banker Adrian Hope. (See: Richmond Hill.)

Ancient Society of Cogers - Held in the White Lion Tavern, upper Thames Street (at least according to a 1947 source.) Founded in 1755. Its purpose was for the members to gather to debate the events of the week. (See: coger, under C.)

anesthesia - First use of: 1846. Prior to then, for any kind of surgery or amputation, the patient was provided with some combination of: a blindfold, liquor, and/or strong men to hold you down.

- See: antibiotics.
- See: ether - 1846.

- See: laudanum.
- See: medicine - Notes at.

Angel Road - Enfield. In 1557 it was called Watery Lane, and then Marsh Lane. Current name dates from the 1870s.

Angel Square - Islington High Street, Islington. The square's name came later, but this part of Islington was a very busy traffic area since ca. the 1670s (or earlier) and generally was called Angel after the busy coaching inn here of the name. Thomas Paine (d. 1809) wrote *The Rights of Man* while living here in 1791. (See: Angel/Islington, under the INNS/PUBS section.)

anglers/angling - (See: fishing.)

Anglicans - Members of the Church of England. (All churches listed in the CHURCHES/CHAPELS section were Anglican during the Regency, unless otherwise noted.) Anglicanism was the official religion of England during the Regency. If you were not Anglican, you couldn't attend university and couldn't run for Parliament.

By 1772, Dissenters could attend classes at Cambridge, but they could not ultimately graduate with a degree. This was challenged in 1834, but it wasn't until 1856 that some degrees were opened to Dissenters, with almost all remaining blocks removed in 1871. Oxford followed a similar path, allowing Dissenters to obtain degrees in the 1850s.

- See: dissolution of the monasteries.
- See: Church of England - For a description of Anglican clergy.

animals - Meaning, creatures that existed in England at the time of the Regency.

"Fair game" has a British legal meaning: under the 18th century's 32 hunting laws, George III meant to stop landowners from being denuded of their livestock. By the early 1800s no one could take game from owned land except the local squire or his oldest son, with the exception of small birds and vermin, these latter being considered "fair game."

It should also be noted that there were strict poaching laws, going back for many centuries. For instance, it was illegal for anyone but the landowner (or one given his permission) to hunt deer or hares on his land.

This list includes domesticated and wild creatures. (It is not an all-inclusive list.)

badger

bat

~~bear~~ - Extinct in England since at least the Middle Ages. After that, they were only sometimes seen in menageries or imported for bear-baiting (illegal after 1835.)

~~beaver~~ - No longer native to England, having been hunted to extinction well before the nineteenth century; beaver skins for Regency hats (and since) therefore came from Canada. (See: beaver, under B.)

boar

bull* - (See *, below.)

cat

chicken

cow* - (See *, below.)

deer - Fallow deer, red deer; also see: muntjac, below.

- See: poaching, under P.
- See: Wimbledon Chase - For 19th C. stag hunts.

dog - There were quite a few breeds that the modern eye would recognize, but the classification of breeds came post-Regency. Some general breeds you'd be able to spot (looking more or less as you'd expect): beagle, bull dog (taller than today's,) dalmatian (called a: coach dog,) greyhound, hound, mastiff, pointer, setter, spaniel, springer, Shepherd's Dog (looking rather like a Border Collie,) terrier. As you can see, it was more about types/what job they were needed for, than breeds. (Although, some bloodlines were carefully recorded, sort of the beginning of the classification of breeds.)

duck

fox

frog

goat

goose

hare

hedgehog

horse* (See *, below.)

mole

mouse

muntjac - A kind of small deer.

musk rat

otter

ox (oxen)

pig & hog - (Swine.)

rabbit

rat - And water rat.

rooster

sheep - The UK has hosted many, many sheep over the centuries, wool being one of the Commonwealth's most important products.

snake

squirrel

stoat

toad

vole

weasel

~~wolf~~ - Extinct in Britain from the later 17th century.

*Bulls, cows, and horses were collectively called: cattle. For instance, a man might call to have his cattle hitched to his carriage, but of course he means his horses, not his bovines.

- You may care to see: birds.
- You may care to see: cattle.
- You may care to see: fish.

Too, menageries caged any number of exotic animals not native to England.

- See: London School of Veterinary Surgery.
- See: zoos.

Antarctica - It's hard to say exactly when Antarctica was first discovered/ recorded, because back to the late 16th C. various outlying islands were noted. What's clear is the first European to cross it was Capt. James Cook in 1773.

antibiotics - Were not yet discovered/known to Regency era medicine. Indeed, they didn't really understand the concept of germs.

- See: medicine - Comments at.
- See: penicillin - 1928.

Anti-Slavery Society - Founded in 1823, superseding the Society for the Abolition of the Slave Trade. (See under S.) Worked to further the abolition of slavery, already illegal in England, throughout the British colonies.

Antiquaries, Society of - (See: Society of Antiquaries.)

antiques/auction houses - (See: auction houses.)

apartment - (See: flat, a.)

Apothecaries' Hall - For the Worshipful Society of Apothecaries. East side of Blackfriars Lane. Livery Hall, founded in 1617, when the Apothecaries' Society broke away from the Grocers' Company.

The right to practice surgery and to "physic" patients/illnesses was made a matter of examination in 1511. Professional surgeons and physicians resented the lesser (less learned) among them, so in 1543 an Act was passed to give these so-called less learned persons permission to "minister medicines."

In 1606, under a charter from James I, the Apothecaries united with the Grocers', but within eleven years they divided. Up until the split, the Grocers' had been the sellers of drugs.

The first hall was in Cobham House (on the present site,) purchased from Lady Howard in 1632. Destroyed by the Great Fire of 1666. The present hall dates from 1670, of "heavy-lidded" brick.

The present courtyard (it has a very short doorway that leads in) dates from 1671, by Locke. The block facing Blackfriars Lane was built in 1684, being much altered in 1779. Circular windows were added in 1786 as well as a pediment, and the brickwork was then stuccoed. The company's coat of arms is above the door.

The 1815 Apothecaries Act (amended in 1874) required some kind of certification of skills, to help avoid quackery. The Society founded a retail drug business in 1822; closed in 1922.

THE ENCYCLOPAEDIA OF LONDON states: "The Pharmacy Act of 1852 put the chief powers of regulating pharmaceutical chemistry into the hands of the Pharmaceutical Society of Great Britain, so the Apothecaries turned their attention to the licensing of practitioners. They obtained recognition as practitioners under the Medical Act of 1858…."

- ➢ See: doctors/apothecary.
- ➢ See: Society of Apothecaries.

apothecary - (See: doctors/apothecary.)

appendicitis - Was usually fatal until ca. 1902 (at which time a successful appendectomy was performed on Prince Albert Edward, 6/24/1902, just two months before he was crowned as Edward VII.)

apprentices - Their term of service (sometimes fair, sometimes slave-like) usually lasted 7 years, during which they were to learn their trade. They could not marry until service was over. Compulsory apprenticeships were abolished in 1814.

Apsley House - The Duke(s) of Wellington home, with the nickname address of "Number One, London." Probably known by this nickname because it was the first house seen by travelers approaching London from the West; Hyde Park Corner was mere steps from Apsley House; the house so called from the early 19th century. Its *real* address is: 149 Piccadilly. (Is now the Wellington Museum, having been gifted to the nation by the Wellington family in 1947.) The present duke still resides here, using the attic rooms.

The first duke's soldiers (who fought at Waterloo) would drill on a barracks square opposite the house (where a fashionable hotel, The Berkeley, now stands.)

Apsley House is situated in the southeast corner of Hyde Park. Built in 1771-8, by Robert Adam for the patron Lord Bathurst, Baron Apsley (also then the lord chancellor.) Bought by Arthur (later the 1st Duke of Wellington) from his brother, the 1st Marquess Wellesley, who lived here by 1810. Arthur lived here from 1816-52, and from some time until 1829 the Iron Duke had nearly all the Adam's interiors taken out. The crown freehold was presented to him in 1830. At first the house was red brick, but while the Duke owned it, it was resurfaced with Bath stone and given a Corinthian portico, under Wyatt, ca. 1828.

It was originally intended to be the outer entrance to (the new) Buckingham Palace, so at first faced Hyde Park Screen (directly south of Piccadilly); the arch moved to its present location in the 1880s. A controversial bronze equestrian statue (as mentioned above in this paragraph) was added to the arch's top in 1846; this was taken down in the 1880s and replaced with the quadriga currently atop the arch.

IRON DUKE: After stones were thrown at his windows in 1831 (his house was unlighted, which was taken at the time as a sign that the inhabitants supported parliamentary reform (to allow Irishmen and/or Catholics into Parliament,) the Duke put iron shutters on the windows. This action earned him the nickname "the Iron Duke."

The Hall survived WWII.

- Achilles statue: 1822. At the back of the house.
- Waterloo Gallery, the: Built in Apsley House in 1828 by Benjamin Wyatt.
- Wellington Arch: In front of the house. Dates from 1828, to a design by Decimus Burton, and topped by Adrian Jones's bronze quadriga (a four-horse chariot,) ca. 1912-14. Also known by its post-Regency name: Constitution Arch. The statue on top is officially named "Peace Descending on the Quadriga of War."
    - See: Constitution Arch.
    - See: Hyde Park Corner/Wellington Arch.

archaeological studies - First practiced (in a more formal sense) in Britain in the 17th C., although a general interest in the study wasn't strong until into the 20th century.

archery - In addition to men, this sport was deemed an acceptable pastime for ladies. (See: Toxophilite Society.)

arches - There are many architectural arches in London, some ancient and crumbling, some grand.

- See: Admiralty Arch.
- See: Constitution Arch.
- See: Marble Arch.

Archway Road - East of Highgate Hill, Islington. Part of the Great North Road. Built in 1808 (second source said the 1820s,) built so traffic could avoid the steepness of Highgate Hill.

There was a tollgate here from 1813-1864.

➢ See: Highgate Hill/Archway.

➢ See: Holloway/Archway Road.

- Archway Bridge: 1900.
- Archway Tavern: 1888, third public house at this site in 300 years.

Argyle Rooms - (See: Argyll Rooms.)

Argyll House - Chelsea. 1723, by Giacomo Leoni (a Venetian.) Famous tenants have included the 18th C. composer of "Rule Britannia," one Dr. Thomas Augustine Arne; and the 20th C. actor Peter Ustinov. (See: Rule Britannia, under R.)

Argyll Rooms - (Sometimes also seen written as: Argyle Rooms.) Was first the mansion home of John Campbell, 2nd Duke of Argyll, standing on King Street's east side. Part of the house was pulled down in 1736, making way for Little Argyll Street. Changed hands a few times, eventually coming to Henry Greville, who added to the house and updated it, opening it as the Argyll Rooms in 1806. It was a venue for concerts, masquerades, and the like.

During the Regency, hosted the Cyprian's Ball (fashionable impures) once a year.

Tarts aside, you had to have more than just your name in Debrett's to be invited to the Argyll Rooms; membership was select. Corner of Regent Street (which was then Swallow Street) and Little Argyll Street from 1806.

In 1818 it transferred to 246 Regent Street; built for the Philharmonic Society of London, which held concerts here until it burned in 1830. (See: Philharmonic Society of London.)

Not to be confused with a later Argyle Subscription Rooms, a Victorian music hall which became part of the London Trocadero, 1849-1878.

Arlington House - Was situated on the southern portion of land that evolved into Buckingham Palace; occupied by the Earl of Arlington. Demolished in 1703.

Arlington Street - Camden Town. Charles James Fox (Whig statesman) lived here from 1804, where he resided until his death in 1806. (Although he actually died at the Duke of Devonshire's Chiswick House.)

- 22: Wimbourne House. Property now owned by the Ritz Hotel and currently called the William Kent House. (See: Wimbourne House.)

Armourers' and Brasiers' Hall - A brasier is someone who works brass.

➢ See: Coleman Street/Armourers' and Brasiers' Hall.

➢ See: halls/Armourers' and Brasiers' Hall.

army - Britons, due to old offenses (such as seizing of property) were yet in the Regency era generally disenchanted with any kind of standing national army. They preferred the Navy, as it was strong, world-spanning, and (perhaps most importantly) not as likely to invade your home or take your stock. The infamous British red coats (the garment) came into being ca. 1704-14.

While impressment was practiced during war-times, so, too, was the use of militia, which were voluntary home soil civilian volunteers. Not full-time, they served to defend local lands and protect coasts.

- See: impressment - Seizing of men for the navy (and army.)
- See: militia - Civilians.
- See: Royal Guards - All of whom are soldiers in the British Army.
- See: Royal Military College - For officer training.

Army and Navy Club - (AKA: The Rag.) Gentlemen's club, formed for officers of the British and Commonwealth Armed Services, 1837. (See under the CLUBS section.)

Arnold Circus - Post-Regency. (See: London Hospital, the note under.)

art/artists -

- See: Ackermann's Repository of Art.
- See: Adelphi - Homes for artists.
- See: Berners Street.
- See: British Institution.
- See: Dulwich Picture Gallery.
- See: Fleet Street/53/Laurie and Whittle - Print shop.
- See: Royal Society of Arts - For important information on obtaining art in the 18-19th centuries.
- See: Society of Painters in Watercolours.
- See: Southampton/Gallery of Arts.
- See: Temple of Fancy.

Arthur Street - Victorian.

Arthur's - 1832. (See: Carlton Club, under the CLUBS section.)

artificial respiration - For drowning persons, 1773. (See: Royal Humane Society - Notes at.)

Arundel House - Tudor, gone after the 17th century. (See: Roman Bath.)

Arundel Place - A cul-de-sac of Georgian design. (Now the site of the Lyons Corner House, 1908.)

Ascot - (Pronounced: as-cut.) In the town of Windsor, on Ascot Heath. The horse racecourse was established in 1711 by Queen Anne. The first Ascot Gold Cup was run in 1806. In 1825, George IV drove down the course in a coach and four, the Duke of Wellington beside him, prior to the race. Didn't become the wildly popular social event we think of today until Queen Victoria's time. Held in June.

Asgill House - (See: Richmond Green/Asgill House.)

Ashburnham House - Little Dean's Yard. Was first a monastic school attached to a Benedictine abbey. 1665 townhouse, for the Ashburnham family, possibly by John Webb. Now engulfed in Westminster School, hosting its library. Is said to have London's finest 17th C. domestic interior. Named Ashburnham House in 1820.

Ashburton Park - 1788. (See: Woodside/Ashburton Park.)

asparagus - Grown in England from at least 1760, possibly much earlier.

- See: Battersea Fields.
- See: Nine Elms.

Asprey & Co. - (See: New Bond Street/165-9.)

Assize Courts - (Also referred to as: the Assizes.) These were courts held by traveling judges who made a regular circuit through the countryside, hearing both civil and criminal cases. This system was abolished in 1971, and became the Crown Courts in 1972. (See: justices of the peace.)

Astley's Amphitheatre - (AKA: Astley's Circus and the Pantomime. AKA: Astley's Amphitheatre of the Arts.) Opened in 1768 as an open riding school. Burned in 1794; rebuilt; with another fire in 1803, and another rebuild. In 1773, Philip Astley opened the first proper circus in England, here on the Westminster Bridge Road, Lambeth. Converted to a theatre in 1780. Philip Astley died in 1814; his son, John, only lived to 1821. The third (Regency) reincarnation sat 3,000 people. Always had a splendid exterior. Bill of fare ranged from "equestrianised" Shakespeare to medieval plays (often an adaptation of Scott's plays,) to military melodrama. These equestrian dramas were called hippodramas. Had: an orchestra, the glow of lights, smell of horses, choruses dancing, clowns. Had few fire exits. Rebuilt again in 1843. Pulled down in 1893. There only remains today a plaque at 225 Westminster Bridge Road, as the site is (since the 1960s) covered by a St. Thomas's Hospital extension.

(See: Wych Street/Olympic Theatre, for another business owned by Philip Astley.)

Astronomical Society of London - (See: Royal Astronomical Society.)

astronomy -

- See: Greenwich Observatory.
- See: Kensington/Campden Hill Road - For note on Mr. James South.
- See: Kew Observatory.
- See: Royal Astronomical Society.

asylum - Alternate term for "hospital," or "orphanage," or "house of refuge," or even "school." At that time, the use of the term did not imply the patients were suffering from insanity, even though there *were* two asylums in London for those termed insane (Bedlam, and St. Luke's Hospital.)

- See: Bedlam.
- See: hospitals.
- See: Lambeth Asylum.
- See: Old Street/St. Luke's Hospital.

Asylum for Female Orphans - (AKA: Royal Female Orphanage.) Lambeth. (See: Lambeth Asylum.)

Athenaeum, the - Gentlemen's club in Waterloo Place, Pall Mall (116 St. James's.) Founded in 1824; erected 1827-30. Built partly over the site of Carlton House. The upper story was added on in 1899. (See under the CLUBS section.)

Athenian Lyceum, the - A debating society, a less-formal men's club interested in Parliamentary reforms. Came into being ca. 1817. (See: Piccadilly/22.)

attorney - (See: lawyer, where it also describes barristers, solicitors, etc.)

Aubrey House - (See: Kensington/Aubrey Street/Aubrey House.)

auction houses -

- See: Christie's.
- See: Montpelier Street/Bonham's.
- See: Old Bond Street/34/Sotheby's.
- See: Phillips.

Auction Mart, the - St. Bartholomew's Lane. It was a commercial building, built by a joint stock company made up of auctioneers, in 1829. In 1873 the building became the Alliance Bank.

Austin Friars - Street near the Bank of England, north of where Throgmorton and Old Broad Street come to a junction. "Austin" is the corrupted version of "Augustine," its name being derived from a church priory of Augustinian friars who resided here starting in 1253. The church was rebuilt in 1354, to be more elaborate. Henry VIII disestablished the friars during the Dissolution in 1538. By 1550 (with a slip out, and in again, of royal favor) the property was given by Edward VI to Dutch Protestant refugees, whose church in London it remained for centuries. It became the Dutch Church. (See: Dutch Church, under the CHURCHES section.)

Severely damaged in an 1862 fire, but restored by 1865, in Decorated Gothic style. Utterly ruined by a WWII land mine.

Australia - "Discovered" by the Dutch in the 17th C., but not much visited by Europeans until later. At this time it was called New Holland.

Capt. James Cook came to Botany Bay in 1770 (calling the land New South Wales.) There were plans to colonize New South Wales as early as 1779, but the War of Independence in America provided a financial block. After the war, America was no longer available for Britain to use for purposes of transportation of convicts, so New South Wales again became an area of interest to the British Crown (plus a desire to have a counter to Dutch and French presences in the Pacific.) Eleven vessels sailed in 1787 from Spithead, 756 convicts on board; 33 died en route. Arrived in January, 1788.

Botany Bay, being inhospitable, was left behind in favor of settling at Port Jackson, and eventually at Sydney Cove.

The whole continent came formally under the British government in 1829.

There were many referendums on unification (with Britain,) but it wasn't until 1/1/1901 that the Commonwealth of Australia came into existence by royal proclamation.

Australia House - The Strand. 1918. The Australian High Commission/embassy.

- See: Royal Courts of Justice - The final passages concerning the Quit Rent.
- See: Wych Street.

Ave Maria Lane - City. Is the southern extension of Warwick Lane. Purportedly when monks walked toward St. Paul's, by the time they got to this street they were done with the Lord's Prayer and were starting in on the Hail Mary (*Ave Maria*, in Latin.) This street dates back to at least 1670. (See: Stationers' Hall.)

Avery Row - 1720s. (See: Mayfair/Avery Row.)

Axminster carpets - Fashionable. (See: Worcestershire/Humphries of Kidderminster, in the BRITISH COUNTIES section.)

-B-

B & B - "Bed and Breakfast." Often a small hotel-like environment, also often run out of a family home, that provides an overnight room, access to a toilet (and possibly bathing facilities,) and usually includes the next morning's breakfast. Modern term.

baby bottles - If you were unable to nurse your child (or chose not to,) you usually hired a wet nurse (a woman who had had a child and still was producing milk.) Since ancient times there were forms of baby bottles, however. The simplest form was a twist of cloth that could be dipped into milk and put in the baby's mouth to suckle; this may have been more for soothing (like a pacifier) than for feeding. But museums have round or oblong "bottles" made of wood or horn or leather, with a hole in the end, sometimes covered with cloth to slow the flow. They also had feeder cups (rather like today's toddler cups, except with a spout rather than a lid) for older children and invalids. (You may care to see: wet nurse.)

bachelor apartments - During the Regency era, women could not take chambers among bachelors' rooms.

- ➢ See: Adelphi.
- ➢ See: Conduit Street/Limmer Hotel.
- ➢ See: flat, a - For an explanation of how bachelors' rooms were different during the Regency era.
- ➢ See: hotel - For how Regency era hotels differed from modern ideas of hotels.
- ➢ See: Piccadilly/Albany.
- ➢ See: St. James's.

badminton - Takes its name from Badminton, Gloucestershire, where the game was first played ca. 1870. The Badminton Association of England (Bromley, Kent) founded in 1893. Note, though, there were other games with racquets and/or shuttlecocks played from centuries past. (See: tennis.)

Bagnigge Wells - King's Cross. Was a (smaller) pleasure garden, popular as a retreat as early as 1680; formalized ca. 1760. Well into the 18th C. the area is described as being resorted to by the lower sort of tradesman (as a leisure site); many references support that Londoners came here to take the waters, but that it was not the most refined locale (with there being an issue with nearby highwaymen at least as late as the end of the 18th century.) The Fleet flowed through it, which banks were oft sat upon for smoking, drinking, cider, and other leisure activities by those who were otherwise not permitted on the grounds (the lower orders.)

- Bagnigge House: Home to Nell Gwynne, Charles II's mistress. Ca. 1760 two mineral springs were discovered in the gardens, thus leading to the founding of Bagnigge Wells.
- Bagnigge Wells Road - Holborn. In 1863 became known as King's Cross Road.

baked beans - Introduced by Fortnum & Mason in 1886.

Baker Street - Marylebone, near Regent's Park. Some building in 1755, but built mainly between 1785-1800, and named for its builder, William Baker. The northern section of Baker Street (as it is now and has been since ca. 1925) was formerly known as York Place.

She did not settle in Baker Street until 1835.

Her real name was Marie Grosholtz, of Switzerland.

In 1884, there was a fire, so the waxworks moved to its present site on Marylebone Road.

- ➢ See: Portman Square.
- ➢ See: York Place.

- 11: This house is thought to date from the Regency. It was destroyed by WWII bombing. Some "Sherlockians" suppose this was the house Sir Arthur Conan Doyle envisioned as the residence of Sherlock Holmes (under the fictional number of 221b, of course.)

- 14: William Pitt the Younger lived here, 1800-1806.
- 221b: There was no such address, of course, until the postal service created it to handle the yearly influx of letters addressed to Sherlock Holmes and Dr. John Watson. (In truth, the letters go to the nearby Abbey National Building Society, which has a full-time employee just for answering "Holmes'" mail. The actual address is 239 Baker Street, but is marked 221b. Holmes' flat (interior of "his" apartment) was created for the Festival of Britain in 1951, and now resides at the Sherlock Holmes pub on Northumberland Avenue. (See: 11, above in this entry.)
- Madame Tussaud's Waxworks: Was here on Baker Street 1835-84. Is presently located on Marylebone Road. LONDON ACCESS calls Madame Tussaud's waxworks a "British Institution since 1765." MYSTERY READER'S WALKING GUIDE: LONDON says Madam Tussaud escaped to London in 1802 (having been imprisoned in France for making wax models of guillotine victims.) She opened a waxworks shop in the Strand sometime between 1802-35.

bakers - For centuries, on Sundays bakers would fire up their ovens in order to (for a small fee) cook local wives' and bachelors' joints of meat (usually intended to be consumed for the better part of the week.) This practice, in rural areas, even lasted as late as the 1930s. The same was true of some pubs, which heated a griddle for those who bought a steak or cut from the butcher and brought it directly for their supper.

- See: Bakers' Hall.
- See: confectioners.
- See: Gunter's.
- See: Old Bond Street/Stewart's.

Bakers' Hall - For the Worshipful Company of Bakers. East side of Harp Lane. The fraternity of Bakers was thriving by 1155, enough so to share with the government the take on the toll of baking. From AN ENCYCLOPAEDIA OF LONDON: "From before the Conquest, the regulation of bread-baking was strict, and punishment for transgressions severe, a third offence entailing lifelong disqualification." Breaking into two factions, the bakers of brown bread and bakers of white bread were strictly required to bake only one or the other, a rule firmly enforced until 1654 (brown bread being any baked from a "mixture of grains.") The factions reunited in 1645 as the Worshipful Company of Bakers (chartered as: Master and Wardens of the Mystery or Art of Baking of the City of London; 1307.) The first Hall was thought to be at Dowgate, 1490. Bakers' Hall was here (Harp Lane) since 1506. This (or a later version) was destroyed by the Great Fire of 1666; rebuilt in 1675. This burned in 1715 (at which time they spent awhile at the Butchers and the Brewers,) leading to a 1719-22 rebuild, with further wainscoting added in 1772. New roof in 1806. Restored by James Elmes ca. 1825. Totally destroyed by WWII bombs in 1940; rebuilt, same site, in 1963.

Bakewell Hall - Existed by 1356. Located on Guildhall Yard's east side. Purportedly named for a John de Bankewelle. Was a market place for woolen clothing, notably cloth made by foreigners. Rebuilt in 1588. Burned in the Great Fire of 1666; rebuilt in 1672. Demolished in 1820 for the building of the Court of Common Pleas.

Ball Court - An old street. Has avoided Victorian widening and post-WWII reconstruction.

ballad-sellers - Old women or children (sometimes men) who sang in the streets for coins. They provided a way by which new songs and/or lyrics could be learned by low and grand alike.

Balmoral - Scotland. Royal residence. Purchased by Queen Victoria in 1852. (See: Scotland/Edinburgh/Balmoral, (erroneously) under the BRITISH COUNTIES section.)

Baltic Exchange - Originated at the end of the 17th C., and most likely evolved out of the Baltic Coffee House, which moved to Threadneedle Street in 1744. Its business was trade with Russia. Moved into the South Sea House when that establishment went vacant in 1854; there until 1899. Today is the only international shipping exchange in the world. (You may care to see: Exchange, for a list of other kinds of exchanges.)

Bank of England - Threadneedle Street (there since 1734.) The bank was founded with the passage of the Tunnage Act by Parliament, and received its Royal Charter in 1694 to raise money for a war with France; it remained the Government's bank until it became publicly owned (nationalized) in 1946. For a short while it was known as the Tunnage Bank.

In the 18th (and first half of the 19th) centuries, the Bank of England was one of many banks (some of which were financially quite shady,) until beginning ca. 1720 when the disastrous financial ruin of the South Sea Bubble led to the Bank of England's eventual rise as *the* national bank. (See: South Sea Bubble, under S.)

The Bank's first few months were spent at Mercers' Hall, Cheapside; moved near the end of 1694 to Grocers' Hall, Princess Street, the Poultry, where it stayed until 1734, when it moved to Threadneedle Street; the Threadneedle Street property was bought in 1724, and between 1724-34 was developed, a commissioned single-story building.

In 1766 Prime Minister Pitt the Elder put the bank under government control directly.

The Bank of England was the leader, by far, in issuing notes (i.e. paper money,) and alone had the issuance of larger denomination notes. It was obliged to be able to exchange notes for gold until 1797, but this was relaxed thereafter.

In the late 18th C. Sheridan (dramatist) dubbed it "The Old Lady of Threadneedle Street," a nickname still heard today. There is a figure, high in the bank's pediment, that added to this nickname; she holds a model of the bank and is supposedly meant to be Britannia; dates from the 1920s.

The Bank was attacked during the 1780 Gordon Riots; thus began the nightly tradition wherein the Bank was placed under military protection every night, until in 1973 when the Bank secured its own protective force. These guards (gate-keepers) still wear long-tailed pink coats with scarlet waistcoats, as do the messengers (supposedly the livery of the bank's first governor, Sir John Houblon.)

Sir John Soane enlarged the building in 1788; this took ages to be agreed upon, finally producing Soane's masterpiece of Greek Revival in 1808. The eight feet thick outer walls that Soane built still exist; they are windowless. Its entrance doors are described as "foreboding."

In 1844 a law was passed dividing the bank into two parts: 1) the note-issuing function, and 2) the general banking/responsibility for guarding the financial reserves of the country.

It was remodeled on a large scale again in 1924-39 by Sir Herbert Baker, removing the old halls, leaving for view only Soane's outer wall and columns.

A working wind dial was installed in 1805 in the grand courtroom (for determining wind direction, as ships could only come up the Thames when the wind came from the east.)

The bank was privately owned until 1946, when it became nationalized.

- Bank Stock Office: Built in 1792.
- Dividend Office, the: 1818-23.
- East Wing: Added in 1766, by Sir Robert Taylor.
- Hall, the: From which bank notes were issued.
- Rotunda: 1796.
- West Wing: Added in 1786, by Sir Robert Taylor.
    - See: banks/banking.
    - See: money, under M - For descriptions of paper notes and coins.
    - See: South Sea Bubble, under S - For its effect on the rise of the Bank of England.

Bank of Scotland - Based in Edinburgh, Scotland. Incorporated in 1695. Held the monopoly on the issue of Scottish notes (paper money) until 1716.

- See: Royal Bank of Scotland - The Bank of Scotland's rival.
- See: Fleet Street/1.

banks/banking - The origins of banking trace back to merchants of the 13-14th century. Maybe even the 12th century in Florence. They were private banks (and goldsmiths) serving as moneylenders. "Official" banking (more as we know it) began in the 17th C. in England.

- See: Bank of England - Founded in 1694.
- See: Bank of Scotland.
- See: Barclay's - Its emblem: an eagle.
- See: clearing house.
- See: Coutts Bank.
- See: Fleet Street/1/Royal Bank of Scotland.
- See: goldsmiths.
- See: Hoare's Bank.
- See: Lloyd's Bank.
- See: Lombard Street - Long the site for many independent banks.
- See: money - For a list of coins and banknotes.

Bankside - The longest walk in London. Also sometimes seen as: Bank Side. (See: Southwark/Bankside, the latter of which borders on Southwark.)

Banqueting House - (AKA: Banqueting Hall.) Burned in 1619. (See: Whitehall, Royal Palace of/Banqueting House.)

Baptists - (As in the religion.) Formed in the 17th C.; in London by 1612. In 1660 Baptists had flourished, forming 200-300 congregations in and around London.

The Reformed Baptists separated in the 1640s for specific theological differences (among them: doctrine of salvation) from the traditional Baptists.

- See: Corporation for the Propagation of the Gospel in New England.
- See: New Park Street Chapel.

Barbers' Hall - For the Barber-Surgeons' Company. Monkwell Street. In 1163 the clergy were prohibited from practicing surgery, which allowed the Barbers to assume this function. By 1308 there began a "Barbers Gild," which was ruled by a master; it had two masters by 1376 and was prohibiting unqualified practitioners. The guild has held its meetings on Tuesdays since 1308.

The first Barbers' Hall was built in Monkwell Street in 1381.

In medieval times, a barber's place of business would be marked by a striped pole sign (the vestiges of which can be seen to this day, even in America.)

Incorporated in 1540, by statute, with the Surgeons.

Inigo Jones added a court-room and a surgical theatre to the Hall ca. 1636. The Great Fire of 1666 burned most all of the buildings, sparing the court-room and theatre; restored in 1678.

In 1745 the Barbers and the Surgeons were separated, again by statute.

Ca. 1752-3 there were extensive repairs to Barbers' Hall, and a cupola was added. During the 18th C., dissection of criminals' bodies following hangings were carried out here (to learn about the systems in the body.) The surgical-theatre was demolished somewhere around 1753.

Warehouses replaced most of the Hall buildings in 1863-4, excepting the court-room (and which the Barbers' Company retained and consequently then made into the Hall.) Utterly destroyed in WWII. The current Hall dates from 1969, still on the same site. The Barbers' are not much related to that trade anymore, but these days are more closely tied to the medical fields. It is rated 17th in the order of guild precedence.

Barbican Center - 20th C. (1960s) arts complex. "Barbican" derives its name from a barbican (medieval watch tower) that stood in this area in Norman times, the latter pulled down in 1267.

Barclay's Bank - Began at 54 Lombard Street in 1690, developed out of a goldsmith's place of business (John Freame and Thomas Gould,) here in 1694. In 1736, Freame's son-in-law, James Barclay was made a partner, it then being Freame and Barclay. In 1896, Barclay's took over many other banks, at this time having a strong Quaker connection (and some smaller banks of which had themselves been started from goldsmith roots.) Still exists. Its emblem is an eagle. (See: banks/banking.)

Barclay's Brewery - Barclay, Perkins & Co Ltd, Anchor Brewery, Park Street, Southwark. Founded by James Monger in 1616 by James Monger, and became Barclay, Perkins in 1781. Registered in June 1896. In 1955 merged with Courage & Co, forming Courage & Barclay Ltd. Brewing other than lager ceased in 1958 and all brewing ceased in the 1970s. Site now redeveloped for housing. In its day, 12 or 15 barrels of beer were brewed in a day.

bargemen - Those who help push barges. In Victorian times, the men who worked the barges *on the canals* preferred to be called "boatmen" (as opposed to bargemen.) Those canal boatmen were not well-respected, due to having to work seven days a week, with no time off for church, so they were dubbed heathens, or so went the logic of the time. The law was changed later in the 19th C. to allow the men Sundays off.

(You may care to see: watermen.)

Barker & Howard - Watney Street. It still prints navigational books; being one of London's oldest firms (started purportedly prior to 1490, although Christopher Barker lived ca. 1529-1599.) This company descended from Christopher and Robert Barker, father and son printers of the 16-17th centuries, who produced many versions of the Bible (1611,) and were printers to Queen Elizabeth I.

Barker Panorama - (See: Leicester Square/Barker Panorama.)

Barking - Ancient market town on the River Roding, 10 miles/16 km from Westminster. Joined to Ilford on the north, London on the west. Creeks and mud-flats; a fishing village. There once was an abbey here, founded 675, and burned in 870 by Vikings. From the 14-19th centuries it was a fishing community, fishing being especially important to this community up to the 1850s.

- Eastbury Square:
    - Eastbury Manor House: 1572. Red-brick manor house, described as "grim."
- St. Margaret's Barking: Norman, with Early English additions. The churchyard has an ancient gateway that is two stories high, with an embattled parapet and a turret. (See under the CHURCHES section.)

Barnard's Inn - 20-23 Holborn. 16th century. Hall, built as part of John Markworth's London mansion (he was the Dean of Lincoln); thusly the inn, in 1454, was first known as "Macworth Inne." It was soon leased to one Lionel Bernard, from which "Barnard" derived. Lionel Bernard owned it briefly, but he soon leased it to Grays Inn legal students. It was an Inn of Chancery.

In 1888 the lease renewal was refused, the Dean seeing the inn as little more than a dining club; the freehold was bought by Bartle Frere (acting as a trustee,) and who sold it to the Mercers' Company. Demolished in the 20th century (although the remains of an Inn of Chancery remain.) From 1894-1958 it was the site of the newly built Mercers' School, replacing most of the old buildings (but not the Hall.) In 1933, much of the Hall was decaying, so a replica was reconstructed using as much original material as possible.

Barnet - The highest spot (425 feet) on the Great North Road. The village of Barnet existed before 1471; it was an important posting place for outbound London coaches in the 17-18th centuries.

- Barnet fair: Ancient horse fair (for horse-trading,) still held in September. Barnet was in the 19th C. quite a distance for Londoners to come.
- Child's Hill: Hendon. In the early 19th C. was an industrial area, including brick and tile-making. Also known for handling the laundering for Hampstead residents. When railways came in (1840-50s) became known as Cricklewood. By the late 19th C. was a "disgracefully poor" district.
- High Barnet: CHAMBERS LONDON GAZETTEER provides: "Modern maps usually treat High Barnet as the area north of Wood Street, and Chipping Barnet as the part to the south and southeast, but history does not recognize this distinction and nor does the local population." The name did not catch on until after a railway station opened here in 1872.

- New Barnet: Victorian area.
- St. Mary's Church: 1856.
- South Barnet: (See under S.)

Barnsbury - Rural area in Islington. Its name is a corruption of "Villa de Iseldon Berners," medieval manor lords. (See: Islington/Barnsbury.)

- Pentonville Prison: 1842. (See under P.)

barons of London - (See: Court of Aldermen.)

barrister - (See: lawyer/barrister.)

Bartell's Building - (See under: Holborn/Bartell's Building.)

Bartholomew Close - This area escaped the Great Fire of 1666, so it featured timbered medieval buildings. Leads out of Little Britain. William Hogarth (printmaker/cartoonist) was born here in 1697.

- 87-88: Butchers' Hall: At this location since 1885. (See at its own listing.)

Bartholomew Fair - Was an event, not a street. Began ca. 1123; held in summer; traditionally on August 24th, the feast of St. Bartholomew. Existed for some 700 years. The space used by the fair (Smithfield Market) was also used for tournaments in the far past, and for executions. By the 17th C. the fair had been extended to last a fortnight.

Was on-going in Clerkenwell (outside the gates of St. Bartholomew's Hospital) until declared defunct in 1855. The City had wanted to be done with the fair before then, for the City destroyed the booths in 1840. (Note, however, that by 1802 this cloth fair was definitely not fashionable, as it had been. Had turned riotous. In 1822, there was a huge riot here the night before the fair officially opened.) The red brick market hall dates from 1868 (now altered and expanded.)

Bartholomew's Gate - (See: St. Bartholomew's Gatehouse, under S.)

Bartholomew Lane - Near the Bank of England (after 1734); described as a quiet street at the back of the Bank of England. There is a cul-de-sac off it called Capel Court. (See: Stock Exchange.)

Barton Street - Smith Square, Westminster. Originally laid out ca. 1722; Georgian houses still standing there.

Bart's Hospital - Nickname. (See: St. Bartholomew's Hospital, under S.)

baseball - (AKA: British baseball, or Welsh baseball.) This game is mentioned in Jane Austen's *Northanger Abbey* (1798,) but is centuries old. Resembled the game called Rounders. Played with a bat and ball. The American style/game of baseball wasn't established in America until 1838.

Basing Lane - Offshoot of Cannon Street, near St. Paul's Churchyard. Removed in 1853-4. (See: Candlewick Street.)

Basinghall Street - Cheapside. Wool district.

- Coopers' Hall: (See under the C section.)
- Girdlers' Hall: They made girdles in medieval times, which evolved into belts. (See: Girdlers' Hall.)
- Guildhall Library: (See: Guildhall/Guildhall Library.)
- Weavers' Company.

Basket Makers' Company - (AKA: the Worshipful Company of Basketmakers.) The Brewers' Company has records from 1422 that reference basketmaking in the City. Basketweavers were, for political reasons having to do with foreign-made baskets, cast out of the City in the 15th century.

Finally established in 1569 by an Order of the Court of Aldermen. Fifty-second in order of (Livery Company) precedence.

They joined with the Butchers' Company (because the latter extensively used baskets.) The Turners' also used baskets (and sold them.)

The Basket Makers did not obtain a (re)Charter following the restoration of the monarchy in 1660; was granted in 1937 by George VI, However they did exist all along, and obtained the right of Livery in 1825. Has no hall.

Bateman's Buildings - An alley, narrow and nondescript, on the former site of Monmouth House (which was pulled down in 1773.) Here by at least 1799 and at least until 1836. Connected Bateman Street and Soho Square. In the 20th C. the rather squalid premises here were replaced by rather dull commercial businesses.

Bath chair - So named because it was invented in Bath, mid 18th century. It was a sort of precursor to the wheelchair. Had 3-4 wheels (usually just the one in front.) Was propelled by an able-bodied person pushing it, not the invalid. (You may care to see: sedan chair.)

Bath, the City of - In the County of Somerset. (See: Bath, under the BRITISH COUNTIES section.)

bathroom - Not really a Regency term, as most homes did not have a separate room for bathing, nor for the evacuation of human waste, as having a chamber pot under the bed or in a nightstand was far more usual. (See: nightstand, under N.) A very grand house might have a room just for bathing. Or the term "bathing room" could mean a room in a public building where members of one sex would bathe together (clothed in bathing costumes) in what was considered medicinal waters. Such "bathing rooms" were rather rare in Regency England; early 19th C. folk were more likely to "take the water" (drink it) than bathe in it. Although it should be noted that, for one's health, plunges into seawater (also fully clothed in bathing costumes-was called bathing.

As for bathing privately (to cleanse one's self,) a person might take what we now call a sponge bath (washing with a cloth, from a basin of water, while standing,) or have a tub carried up to one's room and filled with water heated in the kitchens; these tubs were small by today's standards, with just enough room to sit with one's legs drawn up; it was difficult to heat and carry a great deal of water, so the hip-baths were quite smallish.

Some inventors were playing with the idea of showers (water from an overhead source,) but the concept did not become perfected or catch on for years past the Regency.

- You may care to see: soap.
- You may care to see: towels.

batman - A soldier-servant for an Army officer. "Bat" comes from the French *bât*, the word for a packsaddle. A batman looked after the pack horses (and by the Regency had come to mean the man caring for an officer's needs.)

Battersea - Southwark. One of the oldest recorded place names in London. Became a borough in 1900; is now part of the Wandsworth borough.

- St. John's School: Founded in 1700 by Sir Walter St. John. The first school in Battersea. Ca. 1858 the school was rebuilt.
- St. Mary's: (AKA: Battersea Old Church.) Rebuilt in 1775. Had a medieval foundation, dating from 1157. William Blake (poet) was married here in 1782. (See: St. Mary's Battersea, under the CHURCHES section.)
- Old Battersea House: Vicarage Road. Brick, built 1699 by Sir Christopher Wren for Sir Walter St. John. Later owned by Samuel Pett, a naval officer.

Battersea Fields - (Now Battersea Park.) Scene of Wellington and Lord Winchilsea's March 21st/1829 duel, (among others, as this locale was known for dueling.) The field's main crops consisted of asparagus and cabbage. It was purchased ca. 1828 by the Marquess of Westminster, who leased it to Cubitt, who perceived it as a park, and in 1848 the conversion to a park began. This conversion consumed the Red House Tavern. (See, below.)

- Red House Tavern: In the late 18th C. was a minor competitor as a pleasure garden to Vauxhall Gardens, but by the time of the Regency it had degraded to drinking, gaming, and donkey races. Was pulled down during the Battersea Park construction in 1848.

Battersea Park - Developed in 1858; opened in 1859. Nearly 200 acres. Created expressly for the people of London (as opposed to or private individual.) Had been Battersea Fields. (See: Battersea Fields, at its own listing.)

Battlebridge - (Also seen as: Battle Bridge.) Prior to 1820 was a dirty, dangerous neighborhood. Dustcarts were emptied here. After 1820, the hovels were pulled down; area was renamed King's Cross, for George IV's statue here. (See: King's Cross.)

Baynard's Castle - Supposedly built by a nobleman named Baynard during William the

Conqueror's reign (and intended as one of William's castles throughout the London area.) Reportedly destroyed in 1212 by King John, but restored along with the king's favor. It was not rebuilt after 1666's Great Fire damaged it, but one tower remained habitable until 1720. The entire site was cleared at the beginning of the 19th century. The site is marked by the Baynard's Castle Tavern on the corner of St. Andrew's Hill Street and Queen Victoria Street.

Bayswater - Westminster. In the early 1820s was described as just a little hamlet; development didn't begin until 1809 and was slow, not really being built up until into the 1850s. A somewhat vague district between Hyde Park's north side and Notting Hill Gate. We know that in 1825 watercress was cultivated here. There was a stone conduit house (near to Craven Hill) which served, via leaden pipes, to convey water to Cheapside and Cornhill in the City. In 1830 this area was yet called Bayard's Watering Place (although a 1659 record had it mapped as "Bayswater.") This area has always been one where foreigners made their homes.

- Bayswater Road: (See: Paddington/Bayswater Road.)
- Blackman Lane: Called thus until 1830. (See: Westbourne Green, below in this entry.) The west side of this street held a row of small houses (later turned into shops.)
- Chapel of Ascension: 1894.
- Orme Square: Built ca. 1815. Named for a Bond Street print-seller, Mr. Orme.
- St. Petersburg Place: Ca. 1815. At first called Petersburg Place. (See under S.)
- Westbourne Green: A hamlet, with a country lane that wandered across the green, called Blackman Lane (which would later be converted into Queen's Road, and later yet into Queensway.) The lane across the green existed until the time of William IV. Beautiful rural area.
- Westbourne Grove: During the Regency it was a quiet street of cottages with front gardens.
- Westbourne Place: Isaac Ware, who had been hired to construct Lord Chesterfield's home (1748,) used some supplies from that employment to build this, his own mansion.

Beacontree - Dagenham. A 20th C. housing development.

beadles - Usually a church warden, they served in a policing capacity for properties belonging to a bishop/the church. (Could also sometimes be ex-military, not associated with a religion.) Beadles wore coats and bowler hats (the latter dating from after 1850.) Some other references to beadles:

- See: Burlington Arcade.

- See: Church of England/Beadles.
- See: Regent Street.

Beak Street - Soho.

- 41: Canaletto, the Italian painter, lived here ca. 1746-53.

bear-baiting - Not a Regency diversion. Had gone out of vogue. Was outlawed (along with all animal baiting) in 1835.

- See: animals/bear.
- You may care to see: bull-baiting.

Beauchamp Place - (Pronounced BEECH-am.) Just off Knightsbridge, Brompton. Regency era street. Short and straight. Is currently an expensive shopping street for clothing and jewelry.

Beaufort House - (See: Chelsea/Cheyne Walk/91-4.)

beaver - Meaning both the animal and the type of men's hat.

- See: animals/beaver.
- See: hats.

Bed and Breakfast - Modern term. (See: B & B.)

bedding shop -

- See: Rathbone Place/Heal & Son.
- You may care to see: blankets.
- You may care to see: quilts.
- You may care to see: sheets.

Bedford Gardens - 1822. (See: Holland Park/Bedford Gardens.)

Bedford House - (See: Covent Gardens/Bedford House.)

Bedford New Town - Camden. 1830s, for the Duke of Bedford. Was the original name of the manor that became Fig's Mead.

Bedford Park - 1895 suburb. (See: Chiswick/Bedford Park.)

Bedford Place - Bloomsbury. In the 18th C., it was described as "old and honorable." 1800, by James Burton. (See: Bloomsbury Square/Bedford Place.)

Bedford Row - (See: Holborn/Bedford Row.)

Bedford Square - Bloomsbury. Adams, started in 1776; took ten years to build. GEORGIAN LONDON says the architects were Robert Scott and William Crewes; LONDON REDISCOVERED says it was "probably built by Thomas Leverton, who lived at No. 1." Built for the Russells, who still own it. "Smart," with uniform doorways of Coade stone, still well preserved. It grew into a thriving residential area in the first decades of the 19th century. The central garden is still surrounded by the original railings; planted in the early 19th century. Remains a bastion of Georgian uniformity of style. First London square designed to have four palace-fronted terraces. The statue of Charles James Fox (on the north side of the square) has been there since 1816. The houses are now all office buildings (no longer residential,) and the occupants still have sole (private) use of the oval central garden.

Bedford Street - Residents here from at least 1638. Off Henrietta Street, Covent Garden.

Bedlam - (AKA: St. Mary Bethlehem, this was its official name; "Bedlam" was its widely used nickname. AKA: Bethlehem Royal Hospital. AKA: Royal Hospital Bethlehem. AKA: Bethlehem Hospital. Also seen as: Bethlem Hospital, but this is just another corruption.)

Founded in 1247. Administered by the Crown (one of five London hospitals to be so administered, the other four being: Chelsea Hospital, Christ's Hospital, St. Bartholomew's Hospital, and St. Thomas's Hospital.)

Referred to on maps as early as the 14th C. as "Bedlam Hospital." A document dating from 1632 referred to the year 1377 as when Bedlam first began being used for "distracted persons"; at any rate, the hospital was firmly established as a lunatic asylum by Henry VIII in 1547-57.

Deteriorated badly by the 17th C., newly built at Moorfields, Bishopgate in 1675, opened in July, 1676. Over the gates were two carved figures: "Dementia" and "Acute Mania." A German visitor, one Sophie von La Roche, wrote of Bedlam in 1786 as "very palatial." It was 540 feet in length "with two large wings either side and fine gardens, where the poor people can enjoy fresh air and recreate themselves amongst trees, flower, and plant."

One source said that the viewing of the inmates was stopped in 1751; yet another says it was an early 19th C. outing. John Wesley (cleric and theologian, d. 1791) wrote that visits to Bedlam "had been prohibited."

LONDON THE AUTOBIOGRAPHY informs us that: "One John Howard wrote of "Bethlam" Hospital (in Moorfields) in 1788: 'The committee room and apartments for the stewards & c. are in the centre; and in long galleries and wings on either side, are the rooms for the patients. The size of these rooms is 12 feet by 8 feet 10 inches, and 12 feet 10 inches high... On the 4 floors there are about 270 rooms: these were quite clean and not offensive, though the house is old and wants whitewashing... The patients communicate with one another from the top to the bottom of the house, so that there is no separation of the calm and quiet from the noisy and turbulent, except those who are chained in their cells... There are sitting rooms with fireplaces properly guarded with iron - a cold bath and airing grounds for each sex - no chapel - bread allowance to patients 1 lb. a day... Visitors are admitted by a governor's ticket, only on Mondays and Wednesdays, between the hours of 10 and 12." At that time hosted 133 men and 139 women.

Moved to St. George's Fields, Lambeth, in 1815 (the old locale then becoming

Finsbury Circus in 1819,) into a domed building by Lewis, at Lambeth Road's east end; (a 2nd and 3rd source says the dome and portico were added as a chapel by Robert Smirke in 1844-5.) In 1816 the hospital accepted criminally insane persons at the request of the government (but these were disallowed in 1864.)

In 1835 the hospital added more blocks in order to house more patients.

Padded rooms were added in 1844.

In 1930, Bedlam moved to Monk's Orchard, West Wickham, Surrey. The old grounds were purchased this same year and gifted to the city as a park (Geraldine Mary Harmsworth Park); the east and west wings were demolished for the park, but the central section remained, the old grounds becoming then the Imperial War Museum (since 1935,) and Liverpool Street Station.

The only other hospital for the treatment of insanity in London was: St. Luke's in Finsbury.

- ➢ See: Chelsea/Belgrave Square.
- ➢ See: Eaton Square.
- ➢ You may care to see: Old Street/St. Luke's Hospital.

- King Edwards School: Took a long-term lease with Bethlehem Hospital in 1806; built its school here in 1830. The school was a reformatory for both boys and girls, and called House of Occupations.

beds - (See: bedding shop.)

beef - Beef was a common-enough food in Regency England...if you could afford it.

- ➢ See: Barnsbury.
- ➢ See: cattle.
- ➢ See: Isle of Dogs.
- ➢ See: meat.
- ➢ See: milk - For note on where cows grazed in London.

Beefeaters - (AKA: Yeomen Warders. Their formal name is: Yeoman Warder of Her Majesty's Royal Palace and Fortress the Tower of London, and Members of the Sovereign's Body Guard of the Yeoman Guard Extraordinaire.) They prefer NOT to be called Beefeaters.

They are the halberdiers of the Tower of London. They have served at the Tower since Henry VII's time, as his bodyguards (1485.) Their undress (that is, informal) uniforms date back to Mary Tudor, being blue, with the sovereign's monogram; on ceremonial occasions the famous State uniform is worn, it is red and gold.

Not to be confused with the Yeomen of the Guard, the monarch's Bodyguard at St. James's Palace (except that in fact the Yeomen Warders are members of the Yeomen of the Guard, Extraordinary.)

Were purportedly designated "beefeaters" because their service assured them a regular allotment of beef. The nickname seems to date from at least as far back as Henry VIII's time. However, don't call them this; it won't be appreciated.

They and their families live in the Tower of London. They pay rent and council tax. (See: Yeoman Warders, more at.)

beer - Beer was long plentiful in London and its environs, with some form thereof dating from the time of the Romans.

From early times, water sources in London were largely contaminated, so a low-alcohol beer was "every man's due" in order to have something safe to drink, ranging from children to duchesses.

- See: breweries.
- See: food/beer.
- See: food/hops.
- See: porter.
- See: small beer.
- See: Staffordshire/Bass Brewing, under the BRITISH COUNTIES section - For the 1822 invention of East India Pale Ale.
- See the INNS/PUBS section - For all the notes under.
- See: water.

Beggar's Bush - Sometimes seen as: Beggars Bush. (See: Russell Hill.)

beheadings - Not practiced in the Regency era.

- See: Newgate Prison.
- See: punishments.
- See: Tower Hill.

Belgrave Square - Belgravia. (Actually, "Belgravia" was a term that grew out of the existence of Belgrave and Eaton Squares.)

Belgrave takes its name from a village on the outskirts of Leicester, on land belonging to the Grosvenors. It was part of the largely swampy area owned by Lord Grosvenor (Viscount Belgrave.)

The land here was drained and laid out in 1825 by Thomas Cubitt, after the Earl of Grosvenor obtained an Act of Parliament allowing him to build on the land. Covers ten acres. George Basevi built the square in the 1840s; the Basevi buildings were meant to compete with Nash's work for George IV.

It is now the home to many foreign embassies.

- See: Belgravia.
- See: Chelsea/Belgrave Square.

- 36 Belgrave Square: Queen Victoria rented this house for her mother, the Duchess of Kent (until the apartments at Kensington Palace were complete.)

Belgravia - (Pronounced Bell-GRAVE-e-ah, not Bell-GRAHV-e-ah.) Until developed, this area was known as Five Fields. (See under F.) Development of the area didn't begin until 1824; laid out by Thomas Cubitt between 1826-31, under a special Act of Parliament that passed in 1826. LONDON REDISCOVERED says Belgravia was designed by James Wyatt and Thomas Cundy the Elder. CHAMBERS LONDON GAZETTEER says it was Thomas Cubitt and his brother Lewis. It was first built to house servants who worked in Buckingham House (Palace,) but soon gave way to homes for the wealthy. (Actually, "Belgravia" was a term that grew out of the existence of Belgrave and Eaton Squares.)

To repeat, prior to development, the area was known as Five Fields. It was rather marshy. Streets of many white or cream stucco houses. Named after Belgrave, Leicestershire, where the Grosvenor family (the area's owners) had one of their residences.

Its boundaries are: Knightsbridge, Sloane Street, Grosvenor Place, (and what is now the Victoria Station.) Is currently home to 25+ embassies (which primarily moved into this area after WWI.)

- ➢ See: Belgrave Square.
- ➢ See: Chelsea/Belgrave Square.

- Belgrave Square. (See at its own listing.)
- Ebury Street. (See under E.)
- Grosvenor Place: The first Belgravia houses were built here ca. 1747-67. (See under G.)
- Lowndes Square: 1836-7. (See under L.)
- Sloane Square: (See under S.)

Bell Alley - Dense houses, cleared in 1835-40 to make Moorgate.

Bell Foundry, the - AKA: Whitechapel Foundry. (See: Whitechapel Road/32-4.)

Bell Green - Lewisham. Modern name for Sydenham Green. (See: Sydenham/Sydenham Green.)

Bell's Library - (See: Southampton Street/Gallery of Arts.)

Bella Court - (See: Greenwich/Bella Court.)

Belle Sauvage, the - Ancient coaching inn. (See: Ludgate Street/Belle Sauvage.)

Belsize House - Camden. Dates from 1496 (as a manor house.) Rebuilt in 1720, where a person referred to as the "Welsh ambassador" opened pleasure gardens here; closed in 1740. Belsize was made into nine leasehold estates in 1808, each with a house and parklands. At this time a grander Belsize House was rebuilt. Demolished 1854 (at which time the land became Belsize Park.)

Belsize Park - (See: Belsize House.)

Belton Street - (See: Endell Street.)

Benedictine Street - (See: Bennet Street.)

Bennet Street - (Sometimes also referred to as Benedictine Street.)

- 4: Lord Byron (poet) lived here in 1813-14.

Bensbury Camp - (See: Wimbledon Common/Caesar's Camp.)

Bentinck Street - Westminster. (See: Hinde Street.)

- 1: Built in 1800.
- 7: Edward Gibbon (18th C. historian) lived here.
- 8: Built ca. 1780.
- 9: Built ca. 1780-90. James Smithson (founder of the Smithsonian Institution, b. circa 1765-d. 1829) once lived here.

Berkeley House - Mayfair.

- See: Berkeley Square.
- See: Devonshire House.

Berkeley Row - Existed at least by 1765, still around in 1789 at which time it was known for being an area of prostitution.

Berkeley Square - (Pronounced BARK-lee.) Mayfair. The square was built piecemeal starting in 1698 through 1738, named for the first Lord Berkeley of Stratton, who built his home here in 1665. In 1737-47 was built to designs by William Kent (on the grounds of the former Berkeley House.) It was not designed with shrubs and trees at it center until the 1760-85 era. Ancient plane trees line the west side of the square.

There are no longer any private residences here (the last sold in 1953,) being now filled with offices, clubs, and high-end businesses.

- 7 and 8: Gunter's. Caterer, maker of ices, cakes, sweets. East side of Berkeley Square until 1937, when it moved to Curzon Street. (See: Gunter's, under G.)
- 11: Horace Walpole (Whig politician) moved here in 1779.
- 44: Town house built by William Kent, 1742-4, for Lady Isebella Finch. Now hosts the 20th century Clermont Club. (See under the CLUBS section.) There was another club, Annabel's, prior, 18th century. This house has a dramatic baroque staircase. LONDON ACCESS calls it "the finest remaining example of a Georgian terraced house in Central London."
- 50: George Canning (Tory politician) lived here sometime prior to his death in 1827, but no one has lived here for over 100 years, due to a series of accidental deaths and suicides that tainted its reputation. Built by William Kent. Described as beautifully preserved.
- Bruton Place: (See at its own listing.)

- Bruton Street: (See at its own listing.)
    - 17: Queen Elizabeth II was born here in 1926.
- Charles Street: This street was most likely named for the first Lord Berkeley's brother, Charles, 1st Earl of Falmouth (d. 1665.)
    - Berkeley Chapel. (See under the CHURCHES section.)
    - 44: Beau Brummell (19th C. fashion trendsetter) lived here at one time.
- Fitzmaurice Place:
    - Lansdowne House: (See under L.)
    - Lansdowne Passage: (See under L.)
- Half Moon Street: Dates back to at least the time of Boswell (at least 1763.)
    - 1 Half Moon Street: Fanny Burney (Madame D'Arbley, also a novelist) was persuaded by her son to move here in 1828.
- Hill Street: Houses yet sport brick Georgian fronts.

Berkeley Square House - Mayfair. 1938.

Berkeley Street - Mayfair. Built in 1684 for Lady Berkeley.

- 9: Alexander Pope (poet) lived here, prior to his death in 1744.

Berkshire House - (See: Cleveland House.)

Bermondsey - Since the year 708, was Bermond's Ei (or marsh.) Resettled by wealthier types following the Great Fire of 1666. Through the Regency era it remained much the same, but by Charles Dickens' time, quite a bit of the area had turned into slums. It was the center of leather trade since the early 1700s, and Bermondsey Market was established here ca. 1833. (See: Leather Market, below.) Antiques have been sold here since 1949. Is now a part of the London borough of Southwark (was formerly a metropolitan borough in Surrey.)

- Bermondsey Square: Still hosts some 16th C. homes.
- Leather, Hide and Wool Exchange: Leathermarket Street. 1870s.
- Leather Market: Weston Street. 1833.
- Morocco Street: As its name implies, there was leather trade practiced here.
- St. John's Church: Horselydown. 1732. (See under the CHURCHES section.)
- St. Mary Magdalene: (See under the CHURCHES section.)

Berners Street - Built ca. 1750. Leads from Oxford Street to Middlesex Hospital. Artists, painters, and sculptors lived here.

- No. 71: Samuel Taylor Coleridge (poet, d. 1834) lived here at one time.

Berry Bros. & Rudd - Wine merchants. (See: St. James's Street/3.)

Berry's Green - Bromley. Regency name for Single Street. (See: Single Street.)

Berwick Street - Soho. Built 1687-1703. Named for the first Duke of Berwick. There are a few 1730s buildings yet here. Is currently a food market that supplies the local gourmet restaurants and Berwick Street Market, dating from the 1840s.

bet - (See: wagering.)

Bethlem Hospital - Yet another version of "St. Mary Bethlehem." (See: Bedlam.)

Bethlehem Royal Hospital - (See: Bedlam.)

Bethnal Green - Whitechapel. At first it was a part of Stepony; separated in 1743. Now a part of the London Borough of Tower Hamlets (named "Tower Hamlets" in 1965.) In the 18th century, Bethnal Green was known for its chair-making and silk-weaving. In the 19th C. was rather notorious for its child labor. By the 1820-30s, it had become more populated and less rural.

- St. John's church. (See under the CHURCHES section.)
- St. Matthew's: In Church Row. Parish church, established in 1740 (or 1746.) (See under the CHURCHES section.)

Bethwin Road - (See: Windmill Lane.)

betrothal - (See: marriage.)

betting -

- See: gaming.
- See: wagering.
- You may care to see: the CLUBS section - Many of which provided wagering for gentlemen.

Bevis Marks - In the ward of Aldgate, the City. Has had various spellings since the 1400s, and probably dates back to the 12th C.; known as Bevis Marks since 1720. Is mentioned in *The Olde Curiosity Shop*, by Charles Dickens.

- Bevis Marks Synagogue: Built in 1701. It is the oldest still used synagogue in the United Kingdom. Perhaps curiously, its builder was the Quaker Joseph Avis; he refused his fee as it being wrong to profit from building a house of God. It burned in 1738; Queen Anne donated an oak beam for the new roof, taken from a royal warship. The building was damaged in 1992 and 1993 by IRA bombings. (See: Spanish and Portuguese Synagogue.)

Bexley - Borough in southeast London. Existed since at least the year 814. It was, however, very little occupied prior to the 19th century; became industrialized in the late 19th century.

- Bourne Road.
    - Bexley National Schools: 1834.
- Hall Place: Manor house, probably since 1241. The present hall dates from ca. 1540.
- High Street: Merchants' homes from the mid 18th century.
- Old Bexley: Also called Bexley Village. "Old" distinguished this area from

Bexleyheath (the latter called Bexley New Town in the 2nd half of the 19th century.)

- Styleman's almhouses: 1755.

bibles - There were no (fully) English language bibles until 1382, with the first *printed* one coming along ca. 1525. There was a "Great Bible" version in 1539.

The Book of Common Prayer was made compulsory under the Act of Uniformity in 1549.

The King James' Bible (also called: the Authorised version, but most correctly called the: New English Bible) was first published in London in 1611. Used for 270 years, until a newer version of the New Testament was published in 1881, and the Old Testament in 1885. (See the INTRO-REIGNS section/British Kings and Queens & Their Reigns/James I.)

- See: Barker & Howard.
- See: British & Foreign Bible Society.
- See: Printing House Square - The note on the King's Printer.
- You may care to see: Church of England.
- You may care to see: Book of Common Prayer.

Big Ben - 1834, by Barry. The term actually refers to the bell itself, rather than the tower spire in which it is hung. The tower is now called: the Elizabeth Tower (21st century, in honor of the long reign of Queen Elizabeth II.) Before that is was: the Clock Tower (20th century.) Victorian journalists called it: St. Stephen's Tower (because MPs used to sit in St. Stephen's Hall; later 19th century.) LET'S GO: THE BUDGET GUIDE TO LONDON says the bell was cast and hung in 1858; the delay between 1834 and 1858 was due to the bell cracking and being recast, and the clock hands being too heavy, and having to be redone. The clock finally was in action on 5/31/1859. The tower is 316 feet tall, and has a 340 step staircase. Big Ben (the hour bell) rings in the key of E, and weighs 13.5 tons. The quarter hour bells rings in the key of F.

- See: Victoria Tower - Across from Elizabeth Tower.
- See: Whitechapel/Whitechapel Bell Foundry.

Bill of Rights - The English Bill of Rights, 1689. Not the American one, 1791. (See: INTRO-REIGNS section/Historical Eras/William and Mary's time.)

Bill of Rights Society - Formed in 1769. It was first called the "Society of Gentlemen Supporters of the Bill of Rights." Centered around supporting the rights of the American colonies, and the founder of British radicalism, John Wilkes (1725-1797.) Faded by 1771, the Bill of Rights Society folded when the founders were imprisoned in that year.

billiards - The table game, resembling the later snooker. (See under S.) Billiards originated in England, ca. 1470, and at first was called the "winning and losing carambole game." Has 2 white balls and 1 red. Players shoot for points and pockets in a 12-point game. Cues used to have a rectangular ivory piece affixed on the shooting end, until 1800 when the straight cue developed.

Billingsgate - (More formally AKA: Billingsgate Market. AKA: Billingsgate Fish Market.) Lower Thames Street, the City. One of London's main harbors. Has hosted a market for over 1,000 years, dating from the 9th century. Besides fish, also known for corn and salt. Takes its name from King Belinus, 12th century, who supposedly built a gateway here.

In the early eighteenth century, the market was housed in a series of "low booths and sheds." First officially recognized as a fish market in 1698, when it was made a wholesale fishmarket by Act of Parliament (before then it had been a general produce market.)

The City put up market buildings in 1849-53, removing the market from the streets surrounding Billingsgate Wharf; replaced in 1875 by a larger building. Closed in 1982 due to severe congestion; this building survives today on Lower Thames Street. The market reopened ca. 1992 at the West India Quay on the Isle of Dogs. (See: docks/West India Docks.)

A "Billingsgate fishwife" was/is a term for a strident/loud-mouthed/uncouth woman.

- See: fish.
- You may care to see: eels - Which were *not* sold at Billingsgate.

Billiter Lane - Aldgate. Corruption of the medieval name "Bell-yetteres" (bell-founders.) Ran northwest from Fenchurch to Leadenhall. Dates from the Medieval Ages. Survived the Great Fire of 1666, but demand was definitely in decline. By the early 19th century Billiter Lane was referred to as: Billiter Street.

- Ironmongers' Hall: (See under I.)

Billister Square - Aldgate. Dates from at least 1746.

biology - The term "biology" was coined in 1802 by Gottfried Treviranus, German naturalist/physician.

Birchin Lane - Cornhill. Corruption of Birchover Lane, named for its first builder. A short street that ran from Cornhill Street to Lombard Street. There were secondhand clothes merchants here in the medieval period. Here were men's "ready-made" (but which would be sewn/altered for fit) clothes shops in the 17th century. By the 18th C. hosted coffee houses. Still exists.

Birdcage Walk - Along the south side of St. James's Park. Named for the aviaries Charles II kept here. (See: St. James's Park/Birdcage Walk.)

- Wellington Barracks: 1834-59. For the household troops' use. (See under W.)

Bird-in-Hand Court - Cheapside. First called Naked Boy Alley, but known as Bird-in-Hand Alley by 1677.

- Simpson's Chop House:
    - See: Cheapside/76.
    - See under S.

birds - During the Regency era, these birds lived in England. This list is not all-inclusive:

blackbird

blackcap

blue-tit

bullfinch

canary - (See: Norwich.)

cormorant

crow

cuckoo

diver - In America called a loon.

dove

duck - Both wild and domestic.

finch

goose

grouse

gull

heron

house-martin

jay

lark

nightingale

nuthatch

owl

~~parakeet~~ - In the UK, called a: budgerigar. From tropical climes. Not wild in the UK until the 20th century, due to a multitude of released pets.

partridge

pheasant - (See: Selsdon.)

pigeon

raven

reed warbler

robin

rook

seagull

sparrow

swan

swift

thrush

tit

turkey

wagtail

woodcock

woodpecker

wood-pigeon

wren

yellowhammer.

Birkbeck College - Began as the "London Mechanics' Institution," at the Crown and Anchor Tavern, on the Strand, 12/02/1823. The next home was in an old meeting-house called Dr. Lindsey's Chapel, Monkwell Street, Cripplegate. Shortly moved to 15 Furnival's Inn, but by 12/02/1824 the foundation stone of 29 Southampton Buildings (their then permanent premises) was laid. Its intent was to serve as a rabble-rouser (as in a liberal venue,) even though nominally to "educate." The Institute was not prospering by the 1850s, until it revived and was renamed to Birkbeck Literary and Scientific Institution in 1866. Moved in 1885 to Bream's Buildings. The name was changed to simply Birkbeck College in 1907. In 1920 it was a college under the University of London umbrella. It was the first college built for the part-time education of students with employment. Moved to Bloomsbury after WWII.

birth control - Was generally frowned upon during the Regency era, usually under religious grounds (that one was to welcome children and/or the use of any kind of birth control just encouraged profligacy.) Too, what little they had, as history assures us, did not work well. In addition to what is immediately below, sometimes a sponge soaked in lemon juice or vinegar was used (supposedly primarily by prostitutes.)

- See: condoms - Mostly used to prevent disease, more than to prevent pregnancy.
- See: money/penny - Nicknamed a cartwheel, was rather large, and so was sometimes used as a diaphragm.
- You may care to see: childbirth.

Bishopsgate - The City. The Bishop's Gate was first Roman. (See: gates.) Mentioned in the

Domesday Book as *Porta Episcopi.* No one is sure from which Saxon bishop it derived its name; it may have come from the fact in medieval times the Bishop of London was allowed one stick from every cart of wood to pass through the gate.

Rebuilt in 1471. Often used to display the heads of executed criminals. Repaired in 1648. Housed many coaching-inns, which survived the Great Fire of 1666, but are there no longer. Also rebuilt in 1731-35, now in a plainer style, the only decoration being the royal arms on a pediment over the arch. Coach-builders resided here. Demolished in 1760. Now houses banks.

- Bedlam: (See at its own listing.)
- Bishopgate Street: In 1830 it was still divided into two sections; the entire street was not referred to simply as "Bishopgate" until the 20th century.
    - Bishopgate Street Within.
    - Bishopgate Street Without.
- Crosby Hall: Relocated to Chelsea in 1910. (See: Chelsea/Crosby Hall.)
- Flower Pot, The: Ancient inn. Pulled down in 1865. (See under the INNS/PUBS section.)
- St. Botolph's: (See under the CHURCHES section.)
- St. Ethelberga: (See under the CHURCHES section.)
- St. Helen Bishopgate: (See under the CHURCHES section.)
- Spital Square: (See under S.)
    - On the south side is Spital Yard, in which stands a 17th C. house wherein Susannah Wesley (mother of John, founder of Methodism) was born.

Bishopgate Institute - Ca. 1850. (See: London and Middlesex Archaeological Society.)

Black Death, the - (AKA: the Great Plague.) 1347-51. Killed 1/3 of the English population, and many more throughout Europe and into Asia. (See: the INTRO-REIGNS section/British Kings & Queens and Their Reigns/Edward III.)

Black Friars, the - Also called the Dominicans. Medieval monks. Wore long black mantles over white robes, hence the nickname. Dissolved in 1538 by Henry VIII's Dissolution. Their priory building did not survive, its stones being used to build Blackfriars Theatre in 1596 (which ceased in 1655.)

Black Lion Lane -

- See: Queen's Road, Kensington.
- See: Queensway.

Black Swan Court - The City. An old street. (See: Byward Street.)

Blackfriars Lane - The City; near the bridge of the same name. Named for the Dominicans ("the

Dominicans of London") who settled here in the 1221 (until the Dissolution when they were disbanded.) At one point this street was called Water Lane. The remains of the priory mostly perished in the Great Fire of 1666; in the 17th C. this district was fashionable, at least until it burned. (See: Apothecaries' Hall.)

- Ireland Yard: The only fragment of the 13th century Blackfriars Priory (above ground, that is) can be found here.
- Playhouse Yard: Dates back to Shakespeare's time, when he performed in the long gone Blackfriars Playhouse that had been here. This street yet exists.

Blackfriars Road - Southwark, leads to the City. Previously known as Surrey Street (or Great Surrey Street); the road was (re)built between the 1760s-1800.

- Christ Church: Built 1738-41. Plain brick quadrangle. The "new" chancel dates from 1870.
- Ring, The: Built in 1783. In the Regency it would have been known as Surrey Chapel. (See: Surrey Chapel, under the CHURCHES section.)

Blackheath - Greenwich. (AKA: Blackheath Commons.) James I introduced the game of golf to England here, to a then less than thrilled crowd. The area, early in the 19th C., had problems with highwaymen, as it was the site of many robberies. By the early 19th C. those of the upper crust were beginning to move west, out of this district. In 1808, this area was rolling hills with bushes and a windmill, not an open meadow. It was still a popular gathering place/staging post when traveling toward Dover and the Continent. Used by orators, at times. (See: Greenwich/Blackheath.)

- All Saints' Church: 1859.
- Blackfriars Bridge: 1769. (See under the BRIDGES section.)
- Blackheath Park: 1957, by Eric Lyons. Is the (private) Cator estate (which began to be built up in the 1820s-30s.)
- Paragon, the: 1793-1807, by Michael Searle. LONDON by Knopf Guides writes: "The English custom of building semi-detached houses dates back at least to the 18th century. The fourteen huge houses that make up this group, designed by Michael Searles around 1790, are linked by Tuscan colonnades. It is one of the finest Georgian housing developments in London." Seven identical units, 4 stories, in a shallow curve. Restored after WWII damage.
- Royal Blackheath Golf Club: Constituted in 1766, but founded and played on the heath "much earlier," at least by ca. 1606. James I (AKA: James VI of Scotland) played here. (See: golf.)

Blacklands Lane - (See: Marlborough Road.)

Blackman Street - Southwark. In Roman times, was Stane Street. Known as Blackman Street until 1889. Its modern name is Newington Causeway.

Blacksmiths' Company - (For the Worshipful Company of Blacksmiths.) First written of in 1325, and first known as "The Fraternity of St. Loie." Records from the 1490s speak of a Hall that was old at that time. It was largely a religious body by the end of the 15th C., more about serving religion than serving governance of Blacksmithing at that time. This was disrupted by the Dissolution of the Monasteries.

Received its letters patent/Royal Charter in 1571 as: the Art and Mistery of Blacksmiths-spurriers (makers of spurs,) the latter being incorporated with the Blacksmiths that year.

The Hall was destroyed in the Great Fire of 1666, as was much of the company's leasehold property; the Hall was rebuilt. Its lease expired in 1785, due to a shrinking of the Blacksmiths' powers, and was not renewed; no longer has a Hall.

Social changes brought about the company's demise, and its lease with the City Corporation ended in 1785. It yet offers prizes, medals, and diplomas for workmanship. Livery Company. 40th in the order of precedence.

- ➢ See: Clockmakers' Company - Which was part of the Blacksmiths until 1631.
- ➢ See: spurriers - Who were part of the Blacksmiths' Company.

Blackwall - Dock, located on the north bank of the Thames, five kilometers (about 3 miles/4.8 km) east of London Bridge. It was the first commercial enclosed wet dock, built by the East India Company, ca. 1660. Used for outfitting, masting, and repairing ships, *not* for unloading cargo vessels. Enlarged in 1789, resulting in **Brunswick Dock**, the nucleus for the development of the East India Docks in 1806, at which time this became the export dock.

- ➢ See: docks/Brunswick Dock.
- ➢ See: docks/East India.

blankets - The term "blanket" is seen in English writings by at least 1373. If the blanket is for a Regency era bed and you mean like what an American calls a bedspread, it's more appropriate to call it a counterpane.

A blanket used inside a carriage is better referred to as a rug. Rugs (that were blankets) were also used for animals, particularly to warm/protect horses.

- ➢ See: Oxfordshire/Early's, in the BRITISH COUNTIES section - Blanket-makers.
- ➢ See: quilt.
- ➢ See: sheets.

Blenheim Palace - (See: Oxfordshire/Blenheim Palace, under the BRITISH COUNTIES section.)

Blewcoat School - 23 Caxton Street. Founded in 1688 as a charity school; present building built on Caxton Street in 1709. Existed until 1926 (or 1939.) (Not to be confused with "Bluecoat School.") Now a National Trust shop.

blood transfusions - Dr. Thomas Blundell, Guy's Hospital, made the first blood transfusions in 1818. Alas, his system failed, out of not understanding the nature of blood.

Bloody Code, the - Nickname for the penal statutes that listed capital offenses punishable by death. In 1700 there were approximately 50; by 1800 there were near 200 (for instance: stealing a handkerchief valued over one shilling.) It should be noted, however, that the number of executions actually went down when the punishable offenses list grew, largely due to the alternative punishment of transportation. NOTE: The term "Bloody Code" is Victorian.

- See: prisons.
- See: punishments.
- See: rough places.
- You may care to see: dueling places.

Bloomsbury - Camden. The estate existed since William the Conqueror; Bloomsbury is a corruption of "Blemonde"; in the 11th century William the Conqueror gave this land to one of his vassals, Baron Blemonde.

In the 1660s, the Earl of Southampton laid out Bloomsbury Square. (See: Bloomsbury Square, at its own listing.) Mostly developed between 1800-1830, it had row houses described as "handsome and elegant."

- Bedford Square: (See at its own listing.)
- Bloomsbury Square: (See at its own listing.)
- British Museum, the: (See: Bloomsbury Square/British Museum.)
- Brunswick Square: Featured in Austen's *Emma.* (See at its own listing.)
- Cartwright Gardens: Built 1809-11, first known as Burton Crescent. Later named Cartwright Gardens after John Cartwright, b. 1740, d. 1824, philosopher. Crescent shaped street and park.
    - 45: Jenkins Hotel. Described as having Georgian charm.
- Church Lane: During the Regency was a squalid rookery. Is now a part of Bucknall Street. It was replaced in the 1840s by New Oxford Street renovations.
- Church Street: During the Regency, it was a rookery (hang out for criminal types.) Its lower end is now known as part of Bucknall Street. Replaced in the 1840s by New Oxford Street renovations.
- Doughty Street:
    - 48: Charles Dickens (who lived in many places in London) lived here 1837-39, where he wrote: *Nicholas Nickleby, Oliver Twist,* and *The*

Pickwick Papers. Is now the Dickens House Museum.

- Gordon Square: (See under G.)
- Gower Street: (See under G.)
- Great James Street: Ca. 1722.
- Great Ormond Street: 1720s.
- Keppel Street: Existed by at least the 18th century. (See under K.)
- London University: Gower Street. Founded in 1828.
    - See under L.
    - See: University College.
- Malet Street: (See under M.)
    - University of London. (See under U.)
- Russell Square: (See under R.)
- St. Giles's in the Fields: (See under the CHURCHES section.)
- Store Street: Mary Wollstonecraft (author) lived here in 1792, when she wrote *A Vindication of the Rights of Woman.*
- Torrington Square: (See under T.)

Bloomsbury House - (See: Montague Street.)

Bloomsbury Square - Built in 1660 (two sources claimed this date, while two others claimed 1665 and 1667 as the founding date.) Was originally "Southampton Square," laid out by the Earl of Southampton. Nothing remains of the earl's palace except the gardens, which are largely intact.

It was the first residential square in London.

Called "Bloomsbury Square" by the time of the Regency. Sometimes called "Judge-Land" for the number of respectable citizens (judges) who lived here.

Shaded garden at its center (now surrounded by a one-way traffic system); at the northern end of the garden is a statue of Charles James Fox (Whig politician,) erected in 1816.

- 3: Sir Hans Sloane (a progenitor of the British Museum) lived here (mid 18th century) with his huge collection of artifacts, until he outgrew his home and bought the residence next door as well. (See: British Museum, below, for more on Sir Hans.)
- 6: From 1817-1825, was home of Isaac D'Israeli (writer, father of Benjamin.)
- Bedford House: (See: Covent Gardens/Bedford House.)
- Bedford Place: Built in the later Georgian period.
- British Library: AKA: British Museum Library. (See at its own listing.)
- British Museum: Founded in 1753 by Act of Parliament following George II's

ascent to the throne, the money to be raised by public lottery, for purchasing Montagu House to house the museum; the lottery began in 1755. Was to promote greater public understanding via the arts, natural history, and science.

The basis of the collection came when Sir Hans Sloane, a wealthy Chelsea doctor, bequeathed his collection of some 71,000 books, manuscripts, natural specimens, and antiquities to the State (receiving a sum of £20,000 for doing so,) forming the foundation that would become the British Museum. Along with Sir Hans' behest, two others' generosity forced the State to find a way to house the growing collection:

1) That of Sir Robert Cotton (the Harleian library of books and medieval manuscripts, which the State had received in 1700);
2) That of Robert Harley, Earl of Oxford; and (as stated above);
3) That of Sir Hans Sloane (collections of antiquities, art, coins, books, medals, and natural history.)

It is the world's first national public museum. The museum opened (in Bloomsbury/Montagu House) in 1759.

The collections were divided into three departments, each with a suite of rooms:

1) coins, manuscripts, medals
2) books, drawings, maps
3) "natural and artificial productions." Sub-divided in 1807, to create a department for antiquities (the Townley Gallery, 1808, opened to accommodate it.)

In its first year (1759,) the museum was open for only three hours per day. Written application was required to get tickets, and even then only ten people per hour were allowed in. (The practice of having to acquire tickets ahead was still in place during the Regency. Unrestricted access to the galleries was not allowed until 1879.) In 1784 a bill to charge for admission was defeated in Parliament.

George IV gifted the museum in 1823 with a large collection of books (inherited from his father, and AKA: the King's Library); this gift finally proved that Montagu House was now too small for the burgeoning museum. (See: British Museum Library, at its own listing.)

The present building dates from 1823-52 period; Nash's designs of 1823 were revamped in 1833, and the job was completed by Robert Smirke in 1850-52, and entered on Great Russell Street. (See: Elgin Marbles, below, the last couple of lines.)

Currently hosts over 6.5 million objects. The museum, today, covers over 13 acres. The east wing moved to St. Pancras in 1998.

- Colonnade: Completed in 1847.
- Duveen Gallery: Dates from 1938.
- Egyptian Gallery, the: The museum had some 10,000 Egyptian artifacts by 1866, though items had belonged to the museum since its beginning. The modern gallery dates from the 20th century. It has three sections: a gallery for sculpture, one for mummies, and a third for a collection of papyri. (Not to be confused with the Egyptian Hall that existed during the Regency, this latter being part of the Mansion House, to be seen under E.)
- Elgin Marbles: ("Elgin" is pronounced with a hard "g" as in "golf," not a soft "jin" sound as in "George.") The Elgin Marbles*, from the Parthenon in Athens, dating from the 5th century B.C., were first purchased by Lord Elgin in 1810, while he served as the ambassador to Constantinople. He eventually sold them to the English government in 1816. The collection was put in a pre-fabricated timber-frame shed surrounded by single brickwork walls. In 1821 it was decided to build a purpose-built building for the collection (along with four other major ones acquired between 1820-25,) with Robert Smirke to design it ("it" being the British Museum.) Work began in 1823; completed 1857, with the museum's current facade.

  (*In modern times, the Marbles are more politically correctly called: the Parthenon Sculptures. There has been/remains some measure of pressure to return them to their land of origin.)
- King Edward VII Galleries: Were added in 1908-14.
- Natural History Museum: Broke away (i.e. got its own building) in 1881, in South Kensington. (See: National History Museum, under N.)
- Reading Room: (AKA: the Library Reading Room.) Was built in 1857 on the site of the old museum courtyard. (See: British Museum Library, at its own listing.)

- British Museum Library: (See at its own listing.)
- Foundling Hospital: (AKA by its full name: the Hospital for the Maintenance and Education of Exposed and Deserted Young Children.) 18th C., built in the fields that became Bloomsbury. Established by Cpt. Thomas Coram, a retired sea captain/philanthropist. Royal charter in 1739, completed in 1752. In 1926 the hospital moved to Redhill, then to Berkhamsted, closed in 1954. (See under F.)
- London University: (See: University of London, under U.)

- Malet Street: (See under M.)
- Montagu House: Occasionally seen as: Montague. (See: British Museum, above.)
- Montague Street: Built in the late Georgian period.
- St. George's: Completed in 1730 with a fine portico and a statue of George I surmounting the spire. Slightly eccentric design, by Hawksmoor. (See under the CHURCHES section.)
- Southampton House: Occupied the north side of Bloomsbury Square until it was pulled down in 1800.
- Southampton Square: Bloomsbury Square was originally "Southampton Square," laid out by the Earl of Southampton. Nothing remains of the earl's palace except the gardens, which are largely intact. It was the first residential square in London. Called "Bloomsbury Square" by the time of the Regency.
- University of London: (See under U.)

Bloomsbury Way - 1910. Contains buildings from at least the 1780s. The street's pre-1910 name was Hart Street. (See under H.)

- St. George's Church: 1731. (See under the CHURCHES section.)

blue coat schools - Built in various parishes, taking the idea from schools first begun in London. They were funded by way of voluntary contributions, to teach poor children to read and write. They were usually free, or had a small fee in order to provide the (often blue coated) uniforms. Children who graduated from these schools were often put out to join a trade or service. Some even sent students on to university. (See: Bluecoat School, below - A frequent nickname for the charity school of Christ's Hospital.)

blue plaques - These plaques indicate a former residence of a person of cultural and/or historical importance or interest. The first such plaque was placed on Lord Byron's birth home in 1867. (See: Holles Street/24.)

Bluecoat School - (Also seen as: Blue-Coat School.) In 1709 was a charity school. Until 1939; ruined in WWII. "Bluecoat" was a nickname commonly used for Christ's Hospital, because the school uniform included a long blue coat. Not to be confused with Blewcoat School. (See: Christ's Hospital.)

Blues and Royals, the - Cavalry. They wear blue tunics and red plumes. (See: Royal Guards.)

bluestocking - Term for scholarly/literary ladies. Originally referred to those women who met at the homes of Mrs. Montagu, Mrs. Ord, and Mrs. Vesey (particularly in the Montagu salon.) The term was first used in 1756, and referred to men who sought such feminine company. By the time of the Regency the term was applied to women and was not complimentary, implying an unsuitable intellect/one who was engaged in (as considered at that time) off-putting non-feminine-appropriate pursuits.

Boadicea - Statue of, on Westminster Bridge. Also seen written as: Boudica (and other spellings.) Commissioned by Queen Victoria in the 1850s, but not at this site until 1902. Boadicea was a Celtic warrior/queen of the Iceni who fought back the Romans; she destroyed London; and she died in 60AD of a self-administered poison, rather than be captured.

Board of Agriculture - (Very quickly took on the expanded name: Board of Agriculture and Internal Improvement.) Founded in 1793, a voluntary association wishing to encourage agricultural improvement. Commissioned a series of county reports. Dissolved in 1822.

Board of Control - Created in 1784 in order to administer the government of India. (For prior to 1784, see: East India Company, largely the British body involved with India up to 1784.) From CASSELL'S COMPANION TO EIGHTEENTH CENTURY BRITAIN: "After the conquest of huge swathes of territory in the subcontinent during the Seven Years War the government of India had become a pressing problem. Previously the British involvement with India had been largely the concern of the East India Company, which maintained a number of factories there. But the Company ran into difficulties attempting to administer a territorial rather than a commercial empire.... When William Pitt the Younger became prime minister, he created the Board of Control by the India Act of 1784; this body took over responsibility for the government of India, but left trade and patronage in the hands of the Company. It also avoided the dubious constitutional innovation of having it answerable to the Commons rather than to the crown."

- See: East India Company.
- See: India.

Board of Trade, the - The Treasury. (See: Treasury.) The Board of Trade started and stopped several times. Began ca. 1668, it failed within 3-4 years; revived in 1696, lasting until 1782, at which time it was abolished. Sprang up again in 1786 as the Board of Trade and Plantations, under Pitt the Younger (and still exists.) CASSELL'S COMPANION TO THE EIGHTEENTH CENTURY says: "...Established by Parliament in 1696 as 'the Board of Trade and Plantations' to replace other ad hoc bodies in the administration of colonial affairs." In 1768 a secretary of state was appointed for the colonies, heralding the abolishment of the Board's role in the colonies in 1782. (Britain had many colonies at that time, including America, Australia, and India.)

Left the Treasury in 1873-4, however mostly remaining in the Whitehall area until 1964, when it moved to Victoria Street. Merged in 1970 with the Department of Trade and Industry.

Board of Work, Metropolitan - Established in 1855. (See under M.)

boating -

- See: activities/entertainments/sports, boating (under A.)
- See: Doggett's Coat and Badge Race.
- See: Henley-on-Thames - Henley Regatta, 1839.
- See: Hyde Park/Serpentine.
- See: Oxford and Cambridge Boat Race.
- See: Thames.

boatmen - (See: bargemen.)

body-snatching - Stealing bodies, to be sold, usually to anatomists (who were usually doctors who illegally wished to learn through dissection how human bodies functioned.)

- See: hospitals - For further notes on dissection.
- See: Pie Corner/Fortune of War tavern.
- See: resurrectionists.
- See: St. Sepulchre, under the CHURCHES section - For a legal method of acquiring bodies for medical study.

Bolsover Street - Marylebone. Was originally part of the Portland Estate. Laid out in the 18th century. In 1815 was taken over as the north part of Regent Street. Significantly rebuilt in the 20th century. (Not to be confused with a later street named Bolsover, which runs parallel to Great Portland Street.)

Bolt Court - Off Fleet Street.

- 6: Dr. Samuel Johnson (lexicographer) spent his last 8 years here, dying in 1784. Now demolished.

Bolton House - (See: Hampstead/Bolton House.)

Bolton Street - Clean and quiet. There at least since 1708.

- 11: Fanny Burney (Madame D'Arblay, novelist) moved here from 1818-1828, as an older woman of 66.

Bond Street - Bond Street is the main street in Mayfair.

NEW BOND STREET: Approximately a half mile/0.8 km long, continues on to Oxford Street. (The northern section.)

OLD BOND STREET: Runs for about 200 yards due north to Piccadilly. (The southern section.)

Note: There is actually no plain old "Bond Street," and there still remains a division of "New" and "Old," despite proposed legislation to combine the two simply under the one name. In common use, however, one part or the other is often referred to simply as "Bond Street."

In 1644 the area was converted from wild countryside to an "imposing palace" for the Earl of Clarendon.

In 1683 the earl's Clarendon House was pulled down in order to make Bond Street; the first part constructed became known as Old Bond Street. Named for Sir Thomas Bond, who died in 1689; the street had been laid out prior to the 1689 date, but was largely undeveloped and described as resembling "the ruins of Troy."

In Georgian times, besides residents it also boasted not just the best shopping, but the best place to be *seen* shopping, (a fact still true.) Rich, idle men who lingered here were referred to as "Bond Street Loungers."

By the early 19th C. there were apartments for gentlemen, often called hotels (but more like flats than today's hotels. See: flat, under F.)

Among the fashion shops, which were exclusively for males, there were other types of businesses here: for instance, boxing lessons could be hired, and one could find wine or books in addition to men's clothing. Women had to go to Covent Gardens to find clothing for their gender. Women could make purchases here for the males in their lives, but feminine customers would have been few and far between; it was said that a decent lady could only be on Bond Street before midday. While the street was appropriate for promenading ladies (supposedly before noon,) Bond Street after dark was a place definitely frequented by "ladies of low quality"; this was a known Regency venue for prostitutes at night.

These days, combining both New and Old Bond Streets, there are more Royal Warrants here than anywhere else in London. (See: Royal Warrant, under R.)

NEW BOND STREET:

- 26: Tessier's, silver- and goldsmiths. Established in 1851.
- 34-35: Sotheby's Auction House. Here since 1907. (See: Sotheby's, under S.)
- 50: Chappell, Samuel: Music publisher, and (from the 1840s) manufacturer of pianos. In the late 19th C. began selling organs. Founded in 1810; had a fast-growing good reputation. In 1980 sold its retail concerns to concentrate on the publishing part of its business. Closed in 1987.
- 63: Fenwick of Bond Street. (Pronounced Fen-ick.) Women's high end fashion store, founded in 1891.
- 101: Phillips. Auction House. Established here in 1796. (See under P.) Is now a part of Bonham's Auction House, since 2001. (See: Montpelier Street/Bonham's.)
- 103, 130, 141 & 147: Admiral Lord Horatio Nelson (naval hero) lived in New Bond Street on four occasions; at 103, age 39, during the winter of 1797-98, being here for seven months. At 130 & 147 with his mistress, Lady Hamilton. And at 141 with his wife (after the loss of his arm at Santa Cruz.)

- 164: Grafton House. One source says it's on the corner of Clarges Street and Piccadilly; a second source says it is on the corner of Grafton Street. In 1811 owned by the firm of linen-drapers called Wilding & Kent (and later the Grafton Fur Company.) As drapers, it was a popular place, as Jane Austen (author) wrote of it to her sister.
- 165-169: Asprey's & Co. Jewelers, goldsmiths, silversmiths. Established by William Asprey 200+ years ago. Came to London from Mitcham in the 1830s. Moved into 165-169 in 1847.
- 175-177: Cartier Jewelers. Here since 1909.

<u>OLD BOND STREET</u>:

- 4: Lawrence Sterne (author of *Tristam Shandy*) died of poverty here, 1768.

  "Gentleman" John Jackson's famous pugilistic establishment was here during the Regency; sometimes called "Jackson's academy." Gentleman Jackson was the much-admired Champion of England (in boxing, b.1769-d.1845,) although it should be noted he only won three prizefights himself prior to setting up this training establishment. He wore a scarlet jacket, lace cuffs, breeches, and silk stockings. Lord Byron (poet) was a regular customer.
- 13: In 1820, Benson & Hedges, Tobacconists, were established here. (Today, is the oldest surviving shop in all of Old Bond Street.)
- 23: Truefitt. Court Hair Cutter/Hair Dresser. Established in 1805 (at that time to men only.) Wigmaker to Prinny. Still makes wigs. In the late 1800s they became the first ladies' hairdressers at their own establishment wherein the lady was expected to come to them instead of the hairdresser going to the lady's home. They also sold their hairdressing products and colognes. In modern times: this address houses Cartier (the jeweler,) and was scheduled to become a Stella McCarthy (designer clothing) store.
- 33: Present location of Yardley Soap. Moved here in 1910. (See under Y.) Atkinson, the perfumer moved here in 1832, although his decorative bear was disallowed at this Old Bond Street location. (See: Soho/Atkinson.)
- Hookham's Book Shop: Existed during the Regency. (See under H.)
- Royal Arcade: 1880. The Arcade links Albemarle Street and Old Bond Street. Replaced the Clarendon Hotel, which had been demolished in 1870.
- Stewart's: A baker's shop since 1688 (however beginning at another location.) Became renown in 1780 (at this location) for its "Uxbridge Rolls."
- Western Exchange, the: Here by at least 1817. Described as a precursor of the

modern department store.

- Weston: John Weston, coat-maker. Was here during the Regency. Beau Brummell (fashion trendsetter) helped make this, his tailor, famous.
- Yardley Soap: (See: 33, above.)

bondsman, being a - Could also be called: a bondservant, or an indentured laborer. Being a bondsman in Britain was different from being a slave. Sort of.

A bondsman (or bondswoman) was an indentured servant; they were bound by a signed (or sometimes signed under force, especially in the further past) contract to work for a particular employer, for a set time. Often it allowed the employer to sell their bondsman's labor to a third party. The bondsman signed the contract in order to refund a debt or to meet some other legal requirement. They were freed once they'd served their contracted time, and sometimes even given a plot of land. This practice was well faded by the time of the Regency era. This system is now banned by the Universal Declaration of Human Rights, 1948, as being a form of slavery. (You may care to see: slaves.)

bone china - As in dishes.

- See: china.
- See: Staffordshire/Spoke, in the BRITISH COUNTIES section.

Bonham's - Auction House. (See: Montpelier Street/Bonham's.)

Bonners Field - Kennington Common (now Kennington Park.) There for centuries. Site of the Chartist Riots (universal manhood suffrage) in 1848, a failed event which pretty much put paid to the Chartist movement in England.

bonnets - Women's headwear.

- See: hats.
- See: hatters.

Boodle's Club - Gentleman's club; "the country gentleman's club." Founded in 1762. Unpretentious. (See under the CLUBS section.)

book clubs - From the 18th C. and increasingly as the 19th C. came along, most towns and many villages had a book club (or several) for the purposes of buying, exchanging, and discussing books. Both genders participated, although the clubs might be gender separated.

book, first in English - The first dated book in English (that was not a bible) was: *The Dictes and Sayenges of the Phylosophers*, 1477, by the Kent merchant/publisher William Caxton (funded by Edward IV.)

Book of Common Prayer - Introduced during Edward VI's reign (doomed son of Henry VIII) in 1549. Many Roman Catholic practices were outlawed, and the Anglican clergy were granted permission to marry. It was rewritten in 1552 to make issues of doctrine clearer, by Thomas

Cranmer (English Reformation leader.) The uniformity of service that resulted is said to have advanced the establishment of England as a Protestant State.

- See: bibles.
- See: Printing House Square - The note on the King's Printer.

Booksellers' Row - Popular nickname for Holywell Street; it no longer hosts any booksellers, but did in Regency/Victorian times. (See: Holywell Street.)

booksellers/bookshops - Booksellers and printers were often one and the same.

- See: Barker & Howard - Bibles and navigational books.
- See: Booksellers' Row.
- See: British & Foreign Bible Society.
- See: Finsbury Square/Lackington's.
- See: Fitzroy Square/Warren Street - For comments on cookbooks.
- See: Gallery of Arts.
- See: Hatchard's.
- See: Henry Sotheran.
- See: Holywell Street.
- See: Hookham's - (See at: Bond Street/Old Bond Street/Hookham's.)
- See: libraries/lending libraries.
- See: Little Britain - For pre-1725 booksellers.
- See: Ludgate Street.
- See: Middle Row.
- See: novels.
- See: Paternoster Row.
- See: Ridgeway's Bookshop.
- See: Sackville Street/2-5/Henry Sotheran.
- See: St. Paul's Churchyard - Not the graveyard, but the adjacent street.
- See: Soho/Wardour Street.
- See: Stationer's Hall - For where books had to be registered.
- See: Temple of Fancy.
- See: Wiley's Legal Bookstore - 1830.

Booth's - Circulating library in Duke Street, Portland Place. Existed in 1804. Existed here until at least 1835.

bootmakers -

- See: Cockspur Street/Edward Rymer - Prinny's bootmaker.
- See: St. James Street/Hoby's.

- See: St. James Street/9/Lobb's.

Borough, the - Is actually separate of Southwark, on which it borders. (All the same, see: Southwark/Borough, the.)

Borough High Street - (AKA: Borough Street.) Southwark and Kennington.

- 77: The George, an inn. Rebuilt in 1676, it is the last timbered, galleried inn in London. (See the INNS/PUBS section.)
- 103: Queen's Head Inn. John Harvard (main contributor/founder of Harvard University) had this inn bequeathed to him by his mother in 1636 (the inns here had existed since Chaucer's time.) He in turn deeded it to the university. Gone now (except for a plaque,) it stood at least until photography had been invented.

Borough Market - Southwark. At the southern end of London Bridge. Oldest municipal wholesale fruit & flower market in Britain, and also claims to be the oldest surviving London market still in London. Records do date back to the 13th century. Moved to its present and slightly more southern place during Victoria's reign (near Southwark Cathedral.) This area also housed Georgian warehouses. (See: Southwark/Borough High Street/Borough Market, under S.)

Borough Street - (See: Borough High Street, at its own listing.)

Boswell Street - Earlier name of Devonshire Street; was still called Boswell Street as late as 1875.

botanical gardens - Bringing plants from abroad and fostering them for British growth was a popular pursuit in the Regency era.

- See: Chelsea/Chelsea Physick Garden.
- See: gardens.
- See: Kew Gardens.

Botany Bay - A community in Enfield Chase.

- See: Australia - For the Botany Bay there.
- See: Enfield Chase.

Bottlemakers' Company - (See: Horners' Company.)

Boudicca - (See: Boadicea.)

Bow - (Rhymes with "go.") Tower Hamlets. An area east of the City, where porcelain was manufactured in the 18th century. Until the industrial growth here, was used by wealthy gentlemen for their country homes. Terraced houses came in in the 1820s. The May Fair (for which the area Mayfair was named) came here in 1764 when it was exiled from Mayfair in the St. James's district.

- Bow Commons: Industrialized in the mid 19th century. Historically was known as a poorer district.

Bow Lane - (AKA: Cordwainer Street; cordwainers were professional shoemakers who made their product from new leather, the word being derived from "cordovan," as in fine leather.) Its name was changed in the mid 16th C. to Bow Lane. (See: Cheapside/Bow Lane.)

- 39: Ye Olde Watling, 1668. Huge, blackened ceiling beams. (See under the INNS/PUBS section.)

Bow Street - A poor, sometimes dangerous area by the later 18th century. Home of the famous Bow Street Runners. (See: No. 4, immediately below.)

- 4: Bow Street Runners.

  Established as a home in 1740, for Sir Thomas de Veil.

  In 1749, Henry Fielding bought the house, and converted it into a magistrate's office/the home of the Bow Street Runners, led by Sir John Fielding (died 1754; blind brother to Henry Fielding the author.) The Runners were a private policing force, and so (not being publicly funded) must be hired to carry out their work. They never numbered more than twelve at this location, but there were more Runners when the organization expanded to nine other offices in later years; (seven offices were established throughout London in 1792.) The Runners were nicknamed Robin Redbreasts because of their bright scarlet waistcoats, which they started wearing in 1822. Also called "officers of the Bow Street magistrates' court." Also called "thief-takers."

  The first six Runners were paid a guinea a week plus a per criminal bounty (which made them relatively well paid.) These first six had been parish constables.

  The Chief Magistrate was James Read from 1806-1813; from 1813-1820 it was Sir Nathaniel Conent.

  Existed until 1829, when the Metropolitan Police force began. (See under M.) The adoption of police forces nationally came in in 1856.

  The Bow Street location remained a magistrates' court until it was closed in 2006.

  Sir John Taylor built a new (now) police station in 1880, on the opposite side of the road, directly opposite the Royal Opera House. This (once-Bow Street) station, the Magistrate's Court, closed in 1992.

  - Horse Patrol, the: Was an off-shoot of the Bow Street Runners. It was mostly made up of ex-cavalrymen, and made a significant reduction in highwayman crimes. (See: Metropolitan Police/Bow Street Horse Patrol.)
    - See: Charlies.
    - See: police.
    - See: Scotland Yard.

- See: Watchmen.

Bow Street Horse Patrol -

- See: Bow Street/4/Horse Patrol.
- See: Metropolitan Police/Bow Street Horse Patrol.

Bow Street Runners - (See: Bow Street/4.)

Bowler hat - Invented in 1850.

bowling green - A place for playing nine-pins (a game similar to the ten pin bowling we know in modern times, absent the head pin.) Bowling greens date in London from at least 1560. (See: Tiger's Head, under the INNS/PUBS section.)

Bowling Green House - (See: Putney Heath/Bowling Green House.)

bowls - A game dating from the 13th C., something like bocce ball or horseshoes. First in London in 1455. From 1511-1845 it was banned, except on Christmas; except for those willing to pay a high license fee for playing on private greens (on their own land.) Ca. 1864 it took off again, in the formation of Bowling Clubs.

- See: bowling green - For an activity somewhat like American-style bowling.
- See: earthenware - For a bowl as in: used for eating.

Bowyers' Company - (AKA: the Worshipful Company of Bowyers.) Longbow-makers. AN ENCYCLOPAEDIA OF LONDON states: "Before 1370; in London the provision of archers' equipment depended on three separate crafts: the bowyers, the fletchers or arrow-makers, and the stringers or longbow string-makers. The first two were originally a single trade but in 1371 the bowyers and fletchers...enforcing an ordinance of mutual exclusion for the two crafts" separated. (See: Fletchers' Company.)

Achieved a coat of arms in the late 1480s.

Due to the invention of the firearm, by the early 1600s there were only four bowmakers left in London.

The Bowyers' trade yet exists (with a resurgence of interest in target archery in the 20-21st centuries,) but is now mostly a charitable organization. 38th in the order of precedence. Has no Hall.

Bowyer's Lane - (Also seen as: Bowyers Lane.) Camberwell and Peckham. Dates back to at least the 16th century. By 1836, was still known as Bowyer's Lane, and had "slum-like dwellings." Today is known as Wyndham Road.

Box Farm - (See: Markham Square.)

boxing - (AKA: pugilism.) This sport was quite popular in the 18th and well into the 19th century. The first prize-fighting champion was James Figg, who successfully defended his title in 1727. Gentleman Jackson (who was also a champion) had a place during the Regency in which to learn pugilism, and to watch boxing matches. (See: Bond Street/4/Gentleman Jackson's.)

There were no gloves at this time; you boxed bare-knuckled (until ca. 1814, and even after that the pugilists may or may not wear somewhat puffy-looking gloves.) They stripped to the waist. They were called prize-fighters, since they fought for cash prizes (although the legal position of holding prizefights was dubious, with fights sometimes being broken up by a local magistrate.)

When boys/men got into a fist fight, the scuffle might be called "fisticuffs"; however, this term was also applied to pugilism as often as not.

The Marquess of Queensberry lent his name for the rules of glove-fighting, devised in 1867.

- See: Bond Street/Old Bond Street/4/Gentleman Jackson's.
- See: Cribb's Parlour.
- See: Five's Court.
- See: Mendoza's - He was the first to write a boxing textbook.
- See: Old Kent Road/320.

Boyle Street - Burlington Gardens. The street is named for the Boyles, the Earls of Burlington. Here from at least 1720.

braille - Tactile system of reading for the blind, via raised bumps embossed on paper. Invented by Louis Braille (French educator/inventor) in 1837.

brain tumor - First identified as such after 1866. (See: Maida Vale/Maida Vale Hospital.)

Brandenburgh House - (See: Fulham/Brandenburgh House.)

brasier - A brasier is someone who works brass.

- See: Coleman Street/Armourers' and Brasiers' Hall.
- See: halls/Armourers' and Brasiers'.

Bread Street - Cheapside. John Donne and John Milton (both poets) were born on this street, the latter in 1608. Known for its cookshops.

- Gresham College: (Also seen as: Gresham's College.) 1597. Housed in (the merchant, and builder of the Royal Exchange) Sir Thomas Gresham's Bishopgate home until 1768; moved several times; ended up in Holborn. (See: Gresham's College, under G.)
- Mermaid Tavern, the: (See under the INNS/PUBS section.)

breakfast - (See: meals.)

breeches-maker -

- See: Charing Cross Road/16.
- See: pants - Not a Regency term.

- See: Romford - Leather breeches.
- See: tailors.

Brentford - Developed early as a trading place; was granted the right to hold fairs/markets in 1306. Was a first stage for coaches leaving London, and so an increasingly important locale as the 17th century advanced. Charter received in 1932. The small River Brent is here, where it blends into the Thames. (See: canals, note under.) In the 19th century Brentford became increasingly industrial, and therefore increasingly working-class.

- Brentford Football Club: 1889.
- Brentford High Street: (See: Great Western Road.)
- Green Dragon Yard: Took its name from a nearby posting inn, which by the 18th C. was a halting place for carriages on their way to Essex. Rebuilt in 1810. Cleared following serious WWII bombing damage.
- High Street: Shops. Victorian. Not a very attractive street.
- Old Brentford: According to CHAMBERS LONDON GAZETTEER: "The south-eastern corner of Brentford, located at the mouth of the River Brent, nowadays more commonly known as Brentford Dock," (ca. 1850s.) CHAMBERS continues: "Medieval Brentford was divided between the parishes of Hanwell and Ealing and the two halves were later distinguished as New and Old Brentford. New Brentford, which is no longer shown on maps, was associated with the manor of Bordeston, which came to be called Boston Manor." The dock closed in 1964, becoming the Brentford Dock marina in 1980.

Brettenham House - (See: Lancaster Place.)

Brewer Street - Soho. First seen on a map in 1664.

- 71: A diplomat, soldier, and spy named Charles d'Eon de Beaumont (b.1728-d.1810) lived at 71 Brewer Street for 33 years; he scandalized London by dressing as a woman (although anatomically a man.)

breweries - Breweries were plentiful in most eras of London life. (See: the opening notes in both parts of the INNS/PUBS section.) In the Georgian era, brewing was a huge business in London; in Southwark, much of the business belonged to the firm of Perkins; Truman Hanbury and Buxton in Spitalfields; Charrington's in Mile End Road; Watney's in Pimlico; and Whitbread's in Chiswell Street. (There were others.)

- See: beer.
- See: Brewer's Hall.
- See: Chiswell Street/Whitbread's.
- See: Chiswick/Fuller's.

- See: Hammersmith.
- See: Mile End Road.
- See: Southwark/Brewery/Barclay & Perkins.
- See: water - For why Regency people drank more beer than water.

Brewers' Hall - (For the Worshipful Company of Brewers. AKA: the Wardens and Commonalty of the Mystery or Art of Brewers of the City of London.) Aldermanbury Square (not a Regency square,) their Hall here for 600+ years (from 1403.) Oldest mention dates from 1292. Of old, brewers were considered to be of low repute, but by 1345 were growing in importance and dignity. Charter in 1438. Burned in the Great Fire of 1666; rebuilt in 1673. Repaired in 1828. Stood until 1940, when destroyed during the Blitz in WWII; rebuilt in 1960. Ranks 14th in precedence. Still closely involved in the trade of brewing (and is also a charitable organization.)

Brewer's Lane - (See: Hungerford Lane.)

Brick Lane - (See: Whitechapel/Brick Lane.)

Brick Street - Piccadilly, Mayfair. Was formerly called "Engine Street," because of a mechanical mill that regulated the rise of the Tybourne (Tyburn) stream. A 1793 source refers to it as: Engine Street; a 1907 one as: Brick Street.

bricks - After the Great Fire of 1666, when London building regulations allowed no buildings be built of (oh-so-burnable) wood, bricks were always in demand.

- See: Barnet/Child's Hill.
- See: Great Fire of 1666 - For more on its resultant change of building laws.
- See: Highbury.
- See: Kensington.
- See: Pot Kilns.
- See: Paddington.
- See: Whitechapel/Brick Lane.

Bride's Lane - (See: Bridewell Prison.)

Bridewell - (See: Bridewell Prison.)

Bridewell Hospital -- (AKA: Christ's Hospital of Bridewell. Also: the City Bridewell.) New Bridge Street, off Fleet Street, Blackfriars. Orphanage, established by Edward VI in 1553. One hundred children were sent from here to Virginia (America) in 1619 (in a kind of foster program); it was a successful project, with another one hundred children following. It was, however, in many respects a prison (as indicated by its very name, and its stated intent to correct the behavior of its residents.) I found one 1844 reference that refers to this place and practice still existing.

Bridewell Place - Hosted the Bridewell Prison. An old Street. Damaged in WWII. (See: New Bridge Street.)

Bridewell Prison - Also referred to simply as "Bridewell." (See: NOTE, below in this entry.) Some referred to it as "Tothill Fields Prison" because of its Tothill Fields, Westminster location. (See the reference, below in this entry: toot hill.)

Originally a royal palace (Bridewell Palace; in the early middle ages, on the banks of the Thames, built for Henry VIII in 1520,) given to the City by Edward VI. Became a hospital; then in 1556 became a workhouse for undesirables; evolved into a House of Corrections for criminals and heretics, retaining its palace-like appearance. First existed in Westminster in 1618 on "toot hill" (meaning the highest hill to be found in the area.)

A whipping post and ducking stool were installed in 1633; it was a "London sight" to come and watch the twice-weekly whippings. A special whipping-room was built and draped in black; a balustrade for spectators was added in 1677. The practice survived to ca. 1767.

Partially burned in the Great Fire of 1666; rebuilding completed in 1676. AN ENCYCLOPAEDIA OF LONDON states: "This (rebuilding) included a new stone bridge built in 1672, to replace the wooden one over the Fleet erected for Charles V." There were 36 sleeping rooms for men in the men's prison building (east side.) The women's building was to the west.

Rebuilt in 1834 in nearby Frances Street, able to house 800; then being known as New Bridewell Prison.

Closed in 1855. Demolished in 1864; the Court Room and some offices yet exist.

Unilever House now also stands on this site.

This Bridewell had three churchyards: one south of the chapel, one south of Tudor Street; the third between Bridewell Place (modern street) and Dorset Street. The last yet remains, sans tombstones.

NOTE: "Bridewell" was often used as a general term to mean imprisonment by a local magistrate (usually for petty crimes,) such as in "He must settle with his creditors soon, or it will be Bridewell for him," even if the debtor would in truth end up at some other prison. Too, it was not uncommon for an area to call its local gaol Bridewell Prison; for instance, Clerkenwell Bridewell. Bridewells were for able-bodied prisoners, who were put to work. Reluctant bridegrooms were threatened with a term in Bridewell if they chose not to marry their impregnated sweethearts.

Contains the Bridewell Pass-room. Pauper women were held here for a week before being sent back to their own parishes under the Poor Laws.

- See: workhouses - For note on the Poor Laws.
- See: prisons - For a list of others, plus mention of Bridewells.

bridge - The card game. (See: Portland Club, under the CLUBS section.)

bridges - (See the BRIDGES section.)

Bridgewater Canal - (Also seen as: Bridgwater Canal.) Opened in 1761. This was the first canal in London, and was considered successful, leading to other canals following. (See: canals/Bridegwater Canal.)

Bridgewater House - (See: Cleveland House.)

Bridgewater Square - Small, neat, 1730s homes, open space, and small garden at its center, built for the Earls of Bridgewater.

- 7-8: Gunter's. Famous confectioners. (See under G.)

bridles - As in, for horses. (See: Loriners' Company.)

Brighton - Located in East Sussex, obviously not in London. (Its full name was: Brighthelmstone. By the time of the Regency, only old-fashioned types would have still called it Brighthelmstone. Approximately 50 miles/80 km from London. (See: Brighton, under the BRITISH COUNTIES section.)

Brintons - Carpet manufacturers. (See: Worcestershire/Brintons, under the BRITISH COUNTIES section.)

Britannic House - Finsbury Circus. By Sir Edwin Lutyens, 1924-7, rebuilding what had been here, now as the Britannic House. The two statues of *Britannia* dates from 1924.

British & Foreign Bible Society - PILGRIMS' LONDON states: "An organization whose purpose is 'to encourage the wider circulation of the Holy Scriptures without note or comment,' the BFBS was founded in London in 1804 by members of the Clapham Sect and other evangelicals. Today, known simply as The Bible Society, it prints and circulates Bibles in hundreds of world languages."

British Academy, the - (Currently AKA: The British Academy for the Humanities and Social Sciences.) Somerset Place. When first established it was "for the Promotion of Historical, Philosophical and Philological Studies." 1899. Charter in 1902.

British and Foreign School Society - Supported free British Schools/teacher training in the 19th century, ca. 1810. It provided the teacher training until the 1970s. The schools they funded were called "British Schools," as opposed to "National Schools." (See: National Society for Promoting Religious Education..., under N - For explanation of National Schools.)

British Armed Forces -

- See: army.
- See: Marines.
- See: Ministry of Defence.

- See: navy.

British Counties - (See: the separate BRITISH COUNTIES section.)

British flag - (See: flag, British - Under F.)

British Forum, the - A London debating society, run by John Gale Jones (radical orator.) Existed at least by 1808 and was still in existence by 1818; one reference refers to a speech Mr. Jones made at: "The British Forum, held at The Crown and Anchor Tavern, in the Strand." So, like many societies, I think this one did not necessarily have a permanent base, but was a body of like-minded men who met at various sites, the *gathering* being the Forum rather than a particular place. Given that Mr. Jones was arrested several times for disturbing the peace (that is, rabblerousing,) this may have been prudence on his part. (You may care to see: debating societies.)

British Gallery - This is a nickname for the National Gallery. (See under N.)

British Institution - 52 Pall Mall. Established in 1805; George III was the patron, along with wealthy subscribers. Opened in 1806. Had two major exhibitions a year, one of works by living contemporary artists, the other of loaned master works (which students could come and copy.) There was a memorial exhibition of Joshua Reynolds' works here in 1813. Closed in 1867, and in 1868 the building was sold to the Marlborough Club (though it was shortly demolished thereafter, that a new clubhouse building might take its place.)

(See: Almack's Club, under A; *not*: "Almack's Assembly Rooms.")

British Library - Formed in 1973 out of the British Museum, the Patent Office, and other museums.

- See: British Museum Library.
- See: Southampton Street/Gallery of Arts.

British Lying-in Hospital - Covent Garden. Established in 1749, London's first maternity hospital. Doctors set up this hospital for married women, the doctors being unhappy with how childbirth was handled at Middlesex Hospital. BUT: keep in mind that in the nineteenth century *most* births occurred at home; to go to a hospital to give birth suggests there were expected complications.

- See: childbirth.
- You may care to see: City of London Lying-in Hospital.

British Museum - (See: Bloomsbury Square/British Museum.)

British Museum Library - (AKA: the Royal Library.) Began as part of the British Museum, but now is its own entity (by an Act of Parliament in 1973) even though its Reference Division is still a physical part of the British Museum; so now is known simply as THE BRITISH LIBRARY. (Not to be confused with the so-called one by John Bell. See: Southampton Street/Gallery of Arts, for Bell's.) Is entered via Great Russell Street. Began in the 1750s as donated books amassed from private collections. Was housed in a basement reading room in Montagu House from 1759. In 1857, the collection moved into the British Museum Library READING ROOM (AKA: the Round Reading Room,) a copper-domed room north of the main foyer of the British Museum, constructed on the site of the old museum courtyard (at that time being 235,000 books strong.)

A new, round purpose-built building was begun in 1854-7 by Sydney Smirke (brother of Sir Robert.) It could shelve 1.3 million books.

By 1945, portions of the collection were stored elsewhere due to growth. In 1973, this was combined with some private collections and the whole of the books were then called the British Library.

In 1982, a new building (which has been some twenty years in the making) was begun on the site of the former Midland Railway on Euston Road in St. Pancras; present address: 96 Euston Road, St. Pancras.); opened in 1997. Described as "massive" and having a "rather brutal exterior."

(See: British Library, the (1973/became its own entity.)

Brittanic House - 20th century. (See: Finsbury Circus/Lutyens House.)

Britton Street - Clerkenwell. Laid out in 1718-24, originally called Red Lion Street. Renamed to Britton Street in 1937.

- 55: Jerusalem Tavern. Small. Atmospheric. Georgian interiors, complete with "intimate snugs." Named for a local pub frequented by persons such as Dr. Johnson (lexicographer) and David Garrick (actor,) although this building's incarnation as a pub of this name is from ca. 1995. The building, however, dates from 1720; started life as a coffee-house.

Brixton - Lambeth. Had been a place for raising game and of market-gardens (to supply London); in the early 19th C. began to become residential. Took on its African and Caribbean flavors in the 1950-60s.

Brixton Hill - Lambeth.

- Brixton Prison: 1830. (See at its own listing.)
- Royal Asylum of St. Ann's Society: School for needy children and orphans. 1829. (Later the St. Pancras Auxiliary Institution.)

Brixton Prison - On Brixton Hill. Started life as the Surrey house of correction; built in 1830. At first it was only for female prisoners, but by 1853 it included males.

Broad Common - (See: Clapton/Upper Clapton/Clapton Common.)

Broad Green - (See: Croydon/Broad Green.)

Broad Sanctuary - Street, built along with Parliament Square (the latter in 1840-50s,) ca. 1868.

Broad Street - Golden Square, Soho, Westminster. (AKA: Old Broad Street. See under O.) First built in 1686. The road was developed by 1736, at which time it was a fashionable address, but by the mid 18th century it was a residential area for tradesmen and shopkeepers. Many 18th C. buildings still remain on this street. It was known as "Old Broad Street" by the time of the Regency. Former name of Broadwick Street, the name change occurring in 1936 (when Broad Street and Edwards Street were combined.) Famous for an outbreak of cholera here in 1854.

- ➢ See: Golden Square.
- ➢ See: Petty France/New Broad Street - Victorian.
- ➢ See: South Sea House.

- 74: Birth home of William Blake (painter/poet,) born 1757.
- Excise Office: (See under E.)
- Gresham College: (AKA: Gresham's College.) After Sir Thomas Gresham's widow died (ca. late 16th century,) his home on this street was willed by him to become Gresham College. (See under G.)

Broadwick Street - (See: Broad Street.)

Brockley - Lewisham. Victorian suburb.

Broderers' Hall - For the Worshipful Company of Broderers. (AKA: The Brotherhood of The Holy Ghost of the City of London.) Broderers practice the ancient art of embroidery. The company existed as early as 1430; chartered in 1561. Early on, their Hall stood in Carey Street. It moved on to Gutter Lane, where it was lost to WWII bombing. This organization held embroidery exhibitions in the late 19th century. The guild yet exists. They were not on the (Court of Aldermen's) list of precedence until 1837, at which time they were dubbed 48th.

Bromley - In records from the year 862 it is written as "Bromleag." King John granted a charter for a town market in 1205; specialized in wool trade. 129 households here by the 1660s. (See: St. Blaise's Well, below - The note under.)

- Berry's Green: (See: Single Street, below.)
- Bromley Common: Its 300 acres were enclosed beginning in 1764; second part of the enclosure dates from 1821.
- Broom Hill: (Also seen as: Broomhill.) 18th C. industry: broom-making, bonnet-making. Remained largely rural into the 20th century.
    - Zion Chapel: 1819.
- Crofton: Described at the end of the 18th C. as "lying in the middle of woods." Possibly had once been a parish, one destroyed by fire. Is now a nature reserve, called Crofton Wood (or Woods.)
- St. Blaise's Well: Rediscovered in 1754. Caused the town of Broom Hill to

flourish (as wells were often attractive to those seeking to drink the waters/seek health/treat an illness.)

- St. Peter and St. Paul: Martin's Hill. Parish church. The wife of Dr. Samuel Johnson (lexicographer) is buried here.
- Single Street: Its Regency name was Berry's Green. (See: Single Street, under S.)
- South Bromley: Not really in Bromley. (See: Bromley-by-Bow/South Bromley.)
- Southborough: Southeast corner of Bromley. Had a few large houses and about 16 cottages by the mid 19th century.
  - South Barrow: 17th C. house. In 1901 became Belmont School; closed in 1922. Became an old folks home, then an office for the War Damage Commission; pulled down in 1954, replaced by Birdham Close.
- Sundridge: (See under S.)
- Swan and Mitre: Pub. On High Street. Edwardian.

Bromley-by-Bow - East End, between Bow and Poplar. Not related to Bromley. In the 17th C. was rural retreats. In the 1820s was workers' housing and "noxious industries." Descended into slums by the late 19th century.

- South Bromley: These days the name is little used. Is the southeast corner of Bromley-by-Bow. Had factories from the mid 19th century.
  - Bromley Hall: Small but elaborate 15th C. manor house of Lower Bromley. Widely remodeled in 1700. Has turned into many things, most recently offices.

Brompton - (AKA: Knightsbridge. See under K.) Developed (as Brompton) in the 1820s. (See: Broom Farm.)

- Queen Street: (See under Q.)
- West Brompton: (See under W.)

Brompton Cemetery - (AKA: the West Brompton Cemetery. See under W.) Opened and consecrated in 1840. Lord Byron (poet, d. 1824) is buried here.

Brompton Crescent - 1840s. Later renamed as Egerton Crescent. (See under E.)

Brompton Grange - Is arrived at via Michael's Grove. Opened ca. 1786. Builder Michael Novosielski built this as his own residence. Pulled down in 1843. A crescent of buildings replaced it in the 1880s.

Brompton Hospital - 1842. Philip Rose (later knighted for his efforts) had a clerk who was sick with consumption (tuberculosis.) The clerk, as was common at the time, was refused entry into a hospital. Concerned and angry, Mr. Rose assembled colleagues and organized the founding of a "Hospital for Consumptive and Diseases of the Chest" in 1842. It moved in 1846 to its present location and took on the name Brompton Hospital. East wing dates from

1846, the west from 1854. This is the same as "Royal Brompton Hospital." (See: Fulham Road/Royal Brompton Hospital.)

Brompton Oratory - 1853. Catholic. (See under the CHURCHES section.)

Brompton Park - 1855 road. Adjacent to the street called Queen's Gate.

Brompton Road - The north side was called Brompton Row during the Regency. The south side was called Brompton Grove, and Queen's Row. It was a suburban district until the 1870s. (See: Knightsbridge/Brompton Road.)

- 235: James Hardy & Co., silversmiths. Here since 1853.

Brompton Row - (See: Brompton Road.)

Brompton Square - Laid out in 1821-35, by builder James Bonnin. The fine houses are of yellow brick. The "square" is actually a long, narrow half-circle rather like a horseshoe shape.

Brook Green - Hammersmith and Fulham. Dates back to the 15th century. There was an annual fair here since 1800, but by 1823 it was banned. As the 19th C. advanced, the area turned into a rookery.

Brook Street - Mayfair. Fashionable thoroughfare that led from Grosvenor to Hanover Square. Took its name from the (once) nearby Tyburn Brook. Built in the first half of the 18th century, typical but individually designed terraced houses. Some are modest, some are rather grand.

- 23: Jimi Hendrix (guitarist) lived here 1968-9.
- 24: Handel (composer's) home from 1729 until his death in 1759. Now the Handel Museum. (In Handel's time, the house number was 57.)
- 25: Claridge's Hotel. Was known as "Mivart's" in the Regency. Claridge's says of themselves: "Two hundred years of refined hospitality." Currently has an art deco decor.

Brook's Club - Less frequently seen as: Brooks's Club. (See under the CLUBS section.)

Brooke House - Upper Clapton Road, Hackney. This property was once a part of the manor of Kingshold, taken by Henry VIII in 1538, at which time it had a manor house called Hackney House. Edward VII gave it to the Earl of Pembroke in 1547. From him it transferred to Henry Carey, first Lord Hunsdon, 1570-83, at which time the house is presumed to have been rebuilt. It next went to Sir Rowland Hayward, and when he died in 1593 the house went to Anthony Redcliffe (one of Hayward's executors.) Elizabeth, Countess of Oxford, got possession in 1596-1609. Fulke Greville (1st Lord Brooke) finally gave the house the name it yet carries. It has undergone renovations at various times since. At some point (at least prior to WWII) it became a mental hospital.

Brooks's Club - More often seen as: Brook's Club. (See under the CLUBS section.)

Broom Farm - Dates from at least 1294. Converted into fruit gardens in the 16th century. During the Regency it was scattered market-gardens. This district developed into Brompton in the 1820s.

- Brompton Park Nursery: 1691. Where the Victoria & Albert Museum is now.

Broom Hill - (See: Bromley.)

Broomwood House - William Wilberforce lived here from 1797-1808. It was demolished in 1904. Now (a little removed from the original property) it is a primary school known as Broomwood Hall.

Brown's Hotel - 30-34 Albemarle Street. Founded as an inn in 1837 by Lord Byron's butler, James Brown. The present restaurant here still has its high Victorian charm (and a very high tea.) Built over some of the foundations of Clarendon House, 1666-1680s.

Bruce Castle - Bruce Grove. (See: Tottenham/Bruce Castle.)

Brunswick Dock - (See: Blackwall, at its own listing, the note there.)

Brunswick Place - Marylebone. In the 1920s was renamed Upper Harley Street, because it was accommodating the overflow of doctors from Harley Street.

Brunswick Square - Bloomsbury. Featured in Austen's *Emma.* Laid out in 1794. Not terribly fashionable; close to the legal quarter of London; built for the bourgeois. A public garden and supplementary streets. Open and airy. (Also see: Mecklenburgh Square, which mirrors Brunswick Square.)

- 40: Founding Hospital, after 1929. (See: Foundling Hospital.)
- 4 Old Burlington Street: Poole, Henry. Tailor. (See: Savile Row/15.)

brushes - For personal care.

- ➢ See: St. James's/Kent & Sons - For hair.
- ➢ See: Middle Row - For combs.
- ➢ See: toothbrushes.

Bruton Place - Mayfair, Piccadilly. Described as a "quaint little mews" off Berkeley Square.

- 30: The Guinea, pub. Dates back to the 15th century.

Bruton Street - Berkeley Square, Mayfair. "Sheridan and his lovely wife" (playwright) lived here in 1786.

- 17: Queen Elizabeth II was born here in 1926.

Bryanston Square - Marylebone. Now an affluent area of London; in modern parlance it gained the nickname "Millionaire Square." (The word "millionaire" was not coined until 1843.) Built 1810-15, on Ward's Fields, part of the Portman estate. Takes its name from the Portman family estate in Dorset.

- Bryanston Court:
    - 5: When Wallis Simpson was married to her 2nd husband (1929) she lived here. She met Edward VII in 1931.

Brydges Place - Tiny alley (London's narrowest; narrows down in one part to just fifteen inches) off St. Martin's Lane; 200 yards long, connecting Bedfordbury, Covent Gardens with St. Martin's Lane. Certainly existed by Dickens' time.

Buckingham Court - (See: Spring Gardens/Buckingham Court.)

Buckingham Gate - Victorian name for this older street. (See: James Street.)

- Queen's Gallery: 1830.

Buckingham House - (Later: Buckingham Palace.)

The Mall, Westminster. Originally on this site there had been a monastery. During the time of the Stuarts this site hosted a spot called Mulberry Garden, because in 1615 James I had an idea to introduce silk production into England. Stands near what was once a Jacobean mansion called Goring House, which was burned, and in the 17th C. was replaced by Arlington House. This Arlington House (located on the southern section of this general location) was demolished when a new brick house was commissioned in 1702 for John Sheffield, the first Duke of Buckingham and Normandy, who used a Dutch architect, Capt. Wynne. (By this time Arlington House had devolved into a notorious brothel.) The new brick house was completed in 1705 (near the original house's site.) The duke died in 1721.

In 1761 it was acquired by George III from the duke's illegitimate son for £28,000 (because the King disliked St. James's Palace, it negatively affected his health.) He moved in to Buckingham House in 1762. He had BH made over into a palace, (although it was not called "palace" officially until declared so by William IV following George IV's death in 1830.)

In 1775, in exchange for Somerset House, by Act of Parliament the property was settled on Queen Charlotte by her husband, George III, and so it was known as "the Queen's House" (not to be confused with other "Queen's Houses" known throughout London history. See under Q.) During the actual Regency, this same lady, Prinny's mama, lived here. The house was not in good repair by the time of his Regency (1811-1820.)

The present palace was started in 1825 by John Nash for George IV (Prinny.) At this time it was sometimes referred to as the King's House, at least in the common parlance. The construction of Buckingham House was so expensive, George IV had to abandon Carlton House, despite having lavished years of effort and money on the latter.

Nash was dismissed (following a government investigation) and replaced by Edward Blore. At this time it retained only the shell of the former house. It was not completed by the time of George IV's death in 1830 (funds ran out in 1828, and work was stopped.)

The house was completed in 1837 (the same year the new king, William IV, died) in the Palladian style, and Queen Victoria was the first monarch to actually live here

(although she left it following Prince Albert's death.)

Currently of Bath Stone (since George V's time,) was originally of red brick. The east facade (Mall side, the side visitors view) had been iron palisades, but was rebuilt in 1846 by Edward Blore (giving the building the well-known look it has generally kept since,) and again in 1913, this time by Sir Aston Webb, with a Portland stone facade. The south wing and the ballroom were added in 1856. (The western facade was done by John Nash, and is visible only from a helicopter.) Has forty acres of garden.

As stated above, Victoria was the first monarch to live here permanently, moving in in 1837 (while sticky windows and dysfunctional plumbing were still being corrected.) Victoria and Albert added the State Supper Room and the Ball Room, and the Marble Arch, which later moved to Hyde Park.

- ➢ See: Marble Arch, below.
- ➢ See: Marble Arch, under M.

Had 600+ rooms; as of the 21st C. it has 775, 19 are State rooms, 52 are bedrooms for Royals and guests, 188 bedrooms for staff, 78 bathrooms, and 92 offices.

The palace was revamped in 1913.

It wasn't used again, since Victoria's time, as the regular London home of the Sovereign until the reign of Edward VII.

The exterior facade lighting began in 1931.

Parts of the interior were opened to the public in 1993.

- Buckingham Palace Gardens: The Palace has a 45 acre park, five of which are covered by a lake. Described as "fine gardens," laid out by William Townsend Aiton ca. 1830. Usually not open to the public.
- Library, the: This was the library from which George IV gave 120,000 volumes to the British Museum.
    - ➢ See: Bloomsbury Square/British Museum/British Museum Library.
    - ➢ See: British Museum Library - At its own listing.
- Marble Arch: (See under M.)
- Mulberry Tree: There still remains one of the original black mulberry trees planted by King James I in 1609. (He was attempting to found a silkworm farm, planting 30,000 black mulberry trees. The experiment was a failure, because no one had told him that silkworms only like to consume the leaves of *white* mulberry trees.)
- Royal Mews: On the palace ground's south side.
    - ➢ See: Buckingham Palace Mews.
    - ➢ See: Royal Mews, under R.

Buckingham Palace - (See: Buckingham House.)

Buckingham Palace Gardens - (See: Buckingham House/Buckingham Palace Gardens.)

Buckingham Palace Mews - Derives from the King's Mews, 14th C., which was at that time at Charing Cross. From 1377 royal hawks were kept here (hence the term "mews," which means "molting"); that burned in 1543, then being rebuilt as stables. From ca. 1762, George III had his stables (re)built here; with George IV fully establishing the stables (and storage of state carriages) here; rebuilt in 1824-5 by John Nash. To this day, yet provides road transport (horse or motor car) to the Royal Family; and is yet a working stable.

Buckingham Street - Built in 1675. (One of several streets built over the site of York House.) The Duke of Buckingham had a mansion here, York House (named for the 13th century Bishop of York, the original landowner,) which the duke remodeled in 1626. When the duke died, the new duke did not often live at York House and ended by selling it to a developer (ca. 1676,) with the stipulation that his name(s) be used in developing the area; hence you get (among others): Buckingham Street, Duke Street, George Street, Villiers Street.

- 12: Samuel Pepys (the famous diarist who recorded the great fire of 1666) lived here in 1679-85; he also lived at 14 at one time.
- Water Gate: (See under W.)

Bucklersbury - A small street, leads from Cheapside to Walbrook. Dates from the 14th century.

- Bucklersbury House - 1954. The ruins of a Roman temple dedicated to Mithras was found at the site at the time of this house's construction, dubbed the Bucklersbury Mosaic.

Budge Row - Near Sise Lane. Dates back to at least the 16th century.

- St. Antholin's: (See under the CHURCHES section.)

bugs - (See: insects.)

Builders Merchants Company - (AKA: the Worshipful Company of Builders Merchants. Also seen written as: Builders' Merchants' Company.) It awards grants to institutions related to building. Surprisingly not ancient, founded in 1961; became a livery company in 1977. 88th in the order of precedence for Livery Companies.

bull-baiting - Not a Regency diversion; had gone out of vogue. It was outlawed in 1835. (You may care to see: bear-baiting.)

Bullock's Museum - (See: Piccadilly/Egyptian Hall.)

Bunhill Fields - (Less frequently also called: Bunhill Fields Dissenters' Burial Ground. AKA: Bunhill Burying Ground.) Corruption of "bone hill." 38 City Road, St. Luke's, Finsbury. The land was granted in 1315 to the Mayor and Commonalty at an annual rent of 20 shillings. First designated as a cemetery after the Great Plague of 1665; enclosed then with brick walls and a gate (although burials took place here from 1315.) In fact, between 1315-1854 some 120,000 souls were put to rest here. Although PIGRIMS' LONDON says: "The property was set apart and consecrated in 1665 as a burial place for plague victims outside the city. However, according to historian William Maitland writing in 1739, the actual ground where a huge pit was dug to bury the victims was elsewhere, and this land was simply held by the city until the restoration. After 1660 rents were demanded, and the city then let the property out for a cemetery." CHAMBERS LONDON GAZATTEER claims that in 1665 it was a Quaker burial ground and "It was popular with Dissenters of various denominations because the ground was unconsecrated." (Quakers are more formally called Friends (members of the Society of Friends. Their founder, George Fox (b.1624-d.1691) is buried here.) Yet another source confirms that in 1685 (or 1695) it was allocated to the religious nonconformists. William Blake and Daniel Defoe are buried here (but Blake did not get his present monument until 1927.) It became so overcrowded by 1800, it was becoming a health hazard; it was closed as a cemetery in 1863, 1867 being the date at which an act for preservation of the grounds passed. Open in 1869 to the public by the Lord Mayor; it is no longer a burial ground, now being a "garden of rest." (See: City Road.)

Bunhill Row - A street in Islington, near Bunhill Fields. John Milton (poet) lived here for a while.

buns - To eat, as in what Americans call "rolls." While there were receipts in the Regency for dishes called rolls, when speaking of a small bread to eat, a "bun" is the better Regency era term.

- See: Cheapside/Bunhouse.
- See: food/buns.

Burberrys - Victorian draper; founded in 1856 by Thomas Burberry in Hampshire; raincoat (and coat) manufacturer. Sir Thomas invented his famous weatherproof cloth ca. 1880. Opened in London, the Haymarket, in 1891.

Burgh House - (See: Hampstead/Flash Walk/Burgh House.)

burials - Being buried was virtually how every Regency era body was disposed of (at least legally.) Cremation was extremely rare, if not unheard of.

- See: cemeteries.
- See: embalming.
- See: suicides.

Burlington Arcade - Piccadilly, Mayfair. Built by Samuel Ware, 1819, for Lord George Cavendish. Built adjoining the garden of Burlington House (supposedly to keep people from tossing their garbage over Lord Burlington's garden wall.) Was from its inception and still is patrolled by beadles, who yet wear coats and bowler hats (the latter of which date from 1850.) Opened on 3/20/1819. Being a covered corridor, which leads from Piccadilly to Burlington Gardens, one of its chief attractions was that you did not have to tramp in mud;

a collection of shops, first shopping district of its kind. Shallow inverted "V" covering has windows set in it (windows meet at the arch.) Ornamental lamps overhead, at about three-quarters of the way to the summit. Shopfronts all had a disciplined regularity, with mahogany-lined interiors. Tiny shops, with quarters above for the shopkeepers. The ostentatious shop facades at either end of the arcade were added in 1911.

- 68-69: Lord's. Looking at a contemporary drawing, below No. 68 it reads "Hosier," and below No. 69 it reads "Glover." (See: Lord's, under L.)

Burlington Gardens - Mayfair. Runs along Burlington House. Burlington Gardens used to be Vigo Lane, then Vigo Street, running from Bond Street to Glasshouse Street, by 1831.

- 6: Built in 1866-7 in a Renaissance style. Part of the University of London until 1972, when it became the Museum of Mankind (part of the British Museum.)
- Boyle Street. (See at its own listing.)

Burlington House - On the north side of Piccadilly, (across from 185 Piccadilly.) Designed in 1664-5 by an architect, to be used as his own home, but was only partially completed. He sold the unfinished house to the first Earl of Burlington. This was remodeled by James Gibb in 1717, for Richard Bayle, 3rd Earl of Burlington. Remodeled (extensively) again in 1811-1816 by Sidney Smirke for Lord George Cavendish; Cavendish did not live here at the time, however, (instead at 1 Savile Row,) and so Lord Elgin was allowed to leave his Elgin Marbles here for this time. (See: Bloomsbury Square/British Museum/Elgin Marbles.)

Cavendish gave the house over to the University of London in 1853. The university's headquarters were here from 1853-66 (having come from its original site in Somerset House.)

It was purchased in 1854 by the government.

The Quadrangle was added in 1869-73.

- ➢ See: Royal Academy of Art, below.
- ➢ See: Royal Academy of Art, under R.

- Royal Academy of Art, the: When the University of London moved out in 1866, this space was leased, from 1868 to the Royal Academy of Art; rent was £1 a year. (See: Linnean Society, for a longer list of societies here.)

Bury Street - St. James's. Beau Brummell's father lent rooms to the Quality here. (There is another Bury Street, in Enfield, which would have been mostly farmland during the Regency era.)

- 30: William Taylor, tailor. Reasonably fashionable. There by at least 1815.
- Wilton's: Founded in 1742; began life as a fishmonger's stall in Cockspur Street; still renowned for their fish and oysters. Wilton retired in 1770. Ca. 1980s Wilton's moved to 55 Jermyn Street.

bus - There were no Regency era buses. They did have wagons, which could be (less elegantly) used to move a group of people; picture servants rather than the upper classes.

- See: double-decker bus - 1902.
- See: omnibus - 1829.
- You may care to see: hackney coach.
- You may care to see: hansom cabs.
- You may care to see: trams - 1861.

Bush House - 1925-35. Aldwych, opposite St. Mary-le-Strand. Designed by Americans.

Bushy Park - Teddington. One of eight Royal parks in London. (See: royal parks, for all eight.) Lies outside the grounds of Hampton Court Palace. Described as being "wilder" (than the average royal park) despite a formal line of spectacular, large horse chestnut trees. Contains rhododendrons, and wild deer. Established in the early 16th C., a hunting ground for Hampton Court.

CHAMBERS LONDON GAZETTEER states: "The second-largest but least-known of the eight royal parks of London, situated between Teddington and the Thames at Hampton Court."

Beautified by the earls of Halifax in the early 18th century, at which time it was enclosed by a wall.

- Bushy House: Built in 1663. Restored and rebuilt 1713-15. Queen Victoria gave it to the Commission of Works in 1900, to be the National Physical Laboratory.
- Teddington Hockey Club: Began here in 1871. The world's oldest hockey club (with a continuous history.)

businesses, owned by women - During the Regency there was no law against a woman owning a business, so long as she was of age (21.) Realize, though, that unless she had a rather clever lawyer, the minute a woman married, all property/money/income belonged to her husband. Such circumstances (a woman owning a business and/or keeping her property/income) would have been more likely to happen with the middling classes, not the aristocratic woman. The latter was often "protected" from worldly knowledge, plus it would have been considered scandalous to her peers to see one of their own in business or as being money-savvy; it wasn't genteel; it would almost certainly cost the woman her social standing. To be clear, a woman of the *haut ton* was not legally restricted from such acts, but she'd have to have her husband's permission and support, in a time when most husbands would have been appalled at such ideas.

All of this might carry less sting/pull, even if the woman were of the upper class, if one were a spinster or a widow.

(You may care to see: Women's Rights.)

butchers - There would have been a butcher in most communities. To this day under existing law, a

City of London butcher who knowingly sells bad meat could be pilloried for a day.

- See: meat, the note under - For how someone could buy a cut at the butcher's and get it cooked.
- See: Newport Market.
- See: Paternoster Row/Newgate Market.
- See: shambles.
- You may care to see: knackers - For the difference between a knacker and a slaughterer.

Butchers' Hall - For the Worshipful Company of Butchers. Some records indicate the presence of organized Butchers as far back as 975AD. Regardless, the Hall first stood in Monkwell Street; moved in 1548 to the one-time parsonage of St. Nicholas Shambles (east end of Newgate Street. "Shambles" is an old word for a butcher's shop or stall.) In 1605 the Guild of Butchers was granted their Royal Charter. The Hall burned in the Great Fire of 1666; rebuilt, up a court, on the south side of Eastcheap (between Botolph Lane and Pudding Lane); finished by 1677. This site was heavily altered in 1828-9, but it was then quickly lost to fire. Rebuilt in 1829, same site. The Company existed before 1180. Their charter was first granted in 1605; it was taken away and returned several times; the current charter dates from 1749. The present Hall dates from 1885, when the Butchers moved to Bartholomew Close.

Butcher's Row - Pulled down in 1790-1815. (See: Pickett Street.)

Butler's Wharf - A 16th C. dock. (See: docks/Butler's Wharf.)

buttons - (For securing garments closed.) Regency era buttons ran the gamut from simple bone with two drilled holes, on up to beautifully painted miniature portraits. They were often a metal ring wrapped in thread (often knotted into a design) or covered with fabric. Some other button materials used were: metal (usually for men, not always,) polished or painted glass, pearls, shells, silk, wood, and stone (such as agate.) This is not an all-inclusive list. Not all women's dresses had buttons, some were held closed with ties, visible or hidden inside the garment. (See: Firmin & Son, for military buttons and accouterments.)

Byron House - 8 St. James's Street. Byron House was built on this site in 1960, commemorating Byron's one time home here. (See: St. James's Street/8.)

Brydges Street - (See: Covent Gardens/Catherine Street.)

Byward Street - The City. Built 1895-1906, replacing the far older Black Swan Court.

-C-

cabbages - Grown in England for eons. Would have been a crop harvested well into the cold time of the year.

- See: Battersea Fields.
- See: food/cabbage.

Cabinet, the - (AKA: the Cabinet Office.) Whitehall. (Not to be confused with the Cabinet War Rooms, which was a WWII complex built seventeen feet underground for Winston Churchill and the members of the War Cabinet.)

The Cabinet, meaning both those who work in the Cabinet and the building itself, is led by the Prime Minister (keep in mind this is now, see below for earlier) and has about 20 members. Came about in the 17th C. and originally housed the Treasury. The building was worked on over the years 1733-1844 by William Kent; Sir John Soane; and Sir Charles Barry, (the current version dating from 1845.) Cabinet members are selected by the Prime Minister (who also advises on the selection of bishops and candidates of honour,) and they are in charge of the major state departments (such as: the Treasury, the Home Office, the Office of the Leader of the House of Commons, the Office of the Leader of the House of Lords, etc.)

At its north end resides the Privy Council, the Queen's (or King's) Private Council. (See: Whitehall/Privy Council.)

Meetings are held at 10 Downing Street in the ground floor Cabinet Room.

- See: Lower House.
- See: Upper House.
- See: Westminster.

To be clearer, the cabinet refers to the persons who make up the inner circle of government ministers, and it refers to where they meet. CASSELL'S COMPANION TO EIGHTEENTH CENTURY BRITAIN states: "Although the expressions 'cabinet,' 'cabinet council' and 'inner cabinet' were used of meetings of ministers in the 18th century, this does not mean that there was such a thing as cabinet government. On the contrary, it could be claimed that there was a movement towards less and less formal consultation between prime ministers and their colleagues as the period progressed." However, the wars with France (1793-1815) created an atmosphere of increased power for the Prime Ministers and their cabinets, with, by 1800, the monarch normally accepting unanimous cabinet advice; in 1812 the Prince Regent (later George IV) allowed the cabinet to select the PM.

Cabinet War Rooms, the - (Also now called: Churchill War Rooms.) 1938. Clive Steps, King Charles Street, Westminster. Described as: "A secret warren of underground rooms" stretching below Westminster.

cabs -

- ➢ See: Corporation of Coachmen.
- ➢ See: hackney coach.

Cadogan Gardens - Near Sloane Square, Chelsea.

- 11: Eleven Cadogan Gardens. (I'm not repeating; this is the name of the place.) Understated luxury. Late Victorian design, for Lord Chelsea, who built four mansions here on his cricket ground in the late 19th century.

Cadogan House - Georgian. (See: Ministry of Defence.)

Cadogan Pier - Cheyne Walk/Chelsea. On the Thames. Demolished in 1873. Rebuilt, because it yet exists, with 2016 being its 175th anniversary, so was first built in 1831. (See: Doggett's Coat and Badge Race.)

Cadogan Place - Chelsea. Developed by Henry Holland, on land leased from Lord Cadogan. Built before 1811. Charles Dickens (presumably a bit tongue-in-cheek) wrote of Cadogan Place as the link "between the aristocratic pavements of Belgrave Square and the barbarism of Chelsea."

- 30: The actress Dorothy Jordan (b.1762-d.1816) lived here at one time.
- 44: William Wilberforce (anti-slavery leader/politician) was lent this house by his cousin, Mrs. Lucy Smith, 9th July 1833, but he died on the 29th. It is a Henry Holland (Georgian) house. Elegant mansion, in a row of them.

Cadogan Square - Knightsbridge. Built in 1877-88, named for the Earl Cadogan.

- ➢ See: Hans Town/Sloane Place.
- ➢ See: Pavilion, the.

Cadogan Street - Chelsea/Knightsbridge.

- St. Mary's: 1812. Roman Catholic. (See under the CHURCHES section.)

Caledonian Asylum - (See: Islington/Caledonian Fields/Caledonian Asylum.)

Caesar's Camp - (See: Wimbledon Common/Caesar's Camp.)

cakes - (See: food/cakes.)

Caledonian Road - (See: Chalk Road.)

calendar -

- ➢ See: rents.
- ➢ See: year, beginning of.

Camberwell - Now part of the London Borough of Southwark; had been an ancient parish that was considered part of Surrey. Kings hunted here. Described in 1801 as a tiny village surrounded by farms and fields. Terraced houses came in in the 1820-30s.

- Camberwell Green: Held an annual fair until 1855.
- Camberwell Grove: An 18th C. road, described as pleasant, which once led to a villa on a large tract of land.
- Camden Chapel: (See under the CHURCHES section.)
- Denmark Hill: Named for George, Prince of Denmark (consort to Queen Anne,) the latter of which had a house nearby.
- Dulwich Village: Still has "an old-world and rather countrified air." (See: Dulwich/Dulwich Village.)
    - Dulwich College: 1616. (See: Dulwich/Dulwich College.)
- Rawlings of Camberwell: Established ca. 1810, for purchasing non-alcoholic drinks such as mineral water and fruit drinks.
- St. George's: Wells Street. (See under the CHURCHES section.)
- St. Giles Church: Parish church, after which the benighted neighborhood was named. (See under the CHURCHES section.)
- St. Giles: Notorious rookery. (See under S.)
- Southampton Way: Robert Browning (poet) was born here.

Camberwell Grove - Southwark. (See: Grove Hill.)

Camberwell New Road - 1820. Runs from Kennington Common to Camberwell Green.

Cambridge - University. East Anglia, on the River Cam; 56 miles/90 km northeast of London. The town of Cambridge has existed some 2,000 years. The school was founded in the 13th century. For centuries, only Anglicans were admitted. The colleges are frequently referred to by a single name, dropping the use of "College." For instance: "I attend King's." -or- "I'm meeting him at Magdalene."

By 1772, Dissenters could attend classes at Cambridge, but they could not ultimately graduate with a degree. This was challenged in 1834, but it wasn't until 1856 that some degrees were opened to Dissenters, with almost all remaining blocks removed in 1871. (See: dissenters, under D.)

Note that seven of the colleges listed below were founded by women.

- Christ's College: God's-house (also seen as: God's House) had stood here since 1436, but was renamed in 1505 by Henry VII's mother, Lady Margaret Beaufort and dedicated by her as Christ's College.
- Churchill College: 1960.
- Clare Hall (NOT known as Clare College until 1856): Seemed to have started life as a convent. Founded in 1326 by Cambridge University as "University Hall."

Lady Elizabeth de Clare (three times a widow at age 29) refounded it as Clare Hall in 1338. Rebuilt in 1636-1715. Name changed in 1856 to Clare College.

- Corpus Christi College: 1352, started by donations from the two guilds of Corpus Christi and St. Mary. It is two groups of buildings: those built by the guilds, and those built by Wilkins in 1823-7.
- Darwin College: 1964.
- Downing College: Founded in 1717 by bequest of Sir George Downing, Bart. (Baronet.) Charter obtained in 1800.
- Emmanuel College: Founded in 1584 by Sir Walter Mildmay, Chancellor of the Exchequer. Chapel and cloister designed by Wren.
    - Addenbrooke's Hospital: 1766.
    - Fitzwilliam Museum: Funds in 1816; the interest from those funds built the museum in 1837-47.
- Fitzwilliam: 1966.
- Girton College: Founded for women, in 1869. Opened (in a hired house in Hitchin) in 1873.
- Gonville & Caius College: (Caius is pronounced: "keys.") Founded in 1348 by Rector Edmund Gonville as Hall of the Annunciation. Moved to its present site in 1351. John Caius renovated/expanded it in 1557.
    - Church of St. Michael: Dates from 1323.
- Homerton: 1976.
- Hughes Hall: 1885.
- Jesus College: The Bishop of Ely (John Alcock) founded this college in 1496 when the convent of St. Radegund was suppressed.
    - Church of All Saints: 1865 (replacing a small church in Trinity Street.)
    - Church of St. Andrew the Less: (AKA: the Abbey Church.) Seems to date from the 13th century. Rebuilt 1854-6.
    - Hospital of St. Mary Magdalen: Founded in 1199 for lepers.
    - Library: Its bookcases date from 1679.
    - Pump Court: (AKA: New Court.) 1870.
- King's College: On King's Parade. Founded in 1441 by Henry VI as houses named St. Mary and St. Nicholas, on its first site. The second site was bought and built in 1443-9. (See: King's College, under K, more at.)
    - Bodley Building: 1893.
    - Chapel Building: 1446.
    - Fellows' Building: 1724.

- Hall; Library; Provost's Lodge; Screen: All date from 1824.
- Kennedy Building: 1928.
- Scott Building: 1870.
- Webb Building: 1908.

- Lady Cavendish: 1965.
- Magdalene College: (Pronounced: Maud-lyn.) Henry VI granted this site to the English Benedictines in 1428; they established a Benedictine hostel. Founded in 1542 as the college, by Thomas, Lord Audley, to replace Buckingham College. Samuel Pepys (diarist) attended here (and eventually left his library to this school.)
    - Church of St. Giles: 1875.
    - Observatory: 1824.
    - St. Peter's by the Castle: Rebuilt from virtual ruins in 1781.
    - Shire Hall: 1842.
- Newham College: A house for women students attending lectures was opened in 1871. Moved to a new building in 1875, this being presently the oldest block in Newham College.
- Pembroke College: Founded in 1347 by Marie de Saint Paul, widow of the Earl of Pembroke.
- Peterhouse College: Trumpington Street. Founded in 1281 by the Bishop of Ely, Hugh of Balsham; moved (by him) in 1284 to its present site. First enrolled scholars in 1284. Cambridge's oldest and smallest college.
- Queens' College: Founded not once, but twice. First in 1448 by Andrew Dokett, whose patron in this venture was Margaret of Anjou (queen of Henry VI.) Founded again in 1465 by Elizabeth Woodville (queen of Edward IV.) Since two queens had influence here, "Queens'" is spelled with the apostrophe following the s.)
- Robinson College: Grange Road. Founded in 1977.
- St. Catherine's College: Founded in 1473 by Dr. Robert Wodelarke (third provost of King's College.)
- St. Edmund's: 1896.
- St. John's College: Founded in 1511 by Henry VII's mother, Lady Margaret Beaufort, when the Hospital of St. John the Evangelist (founded in 1135) was suppressed. Is one of Cambridge's seven colleges founded by a woman.
    - Cambridge Union Society: 1866.
    - Church of St. Clement: 1821.

        - Church of the Holy Sepulchre: (Commonly called the Round Church.) Probably built ca. 1120-1140.
        - Master's Lodge: 1863.
    - Selwyn College: Founded in 1882 as a public hostel; named for George Selwyn, Bishop of Lichfield. Became an Approved Foundation (of the university) in 1926.
    - Sidney Sussex College: Founded in 1596 from a bequest by Lady Frances Sidney, Dowager Countess of Sussex.
    - Trinity College: (AKA: St. John's Trinity.) Founded by Henry VIII in 1546; this founding was a blending of King's Hall (1336) and Michael House (1323) and Physwick's Hostel (had belonged to Gonville Hall) and some other minor hostels. Specialized in Literature.
    - Trinity Hall: 1350, founded by the Bishop of Norwich, William Bateman.
        - Latham Building: 1927.
    - Wolfson: 1965.

Cambridge House - 49 Piccadilly, Mayfair. Built in 1756-61 by the second Earl of Egremont. Late Palladian style. Was first known as Egremont House, then in the 1820s as Cholmondeley House for its then resident, the first Marquess of Cholmondeley. In 1829-50 Prince Adolphus (seventh son of George III,) the Duke of Cambridge, lived here and the house took on its current name. Lord Palmerston (statesman/PM) lived here from 1857 to his death. In 1862 it became the Naval and Military Club.

> ➢ See: Piccadilly/49.
> ➢ See: Naval and Military Club, under the CLUBS section.

Cambridge Square - Post-1840. (See: Hyde Park Square, note at.)

Cambridge Terrace - On the southeast side of Regent's Park. Built in 1825, designed by John Nash. Described as a "short line of houses." (See: Park Crescent/Cambridge Terrace.)

Cambridge University Press - (AKA: Bentley House.) 1931.

Camden - (AKA: Camden Town.) Islington. Named for the 18th century Earl of Camden. Just northeast of Regent's Park. Started to develop by the 1790s, although parts date from as late as 1828 (especially after Regent's Canal was built.) In the mid 18th C. it had been a part of the area known as Kentish Town. By the mid 19th century, it was a solid working class district. Is now known for antique shops, and a twice-weekly street full of stall-holders. (See: Camden Market, below.)

- Arlington Street: (See under A.)
- Bayham Street:
    - 16: (Now number 141.) Charles Dickens (author) spent his childhood here

in a crowded four room tenement.

- Camden High Street: A short street, goes one way toward the north, originally called Southampton Place.
- Camden Market: This location has a 200+ year history. In 1974 the area was purchased and then called Camden Lock Market, having only 16 stalls. Now it is a flourishing antiques street with many stalls.
- Morning Crescent: (AKA: Mornington Crescent.) Begun in 1821.
- Mother Red Cap: Pub. Built mid 17th C., on the site of the home of an acquitted witch, whose real name was Jinny Bingham, but who was called Mother Red Cap (and also Mother Damnable.) The pub still exists there, although it is now known as The World's End, Camden Town.
- St. Nicholas: Parish church. 15th C., but only the Perpendicular north part of the church remains from that time, the remainder being mostly modern.
- Vale of Health: (See: Hampstead/Well Walk.)

Camden Market - (See: Camden/Camden Market.)

Camden Place - Elizabethan mansion, dates at least from 1609. Napoleon III lived here in 1871-1873.

Camden Road - 1825.

Camden Town - (See: Camden.)

Campden Hill - (See: Kensington/Campden Hill.)

- Campden Hill House: (Sometimes seen as: Campden House.) A Stuart mansion on the hill. Built in 1612 for Sir Baptist Hicks, made Viscount Campden in 1628. Queen Anne lived in it as a princess. Sold in 1751. In 1847 the then owner spent a great deal on renovations (including installing a private theatre.) Burned in 1862. Referred to as "the Dukeries," an apparent comparison to the poor and odiferous "Potteries" area not far away; this nickname was Victorian.

Campden Hill Road - Kensington. Originally called Plough Lane, name changed ca. the 1980s.

- 114: Windsor Castle, a pub. Built in 1828 as a coaching inn. Its look remains consistent with that period.

Canada - Regarding Britain's connection to Canada (and in very quick and simplistic terms,) from before the 18th century Britain had had a long-standing connection with Canada. (See: the INTRO section/British Kings and Queen & Their Reigns/Henry VII.)

When Britain conquered New France, it led to the Treaty of Paris in 1763, which then led to Britain beginning to populate the formerly French-held Canada with English speakers.

Upper and Lower Canada were created by Act in 1791. Upper Canada was land west of the Ottawa River (what is now Ontario), Lower Canada was east of the Ottawa River (what is now Quebec.) They were independent of one another.

Out of improved governance that formed in 1848, now four Canadian colonies chose to federate in 1867, becoming a Dominion (ergo, at that time becoming the one Canada.) Out of that grew Canada's push toward more independence in the matter of world affairs; they were then independent of Britain except for matters of foreign and military policy.

Britain declared in 1926 that it would no longer legislate for any of its Dominions, making them independent states, formalized by the Statute of Westminster in 1931. This codified that all Commonwealth Realms were equal and independent of one another, only yet having allegiance to the King (or Queen.)

Canada's legal separation from Britain continued. The Canadian Citizenship Act of 1946 granted Canadians a legal separate identity from Great Britain, with the last of the constitutional ties between the UK and Canada ending with the Canada Act of 1982.

Canada is a fully independent country, but like other Commonwealth Realms has a head of government AND a head of state, the former being the Prime Minister of Canada and the latter being the monarch of the UK. This form of government has been likened to a company having both a president and a CEO. The Queen of England is also the Queen of Canada (and other Commonwealth countries, such as Australia,) and she is its personification; when a Canadian person pledges to her, that person is pledging to "Canada." In her role as Head of State (the Sovereign of the parliamentary democracy and constitutional monarchy of Canada,) she appoints the Governor General, who is turn appoints the ten provinces' Lieutenant Governors, in conjunction with Canada's Prime Minister. The Queen serves other duties as well, such as supporting national organizations, traditions, and ceremonies.

(See: INTRO-REIGNS section/British Kings & Queens and their Reigns/Henry VII - For the "discovery" of Canada.)

Canada House - Trafalgar Square. Bath stone; "handsome," by Sir Robert Smirke. Completed in 1824-7. Was originally two buildings that made up the Royal College of Physicians, and the Union Club. Besides the National Gallery, it is one of the only buildings that survives from the initial development of Trafalgar Square. Became Canada House, with remodeling, in 1924.

- See: Royal College of Physicians.
- See: Union Club, under the CLUBS section.

Canada Square - Modern. (See: docks/West India Docks/One Canada Square.)

canals - AN ENCYCLOPAEDIA OF LONDON states: "There are three 'mouths' to the London canal system: the mouth of the River Lea, by which barges can proceed northward; at

Limehouse, where admission is given to the Regents' Canal, which goes northward for a while till it takes a westward turn to link up with the Grand Union system; and at Brentford, where the mouth of the partly canalized river, the Brent, is the main 'port' for inland navigation."

The canals really opened up London transportation of goods, most coming in in either the rather late part of the Regency era or later (they generally began to expand/be developed at the same time as the railways.)

The following list of canals is not all-inclusive:

Forth and Clyde Canal: Begun in 1768 by John Smeaton.

Grand Junction Canal: Dates back to the late Regency era. (See under G.)

Grand Union Canal: The chief canal south of the Thames, 1929. (See under G.)

Leeds Liverpool Canal: 1816.

Manchester to Liverpool Canal: 1767.

Sankey Brook Canal (Liverpool): Dates from 1755.

Trent and Mersey Canal: Completed in 1777.

Worsley Canal: (Ran from Worsley to Manchester.) Dates from 1761.

- See: Bridgewater Canal.
- See: Croydon Canal, 1809-1858.
- See: Grand Junction Canal.
- See: Grosvenor Canal.
- See: Limehouse/Limehouse Cut - London's oldest canal, ca. 1770.
- See: Paddington Basin.
- See: Paddington/Grand Junction Canal.
- See: Regent's Canal.

Canary Wharf - 20th century. (See: Docks/West India Dock/Canary Wharf.)

candles - The best were made of beeswax (not often used by the common man, being too expensive, instead he burned tallow candles.) Candles could also be made of spermaceti, a waxy oil derived from sperm whales' heads; both beeswax and spermaceti candles gave off better light and less smell than the alternatives. Tallow candles, with the wick dipped in animal fat, were also (from their nature) called dips. Their light flickered more and was smelly.

There were also rushlights, tended to be used by the poor: rushlights were strips of plant fiber drawn through cooking grease or tallow; a two foot long one might burn for 45 minutes. Their light was decent, and unlike candles, they were not taxed. Rushlights burned best in a bowl, as they needed an angle to burn well.

Similarly, there was also the ancient method of a wick floating in a bowl of oil or grease, but they were smelly and smoky.

All *candles* were taxed.

- See: lamps.
- You may care to see: Tallow Chandlers' Hall.
- You may care to see: Wax Chandlers' Hall.

Candlewick Street - Original name of Cannon Street, Candlewick Street dates back to at least 1180-7. The original name derives from the fact that candle-makers (also called candlewrights) lived here in the Middle Ages (13-14th centuries.)

In the 1666 map by Leake it is written of as "Cannon Street."

Regency era folks would have called it: Cannon Street.

Used to run only to Walbrook, but when Cannon Street was revamped and widened in 1853-4, several off-shooting small streets were removed: Basing Lane, Great Distaff Lane, Great St. Thomas Apostle, and Little Friday Street.

- Cordwainers' Hall: (For the Worshipful Company of Cordwainers.) 7 Cannon Street. Near St. Paul's Cathedral, Great Distaff Lane. "Cordwainer" means a dealer in Cordovan leather, and came to be used equally for "shoemaker."

  The Company dates from 1272. In 1409 Cordwainers were distinguished from Cobblers (who dealt in old leather.)

  The first Hall probably was built in 1393. Another in 1577 (possibly the third, rather than the second); this burned in the 1666 Great Fire. The fourth Hall was constructed in 1670. The fifth Hall on this site dated from ca. 1788, standing on the site of what had once been St. Paul's Garden. The sixth Hall here was built in 1909-10, of gray Portland Stone. Totally destroyed by WWII bombs; not rebuilt. (See: Cordwainers' Hall, at its own listing.)
- Hosier Lane: The Hosiers Company moved to Cordwainer Street in Tudor times, leaving Hosier Street as a legacy of their medieval presence near Candlewick Street.
- Milliarium, the: (Also called: the London Stone.) CHAMBERS LONDON GAZETTEER says: "Sometime in the Middle Ages a limestone monolith was placed in the middle of Cannon Street, where it may have acted as a focus for judicial proceedings. Over the years, it became the subject of various legends... Edward III made it the axis of the City's trade when he granted Londoners the right to hold markets within a seven-mile/11 km radius of LONDON STONE, as it had come to be known. In 1742 a chunk of the original block was set into the wall of St. Swithin's Church. When wartime bombing destroyed the church, the Corporation of London moved the stone to Guildhall. It now sits in a niche in the facade of the Chinese bank that stands on the site of St. Swithins." A central

point from which the Roman roads spread, which was also used to mark distances from London. (See: London Stone, under L.)

- St. Mary Abchurch: Abchurch Yard (off Abchurch Lane) and Candlewick Street. (See under the CHURCHES section.)
- St. Swithin's: (See under the CHURCHES section.)

Cannon Row - Westminster. (AKA: Channel Row. AKA: Canon Row.) Dates from at least the 16th century. Called "Cannon" for the Canons of St. Steven's Chapel who had a residence here.

Cannon Street - (See: Candlewick Street.)

Canonbury Square - (See: Islington/Canonbury Square.)

cant - (See: Cockney rhyming slang.)

Canterbury - (See: Canterbury, at its own listing in the BRITISH COUNTIES section.) Christianity came to England and settled in ca. the year 675, at the time the Church despaired of London's paganism, so choosing instead to make its seat in Canterbury, where it remains to this day.

Capel Court - Short walkway. Dates from at least the 16th century.

- See: Bartholomew Lane.
- See: Jonathan's Coffee House.
- See: Stock Exchange.

Cardinal's Cap Alley - (See: Southwark/Cardinal's Cap Alley.)

Cardinal's Wharf - Bankside/Southwark. Small group of 17th C. houses.

cards - (See: playing cards.)

Carey Street - Holborn. This street existed from the late 17th century. The phrase "on Carey Street" means being bankrupt. It comes from the bankruptcy court being located here (in the 1840s,) but the phrase didn't come into common use until the 1920s.

- Seven Stars, the: Pub, established in 1602. (See under the INNS/PUBS section.)
- Wiley's Legal Bookstore: Founded here in 1830.

Carlton Club - Founded by Wellington in 1831, in Charles Street. Moved in 1832. (See under the CLUBS section.)

Carlton Club - Modern. (See: Thatched House Tavern, under the INNS/PUBS section.) Not to be confused with the "Carlton club" of 1832, above.

Carlton Gardens - St. James's. By John Nash, ca. 1830. Built on the site (as was Carlton House Terrace) of the former Carlton House that George IV had pulled down.

Carlton House - Pall Mall/Regent's Street. Its lovely garden extended along the Mall to Marlborough House. Reportedly built on the site of the old St. Philip's Chapel; (Carlton House's site is now occupied by the Athenaeum Club, and by Carlton House Terrace.)

Built in 1709 by Henry Boyle for Baron Carlton. It then was bequeathed to the Earl of Burlington, Carlton's nephew. In 1732 he presented it to his mother, the Dowager Countess. She sold it that same year to the Prince of Wales (later George III,) who took it as his principal home. The Dowager Princess of Wales considerably enlarged the house by adding on the house next door.

Remodeled (into a far more magnificent building) in 1783-96, by act of Parliament, and given as a separate residence for Prinny (later George IV,) and raised to the status of a Royal Palace. Prinny chose Henry Holland to remodel the exterior, and a Frenchman, Gaubert, the interior. GEORGE IV, PRINCE OF WALES states that Holland began work on Carlton House in the early autumn of 1783... "the Prince was already living there as the work went on around him," and "within a few months of his moving into the house it had already become magnificent." This latter being in reference to the interior, for it is otherwise described as a plain brick building (standing on the site now covered by the Athenaeum Club, the United Services Club, and Waterloo Place and its Duke of York's Column, along with the Duke of York Steps, overlooking St. James's Park.

- See: Carlton House Terrace/Duke of York Steps.
- See: Duke of York Column - 1834.

Holland went on to improve the interior: octagon-shaped hall and handsome double staircase covered by two semi-domes meeting a coffered barrel in the center. Described as having an "august simplicity" of interior design. Predominantly French style, with plenty of gold and silver decoration.

Holland rebuilt the Pall Mall facade in lightly rusticated stone, with a wide classical portico of six Corinthian columns in the center. Then, to screen the Palace from the street, he designed a long colonnade of coupled Ionic columns with two imposing gateways. (Londoners found this odd and rather amusing.) Was done being remodeled by at least 1815, when Jane Austen was invited to call upon the Prince Regent. In 1816 Princess Charlotte (daughter of George IV) was married here to Prince Leopold of Saxe-Coburg.

By 1820, George IV had decided Carlton House was "shabby, inconvenient, and unsafe," (so that in 1821 John Nash was assigned to redecorate Buckingham House as George IV's royal residence.) The furnishings, interior decorations, and other architectural facets of Carlton House were removed by the government (to which the house had reverted) in 1826, and in 1828-9 the house was demolished, and Carlton House Terrace (designed by Nash) was built in its place. (The Corinthian portico and row of Ionic pillars from this structure now decorate the National Gallery. In fact, much was raided from the structure and used in various royal and non-royal locales.)

Carlton House Gardens - (See: Carlton Gardens.)

Carlton House Terrace - Regent's Park, north side of the Mall, St. James's. By Nash, in 1827-33. It is a series of houses, a 1,000 foot long terrace. The center of the terrace is divided by the Duke of York Steps. (See under D.) There is a statue on the terrace of (naturally) the Duke of York (Prinny's brother.) The building occupies the site of the house and gardens that had been Carlton House; along with Carlton Gardens, built also by Nash ca. 1830; and the Athenaeum Club. Prinny lived here while Buckingham House was being renovated.

- See: Athenaeum Club.
- See: Carlton Gardens.
- See: Carlton House.

- 6: The Royal Society of Distinguished Scientists. Here since 1966, but dates back to 1660. (See: Royal Society, The, under R.)
- Duke of York Steps: John Nash, 1828-33. Steps, splitting Carlton House Terrace. NAIRN'S LONDON waxes poetic: "Just steps? Well, no. These are in their more direct way the London equivalent of the Spanish Steps... There are three flights, with two intermediate landings." (See under D.)
- Institute of Contemporary Art, the: Established 1947; here since 1968. (It is NOT another name for the Royal Society of Arts.)

Carlton Mews - John Nash, ca. 1830. Behind Carlton House Terrace. Pulled down in 1969.

Carlyle House - (See: Chelsea/Cheyne Row/5, and 24.)

Carmens' Company - (AKA: the Worshipful Company of Carmen.) Dates back to 1517. Carmen hired themselves out, transporting goods (a carman was a driver of carts.) A certain Fraternity of St. Katherine made an agreement with the Lord Mayor and Aldermen in 1517 governing the carmen's trade. The craft included the Woodmongers, who were sometimes called: the Fuellers (not to be confused with Fullers); the Woodmongers were also drivers of carts (usually filled with wood.) They thrived most in the 17th century, at which time the Woodmongers joined with the Carmen. They were given a Royal Charter, but fell into disgrace, and had to surrender their Charter within 65 years. The Woodmongers went defunct in 1746. The Carmen achieved a Royal Charter in 1946, having been granted Livery in 1848. With carts being replaced by motorized vehicles, the Carmen remain but now as a charitable organization. Livery Company. They have no hall. 77th in the order of precedence.

Carnaby Market - Built ca. 1720. Paddington, on the Craven estate. (See: Paddington/Carnaby Market.)

Carnaby Street - Off Regent Street (and running parallel to.) Dates from the 1680s. At first it was a fashionable address, but had quite lost its cachet by the time of the Regency. Was a trades street by the mid 19th C., descending as the century advanced into including sewing sweatshops (to supply nearby Savile Row.) Came to represent London's "swinging sixties" in the 20th C., with trendy unisex boutiques. Still famous for clothing.

- 45: Inderwick's, since 1797. England's oldest pipe maker.

Carpenters' Hall - For the Worshipful Company of Carpenters. London Wall, where their hall has always been, since 1429. Royal Charter in 1477. The first Master Carpenter mentioned in London records was in 1271. There have been three Halls, today's dating from 1960. Livery company. 26th in precedence. The Carpenters joined wood with nails; the Joiners used adhesives.

- ➢ See: Furniture-makers' Company - To read how carpenters relate to furniture making.
- ➢ See: Joiners' Hall.
- ➢ See: Throgmorton Avenue/Carpenters' Hall.

carpet manufacturers - In the UK, an all-over floor covering is a carpet. A smaller, movable covering is a rug. (See: rugs.)

- ➢ See: Scotland/Whytock, under the BRITISH COUNTIES section.
- ➢ See: Wiltshire/Wilton Royal, under the BRITISH COUNTIES section.
- ➢ See: Worcestershire/Brinton's, under the BRITISH COUNTIES section.
- ➢ See: Worcestershire/Humphries of Kidderminster, under the BRITISH COUNTIES section.

carriages - "Carriages" is a catch-all term for wheeled vehicles. For instance, all coaches are carriages, but not all carriages are coaches. There were many kinds of carriages during the Regency (this is not an all-inclusive list): barouches, cabriolets, carts, chaises, chariots, coaches, curricles, dog-carts, gigs, landaus, phaetons, waggons (spelled with two gg's.)

- ➢ See: coach, and all the "coach" related listings there.
- ➢ See: hackney coach - For details on when inventions came along in coach-building.

Carrier Street - St. Giles, slums. Described as a "rabbit warren."

- 1: Lord Curzon of Kedleston (statesman/Viceroy of India) lived here (b. 1859-d.1925.)

Carrington House - Whitehall. By Sir William Chambers, 1765-74, for the 2nd Earl Gower; first known as Gower House. Lord Carrington bought the house in 1810, lived there until 1863. Demolished in 1886.

Carrington Street - Mayfair.

- 2: There by at least 1786, when Harriette Wilson (famous mistress of many) was born and resided there.

Carr's of Carlisle - Founded in 1831 in Carlisle, England. Started as a bakery and mill that expanded into an agricultural brand begun by Jonathan Dodgson Carr. Royal Warrant from 1841. Is now widely marketed, and is best known for their biscuits (what Americans call cookies.)

Carshalton - A village, between Croydon and Sutton. Thriving market-gardens in the 13th C., but then declined until a resurgence in the 17th and early 18th centuries when mills banked on the River Wandle.

- Anne Boleyn's Well: Supposedly Anne stopped here to drink and found the water to be sweet. She gave money for it to be welled over.
- Wandle, the: River, stocked with trout.

Carter Lane - Records indicate this street existed by the 12th century. First known as Shoemakers' Row; name changed to Carter Lane in the 13th century when it was divided into Great Carter Lane and Little Carter Lane, probably renamed thus because it was used by carriers (those who operated handcarts.) Yet exists.

Carthusian Order, the - Resided in what is now the Charterhouse. Long gone as an order by the time of the Regency. The Carthusians were a contemplative and austere Catholic order established in France in 1084; they were also vegetarians. (See: Charterhouse.)

Cartier - Watches, jewelry. (See: Bond Street/New Bond Street/175-177.)

Castle Street - Is now Eastcastle Street, since 1887.

- ➢ See: Charing Cross Road.
- ➢ See: Fitzrovia/Castle Street.

Castrol House - 1958, offices. Marylebone Road.

Cateaton Street - (See: Gresham Street.)

Catherine Street - (See: Covent Garden/Catherine Street.)

Catholics - During Elizbeth I's reign it was outright illegal to be a Roman Catholic priest in England.

There were some 100,000 Catholics in England and Wales in 1800, primarily of Irish descent. This faith was still rather actively suppressed in England during the Regency. For instance, *Catholic* lords (as in landed men of title) could not vote or take office in Parliament.

Catholic churches are so designated in the CHURCHES section (although you have to read the individual listings to spy them.)

- ➢ See: Ireland - For details on Catholic rights in England.
- ➢ See: Irish immigrants.
- ➢ See: Society of Jesus - Jesuits.
- ➢ See: Soho/St. Patrick's.

Cato Street - Marylebone. In 1820 the street name was changed (until 1937) to Horace Street, because of the infamous "Cato Street Affair," wherein on 2/23/1817 the followers of the late Thomas Spence planned an overthrow of the government, but were instead apprehended in their headquarters on this street.

Cat's Hole - Slum. (See: St. Katherine's, Tower Hamlets.)

cattle - British usage encompasses both bovines and equines. Example: "See that my cattle are readied for the coach at eight." Bulls, cows, horses, oxen. (You may care to see: meat.)

Cavendish Square - Laid out in 1717-1719 by John Prince, for Edward Harley, second Earl of Oxford; the square was named for the earl's wife, Lady Henrietta Cavendish-Holles. A building slump slowed the square's development, but in the later 18th C. it was developed further. There are two Palladian buildings, connected by an archway with a Madonna by Epstein, on the north side of the square, with columned facades; these are the remaining signs of a large mansion once owned by the Duke of Chandos. Admiral and Mrs. Horatio Nelson lived in Cavendish Square in 1791.

- 21: Lord Byron (poet) lived here at one point. Located on the square's south side. It is now a department store.
- Harley Street: (See under H.)
- Margaret Street: Leads from Fitzrovia to Marylebone. Built in 1734.
    - 11: Schweppes soda water. (See under S.)
- Statue of Lord (William) George Bentinck, second Duke of Portland (married to a Cavendish daughter) dates from 1851.
- Wigmore Street: Leads off the square. (See under W.)

Cavendish Street - Marylebone, off Oxford Street. (See: New Cavendish Street.)

Cawthorne's - Circulating library in the Strand. Existed by 1804. Lasted until at least 1874.

Caxton Hall - (See: Almonry/Caxton House.)

Caxton Street - Westminster. Dates from at least the early 18th century.

- 23: Blewcoat School, charity school, 1709. Is now a National Trust shop. (See under B.)

Caxton's House - AKA: Caxton Hall. (See: Almonry/Caxton House.)

Cecil Court - Covent Garden. Runs west from St. Martin's Lane. Dates back to the end of the 17th century. Suffered a devastating arson fire in 1735. Once films had been invented, it took on the nickname "Flicker Alley" because of early film companies here. Now is known for its booksellers, including secondhand books, maps, prints, often with Victorian shop frontages.

Ceilers - (See: Joiners' Company.)

cemeteries - Nearly every London church had a cemetery. In 1852, under the Act of Burial of the Dead in the Metropolis, burial in City churchyards ceased (at least technically, but an

Order in Council had to be made in each churchyard's case for exceptions.) The always popular crypt burials were outlawed in 1854. The Disused Burial Grounds Act of 1884 protected those closed churchyards from being built on.

- See: Brompton Cemetery - 1840.
- See: Bunhill Fields.
- See: burials.
- See: Chelsea/Old Church Street/Jew's Burial Ground.
- See: Highgate.
- See: resurrectionists - For stolen corpses.
- See: St. Pancras.

Cenotaph, the - 1920 war monument. Whitehall.

census - The first official British census (of England, Scotland and Wales, and not counting 1086's Domesday book) occurred in March, 1801; the populace of London at the time was deemed to be 959,000 in greater London; 128,000 in the City. Censuses were conducted every ten years thereafter.

- You may care to see: Domesday book.
- You may care to see: literacy.

Center Pointe Street - 36 story high, massive block; corner of New Oxford Street. 1963-67. Built over part of a famous slum, St. Giles. (See: St. Giles.)

Central Criminal Court - Post-Regency term.

- See: Newgate Prison.
- See: Old Bailey.

Central Middlesex Hospital - Brent. 1903.

cesspits - Digging large holes and burying waste was an ancient method of dealing with human waste. This became increasing difficult in the 18-19th centuries, as places for digging became increasingly scant in crowded London. (See: sewers.)

Chalk Farm - Northwest of London, a traditional dueling ground, near Primrose Hill (the latter of which was also known for dueling.) The area had been owned by the Chalcott family, whose name was abbreviated to "Chalc's," and then further corrupted to "Chalks." The dead and wounded (from dueling) were taken to the Chalk Farm Tavern (until it was demolished in 1853.) There was a row of trees behind the tavern, which duelists made use of for their affairs of honor after ordering breakfast at the tavern. (See: Primrose Hill.)

Chalk Road - Islington. Built in 1826-7, a toll road. Originally called Chalk Road, in 1861 it was renamed Caledonian Road.

champagne - Through much of the 17-18th and into the 19th centuries England was at war with France. True champagne must come from the district of Champagne in France, so it was often unobtainable for Britons (except via smugglers.) Ca. 1662 Britain developed champagne's equivalent: sparkling wine. (See: food/drinks/champagne.)

Chancellors Lane - (See: Chancery Lane.)

Chancery Lane - The City/Camden/Westminster. Once called New Street; but took on the name of "Chancellor's Lane" following Edward III's presentation of a house here to the then Lord Chancellor in 1377. This house was demolished in 1896, and on the site was built the Public Record Office, 1838. (See under P.)

While it retained its Georgian buildings, by the 1770s Chancery Lane was increasingly urban, with lawyers moving in and the businesses to support them. The Inns of Chancery disappeared, one by one.

- ➢ See: Inns of Chancery.
- ➢ See: Serjeants' Inn.

Persons in the Legal field can yet buy their wigs and robes along this street.

- Law Society: (East side of street.) Formed in 1822, building completed in 1827. Royal Charter in 1831, institution opened to members in 1832. The Law Society is the regulatory body for the solicitors.
- Public Record Office: 1896. (See under P.)

Chandos House - Chandos Street, 20 St. James's Square. Built by Robert Adam, 1771, of Scottish stone; described as a beautiful example of Adams' best work. Four bays, three stories, "severe" brown stone. (See: St. James's Square/20.) In the 19th C., was for a while the Austrian Embassy, with their lease expiring in 1866.

Chandos Street - Marylebone. East of St. Martin's Lane, west of Bedford Street. Built ca. 1750.

Change - Change or 'Change was often used in abbreviation for "Exchange," meaning a place where commodities, currencies, products, or shares could be traded.

- ➢ See: Baltic Exchange.
- ➢ See: Corn Exchange.
- ➢ See: Exeter Exchange.
- ➢ See: Royal Exchange.
- ➢ See: Stock Exchange.

Change Alley - (AKA: Exchange Alley.) Serves as a shortcut between the Royal Exchange to the Post Office on Lombard Street.

- ➢ See: Jonathan's Coffee House.
- ➢ See: Lloyd's of London.

- Garraway's Coffee House: Here until 1866, opened ca. 1650. First (what Americans call the second) floor contained the sale room, where business was conducted. Ground floor was for food and drink service. The founder, Thomas

Garraway, was the first man in London to sell tea. (See: Garraway's, under G.) Garraway's burned in 1748. Its last 120 years was at its final address in Change Alley. Next door to Jonathan's Coffee House.

Channel Row - (See: Canon Row.)

Channel Tunnel - (Familiarly called: the Chunnel.) Links England and France, and runs under the channel. Opened in 1994.

Chapel Royal - There are five Chapels Royal in London. Such are not subject to a bishop, but rather directly to the sovereign. The five are:

- Buckingham Palace: While in residence the monarch has a private service here.
- St. James's Palace/Chapel Royal: The monarch attends several special ceremonies per year here. (Not to be confused with St. James's Palace/Queen's Chapel.)
- Tower of London/St. Peter ad Vincula.
- Westminster Palace.
- Windsor Castle/St. George's Chapel: Used when the monarch is in residence.

LONDON STEP BY STEP states: "...the Chapel Royal...is not a building but an establishment, founded in Saxon times to serve the spiritual needs of the sovereign. The Chapel Royal is regarded as the cradle of English church music, and its organists have included the composers Tallis, Byrd, and Purcell."

- ➢ See: Hampton Court Palace/Chapel Royal.
- ➢ See: St. James's Palace/Chapel Royal.
- ➢ See: Whitehall Palace/Chapel Royal.

Chapel Street - Belgravia. There are Georgian homes here still.

charcoal - (See: coal.)

Charing Cross - Westminster. A production area for guns, swords, and scientific, medical and surveying equipment, clockmaking, and other shops. In 1732 was the site of the King's Mews. (See: Charing Cross Road, as that was the more specific site of the Royal Mews.)

Eleanor Crosses: Site of one of the 12 crosses erected after Eleanor of Castile died in 1290, ordered placed by King Edward I. These were constructed along her funeral route, which took 12 days. (The stopping points: Lincoln, Grantham, Stamford, Geddington, Hardingstone, Stony Stratford, Woburn, Dunstable, St. Albans, Waltham, West Cheap (Cheapside,) and Charing.)

Charing Cross did not become a book-selling center until about 100 years ago. Has had an Equestrian statue here of Charles I since 1646 or 7 (restored to the site in 1675); the practice of decorating the statue began in 1892.

Samuel Johnson (18th C. author) once said "the full tide of human existence is at

Charing Cross." It is the point from which all distances from London are measured.

In the 16th and 17th centuries some executions (hangings) occurred here.

By the time of the Regency, this was a bustling locale.

Later a portion became Trafalgar Square.

The "Eleanor" cross was rebuilt in 1863-4, replacing the medieval original, which had been pulled down by Puritans in 1647. The present cross is a memorial, not a reflection of how the original was designed (although one source implied this remake *attempted* to resemble the medieval cross); it is 70 feet high, Gothic style, and in its upper stories are eight statues of Queen Eleanor. The original thirteen crosses were erected at the sites where the departed Eleanor of Castile's body rested on its way in 1290 to Westminster Abbey for burial, this one being the 13th and last one constructed. It is often believed that "Charing" is derived from the French for "beloved queen," but AN ENCYCLOPEDIA OF LONDON declares: "The derivation does not imply a dear queen. Canon Westlake found evidence of a smithy kept by one Richard at Charing at the end of the 12th century. A manuscript entitled *Liber de Antiquis Legibus* in Guildhall Record Office mentions the village of Charing in 1260, thirty years before the death of Queen Eleanor." It is possibly derived from "char," the Anglo-Saxon word for wood burned down into coal. In fact, the final cross was really located at the top of Whitehall (which is immediately south of Trafalgar Square.)

- See: King's Mews.
- See: Trafalgar Square.

- 36 Craven Street: (See: Craven Street/7.)
- Charing Cross Road: (See at its own listing.)

Charing Cross Hospital - (AKA: Charing Cross Hospital and Medical School.) Fulham Palace Road. Founded in 1818 by Dr. Benjamin Golding, as a charity hospital, as the West London Infirmary and Dispensary, in Suffolk Street. Care for the poor. It moved in 1823 to Villiers Street, having then twelve beds. The name changed to Charing Cross Hospital in 1827.

A new, much bigger facility was obtained in 1834, on Agar Street, designed by Decimus Burton, now having sixty beds. The medical school was in the hospital.

Moved five miles/8 km to Hammersmith in 1959.

Charing Cross Road - Leicester Square. Had been Crown Street and Castle Street; renamed as Charing Cross Road in 1887, when it was significantly rebuilt/conceived anew (and when the booksellers would have begun concentrating in the area.)

In 1732 housed the King's Mews, and also a slum area that grew up around St. Martin's Church, the area being known as the Bermuda and Caribbee Islands, and Porridge Island.

During the Regency, this street was known as: Hog Lane.

- 16: Francis Place, master breeches-maker. By 1820 had made his establishment into "the head-quarters of English Radicalism," reformist politics.
- Hungerford Market: (See under H.)
- Royal Mews: (See under R.)
- Smith's: Snuff and tobacco suppliers, established 1869.

charities - The idea of the State financing benevolent charities/hospitals/organizations/schools for social relief was little practiced in the Regency era (or before.) About the only time this happened is when a royal personage chose to take up a cause and finance it (in full or in part) personally. Otherwise, a religious organization or a private person of means would provide the funding and/or raise money through solicitations of friends and/or the public. You will find throughout this listing many examples of a charity begun or funded under the auspices of a religious order or private individual. For examples:

- See: blue coat schools.
- See: charity schools.
- See: Foundling Hospital.
- See: Lambeth Asylum.
- See: Southwark/St. Thomas' Hospital.

For examples of charities with a royal patron:

- See: Royal Humane Society.
- See: Royal Military Asylum.
- See: Royal Society of Literature.

charity schools - Charity schools sprang up in the early 1700s, funded by private citizens or religious organizations, their intent to relieve the terrible poverty and/or educate children of the poor. In the later 1700s the Church of England added to their number with the "National" schools. (See: colleges, for non-charity school information. Also: schools.)

- See: Bluecoat School.
- See: Charterhouse.
- See: Holborn Charity School.
- See: Royal Military Asylum.

Charles Street - (See: **Berkeley Square**/Charles Street.)

Charles Street - **Covent Garden**, off St. James's Square, Mayfair, 1631. In 1846 became known as Wellington Street. (See under W.)

- I am the Only Running Footman - Pub. (See under the INNS/PUBS section.)

Charlies - (Also seen as: Charleys.) Common nickname for 18-19th century Watchmen, the "police" of London prior to the establishing of the Metropolitan Police (1829,) and in addition to the hired investigators called the Bow Street Runners (1747,) and in addition to the parish or church wardens (beadles, who were usually privately hired.)

The night watchmen began ca. 1660-1685, during Charles II's reign, hence the "Charlie" nickname.

The Charlies (who were more properly called constables) were largely old men who walked the streets armed with nothing more than a staff (or cudgel) and a bell to ring. They were fairly ineffective at catching criminals or even discouraging crime, and were often ridiculed, but in a time when most people did not have a watch or clock, the calling out of the time on the hour was largely considered useful. The Watchmen of medieval times wore red and white cloaks, though this practice was long gone by the time of the Regency.

- ➢ SEE: POLICE.
- ➢ See: Watch, the.
- ➢ See: Watchmen.

Charlotte Street - Soho and Bloomsbury. The street was named for George III's Queen.

- 76: John Constable (painter) lived here with his wife and young family from 1822 to his death in 1837.

Charlton Hornfair - (Also seen as: Charlton Horn Fair.) Bermondsey. Was a fair, begun probably in the 13th century. Not abolished until 1874, due to open drunkenness. People wore horns on their head-dresses, the practice going back to a connection with St. Luke's Day, October 18th (because in paintings of St. Luke there was usually included horned animals in the background.) Called "riotous" and "impudent," the modern Horn Fair is a far tamer event.

Charlton House - Greenwich. Jacobean mansion. Built in 1607-12 for Sir Adam Newton, tutor to Price Henry (eldest son of James I.) On the grounds is a mulberry tree planted by James I in 1608. Described in LONDON by Knopf Guides: "...as the finest Jacobean facade in London." Now used as a Community Center.

Charlton Village - Greenwich. The old center of Charlton, not the newer community that has surrounded it.

- Charlton House: (See at its own listing.)
- New Charlton: Grew up when factories came in ca. the 1850s.
- St. Luke's Church: First mentioned in 1077. Rebuilt in 1629.

Charterhouse - Charterhouse Square, Clerkenwell. (AKA: Sutton's Hospital in Charterhouse. AKA: Charterhouse School.) The name supposedly derives from Chartreuse in France, where commenced the Carthusian Order in 1084; at any rate, all the Carthusian monasteries in England are known as Charterhouses. The Carthusians founded this one here in the 14th C.; in 1371 another thirteen acres were added. NAIRN'S LONDON calls it: "A rambling nest of medieval and Renaissance buildings, an equivalent of Lambeth Palace..." From PILGRIMS' LONDON: "...traces its history back to a terrible plague which occurred in

1348. People died so rapidly that the bodies were simply thrown into pits outside the city walls. The bishop of London...grieved that these burials were in unsanctified ground, consecrated three acres of land not far from the Smithfield for a burying ground... The place was called Pardon Churchyard... A few years later, in 1361, another bishop...left in his will a large sum of money to endow a Carthusian monastery at Pardon Churchyard."

Thomas More (saint/counselor to Henry VIII) lived here from 1499-1503. Thomas Cromwell (lawyer/statesman to Henry VIII) stayed here in 1535, upon the dissolution of the monasteries. The monks/brothers here had refused to take an oath acknowledging Henry VIII as head of the Anglican church, or renounce the Pope. In the remains of the 16th C. it changed ownership many times, a kind of royal bauble that bounced around. (You may care to see: Dissolution of the Monasteries.)

Eventually, in 1611, it was sold by the Earl of Suffolk to Thomas Sutton, who became known for his philanthropy and who bought the Charterhouse to found a charity hospital for boys of poor parents and old pensioners, the Hospital of King James, and a charity school. It is the only remaining monastic complex in London that was converted to a private mansion after the Dissolution. The archway and oak doors are 15th C.; the house overhead dates from 1718. John Wesley went here. These kind of schools (often called academies) were private schools (which an American would call a public school,) and were attended by essentially "middle and high school" age students. To get into one, a boy had to be sponsored by someone of influence. Ca. 1792, the annual fee to attend was approximately £50 per year, although sons of poor gentlemen could attend with financial support of a sponsor.

The boarding school for boys moved to Godalming, Surrey, in 1872; the old site was taken over by the St. Bartholomew's Hospital medical school in 1935. The pensioners (bachelors or widowers - called brethren - over age 60, numbering about 40, of the Church of England, and retired from: the arts, the clergy, doctors, lawyers, military, or professional men) remain, though the school has moved.

Note: Charterhouse was located in Charterhouse Square.

Some of the components of Charterhouse are:

- Brothers' Library: The brothers being the Charterhouse brothers/monks. Is housed in a refurbished Victorian building.
- Chapel: Hosts Thomas Sutton's elaborate tomb, from 1611, described as "sumptuous."
- Chapel Cloisters: Jacobean.
- Doctor's House, the: Dates from the 18th century.
- Gown Boys: For reasons unclear this was the name of the schoolrooms for the

boys, Elizabethan. A hall and a writing room.

- Great Hall, the: Oldest part of Charterhouse, dating from 1571.
- Guesten Hall: Dates from the early 16th C., and was improved in ca. 1564, at which time the lovely staircase also was built.
- Pensioner's Court: 1825.
- Preacher's Court: 1825.
- Wash-house Court: (Also seen as: Washhouse Court.) Was originally and anciently called Kitchen Court, but was Wash-house Court by the time of the school, and is the oldest court of Charterhouse.

Charterhouse School - (See: Charterhouse, above.)

Charterhouse Square - Is a wooded green. (See note under: Charterhouse.)

- London Dispensary for the Relief of the Poor Afflicted with Diseases of the Eye and Ear: Established in 1805. Moved to Moorfields, becoming: Royal London Ophthalmic Hospital (AKA: Moofield's Eye Hospital.)

Charterhouse Street - Victorian.

Chatham House - (See: St. James's Square/9-10-11.)

Cheam - Sutton. Known for its potteries in the 14-16th centuries, particularly jugs. Henry VIII acquired Cheam ca. 1538 in order to build Nonsuch Palace. The manor house here was pulled down in 1796.

- ➢ See: Cuddington.
- ➢ See: Lower Cheam.

- Cheam Common: Enclosed in 1810.
- Cheam Old Church: Built for Lady Jane Lumley, d.1577. Now only fragments with a sculpture of Lady Lumley.
- Lower Cheam: (See under L.)
- North Cheam: East of Worcester Park on London Road. Farmland into the 20th century.

cheap - A medieval term for a market, derived from the Saxon word "ceap," meaning "to barter" or "price" or "sale." Seen in place names. (Example: Cheapside.)

Cheapside - The City. Earlier known as Westcheap; was first known as "Chepsyde" by 1510. The commercial quarter of London; described as the "City of London's main shopping street for the past millennium." Started as the medieval shopping center of London (was the medieval City's High Street.) Along with East Cheap, these were the two largest roads in London, wide enough to host tournaments, with West Cheap being quite a bit the larger of the two. The low roofs of the market buildings were used for viewing the tournaments.

Goldsmithing was centered here in medieval times.

Westbound traffic *had* to pass through here to get to London Bridge.

A 1775 visitor thought the (nighttime) street was candlelit for some kind of festival, but it was merely the ordinary light from the many businesses here.

Jane Austen had exemplary characters live here. Still thriving during the Regency.

From the late 19th C. it turned to hosting mostly housing offices.

- 76: Simpson's Restaurant. (AKA: Simpson's Chop House. See under S.)
- Bow Lane: Yet retains quaint 18-19th C. shop facades.
- Bread Street: Named for what it sold. John Milton (Commonwealth poet) was born here in 1608. Joins Cheapside to Queenhithe Dock. Name reflects its medieval trade.
- Cheapside Cross: One of the thirteen crosses marking where Eleanor of Castile's bier rested while traveling from Nottingham to Westminster in 1290. Mutilated in 1581 by Puritans; rebuilt. Parliament ordered its destruction in 1643, not to be replaced. (For another of these crosses, see: Charing Cross.)
- Cheapside Market: Produce market. Was yet a bustling place in Charles Dicken's time. Still exists, but is now offices and retail shops.
- City of London School: Built 1835, opened in 1837.
- Friday Street: So named from Catholic medieval times, because fish were sold here (and Catholics did not eat meat on Fridays,) but probably not sold here past medieval times. (See under F.)
- Goldsmith Street: (Also seen as: Goldsmiths' Row.) Famous enough to be heard of throughout Europe.
- Guildhall: (See under G.)
- Gutter Lane: (See under G.)
- Honey Lane: Named for its medieval trade. Built at the south end of Milk Street, where St. Mary Magdalen church had stood until it was destroyed in the Great Fire of 1666 (and not rebuilt.) By 1708 it was hosting not honey but fish, meat, and poultry. Honey Lane was utterly wiped out by WWII bombing; the current lane is about 100 yards east of where it had been.
- Ironmonger Lane: (See under I.)
- Lombard Street: Goldsmiths. (See under L.)
- Love Lane: Where medieval prostitutes plied their trade. Branches off Wood Street. (See: Gresham Street.)
    - St. Mary Aldermanbury: North side of Love Lane. In 1965 was moved brick by brick to Fulton, Missouri, USA.
- Mercers' Hall: (See under M.)

- Mermaid Tavern: Elizabethan. Near St. Paul's. Famous haunt of Shakespeare and of Ben Jonson (playwrights.) Gone after burning in the Great Fire of 1666.
- Milk Street: Hosted medieval milk-sellers. Thomas More (sainted king's advisor) was born here in 1478. Existed until bombed in WWII. (See under M.)
- The Poultry: (See under P.)
- Playhouse Yard: (See: Blackfriars Lane/Playhouse Yard.)
- Poultry, The: Named for what it sold. (See under P.)
- Saddlers' Hall: (See under S.)
- St. Mary Aldermanbury:
    - ➢ See: Love Lane/St. Mary Aldermanbury, above.
    - ➢ See under the CHURCHES section.
- St. Mary-le-Bow: South side of Cheapside. (See under the CHURCHES section.)
- St. Paul's School: For young men. (See under S.)
- Wood Street: Named for its medieval trade. (See under W.)

cheats - Captain Sharp: One who will beat you at cards, not necessarily by cheating (but certainly by having you overplay your means.) Also called "sharpers."

cheap-jack: A huckster.

quack: Unflattering term for a medical man (but not as awful as it is to modern ears.) One might refer to a quack meaning having less medical knowledge (as opposed to being a flim-flam oil-selling sort of quick-talker.)

- ➢ You may care to see: police.
- ➢ You may care to see: punishments.
- ➢ You may care to see: rough places.

cheese - Cheddar cheese, named for where it originated, dates back to at least the 12th century, but it wasn't that well known to Regency Londoners. There were some 40 kinds of cheese available during that era.

- ➢ See: Cheshire, under the BRITISH COUNTIES section.
- ➢ See: food/cheese.
- ➢ See: Jermyn Street/93/Paxton and Whitfield.

cheesecakes -

- ➢ See: food/cheesecake.
- ➢ See: Holloway.

Chelsea - Began its existence in Saxon times. Is mentioned in an 8th C. charter.

In the 16-18th centuries a series of grand retreats were built here for the wealthy and for royals.

In the early 19th C. it had only 10,000 residents (40,000 by 1841.) There were fields between it and London, known as the Five Fields. (See under F.) Rural; people moved here for the air, although one could still walk to visit London shops. Tumbled down to the very edge of the Thames. Did not really meld into London until after the 1820s development of Belgravia. About 1825, a way of draining the soggy fields was put in place, and then the area was built up, using the soil from the St. Katherine's Dock construction, by Thomas Cubitt.

- "Atlanta" statue: Albert Bridge, 1926.
- Beaufort House: (See: Cheyne Walk/91-94, below.)
- Beaufort Street: Connects King's Road to Battersea ridge.
- Belgrave Square: Not until 1827. (See note on drainage in "Chelsea" data above. This was part of what is referred to as Belgravia.) Town houses by George Basevi. (See: Belgrave Square, under B.)
- "Boy with a Dolphin" statue: 1975. At the bottom of Oakley Street.
- Bunhouse, The: (AKA: The Old Bun House.) Jew's Row. Known for selling Chelsea buns (Jane Austen bought them here.) Started by a Mr. and Mrs. Hand in the 18th C, patronized by royalty. On Good Fridays huge crowds besieged the place, demanding buns. Was on what is now called Bunhouse Place. It was a one story building, with a colonnade projecting over the footpath.

  Chelsea Buns are quite a bit like what Americans call cinnamon buns (or rolls); although Chelsea buns don't necessarily have to have cinnamon in them, but do have fruit (such as currants,) and the thin glaze isn't visible except as a sheen.

  Sometimes George III bought buns here.

  Closed in 1839.
- Cadogen Place/44: (See at its own listing in this C section.)
- Carlyle Square: During philosopher/writer Thomas Carlyle's lifetime, this became the name of Oakeley Square. He lived at 5 (now 24) from 1834-81. At the turn of the 19th century, and up until ca. 1845, this square would have been known as Oakeley Square. (See under O.)
- Chelsea Arts Club - 1891.
- Chelsea Barracks: 1861-2. The headquarters of the Coldstream and Grenadier Guards. (See: Royal Guards.)
- Chelsea Bridge Road: 1853.
- Chelsea Embankment: 1874.
- Chelsea Flower Show: (See: Chelsea Physick Garden, at its own listing.)
- Chelsea Hospital: (AKA: Royal Hospital, Chelsea.) On Royal Hospital Road.

Was first a theological college, dating from 1609.

Founded as a hospital in 1682 by Charles II; the building was finished in 1692; Wren was the architect. Old records refer to "The Hospital for Maymed Soldiers" (British Army Pensioners.) It was founded to serve military veterans, known as Chelsea pensioners, who had been disabled by war, by housing, clothing, and feeding them. Still houses army veterans, as opposed to naval. (For *naval* pensioners, see: Royal Hospital, Greenwich.)

Some alterations in 1765-82, by Robert Adam, and in 1809-22 (adding the Infirmary buildings in 1814,) but otherwise the building is largely unchanged since its origin. Built of red brick, plain, stately. Had large, formal gardens, which now annually house the Chelsea Flower Show (See: Chelsea Physick Garden, at its own listing.)

The organist at the chapel here from 1783 to 1814 was one Dr. Charles Burney (father of the author, Fanny Burney.)

There were more renovations after WWII damage.

The pensioners' winter uniform is black, with a tri-cornered hat. The summer uniform has a red coat.

Houses up to 558 pensioners (with many thousands of out-pensioners,) who still wear the recognizable coats.

- Chelsea Hospital Stables: 1814-17. (See: Clerk of Works' House, at its own listing.)
- Chelsea House: (Is now the Elm Park Gardens, has been since the 1870s.) 32 acres facing on the south side of Fulham Road. Circa 1721 the grounds were planted with over 2,000 mulberry trees, as a manufactory of raw silk did business here (the business being soon abandoned as a failure.)
- Chelsea New Church: Robert Street. 1820.
- Chelsea Old Church:
    - ➢ See: Chelsea Old Church, under the CHURCHES section.
    - ➢ See: Cheyne Walk/Chelsea Old Church, below.
- Chelsea Physick Garden: (See at its own listing.)
- Chelsea Town Hall: 1860.
- Chelsea Square: (See at its own listing.)
- Cheyne Row: (Pronounced "Chain-ee.") By 1830 this street was described as having become unfashionable: "at once cheap and excellent" (as said by the author/philosopher Thomas Carlyle.)
    - 5: (Later became 24.) From 1834-1881 was the home of Thomas and Jane

Carlyle, paying £35 per annum rent; (Thomas Carlyle was author of *The French Revolution*, which he had to write in its entirety a second time after a maid accidentally burned the first manuscript.) This house is now the Carlyle Museum; also referred to as Carlyle's House. It is a small Queen Anne era house. (See: 24, below.)

  - 7: Holy Redeemer. 1895. (See: Holy Redeemer, below.)
  - 24: Carlyle House. 1703, Queen Anne red brick terrace house. Thomas Carlyle lived here in 1834. In his day this address would have been known as number 5 (see above.) Is now known as Carlyle's House, and also as the Carlyle Museum.

- Cheyne Walk: Built in 1708. Named for Lord Cheyne, who had owned this stretch of river bank in the 18th century. The street took the place of the manor house when the latter was pulled down in 1753. In the Regency was a very fashionable, pleasant riverside promenade of elegant Georgian brick town houses (many still remaining,) directly overlooking the Thames. Peaceful and narrow. From about the mid 19th C. it was known as a residential area frequented by writers and artists. The street ends at Chelsea Old Church.
  - 2: The female Victorian writer George Eliot (pen name) lived here. (See: 4, below.)
  - 3 thru 6: Built ca. 1717, still exists, privately owned.
  - 4: The novelist George Eliot (pseudonym of Mary Ann Evans) died here in 1880. (See: 2, above.)
  - 5: (See: 24, below.)
  - 16: Queen's House. 1717. Takes its name from the initials "RC" atop the iron gateway, it was presumed to stand for (Regina) Catherine of Braganza, Charles II's queen. However, it actually was the builder's initials: Richard Chapman. The painter Dante Gabriel Rossetti lived here starting in 1862. Not to be confused with any royal Queen's House(s.)
  - 18: Don Saltero's. Coffee-house. Closed down in 1867. The coffee-house had contained a museum.
  - 23: Has a plaque that shows this as the site of Henry VIII's Manor House, which would have stood over numbers 19-26.
  - 48: A 1711 Queen Anne town house. In the 20th C., The Rolling Stones' Mick Jagger lived here and wrote *Street Fighting Man.*
  - 50: King's Head and Eight Bells. Pub, dates from ca. 1580. Still has its 18th C. interior decor.

- 91-94: Beaufort House, 1771. One of Sir Thomas More (king's councilor/humanist's) homes, purchased 1520, resided in by 1532, although three other Chelsea houses claim the same. Purchased in 1736 by Sir Hans Sloane. Was rebuilt from about 1700, and called Beaufort House. Pulled down in 1739-40. Eight acres.
- 93: Elizabeth Stevenson born here in 1810. Later wrote novels as Mrs. Gaskell, married to the Reverend Gaskell.
- 95-100: (Some sources say "96-100.") Lindsey House. (See: Lindsey House, below in this sub-section of Cheyne Walk.)
- 114: King's Arms. (See: King's Arms/Cheyne Walk, under the INNS/PUBS section.)
- 118-119: J. M. W. Turner (the painter) died here in 1851, having lived here for 10 years (under the name of Booth.) The building was WWII damaged; restored to its prior appearance.
- Cadogen Pier: Off of Cheyne Walk.
  - See: Doggett's Coat and Badge Race.
  - See: Cadogen Pier, at its own listing.
- Chelsea Old Church: Cheyne Walk; stands on the river side at the south end of Church Street. (AKA: All Saints, Chelsea.) Goes back to 1290. Sir Thomas More (king's adviser/saint) has a chapel here, and he partly designed the church. In 1532, Sir Thomas had the statue of himself built against the south wall of the chancel. The nave and chapel were rebuilt in 1667-74, adding a steeple with a peal of six bells. It is the only church in London to have chained books, gifts of Sir Hans Sloane. Partly restored in 1910. (See: All Saints/Chelsea, under the CHURCHES section.)
- Crosby Hall: (See under: Chelsea/Crosby Hall, below.*)*
- Lindsey House: (Also sometimes seen as: Lindsay House.) 96-101 Cheyne Walk. Built ca. 1640-74. On the site of Sir Thomas More (king's adviser/humanist's) garden. Described as vast. Robert, 3rd Earl of Lindsey, bought and rebuilt it in the 1660s. It was divided into separate dwellings in the late 18th century. (See: Inns of Court/Lincoln's Inn Fields/59-60.)

(End of Chelsea/Cheyne Walk Listing;
Resumption of "Chelsea" Alpha Listing):

- Church Lane: Until the King's private road was opened in 1830, this was the only way into Chelsea by coach, although you could reach it by river. (See: King's Road, below.)
- Church Street: Same as: Old Church Street. (See, below.)
- Common, the: In ancient maps, it was referred to as Chelsea Heath. Existed until 1815, but in 1810 the Lords of the Manor (and other proprietors, such as the rector) leased pieces of the common for building, which led to full development.
- Cremorne Gardens: Closed 1877. Summer pleasure resort. (See at its own listing.)
- Crosby Hall: Cheyne Walk, Chelsea (by Bishopgate.) A Tudor mansion built in 1466-75 for a grocer and wool merchant named Sir John Crosby. It moved here in 1910. Was originally in Bishopgate; its frontage was some 240 feet long, and in places went back from Bishopgate Street approximately 300 feet.

  From 1621-38 it was the headquarters for the East India Company.

  From 1672-1769 it was a Presbyterian chapel. In 1778 Messrs. Holmes and Hall (they were packers) took possession, remaining here until 1831; they added a third floor ca. 1778. After 1831 the house became dilapidated; was restored to its prior appearance.

  In 1908-10 its hall was moved, stone by stone, to Cheyne Walk and stored until 1926 when it was rebuilt in full in Chelsea, near Battersea Bridge. Converted into the dining room of the British Federation of University Women.
- Earl's Court: (See under E.)
- Eaton Square: Not until 1828.
- Elm Park Gardens: 1870s, on the site of Chelsea House.
- Five Fields: (See under F.)
- Five Fields Row: (Is now: 180 Ebury Street.) Mozart lived here as a boy in 1764, living in a doctor's house. (The Chelsea Bun House was just around the corner.)
- Fulham Road: The dividing line between Chelsea and Kensington.
  - See: Chelsea House, above.
  - See under F.
- Gough House: Built early in the 18th century. In 1866, was converted to the Victorian Hospital for Children. At some point was a school for young ladies.
- Grosvenor Road: (See under G.)
- Hans Place: (See: Hans Town/Hans Place.)
- Holy Redeemer: 1895. Catholic Church, 7 Cheyne Row.

- Jew's Burial Ground: (See: Old Church Street/Jew's Burial Ground, below.)
- Jew's Row: Former name of the western end of Pimlico Road (name change ca. 1850.) A rough district.
  - The Bunhouse was here. (See: Bunhouse, above.)
- Jubilee Place: 1809.
- King's Parade: 1810, erected on a farm site. Two rows of 4-story houses with front gardens. (Is between Arthur Street and Carlyle Square; now merged into King's Road.)
- King's Road: Not open to the public until 1830; until then a special pass was required to use it. This was a royal coach road, to get from Chelsea to Hampton Court Palace, from the time of Charles II's restoration to the throne.
    - ➢ See: Church Lane, above.
    - ➢ See under K.
  - 152: There was an early 19th C. building here; now a restaurant/nightclub called the Pheasantry. (See: King's Road/Chelsea/Pheasantry.)
  - Duke of York's School: (See: Duke of York's Headquarters.)
- Lawrence Street: Named for the Lawrence family. This street dates back to at least the 15th century.
- Lindsey Row: (See under L.)
- Little Chelsea: (See under L.)
- Lower Sloane Street: Lease granted in 1790. Widened in 1886.
  - Rose and Crown Tavern: Ca. mid 1700s. Rebuilt in 1933. (See under the INNS/PUBS section.)
- Market Garden: Here for 300 years, on north side of King's Road.
- Nell Gwynn House: 1937. NOT her house, just named for her. (See: Highgate Hill/Lauderdale House, for her actual house.)
- Oakeley Square: (See: Carlyle Square.)
- Old Church, the: (See: Chelsea Walk/Chelsea Old Church.)
- Old Church Street: West of Carlyle Square. Still hosts some 19th C. terraced houses. This was the main road through Chelsea until the King's Road was built/opened to public use.
  - 43: Chelsea Arts Club. 1891.
  - 46: The Old Dairy, built in 1796.
  - Jew's Burial Ground: On the east corner of Old Church Street. Bought in 1813 by a society of Jews. Those families who paid a fee could be interred

here.

- Old Swan House: Chelsea Embankment, 1876.
- Old Town Hall: 1885-1907.
- Park Walk: Late 18th century. Houses described as "immaculate" dark red brick terraces. Would have housed middle class persons (although now considered fashionable.)
- Pelham Crescent: Original houses still there. 1840s, although the houses were built to look Regency style. (See under P.)
- Ranelagh Gardens: To the rear of the Chelsea Hospital. Closed in 1805. Another source said 1803. Yearly opened in April and closed in July. The rotunda dates from 1740. Redesigned in 1860, long after it had fallen out of popular use. (See under R.)
- Royal Avenue: (See under R.)
- Royal Botanical Gardens: (See: Kew Gardens.)
- Royal Hospital: AKA: Royal Hospital, Chelsea. AKA: Chelsea Hospital. (See: Chelsea Hospital, above.)
- St. Luke's: Second church in Chelsea, built to accommodate the growing population, built in 1820-4.
- St. Mary's Church: Cadogen Street. Roman Catholic. 1812. (See under the CHURCHES section.)
- Shaftesbury House: 1635 to 1856 (its last years were as the parish workhouse.)
- Sloane Square: (See under S.)
- Sloane Street: (See under S.)
- statue: "Atlanta," (nude female,) 1926, Albert Bridge.
- statue: "Boy with a Dolphin," 1975. At the bottom of Oakley Street.
- Upper Cheyne Row:
    - 22: Victorian home of journalist and critic Leigh Hunt.
- Upper Manor Street: (See: Wellesley Street, below.)
- Wellesley Street: Ca. 1850 the name was changed to Upper Manor Street.

Chelsea Embankment - 1934.

Chelsea Flower Show - 1913. Held at the Chelsea Physic Garden. (See: Chelsea Physic Garden.)

Chelsea Hospital -

- ➢ See: Chelsea/Chelsea Hospital.
- ➢ See: Royal Hospital/Chelsea.

Chelsea Physic Garden - (Also seen as Chelsea Physick Garden.) 66 Royal Hospital Road. 4

acres. Strong on herbs; many other plants as well. Established in 1673 by the Worshipful Society of Apothecaries, it is England's second oldest surviving botanical garden (Oxford has the oldest.)

The first greenhouse in England was built here in 1681.

Since 1722 (a second source said 1772,) a continuous lease was granted, contingent on the garden providing fifty plant species a year to the Royal Society, up to a grand total of 2,000. One of Britain's first rock gardens was put in in 1772. The garden's doors were open to the public only after 1983.

Chelsea Square - In ca. the 1840-50 this area was known as Trafalgar Square; the name was changed to Chelsea Square in the 1920s to avoid confusion with the far more famous Trafalgar Square in Westminster.

Chelsea Waterworks Company - (Also known simply as: Chelsea Company.) Founded in 1723, to deliver water into London. In 1824 the water coming from the Thames at Chelsea Waterworks is described as thoroughly "offensive and destructive to health." In 1829 they were the first to introduce to London slow sand filtration. Via the Metropolitan Water Act of 1852 drawing water from the (polluted) Thames (below Teddington Lock) was forbidden. The CWC moved from Seething Wells in 1856. Taken over in 1902 by the Metropolitan Water Board.

Chelsfield Village - Bromley. (Not to be confused with the more modern Chelsfield that is sometimes referred to as New Chelsfield, even though they are both in Bromley.) Dates from at least 1145. Ca. 1290 there was a weekly Monday market, and a yearly 3-day fair; there is a current fair held here, but I can find no confirmation that the Chelsfield Fair lasted from on old into the Regency era.

- Court Lodge: House and farm here since at least the 18th century. Much destroyed by fire in 1857.
- Five Bells public house: Named for the bells of St. Martin of Tours church.
- St. Martin of Tours: Early Norman origin; altered and enlarged in the 13th century. The church had five bells (thus lending a name to the public house, above.) Restored in 1950 after war damage.

chemist - A chemist carries the kinds of supplies for which an American would go to a drugstore. In the 1700s chemists and druggists "battled" with the apothecaries on who would sell medications. A Regency era person would go to an apothecary. In modern times, one would refer to the clerk at a chemist's as a pharmacist, or a dispensary chemist.

- See: doctors/apothecary.
- See: St. James's Street/29.

cheques - That is, a printed writ (not unlike checks in America) on which a particular bank's customer would write the name of the person being paid, a date, and an amount, from the early 18th century. Uncommon. Used by the well-to-do, more for large purchases or private debts, because your average vendor would find a cheque suspect, ever preferring cash. (See: Child's Bank.)

chess - The ancient game.

- See: activities/entertainments/sports - parlor games, under A.
- See: Simpson's Tavern, under S.

Chester House - Wimbledon Commons. Thomas Paine (American writer) visited John Horne Tooke (clergyman/politician) at the latter's home here, probably in the 1790s.

Chester Row - Belgravia. 1968.

Chester Square - Belgravia. Small garden square, residential. AN ENCYCLOPAEDIA OF LONDON says Chester Square "was commenced (in) 1840." The gardens are not open to the public

- St. Michael's: 1847.

Chester Terrace - Regent's Park. 1824-5. (See: Park Crescent/Chester Terrace.)

Chesterfield House - Mayfair, Westminster. (See: South Audley Street/Chesterfield House.)

- Chesterfield Gardens: Victorian mansions.

Chesterfield Street - In 1799, Brummell (age 21) took up residence here.

- 4: Built in the 1740s or 50s.

chewing tobacco - (See: tobacco.)

Cheyne Row - Cheyne is pronounced "chain-ee." (See: Chelsea/Cheyne Row.)

Cheyne Walk - (See: Chelsea/Cheyne Walk.)

Chick Lane - West Smithfield. During the Regency this street was called West Lane. West Lane was also destroyed when the Red Lion Tavern was taken down, see below. (See: Stinking Lane.)

- Red Lion Tavern, old pub, demolished in 1844. A thieves' lodging-house, had concealment passages.

Chigwell Road - Three miles/4.8 km north of Woodford/near Epping Forest.

- King's Head Inn: Ancient hostel. The Verderers' (or Foresters') Courts were held here until 1855. Was mentioned in Charles Dickens's *Barnaby Rudge.* (See: Verderers/Verderers Court.)

Child's Bank - (AKA: Child & Co, from the 17th C.) 1 Fleet Street, the City. Oldest bank in Britain. Began life in the 16th C. as a goldsmith (who were the form of banking at that time.) Founded in 1664. From 1713, had been an independent bank (as was common in Regency England, before the Bank of England rose to dominance) but is now part of the Bank of Scotland group.

They claim they were the first to issue pre-printed cheques (early 18th C.); before then a customer would merely write a letter, and the holder would present it to the appropriate bank for compensation.

- See: cheques.
- See: Fleet Street/1.
- See: money/cheques.

Child's Hill - (See: Barnet/Child's Hill.)

childbirth - Usually occurred at home, usually attended by female family members, sometimes by midwives (who were female.) As the 19th century advanced, man-midwives were increasingly known.

Being "brought to bed" meant going into labor/the birthing process. "Confinement" meant the birth, but also the month following, in which all social (and management of the household) obligations were suspended and the mother given time to recover and receive visitors/well-wishers.

Caesarean sections were known from Roman times, but surgeons were very reluctant to perform the procedure, and the first (recorded) English survival (of the mother, not just the child) dates from 1774.

Before 1800 about 1.5% of expectant mothers died from childbirth, but that soon dropped to 1% with improvements of techniques and a call for cleanliness and fresh air. The average mother bore 6-7 live children.

Wet-nurses were frequently employed for nursing the infant in the 18th C., although less so as the 19th C. came around.

Births were not registered, but baptisms were required. There was the practice of a child having godparents.

Middle names, during the Regency era, were rare (although they might have two first names, such as Sarah Anne.)

- See: birth control.
- See: British Lying-in Hospital.
- See: City of London Lying-in Hospital.
- See: condoms.
- See: diseases/sepsis.
- See: maternity.
- See: Middlesex Hospital - First to have a maternity ward.
- You may care to see: baby bottles.
- You may care to see: wet nurse.

children's games -

- See: games, children's.
- See: toy stores.

chimney-sweeps - The "chimney-sweep" is the adult; the "climbing boy" is his apprentice; "apprentice" not necessarily meaning they were treated well, and was the far more likely of the two to actually go up the narrow chimneys; injuries and burns were common. An 1840 Act of Parliament prohibited the employment of minors in removing soot or extinguishing flames in chimneys. The use of climbing boys was banned entirely in 1875.

- See: Society for Superseding the Necessity of Climbing Boys.
- See: United Society of Master Chimney-sweepers.

china - As in tableware. Note that china differentiates from earthenware; earthenware is made from common rough clays, while bone china is made from finer-particle, harder to manipulate, and smoother clays. China was less seen in the homes of commoners.

- See: bone china.
- See: Derby/Crown Derby, under the BRITISH COUNTIES section.
- See: Doulton Fine China.
- See: earthenware shops - These were more "everyday" tableware.
- See: Limehouse.
- See: Mill Street/Thomas Goade.
- See: St. James's/Wedgwood & Byerley's.
- See: St. James's Square/York Street.
- See: Soho/Wedgwood.
- See: Staffordshire/Spoke, under the BRITISH COUNTIES section - For the invention of bone china.

Chinatown - From before 1850 this phrase meant the Limehouse area. (See under L.) But now refers to the areas around Gerrard Street and Lisle Street, Westminster.

Chinese immigrants - First arrived in London via having served as cooks on British ships; a Chinese community sprang up around the docks at Limehouse. London's modern "chinatown" centers around Gerrard Street/Soho.

- See: Limehouse.
- See: rough places.

Chippendale's - Furnituremaker.

- See: Goodwin's Court.
- See: St. Martin's Lane/60-62.

Chiswell Street - Finsbury Square.

- Whitbread's Brewery: In 1742 Samuel Whitbread, brewer, moved to a small brewery used to make porter. (See: porter.) King George II visited and was feasted here (at a cost to Whitbread of some 1,200 pounds.) The elder Samuel died in 1796. Ca. 1800 the brewery, inherited by his son Samuel, was described as huge. The business merged with Martineau & Bland in 1812. They were brewing ale by 1834. Many of the original buildings remain, although the brewery ceased in 1976. (See under W.)

Chiswick - (Pronounced Chizzik.) Chiswick derives from "cheese." Existed by the year 1000. Area of country estates, six miles/9.6 km west of central London; begun to develop ca. 1760s. An area for breweries.

- Bedfork Park: 1870-90s.
- Chiswick House: (See at its own entry.)
- Fuller's Brewery: Chiswick Lane. Beer brewed in Chiswick since the 17th C., but John Griffin Fuller's brewery here dates from 1816.
- Hogarth's House: William Hogarth (artist.) Red brick. Bought in 1749. Hogarth died here in 1764. Is now the Hogarth Museum, since 1909. (See: Chiswick House, at its own listing.)
- St. Nicholas: Chiswick's parish church. Existence dates back to 1181. Rebuilt in the 15th C., and renovated in 1884.

Chiswick House - Burlington Lane, Chiswick. Built for the third Earl, Lord Burlington (also was Lord Cork.) He had the house designed to be used for entertaining, as opposed to living in (although the ground floor did provide a private apartment for him.) Built to his own designs. Begun in 1725, completed in 1729; a well-preserved model of a Palladian style villa. The park and pleasure grounds cover 190 acres, containing many follies. The gateway was by Inigo Jones, having been brought here ca. 1730 from the demolished home of Sir Thomas More (author/king's adviser.)

It was the painter William Hogarth's country residence ca. 1730-1760s. Charles James Fox (Whig statesman) died here in 1806, as did George Canning (Prime Minister) in 1827. Alexander I of Russia stayed here in 1814 (along with other allied sovereigns,) visiting the Duke of Devonshire.

It later became an asylum, and then public property. Wings removed and reconstruction done in the 1950s.

Chiswick Mall - Hounslow. Georgian and Regency houses. So near the Thames that it has a tendency to flood. Artists liked to reside here for the past 200+ years.

chit - (Starts like "child", rhymes with "it.") Used mostly despairingly, as in "a chit of a girl." It is applied to women. It might be a gentle scold, or it might be used to show a woman is considered to be impudent, or above herself. Not to be confused with "cit." (See: cit.)

chocolate - (See: food/chocolate.)

chocolate-houses - Different from coffee-houses only in the primary beverage served (although either kind of establishment served both, as well as tea.) The term was heard more in the 17-18th centuries than in the 18-19th centuries. When Regency persons asked for "chocolate" they meant a drink rather like what Americans call "hot cocoa."

- See: coffee-houses.
- You may care to see: food/chocolate - To learn more about chocolate.

cholera - It wasn't understood that cholera was caused by polluted water until 1854, and even then resisted as a concept until 1866.

- See: sanitation.
- See: sewers.
- You may care to see: diseases.

Cholmondeley House - (See: Cambridge House.)

chop house - (Also seen as: chophouse.) An 18-19th century version of a restaurant. So called because "chops" (cuts of meat) were served (along with other food choices.) In the Regency era, chophouses were more commonly associated with bachelors (who lacked not only a wife but possibly a functional cooking space,) although it was known that couples, too, would visit a chophouse. Keep in mind, though, that in the 19th C. most dining took place in one's home, or the home of friends or family. The term "chop house" was much more common during the Regency than was "restaurant." An older term for much the same was: cook-shop.

- See: baker - For another source for meal preparation/an oven to be used.
- See: Bread Street.
- See: cookshops.
- See: Eastcheap.
- See: INNS/PUBS section - The notes at the beginning.
- See: Panton Street/Stone's Chop House.
- See: restaurant.

Christian's - A draper's in Wigmore Street at which Jane Austen shopped. (See: Wigmore Street/Christian's.)

Christie's Auction House - (Now simply known as 'Christie's,' but its more formal name evolved over time into Christie, Manson and Woods, Ltd.)

Founded in 1766 by James Christie. At that time, the firm's office was in Castle Street, Oxford Street, and the "Great Room" in Pall Mall (where the United Service Club later resided from ca. 1828-1974) and was where sales took place. Moved to 125 Pall Mall in 1770, adjoining Schomberg House; James Christie died here in 1803; the business went to sons and grandsons.

The business moved to: 8 King Street, St. James's, since 1823.

In the 19th C. it was more of a clearing house in nature; not as preeminent as it is now.

Woods joined in 1859; Manson in 1889.

In 1941 was destroyed by WWII bombs, and Christie's moved to Spencer House, St. James's Place; it has since returned to 8 King Street.

Christopher and Co. - No longer in business, since the 1980s. Spent most of its London history at Jermyn Street, St. James's, coming there in the 20th century. Royal Warrant in 1902. Their sign read: "Wine merchants in the parish of St. James's. Established since the Great Fire of 1666." Supplied mostly wine, but also did their own spirits.

Christ's Hospital - (AKA: Christ's Hospital Bluecoat School.) Boys' school situated on the north side of Newgate Street; is a Church of England independent school, endowed (at first) by public money.

The building was first the Greyfriars monastery, but following the Dissolution, was reused/founded in 1553 by Henry VI as a hospital for foundlings and fatherless children.

Christ's Hospital burned in the Great Fire of 1666; rebuilt on the same site before the end of the 17th century.

Taylor Coleridge (poet/literary critic) and Charles Lamb (essayist) went there.

The boys of Christ were always known as "Bluecoats" because of their uniforms, which consisted of a long blue coat, dating back to its time of origin. Consequently the school, in popular vernacular, is referred to as Bluecoat School. The boys intended to go on to University were called "Grecians" (and they sat in the high pews in the galleries of the chapel); this "title" pre-dates the Regency (and out-lasted it as well.)

Started as co-educational, but girls no longer attended here after 1778 (their portion moving to Hertfordshire at that time.)

In 1902 the boys moved to Horsham, Sussex. The girls' Hertfordshire site was closed down in 1985, the girls then also moving to Horsham.

The site is now occupied by the Post Office building and part of St. Bartholomew's Hospital.

Not to be confused with "Blewcoat School."

(See: Blue-Coat School.)

Chunnel - (See: Channel Tunnel.)

church - (See: churches.)

Church Commissioners for England - Established in 1948 to look after the Church of England's assets (among which are some 150,000 acres of British agricultural land.)

Church of England - Its members are known as: Anglicans. Most of the churches/chapels under the CHURCHES section of this work are Anglican, although they many times started life as Catholic, until Henry VIII broke from the Church of Rome in the 16th century. (See: Dissolution of the Monasteries.) The Act of Supremacy in 1534 declared England a sovereign state, and the king (at that time, Henry VIII) as both head of the church and of the country.

Anglican clergy were men only. They wore no distinctive collar; the only thing that set their dress apart from the average was that they tended to wear white shirts under otherwise black garments. Churches were unheated. Box pews (as opposed to bench pews) were increasingly added through the 18th C., and were often of differing designs as suited their (usually important or rich) owners.

There were no confessionals in Anglican churches (as there were in Roman Catholic ones.)

(You may care to see: Parish Clerks' Hall.)

SOME OF THE ANGLICAN CLERGY:

- RECTOR: The head clergyman in a country parish, the word literally means "governor." This was a desirable living, because the rector owned the tithes and had rights to the land on which he resided. By the time of the early 19th C. he was most likely an educated man, possibly a younger son of a noble, and considered to be on a social scale with the local squire, from whom he could expect invitations to dine, attend gatherings, play cards, and go hunting. Rectors could raise crops on their lands, but if they did not have the wherewithal to turn a profit from their lands (and therefore become quite comfortable) they could instead live off the monies provided by a patron (and so, accordingly, might be treated by the patron as rather like a poor relation.)
- VICAR: This is a parson who heads a parish in which he does not own the land. He may be standing in for an absent or dead rector, having no rights to the tithes, land, or its profits, because these things belong to someone else (presumably the local squire.) He lived in a vicarage (rather than a rectory,) collected an allowance (i.e. a salary) instead of the tithes, and was considered transient (even if he resided there for years.) He was as well-educated as a rector, and if he had an independent income, could be even more socially acceptable. In 1936, tithes were abolished in England, so the two words (rector and vicar) became then largely interchangeable.
- PARSON: A general term, signifying the head of a parish, or any minister below the rank of bishop who had enough authority to conduct religious services. While

not strictly correct, the populace often called rectors and vicars by the term "Parson."

- CURATE: A rector or a vicar's assistant, who usually ended up doing a great deal of the actual business of the parish (especially if the Rector was occupied with crop-growing.) Curates were considered, socially, to be "inferior clergy," usually being insecure in their position, poor, and not as polished as their senior brethren. In the average 19th C. novel, the poor curate is often seen as having a lot of children, on whom the heroine bestows boiled treats, or clothing, or baskets of foodstuffs.
- BEADLE: A parish officer of minor status, he ushered people in and out of services, delivered messages, and kept unruly boys in line. It is not inappropriate to think of him as a church constable. He also served a civic purpose, supplementing the Watch. In fact, to this day there are still beadles, complete with frock coats and top hats, guarding the private road known as Ely Place.
  - See: beadle.
  - See; Watch, the.
- SEXTON: He rang the church bells, took care of church property, and dug graves for a fee. He was a little something more than a janitor.

PLEASE NOTE: You might say, "Good morning, Rector." (Or Vicar.) But you would never say, "Good morning, Rector Jones." It'd be like saying, "Good morning, Priest Jones."

Church Lane - St. Giles, slums. Old street.

Church Missionary Society - Founded in London in 1799 by members belonging to the Clapham sect. (See under C.) It is now (from PILGRIMS' LONDON): "One of the two great missionary arms of the Anglican Church and Britain's largest missionary society…."

Church Row - Bethnal Green.

- St. Matthew's: 1740. (See under the CHURCHES section.)

Church Street - NOTE: almost every little town and village had a Church Street. Not surprisingly, it was a street that contained, or had contained, a church.

Church Street - Chelsea and Chiswick.

- The Old Burlington: Pub. Purportedly where highwayman Jack Turpin's (d.1739) wedding breakfast was served.

Church Street - **Hampstead.** (Now called Church Row.)

- St. John-at-Hampstead: (See: St. John/Hampstead, under the CHURCHES section.)

Church Street - **Limehouse** district. (Now known as Newell Street.)

Church Street - Westminster, on the west side of Lisson Grove. 1790s. Had a haymarket from 1830.

Church Street - Whitechapel. "A cobbled lane." This street is now known as St. Clare Street.

- Holy Trinity Church: (See: Holy Trinity/Whitechapel, under the CHURCHES section.)

churches - There are many, many entries in this entire work, listed under their own entries, or under the part of the city in which they reside(d); but the ones of particular import or interest are separately listed in the CHURCHES section.

- ➢ See: Church of England - Contains a list of the clergy.
- ➢ See the CHURCHES section.

cigars - (Sometimes seen spelled as: segars.)

- ➢ See: Fribourg & Treyer.
- ➢ See: St. James's Street/19.
- ➢ You may care to see: tobacco.

Cinnamon Street - Wapping. From at least the 17th century; cinnamon was most likely sold here then.

- Pear Tree Inn: Here by at least 1811, when a murderer hid here.

circulating libraries - The first circulating library in London was purportedly established in 1740, a bookseller by name of Batho, at 132 Strand. (The first one in the UK was in Edinburgh, Scotland, in 1726.) Besides being able to get books, coffee, chocolate, and conversation here, one could also get jewelry and other gewgaws, up to and including gloves, rings, brooches, and parasols. Despite there being public (free) circulating libraries in cities such as Bristol and Liverpool, in 1804 London had none (although it had plenty that charged fees.)

- ➢ See: Booth's.
- ➢ See: Cawthorne's.
- ➢ See: Lending Libraries - The note under.
- ➢ See: libraries.

circus - A term that can mean a curved street (a full or half-circle,) but here I'm referring to the form of entertainment.

Circuses were much more like "Barnum and Bailey/performing animals" than they were like zoos/menageries. Circuses tended to have a lot of equestrian acts. Also to be seen during the Regency era: animal acts (such as dogs doing tricks,) clowns (tended to look more like a harlequin than a modern clown,) dancers and/or singers, military reenactments, music, parts of plays (even the occasional bit of Shakespeare,) sea-battles (undersized "ships" in several feet of water,) sword-swallowers, wirewalkers. (This list is not all-inclusive.)

- See: Astley's Amphitheatre.
- See: Royal Circus.
- See: Sadler's Wells.

Cistercians, the - Their Abbey of St. Mary Graces, East Smithfield, was destroyed in the Dissolution.

cit - (Pronounced just like "sit.") A mildly derogatory term for shopkeepers and people from the City, usually used by "the quality" to refer to the *nouveau riche*/upstarts. Not to be confused with "chit." (See: chit.)

City - (See: City, the, below.)

City and Guilds of London Institute - In 1878 the City Livery Companies incorporated this joint central body for promoting technical and scientific education.

- See: halls - For more information on the ancient guilds.
- See: Livery Companies.

City Canal - (See: docks/West India Docks.)

City Corporation - (See: City, the.)

City Hall - Since 2002 the new business home for the Lord Mayor, as opposed to where he resides. (See: Lord Mayor, for where he resides.) Has a geometrical/roundish shape. (See: Guildhall, for years prior to 2002.)

City of London Club - 1832-33. Built on the site of the South Sea House, destroyed in 1826 by fire. (See under the CLUBS section.)

City of London Lying-in Hospital - City Road. A lying-in hospital was for giving birth (in the Regency this would likely be used only by women expecting a difficult birth; most births took place at home.) Established in 1750 with the City, but moved outside the City's borders later, in an austere Victorian building. It moved to north London in the 1950s, then called the City of London Maternity Hospital.

- See: childbirth.
- You may care to see: British Lying-in Hospital.

City of London Police Force - 26 Jewry Street. From 1839. Answered to the Corporation of London only. Not to be confused with the Metropolitan Police, with whom the City Council had flatly refused to coalesce. (You may care to see: Metropolitan Police, under M.) The City of London Police are very much like the Metropolitan Police in structure, except in that they answer only to the Corporation of London, not to the monarch via the Home Secretary.

- See: New Scotland Yard - The note near the bottom of the entry.
- See: Watch, the - For what existed before the City of London Police Force (and the Metropolitan Police.)

City of London Regiment -

- See: Royal Fusiliers.
- See: Tower of London/Waterloo Barracks.

City of London School - Was at Mill Street, Cheapside. Opened 1837. Moved to John Carpenter Street in 1882. Since moved to Paul's Walk.

City Press, the - Founded in 1857. Newspaper specifically for the City, named for an old publishing house, with an emphasis on ancient and/or historical interests.

City Road - Goes through Finsbury. Opened in 1761, described as an easy and pleasant run from the eastern parts of the City to the roads between Islington and Paddington. However, has also (in its entire life) been described as "one of London's most featureless thoroughfares." Was a series of individual sections until it was unified in the 1860s as the City Road (when the toll-gate was removed following the 1864 abolition of all toll-gates.)
(See: New Road, as this was an extension on to the same.)

- 47: Wesley's house, ready in 1779. He died here in March, 1791. (John Wesley founded Methodism.) Wesley's Chapel, built ca. 1778, is at this same address, rebuilt after an 1880 fire.
- Bunhill Fields: On the west side of City Road, just down from Old Street. A burial ground. Bunhill is a derivation of "Bone Hill." Between 1315-1854 some 120,000 souls were buried here. (See: Bunhill Fields, under B.)
- City Road Chapel: (AKA: Wesley's Chapel.) Established April 1777 by John Wesley, opened in 1778. The only 18th century Nonconformist chapel still standing in London.
- Eye Hospital: 1805. (See: Moorfields/Eye Hospital.)
- Finsbury Barracks: Headquarters of the Royal London Militia, from 1857. Rather has the look of a small castle. It went through several hands since, finally becoming the home of the Honourable Artillery Company, a charity for British forces. (See: militia.)
- Shepherd and Shepherdess, the: Ale house and tea-garden, before 1745, when it was replaced by the Eagle Tavern (the latter of which is of *Pop Goes the Weasel* fame.) Rebuilt as the Eagle (and attached to a "Grecian theatre") in the 1820s. (See: Finsbury/The Eagle.)

City Temple - Holborn. A Dr. Thomas Goodwin founded, in 1640, a church in Anchor Lane, Lower Thames Street. Circa 1650 the assemblies moved to a meeting house in Paved Alley (located at the Leadenhall Street end of Lime Street.) A new church was built on an adjacent site in 1672. Demolished in 1755; the congregation acrimoniously divided, the minority going to a meeting house in Artillery Street and the majority to Miles Lane,

Cannon Street. A new church opened in Camomile Street in 1766. It moved to the Poultry in 1819, being at that time called the Poultry Street Chapel.

Dr. Joseph Parker's famous ministry commenced here in 1869; it was so successful the City Temple was built at Holborn Viaduct.

(Not to be confused with the Temple Church in the Inns of Court.)

City, The - (AKA: The City of London. AKA: the Square Mile. AKA: Old London.) Not to be confused with the sprawling expanse we now consider to be London, but rather, the area once confined by its ancient walls. Loosely speaking, it is the area between St. Paul's and the Royal Exchange, St. Mary-le-Bow and the Thames.

Despite its nickname of "the Square Mile," these days it actually encompasses 1.16 square miles since a 1990s incorporation of land north of London Wall.

It is both a private landowner and a government appointed local authority.

It is divided into 25 districts, known as wards. (See: wards.)

Just to be clear, "the City" (note the capital C) is how one usually refers to the actual and ancient city of London. It also now is particularly used as a shorthand way of speaking of London's financial district.

The City is the oldest part of London. The Romans settled here ca. 43AD, building in the 3rd century the surrounding wall that encompassed 330 acres.

- See: gates.
- See: London Wall.

The City was given special status by William the Conqueror (he wanted to pacify the citizens.) As described in AN ENCYCLOPAEDIA OF LONDON: "Next comes Henry I's charter, granting the City the right to elect its own justiciars, the foundation of the City's present privilege of holding the trials of the King's Pleas in the chief court of criminal justice in the realm, the Central Criminal Court, commonly called 'the Old Bailey,' which is maintained by the City Corporation." So the City has kept its own freemen, police force, liverymen, etc. ever since that time. In other words, it has its own system of government, independent of the Crown and of Westminster; it is a self-governing corporation, albeit under royal rule; this self-government is referred to as the City Corporation. It has played an important part in restraining those sovereigns who would have bullied their subjects.

One of the City Corporation's other processes is: controlling the City's markets (assuring quality, etc.) There could be no non-City markets within 7 miles (the distance judged fair to be a man's walk to the market and home again in one day.) 7 miles = 11.3 km.

Here in the City there is a seven-way junction of streets which, oddly, has no name; the streets that corner together here are: Cornhill, Lombard Street, King William Street,

Queen Victoria Street, Poultry, Prince's Street, and Threadneedle Street. (See: each at its own listing.) Very much an automotive junction, as opposed to a pedestrian one.

In the 1990s the City still claimed some 6,000 private citizens living there.

Four-fifths of the City burned in the Great Fire of 1666.

Here is a small list of some important City buildings:

- Bank of England: (See under B.)
- Mansion House: (See under M.)
- Royal Exchange: (See under R.)
- St. Andrew-by-the-Wardrobe: Rebuilt in 1695 by Wren. (See under the CHURCHES section.)
- St. Sepulchre's: Was connected to Newgate Prison by a tunnel. (See under the CHURCHES section.)
- Simpson's Tavern: Since 1757 has been serving traditional British fare. (See under S.)

> ➢ See: Common Council.
> ➢ See: Court of Aldermen.
> ➢ See: gates.
> ➢ See: Lord Mayor.
> ➢ See: Lord Mayor's Show.
> ➢ See: Wards.
> ➢ See: Wards Without.

City Wall, the -

> ➢ See: gates.
> ➢ See: London Wall.

civil list - This is the designation for monies voted by Parliament to support the royal family and its household. Following the Glorious Revolution (1688; the ousting of James II) there evolved a separation of funds for the crown and for the state; this allowing for the monarch's "ordinary expenses" (£700,000 per annum in 1698) became known as the civil list. (See: INTRO-REIGNS/Reigns of British Kings & Queens/George III.)

Civil Service, the - So called at least by the mid 17th century. Such portions of the government as: the Admiralty, Land Management, Treasury, etc.

Clapham - Wandsworth/Lambeth. (Pronounced Clap-um.) After the Great Fire of 1666 a goodly number of Londoners resettled here. Samuel Pepys (diarist) died at his home here in 1703. By 1800 there were large detached homes all around the Common, serving as country retreats for the merchant class, although in 1801 it was yet described as a "tiny village surrounded by farms and fields." Didn't really expand until after the 1820s.

- Clapham Commons: Ancient uncultivated land (its soil's poor quality kept it from being exploited.) Up to the 17th C. there were squabbles over who maintained the area, so it was often overgrown and/or boggy. In the 18th C. the north side became favored for country estates. Up to the mid 18th century. it was an important place for the people of Clapham in terms of water, wood, and cattle-grazing. Eventually villas, girls' schools, and sporting clubs came in (the latter more deeply into the 19th century.)
- Clapham Park Estate: 1825.
- Crescent Grove: 1824.
- Elms, The: 1754 house.
- Holy Trinity: 1774-6, on the edge of the Common. Is now the parish church. (See: Holy Trinity/Clapham, under the CHURCHES section.)
- Old Town:
  - 39-43: A Queen Anne terrace, 1707.
- St. Paul's: Parish church. (See: St. Paul/Clapham, under the CHURCHES section.)

Clapham Sect, the - (A group, not a street.) Clapham was where a group of wealthy and influential Christians assembled for Bible study and prayer, beginning in the early 1780s. The group accomplished many religious-minded acts, such as anti-slavery discussions that led to changes in law, and the development of missions.

Clapton - Hackney. Farmland until the railways came in.

- Upper Clapton: Wasn't divided into "upper" and "lower" until ca. 1800. And most of the area is in Upper Clapton anyway.
  - Clapton Common: Before ca. 1800 was known as Broad Common.
  - Upper Clapton Road: Before ca. 1800 was known as Hackney Lane.

Clarence House - Stable Yard Road, adjoins on to the west side of St. James's Palace (in fact, is actually a part of St. James's Palace); west of the Queen's Chapel. 1825-7, by Nash. Painted, stuccoed. Built for the Duke of Clarence (later William IV; he lived here after 1830.) The top story added in 1873; and the entrance moved from the west side to the south, along with a new porch. (See: St. James's Palace/Clarence House.)

Clarence Terrace - Regent's Park. (See: Park Crescent/Clarence Terrace.)

Clarendon Hotel - (See: Bond Street/Old Bond Street/Royal Arcade.)

Clarges Street - (See: Mayfair/Clarges Street.)

Claridge's Hotel - 25 Brook Street, Mayfair. Liveried retainers. Founded 1812 as Mivart's, named for the French chef and first owner. Mivart was known for his joints and steam puddings. Mr. Claridge, the subsequent manager/owner, was a former butler to the nobility, taking over in 1838. Founded in Brook Street, but probably moved to 25 sometime after 1838. (See: Brook Street/25.)

In the Regency, it was known as "Mivart's."

It expanded to five adjoining properties in the 1830s. Acquired by the Savoy in 1893. Rebuilt by Richard D'Oyly Carte (of Gilbert and Sullivan fame) in 1895-9. Royal guests stay here now (following any few days spent at Buckingham Palace.) Now has a 1930s-style restaurant.

Clay Hill - Bromley. (See: Shortlands.)

Clay Hill - **Enfield**. So called by 1754 (before then was known as Bridge Street.)

- St. John the Baptist: 1858.

clearing house - A term that loosely means "bank," but refers to the practice of clearing, that is, each day adjusting the accounts between the many banks. This practice dates from the 18th century.

In 1810 an official building was established in London for this purpose (which had moved inside into a rented room in 1773, whereas business had used to be done in the street); it is the London Clearing House of today (founded in 1888.)

- See: Bank of England - For more on banking.
- See: goldsmiths - For the time before the 18th century.
- See: London Clearing House.

Cleaver Square - South of the Thames (first square that was built to the south.) Georgian, 1789.

- 34 through 41: These houses were built in 1792. Mostly unchanged.

Clement's Inn - Gets its name from the parish of St. Clement Danes. Was attached to the Inner Temple. Its founding date is unknown. It was a house of law in 1479. Leased, probably for legal students, in 1486. Described as being near 'the fair fountain called Clement's Well.' Its hall was rebuilt in 1715. Taken down in order to build the Royal Courts of Justice, 1868. West of the new courts, a new Clement's Inn sprang up (being a row of buildings.) The old hall was demolished in 1893.

Clement's Lane - At the Lombard Street end of this street, there was a purpose-built block of chambers (built particularly for offices,) was erected in 1823. Such purpose-built offices were a new idea at the time. This street dates from at least 1677.

Cleopatra's Needle - The Embankment, Westminster. 60 foot tall granite pillar, one of a pair dating from 1475 B.C., 1,000 years before Cleopatra lived (the other is in Central Park, New York.) Given to Britain in 1819 by the Viceroy of Egypt and Sudan, Mohammed Ali. It was not erected in London until 1878. Misnamed; the deeds recorded on the two pillars are not of Cleopatra, but rather of Thothmes and Ramses II.

clergy, of the Anglican church - (See: Church of England.)

Clerk of Works' House - Was adjacent to Chelsea Hospital. When the hospital added new stables in 1814-17 the addition "greatly modified" the Clerk of Works' House. Demolished in 1858.

Clerkenwell - Once in the borough of Finsbury (now in the borough of Islington.) Dates back to the 12th century. Takes its name from Clerk's Well, a medieval spring; it can still be seen when a well cover is lifted, although now it trickles where once it gushed. The well was in public use up to the 19th C. when pollution caused city officials to cover it over.

Clerkenwell was a gathering place of French Huguenots, who opened jewelry and silver workshops in Hatton Garden, as well as locksmiths, and cutlery shops. Also, later, clockmaking (by 1800.) By the time of Charles Dickens it was mostly slums.

- Charterhouse, the: (See under C.)
- New River Canal: (See under N.)
- Sadler's Wells: (See under S.)
- St. John's Priory: In St. John's Square. (See under the CHURCHES section.)
- Sessions House, Clerkenwell: (See: Clerkenwell Green/Middlesex Sessions House.)
- Spa Fields: Open field used for walking and amusements, laid out ca. 1603-25. Scene of an 1816 riot.

Clerkenwell Green - By the end of the 18th C., the 'green' was no longer green, as all the grass and trees were gone. By the mid 19th C., it was a crowded and poverty-stricken residential area. Had a reputation for being a radical's meeting place. In 1826, William Cobbett (pamphleteer/MP) spoke here, condemning the Corn Laws. Site of the 1832 'Clerkenwell Riot,' a violent clash between the new Metropolitan police and unemployed workers. Some Georgian houses yet remain.

- Clerkenwell House of Detention: Built in 1615. In the next 60 years was rebuilt. 100,000 prisoners a year. Evolved into a debtor's prison over time. Talking among the prisoners was forbidden and resulted in solitary confinement and meals of bread and water. Before 1845, was a "Bridewell" prison. (See: Bridewell Prison, for a description of the term.) Closed in 1877. In 1890 was demolished and replaced with the present school buildings.
- Middlesex Sessions House: (AKA: Sessions House.) Off Farringdon Road. 1782, Palladian, by Thomas Rogers, replacing the local Courthouse (which had been at Hick's Hall in St. John's Lane.) Enlarged in 1860. A PORTRAIT OF GEORGIAN LONDON says the session house was "somewhat more powerful than an ordinary magistrates' court." This session house served as a supplement to Old Bailey. For whatever reason, stiffer sentences were handed out here.
- St. James: (See: St. James Church/Clerkenwell, in the CHURCHES section.)

Clerkenwell Street - 1878.

Clermont Club - Modern.

- See: Berkeley Square/44.
- See: Clermont Club, under the CLUBS section.

Cleveland House - 33 King Street. Southeast corner of St. James's Park, erected in 1630 by Thomas Howard (first Earl of Berkshire); called at that time "Berkshire House." In 1668 Charles II gave the house to Barbara Villiers, who renamed it Cleveland House in 1670 (when she became the Duchess of Cleveland.) Redesigned in 1840 by Sir Charles Barry. Finished in 1854 and renamed Bridgewater House (also seen as: Bridgwater,) for its occupant the 3rd Duke of Bridgewater.

Cleveland Row - St. James's. Rebuilt in 1850.

Cleveland Street - Fitzrovia. Some 19th C. houses remain.

- 19: There was a famous scandal at a male brothel here in 1889, supposedly involving aristocrats and royals.

Clifford Street - Early 18th century. Named after the Clifford family, the Earls of Cumberland.

- 10: Stultz (first spelled "Stulz," and later as I have it here.) Tailor for both men and women, established 1809. There at least until WWI. He gave a discount for cash.
- 141: Samuel Morse (American inventor) lived here 1812-15.
- Long's Hotel: At the Bond Street end of Clifford Street. Much patronized by country gentlemen who came to town out of season, when their own town homes were closed up. Sir Walter Scott (author) lived here for a while, joined sometimes for meals by Lord Byron (poet.)

Clifford's Inn - Fleet Street. Leased by lawyers from a widow (Lady Clifford) in 1345. Was an Inn of Chancery, "entirely independent." Had a constitution of its own, was governed by a principal and twelve "Rules" (older students.) The juniors sat at a table called the "Kentish Mess," this name having no known explanation. The Inn was only damaged a bit in the Great Fire of 1666. A new hall was built in 1767 (keeping some of the medieval work intact.) Ceased taking members in 1877. The building was sold in 1903, but the buyer's plans did not materialize and lawyers continued to live here. It was demolished in 1935 (except for the 1840 gateway.)

- 3: Had finely carved woodwork similar to the work of Grinling Gibbons.
- 12: Purportedly dated back to 1624.

Clifton Hill - St. John's Wood. Leafy. Victorian.

climbing boys - (See: chimney-sweeps.)

Clink Prison - Clink Street, Southwark. First resided under Winchester Palace as a dungeon in

1127, then built next to it (long before the Regency.) Built to hold those convicted of religious misdemeanors, and religious nonconformists, especially in the 16-17th centuries. It last resided at Deadman's Place, Park Street. Destroyed in the 1780 Gordon Riots, and not rebuilt. Is the source of the saying "in the clink" to mean imprisonment.

- See: Southwark/Liberty of the Clink.
- See: Winchester House.

Clink Street - So named for the prison. Southwark. Narrow and dark. Ca. 1340 the Bishop of Winchester's Palace stood here.

Clissold Park - Stoke Newington. Not much developed until 1889-99.

Cloak Lane - In the early 15th C. this street was called Horseshoe Bridge Street; it was "Cloak Lane" by the late 17th C., a corruption of Latin "Cloaca" (sewer.)

- Cutlers' Hall: Located here, until it moved in 1887 to Warwick Lane. (See: Cutlers' Hall, at its own listing.)

Clock Tower - Bridge Street. The iconic Clock Tower is attached to the Houses of Parliament, and houses the bell known as Big Ben. Is now called: Elizabeth Tower. (See: Big Ben.)

Clockmakers' Company - (AKA: the Worshipful Company of Clockmakers.) At first belonged in the Blacksmiths' Company. Got their own Royal Charter in 1631. Livery in 1766. 61st in the order of precedence. Never had a hall, but the Company's Museum had been housed in the Guildhall Library; now housed in the Science Museum in London, since 2015. (Though their archive and library are still at Guildhall.)

clockmaking -

- See: Charing Cross.
- See: Clockmakers' Company.
- See: clocks.

clocks - Mechanical clocks were invented in the late 13th century (as opposed to devices such as sundials or water clocks.) Mechanical clocks must be wound with a key in order to run. These early mechanical clocks weren't terribly accurate, but the invention of the pendulum in 1657 had them keeping better time. In that same century long case clocks came along (and in the 20th C. were dubbed as Grandfather clocks, after a famous poem.) The cuckoo clock came into being ca. 1775.

London's oldest clockmakers, Thwaites & Reed, date from before 1768, at least. They made the clock that is in the tower of the Horse Guards.

Stopwatches were invented in 1776.

In 1800, skeleton clocks (exposed movements under a glass dome) began to be popular.

The electric clock was an 1840s development. In Britain, towns did not necessarily keep the same time; this was not regulated into standard times until the rails came in (also in the 1840s.)

In 1884, International time zones (including Greenwich Meantime) were formed.

- See: Greenwich - For Prime Meridian (Greenwich Meantime) information.
- You may care to see: watches.

cloth -

- See: bedding.
- See: Cloth Fair.
- See: clothing.
- See: clout - Diapers, to Americans.
- See: drapers.
- SEE: FABRICS.
- See: fabrics threads.
- See: fullers - Those who stretch cloth.
- See: milliners.
- See: Spinning Jennies - Factories, and home versions.
- See: textiles.
- See: Wandsworth - Dyeing of cloth.

Cloth Fair - (Street.) Spitalfields. 1604. Named for the raucous Bartholomew Fair. (See under B.) It was the main cloth fair for centuries. Yet contains early 17th C. gabled houses, some of London's few to survive the Great Fire of 1666.

- 38: Rising Sun, the. Pub, 18th century. (See under the INNS/PUBS section.)
- 41-42: Ca. 1670 home, still there. Built just after the Great Fire. (A second source says this home was built *before* 1666, and survived the Fire.)
- 43: Currently a tiny hotel, but for a very long time was a private home, 18th century facade.

clothing -

- See: Bond Street.
- See: Carnaby Street.
- See: cloth.
- See: coat-maker.
- See: Conduit Street/Meyer.
- See: drapers.
- See: Ede & Ravencroft - Robe-makers.

- See: fabric.
- See: fabric threads.
- See: Friday Street/Meaker's - Men's outfitters.
- See: hats.
- See: Mason's Yard/Maxwell, Henry - Boot/shoes/clothing, including Hunting pink.
- See: milliners.
- See: Monmouth Street.
- See: old clothes - A list of where to buy them.
- See: Petticoat Lane.
- See: St. James's.
- See: sewing - There were very little ready-made clothes, and even the little there were, were expected to be fitted and re-sewn to fit.
- See: stockings - (Hose.)
- See: tailors.
- See: uniforms, military.

Clothworkers' Company - (AKA: the Worshipful Company of Clothworkers.) Formed in 1528 by blending the Fullers (who'd formed in 1480) and the Shearers (1508); the Clothworkers assumed the Shearers' rank and thus are 12th in precedence among the halls. (12th of the Twelve Great Companies.) As opposed to the Drapers, the Clothworkers originally did the finishing on woven woolen cloth; "fulling it" meaning to mat the fibers and remove the grease; they shaped it to a uniform finish. Is a Livery Company.

- See: Clothworkers' Hall.
- See: Drapers' Hall.
- See: halls/Drapers' Hall.
- See: Mincing Lane/Clothworkers' Hall.

Clothworkers' Hall - Dunster Court, Mincing Lane. Sixth Livery Hall at this same location; it first belonged to the Shearmen, building their Hall here in 1472. When the Shearmen and the Fullers combined in 1528, the Hall came to the new Clothworkers' Guild. Halls were built, pulled down, and the third Hall here burned in the Great Fire of 1666. A Victorian era Hall burned in 1941. The present Hall was built between 1955-58, its brick and Portland stone facade described as having "Victorian dress."

- See: Clothworkers' Company.
- See: fullers.
- See: Mincing Lane/Clothworkers' Hall.

clout - (Rhymes with out.) What Regency folk called a diaper; "nappies" was a later term.

clubs, gentlemen's - (See under the CLUBS section.)

coach - The first coach (an enclosed type of horse-drawn carriage) in England probably came from France, in 1564. The idea of carriages quickly became fashionable, and coach-building blossomed almost as once. Before then, travel was by walking, horseback, or (rarely) litter (cloth suspended between horses, for ill persons, rather dangerous.) The first coaches were clumsy and heavy, and had no kind of spring or other device to soften passage over the roads (which were often very rough/muddy in themselves.) By 1614 coaches started to become a popular form of transportation throughout London, thereby angering Watermen, and eventually leading to more bridges over the Thames in the 19th century. In 1804, elliptic carriage springs were invented by Obadiah Elliot, a coachbuilder in Lambeth. This provided suspension, making carriage rides much more comfortable.

- See: carriages.
- See: coach-builders.
- See the INNS/PUBS section - The many coaching inn listings there.
- See: Watermen, under W - For another form of transport.

coach-builders -

- See: Bishopsgate.
- See: coach - For details on when inventions in carriage-building came along.
- See: Coachmakers' and Coach Harness Makers' Hall.
- See: Long Acre.
- See: Queen Street, Regent's Street.

coaching halts - Essentially the same thing as a coaching inn. (See: coaching inn - At its own listing.) Except for the small distinction that a coaching halt was on a road everyone knew led (in large part) to a specific destination, such as Bath, or Brighton, or Dover, etc. (This list is not all-inclusive.)

- See: Edgware - Northwest out of London.
- See: Elephant and Castle - Roads coming into London from the Southwest, South, and Southeast.
- See: Longford - Coaching halt on the way to Bath.
- See: Romford - Coaching halt on the London-to-Colchester road.
- See: Snaresbrook - Was a 17th C. coaching halt on the way to Epping.
- See: Turnham Green - Coaching halt on the way to Bath.
- See: Uxbridge - Was a flourishing coaching halt in the 18th century.
- See: Welling - A coaching halt on the way to Dover.

coaching inns - (See many entries in the INNS/PUBS section.)

Many coaching inns had alighting stones (mounting blocks, to aid in getting in and out of carriages,) as did places such as market squares and churches. Circa 1730 there were approximately 200 coaching inns in London.

- See: Ludgate Street/Belle Sauvage.
- See: Southwark/George, the.

Coachmakers' and Coach Harness Makers' Hall - For the Worshipful Company of Coachmakers and Coach Harness Makers. Noble Street. Quoting from AN ENCYCLOPAEDIA OF LONDON: "By reason of the badness of English roads, coach-making was unknown here in the Middle Ages. The Company, before obtaining its charter..." (in 1677, from Charles II) "...was called the Chariot-makers' Company. When its powers were exercised in the 17th and 18th centuries, they...tried to limit coach-making and harness-making to British-born persons, and succeeded in making the craft very exclusive in the 18th century."

The earliest hall was located in Cow Lane, West Smithfield. At Noble Street since 1703, when they occupied the building that had been used by the Scriveners. Greatly altered in 1841-3. Rebuilt also in 1867-70. Totally destroyed by WWII bombs; rebuilt. Is a livery company. 72nd in the order of precedence.

Note: In 1806, a two-year-old *used* chaise cost £150.

- See: carriages.
- See: coach.
- You may care to see: Wheelwrights' Company - With which the Coachmakers had an affiliation until the 17th century/establishment of both as incorporated Guilds.

coade stone - A kind of decorative material, man-made. Weathers extremely well. Popular with builders. (See: Lambeth/Coade's.)

coal - The phrase "carrying coals to Newcastle" to imply a foolish act stems from the fact that coal was Newcastle's prime resource, and it would therefore be absurd to take the product to the place where it is exceedingly plentiful.

Coal was brought to London from Newcastle by at least the 13th century.

Any place supplied by canal, river, or sea was likely to burn coal for fuel, as it could be cheaply gotten. Coal burning was in large part to blame for 18-19th century London's famously thick fogs. Londoners used coal as their main source of heating (wood for burning would be hard to come by in the city,) until it was banned in 1956.

"Sea-coal" meant it was mined (predominantly in northeast England); "coal" generally meant: charcoal.

- See: all the "coal-ish" entries, below.

- See: Great Ryder Street/10.
- See: Seacoal Lane.
- You may care to see: fog - (Generated by coal burning.)

Coal Exchange - Lower Thames Street. The first exchange was built over a tavern, the Dog, where coal purchases had already been conducted; first mentioned in 1758. The Coal Factors' Society owned the exchange, until 1803 when the City obtained from Parliament the right to (compulsorily) purchase the exchange. The exchange's business was run by 15 gentlemen called the Board of Sea-Coal Meters. Rebuilt at the corner of Lower Thames Street and St. Mary-at-Hill in 1846-9, at which time it got its "remarkable" floor designed as a mariner's compass. Pulled down ca. 1960.

Coal Hole - 15-16 Fountain Court, off the Strand. A tavern, once called the Unicorn, 1815. Companies from the theatres whooped it up all night with chops and kidneys and rum-punch and song here. (See: Coal Hole, under the INNS/PUBS section.)

Coal Yard - Off Drury Lane. Actress/Charles II's mistress, Nell Gwyn's birthplace. Later known as Stukeley Street, named for the 18th C. clergyman/archaeologist who lived nearby. A slum by the mid 19th century.

Coast Guard, the - Established in 1824. Before that, there were Marines, red-coated men who served on Naval ships, as fighters, not in running the ships; that was left to the sailors. (See: Marines.)

coat of arms - (See: College of Arms.)

coat-maker -

- See: Bond Street/Old Bond Street/Weston.
- See: tailors.

cobbles - (Also called: cobblestones.) Small blocks of granite for road-building, usage dates from the 15th century, (although Romans were also known to build cobbled roads.)

cobblers - Traditionally, one who works with old leather to make shoes (as opposed to a cordwainer, who used new Cordovan leather. By the time of the Regency, this distinction no longer mattered; and virtually everyone would have referred to a shoe-repairer or -maker as a cobbler. (See: Cordwainers' Hall.)

cock and hen club - Slang. Means: a flash-house (lewd & riotous place.)

Cock Lane - Smithfield. It is believed that birds were bred here from the 12th C. for cockfighting. During medieval times, this was the City's only street licensed for prostitution. Was supposedly haunted by an 18th C. ghost with the unfortunate name of "Scratching Fanny."

- Fortune of War tavern:
  - See: Fortune of War tavern, under the INNS/PUBS section.
  - See: Pie Corner/Fortune of War.

- Saracen's Head Buildings: (See: Saracen's Head/Aldgate, under the INNS/PUBS section.)

Cock Pit, the - 70 Whitehall. Was where the Old Treasury Building was until it was rebuilt in 1734 (at 1 Horse Guards Road,) and significantly altered in 1816 or 1824. Stands today. (See: Treasury - A little below the "Exchequer" paragraph.)

(Note: There are other "cockpit" entries, below, where the word is one instead of two.)

cockfighting - One of the oldest sports known to Londoners, popular across the social spectrum (who sat undivided by class,) until 1849. In a 1710 letter a writer notes that once his bird has lost, if a man cannot immediately pay his wager, he is hoisted in a basket to the ceiling and laughed at.

- See: Cock Lane.
- See: cockpit.

Cockney - A native of the East End of London. To be considered a true Cockney it's said you have to have been born within the sound of the bells of St. Mary, a fact difficult to achieve in modern times as the area is mostly just offices now.

- See: Cockney rhyming slang.
- See: St. Mary-le-Bow, under the CHURCHES section.

Cockney rhyming slang - (Most often called: cant.) This was a manner of speaking in code, primarily by East End thieves, meant to confuse constables and secretly parlay information to one's fellow rough types. Widespread by the 19th century. An ever-evolving "language." Here are but a few of its better known examples (that were used in the Regency era, if not earlier):

- apples and pears = stairs
- bees and honey = money
- cat and mouse = house (Example: "He'll never find the bees and honey. It's stashed under the apples and pears at me old cat and mouse.")
- dog and pup = cup
- fisherman's daughter = water
- needle and thread = bread
- north and south = mouth
- plates of meat = feet
- rats and mice = dice
- tea leaf = thief
- trouble and strife = wife

Over time, paired words such as "apples and pears," used so often the compatriots knew what was meant, might be abbreviated to merely "apples." (Example: "He'll never find the bees. It's stashed under the apples at me old cat.") Of course, each particular gang could develop their own cant phrases, all the better to baffle rivals as well as the law.

cockpit - Cockfighting was banned in 1833, and declared illegal in 1849, but was already falling out of favor as a pastime during the Regency.

- See: Cock Pit (above, spelled as two words.)
- See: St. James's Park.
- See: Royal Cockpit - For when cockfighting was ended in London.
- See: Tufton Street.

Cockpit Steps - Westminster. There at least until 1810. (See: The Two Chairmen, under INNS/PUBS section, the note under.)

Cockspur Street - This street was probably named for the nearby cockpit at Westminster. (See: Tufton Street.) Today, leads west off Trafalgar Square.

- Edward Rymer's business was here; bootmaker to Prinny. Rymer was owed a great deal of money, and complained because Prinny insisted he must have a different shoe pattern for the right and left foot.

Cocoa-Tree Club - Gentleman's club. (See under the CLUBS section.)

coffee - Came to England first circa 1637. Some are surprised to learn that coffee was as popular during the Regency (at least among the upper classes) as was tea. (See: coffee houses.)

coffee houses - (AKA: coffee-houses.) The first coffee house in London opened in 1652, in St. Michael's Alley, Cornhill. The coffee houses were, in the 17-18th centuries, the equivalent of the 19th century's men's clubs (although women were allowed in coffee houses.) A 1722 source notes that despite the coffee house title, other beverages were served: liquors, wine punch, ale, drinking chocolate, tea.

For a penny you could sit at the bar, smoke your pipe, read the newspaper without paying (a huge part of the houses' draw was the news sheets,) and join in the conversation as you pleased. Traders used coffee houses as business addresses. Proprietors handled their correspondence, advertised thefts and rewards, arranged passages on ships bound for the West Indies, Turkey, and the Far East, and conducted auction sales "by Inch of Candle": the last bid before the candle went out secured the lot of sale.

Change Alley held the coffee-houses frequented by stock traders; shipowner's went to Lloyd's; Wills was the haunt of poets and writers; and Man's was where persons of fashion mingled (it became known as the Royal Coffee House.)

By 1663 there were some 80 coffeehouses in London. By 1714 there were 650. In 1770 this number had grown to over 2,000. The coffeehouses (and, their earlier versions, being called chocolate-houses) were a vitally important part of trade in London (and greater

Britain.) However, while still existing, their heyday was definitely passing by the time of the Regency (at least as a center for conducting business.)

- See: Adelphi Hotel.
- See: Britton Street/55.
- See: chocolate-houses.
- See: Cornhill/St. Michael's Alley.
- See: Garraway's Coffee House.
- See: Jonathan's.

Cogers - (AKA: Cogers Debating Society. AKA: Cogers Discussion Hall.) Pronounced with a long "o" sound; the short "o" (as in codger, rhymes with dodger) is considered a gross offense. The name came from the Latin "cogito," meaning "I think." The Society of Cogers was founded in 1755, the oldest debating society in London, at a front room on the ground floor of the White Bear Tavern, 15 Bride Lane. Founded by Daniel Mason, a freeman of the Tallow-chandlers' Company. There was a lamp with the words "Cogers Hall" over the entrance. It had 1,192 members between 1756-68 and met in order to "watch the course of political events." Promoted free speech and other concepts of freedom.

It left Bride Lane in 1856 and went to Shoe Lane. In 1871 it moved to the tavern Barley Mow, Salisbury Square. Briefly moved to the Oriental Hotel in 1887, but went back to the Barley Mow, where it stayed until 1904, and had about a half-dozen other later moves. The old "hall" (in Bride Lane) was remodeled in 1887 and demolished in 1903. (You may care to see: debating societies.)

Colby House - (See: Kensington/Colby House.)

Cold Bath Fields Prison - (Also seen as: Coldbath Fields. And: Cold-Bath Fields.) Clerkenwell, off Farringdon Road. Rebuilt in 1794. Gave "the devil ideas on how to improve his prisons in hell," because it was known for its hard labor and enforced silences (although the sentences tended to be short, due to the fact it was a House of Detention, which means it was a county jail run by local magistrates, who tended to hand out direct punishment, like the stocks, or shorter sentences.) Built to house 1800 inmates, the largest gaol of its time. Named for a local cold water well. Restricted to males only over 17, in 1850. By the mid 19th C. the prison's name was changed to the Middlesex House of Correction. Closed in 1877. In 1886 it was converted into a sorting office for the Post Office. (See: Mount Pleasant/Camden/Cold Bath Fields Prison.)

Colebrooke Row - 1768. Charles Lamb (essayist) lived here after 1825, until his death in 1834. The New River flowed along this row until it was covered over ca. 1850.

Coleman Street - City, the. Takes its name from medieval charcoal burners here In 1642 this street was a bit of a Puritan stronghold. One way street. It is also one of the wards of London. (See: wards/Coleman Street.) Coleman Street's symbol: a rooster.

- 25-29: The Wool Exchange. 1874. (See at W.)
- Armourers' and Brasiers' Hall: The Armourers' existed long before they incorporated, being in Coleman Street since 1346; their first charter being granted in 1453; renewed by Elizabeth I in 1559. Did not burn in the Great Fire of 1666. In 1685 James II ordered any edged tools, armour, and copper, and brass work that was hammered out within the City was to be approved by the Armouries Company; at this time the Brasiers were not a Livery Company, and their work conflicted with the Armourers. The 1709 charter, under Queen Anne, combined the Brasiers with the Armourers; it also gave control of all brass and copper work, and weapons, to the Company (for the City and for "eleven miles round.") Was entirely rebuilt in 1795, this standing until 1840. Rebuilt in 1840-1, on the same site as the 1453 original, to a design by Joseph Henry Good. Interior was largely altered in 1872.

college - Means a body of persons, as opposed to an edifice/building.

- See: colleges/universities.
- See: schools.

College Hall - (See: Deanery Courtyard/College Hall.)

College Hill - Dick Whittington (four times Mayor of London, lived ca. 1354-1423) resided here. It is still a cobbled street.

College of Arms - 1688. Fronts on Queen Victoria Street, on the site of Derby House. (See, below.) Originally known as the College of Heralds, in the 13th C., probably established by Edward I. (See: Herald's College of Arms.)

- Derby House: (Not to be confused with another Derby House, Grosvenor Square.) Built by Thomas Stanley, first Earl of Derby. Was given to the college in 1555 by Mary Tudor. Had been housed in Poultney Lane prior to this, and at Rouncevall Priory near Charing Cross. Burned in the Great Fire of 1666; it was subsequently rebuilt, now forming an open quadrangle, 1688, by M. Emmett and F. Sandford. According to AN ENCYCLOPAEDIA OF LONDON: "The college, whose business it is to deal with all matters of heraldry, consists of three kings of arms - Garter, Clarenceux, and Norroy; six heralds - Somerset, Richmond, Lancaster, Windsor, Chester, and York; and four pursuivants - Rouge Dragon, Blue Mantle, Portcullis, and Rouge Croix. All these officers are appointed by the Duke of Norfolk, in the capacity of Earl Marshal."

College of Physicians - (See: Royal College of Physicians.)

colleges/universities - Note: If you do not see a college listed here or under its given name, also try looking under "Royal College of."

There were many colleges (which might be under the umbrella of a university,) but during the 18th century, Britain boasted only six universities; five of which existed from medieval days:

Aberdeen: 14th C./Scotland

Cambridge: 13th C./England

Edinburgh: 1580s/Scotland

Glasgow: 14th C./Scotland

Oxford: 12th C./England

St. Andrews: 14th C./Scotland

ON THE EDUCATION OF WOMEN: See the notes under: education.

- See: Birkbeck.
- See: charity schools.
- See: college - For a definition of.
- See: Dulwich.
- See: education.
- See: Gresham's.
- See: King's College.
- See: Medical College.
- See: Oxford.
- See: Royal Military College.
- See: Royal Naval College.
- See: schools.
- See: Trinity College.
- See: University College.
- See: University of London - AKA: London University.
- See: Winchester College.

colliers - An occupation (not a street.) Burners of wood (i.e. charcoal-makers,) *not* miners.

- See: Croydon.
- See: Thornton Heath.

cologne, men's -

- See: Jermyn Street/89.
- See: Bond Street/Old Bond Street/Atkinson.

Colosseum - (See: Regent's Park/The Park/Colosseum.)

combe - Old English word for a valley or hollow. Seen in place names.

combs - For hair.

- See: brushes.
- See: Middle Row.

Commercial Road - Whitechapel, near. Built 1800. In 1803, it connected the West India Dock to the City. Went across what had been Stepney Fields. Later in the 19th C. was said to have the heaviest traffic in London.

- 135-153: Built in 1864.

Commercial Street - Tower Hamlets. It lived up to its name, with commercial and shop spaces here. The area is ancient, but much of it now dates from the mid 19th century. An 1838 report described it as hosting the "extremely poor and immoral." The southern part was built in 1843-5, in an effort to clear out slums.

- Christ Church, Spitalfields: (See under the CHURCHES section.)
- Spitalfields Market: (See under S.)

Commission of Sewers - Established in 1669. Housed in the Guildhall. Today's London sewer systems began in the late 19th century. (See: sewers.)

common - Often also called "the heath." From medieval times, a term for a stretch of verdant land held "in common" for district members. (All commons throughout London are now public land.) The lord of the manor was the only one (usually) who could exploit this common land for farming, clay, gravel extraction, etc., whereas the common (public) uses were for things such as grazing cattle, digging peat, drying washing, and gathering firewood.

Enclosures took away the common land, thereby "robbing" the smallest landowners or the poor of land for their own bit of crops, orchards, grazing land, etc. To further define, CHAMBERS LONDON GAZETTEER states: "The process by which common land was closed off to public use and ownership passed to individual landowners... Enclosure was the single most influential factor in the development of outer London before the coming of the railways." Whereas 9-12 men had survived on an area, instead now only 3-4 of the wealthiest kept rights to the same land, thereby forcing those squeezed out to become day laborers or to work in factories. (Although, some say enclosure improved the fields and their yield.)

The common also often served as a rallying point for discontented crowds.

Many, many cities, towns, and villages had a common. Until well into the 19th C. much of London was for "common" use.

(You may care to see: Verderers - For those who dealt with forested common land.)

Common Council - (See: Court of Common Council.)

Common Hall - What the assembly was called when the liverymen of the Guilds met (on

Michaelmas day) every year, at Guildhall, to elect the new Lord Mayor; a practice still in place. (See: Livery Companies.)

Commons, The House of - The Government (majority) sits on the left, the Opposition (minority) on the right, with the Speaker presiding between them.

- See: Lower House.
- See: Westminster.
- See: Westminster/Chapter House.
- See: Westminster Palace.

Commonwealth, the - (See: constitutional monarchy.)

Commonwealth Office - Had been at Marlborough House. (See: Foreign Office.)

Companies, of the City of London - As in the ancient Guilds. Many are listed at their individual entries, such as the Barbers, Lightermen, Mercers, etc.

- See: Canada - Which has an explanation of the modern Commonwealth.
- SEE: HALLS.
- See: Livery Companies.

Company of Surgeons - Separated from the Barbers in 1745. (See: doctors/ surgeon.)

compters - Medieval prisons, directly under the control/supervision of the sheriffs. Essentially a hole or a pit in the ground. For instance, during medieval times a lower level of the Tower of London was a compter. AN ENCYCLOPAEDIA OF LONDON states: "The Liber Albus gives various orders of Henry VI's reign for proper conduct, and it appears that the compters were sometimes designated by the names of the respective sheriffs who presided over them. Probably they were sometimes in the sheriff's own house." These compters (as in Poultry Compter - the entrance to it was through a row of shops and houses - or Wood Street Compter, erected in 1555) existed at least as late as 1817, some to 1855. Usually were not purpose-built, but rather adapted from local buildings. Generally for lesser crimes such as public fighting. (See: Tun, the.)

Compton Street - Soho. Parts known as Old Compton Street until 1896.

condoms - (Also called: armour, cundums, French letters, preservatives, and many other nicknames.) Made of animal intestines, they were not at all widely used, and then primarily in hopes of avoiding venereal disease rather than to avoid impregnation. They were usually rinsed and reused. Breakage was fairly common. They tied on with a ribbon. First seen in Britain in 1640. (You may care to see: birth control.)

Conduit Street - Named after a 1500s wooden conduit that used to carry water from Oxford Street to the City. Charles James Fox was born here, 1749, while Holland House was undergoing repair. Branches off Regent Street, leads to Bond Street.

- 52: (Off Bond Street.) Thomas Edwards, tailor. When Mrs. Byron (the poet's mother) died, Lord Byron provided black clothing for his servants via this shop - not paying the bill for several years.
- Limmer Hotel: Young single men resided here; there by at least 1811.
    - ➢ See: flat, a - For an explanation of Regency era bachelor homes.
    - ➢ See: hotel - For an explanation of how Regency era hotels differed from today.
- Meyer: A tailor named Meyer worked on this street. Tailor to Beau Brummell and Prinny. Meyer was sometimes summoned to Carlton House to attend the Prince, at which time Meyer dressed as a page. Meyer's shop was bombed in 1942 and is now the site of the Westbury Hotel.

confectioner - Maker of sweets, ices, baked goods, etc.

- ➢ See: Bloomsbury/Store Street.
- ➢ See: Gunter's.
- ➢ See: Kensington/Herbert & Jones.

Connaught Place - Street of surviving Regency homes, with balconies and canopies, built during the Napoleonic wars. Built over the site of Tyburn Gate. (See under T.)

Connaught Square - Bayswater, Paddington. 1820s. Described as elegant; also as late Georgian, unremarkable brick, plain. The earliest square in the Bayswater area. Named for the Earl of Connaught (whose greater title was Duke of Gloucester,) who had a home near here. The square in now known as the Hyde Park Estate.

Connaught Terrace - (See under: Paddington.)

constable - A policeman (although the word policeman was much more Victorian than Regency, growing out of the formation of the Metropolitan Police in 1829.) Constables were officers of the parish. Constables, who were unpaid, did not have a huge connection to "the law," per se, being more about rousting troublemakers locally than seeing that persons were prosecuted; this changed when paid constables came along in 1829 with the founding of the Metropolitan Police.

- ➢ See: Charlies.
- ➢ See: justices of the peace - The final note at.
- ➢ See: law.
- ➢ See: Metropolitan Police - 1829.
- ➢ See: PC, under P.
- ➢ See: police.
- ➢ See: Watch.

constitution - While it is often stated that Britain has no written constitution, it is more correct to say it has no codified constitution. That is, no single core document. Most of the "English constitution" is composed of: written documents; is found within statutes, court judgements, and treaties. It is also influenced by things such as constitutional conventions and royal prerogatives.

Britain has a constitutional monarchy, which means the Queen (or King) does not create or pass legislation. (You may care to see: constitutional monarchy.)

Constitution Arch - (See: Hyde Park Corner/Wellington Arch.)

Constitution Hill - Early in its existence it was also known as "Constitutional" Hill. At its very beginning it was referred to on maps as "the King's coachway to Kensington." Charles II took his "constitutional walk" up this hill every day.

constitutional monarchy - Britain has a constitutional monarchy, which means the Queen (or King) does not create or pass legislation. That is the task of the Houses of Parliament.

- See: constitution.
- See: Great Britain.
- See: Houses of Parliament.
- You may care to see: Canada - Which has an explanation of the modern Commonwealth.

Constitutional Society - (See: Bill of Rights Society.)

consumption - Term used for what we know as Tuberculosis. Too, though, it was an over-used word for vague maladies otherwise unnamed. (See: Brompton Hospital.)

Cook, Captain James - 18th century cartographer/explorer/navigator/Royal Navy captain/voyager, b.1728-d.1779 (was killed by Hawaiians.)

- See: Antarctica.
- See: Australia.
- See: Hawaii.
- See: Mile End Road/88 - Lived here for a while.
- See: New Zealand.
- See: Piccadilly/Egyptian Hall.
- See: St. Margaret's Barking, under the CHURCHES section. - Where Capt. Cook was married.
- See: Soho Square/32 - For Joseph Banks' home, a fellow explorer.

cook house -

- See: Bread Street.
- See: chophouse.
- See: cookshops.

cookbooks - Note: It was extremely common during the Regency that recipes were called "receipts."

Cookbooks (or cookery books) became increasingly desired/used as the 18th C. passed. A popular one from 1747 was called: *The Art of Cookery Made Plain and Easy*, by Hannah Glasse, designed for a home manned by servants. One John Farley published *The London Art of Cookery* in 1783. In 1788, Richard Brigg published *The English Art of Cookery*, and *The Universal Cook* in 1792. (There were others.)

- See: Fitzroy Square/Warren Street/43.
- See: food - Opening notes at.

Cooks' Company - (AKA: the Worshipful Company of Cooks.) Can be traced back to 1170, and noted as a Company as early as 1311, and may have been combined early on with the pastelers and the pie-bakers, although each had its own mistery. At any rate, the Cooks' absorbed them all by the 16th century. Charter in 1482. Unlike many of its males-only contemporaries, the Cooks had freemaidens (women cooks) as early as 1495. Never had a hall. The smallest of all the Livery Companies.

cookshops - This is a bit of an older term (see the note at the end of this listing.) Cookshops date back to at least Roman times. They might sell prepared food (rather like a restaurant - See under R - although usually the food was taken away, not eaten there,) and they might prepare your foodstuffs for you. This was common in big cities (such as London) where many residences provided no kitchen or oven. In essence, any place that hosted cooking facilities might rent out their oven and/or staff's time in order to cook a paying customer's food (in other words, you'd bring the cut of meat and they'd sear it for you, or bake your oat cakes, etc.) This would have been more common among the lower classes and in crowded areas. Any spit, oven, or fireplace with cooking tripod could constitute a cookshop. If a pub or inn served food (they usually did) it could also serve as the local cookshop. (See: chop house, a more common term for this kind of service by the time of the Regency.)

cookware - (See: Wandsworth.)

Coopers' Hall - For the Worshipful Company of Coopers. Basinghall Street, Cheapside. Makers of wooden casks (or tubs) for beer, spirits, and wine. The Coopers were first mention in the Mayor's Court records in 1298; at any rate the Guild existed in 1422. AN ENCYCLOPAEDIA OF LONDON notes: "A long Latin charter was granted the Company by Henry VII in 1501. Its second and governing charter was granted by Charles II in 1661; it had a regrant in 1685."

The first hall, 1522, was at the Swan Tavern, but in 1547 built a Hall in Basinghall Street, of wood; it burned in the Great Fire of 1666. Replaced and enlarged in 1669-78.

Lotteries were drawn here in Georgian times, until 1826.

A third version was rebuilt in 1865-8, with part of the site being given over to the City of London for the Guildhall extension.

Totally destroyed by WWII bombs in 1940. The Guild shared quarters with other Companies until they built the current headquarters in Devonshire Square.

Livery company. 36th in order of precedence.

Copenhagen Fields - Islington. Replaced in 1855 by the Metropolitan Cattle Market (AKA: the Smithfield Market.) Although not a term used often now, during the Regency the area between Barnsbury and Thornhill (northeast of King's Cross) was called Copenhagen. In the 18th century Copenhagen Fields was a popular site for radical demonstrations. For instance, in 1795 there were two protests here with crowds of over 100,000. Is now called Caledonian Road, since 1861.

- ➢ Islington/Copenhagen Fields.
- ➢ See: Smithfield Market.

- Copenhagen House: (See: Islington/Copenhagen House.)
- Newgate Market: 1855. (See under N.)
- Royal Caledonian Asylum: Founded in 1815. Moved to Copenhagen Fields in 1827. (See under R.)

Copenhagen House - (See: Islington/Copenhagen House.)

copper -

- ➢ See: money/penny.
- ➢ See: police.

Coppermills - Waltham Forest. A "watery area," with a mill here for many centuries. The Coppermills building was built ca. 1800, minting copper coins during the Napoleonic wars. In 1860 became a pumping station.

Coppice Row - Holborn.

Copthall Avenue - 1890.

Copthall Court - Near the Bank of England.

Coptic Street - Renamed from Duke Street in 1894 (because there were so many streets called Duke.)

Coram Street - Bloomsbury. William Makepeace Thackeray lived at number 13, (at any rate, at the time of Dickens.)

Coram's Fields - On the site of what had been the Foundling Hospital.

- ➢ Foundling Hospital.
- ➢ See: Lamb's Conduit Fields.

Coram's Hospital - (See: Foundling Hospital.)

Cording's - 1839. 19 Piccadilly. Woolens and waterproof items.

Cordwainer Street - Cheapside. Professional shoemakers who make shoes from new leather (derived from "cordovan," as in fine leather.) Name changed to Bow Lane in the mid 16th century.

Cordwainers' Hall - For the Worshipful Company of Cordwainers. 7 Cannon Street. "Cordwainer" derives from "cordwane," a leather from Cordova, Spain, and was often used for shoes. The Company dates back to at least the 14th century.

- See: Candlewick Street/Cordwainers' Hall.
- See: cobblers.

Cork Street - Mayfair. At least by mid 18th century.

- 1: During most of Brummell's reign, Sir Robert Macbreth, whose talents ran to bookmaker, usurer, Billiard marker, waiter, owner of White's, and on to Parliament, lived here. He had convictions for assaulting a lord and taking advantage of a minor, but still contrived to be knighted.
- 9: 1790, tailor by the name of John Levick did business here. Is this the same tailor (Schweitzer and Davidson) to Prinny and Brummell? Schweitzer and Davidson certainly also had a shop on this street.

corn - A term that, to the British, doesn't mean corn as in maize; it is used to mean "grains," therefore the speaker may be referring to barley, rye, wheat, etc. (Oats are the exception, usually singled out simply as "oats.") Of course, if you asked someone what was planted in his field, he'd name the particular grain; but when he took it (plus any other of his grains) to market, he'd collectively call them "corn."

Corn Exchange - Mark Lane. Near Cornhill, where since the Middle Ages grain was marketed. AN ENCYCLOPAEDIA OF LONDON says: "To prevent cornering of wheat, in 1438 Stephen Broun (Lord Mayor) established a public granary, and a few years later Simon Eyre set up another in Leadenhall. The City Livery Companies were required to supply certain quantities of corn* to these granaries. At length they turned stubborn, and refusing to buy corn, provoked much friction with the City Corporation. This was terminated by the Great Fire (of 1666) which burnt the Bridghouse (immediately to the east of St. Olave's Church, Tooley Street,) this having been the main store, and the granary of the Companies."

(*See: corn - The note explaining the term.)

The Corn Exchange was London's only corn, grain, and seed market for 240 years, starting in 1747.

A meeting was called in 1747, and it was agreed to build a market in Mark Lane; by J. W. Wood. Founded by corn factors who wanted a bigger space than they'd had in Thames Street. Built in the 1747. Described as very handsome. Was shaped as a quadrangle; three sides had piazzas with pillars, containing 64 stalls. Partially rebuilt in 1828, and enlarged 1852. In A PORTRAIT OF GEORGIAN LONDON, Fiona St. Aubyn writes: "A new Exchange was added to the north of the Mark Lane exchange in 1827. In spite of this expansion as well as several alterations and enlargements, the old Exchange was rebuilt by Edward I. Anson in 1881. In 1929 both Exchanges were amalgamated..."

Damaged in WWII; closed and pulled down in 1987 when the Corn Exchange moved into the Baltic Exchange.

Site now hosts the London Commodity Exchange.

Mark Lane was originally known as Mart Lane; not sure when the switch came in, but certainly by the time of the Regency, and possibly as far back as in Medieval times.

(See: Exchange.)

Cornhill - The City. Site of a medieval grain market. An area of dark brick Georgian houses, none of which went higher than five stories. During the Regency, publishers existed here. (See: Old Jamaica Inn.)

- 32: Smith and Elder, publishers who published the likes of the Brönte sisters and Thackery. Here from 1816-68.
- Castle Court: Not sure this was a Regency era street name.
    - George and the Vulture, the: (See under the INNS/PUBS section.)
- Lime Street:
    - East India House: 1600-1862. (See under E.)
- ROYAL EXCHANGE: (See under R.)
- St. Michael's Alley: Hosted London's first coffee house (see: coffee houses, at its own listing) in London, in 1652.
- St. Michael's, Cornhill: (See under the CHURCHES section.)
- St. Peter's-Upon-Cornhill: Wren, 1677-81. (See under the CHURCHES section.)
- The Swan and Hoop Inn: Mozart played here as a boy in 1764-65, having had to move from Chelsea as the "wonder" of his talent became less remarkable to a fickle London. (See under the INNS/PUBS section.)

Cornmarket - Oxford. There was a pub there (at least by 1811) called the Blue Boar.

Cornwall Terrace - Regent's Park. 1821. (See: Park Crescent/Cornwall Terrace.)

Coroner - Called in for suspicious deaths. He would conduct the post-mortem if he was a physician, otherwise another medical man would be brought in. (See: doctors/physician.)

Corporation, the - (See: Wards Without.)

Corporation for the Propagation of the Gospel in New England - Created in 1649 by Act of Parliament, this was the first English foreign missionary society. John Eliot was working with Native Peoples in the New World, and this Act came about to support his work.

As stated in PILGRIMS' LONDON: "The first" (mission) "in the modern sense was the Baptist Missionary Society (1792)... The first in London was the London Missionary

Society (1795,) which sent Robert Morrison to China, John Williams to the South Pacific, Robert and Mary Moffat and their celebrated son-in-law David Livingstone to Africa, and James Chalmers to New Guinea."

Corporation of Coachmen - Charter in 1639. Licensed by Parliament. The Coachmen's "cabs" got their name from the French "cabriolet de place." Cabs were barred from royal parks until ca. the 1920s, due to objections to the occasional drunken driver and/or lewd patrons. (See: hackney coach.)

costermonger - Someone who sold fruit, vegetables, cockles, etc. from a barrow on the street. They were known to call out the nature of their wares.

Cotman's Town - (See: Hayes Town.)

Coulsdon - Had a fairly busy coaching road in the 1820s. (See: Old Coulsdon.)

counselors - (See: lawyer/counselor.)

Counties, British - (See: the separate BRITISH COUNTIES section.)

counting house - A private deposit bank; there were plenty yet during the Regency. (See: clearing house.)

County Fire Office - Regent's Circus South (which was renamed Piccadilly Circus in 1880.) 1819-20, by Robert Abraham, it was meant to resemble the facade of the old Somerset House. (Also see: Regent Street/Lower Regent Street/County Fire Office.) NAIRN'S LONDON says the CFO dates from 1924, by W. G. Newton; a rebuild.

County Hall - South Bank, across the Thames from Westminster (just north of Westminster Bridge, at the junction of Belvedere Road, Lambeth, and Westminster Bridge.) Five stories. Begun in 1912; opened in 1922 as the home of The London County Council (later known as the Greater London Council-SEE UNDER G,) headquartered here from 1913 to 1965; then it became the Greater London Council, until it was abolished in 1986. Has 2,930 rooms, with ten miles/16 km of corridors; crescent-shaped sweep of a building.

In the 18th C. this site was a stoneworks, whose terracotta was improved upon by Mrs. Eleanor Coade, thus inventing the hearty, weather-resistant Coade stone so often seen on door entries and window trim. There is a stone lion, from 1837, before the building. The stoneworks closed in 1840.

In 1889 the Council took over the offices of the Metropolitan Board of Works, in Spring Gardens. Obtained the site of the present (South Bank) location in 1906, built in 1913. Has a massive riverfront facade, in the Renaissance mode.

Converted since its abolishment into hotel accommodations, an art gallery, and the London Aquarium.

- London Aquarium: Here since 1995.
    - ➢ See: London County Council.

➢ See: Metropolitan Board of Works.

Courage's - A brewery, Southwark (see under S.)

courgette - What Americans call: zucchini. Rare during the Regency. (See: food/courgette.)

coursing - Greyhounds chasing hares. Dates back to generally the mid 19th C., but its premier event, the Waterloo Cup (in Altcar, Lancashire) dates from 1838 (at an oval.)

Hares had long since been "coursed" (chased, either on foot or horseback. Greyhounds chased (sight hounds,) rather than the scent hounds used in foxhunting. Hare coursing took the place of deer hunting (there weren't enough deer left to hunt); foxhunting took the place of hare coursing, although the latter lived on via the greyhounds racing at courses.

➢ See: greyhound racing.

➢ See: National Coursing Club.

court of - (If you don't see the Court you're looking for, try looking under the plural: Courts of.)

Court of Aldermen - (AKA: the barons of London. AKA simply as: Aldermen.) The position dates from at least the 14th century. Along with the Lord Mayor, the Aldermen have helped run the City for centuries. (Note that I mean "the City," not larger London. See: City, the - Under C.) They meet 12-15 times a year in their own courtroom (or sometimes at the Mansion House.) The Aldermen must first have been Freemen of the City (and even though then elected as an alderman, can be rejected by the others.) They are also Justices of the Peace, and so deal out judgment at either the Mansion House or the Guildhall. These are the ones of whom the monarch must ceremoniously ask permission to enter the City. Their existence dates from the Middle Ages.

By the 15th C., and with the rise of the Guilds, those leading the Guilds had replaced the Aldermen as the most powerful and wealthy men in London.

The wards number at 24; therefore, there are 24 Aldermen. They hold office for life.

One of the Aldermen's duties include: determining the rank of precedence among the City's Livery Companies. The list does not change often, but rank can change when the list is revised due to new companies rising or others fading, and seniority is based on the date of when a Company was granted its letters patent (by the Court of Aldermen.)

(See: Court of Common Council - Of which the Court of Aldermen is a part.)

Court of Common Council - Made up of the Mayor; 24 Aldermen (Court of Aldermen,) who hold office for life; and 134 to 206 Common Councilmen (commoners,) who are elected by ratepayers annually.

The first list of members dates from ca. 1285 as "...the good men of all the wards sworn to consult with the aldermen on the affairs of the City of London." These were leading citizens elected by the City's wards. The court of Common Council has from time to time fixed the number of annually elected representatives, has settled the qualifications required for electors and elected, and has made changes to the machinery of the City's municipal government. It replaced the medieval practice known as a folkmoot. (See under F.) Can be referred to collectively as the commonalty.

- See: Common Council.
- See: Courts of Common Law and Equity/Court of Common Pleas - Note that "courts" is plural.
- See: Guildhall.
- See: wards.

Court of Common Pleas - (See: Courts of Common Law and Equity/Court of Common Pleas. Note that "Courts" is plural.)

Court of Requests - (See: Courts of Common Law and Equity/Courts of Requests.)

Courtauld Institute - (AKA: Courtauld Institute Gallery.) Somerset House, housed where the Royal Academy of Arts used to be (in the Fine Rooms); moved here in 1990 (having moved from Portman Square.) This Institute was created in the early 20th C., and ca. 1940-90 was housed in Woburn Place in "cramped premises."

- See: Portman Square/20.
- See: Somerset House.

Courtenay Square - Kennington. Looks Georgian, but was built shortly before WWII for the Duchy of Cornwall, 1913.

courts of - (If you don't see the "Courts" you're looking for, try looking under the singular: Court of.)

Courts of Chancery -

- See: Courts of Common Law and Equity/Court of Chancery.
- See: Inns of Chancery, under I - For where lawyers were schooled.

Courts of Common Law and Equity - (AKA: Courts of Law. AKA: Law Courts, the.) Westminster Hall. These courts were first housed (for some 600 years) in Westminster Hall, separated only by flimsy partitions. By the 18th C. they had separate rooms (with real walls) each. (See: Westminster Hall/Common Law Courts.)

The current court structure dates from and was created by the Judicature Acts of 1873-5; in 1882 moved to the Strand. (See: Law Courts, the.)

Matrimonial and probate matters were under the auspices of the Church courts until 1857.

The High Court now has three divisions:

Chancery Division: Estates, mortgages, trusts.

Family Division: Adoption, guardianship & wardships, matrimonial matters.

Queen's Bench Division: Most other litigation.

(See: Doctor's Common - For Special Licenses, for marrying.)

- Court of Chancery: Lincoln's Inn Fields. A PORTRAIT OF GEORGIAN LONDON states: "From 1773 onwards the Court of Chancery also sat at the fine Old Hall in Lincoln's Inn." It goes on to say: "In term-time, the business of this court is transacted in the Court of Chancery at Westminster Hall." In EYEWITNESS TRAVEL GUIDES-LONDON it says: "The Court of Chancery sat...in Old Hall, from 1835 until 1858." Chancery comes from "Chancellaria", to judge or preside. From the 14th C. to the end of the 19th C. it was the principal court of equity, the idea being that ethics and fair play overruled legal precedents and procedure (this being called equity law.) Moved in 1882 to the Law Courts, the Strand, following the 1873 Act of Judicature that revamped British Law. (See: Inns of Chancery, under I.)
- Court of Common Pleas: The room was centered in about the middle of Westminster Hall. Civil cases between Subject and Subject.
    - See: Bakewell Hall.
    - See: Court of Common Council.
- Court of Exchequer: The room was in the northwest corner of Westminster Hall. Its architecture was described as "mean" and "with little to recommend it." Named for the chequered cloth that once covered the tables for the judges or chief officers. Founded by William the Conqueror, to try all cases relating to the Crown's revenues.
- Court of King's Bench: The room was in the southeast corner of Westminster Hall. The supreme common law court in England. Takes its name from the fact the monarch was once literally present (as, indeed, he or she is in all his/her courts, by "contemplation of law.") Rules over other courts (is a court of appeal,) keeps the lower courts within their bounds. Controls magistrates. Both criminal and civil cases were tried here.

    Wigs for court wear were introduced in the 17th century.

    This court was attached to Westminster Hall, of course, but along with the Court of Common Pleas, and the Court of Exchequer, also met at times in the Guildhall (see,) from the middle ages all the way up to Victoria's time.

    (See: Royal Courts of Justice-for contrast, royal laws as opposed to the laws of the City/public.)
- Courts of Requests: Westminster. Had been in Westminster Hall. As stated in PARLIAMENT HOUSE: "Also known as the White Hall and the Little Hall it

was one of the old halls of the Norman Palace. Later, the Masters of Requests sat in it to hear petitions. In 1801 the House of Lords moved into it" (there at least until 1808.) "In 1835 it was converted into a temporary House of Commons" following the 1835 destruction by fire of the Houses of Parliament."

- King's Bench: (See: Court of King's Bench, above.)

Courts of Law - (AKA: The Law Courts. AKA: Courts of Common Law and Equity.)

> ➢ See: Courts of Common Law and Equity.
> ➢ See: Westminster Hall.

Courts of Requests - (See: Courts of Common Law and Equity/Courts of Requests.)

Coutts Bank - 440 Strand. Originally were goldsmiths. Bankers to the Royals. The bank itself was established in 1692. The Coutts name came in in 1755, when the founder's granddaughter married James Coutts, who became the sole management in 1775. Has been on the Strand since 1692; present build dates from 1825, Nash, with 1970s renovations. (See: Lloyd's of London, paragraph about Coutts.)

Covent Garden - (Here I am writing of both the street and the market.) Westminster/Camden. Originally was "Convent Gardens," as the convent (the Benedictine convent of St. Peter of Westminster) there provided food for Westminster Abbey from the 13th century.

Has no formally listed boundaries. Some sources refer to the Strand as being another way to call the Covent Garden area.

After the Dissolution of 1540, the Earl of Bedford was given the land, seven acres of garden. The Earl, Francis Russell, drained the East Anglian fens, and laid out the square ca. 1630. He employed Inigo Jones. Circa 1631-37, Inigo Jones laid out London's first residential square here, his famous piazza, of which only St. Paul's/Covent Garden remains. (None of the houses laid out by Inigo Jones in the Stuart era exist today.)

An unofficial market sprang up in 1649, the first inklings of the market to come.

The first Punch and Judy show (would have been Punch and Joan, as she was then known) in England was performed in the Piazza in 1662, by Pietro Gimonde, an Italian puppeteer.

The 5th Earl of Bedford got a flowers/fruit/herbs/vegetables market license in 1670, and in 1678 traders were allowed to put up a row of shops against the convent's garden wall.

In 1705-07 Bedford House was pulled down, and Southampton Street & Tavistock Street were built over the space, so that Covent Garden Market moved closer to the center of the piazza, being then 48 timber booths.

It was rebuilt in 1748, resulting in 160 more shops in two rows, with cellars.

The district known as Covent Garden was firmly centered there by 1750. It became a haunt for prostitutes at night, being known then by the nickname "the great square of Venus" because of the gambling dens, Turkish baths, and houses of prostitution that had settled there. Despite the "darker" side of the area, its reputation did not keep respectable people from living here.

Covent Gardens' northwest corner is the infamous St. Giles slum district. (See: St. Giles.)

A subsequent Earl of Bedford had market buildings added in 1828-30, to relieve the extreme overcrowding (making this the oldest surviving 19th C. market building hall.) Built in the Greek Revival style (its glass roof was added during Victoria's time, but the roof aside, the buildings existed virtually unaltered until 1974.) The covered central market (still there) was designed by Charles Fowler, 1831-3. A second source said the north range was completed in 1829.

The outer courts' cast-iron roofs date from 1875 and 1888. The Floral Hall dates from 1860. The Flower Market (building) dates from 1870-71. The Jubilee Market (building) dates from 1904.

Due to woefully inadequate space, in 1974 the wholesale vegie, fruit & flower market stalls were moved from this space to south of the Thames: Nine Elms. (See under N.) This is about three miles/4.8 km southwest of the old location, and is called: New Covent Garden Market. Note, though, that the Covent Garden buildings and craft and antique stalls remain at the original location; this original site has been declared a "historically interesting" area, ensuring preservation, and is now a specialty shopping center.

- Bedford House: Since 1630. Pulled down in 1704. Stood where Southampton and Tavistock Streets now roughly run. About this time, this area lost its luster as a residential area, because of the now established market. There was a shop here in the author Jane Austen's time, a draper's where she shopped, called Layton & Shear of Bedford House, on Henrietta Street. She would have called this business a warehouse.
- Brydges Street: (See: Catherine Street, below.)
- Catherine Street: First known as Brydges Street. Built in the 1630s. The name change took place in the mid to late 19th century, and nothing much of its original appearance remains.
- Drury Lane (the street, not the theatre):
    - 191: White Hart. Pub. (See: White Hart/Covent Garden, under the INNS/PUBS section.)
    - Drury Lane Theatre: (See under the THEATRES section.)
- Floral Hall: 1860. (See note, in the general section, above.)

- Garrick Street: (See: King Street, below.)
- Henrietta Street: (See under H.)
    - 10: When visiting London in 1813 and 1814, Jane Austen stayed here with her brother, Henry.
- James Street: (See under J.)
- Jubilee Market: Jubilee Hall. Street Market. Built in 1904. Redeveloped in 1987.
- King Street: The Piazza. Built 1633-37. There are yet some 18th C. facades, but most of the historical buildings that yet exist date from the late 19th century. Since 1864 called Garrick Street.
    - 43: Existed by at least 1690. Torn down and rebuilt in 1716-17, possibly by Archer (or someone good at imitating his style.) North side of Covent Garden. The top story is a 19th C. addition.
- Maiden Lane: (See under M.)
- Market, the: Term can refer to the whole area, or more pointedly to the 1830 building built to house the flourishing vegetable market centered in the Covent Garden area. It is divided by five parallel streets: Central Avenue, North Avenue, North Row, South Avenue, and South Row. Covent Garden Market moved in 1973 to Nine Elms, Vauxhall. (See note, above, in the general section.)
- Monmouth Street: Seven Dials area. (See under M.)
- Piazza, the: (See note, above, in the general section.)
- Royal Opera House: (See under the THEATRES section.)
- Russell Street: (See under R.)
- St. Martin's Lane: One of Covent Garden's borders. (See under S.)
- St. Paul's: (Not to be confused with St. Paul's Cathedral, Ludgate Hill, the City.) Built by Inigo Jones, completed 1633. Is on Covent Garden's west side; has a false front (called the Tuscan portico,) that actually faces away from the piazza. The entrance is through a courtyard. The interior burned in 1795, but was rebuilt in the Inigo Jones's style by Philip Hardwick; the stone portico and east doorcase survived the fire, and are original. Known as "the Actor's Church" due to its proximity to several theatres. (See: St. Paul/Covent Garden, under the CHURCHES section.)
- St. Paul's Churchyard: Inigo Jones's walls were stuccoed brick; Hardwick's subsequent stone walls (ca. 1795) were replaced by Victorian brick. (See under S.)
- Seven Dials: Infamous rookery/slum. (See under S.)
- Tavistock Street: Ca. 1707. Had the most elegant establishments in Covent

Garden. (See under T.)

Covent Garden, Theatre Royal - (Now known as the Royal Opera House.) Courtesans occupied front-line boxes at the rich sum of £200 per season, to display their charms. (See: Covent Garden, Theatre Royal, under the THEATRES section.)

Coventry House - (See: Piccadilly/106.)

Coventry Street - Off Haymarket.

- David Wishart: Had a snuff shop here, ca. 1720. The premises were pulled down in 1880, when the then tobacco shop moved to Panton Street.

Cowcross Street - Clerkenwell. Here by the 13th century. A poor area by the 16th century. By the 19th century it was known for its knackers/slaughterhouses. After Farringdon Road was completed, this street was called Cowcross Street (through the Regency period.) Later was: Peter's Lane.

- The Rookery Hotel, the: 12 Peter's Lane. Currently a "hidden gem" of a chic hotel, 33 bedrooms, made up of four Georgian era houses. The terraced building dates from 1764. Became the Rookery Hotel ca. 1989.

Cowley Street - Smith Square, Westminster. Georgian houses there still.

Cowper's Court - Off Cornhill. Dates from the time of James I (b.1566-d.1625.)

Cox's Museum - At Spring Garden. 18th C. museum of mechanical arts (with precious and/or semi-precious stones, such as a peacock with a tail that fanned.) Sold in 1772. Used by the Society of Painters in Watercolours (three months out of each year) from 1809-20. Building demolished in 1825.

- ➢ See: Society of Painters in Watercolours.
- ➢ See: Spring Garden.

Craig's Court - Street built at the end of the 17th century.

- Harrington House. (See under H.)

Cranbourn Street - (AKA: Cranbourne Alley, despite the different spellings of "Cranbourn/e.") Built in the 1670s, completed ca. 1681-82, to connect Castle Street and Leicester Square. There were a great many lovely ladies' caps in the milliners' shop windows along this street by at least 1814, as Jane Austen wrote to her sister. She may have been surprised to find nice products here, as these shops were generally considered to be cheap, due to being too close to the infamous and dangerous Seven Dials area. Widened in 1843.

Cranleigh Street - Camden. (See: Somers Town/29 Johnson Street.)

Craven Hill - (See under: Paddington/Craven Hill.)

Craven House - (See: East India House.)

Craven Street - Charing Cross/the Strand.

- 7: (Now 36.) Benjamin Franklin (American statesman) lived here, 1757-62, and again in 1764-72, in the house of a Mrs. Margaret Stephenson. Brick facade, three stories plus a basement.
- 30: Ca. 1807 Aaron Burr (American politician) moved here (in disgrace, after the duel in which he killed American founding father Alexander Hamilton in 1804.) Soon, for lack of funds, Burr moved to Clerkenwell Close, where he lived until ca. 1811 (when he returned to America.)

cremation - Pretty much didn't exist during the Regency; everyone was buried. (See: burials.)

Cremorne - Chelsea. Pleasure garden/summer resort. Was originally known as Chelsea Farm. Came to the Dowager Countess of Exeter in 1751. In 1803, it came to Viscount Cremorne, at which time it took on the name of Cremorne House. 16 acres. Came into popularity just as Vauxhall's was waning. From 1845 to 1877 it was Cremorne Gardens; in THE FACE OF LONDON by Harold P. Clunn, it reads: "It was much gayer than Vauxhall even on its most brilliant nights, and splendid displays of fireworks were given here. Amongst other attractions were a theatre, a circus, an outdoor orchestra, grottoes, and dining-hall." It was "the last pleasure garden in London," still enjoyed into Queen Victoria's time. As at Vauxhall, there were balloon ascents here (in the summer of 1845.) Sometime before it closed it became a sporting club. Closed 1877.

Crescent Grove - Clapham, Southwark, 1824.

Crewe House - (See: Curzon Street/Crewe House.)

Cribb's Parlour - A boxing saloon. Named for a former boxer named Thomas Cribb (b.1781-d.1848.) He bare-knuckle boxed in 1805-12.

cricket - A version of the game has existed since the 16th century. Early on, townsmen of Boxgrove, England were prosecuted for playing the game on a Sunday.

Historically, played by men only. Cricket matches were an acceptable viewing matter for ladies; contemporary images show ladies viewing the games, plus the Austen women write of matches they had enjoyed seeing. Overarm bowling was introduced in 1864; before then bowling was underhand. Of the county clubs, Sussex (Cricket Club) was founded in 1839; Surrey in 1845.

Georgian era wickets had only two stumps, until 1775. The Coulson Cricket Club was the first to play using three stumps, on their opponents' green in Chertsey.

Cricket has laws (rather than rules.) The laws were formalized in 1744.

The first play vs. Australia took place in 1861 (in that country.)

The first cricket Test Match, 1880, England vs. Australia, was played in London, Surrey Cricket ground, the Oval.

The season runs from April to September.

Cricket might also be played informally, such as at house parties. Women and children could attend, but still the game itself would have only been played by men.

- See: Islington/White Conduit Fields - Where English cricket was first played, up to 1787.
- See: Lamb's Conduit Fields - Cricket played here until ca. 1739.
- See: Lord's Cricket Ground.
- See: MCC (Marylebone Cricket Club,) under the CLUBS section.
- See: Mitcham/Mitcham Commons - England's oldest cricket green.
- See: St. John's Wood.
- See: Uxbridge/Uxbridge Moor.
- See: Walworth.
- See: Westbourne Terrace.
- See: Woodford/Woodford Green.

Cricklewood - (See: Barnet/Child's Hill.)

crime -

- See: Bloody Code.
- See: cheats.
- See: dueling spots.
- See: fingerprints.
- See: Old Street/Finsbury.
- See: poaching.
- See: police.
- See: prisons.
- See: punishments.
- See: rough places.
- See: Watch, the.

cripple - While the word was used to refer to persons who had suffered debilitating injuries or birth defects, in place-names it more likely derived from an ancient Anglo-Saxon word that referred to a covered walkway or burrow.

Cripplegate - The City. "Cripplegate" may have been derived from the Hermit of the Rhone, the patron saint of cripples. Or it may have derived from an Anglo-Saxon word that means a burrow or covered walkway.

Cripplegate is referred to in a 1068 document as "Crepelesgate." AN ENCYCLOPAEDIA OF LONDON says: "Maitland (1739) was of opinion that in 1010 it was the only gate in the north wall of the City, and that it was originally erected over a Roman military way, which led from London to Hornsey." Also: "Stow called Cripplegate a postern, and said: 'It was sometimes a prison'...and adds it was rebuilt by the brewers of London in 1244." Stood at what is now the corner of Wood Street and St. Alphage Gardens.

Repaired in 1336-7, using wood from the Guildhall. Rebuilt again in 1491. Repaired (and "beautified") again in 1663. Did not burn in the Great Fire of 1666.

The area was known for its leatherworkers.

In the 18th C. the wealthy residents were long gone from this densely populated area. Besides the busy market, also provided residences for religious dissidents, and journalists.

The materials of Cripplegate were sold in 1760, and by 1761 the gate was demolished. A fragment of the old gate remained in the White Hart Inn on the north side of Fore Street for a while longer, but now nothing remains. One source said that even the City Corporation marker disappeared in WWII, but a second source says that Cripplegate (and St. Giles Church) were both restored after extensive war damage. (See: gates.)

- Grub Street: (See under G.)
- St. Giles, Cripplegate: (See under the CHURCHES section.)

crocheting - An art practiced in the Regency era. (See: activities/entertainments/sports - knitting, under A.)

Crockford's - The "queen of the gaming-clubs," built 1827. Later: became the Devonshire Club. (See under the CLUBS section.)

Crofton - (See: Bromley/Crofton.)

Cromwell House - Now gone.

- See: Highgate Hill/Cromwell House.
- See: Ministry of Defence.

croquet - Did not become fashionable until the 1850s, at which time it was played by both genders. (You may care to see: tennis.)

Crosby Hall - (See: Chelsea/Crosby Hall.)

Cross Street - Southwark. (See: Southwark/Cross Street.)

Cross's Menagerie - Claims to have been the first wild animal menagerie (zoo) in London. Run by Edward Cross. Opened in 1773 in the Strand (near the later Waterloo Bridge.) Hosted at least one elephant, a hippopotamus, lions, monkeys, a sloth, and tigers. The menagerie closed, its animals sent to Surrey Zoological Gardens, and this site was demolished in 1829.

crown jewels - (See: Tower of London/Crown Jewels.)

Crown Passage - St. James's. Described as picturesque, with old shops and inns. Apparently it was designed to hide less grand shops from the eyes of the upper crust. Researchers believe it was built ca. 1673 or a bit earlier. It's had several names, depending on which map you look at: Golden Lion Court (ca. 1681,) Crown Court (ca. 1689,) Old Pav'd Alley (ca. 1746.)

- Red Lion Pub: (See: Red Lion Pub/Crown Passage, under the INNS/PUBS section.)

Crown Street - (See: Charing Cross Road.)

Croydon - This district was known for its charcoal burning since medieval times, from the nearby woods.

By the 18th C. the area was a place for coaches to rest on their way to southern resorts. The town had a close affiliation with the Archbishop(s) of Canterbury. The existing portion of the Archbishop's palace, on Old Palace Road, was sold in 1780 and made into a bleaching factory; used thus until 1887. The Archbishop(s) had given up the building in 1758, moving to Addington. Dozens of factories (metals, textiles) were here (on the River Wandle) by 1800.

Became a borough in 1889; originally a town divided into old town and new town, each about one mile/1.6 km long.

- Almhouses, the: George Street, 16th century. Still exist.
- Broad Green: Small settlement from the 16th C., but began to attract large houses in the early 19th century.
    - Broad Green House: 1807.
    - Christ Church: 1850s.
- Croydon Canal: Opened in 1809, joining the Grand Surrey Canal near New Cross Gate. Closed in 1835; its route being turned into the London and Croydon Railway.
- St. John-the-Baptist: Mentioned in Domesday Book. Rebuilt in 1867 after a fire.
- South Croydon: (See under S.)
- Town Hall: High Street. Built in 1808, replacing a 1609 structure. (The newer town hall was built in 1893-4 in Katherine Street.)
- Whitgift Hospital: Erected 1596-99 by Archbishop Whitgift. Home for the indigent, infirm, and old persons. Also a school for poor children; another school was founded here in 1881 (rebuilt in red brick.) The entrance is in North End.

Cruciform, the - (See: University College Hospital.)

Crutched Friars - Near St. Olaves, Hart Street. Used to be a monastery here, hence the area name of 'friars,' and 'crutched' referred to the monks caring for the lame and injured; however, PILGRIMS' LONDON says "crutched" means the friars wore a cross sewn on the backs of their cloaks. AN ENCYCLOPAEDIA OF LONDON notes: "The Order (of Crutched Friars) is said to have been instituted by Gerard, Prior of St. Mary of Morella at Bologna, and confirmed in 1169 by Pope Alexander III, who brought them under St. Augustine's rule. They came to England in 1244, and had their first house at Colchester. About 1298 they came to London, and settled in the parish of St. Olave, Hart Street. The name was derived from the cross, forming part of the staff carried by them, which was called a crutch... This was afterwards given up, and a cross of red cloth placed upon the breast of the gown." Reportedly built their monastery in 1319.

- 42: A very fine example of an early 18th C. London house. (See: French Ordinary Court.)

Crystal Palace - Built for the Great Exhibition of 1851. Utterly destroyed by fire in 1936.

Cubitt Town - (Pronounced Kew-bit.) William Cubitt bought this area (southeast quadrant of the Isle of Dogs) in the 1840s. He had built here: wharves, mills, and related industries. Residents followed on the heels of a church and public houses. (See: Isle of Dogs.)

Cuddington - Sutton. St. Mary became the parish church in 1538, built anew in 1867. Cuddington was changed forever when Henry VIII bought the entire manor to build Nonsuch Palace. (See under N.)

Cumberland Gate - Bayswater, Westminster. A street that runs very near Marble Arch.

- See: Hyde Park/Cumberland Gate.
- See: Marble Arch.

Cumberland House - Pall Mall. Built in the 1760s, at first called York House. (See: York House.)

Cumberland Market - (See: Haymarket.)

Cumberland Terrace - Built ca. 1826-7. 800 feet long.

- See: Park Crescent/Cumberland Terrace.
- See: Regent's Park/Cumberland Terrace.

Curate - (See: Church of England/Curate.)

curfew - Ran from the 14th C. to 1847. In medieval days, the curfew being rung also caused the gates of London to be closed for the night and the streets cleared. (See: gates.)

You had to have permission or a good reason (such as fetching a doctor) to be on the streets after dark, although a blind eye might be turned toward those with higher social standing.

- See: impressment - A good reason to obey curfew.
- See: lamps - For why, in addition to the curfew, the populace tended to go to bed at dark.
- See: St. Mary-le-Bow, in the CHURCHES section - Which rang the curfew.
- See: Tower of London/"The Towers"/Bell Tower.

Curriers' Company - (AKA: The Worshipful Company of Curriers.) Their Hall was in London Wall. Curriers scraped, beat, and colored tanned leather. First began as part of the Cordwainers' guild, until a 1272 civic ordinance foreshadowed the Curriers' separation from the Cordwainers, with full separation in 1415. Charter in 1606. The London Wall Hall sold in 1920, so the Curriers no longer have a hall. (You may care to see: tanners.)

curry - As in: east Indian dishes/spices. London's first curry house opened in Portman Square in 1809; it was the Hindostanee Coffee House at 34 George Street. While it should be noted that the now ubiquitous presence of take-away curry houses is far more of a 20-21st centuries occurrence, most cookery books of the 18-19th centuries had a receipt (recipe) or two for curried dishes. Curry (as spices, and as dishes, and due to a British presence in India) were known to Regency era cooks/diners. (See: food/curry.)

Curtain Road - Shoreditch. Formerly was part of Holywell Street, which dates back to earlier than 1576. Was known as Curtain Road by at least Shakespeare's time.

curtains - In the UK, window coverings are curtains, not drapes.

Curzon Street - Mayfair. Described by LONDON REDISCOVERED as being "unequivocally aristocratic."

- 9: Geo F. Trumper, gentlemen's fashion, barbers, and perfumers since 1875. (Always seen written just as "Geo," but it was established by one *George* Trumper.)
- 19: Benjamin Disraeli (prime minister in 1868, and 1874-80) died here in 1881.
- 38: Sunderland House, 1901. (See under S.)
- Crewe House: Built ca. 1735, as Howe House. Renamed to Crewe House in 1899. Still surrounded by its lush gardens. Now part of the Saudi Arabian embassy.

Custom House - (Also see written: Customhouse. Also as: Customs House.) Now at: 20 Lower Thames Street (north bank of Thames, east of London Bridge.) The practice of Customs existed since 1272. The idea of the Customs was to collect duties on goods shipped into England via the Thames. That is, to levy duty on goods that were imported, with a secondary purpose of controlling smuggling. First building built in 1382 (at a location east of the present building, there until 1820) and it was also rebuilt in 1559. Gutted in the Great Fire of 1666. Wren rebuilt in 1671, two stories; burnt in 1715 because of an accidental gunpowder explosion; Thomas Ripley rebuilt it to Wren's designs in 1722-5. Building destroyed by fire, again, on Feb. 12th, 1814. Present building was completed from 1814-17, under David Laing. The foundations were found to be defective, so Sir Robert Smirke revamped in 1825, but otherwise it is the building as we see it today. Its river frontage (488 feet long) dates from the 19th century.

- Custom House Quay: Ship masters, merchants, and brokers had to attend Custom House on the matter of import/export of goods, and used this dock often in so doing. (Was once known as Wool Quay.)

Cutlers' Hall - For the Worshipful Company of Cutlers. Cloak Lane. Knife-makers or dealers. Also made forks.

Existed as early as 1285 as a guild. Ca. 1380 there were recorded women cutlers. Ca.

the 14-15th centuries the Cutlers were supplied by the Bladesmiths (melded into the Cutlers in 1515); the Hafters; and the Sheathers; with the Cutlers assembling the assorted knife parts. Late in the 15th C. the Sheathers appear to have been absorbed into the Cutlers. There was controversy versus the Goldsmiths at this time as well, since precious metals were also used by the Cutlers; it was settled when the Goldsmiths were given the right to assay the Cutlers' silver and gold work.

The first Hall was near the present Mercers' Hall. In the early 15th C. the Cutlers moved to Cloak Lane (then known as Horseshoe Bridge Street); the Cutlers owned the site by 1451. This building was in the Tudor style; it was already an old house. Rebuilt shortly before the Great Fire of 1666, in which, alas, it burned. Reopened in 1670. There was an 1803 partial fire. "Repairs" (so extensive it's probably more correct to call it a rebuild) were in 1853-4.

The site was acquired for the District Railway in 1878, the Company leaving in 1882. From 1882-6 they had space with the Salters' Company. In 1887 they built a new Hall in the west side of Warwick Lane (the same that had been the home of the Royal College of Physicians from 1674-1825); built in a "modern Tudor style"; still exists.

The symbol of an elephant with a castellated tower on its back is associated with the Cutlers' Company because they could use ivory in the making of knife handles.

cutlery -

- See: Cutlers' Hall.
- See: household utensils.
- See: Middle Row.

Cyprian's Ball - A Cyprian was a prostitute. (See: Argyll Rooms - Which hosted the yearly Cyprian's Ball.

-D-

Dagenham - Borough of Barking and Dagenham. In 1703 the Thames formed a breach here, putting nearly 5,000 acres under water. By 1716 the breach had been repaired. Dagenham was a mere village on London's eastern fringe during the Regency. Market-gardens, corn fields, and scattered cottages.

- Dagenham Church: 1800, by William Mason.
- Dagenham Idol, the: Possibly from the Bronze Age, this wooden relic was dug

out of the marshes in 1922, probably buried in order to entice crops to grow.

- William Ford's School: 1825.

Daily Courant, the - London's first daily news sheet (newspaper,) founded in 1702.

- ➢ See: Ludgate/Daily Courant.
- ➢ See: newspapers/news sheets.

Daily Telegraph - 1855. (See: newspapers/news sheets.)

dairy - (See: milk.)

Dalston - Hackney district hamlet. In 1774 was a small, pleasant village. Became famous for its nursery-gardens, some of which continued until 1860.

- Kingsland Road:
    - 41: F. Cooke, still an eel and pie shop, since 1862.

damask - A type of fabric, jacquard woven, reversible with a pattern on each side, either both sides of the same colors or two different ones. (See: Scotland/Whytock, in the BRITISH COUNTIES section.)

Danson Park - Bexley, south side of Dover Road. The original grounds were laid out by Capability Brown (or at least in his style.) Acquired for public use in 1925.

Dark Entry - Slum. (See: St. Katherine's/Tower Hamlets, under S.)

Dartmouth House - 37 Charles Street, Mayfair. 1890.

Davies Street - Mayfair, off Grosvenor Street. There at least by the 18th century.

De Beauvoir Town - After 1852. (See: Hackney/Balmes House.)

Deaf and Dumb Asylum - 1807. (See: Old Kent Road/Deaf and Dumb Asylum.)

dean - (or dene) An old word meaning a wooded vale. Used in place names.

Dean Street - Off **Oxford** Street. Existed by at least 1765. (See: Soho/Dean Street.)

Dean Street - Off **Tooley** Street, Bermondsey. John Keats (poet, d.1821) lived on this street.

Dean's Yard - Westminster. A courtyard adjoined to Little Dean's Yard. It is most of the area around the old monastery of Westminster that's not otherwise occupied by Abbey buildings; those who attend Westminster School call it simply: Green (no "the,") and where they play football (soccer.) No public traffic.

- ➢ See: Westminster/Dean's Yard.
- ➢ See: Westminster School.

Deanery Courtyard - Adjoining Westminster Abbey. Medieval. These buildings used to be the abbot's lodging, and later the Westminster School Dean's place of residence. (See: Deanery, below.)

- College Hall: 1376, by Yevele. Was where the abbot dined; now used by the school as a dining room.
- Deanery, the: 17-18th C. work remains; is now the Dean's residence.

debating societies - They began to flourish in London in the 17th century, being a prominent factor in society well into the end of the 18th century. Due to a shift in policies (influenced by the French Revolution) governmental restrictions on such societies tightened, and they all but disappeared in the very early 19th century. (Although that is not to say there were no longer any such things; See: British Forum.) They covered all manner of subjects from politics, to current events, to issues of love and marriage, and much more, with each society usually having a particular focus.

- See: British Forum.
- See: Cogers.
- See: Piccadilly/22.

Debating Society, the - (See: Piccadilly/22.)

Debenham House - 8 Addison Road, Holland Park. 1905-7. Had the nickname: Peacock House. (See: Holland Park/Debenham House.)

Debtor's Prison - In London, the main places of confinement for debtors were: the Fleet, King's Bench, Ludgate, and the Marshalsea. (See: each under its own listing.) Debtor's prison makes more sense when you know the prisoners could: have visitors, live there with family, weren't usually thrown in with general prisoners, and could oversee the running of their businesses; some could even leave for a day's work.

ENGLISH PEERS (lords/titled persons) COULD NOT BE PLACED IN DEBTOR'S PRISON. Neither could Members of Parliament, at least not while Parliament was in session (Nov-May.) Peers, however, could still be plagued by duns and bailiffs at their homes.

Imprisonment for debt was abolished in 1860.

- See: Fleet Prison.
- See: Newgate Prison.
- See: prisons - Paragraph on Debtor's Prison.
- See: Queen's Bench Prison.
- See: Southwark/Borough High Street/King's Bench Prison.
- See: Southwark/Marshalsea.

debutante - This word dates from 1801, but I've never seen it used in any primary Regency source. (You may care to see: Queen's drawing-rooms.)

delope - There is controversy over if this word actually exists. Well, clearly it exists, but it's thought that the author Georgette Heyer invented it. Ms. Heyer (b.1902-d.1974) was an excellent writer and researcher; but it is said, in order to put one over on fellow authors who possibly "borrowed" her research, she invented some terms. The word delope exists in none of my dictionaries. I've never found it in any contemporary descriptions of duels. Its meaning: to deliberately fire one's pistol into the air during a duel (and thereby not fire upon one's opponent.) Regardless of whether it was invented as a word in the 20th century or not, certainly the *practice* of deloping was long known to duelists; Wellington did so in a duel in 1829.

dene - Meaning a seaside dune or wooded valley. Seen in place names.

Denmark Hill - Lambeth/Southwark. Named for Prince George of Denmark (b.1653-d.1708,) Queen Anne's consort. He kept a hunting-box here. Limited residential building began here starting ca. 1780.

Dennis Severs's House - 20th century name. (See: Folgate Street/18.)

dentist - Often enough referred to as a tooth-drawer; even by the time of the Regency this occupation was most likely filled by the local barber.

- See: doctors/barbers.
- See: Southwark/Guy's Hospital - Note on a dental surgeon, a new wonder in 1799.
- See: toothbrushes.

deportation - (See: transportation.)

Deptford - Tudor hamlet, was first known as Mereton (the town "in the marsh,") It was also known as West Greenwich. Became "Deptford" after the Norman conquest. It is now part of the London borough of Lewisham.

Chemical supply district, such as copperas (iron salt) since 1678.

Dockyards/shipyards also there by at least 1698, closed in 1869. This is where London's powerful and vast force of ships was built; author L. M. Bates described Deptford as "the ground from which, more than any other, grew the British empire." Accordingly, it became one of London's leading ports.

- See: docks.
- See: Tower Hill.
- See: Trinity House.

- Albury Street: The whole street, a set of row houses, was built in 1706-14 by a local mason.
- Deptford Bridge: There was a ford here in ancient times, which became a wooden bridge, then a stone one. In 1497 the Battle of Deptford Bridge was here. The current bridge dates from 1883.
- Deptford Dockyard: Founded in 1513; closed in 1844. (See: docks.)
- Deptford Town Hall: 1905, by C. E. Richards.
- Master Shipbuilder's house remains, 1708.
- St. James': Hatcham. 1854.

- St. Nicholas: Deptford Church Street. Was in Deptford Green, but was later considered to be in the Borough of Greenwich. Dates from the 12th century. Rebuilt in 1697 (except the tower.) Burned in WWII, but much was saved. Brick. Was described as chubby.
- St. Paul's Church: Built in 1712 or 1730, by Thomas Archer. Altered in 1883. (See: St. Paul/Deptford, under the CHURCHES section.)

Derby House - At the **College of Arms**. (See: College of Arms/Derby House.)

Derby House - **Grosvenor Square**. (See: Grosvenor Square/Derby House.)

Devil's Acre - Slum area, made up of Great St. Anne's Lane, Duck Lane, New Pye Street, and Old Pye Street, Westminster.

- ➢ See: Duck Lane.
- ➢ See: St. Katherine's/Tower Hamlets, under S.
- ➢ See: Victoria Street.

Devonshire House - 78 Piccadilly, Mayfair. John Berkeley (the first Lord Berkeley) built Berkeley House ca. 1649 (2nd source said in the 1660s); described as "low and unpretentious." Sold by his descendants in 1696, to the first Duke of Devonshire; Berkeley House was demolished in 1733. On the same site, the 3rd Duke built Devonshire House in 1740, described as "grand." The Dukes of Devonshire lived here through the 18-19th centuries. After WWI it was unoccupied. It was pulled down in 1924. An office building stands there now, under the (re-used) name Devonshire House.

Devonshire Place - Marylebone, Westminster. Built ca. 1791. (See: Marylebone/Devonshire Place.)

- 2: Arthur Conan Doyle (*Sherlock Holmes* author, b.1859-d.1930) had his first doctor's offices here.

diamond - The gem. Side note: While some wedding rings contained diamonds, during the Regency wedding rings were very often just plain bands; the diamond had yet to be affiliated with marriage.

- ➢ See: Hatton Garden.
- ➢ See: jewelry.

diapers - Not called diapers; were called clouts. "Nappy" was a later term, post-Regency. The poor might have used rags, or, if it was warm, no clouts at all. (See: clouts.)

Dick Whittington - The four times Lord Mayor of London. (See: Highgate Hill/Statue of Dick Whittington.)

Dickens Museum - As in the writer, Charles Dickens, b.1812-d.1870. (See: Bloomsbury/Doughty Street/48.)

Dickins & Smith - Drapers, haberdashers. (See: Oxford Street/54.)

dictionary - Dr. Samuel Johnson compiled his *Dictionary of the English Language*, the first of its kind, and published it in 1755. (See: Gough Square/17.)

The first *Oxford English Dictionary* dates from 1857.

The first *Encyclopaedia Brittanica* dates from 1768.

dinosaurs - (See: paleontology.)

diorama - A model of a scene; three-dimensional; can be miniature or large-scale. Popular in the entire 19th century. (See: Park Square/diorama.)

direction - During the Regency era, one was unlikely to ask for a person's "address," but rather instead their "direction." (Example: "I will need your direction in order to call upon you tomorrow.")

Dirty Lane - So known by at least 1807. Apparently the name was appropriate. Later known as Great Suffolk Street.

diseases - Ones known to have existed during the Regency. (This list is not all inclusive.) Some of the following have more information in their appropriate Alpha section.

- appendicitis - (See.)
- bladder stones
- brain tumor - While Regency era doctors understood the body developed tumors, they didn't know what to do about brain tumors until 1866.
    - See: brain tumor, under B.
    - See: Maida Vale/Maida Vale Hospital.
- cancer - (See: Middlesex Hospital - Had a cancer ward by 1792.)
- cholera -
    - See: sewers - Thames River/cholera/1849.
    - See under C.
- conjunctivitis - Known then as: Egyptian ophthalmia.
- constipation - Usually treated by ingesting salts.
- consumption - Its modern name: tuberculosis. (See under C.)
- diphtheria - Is isolated by Pierre Fidele Bretonneau (French physician) in 1820; it gained its name in 1826. Until then it was called: putrid throat. (See, below.)
- dropsy - Modern term: edema. (See under D.)
- food poisoning
- gaol fever - A form of typhus, often spread by lice. (See: typhus, under T.)
- gonorrhoea - American spelling: gonorrhea.
- Gout
- grippe, the - (See: influenza, below.)
- hernias - Usually then known as: ruptures.

- influenza - Often called: the grippe. Outbreaks could be deadly.
- intestinal worms
- jaundice - AKA: yellow jaundice.
- leprosy - No longer an issue to Regency London. (See.)
- lice - (See: haircutters.)
- malaria
- measles
- Parkinson's Disease -
    - See: Parkinson's Disease, under P.
    - See: Shaking Palsy, below - Its Regency name.
- plague - Medieval disease. There were no plagues in Regency Britain, (although there were cholera and influenza issues that killed many.)
    - See: Black Death, under B.
    - See: Great Plague of 1666.
- pox -
    - See: pox, under P.
    - See: smallpox, under S.
- putrid throat - What doctors called diphtheria during the Regency; they also used this name for a strep-throat condition of inflamed throat, destruction, and/or foul odor.
- rabies
- rheumatism
- scarlet fever
- scurvy - (See.)
- sepsis - Infection, often after childbirth, which was usually called: puerperal fever. (See under S.)
- shaking palsy - How Parkinson's was known in the Regency. (See: Parkinson's Disease, above.)
- smallpox - (See.)
- syphilis - (See: Lock Hospital.)
- tuberculosis - (See: consumption, above.)
- tumors - George IV had a tumor removed from his head in 1821, by his reluctant surgeon, Astley Cooper, who feared a poor result. But he was successful, and was given a knighthood for it. (See: brain tumor, above.)
- typhus - AKA: gaol fever. (See under T.)
- whooping cough - Also then known as: chin cough.

TREATMENTS/MEDICINES: The following may have more information in their appropriate Alpha section.

- amputation - Of damaged or diseased limbs.
- anesthesia - (See.)
- apothecaries - (See: doctors/apothecary.)
- asylums - "Asylum" meant more than just places for the insane. (See under A.)
- Bath chair - A kind of wheelchair. (See under B.)
- blood transfusions - (See.)
- chemists - A more modern term for an apothecary. (See.)
- Company of Surgeons - (See.)
- doctors - (See under D - For a good delineation of Regency era medical men.)
- ether – 1846.
- hospitals
- hypodermic needle and syringe - Invented in 1855.
- Hunterian Medical School
- inoculation - Largely misunderstood/feared during the Regency era. (See: smallpox, under S.)
- iodine - Invented in France in 1811.
- laudanum - Like morphine, is a tincture of opium. (See.)
- morphine - An opium derivative; opium was in England (from India) by 1700. In 1805, an apothecary of Hameln, Germany (Friedrich Wilhelm Adam Sertürner) introduced morphine as a painkiller (in pure form is ten times stronger than opium.) Whereas laudanum (also derived from opium) was used by the general populace during the Regency, morphine did not become widely used until the invention of the hypodermic needle and syringe in 1855.
- nursing - (See.)
- operating theatre - (See.)
- opium - (See.)
- penicillin - 1928. (See.)
- Royal College of Physicians - (See.)
- stethoscope - 1816. (See.)
- still-room - Where one made one's own cordials/remedies. (See.)
- surgery.

dissection - Of human bodies, for medical study purposes.

- See: hospitals - Notes under.
- See: resurrectionists - Those who stole bodies for dissection.

Dissenters - Those who dissented from the official church, Anglicanism (Church of England.) Were often barred from privileges, such as earning diplomas, holding offices, etc.

- See: Bunhill Fields.
- See under the CHURCHES section - Notes at.

Dissenter's Burial Ground - (See: Bunhill Fields.)

dissolution of the monasteries - This occurred as the Commonwealth developed, with, alas, many buildings being pulled down (monasteries, churches, and sometimes the homes of dissenters who objected to the change in the national faith from Catholic to Anglican.) London lost much pre-16th C. architecture; while not on a level with the losses from the Great Fire of 1666, still from an architectural point of view the Dissolution scarred not only the "face" of London, but all of England.

The resistance to the Dissolution of the Monasteries was called the Pilgrimage of Grace, also called the great northern rising, and was cruelly repressed. (See: Dissolution of the monasteries, under the opening part of the CHURCHES section.)

Distaff Lane - An old street, although the present Distaff Lane lies near but not atop the ancient one. A distaff is a handheld stick or spindle used in spinning wool (or flax) thread.

- St. Nicholas Cole Abbey. (See under the CHURCHES section.)

Distillers' Company - (AKA: The Worshipful Company of Distillers.) Got their Charter in 1638 from Charles I, but it was disputed until 1658. The guild included makers of vinegar, spirits, alegar (malt vinegar,) in addition to wine and spirits. Never had a hall. Livery company. 69th in precedence.

docks - In 1515 there were royal dockyards established at Deptford and Woolwich. (See: Deptford.)

Some of the other locations for London's docks were: Blackwall, Greenwich, Limehouse, Rotherhithe, and Wapping.

The number of unloading ships at London docks nearly trebled over the course of the 18th century. Until the 19th C. docks came along, the existing quays were so busy and crowded that sometimes ships had to wait up to six weeks to unload their cargo. CHAMBERS LONDON ENCYCLOPAEDIA relays this information: "...with this growth came overcrowding and increased pilferage. Liverpool had shown that wet docks provided a solution and a group of merchants, together with the West India Company and the Corporation of London, chose the Isle of Dogs as their preferred site..."

Of the new docks, each was ringed by forty foot high walls and were patrolled by watchmen.

The London docks all came under the Port of London Authority in 1909 (with the exception of the Regent's Canal Dock.)

The LONDON DOCKLANDS DEVELOPMENT CORPORATION (LDDC) was formed in the 1980s (to re-develop the abandoned, derelict docks into meaningful property such as shopping, flats, etc.

NOTE: The term "docklands" (for the area of the ports of London) is a 20th C. term (and more recently has come to mean Canary Wharf in particular.)

NOTE: "Quay" is pronounced: key.

Here is a list of the docks (and/or buildings in the dock areas):

- Blackwall:
    - See: East India Docks, below.
    - See under B.
- Brunswick Dock: Blackwall was enlarged in 1789, resulting in Brunswick Dock, the nucleus for the development of the East India Docks in 1806, at which time this became the export dock.
    - See: Blackwall, under B.
    - See: East India Docks, below.
- Butler's Wharf: Is located between Shad Thames (a street) and the Thames Path. Known for shipping cloth, eels, hemp, iron, skins, tar, and timber. From at least 1588.

  In 1873 had become warehouses of coffee, dried fruit, spices, tea, and more.

  When the old docks closed in ca. 1968, the whole docks area fell into sad disuse, until the Docklands regeneration project of the 1980s. Butler's Wharf, yet a warehouse, was one of the results, being hosted in the updated but still Victorian buildings existing at that time. Now houses luxurious flats and restaurants.
- Canary Wharf: A modern skyscraper. (See: West India Dock/Canary Wharf, below.)
- Custom House Quay: Not part of the docklands, per se. (See: Custom House/Custom House Quay, under C.)
- East India Docks: (Also seen written simply as: the East India.) There was at least one dock here before 1806, going back to at least 1606. (See: Brunswick Dock, above.) For commercial traffic. On the Isle of Dogs; completed 8/4/1806, an inner and outer dock. In 1838 blended in with the West India Dock, becoming

the "East and West India Dock Company," and establishing together the Tilbury Docks, Gravesend, 1866. The dock closed in 1967. (Not affiliated with the East India Company.)

- Execution Dock: On the Thames between Wapping New Stairs and King Henry's Stairs. One of the pre-19th C. docks (probably dates from the 16th century.) Mutineers and pirates were hanged here in the 16-17th centuries, and their bodies left on the Thames bank until three tides had washed over their remains. The last hanging (for murder and mutiny) here took place in 1830.
- Greenland Dock: (See: Surrey Commercial Dock, below.)
- Hay's Wharf: 1857. (See under H.)
- Howland Great Wet Dock: (Also simply called: Howland Dock.) At Rotherhithe. Created in 1696. Opened in 1699 for the refitting of East India Company ships. "A harbourage for sailing vessels." Later a part of Surrey Commercial Dock. It was the only commercial dock in London until ca. 1800. (See: Surrey Commercial Dock, below.)
- Isle of Dogs: Where the West India and Millwall Docks are located; the East India Docks had been here.
    - See: East India Docks, above.
    - See: Isle of Dogs, under I.
- King George V Dock: Begun in 1912, finished in 1921. One of the three royal docks. (See: Royal Docks, below.) 64 (water) acres. Closed in the 1980s.
- London Docks: Aptly named, due to location. At Wapping. Built by D. A. Alexander and John Rennie. Was two main basins that could handle 300 ships. Comprised of three interlocking docks. Completed in 1800-1805. Closed in 1968.
    - Queen's Warehouse: Housed tobacco.
- Millwall Dock: 1868, opened to handle timber and grain imports. On the Isle of Dogs, Tower Hamlets; connected to the south West India Dock. Name comes from the mills that used to sit on the western embankment.
- Queenhithe Dock: For small boats and barges only; upriver from other Thames docks. (See: Queenhithe, under Q.)
- Regent's Canal Dock: 1812. In the 1980s became Limehouse Basin, a marina.
- Rotherhithe: Is now chiefly the Surrey Commercial Docks.
    - See: Rotherhithe, under R.
    - See: Surrey Commercial Docks, below.
- Royal Albert Dock: 1880. One of the three Royal Docks. (See, below.) In the 21st century, being developed into some 1,550 homes.

- Royal Docks: Collective name for: King George V Dock, Royal Albert Dock, and Royal Victoria Dock. Situated between Beckton and Canning Town and the riverside districts of Silvertown and North Woolwich. The three royal docks closed to commercial traffic in the 1980s.
    - See: King George V Dock, above.
    - See: Royal Albert Dock, above.
    - See: Royal Victoria Dock, below.
- Royal Victoria Docks: In 1855. Closed in 1981. (See: Victoria Docks, below.)
- St. Katharine's Dock: (Also seen written as: St. Katherine's.) Was begun in 1825, and opened on October 25th, 1828. Twenty-three acres; ten are water, and thirteen are land. The area used to be mud basins, ramshackle wharves, and "legal quays" that hampered rather than helped the flow of traffic on the Thames. Although it also should be noted that 1,250 houses were demolished to make way, along with the church of St. Katharine (dating from 1148) and St. Katharine Hospital, (the latter two being collectively known as the Royal Foundation of St. Katharine.) St. Katharine's Hospital relocated to Regency Park. (See: St. Katherine - Tower Hamlets, under S.)

  Described as a miniature port. The docks were around two connected basins, giving the relatively small area of enclosed water a rather long quayside.

  Additional warehouses were added in the 1850s.

  Described as austere yellow-brick warehouses.

  It had tight security; this allowed for protection for high-end goods like: feathers, indigo powder, ivory, shells, tea, and wool.

  Closed at 4 pm, with the shutting of the great gates by the gate-keeper, who said he wouldn't wait another minute, "not even for the King."

  St. Katherine's and London Docks were amalgamated in 1864. Severely damaged by WWII bombs. Lingered, until they closed in 1968, the area being rebuilt for businesses.

  (See: St. Katherine's, under S.)
    - Dickens Inn: Modern structure, built in antique style.
    - Ivory House: 1858-60, by George Aitchison. (Actually sitting on the dock.) Is now flats.
- South-West India Dock: (See: West India Dock/South-West India, below.)
- Surrey Commercial Docks: (AKA: Surrey Docks.) At Rotherhithe. Wriothesley Russell (later the 2nd Duke of Bedford,) at age 14 married Elizabeth Howland (age 11) in 1695. He excavated for the Howland Great Wet Dock by 1700. The

1790s brought congestion (and theft,) and over the next hundred years a bunch of rival dock peninsulas grew up in the area, resulting in "ruinous completion"; the Great Howland Wet Dock was then known as Surrey Docks, until the south bank merger of smallish docks in 1864, then taking on the name of *Surrey Commercial Docks Company.* 300 acres. Is the oldest London dock; the only one on the south side of the Thames. Specialized in Scandinavian timber, grain, wood pulp, Canadian grain, cheese, and bacon. Closed in 1970. Now called Surrey Quays, and is a leisure/shopping center, following vast alterations.

The Surrey Commercial Dock's oldest dock is the Greenland Dock, 1696 (at one time called the Howland Dock, but was known as Greenland Dock by the mid 18th century (at that time being a base for Arctic whalers.) Described as "massive." Lasted into the 19th century.

- See: Howland Great Wet Dock, above.
- See: Rotherhithe, above.

- Tilbury Dock: Gravesend, 26 miles/42 km downriver from London Bridge. 1886. Owned by the East and West India Dock company. Main port for the importing of paper. Also the spot for cars, containers, grain, plus other bulky items.
    - River Cargo Jetty: Adjacent to Tilbury Docks. Used by vessels only partially unloading.
- Tobacco Dock: A huge Thames-side warehouse, built 1811-14, for storing tobacco and wine. Built of timber and cast-iron framing. Still exists (but not as a warehouse per se, is now a shopping mall.)
- Victoria Dock: Plaistow Marshes, opened in 1855. First to accept steamships. In 1880 it added/became the *Royal* Victoria Dock (as part of the three Royal Docks.) A new airport was built on this site in 1987, the London City Airport.
- West India Docks: (Also seen referred to simply as: the West Indias.) Wapping. Built in 1800 for the West India Company, opened in 1802 (brick warehouse on stone foundation) on the Isle of Dogs, by William Jessop and John Rennie. 242 acres.

It was the first wet dock in London for commercial/cargo use; that is, the Howland Dock had been London's sole commercial dock, but with the advent of the West India Docks it was no longer necessary to ferry goods to the ships via smaller boats, but now the ships could load and unload directly in dock. Had iron cranes for loading and unloading the ships.

The preponderance of sugar shipped into London was stored here. These docks also stored hardwoods.

In 1829 became the West India Dock Company. The West India Dock Co. purchased a canal cutting off a bend in the river, converted it into the South-West India Dock in 1870, and devoted it to the timber trade. (See: South-West India Dock, below.) Combined in 1838 with the East India Dock Company. (See: East India Docks, above.) The West India Docks closed in 1980.

- Billingsgate Market: Moved from Lower Thames Street to here (on West India Quay) in 1989.
- Canary Wharf: (AKA: 1 Canada Square: the tallest building in Britain, 2nd in Europe, 243 meters/830 feet tall. Nicknamed "Vertical Fleet Street."

  The wharf is a 1937 strip of land centered in the old West India Docks for unloading/storing fruit from the Canary Islands. The first part of the massive rebuild came in 1991. (Before this, it had been used as a dock for rum and mahogany.)

  CHAMBERS LONDON GAZETTEER notes: (Canary Wharf is now) "the world's largest commercial development and this is probably the only part of London that is indistinguishable from the downtown district of a modern American city."
- South-West India Dock:
  - See: South Quay, under S.
  - See: West India Docks, above - The note under "In 1829..."

doctors - Sometimes hospitals served as teaching centers, so doctors could learn/share information.

The term "quack" existed during the Regency, and would have been used perhaps for the barber, or even the apothecary (if he wasn't much liked,) but it wasn't quite as derogatory a term as it is now.

Some women practiced medicine during the Regency era (aside from midwives,) usually alongside their husbands, or when he had died she assumed his place in a community; such a woman could not rise above surgeon. The first woman to qualify in Britain as a doctor in her own right was: Elizabeth Garrett Anderson (b.1836-d.1917) - whereas first before her was Elizabeth Blackwell (b.1821-d.1910) by virtue of coming *back* to Britain after qualifying as one in New York, America.

- See: coroner.
- See: doctors, streets known as hosting residences for, under D.
- See: Great Windmill Street School - For a school that taught dissection.

- See: hospitals.
- See: surgical training.

Regency England had four kinds of doctors. Medical persons as a whole were referred to as doctors, but there were sharp divisions when it boiled down to referring to a specific person (and his skill level.) Unless people lived in a rather large city, they were unlikely to ever be seen by a physician. Most Regency folk would have called for the surgeon or gone to get a physick from the apothecary. In very small towns, they might have to make do with only a barber's care (who as often as not also served in a veterinarian role.) The four kinds of doctor were:

PHYSICIAN: "Hands off" pusher of pills. Listened to hearts; checked urine; felt the pulse, that was virtually all he did physically. He was university trained ("read for the university", i.e. studied at and took its exams.) He was expensive to hire; usually only found in large cities. He was socially acceptable, rather more so than his fellow caregivers.

Physicians were called "Dr.," unless their training/education was very extensive, at which time they again became "Mr."

They were higher in social status than surgeons (because they did not do manual labor.) To belong to the Royal College of Physicians, one must belong to the Church of England and have graduated from Cambridge or Oxford; if you graduated from any other university you could only be admitted to the College of Physicians as a licentiate. Cambridge and Oxford did not teach practical training; for medical training one went to Edinburgh in Glasgow, Leiden, or other like universities, or into hospitals, or (in London) private anatomy schools.

- See: Coroner.
- See: diseases.
- See: Medical College.
- See: physicians.
- See: Royal College of Physicians.

SURGEON: "Hands on." Did all the surgeries, bone-sawing, stitching, setting of fractures, wound dressing, skin diseases - the physical labor of doctoring. He took care of anything that could not be taken care of by the drugs the physician would prescribe. Schooled, but not necessarily at a university. His training did not cost as much as that for a physician, and he did not require a license to practice his calling.

He was "the doctor" but he was properly referred to as "Mr.," as in, "Our surgeon, Mr. Peabody, will be arriving shortly."

The Surgeons' guild was linked with the Barbers up until 1745.

Were apprenticed for 3-7 years, starting in their teens. They could continue to practice without formal status, or could be examined in London in order to become a member of the Company of Surgeons.

All doctors of the Royal Navy were surgeons, because sea battles required practical skills. By necessity, Royal Navy surgeons would also act as apothecaries, barbers, and physicians. Their skill levels varied.

- ➢ See: Barbers' Hall.
- ➢ See: Hunterian Medical School.
- ➢ See: Royal College of Surgeons.

APOTHECARY: Technically just a dispenser of pills/drugs, but since a lot of villages had no formal doctor, the apothecary often acted as one. He often was a medical adviser, too, for which he was, in theory, not supposed to be paid (but rather only for the dispensing of tinctures and such); by the early 19th C. the theory of limited practice was little in practice. The apothecary often had little formal learning. He would have been a "Mr."

The apothecary might well make many of his own powders and tinctures.

In 1815 the Apothecaries Act brought in some regulation, creating qualified apothecaries.

- ➢ See: Apothecaries' Hall.
- ➢ See: chemists.
- ➢ See: Society of Apothecaries.

BARBER: He cut your hair, shaved your face, pulled your teeth, and could tend the illnesses in your family. He was what most villages had in the way of a doctor. He might have some learning, or he might be the male equivalent of the country midwife, having orally learned what he knows. He was a man-of-all-medical-work, sometimes including seeing to animals. He was also a "Mr.," if thought well enough of to deserve being called by more than his last name, as in, "Jones here will put that leg right."

- ➢ See: Barbers' Hall.
- ➢ See: doctors, streets known as hosting residences for.
- ➢ See: man-midwife.

Doctor's Commons - Great Rider Street (south of St. Paul's Cathedral; approx. 1/2 mile/0.8 km east of the Inns of Court.) Was first situated in Paternoster Row ca. 1530; AN ENCYCLOPAEDIA OF LONDON says of this first residence: "The civilians and canonists then lodged in a small, inconvenient house in Paternoster Row, afterwards the Queen's

Head Tavern. It was a common house for the doctors of law, for the study and practice of the civil law."

Moved to Great Knight Rider Street in 1567, into a house known before as Montjoye Place. Rebuilt following the Great Fire of 1666. It has a stone courtyard, around which was built the buildings, including a big courtroom.

Ecclesiastical graduate lawyers of Cambridge and Oxford made up its society, being admitted to this college to practice canon and civil law. Its litigations proved to be extra long and expensive, so even though it was incorporated in 1768, the institution was viewed with skepticism.

Marriage licenses (including the infamous Special Licenses,) divorces, and wills were granted/registered here. Gentlemen went to Doctor's Commons to get a Special License; only the Archbishop of Canterbury could grant it. Therefore Special Licenses were fairly difficult to come by, since the Archbishop could grant, or not grant one, entirely at his discretion. A special license was considered to be very expensive; I know that by the middle of the 19th C. it cost an expensive 28 pounds.

Doctor's Commons hosted five courts:

- Court of Arches
- Court of Admiralty
- Court of Delegates
- Court of Prerogatives
- Faculty and Archdeacons' Court.

Doctors' Common was made obsolete by the Probate Act of 1857 (its business being transferred to the High Court of Justice, with wills and Testaments moving to Somerset House.) The buildings were demolished in 1867.

doctors, streets known as hosting residences for - Harley Street (not until the mid 19th century. Wimpole Street (also not until Victorian times.) During the Regency era: Savile Row; and Welbeck Street.

Dog Cemetery - 1880-1915 (when pet burials were stopped here.) Near Victoria Gate/Kensington Gardens.

dog - (See: animals/dog.)

dog shows - As in the showing of breeds. First one in England was in 1852 at Newcastle-on-Tyne.

Doggett's Coat and Badge race - Thames. A sculling race; the oldest annual contested sporting event in the world. Irishman, actor, and theatre manager Thomas Doggett introduced the prize (AN ENCYCLOPAEDIA OF LONDON gave the date as Aug. 1st, 1716,) being grateful for the services of the lowly watermen. The theatres were dependent on the watermen to bring their customers across the Thames to them. The race is usually held at the end of July. Ran almost five miles/8km, from the Old Swan Inn at London Bridge to the site of the White Swan Inn at Cadogan Pier, Chelsea (which was demolished in 1873.) Administered by the Fishmongers' Company. Winner gets a red coat, breeches, cap, and a silver arm badge (and is allowed to wear the same to public events.) Is still competed for each year, commemorating George I's ascension to the throne.

Dolphin Square - Pimlico. 1937. A block of private flats.

Domesday Book - (Pronounced dooms-day.) Begun in 1085; published in 1086. It was the most important record from medieval England. It was essentially a census for William the Conqueror, who wanted to know not only what revenues were due to him, but the overall extent of his nation's resources; it measured 13,418 settlements in England (everything south of what was Scotland's border at the time.) It was so extensive that people claimed it was as unchallengeable as the Last Judgement (when the deeds by Christians that were written in the Book of Life would be put before God for judgment; by the late 12th C. this claim led to its being named for Doomsday. It is not one book, but actually two, the second of which for reasons unknown was never summarized and added to the first. (You may care to see: census.)

Dorchester Hotel - 1930s. Park Lane. (See: Dorchester House.)

Dorchester House - Park Lane, Mayfair, Westminster. "Grand as a palace." Built in 1751, but not called Dorchester House until after it was bought by Joseph Danner (who became the 1st Earl of Dorchester in 1792.) Rebuilt to look like a Renaissance Palace, in 1869. Became the Dorchester Hotel (and had an Art Deco facade in 1931, on the site of the old Dorchester Hotel.

Doric Villa - Outer Circle, south end of Regent's Park. Designed by John Nash. Was first lived in: in 1828. Made up of two houses standing together at the east end of York Terrace, although they appeared to be just one house.

Dorset House - (See: Salisbury Court.)

Dorset Square - Marylebone. 1811. The square still has at least one Regency era building (the Dorset Square Hotel.) Where the Hotel now stands were two early Regency homes, 39-40 Dorset Square. (See: Lord's Cricket Ground.)

- Dorset Street:
    - 1: Charles Babbage (b.1791-d.1871) lived here from 1829-71. Mathematician and modern computer pioneer.

Dorset Street - Spitalfields, in the rookery (meaning: rough, poor) area of. (Not to be confused with another Dorset Street. For that, see: Dorset Square/Dorset Street.) Built in 1674, originally called "Datchet Street," the name changed very soon. Associated with one of the Jack the Ripper murders, 1888. Name changed in 1904 to: Duval Street. (See.)

double-decker bus - The first *motorized* double-decked bus ran in London in 1902. They are famously red simply because circa the 1920s the company competed with other (private) bus services, and chose red paint to make theirs stand out.

Doughty Street - A "charming terrace of houses" (terraces on both sides of the street,) built about 1801. Was a private road patrolled by uniformed commissionaires (door attendant.) The bells of St. Paul's proved annoying to those who lived at this location.

- 48: Charles Dickens (author) lived here after marrying Catherine Hogarth, 1837-39. (Is now a Dickens museum.)

Doulton Fine China - Operating at first in the Potteries. (See under P.) In 1815 the widowed Mrs. Jones gave up waiting for her wayward sea-faring son to return to England, and offered a partnership in her pottery to 22-year-old John Doulton. Royal Warrant granted in 1901. Merged with Royal Crown Derby, and with Minton, to create the Royal Doulton Group. Now based in Barlaston, near Stoke-on-Trent.

Dover House - Piccadilly. Stately mansion from 1758, by Paine; the original house being screened from Whitehall by a colonnade and rotunda, 1787, by Henry Holland (for the Duke of York.) The Duke of York had acquired it in 1787, and hired Holland to re-do the entrance. Named for Lord Devon, who bought the house in 1830. Now the Scottish Office, used by Scottish ministers. (See: Piccadilly/Albany.)

Dover Road - (AKA: The London to Dover Road.) Ancient turnpike. Dover Road was the first bit of what would become: Watling Street. The city of Dover was a significant approach/port to leave for the continent. Coachmen who drove Dover Road wore red coats. In the 1840s railways replaced Dover Road.

Dover Street - Mayfair. Laid out ca. 1678.

- 37: Was first the town house of the Bishop of Ely. By Sir Robert Taylor, 1772. Three stories; three bays.
- Brown's (hotel,) 1837. (See under B.)

Doves, The - Coffee-house, until 1860. (See: Fulham/Mall, the.)

Dowgate Hill - The City. Dowgate is one of the 25 wards of the City. (See: wards.)

- Dyers' Hall: (See at its own listing.)
- Innholders' Hall: (See under I.)
- St. Michael Paternoster. (See: St. Michael Royal, under the CHURCHES section.)
- Skinners' Hall: (See under S.)
- Tallow Chandlers' Hall: (See under T.)

Downe House - Richmond Hill, Surrey. Built in 1780 of brick and stone. (See: Richmond Hill.) Was owned at one point by the playwright Richard Brinsley Sheridan (b.1751-d.1816.) Is also known for housing Mick Jagger and family in the 1990s.

Downing Street - Whitehall, St. James's. Short terrace of four 18th C. houses in dull brown brick. Named for Sir George Downing, who was not only a Lord Treasurer and diplomat, but whose home was also on this street (he built the street. See: 10, below.) This property/street came to the British government upon his death in 1684. James Boswell (biographer) lived here briefly as a lad in the 1760s.

- 10: Built as a residence in 1681-3 for Sir George Downing. Became the residence of the Prime Ministers of England in 1732, when it was presented by George II to Sir Robert Walpole, then the First Lord of the Treasury (and since dubbed the first ever British Prime Minister. See: Prime Ministers, under P.) The PM's residence was formed from Downing's home and a second one developed by him at the same time (the latter being described as "much grander" than number 10); both being altered in 1732-5 by William Kent, at which time Walpole moved in.

  In 1766 a new facade was added. Altered again in 1825, by John Soane.

  The PM was also always given the post of First Lord of the Treasury and it is actually in this capacity s/he occupies number 10. Has an internal link to numbers 11 and 12.

  - See: 11, and 12, below in this entry.
  - See: Cabinet, the.
- 11: In 1828 became the residence of the Chancellor of the Exchequer.
- 12: Ground floor is the Office of the Government Chief Party Whip since at least 1723. Belonged in 1803 to the East India Company, which that year sold it to the Crown, was used by the Judge Advocate General at first. In 1827 the Colonial Office took over here. Joined with 10 Downing Street in 1846.

drapers - Sellers of cloth and wool primarily intended for clothing. They might also take on the roles of cloth merchant and/or haberdasher (seller of men's clothing.) In America they might be called a seller of dry goods. (19th century sources use the terms "drapers" and "haberdashers" rather interchangeably.)

- See: Berkshire/Caley's, under the BRITISH COUNTIES section.
- See: Covent Garden/Bedford House/Layton & Shear.
- See: Drapers' Hall.
- See: haberdashers.
- See: Harrod's.
- See: Knightsbridge/Harvey Nichols.
- See: Leicester Square/Gedge's.
- See: Leicester Square/Newton's - Irish linens.

- See: milliners - Sold more than just hats. (See under M.)
- See: New Bond Street/164/Grafton House.
- See: Oxford Street/54.
- See: Pall Mall/Schomberg House - Harding, Howell & Co.
- See: St. Paul's Churchyard.
- See: tailors - Men's clothing.
- See: Wigmore Street/Christian's.

Drapers' Gardens - Throgmorton Avenue. Near the Bank of England. (See: Drapers' Hall/Drapers' Garden.)

Drapers' Hall - For the Worshipful Company of Drapers. Throgmorton Street. Sellers of cloth, and wool. (The Drapers' Guild was AKA: the Master and Wardens and Brethren and Sisters of the Guild or Fraternity of the Blessed Mary the Virgin of the Mystery of Drapers of the City of London.)

The Drapers from the Middle Ages; became a Company in 1438. As opposed to the Clothworkers' Company, the Drapers were originally a trade association of wool and cloth merchants. Is a Livery Company.

The building was bought in 1541 from Henry VIII (who possessed it following its owner's execution, being Thomas Cromwell, Earl of Essex.) The hall burnt in the Great Fire of 1666. Rebuilt to designs by Edward Jarman, this version being rebuilt in 1774 after a partial fire.

Today's Hall (the 4th) was built in 1870, with 28 detached columns of Devonshire granite. (See: drapers, at its own listing.)

The Drapers are 3rd in the order of precedence; one of the Great Twelve Livery companies of London.

- Drapers' Garden, the: Adjacent to the Hall. Probably existed since Cromwell's time. Described as a "dismal yard, containing as much gravel as grass."

drapes - In the UK, window coverings are curtains, not drapes.

drawers - As in underwear. (See: undergarments.)

drawing rooms - In this case I mean those held by the reigning queen: assemblies at which young misses making their come outs were presented to her royal person. The misses were required to wear court dress, which still during the Regency was rather old-fashioned versions of Georgian styles. (See: levees - For men.)

The term "drawing room" is a shortening of "withdrawing room", where persons withdrew following a meal (although they were used for other purposes as well, of course.) Most fine homes claimed a drawing room.

Anyone could host a drawing room, but it usually refers to a more public event, such as would be held by an entire city (say, Bath) or a renowned hostess. (See: Queen's drawing-room, under Q.)

drawn and quartered - Hanged until almost dead, the head cut off, the bowels cut out (and possibly the heart.) The corpse was quartered, then buried (or burned, or mounted above the road as a warning.) The practice had pretty much ended by the late 17th century; the last man to have this punishment fully carried out was one David Tyrie, a traitor, in August, 1782. Later, others were issued the same sentence but only were hanged, and sometimes also beheaded. (You may care to see: punishments.)

dresses, women's - An entire book could be written on the subject of Regency era women's dresses. Here I only seek to define a few particulars. *One important note*: Young women during the Regency, until they married, almost exclusively wore gowns made in white, cream, or pastels.

- Dress and gown are basically interchangeable terms.
- *Day dresses* were just that, made for the day (not the evening,) having higher necklines and usually long sleeves, and were made of less luxurious fabrics than evening dresses. Still, one tried to make one's day dresses as fashionable as possible.
- Any dress could be worn with gloves. In a time without central heating, gloves (and hats) helped provide warmth. (Long gloves were usually reserved for the evening.)
- All dresses could be dyed black for mourning, or be styled with black trimmings for half-mourning. (Half-mourning also allowed for gray or lavender dresses.)

What makes it an afternoon dress? - Intended to be seen. Worn for calling on others, tea parties, walks in the park. A walking dress was an afternoon dress.

What makes it a ball gown? - Was an evening dress. It tended to have more of a bell or fuller shape. Her ball gowns were a lady's most embroidered, trimmed, and impressive dresses. Could be two gowns in one, with a sheerer one worn over an opaque gown, with the sheer one perhaps full length or three-quarters long. You could call a ball gown an evening gown.

What makes it a carriage dress? - (Also called: a traveling dress.) They were made of heartier fabrics, to withstand the stresses of travel. Had less trim, (which could be crushed in a carriage's close quarters.)

What makes it a court gown? - (AKA: court dress.) Only worn when one went to the royal court, particularly for one's presentation at the Queen's drawing-room (a young lady's entry into society.) Court gowns weren't Regency fashions at all, but a specific look dating back to Georgian days (and were required; one could not substitute a more modern look): hooped skirt, lappets, long train, and hair done in an elaborate, old-fashioned style.

What makes it a dinner gown? - Was an evening dress. Not as ornate as a ball gown, but still finely made, and more revealing (think décolletage) than a day dress, although they could also have long sleeves, if desired. Note: gloves were removed in order to dine.

What makes it an evening dress? - An evening gown was worn for more formal occasions (such as a party, or a musicale,) and was often made from more luxurious fabrics. They were a lady's finest gowns (particularly her ball gowns.) Thinner than afternoon dresses, with lower necklines and sleeves often shorter (which allowed for long gloves.) Evening dresses were made of fine muslin, satin, silk, light taffeta, and other fine fabrics. (See: *ball gown*, above.)

What makes it a morning dress? - A day dress, they weren't intended for having company nor for going out. (See: *walking dress*, for the latter.) Morning dresses were less decorated, possibly cheaper, possibly repaired, intended for being at home/not being observed by others outside the family. An old afternoon dress might be turned into a morning dress (often by removing and reusing decorations.) It was the Regency equivalent of sweats and a hoodie (although that comparison is a bit tongue in cheek, as you must recall that the standard of dressing was much higher in the past.)

What makes it an opera gown? - Much like a dinner dress, it was for the evening. Not as ornate as a ball gown, but still finely made, and more revealing than a day dress. One would almost certainly wear long gloves with an opera dress.

What makes it a promenade gown? - (See: walking dress, below.)

What makes it a riding habit? - (Also called: riding dress.) Tended to be modest, simple, and sturdy. There was a fashion for imitating the style of men's uniforms (and hat styles, while riding.) Had a very full skirt, to cover the lady's legs while riding sidesaddle. She would have to carry the excess fabric over her arm while not mounted.

What makes it a round gown? - Started as a Georgian era dress, and stuck around until the empire-waist styles of the Regency, lasting until ca. 1806-10, but after that would have been outmoded. It had a soft, rounded silhouette, full where it was gathered, straight sleeves that stopped at the elbows, and a train. Think Marie Antoinette; also think what it would look like if a dress and a robe were combined into one garment.

What makes it a walking dress? - Also called a promenade dress, a walking dress was intended to be worn outside. Therefore, one's walking dress ensemble must include the dress, a head covering, an outer garment (pelisse, redingote, spencer, or wrap) and gloves. A walking dress was the most decorative day dress. Often made of cotton muslin.

- See: fabrics.
- You may care to see: buttons.

dressmakers -

- See: Aldgate.

- See: clothing.
- See: drapers.
- See: mantuamaker.
- See: milliner.
- See: modiste.
- You may care to see: dresses, women's.

drinking water - Was provided in London via: fountains; piped in from outside the city; and wells. One *did not* drink from the Thames River, it was too polluted.

- See: Metropolitan Drinking Fountain and Cattle Trough Association - For watering horses.
- SEE: WATER.
- See: Thames, the.
- See: the INNS/PUBS section - The notes at the start of.

drinks, alcoholic -

- See: beer.
- See: breweries.
- See: food/drinks.
- See: the INNS/PUBS section - All the notes under.

driving on the left - On roads, the British practice of. (See: London Bridge, under the BRIDGES section, the paragraph on: driving on the left.)

driving tests - The testing of automobile drivers began in Britain in 1934, and were voluntary. Compulsory testing dates from 1935. (You may care to see: traffic lights/signals.)

dropsy - An ailment that today would be called edema, organ swelling due to fluid increase. Term dates from at least the 16th century.

Drury House - Built in the 16th century. John Donne (poet/cleric) once lived in a building adjoining this house. Demolished in the early 19th century. Area became known as Covent Garden. (See: Drury Lane.)

Drury Lane - Covent Garden. It was the main thoroughfare between High Holborn and the Strand (at least until Kingsway was built in 1905.) This street was described as "old" when its first record appeared in 1199. Prior to the 16th C. it was known by several names, such as Via de Aldewych, and Fortescu Lane. Drury House was built in the mid 16th C., and from then this street took the Drury name. Gentlemen's homes were here by 1650. Piece-brokers worked here, buying ragged garments to cut out the better pieces, which they in turn sold to jobbing tailors for patches. During the Regency era, Drury Lane (*the theatre*) was here.

- See: Drury House - At its own listing.
- See: Drury Lane, Theatre Royal, in the THEATRES section.

- Coal Yard: (See under C.)
- Princes Street. (See under P.)

Drury Lane Theatre - Russell Street, Covent Garden. (See: Drury Lane, Theatre Royal, in the THEATRES section.)

Duck Lane - Westminster. Was part of the notorious slum Devil's Acre. (See at its own listing.) Now called: St. Matthew Street.

Dudley Street - Seven Dials, Covent Garden. Described as squalid. (See: Seven Dials/Monmouth Street, in the list.)

dueling spots - Dueling (British spelling: duelling) was technically illegal in England, which is why the combatants almost always met in isolated areas. Dueling was generally not considered murder until the 1840s.

- See: Barn Elms.
- See: Battersea Fields.
- See: Belgravia/Five Fields.
- See: Chalk Farm.
- See: delope - To fire one's dueling pistol into the air.
- See: Five Fields.
- See: Hampstead Heath.
- See: Hyde Park. (See: Hyde Park/duels.)
- See: Kensington Palace/Kensington Gardens.
- See: Pickering Place - Purportedly the site of the last English duel.
- See: Primrose Hill. (See: Regent's Park/Primrose Hill.)
- See: Putney Heath.
- See: Red Lion Square/Rathbone Place.
- See: Sloane Square/Bloody Bridge.
- See: Wimbledon Common.

Duke of Wellington Place - Official title of Hyde Park Corner. (See: Hyde Park Corner.)

Duke of York Column - 1834. Waterloo Place. Bronze statue. This Duke of York was: Prince Frederick Augustus (George IV's brother, 2nd son of George III) Commander-in-Chief of the British Army. He instigated much needed reforms within the army. He is the duke from which derived the nursery rhyme: "The grand old Duke of York, he had ten thousand men..." The column is designed in the Tuscan style; atop it stands the duke in uniform. 40 meters (131 feet) high. Because the duke was deep in debt when he died, it was joked they had to build the column high enough that he could escape his debtors. Still, the duke was rather well thought of by his men, and when he died in 1827, British soldiers donated one day's wage to help build the column.

Duke of York Headquarters - Chelsea, the King's Road. 1801, established by the Duke of York; built by John Sanders (pupil to Sir John Soane.) During the Regency it would have been known as the ROYAL MILITARY ASYLUM,) a children's charity school wherein the pupils were dressed in bright red-and-blue uniforms. These were children of soldiers killed in battle.

In the early 19th C. there were 1,000 children housed here. The children either were eventually returned to their families, or else sent into the army.

In 1846 it became a boys' school.

In 1892 it was renamed the Duke of York's Royal Military School.

(See: Royal Military Asylum.)

Duke of York Steps - Carlton House Terrace, Westminster. 1828-33. Steps down from Waterloo Place to the Mall, where the Duke of York Column resides, and which the steps lead to.

- See: Carlton House Terrace/Duke of York Steps.
- See: Duke of York Column.
- See: Regent's Park.

Duke of York Street - St. James's, off Portman Square, Mayfair. 18th century residential street; is now elegant shops, petite restaurants, and flats.

Duke's Place - St. James's. This area was first occupied by the Priory of Holy Trinity, Christ Church, until it was dissolved in 1531. Henry VIII gave the land to Sir Thomas Audley, who built homes here (although there were yet in the early 19th C. some fragments of the old priory yet to be seen.) Audley's son-in-law inherited; he was the Duke of Norfolk, and that is when the street took on the name Duke's Place.

- See: Houndsditch.
- See: St. James's, Duke Place, in the CHURCHES section.
- See: Synagogue.

Duke's Row - (See: Somers Town/Duke's Row.)

Dulwich - Southwark. (Pronounced "DULL-idge" or "DULL-itch.") Georgian houses/village setting. The college, chapel and almshouses built by Edward Alleyn (contemporary of Shakespeare) are still standing. Restful, beautiful district; country aspects. The common was enclosed in 1805.

- Dulwich College: (See at its own listing.)
- Dulwich Picture Gallery: (AKA: Dulwich College Art Gallery, which part of the gallery is in the adjoining 17th C. building. AKA: Dulwich Art Gallery.) College Road. England's oldest public art gallery, begun in 1811, completed in 1814 by Sir John Soane (the art collection was truly begun when Edward Alleyn left 39 paintings to the college; the school's legacy was expanded in 1811 by 371 more

paintings from the art dealers Noel Desenfans and Sir Francis Bourgeois.) Had skylights to provide better viewing. It was Britain's first public (that is, publicly funded) art gallery.

- Dulwich Village: "Storybook hamlet," north of Dulwich College. Until 1619 this area was mostly cornfields. The college's success enticed monied men, who built "substantial" houses here.
    - Belair: 1765 villa. Now a restaurant.
- Horniman Museum: 1901.
- North Dulwich: Edwardian housing.
    - Dulwich House: In the early 19th century Thomas Lott (timber merchant) lived here.
- West Dulwich: Borders Dulwich, Tulse Hill, and West Norwood. Not known by this name until 1926. (See under W.)

Dulwich College - (Full name: College of God's Gift.) Established in 1619 by Edward Alleyn (actor,) in Dulwich Manor, which he had bought in 1605. Designed by Inigo Jones. The school was for the education of poor boys, plus almshouses. Its eastern wing dates from 1739-40. This old corporation was dissolved in 1857, its members pensioned off for life. Moved in 1866-70, about 1/4 mile/0.4 km from where the founding building was, into a building "much restored" by Barry. Extensive playing-grounds lie to the north of the "new" college grounds.

Dulwich College Picture Gallery - (See: Dulwich/Dulwich College Picture Gallery.)

Dunraven Street - Known as Norfolk Street after 1840, a block between Green Street and Marble Arch.

- 22: Dates from ca. 1820. It faces onto Park Lane, so it has been suggested its address ought to have been 132 Park Lane.

Durham House - The Strand. Built in 1345; described as a noble palace, for Bishop Thomas Hatfield. Passed through royal and notable hands, until in ca. 1768 when it was pulled down so that brothers Robert and James Adam (architects) could build the Adelphi Buildings. (See: Adelphi, the.)

Durham Place - Started life as the Bishop of Durham's medieval mansion, along the Strand, parish of St. Margaret, Westminster, dates from at least 1220. Still belonged to the Bishop(s) of Durham through the 15-16th centuries, until Edward VI lived here before he became king; indeed, over the years many famous names resided here, including Sir Walter Raleigh (author), King Philip of Spain (while visiting England,) and Philip, the 4th Earl of Pembroke. The 5th Earl of Pembroke pulled down the house, and erected here new homes. Also, the Earl of Salisbury managed to get his hands on land here, and built a "beautiful" building here, said to echo the Royal Exchange, a market with an arcade and shops, ca. 1609. James I wanted it called Britain's Burse, but the name didn't stick and it was usually called the New Exchange. It had a brief vogue, but didn't do as well as anticipated, existing only until 1737. Eleven houses were built on its site, but were demolished in 1923.

Durham Place became known as Lambeth Road in 1876.

- 3: Ordinary 3-story house bought by William Bligh (Vice-Admiral/of *Mutiny on the Bounty* fame) in 1794. Lived here (or at least his wife did, while he sailed and was imprisoned,) until he moved to Kent after his wife's death in 1812. (Now known as 100 Lambeth Road.)

Dutch House - (See: Kew Palace.)

duties - (See: taxes.)

Dutton's - Circulating library in Gracechurch Street. Existed by 1804.

Duval Street - Marylebone.

Duval Street - Spitalfields. Rookery/slum area. Built in 1674, first called Datchet Street; but soon called Dorset Street. Short and narrow. Site of one of the Jack the Ripper murders, 1888. Renamed (no doubt due to its infamy) in 1904 to: Duval Street. (See: Dorset Street.)

Dyers' Hall - For the Worshipful Company of Dyers. The present hall on Dowgate Hill, off Upper Thames Street, was built in 1840; had new/more buildings by 1856.

First mentioned in 1188. The Dyers dyed wool, silk, and leather. In 1372 Dyers' wives were "associated as parties" (since they contributed as much labor as their husbands.) In 1704 Queen Anne granted the Dyers a new charter that gave them authority for London and ten surrounding miles (16 km.)

The first hall (1483) was in Anchor Lane, in the Vintry. Its second locale west of London Bridge (given to them in 1545,) is now marked by Dyers Hall Wharf; that hall burned in the Great Fire of 1666. Burned again in 1681. By at least 1731 they were located in two houses (they'd owned and leased to the Salters' Company until 1731); these two houses were located on College Street (at one time called Elbow Lane); the two houses were rebuilt into a Hall; it fell down in 1768. Hall rebuilt in 1770, same site; unusable by 1831, and taken down by 1838. That's when (in 1840) the Dyers moved to 11-13 Dowgate Hill.

Livery company. 13th in the order of precedence.

(See: Vintners' Hall, note on swans.)

Dyott Street - Bloomsbury. Named for a Stuart-era family who had a house here; its early name had been Maidenhead Close. It was known as Dyott Street during the Regency. Ca. 1884 this street was renamed as George Street.

-E-

Ealing - Middlesex. A quiet village, with no real urban spreading until the late 19th and early 20th centuries. In 1902 was dubbed "the Queen of the Suburbs" because of its greenery and half-city/half-country feel.

- Ealing Broadway: Shopping and leisure area, 1838.
- Ealing Common: 40 acres, open space, from the Middle Ages (at which time it covered 70 acres); the difference was lost to encroachment.
- Little Ealing: (See under L.)
- North Ealing: Described as being "barely in Ealing at all." The name is little used. Early building here was mainly in the Castlebar Hill and Cuckoo Hill areas, with a wider expanse (Brentham, Castlebar, Hanger Hill, and Pitshanger) not coming along until the 20th century.
- Northfields: CHAMBERS LONDON GAZETTEER says: "The south-western corner of Ealing, with a history of fruit-growing and tightrope-walking..." (as in entertainment) "...From the 14th century this area was part of the manor of Coldhall, or West Ealing. Great and Little Northfields were two large fields in the late Middle Ages, lying in the extreme west of Ealing parish. By the mid 17th century Northfield Lane (later Avenue) linked Little Ealing with the Uxbridge road and the manor house of Coldhall probably stood near the southern end of the lane at that time." The Steel family had near-industrial apple orchard market-gardens here in the 19th century (probably mid.)
    - Little Northfield: Orchard here by 1738.
    - Plough Inn: Existed by at least 1722, rebuilt several times. Still exists.
- Pitshanger Manor: In 1800 Sir John Soane (architect) bought and rebuilt it. (See under P.)
- St. Mary's: South of Uxbridge Road. The old 12th C. church fell down in 1729, a new one being built prior to 1820. New church rebuilt in 1873, by S. S. Teulon.
- South Ealing: (See under S.)
- West Ealing:
        - ➢ See: Ealing Dean - At its own listing.
        - ➢ See: Northfields, above.
    - London County Mental Hospital of St. Bernard. 1829-30.

- St. Mary: 1782. Rebuilt 1841.

Ealing Dean - Ealing. (Ancient name: Ealinge Dene.) This was the 18th C name for what is now known as West Ealing. "Dean" means a wooded vale. Was mostly farmlands and a few orchards, with two coaching inns. One of the inns, the Green Man, bragged it could stable 100 horses. Gentlemen's villas came later in the 19th century.

Ealing Park - (See: Little Ealing/Place House.)

Earl's Court - Chelsea. (Also seen as: Earls Court.) The DeVeres owned much of Chelsea land. When the DeVeres were elevated to an earldom, the manor house became known as "Earl's Court," which centered in the area that now bears its name. John Hunter (Scottish surgeon/founder of the Hunterian School of Medicine) lived here in 1783.

The square was built in the 1820s; currently described as a "Victorian square." In the present day, it is a bit of a rough area. It is also known for its exhibition center and concert venue.

- Ferris wheel: 1895. (See: Ferris wheel, under F.)

earthenware shops - What the British generally call china shops. Also sold coffee, tea, chocolate. Note, however, that earthenware is made from common rough clays, while china is made from finer-particle, harder to manipulate, and smoother clays. (See: china.)

East Acton - Ealing/Hammersmith/Fulham. A farming village by 1294. Some country retreats here by the mid 17th century.

- John Perryn (goldsmith) lived here in 1654. He bequeathed his land to the Goldsmiths' Company, which went on to acquire more land nearby, established 20 almshouses (and later helped promote a train station here.)

East Cheap - (See: Eastcheap.)

East End Road - (See: Finchley/East End Road.)

East End, the - A later 19th C. term (still used) that once loosely encompassed Spitalfields, Stepney, and Whitechapel - those areas east of the City. Regency folk would most likely have referred to the area as "east of Moorfields."

The Huguenots lived here (late 17th century.) Because the wind blew from the east, the traditionally poor area did not burn in the Great Fire of 1666. The East End is famous as a garment district (ever since the fleeing-to-here Huguenots brought their weaving skills into the district.) It was also (up to the 18th C.) known for soap boiling, and tanning. During the 18th C. distilling, brewing, and sugar-refining came in.

Up to the mid 1800s the area was just a few villages, not yet considered a byword for living in an impoverished state. After the mid 1800s the term "East End" gained the connotation of a "poor" or "immigrant" area, since the poor and "colorful" were often pushed into London's lesser desired districts, with the East End being one of them (being in the mid 19th C. more industrial than decorative.)

The 19th C. brought in the docks, and consequently dockworkers. So it is fair to say that throughout the 17-19th centuries, this area continually provided employment opportunities, but it consistently also resulted in overcrowding.

"East End" and "West End" have become shorthand ways of saying: blue-collared/underprivileged, and fashionable/privileged.

- ➢ See: Cockney.
- ➢ See: Mile End Waste - For the East End's open space.
- ➢ See: West End - The East End's antithesis.
- ➢ See: Whitechapel.

East Ham - Newham. Remained rural until the late 19th century. Its Bangladeshi and Pakistani residents came in in the 20th century.

- St. Mary Magdalene: (See under the CHURCHES section.)

East India Company - (AKA: The British East India Company.) Founded by British merchants. Charter granted by Elizabeth I in 1600.

It was headquartered from 1621-38 at the location that became Crosby Hall. (See: Chelsea/Crosby Hall.)

The Company traded with India and the Far East. Spices, cotton, indigo, saltpeter, silks, tea, and more.

It isn't much of an exaggeration to call the East India Company the virtual ruler of India in the 18th century. Yet they had their troubles. The EIC had rivals, but the Company managed to monopolize British trade with the Far East until 1698, when a second East India Company emerged; war forced a 1709 merger, however, under the name United East India Company. Then, DISCOVERING AMERICAN HISTORY IN ENGLAND notes: "The Colonial unrest in America..." (the Boston Tea Party ships were of the East India Company line) "...resulted in serious financial difficulties for the EIC and led to restructuring in 1773 and 1784 that gave the British government more direct involvement in the company."

The company was abolished by the India Act in 1858, and the company was dissolved in 1874. The site is now occupied by Lloyds of London (since 1986.)

- ➢ See: Board of Control.
- ➢ See: docks/Howland Great Wet Dock.
- ➢ See: East India House.
- ➢ See: India.

East India Dock - Completed in 1806. (See: docks/East India Dock.)

East India House - Corner of Leadenhall Street and Lime Street, the City. The site was first an

Elizabethan mansion called Craven House. The East India Company was first here in 1648. DISCOVERING AMERICAN HISTORY IN ENGLAND writes: "From 1648 to 1746 East India House occupied the former mansion house of Sir William Craven on Leadenhall Street, the site where Lloyd's of London now has its modern office building." Entirely rebuilt in 1726-29. Enlarged in 1799, its building was called humble and unpretentious. Pulled down in 1862, four years after the abolition of the East India Company. (See: East India Company.)

East London Mission - 1865. (See: Salvation Army.)

East Smithfield - Tower Hamlets. In ancient days the open land south of Aldgate was called East Smithfield, near to the Tower of London. There were 14th C. cemeteries here, following the Black Death. The land became the property of the Crown following the Dissolution of the Monasteries. The Royal Mint was here briefly ca. 1809-15 (when it burned,) with little of its building remaining today. (See: Smithfield, comment at.)

Eastbury Square - (See: Barking/Eastbury Square.)

Eastcastle Street - In the Regency would have been called Castle Street. (See: Fitzrovia/Castle Street.)

- 88 Castle Street: Chopin gave his first London recital here.
- King's Road: (See under K.)
- St. Peter's: 1826.

Eastcheap - (Name chosen to distinguish the area from Westcheap, the latter long since called Cheapside.) First mentioned in 1214 records as "Estchepe." Continuation to the west, of Great Tower Street. By 1827 references to the area as "Great Eastcheap" had all changed over to just "Eastcheap," (when King William Street eliminated the "Great" part.) Medieval meat market; long gone by the time of the Regency.

Eaton Place, 165 - Belgravia. The invented address of the Bellamy family of BBC's *Upstairs, Downstairs* television fame. (There is actually an Eaton Place in Eaton Square, but the filming was of the real number 65, with a "1" painted on for the purposes of the program.)

Eaton Square - Belgravia. Takes its name from Eaton Hall, Cheshire, the country seat of the landlords (the Grosvenors.) The square was begun in 1826, but not completed until 1855. Currently described as a parkway with two long, narrow green strips divided by King's Road traffic. The houses tended to be big and gracious, were built around a fenced garden, had minute patio gardens to the rear, which opened on to mews. Has a long connection to legal/parliamentary circles.

Ebury Square - Pimlico. The square (and Ebury Street) are both named for Ebury Farm, which resided here in the 16th C., and which once belonged to Elizabeth I. Became part of the Grosvenor estate in 1676. The square was founded on the 430 acre estate in 1820.

Ebury Street - Ebury Square, north edge of Pimlico. (See: Ebury Square.)

- 22B: Ian Fleming (author of the James Bond novels) lived here in 1936-39. Had been a 19th C. chapel.
  42: Lord Alfred Tennyson (poet) lived here in 1847.
- 180: Mozart (composer) lived here in 1764, writing his first symphony here.
- Coleshill Flats: 1871 tenements.

Eccleston Square - Pimlico. Begun in 1835. Named for one of the Duke of Westminster's country properties at Eccleston, Cheshire.

- 13: Sir Francis Legatt Chantrey (sculptor) lived here from 1811 until the year of his death, 1841.
- 33: Winston Churchill (Prime Minister) lived here from 1908-11.

Ede & Ravenscroft - Presently located at 93 Chancery Lane. Tailoring. Established 1689, as a tailor's shop; became robemakers to the Royal family (since the time of William and Mary.) The robemaking was taken over by Francis Stone in 1770; his son-in-law took over in 1797, running it under his own name of William Webb for 35 years; he moved his business to Fleet Street in 1827. Joseph Ede became his apprentice in 1811; Webb's son took over when Webb died in 1831. Ede's uncle bailed out the then struggling business, which became known as "Adam and Ede." An Ede married a Ravenscroft in 1861, and hence the current name. Humphrey Ravenscroft (the founder's grandson) invented the white horse hair wig (we know to this day) in 1822, before then they had been black. This company had also (in addition to robes) been making wigs for judges and barristers since 1726. They have a tradition of sewing their label in upside-down, presumably so the label will be right-side up when their robes are hung on a peg.

Edgware - Barnet/Harrow. (Before 1965, it was in Middlesex.) Dates from 975. In the far past was also written as Eggesware and Edeworthg. Principally built along ancient Watling Street. By the mid 18th century Edgware was becoming an important coaching halt northwest out of London. (See: Watling Street.)

- Newlands: Barnet. Lies between Brockley Hill and Edgware Way; was a part of Edgware manor, which from 1443 belonged to All Souls College, Oxford.
  - Bromfield House: Early 19th century. Stucco. Now demolished.
  - Green Lane: Now called Piper's Green. Dates from at least 1597. The common land here is now a sports ground.
- St. Margaret's: Parish church. Corner of High Street and Station Road. Dates from 1375. Rebuilt 1705, 1764, and in 1845.

Edgeware Road - (Also written as: Edgware Road.) North of Hyde Park. Later Maida Vale (1830-40s, although the name change was not officially granted until 1868.) Connected Paddington to Marylebone, it is one of London's oldest roads. Long known as a traffic thoroughfare and a shopping district. (Note: There is another Edgware Road to the north; when people spoke of Edgware Road they usually meant this one separating Paddington from Marylebone.)

Edmonton - Enfield. Two miles/3.2 km north of Tottenham. Ancient. Would have been market-gardens here ca. 1800. At the same time the gentry began moving out; described as the area then mostly housing retired weavers.

- All Saints: Parish church. Perpendicular style. In the churchyard Charles Lamb (essayist) and his sister, Mary, are buried.
- Lower Edmonton: (See under L.)
- Pymmes Park: The area dates from 1327; an Elizabethan mansion stood here, built for William Pymme. Belonged to Lord Burghley by 1582; remained to that family until 1801. Owned 1808-1899 by the Ray family. Park open to the public in 1906.
- Salisbury House: Late Tudor. Built for the Bishop of Carlisle. West of Durham Place, opposite side of Ivy Lane. Occupied by a series of lords. Rebuilt in 1602. Torn down; the entire Salisbury estate was sold in 1888, and Shell-Mex House now covers most of the area.
- Upper Edmonton: (See under U.)

education - FOR WOMEN: Primarily educated at home, although a minority attended private schools, either because they came from money, or conversely were so poor or "fallen" (were prostitutes, or had borne children outside marriage) that they qualified for charity-funded schooling.

FOR MEN: In Britain, the terms public school and private school (still) mean the opposite of what they mean in America: a *public* school was *not* free to attend, and its students tended to be well-to-do (or sponsored.) Plus the students tended to board there. There was no *private* school system (such as in the State paid for/oversaw the schools, again private having the opposite of the American meaning) in the 18th and into the 19th centuries.

For those less financially blessed, or with the means but perhaps not so well-born nor inclined toward public schooling, there were also parish schools, charity schools, and endowed grammar schools to choose from; in 1815 the latter numbered around 700. (See: charities - To expand on how the poor might be educated.)

The great public schools included: Charterhouse School, Eton College, Harrow School, Rugby School, Shrewsbury School, Westminster School, and Winchester College.

IT MUST BE NOTED: that in the main, the masses received little or no education. Girls trained for domestic service (often residing *in situ*) and boys were apprenticed out to tradesmen or as farm laborers. In 1800, 40% of (all) men could not write their name at the time of marriage; 60% of women could not. In 1810, three-quarters of agricultural workers were illiterate. School attendance was not mandatory for children in Britain until 1891 (at that time enforced up to age 14.)

For ADVANCED EDUCATION, one attended University (ex: Cambridge or Oxford,) which were Anglican and therefore barred dissenters; the latter who would instead possibly pursue education in Edinburgh or Leiden in Scotland, or on the Continent.

- See: colleges/universities.
- See: pencils.
- See: schools.

Education Dock - (See: docks/Education Dock.)

Edward Street - Off Duke Street, near Manchester Square. By 1815 this street was swallowed up by the construction of Regent Street.

Edwardes Square - Kensington. Built in 1811-19 on 11 acres leased from the 2nd Lord Kensington and named for his father, William Edwardes. The central garden dates from 1820.

- Earl's Terrace:
  - 4: The novelist Mrs. Elizabeth Inchbald lived here in 1816.

Eel Pie Island - Richmond. First called Twickenham Ait (in Medieval times.) The largest island in the Thames. Henry VIII used it as a "courting ground." In the 18th C. it was used by boaters and picnickers, and you could indeed buy pies here made from locally caught eels. Edwardians built summer homes here. In the 20th C. became famous for launching rock groups (who played in the local jazz club) and has been dubbed as "the place where the Sixties began."

eels - A commonly eaten fish in England. NOT sold at Billingsgate Fish Market; sold by Dutch fishermen moored in the Thames; this was allowed because the Dutch eel vendors had fed London after the Great Fire of 1666 when so many resources were destroyed. (You may care to see: Billingsgate.)

Egerton Crescent - Kensington. Designed by George Basevi, built by James Bonnin, 1840s. At first called Brompton Crescent, until 1896. Called the "most expensive street in Britain" in 2013, the houses pricing at an average £7.4 million; 2nd most expensive by 2015 at £7.5 million.

Egremont House - (See: Cambridge House.)

Egyptian Hall - Over time there are/were two:

- See: British Museum/Egyptian Hall - 20th century housing for antiquities.
- See: Piccadilly/Egyptian Hall - The Bullock one, in the Mansion House.

Egyptian House - 1905, built on the site of the old Egyptian Hall. (See, above, the Piccadilly one.)

ei - An ancient word for "marsh." Still reflected in place names such as Bermondsey (that is, Bermond's Ei.)

Elder Street - Spitalfields, 1720s.

- 36 and 75: Built ca. 1725-80.

Elephant and Castle - Southwark. Sometimes referred to simply as "the Elephant." The district's proper name is "Newington," but it's generally referred to as Elephant and Castle to avoid confusing it with Stoke Newington. "Elephant and Castle" is a corruption of: *Infante of Castile.*

"Newington" grew ca. 1200 in support of Lambeth Palace. It remained a farming village until the last half of the 18th C., but with some industry, including making clay tobacco pipes.

A blacksmith's forge was established here in 1641; converted in 1740 to a tavern displaying an elephant with a castle on its back. (See: Cutlers' Company, which also uses the elephant and castle symbol.) In the 19th century this area's architecture was largely made of red brick. The tavern became a busy coaching halt, so that the road junction came to take the same name of Elephant and Castle, and thereby so did the district. (See: Elephant and Castle, under the INNS/PUBS section.)

- Metropolitan Tabernacle: 1861.
- Trinity Church: Newington. 1824, on land that had belonged since 1661 to the Corporation of Trinity House. Became Henry Wood Hall (recording venue) in 1975.

elevators - Post-Regency. In England, called a: lift. (See: Westminster Palace Hotel.)

Elgin Marbles, the - "Elgin" is pronounced with a hard "g" as in "golf", not a soft "jin" sound as in "George."

- ➢ See: Bloomsbury/British Museum/Montagu House.
- ➢ See: Burlington House.

Elizabeth I, Queen - Statue of. Surprisingly the *only* statue of this renowned 16th C. queen, located in St. Dunstan-in-the-West. (See: St. Dunstan-in-the-West, in the CHURCHES section.)

Elizabeth Tower - (See: Big Ben.)

Elliott's Lawn - (See: Westminster Cathedral.)

Elms, The - Clapham, Southwark. Home of William Hewer (manservant/trusted friend to Samuel Pepys, the diarist) here, built 1754.

Eltham Palace - On the slopes southeast of Blackheath, Kent. 14th C. courtyard. In the 16th C. the palace's three parks (Great Park, Horn Park, and Middle Park) were cut down for shipbuilding wood. In the Regency, this was a moldering ruin of a palace. Restored in 1934: Stephen Courtauld restored the banqueting hall (which, along with the bridge, is all that remains from the ancient palace.) The Great Hall had originally been built in 1479 for Edward IV. A former royal residence, although long unused and now managed by English Heritage, which restored it in 1999 and opened it to the public.

- Eltham Lodge: Built in 1664 on leased Great Park land, by Hugh May. In the Dutch style. The park is now the Royal Blackheath Golf Course and the lodge its clubhouse.
- Eltham Park estate: 1900.

Ely Chapel - Pronounced ELL-ee. (See: St. Etheldreda, under the CHURCHES section.)

Ely Court - Off Hatton Gardens. Old.

- 1: Ye Old Mitre Tavern. (See under the INNS/PUBS section.)

Ely Place - Narrow alley, at the sound end of Hatton Garden, gated road, last privately owned street in London. The site had been where Ely Palace had stood, 1290-1772, for the Bishop(s) of Ely. (See: Holborn/Ely Place.)

  - ➢ See: Holborn/Ely Place.
  - ➢ See: Ye Old Mitre, under the INNS/PUBS section.

- 14: St. Etheldreda's Chapel. (See under the CHURCHES section.) In the Regency, would have been known as Ely Chapel.

embalming - The practice was invented by 17th century Dutchmen, but did not become common in the western word until the early 1860s. (You may care to see: burials.)

Embankment, the - (AKA: the Victoria Embankment. AKA: Thames Embankment.) 1864; opened in 1870. Runs from Westminster to Blackfriars. This was the grand Victorian improvement to the waterfront along the Thames, resulting in river flood control, and greenery along the bank's sweep.

- Cleopatra's Needle. (See under C.)
- Sphinx, the: Sculpture. At the foot of Cleopatra's Needle. 1878 (or 1882.)

enclosure - The act of. (See: common, the.)

Encyclopaedia Britannica - Was first published in 1768, in Edinburgh, Scotland. The first edition was three volumes. Second edition was 10 volumes. The fourth edition (1801-10) was 20 volumes. No longer published except online. (Not to be confused with *A Dictionary of the English Language*, the first English language dictionary, written by Samuel Johnson, 1755. See: dictionary.)

Endell Street - West End. First known as Belton Street. Rebuilt in 1846 and renamed as Endell Street.

Enfield - Middlesex. Dates from the Middle Ages. Once was 8,349 acres, which contained a famous

Chase. (See: Enfield Chase, at its own listing.) There were numerous fine gentlemen's homes here by the 18th century. In the 19th C. this area became known for gun-making. (See: Enfield Lock, below.) Enfield was the second largest Middlesex parish by 1831.

- Church Street: From ca. 1632.
- Enfield Chase: (See at its own listing.)
- Enfield Grammar School: 1557.
- Enfield Highway: Dates from at least 1572, at which time it was known as Cocksmiths End. The present name dates from the mid 18th century.
    - St. James's Church: 1832.
- Enfield Lock: 1804. Royal Small Arms Factory, for the manufacture of *muskets*; this began Enfield's association with gunmaking. The first (and renowned) Enfield ***rifles*** were made here in 1853. The RSAF was closed in the 1980s; Enfield Lock was rebuilt in 1922. (See: Royal Small Arms Factory.)
- Enfield Town: (Essentially, the green of Enfield.) The 16th C. brought inns, and houses began to encircle the green. A 1632 marketplace led to a street plan, including Church Street, London Road, and Silver Street.
    - Gentlemen's Row: Georgian and Victorian houses remain here.
    - Trent Park: Given to Sir Richard Jebb, George III's favorite physician. Mansion of brick, rebuilt 1894. 1,000 acres, with a lake of several acres, which the terrace faces.

Enfield Chase - Enfield, Middlesex. Used by kings for deer hunting. Took on this name when the area was enclosed in 1777, disafforested in 1779, at which time its agriculture centered on dairy farming and hay-making. By 1819 it was renamed (after the Australian locale) Botany Bay. First chapel here in 1851.

Enfield Lock -

- See: Enfield/Enfield Lock.
- See: Royal Small Arms Factory.

engagement - (See: marriage.)

Engine Street - Piccadilly, Mayfair. (See: Brick Street.)

engineers -

- See: Society of Civil Engineers.
- See: Well Street.

Englefields - 300+ years as pewterers. (See: Shoreditch/Cheshire Street/Englefields.)

Ennismore Gardens - Knightsbridge. 1848-55.

entertainments - Of the Regency era. (See: activities/entertainments/sports, under A, various listings.)

envelopes - Not used for letters until the 1840s. (See: Post, the.)

Epping Forest - In the county of Essex. Approximately 5,000 acres. Dedicated as a public area in 1882 by Queen Victoria. Called Epping Forest as early as 1600 (if not much earlier; prior to that it was called the Forest of Essex, and apparently was absolutely huge.) Illegal enclosures and land-robbing of park space for housing developments were on-going, being particularly rampant ca. 1850-70 (more land was absconded in these twenty years than in the previous 250 years.) As of 1851 the forest had shrunk to 3,000 acres. With the Epping Forest Act of 1878 - the forming of the Epping Forest Fund (Queen Victoria's dedication of 1882) - this practice of encroachment was severely curtailed. Unlike most London forests, this one is kept entirely natural.

Epsom (horse races) - (AKA: Epsom Downs.) Epsom Downs is in the town of Epsom. In the 17th C., the town was fashionable because of its mineral springs. Horse races/Epsom Derby were run here since 1780. Prinny took Mrs. Fitzherbert (his first, disallowed wife) here in 1787. The Derby, the Oaks, and other races are still run here.

Eros, statue of - 1893. (See: Piccadilly/Eros.)

Essex Court - Temple, the/Inns of Court. (See: Inns of Court/Temple/Middle Temple/Brick Court, and Essex Court.)

Essex House - Essex Street. (There are two Essex Houses, this one at the Strand end of Essex Street, and the "Leyton" one below.) Near St. Clement's Church. Built ca. 1680, known as Essex House. In 1774 it came into the possession of Unitarians, becoming a Unitarian chapel.

Essex House - Leyton. Now known as Walnut Tree House. (See: Leyton/Walnut Tree House.)

Essex Road - (See: Islington/Lower Street.)

Essex Street - Spitalfields. An old street. In 1845 was made an extension of Swallow Street.

ether - For surgeries. The University of London was the first to use ether during surgeries, 1846.

- See: anesthesia.
- See: laudanum.
- See: University of London.

Eton College - Public boys' school. Located across the Thames from Windsor. Built primarily along one long street leading from the college to Windsor Bridge (you can only walk across the bridge; no cars.)

Founded in 1440 by Henry VI (who himself was only 18 at the time.) On one side of the main road resides the Old Schools; on the other side are the New Schools, 1863.

A boy's uniform was a blue coat (with a double row of large brass buttons, the top left open to reveal a bit of white waistcoat underneath, with a ruffled shirt) and blue knee breeches. White cravat tied in a bow. Despite the appellation of 'college,' this school is for younger boys. Boys are aged 13-18; this would be something like High School is in America.

"Pop" is the name for a society of 24 boys who get to wear fancy waistcoats (as opposed to the regulation uniform one,) this kind of select company being founded in the 1820s.

- Eton College Chapel: 15th century. Eton's main chapel. Perpendicular style. Wooden roof replaced in the 1950s with concrete, now vaulted (where it hadn't been before.)
- Green, the: Where cricket, and undoubtedly other sports, were played.
- High Street: (AKA: Eton High Street.) Lined with "ancient and motley" buildings.
  - ➢ See: education - For explanation of private school vs. public school.
  - ➢ See: schools.

Euston Arch - Built 1837. Original entrance to Euston Station. Demolished in 1962-3.

Euston Road - Old road.

- ➢ See: New Road.
- ➢ See: Warren Street.

Euston Square - Camden. Began existence in the 1750s as part of the New Road; in the 1810s Bloomsbury had grown to meet this area. The road as "Euston Square" dates from 1813; not completed until 1831 (a second source said 1827.) Not really a 'square' as it is part of the road (as it was always planned to be.) Southern end was an open garden until 1926.

Examiner, The - A weekly liberal reformist journal, edited by Leigh Hunt (essayist/poet.) Lasted from 1808 to at least 1817.

Exchange -

- ➢ See: Baltic Exchange.
- ➢ See: Change - Explanation of abbreviation at.
- ➢ See: Corn Exchange.
- ➢ See: Exeter Exchange.
- ➢ See: Royal Exchange.
- ➢ See: Stock Exchange - (AKA: London Stocks Exchange.)

Exchange Alley - (AKA: Change Alley.)

- ➢ See: Change Alley.
- ➢ See: Garraway's.
- ➢ See: Jonathan's.

Exchequer, the - A sometimes used term for the Treasury.

- ➢ SEE: TREASURY.
- ➢ See: Westminster/Exchequer.

- See: Whitehall/Treasury.

Excise Office - Old Broad Street. Excise taxes were implemented in England in 1642. Was first housed in a brick mansion-house (it had belonged to one Sir John Frederick.) Needed more room, so in 1767 the offices moved to Gresham College (this site is now covered by a modern block.)

A PORTRAIT OF GEORGIAN LONDON says: "(These offices) receive the duties on beer, ale and spirituous liquors; on tea, coffee, and chocolate; on malt, hops, soap, starch, candles, paper, vellum, parchment and other exciseable commodities..."

Removed to Somerset House in 1848. Blended with the new Inland Revenue department in 1849.

Execution Dock - (See: docks/Execution Dock.)

executions - Public executions were abolished in 1868. Capital punishment was abolished entirely in 1965 (even for treason.)

- See: Marble Arch.
- See: Newgate Prison.
- See: punishments.
- See: Tower of London/"Other Places & Things"/Tower Green.
- See: Tyburn.

Exeter Exchange - (AKA: Exeter 'Change.) "Change" was often used as an abbreviation for "exchange." The Strand, ca. 1689; it was located on the north side, near Catherine Street; it was upstairs. Described as a covered bazaar. For years this exchange challenged (not very successfully) the Royal Exchange in the City. Pulled down in the late 1820s. There was a menagerie here, which was known as Pidcock's Menagerie. In 1826, the elephant was shot after going berserk.

Exeter Hall - 1831. Became the Strand Palace Hotel in 1909.

Exeter Street - Covent Garden. Original name of a portion of Hans Crescent, laid out in 1673, built in 1676. Was called Exeter Street in an 1834 document.

Exmouth Market - Mount Pleasant, Clerkenwell. A market place since the 1890s, 32 stalls. In the 19th C. this was a run-down area.

- 56: Joseph Grimaldi (the clown) lived here at one time.
- Holy Redeemer: (AKA: Our Most Holy Redeemer.) Roman Catholic interior. Italianate campanile, by John Dandro Sedding. Built in 1888.

Exmouth Street - (See: Sadler's Well/Exmouth Street.)

Eye Hospital -

- See: Charterhouse Square/London Dispensary.
- You may care to see: Braille - 1837.

➢ You may care to see: spectacles.

eyot - Denotes small islands, for the purpose of this listing in the Thames. (See: ait.)

-F-

fabrics - (This list is not all inclusive.) Fabrics available to Regency folk:

blonde - (AKA: blonde lace.) Unbleached silk bobbin lace, with a creamy color. Could be dyed, often in black.

bombazine - Seen as: bombazeen. Also as: bombasine.

broadcloth - So called because it was wider than one man could weave; it required two. High quality woolen fabric.

brocade - Jacquard weaving of cotton, with raised patterns showing damasks, florals, paisleys. (Jacquard weaving was invented in 1801.)

calico - Lightweight painted or printed cotton, name derived from Calcutta. (See: Merton.)

cambric - Cotton or linen calendared (treated with rollers or with heated glass tools to create a shiny texture.)

chintz - Came from India, and was expensive. (See: quilting.)

cotton - In 1806 the British cotton industry employed 90,000 factory workers and 184,000 handloom weavers. In the 1820s the power looms overtakes/displaces handlooms; the work shifts out of homes and into factories.

cotton-wool - Imported; was fairly new at the time of the Regency.

crape - (Also seen as: crepe.) Often seen in black, often for mourning. Silk fabric made with twisted yarns to achieve a crinkly surface.

damask - (See under D.)

dimity - Durable cotton woven with 2-3 warp cords woven together, often with checks or raised stripes.

duck - A general term for canvas-like fabrics, cotton, strong, plain.

flannel - Although its use was mostly associated with the old or infirm. Its name derives from Welsh for wool. Plain or twill weave, lightly napped, good for holding in warmth. Used with lineaments to make chest plasters for colds and coughs.

gauze - Cotton, but originally made of silk. Thin, open weave. Name derived from

Gaza, Egypt.

Holland cloth - Also called Irish cloth, used for shirts or to cover stored furniture.

kerseymere - A twilled woolen cloth, fine textured. Medium weight, for warmer weather.

lace

lace net

lawn - Plain weave, very fine. To be French lawn, it had a brittle and stiff finish.

leather - Not a fabric, a tanned animal hide, used for men's breeches.

linen - From flax.

lustring - (Also called: lutestring.) A plain, glossy silk, often seen on women's clothing or in ribbons.

Merino - Wool from the Merino sheep, twilled worsted, very fine.

muslin - Cotton muslin, finely woven, lightweight; although can have heavier thread woven in to create lines, checked appearance, or metallics. During the Regency, it was very often seen in white or pastels. Jaconet muslin (lightweight cotton cloth with a smooth and lightly stiffened finish.)

net - French net was often used in Regency evening gowns.

plaid - Checkered patterns. Despite the fact that wearing of a tartan kilt since the 1745 Scottish Highlander uprising was forbidden, plaid was a highly popular Regency fashion, especially in hats and trims. In 1822, Prinny went to Scotland and wore a kilt, and consequently tartans and plaids were even more popular.

poplin - Lightweight cotton, with a corded surface.

sarsanet - (Also seen as: sarsnet.) Fine, soft silk used for dresses and/or as lining material. For warmer weather. Had a sheen.

satin - Smooth, lustrous.

silk - In the Regency, was imported. In 1830 the Jacquard loom arrived in the UK; it revolutionizes the production of woven silks.

superfine - Woolen coat fabric, fulled (shrunk and thickened) and sheared into a soft finish. Often black.

taffeta

tissue - Gold or silver, a silk lame material. Often used for veils.

towels - As for bathing/drying one's self. (See under T.)

tulle

velvet - For colder weather.

wool - For colder weather.

worsted - Woven wool.

- Fabrics were sold by: drapers. (See under D.) Sewn by: tailors (men) and mantua-makers (an older term,) milliners, or modistes (women.)
- Men's breeches could be made from buckskin (soft leather) as well.
- Thread was usually silk, but cotton thread was becoming more available.
    - ➢ See: cloth.
    - ➢ See: dresses, women's.
    - ➢ See: Lancashire, under the BRITISH COUNTIES section.
    - ➢ See: textiles.
    - ➢ See: Wandsworth - Dyeing of cloth.
    - ➢ You may care to see: buttons.

Fairfield - Croydon. Dates from at least Tudor times, when it hosted a cattle fair, which was abolished in 1868. Fairfield was created as a ward in 1978; before then would have been referred to as Croydon.

fairs - Fairs, as opposed to market-places, were usually only held in their locale once per year. Usually lasted anywhere from 1 day to a week, and were not dissimilar to a modern American fair, in that they sold wares, provided entertainment, and had food and drink for sale. Often were affiliated with a particular interest or craft. Sometimes riotous (although this tendency was more repressed by the time of the Regency era, because by then the truly raucous fairs had long since been shut down.)

There actually was a Scarborough Fair. It was held in the county of Yorkshire, widely attended in medieval times. Was large, and lasted an amazing 45 days each year. Faded in the 17th century, and was gone completely by 1788.

- ➢ See: Barnet.
- ➢ See: Bartholomew Fair.
- ➢ See: Camberwell Green.
- ➢ See: Charlton Hornfair.
- ➢ See: Cloth Fair.
- ➢ See: frost fair.
- ➢ See: Mayfair.
- ➢ See: Mitcham Fair.
- ➢ See: Peckham.
- ➢ See: Rag Fair.
- ➢ See: Uxbridge.

Fan Museum - 10-12 Crooms Hill, Greenwich. 1991.

Fanmakers' Hall - For the Worshipful Company of Fanmakers. Charter granted in 1709, however, according to AN ENCYCLOPAEDIA OF LONDON: "...but increasing pressure by non-freemen and from foreign imports broke down the Company's control of the trade and after a petition of 1806 against the 'extinction by Foreigners of British fan craft' had failed, the Company's powers were finally abandoned. (The Huguenots had brought their fan-making skills.)

The Company was revived in 1877 as a traditional trade guild..." It took a small Hall in Bishopgate in 1950. Has adapted and is now involved with air conditioning and heating. 76th in the order of precedence.

Farm Street - Mayfair, West End. (See: Mayfair/Farm Street.)

Faraday Museum - Modern. (See: Albemarle Street/21.)

Farmers' Company - (AKA: the Worshipful Company of Farmers.) Formed late as a guild in 1938, and "became a voluntary body as the Farmers' Company" (charity) in 1946. Did not/does not have a hall. Livery company. 80th in precedence.

Farriers' Company - (AKA: the Worshipful Company of Farriers.) Horse-shoers. Began in the 13th century. Incorporated in 1685; gained livery in 1692. According to AN ENCYCLOPAEDIA OF LONDON: "Has examined and registered shoeing smiths for over 70 years." Farriers might also treat horse ailments; consists of veterinary surgeons as well as craft farriers. 55th in the order of precedence. Never had a hall.

Farringdon - The City/Islington. William de Farindon (whose name is spelled a number of ways) was a 13th C. goldsmith and City of London alderman who settled here. The village was fairly isolated until the River Fleet was covered over in 1737, Farringdon Street (see) being built over the defunct river. Leading up to the 1840s this area became badly overcrowded; the 1840s and on improvements pushed out some 16,000 slum residents.

- Farringdon Market: Opened in 1829, ran until 1874. Near Stonecutter Street. Replaced Fleet Market.
  - ➢ See: Fleet Market/Stocks Market.
  - ➢ See: Stocks Market - Which had been nearby.
- Farringdon Street: Is built over/follows the path of the defunct Fleet River, so was a nice, wide street. Begun in 1826; completed in 1830. (Previous to 1826, this site was the Fleet Market-see references, immediately above.) At first was called Victoria Street, then Farringdon Road, then Farringdon Street.
- Seacoal Lane: (See under S.)
  - o Fleet Prison. (See at its own listing.)

fellmongering - Dealing in skins.

- ➢ See: Hornchurch.
- ➢ See: Skinners' Hall.

Feltham - (Pronounced Felt-um.) Hounslow. Dates back to at least the time of Domesbook Book.

In the Regency era it was largely rural.

- St. Catherine: 1880.
- St. Dunstan's: Medieval. Parish church. Survived a 1634 fire. Rebuilt in 1802. Plain brick, with an embattled tower and a spire.

Feltmakers' Company - (AKA: the Worshipful Company of Feltmakers.) Dates back to 1180. In medieval times feltmaking was a craft shared by the fullers, hatters, and cappers. The hatters were subordinated to the Haberdashers in 1501. In 1604, James I gave a Charter to the Feltmakers; Livery was granted in 1733. The guild lost a lot of business when silk hats came into vogue in the 19th century. Never had a hall. 63rd in the order of precedence.

Fenchurch Street - The City. A continuation of Lombard Street. There by at least 1283. Corruption of "Foin Church," "foin" being a French word indicating a hay-market (there had been an ancient one nearby in Gracechurch Street.) Described as a gloomy street (although this description may be modern.) The East India Company built bonded warehouses here in the late 18th century. Now filled with offices.

- Elephant Tavern. (See: Elephant and Castle, under the INNS/PUBS section.)
- Fountain: The fountain on this street dates from 1954-57.
- Hall of the Ironmongers' Company: 1751. (See: Ironmongers' Hall, under I.)
- St. Dionis Backchurch: (See under the CHURCHES section.)

fencing - As in the art of swordplay. The place where this skill was taught would be called a fencing salon.

> ➢ See: dueling spots - For information on where gentlemen might meet to test their honor.
>
> ➢ See: Wilkinson - For information on a swordmaker.

Fenton House - (See under: Hampstead/Fenton House.)

ferris wheel - London's first was built in 1895, Earl's Court. Demolished in 1907. (You may care to see: London Eye, a 20th C. wheel.)

ferry - There was a ferry between Fulham and Putney, until it was replaced by a bridge in 1726. (See: Horse Ferry.) There were many ferries (and small boats) used to ferry people across and all along the Thames, less so as the Georgian era advanced into the Regency, and more bridges over the river were built. But the Fulham-Putney ferry was the only one that could accommodate coaches with horses (at least ca. 1706.)

> ➢ See: London Bridge, under the BRIDGES section - The notes under.
>
> ➢ See: Watermen.

Festival of Britain - A fair held in Southwark in 1951, to relieve the gloom left over from WWII. (See: Royal Festival Hall.)

Fetter Lane - Corruption of "fewters" (beggars.) Off Fleet Street. Very old street. (See:

Holborn/Black Swan Distillery.)

- 10: Built ca. 1662, Stuart period home. Had a porch, with a wide front door. Destroyed in WWII.
- Fleur De Lis Court: Located two blocks up Fetter Lane. Now gone (site covered by offices.)
- Moravian Chapel: On the south side of Neville's Court. Possibly as old as the 17th century. Not architecturally pretty.
- Neville's Court: (Also seen written as: Nevill's Court.) Alley off Fetter Lane. Until WWII damage there were ca. 1670 houses here.

Field Lane - Near the Fleet Ditch. Rookeries for pickpockets and mean little shops. Existed by at least 1585.

Fig's Mead - 1830s. (See: Bedford New Town.)

Figge's Marsh - Merton. Nine miles/14.5 km from London. Named for William Figge, who owned the land here in 1357.

- Pound Farm: Grew flowers and herbs for perfume and culinary markets by the 18th century. One James Arthur, of this farm, and his neighbor Major James Moore grew opium poppies here in the early 19th C., to sell for medicinal use.

Financial Times, the - News sheet. Established in 1888.

Finchley - Mostly consisted of common land, although by the 16th C. the east end of Finchley hosted inns, smithies, and other services travelers needed. After the 16th C., and as the woodlands cleared, its agriculture turned to dairy farming and hay-making. The common was enclosed and cultivated in the early 19th C., which curtailed the frequent late 18th C. robberies here.

- East End Road: In Medieval days, part of the area was called Hunts Green. In the 18th C. this road was: Finchley Road. In the 19th C. it was Manor Lane. It connected the two halves of Finchley.
- Finchley Common: Existed before 1660.
- Gravel Hill: 12th century.
- St. Mary's Church: 1274.
- West Finchley: (See under W.)

Finchley Road - Camden. Out of Hampstead. 1826 (but growth in this area was slow for 20-40 years.)

fingerprints - (As in: used in criminology.) First used to solve a British murder in 1905.

Finsbury - Became a metropolitan borough in 1901; is now in the London borough of Islington, since 1965, when the former Metropolitan boroughs of Finsbury and Islington united. (That being said, both Finsbury and Islington are very old areas.)

- City Road (from 1800-1830, filled with pawn shops.)
    - Eagle, the: It was a famous pleasure resort, from ca. 1800 into Charles Dickens' time. Hence the rhyme:

"Up and down the City Road,
In and out the Eagle,
That's the way the money goes,
Pop goes the weasel."

That is, to afford the night of revelry here, one might need to "pawn the weasel" or silverplate. (See: City Road/Shepherd and Shepherdess, under C.)

- Clerk's Well: In Gosswell Street (behind Charter House Square and the Islington Road.)
    - Gordon's: 1769. The Scots-English Alexander Gordon sold his own brand of gin from his home here. (Gordon's Gin eventually becomes the largest seller of gin in the world.)
- Finsbury Square: (See at its own listing.)
- Lackington Street: Named for James Lackington, b.1746-d.1815, bookseller. (See: Finsbury Square/Lackington's.)
- Lloyd Square: (See under L.)
- Old Street: (See: Old Street/Finsbury, under O.)
- St. Luke's: Old Street. 1733.
    - See: Old Street/Finsbury - Several St. Luke's references.
    - See: St. Luke's/Finsbury, under the CHURCHES section.
- Tabernacle Street: (See under T.)

Finsbury Barracks - (See: City Road/Finsbury Barracks.)

Finsbury Circus - East side of Moorgate, Lower Moorfields. Late 18th C., by George Dance the Younger. In 1819, after the removal of Bedlam Hospital from the site in 1815, the square garden was made round and converted into Finsbury Circus. Despite its circular shape, it is still referred to as a "square." None of George Dance the Younger's houses remain.

- London Institution, the: 1815-19. (See under L.)
- Lutyens House: 1924-7, by Sir Edwin Lutyens. (Was first, and briefly, known as Britannic House.)

Finsbury Fields - From 1498 archery was practiced here. Archery had completely fallen away here by the mid 18th century.

Finsbury Park - 1869, a development derived from a surviving corner of Hornsey Wood. Called a green retreat for north Londoners.

Finsbury Pavement - Name of Moorgate Street until 1835. John Keats (poet) was born in

Finsbury Pavement in 1795.

Finsbury Square - Lower Moorfield. The square has four sides. There are Georgian houses, four stories high, designed in 1777 by George Dance the Younger. Known as Moore Place on the west side of the square. The other three sides of the square built in 1789, 90, 91. It is claimed this was the first *square* in London to have gas lighting permanently installed.

- Chiswell Street: (See under C.)
- Lackington's: Had the full title of "Lackington, Allen & Co., Finsbury Square" during the Regency (but commonly called simply "Lackington's.") In the southeast corner of Finsbury Square. Bookshop, run by James Lackington; he had started in Chiswell Street, but moved to Finsbury Square in 1794. His shop was huge in size, and very successful. He would not accept credit, only cash. Whenever Lackington was in residence, a flag flew from the building's dome. When Lackington retired, his nephew ran the bookshop.

  Later called the Temple of the Muses (a sign in 1828, above the shop, reads "Late Lackington's"; Lackington's had been sold to Jones and Company "for distribution of their books and other works."

  Destroyed by fire in 1841.

  There is an 1809 picture that shows many shelves of books, and also books filling the upper rotunda story. At the time it was established it was London's largest bookstore.

fire brigade - Although there were fire companies (run by insurance companies) prior, there was no *publicly funded* fire brigade in London until 1833, when the London Fire Engine Establishment formed (from a gathering of private fire brigades.) The first public fire service in Britain overall (Edinburgh, to be exact) was formed in 1824.

The private fire brigades only put out your fire if your house displayed their particular fire-mark, a metal disk with their "logo" on it. If you hadn't paid them specifically, they did nothing for you - even if your house neighbored on the burning one.

FIRE ENGINES existed from the late 17th C., but they were primitive hand-pumps that were impossible at delivering water to any height. Most fires were fought with bucket brigades.

- See: County Fire Office.
- See: London Fire Establishment.
- See: Metropolitan Fire Brigade, 1866.

Firm, the - A modern, flippant term for the extended Royal family.

Firmin and Sons - Buttonmakers to HM the Queen (Elizabeth II.) Also, has been providing the garments for officers (of many nations) for 300+ years. Their buttons were worn at

Waterloo, and quite possibly by Napoleon as well. Royal Warrant granted by George II. Founded in 1677, by Thomas Firmin. Once was at "the sign of the Red Lion, Norfolk Street on the Strand," though now at 100 Crawford Street. (See: buttons.)

First Lord of the Treasury - (See: Downing Street/10.)

fish - By 2010 it was noted there were 125 species of fish living in the (much cleaner than during the 19th century) Thames River. Some seafoods were seen being sold from push-carts by costermongers, such as: cockles, mussels, oysters. While not an all-inclusive list, these are many of the fish/shellfish available during the Regency (some from the salty part of the Thames, some from the non-tidal waters):

- anchovies
- barbel
- bleak
- bream - Also: bronze bream.
- brown trout
- carp
- caviar - NOT from the Thames, but introduced to England in the 1500s.
- cockles
- cod
- crab
- dace
- eels - (See under E.)
- flounder
- goldfish - 1730. For viewing, not for consuming. (See: goldfish, under G.)
- grayling
- gudgeon
- herring - Too: red herrings, which lent their name to leaving false clues, probably due to criminals burying them to distract tracking dogs. (See: kippers.)
- kippers - Smoked herring. Often served at breakfast.
- lampreys
- lobster - While eaten by both rich and poor, it didn't have the "fine dining" aspect it has today; prisoners who had to eat it too many days in a row were known to riot.
- mackerels
- minnow
- mussels

- oysters - (See: Mile End Road.)
- periwinkles
- pike
- plaice - A European flounder type.
- prawns
- roach
- rudd - Clearwater fish.
- salmon - Killed off in the Thames by pollution in the 1860s.
- shrimp
- sole
- stone loach
- tench
- trout - Also: brown trout.
- turbot
- whelk
- winkles - Same as: periwinkles.
    - ➢ See: food - Various seafoods listed there.

For fishing (the act of), or for purchasing seafoods:

- ➢ See: Alperton.
- ➢ See: Barking.
- ➢ See: Billingsgate - For purchasing fish.
- ➢ See: Bury Street/Wilton's - Known for their fish and oysters.
- ➢ See: fishing.
- ➢ See: Fishmongers' Hall - For fishing as a profession.

fish and chips shop - First one opened in London's East End in 1860, although deep-fried fish was a dish known from the 16th century and on. (See: New Earl Street/Sweetings - For London's first fish restaurant, 1830, although note it wasn't a fish and chip restaurant, per se.)

Fish Street Hill - Lies along the path of a Roman road; originally called Bridge Street. The present dates from at least 1762; it has been called New Fish Street since 1321. (See: Fishmongers' Hall, for more on Fish Street Hill.)

- The Monument: (See under M.) A monument that commemorates the Great Fire of 1666, built in 1677.

Fisher House - (See: Islington/Lower Street/Fisher House.)

fishing - I'm referring to that done with rods, but also sometimes with nets, by sportsmen, as opposed to as an industry. (For industrial fishing, see: Billingsgate.) In the UK this sport would more likely be called: angling (and its practitioners: anglers.)

- ➢ See: Alperton.
- ➢ See: Barking.
- ➢ See: fish.

Fishmongers' Hall - For the Worshipful Company of Fishmongers, one of the twelve Great Twelve livery Guilds of London. Sellers of fish and seafood. This company has existed for over 700 years.

The Fishmongers moved from just north of Queenhithe Dock to Fish Street Hill in 1321, at which time the street took on the name of New Fish Street. The Hall burned in the Great Fire of 1666. In 1671 the second building was erected, and was described as a "stately structure." When water damage to the Hall and the new London Bridge was detected, this led to a whole new Hall. Third building erected in 1831-5, in the Greek Revival style, is described as the "most conspicuous of all the Companies' Halls," by Henry Roberts. Destroyed by WWII bombing, but restored to its "former glory" by 1954.

In olden times, there were two Companies, one for salt fish, one for stock fish (with the salt fish Company coming first.) In Henry III's time, the king restricted the fishing to Queenshithe, with a fish market being on Old Fish Street (later Knightrider Street.) Edward I took the restriction away, at which time the fishmarket moved to Bridge Street (Fish Street Hill,) ca. 1321. When the Stock Fish Mongers came into being, 1399, they were in Lower Thames Street. They went on to have six Halls.

The Fishmongers yet reside at Fish Street Hill. The stock fishers and salt fishers were finally united in 1536 (they had decided to house together in 1504, at "the Lord Fanhope's house" (John Cornwall, Baron Fanhope,) who seemingly granted them the property in 1434. (The Stock-Fish Mongers' old Hall stood until 1615, ca. when they finally combined with the Fishmongers.)

It is one of the few ancient Companies still listed as active as regards to craft (rather than primarily as charities,) with appointed fishmeters who seize fish that have turned unsound.

(See: Gresham College.)

fisticuffs - Term used during the Regency for boxing (too: pugilism,) as in athletic boxing matches. While it might be used to mean a scheduled match, the term tended to more mean an informal street scuffle (like a fistfight in America.)

- ➢ See: boxing.
- ➢ See: Fives Court.
- ➢ See: pugilism.

Fitzherbert House - The name of flats built over Mrs. Fitzherbert (Prinny's disallowed first wife's) townhouse, which was pulled down in 1927. (See: Regent's Park/(*The Park)*/Inner

Circle.)

Fitzmaurice Place - (See: Berkeley Square/Fitzmaurice Place.)

Fitzrovia - Westminster. "Fitzrovia" is a phrase coined in the 1930s. And the name Fitzrovia did not appear on Ordnance Survey maps until 1994. (See: Fitzroy Square.)

- Castle Street: Is now Eastcastle Street. (See: Eastcastle Street.)
- Charlotte Street: Quote: "Bacchus brooded over Charlotte Street; it is still rich in the altars of booze and food.") Now known not just for restaurants but also media companies.
- Middlesex Hospital: 1745. (See under M.)
- Soho: (See under S.)

Fitzroy Square - North of Soho. The east and south sides were built ca. 1790-1794, by the brothers William and Robert Adam, for the first Baron Southampton, who named the square for his grandfather, Charles Fitzroy (second Duke of Grafton.) The north and west sides were built in 1825-9.

By the early 19th C., those of the upper crust were starting to move west, out of the Bloomsbury area.

As the century advanced this area became more a place for immigrants, craftsmen, workshops, studios, and rooms to let.

This (extended) area was dubbed "Fitzrovia" by artist/writers in the 1930s. (See: Fitzrovia.)

- All Saints: Margaret Street. 1850s.
- Chippendale: The furniture-maker. Had a late 18th C. shop here. (See: Goodwin Court, for more on Chippendale.)
- Fitzroy Street: 1780s houses. Is the continuation of Charlotte Street northward from Howland Street to Euston Road. The southern part of this street, prior to 1867, was known as Russell Place.
- Warren Street:
    - 43: Dr. William Kitchiner lived here in 1816; he published in that year his cookbook with exact receipts (recipes,) lists of ingredients, and instructions of the order in which they are used. (There had been recipe books before then, but they usually had vague descriptions such as "add the spice", and were frequently inexact in proportions, length of cooking time, etc.

Five Chimneys - Other name for the Pest Houses. (See under P.)

Five Fields - Chelsea. In what would become Belgravia. AN ENCYCLOPAEDIA OF LONDON describes it thusly: "Down to about 1831 there was an open and rural expanse where now stands Belgrave Square, the heart, as it were, of Belgravia. This rural space was known as 'Five Fields.' They were intersected by mud banks, occupied by only a few hamlets, and, until the beginning of the 19th century, infested by foot pads and robbers." In addition to mud-banks, there was clay and swamps, with a few sheds scattered about. Located southwest of Hyde Park Corner (between Grosvenor Place, Hyde Park Corner, and Sloane Street.) Extended from Chelsea to London. The site of duels. Known as Five Fields until 1824. The Act of Parliament which allowed Five Fields to be drained and raised was obtained in 1826 by the Duke of Westminster. (See: Pimlico - Note under.)

- Bloody Bridge: (So called on an 1810 map.) Crossed the West Bourne River. Name due to the violence of the footpads who struck here after dark.

fives - Fives can be used as slang to mean a fisted hand, but here I mean a type of game. (See: Fives Court.)

Fives Court - St. Martin's Street, Leicester Square. Sparring (boxing, fisticuffs) matches were held here. Was in fact one of the chief locations for boxing in London.

"Fives" is also the name of a kind of game, thought to be a forerunner to Squash. The ball was struck by the hand, played on a three-sided court. It was played at Eton.

When the proprietors of Fives Court saw popularity of the game waning, they took advantage of the name and added boxing matches. A stage, the better to see the match, was added.

In addition to the Fives Court here on St. Martin's Street, during the Regency there were courts also at Cambridge and Oxford, as well as at the Fleet and the King's Bench prisons. The game of Fives lost its popularity after 1810, so after that time the Fives Court reputation for pugilism grew.

flag, British - (AKA: the Union Jack - But see notes below.) England's (as opposed to Great Britain's) first flag was St. George's Cross, from the 13th century. (That same St. George's Cross was worn by the Crusaders.)

The Union Jack was first revealed in 1606, ordered by James I (who had declared himself the King of Great Britain, despite the resistance of both the English and Scottish governments to the term Great Britain.) This naval flag was called: the King's Colours. Its design came from mixing together three flags, those of England, Northern Ireland, and Scotland. This Union Jack flag was flown only at sea, not being flown on land until 1701 (at the Act of Union between England and Scotland.) Never *officially* called the Union Jack. It is believed the "jack" in the Union Jack comes from being flown on a Navy ship's jackstaff (at the stern.)

In 1801, the cross of St. Patrick was added to the national flag, after the Act of Union with Ireland in 1800. (The addition to the flag being: the diagonal red stripes.)

If not flown at sea, this latter flag is more correctly called: the Union Flag (but the distinction is getting lost in common use as the populace tends to call it the Union Jack.)

- You may care to see: Great Britain.
- You may care to see: United Kingdom.

Flamsteed House - (Also sometimes seen written as: Flamstead House.) 1676. Greenwich Park. Observatory, built for the first Astronomer Royal, for whom it was named. By Wren. Appointed in 1675 by Charles II. In that year of 1675 the ROYAL OBSERVATORY (AKA: Greenwich Observatory) was built here, first called Flamsteed House. The top room is a unique octagonal shape. Contains Britain's largest refracting telescope. (See: Greenwich Observatory - Of which this house is the oldest part.)

flash-house - Slang. Means: a lewd and riotous place. Also called a cock and hen club. A drinking and lodging place where thieves and their ilk would be found, making criminal plans and/or fencing goods. (See: Old Street/Finsbury.)

Flask Walk - (See: Hampstead/Flask Walk.)

- Flask, the: Pub. (See under the INNS/PUBS section.)

flat, a - Term means, largely, (in American parlance) an apartment. "Flat" is a 20th century term. During the Regency, single men would have what acquainted to a flat (or a hotel suite,) and would refer to their residence as either "my rooms," or "my accommodations," or his "bachelor rooms." (You may care to see: hotel, under H, to see how the few Regency era hotels differed from modern conceptions.)

Fleet Ditch - A depression marked where the Fleet River used to flow, when the river was covered over in 1769. Slum homes often backed on to the Ditch. It ran from Peter Street to Castle Street. (See: Fleet River.)

Fleet Market - The City. Original name for the Stock Market.

- See: Stock Market, below.
- See: Stock Market, under S.

- STOCK MARKET: (Also seen as: Stocks Market.) This was the area's name until 1737. Originally called the Hales (another word for stocks.) From the 13th C.; the earliest fully recorded market building in Britain. For butchers and fishmongers; built because the Mayor, ca. 1274, made an attempt to move the market from Cheapside in preparation of a royal visit to the City.

  Rebuilt several times, being in the 17th C. a "stone house" divided into sections for fish and meat. The Great Fire of 1666 destroyed it; rebuilt on the site of St. Mary's, Woolchurch Haw. (See under the CHURCHES section.)

  Torn down in 1737, for construction of the Mansion House; The "filthy Fleet" was covered over at about this same time, and the Stock Market was pulled down; replaced by the Fleet Market, designed by George Dance, Sr. The latter was two rows of single-story shops, with a covered walkway with skylights.

Cleared again in 1826, for Farringdon Street, which street was completed in 1829. (See: Farringdon/Farringdon Market.)

Fleet Prison - (AKA: The Fleet. AKA: Fleet Street Prison.) Off Farringdon Street, in Seacoal Lane. This area stank, from a sluggish Fleet River and from river dumpings that came out of Smithfield Meat Market. Dates from ca. 1189-1197; is the oldest building specifically built as a prison. Being a royal prison, it served to hold: those who owed the Crown money, showed contempt of the king or his courts; or just plain old annoyed the king. Rebuilt during Edward III's reign (1327-1377.)

Destroyed in the 1381 (Wat Tyler) rebellion, and in the Great Fire of 1666.

Was a Debtor's Prison only after 1641.

Destroyed again in the Gordon Riots of 1780 (at which rebuild it could hold 300 prisoners and their families); rebuilt immediately. Four story building.

The prison chapel (and surrounding streets) was the site of many a clandestine marriage in the 18th C., but the practice was impossible by the time of the Regency because of Fleet Prison marriages' illegality as declared in the Marriage Act of 1753. (See: marriage.)

The prison was abolished in 1842; sold; demolished in 1846. Now occupied partially by Caronne House.

Fleet River - Flowed from Hampstead to the Thames. Talk of pollution here came as early as 1290. Covered over in 1769. Still exists, but underground, acting as a sewer. (See: River Fleet.)

Fleet Street - The City. The street was named for the river it crossed over (the Fleet, covered over in 1769.)

Fleet Street first began to be associated with printing in 1500 when Wynkyn de Worde set up a workshop here (near Shoe Lane,) bringing in the area's first printing press in 1501.

The first *newspaper* arrived in this street in 1702, when *The Daily Courant* set up offices here. This street contained many taverns, frequented by the working men of the press.

In the 19th C., this street was very much the center of the press. (See: Fourth Estate.)

Connects the City to the West End; busy artery. In the 20th C. the newspapers almost all moved elsewhere, but despite their loss, Fleet Street is still thought of as (and used as a term meaning) the cradle of the press.

Fleet Street: is also the term used to speak of the entire area east of the Strand.

TEMPLE BAR marks where Fleet Street and the Strand meet. (See: Temple Bar, below.)

- 1: Bank of Scotland. Founded in 1671. Oldest bank in London. Was once Child's Bank. It is now part of Williams' and Glyn's Bank, the private banking arm of the Royal Bank of Scotland. The present building dates from 1829.
    - See: Bank of Scotland, under B.
    - See: Child's Bank.
- 3: S. Weingott, tobacconists. 1859.
- 17: Prince Henry's Room. A half-timbered house, built in 1610 as a tavern; the only building in the area to escape the Great Fire of 1666. Is a single room. The ornate (but monochromatic) Jacobean plasterwork ceiling dates from 1610. Also has mahogany paneling, richly carved. It is the oldest standing domestic dwelling in the City. *Is on the top floor of Inner Temple Gateway.* (See: Inns of Court/The Temple (1st)/Inner Temple/Gateway.) The stairs leading up to Prince Henry's room are just to the left of the gate. Is now the Samuel Pepys Exhibition; during his time (1661) was known as the Fountain Inn. Probably not called 'Prince Henry's Room' during the Regency, as in the early 19th C. it was yet a "Mrs. Salmon's Waxworks," with a tavern at the rear. (See: Inns of Court/Temple (1st listing)/Inner Temple/Inner Temple Gateway/Prince Henry's Room.)
- 22: Ye Olde Cock Tavern. Ancient; still there. (See under the INNS/PUBS section.)
- 32: John Murray, bookseller. Began business here in 1768. Published Jane Austen. Acquired by Hodder Headline in 2004.
- 37: Hoare's Bank. Founded in 1672. Private bank (the only one still left in London.)
- 47: El Vino. Wine bar. Founded as "Bower and Co." in 1879. Changed name to El Vino in 1928.
- 53: Richard Homes Laurie (Laurie and Whittle,) toys. ROMANTIC LONDON refers to Laurie and Whittle in the beginning of the 19th century as a print-shop (seller of pictures.)
- 65: Whitefriar's Crypt. 14th C., left from the Carmelite monastery, but not excavated until 1927.
- 95: Old Bell Tavern. Built supposedly by Wren in 1670. There probably had been a pub here since prior to the Great Fire of 1666. Described in LONDON ACCESS as "intimate and warm." It was built to accommodate the workmen

who were reconstructing St. Bride's after the Great Fire in 1666.

- 127: The Morning Advertiser (newspaper) moved from the Strand to here in 1825.
- 145: Ye Olde Cheshire Cheese.
    - ➢ See: below, in this section, under Y.
    - ➢ See under the INNS/PUBS section.
- 201: The Cock Tavern. (See under the INNS/PUBS section.)
- Cheshire Cheese: Pub. (See: "Ye Olde...," below.)
- Crown Office Row:
    - 2: In 1775, Charles Lamb (essayist) was born here.
- Gough Square: (See under G.)
- Hare Court: Dark courtyard. (See: Inns of Court/Temple (2nd entry)/Hare Court.)
- Inner Temple Lane: (See: Inns of Court/Temple/Inner Temple/Inner Temple Lane.)
    - 4: Charles Lamb (essayist) lived here from 1809-1817, while working for the East India Company.
- Middle Temple Gateway - (See: Inns of Court/Middle Temple/Middle Temple Gateway.)
- Old Cock Tavern: (AKA: Ye Olde Cock Tavern.) Still there; since Samuel Johnson's time.
    - ➢ See: 22, above.
    - ➢ See under the INNS/PUBS section.
- Prince Henry's Room: (See: 17, above.)
- Printing House Square: *The Times* (newspaper) was produced here since 1785. (See: Times, the, under T.)
- St. Bride's: At least 300 year old church. "The printer's cathedral," Wren. (See under the CHURCHES section.)
- St. Clement Danes: (See under the CHURCHES section.)
- St. Dunstan in the West: (See under the CHURCHES section.)
- Salisbury Court: (See under S.)
    - Salisbury Square: (See under S.)
- Temple Bar: The gate/archway that once marked the western boundary of the City, between the City and Westminster (where Fleet Street turns into the Strand.) Built by Wren. Moved from Fleet Street in 1878. (See: Inns of Court/Temple/Middle Temple/Temple Bar.)

- Ye Olde Cheshire Cheese: 145 Fleet Street. In Wine Office Court, (an alley off Fleet Street.) A tavern here since at least 1590. The first building rebuilt (1667) after the Great Fire of 1666, apparently for the relief of those men working following the fire. Frequented by Ben Johnson (playwright,) and later by (author) Charles Dickens. (See under the INNS/PUBS section.)

Fletchers' Company - (AKA: the Worshipful Company of Fletchers.) Bowyers were long-bow makers; fletchers were arrow-makers. In 1371 the Fletchers agreed their craft was separate from the Bowyers; they petitioned the Lord Mayor and in 1403 Ordinances were declared. Charter granted in the time of Edward IV. Never had a hall. 39th in precedence. This trade no longer exists, although the Company remains as a charitable organization.

floors - That is, a building's stories (levels/floors.) What Americans call the first floor, Britons call the ground floor. Our "second floor" is their "first floor," etc. If a servant is said to have a third floor room, it would mean she sleeps four stories above street level. Same usage if you substitute "storey" (British spelling) instead of "floor."

Floris - Colognes, perfumes. (See: Jermyn Street/89.)

flour - There were many mills in or near London, for all the various milling needs/purposes.

- See: food/bread.
- See: food/flour.
- See: Three Mills.
- See: Uxbridge - Provided much of London's flour.

flowers - Of Regency England. (This list is not all-inclusive):

anemone
auriculas
black-eyed susans
calendulas
camomile - In America, spelled: chamomile. (See: food/camomile.)
campanulas
carnations
chrysanthemum - Imported from China to London in 1789.
clematis
crocus
cowslip
daffodils
dahlias - First in England in 1804.
daisy

delphinium

dog's mercury

foxglove

hearts-ease - (Also seen as: heartsease.) Also known as: Johnny-jump-up. Wild flower. Is a violet, Viola Tricolor (purple, white, and yellow.)

hellebore

hollyhock

honeysuckle

lavender - (See: Lavender Hill.)

lilac

lily

marguerite

marigold

marsh forget-me-not

monkshood

pansy

peony

pinks

primrose

rose - The national flower of England.

snowdrops

stocks

sweet William

tulip

violet.

- See: Chelsea Physic Garden.
- See: Figge's Marsh/Pound Farm - For a place that grew flowers and herbs.

fog - Being an island, England has always had fogs, and by the 15th C. sea-coal and wood fires in London created an "unnatural mist, ever over the city." And the infamous fogs of Victorian London were, even more so, largely the product of air pollution caused by dense populations burning coal for heat. (See: coal.)

Foley Street - So known until 1864, when its name was changed to Langham Place. (A continuing part of the street is still known as Foley Street.)

- All Soul's Church. (See: All Soul's/Langham Place, under the CHURCHES section.)

- Foley House: House pulled down ca. 1820, to begin construction of Langham Place.

Folgate Street - Shoreditch. Folgate Street was known as White Lion Street until 1938.

- 12 and 14: Built in 1724. Replaced by a 1983 building.
- 18: Dennis Severs's House. Built in 1724. A Huguenot silk-weaving family, the Jarvises, lived here from 1725-1919. It was restored to its original state in the 20th C. by Dennis Severs (who does a performance/tour of the place to showcase the house's historical nature. Hence it is now known as Dennis Severs's House.)

folkmoot - A medieval gathering of city leaders; long since replaced by the Common Council. (See: Common Council.)

follies - An architectural term. 17-19th century landowners sometimes indulged themselves with "ruins" custom-made for their gardens. These could be columns, temples, cascades, etc., usually built to appear aged/ancient.

food - The Alpha list of individual food items is below this opening information, which explains *how* food was cooked and stored. (Note that the list is not all inclusive.)

- See: chophouse.
- See: forcing gardens.
- See: fruits.
- See: markets.
- See: meat.
- See: Mincing Lane - In the Regency era, was known for selling spices.
- See: orangery.
- See: pinery.
- See: restaurant.
- See: the INNS/PUBS section - The notes at the top, in regards to dining.
- See: vegetables.

Keep in mind that foods were very seasonal. While you could store foods like apples and potatoes in a cool cellar for much of the year, things such as oranges and asparagus had a shorter shelf-life. That being said, many foods were imported, for instance, oranges (though expensive) could be gotten at Christmastime as a special treat.

Perhaps more important to the British housewife was that many, many foods could be preserved. Even the grand lady of the manor oversaw that the processes of preserving food went forward, as her family (and staff) heavily depended on that food for the winter.

There were many ways of preserving food. This is a list of some of the methods:

- brewing

- honeying
- icing - During the winter. Or in an ice house, which was usually a straw-lined deep hole.
- jams/jellies/catchups/chutneys - Making of.
- pickling/brining
- potting - Covering the food with melted butter to seal it in a container.
- salting
- smoking
- sugaring - As in coating the item with sugar.
- sugar syrup - Covering the item with.

Notes on preservation:

- Canning was invented in Napoleon's time (although it was at first in reused champagne bottles, so would have been "bottling" rather than "canning"; tin cans were yet a long way off,) but this process of preservation was little understood or utilized until post-Regency.
- Fresh meats were almost always roasted on spits; not every kitchen had an oven, which anyway might be primarily used for baking.

Besides being spitted, these are some of the other methods of food preparation:

baking - Often whole communities shared a bread oven.

boiling

broiling - They had salamanders, which were a length of usually flat metal heated in a fire and then hand-held (with a protective cloth for your hands) over a dish in order to melt or sear its topping.

chops

chutneys - Made into.

drying - Example: peas, which could then be stored all winter.

fricasseeing

frying

forcemeat - Forming rolled balls, sausages.

jugging - Cooking a whole animal in a lidded dish.

mincing - Chopping very small - "minced chicken" was considered a bit of a meager side dish.

molding - Shaping, say, butter. Or forming patties, such as oyster patties.

ribs - Might be sauced, but *not* with BBQ sauce.

steaks

stewing

toasting.

Notes on food service:

- Sweet and savory dishes often were served at the same remove (or course.) They called things "dessert," but the concept of leaving anything sweet exclusively for the end of the meal wasn't yet in place. The end of a meal would be more likely referred to as: the last course (as opposed to: dessert.) "Afters" is a modern term (1909.)
- Many meals (or parts thereof) were served cold; Regency folk (and their forebears) didn't really have the concept of leftovers - except that everyone ate them to avoid waste and because food preparation was so time-consuming, so what was prepared must be consumed (by first family, then servants, and even down to consumption by the animals.)
- These were the meals of the day (at least for the privileged/upper crust):
    - Breakfast: Taken at ten or so. One might rise quite a bit earlier, getting on with one's day but not taking this meal for several hours. Even then, it was often just tea or coffee plus some manner of bread.
    - Dinner: The largest meal of the day. Sometimes also called luncheon, never "lunch."
    - Tea: Taken around four, to stave off hunger until supper. Tea became more and more fixed as a part of a Briton's day as the 19th century stretched on. (See: Langham Hotel, which claims to have originated the afternoon tea.)
    - Supper: Taken at eight or later; it was generally a light meal.

Additional notes:

- IN THE REGENCY (and the prior Georgian) PERIODS, RECIPES WERE CALLED RECEIPTS. In sources from the time, you sometimes see "recipe," but "receipt" is far more common.
- *Baked beans* were introduced by Fortnum and Mason in 1886.
- *Baking powder* did NOT exist in the Regency era. It dates from the 1840s. Cooks provided leavening by using eggs or yeast.
- *Worcestershire Sauce* dates from 1837. (See under W.)

EVERY FOOD ITEM IN THE FOLLOWING LIST HAS BEEN SEEN IN ACTUAL REGENCY ERA RECEIPTS (RECIPES.) Again, this list is not all-inclusive.

Regency era persons were known to eat and drink:

acorns

ale

almond paste - Is primarily what Americans call marzipan.

almonds - Imported. Almond was also a common flavoring. (See: sugar-plums, below.)

anchovies - (See: Strand/Burgess, John.)

anise

apples

apricots

Arrack punch - Distilled alcohol, made from coconut flowers, or fruit, or grain (red rice, for one,) or sugarcane. Came from the Indian subcontinent/Southeast Asia. Vauxhall Garden's drink of choice.

artichokes - You might see it on a bill of fare as: artichoke bottoms.

asparagus

aubergine - In America: eggplant. (The word is also used to describe a purple color.)

bacon - This was more like Canadian bacon or ham; what Americans call bacon would be "rashers," or (less frequently) "streaky bacon." (See: gammon.)

barberries

barley

bay leaves

beans - French beans, what Americans call green beans. Haricot beans (sometimes called by the Italian name: fagioli); Americans call them kidney beans. Runner beans.

beef - Was an oft-consumed food...if you could afford it. The poor might be more likely to obtain their protein via cheese and eggs.

- See: beefsteak.
- See: Smithfield Market.

beefsteak - I've never seen a Regency receipt that simply speaks of "steak," it's always "beefsteak." (Or pork steak.)

beer - Very often was small beer, with a low alcohol content (2%.) Everyone drank beer, especially in the city where it was hard to get clean drinking water. Strong beer was also brewed. (See: beer, under B.)

beets - Also called beet-root.

bergamot - Plant seen in 18th C. gardens and beyond, with its citrus-y fruit, which peel is used.

biscuits - Americans call them cookies. Usually biscuits were not all that sweet, and could even be savory. They were more for tea or having a nibble, usually only seen at supper as part of a last course. (See: wafers.)

black butter - Based on apple pulp. Often was an apple-blackberry spread, but other fruits could be used.

blackberries - Eaten, of course, but also popularly used as a dye.

Blackcurrants - (See: currants, below.)

blancmange - Also seen as: blamange, blanch mange. A gelled dessert made with wine, milk, and sugar. (The gel was derived from animal hooves, or from fish. See: islinglass, below.)

boar

boiled sweet - In America, it'd be called a hard candy.

brandy

brawn - The brains of calves and pigs, boiled and pickled, in jelly. (Called headcheese in America.)

bread - *Everyone* ate bread, it was a staple even for the poorest. What Regency era persons called white bread was actually rather yellow; the bleached wheat of today's white bread was a decade or three away. By the time of the Regency many of the flours of the past had pretty much given way to wheat only, although oat flour, rye flour, etc. still existed. Poor persons tended to eat browner, coarser bread than did the privileged.

(See: toast, below.)

breadcrumbs - Where there is bread, chefs will make breadcrumbs for filler or toppings.

broccoli

broth - Clear soups. Broth was eaten, or used to add flavor to dishes. (See: soups, below.)

brown sugar - Called: golden sugar. (See: sugar.)

buns - That is, what Americans tend to call rolls. While there were rolls in Regency era cookery books, they were less like plain bread and more like what Americans think of as a sweet (lemon, cinnamon, lavender) or a savory (herbed, bacony, cheesy) bun. That is, in Regency-speak, buns were for accompanying meals (supper, sandwiches,) and rolls tended to be more of a treat or a sweet addition to a meal. When in doubt, use the more common term: buns.

- See: Chelsea/Bun House, under C.

- See: wig.

burgundy

butter - Easily obtained in Regency London. (See: milk, below.)

buttermilk

cabbage - Served raw, cooked, pickled. (Also see: savoy.)

cake - Sweet, or savory. Many kinds and flavors. Pretty much the one- or two-layer dessert we think of today. It was fashionable to serve individual-sized cakes. They had pound cake, which was also called heart cake. May or may not have an icing.

A few examples: apple cake, cheesecake, gingerbread (see,) plum cake, rosewater cake.

Too, one might refer to a concoction of (for example) a protein, crumbs, and egg as a cake: "Luncheon today consists mainly of salmon cake."

- See: icing, below.
- See: Islington - The note at the start.

calves - (See: veal, below.)

camomile - (In America, spelled: chamomile.) Used for treating hay fever, insomnia, upset stomachs. Often taken as a tea.

capers

capon - A male chicken castrated to improve growth and flavor.

caraway seeds

cardamom

cardoons - Cousin to the artichoke, it tastes like one combined with celery.

carrots

catchup - Usually seen with this spelling. The Regency era had quite a few kinds of catchups, virtually none of them made from tomatoes. They could be made from fruits or vegetables, and tended to be more savory. (See: tomatoes, below, why it wouldn't be used.)

cauliflower

caviar - Introduced to England in the 1500s.

cayenne - Also sometimes seen as: chyan. In receipts almost always meant the powder, rather than chopped fresh peppers.

celery

chamomile - (See: camomile.)

champagne -

- See: drinks/champagne, below.

> See under C.

cheeks - Of many creatures, such as: cows, oxen, pork, trout.

cheese - Cheesemaking in England began at least with the Romans. England tended to produce harder cheeses; Scotland, often using sheep's milk, tended to produce softer ones. Almost everyone had cheese in their diet. Cheesemaking declined after Henry VIII dissolved the monasteries, the latter having been responsible for a fair amount of cheese production. But in the 17th C. cheesemaking had a revival at home farms. By the end of the 18th C. most farms produced cheese. There were some 40 kinds of cheese available to the Regency table. Cheese might be served with breakfast.

Some types available:

- Blue Vinney - From Dorset. Made from leftover unpasteurized cow's milk; a blue cheese. Crumbly. Around for hundreds of years.
- Cheddar - Originated in Cheddar/ Somerset. Less well-known to Regency Londoners, but it has been seen in England since the 15th century. Now the UK's most popular cheese.
- Cheshire - As its name implies, originated in Cheshire. Dates at least back to Domesday Book. Was the most popular cheese during the Regency era.
- cottage cheese - (See: curds and whey, below.)
- Gloucester - Made from Gloucester cows' milk, first seen in 1498.
- Lancashire - Dates from the 13th century.
- Leicester - (Now known as: Red Leicester.) Hard cheese, from unpasteurized cow's milk. From the 17th century.
- Parmesan - (More correctly called: Parmigiano-Reggiano.) Imported from Italy. Dates from the late 16th century. There was an English version of parmesan.
- Stilton - Dates from the 18th century. Blue Stilton is better known than the other variety: White Stilton.
- Wensleydale - Dates from the 11th century. Made from sheep's milk, a blue cheese. White Wensleydale dates from 1930.

> See: Warwickshire/Cheshire, under the BRITISH COUNTIES section.
> See: curds and whey, below.
> See: Welsh rabbit, below.
> See: Ye Olde Cheshire Cheese, under the INNS/PUBS section.

cheesecake -

- See: cake, above - Reference at.
- See: Holloway.
- See: Richmond Green/Maids of Honour Row - For Maid of Honour cheesecakes.

cherries

chervil

chestnuts

chicken - If one's living environment allowed it, almost everyone kept chickens. Includes roosters.

- See: capon, above.
- See: pullet, below.

chives

chocolate - Regency folk using this term almost always meant what Americans call hot cocoa. "Do send up a pot of chocolate." Chocolate was available for baking, but it wasn't sweet and was used in dishes, not consumed on its own. Sugary chocolate wasn't completely unknown, but developed/came far more into vogue as the 19th century went on; factory-produced blocks of chocolate were produced in 1819, in Switzerland.

chutneys - Preserves made of fruit, spices, sugar, and vinegar.

cider - Mildly alcoholic.

cinnamon - In England by at least the 17th century.

citron - Seen with a variety of spellings. The fruit of an evergreen citrus tree, resembling a large lemon in shape and color, with a thick and well-scented rind. A frequently called-for ingredient.

claret

cloves

cockles

cod - Also seen as: codfish.

coffee - Imported, expensive. (See: coffee-houses, under C.)

comfits - These were nuts, particles of spices, or seeds coated in sugar. (See: sugar-plum, below.)

cordials - Alcoholic drinks, like the cordials of today.

coriander - Referring to the leaves; in America: cilantro.

corn - (See: maize.)

coss lettuce - Romaine.

courgette - What Americans call: zucchini. It existed in early 19th century England, but it would have been rare, only in the gardens of those particularly interested in "foreign" plants (historically it came from America, went to Italy, and returned to America ca. the 1920s/Italian immigrants.)

cowslip - Not the same as the American cowslip, which is poisonous. Sometimes used in brewing.

crabs

cranberries

cream - Where you have cream, you can make: whipped cream. (See: milk, below.) Clotted cream was not a Regency/London food until Victorian times.

cresses (and watercress) - Of the mustard family, used as a garnish and in salads.

crumpets - Around since at least 1382, but the old version was a kind of hard pancake. The soft and spongy version we know today came along in the Victorian era.

cucumbers - A food commonly seen/consumed. Salads were often made up of just lettuce and cucumber, and dressed. (See: pickle, below.)

curds - Usually made from a fruit, like today's lemon curd. What Americans might think of as a rich, fruity kind of pudding/custard.

curds and whey - Curds are like cottage cheese; the whey is the watery substance that's left behind when the cheese curds form. The whey was taken as a drink sometimes (but mostly by children or invalids.)

currants - Seen in many receipts, both sweet and savory. Derived from the tiny Black Corinth grape. Came from Greece in the 16th century. Besides blackcurrants, there were also red currants, and white currants, the latter being sweeter. Often used for cordials or jellies.

curry - Meaning both dishes of Indian derivation and the mixed spices with which to season them. Whereas a person of India makes their own mix of seasonings on the spot each time (i.e. creates their curry spice combination as they cook,) Regency cooks (much as many Americans today) used a prepared jar of curry powder. Curry was mildly in vogue during the Regency due to Britain's interests in India/military men bringing back the spices/receipts. I've seen Curry of Rabbit on a bill of fare. (See: curry, under C.)

custards - Many kinds. (You may care to see: Islington/Copenhagen House.)

dates

deer - (See: venison, below.)

dill

dotterel - A bird of the plover family.

doves

drinks -

- ale
- Arrack punch - (See at A, above.)
- beer - Even children drank small beer, which had a low alcohol level.
    - See: bitter.
    - See: porter, under P.
    - See: strong beer.
    - See under B.
- bitter - A denser, often heavier beer.
- brandy
- burgundy (See: wine.)
- champagne - Must come from France to be true champagne, a country with which Britain was often at war in the 18-19th centuries, so the British figured out how to make: sparkling wine. (However, Regency folk were not scrupulous about the use of the term champagne, using it freely regardless of the origin of such.)
- cider
- claret
- cordials
- frumenty - (See more, below, at F.)
- gin
- ginger beer - Usually non-alcoholic.
- hock - (See below, at H.)
- lemonade - (See below, at L.)
- madeira
- mead - Not common during the Regency, but not unknown.
- milk
- negus - (See below, at N.)
- port
- porter - (See under P.)
- punch - Many kinds, mostly made of wine and fruit. (See: Arrack punch, above.)
- ratafia - A sweet liqueur made from wine of grape juice, usually mixed with brandy, and flavored with almonds or fruit. Considered acceptable for women to drink.

- rum
- sack - White fortified wine.
- sherry - Was drunk, of course, but also used in many receipts.
- sparkling wine - (See: champagne, above.)
- spruce beer - Alcoholic. Often homemade.
- vermouth - (See, below.)
- wassail - (See under W.)
- water - Because of pollution in the Thames (and many bodies of water near London,) water was generally not drunk in the London area unless it could be had from a well on the outskirts of the crowded city; people generally slaked their thirst with coffee or tea, both of which would be boiled and thereby made drinkable, or small beer, or wine.
- whey - (See: curds and whey, above.)
- whisky - (See below.)
- wine - Red. White. Fortified ones, like sack or sherry. Hock. Port. England often looked to Portugal for wines.

duck

dumplings - Sweet or savory, such as apple dumpling, or "ox-cheeks with little dumplings."

dun fowls

eels - Often seen in eel pie. Sometimes referred to as: lampreys. (See under E.)

eggplant - See: aubergine, above.

eggs - Hen, duck, quail. Eggs were hard-boiled, soft-boiled, broiled, made as omelets, coddled, served in egg cups, etc. Hard-boiled eggs were often in many savory receipts, chopped and added to the dish as it cooked, or sprinkled atop as a garnish.

- ➢ See: Chicken, above, note at.
- ➢ See: Scotch egg.

elderberries

endive

fennel

feverfew - A mainly medicinal herb.

figs

filberts

fish (and shellfish) -

- ➢ See: Billingsgate.

- See: fish, at its own F listing.
- See: at their own listings in this entry, such as: cockles, eels, lobster, salmon, etc.
- See: fish and chip shop, under F - For note on fried fish.
- See: New Earl Street/Sweetings.

flour - Towns often had a mill; if you grew the grain, you could pay a fee to have it milled into flour.

- See: bread, above.
- See: Uxbridge - Provided much of London's flour.

French beans - What Americans call: stringbeans.

fruit - Often served as a remove, along with nuts and raisins. Not uncommon to see 3-4 plates piled into pyramids (each with only one type of fruit upon it.)

fruit juices - If you could get juice from it... Example: lemonade (See, below.)

frumenty - Variant spelling: furmity. Was hulled wheat boiled with milk and flavored with cinnamon and sugar, sometimes raisins.

galangal - Also seen often as: galangal root. Ginger-like, with a hot, citrus-y flavor.

gammon - The lower part of a side of bacon.

garlic - Grown in England for centuries.

giblets

gin - Also called: Blue Ruin. (See under G.)

ginger - Also, preserved ginger.

ginger beer - Usually non-alcoholic.

gingerbread - In cake form, not "houses." Sometimes seen spelled as two words.

gizzards

goose - Eaten year-round, but was a winter favorite.

gooseberries - In Britain also sometimes called: goosegog.

grapes - Often from forcing gardens.

gravy - Not the thickened sauce Americans think of; the term meant the juices that came off the meat as it was cooked, more like what Americans think of as "au jus."

green onions - Same as scallions. Both terms were used, but I've seen "green onions" more often.

grouse - Wild birds were often written of as: "I've brought a brace of grouse for the table" - meaning: two.

guinea-fowl

ham - (You may care to see: pork.)

hares - Note: because the animals were protected under poaching laws, usually only landowners dined on their property's hares.

- See: leveret, below.
- See: rabbit, below.

herrings - Often smoked (and called kippers.)

hock - A German white wine.

hogget - (See: lamb, below.)

honey - Beekeeping was fairly common. (You may care to see: sugar.)

hops - For beer-making.

horseradish - If you grew your own, due to its pungency you had to protect your eyes and hands while grating it for use.

hot chocolate - (See: chocolate.)

hyssop - A mostly medicinal herb used for lungs and expectoration.

ice - As in frozen water, was available. It was brought from colder climes in large chunks and, for those who could afford it, placed in an ice house (which was usually underground and lined with straw.) For those without an ice house, ice could be purchased, but it was a bit of an indulgence. (See: ices.)

ices - Also called: ice-cream. Dessert or treat. Popular. The ice cream cone wasn't invented until 1904, in America. (See: Gunter's, under G.)

icing - On cakes. Not called "frosting." On wedding cakes they sometimes had an almond icing, browned in the oven. An icing of white, refined sugar was a sign of affluence, because sugar (and especially refined sugar) was expensive. (See: cakes, above.)

islinglass - A form of gelatin; collagen derived from the swim bladders of fish. Think (American) "jello" but with a mildly fishy taste.

jams and jellies - A jam is always made of fruit. Both often made from fruit, but jellies could also be made from things like rose or lavender. Plus could also mean: a dessert containing jelly; it was frequently called just "jelly" as a remove. (See: marmalades.)

kale

kidney beans

kidneys

kippers - Smoked herring; is split, salted, dried, then smoked. Often seen at breakfast.

lamb - Lamb means young sheep; mutton means older; hogget is a 1-2 year old sheep, which tends to be a darker red meat (also refers to the animal's first shearing coat.)

lard - A fat derived from pork. Lard could be used for making pastries or sweets, whereas suet (see) was more for savory dishes.

larks - The bird.

lavender

leeks

lemonade - Like what Americans think of. (See under L.)

lemons - Its pulp/juice. Also used for decoration, sliced on top of both sweet and savory dishes. Its peel could be candied. In addition to being a dessert ingredient, lemons are seen in many Regency era receipts, often as a last-minute squeeze of flavor enhancement to meats and stews and such. (See: lemonade, above.)

lettuce - Green. Coss lettuce (Romaine.) Leafy salads of the day were often just lettuce and cucumbers. (See: cresses.)

leveret - A young hare. (See: hare, above.)

limes

liver - Of various animals.

lobster - While seen regularly in Regency receipts, lobster didn't have its "ritzy" reputation yet. (See under: fish, at its own F listing.) You might see it on a bill of fare as: Buttered Lobster.

macaroni - While Regency receipts sometimes call for specific types of pasta (for instance, vermicelli,) pasta was generally called by the collective term of macaroni; it didn't mean the elbow-shaped tubes known to Americans. (For what it is worth, "macaroni" was also an 18th century term for a dandy/excessively smartly dressed young man.) Less frequently, it might be called: pasta.

mace - The spice.

madeira

maize - This is what Regency folk called the grain that grows on a cob. "Corn" meant all crops except oats. Sometimes called "turkey corn." (See: corn, under C.)

mangos - Imported.

marjoram - Also called sweet marjoram.

marmalade - All manner of flavors. Often contains the fruit's peel. Apricots, cherries, oranges, quince, etc. Orange marmalade made with oranges from Seville, Spain were prized. (See: jams and jellies, above.)

marrows - Squash.

marzipan - (See: almond paste.)

mead

meats - (See at their individual listings.)

- beef
- brawn
- chicken - Capons, pullets, roosters.
- dotterel
- duck - Includes teals and widgeons.
- dun fowls
- game birds - Many kinds of, such as grouse, guinea-fowl, lark, pheasant.
- gammon
- giblets
- gizzards
- goose
- ham
- kidneys
- liver - Beef, goose, etc.
- ox
- partridge
- pheasant
- pigeons
- pork
- ribs of beef - Or lamb, or pork.
- sausages
- snipes
- swans
- sweetbreads
- tongue
- tripe
- turkey
- veal
- venison
- wheat-ear - A bird.
- woodcocks.

(Also see: fish, at its own F listing.)

medlars - A small apple-shaped fruit not edible until it's over-ripe.

melons - A type: musk melon.

milk - Was easily obtained in London. Cows grazed in many places/on commons, so milk was readily available to Regency era folk. Goat milk was also consumed.

- ➢ See: butter, above.
- ➢ See: buttermilk, above.
- ➢ See: cream, above.
- ➢ See: milk, under M.

mincemeat - A mince pie contained, literally, minced meat, suet, chopped fruits, and spices.

mineral waters - (See: Schweppes, under S.)

mint

muffins - As the song says, sometimes sold by muffin men (street vendors.) Made with yeast, not like a modern American muffin.

mulberries

mushrooms - Fresh, dried, or pickled.

mussels

mustard - Both the plant and the condiment. (See: Uxbridge Moor.)

mutton - (See: lamb, above.)

nectarines

negus - Hot wine, often port, with sugar, water, nutmeg, lemons, and sometimes oranges.

noodles - Not a Regency era word. (See: macaroni.)

nutmeg

nuts - Nuts could be pickled. (Not an all inclusive list):

- Almonds: Imported, but frequently seen on elegant tables.
- Chestnuts.
- Filberts.
- Hazlenuts.
- ~~Peanuts~~: Were an American crop and had yet to catch on outside the U. S.; this was not a term known to the average Briton during the Regency. If they did know of them, they would refer to them as: ground-nuts.
- Walnuts.

See: acorns.

See: chestnuts.

oat-cakes - A handy breakfast.

oatmeal - Oatmeal (as in the hot cereal) is a type of porridge, but not all porridges are made of oatmeal. Porridge is made from grains, vegetables, or legumes, usually boiled with water or milk. (Regency era folk would have called prepared hot oats: porridge.)

oats - A plentiful grain throughout Britain.

- See: corn, under C.
- See: maize, above - Note at.
- See: oats, under O.

oils - Vegetable oil. Olive oil was known and used, but not widely popular; (could be called: oil of olives, or oil olive.) Melted butter, lard, or suet were often used in place of an oil. (See: oils, under O.)

olives - You might see it on a bill of fare as: Preserve of Olives.

onions - Also: green onions, AKA: scallions. (See: Ilford.)

orange-water - Used to flavor many things, often desserts. There were all kinds of flavoring waters: cucumber-water, lavender-water, rose-water, etc.

oranges - Seasonally imported, often from Seville. Or grown in Britain in a hothouse called an orangery. Its peel could be candied. To the average Regency person, considered a treat.

ox - Ox tails can actually be the tail of any bovine.

oysters - (See: fish/oysters, under F at its own listing.)

parsley

parsnips

partridge

pasta - (See: macaroni.)

pasty - (Rhymes with nasty.) What Americans would call a turnover (though perhaps heartier and less flaky.) A hand-pie, favored by laborers because pasties could easily be carried to work for their dinner.

pastries - Many kinds, some savory, often taken for breakfast. (See: puffs.) You might see it on a Bill of Fare as: Baskets of Pastry.

See: Gerrard Street.

See: puffs, below.

peaches

peacock

pears

peas - Were a large part of the British diet, not least because they could be preserved through drying. Also seen as: pease. Pease porridge is, well, pea porridge. Also, of course, served fresh.

pepper - The spice. Imported, expensive. Also, naturally: peppercorns.

pheasant

pickles - Regency folk would have called them: pickled cucumbers, or cucumber pickle. In today's UK, a pickled cucumber would likely be called a gherkin. But cucumbers were just a start - there were many kinds of pickled vegetables (broccoli, carrots,) fruit (Damson plums, lemons,) eggs, nuts, etc. (See: MacKey & Co., under M.)

pies - Sweet, savory. Examples: apple pie, game pies, lemon pie, pigeon pie. Also: hand-pies, convenient for one's dinner, especially for laborers. (See: pasty, above.)

pig - (See: pork.)

pigeons

pineapples - Exotic. First imported to England in 1514. A pineapple was the symbol of hospitality. It was also the medieval sign for a confectioner's shop (still used during the Regency.) Pineapple was imported, although they could be grown in Britain in hothouses called pineries.

plums - Damsons, Greengages, Orleans. (See: prunes.)

poppy seeds

pork - A common-enough meat in the Regency era. It was easier to house pigs than cattle or sheep. (Also: boar.)

- See: Kensington/Notting Hill - For a place people raised pigs for their personal consumption.
- See: St. James's Market/Wall's Meat Co.

porridge - (See: oatmeal, above, for explanation.)

port

porter - (See under P.)

potatoes - Seldom seen as a Regency era *home-grown* crop, for some reason, but they were readily available to buy. They were introduced from South America to Europe in the last half of the 16th century. They were a major crop in Ireland by the second half of the 17th century, and in most of Europe by the end of the 18th century. There were many receipts for potatoes. (See: Ilford.)

poultry -

- See: capon; chicken; duck; goose; pullet; quail; rooster; turkey - in this list.
- See: Leadenhall Market.
- See wild birds such as: pheasant, pigeon, rooks - In this list.
- See the parts thereof, such as: gizzards, liver, tongue - In this list.

pound cake - (See: cake.)

prawns

prunes - Dried plums.

puddings - All manner of, sweet or savory. Dozens, if not hundreds of varieties. Most dinner parties had at least one pudding included, not necessarily sweet or at the end of the meal. Examples: bread pudding, cheese pudding, flour pudding, hasty pudding, rice pudding, suet pudding, vegetable pudding. (Note: plum pudding almost always really was calling for raisins, not plums. Americans tend to call it plum pudding, but Britons tend to call it Christmas pudding.)

In modern times, in the UK the word "pudding" can mean almost any kind of dessert, though it might not have anything to do with a custard-like pudding such as Americans take the word to mean.

puffs - An airy type of pastry.

pullets - A young female chicken, usually yet to have lain eggs.

pumpkin

punch - (See: drinks/punch, above.)

quail

quince - Red quince. White quince.

rabbit -

- See: hare.
- See: leveret.

radishes

ragout - Pronounced ra-goo (the a is short, like in the word rag.) What Americans call: stew. (See: stew, below, to see why it's not called "stew" in the UK.)

raisins - Imported.

rashers - (See: bacon.)

raspberries

ratafia - (See: drinks/ratafia.)

rhubarb

rice - Imported, expensive, but definitely seen on fine tables. One example: sweet rice with stewed apples.

rooks

rooster - (See: chicken.)

rosemary

rum

rutabaga - (See: swedes.)

saffron - Imported.

sage

salads - Salads were not the "highlight" at most Regency era tables, but there was usually at least one salad at formal dinners. It would be odd to serve one's guests just a salad.

- See: cresses.
- See: kale.
- See: lettuce.
- See: sorrel.
- See: spinach.

salmon - Killed off in the Thames by pollution in the 1860s.

salt - They had salt cellars for the table, which weren't shakers; they were open low dishes, and you used a small spoon to scoop and sprinkle the salt crystals on your food.

Often seen: salt beef, salt fish, salt pork - meats heavily salted for preservation. Usually soaked or boiled to reduce the salt taste.

- See: Cheshire, under the BRITISH COUNTIES section.
- See: St. Swithin's Lane/Salters' Hall.

sandwiches - (See: sandwich, under S.)

sauces - Many kinds. Examples: bread sauce, caper sauce, fish sauce, mock oyster sauce, sorrel sauce, white sauce. Usually not made from tomatoes. (See: tomatoes, below.)

sausages

savoury - An herb.

savoy - A crinkly-leafed winter cabbage.

scallions - (See: green onions, above.)

Scotch egg - Hard-boiled egg, wrapped in sausage, then breadcrumbs, then deep-fried. Invented by Fortnum (of Fortnum & Mason) in 1738.

shallots

sheep -

- See: lamb, above.
- See: mutton, above.
- See: Smithfield Market, under S.

shellfish - (See: fish, at its own F listing.)

sherry

skirrets - A sweetish root vegetable similar to carrots.

snipes - A wading bird found on river banks.

sole - Dover sole.

sorrel - A sharp-tasting plant rather like buckwheat, used in salads and sauces. Sometimes called: sorrel spinach.

southernwood - An herb, used in herbal teas.

soups - Many kinds. Barley was often found in a variety of soups. Soup examples: chicken soup, mulligatawny soup, onion soup, pea (or pease) soup, turtle soup, white soup (the latter made of: chicken or veal, bacon, almonds, plus cream.) There were also many broths. (See: broth, above.)

spices -

- See: Mincing Lane, under M - Where many spices were sold.
- See: the various spices alphabetically in this listing, such as: anise, cinnamon, saffron, etc.

spinach

spruce beer - Alcoholic.

squash - (See: marrow, above.)

steak - (See: beefsteak.)

stew - Was slang for a sauna or brothel, not a food dish. (See: ragout.)

strawberries - (See: Whitton.)

strong beer - (See: beer.)

suet - A hard white fat found on the kidneys of cows and sheep. (See lard, for more information.)

sugar - Imported. Expensive. Used by those who could afford it. The poor used honey when they could get it. (Actually, honey was used by everyone.) There was white sugar: called caster sugar or refined sugar, and there was golden (brown) sugar. In being processed, sugar didn't end up as loose grains, it was formed into loaves or cones. When you had need of the cone, you used a sugar cleaver (or a sugar ax, or sugar nippers) to break off the amount needed.

- See: docks/West India Docks - Where most sugar was shipped into London.
- See: sugar, under S.

sugar-plums - Not plums at all. They were sugared almonds. It was a kind of comfit. (See: comfit, above.)

swan - Tended to be protected by landowners (for instance, the King) so were more likely to be seen only on upper class tables.

swedes - What Americans call rutabagas.

sweet, a - More or less, a candy. (See: boiled sweet.)

sweetbreads - The pancreas or thymus, usually of a calf or lamb, often fried.

sweetmeats - Candied fruits, nuts, and other sweet nibbles.

syllabub - A dessert of cream whipped with brandy and sugar.

syrups - Sugar, water, and flavor, cooked and reduced together. Could be either made from fruit, or more savory things such as lavender, rosemary, etc. Used to flavor many dishes. In some receipts that call for lemon or orange juice really are calling for syrups.

tamarind - Imported from India.

tarragon

tart - Sweet, savory. Many kinds and flavors. Examples: apple tart, lemon tart, treacle tart.

tea - Imported, expensive. (See under T.)

teals - A small duck.

thyme

toast - As in browned bread. Often toasted on a long fork held near a fire. A fairly popular morning food.

tomatoes - Tomatoes were at the time of the Regency erroneously considered by many to be poisonous, so while used by some, they were rather uncommon in dishes during the Regency era. When used, they were invariably cooked.

tongue - Beef, pork, even birds (such as: duck tongues.)

treacle - A refined black sugar syrup. Essentially, what Americans call molasses (although the two are refined slightly differently.) Treacle can be tawny, but can also be black; the darkest ones are just this side of edible.

trifle - A dessert of sponge (cake) soaked in sherry or juice, layered with jam or jelly, and topped with custard and/or whipped cream.

tripe

trout

truffles - The mushroom-like delicacy, not the sweet treat.

turkey - Eaten year-round but, like goose, was a winter favorite. It was relatively expensive. Introduced to Europe in the early 16th C., brought back from North America. (See under T.)

turmeric

turnip greens

turnips - Often used much as Americans would utilize potatoes (boiled, mashed, in ragouts, etc.)

turtle - You might see it on a bill of fare as: turtle cutlets.

veal - Also eaten: calf's head.

venison - Deer, like hares, were also protected under the poaching laws. (See: hares, above - The note under.) You might see it on a bill of fare as: Haunch of Venison. The fallow deer was yellowish, bucks taken in the summer; does in the winter.

vermouth - Invented in 1786, in Turin, by Antonia Benedetto Carpano, Italian distiller; became popular at once and was enjoyed in Georgian London (and ever since.)

vinegar - They had distilled (white) vinegar, as well as many flavored ones such as: dill vinegar, malt vinegar (sometimes called alegar,) raspberry vinegar, tarragon vinegar.

- See: Distillers' Company.
- See: South Lambeth/Beaufoy vinegar distillery.

wafer - A kind of thin biscuit (cookie,) often made on a heated iron.

walnuts

wassail - A Christmas drink. (See under W.)

watercress -

- See: Bayswater, under B.
- See: cresses, above.

waters - For flavoring. (See: orange-water, above.)

Welsh rabbit - Melted cheese and butter over toast, absolutely no rabbit in the dish. Was called Welsh Rarebit until 1735. Purportedly evolved to "rabbit" because Welsh wives served it as a kind of consolation when their hubbies came home without a rabbit for the pot.

wheat

wheat-ears - A bird.

whelk - (See: fish/whelk, at its own F listing.)

whey - (See: curds and whey.)

whisky - Whisky (no e) is the Scots spelling. If it has an e in it (whiskey) it is American or Irish.

widgeons - A freshwater wild duck.

wig, a - A cake or bun that rises up out of its pan, forming a "wig" or mushroom-like cap.

wine - Reds. Whites. Fortified ones, such as sack and sherry. Burgundy. Hock. Port.

Woodcocks

Worcestershire sauce - Invented in 1837. Pronounced: WOO-stuh-shur. (See: Worcestershire/Lea & Perrins, under the BRITISH COUNTIES section.)

wormwood - A bitter herb, used to flavor vermouth.

yeast - Receipts tend to call for teaspoonful(s) of yeast.

foolscap - (See: paper.)

Foot Guards, the - (See: Royal Guards/Foot Guards.)

football - (Known in America as: soccer.) Various forms of games with balls handled primarily with the feet have been played for time out of mind. Edward II banned football from London in 1314, saying: "Many evils may arise which God forbid." A set of common football rules was not established at university games until 1849. The Football Association was formed in 1863. Ball handling (with one's hands) was not strictly limited to the goalkeeper until 1871.

forcier - A water pump, 16th century (to carry water up from a river to a residence.) They were still used during the Regency era.

forcing garden - A hot house. Examples: a pinery (for growing pineapples); an orangery (for growing oranges.) Most large country estates had a forcing garden. (See: greenhouses.)

Fore Street - Cripplegate. Daniel Defoe (author) born here in 1660. Today Fore Street is part of the Barbican development, from the 1960s.

- Fore Street Warehouse, the: Founded 1799.
- St. Giles, Cripplegate: (See under the CHURCHES section.)

Foreign Office, the - King Charles Street, Whitehall. (Also now called the Foreign and Commonwealth Office. AKA: FCO.) Responsible for promoting/protecting British interests worldwide/*external* affairs. (As opposed to the *Home Office*, which was for *internal* affairs.) Like the Home Office, the Foreign Office was also formed in 1782.

In a quadrangle building standing between Whitehall, Downing Street, St. James's Park, and King Charles Street, "massive." The building was built on this site in 1868-73, Italianate frontage.

Previous to that, the offices of the Foreign Office were across from 10 Downing Street. This is where the Regency era Foreign Office was; those buildings were demolished to make room for the 20th century FCO.

If the 19th century had spies working for King and Country, the Foreign Office is where they would have reported.

Today's FCO was created in 1968 when the Commonwealth Office and the Foreign Office combined. The Commonwealth Office had been responsible for interacting with the Commonwealth of Nations, starting 1926, the UK's former colonies. Did not include America, because this was the 20th century decolonization of the British Empire. (See:

Commonwealth Office, under C.)

forest - (See: forests.)

Forest Hill - Lewisham. Early on it was Forest Hill, but then it was simply called "the Forest" until the 1780s, (it was the last remnants of the Great North Wood,) and was virtually uninhabited. The Forest Hill name came back in Victorian days.

- Honor Oak Road: Now the name of an area called "Forest Hill," merchants' well-proportioned homes built in the 1780s.

Forest of Middlesex - Ancient. At one time covered much of what became London, Hertfordshire, and Essex. (See: Queen's Wood.)

Forest, The - (See: Forest Hill.)

Foresters - (See: Verderers.)

forests - Most forest areas near London are not "natural," meaning that how the forest had become laid out (in terms of plants, trees, bodies of water) tends to be in rows or otherwise planned or shaped for aesthetic or practical purposes by man's planning. Epping Forest is the rare exception, being allowed to grow and shape itself without (overall) human interference.

Also, note that most British forests have been harvested and replanted many times over, supplying wood and timber for the masses throughout the centuries.

Some of the following were called forests, some called woods.

In the 21st century, the borough of Haringey yet boasts four distinct (and ancient, although now rather smaller) woods:

- Bluebell Wood: This is what is left of Tottenham Wood. At the end of Winton Avenue. In large part consisting of sessile oak.
- Coldfall Wood: Muswell Hill. Near the St. Pancras and Islington Cemetery. Was twice its present size until the 20th century.
- Highgate Wood: 70 acres. Lies between East Finchley, Highgate Village, and Muswell Hill.
- Queen's Wood: (See under Q.)
    - See: Epping Forest.
    - See: Forest of Middlesex.
    - See: Great North Woods.
    - See: Hainault Forest.
    - See: Hampstead Heath/Kenwood.
    - See: Highgate Hill/Highgate Wood.
    - See: Lloyd Park.
    - See: St. John's Wood - Began to be built over in the 1820s.
    - See: Verderers.

forks - Eating utensils. (See: Cutlers' Hall.)

formal acquaintance - One way the upper classes protected women was through the process of becoming formally acquainted. That is, you didn't recognize or talk to someone to whom you had not been introduced by a third party. The role of third party was taken seriously; by introducing someone you were essentially vouching that they were of decent and honorable deportment. Therefore, once an introduction was mutually acceptable (and contrary to some perceptions,) a man and a woman *could* stroll alone together during the Regency era. (Although having a chaperone with you was always suitable, of course.)

Fortnum & Mason - Famed grocery (+ much more) shop. (See: Piccadilly/Fortnum & Mason.)

Foster Lane - Cheapside. "Fosters" derived from "fusters," makers of wooden saddle bows.

- Goldsmiths' Hall: (See under G.)
- Saddlers' Hall: (See under S.)
- St. Vedast's Church: (See under the CHURCHES section.)

Founders' Company - (AKA: the Worshipful Company of Founders.) Founders worked in a foundry. Existed by at least 1365, at which time they cast things such as small brass and copper candlesticks, pots, stirrups, etc. By the time they were granted their Charter (1614) they had gained the right to size and mark brass weights. Their powers dropped off in the 19th century.

They had their first Hall built in 1531; it burned in the Great Fire of 1666. Their second hall yet stands, but it has been office space for decades, at 1 Cloth Fair. Livery company. 33rd in the order of precedence.

Foundling Hospital - (AKA: Thomas Coram Foundation for Children.) Was first in Guilford Street; after 1929 it was demolished and the hospital moved to 40 Brunswick Square, Bloomsbury.

Established in 1736 by one (sea) Capt. Thomas Coram, who was moved when he saw the many orphaned and abandoned "street babies". Received its Royal Charter in 1739; and the hospital was erected in 1742-47 on the site of what is now Coram's Fields (in the Regency, the fields were called "Lamb's Conduit Fields.") It was open only to the mother's first child, under the age of 12 months. The children were cared for by foster parents to the age of 4 or 5, at which time the child returned to the hospital. They stayed to about the age of 14, and were then put into domestic service or the military. At that time, the main entrance gates would have been on Guilford Street.

The hospital was so successful even Parliament eventually established funds for this charity. (Usually charities were only privately funded.)

It turned into a private institution in 1760.

After 1801, due to overcrowding, only illegitimate children were admitted (and then only if the mother first filled out a questionnaire and stated the child was the result of a broken promise of marriage.)

Charles Dickens (author) was "favorably impressed" when he visited.

The hospital moved to the Home Counties in the 1920s and very little of the 18th C. building remains from the almost complete demolition of 1926; what does remain are splendidly restored 18th C. rooms that host a small museum containing items from the hospital's past, and what is now an adoption agency under the title of the Thomas Coram Foundation.

- See: Bloomsbury Square/Foundling Hospital.
- See: Royal Academy of Arts - The note under.

foundry - For making bells, see: Whitechapel Road.

- See: Founders' Company
- See: Whitechapel Foundry.

Fountain Court - Inner Temple. (See: Inns of Court/Temple/Inner Temple/Fountain Court.)

- 3: William Blake (poet, mystic) lived here from 1823 to his death in 1828.

fountain pens - 1827. (See: quill.)

Four-in-Hand Club - Founded in 1856 by the dissolute Lord Barrymore, who ran it along with Lord Sefton (Sefton drove a team of bays,) Sir John Lade, Colonel Berkeley, and the Marquis of Worchester (he drove a team of grays.) Departed off of George Street, Hanover Square; they drove to the Windmill (an inn) at Salt Hill, where they supped on sumptuous dinners.

Fournier Street - Spitalfields. 18th C. houses have wide attic windows to provide light for French Huguenot refugees; the street was named for one of the silk-weaving Huguenot families. Plain Queen Anne facades.

- Christ Church: At the west end of the street. (See: Christ Church, Spitalfields, under the CHURCHES section.)

foxhunting - Originated in the Hanoverian era; before then hare-coursing was the popular hunt. The fox was traditionally a red fox, pursued by scent hounds. If caught, the fox was killed by the hounds. Fox were seen as pests, because they attacked farmyard creatures/their eggs. Foxhunting season ran usually November to March. Women did not hunt much in the beginning of the 19th century, until the leaping horn (also called: second saddle horn) was added to women's sidesaddles in the 1830s. A woman participating in the hunt during the Regency would have to be able to keep her seat (difficult to do, especially in a jump,) might be considered foolhardy, and would not wear the pink; men could be invited to wear "colours," this is the red coat worn by the hunt master, whippers-in, other hunt staff, and others invited to do so by the hunt master. (See: Mason's Yard/Maxwell, Henry - For the foxhunting red coat called a pink.)

Framework Knitters' Company - (AKA: the Worshipful Company of Framework Knitters. AKA: the Society of the Art or Mystery of Framework Knitters of the Cities of London and Westminster and the Kingdom of England and the Dominion of Wales.) Dates from 1589, upon the invention of a way to knit mechanically. Charter granted in 1657 by Oliver Cromwell, Lord Protector of the Commonwealth; the Charter was reissued by Charles II in 1663, after the restoration of the monarchy. Livery Company since 1713.

Framework Knitters primarily produced silk hose. Most of the stockings trade moved to the Midlands in the 18th century. Never had a hall. 64th in the order of precedence.

(See: stockings.)

free house - A tavern that was not under the auspices of one particular brewery. (You may care to see: the INNS/PUBS section - The notes under.)

free tenement - An old term meaning an estate held for life or longer. That which is held rather than owned. For instance, the king might technically own the land, but one granted a free tenement would have the use, farming, grazing, etc. of the estate/property.

Free Vintner - One who serves *wine*, needs no license, and can open and close as he wishes. This right was granted to the Vintners' Company by James I in 1611; the right was abolished in 2006. (You may care to see: Vintners' Company.)

Freedom of the City of London - (Granted this status, you would be: a Freeman of the City of London.) Bestowed upon a valued citizen (or visiting dignitary.) In medieval times it meant freedom from serfdom, AKA: recognizing you as a freeman (as opposed to a vassal to a feudal lord.) You had to belong to one of the Livery Companies. It used to mean you could trade and own property in the City, but in the 20th-21st centuries it has become ceremonial only.

Only three Americans have been granted this privilege: George Peabody (philanthropist, b.1795-d.1869); Theodore Roosevelt (American President); and Dwight D. Eisenhower (American President.)

- See: halls.
- See: Livery Companies.

Freemasonry - The "modern" practice of freemasonry began in England on 6/24/1717, at the Goose and Gridiron alehouse in St. Paul's Cathedral churchyard, where four London fellowships met and founded the first Grand Lodge in the world. Not to be confused with the Livery Companies/Guilds of London. (See: Freemasons' Hall.)

Freemasons' Hall - 60 Great Queen Street. NOT a Livery Company hall. It is the headquarters of the United Grand Lodge of England (of the Society of Free and Accepted Masons,) plus a meeting space for the Masonic lodges in the London area.

The hall was built in 1775-6, the freemasons having previously met in a series of taverns. (See: Freemasonry.) This building was replaced by a larger version in 1864-7, which subsequently burned down. The third version was built in 1883-5; this was expanded in 1898-1900. An even larger version supplanted this in 1927-33 (and still stands, built to commemorate Masons who died in WWI.)

- World Anti-Slavery Convention, the: Held here in 1840.

French - Here I refer to the British Regency era habit of adding "French" before terms, in order to indicate they were risqué or naughty. For instance: a French letter was a condom.

- See: menstruation - The "French lady's visit."
- See: prostitution - For more "French" examples.

French immigrants - Despite some 22 years of war, on and off, with France (during and around the Regency era,) it's not too broad to say that if you were a rich immigrant from France, you would be welcome anywhere in London.

For respectable but perhaps not so rich, see: Gloucester Place; (the farther north one went from this street, the more it reflected the immigrant's lack of available monies and possible lack of accompanying status.)

- See: Huguenots.
- See: Petty France.
- See: South Kensington/Little Paris.
- See: Wandsworth - For Huguenot refugees.

French Ordinary Court - Near Fenchurch Street. "A hole" off 42 Crutched Friars leads to this court. Supposedly took its name because a French eatery sat here once, with an "ordinary" being a fixed price for the meal. Or, it's also said the name comes from Huguenots who settled here. Described in NAIRN'S LONDON as: "...in effect a big and very dark wedge-shaped room carved out under the railway tracks"; private. 18th century. Along this road the northern end is called St. Katherine Coleman, and is open-aired; the southern end is under railway tracks and is called French Ordinary Court, no cars, very narrow, although at its southernmost end it opens up into a car park. (See: Crutched Friars/42.)

Friary Court - St. James's Palace. A courtyard. New monarchs are still announced from a balcony (which is partly Tudor in its construction) in Friary Court. St. James's Palace's State Apartments can be reached via a northeast corner door in Friary Court. It used to be significantly larger, enclosed by an east range which included a chapel built for Queen Anne; the range was demolished by fire in 1809; rebuilt in Neo-Tudor style.

Fribourg & Treyer's - 34 Haymarket. Was conveniently near many gentlemen's clubs. "Foreign snuff, Tobacco and Oriental Segars," there for 250 years, still now has its 18th C. window fronts. Founded in 1720 by Peter Fribourg. Known simply as "Fribourg's" until 1780, when its then proprietor, G. A. Treyer, added his name. In 1803 the business passed through marriage (Mrs. Treyer had been Miss Evans) to the Evans family. Women also patronized this shop. (You may care to see: tobacco.)

Friday Street - Cheapside. Fish were sold here in medieval times, hence the name (because Catholics, from the early days of the church, did not eat meat on Fridays.)

- 6: Saracen's Head Inn. Old coaching inn, from at least 1722. Pulled down in 1844. (See: Saracen's Head Inn, Cheapside, under the INNS/PUBS section.)
- Meaker's: On the corner of Friday Street, it is the oldest building in Cheapside, surviving 1666's Great Fire. Was the City branch of this gentlemen's outfitter until 1965 (when it was pulled down.)

friendly societies - Organizations that provided insurance against sickness, unemployment, and provided pensions to widows. They were a sort of precursor to the mid to late 19th C. labor unions (and were loosely offsprings, by the workers, of any Guild to which they might also belong.) Had subscription fees. Started springing up in the 17th C., with there being 7,200 such societies by 1793. They had memberships of 704,350 by 1803, and 861,657 by 1815. Had nothing to do with the Quakers, who also have the name Friends. (See: union.)

Friends Burial Ground - For Quakers. (See: Bunhill Row/Friends Burial Ground.)

Frith Street - (See: Soho Square/Frith Street.)

Frogmore House - Windsor Great Park (on the grounds of/contained in,) Windsor Great Park/Berkshire. Described as a "sprawling white mansion." Was first built in 1680, being remodeled through the years. Generations of royal ladies had retreated here, with Queen Charlotte (wife of George III) being the first.

Queen Victoria gave the house to her mother (the Duchess of Kent) in 1841. At the Duchess' death the first of several royal mausolea were built, 1861. Prince Albert's mausoleum was also built here in the same year.

- Green Pavilion: Restored prior to Queen Charlotte's death in 1818.

Frognal - Camden. The name derives from the fact frogs really did inhabit here once. In the 17-18th centuries it expanded from one house and farm to cottages and mansions, due to its "salubrious air." Still, there wasn't much urbanization until after 1870.

- 35: 1885 house, by Norman Shaw.
- Frognal Park: 1806.

frost fair - Held only when the slow-moving waters of the Thames above the narrow arches of old London Bridge froze over. (When repairs were made to London Bridge's arches in 1831, this corrected where the ice used to be able to build up, so that the last frost fair was held eighteen years earlier, in the winter of 1813-4.)

There were frost fairs in:

1564-5 - Football (soccer) was played mid river on the ice.

1608 - At which there were football matches, and temporary taverns.

1648-9 - At which a printing press was set up, making an on-going custom for people wanting to buy a "frost fair souvenir certificate."

1683-4 - Called the Great Frost. Charles II bought one of the certificates at this fair, and there was a whole row of booths set up on the ice like a street, and an ox was roasted right atop the ice. Horses and carriages were able to cross the ice as well. There were also: sledding; "sliding with skates"; bull-baiting; horse and carriage races; puppetry; and "lewd places." It must be noted the Great Frost's severe cold had a truly terrible side as well, killing London's people, trees, and crops.

1715-16; 1739-40; 1788-9; and 1813-14 - The last being the last Thames frost fair, with archery matches, dancing, and skating. (There could be no more frost fairs after 1831, when the old bridge arches were demolished, thereby allowing the water to be too fast-moving to freeze over.)

fruit - Eaten fresh, baked, juiced, preserved, stewed, etc. Available in spring/summer/early fall, depending on the fruit. (This is not an all-inclusive list.)

ALSO SEE EACH OF THESE UNDER: food. (Higher in this F section, where there can be additional information.)

apples

apricots

barberries

blackberries

cherries

citron

currants

dates

elderberries

figs

gooseberries - In Britain, also called: goosegog.

grapes

lemons - Surprisingly prolific in Regency receipts.

mangos

medlars

melons

mulberries

nectarines

oranges

peaches

pears

pineapples

plums - Damsons, Greengages.

quince

raisins

raspberries

strawberries - (See: Whitton.)

- See: Fruiterers' Company.
- See: greenhouse.
- See: orangery.
- See: orchards.
- See: pinery.
- See: scurvy - How citrus prevented it.
- See: vegetables - For some vegetable-like fruits such as rhubarb and tomatoes.
- See: Walworth.

fruit drinks and mineral waters -

- See: Camberwell/Rawlings.
- See: Schweppes.

Fruiterers' Company - (AKA: the Worshipful Company of Fruiterers.) In existence since 1463. Royal Charter in 1605. Livery company. Never had a hall. Were concerned with the importation of fruit into the City; also with apprenticeships, mentoring, etc. Declined in connection to the control of fruit by the late 19th C., although restored in the 20th C. as a charitable organization. 45th in order of precedence. (See: fruit.)

Fuellers - Not to be confused with Fullers. (See: Carmen's Company.)

fuels - (To heat one's home.) If you could get it by canal, river, or sea delivery, coal was preferred. However, depending on one's topography, other fuels to burn were: peat, turf, wood - the latter less readily available to city folk.

- See: coal.
- See: wood.

Fulham - Ca. 1085 was a noted fishing village. Had highly cultivated market-gardens, big supplier to Covent Garden. There were still some genteel homes here in the early 19th C., but it did eventually devolve into a seedy part of town (remaining "working class," until a coming into fashion era in the 1970s.) This area, in 1834, became known as part of Hammersmith (i.e. Hammersmith was a portion of the parish of Fulham until 1834.)

- All Saints: Ancient church, built ca. 1440. Has an embattled tower.
- Brandenburgh House: (Post-1834, a part of Hammersmith.) Early 17th century. One-quarter mile/0.4 km east of Hammersmith Bridge. In 1792, was bought by the Margrave of Brandenburgh-Anspach; died 1806. Alterations were then made to the mansion, at which time it took on the Brandenburgh House name.

  George IV's unbeloved Queen Caroline (coming from South Audley Street,) held her court here, trying to rival her unhappy spouse's court, during her House of Lords trial of 1820. A few days before the trial, Caroline moved back to London, staying in the house of Lady Francis in St. James's Square. All the same, when the Bill of Pains and Penalties did not go forward, the locals immediately around Brandenburgh House celebrated and illuminated their homes, and lit a celebratory bonfire before this house. When Queen Caroline died in August, 1821, the house was sold at auction, and pulled down, replaced by a factory.
- Fulham House: Home of the Lords Stourton, and later William Sharpe (a slave trader,) who died here in 1813.
- Fulham Palace: (See its own entry.)
- Hermitage, the: A home. At least by 1770. Located in the little hamlet called North End. Now called Mount Carmel Retreat. Surrounded by walls, it has a large garden.
- High Street: Widened in 1908.
- Hurlingham Home: Georgian build. (See: Hurlingham Club, under H.)
- Mall, the: (In post-1835, became a part of Hammersmith.) This street runs from Hammersmith Bridge to Chiswick. Has the Lower and Upper Malls, divided by a creek. The creek had a wooden footbridge over it, 1751, called High Bridge. A coffee-house, The Doves, stood on Upper Mall until 1860, accessible only via a winding, narrow path that ran through a cluster of houses. The Mall is shaded by 200+ year old elms planted by Queen Catherine, widow to Charles II; she made her summer home here in Fulham.
- meadows, the: In the Middle Ages, villagers grazed their cattle here on the town's marshy meadows (southwest of Sandford manor.) It came to be known as Sands End (perhaps as far back as Henry VII's time, but certainly by the 18th century.) Riverside industries came in ca. the 1820s.
- Munster House: Said to have once been a hunting seat for Charles II. Later

occupied by John Wilson Croker (b.1780-d.1857) essayist, editor, and Secretary of the Admiralty.

- North End: Described as "lowly." In the 1880s was developed under the new name of West Kensington. (See: West Kensington, under W.)
- Red Cow Tavern: A well-known coaching inn. Lasted over 250 years. (Adjoined the grounds of what later became St. Paul's School, at the corner of Colet Gardens.) Rebuilt 1897. Now gone.
- St. Paul's: (Post-1834, was a part of Hammersmith.) Queen Caroline Street. Consecrated 1631. Restored in 1864.
- St. Paul's School: Brought from the City to here in 1884, on 16 acres of land purchased in 1877 by the Mercers' Company. (See: St. Paul's School, under S.)
- St. Peter's Church: 1829. (Post-1834, was a part of Hammersmith.)
- St. Peter's Square: 1839. (See: Hammersmith/St. Peter's Square.)
- Sands End: (See: meadow, above.)

Fulham Broadway - (See: Kensington/Walham Green.)

Fulham Palace - From the 8th C. to 1973, was the home of the Bishop(s) of London. The oldest existing parts today date from ca. 1480, when it became a country retreat for the archbishops, becoming the main residence in the 18th century. Stands among gardens in Bishop's Park, (northwest of Putney Bridge.)

Fulham Road - Chelsea and Kensington. When the Bishop of London wanted Chelsea and Fulham connected, he caused Stamford Bridge to be built, resulting in Fulham Road also being built, 1410. Not a lot of building here until the mid 18th C., when clumps of houses began to appear. Newer developments had street lighting by 1806, and by 1845 added paving.

- Royal Brompton Hospital: 1840s (See: Brompton Hospital, under B.) Was first a cancer hospital under another name. Moved here in 1862. Merged with Harefield Hospital in 1998, then called: Royal Brompton & Harefield NHS Trust (heart and lung disease expertise.)

fullers - Those who shrink and thicken cloth, usually wool. (See: Mincing Lane/Clothworkers' Hall.)

Fuller's Brewery - (See: Chiswick/Fuller's Brewery.)

furnishing trimmings - (See: Henry Newberry.)

furniture/furniture-makers -

- See: Furniture-makers' Company - For useful information.
- See: Goodwin's Court - Where Chippendale's was.
- See: Heals.
- See: Long Acres.

- See: Oxford Street.
- See: Tottenham Court Road - Especially cabinets.
- See: Upholders' Company.
- See: Wardour Street/106.
- See: West End.

Furniture-Makers' Company - (AKA: the Worshipful Company of Furniture Makers.) Company and charity for the furnishings industry.

Founded, amazingly, in 1952. Became a livery company in 1963; Royal Charter in 2013. 83rd in the order of precedence.

In Medieval times (if you didn't make your own humble furniture) furniture pieces came from the Carpenters and the Blacksmiths (the latter for strapped constructions, like a chest.) But, too, the Turners were important for turned chair legs.

Moving into the mid Medieval days, the Cofferers had a part in the sphere of furniture, too, for chests, chairs, and coffers (small chests or strongboxes banded in metal,) by covering wood with textiles. This brought in: Clothworkers, Broderers, etc., plus Basketmakers for woven-material cradles.

It was the Joiners who made furniture, mainly, from the 15th C. and on, (although Turners and Basketmakers still played their part.) There were now more woods (such as Walnut) in use, and less oak (which was heavier.)

Cabinet-making came along in the Restoration era (ca. 1660.)

As time went on, Carpenters were different in that they joined wood with nails, whereas Joiners did so with adhesives.

Despite the experimental and widening styles of 17-18th C. furniture, no Furniture Makers Guild came to be then, possibly because the Upholsterers dominated the world of furniture at that time; fine designers such as Chippendale thought of themselves as Upholders first, furniture-makers second.

Then came Victorian mechanization...so, again, plans for a guild never came into being until 1952. Livery company. Their Hall is at 12 Austin Friars.

- See: Carpenters' Hall.
- See: Joiners' Hall.
- See: Turners' Company.

Furnival's Inn - (See: Inns of Court/Lincoln's Inn/Furnival's Inn.)

-G-

Gallery of Arts - (See: Southampton Street/Gallery of Arts.)

game - As in animals to be hunted/caught. (See: animals - The note at the beginning of.)

games, children's - Many (if not most) "toys" of this time were intended to be instructive. Dolls were meant to teach children how to tend to offspring, and maintain clothing and accoutrements. Dissected maps were to teach the names of countries and their locations, or the order of the alphabet, etc. Word games were to teach grammar, or spelling, or historical facts. The fact that children might be entertained or occupied was not the first consideration. This list is not all-inclusive.

(See: toy store.)

alphabet blocks - From the 1600s and on.

backgammon

balls

bilbocatch - A ball and cup.

board games - Engraved or etched. Might have ivory markers. More likely found in upper class nurseries. Usually meant to teach you your letters, languages, mathematics, or geography.

cards - Traditional, or with child-friendly art. Could be educational, such as teaching the ABCs, musical terms, nature, etc. There were also metamorphosis cards, cut in thirds, so a child could "assemble" odd people (such as an admiral's hat and head, a cleric's torso, and a farmer's legs.)

chess

conundrums - Word games.

dissected maps - Later called: jigsaw puzzles (ca. 1870.) In the Regency they were not yet interlocking, having straight edges, or slightly wiggly ones, or ones that followed shapes such as the outlines of countries and bodies of water.

dollhouses

dolls - Dolls are ancient. The fancy dress-up kind came about in the 17th century. Porcelain or bisque dolls date from ca. the 1840-60s. Prior to the porcelain-faced dolls, they were made of cloth (glue-stiffened,) composition (basically papier-mâché with sawdust mixed in,) leather, or wood.

dominoes

draughts - American: checkers.

hoop and stick

ice skating - For those who could afford skates (blade attached to a plate, and tied with broad ribbons snaking up the shoe/ankle/leg.)

kites

marbles - An ancient toy, but more popular with Victorians than during the Regency era.

marionettes

musical instruments - Child-sized horns, drums, etc.

Nine Men's Morris - A triangle shape with pegs.

painting supplies

paper toys - A jumping jack: Started in 18th C. France, a flat paper figure, cut out, its parts attached by string, so that when a dangling string was pulled, the figure moved.

- panoramas: An image that was moved from one spindle to another, with themes such as "the Thames," or "Race Day."
- paper dolls: There was an 1810 printed set called "Little Fanny," wherein Fanny runs away with gypsies, only to contritely return to the bosom of her family. Paper dolls were fairly inexpensive. They were pre-cut, as scissors were too valuable for children. Earliest sets did not have tabs (by which the clothes could hang from the "doll.") Might have back images as well as front ones, so you could dress the figure from both sides. There was another version, not with figures to be dressed up, but figures to be placed in a scene, such as a fishing town, or a theatre.
- paper ships - You folded them yourself.
- peep shows - You looked through a hole and viewed scenes cut out and lined up to show sections of a garden, menagerie, etc.

puppets - Were mostly a performing art, but some lucky (and well-to-do) Regency era children might be given puppets and/or a puppet theatre. (You may care to see: Punch and Judy puppets.)

rattles - Made of wood or metal.

riddles

sleds

soap bubbles

spillikins - (Pick-up sticks.)

stuffed animals

swings - (See under S.)

tea sets

tops

toy soldiers - Not yet three dimensional; were flat tin. Might be painted.

toy theatre - Also called: miniature theatre. Could be made of paper or wood.

wooden toys - Many kinds, from a doll, to Noah's Ark (with attendant pairs of animals,) to wheeled horses that could be pushed, or pulled on a string.

gaming - While both terms "gambling" and "gaming" were used, "gaming" is the one more frequently seen in Regency era writings. Both men and women gamed (with money stakes) at public venues and/or private homes. (See: CLUBS, in its own section-which were males-only.)

Garent Street - (See: New Gravel Lane.)

gaol - A chiefly British variation of the word "jail" (which is also how it is pronounced, rhymes with mail.) Commonly used term in the Regency era. Gaol Fever was a form of typhus, usually spread by lice.

- See: Cold Bath Prison.
- See: prisons.
- See: punishments.
- See: typhus.

Gardeners' Company - (AKA: the Worshipful Company of Gardeners.) First mentioned in 1345; existed as a mystery (or fellowship) until the Guild was incorporated in 1605. Never had a hall, but has a horticultural library at Guildhall. It is a "living" guild, meaning it yet has to do with the profession of gardening (and with amateurs,) and isn't just a charity as some Companies have become over time. Livery Company. 66th in precedence.

gardens - When speaking of those areas around a home, a "yard" is where the business of the house takes place (such as dealing with horses and coaches.) It may or may not be cobbled or have paving stones. Whereas the "garden" is any part that has some greenery and/or is intended for pleasure/relaxation, whether or not there are any actual flowers there. In other words, it would be highly unlikely a hostess would serve her guests tea in the yard, but completely normal to serve it in the garden.

Pruning shears were invented in 1815, by Bertrand, Marquis of Moleville, France. Quickly became popular throughout Europe. (Before this, gardeners used: hooks, pruning knives, scissors.)

- See: the various parks - Green Park, Hyde Park, St. James's Park, etc.

- See: botanical gardens.
- See: Gardeners' Company.
- See: Royal Horticultural Society.
- See: Westminster/Abbey Garden - For the country's oldest cultivated garden.
- See: yard.

garlic - (See: food/garlic.)

Garnet Street - (See: New Gravel Lane.)

Garrard - 112 Regent Street. Jewelry shop. Opened in 1735. Garrard, in 1802, took sole command of the company. Was the Crown Jeweller (maintained the Crown Jewels) from 1843-2007. In 1911 Garrard's moved to Albemarle Street.

Garraway's Coffee House - Originally in Sweeting's Rents, and afterwards (1657) in Exchange Alley. (See: Royal Exchange, the paragraph under - That refers to how the Stock dealers came to be in the coffee-houses.) Garraway's was the first place in London to sell tea, circa 1657. Was frequented by the most prominent auctioneers and brokers in merchandise. Garraway's was used to sell wool exports in 1821 (until, in 1870, the wool sales moved to the Wool Exchange in Coleman Street. Had sales here until 1866.)

- See: Change Alley.
- See: Jonathan's.

Garrick Club - (See: Garrick Street/Garrick Club.)

Garrick Street - Covent Garden. Built in 1861-4. Previously was called King Street.

- 15: Garrick Club. 1831. Named for the famous 18th C. actor, David Garrick. Is unmarked as a club (but most of the gentlemen's clubs were/are); if you belonged there, you knew where they were situated. (See under the CLUBS section.)
- Lamb and Flag: Pub. (See under the INNS/PUBS section.)

gas lighting - (Of streets.) The London Gas Light and Coke Company was founded in 1816 by Frederick A. Windsor; it was a form of coal, processed to burn better.

The first gas-lit street, June/1807, was Pall Mall; the pipes were made from musket barrels, considered strong enough to withstand the pressure of coal gas. The first square to be fully lighted with gas was: Finsbury Square. The theatre district was gas lit in 1817 (although the Lyceum Theatre was gas lit since 1803, a great rarity that early.) There were 26 miles/42 km of gas mains in London by 1816; 122 miles/196 km by 1823.

Note: The first *street* lighting - in the 1690s-1700s (and not involving gas at all) - was in Hyde Park.

- See: Finsbury Square.

- See: Hyde Park/Rotten Row.
- See: Piccadilly/Fortnum & Mason.
- You may care to see: candles.
- You may care to see: lamps.

gates - The ancient gates of London. The oldest set of London gates numbered only four: Aldgate, Bishopsgate, Ludgate, and Newgate, built in 120AD as part of a Roman fort.

London Wall was built ca. 190-225AD, then surrounding the City and incorporating seven gates, with the wall having the purpose of a defensive barrier for Roman Londinium: Aldgate, Aldersgate, Bishopgate, Ludgate, Moorgate, Newgate, and Posterngate.

The City's eight *medieval* gates included: the seven, plus Cripplegate (which had evolved out of part of the ancient Roman fort.)

Virtually all of the ancient gates are pulled down now, plus newer ones (such as Billingsgate, Gloucester Gate, and Hanover Gate) were demolished in 1760-61 to make way for the ever-increasing wheeled traffic in and out of the city. Only Temple Bar (between Fleet Street and the Strand) remained until 1860.

- See: the various listings, such as:
  Aldgate, under A,
  Bishopgate, under B,
  Cripplegate, under C., etc.
- See: turnpike - To see a wholly different kind of gate that had nothing to do with the ancient gates of London.

Gedge's - Leicester Square. Drapers. 1782. (See: Leicester Square/Gedge's.)

General Board of Health - Created by the British Public Health Act, 1848. Made local leaders responsible for drainage, inspections, and water supplies.

General Post Office - First situated in Cloak Lane (near Dowgate.) Moved to the Black Swan in Bishopsgate Street. Then to Sir Robert Vyner's mansion in Lombard Street, the City, in 1678. Moved to St. Martin's-le-Grand in 1829, built from 1824-9 by Robert Smirke; this building being demolished in 1912-13; the General Post Office had already moved again; its building design dates from 1895, to King Edward Street.

The first of the famous pillar boxes (green post boxes to be found on street corners, etc.) appeared in 1855; they changed to red as a standard color between 1866-79. (See: post boxes.)

General Register of Births, Death and Marriages - Located in Somerset House from 1836-1973.

- See: Public Record Office - 1838.
- See: Somerset House/Public Records.

Gentleman Jackson's - Pugilism. (See under: Bond Street/Old Bond Street/4.)

Gentleman's Magazine - The most famous of the monthly periodicals; first to call itself a "magazine." Began in 1731, and lasted until 1914. Started as a news-reporting writ; evolved to include comments on society and manners, poems, and reviews of books.

- See: St. John's Gate - Where *GM* was published 1731-54.
- You may care to see: magazines.

Gentlemen at Arms - The sovereign's personal guard; another name for the Royal Guards.

- See: Royal Guards, under R.
- See: St. James's Palace/Gentlemen at Arms.

Geological Museum - Craig's Court, Whitehall. Founded in 1835. (Since 1933, has moved to its present site in South Kensington.)

Geological Society of London - (AKA: the Geological Society.) The oldest geological society in the world. Formed in 1807. (See: Linnean Society.)

George Cross, and the George Medal - Instituted in 1940 by King George VI, to award civilians for acts of bravery.

George Square - AKA: St. George's Square. (See under S.)

George Street - Chelsea. Regency era name of the road later known as Sloane Gardens.

George, the - Famous coaching inn, in Southwark, large, with courtyard.

- See: George, the, under the INNS/PUBS section.
- See: Southwark/Borough High Street/77.

George Yard - (See: Gunthorpe Street.)

Germany - (See: Holy Roman Empire.)

germs, concept of - Not understood during the Regency. (See: medicine - Notes at.)

Gerrard Street - Soho. Built ca. the 1670s (after pulling down mansions here.) This street housed pastry cooks during the Regency. Is now the heart of London's "Chinatown."

- 9: Turk's Head Literary Club. (See under the CLUBS section.)
- 43: John Dryden (Restoration poet, dramatist, critic) lived here.

ghosts - Not surprisingly, London claims many ghosts. The Tower of London, not surprisingly, is said to have its ghosts, not least Anne Boleyn.

- See: Cock Lane.
- See: Hall Place.
- See: Lansdowne Passage.

Gibson Square - Islington. 1835-40.

Gieves and Hawkes - Tailors. (See under: Savile Row/1.)

Giltspur Street - Smithfield. Medieval jousts were hosted here (in Smithfield,) hence this street's older name of Knightrider Street.

- Giltspur Street Compter: A prison, small, here from 1791-1855.

gin - From the early 18th C., gin, also called Blue Ruin, was too often the drink of choice among the underprivileged classes, due to its inexpensiveness. Increasingly so into the Victorian age, any seedy part of town was sure to have a gin palace. The widespread consumption of gin was often blamed for social ills such as poverty and thievery. Here, an 18th C. saying of gin: "Drunk for a penny, dead drunk for two pence." (See: Finsbury/Clerk's Well/Gordon's.)

gipsies - (See: gypsies.)

Gipsy Hill - Lambeth/Southwark. The "Norwood Gipsies" lived here in the 17-18th centuries. Its present name derives from that fact (but is a Victorian designation.) The most famous of the fortune-tellers was Margaret Finch (d.1740.) Not much developed until the railways came in.

- Gipsy House: Timber-built. Margaret Finch's descendants lived here until the early 19th century.

Girdlers' Hall - For the Worshipful Company of Girdlers. Still at the north side of Basinghall Avenue. They made the adornment known as the girdle, an important article of clothing in medieval times, as one's sword or purse hung from one's girdle, (which could be made out of metal.) Had its foundation in 1180. Letters Patent were granted in 1327. AN ENCYCLOPAEDIA OF LONDON states: "In 1431 Andrew Hunt, Girdler, gave two tenements and a parcel of land in the parish of St. Michael, Bassishaw, to the wardens of the mistery."

Incorporated/Royal Charter in 1449. Combined with the Pinners and the Wireworkers in 1567. (The Pinners being separated out again in 1640. The ground that became the Hall garden was given to them in 1505. Burned in the Great Fire of 1666. Rebuilt in 1681. The court room (once the ladies parlor) was enlarged in 1735. Entire building restored in 1878-9. Ruined in 1940; rebuilt.

As girdles waned, the Girdlers made belts. They also made garters and bandoliers. By the time of the 18-19th centuries, any girdles would have been ceremonial only. Yet the Girdlers still flourished, being associated with crafts involving leather or metal.

Their patron saint is: St. Lawrence the Martyr. They are associated with the nearby church of St. Lawrence Jewry-next-Guildhall. (See: St. Lawrence Jewry, under the CHURCHES section.)

While its craft is no longer practiced, there is the single exception that the Girdlers provide for each new monarch's coronation a sword belt for the Sword of State. Livery company. 23rd in the order of precedence.

glass windows - Came into general use in London in Tudor times/16th century. (Before then, "windows" were closed, if possible, by skins or shutters, both shutting out light.)

Most glass windows would have tilted out from the top of the frame, or been in two parts, opening outward from the center (like double doors); windows that slid open bottom to top were unlikely. There was a window tax, determined by how many windows fronted the house, so many homeowners tried to restrict the number of windows that showed on the front facade of the home.

(See: Hackney Coach - For windows in carriages.)

glasses - As in eyewear. (See: spectacles.)

Glasshouse Street - Soho, Westminster. North of St. James's Park. Dates back to the 16th century. (See: Burlington Gardens.)

glasshouses - For manufacturing glass.

- See: Aldgate.
- See: glass windows.
- See: glassware.
- See: Whitefriars.

Glass-sellers' Company - (AKA: the Worshipful Company of Glass-sellers.) Also seen as: Glass Sellers. Venetians came to London in the 16th C., producing lots of home-produced glass, so English glass-sellers petitioned for a Charter in 1635; it was granted in 1664 by Charles II, (it took so long due to the civic unrest during the rise and fall of the Commonwealth.) Note: There were already glass-workers who dealt with glazing windows (the Glaziers,) and with spectacles (the Spectacle-makers,) so this Guild was established to cover all the other needs of the glass trade. Livery company. Never had a hall. 71st in the order of precedence.

glassware -

- See: Mill Street/Thomas Goade.
- See: West Midland/Stevens & Williams, under the BRITISH COUNTIES section.

Glaziers' Company - (AKA: the Worshipful Company of Glaziers. AKA: Glaziers and Painters of Glass.) Montague Close, Southwark. Established in the 14th C., when the term "glazier" replaced "verrers." By 1637 it was clear glaziers did glazing, leading, and painting of windows. Livery company. It is the only Livery company to have its Hall south of the Thames, in an early 19th century dockside warehouse (used to be called Hibernia Wharf, and which had been largely destroyed by fire in 1851.) The Hall is shared with two other Livery Companies: the Worshipful Company of Scientific Instrument Makers, and the Worshipful Company of Launderers; this is the Glaziers' (and Launderers, and Scientific Instrument Makers') first Hall.

Globe Theatre - (AKA: Shakespeare's Theatre. He did not own it.) Did not exist at the time of the Regency, had burned down long since. However, it was rebuilt in 1997, to exacting standards, including the only thatched roof now allowed in London. (See: Globe Theatre, under the THEATRES section.)

Globe Town - Tower Hamlets. In the Middles Ages it was a track called Theven Lane. By the early 18th C. it had been renamed Globe Lane. Then it was Globe Road, possibly so called for a local inn. Land was developed beginning in the 1790s. By 1808 it was known as Globe Town. Houses aimed at a more middle-class clientele were built ca. the 1820s.

Gloucester - (Pronounced: GLOS-ter.)

Gloucester Gate - Designed by John Nash; built by Richard Mott in 1826, with design assistance from J. J. Scoles. (See: Regent's Park/"The Park"/Gloucester Gate.)

Gloucester House - 137 Piccadilly. (Also here: Gloucester Lodge. Which is Gloucester House and which is Gloucester Lodge is unclear, even to experts; one of the two, at any rate, used to be called Stratherne Villa.) Built early in George III's reign for the Cholmondeley family, these are a pair of semi-detached houses that appear to be one; they face north. Not particularly wondrous architecturally; had green-painted balconies that are reminiscent of 18th century Brighton houses. Prince William Frederick/Duke of Gloucester and Edinburgh, occupied a house here from 1816-34 (when he died," and then Prince George came here. At one time belonged to Lord Elgin, who actually stored "his" Elgin Marbles here for a while until they found a home elsewhere. (See: Bloomsbury/British Museum, for more on the marbles.) Pulled down in 1904, but rebuilt as a luxury home.

Gloucester Place - Portman Square. North of Mayfair, Marylebone. The street is still lined with Georgian era town houses. In the Regency, French émigrés tended to live in this general area. Mrs. Mary Anne Clarke (mistress of the Duke of York) had a mansion here.

- 51: Hart House Hotel. Had been a Georgian mansion.
- 62: Benedict Arnold (American patriot turned traitor) lived here ca. the turn from the 18th to the 19th century.

Gloucester Road - Kensington/Chelsea. Ca. 1612 originally called Hogmore Lane (also seen as "Hogs Moor," and as "Hogsmire" Lane, and as "Hog Moore" Lane.) Was an unsuccessful pleasure-garden in the late 18th century. In 1805, Maria, the Duchess of Gloucester and Edinburgh, died in the villa she had here, later known as Gloucester Lodge. (See: Gloucester House.) The road took its name from the Duchess, but not until ca. 1850.

Gloucester Square - Bayswater. Post-1840. (See: Hyde Park Square, note at.)

Gloucester Terrace - Bayswater, near Regent's Park. Named by John Nash for the Duke of Gloucester, Prinny's cousin and brother-in-law. On Regent's Park's east side, it is the area's north-most terrace. Built mostly between 1843-1852. (See: Regent's Park/"The Park"/Gloucester Terrace.)

Glovers' Company - (AKA: the Worshipful Company of Glovers.) Long existing as a craft, glove making was first mentioned in 1327, and formed as a Company in 1349. United with the Pursers in 1498, and with the Leathersellers in 1502. Glovers had their Royal Charter from Charles I in 1638 as a separate Company. From 1662 a Hall was established in Beech Lane, Cripplegate. But when the Glovers declined from 120 members to 14 at the end of the 18th C., the Hall was abandoned. Livery company. 62nd in the order of precedence.

gloves - In times when there was no central heating (most of history,) gloves were worn by everyone, including children. Half-hander gloves existed.

Surgical note: Gloves were not used during medical care/surgeries until ca. 1900.

- See: Burlington Arcade/68-69/Lord's.
- See: Glovers' Company.
- See: Piccadilly/185/Swain Adeney Briggs & Son.

God Save the Queen - (*Or King.*) The phrase is ancient. The song is thought to have been first sung in London in 1745, author uncertain. Became the British national anthem in 1790.

godparents - The practice of being/having godparents was practiced during the Regency. (See: childbirth.)

Gog and Magog - Two figures of ancient Druidic gods (or giants,) in a large clock. (See: St. Dunstan-in-the-West, in the CHURCHES section.) There is a set of Gog and Magog statues on either side of the stairs in the Great Hall of the Guildhall - a different set than the "St. Dunstan" ones.

Gold and Silver Wyre-drawers' Company - (AKA: the Worshipful Company of Gold and Silver Wyre-drawers.) Also seen as: Gold and Silver Wyre Drawers. Made gold and silver thread for ceremonial clothing and uniforms, an art still practiced (although the Company is primarily a charity now.) Royal Charter in 1693; granted as a Livery Company in 1780. 74th in the order of precedence. Has no Hall (but is associated with a Masonic Lodge since 1945.)

Gold State Coach, the - Is the oldest royal coach. Drawn by eight horses. Commissioned in 1760; first used by George IV in 1821, in opening Parliament. (You may care to see: coaches.)

Golden Mile, the - (See: Great Western Road.)

Golden Square - Soho. Aristocratic address from the 1760s. (Near Soho Square.)

- 28 Broad Street: William Blake (poet, b.1757-d.1827) lived here as a child.
- King Street: Existed by at least 1674 (and probably earlier.)

goldfish - Imported from China (for the first time successfully) to England in 1730.

Golding Street - (See: Grove Street.)

Goldsmith Street - Cheapside. Named for the goldsmiths' shops there.

goldsmiths - Before there were formal banks, goldsmiths more or less served that purpose. Two banks still in existence (Child's and Hoare's) started centuries past as goldsmiths. There was an Association of Goldsmiths in Henry I's time.

- See: Goldsmiths' Hall.
- See: Lombard Street.
- See: Ludgate Street/Rundell & Bridge.

Goldsmiths' Company - By 1180 (if not sooner.) The Company's Hall, Goldsmiths' Hall is located in Foster Lane, Hatton Garden, Clerkenwell. The Goldsmiths' Company owns 200 acres in East Acton, where they built almshouses.

- See: East Acton.
- See: Goldsmiths' Hall.
- See: Bond Street/New Bond Street/165-169/Asprey & Co.

Goldsmiths' Hall - (For the Worshipful Company of Goldsmiths.) Foster Lane, Hatton Garden, Clerkenwell. First mentioned in 1180; said to have been on the east side of Foster Lane, the building being known as Goldsmiths' Row (but another source said the "Goldsmiths' Row" name belonged to a section of Cheapside from Bread Street to the cross.) The date of 1327 is generally accepted as the year of incorporation/Royal Charter. Burned in the Great Fire of 1666; restored in 1669, of red brick; lasted until 1829. Rebuilt on the same site in 1835, by Philip Hardwick, with an imposing facade. Has the "most sumptuous interior" of all the Companies' halls.

It is 5th of the Twelve Great Livery Companies.

The Trial of the Pyx (wherein a sampling of the coins minted here are examined for accuracy) has been held here since 1871 (before that it was held at Westminster, from the 13th century.)

- See: East Acton.
- See: Hatton Garden.

Goldsmiths' Row - (See note under: Goldsmiths' Hall.)

golf - Introduced into England by James I (AKA: James VI of Scotland.) Golf was played at St. Andrew, Scotland as early as 1414; the Society of St. Andrews Golfers was founded in 1754 (the 2nd golfing club in Britain. I don't know what the first one was, but it was quite possibly the Royal Blackheath Golf Club.)

The headquarters and controlling body is the Royal and Ancient Club of St. Andrews, Scotland; although, the administering body in England is The English Golf Union, Wokingham, Berkshire.

- See: Blackheath/Royal Blackheath Golf Club - Note at.
- See: Mitcham/Mitcham Common.

Goodge Street - Camden. In 1718 John Goodge came by Crab Tree Field via marriage. His sons developed the area in the 1740s. Little developed before 1907. Its modern affiliation with the "hippie drug scene" dates from a mention in a pop song.

Goodman's Fields - A medieval name for this Whitechapel area. (See: Leman Street.)

Goodwin's Court - A tiny alley, near St. Martin's Lane. In the 18th C. it was inhabited by a colony of tailors; these buildings have bow windows. Still has its Georgian appearance. Thomas Chippendale (the furniture-maker, b.1718-d.1779) had his workshops here, ca. 1750. (See: St. Martin's Lane/60-62/Chippendale.)

Gordon Hill - Enfield. Was part of Enfield Chase (see.) Enclosed and divided, 1770s, the land being acquired mostly by Trinity College, Cambridge.

- Gordon House: George Gordon (Lord Byron) lived here. Then came Sir Thomas Hallifax (banker, and Lord Mayor of London in 1776.) Demolished in the late 1850s.

Gordon House - (See under: Petersham.)

Gordon Riots - Not a street, but an event.

- See: Lambeth/St. George's Fields.
- See: St. George's Field.

Gordon Square - Built by Thomas Cubitt. Late Georgian houses (still intact on the east side.) Built in the midst of the London University buildings.

- University Church: 1853.

Gordon's Gin - Famous brand of gin. (See: Finsbury/Clerk's Well/Gordon's.)

Gordon's Wine Cellar - 47 Villiers Street. There was a warehouse for sherry and port here from 1364. A wine cellar here some 300 years. Had been owned by a Free Vintner (one who needs no license, and can open and close as he wishes) until recently, (but the present owner has a standard license.) The door remains from the early 19th century. STYLE CITY LONDON says: "Its origins as a wine bar date from around 1870..." Still has its medieval vaults.

Gore House - South Kensington. As a result of Gore House having stood here, this part of Kensington Road in called Kensington Gore. The Royal Albert Hall now stands on the site of this house where William Wilberforce brought his family in 1808; they moved from here in 1821. Wilberforce hosted anti-slavery meetings here. Was also later the mansion for Lord and Lady Blessington, who entertained here writers such as Charles Dickens and William Thackery.

Walking distance to Westminster. Overlooked Hyde Park and Kensington Gardens.

Auctioned off in 1849, and became a restaurant, and finally the Royal Albert Hall (also known simply as Albert Hall.)

Gough House - (See under: Chelsea/Gough House.)

Gough Square - Fleet Street. Until 1897 it was narrow and cobbled, and already famous for its taverns. Little courts and alleyways.

- 17: Dr. Samuel Johnson lived here (very humbly, it is said to be the smallest house in London) between 1748 and 1759 (at which time the address was number 4.) The doctor compiled his *Dictionary of the English Language* while living here; published in 1755. The building (built ca. 1700) is now a museum of Dr. Johnson's life; four stories; dark brick.

Goulds Green - Hillingdon. John Golde's family is mentioned in 1373 records; Goulds Green in 1592. Was a 20-acre extension of Hillingdon Heath. Was yet a hamlet in 1806 (although significant enough to form one of the four divisions of Hillingdon parish.)

government -

- See: Downing Street/10.
- See: Guildhall - Notes on the City's self-governance.
- See: Lower House.
- See: Royal - Many listings starting with.
- See: Tories.
- See: Upper House.
- See: Westminster.
- See: Whigs.
- See: Whitehall.

Gower House - (See: Carrington House.)

Gower Street - (Rhymes with "power.") Bloomsbury. Built in the 1780s, brown bricks (not particularly admired architecturally at the time, although now is considered a good address.)

- 17-21: Is now the Academy Hotel, residing in three Georgian houses.
- London University, founded in 1828. (Also see: University College.)
- University College Hospital: 1833. (See under U.)

gowns - (See: dresses, women's.)

Gracechurch Street - (Also written as: Grace Church.) City. It runs directly over the ancient sites of the Roman basilica and forum that had been here. In medieval times there was a cornmarket here. It had various spellings of the name, but "Gracechurch" came in after the Great Fire of 1666.

By the Regency, was a low place where "a month of ablutions" would not remove its impurities. Pawnbrokers. Silversmiths. Nearby warehouses. Also a market for corn and oats. In *Pride and Prejudice*, by Jane Austen, it was considered a bit disgraceful that some of Elizabeth Bennet's relations lived here.

- Dutton's Circulating Library. (See under D.)
- Leadenhall Market: (See under L.)
- St. Benet's Gracechurch: There till 1867.

- St. Peter's Cornhill: By Wren. (See under the CHURCHES section.)
- Spread Eagle Inn: (See under the INNS/PUBS section.)

Grafton House - (See: Bond Street/New Bond Street/164.)

Grafton Street - Became known as Grafton Way, but not before 1845.

- Grafton House: On the corner.

grains -

- See: corn.
- See: Corn Exchange.
- See: oats.
- See: rye.
- See: wheat.

Grammar School - Guildford (see) borough. Founded in the mid 16th century.

Grand Junction Canal - Runs from Braunston, Northamptonshire, to the Thames at Brentford, London. Built 1793-1805. It reduced the journey from the Midlands to London by 60 miles (100 km), and helped the shipping of goods to London to thrive. Bought by the Regent's Canal Company in 1927, and since 1929 has formed the Grand Union Main Line's southern half from London to Birmingham. Not to be confused with the 1929 Grand Union Canal. (See: Paddington.)

Grand National Archery Society - (See: Toxophilite Society.)

Grand National, the - Aintree Racecourse, near Liverpool. (See: Lancashire, under the BRITISH COUNTIES section - To learn more about Lancashire and Liverpool.) Horse race, a British institution begun in 1837. Steeplechase. "Grueling." 40 horses, 40 fences, 4-1/2 mile/7.2 km course.

Grand Surrey Canal - Began 1807, running from the Surrey Commercial Docks to Old Kent Road; 1810 to Camberwell; 1826 to Peckham. It transported cargo, mostly timber. Closed in 1971; is now mostly filled in.

grand tour, the - A young man's "education" might include a grand tour, the classic version of which would take him to Paris, Rome, Florence, Naples, and/or Venice. However, depending on wars and politics, he might instead avoid some of those places and include Amsterdam, Berlin, Geneva, and other continental locations. Only the most intrepid travelers, however, braved Russia or the Ottoman Empire.

Grand Union Canal - (Not to be confused with the Grand Junction Canal.) 1929, and extended in 1932, amalgamating several other canals. Starts in London, ends in Birmingham, 137 miles/220 km.

gravel - As in rocks, for building, fill, roadways, etc.

- See: Mitcham/Mitcham Commons/Seven Islands Pond.

- See: Paddington.
- See: Highgate Hill/Pond Square.

graveyards - (See: cemeteries.)

Gray's Inn - West side of Gray's Inn Road. (See: Inns of Court/Gray's Inn.)

Gray's Inn Road - Camden. Leads north from High Holborn. That portion which runs from Holborn to Theobold's Road was known as Gray's Inn Lane, until most of the properties were pulled down; replaced with plain four-story terraced houses (only 55 Gray's Inn Road survives from this 1680s renovation.)

- Gray's Inn: (See under: Inns of Court/Gray's Inn.)
- Horse and Carriage Repository: (See under H.)
- Royal Free Hospital: 1828 (See under R.)
- St. Alban's Church: 1863.

Gray's, Thomas - A London jeweler; Prinny purchased here. Fashionable. In Sackville Street. While Prinny was still the Regent, Gray's was a pub with cockfights; Prinny (knowing of Gray's interest in jewelry) suggested Gray open a jewelry shop, which Gray then did.

Gray's apprentice, Joseph Kitching, started his own shop in Dover Street (1834, in Conduit Street.) This became the still existing Collingwood of Conduit Street, jewelers.

Great Armoury - (See: Tower of London.)

Great Britain - The concept of a combined Scotland and England as Great Britain was first introduced by James VI (AKA: James I of Scotland) when he ascended the English throne following Elizabeth I's death (3/24/1603.) The idea of union was presented to Parliament on 3/22/1604; James VI declared himself (despite Parliamentary resistance) King of Great Britain on 10/20/1604; union rejected in 1607. The concept (plus plague, plus trying to restore Catholicism in England, plus James being deemed cruder/less elegant than the late queen) led to the Gunpowder Plot (now remembered via Guy Fawkes Night, "Remember, remember! The Fifth of November, the Gunpowder treason and plot; I know of no reason Why the Gunpowder treason Should ever be forgot!")

The haughty Charles I (1625-1649) did not tame Parliament's unease with the idea of a union, and this led to civil war and to his own execution, and the reinvention of England as a commonwealth; the monarchy was abolished on 3/17/1649 (along with the House of Lords.) Parliament became the "supreme authority" on national matters. Cromwell was made Commander-in-Chief of the Commonwealth forces.

Opposition forces crowned Charles II on 1/1/1651 as King of England, Scotland, Ireland, and France (the last title being traditional); the Civil War was begun.

Charles II returned to London on 5/29/1660, thereby restoring the monarchy.

A new hybrid of rule called constitutional monarchy came into being under the joint rulership of William and Mary (as requested by Parliament,) 2/13/1689. It exists yet today.

- See: constitutional monarchy.
- See: Canada - Which has an explanation of the modern Commonwealth.
- See: flag, British.
- See the INTRO-REIGNS section/British Kings and Queens & their Reigns/Henry III.
- See the ITNRO-REIGNS section/British Kings and Queens & their Reigns/Edward I.
- See the INTRO-REIGNS section/British Kings and Queens & Their Reigns/James I.
- See: United Kingdom - (1801.)

The union of England and Scotland (as Great Britain) finally came into being in 1707. (See: Act of Union.)

Great Chapel Street - After the Regency, a portion was known as Broadway. Courts, alleys, "nests of vice."

Great Charter - (See: Magna Carta.)

Great Companies, the - Refers to the 12 original (medieval) Livery Companies. The others are called "Minor."

- See: guilds.
- See: halls.
- See: Livery Companies.

Great Cumberland Place - Half a circular terrace built in 1789 (a second source says 1800-1810); the other half never got built. Here is found The Montcalm (Hotel) with the original porticoed facade and 18th C. iron railings remaining out front. Doorman wears dark brown and gold livery, he stands on the three marble steps. During the Regency...? Given its proximity to Bond and Oxford Streets, buildings here were either a business or a residence.

Great Distaff Lane - Small offshoot of Cannon Street, removed in 1853-4.

Great Dover Street - 1809. Parallel to Kent (Tabard) Street.

Great Fire of 1666, the - The infamous and disastrous fire started at 1:00am on Sunday, September 2nd, in a pastry shop in Pudding Lane. (See under P.) Burned until Tuesday night. With the exception of Aldgate and Bishopsgate, virtually all of the City (within the old walls) burned. The fire destroyed over 13,000 houses, and 87 churches, including St. Paul's Cathedral.

Amazingly, various reports tell us few people died, some say 5, 9, or 16 (although, alas, poor people may not have been included in the counting.) Still, some 100,000 people were left homeless by the Great Fire.

There were grand plans to remake the City, but due to lack of funds coupled with a resistance to the loss of old byways (and one's holding thereof,) not as much of the City was altered as had been imagined (it had been hoped it could be rebuilt with a more grid-like pattern.) As a result of the residents' resistance, many of the old roads, albeit with new buildings, remained where they had been. Some 2,800 buildings were rebuilt by 1669; there was an astonishing 70% rebuild within five years. And within ten years, most of the City was rebuilt (if not always grandly.)

Building laws were changed at this time, *requiring* houses of brick or stone must replace the old habit of timbered construction, and upper stories could no longer be built to project out over the street (the upper stories had sometimes come out far enough that, especially opposite a matching oversized upper story, they had sometimes resulted in traffic obstruction.)

There are hundreds of references in these pages to the scars left in London by this widespread and overwhelming fire.

At least the purging nature of the Great Fire brought an end to the Great Plague.

- ➢ See: eels - Why the Great Fire led to them not being sold at Billingsgate.
- ➢ See: Great Plague of 1665 - Which devastation of the city's health was only a year earlier.
- ➢ See: Little Fire of London.
- ➢ See: Pie Corner - Where the Great Fire finally ended.

Great Forest of Middlesex - (See: Hampstead Heath/Kenwood.)

Great George Street - Off Hanover Square. There by at least ca. 1770. NOT the same as George Street. (See: Treasury.)

Great James's Street - Bloomsbury, ca. 1722.

Great Marlborough Street - In Westminster.

- 49: Mrs. Siddons, the actress, lived here from 1804-11.

Great Mews, the - (AKA: King's Mews. AKA: Royal Mews.) By William Kent, under advice of Lord Burlington, 1732-3. Demolished 1830, to make way for the National Gallery. (See: Royal Mews.)

Great North Wood -

- ➢ See: Forest Hill.
- ➢ See: Norwood.

Great Ormond Street - Bloomsbury, 1720s. (See: Hospital for Sick Children.)

Great Ormond Street Children's Hospital - 1852.

Great Park - (See: Windsor.)

Great Plague (of 1347-51) - (See: Black Death.)

Great Plague of 1665, the - Bubonic plague outbreak, widespread, during the reign of Charles II. Began in the crowded slums of St. Giles. Deaths added up to over 100,000, one-fifth of London's population at the time. Ran rampant for about six months. There are many references throughout these pages of areas outside the City where the populace (those who could afford to do so) fled to escape the sweeping epidemic.

- See: Pest Houses.
- You may care to see: Great Fire of 1666.

Great Portland Street - In the 1790s, was a rather squalid and insignificant little street. Felix Mendelssohn (composer) stayed here when he visited in the 1820s and 30s (in the home of a German iron merchant/friend's home.)

- 122: James Boswell (Biographer/diarist) died here in 1795.

Great Prescott Street - (See: Prescott Street.)

Great Queen Street - Lincoln's Inn Fields, West End. Was called Queen Street ca. 1605-09, but by 1670 it was Great Queen Street. Described as St. Giles's eastward extension of the street Long Acre. Named for Henrietta Marie, wife of Charles I. During the Regency this street connected Drury Lane with Lincoln's Inn Fields.

- 37: Bhatti, a modern Indian restaurant, but it resides in a 17th C. building, with original fireplaces, paneling, and stenciling.
- Freemason's Hall: (See under F.)

Great Russell Street - Russell Square, Bloomsbury. Formed by 1682, but there wasn't much here until buildings came in ca. the 1780s. The British Museum and Montagu House are here.

- See: Bloomsbury Square/British Museum.
- See: Montagu House.

- 23-28: Homes here by at least 1857. Currently is the Trades Union Congress House.
- 46: Building built as a private house ca. 1735; revamped in the 1850s. Was a bookshop since at least 1890. Now is: Jarndyce Antiquarian Booksellers.
- 119: Percy Bysshe Shelley (poet) lodged here Feb-Mar/1818.

Great Ryder Street - (See: Ryder Street.)

- 10: (Perhaps also known as number 11.) Barringer and Company, coal-merchants. There by at least 1818; still there in 1840.
- 11: Scrope Berdmore Davies (Regency dandy) lived here ca. Feb/1816.

Great St. Thomas Apostle (street) - Small offshoot of Cannon Street, removed in 1853-4.

Great Scotland Yard - Lies between Whitehall and the Thames. Until 1603, accommodation was provided in the Old Whitehall Palace for the kings of Scotland when in London, thus the name. AKA: The Metropolitan Police, formed in 1829.

- See: New Scotland Yard.
- See: Whitehall/4/Scotland Yard.

Great Suffolk Street - (See: Dirty Lane.)

Great Surrey Street - (See: Blackfriars Road.)

Great Titchfield Street - Fitzrovia, Westminster. Half completed by 1746; fully done by 1793. In the mid 19th C. it was described as dirty and dingy shops and private homes.

Great Tower Street - At first known as Water Lane. (See under W.)

- All Hallows Barking: (See under the CHURCHES section.)
- Great Wardrobe: (See: Royal Wardrobe.)

Great Western Road - Brentford and Hounslow. (AKA: Great West Road.) This road wasn't called this until the 1920s (when it was built); had been parts of the Bath Road, the Great West Road, and London Road. The old roads were dangerous, because of footpads and highwaymen (tempted by the traffic here that went from Kensington to Hyde Park Corner toll-gate (toll-gate removed in 1825.) Apsley House was built on Hyde Park Corner, very near the toll-gate, Lord Wellington's home. (See under A.)

After the 1920s and due to American-funded factories that were built here, it took on the nickname: the Golden Mile.

Is now a part of the A4.

Great Windmill Street School - Another name for the Hunterian Medical School. (See under H.)

Greater London Council - (AKA: Greater London Authority.)

- See: County Hall.
- See: London County Council.
- See: Lord Mayor - Is especially useful.

Greek Street - Soho, Near Frith Street. Some 18th C. houses, but is mostly from the 19th century. (See: Soho/Greek Street.)

green grocers - (Also seen as: green-grocers.) Those vendors who deal in produce. (Grocers vs. green-grocers: GROCERS sell groceries, which includes more kinds of foodstuffs, and can include things such as household items. GREEN-GROCERS sell fresh fruit and vegetables, and are usually a smaller shop or stall.)

Green Lane - Hackney/Haringey/Enfield. (Sometimes seen as: Green Lanes.) One of London's longest roads that carries the same name for its length. CHAMBERS LONDON GAZETTEER points out: "This was part of an ancient route that led from London's Shoreditch through Enfield to Hertford, and may have been in use from the second century

AD. The road connected a series of greens, most of which have since been lost, even in name... Drovers bringing animals to London for slaughter liked the road because it was less busy than other highways. It was formerly called Green Lanes for an even greater length than its present extent, but in the mid 19th century the southernmost part was renamed Southgate Road, and the section that passes through Wood Green became the High Street, which was changed to High Road around 1895." Now known for its Greek and Turkish residents.

- See: Manor House, Hackney, under M.
- See: Warwick Avenue.

Green Park - (Occasionally referred to as: the Green Park, as in: "I'm going for a stroll in the Green Park.") Mayfair, Westminster. The smallest London royal park. In the distant past, it was a burial ground for lepers.

It was adjoined in 1667 on to St. James's Park by Charles II; previously had been Henry VIII's hunting grounds, as were Hyde Park and St. James's Park. Charles II enclosed the park with a wall in 1667, giving it a ranger's house, and stocking it with deer. At this time the park was known as Upper St. James's Park. By the mid 18th C. it was commonly known as Green Park.

It is the only royal park to host no flowerbeds (except for a fringe of daffodils in the spring.) The apocryphal story goes: The lack of flowers is because Charles II, on a walk, plucked a flower for "the most beautiful lady present." Alas, he was supposed to have given it to a milkmaid, not Queen Catherine, his wife. The livid queen purportedly then ordered all flowers removed.

Fifty-six acres; was larger until George III reduced its size in 1767, to enlarge the Buckingham House gardens. Open to visitors sometime in the 18th century. Has leafy paths, with lovely ancient trees (beech, lime, plane,) and green lawns.

In Georgian times the park hosted duels (llegal,) ballooning, and firework displays, in addition to its walks.

During the Regency, the park was ringed by grand mansion homes (now nearly all gone and replaced by luxury hotels.) It has no lake.

- Broad Walk: Covered with grass; lined by plane trees.
- Gates, the: (That is, the gates of the park.) Elaborate. Black metal with much gilding.
- Queen's Library: Built for Queen Caroline, wife of George II. Pulled down in 1855.
- Queen's Walk: Opened in the 1730s (named for the same Caroline as above, wife of George II.

- Ranger's Lodge: Built in the Adam style. Had an ice house and a fountain. The lodge was removed in 1842; its gardens were then absorbed into Green Park.

Green Park Arch - (See: Hyde Park/Wellington Arch.)

Green Street - Mayfair. Was part of the Royal Mews complex until 1829. (See: Royal Mews, note at.) There was a lot of building here in the later 19th century.

Green Street Green - Bromley. First record dates from the 1290s. Green Street took its name from the village green, this not being noted until the 18th C.; at this time the area was rather busy, as coaches came through here from London to Rye on the Sussex coast. Before 1836, it was a sleepy hamlet. John Fox established the Oak brewery (often called Fox's brewery) here in 1836; unlike many local breweries this one truly flourished. In the late 19th C. this area had become an industrial community described as "grim." It was somewhat revived by Edwardian cyclists and tea-rooms.

Greenford - Ealing. First seen in 845AD records. A farming hamlet. Didn't begin to grow until the late 19th century. (See: Wood End - Ealing.)

Greenhill - Harrow. A small hamlet in the 18th C., with modest farms regularly placed around the village green (the green being half its size by 1817.) By 1841 there were 28 houses here.

- St. John the Baptist: 1866.

greenhouse - It might be called a greenhouse, or a forcing garden, or might be called by whatever was primarily grown there, for instance: an orangery (oranges,) or a pinery (pineapples.)

> - See: Chelsea Physic Garden.
> - See: fruit.
> - See: orangery.
> - See: pinery.

greenroom - (Also seen as: green-room.) A theatre term certainly in use by the time of the Regency (and yet today.) Refers to the room where actors await their turn on stage (and where visitors come to call.) One was once literally green in color, but subsequent green rooms need not be green at all.

Green's Pistol Repository and Shooting Gallery - 1836-55. (See: Leicester Square/Savile House/William Green's Pistol Repository and Shooting Gallery.)

Greenwich - (Pronounced GREN-itch.) A part of Chelsea. Perches along the Thames. Greenwich gained prominence in the life of London because the Thames flowed deep and wide here (London's riches lay in its being a port city.)

Elizabeth I was born here, 1533, when it housed Greenwich Palace. (See at its own listing.)

Greenwich became the Prime Meridian in 1884.

> - See: clocks.

    - See: prime meridian, under P.
- Bella Court: Henry V's brother, Humphrey (Duke of Gloucester) inherited riverside land here and built in 1427. When Humphrey died, Margaret of Anjou (wife to Henry VI) enlarged the house and renamed it "Placentia." (See: Royal Naval Hospital, below.)
- Blackheath: Open heath, long a rallying place. James I introduced golf to England here. Still has stately Georgian houses and terraces surrounding it. (See under B.)
- Charlton House: 1607-12. (See under C.)
- Croom's Hill: 17th C., steep and winding residential street. Oldest buildings at southern end, near Blackheath.
    - 10-12: Georgian town house. (Is now the Fan Museum, since 1991.)
    - 66: Older than the Manor House. (See below.)
    - 68: About as old as the Manor House.
    - Grange, the: A home. Has 12th C. timbers.
    - Manor House, from 1695.
- George II Statue: By John Rysbrack, sculptor, in 1735 (depicts the king as a Roman Emperor.)
- Greenwich Hospital: (See: Royal Naval Hospital, below.)
- Greenwich Market: First dates from 1700. 1831 rebuild, by Joseph Kay.
- Greenwich Observatory: (See at its own listing.)
- Greenwich Park: (See at its own listing.)
- Maze Hill: Existed by at least the 15th C., when the common was enclosed. Ca. 1650 known for gravel extraction here, and lime burning. That phased out, and smallholders came in, then gentlemen, naval officers, and scholars.
    - Vanbrugh Castle: 1717 to ca. 1726, for architect/playwright Sir John Vanbrugh. Mock medieval. Restored in 1976 (now four dwellings.)
- Painted Hall, the: 18th C. murals by Sir James Thornhill (who also painted the dome interior of St. Paul's Cathedral.)
- Park Row:
    - Trafalgar Tavern: Pub. 1837.
- Plume of Feathers: Pub. (See under the INNS/PUBS section.)
- Queen's House: Inigo Jones designed this house for James I's wife, Anne of Denmark. (She died while it was being built, so the house was finished for Charles I's wife, Queen Henrietta Maria, in 1635.) Built in 2 halves, one on each side of the Woolwich to Deptford Road, connected by a bridge. (Road was later

diverted.) Palladian style. Since 1937, became the core of the National Maritime Museum. (See: Queen's House, Greenwich, under Q.)

- Ranger's House: (See: Greenwich Park, at its own listing/Ranger's House.)
- Rotunda Museum: 1814-19, by John Nash. Off Repository Road. A gun museum. NAIRN'S LONDON says: "Alias the R. A. Repository, or Nash's Tent. Surely, by now, the oldest tent in the world. Nash put it up in St. James's Park as part of the premature arrangements to celebrate the first defeat of Napoleon, in 1814. It was presented to the R. A. in 1819 and equipped with a lead roof, an inner skin, and a socking great Doric column in the middle. Between the two skins the original sailcloth is apparently still there."
- Royal Naval Hospital: (AKA: Greenwich Hospital.) Was built to accommodate retired/wounded Navy sailors. Built on the site of Bella Court; Henry VI's queen had renamed it Placentia. (See: Bella Court, above.) Henry VII aggrandized Placentia, making it at that time a favorite royal resort. (For a hospital built for Army soldiers, see: Royal Hospital, Chelsea.)

  Henry VIII was born at Placentia in 1491; he went on to add even more improvements. Both daughters (Mary I and Elizabeth I) were also born here.

  During the Commonwealth, the palace descended into being used both as a biscuit factory and a prisoner-of-war camp.

  Demolished by Charles II, with the Queen's House being spared.

  William and Mary turned it into a naval hospital in 1692-1703, by John Webb (1664-onward, the blocks by the riverside) and Christopher Wren (1669-1703, added the domes and colonnades.) The first pensioners were here by 1705. Sir John Vanbrugh added to the structure, 1728.

  Interior painted hall dates from 1707, by Sir James Thornhill, and took 19 years to finish. Chapel completed in 1745, overlooking the Thames from the river's south bank.

  William Newton added to the house, 1789.

  In 1869 the hospital closed; it converted in 1873 into the ROYAL NAVAL COLLEGE, the college coming from Portsmouth. (See: Royal Naval College, under R, for more.)

  Still houses pensioners, who wear red uniforms in summer and dark blue ones in winter.
- Royal Observatory: (See: Greenwich Observatory, at its own listing.)
- St. Alfege (or Alphege, or Alphagh) Church: In Church Street. Rebuilt 1718. (See under the CHURCHES section.)

Greenwich Observatory - (AKA: the Royal Observatory. AKA (from 1957-1998) as: Old Royal Observatory.) Official government observatory from 1675-1948.

Stands at the top of a hill in the middle of Greenwich Park. On this site once stood an old fort, referred to as Duke Humphrey's Tower, built at about the same time as his nearby palace (home,) ca.1427.

While the foundation stone for the Royal Observatory was set on 8/10/1675, the Astronomer Royal, John Flamsteed, was ready to get to work. He went to the Tower of London, working from the northeast corner of the turret of the White Tower; he was trying to solve the question of measuring longitude, a solution to which was still some 50+ years away. (See: longitudes.)

FLAMSTEED HOUSE: (See under F - And note this name was often at first used for the Observatory, as it is the oldest part of the Observatory.) Where Flamsteed, as director of the observatory (and Astronomer Royal,) lived. Next to the House is the Meridian Building. (See under M.)

The Royal Observatory is now housed at Herstmonceux Castle (near Battle, East Sussex,) largely due to London's air pollution. The old observatory building now houses a museum.

The red time ball on the roof dates from 1833. It was used to signal time to ships on the Thames.

GREENWICH MEAN TIME: While it had already been adopted by the railways, Greenwich Mean Time was not adopted generally until after there was an international conference in 1884, held in Washington D. C., USA. The *PRIME MERIDIAN* was awarded to Greenwich because it was home to the clockmaker John Harrison, the man who first solved the naval problem of determining longitude (he invented the marine chronometer, a portable way to measure longitude at sea, starting in 1730 and working on it for 30 more years.)

Greenwich Palace -

- See: Greenwich.
- See: Greenwich Park.
- See: Royal Naval College.

Greenwich Park - Originally was royal palace grounds (Greenwich Palace,) is yet owned by the crown. 200 acres. Used as a burial ground during the plague of 1353. Hosts horse chestnut, caster-oil, cypress, and paper birch trees. Deer were introduced here by Henry VIII, 1515. James I walled the park in, having the gardens laid out in the French style. Opened to the public in 1830. Public rowdiness led to the 1857 abolishment of a bi-annual fair.

- Flamsteed House:
  - See: Greenwich Observatory.
  - See under F.
- Greenwich Observatory: (See at its own listing.)
- Ranger's House: 1688, built for an admiral. Blackheath end of the park. Enlarged ca. 1748, when the fourth Earl of Chesterfield acquired it. In 1815 this house was allotted to the Park Ranger. Today houses the Suffolk Collection of 17th C. portraits by William Larkin, and others.
- Queen's Elizabeth's oak: 12th century. Enormous tree. Had a door and window put into the trunk. Park offenders could be locked in here. The oak died in 1880 or so, but the trunk remains.
- Royal Observatory: (See: Greenwich Observatory, at its own listing.)

Grenadier, The - Pub. (See under the INNS/PUBS section.)

Gresham College - (AKA: Gresham's College.) 1597. At Barnard's Inn Hall, Holborn. Housed in Sir Thomas Gresham's former home in Bishopsgate (he had been the founder of the Royal Exchange.) Hosts some 140 free public lectures per year, and doesn't enroll students or award degrees. The Bishopsgate site is now occupied by Tower 42, the National Westminster Tower (NatWest Tower,) modern skyscraper; the college has operated at Barnard's Inn Hall, Holborn since 1991. (See: Broad Street/Gresham College.)

Gresham Street - Named for the merchant Thomas Gresham, d.1579. Before 1845 the length of this street was known as: Maiden Lane (to Wood Street); as Lad Lane (to the east); and as Cateaton Street (from Aldermanbury to Lothbury.) Runs from Lothbury and Moorgate, to St. Martin le Grand.

- Guildhall. (See at its own listing.)
- Haberdashers' Hall: (See under H.)
- St. Anne's and St. Agnes's Church: (See under the CHURCHES section.)
- Swan with Two Necks, the: 17th century Coaching Inn. (See under the INNS/PUBS section.)
- Waxchandlers' Hall: (See under W.)

Gretna Green - Scotland. Infamous elopement destination. (See: marriage.)

Grey Friars Monastery - (Also called the Franciscans.) Newgate Street, off Warwick Lane. From 1225 to 1538. Important intellectual/theological learning here, until the monks were disbanded under the Dissolution of the Monasteries/Henry VIII. The nuns of this order were known as Poor Clares. It became the "Blue Coat" school of Christ's Hospital. (See: Christ's Hospital.)

Greycoat Hospital - Horseferry Road, Lambeth. Founded in 1698. Queen Anne granted its charter in 1706 (and so the facade bears her arms.) There is also a clock turret on the facade. Severely altered in 1873.

Greycoat School - (AKA: The Grey Coat Hospital Church of England Comprehensive School for Girls.) Westminster. Founded in 1698. In the late 17th C. this was a rather squalid area. First established to educate the poor of the parish; an old workhouse in Tothill Fields was purchased in 1701, and a school was established for boys and girls. There was a scandalous murder at the school in 1773, and an 1801 rebellion against "dreadful conditions" at the school. In 1874 became a day school for girls only, its headmistress earning a glowing reputation for her pioneering ways in the area of girls' education.

Greyfriars - (See: Grey Friars.)

greyhound racing - Evolved from the sport of coursing, in which dogs chased live game animals. (See: coursing.) In 1776 the first official UK coursing meeting was held in Swaffham, Norfolk, in which two greyhounds only were allowed to pursue only one hare. Using a proxy (rather than a live animal) began in 1876.

Griffin statue - (AKA: the London Dragon. AKA: Temple Bar Marker.) It tops Temple Bar, since ca. 1880.

- See: Inns of Court/Temple ("Overall")/Middle Temple/Griffin.
- See: Temple Bar, in the T section.

Grillon's Hotel - 7 Albemarle Street, Mayfair. (See: Albemarle Street/Grillon's Hotel.)

Grimaldi, Joe - Famous 18-19th century clown. (See: Sadler's Wells/Joe Grimaldi.)

grocers - Grocers vs. green-grocers: *Grocers* sell groceries, which includes more kinds of foodstuffs, and can include things such as household items. *Green-grocers* sell fresh fruit and vegetables (and are usually a smaller shop or stall.)

- See: green-grocers.
- See: Grocers' Company - Note at.
- See: market-gardens - Because much of London's shopping took place at these, particularly for produce.
- See: Piccadilly/Fortnum & Mason.

Grocers' Company, the - (AKA: the Worshipful Company of Grocers.) This guild was at first the Pepperers (in Sopers Lane.) The Pepperers existed by 1180.

If you dealt in gross (that is, wholesale,) you were a "Gross-er." Twenty-two Pepperers founded the Grocers' Company in 1345. The Grocers purchased Lord Fitzwalder's town mansion in 1426 and built their hall where it yet stands (near the Bank of England.) They were granted their Charter in 1428. St. Stephen Walbrook's patronage was bestowed on the Grocers' Company in the 15th century.

In the mid 15th C. the Hall moved to Cornet's Tower, Bucklersbury (at that time the

Grocers also included druggists and herbalists.)

In 1607 the Grocers incorporated in the Apothecaries; this union dissolved in 1615. (The Apothecaries formed their own Company in 1617.)

AN ENCYCLOPAEDIA OF LONDON states: "The Great Fire practically destroyed all its house property... It does not appear to have exercised any authority over the craft afterwards."

Debt, in 1679, forced the Company from its hall, after which time its fortunes turned, becoming prosperous. There was a thorough repair in 1681.

Rebuilt ca. 1802, but so poorly that it had to be repaired in 1827.

The present Hall dates from 1893, now on the west side of Princes Street.

Livery Company. 2nd in the order of precedence, being one of the Great Twelve companies of the City of London.

Grosvenor Canal - A former waterworks channel, converted in 1823, near to Pimlico.

Grosvenor Chapel - South Audley Street. (See under the CHURCHES section.)

Grosvenor Gate - (See: Hyde Park/Grosvenor Gate.)

Grosvenor House - (AKA: Grosvenor House Hotel, since 1929.) Park Lane; main entrance in Upper Grosvenor Street. Built on the site of Grosvenor House, London home of the Dukes of Westminster (family name: Grosvenor.) The original house was "grand as a palace," one of the biggest private mansions that existed in London. Requisitioned during WWI. Pulled down in the 1920s.

Grosvenor Place - Belgravia. Built in 1767. It overlooked Buckingham House's gardens (a fact that annoyed George III.) The houses were fashionable although small. Its arterial streets ended at high and uninviting mudbanks. (See: Belgravia/Grosvenor Place.)

- 1: School of Anatomy and Medicine, adjoining St. George's Hospital, 1830. (See: St. George's Hospital.)
- Lock Hospital: There prior to 1767. Moved in 1842; the Grosvenor Place building was pulled down in 1846. "Lock" is another word for "rags," which were used to bind sores, and any hospital that treated leprosy was therefore called Lock Hospital. The first Lock Hospital, 12th C., in London was in Southwark. By the 18th C. there was no leprosy in London, so these institutions began to treat persons with venereal diseases, in particular syphilis. (See: Lock Hospital, under L.)

Grosvenor Road - Chelsea. Was called Grosvenor Road throughout the 19th century. Now called: Pimlico Road.

- St. Barnabus: Built 1847-50, by Thomas Cundy.
- St. Saviour's: George Square. 1864, design by Thomas Cundy the Younger. (See

under the CHURCHES section.)

Grosvenor Square - (Pronounced Grove-nur.) At the end of Upper Brook Street; six acres in the heart of Mayfair, making it the largest purely residential square in London. Completed between 1725-40. Remained a fashionable locale from the 1720s through 1939. Home to those of the highest *ton* and/or titles. Made up of "rather plain" brick houses, flat-fronted. Had a mews lane (for carriages and horses) behind.

Since 1785 it has had the nickname "Little America." (See: number 9, below, for an explanation.)

As described in 1817, the square's center was a garden surrounded by a railing; this spreads over the site once called Oliver's Mount, an earthen barricade erected in 1643 by the people (trying to repel Charles I's royalist army.) Walks, shrubs, flowers, grass were all well arranged and well kept there. Each house around the square was required to pay toward the garden's upkeep, and could then freely enjoy it.

- 1: The American Embassy moved here in 1938-2018; before then moving to 33 Nine Elms Lane. (See: United States Embassy.)
- 9: John Adams (later American President) lived here in 1785, serving as the first American ambassador to England. Ever since this time, Grosvenor Square has had the nickname "Little America." (See: 1, above.)
- 20: General Dwight D. Eisenhower used this as his headquarters when he was Supreme Commander of the Allied Expeditionary Force, Jan-Mar/1944. This location is still used by the U. S. Navy.
- 29: Site of the Cato Street conspiracy. (That is, where it began. The conspirators were *caught* at Cato Street, Marylebone.)
- American Embassy, the: Dominates one side of the square.
    - See: 1 and 9, above.
    - See: United States Embassy.
- Derby House: (Not to be confused with another Derby House. For the second, see: College of Arms/Derby House.) This Grosvenor Square home was built in 1773 for Lord Stanley, later 12th Earl of Derby. Demolished in 1862. "One of Adam's most splendid creations for Lord Stanley." Second largest estate in London, first largest is Lincoln's Inn Fields. (See: Derby House/Grosvenor Square, under D.)
- Diplomatic Gates: Modern. Commemorates the 200th anniversary of the signing of the Treaty of Paris, of 1783 (which formally ended the American War of Independence.)

Grosvenor Street - Mayfair. 1720-25.

- 59: Existed here by at least 1730. This address was later renamed as number 60.
- Milne, James: Tailor. Lord Byron's tailor. Milne had bailed Byron's father out of debtor's prison years earlier.

Grove Hill - Camberwell, Southwark. Built in the mid 1770s. Grove Hill, a mansion; one Dr. John Coakely Lettsom lived here from 1779-1810. Was known for its gardens and for having plant species from around the world. Sold due to his decline in fortunes.

- Grove Chapel: 1819.
- Grove Crescent: Eight Georgian terrace houses.

Grove Park - Lewisham. In the extreme south of the parish of Lee, until the early 18th C. this was merely dense woodland (and the name Grove Park for this area is not found in records until after the railways arrived.)

Grub Street - North of St. Paul's, Covent Garden. Where "hack writers" turned out their work in a "small and dingy thoroughfare." The term "Grub Street" was a derisive way of referring collectively to hack writers overall. Circa 1830 it was renamed Milton Street.

➢ See: Albion Street.

➢ See: St. Paul's Cathedral/Grub Street.

Guards' Chapel of Wellington Barracks - Birdcage Walk. 1839-40. (See: Wellington Barracks/Guard's Chapel.)

Guards Museum, the - Modern. (See: Wellington Barracks.)

Guards, the - (See: Royal Guards.)

Guildford - Became a borough ca. 1131.

- Grammar School: Built in the mid 16th C. under the sponsorship of Edward VI.
- Loseley House: Tudor mansion.

Guildhall, the - Guildhall Yard, King Street, Cheapside, the City. The place where civic government (as opposed to royal or parliamentary government) was enacted. Because it was founded in Saxon times as "Guild Hall," this building has always borne this name, even when it would have been more appropriate to call it City Hall because it had become the seat of municipal power.

It's important to understand that the City of London (the Square Mile) had long seized the right to govern itself (since medieval days.) It has guarded those rights jealously; and, hence, needed institutions such as the Guildhall, the Court of Aldermen, the Court of Common Council, etc. to provide self-governance, rather than answering to the Crown. One example: to this day when the monarch comes to Parliament, he/she must ask permission from the Lord Mayor before passing through Temple Bar on into the City.

(See: guilds.)

The Guildhall was used by the first ever Mayor of London. "Lord Mayor" as a title does not appear in records until 1283, and wasn't commonly used until ca. 1545. (See: Lord Mayor, under L.)

The COURT OF COMMON COUNCIL administers the City's business from here, (the Court developed from the ancient Court of Hustings.) Here was the City's administrative building for 800+ years, a place for meetings, ceremonies, and self-government; first recorded date of existence was in 1128. It was once used for Treason trials, notably Lady Jane Grey. (See: Court of Common Council, under C.)

The crypt and the Great Hall in the present building date from a 1411-40 rebuild, designed by John Croxton, near the site of the prior 1128 cottage-sized building. The Gothic porch was built in 1430, and the main thrust of the building in 1439.

It was greatly damaged in the Great Fire of 1666, being afterward much restored; rebuilt in 1673.

Is where the state lotteries were drawn from 1694-1826. Lotteries were banned in 1826 (and briefly from 1699-1709) for fear of their encouraging mass gambling.

The building that was standing here during the Regency had a front (a facade into which the old medieval porch was set) that was designed by George Dance the Younger, 1788-9; described as "new Gothic fantasy." ROMANTIC LONDON (published in 1928) states: "...though rebuilt by Dance in 1789, it contains the greater part of the old walls of 1411, in addition to the original crypt. The Guildhall was much damaged by the fire of 1666, and what with Dance's reconstruction and later restorations in the so-called Gothic sytle, there is little about it which has not been restored or rebuilt." It still had the outer walls that had survived the Great Fire, with this new front. It had an ugly flat roof (was by Wren) until 1864. The flat roof was replaced by an open one, and a minstrel's gallery added.

- Commission of Sewers: (See under C.)
- Court of Common Council: (See, in paragraph above.)
- Gog and Magog: The figures of Gog and Magog (ancient Druidic tree-dwelling god figures) date from 1708, but were burned in WWII, and remade. They stand on either side of the stairs of the Great Hall. (Not to be confused with the Gog and Magog of St. Dunstan's-in-the-West Church.)
- Library: Founded in 1423 from money left for the purpose by Dick Whittington, (four times Lord Mayor of London.) Partly destroyed in the Great Fire, and is still used. The present Library design dates from 1828, and was opened to the public in 1873. Described as a "fine building." There was an earlier library in a building near the Guildhall, but that collection was carried away by the Duke of Somerset in 1549, (and recovered in 1824.) The Library is now used for state occasions; by 1966 it was located in Basinghall Street.

Guildhall Museum - Founded in 1826. Combined with the old London Museum to form the (new) London Museum in 1976.

guilds - The guilds were bodies of craftsmen and tradesmen, Masters and journeymen. They trained apprentices. They set quality control standards, and often were able to set/fix wages (although some of their powers were lessened from the 16th C. forward, due to legislation.) In the 19th C. a waiving of apprenticeship led to even more influence lost.

In medieval times, the guilds held much power in the City. The Companies often went on to build halls, many of which were large and/or grand. (See: halls - For much more information.)

In the Regency era, the guilds were no longer the heartbeat of London/England, but many still remained/still had influence.

Although there are some 110 guilds now, the twelve "Great Companies" (founded from medieval times) are:

Clothworkers - 12th in precedence
Drapers - 3rd in precedence
Fishmongers - 4th in precedence
Goldsmiths - 5th in precedence
Grocers - 2nd in precedence
Haberdashers - 8th in precedence
Ironmongers - 10th in precedence
Mercers - 1st in precedence
Merchant Taylors - 7th in precedence*
Salters - 9th in precedence
Skinners - 6th in precedence*
Vintners - 11th in precedence

*The Skinners and the Merchant-Taylors disputed their order of precedence, so in 1484 the Lord Mayor declared they would change 6th and 7th positions on a yearly basis, which they do yet to this day, thus supposedly giving rise to the phrase to be "at sixes and sevens" (meaning out of sorts/topsy-turvy.)

There are, of course, many other guilds, but only the original twelve are "Great," all others are "Minor." For instance, some of the Minor Companies are: the Coopers, the Glaziers, the Pattenmakers. There were no new guilds founded from 1709 until 1929 (when the Air Pilots and Air Navigators Guild was founded.) The Information Technologists Guild was established in 1992, being the city's one-hundredth City company.

- See: Common Hall.
- See: Court of Aldermen.
- SEE: HALLS.
- See: Livery Companies.
- See: mystery - How an organization of like-minded craft-persons was styled prior to achieving its Charter.

Gunnersbury House - 7-8 Bridgewater Square. Built in the mid 17th C. as a Palladian mansion for Sir John Maynard (the king's principal serjeant-at-law,) existed by at least 1674. Home to Princess Amelia (George II's daughter) 1762-86, as her summer residence. Sold in 1800 and the house was pulled down. Replaced by 2 houses: Gunnersbury Park and Gunnersbury House (nicknamed the Large Mansion and the Small Mansion.) Later, home to the Rothschilds family. In 1926, became a museum/park, encompassing 200 acres.

Gunmakers' Company - (AKA: The Worshipful Company of Gunmakers. AKA: the Society of the Mystery of Gunmakers of the City of London.) Gunsmiths used to belong to either the Armourers' Company or the Blacksmiths' Company, until the Gunmakers were granted their Charter in 1637. (The Charter, due to opposition, was not enrolled until 1656.) Livery was granted in 1778. Never had a hall; they are located at Proof House, Commercial Road. Note that they are outside the City, (because gunpowder was kept outside the old City walls.) They have kept a link with their trade, because they are yet responsible for proof-testing gun barrels/actions for safety standards. 73rd in the order of precedence.

gunpowder -

- See: Great Britain - About the Gunpowder Plot.
- See: Gunmakers' Company.
- See: Waltham Abbey.
- You may care to see: weapons.

Gunpowder Alley - An offshoot off Shoe Lane. (See: Shoe Lane/Gunpowder Alley.)

guns - (See: weapons.)

gunshot - (See: weapons.)

Gunter's - 7-8 Berkeley Square, Mayfair. Established in 1757 by an Italian pastrycook, Domenico (or Domenicus) Negri. Besides its wet and dry sweetmeats (including ices, for which they were known) Gunter's was also famous for its turtle soup and its elaborate wedding cakes. Originally at 7 Berkeley Square (on the east side of the square.) In 1835, number 8 was added on to 7.

Negri took Gunter as a partner in 1777, and by 1779 Gunter was running the shop by himself.

It was a light eatery, and had the confectioner's sign, a pineapple, hanging outside the establishment, and there were iron railings before the shop. Ladies (or anyone) could, if they desired, pull their carriage up to the rail and conduct their transaction without ever leaving the carriage; waiters brought the orders to them. They also provided refreshments and wine to people's homes.

It was not considered shocking for a lady to dine here on her own.

Lord Alvanley (b.1789-d.1849, an Army officer and a Regency buck) once ordered a luncheon hamper for a boating party from Gunter's for the princely sum of £200.

In 1936-7 the east side of Berkeley Square was pulled down, so Gunter's moved to the Curzon Street and Park Lane corner address. The tea shop part of the business closed in 1956 (although catering continued until 1976.)

Gunthorpe Street - Whitechapel. First known as George Yard, which existed by at least 1676. By 1822 George Yard was known as a notorious area for thieves. One of Jack the Ripper's victims was murdered here. Rebuilt ca. the 1860s. Renamed to Gunthorpe Street in 1912.

Gutter Lane - Cheapside. First mentioned ca. 1199-1216 (during King John's reign.)

- Saddlers' Hall: (See under S.)

Guy's Hospital - (See under: Southwark/Guy's Hospital.)

Gwydyr House - (AKA: Welsh Gwydyr House.) 65 Whitehall. 1772, by Marquand. Built as a private home and named for an early Welsh owner. Privately owned until 1835. Since 1871 it's been used for official needs.

- Welsh Office: 1965, to execute policy in Wales; disbanded in 1999, its powers shifting to the National Assembly for Wales (and some to the Office of the Secretary of State for Wales, the latter of which is now housed at Gwydyr House.)

Gypsies - Also seen spelled "Gipsies" in fact, in source data I've seen it about 50/50 with either spelling. In the 17-19th centuries gypsies were not well thought of by the general populace. In Britain they were often suppressed and denied rights, living a wanderer's existence. Often blamed for thefts and small crimes. They frequently had to contend with the vagrancy laws, and were sometimes accused of stealing children. Into modern times, the Gypsy lifestyle generates controversy.

- See: Gipsy Hill.
- See: Mawney.
- See: Penge.
- See: Smitham Bottom.
- See: Streatham Vale.

-H-

ha-ha - A sunken barrier, a deeper trench usually put along the edges of one's property to keep out wildlife or cattle, arranged so that when the property as a whole is viewed from a distance it appears to be unbroken. Supposedly called a "ha-ha" because this is what a visitor might say when coming upon it unexpectedly.

haberdashers - Dealers in notions/accoutrements, particularly hats. Or, more in the past, one who provides sewing articles such as buttons and ribbons, by the 18th C. it was much more of the former. (19th century sources use the terms "drapers" and "haberdashers" rather interchangeably.)

- See: drapers.
- See: hats.
- See: hatters.
- See: Oxford Street/54.
- See: tailors.
- See: Telegraph Hill.

Haberdashers' Hall - (For the Worshipful Company of Haberdashers.) They were first called Hurrers (cap-makers,) but where the word "haberdashers" comes from is uncertain. The guild was first mentioned in 1381. Got their charter in 1448. The hall was bequeathed to them by one William Baker in 1478, and located in Gresham Street. This burned in the Great Fire of 1666; rebuilt by Wren in 1667 on the site of St. John Zachary (which also burned in the Great Fire.) The Hall remained until 1840, when a large portioned burned again. The most recent Hall dates from 1862-4, and is in Staining Lane. (See: New Cross/Worshipful Company of...)

Hackbridge - Sutton. Dates from at least 1235. There were mills here (on the River Wandle) since the Middle Ages. Tanning and the making of paper here.

- Hackbridge House: By 1820, home to the Goad family.
- Red Lion Inn: 1721. The building yet exists.

Hackney - Existed by at least 1275, at which time rich Londoners were already building country homes here, with large artistic houses making a strong surge in the 16-17th centuries. By the 18th century Hackney's wealth came not just from noblemen but merchants (including Huguenots and Jews.)

- Balmes House: Built ca. 1540. Pulled down in 1852. Brick, two stories, dormer windows, high-pitched roof. Sometime early in the 19th C. the house became a lunatic asylum. The land was developed after 1852, becoming De Beauvoir Town.

- Brooke House: (See under B.)
- Church Street: (See: Mare Street, below.)
- Gravel Pit Chapel: Ram Place, at Morning Lane. Joseph Priestly (scientist) was the minister here ca. 1792-4.
- Hackney New Church: (See: St. John's, below.)
- Hackney Old Church: (AKA: St. Augustine's.) Medieval. Pulled down in 1798 to make way for St. John's. (See, below.) Except the tower of St. Augustine's remained, in the churchyard (the grounds of which were later made into a recreation ground.)
- Homerton: During the Regency, this district belonged to the parish of Hackney, only later becoming its own parish. A quiet village. (See at its own listing.)
- Kingsland High Street:
    - Hospital for lepers in the 18th C., annexed to St. Bartholomew's Hospital as a kind of out-ward.
- London Fields: Close to Mare Street. 26-1/2 acres (2nd source said 31 acres.) East of the field, Lamb Lane and Sheep Lane run. So cropped and traveled over that the grass was slow to grow, being hard and dusty in summer, and swampy in winter. Consequently, became an area for rough types. By the early 19th C. the area had become densely built up. Richer residents tended to reside on the north side.
    - Broadway Market: There was a row of two-storied shops here; the market grew up around them in the 1820s.
- Lower Clapton: Lies south of the Lea Bridge Road and north of Hackney; this area's name dates from the early 19th century. 17th C. country seats for the wealthy here.
    - Clapton House: (On what is now) Lower Clapton Road. Ca. 1680. Became a school. Pulled down in the 1880s.
    - Clapton Square: Laid out in 1816. Now a conservation area.
    - Lower Clapton Road: 113. Built by at least 1792-4 when Jason Priestly (scientist) lived here.
    - Piss Pot Hall: Built in the late 1710s for a manufacturer of novelty chamber pots, hence the name. The house has five bays. Across the road from Clapton House. Became the British Asylum for Deaf and Dumb

Females, for girls over the age of 10, 1851; also had a home for aged and infirm deaf ladies. The Asylum had been elsewhere, but moved to Piss Pot Hall in 1857. Closed in 1986.

    - St. James's Church: 1840.

- Mare Street: Old village high street, lined with homes and shops from the 1720s. The northern part is now called Church Street.
- Pentonville Prison: (AKA: Model Prison.) 1840. When it was built, it stood alone in an open field.
- St. John's: (AKA: Church of St. John-at-Hackney.) Built 1791-7 to replace St. Augustine's. (See: Hackney Old Church, for more on St. Augustine's.)
- St. Peter's Church: Built ca. 1830.
- Shoulder of Mutton: A public-house (now the Cat and Mutton) stood here since at least 1731. (See under the INNS/PUBS section.)
- Stoke Newington Church Street:
    - 172: Edgar Allan Poe (American poet/writer) lived here sometime between 1815-29.
- Sutton House: Mansion built in 1535; still standing. Oldest house in the whole of London's East End. (See under S.)
- Sutton Place: Georgian terrace.
- Whitmore Road: Adjoins Regent's Canal. Built as a carriage drive to connect Balmes House to London. (See under B.)

hackney coach - (AKA: hackney carriage. Of course, all coaches are carriages, but not all carriages are coaches.) A hackney coach was a carriage for hire. ("Hackney" means horse. Or in more common usage, a horse for hire.) Introduced to London ca. 1605, becoming more available/desired by the 1630s. They were built in the Strand at that time.

Springs started to be added to hackney coaches ca. 1625, making travel more comfortable for the passengers, but they weren't universal until the latter half of the 18th century.

Hackney carriage licenses were first issued in 1662.

Glass windows (as opposed to the prior leather flaps) began to appear in carriages in 1685.

Hackney carriages continued as a common form of transport into the Regency era, although considered less comfortable/fashionable than a private coach. By Victoria's reign, they began to be replaced by hansom cabs (and their larger cousins called "growlers"); hansom cabs had the driver up and behind the coach; they were patented in 1834. Hackney carriages survived as a transportation option into the 1940s.

- See: Corporation of Coachmen.
- See: Hansom cab.

Hackney Lane - (See: Clapton/Upper Clapton/Upper Clapton Road.)

Hackney Marsh - (Also called: Hackney Marshes.) Hackney. On the banks of the River Lea. 336 acres, London's largest recreational ground, and second largest common (after Hampstead Heath.) Was true marshes, with occasional flooding by the River Lea. In the 16th C. was also known for its highwaymen. By the time of the Regency, people were trying to turn this area into recreational land, not so successfully, but even so the reputation was improving.

Haggerston - A Shoreditch hamlet/Hackney. Long ago was known as Hergotestane. Country residences. Was built up as the 19th C. advanced, until it became overcrowded.

- Queen's Road: Big, long, straight, busy. Cuts through nice and not-so-nice neighborhoods alike. Was later called Queensbridge Road (ca. the 1840s.)

Hainault Forest - East of the hamlet Chigwell Row. Ancient. Purchased for public use in 1903. It was once a part of the ancient Forest of Waltham.

hair, notes on - (You may care to see: looking-glass.)

- Britons do not say "bangs," they say "fringe."
- Britons do not say "braid," they say "plait," rhymes with flat. (This is true of anything that can be plaited, not just hair.)

hair tonics -

- See: brushes.
- See: combs.
- See: St. James's Street/29.

haircutters - Hair might well be cut at home by one's family, but there were professional haircutters, too. Women tended to grow their hair long, although short cuts were not unknown.

One treatment for lice was to shear the hair off down to the scalp, so the sheared look was unpopular among both genders.

- See: Barbers' Hall.
- See: Bond Street/Old Bond Street/23/Truefitt's - The first hairdressers to have the lady come to them, rather than the other way around, in the late 1800s.

Hale, the - Barnet. First mentioned in 1294 records. By the mid 18th C. had formed into two hamlets: Upper Hale (around the junction of Deans Lane, Hale Lane, and Selvage Lane,) and Lower Hale (smaller, centered on a village green to the northwest.) Was rural deep into the 20th century.

- Green Man Inn: Upper Hale, 1751. Later became a meeting place for boxers (and other sportsmen.)

Half Moon Street - Mayfair. (See: Berkeley Square/Half Moon Street.)

Hall Place - Bexley area mansion. Edward of Woodstock, son of King Edward III, died before his father, and who is also known as the Black Prince: his ghost is said to appear here in the grounds.

halls - *While the trade Companies don't all have halls, I have chosen to put a preponderance of "Companies" data here, in order to avoid too much repetition in this work. Still, much can be found at LIVERY COMPANIES under L, and at each Company under its own name in its Alpha section.*

Many of the City Companies (AKA from medieval times as: Guilds) had/have halls in which to meet/conduct business/set down the restrictions and regulate the rules of their trade, train apprentices, and supply camaraderie. Companies whose duties are no longer as relevant in the 21st century (say, the arrow-making Fletchers,) no longer regulate their industry in London, but still exist and now act as resources and charities.

The Companies number in precedence, the ancient and uppermost ones being called the "Great Twelve," they are the 12 that date from medieval times (in the following order):

1. Mercers.
2. Grocers.
3. Drapers.
4. Fishmongers.
5. Goldsmiths.
6. Skinners.*
7. Merchant-Taylors.*
8. Haberdashers.
9. Salters.
10. Ironmongers.
11. Vintners.
12. Clothworkers.

her Companies are: minor.

*The Skinners and the Merchant-Taylors disputed their order of precedence, so in 1484 the Lord Mayor declared they would change 6th and 7th position on a yearly basis, which they do yet to this day, thus supposedly giving rise to the phrase to be "at sixes and sevens" (meaning in a tizzy/out of sorts/topsy-turvy.)

NOTE: Not all Companies have livery; only those that were chartered to have the ceremonial robes, do. The Parish Clerks, for instance, do not have livery. (Nor do they have a hall.)

Also, while many do, not all the Companies number in precedence, either.

- See: Court of Aldermen - Regarding the Order of Precedence among the Companies.
- See: Freeman of the City - Having the right to work one's trade in the City of London.
- See: Guildhall.
- See: guilds.
- See: mystery - Old term for a pre-Charter guild.
- See: Royal Warrant - Came into being in the Victorian era, in part to fill a void left by the fading influence of the Guilds.
- See: Worshipful Company of..., under W.

THE FOLLOWING LISTS ARE NOT ALL INCLUSIVE, especially as relates to more modern Companies, which are largely neglected in this work, as they didn't exist before or during the Regency era. Too, through the centuries, some Companies have risen, then ceased to exist altogether, leaving little record of themselves behind (for instance: the Longbow String Makers, who are long gone.)

Just to be clear: in order to not repeat the same data at "companies" and "halls" and "Livery Companies," I have chosen to put a preponderance of information here at "halls." The listings below are for the Companies' halls. The halls *do not* have precedence; the precedence (order of ceremonial preeminence) belongs to the Company for which the Hall was built.

And, again, don't forget to look under individual Alpha listings.

THE COMPANIES IN THE FOLLOWING LIST HAVE HALLS:

- Apothecaries' Hall - 58th in precedence. Shares space in their Hall with the Spectacle Makers. (You may care to see: doctors/apothecary, under D.)
- Armourers' and Brasiers' Hall - Brasiers work brass. 22nd in precedence. (See: Coleman Street/Armourers' and Brasiers' Hall.)
- Bakers' Hall - 19th in precedence.
- Barbers' Hall - 17th in precedence. Included barbers and surgeons.
  - See: Barbers' Hall, under B.
  - See: doctors - For more on medical men.
- Brewers' Hall - 14th in precedence.
- Broderers' Hall - As in embroidery. 48th in precedence.

- Butchers' Hall - 24th in precedence.
- Carpenters' Hall - 26th in precedence. (See: Throgmorton Avenue/Carpenters' Hall.)
- Clothworkers' Hall - 12th in precedence. (See: Mincing Lane/Clothworkers' Hall.)
- Coachmakers' and Coach Harness Makers' Hall - 72nd in precedence.
- Coopers' Hall - Makers of wooden casks or tubs. 36th in precedence.
- Cordwainers' Hall - Originally the Cordwainers were the ones who made new shoes; the Cobblers only repaired shoes. Over time, it became that the Cordwainers dealt exclusively in Cordovan leather. 27th in precedence. Had a hall until it was destroyed by WWII bombing. (See: Candlewick Street/Cordwainers' Hall.)
- Cutlers' Hall - Makers of knives, fork, and swords. 18th in precedence. Associated with the elephant and castle symbol.
- Drapers' Hall - Sellers of cloth and wool. 3rd in precedence.
- Dyers' Hall - 13th in precedence.
- Fanmakers' Hall - Dowgate Hill. 18th century. Originally for decorative fans, now connected with heating and air-conditioning. 76th in precedence.
- Fishmongers' Hall - 4th in precedence. Their hall is described as grand, impersonal, and stately, in the Revival style, 1830s.
- Founders Hall - (See under "No Halls" list, below.)
- Girdlers' Hall - Made a kind of Medieval belt called a girdle; when those largely disappeared, also made garters, bandoliers, and other leather items. 23rd in precedence.
- Glaziers' Hall - Glazing and leading of windows. AKA: Glaziers and Painters of Glass. 53rd in precedence. Has had a Hall only since the 1970s.
- Goldsmiths' Hall - 5th in precedence.
    - See: East Acton.
    - See: goldsmiths, under G.
    - See: Goldsmiths' Hall, under G.
- Grocers' Hall - 2nd in precedence.
- Haberdashers' Hall - 8th in precedence. Makers of hats, men's accoutrements, thread, and sewing articles.
- Information Technologists' Hall - Company created in 1992. Unlike many newer companies, the Information Technologists have their own hall (not shared.)
- Innholders' Hall - 32nd in precedence.
- Ironmongers' Hall - 10th in precedence. Dealers in iron and hardware. The

Ironmongers' Company shares its Hall with the Shipwrights' Company.

- Launderers - Actually, their Hall is shared with Glaziers and the Scientific Instrument Makers. (See: Glaziers' Company.) Surprisingly, the Launderers date from only 1960. 89th in precedence. Has been a Livery Company since 1977.
- Leathersellers' Hall - 15th in precedence.
- Master Mariners Hall - 78th in precedence. Has a (literally) floating hall, on the HQS Wellington. The first new Livery Company (1932) formed since 1746. (See under M.)
- Mercers' Hall - Dealers in small wares. Existed by at least 1414. 1st in precedence.
- Merchant Taylors' Hall - 7th in precedence. *See note above, right below the list of the Twelve Great Companies.
- Painter-stainers' Hall - 28th in precedence.
- Pepperers' Hall - Were part of the Grocers from the 14th century. (See: Grocers Company, in the G section.)
- Pewterers' Hall - 16th in precedence.
- Plaisterers' Company - "Plaister" is an ancient way of spelling: plaster. Are 46th in precedence. Went without a Hall for years, but has a new one since 1972. (See under P.)
- Saddlers' Hall - 25th in precedence.
- Salters' Hall - 9th in precedence. The Salters did not produce salt, they salted provisions. Were salt and chemical merchants; but are now connected with the chemical industry. (See: St. Swithin's Lane/Salters' Hall.)
- Scientific Instrument Makers - Founded in the 20th century. 84th in precedence. Doesn't have a Hall of their own; their Hall is shared with the Glaziers and the Launderers.
    - See: Glaziers' Company.
    - See: Scientific Instrument Makers, under S.
- Shipwrights' Company - Ship construction and repair. Don't have a Hall of their own; shares one with the Ironmongers' Company. 59th in precedence.
- Skinners' Hall - Dowgate Hill, there since the late 1200s. Fur trade, worked with pelts. Their hall is described as fine, homely, and intimate. 6th in precedence.* (*See the note above, right under the list of the 12 Great Companies.) Were in earlier times referred to as Fellmongers. (See: Fellmongers, under F.)

    Here's an example of how different Guilds dealt with the same product: Skinners took the hides off cows and pigs.

Tanners treated/turned the hides into leather.

Curriers cured and dyed the leather, making it flexible, strong, and largely waterproof.

So, the same item was handled three times, each Company achieving their different aim/craft.

- Spectacle-makers' Company - Formed in 1563. 60th in precedence. Has no Hall of their own, is housed in the Apothecaries' Hall, Black Friars.
- Stationers' Hall - AKA: Stationers and Newspaper Makers. Established in 1430. 47th in precedence. (See under S.)
- Tallow Chandlers' Hall - 21st in precedence.
- Vintners' Hall - Wine merchants. 11th in precedence.
- Watermen's and Lightermen's Hall - Dates from 1688. Does not have livery. Does not number in precedence.
- Waxchandlers' Hall - Now includes beekeeping and honey production. 20th in precedence.

THESE COMPANIES DO NOT HAVE HALLS. Some of these are modern; some are ancient.

- Air Pilots and Air Navigators, Guild of - 1929. 81st in precedence.
- Basket Makers' Company - Also seen as: Basketmakers. 52nd in precedence.
- Blacksmiths' Company - 40th in precedence.
- Bottlemakers' Company - (See: Horners' Company, under H.)
- Bowyers' Company - 38th in precedence.
- Carmens' Company - Hired themselves out as transporters of goods. 77th in precedence. They had included the Woodmongers, the latter defunct in 1746.
- Clockmakers' Company - 61st in precedence.
- Cooks' Company - Royal Charter in 1482. The smallest guild in London. Never had a hall. 35th in precedence. Included women since 1495. (See under C.)
- Curriers' Company - Scraping, coloring, beating tanned leather. 29th in precedence.
- Distillers' Company - 69th in precedence.
- Farmers' Company - 80th in precedence.
- Farriers' Company - Those who shoe horses. 55th in precedence.
- Feltmakers' Company - Never did have a hall. 63rd in precedence.
- Fletchers' Company - Put the feathers on arrows. Never did have a hall. 39th in precedence.
- Founders' Company - Once had a hall, but the location has housed offices for

decades. They were metal-casters. Some of the things they made: bells, candlesticks, pots, weights. 33rd in precedence.

- Framework Knitters' Company - 64th in precedence.
- Fruiterers' Company - Never did have a hall. 45th in precedence.
- Furniture Makers' Company - 83rd in precedence.
- Gardeners' Company - Never did have a hall, but has a library at Guildhall. 66th in precedence.
- Glass-sellers' Company - Never did have a hall. 71st in precedence.
- Glovers' Company - Had a Hall, but it was abandoned at the end of the 18th century. 62nd in precedence.
- Gold and Silver Wyre-Drawers' Company - 74th in precedence.
- Gunmakers' Company - 73rd in precedence.
- Horners' Company - Originally literally worked with animal horn, used in place of glass for windows, and later boxes and horn-books. They are now connected with the plastics industry. 54th in precedence.
- Joiners' Company - Joined timber; then furniture; then evolved into carvers. Once had a hall. Now called: the Joiners and Ceilers. "Ceilers" refers to wall and ceiling wood panels. 41st in precedence.
- Loriners' Company - Dates from 1261; its present ordinances from 1741. Royal Charter in 1711. Made metal bits for bridles and saddles. 57th in precedence. They take their name from the French for bridle: lormier.
- Makers of Playing Cards Company - 75th in precedence.
- Masons' Company - Those who laid stone or brick. Never had a hall. 30th in precedence. Not to be confused with Freemasons, (although the Freemasons do/did utilize many mason principles/symbols.)
- Musicians' Company - 50th in precedence.
- Needlemakers' Company - 65th in precedence.
- Parish Clerks Company - Charter dates from 1442. Has no livery. Does not number in precedence. Used to have a hall, but was not rebuilt after WWII damage.
- Pattenmakers' Company - A kind of slide-on wooden over-shoe that raised one's shoes out of the water/mud. (See: patten, under P.) The trade dates from the 12th C. or earlier. There was a trade association in 1379. Their Royal Charter came in 1670. As roads improved, pattens were increasingly old-fashioned (but still sometimes seen) during the Regency. Today the Pattenmakers work in orthopedic shoes, particularly for those who have served in the military. 70th in

precedence. No hall.

- Paviors' Company - Road engineers. Never did have a hall. 56th in precedence.
- Plumbers' Company - 31st in precedence.
- Poulters' Company - No longer has a Hall. 34th in precedence.
- Scriveners' Company - Drafted legal forms such as wills and deeds. Charter in 1617. 44th in precedence.
- Solicitors of the City of London Company - (AKA: the London Solicitors.) 1909. 79th in precedence.
    - See under S.
    - You may care to see: lawyer/solicitor, under L.
- Spurriers - Makers of spurs. Women seldom wore spurs because they tangled with their skirts. The Spurriers were part of the Blacksmiths' Company. (See: Blacksmiths' Company, under B.)
- Tin-plate Workers' Company - 1670. Has no hall. 67th in precedence.
- Tobacco Pipe Makers and Tobacco Blenders' Company - 82nd in precedence.
- Turners' Company - Turners of wood, as for chair or table legs. 51st in precedence.
- Tylers and Bricklayers' Company - Roof and floor tile layers. 37th in precedence.
- Upholders' Company - "Upholder" is the ancient version of the word upholsterers, as in those who cover chairs with fabric. Dates from 1360; Royal Charter in 1626. 49th in precedence.
- Weavers' Company - Royal Charter from 1155; the oldest on record, so the Weavers are most likely the oldest London guild. Hall demolished in 1856. 42nd in precedence.
- Wheelwrights' Company - 68th in precedence.
- Woolmen's Company - Began in 1180. "Woolmen" regulated the wool trade, whereas "woolmongers" worked directly with the sheep's wool. 43rd in precedence.

The following are not Companies (as in guilds) but are listed here in order to re-direct the reader to the proper listings:

- *Common Hall: NOT a guild hall, but rather a term for the time when the Lord Mayor was/is elected by the leaders of the guilds. (See under C.)*
- *Freemasons' Hall: NOT a livery company/guild. (See at its own listing under F.)*

ham - An ancient word meaning a homestead or settlement. Seen in many place names. (Of course, it also is a food term for cured pork.)

Ham - Richmond. Called "an extended village," dates from 1150. Henry V acquired the "manor of Hamme Upkyngeston" in 1415. In 1800 this area was fairly rural, with agriculture its main trade.

- Ham House: (See at its own listing.)
- Ormeley Lodge: Georgian.
- West Ham: (See under W.)

Ham House - Ham Street, Richmond, county of Surrey. Across the Thames from Twickenham. Jacobean mansion and garden, built 1610, and rebuilt in 1673. The Dysart family lived here from the 17th century. Little changed and well preserved since at least the 1750s, after which time it took on the Ham House name. Red brick. Leafy avenues. Presented to the National Trust in 1948; now an annex to the Victoria and Albert Museum. (See: Richmond/Ham House.)

Hamley's - Toy store, 1760.

- See: Noah's Ark.
- See: Regent Street/188-196.

Hammersmith - Hammersmith and Fulham. Started out possibly in Roman times. By 1294 it was an established fishing village. Was a part of the Fulham parish until 1834, when it became its own parish. An area for breweries. (See: Fulham.)

- St. Paul's Church: 1631. A chapel of ease. (See: St. Paul/Fulham, under the CHURCHES section.)
- St. Peter's Square: 1839.
- West Kensington: ca. 1880. Is actually *not* in Kensington Borough, but rather in Hammersmith. (See: Fulham/North End.)

Hampden Club - Political men's club, 1811. (See under the CLUBS section.)

Hampstead - North London village, neighbors on Highgate, Camden; (Hampstead and Highgate are connected by a large swath of open heathland.) Hilly. Its name derives from the word "homestead." From THE FACE OF LONDON: "The charming old town of Hampstead is built in a torturous irregular fashion on the slope of the hill leading up to the heath." Dates from the year 990. It was once woodland, but rebuilding following the Great Fire of 1666 pretty much denuded its forest-y nature (although nowadays it is yet described as having a "leafy tranquility.") Was for a while a popular spa (there is a spring there,) but it declined by the 1730s, being too close to London and having attracted too many "common people." By the 1790s it attracted wealthier residents. In 1811, there were 904 houses, and a population of 5,483. In the 1820s it became a popular place of residence with professionals, writers, & artists from the city and the West End. By 1860s was still not a part of London proper; still countrified. Officially joined to the capital in 1888. Is now rather conspicuously wealthy; the streets are described as elegant, charming, and narrow.

- Admiral's House: (See: Hampstead Heath/Admiral's House.)
- Assembly Rooms: 1807. Eventually, as the 19th C. advanced, became discredited because of the excessive gambling here. (See: Romney House, below.)
- Bolton House: Joanna Baillie lived here. She knew literary fame at the time of Keats (poet) and Sir Walter Scott (author,) both of whom visited her here, the latter in 1806. She died here at age 89 in 1851.
- Bull and Bush: (AKA: Old Bull and Bush.) Inn. 17th C., still there, though recently revamped.
- Burgh House: (See: Flash Walk/Burgh House, below.)
- Church Row: Off Heath Street, opposite St. John's. Early 18th century. "One of Hampstead's glories" and "one of London's finest Georgian Streets," ca. 1720-50. Tall, narrow houses.
    - St. John: 1747 (at the end of Church Row, on the corner of Downshire Hill.) John Constable, the painter, is buried here, in the churchyard. (See: St. John/Hampstead, under the CHURCHES section.)
- Downshire Hill: Beautiful, elegant street, largely Regency era houses (1816-ish.)
- Fenton House: 20 Hampstead Grove, Windmill Hill. Hampstead's oldest residence, possibly built by Wren in 1693. It is named for the merchant who purchased it in 1793. Now is in the area named Hampstead Grove. Still has its 17th C. facade and "an exquisite walled garden." Is the oldest surviving example of a merchant's house. It is now a National Trust building that exhibits 18th C porcelain and early keyboard instruments (still occasionally used for concerts.)
- Flask Walk: Narrow street. So named because the spring waters were bottled for sale on this street in flasks.
    - Burgh House: New End Square. Queen Anne style house, built ca. 1702 for a Quaker family named Sewell, but a Dr. William Gibbons, famous Hampstead physician, lived here in 1702. However, the house is named for a 19th C. doctor-resident, Dr. Burgh (the house's tenth owner.) In now a local history museum.
    - Lower Flask tavern: (AKA: The Flask.) At the top of Highgate Hill. Since the mid 18th C., still there. Beyond the pub, the road broadens into an area where Regency homes still can be seen.
- Green Man, the: Pub. (See: Well Walk/Wells Tavern, below.)
- Grove Lodge: 18th century.

- Hampstead Heath: (See at its own listing.)
- Hampstead Square: Some houses here by the early 18th century. Described as being lined with Georgian mansions.
- Highgate Cemetery: 1839.
    - See at its own listing.
    - See: St. Pancras Churchyard, below.
- Holly Bush Hill: On this street resides a timber-built home dating from 1797, built for George Romney (portrait artist.)
- Holly Bush Pub: (Also called: Holly Bush Tavern.) An attractive early 18th C. building. When Romney House became the Assembly Rooms in 1807, Romney House's stables became the Holly Bush Tavern.
- Island Queen Pub: 1848. Noel Road.
- Jack Straw's Castle: (See under: Hampstead Heath/Jack Straw's Castle.)
- Keats' Grove: (See: Wentworth Place, below.)
- Kenwood House: (See under: Hampstead Heath/Kenwood House.)
- Lower Terrace (Street): By at least 1779.
    - 2: Constable (the artist) lived here for a while, before moving to 40 Well Walk. (See: Well Walk/40, below.)
- New End: Before the start of the 19th C. this was rather the poor corner of Hampstead. (See: New End, under N.)
- Noel Road: 1848. (See: Island Queen Pub, above.)
- Old Bull and Bush: (See: Bull and Bush, above.)
- Parliament Hill: Provides a spectacular view of London. A place to fly kites and sail model boats.
- Romney House: 1797. Built for the painter George Romney. In 1807 became the Assembly Rooms. (See: Holly Bush Pub, above.)
- Rosslyn Hill: (See under R.)
- St. John's: Hampstead's parish church. At the west end of Church Row. Built 1744-7 by Henry Flitcroft, of brick. Still has its original pew boxes; was smallish. Castellated steeple and belfry (gives it a faintly medieval air.) The west end was modified sometime in the mid 19th century. Dubbed: St. John-at-Hampstead, but not until 1917. (See: St. John/Hampstead, under the CHURCHES section.)
- St. Mary's: Holly Walk. Abbé Morel, a Frenchman, founded this church; Roman Catholic. Has white exterior walls. (See: St. Mary/Hampstead, under the CHURCHES section.)
- St. Pancras Churchyard: Was replaced in 1839 by Highgate Cemetery. (See:

Highgate Cemetery, at its own listing.)

- South End: (See under S.)
- Spaniards Inn, the:
    - See: Hampstead Heath/Spaniard's Inn.
    - See under S.
- Squire's Mount: Georgian cottages.
- Vale of Health: (See: Well Walk/Vale of Health, below.)
- Well Walk: In the 18th C. there was a working chalybeate spring well here, and the area was a fashionable pleasure haunt. There were Assembly Rooms, built in Queen Anne's time, but by the time of the Regency they were derelict and unused (the site had lost its appeal as a health spa.)

  This part of town was also referred to as the VALE OF HEALTH (after the swamps were drained at the end of the 18th C; prior to that had been called Hatches Bottom.)
    - 1: In March-April,1817, John Keats moved here with his two brothers, into the home of the local postman. Here he wrote part of *Endymion.* (House now demolished.) Keats moved here to be near his friend, Henry Leigh Hunt, who had moved here to Hampstead after being released from gaol in 1815. (He was sent to gaol for libeling the Prince Regent.) Hunt also housed Bryon, Coleridge-Taylor, and Shelley (all poets.)
    - 40: Artist John Constable (b.1770-d.1837) lived and worked here.
    - VALE OF HEALTH: Hampstead Hill/Camden. A bit of village within a village. First known as Gangmoor; later as Hatches Bottom, ca. early 18th century. When in 1777 a pond was dug here, it allowed for houses to be built in prior marshy areas. The area built up after ca. 1850.
    - Wells Tavern: Almost opposite the chalybeate spring. In 1850 changed its name to Wells Tavern (from the previous one of: the Green Man.)
- Wentworth Place: This was the name of Keats' Grove during the Regency; the name was changed, later, to honor the famous poet/resident. Keats lived here in 1818-20. The double-fronted house was built for Keats' friends Charles Armitage Brown and Charles Wentworth Dilke. (See: Wentworth Place, under W.)
- West Hampstead: Built ca. 1890-1905. (See under W.)
- Whitestone Pond: Highest point in north London. Is actually a pond. (See under W.)

Hampstead Garden - (AKA: Hampstead Garden Suburb.) 1907.

Hampstead Heath - (AKA: Hampstead Common.) Camden/Barnet. Separates Hampstead and Highgate. In modern times is still a breezy open space, north London, because it was purchased in 1872 by the Metropolitan Board of Works in order to preserve it as a London open space. 790 acres. It is quite possible to get lost here. Hosts: bathing ponds, meadows, lakes. In the Regency it was formed from several separate properties. While very popular for daytime strolls, it was a dangerous place at night in the 17th through early 19th centuries, due to highwaymen, its most famous one being Dick Turpin, hanged in 1739. Constable (the artist) painted here in the 1810s. Until 1871 there were sand and gravel extractions here. From 1871, there was more farmland, and parkland kept expanding the area, until it was nearly quadrupled in size by the 1920s. It was featured in the 1964 film *Mary Poppins.*

- Admiral's House: On Admiral Walk. From ca. 1700 (although with later additions,) built for a sea captain, meant to resemble a ship (but apparently not very successfully.) While a sea captain lived there, no admiral ever actually did.
- Boudiccea's Burial Mound: (Seen with a variety of spellings. Also simply called: Boudiccea's Mound.) There prior to at least 1725.
- Burgh House: (See: Hampstead/Burgh House.)
- Fenton House: (See under: Hampstead/Fenton House.)
- Jack Straw's Castle: North End Way. Near Whitestone Pond. The original was built ca. 1381 (the year the first poll tax was imposed, hence the name.) A tavern since the early 17th century. Charles Dickens (author) supped here. Revamped in 1962. (See under the INNS/PUBS section.)
- Kenwood: A small wood, a remnant of the Great Forest of Middlesex.
- Kenwood House: Hampstead Lane, Spaniard's Road, Hampstead Heath. 1616. Remodeled by Adams in 1764-9 for Lord Mansfield, the Chief Justice (who was an unpopular public figure); the house was attacked during the Gordon riots (because he lived there.) Brick, Neo-classical style. Still exists. Bequeathed to the nation in 1927 by Edward Guinness, 1st Earl of Iveagh (after buying it in 1925 and filling it with great art.) Currently boasts fine trees and "some of the most beautiful rhododendron gardens in London." (See under K.)
- Kit-Kat Club: 18th C. men's club. (See under the CLUBS section.)
- Old Bull and Bush: Inn. (See: Hampstead/Bull and Bush.)
- Parliament Hill: 319 feet high. Ancient. Until 1800 it was called Millfields Hill (the "Parliament Hill" name dates from 1875.) Also once known as "Traitor's Hill," a reference to Guy Fawkes and his co-conspirators. (See: Traitor's Hill, under T.) The 267 acres of land are now famous for their kite-flying.
- Spaniards Inn: Spaniard's Road. Had a toll-house. Since the 17th C., supposedly

named for the Spanish Ambassador at the time, or two Spanish brothers who killed each other in a duel here. Known to Charles Dickens (author.) Dick Turpin, 18th C. highwayman, frequented here. (See under the INNS/PUBS section.)

- Vale of Health: A part of the Hampstead Heath. (See: Hampstead/Well Walk.)
- West Heath: (See: West Heath - Camden, under W.)

Hampton - Richmond. According to CHAMBERS LONDON GAZETTEER: "The name is used both for the Thames-side locality west of Bushy Park and for the entire district that extends from Marylebone Park and Nurserylands..." (modern) "...in the west to Hampton Wick, 3 miles/4.8 km to their east. The early village surrounded by arable land, would have been centered on Thames Street and Church Street and the southern end of the High Street... By 1500 the population of Hampton and Hampton Wick was over 300, a figure that had doubled by 1600 and doubled again by 1700. By 1840 there were five horse-drawn buses a day to London." Wren (the architect) lived here.

- Hampton Church: (AKA: St. Mary's Parish Church, Hampton.) 1830, replacing an older structure dating from at least 1342. The parish was created in 1863.
- Hampton House: (Later called Garrick Villa.) Home to the actor David Garrick from 1754-79. Connected to the Thames by a tunnel purportedly designed by Dr. Johnson.
- Shakespeare Temple: Commissioned by the actor David Garrick. Hosts a Shakespeare statue.

Hampton Court - (See: Hampton Court Palace.)

Hampton Court Bridge - (See under the BRIDGES section.)

Hampton Court Palace - Hampton Court Road, Twickenham (west of Kingston Bridge; 15 miles/24 km upstream, southwest, from London); in the county of Richmond. Is often simply called: Hampton Court. It is often described as "the English Versailles."

Began its existence as an agricultural estate. The Knights Hospitaller of St. John of Jerusalem obtained the estate in 1236. By 1338 the manor had: a chamber block, church, garden, and hall. Sir Giles Daubney leased it in 1494, building on a kitchen, gatehouse, and a courtyard. (See: Great Kitchen, below.)

In 1514 Cardinal Wolsey came in (he being the Archbishop of York, who had the property on a 99-year lease, starting from 1515, from the Knights Hospitaller.) Built of brick. In approx. 1525, Wolsey "offered" it to Henry VIII, in return for Richmond Palace, in a failed attempt to stave off the king's envy and his own eventual disgrace. Once in Henry's possession, it became a Palace Royal.

Henry VIII built the Houses of Office, the council chamber, new royal apartments, and the Great House of Easement. (See: Houses of Office; Bayne Tower; and House of Easement, all below.) He expanded the kitchens, and rebuilt the chapel and great hall. He had a drinking water system brought in from Coombe Hill in Kingston; he also had sanitation improved. In addition: bowling alleys, gardens, a hunting park, and tennis courts. (See: Indoor Tennis Courts, below.) These improvements would have been in the 1530s, by John Molton.

From there, the buildings stayed mostly the same until 1690, when William & Mary partially rebuilt it, with Wren adding the east and west wings. As previously mentioned, Wren meant it to be a kind of "English Versailles," building 4 magnificent ranges around a new fountain court before his grand plans (which would have meant massive demolition) were abandoned. Wren also built the eastern wing, in a neo-classical style. (See: State Rooms, below.) You will sometimes see references to the "New Palace", meaning this 17th C. (extensive) remodel. This wing was damaged by fire in 1986.

From the time of Queen Anne to George II, it was the preferred royal residence. The (royal) full court was at Hampton Court for the last time in 1737.

Opened to the public in 1838 by Queen Victoria; she gifted it to the British government in 1851. It is no longer a royal residence.

Red brick, with approximately 1,000 apartments. Fielding's BRITAIN 1995 states: "Today approximately 1000 units exist as 'grace and favor' quarters, provided by the crown for families related to heroes who distinguished themselves through service to the nation."

It took six years to repair 1986 fire damage of the King's Apartments.

- Bayne Tower: Henry VIII had new apartments built for himself and his queen (as opposed to the royal apartments Wolsey had had built for himself.)
- Bushy Park: Royal park. (See under B.)
- Chapel Royal: 16th century. Its fine fan-vaulted roof was put in by order of Henry VIII.
- Clock Court: Dates from the original building. Contains a famous astronomical clock built for Henry VIII.
- Gardens, the: Still largely have the flavor from Wren's time. It is the sole remaining palace to remain near London with intact gardens.
- Great Gatehouse: Dates from ca. 1500 (under Cardinal Wolsey.)
- Great Hall: Rebuilt for Henry VIII, where he went on to dine with four of his six eventual queens.
- Great Kitchen: Ca. 1494. Survives under this name to the present day.
- Great Vine, the: A grape vine. Planted in 1768, and is of the Black Hamburg variety.

- Houses of Offices: Ca. 1528, built for Henry VIII. These were a bakehouse and stores.
- Indoor Tennis Courts: Built in 1529. Still used by "real tennis" (i.e. when the game resembled Squash) enthusiasts. (You may care to see: tennis.)
- Lion and Unicorn (the symbols of the monarchy, in statuary) guard the entrance.
- Maze, the: Hedgerow labyrinth dates from 1714.
- State Rooms: Added for William III, by Wren.

Hampton Wick - Hampton/Richmond. A landing place. Probably used to bring supplies by water for the later Hampton Court Palace. Described as an "undistinguished hamlet," growth not coming in until the 1830s.

- Kingston Bridge: 1219. It was the only bridge crossing the Thames (between London Bridge and Staines Bridge) until Putney Bridge was built in 1729.
    - ➢ See: Kingston Bridge, under the BRIDGES section.
    - ➢ See: Kingston-upon-Thames/Kingston Bridge.

hanging signs - (See: signs, hanging.)

hangings - As in punishment. In early hangings, the victims were made to mount a ladder; once the noose was in place, the ladder was turned around and removed - hence the phrase of being "turned off." After this method, next came putting the victim on a cart, which left them dangling once the cart was pulled away. The drop (trapdoor) method came along in 1760 (first used at the Tower of London,) intended to snap the spine and cause instant death, thereby being "more merciful." Members of the House of Lords, if convicted, often did not face hanging; the last to do so was Laurence Shirley, 4th Earl Ferrars, in 1760. (Grammar note: a picture is hung; a person is hanged.)

- ➢ See: Marble Arch.
- ➢ See: Newgate Prison.
- ➢ See: punishments.
- ➢ See: Tyburn.

Hanover Gate - The northwest gate of Regent's Park. By John Nash, ca. 1825, Baroque octagon.

- ➢ See: Abbey Lodge.
- ➢ See: Regent's Park/"The Park"/Hanover Gate.

Hanover Hotel - 30-32 St. George's Drive. Hotel evolved from two 1859 houses.

Hanover Lodge - A mansion designed by Decimus Burton in 1825, for Colonel Sir Robert Arbuthnot. Spacious grounds.

Hanover Square - Mayfair. Laid out in 1714-17, completed in 1719. Named for the new ruling house in England at the time, the Hanovers. It was the centerpiece of the (13 acre) Millfield (also called Kirkham Close) estate. Intended to resemble George I's German House of

Hanover. Became immediately fashionable, housing aristocrats as well as military men. Statue of William Pitt here since 1831.

- 21: Charles Maurice de Talleyrand-Périgord (French diplomat) lived here in 1830-4.
- 24: A Georgian era building still stands here.
- Princes Street: (See: Princes Street, Hanover Square, under P.)
- St. George's, Hanover Square: (See under the CHURCHES section.)
- St. George's Street.
    - 25: John Singleton Copley (painter) lived here 1783-1815.
- St. Peter's, Hanover Square: (See under the CHURCHES section.)
- Tenterden Road: (See under T.)

Hanover Street - From the 1730s.

- 19: 1804, Davies & Son, tailor, moved here. Thrived here until 1979. Now in Old Burlington Street.

Hanover Terrace - Regent's Park. 1822-3. (See: Park Crescent/Hanover Terrace.)

Hans Crescent - Brompton.

- ➢ See: Exeter Street.
- ➢ See: New Street.

Hans Place - (See: Hans Town/Hans Place.)

Hans Road - Brompton. (See: Queen Street, Brompton.)

Hans Town - Chelsea, Knightsbridge. Developed by Henry Holland on land he leased from Lord Cadogen, ca. 1742. (Named for Sir Hans Sloane, whose daughter, Jane, was Lord Cadogan's wife.) 89 acres. Red brick. Professionals from the City liked to live here, as it still had a country feel to it. Many small Hans Town streets were pulled down ca. 1870, wiping out homes for the "respectable poor" with homes for the "fashionable rich" in the Queen Anne style. It is now no more than an electoral ward. Centered on Sloane Street.

- Hans Place: At the end of Hans Place was a building once known as Sloane Place, but at this time known as the Pavilion, in 1814 belonging to a Lady Charlotte Dennis. (See: Pavilion, under P.)
    - 23: Henry and sister Jane Austen lived here August/1814 to 1815.
- Pavilion, the: (See under P.)
- Sloane Square: (See under S.)
- Sloane Street: The west side had spacious 3-story terraced houses (as was done as well on Cadogan Place, Hans Place, and all around Sloane Square,) from the 1790s, by Henry Holland.

hansom cabs - The hansom cab was patented in 1834, a two-wheeled carriage with the driver mounted behind the cab that held two. As the 19th C. progressed there were more and more design versions of the hansom cab. (See: hackney coach, its precursor.)

Hanwell - Ealing. In 1816 the last of Hanwell's open land was enclosed, some terraced houses appearing in the next decade.

- Central London District School: 1856.
- Hanwell Lunatic Asylum: Became St. Bernard's Hospital in 1831. Eventually gained a humane reputation. (See: St. Bernard's Hospital, under S.)
- St. Mary's Church: Dates from the 12th century. Rebuilt three times.

Hanworth - Hounslow. Dates from Domesday Bock. In 1512 the manor of Hanworth came into royal hands.

- Hanworth House: (Sometimes: Hanworth Castle, or Palace.) Was Hanworth Park's hunting lodge; Henry VIII gave it to Anne Boleyn (2nd wife,) then Katherine (6th/last wife.) At age 15, Princess Elizabeth (later Elizabeth I) lived here. When the plague was ravaging London in 1635, Queen Henrietta Maria lived here. Was then owned by Baron Cottington of Hanworth. Destroyed by fire in 1797; rebuilt, but torn down ca. the 1890s.
- Hanworth Park House: 1820s. 100 rooms. (*Not* the same as Hanworth House.)
- St. George's: 1293. Rebuilt in the 19th C., in two phases.

Harding, Howell & Co. - Drapers, located in Schomberg House. (See: Pall Mall/Schomberg House/Harding, Howell & Co.)

hare - As a place name, see the word: "here," below. For the animal, see: food/hare.

Hare Court - (See: Inns of Court/Temple (2nd entry)/Hare Court.)

Hare Street - Havering. This street is now known as Main Road, and has all but been absorbed into a development called Gidea Park. It had inns to serve those coaching between London and East Anglia on the Great Road.

- Hare Hall: Built in 1769-70 for a John A. Wallinger.
- Hare Street: Humphrey Repton lived here in 1786 (shortly before beginning his career as a landscape designer.)

Harefield - Hillingdon. Seen spelled as "Herefeld" in the Middle Ages. Then and up to the 16th C. it was mostly moors and common land; the manor lands around the village were cultivated. CHAMBERS LONDON GAZETTEER WRITES: "The construction of the Grand Junction (now Grand Union) Canal on the western side of the parish at the end of the 18th century changed the character of this part of Harefield. By 1813 lime-kilns and copper mills lay along the northern part of the canal... The industrial area continued to expand throughout the century, but away from the canal Harefield remained one of the few places in Middlesex where the ancient pattern of an agricultural village survived into the second half of the 19th century, mainly because of the absence of a main road or railway."

- Harefield West: (See: Mount Pleasant, Hillingdon.)
- St. Mary's Church: 13th C. origin, has a "wealth of monuments."
- South Harefield: Is south of St. Mary's Church, and is a modern name for the area.

Harley Street - Cavendish Square, Marylebone, Westminster. Edward Harley, later the 2nd Earl of Oxford, started to develop his family estate here ca. 1719, but the street was not completed until 1770. The house exteriors are described as "dull," but the interiors as "sumptuous"; stately Georgian houses. 18-19th C. residents here included: Lady Nelson (wife of the admiral); J. M. W. Turner (painter); William Gladstone (statesman); the (later) Duke of Wellington's wife and children; foreign ambassadors (certainly the Russian ambassador); country families who required rooms for the London season; and Florence Nightingale (1853.) CHAMBERS LONDON GAZETTEER states: "Around the mid 19th century, Cavendish Square became a prestigious location for physicians' consulting rooms and doctors began to colonize the southern end of Harley Street in order to be near the square." Too, the homes of doctors did not segue into homes-with-doctors'-offices until later in the 19th century. Until the doctors moved in, this was considered a fashionable address.

- 43-49: Queen's College. Founded in 1848, the first college in London for ladies. The buildings dates from 1765.
- Upper Harley Street: 1920s. (See: Brunswick Place.)

Harp Lane - Connects with Lower Thames Street, the City. Is an ancient street.

- Bakers' Hall: (See under B.)

Harrington House - 1702. Craig's Court. Queen Anne frontage. The Earls of Harrington lived here until 1917.

Harrod's - 8 Middle Queen's Building, Brompton Road, Knightsbridge. Henry Harrod was a draper turned retailer; began in Stepney in 1834. Harrod bought the (now famous) shop in 1853. It was what would later become known as a department store, meaning a retailer who sold many items. Moved to its present terracotta building in 1905; the building was built in 1901-5 by Steven and Munt in Edwardian splendor.

Harrow - Boys' school (more or less equivalent to high school in America.) Boys start here at about age 13. Located in Harrow-on-the-Hill. Established 1572; Charter granted by Elizabeth I. Schoolhouse completed in 1615; doubled in 1821. At first was a local boys' school, but grew to eminence. The original building is in the Jacobean style. Expanded so that it took up most of the original village area. Lord Byron (poet,) Lord Palmerston (statesman,) and Sir Robert Peel (founder of the Metropolitan Police) were all pupils here. 295 pupils attended here in 1816; only 70-80 by 1836, and then the count was up again to its maximum of 580 by 1895.

Not built on a campus, but rather integrated into the area.

- Chapel: 1839.

Harrow-on-the-Hill - Harrow. (Also seen spelled without the hyphens: Harrow on the Hill.) The hill is the highest in Middlesex county.

- Harrow School: (See: Harrow, at its own listing.)
- Headstone Manor House: Was the archbishop(s) of Canterbury's residence from 1307-1546, when it was confiscated by the Crown; sold within one week. Remodeled in the 1630s. Given another wing in the 1650s. More alterations in 1762. Deteriorated.
- King's Head Inn: 1553; still there.
- St. George's Church, Headstone: Consecrated in 1911.
- St. Mary: Built by Archbishop Lanfranc on the top of the hill during the Conqueror's reign, some parts of which remain yet. Largely rebuilt in the 14th C, and restored in 1847.

Hart Street - **Bloomsbury**. Is the pre-1910 name of Bloomsbury Way. (See under B.)

Hart Street - **Tower Hill**, the City.

- St. Olave's: (See: St. Olave, Hart Street, under the CHURCHES section.)

Harvie & Hudson - 97 Jermyn Street. 1929. (See: Jermyn Street/97.)

hat - (See: hats.)

hatch - An old word for a gate that kept forested cattle from getting onto roads. Seen in place names.

Hatch End - Harrow. Part of Pinner, called Pinner after 1842, when the rails came in.

- Dove House Farm: At least by 1547.
  - farmhouse, its: By 1759 "occupied a moated site." Tilbury, a horse dealer, lived here in the early 19th C.; he invented the Tilbury, a two-wheel carriage.

Hatcham - Lewisham. East of Peckham and north of Nunhead. Existed from the time of Domesday Book, well into the 20th C., but is now called New Cross Gate. (See: New Cross/New Cross Gate.)

Hatchard's - Popular Regency era bookshop. (See: Piccadilly/187-8.)

Hatches Bottom -

- See: Hampstead/Well Walk.
- See: Hampstead/Well Walk/1.
- See: Hampstead/Well Walk/Vale of Health.

Hatfield House - Hertfordshire. Once belonged to Elizabeth I; sold in 1607. More recently belonged to Barbara Cartland (deceased Romance novelist.)

hats - Everyone wore hats, rich or poor; young and old; indoors, outside; daytime and at night. There was no central heating, so hats were often essential for warmth. Both sexes wore night caps to bed, a defense against the cold. (These lists are not all-inclusive):

Men of the Regency wore:

- beavers - Expensive top hats covered in water-resistant beaver fur. (See under B.)
- caps - A softer, casual hat, rather like caps of today.
- chapeau bras - A flattish, not-high crowned hat.
- cloth hats
- top hats - First seen in London in 1797.
- tricorn - Old-fashioned by the time of the Regency.

For outdoors/calling on others, women wore:

- bandeau - A thin circlet that went around the forehead, or from nape to crown. Could have decorations (particularly feathers) attached. Could be made of gems. This was more evening dress than day wear.
- bonnet - Think of a "Little House on the Prairie" hat. It covered the hair closely to the nape (this part could be soft or hard,) then had a flaring brim that formed a "U" around the face, tied under the chin. Made from many kinds of materials. Could have shapes, such as squaring it off around the face, or a rippled edge. Could be close to the face, or built to stand away from the face a bit (to show off curled hair across one's forehead). A chip (or chip straw) bonnet was not really made of straw, but thin strips of wood. (See: poke bonnet, below.)
- caps - More casual, softer than bonnets, and might have no ties. Almost always white, often made of lace (especially if worn for fancier occasions.) Could have embellishments. Virtually every kind of woman, regardless of status, wore caps. Children, too.
- chip bonnet - (See: bonnet, above.)
- cornette - A kind of wimple (like nuns wear); caps with pointed or rounded cauls (cloth that covered the hair,) they fastened under the chin and covered the ears. Could be worn under a hat.
- hood - Think of the head part of a cloak. Had ties (in order to stay on.) Were worn outdoors and sometimes indoor for warmth. Might have a frill of lace around the face.
- Leghorn hat (or bonnet) - Began being made from straw in 1815; the best ones came from Leghorn, Italy.

- Mameluke - A turban.
- poke bonnet - A bonnet that typically extended beyond the face. All of one's hair could be contained, even the curls at the forehead, part of what made them popular.
- riding hat - Often resembled men's hats, particularly the top hat. Could be made from beaver pelt. Often had a veil attached, attractively draped.
- round hat - More a description than a type. Looked rather like an inverted bucket when worn, smaller and closer to the head than some other hats.
- scarves, and handkerchiefs - Usually more of "home" wear, but a lady might care to show off a particularly pretty scarf by draping it over her head and shoulders.
- silk hats
- straw bonnets - Just one material (straw) with which to make a bonnet. (See: bonnets, above.)
- toque - Had a very small brim (or none,) was a vertical shape, rising some 6-8 inches straight up on one's head.
- turbans - Many kinds. Fashionable among young and old (but were less popular among the young as the Regency went on.) Some sat atop the head, looking like folds or twists of fabric. Some had an attached, decorative flat band across the forehead.
- veil - Often fell to thigh length. Held in place by combs. For evening wear or mourning.
- walking hat - Rather similar to a man's brimmed hat, with a larger brim, and ornamented.
- wreaths of silk flowers - More common for fancy dress affairs.

<u>Indoors, women wore:</u>

- caps - (See: outdoors, above.)
- house bonnets (AKA: cloth bonnets.) Made of cloth, brimless, tied under the chin.
- mob caps - Close fitting to the head, often worn for warmth. Also often seen on servants.
- scarves, and handkerchiefs.

▪ Both men and women wore caps to sleep in, (trying to stave off the cold.)
▪ There was a tax between 1784-1811 on men's hats, for which neglect of paying was punishable by fine (or, for forgers of the tax revenue stamp, death.) The more expensive the hat, the higher the tax.
▪ Women could wear hats pretty much anywhere, but they sometimes chose not to wear a

hat (or removed their hat and gave it into the care of a servant) at balls or other evening entertainments (where they might wish to show off their hair and any embellishments thereupon, especially if they were young.) Regency women's hats were generally not as large as were hats of the Georgian era.

- Women's hats were made of: chip (strips of wood,) cork, felted wool, straw. These materials might be mixed with (or completely covered by): fabric, many kinds. Hats might well be deliberately designed to accommodate a hair style.
- Women's hats were decorated with any manner of things. Seen: Artificial fruit. Brooches. Buckles. Cords. Embroidery. Fringes (gold or silver were the most usual.) Gems, such as diamonds, jet, or pearls. Net. Plaits formed from straw or trim or fabric. Silk flowers. Tassels. But mostly: feathers (particularly ostrich,) or ribbons (all manner of, in bows, rosettes, streamers, etc.) Hats were often lined with fabric, for contrast or comfort. Whole ensembles would be sewn at one time, so hats often matched the fabric and/or decoration on the dress and/or outer garment with which it was to be worn.
- Men's Bowler hats did not exist until 1850.

hatters - Most establishments would refer to themselves as "haberdashers." (See at its own listing.)

- See: Milsom Street.
- See: Pall Mall/Schomberg House.
- See: Piccadilly/10/Swan & Edgar.
- See: St. James's Street/2/James Swallow.
- See: St. James's Street/6/Lock & Co.
- See: St. James's Street/8.

Hatton Garden - Clerkenwell/Holborn. Dates back to the time of Elizabeth I. CHAMBERS LONDON GAZETTEER notes: "...takes its name from Sir Christopher Hatton, who acquired the property from the diocese of Ely. Hatton was both knighted and made chancellor by Elizabeth I, who had originally been attracted to him by his graceful dancing at a ball. Accordingly nicknamed the 'dancing chancellor,' he was a major sponsor of Sir Francis Drake's round-the-world voyage... From an early role as a cutting centre for Indian diamonds, Hatton Garden developed a trade in gold and platinum during the 19th century." Ergo, home to the Goldsmiths' Hall, and to diamond and gem merchants/jewelers ever since.

- Leather Lane: A market. (See under L.)
- Ye Olde Mitre Tavern. Ely Place. (See under the INNS/PUBS section.)

Havering-atte-Bower - Havering. Stands on high ground. There is a highly unlikely tale that a beggar asked Edward the Confessor for alms, and Edward answered, "I have no money, but

I *have a ring,*" (which he gave to the beggar); most scholars doubt this is actually the genesis of the Havering name.

- Bower House: 1729, perhaps using stones from a 12th C. royal home nearby. Still exists (owned by the Ford Motor Company.)
- Church of St. John the Evangelist: 1878, on the site of a prior church that may have stood on the site of an even earlier royal chapel.
- Round House, the: Broxhill Road. 1794. Oval. Three stories. Stuccoed villa.

Haverstock Hill - Camden. Pronounced: Have-vuh-stok. Dates from 1741-5; until about this time the road had been known as Hampstead Road or London Road. Almshouses, a church, and an orphanage came along in the mid 19th century, at which time most of this area took on the name Maitland Park. (See under M.)

- Load of Hay Tavern: 17th century. Until the mid to late 19th C., this tavern and a few cottages were the sole occupants of Haverstock Hill. Rebuilt in 1863, and now called the Belrose.

haw - An ancient word that means a yard (as in property, not measurement.) Seen in place names.

Hawaii - Captain James Cook first saw the Hawaiian Islands on January 1st, 1778. Twenty-seven days later he was killed by natives. No Europeans came back to the islands until 1786. Cook had dubbed them the Sandwich Islands (which is what most Regency era folk would have most likely called them.) UK-Hawaiian relations were finally struck up by Capt. Vancouver in 1793-4.

hay - For London horses.

- See: Haymarket.
- See: haymarkets.
- See: Northolt.
- See: West Finchley.
- See: Whitechapel.
- See: Woodside Park.

Hay Hill - Mayfair. Not named for the crop, but a mispronunciation of the Aye bourne (a stream,) which in itself was corrupted to T'Aye bourne, and then to Tyburn (which once flowed nearby.) Dates back at least to 1554. The famous Tyburn gallows stood here. (See: Tyburn.) A rough part of London. As a young man, Prinny (and his brother the Duke of York) were robbed here while riding in their hackney carriage.

Hayes - Bromley. (AKA: Hayes Village.) A picturesque village, which in the early 19th C. was surrounded by an uncultivated waste that was prone to hosting footpads.

- St. Mary: Hayes parish church. 13th century. Square tower of flint and stone; 16th C. wooden roof; and a lych gate. Restored in 1873-4.

Hayes - **Hillingdon**. A 20th C. agglomeration of once medieval hamlets; 2 miles/3.2 km west of Southall.

Hayes Town - Hillingdon. First called by this name in 1817; before then was called Cotman's Town (the old name took about a century to fade away.)

Haymarket - Founded in the 17th C, a hay market here until 1830, when it removed to Cumberland Market. Existed where the St. James's Street area is now. Thrice-weekly market for hay and straw. Not disturbed by the Regent's Street renovations. Mostly buildings here were inns and livery stables. The street was paved in 1692, at which time a tax was put on the carts using the road, the fee being dependent on their load.

- Covent Garden Theatre: Called the Royal Opera House when rebuilt in 1858. (See: Covent Garden, Theatre Royal, under the THEATRES section.)

Haymarket, the (Theatre Royal) - (See under the THEATRES section.)

haymarkets -

- See: hay.
- See: Haymarket.
- See: Smithfield.
- See: Whitechapel.

Hay's Wharf - Southwark, 1857. Now filled in and covered over to create Hay's Galleria, 20th century.

hazard, the card game of - Was officially illegal in England, but was very widely played anyway, both at clubs and in private homes.

Hazlitt's (Hotel) - (See: Soho Square/Frith Street/6.)

Headstone - (See: Harrow/Headstone.)

Heals - Furniture-makers in the West End, established 1810, originally as a feather-dressing business. Presently in Tottenham Court Road, 1818, expanding then into furniture and bedstead manufacture. Its heyday was near the end of the 19th century. (See: Upper Rathbone Place/Heal & Sons.)

Heathrow - Hillingdon. (Now contains: Heathrow Airport.) The area first appears in 1453 records. Aviation began here in 1930; first used as a commercial airport after WWII, 1946. The airport construction wiped out the hamlets of: Heathrow, King's Arbour, and Perry Oaks.

hectare - A unit for measuring plots of land. Five hectares equal about 13 acres.

hedgerows - A (vegetative) way of dividing fields. A hedgerow can be of various heights, usually bushy (to dissuade animals passing through) and planted from any number of bushes: blackberry, crabapple, dog roses, elder, hawthorn, honeysuckle, and more.

Hell-fire Club - (See under the CLUBS section.)

Hendon - A district, blended with Wilsdon and Paddington. Described as "a scattered village." Its charter of incorporation was received in 1932.

- Hendon Hall: Garrick's manor home (now privately owned.)
- West Hendon: (See under W.)

Henrietta Place - (See: Henrietta Street.)

Henrietta Street - Covent Garden area. Laid out in 1729; fell out of favor as the 19th C. advanced. Is now called Henrietta Place; Jane Austen (author) wrote of it as: Henrietta Street. An area of tightly packed streets, no gardens, in the middle of a business area.

- 10: Jane Austen occasionally stayed here with her brother Henry. (See: Covent Garden/Henrietta Street.)
- Layton & Shear's: A fashionable mercer's shop at which Jane Austen shopped. (See: Covent Garden/Bedford House.)

Henry Maxwell - Spurmaker. (See: Savile Row/11, where they are now shoe and bootmakers.)

Henry Newberry - (Also seen as just: Newberry's.) Established 1782, furnishings trimmings. Open to trade only.

Henry Poole & Co. - Tailors. Established ca. 1834. (See: Savile Row/15.)

Henry Sotheran - Bookshop, dates from 1761 in York; in London by 1815. (See under: Sackville Street/2-5.)

Henry VIII statue - Surprisingly, there is only <u>one</u> statue of Henry VIII in all of London.

- See: St. Bartholomew's Hospital.
- See: West Smithfield.

heraldry - College of Arms and Herald's College are the same thing.

- See: College of Arms.
- See: Herald's College.

Heralds' College - (AKA: the College of Arms. AKA: the Royal College of Arms. AKA: Heralds' College of Heralds' Office.) A PORTRAIT OF GEORGIAN LONDON reads: "The Heralds of the Kings of England have been part of the royal household since early times. The Officers at Arms* are still appointed to the College of Arms...by the Crown on the advice of the Earl Marshall. His title is hereditary and it has been held by successive Dukes of Norfolk since 1672."

*The Officers of Arms (13) arrange the opening of Parliament, coronations, and other state ceremonies of historic nature.

Richard III granted its royal charter in 1484. (It was known to function prior to 1484, for the Draper's received their grant in 1439.) Henry VII took the charter away; a 2nd charter was granted by Mary Tudor in 1555.

Moved from Coldharbour House, Upper Thames Street in the 16th C.; moved to the mansion (Queen Victoria Street) where it remains yet. Destroyed in 1666; rebuilt 1672-88, by Wren. Part of it was pulled down in 1867-8 (to make way for Queen Victoria Street); the college had been built around a courtyard in the 1670s, but when Queen Victoria Street went in, the college went a little to the south of that site. Sits behind ornate gates.

The College of Arms is the authority for official heraldic matters in most of Britain; they still assess who has a right to a British Coat of arms & livery. Is directed by the Earl Marshal, the Duke of Norfolk.

(See: College of Arms.)

- Court Room: The officer-in-waiting can look up one's claims to a British family coat-of-arms.

herbs - Would have been grown in almost every garden and/or village.

- ➢ See: Figge's Marsh/Pound Farm.
- ➢ See: food - By alphabetical listing there.
- ➢ See: Mitcham - For a commercial herb venture.

here - An old English word for an army. Survives in place names, such as: Hereford. Also seen as "hare," as in Harewood House.

Hereford House - Mayfair. 1928. Built over Hereford Garden. (Not to be confused with Hertford House.)

Hereford Square - 1847, by Edward Blore.

- 24: 1959.

Hermitage, the - (See: Fulham/Hermitage.)

Herne Hill - Lambeth/Southwark. First mentioned in 1789. A few large houses, but was mostly rural until ca. the 1860s.

- Velodrome: 1891. Bicycling racetrack.

Hertford House - (Not to be confused with Hereford House.) Manchester Square. A large, reddish mansion. 1770s, built for the Duke of Manchester. In the 1790s it was leased by the Spanish ambassador. Since 1900 has housed the Wallace Collection, of various arts. (See: Manchester Square/Hertford House.)

Hertford Street - Mayfair. Built in the mid 1760s.

- 4: Dr. Jenner (discoverer of how to vaccinate against smallpox) lived here from 1804.
- 10: General John Burgoyne (British general who surrendered to the Americans at Saratoga) lived and died here in 1792.

Hertford Villa - Built in 1825 by Decimus Burton for Charles Francis Seymour Conway, 3rd Marquess of Hertford. The name changed to Saint Dunstan's in 1836, because the marquess had purchased the Gog & Magog figures from the clock of St. Dunstan's church, Fleet Street. (It returned to the church a century later.) The marquess died in 1842, the villa going to his ward, Charlotte Strachan, Countess Zichy-Ferraris; she sold it in 1855.

Heston - Hounslow. Once had been marshland separating the great forest north of Middlesex and the bordering marshes on the Thames. In the 13th C. became a parish separate from Isleworth. Known for the quality of its wheat. The heathland was enclosed in 1813, but there wasn't much growth here until the 20th century.

hide - (Also sometimes spelled: hyde, especially in place names.) A hide is the amount of land deemed adequate for the support of one free family with dependents, between 60-120 acres. Manors were often laid out in 100 hide increments. An ancient term. (Of course, "hide" also refers to the pelt of an animal.)

Higgler's Lane - A higgler was an old word for a peddler who traveled around, selling small items. Street so known at least by 1807; later known as Webber Street, ca. the 1820s.

High Barnet - (See: Barnet/High Barnet.)

High Court of Chancery - Was a court of equity in England and Wales. The idea was to avoid the slow pace of change and "inequity" by having a set of loose rules of the common law, such as in cases of lunacy, guardianship of infants, land law, trusts. They were to use "conscientious law"; it could overrule many decisions made by the common law courts. Lost its jurisdiction under the Administration of Justice Act of 1841.

- See: Inns of Chancery.
- See: Law Courts.

High Court, the - Alternate name for the Royal Courts of Justice.

- See: Courts of Common Law - For the converse.
- See: Royal Courts of Justice.

High Cross, the - (See: Tottenham/High Cross.)

High Holborn - Anymore most people do not distinguish High Holborn from Holborn, meaning the two when they say Holborn. Until 1783 the condemned were led along this road on their way to Tyburn.

- See: Inns of Court/Lincoln's Inn.
- See: Tyburn.

- 22-23: Cittie of Yorke, the. 17th. C. building, built on the site of a 15th C. tavern. It is currently a pub, dating from 1890. (See under the INNS/PUBS section.)
- 335: Staple Inn. (See: Inns of Chancery/Staple Inn.)
- Middle Row. (See under M.)
- Noah's Ark: Toy store. (See under N.)

High Road - Hackney. (See: Green Lanes.)

High Street - Most every district had/has a high street, usually where market shops and businesses were/are centered.

Highbury - North Islington. The Knights Hospitallers had possession of this area in the 13th century. During the 17th C. most of the woods here were denuded, and the area was known as "Highbury" by this time (due to being relatively elevated.) Brickfields here ca. the 1820s. Developed for residents ca. 1859-60. (You may care to see: Islington.)

- Cream Hall Farm: 17th C. villa. In a later development now called Highbury Vale, where Riverside Road is now. 1780s-1880s, provided milk to north Londoners.
- Highbury Barn Tavern: In 1740 Highbury Barn was a tea and ale-house. (See: Islington/Highbury Barn.)
- Highbury New Park: 1850s.
- Highbury Park: 1820s, by Thomas Cubitt.
- Highbury Place: Mid 1770s. The first part of Highbury to be built up.
- Highbury Terrace: (See: Islington/Highbury Terrace.)
- Highbury Vale: 1823, a road that was renumbered, as part of Blackstock Road, in the 1880s. (See: Cream Hall Farm, above.)
- St. John's Church: Highbury Vale. 1881. Demolished in 1980.

Highgate - Camden/Haringey. Neighbors onto Hampstead; (Hampstead and Highgate are connected by a wide swath of heathland.) Described in 1801 as a tiny village, surrounded by farms and fields. The village green was peppered with ponds and elm trees. Was atop a 426 foot high hill. (See: Highgate Hill.)

- Highgate High Street: Crosses over Highgate Hill (see); built in 1386 by order of the Bishop of London.
- Queen's Wood: (See under Q.)

Highgate Cemetery - Swain's Lane, Dartmouth Park, Highgate, Hampstead. (See: Highgate Hill/St. Michael's.) Consecrated and opened in 1839. Built by Stephen Geary to replace the old St. Pancras churchyard, which due to overcrowding and bodysnatching had taken on an undesirable reputation. Is now two parts: the western (original) and the eastern (1854,) separated by Swains Lane. Described as having many "gothic" mausoleums, memorials, and catacombs. Karl Marx (philosopher/Socialist's) grave is here.

Highgate Hill - At the top of which is a stone commemorating Dick Whittington, placed in 1821, the third one there. Still to be seen. (See: Statue of Dick Whittington's cat, below.) The hill is rather steep. Up near the top, on the right, is a terrace of attractive 17th C. houses; Lauderdale House is to the left. (See: Highgate.)

- Archway, the: Archway Road. Built by Nash, 1813, to take Hornsey Lane across the new line of the Great North Road. (See: Archway Road, under A.)

- Bull, the: On North Hill. 18th C. tavern.
- Cromwell House: 1638. Faces Lauderdale House, on the east side of the summit of Highgate Hill. First house since 1294 to be owned in England by a Jewish family, when they moved in in 1675. (The family name was: Mendes da Costas.) According to THE LOST TREASURES OF LONDON: "...its chief glory is its staircase, with carved figures representing various grades in the army of Cromwell - hence its name."
- Grove, the: Still a fashionable address. Still has ca. 1670 houses, shaded by "magnificent" elms. (See: South Grove, below.)
    - 3: Samuel Taylor Coleridge (the poet) lived here from 1816 until his death in 1834, living with the local doctor and his wife, James and Ann Gillman. (See: South Grove/Moreton House, below.)
- High Street: Steep. Described as having "remarkable homes," Georgian mixed among discreet shops.
    - Angel, the: Pub since the 15th century.
- Highgate Cemetery. (See at its own entry.)
- Highgate School: Founded in 1564, opened in 1565. Was founded for "good families" as well as to serve the village's needy. Opposite Highgate's gatehouse. Present building is of Victorian construction, dating from 1865-8, when it was designed in a French neo-Gothic style.
- Highgate Toll: (See at its own listing.)
- Highgate Woods: 70 acres. Ancient woodland, originally part of the Forest of Middlesex. Still exists.
- Holly Village: 1865 cottages.
- Hornsey Lane: (See: Archway, above.)
- Kenwood House: Earl of Manfield's great house. (See: Kenwood House.)
- Lauderdale House: Dates from the 16th C.; rebuilt in 1661 by the Duke of Lauderdale (Charles II's minister.) Nell Gwynn, mistress to Charles II lived here (one of many homes she shared with Charles II.) Given to the public in 1889 by Sir Sidney Waterlow, and the grounds then became known as Waterlow Park. The grounds contain azaleas and mature trees.
- Moreton House: (See: South Grove, below.)
- Pond Square: Is at the top of the Hill (and the middle of the village.) Described as having "remarkable homes" around the square. The pond had been formed as gravel was removed from the site to mend roads. The pond was filled in in 1864.
    - Highgate Literary & Scientific Institution. Founded after 1834.

- Queen's Wood: Ancient woodland.
- St. Michael's: 1830-32, by Lewis Vulliamy. Neo-Gothic. Built over the site of a home lived in by Sir William Ashurst (Lord Mayor in 1694,) and which appears to have been built over an ancient chapel of ease. Shortly after 1830, the remaining land was bought for the London Cemetery Company. In 1839 it opened as Highgate Cemetery.
- South Grove: 18th C. homes yet remain here. (See: Grove, above.)
    - 17: Old Hall. Replaced Arundel House, which was pulled down in 1691 or 94. Old Hall is still here.
    - Moreton House: Owned by the same family as Cromwell House. 18th century.
- Statue of Dick Whittington's cat: The stone was put up in 1821; the stone cat was added in 1964. Stems from the tale that supposedly Dick Whittington sat upon a milestone on Highgate Hill (which, alas, was not the route to his Gloucestershire home) and, hearing the distant sound of Bow Bells (as in St. Mary-le-Bow Church,) turned back to find fame and fortune in London. The cat comes in, in that Whittington sold it to an outgoing ship, which in turn sold it for a large sum in rat-infested Bombay. When Whittington returned to London, he retrieved these proceeds and built his career (he was a mercer.) He did, in fact, become the city's Lord Mayor (four times, actually.) The statue is atop a replica of the supposed milestone.
- Whitanhurst: 1913 Neo-Georgian mansion. Said to be the largest private house in London.

Highgate Toll - Erected 1386; removed in 1769. Atop Highgate Hill.

Highgate Woods - Purchased for public recreational use in 1885. 6.7 acres.

highway robberies - (See: Metropolitan Police/Bow Street Horse Patrol - For serious reduction of highway robberies.)

highwaymen, districts for - (See: rough places.)

Highwood - Barnet. Northern corner of Mill Hill. Now known as Highwood Hill. In the 17-18th centuries, was a fashionable country retreat area.

- Highwood House: Bought by Sir Stamford Raffles (of Singapore fame) in 1825; he died in 1826. His wife lived here until 1858.
- Holcombe House: 1778 villa. Built for a City glove merchant. Herbert (later Cardinal) Vaughan bought it in 1866 and founded a Catholic missionary college here. Soon outgrown, so he built the nearby St. Joseph's College. Franciscan nuns moved in here, but were soon also gone to larger accommodations.

- Rising Sun Inn: (See under the INNS/PUBS section.)

Hill Street - Berkeley Square, Mayfair. Brown brick Georgian fronts, "patrician calmness."

Hillingdon Heath - Hillingdon. Rural until the 20th century.

- Hillingdon House: Built in 1717. Present house dates from 1844. Mary, Marchioness of Rockingham died here in 1894. Still there.
- Red Lion Inn: Has been here since the 16th century. Charles I stopped here in 1646 while fleeing from besieged Oxford (to Nottingham and the Scottish army sitting there.) Still there. (See: Red Lion Inn, Hillingdon, under the INNS/PUBS section.)
- St. John the Baptist: Parish church. Dates from 1100; parts date back to the 13th century. Decorated in the Gothic style. Tall, massive tower. Restored in 1848.

Hinde Street - Near Manchester Square. Westminster. Still has 18th C. houses (but now mostly offices.) Hinde Street (at Thayer Street) turns into Bentinck Street. (See: Bentinck Street.)

Hindu temple - Modern. (See: Shri Swaminarayan Mandir.)

Hippodrome, the - Notting Hill. Horse race course. Opened in 1837. Closed in 1841.

His Majesty (or *Her Majesty*) - The term had been applied to the Roman emperor; it was first used by a king in 1534, by Henry VIII, in seeking authority during his battles with the Pope. (Up until then, the monarch would have been: His Grace.)

hithe - A cut into a riverbank, lined with stakes. Ships tied to the stakes and then unloaded onto wooden platforms. Essentially, smaller harbors; is a Roman and medieval term. Some ancient London hithes have been recently uncovered by archaeologists. More simply, it also means a wharf. (Example: Rotherhithe.)

Hither Green - Lewisham. 18th C. hamlet, built very near where the prior hamlet of Romborough had been. The latter was virtually wiped off the map by the Black Death. Nursery-gardens, from the early 17th century. The villas of successful merchants came in here ca. the 1780s.

Hoare's bank - 1672. (See: Fleet Street/37.)

Hoby's - Royal bootmaker, to George II. George Hoby was b.1759-d.1832. On the corner of Piccadilly and St. James's Street. In consultation with the Duke of Wellington, made a Hessian boot a bit higher, creating the Wellington boot. He also was bootmaker to the dandy Beau Brummell. (See: St. James's Street/Hoby's.)

hockey - 1871. (See: Bushy Park/Teddington Hockey Club.)

Hog Lane - Near Soho Square. In 1879 was redeveloped as Charing Cross Road. Dates back to at least the 16th century. (See: Charing Cross Road.)

Hogarth's House - (See: Chiswick/Hogarth's House.)

Hogmore Lane - (See: Gloucester Road.)

Holbein Place - Sloane Square, Belgravia. Ca. 1886.

Holborn - (Is usually pronounced "HO-burn.") "Holbourne" was the local name for the Fleet River. It is said it is "difficult to describe what or where Holborn is." Lies between Covent Garden to the west, Bloomsbury to the north, Clerkenwell & Smithfield to the east, and the Strand and Fleet Street to the south. Existed by 1249.

The borough of Holborn was subsumed into that of Camden in 1965. Contains few residential areas (now,) although it had more in Victorian times (mostly slums.) Never was an elegant address. The street Holborn becomes High Holborn west of Gray's Inn Road, but these days the distinction is little made. (See: High Holborn.)

It was a three hour cart ride from Newgate, up High Holborn, to the hangings at Tyburn.

Most of the medieval buildings were destroyed in the late 18th C., and those that remained were treated poorly.

- Barnard's Inn: Inn of Chancery. Its address is 20-23 Holborn. (See a fuller description under B.)
- Bartlett's Buildings: Possessed the oldest (in situ) name plate in the City, until it was broken in the 20th C., in the building's demolition: "Bartlett's Bvildings 1685." Located in Holborn Circus (the Circus itself dates from Victorian times.)
- Bedford Row: Built ca. the 1670s. Dark red brick homes.
- Black Swan Distillery: Backed on to Fetter Lane. There by at least 1780, during which it was burned in the "No Popery" (Gordon) riots. The Black Swan started life as a coaching-inn, by at least 1706.
- Ely Place: (Pronounced ELL-ee.) 1773. 18th C. houses yet remain. Built by Cole, over the 13th C. site of Ely House (AKA: Ely Palace,) home of the Bishop(s) of Ely. In the 17th C. the house became the Spanish Embassy; demolished in 1772. Still a private road guarded by beadles in top hats and frock coats. There is an iron bar at the entrance to stop horses from using the cul-de-sac as a turnaround. The land belongs to Ely Cathedral yet, hence the beadles; it is the last privately owned street in London. (See: Ely Place, under E.)
    - 14: St. Etheldreda's Chapel. The Bishop of Ely's chapel. Bought back by the Catholics in 1874. Parts of it dates back to the Middle Ages. It is the oldest Catholic church building in Britain. (See under the CHURCHES section.)
- Farringdon Road, and Farringdon Street: Their construction covered over the River Fleet. 1830. (See under F.)
- Fetter Lane:
    - See: Black Swan Distillery, above.

- See under F.

- Gray's Inn: Sits on the north side of High Holborn. (See: Inns of Court/Gray's Inn.)
- Gresham's College: (See: Bread Street/Gresham College.)
- Hatton Garden: Presently is London's diamond and jewelry district, a concern that spawned in the early 19th century, having spread out of Clerkenwell. (See: Hatton Garden, at its own listing.)
- High Holborn: (See under its own listing.)
- Lambs Conduit Street: (See under L.)
- Leather Lane: (See under L.)
- Middle Row: (See under M.)
- Mitre tavern: (Back of St. Etheldreda's,) Mitre Court (the court dates from 1830.) 1546. In the bar is the trunk of a cherry tree, around which Elizabeth I is supposed to have danced with a favored courtier. (See: Ye Olde Mitre Tavern, in the INNS/PUBS section.)
- Old Hall of Lincoln's Inn: (See: Inns of Court/Lincoln's Inn/Old Hall.)
- Rugby Estate, the: (See under R.)
- St. Andrew's: Holborn Square. Survived the 1666 Great Fire, redesigned by Wren in 1686. (See under the CHURCHES section.)
- St. Etheldreda's Chapel: (See: Ely Place/14.)
- Staple Inn: (See: Inns of Chancery/Staple Inn.)
- Ye Olde Mitre tavern: (See: Mitre tavern, above.)

Holborn Bars - Late 19th century. Is located very near Staple Inn. Holborn Bars are two stone obelisks that mark one boundary of the ancient City. (142 Holborn Bars can be seen at: Inns of Court/Lincoln's Inn/Furnival's Inn.)

Holborn Circus - A junction of five highways, uniting Hatton Garden, Holborn, and Smithfield. 1867, by architect William Haywood.

Holborn Viaduct - Road bridge. Not until 1863-9, by William Haywood. Precursor was Skinner Street. (See under S.)

Holford House - Regent's Park. Built in 1832, designed by Decimus Burton for James Holford (a wine importer/merchant.) Holford lived here until his death in 1853, when the house became Regent's Park College. (See under R.)

Holland House - Holland Park, Kensington. Built in 1605-7 by John Thorp. At its first construction it was called Kensington House (no relation to Kensington Palace.) Then called Cope House (and sometimes Cope Castle); named for Sir Walter Cope, Chancellor of the Exchequer. The property passed to his son-in-law (Henry Rich, first Earl of Holland) when

Cope died in 1614. Rich enlarged the house, at which time it took on the Holland House name.

Was enlarged in 1638-40; 1704; 1748; 1796; and sometime in the 19th century, perhaps when the 3rd Lord Holland owned it ca. 1812.

Was dubbed "the centre of intellectual society" in the first half of the 19th century. During the Regency this area (Kensington) was considered quite rural, Holland House was at that time a country seat estate. The early 19th century Lady Holland is described as having a fearsome eye and a scathing tongue, and was very present at the intellectual gatherings here at her home. (It must be noted, however, that gatherings at Holland House were considered highly fashionable, at least among those of the same political ideology.) Lord Byron (poet) was known to come to Lady Holland's garden parties.

The house came to the Ilchester family in the 20th century.

Only the east wing yet survives, following extensive WWII damage. Parts of its garden are now a public park.

- Gardens: Has three - the Dutch Garden, the Iris Garden, and the Rose Garden.
- Ice House: Dates from the 18th C.; still exists.
- Orangery: Its modern incarnation is as a restaurant.
- Stables, the: Were built in 1638-40.

Holland Park - Off Kensington High Street. Formal style. Not known as Holland Park until 1866-73. On the site of parts of Holland House's gardens (because Baroness Holland needed to sell land in response to her extravagant entertaining expenses.) Oddly, Holland Park is not one road but made up of three, all collectively thus named.

- Bedford Gardens: 1822, by William Hall.
- Campden House: 17th century. Described as "the second finest house" in the district. Is now flats.
    - See: Kensington/Campden Hill House.
    - See: Campden Hill/Campden Hill House, under C.
- Debenham House: 8 Addison Road. 1905-7. (Had the nickname: Peacock House.)
- Holland House: (See at its own listing.)
- Japanese Garden: Opened in 1991.
- Leighton House: 1879, for Frederick, Lord Leighton, painter, and president of the Royal Academy 1878-96, and member of the Holland Park Circle, a group of artists and architects. (See: Leighton House, under L.)

Holles Street - Westminster. It is "Holles Street" north of Oxford Street; "Lower Holles Street" on its south side.

- 24: Birthplace of George Gordon Byron, Lord Byron (poet), 1788. The first residence in London to receive a Blue Plaque (1867.)

Holloway - Near Islington and Highgate. Before the 14th C. this area was known as Tollington. Lower Holloway, up to the beginning of the 19th C., was famous for its cheesecakes. A man on horseback rode through London to hawk them; also sold at local taverns. There were a few villas and terraced housing here by 1800, but didn't really develop until the 1840s (although the addition of Archway Road in the 1820s ended the area's aspect of being rural.)

- Archway Road: 1820s. This road's construction ended Holloway's rural tone. (See under A.)
- Holloway Prison: 1852. Built on the site where cholera victims were once buried. Exclusive to female prisoners from 1903.
- Holloway Road: From the 14th C., was the main route from the City to the north. In the 17th C. it was famous for its highwaymen, but this faded with the century's advance and additional housing.
- Lower Holloway: (See under L.)
- Seven Sister Road: 1832. (See: Seven Sisters/Seven Sisters Road.)
- Upper Holloway: (See under U.)

Holmes - (See: Regent's Park/Holmes.)

Holwood - Bromley.

- Caesar's Camp: Site of an Iron Age hill fort; also the source of the River Ravensbourne.
- Holwood House: Early 17th century. Called "modest." Was extended on over time. William Pitt the Younger was here in 1784; Sir John Soane remodeled and extended the house more for him; Humphry Repton improved the grounds. CHAMBERS LONDON GAZETTEER states: "Holwood House became an important meeting place for political figures of the time... The hollow trunk of the 'Wilberforce Oak' stands where William Wilberforce gave notice to Pitt that he had resolved to raise the question of the slave trade in the House of Commons." Burned down. Rebuilt by Decimus Burton in 1826. Restored in the very late 20th century.

Holy Land - Nickname of a low roost inhabited mainly by Irish Catholic poor (immigrants seeking a better life, but surely not finding it here,) close to Buckeridge Street in St. Giles, not far from Bloomsbury. Known as a meeting place for beggars, conmen, tricksters, and mountebanks. (See: Seven Dials, which neighbored on the Holy Land.)

- Noah's Ark: Described as being in "the back slums of the Holy Land." This appears to have been a pub/gin palace. Notorious for the beggars, mock-beggars, and charlatans who frequented it. (Not to be confused with Noah's Ark toy store.)

Holy Roman Empire - From the Middle Ages, was a complex of ethnicities and territories in Central and Western Europe. In 1806 the Holy Roman Empire dissolved (in part, under the weight of the Napoleonic wars.) Included Germany, the Kingdom of Italy, the Kingdom of Bohemia, and the Kingdom of Burgundy (plus additional territories.) Replaced by a new German Confederacy, 1815, at the Congress of Vienna.

Holyrood House - The present queen's Scottish residence. (See: Scotland/Edinburgh/Holyrood House, under the BRITISH COUNTIES section.)

Holywell Street - An old street. Also known by the popular name of: Booksellers' Row.

- See: Booksellers' Row.
- See: Curtain Road.

Home Counties, the - This term dates from 1898. Those counties immediately adjoining London, not including London itself. It's not an exact term, and has encompassed different areas affected by differing laws, but generally the home counties might include: Berkshire, Buckinghamshire, Essex, Hertfordshire, Kent, Middlesex, Surrey, Sussex (East,) and Sussex (West.)

Home Department, the - (Not to be confused with the Home Office.) In charge of internal affairs in England; that is, affairs of the State. In 1812 the Principal Secretary of State was the Right Honorable Richard Ryder, making £6,000 per annum at this post. Had *internal* spies (operated/surveilled British subjects.)

Home House - (See: Portman Square/20.)

Home Office, the - (Not to be confused with the Home Department.) Was in charge of domestic intelligence (or spying,) immigration (1793,) security, and law and order (1824.) Formed in 1782, having previously been called: Southern Department. Was housed in the Foreign and Commonwealth Office Main Building, Whitehall, until 1978. Was situated at 50 Queen Anne's Gate, 1978-2004 (now known as 102 Petty France.) Since 2005, at 2 Marsham Street, Westminster. There was a Home Office during the Regency; from 1812-22, Viscount Sidmouth was the Secretary of State for Home Affairs. Presently also provides pathological services/forensics. (Had *external* spies; foreign lands.)

Home Park - (See: Windsor/Windsor Great Park.)

Homerton - (Pronounced: HO-mah-ten.) Dates from 1343. Was the most populous part of Hackney in the 17th C., with homes for knights and lords. Building beyond the High Street began in the mid 18th century. When industrialization set in here (ca. 1780) most of the gentry moved away; by the mid 19th C. the place had "cramped terraces." (See: Hackney/Homerton.)

- Berger's paint factory: 1780.
- Eastern Hospital: 1871, for smallpox victims.
- Sutton House: High Street. Built in 1535 for Sir Ralph Sadlier, a principal secretary of state to Henry VIII. Later owned by Thomas Sutton. Is now a National Trust building, a museum, and art gallery. Retains Tudor details. (See: Sutton House, under S.)

homosexuality - Not legal in England and Wales until 1967; in Scotland, not until 1980. Penetration was required to constitute an act of homosexuality/sodomy; practices other than that were not covered under the law. Regency era society was not kind to those suspected of homosexuality; they were often ostracized/forced to go abroad. It could result in imprisonment, although hanging had not been removed as a consequence; sodomy was punishable by death. (You may care to see: punishments.) In the 19th C. lesbianism was largely considered more of a rumor/joke than an actuality.

Honey Lane - Cheapside. There was a Honey Lane Market after 1666; now covered over. (See: Cheapside/Honey Lane.)

honeymoon - (See: marriage.)

Honor Oak Road - (See: Forest Hill/Honor Oak Road.)

Honourable Society of Knights of the Round Table - Formed by actors who bemoaned the loss of chivalry, in 1720. Lasted at least until Charles Dickens (author) became a member.

Hookham's Book Shop - Existed during the Regency. Bond Street/Old Bond Street. Thomas Hookham, b.1739-d.1819, bookseller/publisher. His circulating library was established in 1764, preeminent in London by 1800. In 1871 was acquired by Mudie's.

Hop Exchange - Southwark Street, Southwark. 1866. Is now offices.

Hopton Street - Almshouses dating from 1752. (See: Southwark/Hopton Almshouses, which are the same almhouses.)

Horace Street - (See: Cato Street.)

Hornchurch - Havering. Into the 19th C. this area was known for its leather currying, tanning, and shoemaking.

- Dell, the: A gently sloping bowl/setting for 18th C. sporting events, wrestling matches, and a cockpit. Is now a recreational ground.
- Emerson Park: Ca. 1895.
- Fairkytes: Georgian house. Is now the Hornchurch Arts Centre.
- North Ockendon: (See under N.)
- St. Andrew's Church: Medieval. Partially rebuilt in 1802. Again in 1869. And in the 20th century.

Horners' Company - (AKA: the Worshipful Company of Horners.) Animal horn is a "natural plastic," keratin, which can be molded into beakers, boxes, buttons, combs - but right up to the 18th C. its primary use was as (beaten into translucence) lantern sheets, and as a kind of window "glass." The craft is ancient; first written mention of it in London dates from 1284.

The Horners united, via mutual request, with the Bottlemakers (the latter made leather bottles) in 1475.

As glass production improved, the need for horn declined, but resurged when horn snuffboxes and horn-books came into demand. Charter dates from 1638.

The Company is now strongly linked with the plastics industry. Livery Company, full rights in 1846. Never had a hall. 54th in the order of precedence.

Hornsey - Haringey. Belonged to the Bishop of London from at least 1321. Densely wooded until the 18th C., at which time it was a good-sized village, with Londoners' retreat homes here. Suburban streets by the 1810s, but significant growth didn't come until the railways did.

- Hornsey Wood: Today it is Finsbury Park.

Horse and Carriage Repository - (AKA: London Horse and Carriage Repository. AKA: Aldridge's Horse and Carriage Repository.) 277 Gray's Inn Road. Upper Saint Martin's Lane (near Leicester Square.) Owned from 1776-1826 by the Aldridge family. All manner of horses were traded here, with the exception of race horses. The facade was demolished due to the street being widened in 1843, and moved the door to the north side of the building.

Horse Armoury - (See: Tower of London/"Other Places & Things"/Great Armoury.)

Horse Ferry - LONDON by Knopf Guides states: "Until the 19th century, a ferry plied between Lambeth Palace and the Palace of Westminster on the other side of the river. It was known as Horse ferry, and was the only boat licensed to carry wagons and horses."

- See: ferry.
- See: Horseferry Road.
- See: Lambeth.

Horse Guards, the - (ABSOLUTELY SEE: ROYAL GUARDS, under R.)

Horse Guards Parade - (See: Royal Guards/Parade Grounds.)

horse racing - Popular in all of Britain since at least Tudor times. There were racecourses everywhere throughout England and its environs. They weren't always all official/formally arranged. There might well be a winning post, a little machine upon wheels. Those who came to watch in their carriages might sit in them the entire time of race viewing. Women (and older children) attended horse races, remaining in their carriages. As the men tended to leave when the races were over and find their way to taverns, coffee-houses, or cockpits, the ladies then left for home.

- See: Jockey Club, under the CLUBS section.
- See: Newmarket.

- See: racing.
- See: steeplechasing.
- See: Tattersall's - Where gentlemen paid off their wagers.

Horseferry Road - Westminster & Lambeth. (See: Horse Ferry.)

- Greycoat Hospital: (See under G.)

Horselydown - (See: Shad Thames.)

Horsemonger Lane - Ran near the prison. (See: Horsemonger Lane Gaol.)

Horsemonger Lane Gaol - (AKA: Surrey County Gaol. AKA: New Gaol.) Southwark. Built in 1791-9 as a model prison (meaning one built with the intention of corrective learning, not just punishment.) By George Qwilt the Elder. Surrey's principal prison and place of execution. Held both criminals and debtors. Could hold about 300. The poet Leigh Hunt was imprisoned here for two years starting in 1813, for insulting the Prince Regent. There were public executions outside this jail for years (at least into 1849, when Charles Dickens witnessed a double hanging here.) Renamed in 1859 as Surrey County Gaol (and also then called New Gaol.) Closed in 1878; demolished in 1880. Is now a park, Newington Gardens.

horses - "Nag" was originally used to mean a horse for riding (as opposed to a draft animal, or a racing horse.) Came, over time, to mean the more modern usage representing a broken-down horse. A nag could also be called a mount, or a saddle horse, or a hack. A pony is a small breed (not a baby horse.)

- See: Horse and Carriage Repository.
- See: Loriners' Company - For the makers of saddles and other equine tack.
- See: Metropolitan Drinking Fountain - For watering horses.
- See: mews.
- See: Newmarket.
- See: Royal Mews.
- See: Smithfield Market.
- See: Tattersall's.
- You may care to see: polo - 1860s.

- To buy a horse, see: Barnet Fair. - A September fair, would have been a distance for Londoners to travel to.

- To hire a horse, see: Mount Street.

- For racing, see: Jockey Club, under the CLUBS section.

- See: horse racing.
- See: Newmarket.
- See: racing.

Horticultural Society of London - (See: Royal Horticultural Society.)

hose - (See: stockings.)

hosier - A maker of hose/stockings.

- See: Burlington Arcade/68-69/Lord's.
- See: Candlewick Street/Hosier Street.
- See: St. James's Street/8.
- See: stockings.

Hosier Street - Named for the manner of shops there; ancient. (See: Candlewick Street/Hosier Street.)

Hospital for Consumption - 1841. North of Pelham Crescent, Chelsea.

Hospital for Sick Children - Great Ormond Street (south of Coram Fields,) Bloomsbury. Founded by Dr. Charles West. Charles Dickens (author,) in 1858, gave fundraising public readings here in order to draw attention to the organization.

(See: hospitals - The note on children under.)

In that same year, Ormond added 48 Great Ormond Street to the hospital, bringing its capacity to twenty beds. It was reconstructed on the same site in 1877, now having 120 beds. Is now the UK's largest center for child heart surgery.

Hospital of King James - (See: Charterhouse, about halfway down in the entry.)

hospitals - During the Regency, if you had money, you *avoided* being in hospital. It was an unhealthy place, usually where the poor or unwanted went hoping for a cure, but most likely to die (with some measure of comfort/aid.) With money, you could and would obtain your doctoring at home.

As stated in PILGRIMS' LONDON: "the name of modern medical facilities comes from the medieval 'hospices,' or places of shelter for aged and infirm persons operated by the church."

It was a centuries-old practice to use executed criminals' bodies for the purpose of dissections - that is, anatomical study on real human bodies; this practice was strongest in Britain in the 18-19th centuries, as private anatomy schools flourished in England and Scotland. Those who dug up the recently dead were acting illegally, because as noted until 1836 (the passage of the Anatomy Act) the only legally available bodies were those of condemned criminals (as it was not until then legal to voluntarily offer your mortal remains to science.) The act of stealing the interred was called body snatching, distinct from grave-robbing because the latter meant taking the deceased's jewelry or heirlooms that might be in their grave.

- See: body-snatching.
- See: resurrectionists.

William Harvey, a 17th C. surgeon, was renowned for discovering the nature of the human circulatory system.

In the Georgian era, hospitals shifted away from mostly being ways of housing/caring for veterans and the aged, to being more about healing and caring for groups such as the poor.

In the early 19th C., the word "hospital" might mean a place for care and comfort (even though notions of *curing* were more remote than they are today,) but could also mean a charitable institution for those who were aged, young, infirm, or needy. Hospitals might also be called asylums - not necessarily for the insane, as we tend to associate the word "asylum" these days. There was little more stigma about going into an asylum than there was going into a hospital. Asylums/hospitals might be dedicated to a specific problem: children of the poor; cripples; sailors; etc. (See: asylum.)

<u>CHILDREN</u> were not expected to be tended in hospitals (but rather at home.) It was a real innovation when the Hospital for Sick Children opened ca. 1850. (See under H.)

An <u>endowed</u> hospital meant it was financed by benefactors (other than royals,) and not in need of public funds (from the State or interested royal persons.) In fact, most charities were not funded by State/royal money. (See: charities.)

- See: Bedlam - To treat the insane. (AKA: St. Mary Bethlehem.) IF YOU READ ONLY ONE OTHER HOSPITAL REFERENCE, MAKE IT THIS ONE.
- See: British Lying-in Hospital - 1749, for married women giving birth. (See under B.)
- See: Caledonian Asylum - (See: Islington/Caledonian Field/Caledonian Asylum.)
- See: Charing Cross Hospital.
- See: charities - To understand how charities such as hospitals were funded.
- See: Charterhouse - (AKA: Sutton's Hospital. AKA: the Hospital of King James.)
- See: Chelsea Hospital - (AKA: Royal Hospital.) To house and assist disabled soldiers.
- See: Christ's Hospital - For the care of orphaned children.
- See: City of London Lying-in Hospital - A birthing hospital. (See

under C.)

- See: doctors.
- See: Duke of York's Headquarters.
- See: Foundlings' Hospital.
- See: Greenwich Hospital - (See: Royal Naval Hospital.)
- See: Greycoat Hospital.
- See: Grosvenor Place/Lock Hospital.
- See: Guy's Hospital - An endowed hospital. (See: Southwark/Guy's Hospital.)
- See: Hospital for Sick Children.
- See: Hospital for Women, 1843.
- See: Hunterian Medical School - Not a hospital, but a training school.
- See: infirmary.
- See: Islington Lunatic Asylum. (See: Islington/Caledonian Asylum.)
- See: Lock Hospital - For venereal diseases. (See under L.)
- See: London Hospital - For the poor of Aldgate.
- See: lying-in hospitals. - For the delivery of babies. London housed several, although most births happened at home, rich or poor. The lying-in hospitals were generally small, 40-50 beds.
    - See: British Lying-in Hospital, above.
    - See: City of London Lying-in Hospital, above.
- See: Middlesex Hospital - For the poor of Soho.
- See: Royal Free Hospital - 1828.
- See: Royal Military Asylum. (See: Duke of York Headquarters.)
- See: Royal Naval Hospital - (AKA: Greenwich Hospital.)
- See: St. Bartholomew's - For the ill and the incurable; endowed.
- See: St. George's - For the "sick and lame."
- See: St. Katherine's Hospital - For the "maintenance of poor persons"; leaning more toward a church and charity than a hospital.
- See: St. Luke's Hospital - For "lunatics." (See: Old Street, Finsbury/St. Luke's Hospital.)
- See: St. Mary Bethlehem (See: Bedlam.)
- See: St. Thomas's/Southwark - For the ill and the incurable; endowed.
- See: Southwark/Guy's Hospital.
- See: Trinity Hospital.

- See: Westminster Hospital.

Hôtel de la Sablionère - 1801. (See: Leicester Square/30.)

hotels - There were very few in England before the 1860s; people stayed at inns, or with friends or family. Until Victorian times, the few hotels in London were mostly centered in Mayfair. You will see Regency notes in which a person asks if the receiver knows of a good hotel, but they are using this French word with more of a meaning of "inn" than of our modern idea of what constitutes a hotel.

- See: Albemarle Street/Grillion's - Notable exception to the "no 19th century hotels" fact.
- See: Brown's.
- See: Clarendon's - (Under: Bond Street/New Bond Street/169.)
- See: Claridge's - (Under: Brook Street/25.)
- See: Conduit Street/Limmers.
- See: flat, a - For an explanation of Regency era bachelor homes.
- See: Hôtel de la Sablionère - (Under: Leicester Square/30.)
- See: Inns, under the I section - Beginning notes under.
- See: Long's - (Under: Clifford Street/Long's Hotel.)
- See: Pulteney's - (Under: Piccadilly/105.)
- See: Richmond Hill/Star and Garter Hotel.

hothouse -

- See: forcing garden.
- See: greenhouses.

Houghton Hall - Not in London, in the county of Norfolk. (See: Norfolk/Houghton Hall, under the BRITISH COUNTIES section.)

Houndsditch - The City. One-way street, running from parts of the Bishopsgate Without and the Portsoken wards. Long ago used to be a ditch outside the London Wall, particularly known as a place to dispose of dead dogs, hence the name. By the early 20th C. it had become a thriving area for clothing and novelties. (See: Rag Fair.)

Hounslow - By 1635 was a significant coaching halt, the first stop outside London for most westbound locations. Although the village wasn't much more than its High Street, it had a hundred residents and at least five inns.

- Hounslow Field: (See: Woodlands.)
- Hounslow Heath: On occasion, hosted large armies (such as Cromwell's.) There are still military barracks here (the Hounslow Barracks, 1793, which could accommodate 400 men and their horses and gear.) In the 18-19th C. it was often

used as a parade ground. The heath ran westward for five miles/8 km. In the 17th and through the early 19th C., it was bedeviled by highwaymen and footpads.

- St. Paul's: 1874.

house - Ca. 1800, to rent a country cottage for a year might be £50.

Speaking of renting, the practice was common in London during the season (while Parliament sat) if you otherwise owned a home to retreat to when the season was over; if you could travel, you usually chose to escape the heat and smells of a London summer. (See: money - Near the bottom of the entry: "Here is a list of some approximate pricing..." for more on the price of homes.)

House of Commons - Westminster. (AKA: one of the two Houses of Parliament. AKA: the Lower House.) Independent of, but complementing, the House of Lords. Both Houses must consider bills before they can become law.

Unlike the House of Lords, the members of the House of Commons must be elected. There are roughly 650 members in the House of Commons.

This House got its very beginning under King Henry III, in 1264. (See: INTRO-REIGNS/British Kings & Queens and their Reigns/Henry III.)

From 1547-1834: Was housed in St. Stephen's Crypt, Westminster. In 1834, both of the old houses of Parliament burned, necessitating a new building.

Open to continuing debate and although it can be argued that the House of Lords exercised more control/power, it is generally held that the House of Commons has never simply rubber-stamped policies of either the monarchy or its ministers. In light of which it should be noted, the House of Commons is responsible for all finance bills to come before Parliament, a power surely all its own.

The first woman to be seated in the House of Commons as an MP (Member of Parliament) was Nancy Langhorne Astor in 1919. She was the only woman until 1921. She served in the House until 1945.

The House of Commons is the only British building the Queen (or King) cannot legally enter, because she is not a commoner.

- See: Houses of Parliament.
- See: Lower House.
- See: St. Stephen's Chapel.
- See: Westminster.

House of Detention - A county jail run by local magistrates, usually for shorter terms of imprisonment.

- See: Clerkenwell Green.

- See: Cold Bath Fields Prison.
- See: gaol.
- See: prisons - Keeping in mind that Houses of Detention were county gaols, as opposed to their rougher city cousins.

House of Lords - Westminster. (AKA: one of the two Houses of Parliament. AKA: the Upper House. AKA: the House of Peers.) Independent of, but completing, the House of Commons. Both Houses must consider bills before they can become law. Unlike the House of Commons, the members of the House of Lords are appointed (not elected): they are drawn from the peerage (i.e. those who hold a hereditary or honorary title.) This used to be a privilege granted to all hereditary peers, but following the House of Lords Act of 1999, membership is restricted to 92 hereditary peers (whereas there are some 790 present sitting Lords.)

- See: Houses of Parliament.
- See: Upper House.
- See: Westminster.

House of St. Barnabas - (See: Soho/Greek Street/House of St. Barnabas.)

house painting - (See: Painter-Stainers' Hall.)

household provisions -

- See: Cutlers' Hall.
- See: Mercers' Hall.
- See: household utensils.
- See: Hungerford Market.

Household Regiments, the - (See much more at: ROYAL GUARDS, under R.)

- the Coldstream Guards
- the Grenadier Guards
- the Irish Guards
- the Scots Guards
- the Welsh Guards

household utensils -

- See: household provisions.
- See: Hungerford Market.
- See: Temple & Crook.

Houses of Parliament - Still officially known as "the New Palace of Westminster" (from 1834,) reflecting the latter's origins as a royal residence. Parliament had been in Westminster Palace; since 1834 in their own Parliament building, in Parliament Square.

Edward the Confessor's Westminster Palace (the previous building on this site) was the locale of the two houses of Parliament from 1512 to until they were destroyed in 1834, burned to the ground, all but Westminster Hall and a few other bits. The fire had started with a careless burning of small tally sticks (used to aid with accounting,) which caused a chimney fire. The night-long conflagration attracted many viewers, and was drawn by artists who were there watching.

Due to the catastrophic 1834 fire, the current impressive "new" buildings are less than some 200 years old; foundation laid in 1839; completed in 1860. Although rebuilt strictly for parliamentary use, it remains a royal palace officially. (See: Westminster, Palace of, for more on the original building here.)

The House of Commons is in the northern end of this marvelously gothic building; the House of Lord the southern.

- ➢ See: House of Commons.
- ➢ See: House of Lords.
- ➢ See: Lower House.
- ➢ See: Parliament Square.
- ➢ See: Upper House.
- ➢ See: Westminster.
- ➢ See: Westminster Palace.

- Clock Tower: In the 20th C. renamed the Elizabeth Tower.
    - ➢ See: Big Ben, under B.
    - ➢ See: Clock Tower, under C.
- St. Stephen's Porch: The public entrance to the Houses of Parliament.

Howard Street - Westminster. Now gone (since the 1970s,) but had run south from the Strand, between Arundel Street and Essex Street.

Howe House - (See: Curzon Street/Crewe House.)

Howland Dock - Now part of Surrey Commercial Dock. (See: docks/Howland Great Wet Dock.)

Hoxton - A part of the borough of Shoreditch/Hackney. Marshy. Rather far outside London. Known for its medicinal wells. (This district considered as being adjoined to the City as early as 1598.) CHAMBERS LONDON GAZETTEER says: "There were attempts in the 1680s to make Hoxton a sort of 'North End' to rival the West End, but the creation of Hoxton Square and Charles Square failed to spark an inrush of wealthy homebuyers. Instead, Hoxton's open spaces retained their market gardens and gained hospitals, schools and public houses."

Ben Jonson (playwright) killed his fellow actor Gabriel Spencer, in 1598 on Hoxton Fields in a duel.

Mary Wollstonecraft (proto-feminist author) was born in Hoxton (b.1759); her father was a silk weaver here.

- HAC, the: (Honourable Artillery Company.) Military body here since 1642.
- New Chapel: Built by John Wesley in 1778. He is buried here, behind the chapel in a little garden.
- Old Street: John Wesley (Methodist cleric) used to run around the grounds of a former gun foundry, to keep fit, in 1739.

Huguenots - 16-17th century persecuted (in France) French refugees/weavers, who fled to England when Louis XIV made Protestantism illegal in France. Became famous for their silkweaving.

- See: Clerkenwell.
- See: Folgate Street/18.
- See: Fournier Street.
- See: Petty France.
- See: Soho/Old Compton Street.
- See: Spitalfields.
- See: Wandsworth.

Hughes - (AKA: St. George's Fields Circus.) Circus and equestrian acts. (See: Royal Circus.)

hulks - Old ships, beached and converted into either prisons or as a holding site until enough prisoners were sentenced to transportation. (See under T.) The practice of using hulks for holding prisoners continued until 1857. Miserable conditions.

Humane Society - Not to be confused with the Royal Society for the Prevention of Cruelty to Animals. Note: In the UK, "the Humane Society" can now mean for rescuing animals, but also can be an organization for rescuing/preventing drownings.

- See: Hyde Park/Serpentine/Humane Society.
- See: Royal Humane Society - For drowning/rescues.
- See: Royal Society for the Prevention of Cruelty to Animals - For animal rescues.

Humphries of Kidderminster - Carpets. (See: Worcestershire/Humphries of Kidderminster, under the BRITISH COUNTIES section.)

Hungerford House - The house burned in 1669. Demolished and replaced by an updated Hungerford Market, 1830-1833; in 1863 this area was revamped for Charing Cross Station; Charing Cross Hotel was built over the Hungerford House site in 1864.

Hungerford Lane - Charing Cross. Now runs under Charing Cross station. Possibly 500 years old, and only recently (early 20th century) known as Hungerford Lane. Before then it was: Brewer's Lane.

Hungerford Market - Where Villiers Street, Charing Cross is now. Market here since at least 1680. Still there in the Regency. Charles Dickens (author) worked here as a lad. Described as "bustling." Rebuilt in 1833 and grandified. (See: Hungerford House, notes under.) But in the mid 1800s Hungerford Market was closed and replaced by Charing Cross Railway Station and Hotel. The market had been where one went for household provisions.

Hunterian Medical School - (AKA: Great Windmill Medical School. Also, in modern usage, as the: Hunterian Museum.) Royal College of Surgeons. 16 Great Windmill Avenue. Built in 1767 for the Scottish physician Dr. William Hunter, designed by Robert Mylne. It was Dr. Hunter's home, and also contained his "extensive anatomical museum" and his new medical school. Had a basement and three stories. Dr. Hunter taught anatomy and surgery here, starting in October, 1767. Closed in 1838. In 1887, after being other things, it was merged into the Lyric Theatre.

hunting clothes - AKA: pink, meaning the red coat some were allowed to wear during foxhunts. (See: Mason's Yard/Maxwell, Henry.)

Hurlingham - Hammersmith and Fulham. Was a field of "little significance" until the late 17th C., when the field was divided into Little Hurlingham and Great Hurlingham. In the 18th C. a plague pit was dug here.

- Hurlingham House: (See: Hurlingham Club.)

Hurlingham Club, the - Ranelagh Gardens, Fulham, not quite 6 miles/9.7 km from London's center. Built onto Hurlingham House, which still forms a portion of the club and which was built in 1760 for a well-known physician, Dr. William Cadogan. Later went to the Duke of Wellington's older brother, and on to several governors of the Bank of England. It was leased in 1867 as a pigeon-shooting club, this being the foundation for today's polo club. It became the sport's headquarters in Britain, until 1939 when the Hurlingham Polo Association moved to Oxfordshire. (These days the club also accommodates: bowls, cricket, croquet, gymnastics, squash, swimming, and tennis.)

Hurrers - Old term for cap-makers. (See: Haberdashers' Hall.)

hyde - Also seen as: hide. (See.) A Saxon word, an ancient term for a measurement of cultivatable land.

Hyde, The - Barnet. CHAMBERS LONDON GAZETTEER writes: "First identified separately from its parent manor of Hendon in the 13th century, the Hyde had around a dozen dwellings in 1597. The village grew with the appearance of coaching inns during the 18th century, by which time it had become the principal settlement on the road between Cricklewood and Edgware."

- Hendon Brewery: Established in 1860 (but this name came later.) Gone ca. 1960. Now an office block called Hyde House.
- Hyde House: Oliver Goldsmith (playwright) lived here 1771-74. A farmhouse. Not the same as the Hyde House mentioned in the "Hendon Brewery" entry immediately above.

Hyde House -

- See: Hyde, the/Hendon Brewery.
- See: Hyde, the/Hyde House.

Hyde Park - Mayfair, Westminster.

Its name is derived from "hide," a Saxon word for the measurement of a unit of cultivatable land.

Known as: the Park. All others need their name affixed (Green Park, St. James's Park, etc.,) but Hyde Park can/could be referred to just by the simple appellation of: the Park.

According to Domesday Book (1086AD,) this was farmland known as the manor of Eia.

When first royally acquired, it was almost twice its present size, and included the present day Kensington Gardens, (which became its own park, 1705); Hyde Park started its royal existence as a hunting ground for Henry VIII after he confiscated it from the church.

The roadway dividing Hyde Park and Kensington Garden is a five-arched stone bridge built by Rennie in 1826. The southeast edge of Hyde Park joins to Green Park.

It is 350 acres; London's largest open space. If you rode straight across it (northeast corner to southwest corner,) it would be an almost 2 mile/3.2 km ride. Situated on Mayfair's western border.

Public access to the park was a favor that was given and withdrawn at different times. It was first opened to the public by Charles I. CHAMBERS LONDON GAZETTEER writes: "In the early 1630s Charles I opened the park to the public without any of the public pressure that usually presaged acts of royal generosity. After the king's execution the park was seized by the state but citizens continued to use it as a pleasure resort. At the Restoration, Charles II replenished the stock of deer in a newly created enclosure and surrounded the park with a high wall."

From 1695 only private carriages were allowed to drive here, stemming from an event with a public hackney coach full of masked men who drove about the park with no higher aim than to annoy the aristocracy. (See: Hyde Park Corner, for more on park robbers.)

The park was re-opened to the public by George I. But George II closed it again, and built a new wall around it, only to reopen it to the public once again. (But only on Sundays, and only to "those in formal dress" not to include sailors, soldiers, or servants in livery.) Complete unrestricted access came during Victoria's time (it was made truly public in 1861,) although it was open to "the middle classes" (who were thought likely to behave themselves and dress "properly") before then.

Captain Gronow says (in his memoirs) in 1814: "Under the trees cows and deer were grazing, the paths were fewer" (than they were at the later date from which he was commenting.)

Cows grazed in the park, at least as late as 1814. (As was common, London making the most of such grazing ground. See: milk.)

The park is enclosed by large, beautiful trees.

Well into the 19th C. the park was still plagued by thieves and rough types after dark. The park-keepers proved to be ineffective against them.

When the Victorian craze for bicycling came along (ca. 1850) the act was forbidden in Hyde Park (but was acceptable in 1853's Battersea Park.)

Political meetings have been allowed in the park since the late 1860s.

Taxis (motorized) were finally allowed in to Hyde Park, in the early 20th century.

- "Achilles" statue: (Near Hyde Park Corner.) Was erected in June, 1822. (It is not really Achilles at all, as often supposed, but a copy of a figure on Monte Cavallo at Rome.)
- Apsley House: (See under A.)
- Birds' Sanctuary: Dates officially from 1925.
- Cumberland Gate: 1851. (See under C.)
- Duels: Purportedly the last duel in Hyde Park was fought in April, 1817.
- Exhibition Grounds: For the Great Exhibition, 1851. (The Crystal Palace part of the grounds was moved in 1852-4 to Sydenham.)
- Grosvenor Gate: Hyde Lane. Dates from 1725, built to form a carriageway. One of the entranceways to Hyde Park.
- Hyde Park Corner: (See at its own listing.)
- Italian Garden: Came into being in 1860-1. Previously the area had been a one-foot deep (and often polluted) duck pond.
- Long Water, the: Formed in 1731 by simply damming up the Westbourne River. Note: Whereas the Long Water is in Kensington Garden, and the Serpentine is in Hyde Park, they are generally considered to be the same lake. (See: Kensington Palace Gardens.)
- Marble Arch: Was not placed in Hyde Park until 1850. (See: Marble Arch, under M.)
- Old Road: (See: Rotten Row, below.)
- Queen Elizabeth Gate: (AKA: Queen Mother's Gate, so called for the late "Queen Mum," Elizabeth II's mother, Elizabeth (nee) Bowes-Lyon. Dates from 1993.
- Ranger's Lodge: A ranger being one who tended to the park, a park keeper. In

the park, opposite Down Street. Stood until 1825.

- Ring, the: There from at least the time of Charles I. Was midway between Stanhope Gate and Grosvenor, and is now a garden. It had been a circular reservoir (ca. 1725 it was described as "ugly") with a low wall and iron railings. Seems to have been somewhat passé (unfashionable) by the Regency. Foot and horse races were held here. The reservoir was abolished in 1861. Pertaining to the Ring Road, the oldest version of it was farther west than the one there now (being displaced by the formation of the Serpentine in 1730.)
- Rotten Row: Is most likely a corruption of "Route de Roi" (the King's Way.) One mile (1.6 km) long, hence its nickname: The Mile. Established as a bridle path, it connected Westminster and Kensington Palace. William III liked to walk here to Kensington Palace (and so began the "route de roi" nickname.) Prior to then would have been called: the Old Road; William had the path lit with 300 oil lamps (they hung from the trees) to discourage robbers, thus providing London's first streetlighting. Was also often referred to as the King's private road, as only he truly "owned" the right to ride down it (and merely allowed those of the aristocracy to make use of it.) This equestrian road was doubled in width in 1853; *carriages* were not allowed here - horses and riders only. (Aside from the king, it always was intended just for riders, never for strollers.) Railings were added in 1793, and iron rails replaced the brick wall in 1828.
- Serpentine, the: A 28 acre boating and bathing lake was formed in 1730, by Queen Caroline, who ordered the River Westbourne dammed up. (See: Hyde Park/Long Water, above - The note under.) The soil excavated to form the Serpentine was used to make a mound at the southeast end of Kensington Gardens, and is still there. The head of the Serpentine is called the Dell, described as a sheet of water flowing from a waterfall, connecting with the east end of the Serpentine. The serpentine's excess waters go into an underground passage to form a man-made cascade over rocks, this being formed ca. 1817. (See: Kensington Palace/Long Water.)

  In 1814 the Regent's Fête was held here, to celebrate the centenary of the House of Hanover's rise to the British throne (and also to honor the visits of the King of Prussia, and the Tsar of Russia.) Lasted for a week, with booths, side-shows, and swings being allowed in the park.

  In 1815, it was the scene of rejoicing following the Battle of Waterloo.

  In 1816, Shelley's first (and pregnant) wife, Harriet Westbrook, drowned herself here.

Two branches of the Ranelagh sewer flowed into the head of the Serpentine, leaving the water polluted (until this was corrected in 1855.) It smelled of sulfur and ammonia. (Yet, people boated and swam here.)

- Humane Society: In 1794 Prinny gave a plot of land on the Serpentine to the Humane Society (later Royal Humane Society,) where they erected a house for giving aid to drowning persons; replaced in 1844 by the present Decimus Burton building. (See: Royal Humane Society, under R - Not to be confused with the animal rescue organization of the Royal Society for the Prevention of Cruelty to Animals.)
- Ladies' Mile: Is situated on the north side of the Serpentine; a carriage-drive; widened in 1852.

- Serpentine Gallery: 1908, a tearoom.
- Speaker's Corner: (AKA: Orator's Corner.) Was not guaranteed in Hyde Park under law until 1872, and such political/dissenting (or just plain rants) oration was not much tolerated by officials until well into the 2nd half of the 19th century. (See: Speaker's Corner, under S.)

Hyde Park (Tyburnia) - An alternative name for the district known as Tyburnia. (See under T.) Not to be confused with the park of the same name. Also not to be confused with The Hyde in Barnet.

Hyde Park Corner - Westminster. (The street's official name is: Duke of Wellington Place, keeping in mind that Arthur Wellesley was made the Duke of Wellington in 1814.) Southeast corner of Hyde Park; the official entrance to the park. Moved to its present location in the 1880s.

During the Regency era, this area was called Hyde Park Corner, but it was not completely surrounded by roadways (as it is now, where six streets meet: Constitution Hill, Grosvenor Crescent, Grosvenor Place, Knightsbridge, Park Lane, and Piccadilly.)

It was dangerous to travel past the turnpike here at Hyde Park Corner through Knightsbridge after dark. A bell was rung here at 7:00pm and at 9:00pm, to call wayfarers together that they might travel more safely, en masse, between Kensington and the City. George II was stopped and robbed here, after which a troop of armed horsemen were set to patrol the streets at night. (This was the very beginning of what would eventually become the Metropolitan Police ca. 1825.) Until ca. 1820, Hyde Park Corner was more-or-less viewed as the western border of the City.

Hyde Park Corner (since 1855, and officially since 1872) is renowned for its public soapbox speakers, because anyone was/is free to speak here, on any topic.

- Apsley House: The Duke(s) of Wellington still have their home near to Hyde Park Corner - Apsley House, at 149 Piccadilly. (See under A.)
- Goddess of Peace: Statue on the top of the arch. Added in 1912. It was built by Capt. Adrian Jones. Bronze. Its real name is: Peace Descending on the Quadriga of War, replaced in the 1880s with the present version of the quadriga. This displaced a precious (and huge) equestrian statue of Lord Wellington. (See: Apsley House/Wellington Arch.)
- St. George's Hospital: (See under S.)
- Wellington Arch: The triumphal Arch here has had the names:

  - Constitution Arch: A post-Regency designation. Is yet an alternative name for the Arch.

  - Green Park Arch: Its original name, 1830, when it was first finished.

  - Wellington Arch: Its present name.

  The Arch was ordered by George IV, 1825, to commemorate victory in the Napoleonic Wars. The arch was designed by Decimus Burton, neo-classical; built 1826-30. It first faced north (toward Constitution Hill, and faced Hyde Park Screen,) and was neither beloved nor particularly admired. It was meant to be an entrance into Buckingham Palace, but never was. A statue of Lord Wellington was added in 1846, and has been called gloomy and oversized for the arch's dimensions. After Wellington died, the monument was moved to Hyde Park Corner, and the Quadriga statue was substituted for the Wellington one. Has been called "England's answer to the Arc de Triomphe." (Not to be confused with Marble Arch.)

Hyde Park Corner Lodge - Dates from the 1820s.

Hyde Park Corner Tollgate - Was mere steps from Apsley House. It was a gate and a gatehouse. Lasted until at least 1810. (See: Hyde Park Screen.)

Hyde Park Gardens - Laid out ca. 1845. (Earlier, was called Hyde Park Terrace.) Not to be confused with Hyde Park, which is, of course, a (royal) park.

Hyde Park Gate - Kensington Gore. Two parallel streets in Kensington Gardens, running south, but "Hyde Park Gate" also is applicable to the houses between Queen's Gate and DeVere Gardens. The land dates back to at least 1811, but the homes there now are not nearly so old. Not to be confused with Hyde Park Corner, or Hyde Park Screen, or Hyde Park Tollgate.

- 28: Winston Churchill (Prime Minister) died here in 1965.
- 39: Herbert Hoover (later American president) lived here 1901-7. At the time he was a petroleum engineer.

Hyde Park Screen - Built in 1828 by Decimus Burton, intended as part of a grand approach to Buckingham Palace. It was built over the tollgate that had been here. Its frieze is thought to be meant to put one in mind of the Elgin Marbles. It is sometimes misidentified as Hyde Park Gate, but that is a housing development. (See: Hyde Park Gate.)

Hyde Park Square - North of Hyde Park. Westminster. Name of a square planned in 1827 but developed after 1840. The space it occupied had previously been part of a large market-garden (as were Cambridge Square; Gloucester Square; Oxford Square; and Sussex Square.)

hythe - (See: hithe.)

-I-

ice -

- ➢ See: food/ice - Frozen water.
- ➢ See: food/ices - Ice cream.

ice skating - Existed in Britain by at least 1683 (and bone skates have been uncovered from the 12th century.) London did not have an official ice skating rink until the 1840s.

- ➢ See: frost fairs.
- ➢ See: Moorfields.

Ickenham - Hillingdon. Small village near Uxbridge.

- Ickenham Hall: Mid 18th century. Still exists (now attached to the Compass Theatre and Arts Centre.)
- St. Giles' Church: By at least the mid 13th century. In the present building, the oldest parts date from the 1330s.
- Swakeleys House: 1638. Ostentatious. Still exists.

Ilford - Redbridge; was a part of Barking parish until 1830. Had onion and potato fields. (See: Redbridge - For the different between Great Ilford and Little Ilford.)

- St. Mary: 1831.

illnesses -

- ➢ See: diseases.
- ➢ See: hospitals.

immigrants (to London) -

- ➢ See: Chinese immigrants.
- ➢ See: East End.

- See: French immigrants.
- See: Gloucester Place.
- See: gypsies.
- See: Irish immigrants.
- See: Jewish immigrants.
- See: Kensington/Notting Hill.
- See: Limehouse - For Chinese immigrants.
- See: Little Italy.
- See: Little Venice.
- See: New Malden - For Koreans; 1970s. And for - Tamil; 20th century.
- See: Old Jewry.
- See: rough places.

Imperial College - Corner of Prince Consort Road and Exhibition Road, South Kensington. Part of London University. A leading scientific institution. In 1907 it combined with the Royal College of Science, Royal School of Mines, and City and Guilds College, into this one college.

Imperial Gas Works, the - Formed 1821. Regent's Canal. Francis Edwards.

Imperial War Museum - Lambeth Road. Dome and portico added by Sydney Smirke in 1838. In terms of serving as the Imperial War Museum, dates post-Regency, 20th century. Its collection of war implements dates from 1914 and onward.

impressment - (AKA: conscription. AKA: press-ganging. Also as: the press.) Impressment was the taking of men by force into British army or naval forces, with or without notice or consent. Often used in wartimes. The public in general objected to the practice of young men being seized and forced into military service, but conscription was upheld in the courts. Yet another reason to obey the curfew, as men were often seized at night/while drunk.

- See: America - Note at, regarding the War of 1812.
- See: curfew.
- See: Marine Society.

Inderwick's - Pipe-makers. (See: Carnaby Street/45.)

India - In very quick and simplistic terms, relations began in 1600 between Mughal India and Tudor England, growing out of Elizabeth I granting a Royal Charter to the East India Company.

The Mughal Empire declined by 1707, and the East India Company gained a great deal of influence in India.

The East India Co. dissolved in 1858, but the British Empire stepped in to take up its huge influence, using India as their base of Asian expansion. Queen Victoria was named the Empress of India in 1876. (She was the first; George VI was the last, as India gained independence in 1947.)

Opposition to British rule only continued to grow as the 19-20th centuries went on, leading to India's independence in 1947.

- See: Board of Control.
- See: curry.
- See: East India Company.

infirmary - A hospital is a place where there is diagnosing and treatment of the sick. An infirmary is a place where the sick are lodged while receiving care and treatment; the terms are/were largely used interchangeably. (See: hospitals.)

influenza - Often called: the grippe. (See: diseases/influenza.)

Information Technologists, the - (AKA: the Worshipful Company of Information Technologists.) Guild, founded in 1992. Became the City of London's 100th livery company. Unlike many other modern companies, the Information Technologists have their own Hall, on Bartholomew Close. They rank 100th in the order of precedence.

ink - Ink is seen on papyrus from the 26th century BC; in China since the 23rd century BC; in India since the 4th century BC. India ink (carbon based) was invented in China, but the ingredients to make it often came from India, hence the term India ink. By the 4th century AD, ink could also be made from treating iron salts with sulfuric acid; this made a bluish-black ink (that famously fades to a dull brown.) Iron gall ink (AKA: common ink, made with the iron salts) was either purple-black or brown-black. Over the years, many ink recipes were developed, using various combinations of dyes, egg white, glue, oak galls (the bumpy parts of an acorn,) oil, pounded bark, resins, soot, wine, and more - but a new one had to be found in the 15th century when the printing press was invented, because the print blurred when using the prior types of ink. The subsequent printing ink is said to be closer to a varnish than an ink.

Homemade inks were common, as commercial ink could be hard to come by and was expensive. Ink was held in stoppered bottles, or in inkwells. It could be carried as a powder, and mixed with a little water when needed for use.

The typewriter was invented in the 1860s.

- See: pencils - Note at.
- See: pens.
- See: quill.
- You may care to see: paper.

Innholders' Hall - (For the Worshipful Company of Innholders.) College Street, south of St. Michael, Paternoster Royal. AN ENCYCLOPAEDIA OF LONDON explains:

"...on the south side of Elbow Lane (i.e. College Street, just east of Little College Street) in Dowgate ward." Charter granted in 1515. Land for the Hall was received in 1613. Rebuilt ca. 1670 following damage in the Great Fire of 1666. Rebuilt again in 1886.

Also according to AN ENCYCLOPAEDIA OF LONDON: "In 1327, Hostelers and Haymongers, apparently one body, were cited in a petition regarding the irregular sale of hay... In 1446 certain Hostelers of the City petitioned the Lord Mayor for confirmation of ordinances. In 1473, the warden and others of the mistery of Innholders represented that they had been theretofore improperly designated Hostelers, a word that signified their servants: since then the Hostler or Ostler has been the underling."

inns - (SEE: the separate INNS/PUBS section.)

Inns were where people stayed while traveling (if not with friends or family.) Inns were the past's version of a motel. They weren't the same as a pub (public house,) in that a pub was for meeting in and lingering and sharing a pint or two - but that happened anyway sometimes at inns, particularly with locals. Inns were very important for those who had to travel more than one day's journey.

Food and drink were served to travelers, and rooms provided in which to sleep. The more you paid, the better your chambers would be. There would be chamber pots under the beds, or otherwise available. It was not uncommon for those with little funds/of the lower classes to push back the tables and sleep on the common rooms' floors (for a smaller fee than for a room.)

Purportedly the oldest inn in all England is "The Olde Trip to Jerusalem," near Sherwood Forest, Nottingham; established 1129.

Presuming the traveler was bound for London, once you got there you didn't remain in inns; it was more common during the Georgian-Regency eras to rent lodging in apartments (which were rather like modern flats) once one got to town, than it was to stay in a tavern or inn for a length of time. That is, inns were for those on the move, but once arrived, they would usually rent a home or apartment for the duration at their destination (if they couldn't stay with friends or family.)

Carriages and roads were less terrible (relatively) in the Regency time period, so inns thrived.

Some mansions have "inn" as part of their name, a leftover medieval reminder that these grand homes did not face the street but an inner courtyard, with visitors having to enter through a gate-house.

(See: coaching inns, by and large a fancier, bigger version of an ordinary inn, dedicated to travel, and with horses to hire.)

Not to be confused with: the Inns of Court (which are/were inns, but reserved only for those practicing/studying in the legal field.)

Inns of Chancery - Founded by Henry III in the 13th C. when he repressively closed the schools of law in the City.

CHAMBERS LONDON GAZETTEER states: "The Inns of Chancery ceased to serve an educational role after the Civil War and thereafter functioned as professional clubs."

NOTE: Beginning ca. 1320 and over the centuries, the *Inns of Court* became where barristers are taught/trained; the *Inns of Chancery* are for solicitors.

- Barnard's Inn:
  - See: Gresham College.
  - See under B.
- Chancery Lane: (See under C.)
- Clifford's Inn: (See under C.)
- Staple Inn: 338 High Holborn, (on High Holborn's south side.) Into the 19th C., but now defunct. It was the only Inn of Chancery surviving from the original nine. Erected ca. 1560. (Is now offices and shops, and since 1884 has housed the Institute of Actuaries.) In the 14th C., it was a hostel/marketplace for wool traders (known as Staplers, or more formally "the Wool Trade's Merchants of the Staple"; hence the name of Staple Inn.
  - See: staplers.
  - See: Wool Staplers.

  The Staple was the name originally given to the King's dues on exported material such as lead, hides, and wool - that is, those products which were "English staples." (However, see: stapler - For another explanation.) However, the Wool Merchants were not long here; in 1378, Richard II ordered them back to Westminster, and Staple Inn became an Inn of Chancery.

  It is a pair of black and white timbered Elizabethan buildings dating from ca. 1581-9. Irregular quadrangles. (The Chambers probably date from the late 17th century.) The garden was laid out in 1886 (when the property was bought by the Prudential Assurance Company.) The interiors are completely rebuilt now. Known to Charles Dickens (author,) which he describes as a "nook, contain(ing) a little Hall with a little lantern in its roof."
  - 1 Staple Inn: Burned in 1756, along with ancient archives and documents stored here. Rebuilt.

- 2 Staple Inn: Dr. Samuel Johnson lived here in 1759.
- Court, the: In 1803 was described as "clean, dry and pleasant" (description taken from "Londinium Redivivium" by Malcolm.
- Garden, the: Also described by Malcolm in 1803, as "prettily disposed with trees and walks."
- Hall, the: Again in Malcolm's 1803 words: "...has four buttresses of four graduations with angular mullioned windows, and an enriched Gothic door," (the door dating from 1753, and described as a fine example of "Churchwarden's Gothic") "...shaded in rather a picturesque way by shrubs and foliage."
- Shops: Staple Inn had a row of shops, housed in the last surviving Elizabethan domestic buildings in London, built in 1586. Among them: Ye Olde Tobacco Shoppe, established 1864.

Inns of Court - Holborn. Theobald's Road, near Fleet Street. Very near the Thames. Scarcely a half-mile/0.8 km square. Medieval gathering spot for the lawyers' guilds, 14th century.

This area first belonged to the Knights Templar. (See: Knights Templar, under K.) After the Templars were disbanded in 1312, the area passed into the lawyers' hands. It became known as the Inns of Court because when lawyers first came to attend the sessions of the Royal Courts of Justice, they stayed at local taverns (inns.) In short order the schools became known under the appellation of "the Inns."

When these courts were first founded, English Common Law was not taught at the universities, hence the need for this legal center. Each of the four courts has its own chambers, chapel, common rooms, dining hall, gardens, and library.

These learning centers were intended for England and Wales, and over time, the Inns of Court became where barristers trained/became the professional association for such. (Whereas solicitors are trained at the Inns of Chancery, the latter of which are *affiliated* to the Inns of Court; they deal with commercial law.)

- See: Inns of Chancery.
- See: lawyer - To define different kinds of UK lawyers.

As of the 20th century, many lawyers have moved elsewhere, seeking more modern accommodations, with the inns mostly now serving as offices.

The four inns (Lincoln's Inn, Inner Temple, Middle Temple, and Gray's Inn) have long been designated as equal in order of precedence.

The study of common law was first recognized as needing to be an area of study in the mid 18th century. (Prior to that, law was mostly learned by networking, sharing dinners, and being in court.)

Bar examinations first became compulsory in 1872 (in order to practice law.)

The grades of membership: students, then becoming barristers, then Masters of the Bench. The "benchers" make up the governing bodies.

The Inns of Court (along with Fleet Street) are in a kind of no man's land, being situated between the City of London (which technically ended at Ludgate) and Temple Bar, the beginning point of Westminster.

Courtyards are free of vehicular traffic.

Over the centuries there have been over 30 inns - now numbering only four, those four (to repeat myself) being GRAY'S INN (Holborn,) INNER TEMPLE (off Fleet Street,) LINCOLN'S INN (Holborn,) and MIDDLE TEMPLE (off Fleet Street.) Each of the four yet has a high-ceilinged hall, with oak beams and panels, coats of arms, and portraits about the walls, where lunch and dinner are still served. (To be called to the bar, an aspirant must have eaten 24 dinners here; this practice goes back for centuries.) To re-state the obvious from the above: the members lived communally.

FOR STAPLE INN, SEE: INNS OF CHANCERY/STAPLE INN.

***

THE INNS APPEAR, BELOW, IN THIS ORDER:

Gray's Inn

Lincoln's Inn

Lincoln's Inn Fields

Temple, The

GRAY'S INN: (AKA: The Honourable Society of Gray's Inn.) Gray's Inn Square. Is at the north end of Fulwood Place, off High Holborn. In the 13th C. this area belonged to Sir Reginald de Grey (Chief Justice of Chester, and Constable and Sheriff of Nottingham. Died in 1308.) Gray's Inn (note Grey changed to Gray) was established as the lawyers came in ca. 1360-70, an inn to house legal students. The Hall dates from 1556-60, Tudor architecture. Bombed in WWII. Restored to much of its former glory in the 1950s.

- Field Court: Connects Gray's Inn Garden and Gray's Inn Square. There is an ancient catalpa tree here that dates from the time of Francis Bacon (who was Gray's Treasurer.)

- Gray Inn's Gardens: 1606, were laid out by Sir Francis Bacon. On the north side of the inn; a wide green expanse. The fine wrought-iron gateway is dated from 1722, and is designed so that it is always open. These are the only Inn gardens open to the public. Often described as the Inns of Courts' best garden.
- Gray's Inn Hall: Of Elizabethan origin. Retains its 1580 stained glass, and the majority of its ornate screen. In 1814, Percy Bysshe Shelley (poet,) at this time deep in debt, used to secretly meet his lover Mary here.
- King's Road (now known as Theobald's Road): King's Road led from Gray's Inn Road to Bloomsbury Way.
    - 4: (Now known as 22 Theobald's Road.) Benjamin Disraeli (Prime Minister's) birthplace, 1804. Four stories and a basement, conventional late Georgian terrace. Highly fashionable district. Disraeli left in 1818, to move to 6 Bloomsbury Square (where his father, Isaac, lived.)
- Raymond Buildings: Off Theobold's Road, you find this long Georgian bulk, with gardens. There are boards on every doorway (known, for some reason, as staircases) which had the resident's name written on them.
- Walks, the: (Not their name, just a way to refer to the paths.) The walks, where once Society met, are now mostly gone. This fashionable choice seems to have been mostly favored during the 17-18th centuries. There were also sometimes duels here.

***

LINCOLN'S INN: (AKA: The Honourable Society of Lincoln's Inn.) Is the most collegiate looking of the four Inns of Court, and the most beautiful, as well as the largest in London. It was also the only one to escape extensive WWII damage/restoration. Situated along High Holborn (the large entryway is in Chancery Lane, dating from 1518.) Built on the site of the Knights Templar tilting ground; their order was dissolved in 1312.

CHAMBERS LONDON GAZETTEER tells us: "The land" (then) "belonged to the Dominican priors who subsequently decamped to Blackfriars, whereupon the Earl of Lincoln built a house here. The earl bequeathed his home to a college of lawyers, who moved in some time in the 14th century. The earliest buildings have not survived but the complex that evolved on the site has elements from every century since the 15th…"

General information on Lincoln's Inn: The central part of the fields was, in the 1600s, declared to "for ever and hereafter be open and unbuilt" (as it has remained.) Has retained, for the most part, its identity as the Inn for barristers at the Chancery bar. Its members have the rare privilege of being allowed to remain seated while the loyal toast to the monarch is raised, conferred on them by Charles II after he supped there one night. Railed in in 1735.

(You may care to see: Lincoln's Inn Fields, at its own listing.)

- Chancery Lane: The old east gateway leading from Lincoln's Inn to Chancery Lane was built in 1518, restored in 1899. (See: Chancery Lane, under C.)
- Chapel, the: Dates from 1619-23. In the Gothic style. Renovated in 1685 by Wren; again by Wyatt in 1791. The western extension was added in 1882-3, by Salter.
- Court of Chancery:
    - See: Court of Chancery - At its own listing.
    - See: Old Hall, below - Where the Court of Chancery was sometimes held.
- Furnival's Inn: Attached to Lincoln's Inn. The 4th Lord Furnival leased this space to law students as a place of boarding in 1383. A long-term lease came into being between this inn and nearby Lincoln's Inn, the latter of which declined the lease in 1817; Furnival's Inn was then demolished. Replaced by a new building, which retained the Furnival's Inn name; Charles Dickens (author) lived here in 1834-7. It is now the Prudential Assurance Building, 142 Holborn Bars.
- Holborn Bars: Late 19th century. Is located very near Staple Inn. Holborn Bars are two stone obelisks that mark one boundary of the ancient City. (See under H.)
- Library: Established in 1497. Present building dates from 1845. Is London's oldest library.
- New Hall: Dates from 1845. Is Victorian red brick, designed by Philip Hardwick.
- New Square: Dates from 1697. Faces toward Lincoln's Inn Fields. Described as pretty and tranquil. Is terraced 4-story houses built around a central lawn. (See under N.)
- Old Buildings: Dates from Tudor times. An irregular brick square building.
- Old Hall: Located in Old Square; east of New Square. Dates back to 1485-92; (apart from St. Etheldreda's, the oldest building in Holborn.) It was sometimes used as the High Court of Chancery from 1733 to 1873. Largely rebuilt in 1926-8.
- Stone Buildings: An 18th C. court, built in 1774-80 by Robert Taylor, on the Inn's northeast corner, near Chancery Lane. NAIRN'S LONDON describes it: "Taylor...set out his attached columns with real gusto and exquisite masonry technique."

- Treasury: Built in 1497. Current one dates from 1845.
  - See: Law Courts.
  - See: Whitehall/Treasury.

***

LINCOLN'S INN FIELDS:

(See: Lincoln's Inn Fields, under the L section.)

Lincoln's Inn Fields is the largest square in London. William Newton meant to build on the twelve acres here in 1620, but angry lawyers protested to the House of Commons - and won the day, leaving the space open. Lincoln's Inn Fields were not laid out, therefore, as a square until in the early 1640s. There is a mock-Tudor archway leading into the gardens of Lincoln's Inn Fields, this archway being built in 1845. Handsome buildings surround the square. The west and south sides were built to designs by William Newton in the 1930s.

To this day, a bell is tolled from 12:30-1:00 when a bencher of the Inn dies, a custom dating back to the days of John Donne. ("Ask not for whom the bell tolls...")

- 12 Lincoln's Inn Fields: Sir John Soane (architect) bought this for his own family home in 1792. Subsequently bought numbers 13 and 14. Remodeled all three by 1824.
- 13: (See: Soane Museum, below.)
- 56-60: Lindsey House. On the West side, numbers 56-60 make up Lindsey House, believed to have been built by Inigo Jones ca. 1640, or at least styled after him. It is the only building from William Newton's plans for Lincoln Inn Fields to survive. It was the Earl of Lindsey's home in the early 18th century. (See: Chelsea, Cheyne Walk, Lindsey House.)
- 57-58: Built ca. 1730 by Henry Joynes. Deliberately designed in Portland stone to complement Lindsey House, next door. Charles Dickens' friend/biographer, John Forster, lived at 58.
- 59-60: Now one house. The right-hand part was built in 1640 in the Inigo Jones style; in 1730 the left-hand one was built to match (if rather a bit better.) At the 18th century's end Soane put on the double porch.
- Chapel: Dates from 1592, inaugurated by John Donne.
- Lindsey House: (See 56-60, above.)
- Newcastle House: (See under N.)
- Portsmouth Street: Southeast corner of Lincoln's Inn Fields. (See under P.)

- Royal College of Surgeons: On the south side of the square. 1800. Still located there. (See under R.)
- Soane Museum: 13 Lincoln's Inn Fields. This house was left, by virtue of Sir John Soane's will as he gifted the property to London, exactly as he left it upon his death in 1837, with the stipulation that nothing be changed (and it never has.) The house was built to his designs in 1792. Rebuilt (still to Sir John Soane's designs) in 1824. Has a good collection of Hogarth and Turner paintings.

***

1. **TEMPLE, THE (OVERALL):**
   Featuring:
   The Inner Temple
   The Middle Temple
   The Outer Temple

HERE I MEAN: THE OVERALL AREA CALLED "THE TEMPLE," (WHICH INCLUDES THE INNS, THE INNER TEMPLE, MIDDLE TEMPLE, AND TEMPLE AREAS.) PLEASE ALSO SEE "**THE TEMPLE**" (MEANING THE AREA OF THE TEMPLE CHURCH) AT #2, BELOW.

The larger area often referred to simply as "The Temple" is in the area of Lincoln's Inn. Fleet Street, the City. Lawyers have been here since 1320.

"The Temple" (as an area) incorporates both the Inner Temple and the Middle Temple, with no obvious division between the two. They have their own halls and libraries, but share the church. (See: Temple Church, below.) You will find some entries are listed twice, in both locales, since the division between the Inner Temple and the Middle Temple is hard to divine. Although the dividing line is convoluted, the main portion of Inner Temple lies to the east of Middle Temple Lane, with Middle Temple primarily lying to the west.

According to CHAMBERS LONDON GAZETTEER (regarding the Knights Templar here): "The order's clergy occupied a consecrated precinct on the east side of the church and the knights, squires and various lay brothers lived to the south and west. The Order was suppressed in 1312 and Parliament voted its buildings" (be given to) "the Order of the Hospital of St. John of Jerusalem, which leased them to students of law." There is some debate about when, why, and even *if* the college divided itself into two separate Inns of Court.

The Temple (area) became crown property after the Dissolution, and in 1609 James I granted the land in perpetuity to the lawyers (as said at the opening part of "Inns of Court," above in this entry.) The Temple was rebuilt following WWII damage, to designs by Sir Edward Maufe, to a neo-Georgian style.

Most of the medieval buildings were destroyed by the 1666 Great Fire of London (and through other 17th C. fires.) The Temple area then was largely rebuilt in a collegiate style.

To this day, the courtyards are lit by gas lamps.

<u>THE **INNER TEMPLE**</u>: (AKA: The Honourable Society of the Inner Temple.) Its symbol is the Pegasus. Here from 1337; this is where the lawyers first resided. The wrought-iron gate dates from 1730.

- Buttery, the: A 14th C. building. Two-story. Built as part of the original monastic refectory, and was probably a provisions store.
- Charles Lamb Memorial: Lamb was an antiquarian/essayist/poet. Dates from 1930.
- Clement's Inn: (See under C.)
- Fountain Court: Near Middle Temple Hall. Has a round pond and mulberry trees. This court is named for the 1681 fountain still there (restored in 1919.)
- Inner Temple Garden: Is protected, huge, and said to be "immaculate." Three acres, was there by at least Shakespeare's time. Was the Inner Temple's private garden (for the lawyers only.) The kneeling black figure here dates from ca. 1700, but not in this locale until 1905.
- Inner Temple Gateway: 17 Fleet Street. Leads to the Strand. Half-timbered three-story house, 1610, (described by LONDON ACCESS as looking "rather like a stage set.") The Jacobean woodwork all had to be revamped in 1906 (with the exception of the carved panels between the windows.)
    - Prince Henry's Room: 1610. Is on the top floor of the gateway. Prince Henry was the oldest son of James I. It is considered unlikely that the prince actually resided here, as there was a tavern (the Prince's Arms) below, but was probably called Prince Henry's Room to commemorate his investiture as Prince of Wales in 1610.
        - See: Fleet Street/17.
        - See under P.
- Inner Temple Hall: Southeast of Temple Church. Ancient. The 1870 rebuild was

on the site of a far earlier version of the hall, retaining the ca. 1500 stone brackets, two Elizabethan doors, a wall painting of Pegasus (1709, by Sir James Thornhill,) four effigies (two of Knights Templar and two of Knights Hospitallers.) Extensively rebuilt after WWII damage.

- Inner Temple Lane: Dr. Samuel Johnson was born here.
- Inner Temple Library: Private law library. Established in the late 15th century. (Not to be confused with the Middle Temple Library.)
- King's Bench Walk: Existed at least since Christopher Wren's time. Near Inner Temple Gardens. The offices of the King's Bench burned in the 17th C., replaced by the present buildings.
    - 4-5: Built 1677-8, designed by Wren.
    - 7: Built 1685.
    - 8: Built 1782. Novelist George Moore lived here.
    - 9: (Also called Staircase 9.) Montague Druitt, a barrister, lived here until he drowned himself in the Thames; he is one of the persons proposed to have been Jack the Ripper.
- Temple Church: (See: Temple (2nd entry)/Temple Church, below.)

THE **MIDDLE TEMPLE**: (AKA: The Honourable Society of the Middle Temple.) Fleet Street. Lawyers here from 1346. Built 1560-70. Its symbol, seen on the weathervane, is the gilded lamb and flag. Although the dividing line (between the Inner Temple and Middle Temple) is convoluted, most of Middle Temple is west of Middle Temple Lane; Inner Temple to the east.

- Brick Court, and Essex Court: 17th century. There was a range that divided these two courts off Middle Temple Lane, but it was destroyed in WWII, leaving the two courts to seem as one now.
    - 1 Essex Court: The diarist John Evelyn lived here in 1640.
- Crown Office Row:
    - 2: Charles Lamb (essayist/antiquarian/poet) was born here.
- Essex Court: (See: Brick Court, above.)
- Griffin, the: Dates from 1880, marking (as did Temple Bar) the entrance to the City from Westminster. (See: Temple Bar, below.)
- Middle Temple Gateway: 1684, by Roger North (a lawyer and senior member of the Inn.) This is the main entrance by foot to Middle Temple. Has four Ionic pilasters and a pediment that fronts on Middle Temple Lane.
- Middle Temple Hall: 1562-73 interior, Tudor style. Repairs done in 1699, and in

1745; in 1757 the original red brick exterior was changed (some say destroyed) by an "improvement" of casing stone. The tower and east section are from 1832. The roof is a double hammerbeam design, rare. The hall measures 100 feet x 40 feet. Yet has a functioning dining hall, still with its Tudor era appearance. Student barristers are required to (and have been for a very long time) dine here a minimum of 24 times. Carefully restored following WWII damage.

- Middle Temple Lane: Gloomy, narrow walk that connects the Inns.
  - 1, 2, 3 Middle Temple Lane: Built ca. 1693. Overhanging upper stories, which while attractive broke the post-Great Fire building requirements.
- Middle Temple Library: A small library here by at least 1540 (which books were eventually all stolen, as the library was unlocked.) Re-established in 1641. Today hosts some 250,000 volumes. Immediately south of Fountain Court. (Not to be confused with the Inner Temple Library.)
- Temple Bar: A flamboyant entry to Middle Temple Lane. Built in 1672. Made of Portland stone. Pulled down in 1878 as being a traffic obstruction, and moved in 1888 to Theobald's Park, Waltham Cross. Where the visitor now finds the Griffin rearing its head near the Thames (and known as the Temple Bar Memorial,) was the site of the old Temple Bar.
  - ➢ See: Griffin, above.
  - ➢ See: Temple Bar, under T.
- Temple Church: (See under: Temple (2nd entry)/Temple Church, below.)

<u>THE OUTER TEMPLE:</u> There is no OUTER TEMPLE now. It used to be lands which lay outside the City boundary, also was known as Stapleton (or Exeter) Inn. The outer Temple was long gone by the time of the Regency.

2. **<u>TEMPLE, THE</u>** (HERE I MEAN THE ACTUAL AREA OF THE TEMPLE, RATHER THAN THE LARGER AREA THAT INCORPORATES ALL THE INNS, HALLS, WALKS, ETC. THAT IS, THE ACTUAL TEMPLE CHURCH AND ITS SURROUNDINGS, THE FORMER ALSO KNOWN AS: ST MARY THE VIRGIN CHURCH.)

"The Temple" is a complex of ancient buildings and courtyards given over to lawyers. Dates from ca. 1160.

During the struggles of the Christians to obtain the Holy Land, two celebrated military orders of monks were instituted, the Knights Hospitallers of St. John of Jerusalem, and the Knights Templar (who specialized in protecting pilgrims on their way to the Holy Land, Jerusalem.) The Knights Templar settled here ca. 1160, until they were suppressed and disbanded in 1312. The Knights leased this area to the lawyers.

In 1608, James I granted a freehold charter to the Benchers of the Inner, and Middle, and Temple, and thus came the lawyers *permanently* to these courts; James I had this property available for such a granting due to the fact that Henry VIII confiscated it during the Reformation. A condition of the charter is that they must maintain the Temple Church. (See: Temple Church, below.)

- Choir, the: Finished in 1240.
- Hare Court: Charles Lamb (essayist/poet) described it as a "gloomy churchyard-like court."
- King's Bench Walk: (See: Temple (1st entry)/Inner Temple/King's Bench Walk.)
- Law Courts, the: 1874-82. Before this was built, the courts were divided between Lincoln's Inn and Westminster.
    - See: Courts of Common Law and Equity, under C.
    - See: Law Courts, under L.
- Pump Court: Runs out of Middle Temple Lane.
    - Temple Church: (See, below.)
- Round Church: (See: Temple Church, below.)
- **Temple Church:** (AKA: St. Mary the Virgin. Also known, in more common parlance, as the Round Church.)

  In Pump Court, in the Inner Temple (but it serves both Inner and Middle Temple.) Built in two phases; completed in 1240. It is a "Royal Peculiar," which means it is directly responsible to the sovereign (not an archbishop.) The nave (that part of the church called "The Round") dates from 1185, round design, to emulate the round temple in Jerusalem (called the Sepulchre, as it was reputed to have been built over the tomb of Jesus.) It is the only part of the Inns of Court still remaining from the time of the Templars. The carved grotesque stone heads which circumnavigate the wall were here before the Regency era. The conical roof dates from 1840.

  The rectangular Chancel (also known as "The Oblong") was added in 1240, and its style is Early English; replaced the first chancel that had dated from 1185. Here were the effigies of nine 12th and 13th century Knights, probably thought by Regency London to have been Knights Templar, but now no longer so thought; restored in 1840.

  The church was damaged in 1580 by an earthquake, but repaired.

It was not burned in the Great Fire of 1666, but Wren chose to refurbish it in 1681-3 (following a 1679 fire.)

It was "beautified" once again in 1706, being then whitewashed.

In 1828 Robert Smirke restored the lovely arcading.

It was tinkered with two more times until it was "restored" in 1839-42 by over-enthusiastic Victorians, who (among other things) lowered the chancel floor by 16 inches. It was restored again after extensive WWII damage.

Inns of Court Hotel - 1866.

inoculation, from diseases - Was known of in a limited sense, and throughout the Regency remained largely misunderstood/feared. (See: smallpox.)

insects - In England at the time of the Regency. (This list is not all-inclusive):

ants

bees

beetles

butterflies

cockroaches - Note: There is a type of fish in England called a roach, clearly no relation to cockroaches.

crickets

damselflies

dragonflies

earwigs

fleas

flies

grasshoppers

ladybirds - In America: ladybugs.

lice

mayflies

mosquitos

moths

spiders

wasps

worms - Many kinds.

Institute of Actuaries - July/1884. Based in England; the Faculty of Actuaries based in Scotland; they are separate but work together. Bonded by vote in 2010, they've become the Institute and Faculty of Actuaries.

Institute of Civil Engineers - 1 Great George Street, Westminster (from 1839 to the present.) Independent, professional association, and charitable body. Founded in 1818, the world's first *professional* engineering organization. In 1818 they met in the Kendal Coffee House, Fleet Street. Royal Charter in 1828. (You may care to see: Society of Civil Engineers.)

Institute of Contemporary Arts - Established in 1947; located at Carlton House Terrace since 1968.

Institute of Directors - 116-119 Pall Mall. Nash, 1828. The United Service Club (here until 1974) commissioned this building in 1815 (only was number 116; number 117 was acquired in 1858; numbers 118 and 119 in 1912.)

instruments, musical - Played during the Regency era. (This list is not all inclusive):

accordion - Invented in 1822.

bassoon

cello

clarinet

clavichord - Fell out of use in the 1850s.

concertina - Invented in 1826.

drums

dulcimer

flute

guitar

harp

harp-lute - Invented in 1798, refined in 1810, popular with ladies in the Regency. Its precursor was the English guitar. The harp-lute was shorter. Had a dual neck, on the side near the player had a fret board that ended in a curved harp-like string support. Had twelve strings, but only some of them stretched over the fret board, played like a guitar; the other strings were played like a harp.

harpsichord - Old-fashioned by the time of the Regency, but still seen.

mandolin

oboe

organ

pianoforte - This is the formal name of the piano. Regency folk sometimes used the foreshortened term "piano."

spinet

trombone

trumpet

viola

violin - Sometimes called a fiddle.

International Epidemiological Association - Founded in 1850, housed in Hanover Square.

International Standard Book Number - AKA: ISBN. (See: W. H. Smith Company, under W.)

International Working Men's Association - Formed on 9/28/1864 in St. Martin's Hall; French and British trade union workers, with Karl Marx as their general secretary; the center, perhaps, of Communism in mid 19th century London.

Ireland - In short and simplistic terms: Ireland was under English control from 1653 (with a conquest of Ireland having been often pursued since 1169.)

The Irish Parliament was granted legislative independence in 1782; in 1793 the Dublin Parliament voted in a Catholic Relief Act, trying to satisfy Catholics (who felt disenfranchised from the act of governing; England was strongly disinclined to like the idea of a Catholic-led Ireland.) The Act allowed Catholics to vote (although they still could not sit as Members of Parliament.) Unrest continued, leading to the (crushed) Irish Rebellion of 1798, at which time the Prime Minister, Pitt the Younger, felt the only way to keep Ireland "safe" was to bring it into the United Kingdom.

The Union of Britain and Ireland was enacted 7/2/1800 (effective from 1/1/1801.)

The issue of Catholic rights was not resolved (well, *improved*) until Parliament passed the Catholic Emancipation Act of 1829.

The Home Rule Act (limited independence for Ireland) had to wait until 1914, and even then was delayed until after WWI, 1922. (You may care to see: Order of St. Patrick.)

Ireland Yard - Small alley, off Blackfriars Lane. During Shakespeare's time, was a popular place for actors to reside, because it sat within the City but was a Liberty, and so did not have to answer to City laws. (You may care to see: liberties.)

- Blackfriars Priory: A fragment of its 13th C. monastic wall is all that remains above ground. Ireland Yard had once been a major entry into the priory (until the Dissolution.)

Irish immigrants - London hosted some 23,000 Irish by 1780, alas mostly in the infamous slum area of St. Giles. In 1845-50 the potato blight in Ireland increased the Irish population in London to over 100,000.

- See: Holy Land.
- See: Kensington/Notting Hill.
- See: rough places.
- See: St. Giles.
- See: Soho/St. Patrick's.

Irish linens - (See: Leicester Square/Newton's.)

Iron Duke, the - (See: Apsley House, for an explanation of how Arthur Wellesley, 1st Duke of

Wellington, came to be known as "The Iron Duke."

Ironmonger Lane - Cheapside. Narrow. One-way. This street has held this name since at least the 12th century. There were probably ironmongers here at one time, but by the end of the 16th C. they'd moved on. Thomas à Becket was supposedly born here.

- St. Olave Jewry: (See under the CHURCHES section.)

Ironmongers' Hall - (For the Worshipful Company of Ironmongers.) Dealers in iron and hardware. The guild is first mentioned in the 14th century. Their charter dates from 1463. AN ENCYCLOPAEDIA OF LONDON states: "There is no record of any hall until 1457, when, under the will of Alice Styward, they obtained the site on which their halls successively stood for about 460 years. It was on the north side of Fenchurch Street, at the corner of Fishmonger Alley, between that and Billiter Street." That Hall dates from 1750-51. After WWI/1917 damage, the hall was rebuilt in Shaftesbury Place, Aldersgate Street; dates from 1925, with a Tudor look. Ironmongers produced the type of objects an American might expect to go to the hardware store to buy. (See: Shipwrights' Company - Who share the Ironmongers' Hall.)

Isis, the - In Oxford the Thames river is known as the Isis.

Island of Thorney - The land between the two tributaries of the Tyburn River.

This is where Westminster now stands.

- See: Westminster.
- See: Westminster Palace.

Was in ancient times a rather marshy island of thorn trees, hence the name. Was a place of worship from at least the 2nd century (perhaps earlier.) CHAMBERS LONDON GAZETTEER explains: "From 785 it was the site of a monastic foundation which Edward the Confessor re-endowed and to which he added a large, stone abbey church, consecrated in 1065; this was referred to as the 'west minster' to distinguish it from the 'east minster,' St. Paul's Cathedral in the City of London." (See: Tyburn River.)

Isle of Dogs - Since at least 1588. Reclaimed in the 17th C. by Dutch engineers. 800 acres, a tongue of land out into the Thames (across from Deptford and Greenwich); was a peninsula, in truth, until it was made an island in 1802 by cutting a new canal. Was once called Stepney Marsh. Supposedly Charles II (b.1630-d.1685) kenneled his spaniels there, hence the island's name as we know it. Millwall Dock and Cubitt Town are here. Was not a "nice" neighborhood, although it was considered a richly healthful place to graze cattle. One of London's main centers for naval shipbuilding. In the 19th C. had docks and factories here. Its government is/was independent of London rule, being self-governing.

- Billingsgate Market: Since 1989. (See: docks/West India Dock/Billingsgate Market.)

- Canary Wharf: Canary Wharf now consists of a modern skyscraper. (See: docks/West India/Canary Wharf.)
- West India Docks: (See: docks/West India Docks.)

Isle of Thorney - (See: Island of Thorney.)

Isle of Wight - Has artifacts from: dinosaurs, fossils, the Bronze Age, Iron Age, and the Romans, the latter of which occupied here for 400 years. The history of the "Wight" name is unsettled. It has had a long history of invaders, kings fleeing here, and hosting troops.

- J. Samuel White, boat-builder: 1802. His successful business attracted more marine manufacturers here through the 19-20th centuries, and marine interests yet continue here.
- Nash, John: Famous architect, lived here in Regency days.
- Osborne House: 1851. Royal residence for Queen Victoria. (See under O.)

Isleworth - (Pronounced "Izle-woth.") Hounslow. Dates from the year 677. By the mid 13th century, it was a village on a manorial estate. Remained through the 19th century as a quiet village, with titled residents who did not move out until the railways came in. (You may care to see: Old Isleworth.)

- All Saints: Rebuilt inside the shell of the 14th C. building, which burned in 1943.
- Old Isleworth: The original settlement part of Isleworth. (See under O.)
- Osterley Park: (See under O.)
- Spring Grove: Northwest corner of Isleworth. (See under S.)

Islington - Hounslow.

Surprisingly, Islington was established in 1965, when the former Metropolitan boroughs of Finsbury and Islington united.

That being said, Islington is very old, existing since before the 11th century. It started to be a less wild place when it became a royal hunting ground. People fled here during the Plague. By the 16th century it was frequently used as a grazing place while driving cattle to Smithfield Market; by the late 18th century, every year tens of thousands of oxen and hundreds of thousands of sheep passed through Islington High Street, on their way to the meat market.

In the 17th C. the area had become a "trendy" place for alehouses and cream teas. (See: Copenhagen House, below, for cakes and custards.)

By the 18th C., however, the upper classes had abandoned the area, and it deteriorated, clear into the 20th century.

By 1800 the population here was around 10,000, not yet a part of the metropolis. Pleasant countryside, if not the "in" place it once had been. By the 1820s the squares and terraces of Barnsbury appeared. Circa the 1840s, Islington became a bit of a "walking suburb" for thousands of clerks who literally walked to work in the City.

Modern Islington boasts no parks.

- Angel the: 3-5 Islington High Street. Now a hotel, was a coaching inn since the 17th century. Was the first overnight stop for those traveling north out of London. (See under the INNS/PUBS section.)
- Barnsbury: Squares and terraces, 1820s. Between Caledonian Road and Upper Street. In the parish of Holy Trinity. Until 1842 it was known as Barnsbury Fields and Caledonian Fields. Rough sports were staged here (such as boxing, cock-fighting.)
- Caledonian Fields:
    - Caledonian Asylum: Founded in 1815, for Scottish children, age 7-10. Moved here to Caledonian Fields in 1827.
- Caledonian Road: Connects Islington to Holloway. 1826-7. Originally called Chalk Road. Toll road. Renamed to Caledonian Road in 1861. In the 20-21st C., locals called it the Cally.
    - Copenhagen House: ca. 1650s (or older.) Demolished 1853. Site became a cattle market.
    - Pentonville Prison: (See under P.)
- Camden Market: (See under C.)
- Canonbury Manor: Built by the canons of St. Bartholomew's Priory. Later known as Canonbury House. The still existing Canonbury Tower (60 feet high) dates from 1562. Tower would have been familiar to Sir Walter Raleigh (1580s.) In the 18th C. it was converted into apartments. (See: Canonbury Square, below.)
- Canonbury Square: Laid out in 1800, over the site of Canonbury Manor. Until this, the area was largely open fields.
- Chalk Road: (See: Caledonian Road, above.)
- Chapel Market: Started as (unwanted) costermongers selling their wares, but despite the grumbles of residents it grew into a full-fledged street market ca. the 1860s. Made official in 1879. Is currently known for its fruits and vegetables.
    - 45: Charles Lamb (essayist/poet) lived here briefly in 1799.
- Colebrook Row: Begun in 1710. A long row of handsome, if simple, terraces.
    - Colebrook Cottage - (Now 64 Duncan Terrace.) Charles Lamb (poet/antiquarian) lived here for a while in the 1820s.
- Copenhagen Fields: Was in 1834 the site for large-scale demonstrations against the jailing of unionized agricultural workers. Replaced in 1860 by the

Metropolitan Cattle Market. Also hosted at various times such events as cardplaying, bulldog fights, and mass protest meetings.

  - See: Copenhagen Fields, under C.
  - See: Newgate Market.

- Copenhagen House: Thought to have been constructed in 1606 as a place for visiting Danes to stay while the King of Denmark came to England for a visit. Definitely affiliated with the 17th century Danish ambassador to Britain. In the 18th C., it was a famous tea garden, with cakes and custards, which lasted until pulled down in 1852; demolished so as to build the Metropolitan Cattle Market, 1855.
- Cross Street: Between Lower Street and Upper Street. Georgian houses built on a raised pavement.
- Duncan Terrace: Row houses, built late 18th century. (See: Colebrook Row/Colebrook Cottage, above.)
- Essex Road: (See: Lower Street, below.)
- Finsbury:
  - See: Islington, above - The note at the start of.
  - See under F.
- fire-engine house, a: 1792; heightened in 1822. Although in poor shape, it yet survives.
- Highbury Barn: A pleasure resort, most fashionable in the 1700s. Five acre grounds. Various indoor entertainments. Around 1820 it was a noted tavern with tea gardens, popular in the summer months. In Victorian times took on "dancing" which was considered so scandalous that it was closed down. The concert hall was added during Victorian times.
- Highbury House: 14th C., built for the Prior. Revamped and built into a mansion in 1781.
- Highbury Place: Built 1774-79.
- Highbury Terrace: Building began here in 1794. 22 houses here by 1829.
- Islington Church: Same as St. Mary's. (See: Upper Street/St. Mary's, below.)
- Islington Green: The lord of the manor of Canonbury, the Marquess of Northampton, gave the triangle of land at the center of Islington to the vestry in 1777. This green was cleared, then enclosed with posts and rails. Soon acquired a watch house, and in 1808 trees were planted on this former waste area.
  - Statue of Sir Hugh Myddleton: At the south end of the Green, there since 1862. Sir Hugh built the 40 mile/64 km long New River Canal in 1613.

(See: New River Canal, below.)

- Islington High Street: Contained several inns where travelers would make their stop before the last bit of journey into London. Most famous of these was: the Angel, on the corner of Pentonville Road. Here in 1790, Thomas Paine is supposed to have written the beginning of his *Rights of Man.*
    - ➢ See: Angel, above.
    - ➢ See: Angel, under the INNS/PUBS section.
  - o Peacock, the: Coaching inn. (See under the INNS/PUBS section.)
- Islington Lunatic Asylum: Where Charles Lamb's sister Mary was occasionally placed after having killed their mother with a knife in a fit of insanity, 1790s. (Charles looked after Mary for the rest of her life.) He and she moved from Islington in 1827.
- Islington Tunnel: 1820. Built to bring Regent Canal into Islington.
- Lower Street: May be of Roman origin; certainly existed by the Middle Ages. Lower Street was the name of Essex Road until the later 19th century. (Other names that the road, or parts of it, have gone by: Lower Road, and Seveney Street.) By the late 17th C., houses that had been made over into inns existed here. There was a row of cottages by 1760. As the 18th century advanced, this area became increasingly dense and poor, with a "network of side streets" by the early 19th century. Slum clearings came along in the 1870s.
  - o Fisher House: Early 17th C. mansion. Large garden. There was an academy for young ladies here in 1660. Was an asylum for the insane in 1806. Was unoccupied during the Regency. Demolished in 1845.
- Mildmay Park: Henry VIII hunted here. The Mildmay estate was leased in the 1840s to build middle- and working-class homes.
- Milner Square: 1835-41, by Roumieu & Gough.
- Model Prison: Caledonian Road, 1840. (More often known as Pentonville Prison.)
- Myddleton Square: (See under M.)
- Myddleton Terrace.
- New River Canal: 1609, opened in 1613, by Sir Hugh Myddleton (a Welsh jeweler.) To obtain fresh water for London, he built a river that brought water from Ware in Hertfordshire, a distance of nearly 40 miles/64 km. The River ended at a reservoir near Sadler's Wells (now of the Thames Water Authority.) Taylor Coleridge and Charles Lamb used to walk here when boys to swim. Covered over to prevent cholera in the Victorian period. (See under N.)
- Newington Green: Overlaps Hackney and Islington. Dates back to at least the

year 1086, first known as Newton; Newington by the 13th century. Henry VIII used a house on the south side of the green while here hunting boars and stag.

  - 52-5: Are some of the oldest surviving houses in London, dating from 1658.

- Old Queen's Head: In Essex Road (since 16th C.,) rebuilt in early 19th C., contains the original parlor chimney.
- Peacock Inn, next door to Chapman's apothecary and a sweet shop. (See under the INNS/PUBS section.)
- Pentonville Prison: (AKA: Model Prison.) Caledonian Road. (See under P.)
- Pied Bull Pub: In Upper Street since 16th century. (See under the INNS/PUBS section.)
- Royal Agricultural Hall: (See: Upper Street/Royal Agricultural Hall, below.)
- Sadler's Wells: Joe Grimaldi, the famous clown, performed here during the Regency. (See: Sadler's Wells, under S.)
- St. Mary's:
    - ➢ See: Islington/Upper Street/St. Mary's, under I.
    - ➢ See: Upper Street/St. Mary's, below.
- Thornhill Crescent: Ca. 1849.
- Thornhill Square: Was conceived in 1808, but begun in 1813. For George Thornhill, who died in 1827, at which time his son took over developing this Islington property. Didn't become a square until ca. 1847, 33 houses on the west side, "opulent." Railings for the center garden date from 1852.
- Upper Street: CHAMBERS LONDON GAZETTEER describes it as: "...stretching for one mile/1.6 km between Highbury Corner and the junction with Liverpool Road at its southern end." Almost completely built up by 1735. In Victorian times it was particularly known for its trousseaux and undergarments. Dubbed as the "heart of Islington." It currently houses bars, cafes, and restaurants.
  - St. Mary's: Islington parish church, here from 628AD, first called Our Lady of Islington. Rebuilt 1754, from whence the steeple dates, by Launcelot Dowbiggin. (See: Islington/Upper Street/St. Mary's, under I.)
- White Conduit Fields: Some of the first English cricket games were played here in the 1770-1780s. By 1787 the players thought the grounds too public, and delegated Thomas Lord to find another spot, hence Lord's Cricket Grounds.
    - ➢ See: Lord's Cricket Grounds, under L.
    - ➢ See: White Conduit Street, below.

- White Conduit Street: Ran near or by White Conduit Fields, still exists, whereas the Fields do not. Built in the late 18th C. or early 19th century.

Italian immigrants -

- ➢ See: immigrants - At its own listing.
- ➢ See: Little Italy.
- ➢ See: Lombard Street.

Ivy Lane - The City. Dates from at least 1285. "Ivy" is a corruption of its original name; it was called Ivy Lane from at least 1666. Named for the type of plant growing on houses here.

-J-

Jack Ketch - How executioners were known, named for the man who bungled the beheading of the Duke of Monmouth (d.1685.) It took five blows of the axe to finally do the job, although even then it required a surgeon's knife to completely separate his head and body. While technically still legal, people were no longer beheaded by the time of the Regency, although there were still executions. (You may care to see: punishments.)

Jack Straw's Castle -

- ➢ See: Hampstead Heath/Jack Straw's Castle.
- ➢ See under the INNS/PUBS section.

Jack the Ripper - Began his Whitechapel and Spitalfields murders in 1888. His identity yet remains unknown. (See: Inns of Court/Temple (1st entry)/Inner Temple/King's Bench Walk/9.)

Jackson's, "Gentleman" - Pugilism establishment.

- ➢ See: Bond Street/Old Bond Street/4.
- ➢ See: Gentleman Jackson's, under G.

Jacob's Island - East Southwark. By the early 19th century, this area was beginning to decline; by the 1840s, this area was derelict slums. Now Jacob Street. (See: Southwark/Jacob's Island.)

- London Street: (See under L.)

jail - (gaol; the two words are pronounced the same, rhymes with mail.)

- ➢ See: gaol.
- ➢ See: prisons.

Jamaica Wine House - (See: Jamaica Inn, under the INNS/PUBS section.)

James Lock Co. - Hatters/haberdashers. (See: St. James's Street/6.)

James Smith & Sons - At the junction of Bloomsbury Street and New Oxford Street. Walking stick and umbrella shop, from 1856. (See: New Oxford Street/55.)

James Street - Covent Garden. Dates from 1635. Later called Buckingham Gate (the name change came about in Queen Victoria's time.) Now hosts some foreign embassies.

- Queen's Gallery: Nash, ca. 1830. Built as a conservatory, but converted in 1893 to a chapel; an art gallery by 1963.

Jaques of London - Originally known as: John Jaques of London, and then as Jaques and Son of London. Makes game and sports equipment, since 1795. Founded by a descendant of a French Huguenot. The grandson developed the family company's reputation as makers of bone, hardwood, ivory, and Tunbridge Ware (intricately inlaid woodwork, usually as boxes) games, from about 1849 and forward. Moved to Edenbridge, Kent in 2000.

Jericho - Oxford (not London.) A working-class neighborhood in the 19th century, an Oxford suburb outside its ancient city walls. It's thought the name "Jericho" reflected that this area was "remote," that is, outside Oxford's walls. Mostly Victorian; grew following the 1790 Oxford Canal coming in.

Jermyn Street - St. James's Square, Mayfair, Westminster. Built ca. 1667. Elegant street of tailors, shirtmakers for men (which came to the district in the 19th C.,) jewelers, perfumers. Described as quiet and charming.

- 71-72: Turnbull & Asser, shirtmakers. Very high end. Founded in 1885 at 3 Church Place, St. James's, by John Arthur Turnbull, hosier and shirtmaker. Asser joined in 1893, and his name was added in 1895. Located here in Jermyn Street since 1903.
- 76: St. James's Royal Hotel. (See under S.)
- 87: Sir Isaac Newton lived here 1697-1709. (May have lived at 88 for a short while before then.) Number 87 no longer exists.
- 89: Floris. (Also known as: J. Floris.) The barber Spaniard who founded it in 1730 was named Juan Famenias Floris; he was so successful at selling perfumes (that were reminiscent of Spain) that he eventually ceased cutting hair to just sell scented items. Sold bath oils, perfumes, soap, and toiletries; still today. World renown perfumer. The premises began here, although were extended over the years to the space it occupies today.
- 93: Paxton & Whitfield. Cheeses. Established in 1797 (from a 1742 cheese stall in Aldwych Market.) Small shop. Would have had another name in the Regency, perhaps named for the then-owner Sam Cullum, who took on the partners Paxton and Whitfield. Royal Warrant since 1850.
- 97: Harvie & Hudson, shirtmakers. Established in 1929 in Duke Street. Moved in

the 1960s to Jermyn Street, at which time this shirtmaker blossomed as a business. Its shop front dates from Victorian times.

- Davidoff: Cigar merchant, from 1980.
- Grima: 20th century jewelers.

Jerusalem Chamber - Westminster Abbey. A 14th C. abbot's retiring room, where Henry IV died. Bible revision committees have met here.

Jewels, Crown - (See: Tower of London/Crown Jewels.)

Jewel House, the - Through the centuries and a good half dozen moves, wherever the crown jewels have been stored becomes known as the Jewel House, even if it has another name such as Wakefield Tower. (See: Tower of London/Crown Jewels.)

Jewel House - Westminster. An ancient building, not to be confused with the Jewel House (and other places of storage) in the Tower of London. This Jewel House was a small stone building located across Abingdon Street (from what would later be the 1834 Houses of Parliament.) It is set in a tiny moat. Along with Westminster Hall, this building is the only other remaining vestige of the old Palace of Westminster. Built in 1366 by Edward III to house his treasure - royal plate and jewelry, the first set of Crown Jewels. Due to the theft attempt here, his successor, however, sent the crown jewels to the Tower of London. (See: Tower of London/Crown Jewels/First Set.)

Served as the Weights and Measures Office from 1869-1938. This location is now a small museum.

jewelry - There were shops specifically for jewelry, but it could also be bought at some circulating libraries.

- See: Bond Street/New Bond Street/165-169.
- See: diamond.
- See: Garrard.
- see: Gray's, Thomas.
- See: Hatton Garden.
- See: Jermyn Street.
- See: Ludgate Street/Rundell & Bridge.
- See: Pall Mall/Schomberg House.
- See: Soho/Church Street.

Jewish areas - Parts of the city where a Jewish population tended to reside.

- See: Jewry Street.
- See: Kensington/Notting Hill.
- See: Mile End Road - London's first Jewish burial ground.
- See: Old Jewry.

- See: Stamford Hill.
- See: synagogue.

Jewish immigrants - In 1796 there were some 20,000 Jews in London, with 5-6,000 more in port towns. The Jewish were not given a lot of rights in 18-19th century Britain (nor were they before then); for centuries they were allowed in London only under the tolerance of whichever king/queen reigned, and the privilege was sometimes withdrawn. The notable wave of Jewish immigrants into the East End followed the Industrial Revolution. The Jewish Disabilities Bill passed in 1859. The first Jewish baronet was created in 1841, Sir Isaac Lyon Goldsmid (one of the founders of the University of London.)

- See: Highgate Hill/Cromwell House.
- See: Kensington/Notting Hill.
- See: rough places.

Jockey Club -

- See: jockeys.
- See: Newmarket/Jockey Club.
- See under the CLUBS section.

jockeys - Those who rode horses in races. Existed by (and before) the Regency. Have always worn a kind of "uniform" very like what jockeys wear now: breeches with stockings (rather than trousers,) a fitted, button-up-the-front short coat with long sleeves, and a cap with a little brim (somewhere between a baseball cap and a beanie in appearance.) They have worn, at least sometimes, specific colored shirts to designate the owner of the horse they were riding; by at least 1841 a person's racing silks (colors) had to be registered. Of course, not all horses in races were ridden by jockeys, as Regency era men often enough raced their own horses, especially in less formal races. (See: Jockey Club, in the CLUBS section.)

John Adam Street - At first known as: John Street, 1760s. Is now known as John Adam Street. Runs parallel to the Strand; is on the west side of Adam Street. Hosts the Royal Society of Arts, the fine front entrance hall of which was built by John Adam.

- Adelphi/John Street: (See under A.) John Adam Street is one of the four streets built as part of the Adelphi complex.
- Society of Arts Hall: Built by the Adams brothers in 1772-4 as part of the Adelphi complex. (See: Royal Society of Arts, under R.)

John Bull - A character used to denote Britain overall, much as Uncle Sam represents America, albeit more a "beer, dogs, and the quiet life" everyman. Created in 1712 by a political satirist.

John Lobb - Shoes. (See: St. James's Street/9.)

John Murray - Publisher. Some of its authors: Jane Austen, Lord Byron, Sir Arthur Conan

Doyle.

- See: Albemarle Street/50.
- See: Quarterly Review.

John Street - (See: Adelphi.) This was the street's original name, but is now known as: John Adam Street. (See at its own listing.) Some 18th C. parts still exist here.

Johnson Street - Camden. (See: Somers Town/29 Johnson Street.)

Joiners' Company - (AKA: the Worshipful Company of Joiners and Ceilers.) Grew out of the Guild of St. James Garlickhythe, in 1375. Over time, those who worked with wood were called: fusters, carvers, or joiners. They received their Royal Charter in 1571, granted to the Joiners and Ceilers. ("Ceilers" is from Italian for "carvers"; they made ceiling and wall wood paneling.)

At first (medieval) Joiners joined timber (by mortice and tenon, there were no nails,) but since on a larger scale such work belonged to the Carpenters' Company, the Joiners evolved into persons who did furniture work and carving.

Traditionally, the Joiners were different from the Carpenters in that carpenters used pegs (later, nails) while joiners used adhesives to join wood. They have no Hall. 41st in the order of precedence. (See: Furniture-makers' Company - The notes at.)

Jonathan's Coffee House - (Also seen spelled as "Jonathen" and Johnathen.") Opened in 1680. Next door to Garraway's Coffee House in Exchange Alley.

(See the paragraph under: Royal Exchange, that refers to how the stock dealers came to be in the coffee-houses.)

Stock-jobbers (dealers) moved from the Royal Exchange to this corner location on Threadneedle Street (in Exchange Alley, soon shortened to Change Alley) about the middle of the 18th century. In 1748, the alley burned.

In 1773 Jonathan's ceased to be available, so the newly called "Stock Exchange" moved to Sweetings Alley (in Threadneedle.) A larger building was acquired in Capel Court and opened in 1802 by some disaffected brokers. It quickly grew to a number of 500 (this being most of the original dealers at Threadneedle Street.) In 1812 the rules of the Stock Exchange were printed for the first time, and the control of stockbroking was on its way.

A new building was needed by 1888; again in 1972. Women weren't allowed on the floor until 1973.

- See: coffee houses.
- See: Stock Exchange.

Jordan's Meeting House and Burial Ground - Built in 1688. Still preserved by the Society of Friends (Quakers,) because this was the Friends' first meeting place in London. William Penn, founder of Pennsylvania/USA and his family are buried here.

journals - That is, those printings that would later evolve into magazines, although sometimes the terms were used interchangeably. Also called "monthly periodicals." (See: magazines.)

Jubilee Gardens - 122 Belvedere Road, South Bank. Laid out in 1977 for Queen Elizabeth II's silver jubilee.

Justerini and Brooks - Wine merchants. (See: St. James's Street/Justerini.)

justices of the peace - (AKA: magistrates.) First mentioned in 1361 (but had existed prior, possibly from Richard I's time.) Voluntary and unpaid (and always were) lay magistrates; were local; largely country gentlemen and, as the 16th century advanced, more and more a JP might be a local clergy. Handled non-capital offenses. The magistrates were crown appointments made through the lord chancellor, who usually selected via the advice of the county's lords lieutenant. They could judge local problems such as drunkenness, Sunday trading, vagrancy, etc., punishment consisting of fines or public chastisement. Two justices, and on to three, could band to judge more serious crimes, with the more serious (such as unlicensed alehouse keepers or runaway servants) being held for the King's judges/Assize Courts (which were abolished and became the Crown Courts in 1972.) The justices didn't just judge, but were responsible for things such as licensing, road-building, regulating fairs, and appointing constables. (See: Quarter Sessions.)

-K-

Keats Grove - Not so known during the Regency era. (See: Hampstead/Wentworth Place.)

Kempshott - (See: Hampshire/Kempshott Park, in the BRITISH COUNTIES section.)

Ken Wood - Park. Obtained for public use in 1922-27. Not to be confused with Kenwood.

Kennington - Lambeth/Southwark. (Not to be confused with Kensington.) A royal palace was built here in 1337, when Kennington was given to Edward, the Black Prince. No longer exists, but the manor yet belongs to the eldest son of the monarch as part of the Duchy of Cornwall. Leases were granted to residents beginning in 1622. When Westminster Bridge (1750) brought easier access, Kennington became popular. Elegant 18th C. terraces; became truly respectable in the 1820s.

- Borough High Street: (See under B.)
- Kennington Common: Executions and fairs were held here. In 1852 it was converted into a recreational area, called Kennington Park.
- Oval Cricket Ground: (AKA: Kennington Oval. AKA simply as: the Oval.) This

is the Surrey County Cricket Club's grounds. (See under S.) In the 17th C. flowers, fruits, and vegetables were grown here. The "oval" name comes from a street layout design of 1790 (although never fully executed.) Converted from a market-garden in 1844 when the Montpelier Cricket Club leased ground here following eviction from Walworth. Opened in 1845. The Surrey Cricket Club started in the nearby Horns Tavern; the latter first played at the Oval in 1846.

- St. Mark's: Kennington Park Road. 1822-4. On the site where the gallows had been.
- Surrey Zoological Gardens, August, 1831.
- Trinity Square: 1823-4. (See: Trinity Church Square, under T.)

Kennington Park - (See: Kennington/Kennington Common.)

Kennington Park Road - Row of Georgian houses. (See: Kennington/St. Mark's.)

- Kennington Tollgate - Junction at the Clapham and the Brixton Roads. Dates from ca. 1773.

Kensal Green Cemetery - Formed in 1832, in response to the overcrowded cemeteries already in existence, which had caused the latest cholera outbreak. (Kensal Green, as a district, is on the north side of Harrow Road, but the cemetery is on the opposite side, within Kensington.)

Kensington - Kensington/Chelsea. (Not to be confused with: Kennington.) Began its existence in Saxon times; is listed in Domesday book, 1086. Surprisingly, did not develop and was a rural village well into the 19th century (however Kensington Square dates from William III's reign.) One hour from London on horseback. A place for brick and tile manufactories.

The population in 1811 was 10,886 (by the 1840s it was seven times more.)

Not made a Royal Borough until done so by Edward VII to honor his mother, Victoria's, death, 1901.

- Abbey House: 1860s. Currently a Bed & Breakfast (hotel.)
- Addison Road: Built 1820s. West of Holland House.
    - 23: St. Barnabas's Church: North Kensington, 1830.
- Allen Street: Ca. 1820.
- Aster House: Part of a Victorian terrace. Now a Bed & Breakfast (hotel.)
- Aubrey Street.
    - Aubrey House: Medieval origins. 18th C. rebuild. Large. Garden is two acres. The house was built on the site of Kensington Wells. Never open to the public. (See: Kensington Wells, below.)
- Campden Hill: On the north side of Kensington High Street. Has several old mansions, including Campden House. Their residents were so grand that the area

was given the nickname "The Dukeries" by locals in Victorian days.

  - See: Campden Hill, under C.
  - See: Holland Park/Campden House.

- Campden Hill Road: James South (b. 1785-d.1867) lived here in 1831, building in his garden the world's largest telescope (at that time.) He was a co-founder of the Astronomical Society of London; became the Royal Astronomical Society in 1831.
- Campden Hill Square: Later name of Notting Hill Square; name changed from Notting Hill Square to Campden Hill Square in 1893.
- Campden House:
  - See: Campden Hill/Campden Hill House.
  - See: Holland Park/Campden House.
- Campden House Court: Row of houses, 1897.
- Campden Place: A rookery/slum area since 1651 when it was purchased for use as a parochial charity. Cleared in 1868. Its two side streets were Anderson's Cottages and Pitt's Cottages (with 50 houses between them, of very poor quality.) Is now a tall home called Clanricarde Gardens, 1869-73.
- Church Lane: Name of a portion of the street later known as Kensington Church Street (along with Silver Street.) Linked Kensington to Notting Hill Gate. Still has some fine 18th C. homes along here.
  - 128 Kensington Church Street (known as Church Lane during the Regency): Muzio Clementi, Italian-born English composer, lived here sometime prior to 1832 (the year of his death.)
- Colby House: Replaced by Victorian flats in 1873, but had stood for two centuries.
- Coleherne House: Home to Lady Ponsonby, widow of Major-General Sir William Ponsonby, KCB, killed at the battle of Waterloo on 6/18/1815. (Now is Coleherne Court, 1901-3 flats.)
- Cromwell Road: Originally called Cromwell Lane (after one of Oliver Cromwell's son, Richard, who lived here.) Took on "Road" (over "Lane") at the time of the railway lines.
- Derry Street: Current name of King Street, since 1938. (See: King Street, below.)
- Devonshire Arms: Mid 19th C. pub; still exists.
- Drayson Mews: (See under D.)
- Dukeries, the: (See: Campden Hill, above.)
- Earl's Court House: Home of the anatomist John Hunter. He died in 1795. Had

4-5 succeeding owners; now flats.

- Earl's Court Road: Formerly called Earl Street and Earl's Court Lane.
- Fulham Broadway: (See: Walham Green, below.)
- Gore House: (See under G.)
- High Street: Kensington/Chelsea. In modern times is sometimes referred to as "High Street Kensington." Not really known as a shopping venue until the mid 19th C., at which time it is described as narrow and crowded with traffic. Cleared and bettered in the 1860s.
    - Messrs Herbert & Jones, confectioners. (See: Herbert & Jones, under H.)
- Holland House: (See under H.)
- Holland Park: (See under H.)
- Horticultural Society of London: (See: Royal Horticultural Society, under R.)
- Imperial College of Science and Technology: 1909-12.
- Imperial Institute: 1893.
- Independent Chapel: 1793. Pulled down in 1929.
- Kensington Canal: 2-1/4 mile (3.6 km) long, 100 feet wide. Opened August, 1828. Filled in ca. 1863 to form the West London Railway.
- Kensington Church Street:
    - ➢ See: Church Lane, above.
    - ➢ See: Silver Street, below.
- Kensington Court: (See: Kensington House, below.)
- Kensington Gardens: (See: Kensington Palace/Kensington Gardens.)
- Kensington Gate (Square): 1847.
- Kensington Gore: (See: Gore House, under G.)
- Kensington High Street: In the early 19th C. was little more than a country lane, and was called Kensington Road. Now houses a collection of high end and fashion businesses.
    - Our Lady of Victories' Church: 1869. Roman Catholic.
    - St. Mary Abbot's: (See, below.)
- Kensington House: 1882-83, replaced by Victorian flats, but had stood for two centuries. (Kensington Court was later erected in its place.)
- Kensington Palace: (See at its own listing.)
- Kensington Road: (See: Kensington High Street, above.)
- Kensington Square: 1681-5, by Thomas Young. Located on the south side of Kensington High Street. Communal garden added in 1698, not open to the public. Surrounded by fields until 1840. Has always been a fashionable address.

(See: Kensington Square, at its own listing.)

  - 11 and 12: Built in the late 17th C, particularly attractive.

- Kensington Wells: An early 18th C. spa. Replaced by Aubrey House sometime prior to 1845.
- Kensington Workhouse: Kensington Green. 1849. Then became St. Mary Abbot's Hospital. Now is Stone Hall (a residential complex.)
- King Street: Dates back to at least the mid 17th century. Is now called Derry Street, since 1938.
- Ladbroke Grove: (See under L.)
- Lindsey Row: (See under L.)
- Mall, the: 1868 houses.
- Melbury Road: Victorian.
- Norland Square: 1845.
- North Kensington: Kind of a vague area, generally west of Ladbroke Grove and north of Westway. Was always a poorer district. Not much here until the mid 19th C., after which it was nicknamed "Soapsuds Island" because of its laundries. CHAMBERS LONDON GAZETTEER notes: "North Kensington was a genuine part of the medieval parish" (as opposed to West Kensington, which was not) "but has never been a prestigious locality." (See: Potteries, below.)
  - Notting Barns Farm: Here until at least the mid 19th century.
- Notting Hill: Called Notting Dale in Georgian/Regency times; would have been home to poor Irish and Jewish immigrants. Ca. 1823 was called Ladbroke Grove, then later sometimes called Kensington Park. An area where the few houses (very rural, despite being only 3 miles/4.8 km from London,) all had pigs in the yard; described at the time as housing "farms, potteries, and piggeries." The Saturday night markets were not here until the late 19th century. Began to develop after the railway came in. In modern times the area is known for its racial and ethnic diversity. (See: Ladbroke Grove.)
  - Kensington Park Gardens: 1840s-50s. A housing development, not to be confused with the gardens of Kensington Park. (See: Queen's Road, Kensington, under Q.)
  - Notting Hill farmhouse: In 1845 St. John's was built on this farmhouse's site. (Also was briefly a racing course from 1837-41.)
  - Notting Hill Gate: Slum area/poor.
  - Portobello Road: Victorian road. (See under P.)
- Notting Hill Square: Former name of Campden Hill Square. (See, above.)

- Nottingham House: 1689. (See: Kensington Palace, in the first paragraph.)
- Oakwood Court: Built ca. 1900-3.
- Olympia: First called the National Agricultural Hall, aiming at being the largest UK covered show center. Renamed in 1886 to: Olympia. Was extended in the 1920s.
- Phillimore Terraces: Four terraces, ca. 1787. The one remaining terrace is nicknamed "Dishclout Terrace" because of a drapery swag carved on a high stone on each house; three-quarters of the terraces were pulled down in 1931.
- Potteries, the: Later also known as North Kensington, suburb to Kensington. (See: North Kensington, above.)
- Queen's Road: (See: Kensington Palace Gardens, the 1st entry of that name.)
- Queensberry Place:
    - 8-10: The Gallery (hotel.) Had been Georgian residences.
- Royal Crescent: 1845.
- Royal Geographical Society: Founded in 1830. (See under R.)
- St. Mary Abbot's: (Also seen as: St. Mary Abbots.) 278 foot spire; 1696 building; present building from 1869-72, by Sir Gilbert Scott, in Modern Gothic style. Kensington High Street. There was a church here since before the year 1111 (when it added "Abbot's" to its name, being annexed to the Abbey of Abingdon.) Is the Kensington parish church. (See under the CHURCHES section.)
- Silver Street: Name of a portion of the street later known as Kensington Church Street.
    - St. Olave, Silver Street: (See under the CHURCHES section.)
- South Kensington: Mostly built 1862-77. (See under S.)
- Walham Green: Hammersmith & Fulham, (now West Kensington.) North side of Fulham Road. First mentioned in 1383. Before 1688 it was known as Wansdown Green (from the Manor of Wendon.) Was a traditional English village green through the 17th C. with a pond, pub, stocks, and a whipping post. In the 18th C., gave way to rows of houses. In the 19th C., became terraced streets. Called Walham Green into the late 19th C.; now called Fulham Broadway.
    - Butchers' Almhouses: 1840.
    - St. John: In North End Road, 1827-8.
- Walnut Tree Walk: Earlier name of the 1869-72 Radcliffe Gardens.
- West Kensington: Ca. 1880. Is not in Kensington Borough, it is actually in Hammersmith. It had formerly been Fulham's lowly North End.

- Wright's Lane: In the 1690s, this was little more than a footpath. Broadened in the 1770s.
- Young Street: Built ca. 1680.
    - 13: William Makepeace Thackery (author, b.1811-d.1875) lived here for a large part of his life.

Kensington Church Street - (See: Kensington/Church Lane.)

Kensington Gardens - (See: Kensington Palace/Kensington Gardens.)

Kensington Gore - (See: Gore House.)

Kensington High Street - Currently houses many high end and fashion stores. (See: Kensington/Kensington High Street.)

Kensington New Town - 1840s. Described as "delightful streets" around Albert Place, Launceston Place, and Victoria Road; also as a very large cul-de-sac.

Kensington Palace - First built for Sir George Coppin (clerk of the Crown to James I) as his manor house. Later, was bought by the Earl of Nottingham, who then named it *Nottingham House.*

Wren (with Hawksmoor) converted the house into a Royal Palace (Kensington Palace, but called simply "Kensington House" up to about 1750) for William of Orange (AKA: William III) and Mary in 1689-91. Before this rebuild of the house, however, Wren had already reshaped the gardens - Queen Anne didn't care for the severe Dutch style he developed, so Wren's first work was dug over and redone. (See: Kensington Palace/Kensington Gardens, below.) William III moved here because of his health and need for clean air.

George I extended the palace; it has changed significantly little since. It is said of the palace's design: "Very noble, though not greate." Plain red brick, 2 stories high. The State Rooms date from George I, as do the murals you see today in the King's Staircase.

The palace, although located in Kensington, is attached to the City of Westminster.

George III chose to live in Buckingham House instead of here, so Kensington Palace was then pretty much abandoned, at least until some royal children took apartments here in the early 19th C.; at this time James Wyatt made extensive neo-classical alterations.

At the beginning of the 19th C., part of the park was still swampy, and keepers still hunted fox here.

Queen Victoria was born here in 1819; brought up here.

The park's trees include: sweet chestnuts, red oaks, ash, and weeping willows.

- Albert Memorial: 1863. Enlarged in 1872.
- Broad Walk: 50 feet wide, lined on both sides by large elm trees. Runs from

Palace Gate to Bayswater Road.

- Dog's Cemetery: 1880.
- Flower Walk: 1843.
- Kensington Gardens: The land had been part of Hyde Park (which in Tudor times was twice as large as it is now.) Was separated from Hyde Park in 1728, by request of Queen Caroline. Was at first a private garden for Kensington Palace. Shared by the City of Westminster and with Kensington and Chelsea Borough. 270 acres.

  George II opened the park to "the public," but this meant "respectable persons," not just anyone: "No soldiers, sailors or servants were permitted." (The select few would be given a key by which to open the park gates.)

  Then, in the early 19th C. George III opened the park up to the general public (but again it was stressed these were to be "respectably dressed people,") but only on Saturdays. Jane Austen used to stroll on the grounds here in 1811.

  The last duel fought here was in 1822.

  William IV opened the park fully to the public for any day of the week, although several sources say it was Victoria who did this in 1841.

  The land around Kensington Garden remained largely undeveloped until following the Great Exhibition of 1851.

  - Elfin Oak: 900 year old stump, elaborately carved with animals, gnomes, and the like, moved to Kensington Gardens in 1928.
- Lido, the: A swimming area and its attendant building, 1930.
- Long Water, the: Was created by diverting the Westbourne Stream, done under Queen Caroline's direction, ca. 1730. The Long Water is the same as the Serpentine (as it extends out of Hyde Park, essentially six connected pools) but here it is known as the Long Water. Wooded. This is where Harriet Westbrook (wife to Percy Blythe Shelley) committed suicide in 1816.
- Orangery, the: Added by Queen Anne. Supposedly built by Sir Christopher Wren, 1704 (during the time Hawksmoor ran Wren's offices.) Was, as its name implies, used as a forcing garden for oranges. Is currently a tea room of the same name. (See: Orangery, the, under O.)
- Peter Pan statue: 1912. In a small dell near the Long Water.
- Refreshment pavilion: (By the stone bridge dividing it from Hyde Park.) 1930. There was a "rustic teahouse" here prior to then.
- Rotten Row: Led through Hyde Park to the Palace. (See: Hyde Park/Rotten Row, under H.)

- Round Pond: Dates from the 18th C., at which time it was octagonal. Is in the park's center.
- Serpentine: (See: Long Water, above.)
- Sunken Garden: 1909.
- Temple: In 1726-7, a small temple was built at the southeast corner of the gardens, probably by William Kent. It became part of Temple Lodge.

Kensington Park Gardens (street) - 1850s. (See: Kensington/Notting Hill/Kensington Park Gardens.) Not to be confused with Kensington Gardens, part of Kensington Palace.

Kensington Square - Laid out in 1685. The oldest square in Kensington. House numbers 11, 12, 18, and 41 yet remain. Gardens laid out in 1698. This area remained rural until the 1840s. Was originally called King's Square, and on some maps the original name of King's Square lasts "late," (otherwise showing the area as simply labeled "Square.") There is definitely an 1890 map that labels it "Kensington Square." The name Kensington Square probably was used far earlier, influenced by the nearby Kensington Palace, but evidence is elusive.

- See: Kensington/Kensington Square.
- See: King's Square/Kensington.

Kent - (The county of.) The oldest surviving place name in Britain. (See: Kent, under the BRITISH COUNTIES section.)

Kent House - Bromley. Takes its name from a house that once was the first building seen in Kent on the road from London. Had been a Norman owned estate, half of which was leased in 1240 to the Hospital of St. Katherine by the Tower; Kent House stood at this time. City merchants owned the house over the next few centuries. In 1784 John Julius Angerstien (Russian banker, and Lloyds insurer) bought the house. In ca. 1806 it became a farmhouse, 178 acres. There was middle-class housing on this estate ca. the 1880s. Kent House went on to be a nursing home, then a private hotel. Demolished in 1957, its site covered by Beckett Walk.

Kent Street - Southwark. Existed by at least 1756.

Kent Street - Tabard Street. Kent Street was the original name of Tabard Street. It was the old road (medieval) to Canterbury, Dover, and Greenwich. Near the Lock Hospital/Hyde Park Corner. Renamed to Tabard Street in 1877.

Kent Terrace - Designed by John Nash; built by William Smith in 1827. Named for Prinny's brother Edward, Duke of Kent. It is considered part of the Regent's Park development by Nash, but it faces toward Park Road, away from the park. The flat roof was covered in zinc, a then new invention.

Kentish Town - Dates from at least 1416. In the 1820s was an outlying village to the south of Hampstead, not built up until the 1880s. (See: Camden - The note under.) CHAMBERS

LONDON GAZETTEER states: "The settlement evolved as a ribbon development on the road to Highgate and there is some evidence that it moved northwards to its present location, having first begun near St. Pancras Church; indeed, it may be that St. Pancras and Kentish Town were originally one and the same place." In the 17-18th centuries, was known for its highwaymen attacks here. In the 1860s the last of the grazing land disappeared.

- 2 Wesleyan Place: John Keats (poet, d. 1821) lived here in summers in the last few years of his life.

Kenton - Harrow, and Brent. Northwest London. An ancient hamlet, 13th century. Was still an agricultural village by the late 19th century; was somewhat inaccessible, so gentlemen's country seats did not spring up here. (See: South Kenton - Which is distinct from Kenton.)

Kent's Treasury - (AKA: Treasury, the.) In Horse Guards Parade. (See: Whitehall/Treasury.)

Kenwood - Not to be confused with Ken Wood. (See: Hampstead Heath/Kenwood.)

Kenwood House - Hampstead Lane, on the edge of Hampstead Heath, on Hampstead Hill. First built in the 1600s. Rebuilt in 1767-9, by Robert Adam, for the Chief Justice, Lord Mansfield. Again, ca. 1795 by George Saunders (including the Marble Hall.) LET'S GO-THE BUDGET GUIDE TO LONDON says: "...a picture-perfect example of an 18th century country estate." Bequeathed to the nation in 1927. Neoclassical. (See: Hampstead Heath/Kenwood House.)

Keppel Street - Russell Square, Bloomsbury. Existed since at least the 18th century. Circa 1810 this street was peopled with the working classes - for instance, lawyers.

- 16: Anthony Trollope (author) was born here in 1815.

kerosene - Came along in the 1850s. (See: lamps.)

Ketch, Jack - Famous executioner. (See: Jack Ketch, under J.)

Kevington - Bromley. (AKA: Kevingtown.) Rural hamlet. CHAMBERS LONDON GAZETTEER says: "The Ordnance Survey map of 1876 shows Kevingtown and Kevinton as two separate places, the former at the top of the hill, the latter on its western slope. However, this distinction no longer applies. The manor of Kevington was in the hands of the related Manning and Onslow families from the late Middle Ages to the mid 18th century, when Middleton Onslow sold it to Herman Behrens, a City merchantman from Amsterdam who commissioned the construction of Kevington Hall, completed in 1769 by the architect Sir Robert Taylor." Held by the Behrens until WWII.

Kew - Richmond. Described as an attractive village. First records from 1327. The Tudors made Richmond upon Thames one of the court seats, and Kew provided housing for their courtiers.

- See: Kew Gardens.

  - See: Kew Palace.
- Kew Green: Surrounded by old mansions.
  - St. Anne: 1714, Kew Palace; near the gardens. Queen Anne granted the land, and public subscription provided the funds to build the church. (There had been a 16th C. chapel, not necessarily exactly here.) The painter Thomas Gainsborough was buried in St. Anne's churchyard in 1788.
- Public Record Office: Ruskin Avenue. Mid 1870s. Replaced a Chancery Lane building. (See under P.)
- St. Anne's Chapel: (See: Kew Green/St. Anne's.)

Kew Bridge - Present version: 1903. (See under the BRIDGES section.)

Kew Gardens - ("Kew" means a "neck" jutting out, in this case into the Thames.) Kew, Richmond, Surrey. A mile (1.6 km) from Richmond, on the south side of the Thames.

CHAMBERS LONDON GAZETTEER notes: "The gardens are a convergence of three 17th century projects: the Dutch House and the White House and their grounds, and the northward expansion of the royal gardens of Richmond upon Thames. Over the first three decades of the 18th century, and especially during the reign of George II, several properties in Kew were acquired or built for members of the royal household either as permanent residences or places of leisure. The Dutch House became Kew Palace, while the White House was rebuilt as the home of Frederick, Princes of Wales and his wife Princess Augusta."

Charles Bridgeman and William Kent were appointed in the early 1730s by Queen Caroline to add decorative buildings and enhance the landscape.

Capability Brown heavily altered the grounds in 1770. Ca. the 1770s, the director of the gardens was Joseph Banks; he imported, cultivated, and exported exotic plants from/to Britain's colonies.

Kew's various gardens were united in 1802. The Royal Botanical Society of London was founded in 1839. (See, below.) It is in charge of the Royal Botanical Gardens, Kew Gardens; as such, is still used for botanical studies.

Became a national botanical garden in 1841, at which time it was also designated a royal park. (Note: it had included a public pleasure garden since the 17th century.)

Victorian directors added the commodities of tea, coffee, rubber, quinine, cotton, and more, and kept the gardens scientific, as opposed to a pleasure garden.

(See: Kew Palace.)

- Follies: A series of garden follies were added in the 18th C.; still to be seen.
- Great Palm House: Built in 1848; Decimus Burton claimed the build, but really

the credit goes to Richard Turner of Dublin.

- Kew Green: (See at its own listing.)
- Kew House: (See at its own listing.)
- Kew Observatory: (See at its own listing.)
- Kew Palace: (See at its own listing.)
- Maids of Honour: Still the home of the tarts (as in treats, not doxies) named for the position of the woman who originated them. Described as a quaint, rambling cottage, its address is 288 Kew Road.
- Observatory: (See: Kew Observatory, at its own listing.)
- Pagoda: (AKA: the Chinese Pagoda.) In the southeast corner of the park. Dates from 1757-62. 165 feet (10-stories) high; octagonal; designed by Sir William Chambers.
- Palm House: (See: Great Palm House, above.)
- Princess of Wales Conservatory: 1987. Named for Diana, late wife of Prince Charles.
- Rhododendron Dell: Built by Capability Brown. Still there.
- Richmond Lodge: Prior names were: Ormonde Lodge; the Keeper's Lodge. Capability Brown redesigned its gardens for George III and Queen Charlotte in 1765, although the lodge itself was pulled down in the 1770s. (See under R.)
- Royal Botanical Society of London: (AKA: Royal Botanical Society.) Founded in 1839. It is in charge of the Royal Botanical Gardens; Kew Gardens, as such, is still used for botanical studies.
- Syon House: (See under S.)
- Temperate House: Victorian, designed by Decimus Burton, 1860-63. First called the Winter Garden.

Kew House - During George II's reign (1727-1760,) Kew House was an alternate name for Kew Palace. AKA: the Old Palace. (See: Kew Palace.)

Kew observatory - Old Deer Park (n. of Twickenham Road,) Kew Gardens, Richmond. 1769. Designed for George III, by Sir William Chambers.

Kew Palace - Richmond. (During George II's reign, Kew House was an alternate name for Kew Palace. AKA: the Old Palace.) A red brick, 3-story Jacobean mansion built in 1631 by Sir Hugh Portman, a Dutch merchant; because it was built for a Dutchman and had distinctive Dutch-style gables, this house was at first called the Dutch House. It was leased as a royal residence since 1730.

LONDON by Knopf Guides says that Augusta, dowager Princess of Wales, owned this estate in 1759, at which time she allotted some of the property to a botanical garden.

Bought by Queen Charlotte (wife to George III) in 1761 as a summer home. George III was the only monarch to live there, confined from 1802 while doctors tried to manage his "madness."

Kew Palace was demolished in 1802, at which time the nearby White House became known as Kew Palace; during George III's time here (1802-1818, the latter date being the year Queen Charlotte died) he wanted a rebuild, but it was left undone as the house closed in 1818. Prinny spent most of his childhood here (and did not have fond memories of its dankness.)

Acquired by Kew in 1898. Opened to the public, with an April 4th, 2019 reopening. (See: Kew Gardens.)

Kidbrooke - Greenwich. Ancient manor, decimated in the 14th C. by the Black Death. Provided quality timber in the early 19th C. to London. Also hosted some market-gardens, but mostly used as grazing land until the 1860s.

Kilburn - Brent/Camden. District north of Maida Vale, 2 miles/3.2 km from Oxford Street. Principally was one long street forming a portion of Edgeware Road. To its east was mostly open country. Once was a hermitage here, converted into a convent called Kilburn Priory, now gone. During the Regency it would have been known as Kilburn Wells (also seen as: Kilbourn Wells.) The area did not really develop until the 1850s.

- Kilburn Wells: (See at its own listing.)
- Old Bell Tavern: (Also seen as: Bell Inn.) Dates from at least the early 18th century. As of 1957, was still standing, though rebuilt. Built on where the old Kilbourne manor house had been. There was a turnpike gate nearby, abolished in 1868.
- Queen's Park Estate: 1870s.

Kilburn Park - Brent/Westminster. 1850s development.

Kilburn Wells - A spring off of the Westbourne; in 1714 there was discovered a well here; became the Kilburn Wells spa. Was popular into the 19th century.

kilt, Scottish - The Scottish short or walking kilt (as opposed to the full length cloak from which it developed) came along in the 18th century. After Bonnie Prince Charlie's 1745 uprising, all forms of Highland dress were banned (excluding for Highland troops serving in the British army;) lifted when kilts and clan tartans were given a royal thumbs up when George IV wore one in an 1822 visit to Scotland. The (short) kilt was practical battle gear, in that it was less likely to get caught up in the thistles and thorns of the battlefield.

Irish kilts: The subject is debated, but Irish kilts are generally said to have originated in the 1890s.

King Edward Street - (See: Stinking Lane.)

King George V Dock - 1921. (See: docks/King George V Dock.)

King Square - Islington. Built 1822-25, on land belonging to St. Bartholomew's Hospital. Named for George IV. During Victoria's reign, this area became a poorer one, with the homes being divided into smaller dwellings. WWII damaged much of the area, and it was pulled down in the 1950s. Finsbury Borough built the new King Square Estate in 1965, a little west of the original King Square Gardens.

King Street - Covent Garden. (See: Covent Garden/King Street.)

King Street - Golden Square. (See: Golden Square/King Street.)

King Street - Hammersmith & Fulham. Runs west from Hammersmith Broadway to Stamford Brook, and meets Chiswick High Road and Goldhawk Road. From 1717 it was a turnpike road, adding a brewery, houses, inns, and stables as the century progressed. Part of the Great West Road (until the 1950s.) Shops came in the late 19th century.

King Street - St. James's. (See: St. James's/King's Street.)

King Street - Shaftesbury Avenue, a portion of same, the latter being formed in 1886. King Street was laid out in ca. 1670 (after the Great Fire of 1666,) to connect Guildhall with the Thames, as was Queen Street.

- See: Dudley Street.
- See: Shaftesbury Avenue.

- 8: Christie's Auction House. (See under C.)

King Tudor Street - (See: Tudor Street.)

King William Street - On Fish Street Hill. 1831-5. New northern approach to the new London Bridge.

King's Arbour - Hounslow. (See: Heathrow.)

King's Bench Court - (See: Courts of Common Law and Equity/Court of King's Bench.)

King's Bench Prison - (See: Southwark/Borough High Street/King's Bench Prison.)

King's Bench Walk - (See: Inns of Court/Temple (1st entry)/King's Bench Walk.)

King's College - Cambridge; south side of the Strand; housed in the east wing of Somerset House. (See: Somerset House/King's College.) Designed by Robert Smirke in 1828-9; opened in 1834; founded by the Duke of Wellington, archbishops, and 30 bishops belonging to the Church of England. They wanted a rival for the "irreligious" University College. Students need not be Anglican, although the governors and professors must (with linguists being excepted.) It had its own building by 1831, basically an extension off the east wing of Somerset House. Pioneered evening classes in London in 1849. Became a constituent College of the University of London in 1908.

- King's College Hospital: Founded in 1840. A few blocks north of King's College.

King's Cross - Camden/Islington. Had been called Battle Bridge, (also seen as: Battlebridge.) The

King's Cross name came from the 1830 George IV statue here; the statue proved unpopular (as largely was the monarch) and was removed in 1845; the name, however, stuck. Is currently a poor district. Railway terminal, 1851-2, now made famous by J. K. Rowling's *Harry Potter* books and their tales of Platform 9-3/4.

King's Cross Road - (See: Bagnigge Wells/Bagnigge Wells Road.)

King's Library, the - The King's Library was the genesis of the British Museum Library. (See under B.)

King's Mews - (See: Royal Mews.)

King's Printer - (See: Printing House Square.)

King's Road - Through Belgravia and Chelsea. Until ca. 1829-30 was a private royal road leading from Hampton Court to the City court of the king, Whitehall. (Had to have a ticket, a special copper pass, to use it; patrolled by 29 men.) The nurseries along King's Road were considered "the best" in the 18th C., the reputation of these market-gardens was so strong that outsiders had to have "showrooms" here in order to compete. In 1830 George IV gave permission for it to be used by the public, at which time the road was largely lined with homes and inns. Shops came later in the 19th century. At Fulham, it becomes New King's Road. (See: Chelsea/King's Road.)

- 152: The Pheasantry: A private home. Described as "magnificent." Built in 1881.
- Royal Avenue: (See at R.)
- Royal Military Asylum: 1801. (See: Duke of York's Headquarters - The note under.)

King's Square - (Also seen as: Kings Square.) **Kensington Square**, original name of. Built in 1685 as King's Square. Soon known as Kensington Square, due to Kensington Palace being built nearby in 1689-91; certainly known as Kensington Square during the Regency. (Not to be confused with King's Square/Soho Square.)

- See: Kensington Square - At its own listing.
- See: Kensington/Kensington Square.

King's Square - (See: **Soho Square**.) Not to be confused with the one-time King's Square in Kensington.

King's Street - (Also seen written as: King Street.) Westminster. 1673. It is presumed it was named in honor of Charles II. Between St. James's Square and St. James's Street.

- 8: Christie's, 1823. (See under C.)
- Almack's: 1682. (See under A.)
- St. James's Theatre: 1835.

King's Weigh House Chapel - West end of Eastcheap. An early Presbyterian chapel in London (1695,) housed in a building over what used to be a royal weigh-house where "merchants stranger's" goods were measured on official scales; this weigh house had been rebuilt after the Great Fire of 1666. There was a Presbyterian congregation that went by this name well into the 19th century (although it had to move to Fish Street Hill in 1833-4 when this site was needed to improve the approach to London Bridge.) Today it is the Ukrainian Catholic Cathedral of the Holy Family in Exile.

Kingsbury - Brent. Its ancient name was Tunworth, although Domesday Book labels it Chingsberie (King's manor.) Was decimated by the Black Death in the 14th C., leaving the old village abandoned. Grew up anew around Kingsbury Green, with the old village all but forgotten by the time of the early 19th century. Little developed until 1900.

- Kingsbury Green: Several roads converged on the green in the Middle Ages. A few modest villas here by the early 19th century.
- St. Andrew's Church: Old Church Lane. Medieval. Yet exists. (There is also a newer St. Andrew's, also in Kingsbury, transported stone by stone from its Wells Street location in 1933.)

Kingston - (See: Kingston-upon-Thames.)

Kingston Bottom - Kingston. Name changed in Victorian times to Kingston Vale. Henry VIII enjoyed archery displays here, put on by locals who dressed as Robin Hood's Merry Men (despite the fact there's no such local connection.) All the same, the Tudor play-acting resulted in many Robin Hood place names locally. It boasted little more than a smithy, a few taverns, and some cottages until the early 19th century. Grand homes came in next, quickly matching (or passing) the cottage count.

- St. John the Baptist: 1847. New structure built in 1861.

Kingston House - (See: Listowel House.) Not to be confused with a later block of flats of the Kingston House name.

Kingston-upon-Thames - (Also known simply as Kingston. AKA: Kingston-on-Thames.) Was in Surrey, but since 1965 is considered to be an outlying area of London. In existence for over 1,000 years, it was a medieval marketplace. Was the coronation place for Saxon kings. Edward the Elder was crowned on the Coronation Stone (AKA: the Kingstone, it still stands near the marketplace); here since the year 900. (See: Westminster Abbey/Stone of Scone - For the later coronation stone.) Kingston is now described as "upscale suburbia."

- All Saints: Clarence Street. Some 13-15th C. parts remain. Parish church.
- Bentall & Sons, Messrs.: Departmental store, 1867.
- Clattern Bridge: 12th century. Over the River Hogsmill. Built of stone, in 1828. (See under the BRIDGES section.)
- Druid's Head: Still existing 18th C. inn.
- Kingston Bridge: 1828. (See under the BRIDGES section.)

- Kingstone:
  - ➢ See: Westminster/Stone of Scone.
  - ➢ See: Kingston-upon-Thames, above - Note at.
- Market Hall: 1840. "Fussily Victorian."
- Seething Wells: (See under S.)

Kingstone, the - Kingston-upon-Thames.

- ➢ See: Kingston-upon-Thames - Note at.
- ➢ See: Westminster Abbey/Stone of Scone.

Kingsway Theatre - (AKA simply as: the Kingsway.) 1905. (See: Great Queen Street, under the THEATRES section.)

knackers - An ancient term. Renderers of old horses/cattle. Knackery is different from slaughter in that the latter results in edible product.

Kneller Hall - 1710 mansion, by an artist named Sir Godfrey Kneller. He died here in 1723. In 1856 it became the Royal Military School of Music. Sits in the 20th C. suburb of Whitton. (See: Whitton/Kneller Hall.)

Knightrider Street - The City. Since at least 1322. (See: Giltspur Street, its older name.) Mostly demolished in the 1860s to build Queen Victoria Street.

- Horn Tavern: "Unspoiled" early 19th C. tavern. During Charles Dickens' time it was known as Horn Coffee House.

Knights of St. John of Jerusalem, the - (AKA: the Knights Hospitaller.) Their mission was to provide care of travelers. The second great order of knights (the other was the Knights Templar.) Founded their priory in Clerkenwell. Largely disbanded under Henry VIII; somewhat revived in 1888.

- ➢ See: Inns of Court/Temple (1st entry)/Inner Temple/Inner Temple Hall.
- ➢ See: Inns of Court/Temple (2nd entry.)
- ➢ See: St. John's/Clerkenwell, under the CHURCHES section.

Knights Templar - (AKA: the Poor Fellow-Soldiers of Christ and the Temple of Solomon. In Latin: Pauperes commilitones Christi Templique Salomonici. AKA: the Order of Solomon's Temple. AKA: the Templars.) They were a military order, founded in 1119, Catholic. Given papal recognition in 1139. Disbanded in 1312. (There are several references to the Knights Templar under the "Inns of Court" section.)

Knightsbridge - Westminster. West route out of London, separated from Hyde Park Corner by marshy and undeveloped land. In the 11th C. a village sprang up, taking its name from the bridge over the River Westbourne, where the unlikely tale has it that two knights battled to their deaths. The village took in work that London didn't want: the slaughter of livestock and a leper hospital.

The area between Knightsbridge and Brompton Road, during the Regency, was undeveloped and primarily occupied by nursery gardens. (At that time was known as part of Brompton.)

When this area was being (re)developed in the 1820s it was at first known as Brompton New Town; rather shabby. It seems the Brompton New Town name didn't stick much. Handsome terraces along Brompton Road (this road known then as Knightsbridge Terrace) from the 18th century. Now known for its upscale West London shopping.

- barracks, Knightsbridge: 1795. Housed up to 600 men and 500 horses. Pulled down in 1878.
- Brompton Road: (See under B.)
- Half Way (or Halfway) House: Notorious pub. Is opposite Rutland Gate.
  - ➢ See: Rutland Gate, below.
  - ➢ See under the INNS/PUBS section.
- Harrod's: (See under H.)
- Harvey Nichols, Ltd.: Linen-drapers. Corner of Knightsbridge and Sloane Street. Established 1813, "a small draper's shop." Really grew to prominence in the Victorian era. Attracted trade from ritzy customers going to Bath. Present building dates from the 1880s.
- Rutland Gate: Begun in 1838. (Opposite Knightsbridge barracks.) Opposite the western end of Rutland Gate stood, at least from 1740, an inn of poor repute, Half Way House. (See, above.) Along this road stood stables, troughs, pigsties, and other poor buildings all higgly-piggly (and unattractively) along the roadway. Surprisingly, however, it was not often frequented by footpads, possibly because of the rural nature of the surroundings (and therefore the lack of easy pickings.) Though, it must be noted that the Knights-bridge mail coach ran past here and was sometimes robbed.
- Rutland House: Large, red brick mansion, pulled down in 1833. (See under R.)
- St. George's Hospital: (See under S.)
- St. George's Place: Six houses, replaced in 1863 by the Alexandra Hotel.
- Scotch House: 1830, shopping.
- Sloane Street: Was part of the area Henry Holland built up called Hans Town. (See: Hans Town/Sloane Street.)

knitting - Knitting is an ancient art, much practiced as a home art.

- ➢ See: activities/entertainments/sports - knitting, under A.
- ➢ See: Framework Knitters' Company.

knives -

- See: Cutler's Hall -F or forks.
- See: Middle Row.
- See: weapons.

-L-

La Belle Assemblee - A publication, not a street. Regency ladies would have been familiar with this fashion periodical, from 1805. It was not devoted just to news of fashion, including other types of articles. (See: Southampton Street/Gallery of Arts.)

Labor Party - 1906. (See: Lower House, note under.)

lacemaking - Lace could be expensive, as it was handmade. In 1808, John Heathcote (inventor) presented the Cotton-Lace Bobbin Net machine, making it possible to obtain a less expensive lace.

- See: activities/entertainments/sports - knitting, under A.
- See: St. George's Street/29.
- See: St. Martin-le-Grand.

Lackington's - Bookseller. (See: Finsbury Square/Lackington's.)

Lad Lane - From at least 1561. Now part of Gresham Street, its name since 1845. (See: Gresham Street.)

- Swan with Two Necks Inn: (See under the INNS/PUBS section.)

Ladbroke Grove - Kensington & Chelsea. Sir Richard Ladbroke (MP, and Lord Mayor in 1747,) in 1750 bought four large parcels of land here. An extravagant estate was planned by his heir in 1823, but was slowed by a lack of funds. The luxury housing here now is known as Notting Hill*, and the Ladbroke Grove name is now primarily associated with the train station.

(*Notting Hill was built up in the later 17th C., growing out of the Ladbroke Grove, Norland, and Pembridge estates.)

- Hippodrome, the: Horse racecourse, opened in 1837. Closed in 1841.

Lady Day - March 25th.

- See: rents.
- See: year, beginning of.

Lady Mico's Almhouses - Stepney. Founded by the Mercers in 1692; rebuilt in 1857.

Lady's Magazine, The - (AKA: The Lady's Magazine; or Entertaining Companion for the Fair Sex, Appropriated Solely to Their Use and Amusement.) Published monthly, from 1170 to 1847. In 1770 its price was sixpence (per copy.) Like other women's magazines in England, it offered more than just fashion, including fiction, music, poetry, and social news.

Ladywell - Was once a twin village to Lewisham (on its western side, separated from the High Street by the River Ravensbourne. Sometime during the 18th C. the Ladywell area was called Bridge House (after a farmhouse.) Chambers London Gazetteer says: "From the 1780s smallholders enclosed strips of waste bordering Ladywell Road, often applying to the manor court for squatters' rights and being granted 21-year leases. On the expiry of these leases the farmers became the direct tenants of the lord of the manor." The wooden bridge that connected Ladywell to Lewisham was rebuilt in brick in 1830. (See: Lewisham/Ladywell.)

- 148 Ladywell Road: Our Lady's Well, a spring known of since at least 1472, with supposed healing properties. Covered over ca. the 1860s.

Lamb and Flag - Cover Garden pub. (See under the INNS/PUBS section.)

Lambeth - South Bank. Until the building of the embankment of the Thames, this area was frequently flooded, but by early 19th C. was starting to become populated. Lambeth was notorious as an area to furtively dispose of corpses. This was a manufacturing district from ca. 1670 and on.

The archbishop(s) of Canterbury was the lord of the manor here from 1197.

In Stuart times (1566-1665) Lambeth boasted London's only horse ferry, a ferry equipped to carry horses with coaches. (See: Horse Ferry.)

- Astley's Amphitheatre: (See under A.)
- Bedlam Hospital: (See under B.)
- Coade's, Eleanor: Coade stone manufacturer, 1769-1840. Coade stone is an artificial architectural ornamentation. Weathered extremely well. (See: County Hall, below.)
- County Hall: In 1720 this County Hall site hosted a factory for artificial terracotta (used for sculptures,) which was later bought by Mrs. Coade. (See: Coade's, above.) The Coade Co. ceased in 1840, as so apparently did the secret of producing Coadestone. County Hall was built here in 1909, opening in 1922.
- ferries: Despite some bridges, ferries were the easiest way to access Lambeth; the ferries here existed until 1862. (See: Horse Ferry, under H.)
- Greycoat Hospital: (See under G.)
- Hercules Road: Just east of Lambeth Palace. William Blake (author/poet, b.1757-d.1828) lived here for ten years. (See: Lambeth Asylum, which was at Hercules Inn.)

- Lambeth Palace: (See at its own listing.)
- North Lambeth: (See under N.)
- potters, the (meaning those who work with pottery/earthenware): Moved here (from Southwark) at the end of the 17th C., lasted until the 1970s. John Doulton (as in Royal Doulton) opened his pottery here in 1815.
- Royal Coburg Theatre: Built in 1816. Princess Charlotte's husband, Leopold of Saxe-Coburg, laid the foundation stone. Completed in 1818. (Today known as the Old Vic Theatre.) Its clientele, living away from London as they did, were rowdy and perhaps a little seedy. Described as seating "1,200 deep, wedged in, sweating." (See under the THEATRES section.)
- St. George's Fields: It was here that the Gordon riots took place; this was when an anti-Catholic mob stormed Newgate Prison (and others,) 1780, the politician Lord George Gordon lending his name to these riots. The Gordon riots were the worst in London's history, leaving some 850 dead.

  A poem from 1812 reads:
  "Saint George's Fields are fields no more,
  The trowel supersedes the plough;
  Huge inundated swamps of yore
  Are changed to civic villas* now."

  (*"Villas" is an exaggeration, these homes were mostly cheap and shoddy.)
- St. Mary-at-Lambeth: Stands beside Lambeth Palace. From at least the 17th century. Captain Bligh is buried here. Closed in 1972, but saved by the Trandescant Trust. Was deconsecrated, and is now the Museum of Garden History. Tower is 14th C., but the rest of the church is an 1851 reconstruct. (See under the CHURCHES section.)
- St. Thomas's Hospital: (See: Southwark/St. Thomas's Hospital.)
- South Lambeth: (See under S.)
- Vauxhall Gardens: (See under V.)

Lambeth Asylum - (AKA: the Lambeth House of Refuge.) 1758; founded by Sir John Fielding; orphanage for fatherless or orphaned girls, ages 7-10, to help such avoid prostitution. Was a popular charity for royals and important patrons to support. First housed in Hercules Inn, Lambeth. Ca. 1764 it removed to a newly built building on the corner of Westminster Bridge Road and Kennington Road, Lambeth (which is now Morley College.)

The girls were released into domestic service at age fourteen.

Moved to Beddington Park, Surrey, in 1866 (at which time it took on the simple title of "Beddington," and as it was thereafter always known, despite Queen Victoria's renaming it in 1897 to "The Royal Female Orphanage."

Moved again in 1943 to High Wycombe, Buckinghamshire (still known as "Beddington.") Closed in the mid 1960s. Not to be confused with Bedlam. (You may care to see: asylum, for an explanation of how the word was used.)

Lambeth Palace - Lambeth Road; West Bank; across the Thames from Westminster. (AKA: the Archbishop's Palace; a bishop's primary residence was often referred to as a "palace"; Lambeth Palace is London's only remaining ecclesiastical palace.) London seat of the Archbishop(s) of Canterbury for 800+ years, from ca. 1190. 10 acres. Buildings appeared from then onward, being more substantial from 1207-29; the chapel dates from 1229 and yet survives. Most recent renovation: 1828-34, in the Gothic style, by Edward Blore. Mellow red brick.

- Gateway: (AKA: the Morton Tower.) Large red-brick, Tudor style, built 1486-1501. Riverside.
- Great Hall: Rebuilt in 1663, Gothic style.
- Guard Room: Here since before 1534 (the year Cromwell questioned Sir Thomas More here regarding More's refusal to sign the Oath of Supremacy.)
- Lollards' Tower: Built in 1435, a water tower.
- St. Mary-at-Lambeth: Stands beside the palace's gateway. (See under the CHURCHES section.)
- St. Thomas's Hospital: Here since 1871. (See: Southwark/St. Thomas's Hospital.) Its library has been open to the public since 1610.

Lambeth Road - 1875-6. (See: Durham Place.)

Lambeth Wick - The first Baron Loughborough, Henry Hastings, gained the old manor house here in 1660, plus its 234 acres of farmland. Later became an academy for boys labeled as "superior." The estate sold in three parts, and was built up in the 1820s and on. The house was pulled down in 1854, becoming the Loughborough Park estate (315 houses, varying in splendor.) Is now the Loughborough Hotel.

Lamb's Conduit Fields - Holborn. This was the name of Coram Fields during the Regency. By the first half of the 18th century, this area was known as a cricket field. (See: Coram Fields.)

- Foundling Hospital. (See under F.)

Lamb's Conduit Street - (Also see written as: Lambs Conduit Street.) Holborn. Named for William Lambe, a Tudor man, was the sponsor of (plumbing) pipes (either of elm or leather) that carried water in from an outlying spring into London. Rebuilt by Wren after the Great Fire of 1666.

- 94: The Lamb. Still exists. (See under the INNS/PUBS section.)

lamps - In addition to candles, most Regency households would have had at least one oil lamp, which tended to provide a steadier light than did candles. Whale oil was preferred, but was more expensive (but less so as the 19th century went on); the alternative was animal fats, which tended to smoke. Artificially lighting one's home at night was considered a bit of a luxury; most poor people - and farmers, and indeed many people - went to bed with the sun. (You may care to see: curfew.) Most lamps would have been metal, often brass, with glass lamps becoming more widely seen by the 1830s. There were many styles, and some could be shuttered (to direct or minimize the amount of light provided, popular with smugglers.) Kerosene came along in the 1850s.

- ➢ See: candles.
- ➢ See: gas lighting - For public street lamps.

Lancaster Gate - 1866, Paddington Street. Named for Queen Victoria (who was also the Duchess of Lancaster.)

Lancaster House - (See: Stable Yard Road/York House.)

Lancaster Place - Covent Garden. Row of Georgian houses. Somerset House's west front is here. Short piece of road connecting Waterloo Bridge to the Aldwych and Strand junction.

- Brettenham House: Large, called "magnificent." Art Deco facade, 1930s, clad in Portland Stone.

Lancashire Court - (See: Mayfair/Lancashire Court.)

Lane's - Bookseller/publisher at 33 Leadenhall Street; William Lane (b.1746-d.1814,) established the Minerva Printing Press here ca. 1790 (after having had a circulating library elsewhere.) Minerva was known for its Gothic and sentimental novels, with titles such as: The Haunted Castle, The Maid of Hamlet, and The Orphan of the Rhine. After Lane's death in 1814, Minerva lost its appeal, and the Minerva name was dropped in the 1820s, although the business continued for awhile under his partner, Anthony King Newman.

Lanesborough House - (See: Lanesborough, the hotel.)

Lanesborough, the (hotel) - (AKA: Lanesborough House, from its earlier existence.) Overlooks Hyde Park Corner. The building dates back to at least 1723 (when Lord Lanesborough died.) In 1733 the house became an infirmary (St. George's Hospital) because of the neighborhood's "salubrious air." Its present appearance dates from 1829-35; built of Portland stone, by William Wilkins.

- ➢ See: St. George's, Hyde Park Corner, under the CHURCHES section.
- ➢ See: St. George's Hospital, under S.

Langham Place - So renamed in 1864. Prior name was Foley Street. (See: Foley Street.)

- All Souls: (See under the CHURCHES section.)
- Queen's Hall: 1893.

Langham, the - (Hotel.) Victorian, 1864. Portland Place, Marylebone. Called Europe's first "grand hotel." They claim to have been the originators of afternoon tea.

Lansdowne House - 9 Fitzmaurice Place, Berkeley Square, Mayfair. Robert Adam began building the house for the Earl of Bute in 1762, who sold it in 1768 to Lord Shelburne (2nd Earl of Shelburne, later 1st Marquess of Lansdowne) prior to its completion; Lansdowne lived there as it was completed. (See: Lansdowne Passage.)

Lansdowne Passage - 18th century (at least.) Runs between Berkeley and Curzon Streets. (Now closed and replaced by Lansdowne Row, which runs parallel.) It was separated from Berkeley Street by an old door and an iron bar. (Fitzmaurice Place, in the Regency, was a narrow walkway leaving the southeast corner of Berkeley Square, to Curzon Street; this is where Lansdown House is.) During the Regency, Fitzmaurice Place was too often the site of robberies, and is said to yet host ghosts. (See: Lansdowne House.)

laudanum - Syrup of poppies (opium is derived from poppies); active ingredients were opium and alcohol. Blended with cinnamon and cloves; sometimes mace or saffron were added. It is described as whitish/clear/translucent, was volatile, and sensitive to light (therefore was stored in brown glass bottles sealed with corks.) Dose: 3-25 drops, diluted in water or wine. Was sold without a prescription until the early 20th century. While used for all manner of ailments (primarily for suppressing coughs, and diarrhea, and pain,) its analgesic effects were low; it was more likely to be used after a surgery, not before.

- See: anesthesia.
- See: Figge's Marsh/Pound Farm.
- See: medicine - Notes at.
- See: morphine.

Lauderdale House - (See: Highgate Hill/Lauderdale House.)

Launderers' Company - (AKA: the Worshipful Company of Launderers.) Surprisingly, was founded in 1960. Became a Livery Company in 1977. It ranks 89th in the order of precedence. Shares a Hall with the Glaziers, and with the Scientific Instruments Makers. (See: Glaziers' Company.)

Lavender Hill - Battersea. Named for that flower grown here, for the nearby 18th C. market garden; lavender was grown on the north-facing slopes of the hill. Dates from at least 1717, when the road was part of the Southwark to Kingston Turnpike - but the area wasn't generally referred to as Lavender Hill until the later 19th century; very busy commercial district ca. 1885.

- Lavender Hall: 1790.

law - (Things legal.) "The law" in England is not as codified as it is in America; it is a mix of Common Law and laws passed by Parliament. Courts cannot cancel a Parliamentary law.

A fact sometimes overlooked: in the 18th century English courts tended to take one of only three actions: setting the accused free, transporting (exiling) them, or hanging them. "Setting them free" might mean they first had to pay a fine or be subject to a public shaming - but imprisonment wasn't at all common. (The grisly punishments had mostly faded away. See: punishments - For a list of penalties more common before the 18-19th centuries.) Gaols and prisons were for holding criminals only so long as it took to take them to court. The exception was Debtor's Prison; you stayed there until your debts were settled. In some cases Debtors were allowed out of gaol during the day in order to work; otherwise you stayed until you, or your friends or family settled your debts for you. This did change as the 19th century dawned; imprisonment became more common, if still unusual, as the era of paid policemen came along ca. 1829 in London - and a little later in the rest of England. (Earlier constables, who were unpaid, did not have a huge connection to "the law," per se, being more about rousting troublemakers locally than seeing that persons were prosecuted.)

Britons were not fond of the idea of either a standing army or a formal set of police. Through the 18th C. and the first quarter of the 19th, efforts to establish a police unit were resisted. So, before then if, as a victim of a crime, you wanted persons apprehended, you were expected to pay the costs to do so, and to file charges with the local magistrate. (See: Bow Street Runners.)

- See: Assize Courts.
- See: beadles - Church wardens.
- See: Bloody Code.
- See: Bow Street/4 - Bow Street Runners.
- See: Compters.
- See: constables.
- See: dueling spots.
- See: Inns of Court.
- See: justices of the peace - (AKA: magistrates.)
- See: lawyers.
- See: Metropolitan Police.
- See: pillory.
- See: police.
- See: prisons.
- See: rough places.
- See: Royal Assent.
- See: Watchmen.

Law Courts, the - (More properly AKA: the Royal Courts of Justice. AKA: the Courts of Law.) Were situated in Westminster until they moved to the Strand in 1882; by the architect G.

E. Street, 1868-92. (See: Courts of Common Law and Equity/Court of Chancery, notes under.)

Law Society, the - 1830s. (See: Chancery Lane/Law Society.)

lawn chairs - (See: St. James's Park.)

lawn mower - Created in 1830 by Edward Beard Budding (inventor,) the cylinder (or reel) lawnmower. Before then, servants scythed the lawns (or grazing animals kept them low.)

lawn tennis - (See: tennis.)

Lawrence Street - Chelsea. (See: Chelsea/Lawrence Street.)

lawyer - In the UK "lawyer" is a general term for someone who grants legal aid or advise, and who conducts suits in court; a practitioner of the law.

NOTE: Beginning ca. 1320 and over the centuries, the Inns of Court became where barristers are taught/trained; the Inns of Chancery are for solicitors.

These are the divisions thereof:

- *advocate* - A solicitor advocate is qualified to represent a client as their advocate, in the higher courts. May, as a special advocate, appear in court to offer expert advice.

- *attorney* - (AKA: attorney-at-law.) A person who represents a client in a court of law, pleading or defending. Attorneys in the UK are divided into:

    - barrister* - Represents a client in open court, and may appear at the bar (i.e. has been deemed educated/qualified to argue in court.) Both defense and prosecution. Until 2004, could not accept "instructions" (i.e. could not be directly hired by the client.) The idea was to free the barrister to be "clearer" at viewing the client's case.
    - solicitor - Traditionally did not appear in court (although that distinction has begun to fade in modern times,) appearing only in lower (county) courts or tribunals, hiring barristers to make the needed court appearance(s.) If a barrister was retained, per force so would be a solicitor (who alone was allowed to solicit funds for the lawyering services.) Conducts litigation and practices law outside the courts.

- *counselor** - (AKA: counselor-at-law.) Term for a single person or group pleading a cause. Usually applied to a barrister-at-law.

*"Barrister" is a professional title; "counsel" or "counselor" is used in court, such as: "Counsel is instructed to..."

- See: Chancery Lane.
- See: Courts of Common Law.

- See: Ede and Ravenscroft - For lawyers' robes and wigs.
- See: Inns of Court/Lincoln's Inn/New Square.
- See: law.
- See: money/guinea - Lawyers use of.

Layton & Shear - Drapers. (See: Covent Garden/Bedford House.)

L. C. C. Architect's Department - South Bank. Ralph Knott, 1911. (See: London County Council.)

Lea, the river -

- See: canals - Note under.
- See: rivers (and brooks) of London/Lea.

Lea Bridge - Waltham Forest/Hackney. CHAMBERS LONDON GAZETTEER tells us: "An industrial and working-class residential district straddling the River Lea east of Clapton. There has been water-related industry here since the time it was called Jeremy's Ferry. The first waterwheel was erected in 1707 and this was followed by mills grinding corn and even pins and needles, and a water pumping station." Hackney Cut (Lea Bridge to Old Ford) was opened in 1769, solving navigation problems the mills had created. The Lea Bridge turnpike came in next, making the Lea Bridge area moderately poplar with City merchants and bankers, at least until the rails brought industrialization.

Leadenhall Market - Whittington Avenue. Lies between Leadenhall and Lime Streets, the City. (Its address is formally listed as Grace Church Street.) Poultry (and corn and hay) market, here since medieval times, dating back to the 14th century. There was a manor house (a mansion called Leaden Hall) here in the 14-15th C.; it had a lead roof, from which derived the market's name. In 1327 the specialty here was poultry; cheese was added in 1397. The manor house burned in 1484; the market was re-established on its site, now adding fish and meat. Was destroyed in the Great Fire of 1666; new buildings were erected again on the same site. (At this time, the market became generalized, no longer just primarily a poultry market - but still a food items only market.) The Regency version would have dated from 1730.

Presently the building is later 19th century; the existing covered and ornate cream-and-maroon buildings were built in 1881, by Sir Horace Jones, at which time it was discovered that the Roman Basilica had been built here ca. 80-100AD. Wrought iron and glass roofs.

Restored to its "Victorian glory" in the 1980s.

There was a gander that had escaped his fate; "Old Tom" was allowed to wander freely through the market, fed by vendors. He purportedly lived 38 years, and was "laid in state" in the market in 1835.

Leadenhall Street - Named after the building on the street that had an unusual lead roof. (See: Leadenhall Market.) The Wool Merchants came here sometime after 1378. According to STAPLE INN AND ITS STORY (speaking of Leadenhall, and quoting Stow): "...'the common beams for weighing of wool and other wares as had been accustomed'...'the remnant of the sides and quadrants was employed for the stowage of wool and sacks, but not closed up, the residue and the lofts were letten out to merchants, to wind and pack their wools.'" STAPLE INN AND ITS STORY goes on (of the wool-staplers): "...they never had a Hall or Office of their own within the City of London like other trading companies..." Over time, the Wool-staplers simply faded out of importance.

Now Leadenhall Street is filled with big City banks.

- 33: Minerva Press. (See: Lane's.)
- 86: (See: St. Katherine Cree, below.)
- East India Office: One of the clerks who worked here was Charles Lamb (essayist,) between 1792 and 1825. The building dates from 1800.
- Lime Street: (See at its own listing.)
- Lloyd's: Leadenhall was the site for Lloyd's after 1928.
    - ➢ See: Jonathan's.
    - ➢ See: Lloyd's of London - At its own listing.
- St. Andrew Undershaft: (See under the CHURCHES section.)
- St. Katherine Cree. 86 Leadenhall. (See under the CHURCHES section.)
- Ship and Turtle Tavern: Built 1377, enlarged 1735. Could seat 750, 130 at the great circular counter. Once known for its Masonic banquets and public dinners. Until 1919.

Leather Lane - Hatton Garden, Holborn. Ancient street, with market for shoes and clothing here for over 400 years. (Not named necessarily because of leatherwork here, was originally called Le Vrune Lane, which became corrupted.) The market is more about street foods these days.

- 36: William Felton, coach-builder. Here in 1794, lasted until at least 1803; appears to have gone bankrupt before 1823.

leather/leatherworkers -

- ➢ See: Bermondsey.
- ➢ See: Cripplegate.
- ➢ See: Hornchurch.
- ➢ See: Leathersellers' Hall.
- ➢ See: Norwich.

- See: Romford - Particularly known for its leather breeches.
- See: Swaine Adeney Brigg.

Leathersellers' Hall - Sometimes seen as: Leather Sellers'. (For the Worshipful Company of Leathersellers.) 5-7 St. Helen's Place, Bishopsgate. Here since 1543. A two acre site.

First noted in 1372. Incorporated in 1444. Livery Company. Existed at London Wall (at a place that was henceforth known for centuries as Leathersellers Buildings,) and which is now covered over by a part of Copthall Avenue. Incorporated in 1502 with the Glovers-Pursers. The Pouchmakers (who made all manner of bags and trunks) joined in 1517.

During Henry VIII's Dissolution, the Leathersellers acquired the dissolved priory of the Benedictine convent at St. Helens, Bishopgate, 1543, where they moved to. The building survived the Great Fire of 1666, but was utterly pulled down in 1799. The Company moved to an old house on the property (east end of Little St. Helen's, which road became St. Helen's Place); burned in 1819. A new hall (built on the old site) opened in 1822. The present Hall dates from 1878, built "immediately opposite" the old site.

The Leathersellers' own almshouses in Barnet and Lewisham.

Leatherworkers worked with leather. ("Cordwainer" derives from "cordwane," a leather from Cordova, Spain, and was often used for shoes. The Cordwainers were separate from the Leatherworkers. Too, just for clarity, know that Skinners worked with pelts; Woolmongers with sheep's wool.)

lectures - Many hospitals had a teaching aspect, and so offered lectures to medical students. Where known, I've noted it at the various applicable hospital/medical entries.

Too, many subjects beyond medical issues were covered by any number of lecturers, often attended by the populace as a form of improvement/entertainment/learning. Both sexes attended a variety of lectures - but not all lectures were open to women.

- See: Leicester Square.
- See: London Institute.

Lee - Lewisham. Ca. 1814 became a popular retreat for City merchants.

- Christ Church: In Lee Park. 1855, by Sir Gilbert Scott.
- Lee New Town: (See: Lee Place, below.)
- Lee Place: Moated mansion. North side of Old Road. Pulled down in 1824. By 1825, Lee New Town covered its gardens; homes for those supporting the local gentry; rather shabby; torn down in the 1930-60s.
- Manor House: Ca. 1771. Sold in 1796 to Sir Francis Baring (of the Baring Brothers banking house.) 14 acres of garden. A lake. Became a military college, and now a public library.
- Pentland House: Mid 1680s. In the second half of the 19th C. (ca. 1860) it was

briefly called Foclallt House. Is now a Goldsmiths College hall of residence.

- St. Margaret's: Middle Ages. At the east end of Belmont Hill. Rebuilt in 1814. A new St. Margaret's was built across the road in 1841, due to the area's growth; the old church's ruins remain. Sir Edmond Halley (d. 1742,) he of comet fame, is buried here.
- Tiger's Head: Lee Green. 1766. Had a bowling green. Known as a smugglers' haunt. (See under the INNS/PUBS section.)

Leicester House - Leicester Square, Soho. (Pronounced Les-ter.) The townhouse of the Prince of Wales. 1630s. In 1771 became a "museum of curiosities"; not successful, sold the house by lottery. Became a cheap theatre, then a draper's shop, then a hotel. Pulled down in 1806, swallowed up by the new Essex Street; Lisle Street was built (by at least 1683) on the site of the Leicester House's gardens. There is also a Leicester House in Sutton, but that is not to be confused with this structure.

- See: Leicester Square.
- See: Toxophilite Society - 1781, archery.
- See: Wrythe - For the Sutton Leicester House.

Leicester Square - (Pronounced Les-ter.) In the middle of Soho, Covent Garden, and Westminster districts, rather like a hub to the three. The land was owned by St. Peter's Westminster until the Reformation, when it was confiscated in 1536 by Henry VIII.

Centered in what was once the handsome 17th C. garden/park (in the center of the square) was a statue of George I on a horse, there since 1784, and not moved until the late 19th century (now the site of the Empire Theatre.)

The Square was established in 1630-48, at which time it became affiliated with the Leicester family when the second earl, Robert Sidney, bought the land from the crown. Sidney built his home to the north in 1636, and developed the property to the south as Leicester Square; an early version was laid out in 1665, with houses resembling those in Pall Mall; the square was built in part over the former royal residence that had been here.

Leicester House was a palace for two princes of Wales, 1712-60, which led to Leicester Square becoming a fashionable address/promenade.

The square's center was laid out as a garden in 1874; before then it was used for exhibitions and public lectures.

By the time of the 19th C., this area was moving toward becoming a slightly seedy theatre district. It was favored by artists and painters as a residence.

Has tall plane trees.

Nowadays is pretty much the heart of the West End. Some of the Georgian and Victorian buildings still remain, but most of the square now dates from the 1930s and is known for its cinemas.

- 28: John Singleton Copley (painter) lived here 1776-83.
- 30: The 18th C. painter, Hogarth lived here from 1733 to his death in 1764. In 1801, Hogarth's house became the *Hôtel de la Sablionère*, which might have been the area's first public restaurant. It was on the east side of the square, from 1788-1867. It had a plain frontage, with an iron-railed balcony on the second floor.
- 46: The painter Joshua Reynolds lived here from 1760-92.
- Barker Panorama: Robert Barker, an Irish artist, opened his panorama* just off Leicester Square in 1792, in a large circular building.

(*A panorama is a view that surrounds the viewer. Some of them were designed to move so that one long scene unfolded before the viewer's eyes. They could be large, or small enough to be portable.)

Barker died in 1806, and the business went to his son, Henry Aston Barker. He ran it until 1826. When he retired, Henry passed it on to his assistant, John Burford (at which time it became the Barker/Burford Panorama.) Burford died a year later, the business going to his brother, Robert, who ran it until 1865 (at which time the building became a French Catholic church/school, the Church of Notre Dame de France, which still survives.)

- Empire Theatre: Opened in 1884; reopened as a cinema in 1928. New interior in 1962.
- Gedge's: 1782. Drapers. Was the first London store with a large glass shopfront.
- Leicester House: (See at its own listing.)
- Long Acre: Westminster. Runs from St. Martin's Lane (to the west) to Drury Lane (to the east.) Built in the early 17th century. Coachbuilding was here in the 18-19th centuries. (See: Long Acre, at its own listing.)
    - 12-14: Stanfords. 1852. World's largest map store.
- Martin's Street: Fanny Burney (novelist, d.1840) lived here as a girl, in a house formerly occupied by Sir Isaac Newton.
- Newton's: Drapers. Where Jane Austen's niece bought her Irish (linens.)
- Sablionière Hotel: (See: 30, above.)
- Savile House: Used sometimes by royalty in the 17-18th centuries. By 1809 the house was run down; it was leased in that year to one Mary Linwood (and her associates,) and rebuilt/refurbished. From 1809-1845 (the year of her death) Linwood displayed her needlework here for sale. Destroyed by fire in 1865.
    - William Green's Pistol Repository and Shooting Gallery: Was upstairs in the Savile House, 1836-55.

- Western Literary and Scientific Institute: Founded in 1825 to spread "useful knowledge among persons engaged in commercial and professional pursuits." Opened in Leicester Square in 1828. Open to members only. Existed until 1852.
- Whitcomb Street: Follows an ancient pathway known as Hedge Lane or Colman Hedge Lane, since at least the time of Henry VIII. Part of its length was renamed to Whitcomb Street by 1682, with the whole street taking on the name by 1780.

Leighton House - 12 Holland Park Road, Kensington. Victorian artist Frederick, Lord Leighton lived here from 1866-1896, and the house is preserved in that period's style; it includes the Arab hall, in its current museum and gallery, in Islamic tiles inspired by 12th century Sicily's Moorish palace. (See: Holland Park/Leighton House.)

Leinster Gardens - Victorian terraced homes.

- 23 & 24: Are merely facades, built in the 1860s to provide an open air stretch for steam-driven underground trains passing underneath.

Leman Street - Whitechapel. (Pronounced Lee-mun.) At least since 1720. CHAMBERS LONDON GAZETTEER notes: "Together with Dock Street, Leman Street connects Wapping with Whitechapel and the eastern part of the City of London. Although not the name of the locality…" (it is in Tower Hamlets) "…Leman Street is used as the main point of reference in a rather anonymous district… The area's medieval name was Goodman's Fields. Sir William Leman added houses ca. 1710. Described as now little changed.

lemonade - If you order lemonade in modern Britain, you'll likely be served a lemon-lime carbonated soda drink that is commercially made. During the Regency, however, lemonade was the same drink Americans think of: made of the juice of lemons, sugar, and water. (Today, to get the Regency-style drink, you'd order "lemonade, still," as opposed to "lemonade, fizzy.")

lending libraries - (AKA: circulating libraries.) Developed in the 18th C., commercial establishments run by booksellers. Earliest dates from 1725, in Edinburgh.

- ➢ See: bookshops.
- ➢ See: circulating libraries.
- ➢ See: libraries.
- ➢ See: subscription libraries.

leprosy - The causative agent of leprosy was discovered in 1873 by one G. H. Armauer Hansen, of Norway. Effective treatment became available in the 1940s.

- ➢ See: lock.
- ➢ See: St. Giles-in-the-Fields, under the CHURCHES section.

letters - As in written communications.

- See: activities/entertainments/sports - writing letters, under A.
- See: post, the.

levee - The king's formal assemblies, a sort of launching event for young men entering society. (See: Queen's drawing-room - For women.)

Lewes (races) - County town in East Sussex (not London.) Prinny attended horse races there with Mrs. Fitzherbert (his disallowed wife) and her circle of friends.

Lewisham - (Had been pronounced Luiss-um; now is pronounced Luish-um.) South London borough (and the principle settlement in the borough.) Dates from the 6th century; ancient manor granted to the Abbey of St. Peter at Ghent by Elthruda (niece of King Alfred.) Six almshouses, a grammar school (see below,) and a primary school were built here in the mid 17th century, by the then vicar of Lewisham. Attractive village. Rural, hemmed by green fields. The River Ravensbourne ran alongside the main street. Little growth here until the rails came.

- Grammar school: Founded sometime between 1610-1657 by the Vicar of Lewisham, Rev. Abraham Colfe.
- High Street: Old. Described as an elm-lined ribbon.
- Ladywell: Once a twin village to Lewisham (its western side, separated from the High Street by the River Ravensbourne,) now a part of this borough. (See: Ladywell, at its own listing.)
- New Cross: (See under N.)
- St. Mary: The 15th C. church was pulled down in 1774, and rebuilt. Oblong; stone; plain; square tower at the west end (the base of which remains from the 15th century.) Portico on the south with four Corinthian columns. Parish church. (See under the CHURCHES section.)

Lewisham Armoury - Repurchased by the government in 1807, to use as a gun works. In 1816, production largely moved to Enfield Lock - AKA: Royal Small Arms Factory. (See under R.)

Leyton - Waltham Forest. (AKA: Low Leyton.) Was a hamlet between Walthamstow and Stratford. Includes the district of Leytonstone. Close by to the south edge of Epping Forest. Was marshland, until the 18th C. when most of the marsh had been altered into fertile farmland. It doubled its population every ten years after the rails came.

- Leyton Church: (See: St. Mary, below.)
- Leytonstone: According to CHAMBERS LONDON GAZATTEER: "...(Took) its name from an old milestone, which is now topped by a 19th-century Portland stone obelisk known as the 'high stone.' ...The village evolved early as a roadside halt. A Rose inn was in existence in 1585 and Leytonstone High Road was more

important than the High Road in Leyton by the end of the 16th century." Was a farming village up to the 1850s. Alfred Hitchcock (film director) was born here in 1899.

- Leytonstone House: Ca. 1800. Yet exists, after being a brewery, a school, a hospital, and now offices (on the grounds of a Tesco superstore.)
- Pastures, the: Large 17th C. house; now a youth center.
- St. John the Baptist: Early 1830s. (Leytonstone became a separate parish in 1845.)

- St. Mary: (Sometimes AKA: Leyton Church.) Rebuilt in 1821, except for the older tower. The church there by at least 1737. Still exists, much extended and altered.
- Walnut Tree House: (AKA: Essex Hall.) Built ca. 1500, wings added later. Not known for whom it was built. Still exists, and like St. Mary's is much extended and altered; obtained its Georgian appearance in the early 19th century. Called Walnut Tree House by at least 1804.

liberties - (In ancient times also called: sokes.) Medieval. This term was reserved for important people, giving them the right to hold court over their own people; they did not have to answer to the Aldermen of London. All lands belonging to the church were also liberties, and some of them had sanctuary status (refuge, where neither the Watch nor the king could molest them.) St. Martin-le-Grand's status as a liberty was abolished by Act of Parliament in 1815. (You may care to see: Tower of London/"Other Places & Things"/Liberty, the.)

Liberty - 1875 ornamental goods store. (See: Regent Street/214-220.)

libraries - The first *public* library in *Britain* dates from 1423. For the oldest library in *London*, see: Inns of Court/Lincoln's Inn/Library.

- See: Bloomsbury Square/British Museum/Reading Room.
- See: Bond Street/Hookham's.
- See: Bond Street/Sam's.
- See: booksellers.
- See: Booth's.
- See: British Library - 1973.
- See: British Museum Library.
- See: Cawthorne's.
- See: circulating libraries.
- See: Dangerfield's.
- See: Dutton's.
- See: Earle's.

- See: Guildhall - Hosts several Companies' libraries.
- See: Hookham's - (See: Bond Street/Old Bond Street/Hookham's.)
- See: Inns of Court/Lincoln's Inn/Library - London's oldest library, 1497.
- See: Lackington's.
- See: Lane's - Founder of the Minerva Press.
- See: lending libraries.
- See: London Institute.
- See: London Library, the.
- See: Ogilvy's.
- See: Parson's.
- See: Piccadilly/Hatchard's - Was highly fashionable.
- See: Ridgeway's.
- See: Southampton Street/Gallery of Arts.
- See: subscription libraries.

Licensed Victuallers' Asylum - (AKA: Licensed Victuallers Benevolent Institution.) Founded in 1826-7. Six acres, just off the Old Kent Road. Houses, chapel, etc. for the use of distressed members of the trade association, the Victuallers, plus their wives or widows. Described as "Grecian" in design. Victuallers being self-employed licensees of public houses (that is, pubs not affiliated with a particular brewery or brand.) The name derived from: a victualler of goods.

Lichfield House - 15 St. James's Square. By Athenian Stuart, late 18th century.

Life Guards, the - The part of the military who guard the monarch. They wear red tunics and white plumes. (See: Royal Guards/Horse Guards/Life Guards.)

life peerages - Introduced in 1958. Not hereditary. Introduced to dilute hereditary power in the House of Lords.

lifeboats - Invented in 1790 by William Wouldhave.

lift - What in America is called an: elevator. A post-Regency invention. (See: Westminster Palace Hotel.)

Lightermen - Provided loading and unloading of ships, on flat-bottomed barges called lighters. By Act of Parliament the Lightermen were granted the right to work on the Thames in 1555. (See: Watermen's and Lightermen's Hall.)

lighthouses - Ancient, these structures were an aid long known to those at sea. (See: Trinity House.)

lighting, gas - (See: gas lighting, under G.)

Lime Street - South side of Leadenhall Street. In the 18th C. it was home to wealthy city merchants. By the 19th C. it had moved over to being a financial district.

- Pewterers' Hall: Until 1840. (See under P.)

lime trees - In England (and Europe) these are large deciduous trees. They have nothing to do with the citrus. Not native to North America.

Limehouse - An East End district, Tower Hamlets. Dates from the 1350s. Not fashionable, certainly not during the Regency era, although in the 20th C. the area did begin to take on a more "gentrified air" than it had ever possessed before (and guidebooks are quick to point out that "gentrified" is not the same as "exclusive.")

In the 14th C. there were lime kilns here, used to convert Kentish chalk into quicklime for London's building needs; it is from these that Limehouse derives its name.

In the 16th C. ships were built here, and there were many traders providing for voyages.

In 1801, the inhabitants numbered at approximately 500. Canal traffic, shipwrights, merchants, seafaring men. Porcelain manufacture. Area of growing industry. In the late 18th C. and early 19th C. this is where the Asian populace tended to be concentrated (having been sailors who traveled to London via the East India Company, forming London's first Chinatown.) Limehouse provides admission to the Regent's Canal.

- Limehouse Cut: London's oldest canal, ca. 1770, linking the River Lea at Bow with the Thames at Limehouse.
- Limehouse ware: A soft-paste porcelain invented in Limehouse in the 1740s (first of its kind.)
- Narrow Street: Handsome 17-18th C. houses, built for merchants, yet remain (because it is an official architectural conservation area.) This street's houses were "gentrified" in the late 1950s.
    - 76: The Grapes. A pub described by Charles Dickens in "Le Jolly Fellowship Porters." (See under the INNS/PUBS section.)
- Newell Street: An old street, it yet retains some of its Georgian houses. At one time known as Church Row. The author Charles Dickens' godfather lived here. (See: Wapping/Newell Street.)
- Poplar High Street:
    - St. Matthias: (See: St. Matthias/Poplar High Street, under the CHURCHES section.)
- St. Anne's: (See: St. Anne/Limehouse, under the CHURCHES section.)

Limehouse Basin - 1980s. (See: Docks/Regent's Canal Dock.)

Limehouse Cut - A short canal, Bromley. 1770. (See: Limehouse/Limehouse Cut.)

Limeys - Pejorative for British sailors, beginning ca. 1797, because they drank the juice of limes to prevent scurvy. (See: scurvy.)

Limmer Hotel - (See: Conduit Street/Limmer Hotel.)

Lincoln's Inn - (See: Inns of Court/Lincoln's Inn.)

Lincoln's Inn Fields - West of Lincoln's Inn buildings. There is actually a field with grass and shade trees, there because in the 1640s the residents held the developer to his promise that he would keep the field open to the public. Built in the 1660s. (See: Inns of Court/Lincoln's Inn Fields.)

Lindsey House - (Also sometimes seen spelled as: Lindsay.) Not to be confused with the modern restaurant Lindsay House.

- See: Chelsea/Cheyne Walk/Lindsey House.
- See: Inns of Court/Lincoln's Inn Fields/56-60.

Lindsey Row - Kensington/Chelsea. Built in 1674 by the third Earl of Lindsey, over the top of Sir Thomas More (saint's) garden.

- 4: One Marc Brunel, "a brilliant civil engineer," lived here from 1806. (Now the address is 96-100 Cheyne Walk.) Beautiful 17th C. facade. His son, Isambard (an engineer and visionary, who was part of building the first tunnel under the Thames, begun in 1825) lived here at least until 1825.

linens -

- See: bedding shop.
- See: blankets.
- See: drapers.
- See: fabrics.
- See: fabrics/Holland cloth.
- See: Leicester Square/Newton's - For Irish linens.
- See: sheets.
- See: towels.

Linnean Society - To promote the study of natural history in the British Isles; a biological/life sciences society. Its Fellowship is international. Founded in 1788. Named after the Swedish naturalist Carl Linnaeus (b.1707-d.1828,) whose collections have been retained by this Society since 1829. Charles Darwin first presented his theory of evolution here, 1858. They leased space in Soho Square from 1821-51. Since 1854 it was in Burlington House - as well as: the Geological Society of London (1807,) the Royal Academy of Arts (1768,) the Royal Astronomical Society (1831,) the Royal Society of Chemistry (1980,) and the Society of Antiquaries (1577.)

(You may care to see: paleontology.)

Liquorpond Street - (Also seen as: Liquor Pond Street.) Clerkenwell. Existed by at least 1805. Small, unpleasant street leading out of Gray's Inn Road. Was widened ca. 1856.

liquors - (Not an all inclusive list.) Brandy, claret, gin, madeira, port, ratafia, rum, sherry, vermouth, whisky. Note: Wine was little drunk by the lower classes, due to taxes. (See: food/drinks - Various alphabetical listings at.)

Lisle Street - Existed by at least 1683. Built on the site of the gardens of the pulled down Leicester House. (See: Leicester House.)

Lisson Green - Marylebone, Westminster. 1790s. Now more commonly known as Lisson Grove. London's bypass, the New Road, stretched to here in the mid 18th C., leading to area growth. That was enhanced when Regent's Canal was built (1810,) leading to today's street plan and stuccoed houses. After the 1820s the area grew, becoming increasingly poor and, in parts, criminal. Slum clearing began after the 1850s.

Listowel House - Built ca. 1770. Knightsbridge. (AKA: Kingston House.) Mansion; conservatory; private grounds behind a high brick wall. Pulled down in 1937. Owned by the Listowel family from 1842-1937. (See: Kingston House.)

literacy - In 1800, 60% of (all) men could write their name at the time of marriage; 40% of women could. In 1810, three-quarters of agricultural workers were illiterate. (See: signs, hanging - Medieval method, used for those unable to read.)

Little Britain - Hillingdon. Runs from St. Martin's le Grand to West Smithfield. Was, since the 16th century (and like Fleet Street) a home to printers and booksellers, but only up to ca. 1725 (at which time Paternoster Row became Fleet Street's main competitor.) Little Britain supposedly got its name from possessing a vaguely Britannic shape. Was mentioned in Charles Dickens' writings. Failed to develop much before the 1860s. Is now primarily a 15 acre park.

- St. Bartholomew-the-Great: Near the Barbican Centre. (See under the CHURCHES section.)

Little Burlington Street - (See: New Burlington Street.)

Little Chelsea - District north of King's Road, Chelsea. Until 1860 was a rural area.

Little Cyprus - (See: Palmer's Green.)

Little Dean's Yard - A courtyard adjoined to Dean's Yard.

- See: Ashburnham House.
- See: Westminster/Little Dean's Yard.
- See: Westminster School.

Little Ealing - Ealing. Mid 17th century. (See: South Ealing, under S - The notes at.)

- Place House: Was Little Ealing's largest dwelling. Sir Francis Dashwood (of Hellfire Club fame) got the house in 1745 through marriage. Dashwood sold it in 1746. It was rebuilt later in the 18th century. In the early 19th C. Humphry Repton (architect) revamped this locale and it became Ealing Park. Even so,

William Lawrence got the house in 1838. Ealing Park (plus 70 acres of these grounds) were sold in 1882. This area is now again called Place House.

- Rochester House: Probably dates from the 1710s, built by John Pearce (London distiller); he named it after his son, Zachary Pearce (Bishop of Rochester, who died here.)

Little Fire of London, the - 1676. As opposed to the Great Fire of 1666. (See under G.) Most of the Borough burned at this time. (See: Southwark/Borough, the.)

Little Friday Street - Out of Basing Lane, running west, to Friday Street. Dates from at least 1722. Small offshoot of Cannon Street, removed in 1853-4.

Little Italy - Clerkenwell/Camden. Late 19th C. area, created by an influx of Italian immigrants at that time. Also once known as: Italian Hill. Its boundaries are Clerkenwell Road, Farringdon Road, and Rosebery Avenue. The *Processione della Madonna del Carmine* (a ceremony involving a procession of a statue of the Madonna) has been held here for more than a century.

- St. Peter's Italian Church: 1863. (AKA: Italian Church of St. Peter.)

Little Jerusalem - Nickname for Spitalfields after ca. 1880.

Little Newport Street - Leicester Fields.

- 7: Gillray (the painter) was in business here ca. 1770.

Little Paris - AKA: Petite Paris. (See: South Kensington/Little Paris.)

Little Ryder Street - City. Just off St. James's Street. The west arm of Ryder Street was Little Ryder Street until 1863; the east arm was Great Ryder Street until 1863. (See under G.) Ryder Street dates from at least 1683.

little season, the - (See: season, the.)

Little Stanmore - Harrow. Significant medieval parish, although now it is practically lost among neighboring suburbs (most notably Canons Park.) Canons estate provided most of the employment locally until the late 19th century.

- St. Lawrence's Church: 12th C., white stone. From its stones' color, it got the alternate name: Whitchurch. The oldest surviving part dates from the 14th C. (the tower.) Rebuilt in 1715 with a "startingly ornate interior." Woodcarvings supposedly are by Grinling Gibbons. It is likely Handel first performed his *Chandos Anthems* here.

Little Trinity Lane - City. Dates back to at least 1773. Was originally called Trinity Lane. Was called Little Trinity Lane by at least 1811.

- Painter-stainers' Hall: (See under P.)

Little Venice - Westminster. CHAMBERS LONDON GAZETTEER informs us: "A pool was created here in the 1810s at the meeting point of the Regent's Canal and the Paddington arm of the Grand Junction (now Grand Union) Canal, and was originally known as Paddington Broadwater. A small island with willows and wildfowl makes a kind of roundabout at the junction, which was always intended as a spot for pleasure boats."

In the later 19th C. the area grew with nice terraces, albeit in a piecemeal fashion.

In 1934 Margery Allingham (mystery writer) called a house set on the canal here "Little Venice" - and the name caught on with real estate agents.

- Prince Alfred Pub: Dates from 1890.

Liverpool Grove - 1827. (See: Walthamstow/Liverpool Grove.)

Livery Companies, the - Special Note: Not every Company (Guild) was allowed Livery (ceremonial robes and gear.)

Of all the Companies, not all of them had/have halls. Some no longer exist. Some have existed for centuries. Some didn't exist until the 20th century. I have chosen to make the most extensive list of the City's Companies at: halls.

So be sure to see: halls, under H.

The Companies descended from the medieval craft guilds. They regulated apprenticeship and product quality, and became strong in the business matters of the City. In the 12th C. they took over the task of governing The City, that area of London defined by Medieval measure; AKA "the Square Mile" although it must be noted that their role in government is now much reduced. Yet note, they are still the ones to elect the sheriffs and the Lord Mayor. (See: City, the, under C.)

The Livery Companies as a whole body are called the COMMON HALL, especially when they meet as a body once a year to elect (usually from among their number) the Lord Mayor. (See: Lord Mayor, under L.)

They built halls (increasingly grand) to hold meetings and, of course, demonstrate their collective power, wealth, and influence. For these meetings, the wealthiest members wore uniforms (i.e. liveries,) hence the title "Livery Companies." To this day, members of the Livery Companies still dominate the Court of Common Council.

"The Livery" (those members of designated guilds allowed by the monarch to wear certain distinguished robes) used to be the ruling body of the Companies, but the livery is now limited to a select few (the larger, now non-liveried body of the members being called the "freedom.") Only the Ironmongers' Company has the livery as its governing body. THE ENCYCLOPAEDIA OF LONDON states: "The court is usually by a master and two, three and sometimes more wardens, taken from its own members; each step upward is usually a matter of seniority."

Also according to AN ENCYCLOPAEDIA OF LONDON: "As the Companies became richer and thereby more unrepresentative, the exercise of their powers was resented and resisted... Therefore, for the most part, the Companies retired from business. The Fishmongers', the Goldsmiths', and the Gunmakers' have maintained their chief functions uninterruptedly...but by the 18th century, the Companies of the City of London were as a rule friendly societies, with fancy names and imposing armorial bearings." (Virtually all of the Companies are now charitable organizations, with limited control over their named craft. This is not to say they have no involvement with learning and expertise, just that their role/power has changed or waned.)

The twelve original (medieval) Companies are called the Great Companies. All others are "Minor." Be sure to see the various halls' listings, such as under "A" for the "Apothecaries' Hall," etc.

As indicated above, many have long given up practicing their ancient (and/or no longer required) arts or practices, but are still active in pageantry and charities.

AGAIN, SEE THE EXTENSIVE LIST (OF VARIOUS COMPANIES' HALLS) AT: halls, under H.

The order of precedence is also at: halls.

(See: Worshipful Company of..., under W - Which is usually part of a Company's formal name.)

Lloyd Park - Waltham Forest. CHAMBERS LONDON GAZETTEER says: "A public park located north of Forest Road in Walthamstow. In the Middle Ages the park formed the grounds of a moated house called Cricklewoods. The moat gave its name to Water House, which was built in the mid 18th century, and was also known as Winns."

- Water House: By as late as 1911 this became known as Lloyd Park Mansion. 1911-43, was a clinic.

Lloyd Square - Finsbury. 1819 and onwards. Houses are linked pairs.

Lloyd's - (See: Lloyd's of London.)

Lloyd's Bank - 1765, started in Birmingham. Not to be confused with Lloyd's of London. (See: Strand/222-225.)

Lloyd's of London - (Often seen as just: Lloyd's.) Moved to Lime and Leadenhall Street in 1928 (but read on for a better description of location over time.) Too, a better description is provided under: Jonathan's. (See under J.)

Has been in the insurance business (an association of underwriters) since 1686, out of a coffee-house near the docks that existed at the time; run by Edward Lloyd; in Abchurch Lane.

LONDON by Knopf Guides explains: "Lloyd's is not an insurance company but a stock exchange for insurance contracts. Two types of people work here: the Lloyd's members (underwriters) have the sole right of selling risk insurance, and the annual subscribers (Lloyd's names) are "invited" to stand surety. Contracts are drawn up between a company or individual and a member, who then distributes both the dividends and risks between a number of subscribers."

First rate maritime news was to be had at Lloyd's. (See: Lloyd's List, below.)

In 1769, removed to New Lloyd's Coffee House (the latter being in business from 1691 thru 1785,) in Pope's Head Alley, off Lombard Street, where Coutt's Bank now stands. Quickly became too cramped. In 1771, Lloyd's of London Insurance moved in over the northwest corner of the Royal Exchange, staying there until 1928. From there it went to Leadenhall Street.

A PORTRAIT OF GEORGIAN LONDON states: "In 1811 a trust deed was adopted giving Lloyd's a 'constitution,' and it was incorporated by Parliament in 1871 for the promotion of marine insurance and the diffusion of shipping intelligence.

Lloyd's Coffee-House burned in 1838, along with the Royal Exchange. So from 1838-44 they were in the South Sea House, awaiting a rebuild.

Used to only provide insurance for shipping; but since 1911 will "insure anything" (except long term life insurance.) Purportedly in 1939 Betty Grable (the actress') legs were insured here.

In 1986, moved to Richard Roger's post-modernist building on Leadenhall Street (on the site of the demolished East India House.)

- ➢ See: East India House.
- ➢ See: Royal Exchange.

- Lloyd's List: A news sheet, aimed at shipping news. To be had from Lloyd's of London. Has been published since 1734.
- Lutine Bell: In 1799 the Lutine Bell (salvaged from a French ship by the name of *La Lutine* that sank in 1793 with all hands on board and a cargo of bullion) was installed - one stroke of its great hammer announced that a vessel was missing at sea, two that it was safe. (A second source says the Lutine Bell was not used by Lloyd's until 1859.)
- Subscription Room: Opened in 1802. During the Peninsular wars, subscriptions for widows and orphans were raised here.

Lobb's - Victorian shoemakers. (See: St. James's Street/9.)

lock - "Lock" is another word (medieval) for "rags", which were used to bind sores, and any hospital that treated leprosy was therefore called Lock Hospital. The first Lock Hospital, 12th C., in London was in Southwark. Another nickname for hospitals for lepers was: Lazarus Houses. Lepers were formally banned from London in 1346, although the afflicted were known to try to re-enter. By the 18th C. there was no leprosy in London, so these institutions began to treat those with venereal diseases. The Southwark Lock Hospital closed in 1760, but the name lived on in the Paddington VD-treating area hospital, near the Paddington Workhouse. (See: Lock Hospital.)

Lock Hospital - Grosvenor Place, Belgravia. (AKA: London Lock Hospital.) Founded in 1746. It was meant to specialize in leprosy, but by the Regency era leprosy was no longer an issue, so it treated venereal diseases, in particular syphilis.

- ➢ See: Grosvenor Place/Lock Hospital.
- ➢ See: London Lock Hospital.

Lockbottom - (Also seen as: Locks Bottom.) Bromley, near Orpington. Named for the Lock family, 18th C. landowners. The mock-Tudor shops date from the 1930s.

- Ye Old Whyte Lyon: A 17th C. coaching inn, still standing. (See under the INNS/PUBS section.)

Lock's - (AKA: Lock & Co.) 6 St. James's Street. Hatters. Gave a shilling on the pound discount for settling the bill immediately (although this practice would, heaven forbid, never actually be mentioned.) It should be noted that very few were cash customers. (See: St. James's Street/6/Lock's.)

Lollards - Early religious reformers inspired by John Wycliffe (d. 1384,) who thought the church should reject wealth by adopting poverty, and that every man should be able to read the Bible in his own language, and interpret it for himself. The name "Lollards" derives from the Dutch, a word meaning mumblers (because followers often prayed aloud.) Were often persecuted. Long gone by the time of the Regency.

Lombard House - 1901. (See: Sunderland House.)

Lombard Street - Cheapside. The "Bankers' Clearing House." Still a banking center. Also a street for goldsmiths. Named for the Italians who settled there in the 13th century. The Lombards got around usury laws by acting as pawnbrokers; they served as an early form of banking. The medieval businesses here had once boasted hanging signs (the signs bore pictures, so those who could not read could still find the businesses they required) were banned by Charles I. They did not return until it was time to decorate for Edward VII's coronation (that is, the coronation that never took place, as Edward VII abdicated to marry Wallace Simpson.)

Lombard Street was replaced as the merchants' center of finance when the Royal Exchange was built (16th C.,) although to this day it is still known as a banking center.

- Plough Court: Off Lombard Street since at least 1688.

London - Is primarily situated in the county of Middlesex. London is essentially situated in a river valley, or at least its original confines were (the Square Mile of ancient London.) The river being: the Thames. (See under T.) In ancient times, much of the area that would become London was covered by the Forest of Middlesex. (See under F.)

The city's name derives from either the Welsh king Lud, or from a Celtic word "Llyn-din" (meaning "the hill by the pool.") Certainly, by 61AD the Romans wrote of it as Londinium.

Although the Romans made note of its merchants and trading vessels, London did not start to take on its reputation as a great and growing port until ca. the 9th century.

By 1810, the population of London was over one million, at that time the biggest city in the world.

- ➢ See: City, the.
- ➢ See: gates.
- ➢ See: London Wall.

- 1 London: Home of the first Duke of Wellington. "Number 1 London" is actually only a nickname. (See: Apsley House.)

Loosely speaking, London has some districts where "like" interests have tended to congregate. Listings here are meant to steer you toward general areas, (primarily as they could have been found in the Regency era.) These are only a few suggestions, hopefully to get you started in finding areas of interest within London/this guide:

- bridges of London - Note: there weren't as many bridges across the Thames as you'd think (due to the river needing to be accessible to sea-going vessels.) There were more in the advancing 19th C. than ever before, but early in that century to access different sides of the Thames there was still a fair amount of ferrying by the Thames Watermen instead.
  - ➢ See: the BRIDGES section - And the notes at the start thereof.
  - ➢ See: Watermen, under: W.

- "business" London -
  - ➢ See: City, the.
  - ➢ See: "financial" London, below.
  - ➢ See: halls.

➢ "churchy" London - (See: "religious" London, below.)

➢ "clubby" London (As in Gentlemen's clubs, not dancing.) -

- ➢ See: Pall Mall.
- ➢ See: St. James's.
- ➢ See the CLUBS section.

- "dining" London - While there are references of places to dine throughout this work, 19th C. dining usually happened at home or in the homes of friends. Unlike modern London, there were no concentrated areas for dining out, even given the existence of pubs and inns.
    - ➢ See: chophouses.
    - ➢ See: restaurants.
    - ➢ See: the INNS/PUBS section.
    - ➢ You may care to see: food, under F.

- "downtown" London - Of course, London doesn't really have a downtown, but the West End and the following districts rather give that feel/serve that purpose:
    - Bloomsbury
    - Holborn
    - Marylebone
    - Mayfair
    - St. James's
    - Strand, the
    - Westminster

- "dueling" London - (See: dueling, under D.)

- "educational" London -
    - ➢ See: Bloomsbury - For publishers/booksellers.
    - ➢ See: Cambridge.
    - ➢ See: education.
    - ➢ See: Eton.
    - ➢ See: Oxford.
    - ➢ See: schools.

- "entertainment" London -
    - ➢ See: activities/entertainments/sports, under A.
    - ➢ See: Gunter's - Confectioner.
    - ➢ See: museums.
    - ➢ See: parks.

- See: the INNS/PUBS section.
- See: the THEATRES section.
- See: Vauxhall Gardens.
- See: zoos.

- "financial" London -
  - See: Bank of England.
  - See: coffeehouses.
  - See: Fleet Street.
  - See: money - This is a helpful list of coins and paper money.
  - See: Royal Exchange.
  - See: Stock Exchange.

- "food" in London -
  - See: food, under F.
  - See: "dining" London, above.

- "governmental" London -
  - See: Downing Street.
  - See: Lower House.
  - See: Upper House.
  - See: Westminster - Parliament.
  - See: Whitehall - Government.

- "horsey" London -
  - See: "coach," at C - Several listings under.
  - See: Horse and Carriage Repository.
  - See: horses.
  - See: Tattersall's.

- "imprisoned" London -
  - See: Beadles.
  - See: gaols.
  - See: Metropolitan Police.
  - See: police.
  - See: prisons.
  - See: Tower of London.

- See: Watchmen.

- "journalistic" London -
  - See: booksellers.
  - See: Fleet Street.

- "legal" London -
  - See: "court" and "courts," under C - Multiple listings at.
  - See: Holborn.
  - See: Inns of Court.
  - See: Old Bailey.
  - See: punishments.

- "market" London - Although the markets were mostly about food products, often other things besides produce (or meat or fish) could be purchased at the street markets, depending on which you went to: clothes, furniture, pins, pots, etc. Wealthy and lowly alike shopped at these outdoor vendors (although the wealthy might be inclined to send their servants.)
  - See: markets.
  - See: market-gardens.
  - See: "shopping" London, below.

- "marriage-minded" London -
  - See: Doctor's Common.
  - See: marriage, under M.

- "medical" London -
  - See: Bedlam.
  - See: doctors.
  - See: hospitals.
  - See: Marylebone.

- "military" London -
  - See: army.
  - See: militia.
  - See: naval matters.
  - See: Royal Guards.

- museums of London -
    - See: Bloomsbury/British Museum.
    - See: museums, under M.

- "musical" London -
    - See: music, under M.
    - See: the THEATRES section.

- "old" London -
    - See: City, the.
    - See: gates.
    - See: halls.
    - See: Livery Companies.

- "overnight" London (as in, arriving by coach and/or hiring lodgings) -
    - See: hotels, under H.
    - See: the INNS/PUBS section.

- parks of London -
    - See: parks.
    - See: Royal Parks - Which will lead you to individual listings such as Hyde Park.

- "parliamentary" London - (See: "government" London, above.)

- "post" (that is, the mail) London - See: post, the, under P.

- "reading" London -
    - See: bookshops/booksellers.
    - See: Fleet Street.
    - See: libraries.

- "religious" London - To this day churches abound in London, in keeping with its ancient roots. Most of the churches this compendium lists are/were Church of England, at least after Henry VIII's Dissolution (usually Roman Catholic before then.)
    - See: Church of England - To see a list of the kinds of Anglican clergy.
    - See: dissolution of the monasteries.

- See: districts by name - As virtually every community had at least one church. Such as:

  Acton (St. Mary's.)

  Bermondsey (St. John's; St. Mary Magdalene.)

  Camberwell (St. George's; St. Giles.)
- See: the CHURCHES section.

- "rough/dark" London -
  - See: cemeteries.
  - See: dueling spots.
  - See: "imprisoned" London, above.
  - See: poaching.
  - See: prostitution.
  - See: rough places.
  - See: smugglers.

- "royal" London -
  - See: Buckingham House - Later Palace.
  - See: Hyde Park.
  - See: Kensington Palace.
  - See: Kew Gardens.
  - See: "Royal," under R - Many listings under.
  - See: St. James's Palace.
  - See: Whitehall.
  - See: Whitehall Palace.

- "rural" London - Reminder: we're talking primarily about the 19th century here, so you didn't have to go all that far outside the walls of old London to find pastoral views and to breathe healthier air.

  - See: Blackheath.
  - See: Chelsea.
  - See: Kensington.
  - See: Paddington.

- "shopping" London - "s*hopping London*" is separated from "*market London*" in this list because the following places would more likely be frequented by those of the upper classes. At these more exclusive addresses, the lower classes of the 19th century would have most likely been chased away by shop-owners, Beadles, or Watchmen.

- ➢ See: Bond Street.
- ➢ See: Cheapside.
- ➢ See: Covent Garden.
- ➢ See: Jermyn Street.
- ➢ See: markets - For food items.
- ➢ See: Royal Exchange.
- ➢ See: St. James's Street.
- ➢ See: shopping - Under S.
- ➢ See: various listings - Such as: drapers, hatters, tailors, etc.

- "society" London - (See: "upper crust" London, below.)

- "sporting" London -
    - ➢ See: Activities/Entertainments/Sports, under A.
    - ➢ See: under various sports listings - Examples: archery, cricket, tennis, etc.

- "theatre" London - (See: the THEATRES section.) Note: in modern British usage "theatre" means live performances, "cinema" refers to movie films.

- "upper crust" London -
    - ➢ See: Bloomsbury.
    - ➢ See: Grosvenor Square.
    - ➢ See: Marylebone.
    - ➢ See: Mayfair.
    - ➢ See: Piccadilly.
    - ➢ See: Regent's Street.
    - ➢ See: "royal" London, above.
    - ➢ See: "shopping" London, above.
    - ➢ See: St. James's.

- "watery" London -
    - ➢ See: canals.
    - ➢ See: docks.

- See: Thames, the.
- See: water - For drinking water.
- See: Watermen.

- "working" London - London has for centuries been a busy, bustling place, and so my list here could be very long. Instead, here are perhaps the most pertinent suggestions:
    - See: Cheapside.
    - See: Guildhall.
    - See: halls - To learn about the guilds that ran the complex engine that was ancient-to-19th century London commerce.
    - See: Livery Companies.

London A to Z, the - Essential map guide for visiting/touring London, first developed in the 1930s.

London and Middlesex Archaeological Society - (AKA: Bishopgate Institute.) 230 St. Helen's Place. Founded ca. 1850.

London Aquarium - South Bank. Housed in the old County Hall since 1995. (See: County Hall.)

London Auction Mart - (AKA: New Auction Mart.) An exchange established by London auctioneers. They sought to organize property sales, to bring order and clarity to a group of informal institutions. Built in 1810 (behind the Bank at the corner of Throgmorton Street and Bartholomew Lane at a cost of 40,000 pounds.) This bit of competition, however, did not diminish the prestige of Garraway's for auctioneers. (See: Garraway's Coffee House.)

London Bridge - (See under the BRIDGES section.)

London Bridge City - 1980s development between London Bridge and Tower Bridge.

London Bridge Sewer - (See: Walbrook River.)

London City Airport - 1987. Not to be confused with Heathrow. (See: docks/Victoria Dock.)

London, City of -

- See: City, the.
- See: London.

London Clearing House - (Also seen as: LCH.) Founded in 1888. Serves major international exchanges, dealing in bonds, commodities, rate swaps, etc. Largely owned by the London Stock Exchange group. (See: clearing house, under C.)

London County Council - (Nickname: LCC.) Created in 1888, (replacing the Metropolitan Board of Works) to deal with the conflicts arising as "non-City" areas were added to the City of London (because the City Corporation was restricted to the City only.) In 1965 it became the Greater London Council (this then being abolished under Margaret Thatcher in 1986.)

- See: City, the.
- See: County Hall.
- See: Lord Mayor. - Especially see.
- See: Metropolitan Board of Works.

London County and Westminster Bank - 1834. (See: Westminster Bank.)

London Dispensary for the Relief of the Poor Afflicted with Diseases of the Eye and Ear - (See: Charterhouse Square/London Dispensary.)

London Dock at Wapping - (See: docks/London Dock.)

London Docklands Development Corporation - Established in 1981, but funding didn't come into play until 1987.

London Dragon - (See: Griffin.)

London Dungeon - Modern. (See: Tooley Street/London Dungeon.)

London Eye - Jubilee Gardens, on the South Bank. 1999 oversized Ferris wheel, made up of smooth-riding capsules that provide a 30 minute view ride.

London Fields - (See: Hackney/London Fields.)

London Fire Brigade - (See: Metropolitan Fire Brigade.)

London Fire Establishment - London's *public* fire service, founded 1833. There were fire brigades prior to this, to which landowners could pay a fire protection fee, and which were private companies. Renamed in 1904 as the London Fire Brigade.

- See: Fire Brigade - Notes at.
- See: Metropolitan Fire Brigade.

London Foundling Hospital - (See: Foundling Hospital.)

London Gas Light and Coke Company - (See: gas lighting.)

London Hospital - (Is now known as: Royal London Hospital.) Founded in 1740 in Prescott Street, a quiet road that led to the village of Mile End. Established for Aldgate's poor.

It was four houses with 30 beds, called at first the London Infirmary. It moved outside the City's eastern boundary in 1741 (into an area peopled by prostitutes and drinking houses.)

It was replaced by a Whitechapel building in 1753; finished in 1757 and renamed the London Hospital, with 130 beds and a water flushing system. East wing added in 1775.

A house for wounded or sick dock laborers, seamen and watermen. It is London's oldest "teaching hospital." In 1759, the charter of incorporation was received, and the building on the Whitechapel site commenced.

Just west of the hospital was a huge dump pile formed by rubble after the Great

Fire of 1666; supposedly it was 182 feet by 329 feet, and taller than the hospital. The value of the surrounding land increased over the years, so in 1807-8 the Mount was pulled down, creating Mount Place, Mount Street, and Mount Terrace. Later (post-Regency) became Arnold Circus. (See: Medical College.)

London Institute, the - 1815-19. Finsbury Circus. By William Brooks. Library for foreign and domestic periodicals, and lectures. Later housed the School of Oriental Studies. Demolished 1936.

London Institution for the Gratuitous Care of Malignant Diseases, the - (See: Royal Free Hospital.)

London Library, the - 14 St. James's Square. A private Subscription library. Not founded until 1841, but the building (into which the library was moved in 1845) dates from the 1760s. The private gardens have had an equestrian statue of William III since 1808. It currently has over 1,000,000 books.

London Lock Hospital - (AKA: Lock Hospital.) Moved in 1842 to Harrow, near the canal bridge. From the 1860s also began treating, via a government grant, military patients. (See: Lock Hospital.)

London Marathon, the - Long distance running race situated in London. The first was held in 1981.

London Mechanics' Institute - Founded in 1823. Opened in 1828. Under the University of London umbrella by 1920. Name changed in 1866 to Birkbeck College.

London Missionary Society - London. Founded in 1795. (See: Corporation for the Propagation of the Gospel in New England.)

London Museum, the - The old London Museum was founded by Viscount Esher and Viscount Harcourt in 1912 in Kensington Palace; moved to its home in the Barbican (on London Wall) in 1976. (See: Guildhall Museum.)

London Museum - Alternate name for the Egyptian Hall. (See: Piccadilly/Egyptian Hall.)

London Orphan Asylum - Established in 1813. First at Shoreditch; then Bethnal Green; then Clapton in the 1820s. For "children of married decent parents."

London Passenger Transport Board - 1933, public, replacing the Underground Group (which had been privately run.)

London Planetarium - 1958. Marylebone Road.

London Police Force - (See: City of London Police Force.)

London School Board - Established in 1870.

- See: education.
- See: schools.

London School of Economics - Founded in 1895 at 9 John Adam Street. Moved in 1896 to 10 Adelphi Terrace. Was always open to both men and women.

London School of Veterinary Surgery - 1791. The oldest and largest veterinary school in the UK. Camden Town. Began mostly treating horses, but the type of animals treated expanded over time. Joined the University of London in 1949, and is now called: the Royal Veterinary College.

London Scottish Golf Club - 1864.

- See: golf.
- See: Wimbledon Commons/London Scottish Golf Club.

London Society of Licensed Victuallers - A Licensed Trade Charity. (Not a Guild.) For people working or retired from the trade of selling licensed drink (and their dependents.) Founded in 1836. (See: Strand/Morning Advertiser - To learn the Victuallers were already functioning, however, by at least 1794.)

London Stock Exchange - (See: Stock Exchange, under S.)

London Stone, the - Supposedly placed by the Roman, Brutus. In 1720 it was encased in a stone cavity. Today it can be seen, tucked behind an iron grill, in a wall of the Bank of China (also known as the Overseas Chinese Banking Corporation) on Cannon Street, north side. This is meant to approximate where it had been placed in 1798 in the south wall of St. Swithin's church (the latter demolished in 1962.) Until 1742, the position had been on the south side of Cannon Street (before the street was widened.)

Once described as a "great stone" (being a large pillar of oolite limestone,) it is now only about three feet square. Was a place where pacts and proclamations were made (in the 14-16th C. time frame.)

It is also known as the Milliarium. (See: Candlewick Street/Milliarium.)

Not to be confused with the Stone of Scone. (For that, see: Westminster Abbey/Stone of Scone.)

London Street - Ancient houses. Written of in Charles Dickens' *Oliver Twist.* THE FACE OF LONDON describes this street as being: "amongst the fastnesses of Jacob's Island." So close to the docks the inhabitants could lower buckets from their windows to pull up water. Small, dirty, crowded.

London Symphony Orchestra - 1904. The first self-governing (independent) group of its kind in Britain (but certainly not the first symphony orchestra.)

London to Dover Road - (See: Dover Road.)

London Trades Council - Established in 1860, it brought a number of trade unions together.

- See: halls - For how the guilds supported their members before unions.
- See: union.

London University - Gower Street. Is the same thing as the University of London. (See under U.)

London Wall - (AKA sometimes: City Wall.) While this means the Roman wall that surrounded the original confines of London, in this entry I also refer to the *road* that is named London Wall.

The Roman wall was built by King Lud, whose reign began in 72BC. It contained the ancient gates that allowed entrance into walled London, until they were all pulled down ca. 1760. Despite being pulled down, some scattered remains of the wall can yet be seen. (See: gates.)

The *street* of London Wall: runs the path of the old City wall's northern border; it is a currently sunken garden, which was the ground level during Roman times. Coins found here date from 190-220AD. Last known to have been rebuilt in 1476.

- 150 London Wall: Museum of London. 1976.

London Zoo -

- See: Regent's Park/Zoological Society.
- See: Zoological Society.

Londonderry House - Park Lane, Mayfair. 1850, for the Marquess(es) of Londonderry. Now demolished, when it was sold to the Hilton group in the 1960s.

Long Acre - (Also seen as: Long-acre.) Once a medieval market-garden. By the Regency, it was a rough part of town. Coach-builders and furniture-makers were here by the mid 18th century, (and were here for a 300 year span.) Northwest-ish to Covent Garden, near Drury Lane. This street is a gentle curve. (See: Leicester Square/Long Acre.)

Long Fields - Several squares were built over these fields.

- See: Russell Square - 1801-04.
- See: Torrington Square - 1800.

Long Water -

- See: Hyde Park/Serpentine.
- See: Kensington Palace/Long Water.

Longford - Hillingdon. Near the present day Heathrow Airport. In the past the name was written Long Ford, and was pronounced that way, too. Thirty houses here by 1337. Became a coaching halt on the Bath Road. There were mills here, where farmers had their corn, barley, and wheat ground. Later came paper mills. Later yet came the printing industry.

- Ash Tree Cottage: Bath Road. 18th century.
- Longford River: Charles I had this artificial watercourse built to provide water for the Bushy Park and Hampton Court lakes.
- White Horse Inn: 17th C., yet standing. (See: White Horse Inn/Longford, under the INNS/PUBS section.)

longitudes - The angular distance of a place east or west of the meridian. (See: Greenwich

Observatory.)

Longman's - Publisher. (See: St. Paul's Churchyard/Paternoster Row.)

Lonsdale Square - Barnsbury, Islington. 1838-45. Tall brick townhouses, Gothic Revival style, distinctive steep gables. The land here had previously belonged to the Drapers' Company.

looking-glass - In referring to mirrors used for viewing one's appearance, "looking-glass" leans closer to being correct Regency usage. This is not a hard and fast rule, but "mirror" is more about industry-related silvered surfaces, such as a dentist's tooth mirror.

looms -

- See: activities/entertainments/sports - weaving, under A.
- See: fabric/cotton.
- See: fabric/silk.

Lord Chancellor, the - Presides over the Lords, in the House of Lords. (See: Upper House.)

Lord Mayor, the - (AKA: The Lord Mayor of the City of London.) An 800+-year-old position (not a street.) Born ca. 1135, the first Mayor of London was Henry Fitz Ailwin de Londonstone (Ailwin is sometimes also seen as: Ailwyn.) Elected in 1189, when King John granted London the right to select a Lord Mayor.

The man in the position was just called "Mayor of London" until the change to "Lord Mayor" ca. 1283; another source said the term became more common usage in the 15th century.

He holds office for a year, being for that year the Chief Magistrate of the City; the Admiral of the Port of London; and the Viceroy of the City (in which capacity he is the first to be informed of the death of the sovereign.) While in office, he is deemed an Earl (and if he dies in office, remains so, with all attendant privileges extended to his family.) He has precedence (in the City) over every other person except the sovereign.

The Lord Mayor's Show (a parade, complete with a gilded coach that has been used since 1755, drawn by six dapple-grays) is in November. He is sworn in at the Guildhall.

His wife is called the Lady Mayoress.

NOTE, HOWEVER, SINCE 2002, THERE IS ANOTHER POSITION THAT HOLDS THE WORD "MAYOR": <u>THE MAYOR OF LONDON</u> (as opposed to the Lord Mayor of the City of London.) This person heads the Greater London Authority. (See under G.) According to THE TIMELINE HISTORY OF LONDON: PEOPLE, PLACES, PAGEANTRY: "The refusal of the City authorities to have any responsibilities for the districts that grew up around the Square Mile created a crisis in the capital... It was not until 1889, when county councils were created, that London beyond the City got an authority with overall responsibility, the London County Council (LCC)... The LCC was replaced by the Greater London Council in 1965, and when this was abolished by Margaret

Thatcher in 1986 a government department took on the GLC's responsibilities, though local borough councils remained. In 2000 the Greater London Authority was created with a new Mayor of London in charge... To avoid confusion, the Lord Mayor of London is now referred to as the Lord Mayor of the City of London, an office that is rather different from that of the Mayor of London." Just to be clear: the Lord Mayor tends to the requirements of the City (capital C,) and the Mayor of London tends to the requirements of the boroughs beyond the City.

- See: Common Hall.
- See: Guildhall.
- See: Highgate Hill/Statue of Dick Whittington - "Four times Lord Mayor of London."
- See: Mansion House.
- See: Mayor - For an explanation of borough mayors.
- See: sheriff.

Here is a limited list of Lord Mayors of London:

1800 - Sir William Staines

1801 - Sir John Eamer

1802 - Charles Price

1803 - John Perring

1804 - Peter Perchard

1805 - James Shaw

1806 - Sir William Leighton

1807 - John Ansley

1808 - Charles Fowler

1809 - Thomas Smith

1810 - Joshua Smith

1811 - Claudius Stephen Hunter

1812 - George Scholey

1813 - William Domville

1814 - Samuel Birch

1815 - Matthew Wood

1816 - Matthew Wood

1817 - Christopher Smith

1818 - John Atkins

1819 - George Bridges

1820 - John Thomas Thorp

1821 - Christopher Magnay

1822 - William Heygate

1823 - Robert Wiathman

1824 - John Garratt

1825 - William Venables

1826 - Anthony Brown

1827 - Matthias Prime Lucas

1828 - William Thompson

1829 - John Crowder

1830-31 - John Key (served for 2 years.)

Lord Mayor's House - (See: Mansion House.)

Lord Mayor's Show - This is the medieval practice, first held in 1422 (and still on-going) of the newly elected Lord Mayor presenting himself before the justices of the king at Westminster, wherein he proclaims the privileges and rights of the City. From the mid 15th C. to 1856, the pageant procession returned by water in gilded barges that belonged to the City Companies.

Lord North Street - Smith Square, Westminster. Early Georgian terraced houses are still there; prestigious residence. Built ca.1720-5. Described as "later and plainer" than nearby Barton Street. (See: Westminster/Smith Square.)

Lord's - Hosier, gloves. (See: Burlington Arcade/68-69.) Note: "Lord's" is also a shorthand way of referring to Lord's Cricket Ground, which has nothing to do with this 19th C. business.

Lord's Cricket Ground - (AKA: Lord's Cricket Club. AKA: Lord's.) St. John's Wood, Marylebone, Westminster. CHAMBERS LONDON GAZETTEER provides: "By the late 18th century cricket had acquired a substantial following in north London and the game's upper-class followers wanted a more exclusive venue than the open meadow at White Conduit Fields. Accordingly, Thomas Lord - a Yorkshire-born bowler and a prosperous merchant - laid out a ground at Dorset Fields (now Dorset Square) and founded the Marylebone Cricket Club. In 1814 he moved the operation to the site of a former duck pond in St. John's Wood, and the success of the venue prompted him to build a pavilion and a tavern."

To expand on that just a bit: In 1787, Thomas Lord fenced in 7 acres (in what would later, ca. 1811, become Dorset Square,) and founded here the Marylebone Cricket Club. (See: MCC, under the CLUBS section.) "Marylebone Cricket Club" is how Lord's is officially called. (Also often referred to simply as: Lord's.) It is the international headquarters for the game of cricket.

The first cricket match here was played in 1787, Middlesex versus Essex. Matches were played regularly and reported in the press. The rules must have been looser, or at least on one occasion, for it is said a team of 11 played against a Surrey team of 22, and won by three wickets.

In 1802, Monsieur Andre Jacques Garnarin, who made the first parachute jump, ascended from here (in the hot air balloon from which he jumped,) his ascent viewed by the Prince of Wales and "Persons of Fashion."

In 1805 the first Eton versus Harrow match was played here; in 1806 the first Gentlemen versus Players.

In 1810, Mr. Lord's lease expired (in 1811, this area was developed into a square, named for a former patron of the sport, the Duke of Dorset: Dorset Square,) so Thomas Lord packed up (including the turf!) and moved to Regent's Park in 1811 (but this site proved for some reason less popular, and besides the government had plans to build Regent's Canal through its center,) so then in 1814 it moved to its present location in St. John's Wood, on St. John's Wood Road. The first match here was on June 22nd, 1814, MCC versus Hertfordshire.

The first pavilion burned in 1825, the second dates from 1889-90.

The grandstand dates from 1925.

Lawn tennis was also played here from 1838 (with the MCC later formulating lawn tennis' first laws.)

- Middlesex County Cricket Club was invited in 1878 to also make its home here at the LCC (as opposed to the founding club of Marylebone Cricket Club.)

Lord's Day Observance Society, the - 1831. An anti-pub-houses-open-on-Sunday movement, begun by an Islington vicar.

Lords, The House of - (AKA: the Upper House.)

- See: Lower House.
- See: Upper House.
- See: Westminster.
- See: Westminster Palace.

Loriners' Company - (AKA: the Worshipful Company of Loriners.) A loriner makes/sells bits, bridles, saddle trees, spurs, stirrups, and other metal items required for a horse's harness. According to AN ENCYCLOPAEDIA OF LONDON: "The Loriners' Ordinances of 1260 are among the oldest known rules of self-government granted by the Lord Mayor to the City misteries." Every Easter the Loriners' supply a bridle and bit to the Lord Mayor. Royal Charter granted in 1711, but it wasn't too many years before control of the industry was lost. It exists mostly now in an association with horse shows. Livery Company. Never had a hall. 57th in the order of precedence.

Loseley House - Guildford. Tudor mansion.

Lothbury Street - Near the Bank of England, (after 1734.) The name is said to derive from the "loathsome" noise the pewterers and metal-workers made here.

- St. Margaret Lothbury: Built by Wren. (See under the CHURCHES section.)

lotteries -

  - See: Coopers' Hall.
  - See: Guildhall.

Loughborough Hotel - (See: Lambeth Wick.)

Love Lane - Runs from Wood Street to Aldermanbury. (See: Gresham Street.)

- Swan with Two Necks: Coaching inn. (See under the INNS/PUBS section.

Lower Belvedere - Bexley. (See: Picardy.)

Lower Cheam - Sutton. The eastern part of Cheam. Originally called East Cheam (this name gathering some new interest of late.) The archbishop(s) of Canterbury owned the manor; Thomas Cranmer swapped it with Henry VIII (who in exchange gave Chislet Park in Kent to Cranmer.) This trade allowed Henry to add more hunting park land to Nonsuch Palace.

  - See: Cheam.
  - See: Nonsuch Palace - For more on who gained the manor after Henry VIII's time.

- East Cheam manor house: Built by one of Cranmer's tenants. Demolished in 1800. Lower Cheam House then built here.
- Sutton Cricket Club: Gander Green Lane. 1858.

Lower Clapton Road - (See: Hackney/Lower Clapton/Lower Clapton Road.)

Lower Edmonton - Enfield. You could call this area "downtown Edmonton." (See: Edmonton, under E.) Is where Church Street, Fore Street, and Hertford Road converge. 101 residences by 1801.

- All Saints' Church: 1140. Present building from the 15th century (although severely altered since.)
- Marsh Side: Rarely used, this is another name for the eastern edge of Lower Edmonton (locals prefer "Pickett's Lock.")

Lower Holles Street - (See: Holles Street.)

Lower Holloway - Holloway, Islington. (AKA: Nether Halloway, in the further past.) 1553. Now most often referred to as Holloway Road or Caledonian Road, with a sizable Ghanian and Nigerian population.

- Copenhagen Fields. (See under C.)
- Copenhagen House. (See: Islington/Copenhagen House.)
- Holloway Road: Ca. 1800.

- Paradise Row: 1767. 31 houses (this was the count until approx. 1800.)

Lower House - (AKA: House of Commons.) Located in the northern end of the Houses of Parliament, Westminster.

The Commons had its origin in the King needing money: land-owners (the Lords) had land, but little cash. The Merchant class (the Commoners) had the cash - and gave/loaned it to the King in exchange for being allowed representation (this being a gradual process, not one sudden or specific event.) However, by the 17th C. (at least) it was firmly established only the Lower House could introduce financial Bills (that is, any Bills regarding crown or state monies.) The Upper House couldn't amend them, could only accept or reject them.

The Commons were granted the use of St. Stephen's Chapel for a meeting space in 1547 by Edward VI. There until the fire of 1834, which necessitated the building of new quarters. (See: Westminster.)

Rebuilt after WWII bombing, by Giles Gilbert Scott in 1951.

The Monarch has not been allowed to enter these chambers since 1642 (when Charles I stormed in, demanding five members be arrested.)

The two opposing sides, government and opposition must face each other across two red lines on the floor - they are two sword-lengths apart. No member may cross over these lines from his side. The government and supporters sit to the right, the Opposition to the left (this pattern is repeated in many European governments, and is the origin of saying one party is either "to the right" or "to the left" in terms of conservatism vs. radicalism.) Senior members of both sides sit on the front (lowest, closest to the red lines) benches.

The Speaker presides over the House, wearing a wig.

The Commons were again destroyed in WWII (1941); the rebuild was by Sir Charles Gilbert Scott, 1948-52, on the same site.

The Labour Party was created in 1906.

In 1928 women in the House were finally given a vote equal to a man's.

- See: Cabinet, the.
- See: Houses of Parliament.
- See: Tories.
- See: Upper House.
- See: Westminster.
- See: Westminster/Chapter House.
- See: Whigs.

Lower Norwood - (See: Norwood/West Norwood.)

Lower Pool - Relates to London Bridge. (See: Pool of London.)

Lower Regent Street - (See: Regent Street/Lower Regent Street.)

Lower Robert Street - (See: Adelphi/Lower Robert Street.)

Lower Sloane Street - (See under: Chelsea/Lower Sloane Street.)

Lower Terrace - (See: Hampstead/Lower Terrace.)

Lower Thames Street - Thames Street was/is made up of two parts, Upper Thames Street and Lower Thames Street. The latter was first called Lower Thames Street in 1799. Much destroyed by the Blitz in WWII.

- 17: Is Harp Lane. (See under H.)
- Bakers' Hall: Harp Lane, off Lower Thames Street. (See under B.)
- Billingsgate: No longer there. (See under B.)
- Custom House: (See under C.)
- St. Dunstan-in-the-East: (See under the CHURCHES section.)
- St. Magnus the Martyr: (See under the CHURCHES section.)
- Tower of London: (See under T.)
- Watermen's and Lightermen's Hall: (See under W.)

Lowndes Square - Belgravia. Developed in 1836-7; completed in 1849.

Lowther Lodge - Kensington. Built 1873-75. In 1913 the building was occupied by the Royal Geographical Society.

Lucifers - 1826. (See: matches.)

Ludgate - (Also occasionally seen as: Lud Gate.) Tradition says that the gate was built by King Lud in the 1st century. One of the six ancient gates of the ancient City; the western gate of the medieval City. Venue of mercers. Demolished 1760. "Lud" means "back" or "Postern" in Old English. (See: gates.)

Ludgate Circus - After 1829. Although, ca. 1702 this was the site from whence issued England's first daily newspaper *The Daily Consort.*

Ludgate Hill - Part of the traditional route for processions between the City and Westminster. Nowadays "Ludgate Hill" refers to the entire length of the street (Ludgate Street,) but only the hill itself was so referred to until 1865. During the Regency, this was one of the prime sites for book buying.

- See: Ludgate Street - Note under.
- See: Ludgate Street/32 Ludgate Hill/Rundell & Bridge - Goldsmiths/jewelers.

Ludgate Prison - (Often referred to simply as "Ludgate.") For serious criminals, as opposed to Newgate for pirates and debtors, or compters for minor crimes. (See: compters.)

Its name is assumed to have derived from the Old English "hlid-geat" (hlid meaning lid/cover/opening/gate.) Although some still claim it was named for the Welsh king Lud

(who supposedly gave his name to form "London" as well.)

It guarded the western road into London, almost opposite what is now St. Martin's Church. The area is now called Ludgate Hill.

Rebuilt (from Roman origins) in 1215, at which time the upper rooms were used as a prison for minor offenders. Became a prison ca. 1377; in 1378 it was deemed any serious prisoners would be held at Newgate Prison, reserving this site for holding Freeman of the City or clergy held for lesser crimes.

The gate was rebuilt in 1586, this time with a statue of King Lud on the east, and Queen Elizabeth I on the west (these statues are now outside St. Dunstan's Church, Fleet Street.)

Rebuilt again, but destroyed in the Great Fire of 1666. What was left was demolished in 1760.

Ludgate Street - (See: Ludgate Hill.)

- 32 Ludgate Hill: Rundell & Bridge, established 1788, very fashionable goldsmith and jeweler. There until 1843. (See under R.)
- Belle Sauvage: Ludgate Hill. Famous coaching inn. It was a playhouse during the Elizabethan era, with "miracle plays" performed in its courtyard. Stood from the 15th century to 1873. In its lifetime it had these names: Bel Savage, Bell on the Hoop, Belle Savage, Belle Sauvage, Belly Savage, Old Bell Savage, and more.
- Rundell & Bridge: (See: 32, above.)
- St. Martin Ludgate: 1677-84, Wren. (See under the CHURCHES section.)
- St. Paul's Cathedral: Ludgate Hill.
    - See: St. Paul's Cathedral, under S.
    - See: St. Paul's Cathedral, under the CHURCHES section.
- Wilkinson, sword makers: (See under W.)

lumber - (See: wood.)

Lunar Society - (See: Birmingham/Lunar Society, in the BRITISH COUNTIES section.)

luncheon - (See: meals.)

lush - As in, a drunkard. Term in use since ca. 1790. While the origin of this word is unclear, some say it relates back to the City of Lushington, a London men's club, whose members were known as a "lush." (See: City of Lushington, under the CLUBS section.)

Lutyens House - Finsbury Circus. 1924-7. Was first known as Britannic House (but only briefly.)

Lying-in Hospital - A hospital for giving birth. Please note, however, most women gave birth at home.

- See: British Lying-in Hospital.
- See: childbirth.

➢ See: City of London Lying-in Hospital.

-M-

Macclesfield Bridge - Rather serves as the north gate of Regent's Park. (See under the BRIDGES section.)

MacKey & Co. - Makers of pickles and preserves. Existed from at least 1812-17.

Madam Tussaud's - Waxworks. (See: Baker Street/Madame Tussaud's.)

Maddox Street - Mayfair. Built in 1720. In the 1730s had some tailors here. Associated with Savile Row.

- 38: Mason's Arms, pub. Built in 1721. Rebuilt in 1934, still there.

madness - Unfortunately, a common Regency term for those suffering from mental illness. (Also: insanity, lunacy.)

➢ See: Bedlam.

➢ See: Old Street/St. Luke's Hospital.

magazines - Could also be called: journals, or periodicals. Too, this list includes almanacs, and reports.

➢ See: Examiner, The - Liberal reformist weekly journal. From 1808 to at least 1817.

➢ See: Gentleman's Magazine - For men.

➢ See: journals.

➢ See: La Belle Assemblee - Women's periodical.

➢ See: Lady's Magazine, the.

➢ See: Nautical Almanac, the.

➢ See: New British Ladies' Magazine - 1818, but only lasted a bit over one year.

➢ See: Pall Mall East/Charles Knight - The Penny Magazine, 1832.

➢ See: Philosophical Transactions - Scientific.

➢ See: Political Register, the - Tory report.

➢ See: Quarterly Review - 1808-1967 periodical.

➢ See: Sporting Magazine, the - 1792-1870.

➢ See: Strand Magazine, the - 1890.

➢ You may care to see: newspapers/news sheets.

Magdalen House - (AKA: Magdalen Hospital.) Pronounced MAUD-lin. Founded by Jonas Hanaway and Robert Dingley in 1758 for "penitent female prostitutes," and incorporated in 1769 (when it moved from Whitechapel to four houses around a quadrangle in St. George's Fields, Southwark.) It was attempted to return the girls to their families. That lacking, they were trained for honest service during their maximum two-year stay. In the 18th C. the median age for the attendant girls was fourteen. Moved a final time in 1866, to Streatham High Street (four miles/6.4 km away.)

magistrates - (See: Justices of the Peace.)

Magna Carta - (AKA: the Great Charter.) Forced upon King John in 1215, it was the foundation document in citizens' rights. (See: The INTRO-REIGN section/British Kings and Queens & their Reigns/John.)

Magpie and Stump - Served "execution breakfasts" - that is, a meal to be enjoyed before viewing a criminal's execution - until 1868.

- See: Old Bailey/Magpie and Stump.
- See under the INNS/PUBS section.

Maida Hill - Westminster. Described as a locale that shifts somewhere to the south of Maida Vale. Little happened here until a branch of the Grand Junction (now Grand Union) Canal came in 1801. The "Maida Hill" name faded after 1868. (See: Edgware Road.)

- Maida Hill Tunnel: Begun in 1812. The first tunnel canal in London, and (after Islington's) is the second largest.

Maida Vale - Westminster. Boundary between Marylebone and Paddington. Formerly was (and still abuts to) Edgware Road, the section taking on the Maida Vale name in 1828 (although the greater area was slow to take on the name.) In 1647 the area belonged to the diocese of London, and was pasture and woodland; no buildings other than a few farms until the 18th century. Built up in the 1830s-40s. A Jewish population moved in ca. the 1880s. (See: Edgware Road.)

- Maida Vale Hospital: 1866. For nervous disorders. First hospital to identify and (successfully) operate on a brain tumor.
- Warwick Avenue: (See under W.)

Maiden Lane - Covent Garden. Ancient. Built up in 1631-1728. J. M. W. Turner (landscape painter) was born here in 1775. (See: Gresham Street, which name it took on in 1845.)

- 35: Rule's, restaurant. 1798.
  - See: restaurants.
  - See: Rule's.

Maidenhead Close - Old pre-Stuart name for Dyott Street. (See under D.)

Maids of Honour Row - (See: Richmond Green/Maids of Honour Row.)

mail - Unlike what Americans call "the mail," in Britain the letter delivery system is called "the post." (See: post, the.)

Maitland Park - Camden, west side of Kentish Town. Victorian and post-war buildings. Most of this area, prior to 1847, had been known as Haverstock Hill.

Makers of Playing Cards Company - (AKA: the Worshipful Company of Makers of Playing Cards.) Guild existed by at least the early 15th century. During Queen Elizabeth I's reign, playing card manufacture was largely monopolized by Sir Walter Raleigh. Charter in 1628. Livery granted in 1792. Has a "fine collection" of playing cards in the Guildhall Library. Never had a hall of their own. 75th in the order of precedence.

Malden - (See: Old Malden.)

Malet Street - Bloomsbury. Small street. Mostly developed in the Victorian era.

- University College: 1828. First to admit Jews and Roman Catholics.
    - See: Gower Street/University College.
    - See under U.
- University of London, 1836. First to admit women, 1878.

Mall, the - Westminster. Laid out in 1662 for Charles II as a leafy alleyway in St. James's Park in which to play "paille maille" (pell mell, a croquet-like game.) LONDON REDISCOVERED says: "Along the north side, behind an earlier Mall where fashionable London paraded in the eighteenth century, stand Clarence House and Marlborough House..." Used to dead-end at the village of Charing (this was yet true during the Regency.) In the early 20th century, the Mall was envisioned as a royal processional road, the carriage drive for all royal processions, as well as the arrival of foreign dignitaries to Buckingham Palace. Double rows of plane trees line the road. Now stretches from the Queen Victoria Memorial (before Buckingham Palace) to the 1910 Admiralty Arch in Trafalgar Square. This road was remodeled in 1910, its current lay-out a tribute to Victoria. Is described as "pink-surfaced."

Became even more formal when the following were added at either end of the boulevard:

- Admiralty Arch: 1910. (See under A.)
- Victoria Memorial: 1911. (See under V.)

man-midwife - During the Regency, childbirth was usually a women-only affair, but man-midwives became more seen as the 19th C. advanced. (See: childbirth.)

Manchester House - (See: Manchester Square/Hertford House.)

Manchester Square - Begun in 1776, completed 1788. Despite London's habit of calling a collection of homes a "square," LONDON by Knopf Guides says of Manchester Square: "...it is in no sense a square." It is round.

- Hertford House: Built in 1776-88, was lived in by the Marquess(es) of Hertford into the 19th C.; the 2nd marquess lived here 1743-1823, acquiring the lease in 1797 (at which time the mansion's name changed from "Manchester House" to "Hertford House.") Yet remains; is now the galleries for the Wallace Collection (since it opened to the public in 1900.) (See: Hertford House, under H.)

Manor House - Hackney/Haringey. CHAMBERS LONDON GAZETTEER explains: "Before the creation of Seven Sisters Road, and thus of the crossroads, this was the site of a tollgate on Green Lanes." Seven Sisters Road: 1832. (See: Green Lane.)

- Manor Tavern: 1832, public house. Demolished in 1932; rebuilt in its current mode.

Manor Lane - (See: Finchley/East End Road.)

Mansell Street - Built in the 17th century. Its north end is in Aldgate; its south end in East Smithfield. It is part of the London Inner Ring Road. The Mansell Street estate was constructed in 1977.

Mansion House - (AKA: the Lord Mayor's House.) In the City; it is on Mansion House Street, at the east end of Poultry Street. Built 1739-52. Palladian style. Took over the area that had been the Stocks Market.

This is the Lord Mayor's (who is the Chief Magistrate of the City, highest in precedence in the City except for the monarch) official residence, and he is required to live here for his year as Lord Mayor. (There has been a Mayor since the 12th C., but they had no particular residence until this was built, up to that time being obliged to run the City's business from one's own home.) CHAMBERS LONDON GAZETTEER says: "The idea of commissioning a grand house for the mayor was first discussed after the Great Fire of 1666, but nothing came of it and the stocks market was built here instead. Only when other large cities started to build such mansions did London decide it was not to be outdone."

Begun in 1739, completed in 1753, by George Dance the Elder (who also made his home here.) Portland stone; Palladian front with six large Corinthian columns. In the later 18th C. it was refurbished by George Dance the Younger. Has a 90 foot tall Egyptian Hall on the ground floor (not to be confused with the Egyptian Hall in Piccadilly); it is the Lord Mayor's reception room, used for banquets. On the first floor (second floor, to Americans) there is the Dancing Gallery (also called the Ball Room.) The mayor's private entrance was added in 1845.

There is one woman's and ten men's prison cells in the cellar, known as the "birdcage." The mansion also contained a court of justice, built in 1849 and called the Justice Room. (It is above the cells.)

- See: Court of Aldermen.
- See: Lord Mayor.

- Egyptian Hall: A reception room, the grandest and "most sumptuous" in the Mansion House.
    - ➢ See: Egyptian Hall.
    - ➢ See notes above in this entry.
- St. Mary Woolchurch Haw: Burned in the Great Fire of 1666. Rebuilt as St. Mary Woolnoth. (See both entries under the CHURCHES section.)

Manton's - Dover Street. Shooting gallery and gun shop. In THE RISE & FALL OF A REGENCY DANDY it states that Manton's entry in the Office London Directory of 1819 read: "Patentee for Detonating Guns, Gravitating Stops, and for Chronometers going in Vacuo, Gun-maker to their RH the Prince Regent, the Dukes of York, Cambridge, Gloucester, etc." Also: "...(Manton) kept a gallery behind his premises where gentlemen could practise shooting, or challenge each other to a pacific contest firing at targets." Joseph Manton was renowned as a gunsmith; in 1814 he sold a gun he constructed to famous dandy Scrope Berdmore Davies. (See: weapons.)

mantua-maker - Made women's clothing. An older term by the time of the Regency, but still sometimes used; Regency ladies would probably say modiste. (A mantua was a 17-18th C. garment, at first a loose gown, but evolved into more of a robe; the word comes from the French *manteuil*, meaning mantle.)

- ➢ See: milliners.
- ➢ See: modiste.

maps - Have existed since the time of the ancient Egyptians, but they weren't much preserved until ca. the 15th century. At first were produced by engravers; by the 17th C. they could be had from print shops. (See: Leicester Square/Long Acre/12-14, from 1852.)

Marble Arch - Westminster. It originally stood near the three-bayed, central projection of Buckingham Palace, where the famous balcony from which royalty is seen to wave is situated, 1833-47. (Not to be confused with Constitution Arch, also called Wellington Arch.)

Built of white Italian Carrara marble; its design was based on the Arch of Constantine in Rome.

In 1851 it was relocated to Hyde Park. Then it landed on an isolated traffic circle in the 1860s, at the junction of Edgware Road, Oxford Street, and Park Lane.

Walking through the arch is a privilege reserved for senior members of the royal family and for the monarch's Troop of the Royal Horse Artillery on ceremonial occasions.

- ➢ See: Buckingham House/Marble Arch.
- ➢ See: Cumberland Gate - Along which Marble Arch stands, Cumberland Gate marking the northeast corner of Hyde Park.

Marble Hill House - Richmond. Built 1724-29, by Roger Morris from designs by Lord Herbert, for Henrietta Howard, Countess of Suffolk (George II's mistress.) Elegantly simple Palladian villa. LET'S GO-THE BUDGET GUIDE TO LONDON says: "The Great Room, on the first" (to Americans, the second) "floor, is lavishly decorated with gilt and carvings by James Richards and the original Panini paintings of ancient Rome." Three story. Still there. Bought in 1902 by the London County Council; parklands open to the public in 1903. Restored in the mid 1960s. (See: Richmond/Marble Hill House.)

Mare Street - (See: Hackney/Mare Street.)

Margaret Street - (See: Cavendish Square/Margaret Street.)

Marine Pavilion - AKA: the Brighton Pavilion. (See: Brighton/Brighton House, under the BRITISH COUNTIES section.)

marine police - (See: Wapping/Wapping Police Station.)

Marine Society - Founded by Jonas Hanaway (philanthropist) in 1756, an organization that trained poor street boys for the Royal Navy, lessening the need for press-ganging. (See: impressment.)

mariners - (See: Master Mariners.)

Marines - (AKA: Royal Marines, from 1802.) As stated in A SEA OF WORDS, a Marine was: "A specialized soldier who serves on a Man-of-War and at dockyards, or on shore in certain cases. In Britain, a radical reorganization of the marines brought them under the control of the Admiralty in 1755. During the Napoleonic War, the complement of a large ship of the line often consisted of over 20 percent marines, who served in gun crews and boarding parties and as sharpshooters and sentries." (See: Coast Guard.)

maritime matters - At least in this listing, the difference between maritime issues and naval issues being: "maritime" meaning all things relating to sea-going business or vessels; "naval" relating to the Royal Navy specifically.

- See: Admiralty, The.
- See: Lloyd's of London.
- You may care to see: marine - Various listings at.
- You may care to see: naval matters.
- You may care to see: Thames River.

Mark Lane - City. Links Fenchurch Street and Great Tower Street. Dates from at least 1747.

- All Hallows Staining: (See under the CHURCHES section.)
- Corn Exchange: (See under C.)

market-gardens - The difference between market-gardens and markets is: the former (existing outside greater London) grew the produce; the latter (often within greater London) sold it.

- See: Broom Farm.
- See: Dagenham.

- See: Fulham - Supplied Covent Garden.
- See: Hyde Park Square.
- See: Kidbrooke.
- See: King's Road.
- See: Mitcham.
- See: Nine Elms - Vegetables, including asparagus.
- See: North End.
- See: Pimlico.
- See: Putney.
- See: Queen's Road, Peckham.
- See: Stepney.
- See: Welling.
- See: Woodlands.

markets - In medieval times, a market might be referred to as a "cheap"; hence City names such as Cheapside. Until the mid 19th C. virtually every market was made up of stalls in an open-air space; the stalls themselves might have roofs, but they were not enclosed under a larger protective roof. The markets were utilized by every level of society, rich and poor alike.

- See: Billingsgate - For fish.
- See: Borough Market - For wholesale flowers, fruit.
- See: Carnaby Market - Under "Paddington/Carnaby Market" below.
- See: Corn Exchange - London's only corn, grain, and seed market for 240 years, from 1747.
- See: Cornhill - Had been a medieval grain market; in the Regency known for its publishers.
- See: Covent Garden - Had been a fruit, vegetable, and food market - and by the time of the Regency perhaps as well known for opera, and prostitution (at night.) Revamped in 1828. (See under C.)
- See: Cumberland Market, The Haymarket - Which had been near the St. James's Street area, was pulled down in 1830 and moved here. (See: Haymarket, under H.)
- See: Fleet Market - Was a stock market, as in butchery; pulled down in 1826. (See: Stock Market.)
- See: Hatton Garden/Leather Lane - For diamonds, gems, gold.
- See: Haymarket - Hay and straw market near St. James's Street until 1830. (See: Cumberland Market, above.)
- See: Hungerford Market - For purchasing household provisions.

Described as "bustling."

- See: Leadenhall Market - Had been a poultry market, but turned into a general foodstuffs market after 1666.
- See: Newgate Market - Meat market.
- See: Newport Market - A country market, all manner of items for sale.
- See: Oxford Market.
- See: Paddington/Carnaby Market - Re-established in 1823; presumably remained a fish, meat, and vegetable market.
- See: Rosemary Lane - Rag Fair; for cloth, clothing.
- See: St. James's Market - Meat, fish, vegetables; where servants shopped for their masters.
- See: Shepherd's Market - For fish and game. (See: Mayfair/Shepherd's Market.)
- See: Smithfield Market - Meat; live animals.
- See: Spitalfields - Fruits and vegetables.
- See: Stock Market - Had first been Fleet Market, until 1826. For: meat and fish.
- See: Uxbridge/Uxbridge market-house - For flour.
- See: Whitechapel Road Market - (AKA: Whitechapel Market.) For hay. Thrived during the Victorian era. Eventually there were many "nuisance traders" here, so in 1904 the market was refurbished; was/is known as "the Waste."

Markham Square - Laid out in 1836, on farmland that had been part of Box Farm. Named for the last owner of Box Farm, Pulham Markham Evans.

Marks and Spencer's - (Department store.) 1912, with thirty branches in the London area by 1914.

Marks Gate - Barking and Dagenham. Had a fortified hilltop presence here ca. 600BC. CHAMBER LONDON GAZATTEER tells us: "The medieval manor of Marks was one of Barking's oldest free tenements (an estate held for life or longer,) with its own manor court from the 14th century and special rights in Hainault Forest." The (much reduced) estate sold to the Crown in 1855; now part of Warren Farm.

- Marks Hall: Mid 15th century 20-bedroom moated manor house. Pulled down in 1808.

Marlborough Gate - St. James's Park. 1828. Pedestrian and carriage gates, cast iron. The gates run between Marlborough House and St. James's Palace.

Marlborough House - The future King George V was born here in 1865.

- See: Pall Mall/Marlborough House.
- See: Royal College of Art.

Marlborough Road - By 1828 most of what had been called Blacklands Lane (which dates from at least the 18th C.) was then called Marlborough Road.

- Queen's Chapel: (See: St. James's Palace/Queen's Chapel.)

marriage - On becoming engaged: it would not occur to a Regency gentleman to bring an engagement ring. (A bride wore only a wedding ring.) He would approach the young lady's father or guardian, and upon receiving permission, would propose to the lady herself. (Sometimes, particularly where the gentleman was unsure of the lady's affections, they might first have a conversation, and then he'd seek out parental permission.) Remember, during the Regency, marriage was still at least as much about being a legal agreement between families, as it was a romantic event.

After March 25th, 1754, Lord Hardwicke's Marriage Act (of 1753) decreed marriages were valid only if they had been advertised by banns for three consecutive Sundays or holy days, or sanctioned by a special license; they also had to be conducted by an Anglican clergyman, in a church, and recorded in a register. (See: Doctor's Common - For Special Licenses.) This Act was deemed necessary in order to end the practice of heiresses (or any female) being kidnapped/forced into marriage. Also under the Act, handfasting (marrying by declaration, not by a religious ceremony, practiced sometimes by the lower orders) was made illegal; one *must* be married by clergy for it to be a legal union.

A marriage in just a registrar's office (or a landowner's private chapel) was not legal until 1837; after 1837, a civil registrar must be in attendance (at these two options.)

You could marry on any day of the week, although Sunday services made Sundays more difficult.

After the ceremony, you went to the vestry and signed your marriage lines, into the parish register. (You didn't get a marriage certificate, but being entered into the parish register served the same purpose of proof of marriage, and was required by Hardwicke's Marriage Act.)

JANE AUSTEN'S ENGLAND tells us: "For anyone with an urgent need to marry or who did not wish to obtain a licence, for which an 'allegation' had to be sworn, usually by the groom, giving details of the couple and assurances of no impediments to the marriage. Normally, common licenses were issued by archbishops, bishops and some archdeacons, or by clergy in certain parishes and officials acting on their behalf. A marriage was then permitted to take place within the jurisdiction of the person issuing the licence, in one of the parishes named on the licence, but the requirement to be married in a named parish was often ignored. The wedding could take place later that day, but usually happened the day after."

Rich or poor, you married in a church (unless you eloped.)

Speaking of elopement: the famous Gretna Green in Scotland (and other locales) for elopement was an option for couples lacking parental consent. Scottish marriage law called for only a simple declaration before witnesses (not necessarily a vicar or parson.) In the eyes of English society, however, elopement was a shocking thing (no doubt in part due to the implied lack of parental approval,) and was much frowned upon. If one eloped, one might find oneself unacceptable to the highest society.

To marry by (normal) license, the participants must be 21 (to not require parental permission); minors could marry by publishing the banns, although parents were yet free to set up objections. The age of consent to be married (with parental permission) for boys was 14, 12 for girls, although records show most Regency couples married in their 20s. (You may care to see: age of consent - Regarding sexual activity.)

Apprentices could not marry until their (normally) 7 years of apprenticeship were completed.

By today's standards, most Regency era weddings were small and simple. One married in the morning; canon law required solemnization between 8am and noon (until 1886); to celebrate, you might host a following wedding breakfast.

The bride usually simply wore her best gown; the practice of wearing white would not be popularized until Queen Victoria wore white as she married Prince Albert in 1840. Veils were not seen at this time; brides usually wore a bonnet, perhaps trimmed with lace.

Two things existed from ancient times: the bride's wedding ring (only about half of married Regency era men chose to wear a wedding ring,) and cake. (You may care to see: diamond.) The cakes were more like fruitcake, often liquor-soaked. It might be covered with almond icing, browned in the oven.

There could be bridesmaids.

You could ride in a carriage, but most folk walked to their wedding.

While a couple might take a bridal trip after the wedding, there wasn't such a thing as the modern meaning of "honeymoon" - the term simply referred to the first month after the wedding.

- See: Courts of Common Law and Equity - Regarding courts that governed marriage matters.
- See: Doctor's Common - For special licenses.
- See: weddings.
- You may care to see: literacy - For ages of brides/grooms who could

sign their names.

Mars - (See: planets/Mars.)

Marshalsea Prison - Always written of in this manner: "he was imprisoned in the Marshalsea," sometimes with "Prison" tacked on, but always with the "the." (See: Southwark/Marshalsea.)

Martin Lane - Near London Bridge, the City. Existed since at least 1663.

- Olde Wine Shades: (See under the INNS/PUBS section.)

Martin's Street - (See: Leicester Square/Martin's Street.)

Marylebone - (Pronounced MAR-lee-bun.) A corruption of the name "St. Mary-by-the-Bourne" ("bourne" representing the river, the Tyburn.) Westminster. 18th C. district; Georgian houses with iron railings; behind the houses are mews but no gardens. In current times, this is not really a residential area anymore. Building/expansion came to the area ca. 1811-13 (and on,) in step with the new Park Crescent buildings.

- Baker Street: (See under B.)
- Bentinck Street: (See under B.)
    - 7: The historian Edward Gibbon lived here from 1773-1783.
- Cato Street: Due to the infamous "Cato Street Conspiracy" this street's name was changed in 1820 to Horace Street. (See: Cato Street, under C.)
- Chandos Street. (See under C.)
- Devonshire Place: Built ca. 1791.
    - 2: Sir Arthur Conan Doyle (author) practiced medicine here in 1891.
- Dorset Square: Square dates from 1811. (See under D.)
    - 39-40: Dorset Square Hotel. (See: Lord's Cricket Ground, note under.)
- Gloucester Place: (See: Portman Square/Gloucester Place.)
- Great Marylebone Street: (See: New Cavendish Street.)
- Harley Street: (See under H.)
- Hertford House: 1770s, for the Duke of Manchester. (See under: Manchester Square.)
- High Street: (AKA: Marylebone High Street.) Medieval. Follows along the Tyburn's stream.
- Horace Street: (See: Cato Street, above in this section.)
- Lord's Cricket Ground. (See under L.)
- Marylebone Gardens: At least since 1668, pleasure garden. Redesigned and expanded in 1737. Closed in 1776. (Second source says it served as a pleasure garden until 1790.) On the site of what is now Devonshire Street and Beaumont Street.

- Marylebone High Street:
    - 83-84: Daunt Books: Opened in 1912.
    - Marylebone Lane: East of Manchester Square, Westminster. Marylebone Lane is the southern end of Marylebone High Street. Dates back to Tyburn, the medieval village.
- Marylebone Lane: The southern end of Marylebone High Street. (See at its own listing, under M.)
- Marylebone New Church: Built 1813-17, by Thomas Hardwick, on land donated by the Duke of Portland. The original site of St. Mary-le-Bourne (see below in this section) was on what is now Marylebone High Street. (There had been a prior church near present-day Oxford Street, but it was frequently vandalized and was abandoned.) Heavy portico, in the Corinthian style.
- Marylebone Park: Former name of Regent's Park. (See: Regent's Park/(The Park,) under R.)
- Marylebone Place: The manor house. In 1737 it became a pleasure garden; closed in 1778. Pulled down in 1791.
- Marylebone Road: Was originally called New Road. This section of road was built in the mid 1800s, connecting Islington/Paddington to north London.
    - Madame Tussaud's: Moved here in 1884. (See: Baker Street/Madame Tussaud's.)
    - Marylebone New Church: (See, above.)
    - Royal Academy of Music: 1822. (See under R.)
- Marylebone Watch House: Marylebone Lane (Oxford Street end.) Established in 1753; where the Marylebone district watchmen met to equip themselves for the evening (with a lantern, a long stick or bludgeon, and a rattle.) Was also used as a holding cell for anyone apprehended. Rebuilt in 1803, and in 1825. Closed in 1921, becoming a bookshop until it was pulled down in 1935.
- New Cavendish Street: (See under N.)
- Park Crescent:
    - See: Portland Place, below.
    - See under P.
- Portland Place: Incorporated in Nash's plans/way from St. James's to Regent's Park. This street was primarily built in 1776 (or 1778, depending on your source) by the Adam brothers. Ten of the original Adam houses yet remain. Its northern end is Park Crescent. (See: Portland Place, under P.)
- Portman Square: (See under P.)

  - Gloucester Place: (See: Portman Square/Gloucester Place.)
  - Gloucester Square: 1840s.
- Queen Anne Street: Built in the late 1760s. J. M. W. Turner (the artist) lived on this street from 1799-1851.
  - Chandos House: 2 Queen Anne Street. 1770-1, by the Adam brothers, of Scottish stone that was imported. (See: Chandos House, under C - The note at.)
- Regent's Park: (See under R.)
- St. Mary's-on-the-Burn (or Bourn, or Bourne): There for years, but rebuilt in 1813-1817, with a fine Corinthian portico as seen today, by Thomas Hardwick. Had a reputation for speedy marriages, because was "away" from supervising eyes. This is the third church; also called Marylebone New Church. (See, above.)
- St. Peter, in Vere Street: Built 1722-1724, design by Sir Robert Harley, 1st Earl of Oxford. (See under the CHURCHES section.)
- Seymour Place: (See under S.)
- Upper Marylebone Street: (See: New Cavendish Street.)
- Vere Street: (See under V.)

Marylebone Cricket Club - Founded in 1787; headquarters is at Lord's.

- ➢ See: Lord's Cricket Ground, under L.
- ➢ See: MCC, under the CLUBS section.

Marylebone Lane - (See: Marylebone/Marylebone High Street/Marylebone Lane.)

Marylebone Park - (See: Regent's Park/"The Park.")

Marylebone Road - (See under: Marylebone/Marylebone Road.)

Masons' Company - (AKA: the Worshipful Company of Masons.) Those who laid stone or brick. First references date from 1376. Ordinances in 1481. Guild powers (of all the building crafts) declined because of the Great Fire of 1666 (because the vast rebuilding needs of the City stripped away guild restrictions); even achieving a Charter in 1677 did not restore much of the Masons' control of their trade. The Company's entire membership is admitted into the Livery. Never had a hall. 30th in the order of precedence. (Not to be confused with Freemasons.)

Mason's Yard - Mayfair. Began as Mason's Mews, but by 1740 was being called Mason's Yard.

- Fortnum and Mason, grocers. (See: Piccadilly/Fortnum & Mason.)
- Maxwell, Henry, and Co., Ltd.: South Audley Street. Established in 1750. Hunting clothing, including hunting pink (the famous red coats.) Also boot- and shoemakers. One of the premiere makers of hunting clothes was a gentleman with

the surname "Pink"; (despite being a shade or two off,) nonetheless his name became synonymous with the red coat. This may well be a folktale. From every source I have seen, it appears that hunting pink came along later in the 19th century, post-Regency.

- See: Maxwell, Henry, under M.
- See: Savile Row/11.

Master Mariners - (AKA: the Honourable Company of Master Mariners. They are not "Worshipful" like many other companies; George V granted them the "Honourable" in 1928.) Formed under the Companies' Act, in 1926. It was incorporated in 1930. Became a Livery Company in 1932. (It was the first Livery company to be formed since 1746.) The first Company to have a floating hall (1947,) on a 900 ton sloop named "HQS Wellington." HQS = Head Quarters Ship. 78th in the order of precedence.

matches - As in, fire starting. Friction matches didn't exist until 1826, when they were invented by John Walker (chemist,) accidentally. He went to clean a mixing stick, tried to scrape it off, and it ignited. He called them "friction lights." They were cardboard coated with potash and antimony, packed by the 100 in tin tubes. They were three inches long, with a piece of sandpaper in the tube on which to scrape them. These were nicknamed: Lucifers.

The "waxed vesta," the first match to contain phosphorous as the igniting agent, were invented in 1830, in Germany. They were carried in metal containers, as it was too easy to ignite them accidentally.

That being given, throughout the Regency era (1811-1820,) you mostly lit a flame by borrowing fire from a secondary source such as a lamp or a fire on the grate. (Or used a tinderbox.)

- See: tinderboxes.
- You may care to see: candles.
- You may care to see: gas lighting.
- You may care to see: lamps.

material - (See: fabrics.)

maternity -

- See: British Lying-in Hospital.
- See: childbirth.
- See: City of London Lying-in Hospital.
- See: condoms.

Mawney - Havering, between Romford and Collier Row. A corruption of the name Sir Walter de Mauny (a 14th C. celebrated soldier who had a manor house here.) The name of Mawney (or Mawneys) is used by locals, but is found on few maps. In the mid 19th C. this area was known for its gypsies, who worked fields, and sold doormats and brushes. The area grew after 1883.

Maxwell, Henry - Spurmakers, who became boot and shoemakers.

- See: Mason's Yard/Maxwell, Henry.
- See: Savile Row/11.

Mayfair - St. James's, Westminster. Bounded by Hyde Park, Oxford Street, Piccadilly, and Regent Street.

Was/is called "Mayfair" by everyone, although Mayfair has never been an official name for this district. It has also never been officially recognized as a postal district. Called by the name of the livestock and grain fair that was held here yearly, in the first week of May, from 1686. Each year's fair lasted two weeks. Also included fencers, gaming tables, gingerbread cake, jugglers, pugilists, puppet shows, many stalls, swings, theatre, and toys. The May Fair had moved here from Haymarket, to Great Brook Field (where Curzon Street and Shepherd Market are now.) Due to its disorderly crowds, it was exiled in 1764 to Bow.

The area's origins: in 1677, the lands of what would become Mayfair came to Sir Thomas Grosvenor via marriage.

In 1735, Edward Shepherd was granted by George II the right to build a market.

Mayfair's three main squares are Berkeley, Grosvenor, and Hanover. People mostly only dwelt here during the Winter/Spring Parliamentary season.

All the 18th C. homes of Mayfair were built on seven estates: the Burlington, Millfield, Conduit, Albemarle, Berkeley, Curzon, and Grosvenor estates (the latter being the largest.)

LONDON, FROM THE EARLIEST TIMES TO THE PRESENT DAY says that once the Mayfair squares were laid out, hackney coaches were not allowed to "ply in the squares."

Until they began to thrive in Victorian times, London's few (and "boastable") hotels were mostly centered in Mayfair.

- See: Brook Street/25/Claridge's Hotel, below.
- See: Piccadilly/105/Pulteney's Hotel, under P.

Middle class families put up in lodging houses in the Mount Street part of Mayfair.

By the 1720s Mayfair had also become a "smart" shopping center, being fashionable and exclusive.

Was (still is) owned by the Dukes of Westminster, the Grosvenors.

- Albany: (It is considered ignorant to refer to these bachelor chambers as "The" Albany, or to refer to the rooms as flats.) The poet Lord Byron lived here at one time.

- Albemarle Street: (See under A.)
    - 50: The firm of John Murray has been here since 1812 (publishers.) The John Murray of that time published Lord Byron, also burning Byron's autobiography in 1824 in response to his friends having found it supposedly immoral/shocking.
- Avery Row: Built in the 1720s.
- Berkeley Square: (See under B.)
- Bond Street: Was the main street in Mayfair. (See under B.)
- Brook Street: (See under B.)
    - 24: George Frederick Handel (musician's) home, until 1759.
    - 25: Claridge's Hotel. (See under C.)
- Bruton Street: (See under B.)
- Burlington House: Now home of the Royal Academy. (See under B.)
- Carrington Street: (See under C.)
- Chesterfield House: Built for Lord Chesterfield in the 1730s. Pulled down in 1934. (See: South Audley Street/Chesterfield House.)
- Clarges Street: The street is named for George Monch's (d. 1670) wife Anne Clarges. Lady Hamilton (paramour to Lord Nelson, and society lady) lived here at one time following her husband's death in 1803.
    - 46, Charles Fox (Whig statesman) lived here briefly from 1803-4.
    - A moneylender called, in the parlance of the time, "Jew" King lived on this street, ready to lend large sums to those gentlemen who arrived here after having suffered heavy losses at their nearby gentlemen's clubs. Mr. King lived opulently, drove a flamboyant yellow carriage, and finely dressed his handsome wife as a result of his business dealings.
- Curzon Street: Still has some 18th C. houses here. (See under C.)
    - Crewe House: (Also sometimes seen spelled as: Crew House.) Rebuilt by Sir John Soane in 1730 for Edward Shepherd. (See: Curzon Street/Crewe House, under C.)
- Farm Street: There had been an 18th C. farm here.
    - Farm Street Church: Jesuit church, Catholic. Built in the 1840s, opened in 1849.
- Green Park: (See under G.)
- Grosvenor Chapel: "Attractive, little," built in 1730 in South Audley Street. (See under the CHURCHES section.)
- Grosvenor Square: (See under G.)

- Hanover Square (See under H.)
- Hyde Park: (See under H.)
- Lancashire Court: A twisty-turny lane. Now with cute shops and restaurants. Still has Georgian buildings here.
- May Fair, the: (See the opening section, above.)
- Mount Street: (See at its own listing.)
- New Bond Street: (See: Bond Street/New Bond Street, under B.)
- North Audley Street: (See under N.)
- Old Bond Street: (See: Bond Street/Old Bond Street, under B.)
- Oxford Street: Was Tyburn Turnpike until ca. 1783. (See under O.)
- Pall Mall: (See under P.)
- Park Lane: Had been Tyburn Lane. (See under P.)
- Piccadilly: (See under P.)
- Regent Street: Sealed off Mayfair to the east. In 1810 John Nash bluntly said it was intended to keep the squares and homes of the nobles from the "mechanics and the trading part of the community." (See under R.)
  - St. George's, Hanover Square: (See under the CHURCHES section.)
- Shepherd's Market: (Also sometimes seen written as: Shepherd Market.) Angled in between Piccadilly and Park Lane. From 1735. A fish and game market. The houses and shops were altered in 1860. A tiny square; a jumble of narrow streets and ancient buildings. Was built on the site of the May Fair, the latter having begun in 1686.
  - Shepherd's Tavern: 50 Hertford Street, Shepherd Market. 300-year-old; paneled; 18th C. building; was a shop before it became a pub. WWII RAF pilots found it to be a favorite watering spot.
- South Audley Street: (See under S.)
- South Molton Street: (See under S.)
- Tyburn (gallows): Public hangings ended here in 1783, the gallows being moved at that time to Newgate Prison. (See under T.)
- Upper Grosvenor Street: (See under U.)

Mayflower Barn - A barn was built in 1625-6 on the property of Jordan's Meeting House. It was supposedly in part built of timbers taken from the famous Mayflower ship (that brought the pilgrims to the New World.) The Mayflower ship was dismantled in 1624, and there is some evidence its parts could indeed have been used here. (You may care to see: Jordan's Meeting House.)

Mayflower, the - Southwark. 17th C. inn. (See under the INNS/PUBS section.)

Mayor, the - While this title refers to the Lord Mayor of the City, and since 2002 also the Mayor of London (who heads the Greater London Authority,) it should also be noted that all of the boroughs in the capital also have a mayor (with the exception of Richmond.) They're appointed rather than elected, and carry out ceremonial needs for their respective boroughs. They should not, however, be confused with the historic position of Lord Mayor of the City. (See: Lord Mayor, under L.)

Maypole Alley - So called because there really was a maypole here at one time; St. Mary-le-Strand was built over its site, although not the original one. (See: St. Mary-le-Strand, under the CHURCHES section.)

Maze Hill - (See: Greenwich/Maze Hill.)

Meaker's - Gentlemen's outfitter. (See: Friday Street/Meaker's.)

meals - (See: food - Paragraph: "These were the meals of the day…")

- Breakfast.
- Luncheon. (*Never* lunch, a later term.) Could also be called: dinner. The heaviest meal of the day.
- Tea. (Not a factor until later in the 19th century. That is not to say nobody ever took a bit of tea and a munch or two somewhere around 4pm during the Regency era - but it wasn't a structured event/wasn't the institution it is now.)
- Supper. (Evening meal.) Lighter than modern evening meals.

Meard Street - Ca. 1722-32. (See: Soho/Meard Street.)

measurements - Until the UK adopted the metric system in the 20th C., they used measuring units derived over many centuries; America shared/shares many of the same terms, such as: bushel, fathom, foot, gallon (US and UK are a bit different,) inch, mile, pint, pound (as in weight, not the coin,) quart, yard.

The British Imperial System was used from 1824-1965 (a more formalized system of measurements than had come down from ancient days,) with the metric system being adopted in 1965. (You may care to see: mile.) But keep in mind: standardization of sizes wasn't common. One man's snooker table might be quite a bit larger than the one at his club. An earthenware plate would largely match the size of its mates, but a different plate made down the street might well be thicker, or an inch or two smaller or larger. Dresses/shirts/most clothing was made to measure, literally; you couldn't order a "size 9"; you must be measured with marked cords and the garment created. There were very few ready-made clothes, and even those were expected to be fit to the buyer via alterations.

Still, some things were set in size. If you paid for a pound of cheese, you expected a true one pound weight of cheese.

Here are some terms used in the Regency that you may be less familiar with:

- dram = 1/8 of an ounce - Usually related to liquor, or an apothecary's work.
- ell = About 18 inches - The length between a man's elbow and the tip of his middle finger. Used in measuring fabrics. (Banned in 1824.)
- gill = Five fluid ounces.
- hectare = A unit of land. Five hectares equals approximately 13 acres.
- hogshead = A cask, equal to 63 gallons/238.7 liters. Often used for beer. (See: Tun, below.)
- pint = 2 cups, sort of. (See: pint, under P.)
- quire = 24 pieces of paper. 1/20th of a ream. (See: paper.)
- stone = 14 pounds.
- tun = A cask, an ancient way of measuring liquid volume, rather than weight. A tun equals 4 hogsheads. For: honey, oil, or wine. Typically held the equivalent of 252 gallons. Still used in the Regency era.

meat - All kinds of meat were part of the Regency diet...if you could afford them.

- ➢ See: baker - For the cooking of meat in the city, for the many who did not have access to a kitchen/oven. Bakers often seared meat for locals; the same was possible at some pubs, who kept a griddle for this purpose.
- ➢ See: Barnsbury - For beef cattle.
- ➢ See: butchers.
- ➢ See: fish.
- ➢ See: food - Individual listings at, such as: pork.
- ➢ See: Leadenhall Market - For poultry.
- ➢ See: Paternoster Row/Newgate Market.
- ➢ See: Smithfield - For various meat.
- ➢ You may care to see: knackers - For disposal of carcasses.

mechanical engineers - (See: Well Street.)

Mecklenburgh Square - Bloomsbury. Laid out in 1794. Grand eastern terrace. This "square" only ever had three sides of houses. A mirror image to Brunswick Square - each looked toward the Foundling Hospital grounds in-between them; like Brunswick Square, Mecklenburgh Square was built for the bourgeois. Built on the Foundling Hospital estate.

Medical and Chirugical Society of London - (See: Royal Society of Medicine.)

Medical College - About the same time the London Hospital was founded, the Hospital Board of Governors awarded to Blizard and Thomas Maddocks a site just east of London Hospital. They founded the Medical College in 1783; students began here in 1785. Was a teaching body. It was connected with London Hospital, but not part of it (until a formal link was finally made in 1879.) A new Medical College, still adjacent to London Hospital, was opened in 1854.

medicine - Antibiotics (or indeed even the idea of germs) were not understood/discovered at the time of the Regency. Iodine was invented in France in 1811. Joseph Lister (surgeon) began spreading the idea of (germs and) antiseptic processes ca. 1861, which practices became wider-spread by Florence Nightingale's nursing revolutions ca. the 1850-60s.

- See: anesthesia.
- See: antibiotics.
- See: appendicitis.
- See: Company of Surgeons.
- See: diseases - Includes a list of treatments.
- See: doctors - For a list of Regency era doctors.
- See: food - For medicinal herbs, like feverfew and hyssop.
- See: hospitals.
- See: laudanum.
- See: lectures - There were all kinds of lectures, attended by the public, and a good number of them were on medical issues.
- See: operating theatre.

Melbourne House - Piccadilly. Renamed Albany ca. 1803. (See: Piccadilly/ Albany.)

Melbury Road - Kensington. Famous as a street for artists' and aesthetes' houses, 1870s.

- 29: Tower House. Built in 1876-81. (See: Kensington/Tower House.)

Menagerie, the - (See: Royal Menagerie.)

menageries - "Menagerie" is a more common Regency era term, but I have chosen to put all listings at: zoos. (See: zoos.)

Mendoza's - A Regency era London boxing establishment, located possibly at the Admiral Nelson pub in Whitechapel (where he at least gave impromptu lessons.) Daniel Mendoza billed himself as "Mendoza the Jew." He is credited with establishing the "scientific method" of boxing. He also wrote the first ever boxing textbook. Mendoza died in 1836.

men's apparel -

For boots/shoes:

- St. James's Street/9.
- St. James's Street/Hoby's.

For buttons:

- See: buttons, under B.

For ensembles (coats, or entire outfits):

- See: Bond Street/Old Bond Street/Weston.
- See: Friday Street/Meaker's.
- See: Piccadilly/14.
- See: Savile Row.

For hats:

- See: hats.
- See: Piccadilly/10.
- See: St. James's Street/2.
- See: St. James's Street/6.

For shirts:

- See: Jermyn Street/71-72.
- See: Jermyn Street/97.

menstruation - (AKA: the "French lady's visit." To be having one's period was "being the French lady," that is: being one's self, but different.) During the 19th century (and before,) women tended to menstruate less frequently than do modern women, due to all kinds of stresses such as poor diet and frequent pregnancies.

Rags were used for absorbency; they were washed and reused; they are the source of the term "on the rag." They were folded into a kind of pad, wrapped in a larger rag, and tied in place with others (if one didn't just sit upon the assembled rag-pad.) Women did not wear underwear during the Regency; bloomers didn't come along until the Victorian age. It has been noted that some doctors felt "bleeding onto one's chemise for days in a row" could prove unhealthy. Women often excused themselves from social obligations during one's cycle. Disposable sanitary napkins didn't come along until ca. the 1880s, and weren't commercially very viable until into the 1930s. (You may care to see: childbirth.)

mercers - Everyday term for sellers of small goods, and eventually meant someone who sells textile fabrics. The medieval sign for a mercer's place of business was a golden ball.

- See: Henrietta Street/Layton & Shears.
- See: Mercers' Hall.

Mercers' Hall - (For the Worshipful Company of the Mercers.) Ironmonger Lane, Cheapside.

AN ENCYCLOPAEDIA OF LONDON states: "...mercer means simply a merchant," (although in common usage) "a mercer is one who deals in textile fabrics - especially in silks, velvets, and other costly materials. For a long time mercer meant a dealer in small wares, 'the stock of a general country shopkeeper.'"

By 1172, the Mercers were a guild. Received its charter by 1349.

Hall here in Cheapside since 1414. The second-to-last version of their Hall was once attributed to Wren, but in later years thought to be a product of Edward Jarman; it was replaced in 1879. Totally destroyed by WWII bombs in 1941; rebuilt and its front is now part of the Swanage town hall. It was the only Company to have its own chapel.

The Mercers' Company owns a large amount of land in Covent Garden, around Mercer Street.

The difference between Mercers and Merchant Taylors is - Mercers: at first was a trade association of general merchants, particularly exporters of wool and importers of silk, velvets, fine linens, and other luxurious fabrics. Merchant Taylors: They sewed fabrics; was at first an association of tailors, but by the late 17th C. was a philanthropic/social association. Livery Company. 1st in the order of precedence; 1st of the Great Twelve companies.

- See: Lady Mico's Almhouses.
- See: Ludgate - A venue for mercers.

Merchant Taylors' Hall - (For the Worshipful Company of Merchant Taylors) Originally known as: the Guild and Fraternity of St. John the Baptist in the City of London.) 30 Threadneedle Street, which property was acquired in 1331. Before then they were at the Red Lion in Basing Lane, having been founded ca. 1300. Royal charter granted in 1327; the only Livery Hall that can still boast architectural traces of its medieval origins (a crypt from 1375, and a kitchen that dates back to 1425.) This location was situated between Threadneedle Street and Cornhill, where the Hall remains.

It was an association of tailors, but by the end of the 17th century it had already shifted to being a philanthropic organization (as most guilds are in modern times) - although, its links to Savile Row have been rekindled in the 21st century.

Livery Company. 7th in the order of precedence. (The Skinners and the Merchant-Taylors disputed their order of precedence, so in 1484 the Lord Mayor declared the two guilds would change 6th and 7th position on a yearly basis, which they do yet to this day.)

The Hall was much destroyed by the Great Fire of 1666, and carefully rebuilt to its original design, 1671. At some point it provided schooling for members' sons and/or the poor. Was in Charterhouse Square until it moved to new buildings in 1933, situated at Moor Park in Watford, Hertfordshire. It was bombed and greatly damaged in WWII, and rebuilt in 1959.

The Merchant-Taylors' Company owns most of the triangle of land which is bounded by Bishopgate, Cornhill, and Finch Street; also almshouses in Barnet and Lewisham. Its charities tend to support London elderly, isolated persons, and those with disabilities. (See: Mercers' Hall, above - To learn how the Merchant-Taylors differ from the Mercers.)

Mercury - (See: planets/Mercury.)

Meridian Building - Next to Flamsteed House (the Greenwich Observatory.) The building is 18th century, but the term of "Meridian Building" didn't come along until at least 1851. Now houses early astronomical instruments.

The PRIME MERIDIAN (Greenwich Mean Time) was established at Greenwich in 1884; it is marked by a brass strip in the old observatory courtyard. (See: Greenwich Observatory - Notes at.)

Mermaid Tavern, the -

- See: Cheapside/Mermaid Tavern.
- See under the INNS/PUBS section.

Merton - Formed in 1965 by combining the boroughs of Mitcham, and Wimbledon, and the Merton and Morden Urban District (all of which had been considered to be in Surrey.) There had been a historic parish called Merton (on what is now called South Wimbledon.) The old town grew around the abbey founded during Henry I's reign. The abbey was demolished in 1680, a calico manufactory then being built on the site in 1724. From 1823 on, the area hosted shops, alehouses, carpentry, saddlers, and the building trade.

- Hotham House: Ca. 1764 Richard Hotham built his house northwest of Moat House Farm. It was later called Merton Grove. Merton Grove was demolished in 1913.
- Merton Abbey Mills: Where Merton Priory was until 1538. By 1724 this was a calico-printing mill, on the bank of the River Wandle. A new mill by 1802; this mill produced all the cloth for Liberty's department stores, in the later 19th C.; "Liberty's printworks" (they took control eventually of the mill) closed in 1972.
- Merton Grove: (See: Hotham House, above.)
- Merton Park: 1870s.
- Merton Place: (See: Moat House Farm, below.)
- Merton Priory: Founded in 1115. It was an Augustinian house. A Great Council was held here in 1236, with leading barons forcing the Statutes of Merton onto a reluctant Henry III. Demolished in 1538, its stones were used to help build Nonsuch Palace. (See: Merton Abbey Mills, above.)
- Moat House Farm: Bought in 1764 by Richard Hotham (East India merchant.) He enlarged the house, renaming it Merton Place. Horatio Nelson (naval hero) bought Merton Place in 1802 (living here until he died at Trafalgar in 1805.) His mistress, Emma Hamilton (who lived here with Nelson *and* her own husband, Sir William Hamilton, in an almost open *ménage a trois*, until Sir William died in 1803,) called the house "Paradise Merton," but all the same sold it in 1808. Pulled down in 1823.

Methodist Central Hall - Westminster (opposite the Palace of Westminster.) 1912. Hosted the first meeting of the United Nations, in 1946.

- The Two Chairmen: Dartmouth Street. An 18th C. pub. (See under the

INNS/PUBS section.)

Methodists - The name Methodists was derived from the precepts of discipline and regular practice of one's Christian exercises (practices.)

- See: Foundry Chapel.
- See: Spa Fields Chapel.
- See: Wesley's Chapel, under the CHURCHES section.

Metropolitan Board of Works - Established in 1855. It was the first London-wide (as opposed to City-wide) authority, (although it is also said this Board never really had control over all the smaller parish interests.) Abolished in 1889; replaced by the London County Council. (See: London County Council.)

Metropolitan Cattle Market - (AKA: Metropolitan Meat-Market. Also seen as: Metropolitan Meat Market. AKA: London Central Meat Market - Its formal name.) 1860.

- See: Islington/Copenhagen Fields.
- See: Newgate Market.

Metropolitan Drinking Fountain and Cattle Association - Founded in 1859. Until then, water for horses (or cows being driven into town) could be hard to come by; was usually provided in troughs in front of pubs, but not for free - you paid for water usage or bought beer to earn the use thereof.

Metropolitan Fire Brigade - Formed in 1866. Replaced the prior system of insurance companies' brigades. Renamed in 1904 as the London Fire Brigade. (See: fire brigades.)

Metropolitan Meat-Market - (See: Metropolitan Cattle Market.)

Metropolitan Police - (AKA: Scotland Yard.) Created in early October, 1829.

(See: Hyde Park Corner - Note on the very beginnings of the Metropolitan Police.)

The month The Metropolitan Police began, the rate of pay for a constable was 3-4 shillings per day (considered low, as opposed to 5-10 shillings per day for other kinds of workers.)

When the constables first canvassed London streets in 1829, they wore tall, reinforced top hats; the now iconic police helmets came along in 1865. These first peelers (also called bobbies, both these nicknames derived from the founder, Sir Robert Peel) first wore civilian clothing (except for their hats) and were armed only with truncheons.

A later Victorian nickname was: coppers, due to their copper-colored uniform buttons.

CHAMBERS LONDON GAZETTEER informs us: "In 1830, Somers Town saw the first ever Metropolitan Police fatality when PC Joseph Grantham was kicked to death while trying to break up a street fight." (PC = Police Constable.)

The Metropolitan force absorbed the Bow Street Runners in 1836. (See under B.)

Soon after, the first plainclothes detectives were established.

- Bow Street Horse Patrol: Is now the Metropolitan Police's Mounted Branch. Began as a division of Bow Street in 1760, when Sir Fielding set mounted patrols against highway robberies, 8 men. 60 men by 1805. Had a significant influence on highway robberies, to the point where by 1816 such robberies were pretty much wiped out. Now some 140 officers. (See: Bow Street/4/Bow Street Horse Patrol.)
- Royal Parks Constabulary: Formed in 1872, made up of Royal Parks Keepers (thus called until 1974, when they were renamed the Royal Parks Constabulary.) Became Metropolitan Police in 2004.
- Women Police Constables: There were none in 1829 (when the Metropolitan Police formed,) and it wasn't until 1973 that they were fully integrated. There was, however, in 1914 the Women Police Service, which was formed to discourage London women from going into prostitution.

Police forces were adopted nationally in 1856.

- ➢ See: City of London Police Force - From 1839, and who answer to the Corporation of London, not to the Metropolitan authorities.
- ➢ See: Great Scotland Yard.
- ➢ See: police.
- ➢ See: prison.
- ➢ See: rough places.
- ➢ See: Watchmen.
- ➢ See: Whitehall/4 Whitehall Place - Scotland Yard.

Metropolitan Tabernacle - (See: New Park Street Chapel, under N in the Alpha section.)

Metropolitan Underground Railway - 1863, from Paddington to Farringdon. Went from steam-powered to electric in 1890. This was the foundation of the system now nicknamed "the Tube"/the Underground. (See: Tube.)

Metropolitan Water Board - (See: Chelsea Waterworks Company.)

mewing - The molting of birds of prey. Ergo, the Royal Mews were originally built for birds (Edward I's hawks) rather than horses. But by Henry VII's time, ca. 1500, horses had replaced birds there.

- ➢ See: mews.
- ➢ See: Royal Mews.

mews - Originally a term for where sporting birds of prey were kept, but as interest in falconry fell away, the buildings were re-used; well before the Regency the term came to mean: an alley between (or near) rows of homes, used for stabling horses. They were very like their "country cousins," stables (including rooms above in which grooms and servants could be housed,) except in crowded London they were usually used by the many local residents, not just one estate/family. There were many, many mews throughout London during the reign of the horse - almost anywhere where more than a few homes that could support the expense of horses were centered.

- See: mewing.
- See: Royal Mews.

Meymott Street - (See: Southwark/Cross Street.)

Michael House - East corner of Dorset Street, 1813. Shops and offices.

Michaelmas - September 29th. (See: rents.)

Michael's Place - Brompton. 1786. Small, uniform houses of brick. (44 houses railed off from the main Brompton Road.)

middle class (areas) - "Middle class," as a term, while dating from 1766, wasn't likely to be heard much before the 20th C., especially as it was a class of people just gaining any numbers as the 19th C. advanced. While there have always been gentry and the merchant class, before the 19th C., the vast majority of people were simply either rich or poor.

Soho Square was considered a "serviceable" neighborhood, but not highly fashionable.

- See: Mecklenburgh Square - For the bourgeois. The bourgeoises settled many places, but this particular square was noted for it.
- See: working class neighborhoods, under W - For neighborhoods that housed doctors, lawyers, etc.

middle names - In the Regency period, they were rare. (See: childbirth - Note at.)

Middle Row - Holborn. This street was considered an obstruction in Holborn as early as 1657. Shop-owners there included: booksellers, brokers, comb-makers, and cutlers. Demolished 1867.

Middle Temple Hall - (See: Inns of Court/Temple (1st entry)/Middle Temple/Middle Temple Hall.)

Middle Temple Lane - (See: Inns of Court/Temple (1st entry)/Middle Temple/Middle Temple Lane.)

Middlesex County Cricket Club - (See: Lord's Cricket Club.)

Middlesex County Industrial School - Feltham. 1859; different use by 1919.

Middlesex County Lunatic Asylum - Barnet. 1851.

Middlesex Guildhall - 1913.

Middlesex Hospital - Fitzrovia, Marylebone. Founded in 1745 as Middlesex Infirmary, to care for the lame and ill of Soho. Two small houses in Windmill Street, off Tottenham Court Road.

A foremost teaching hospital since 1746.

It set up the first maternity ward, 1747.

More land was purchased in 1754, and in 1755 Middlesex Hospital was built. Had 64 beds. West wing was added in 1766; east wing in 1780.

In 1788, there were 16 wards; had an "air of poverty."

Had a cancer ward by 1792.

In the early 19th C. it could accommodate 180 patients.

The hospital was rebuilt in 1835, and the adjoining medical school was founded at that time. In 1848 the hospital added an extension.

Florence Nightingale nursed here for a while ca. 1854.

Reconstructed in 1926-35.

Women were admitted to the school as medical students in 1947.

Affiliated with the University of London since 1900.

Middlesex House of Corrections - Built in 1794 as: the Cold Bath Fields Prison. Name changed in the mid 19th century. (See: Cold Bath Fields Prison.)

Middlesex Sessions House - (See: Clerkenwell Green/Middlesex Sessions House.)

Middlesex Street - (See: Petticoat Lane.)

Midland Bank - Founded in 1836 in the county of Birmingham. Not in London until 1930.

Midsummer Day - June 24th. (See: rent.)

midwives - (See: childbirth.)

Milbank Prison - Alternate spelling for Millbank Prison. (See: Millbank Prison. Note the double l's.)

mile - Despite switching to the metric system (from imperial units) in the 20th C., distances on UK roads are still measured in miles, which is not to say you won't see the kilometer distance listed as well. (You may care to see: measurements.)

Mile End - Tower Hamlets. During the Regency era, would have literally been a hamlet. There by at least 1228.

Mile End Green - (See: Stepney Green.)

Mile End Road - Stepney. Ancient road. Oliver Cromwell gave permission for London's first Jewish burial ground here in 1657. In the early 19th C. this area was largely inhabited by poor Jewish citizens. Breweries here. By author Charles Dickens' time, oyster stalls were everywhere.

- 88: Capt. James Cook (military leader/explorer) lived here 1783-88. Taken down in 1959.
- Mile End Waste: (See at its own listing.)

Mile End Waste - Whitechapel. An open area, used for speeches and the East End's answer to Hyde Park. Before the 19th C. it was just an open area. (See: Trinity Almhouses.)

milestones - (Also seen as: mile-stones.) Turnpike roads had milestones, a true convenience for travelers, with every milestone listing the distance from London, and the distance to the next place, and marking crossroads. (You may care to see: turnpike.)

military regalia -

- See: Firmin & Sons.
- See: Savile Row/Henry Poole - Note, though, that during the Regency Mr. Poole's business would have been in Brunswick Square.
- See: uniforms, military.

militia - The obligation to serve in a militia made up of ordinary Englishmen (during emergency situations or times of great civil unrest or wars) was long-standing in Britain, since at least Elizabethan times. All the same, the British as a whole have a long, deep mistrust of a standing army (preferring to look to the Navy as the national protectors,) and this sentiment flourished in the Georgian era and beyond. Still, during the Seven Years War (1756) the call for a militia to supplement the regular army rose again. It was never popular, however, and frequently led to riots. When militias were raised, it was to provide alternate troops at home, thereby freeing regular army men for problem areas abroad. Between 1805-25 there were 100,000 men in the regular militia in Great Britain. (See: army - More at.)

milk - There were plenty of cattle grazed in/around London, often even including on commons and within the parks, even Royal parks. (See: Hyde Park - The note about cows.) Milk would have been fairly easy to come by during the Regency era; it was estimated in 1805 that London's surrounds hosted some 8,500 milk cows.

Of course, where there is milk, there is cream and butter to be had, too.

- See: Enfield Chase.
- See: food/milk.
- See: Highbury/Cream Hall Farm.
- See: Milk Street.
- See: Old Church Street/46.
- See: St. James's Park - Low in the entry.
- See: Woodberry Down - Dairies.

Milk Street - Cheapside. Hosted medieval milksellers in a milk market. Sir Thomas More (adviser to Henry VIII) was born on this street in 1478. Nothing of the original street remained following WWII bombing.

- St. Mary Magdalen, Milk Street: Ruined in the Great Fire of 1666. (See under the CHURCHES section.)

Mill Hill - Barnet. First on record in 1374. CHAMBERS LONDON GAZETTEER notes:

"...possibly the London district most influenced by the Christian faith... A tradition of religious nonconformity began with Quaker and Presbyterian communities in the 17th century. Quakers met at Rosebank, on the Ridgeway, from 1678 to 1719 and the weatherboarded building survives today. Across the road, in 1807 a group of Nonconformist ministers and city merchants founded a Protestant dissenters' grammar school, now Mill Hill School, in the former home of botanist Peter Collinson. New buildings were added in 1827 and have been supplemented by at least one additional structure in almost every decade since. Mill Hill did not acquire a separate Anglican church from Hendon until 1833..."

- Littleberries: 17th C. house. Much altered.
- St. Joseph's College: Lawrence Street. 1869. Roman Catholic.
- University of London observatory: 1929.

Mill Street - Off Hanover Square.

- Thomas Goade: Established 1827. China and glassware. Now located in South Audley Street, since 1845. They were granted their Royal Warrant in 1863.

Millbank - (The road.) Westminster. Very near the Thames. When it was first recorded in 1546, the area belonged to Westminster Abbey. In the early 18th C. it was an ordinary road across crop fields and meadows. Sir Robert Grosvenor built a mansion here in 1736 (on the site of the mill from which Millbank derived its name; the mill that gave the name was pulled down in the early 18th century.) This mansion was demolished in 1809, so that the Millbank Penitentiary could be built. (See: Millbank Prison.)

- Castle's Yard: 1838.

Millbank Prison (or Penitentiary) - (Also seen written as: Milbank.) Pimlico. 1809. Designed by Sir Robert Smirke. A second source says it opened 1811, following delays; completed in 1821. Third and fourth sources say it opened in 1816; at any rate the first convicts arrived in 1816 (coming from Newgate.) Built in the shape of a six-pointed star, to the reformer Jeremy Bentham's designs. It looked like a fortress, and was a "warren of tunnels," so much so that the turnkeys wrote directions in chalk on the walls to prevent getting lost. Surrounded by an octagonal wall. On 18 acres (a second source said seven acres.) The building was brick. Designed for 1,120 prisoners, under the new theory of individual cells. Used for both men and women, until it was limited to just men in 1823 by Act of Parliament (due to sanitation and diet problems.) Convicts intended for transport to Australia were brought to this location.

The prisoners worked at making boots and sewing postbags. For the first half of the prisoners' sentence they were strictly forbidden from conducting any manner of communication.

The governor's house was at the center (hub) of the star-shaped building.

Jeremy Bentham's ideas on prison reform were never completely carried out here, and the prison reverted in 1843 to one of ordinary ideas and procedures on how to manage a prison; and became famous for its harshness.

In 1868, it was in disrepair; the prisoners were sent to Wormwood Scrubs Prison (See under W.)

Closed in 1890. Demolished in 1903, (a second source says it was pulled down in 1892.) Now partially the site of the Tate Gallery, and partially the Royal Army Medical College. (In 2005 the RAMC became home to the Chelsea College of Art and Design, part of the University of the Arts London.)

Millfields - Hackney. CHAMBERS LONDON GAZATTEER says: "The Borough of Hackney's side of the Lea Bridge area, usually considered to be an eastern part of Clapton. The great corn mills that gave the fields their name burned down in 1796."

- Pond Farm: 1950s.
- Pond Lane: Renamed Millfields Road in 1887.

Millfields Hill - (See: Hampstead Heath/Parliament Hill.)

Milliarium, the - (See: Candlewick Street/Milliarium.)

milliners - Provided more than hats; at the time of the Regency, milliners specialized in hats but provided any garment and accessory a woman could need. Some milliners had a business you could visit, but most often the milliner came to you, carrying illustrations and fabric samples.

- ➢ See: Berkshire/Caleys, under the BRITISH COUNTIES section.
- ➢ See: Cranbourn Street.
- ➢ See: fabrics.
- ➢ See: gowns.
- ➢ See: hatters.
- ➢ See: modiste.

Millionaire Square - The word "millionaire" was not coined until 1843. (See: Bryanston Square.)

mills - For the milling of grains/flour. (See: flour.)

Millwall - (See: docks/Millwall.)

Milne, James - One of Lord Byron's tailors. (See: Grosvenor Street/Milne.)

Milner Square - Islington. 1835-40. By Roumieu & Gough.

Milton Street - Renamed to this ca. 1830.

- ➢ See: Albion Street.
- ➢ See: Grub Street - This street's Regency era name.

Milton Terrace - (See: Albion Terrace.)

Mincing Lane - Corruption of "Minehuns" (nuns of St. Helen's.) Circa 1799 began to be the "spice-trading center of the world."

- All Hallows Staining: North end of Mark Lane. (See under the CHURCHES section.)
- Clothworkers' Hall: (For the Worshipful Company of Clothworkers.) Dunster Court, Mincing Lane. The Clothworkers began as two separate guilds: the Shearmen, and the Fullers. Contrary to what you might surmise, Shearmen were not sheep shearers but those who sheared away the superfluous nap of cloth. Fullers shrank and thickened cloth (usually wool.) The Fullers were housed at Whitechapel, in Billiter Street.

  The Shearmen and Fullers united in 1528, at which time they were named Clothworkers. Their first mutual hall was a small red brick building; its cellars were full of oil during the Great Fire of 1666, so the hall blazed rather spectacularly. Had a new building by at least 1708, which was described as "a noble rich building"; taken down in the 1850s. Rebuilt in 1856-60, with a Portland stone front with Corinthian pilasters. Destroyed by air raid in 1941. Rebuilt in 1958 in a neo-Georgian design. (See: Clothworkers' Hall, under C.)

Minerva Printing Press - Late 18th-early 19th century publisher, known for its Gothic novels. (See: Lane's.)

Ministry of Defence, the - (AKA: the Old War Office. Nickname: the Quadragon, in parody of the U.S.'s "Pentagon.") Whitehall. 1898. Across the street from the Old Admiralty.

Implements the policies established by the monarch's government. Also is the headquarters for the British Armed Forces.

The New Ministry of Defence was built between 1939-1959; built over Henry VIII's wine cellar, Whitehall - which same locale had hosted three Georgian era houses: Cadogan House, Cromwell House, and Pembroke House until pulled down for this new structure. (See: New Ministry of Defence.)

In the gardens behind the building lie the remains of Queen Mary's Terrace, built for Queen Mary II (co-reigned with her husband, William III, from 1689, until she died in 1694); marks the water level in the 17th century.

Minories, The - (More often referred to simply as: Minories. AKA: Minories Holy Trinity.) The name is derived from the nuns of the Order of St. Clare the Minoress, who were here in 1293. The Abbey dissolved in 1539, the property going to the Crown. Was abolished in 1895 as a civil parish, absorbed into Whitechapel.

- Holy Trinity Church: (See under the CHURCHES section.)
- James Taddy & Co.: Tobacco and snuff. Established ca. 1740 in Fenchurch

Street. Moved to The Minories ca. 1820, where it existed until 1920. Probably the best known tobacco and snuff manufacturer in London during its time.

- Mitre Street: (See at its own listing.)

minster - Term for an Abbey (that is, mission) church. Seen in place names, such as Westminster.

Mint Street - Very near the Tower of London. HIS MAJESTY'S TOWER OF LONDON states: "Standing beside the Bell Tower and looking northward the visitor will see Mint Street, beside which are the Casements where some of the Yeoman Warders" (of the Tower) "and their families live. This street proceeds around the north and east sides of the Tower forming a portion of the Outer Ward, and is named after the Mint which was situated therein until 1810." (You may care to see: Tower of London/"Other Places & Things"/Royal Mint.)

Mint, the -

- ➢ See: Royal Mint.
- ➢ See: Tower Hill/Mint, the.
- ➢ See: Tower of London/"Other Places & Things"/Royal Mint.

minting (of coins) - In Regency times only the crown could mint coins, rather than the secular government.

- ➢ See: money/Coinage - Near the start of the Money entry.
- ➢ See: Royal mint.

mirror - (See: looking-glass.)

missionaries -

- ➢ See: Clapham Sect - For a group that helped develop missions.
- ➢ See: Corporation for the Propagation of the Gospel in New England.

mistery - (See: mystery.)

Mitcham - Merton. Ancient, sprawling village. Has held an annual fair here on August 12-14 for centuries; it is said Elizabeth I granted a charter for a fair after having enjoyed it in its unofficial capacity.

Gentlemen built retreat homes here in the mid 17th C., to escape London's air and plagues.

From the mid 18th C. the district was known for its market-gardens, with an emphasis on lavender, poppies, anise, oil of peppermint, oil of rose.

- Canons manor house: 1680. Is now a borough leisure center.
- Mitcham Common: Early site for golf (once the game was introduced into England by James I.) Also for cricket (in the lower green); it is the country's oldest cricket green, with good evidence the game was played here as early as 1685.

    - Seven Islands Pond: In the 19th C. gravel was extracted here, resulting in depressions and ponds; this was the largest of those depressions. Gravel extraction was stopped in 1891.
- Mitcham Fair: (See at its own listing.)
- St. Peter and St. Paul: Rebuilt 1821, in the Perpendicular style.
- Surrey Iron Railway: 1801. Horse-drawn. Used to move Mitcham's horticultural goods to London. This railway ceased in the 1840s.

Mitcham Fair - London, 1732 or earlier; still active fair. (See: Mitcham.)

Mitre Court - 1830. (See: Holborn/Mitre Tavern.)

Mitre Street - The Minories. According to THE LOST TREASURES OF LONDON: "On the right is the shop of J. E. Sly and Son, Dealers in Sacks, Ropes, etc. It is said to date from 1650..."

Mivart's Hotel - (See: Claridge's.)

mob - As in an unruly gathering of people. The term dates from the 1680s.

Model Prison - (More commonly called: Pentonville Prison.) Barnsbury, Islington. Built in 1840. Note: A "model prison" meant it was intended to provide corrective learning rather than just punishment. Model prisons were a new (and rare) idea in the Regency era. (See: Pentonville/Pentonville Prison, under P.)

modiste - A dressmaker; a fashionable milliner. Usually came to the client's home with samples of fabric and patterns. (See: milliners.)

Molton Street - (See: South Molton Street.)

money - The British monetary unit is/was the pound sterling (AKA, much more commonly as: the pound.) The "£" symbol derives from librae (Latin for scales or balance.)

At the turn of the 19th C. the lowest laborer could earn as little as £12-25 per year; the wealthy: £10,000; the extremely wealthy: £50,000.

BANK OF ENGLAND**:** The Bank of England became the dominant bank by the end of the 18th C., becoming the main issuer of bank notes (i.e. paper bills,) and the *official* national bank in the 19th century. The standardization of a national bank note did not become fully established until 1833 - and even then, it was some 40 more years before other banks stopped issuing their own bank notes. (See: Bank of England, under B.)

BANK NOTES: Being paper money - (they were called notes, not bills as Americans would say) - were more suspect to your average merchant. Even paper money *within Britain* was not as regulated as it is now (and could be printed from sources other than a bank or government,) and too often did not maintain value; therefore foreign bank notes probably would not be accepted as payment. Foreign *coins,* however, had a more tangible value to the standard Regency vendor. With London being both a port and a major trading city, a merchant/vendor might well be more accepting of non-British coinage (and there were, in fact, many kinds of foreign coins that passed hands during the Regency era.)

- SEE: BANK NOTES, below, at the end of this entry.
- See: Royal Mint, under R.

CHEQUES: Uncommon. Only the well-to-do would have them (because they were usually only used for rather large sums.) Not too dissimilar to modern bank account checks, if larger and a bit flimsier, on which was written the name of the recipient and the amount.

- See: cheques, under C.
- See: Child's Bank - For more on cheques.

COINAGE: Since before the Regency, coinage wasn't regulated or standardized. There were all kinds of coins minted by local banks (and other organizations) - the problem was getting people to accept them. It helped that the coins had intrinsic value from the metals they were made of (until the gold standard was put aside, much later.) A Regency era person might refuse to accept coins (and paper notes) unfamiliar to them, or stamped locally, preferring London minted coins, which led to various coins essentially serving as local tokens only (if they were even accepted under those conditions.)

A "light coin" was one that was chipped or mutilated. Example: the old Spanish Piece of Eight could literally be broken into 8 pieces. A light coin probably wouldn't be rejected by traders/vendors, but of course had less value.

As noted, neither were foreign coins necessarily rejected out of hand. As noted, with London being a port city, Londoners saw a fair number of foreign coins, and if vendors were familiar with them and held them as having value, might accept them as payment, although there could be much haggling over their worth.

Note: (on the matter of foreign coins): From household and business records, those record-keepers, while making note of the foreign coin received, would convert them into their value (into pounds(£)/shillings(s)/pence(d) format) in order to make tallying a day's income/expenditures easier.

(See: Piccadilly - The paragraphs at the start of, that talk about exchanging money, particularly foreign coins like Napoleons and Louis d'ors.)

THE POUND SCOTS: Ceased to be legal tender after the 1707 Act of Union between England and Scotland. Scotland then used British pounds.

The coins below are listed in (generally) descending value. Here is an Alpha order to make location easier:

crown - entry 9.
farthing - entry 17.
five guinea - entry 2.
guinea - entry 4.
half crown - entry 10.
half-guinea - entry 5.
halfpenny (ha'penny) - entry 16.
half-sovereign - entry 6.
one-third guinea - entry 7.
penny (copper) - entry 15.
pound (quid) - entry 1.
quarter-guinea - entry 8.
shilling - entry 11.
sixpence - entry 12.
sovereign - entry 3.
threepenny (thruppence) - entry 13.
twopence (tuppence) - entry 14.

THE FOLLOWING VALUES WERE PRIOR TO THE MODERN DECIMAL SYSTEM (1971.)

1. The **pound** = 20 shillings. (AKA: pound sterling; quid.)
I repeat from above, the £ symbol derives from *librae* (Latin for weight, scales, or balance.)

- The pound's nickname: quid, possibly derived from the Latin "quid pro quo." It remains "quid" (no "s") even when used in the plural: "He owes me ten quid."
- The pound came in two forms: a paper bill, called a note; and a gold coin called a guinea (until 1820; then known as a sovereign from 1821.) THE ONE POUND NOTE (paper money) wasn't seen until 1797. (See: Bank Notes, at the bottom of this entry.)
- In the early 19th C. people were more likely to pay a pound's equivalence

via shillings and crowns. That is, to the common man, it was rarer to possess and use an actual pound. In a time when £50 could rent you a country cottage for a year, a pound was a lot of money.

- 1 £ = 4 crowns
  = 8 half-crowns
  = 20 shillings
  = 240 pence
  = 960 farthings
- Written as: £1.

2. The **five guinea** = Its original value was 2£ (forty shillings,) but its value fluctuated until 1717. (See note - Immediately below.)
   - Was gold. Existed from 1664-1777. Now known as a "five guinea" piece, but in the 17-18th centuries it was also called a "five-pound" piece (because during Charles II's time a *guinea* was worth twenty shillings, until it was fixed at the value of twenty-one shillings in 1717 by Royal Proclamation.)
   - Written as: £5.1s.

3. The **sovereign** = one pound (dates from 1817.)
   - Note: The (new) sovereign coin was meant/desired to replace the guinea (the latter being valued at 21 shillings, instead of the sovereign's 20 shillings.) Named for the 1603 English gold sovereign (which would have been, until 1817 when this new sovereign came along, the Regency era coin.)
   - A gold coin, approximately .24 ounces of 22 carat gold. Is no longer in circulation.

4. The **guinea** = 21 shillings.
   - First issued in 1663. It was a gold coin, the gold literally brought from Guinea. Due to the stability of its value, it was often used in conducting legal profession business or in accounting transactions. It's been said a gentleman paid his tailor with shillings, but his barrister with guineas. It was a coin version of a pound (1£,) despite being +1 shilling more valuable. (It was formally set at the value of 1 pound + 1 shilling in 1717.) Its use was discontinued in 1813, and it went out of circulation by

1820. Despite its absence, the term lingered; it remained a pricing unit for luxury items long after the coin disappeared.

- Guinea = 1 pound + 1 shilling
  = 4 crowns + 1 shilling
  = 252 pence (240+ 12)
- Written as: £1.1s.

(See: sovereign - Note at.)

5. The **half-guinea** = 10 shillings + 6 pence.
   - Was gold. From 1669-1816.
   - Written as: 10s.6d.

6. The **half-sovereign** = ½ a sovereign (functionally, ½ a pound.)
   - Half-sovereign = 10 shillings
     = 120 pence
   - Dates from 1817. A gold coin. No longer in circulation, except occasionally issued as a commemorative coin, in excess of its face value.
   - Written as: 10s.

   (See: sovereign, above.)

7. The **one-third guinea**. (AKA: third guinea.) = 7 shillings.
   - Was gold. From November, 1797; minted only in the reign of George III (who reigned 1760-1820.)
   - Written as: 7s.
   - One-third guinea = 84 pence

8. The **quarter-guinea** = five shillings + threepence.
   - Was gold, small. Only issued in two years: in 1718, and in 1762 (the coins were small, impractical, and proved unpopular.) Would not have been seen much, if at all, in the Regency era.
   - Written as: 5s.3d.

9. The **crown** = ¼ of a pound.
   - Originally known as the "crown of the double rose." Was at first a gold coin, 1526. A silver coin began in 1551, but some crowns were yet minted in gold until 1662. No crowns were minted during Mary I's reign, but

resumed in Elizabeth I's. In 1707 the English crown was superseded by the British crown; the latter is yet minted, but now has a value of five pounds.

- Crown = ¼ of a pound
  = 5 shillings
  = 60 pence
  = 240 farthings
- Was written as: 5s.

10. The **half-crown** = 2 shillings & 6 pence.

- It was silver. First issued in 1549.
  Important Note: the coin itself was called a "half crown," but the amount you paid over for an item was called "half a crown." Now obsolete; withdrawn in 1969; demonetized in 1970.
- Half-crown = 1/8th of a pound
  = 2 shillings + 6 pence
  = 30 pence
  = 120 farthings
- Written as: 2s.6d.

11. The **shilling** = 12 pence. 1/20th of a pound.

- It was silver, from ca. 1503-1947, introduced by Henry VII; after 1947 it was made from cupronickel.
- First minted as: the testoon, in Henry VII's reign (1509-1547); called the shilling by the mid 16th century. Circulated until 1990.
- The shilling's nicknames: twelvepence (not frequently seen in contemporary works of the time.) Also called: bob. "Bob" was not used in the plural; correct example: "He paid twelve bob for that." You wouldn't say: one bob (that is, bob is always used for more than one.) Bob would have been used by the lower classes, and some dashing young men, but not by ladies or older persons; it was definitely slang.
- 1s = 1/20 of a pound
  = 1 shilling
  = 12 pence
  = 48 farthings
- Written as: 1s.

12. The **sixpence** = ½ a shilling.

- A silver coin until 1947; after 1947 made from cupronickel. Existed from 1551 to 1971 (after which time it was valued at 2-1/2 new pence.)
- Its nicknames: bender; sixpenny bit; tanner (from ca. 1811.)
- Sixpence = 1/40th of a pound
  = ½ a shilling
  = 6 pence
  = 24 farthings
- Written as: 6d.

13. The **threepenny** = ¼ of a shilling.

- A silver coin. Minted from 1547-1970.
- Its nicknames: thruppence; threepenny bit. (See: penny, below, about the difference between using pence and penny, or in this case thruppence and threepenny.)
- Thruppence = 1/80th of a pound
  = ¼ of a shilling
  = 3 pence
  = 12 farthings
- Written as: 3d

14. The **twopence** = 1/6 of a shilling.

- Was a large copper coin, 41 mm diameter, minted only in the year 1797. Was silver (and smaller) in a new minting in 1818-20.
- Common name: **tuppence**. AKA: as a cartwheel (because of its size. See note under "penny.")
- Tuppence = 1/120th of a pound
  = 1/6th of a shilling
  = 2 pence
  = 8 farthings
- Written as: 2d

15. The **penny** (or pence, or COPPER) = 1/240th of a pound.

- The "d" (used in old recordkeeping) is Latin for *denarius* while used in writing; *denarius* was virtually never used in speech.

- Pennies were minted (on and off) until George III's reign (1760-1820) out of silver - and were primarily minted/used only for Maundy money (symbolic alms, for a Church of England's Good Friday and some other religious alms givings.) But by George III's time, there was a severe shortage of pennies, to the point that merchants and mining companies were minting their own copper tokens (a practice that ended in 1802, and resurged in 1811-12.) In 1797 the government authorized copper pennies (and twopences); both the pennies and the twopences were significantly larger than the silver versions, and so got the nickname: cartwheels (and were sometimes used, particularly by prostitutes, as a kind of hopeful if not that efficient diaphragm against pregnancy.) The government took on a serious reissue of coins in 1816, of gold, silver, and copper; an Act of Parliament forbade private coining (with severe penalties against) in 1817. Note: eventually, as it devalued, the penny became minted of a copper alloy (as were the halfpenny and the farthing; too, these later pennies were smaller than the "cartwheels" of George III's reign.
- Nicknames: cartwheels (see above paragraph); copper (another slang term that the higher classes would probably not have used.)
- Important Note: Pence was used to denote cost or change, whereas the coin itself was referred to as a penny.
- Pence = 1/240th of a pound
  = 1/12th of a shilling
  = 1 pence
  = 4 farthings
- Written as: 1d.

16. The **halfpenny** - Or ha'penny, a term in common use by all classes. (See: penny, above - The Note at.)

- At first was a silver coin; bronze after 1860. Minted from 1672-1969. (There was a new ha'penny issued in 1971, valued at 1/200th of a pound; this new halfpenny lost its standing as legal tender in 1985 and was deleted from circulation.)
- The old halfpenny is obsolete; withdrawn in 1969.
- Halfpenny = 1/480th of a pound
  = 1/24th of a shilling
  = ½ of a pence

= 2 farthings

- Written as: 1/2d.

17. The **farthing** = ¼ of a pence. It took 960 farthings to equal a pound. Officially issued in 1665 - before then some traders offered their own versions of a farthing. There was much demand for such a coin, but the government dragged its heels in issuing such a small value coin. (See: penny, above - The note at.)

    - A bronze coin.
    - It is now obsolete, having been withdrawn in 1960 (due to inflation.)
    - Farthing = 1/960th of a pound

      = 1/48th of a shilling

      = ¼ of a pence
    - Written as: 1/4d.

BANK NOTES: As noted under "pound," above, the one-pound bank note (paper) was not seen until 1797, being that previously banks were not allowed to issue paper notes under a £5 face value. (Also see: "Bank Notes" at the start of this Money section.)

The Bank of England issued the following bank notes: 10s (yes, ten shillings, or in effect ½ a pound,) £1, £2, £5 (its nickname: a fiver,) and £10 (nickname: a tenner.) Keep in mind that £10 could pay for 1/5 of a year's rent on a country cottage, so that was a huge amount to trust to paper money during the Regency era.

Some nicknames for sums of money (there are more under the listings above):

£25 - A pony. Used as in: "He's utterly mad if he risked a pony on that race."

£500 - A monkey.

<u>Here is a list of some approximate pricing</u> (derived from Regency sources) of common items/expenses. They varied, of course:

average income for a family (what we would now call lower middle class) - £120-£150 per year

average income for a widow (from the gentry) - £100 per year

butter - 1d per pound (remember: "d" means pence, so butter was 1 penny per pound)

cheese - 9d per pound

country cottage - £50 - £100 per year

eggs - 30 eggs for 1 shilling (equals 12d)

female cook - £15 per year (whereas a male French cook would earn as much as £80.)

female servant - £10-£12 per year (includes clothing)

handkerchief, silk, white - 6 shillings (equals 72d)

horses -

£40 to £200 (for a saddle-horse)

£150-£400 (for a pair of coach horses)

£350 (for an "excellent" hunter)

£1,500 and up (for a race horse)

house in London -

rent - £500 per year (for a fine house)/£200 (for a fair house)

purchased - (nice house) £16,000 total

housekeeper - 24 guineas per year

inn (2 people, one night stay, private room) - Between £2-£11

male servant - £40 per year (includes their livery)

meat - 8d per pound

pianoforte - 30 guineas

snuff (Spanish) - £3 per pound

used chaise (carriage), two years old (in 1806) - £150

valet - £35 per year.

Monmouth Court - Between Monmouth Street and Little Earl Street (Seven Dials.) Now gone, eliminated by the 1885 construction of Shaftesbury Avenue.

- Press, a: One James Catnach founded a press here in 1813, producing chap-books and broadsides.

Monmouth House - Soho Square (in the 17th C. called: King's Square.) 17th century mansion. Demolished in 1773.

Monmouth Square - (See: Soho Square.)

Monmouth Street - Covent Garden. Existed by at least 1724. Ran through the infamous "Seven Dial" slums. An area for brokers' shops that sold secondhand clothing and shoes. (Speaking of shoes, there were cobblers who lived in the cellars on Monmouth Street called "translators," they reworked and resold old shoes.) Reportedly, most of the items in these shops were stolen. People of money, during hard times, would sell or buy here. A good place for men just in from the country to equip themselves with city clothes. Was known in the 1840s as Dudley Street; swallowed up in 1885 by Shaftesbury Avenue. (See: Seven Dials/Monmouth Street.)

Montagu House - (Occasionally spelled Montague.) Great Russell Street, Bloomsbury. The original building was built in 1675-80 for the first Duke of Montagu.

It was the site of the British Museum Collections until new (present) building was begun on the same site in 1820 (second source says 1823); finished 1847. Collections begun by Sir Hans Sloane. Mrs. Montagu, aged 80, died here in 1800. (See: Bloomsbury Square/British Museum - For much more information.)

Montagu Square - Marylebone. A bit north of Marble Arch. Built 1810-15. Plain, brown brick homes.

- 23: There by at least 1816.

Montague Street - Bloomsbury Square. 1800-3, James Burton. Placed, along with Bedford Street, on the site of Bloomsbury House.

monthly periodicals - (See: journals.)

Montpelier Place - Kensington. Victorian. Had been Rawstorne Street, which existed by at least 1771.

Montpelier Row - (See: Twickenham/Montpelier Row.)

Montpelier Square - Began ca. 1824, smallish and secluded, but grew over the next three decades. Now described as one of the best squares in London.

Montpelier Street - Between Brompton Road and Knightsbridge. Regency era street.

- Bonham's: 1793. Founded as (and remains) an auction house. There is a 6th-generation Bonham on staff to this day. (See: Bond Street/New Bond Street/101.)

Monument, the - (AKA: the Monument to the Great Fire of London.) Located a few blocks from the Thames, in Eastcheap, on King William Street (which dates from 1831-5,) which is situated on Fish Street Hill. Also sometimes referred to by its description: Roman Doric Column.The Monument is a tall column designed by Wren (with Robert Hooke) to commemorate the Great Fire of 1666. Built in 1671-77. 202 feet high, with 311 steps to the platform (with no halting place) for the view. At the base is a relief of the king and his citizens fighting the fire. The platform was enclosed with rails following an 1842 suicide.

Moorfields - Islington/Hackney/the City. Laid out ca. 1603-25. An open space with pleasant walks. CHAMBERS LONDON GAZETTEER points out: "Moorfields was originally a large open space that stretched from the north side of the City wall towards Hoxton and Islington but the name is now principally used in the context of the Eye Hospital, which is located north of Old Street station. A back street named Moorfields survives nearer London Wall, by Moorgate Station."

In 1415 the fields were marshland, which sometimes froze and provided skating surfaces.

By 1605 drainage had been improved and Moorfields was described as a place of pleasant air and walks. Citizens escaped to here during the Great Fire of 1666.

Bedlam Hospital moved here from Bishopsgate in 1675. Moved to Lambeth in 1815. (See under B.)

- Eye Hospital: (See: Charterhouse Square/London Dispensary...)
- Finsbury Circus: Lower Moorfields. (See under F.)
- Finsbury Square: Lower Moorfields. (See under F.)
- St. Mary Moorfields: (See under the CHURCHES section.)

Moorgate - (Also seen as: Moor Gate.) The City. One of the ancient medieval City gates. (See: gates.) The Moor Gate opened onto Moorfields, in 1415, when the Lord Mayor "caused the wall of the City to be broken towards Moorfield"; the fields were marshland at that time. There was a foundry (for military cannon) here until 1716, when it moved to Woolwich Arsenal. The gate was taken down in the 1760s to ease traffic. The street of this name runs from the northwest corner of the Bank of England northwards to the edge of the City of London, built in the 1830s (See: Moorgate Street.)

- Electra House: Edwardian.

Moorgate Street - 1834-40. Known in the Regency as Finsbury Pavement. (See under F.)

Moravians - (AKA: Moravian Brethren. AKA: the Church of the United Brethren. Note, they refer to themselves as: the Unity of the Brethren.) Refugees from Moravia resettled in Saxony (which is now East Germany) and some came as missionaries to England. Had a chapel on Fetter Lane in the mid 18th century. John Wesley (famous religious convert, b. 1703-d.1791) had his spiritual awakening in the London home of one of the Brethren. (See: Moravian Burial Ground.)

Moravian Burial Ground - Between Milman's Street and King's Road, Chelsea. According to AN ENCYCLOPAEDIA OF LONDON: "...the benevolent Count Nicholas von Zinzendorf, leader of the 'unitas Fratrum,' invited members of that body to settle on his Chelsea estate after their expulsion from Bohemia and Moravia in the first half of the 18th century." The burial ground is separated into designated plots for: married men, single men, married women, and single women. The gravestones list only the name and age of the occupant, and are all flat.

Morley's Hotel - Trafalgar Square. Restaurant, 1831. Later the site became South Africa House. (See under S.)

Morning Advertiser - 1794 News sheet. (Strand/Morning Advertiser.)

Morning Post, the - By the end of the 18th C. this was the leading newspaper in London. Published from 1772-1937. Originally a Whig writ, by 1795 it was a Tory paper. it became known for its vitriolic flavor. (See: newspapers/news sheets.)

Mornington Crescent - Camden Town, at the junction of Hampstead Road and Camden High Street. (AKA: Morning Crescent.) Begun in 1821, named after the Earl of Mornington. Ca. 1911 this street began its stretch of rivaling Cheyne Walk as the "most creative hotbed" of residents.

morphine - (See: diseases/Treatments/morphine.)

Morris dancers - An ancient (perhaps from 1500) tradition of dancing men dressed in white, with flower-bedecked hats, and ribbons and/or bells tied around their calves, and often holding handkerchiefs that are waved as they dance. Still seen at many folklore rituals and festivals. Thought to be a form of a fertility rite. Traditionally for men only.

- You may care to see: mummers.
- You may care to see: Pearly Kings and Queens.

Morse Code - Invented in 1838.

Mortlake - Richmond. Lies to the east of Barnes Village. Until 1619, although the manor was extended, the village was just a few riverside houses on a single street. In 1619 James I financed a tapestry works here, employing Flemish weavers. Charles I bought this concern in 1636. The next year the king made the locally unpopular choice of buying 732 acres of Mortlake manor to be part of his new hunting ground, Richmond Park. The tapestry works closed in 1703. Some fine homes came in the late 18th century. The area was known for its potteries/stoneware and its tapestries (17-18th centuries.)

- St. Mary's: 15th century. Stone and flint building. In the High Street.

mosque - The first in Britain was built in 1890. The London Central Mosque (also called Regent's Park Mosque, due to its location) opened in 1977-8.

Mount Place; and **Mount Street**, and **Mount Terrace** - (See: London Hospital, for the creation of all three of these.)

Mount Pleasant - Camden/Islington, Clerkenwell. Used to be Cold Bath Fields; cold baths were here in 1697; the name changed to Mount Pleasant in the 1730s.

- Coldbath Prison: 1794. (See under: Cold Bath Fields Prison.)
- Exmouth Market: (See under E.)

Mount Pleasant - Hillingdon. (AKA: Harefield West.) Mills and their noxious nature came in ca. the 1840s, probably leading to the irony of using the Mount Pleasant name.

Mount Street - Mayfair. Name derived from "Oliver's Mount," left over from Cromwell's time. The name of "Mount" came about in the Civil War of 1642, because nearby trenches were dug, and the dirt from them piled here. This mound (mount) was increased to a higher height following the Great Fire of 1666. (See: London Hospital - The explanation under.) There are 1890s terracotta frontages here yet.

- One John Tilbury had a business here from which gentlemen could hire a horse for twelve guineas a month (not including its keep.)

- R. Allen & Co.: Butchers. Here (or nearby) since ca. 1840s.

Mount Street Gardens - Mayfair. A public park laid out in the late 19th century.

mounting blocks - (Actually called: alighting stones.) An aid for getting down from a carriage. (See the INNS/PUBS section - The beginning of the Inns section, at the "coaching inns" comments.)

MP - Short for Member of Parliament; one who sits in the House of Commons or the House of Lords. The use of the initials is a more modern usage.

Mulberry Garden - A Stuart haunt. Became the site of Buckingham Palace. (See: Buckingham House.)

mummers - Strictly speaking, people dressed up in disguises. The tradition dates back to at least the 13th century. Often associated with religiously-based holidays/festivals. Were seen/practiced yet in the 19th century (and up to today,) usually with a charity collection to follow.

Museum of Childhood - 1856. Is part of the Victoria and Albert Museum, which was founded in 1852.

Museum of Garden History - Lambeth. 1972. (See: St. Mary-at-Lambeth, under the CHURCHES section.)

Museum of London - 150 London Wall. 1976.

Museum of Mankind - Building dates from 1866. 6 Burlington Gardens. Became the Museum of Mankind in 1972 (extension of the British Museum.) Backs on to Burlington House, behind the Royal Academy of Arts. In 2001 the Royal Academy of Arts purchased the museum's locale.

Museum of Practical Geology - (Is now called the Geological Museum.) Exhibition Road, South Kensington. Founded in 1835. Part of the Natural History Museum of London.

museums - Some pubs (by at least the 18th C.) contained museums, usually sports-related, such as boxing, or to represent a specific historical event or person (and therefore attract customers, of course.)

- ➢ See: Bloomsbury/British Museum - For more on this, also see: Montagu House.
- ➢ See: Egyptian Hall.
- ➢ See: Liverpool Museum.
- ➢ See: Piccadilly/Bullock's Museum.
- ➢ See: St. James's Park/Rotunda.
- ➢ See: Soane Museum.
- ➢ You may care to see: Royal Academy of Arts - For the note on the

lack of 18th C. museums displaying paintings.

music - Rich or poor, if you could sing or play an instrument, you probably shared your talent with those around you, whether to earn money or as a social obligation. Being able to provide entertainment was a valued skill.

- See: ballad-sellers.
- See: God Sing the Queen.
- See: instruments, musical.
- See: London Symphony Orchestra - 1904.
- See: Royal Academy of Music - 1774.
- See: Rule, Britannia.
- See: songs.
- See: the THEATRES section.
- You may care to see: waltz.

musical instruments - (See: instruments, musical.)

music-halls - Victorian. (While of course the Regency era had places where one could go to enjoy music - the theatres, parks, Vauxhall, etc. - those places were not referred to as music-halls, not until later into the 19th century.)

Musicians' Company - (AKA: the Worshipful Company of Musicians.) Ordinances of 1350 refer to a fellowship of minstrels. The Musicians' Company formed in 1500. Royal Charter by 1604. By the mid 18th C. the guild had lost its impact, becoming more of a benevolent/educational body. Livery Company. 50th in the order of precedence. Never had a hall. The Company, since 2013, resides at the Guildhall School of Music and Drama.

Muswell Hill - Haringey. While Muswell Hill is now an Edwardian suburb, it contains ancient woods. Muswell is a corruption of "mossy well."

- See: forests/Coldfall Wood.
- See: forests/Highgate Hill.

Myddleston Square - Finsbury/Islington. 1827. By W. C. Mylne. Prior to 1827 this area had hosted Georgian and Regency farms and gardens, with a smattering of streets and squares.

mystery - (Almost as often, seen spelled: mistery.) This was an ancient term (it actually came from the Romans) that indicated a Guild before it achieved its royal charter, as in "the Mystery of Egg-gatherers in the City of London." (I made up the egg-gatherers; there is no such mystery/guild.) After the 16th century the term was seen less as time went on. "Mystery" being said, in this case, to mean: a religious truth one can only know by revelation and not completely understand, and is generally accepted to represent that the guild held a private secret or practiced special skills.

- See: guild.

➢ You may care to see: Worshipful Company of..., under W.

-N-

Nags Head - Islington. At the junction of Seven Sisters Road and Holloway Road. Named for the public house that stood here since ca. 1800. Ca. 1870 the Nag's Head Inn was remodeled in the Italianate style.

Nags Head Road - (See: Southbury/Southbury Road.)

napkins - What Regency era persons called the cloths for cleaning one's fingers/face while dining.

➢ See: clouts - For: diapers.

➢ See: serviettes - Victorian phrase.

National Agriculture Hall - 1884. (See: Olympia Exhibition Hall.)

National Archives - (See: Public Record Office.)

National Army Museum - Sandhurst, 1960; moved to Royal Hospital Road, Chelsea, in 1971. Shows the history of the British Army since 1845.

National Association of United Trades for the Protection of Labour - 1845. (See: union.)

National Central Library - Malet Place. 1933.

National Coursing Club - Greyhounds pursuing hares. The NCC was founded in 1858. (See: coursing.)

National Gallery of British Art - (AKA: the Tate Gallery.) Millbank. 1897. One Sir Henry Tate gave much of the founding money, so it became known as the Tate Gallery.

National Gallery, the - (AKA: the British Gallery.) St. Martin's Place, off Trafalgar Square, Westminster.

Not to be confused with the National Portrait Gallery, which stands at the *side* of the National Gallery, facing St. Martin's Lane. (You may care to see: National Portrait Gallery, at its own listing.)

Founded in 1824, built to house the art collection donated by Sir John Angerstein. Buildings by William Wilkins in 1834-38, built on the site of the main building of the Great Royal Mews (demolished 1830 for the National Gallery and the construction of Trafalgar Square.) The front portico (by Henry Holland) was moved here from Carlton House when Carlton House was scheduled to be demolished. The initial building was only one room deep. The beginning collection (38 paintings) was hung in the home of the benefactor (one John Julius Angerstein, a Russian) in 100 Pall Mall until moving to its Trafalgar Square home in 1838. It now houses Britain's premiere collection of Old Masters, the number of paintings here now about 2,100.

- Royal Academy of Arts: Moved from Somerset House to here in 1837; here until 1868. (See under R.)

National Institute of Medical Research - Hampstead. 1880.

National Maritime Museum - 1937. (See: Greenwich/Queen's House.)

national park -

- See: Peak District.
- You may care to see: royal parks.

National Physical Laboratory - Bushy Park, Teddington. National measurement standards laboratory. 20th century. (See: Bushy Park/Bushy House.)

National Portrait Gallery - (Not to be confused with the National Gallery, beside which the National Portrait Gallery stands.) Founded in 1856, at 29 Great George Street. Opened in 1859 to the public. Since 1895, has been at 2 St. Martin's Place, Charing Cross Road, built by Ewan Christian and Colling.

National Rifle Association - Begun in 1860.

National Society for Promoting the Education of the Poor in the Principles of the Established Church in England and Wales - (Often AKA: National Society. AKA since 2016: The Church of England Education Office.) Founded in 1811, by Church of England members who were fearful for children who could not read (and therefore did not learn their Bible) started this society. Traditionally, schools founded by this Society were called: "National Schools," as opposed to those founded by the British and Foreign School Society, which were called "British schools." Yet exists. (You may care to see: British and Foreign School Society.)

National Trust, the - 40-44 Queen Anne's Gate. The building itself probably dates back to ca. 1704, but the National Trust was formed in 1895 (at a meeting in Grosvenor House.) It was formed to buy up historic homes and land, to preserve them for the nation. (See: protected London properties, under P.)

National Union of Women's Suffrage Societies - 1897. This was followed by Emmeline Parkhurst's organization in 1903, (the radical) Women's Social and Political Union. British women won the right to vote in 1928. (See: votes, for women.)

National Westminster Bank - (See: Westminster Bank.)

Natural History Museum - Cromwell Road, South Kensington. 1873-80, by Alfred Waterhouse, built on the site of the 1862 International Exhibition Building. In 1860, to manage its ever-expanding exhibits, the British Museum determined the Natural History Collection needed to be moved - that is, out of the British Museum to this location on Cromwell Road. (See:

Bloomsbury Square/British Museum/Natural History Museum.)

Nautical Almanac, the - First published in 1766, by Nevil Maskelyne. Explored naval and scientific advances. Was published annually for 45 years (until 1811, the year of Maskelyne's death.)

naval matters - Naval ships were built at extensive royal and private dockyards. While the British populace was largely suspicious of any standing army, the Royal Navy was always popular. Although naval pay was poor, there were always volunteers (in addition to men who were pressed into service, especially during times of war) because of the possibility of bounties and sharing in prize money (derived from captured ships.)

- See: Admiralty.
- See: army - Note on how Britons long preferred the navy over the army.
- See: Coast Guard.
- See: doctors/surgeons - All naval doctors were surgeons.
- See: Greenwich Observatory - Note on determining longitude.
- See: impressment.
- See: lifeboats.
- See: lighthouses.
- See: Marines.
- See: maritime matters.
- See: Royal Naval... - Several listings.
- See: scurvy.
- See: Somerset House - Note about halfway down from the beginning.
- See: Telegraph Hill - Final note, on semaphore signals.
- See: Trinity House - For: pilots (navigators); construction of naval things like buoys.

navigators - (See: pilots.)

Needlemakers' Company - (AKA: the Worshipful Company of Needlemakers.) Needles and bone awls date back to the stone age. A guild was slow to form, so needlemakers tended to join other guilds in order to qualify as a Freeman of the City, such as the Blacksmiths, Drapers, Merchant Taylors, etc.

Oliver Cromwell granted a Charter to the Needlemakers' Company in 1656; a second was granted by Charles II in 1664. According to AN ENCYCLOPAEDIA OF LONDON: "By the 18th century the centre of the trade had moved to Redditch but the Company still maintains close associations with the modern trade." Livery Company. 65th in the order of precedence. Never had a hall.

Nelson Column, the - (AKA: Nelson's Column. AKA: Nelson Monument.) 1840-3, for the naval hero. (See: Trafalgar Square/Nelson Column.)

Neptune - (See: planets/Neptune.)

Neville's Court - Alley off Fetter Lane, Holborn. Houses, built ca. 1670.

New Addington - (See: Addington Temple.)

New Auction Mart - (See: London Auction Mart.)

New Barnet - Barnet. Victorian.

New Bond Street - (See: Bond Street/New Bond Street.)

New Bridewell Prison - 1834 rebuild. (See: Bridewell Prison - Paragraph under.)

New Bridge Street - Led from the Thames to Ludgate, 1765. Named for the "new" Blackfriars bridge (at that time built in 1760-69.) Bridewell Place (where Bridewell Prison stood) was off this road.

New British Ladies' Magazine - Fashion/gossip magazine for women. Published in 1818, but it only lasted a little over one year.

New Broad Street - (See: Petty France/New Broad Street.)

New Burlington Street - Built ca. 1735-9. Was originally called Little Burlington Street, name change came in ca. 1763. Today's street little resembles the one built in the early 18th century.

New Cavendish Street - Marylebone, one of this district's longest streets. In the second half of the 18th C. construction began. By 1799 the street had three distinct names and sections: Great Marylebone Street, New Cavendish Street, and Upper Marylebone Street. In 1904 Great Marylebone Street and New Cavendish Street were combined, and the house numbers consequently reordered. A reordering occurred again in 1937 when Upper Marylebone Street was also combined in, and the lot were called New Cavendish Street. There are yet some Georgian, Regency, and Victorian houses here.

New Charlton - Greenwich. (See: Charlton Village/New Charlton.)

New Court - St. Swithin's Lane, the City.

- Rothschild's Bank: 1810. The Rothschilds banking system was founded in England in 1798, by Nathan Mayer von Rothschild (b.1777-d.1836,) was first in Manchester.

New Coventry Street - Soho. Built in 1843-46.

New Cross - Lewisham. New Cross Heath was in 15th C. records, heavily wooded then. (See: Lewisham.)

- New Cross Gate: 1820s. Western part of New Cross. Takes its name from a 1718 tollgate here, the tollgate being relocated in 1813 from Clifton Rise to the junction of New Cross Road and Peckham Lane, now Queen's Road. (See:

Hatcham.)

- Royal Naval School: 1843. The Goldsmiths' Company Technical and Recreative Institute took over the building in 1891; later became Goldsmiths College (as part of the University of London.)
- Worshipful Company of Haberdashers: Acquired much of the land here in 1614. Not to build their Hall; the land was used as an endowment for the Haberdashers' charity. In the 18th C. the Company leased land to members and to gentlemen. More developed from the mid 19th century on.

New Earl Street - That portion of the road connecting Trinity Lane and Cannon Street; became a portion of Queen Victoria Street ca. 1860-70s.

- Sweetings: 39 Queen Victoria Street. Tiny. London's first fish restaurant, begun in 1830. (You may care to see: fish and chip shop - For the origins of same.)

New Eltham - Greenwich. Rural until the late 19th century. Most of the present buildings date from the 1930s.

New End - Hampstead/Camden. Up to the start of the 19th C. this was rather the poorer corner of Hampstead; humble cottages, housing artisans. Grew into/was engulfed by Hampstead in the late 19th century.

- Burgh House: (See: Hampstead/Burgh House.)
- parish workhouse, a: 1800. Rebuilt in 1845. Later became New End Hospital, now closed.

New Exchange - Shopping area across the Strand (from Covent Garden,) east of what is now Charing Cross station. It was rather like today's American shopping venues/malls. Designed by Inigo Jones, opened in 1608 or 1609. Facade of stone, Gothic style. Taken down in 1737.

New Fish Street - (See: Fish Street Hill.)

New Gravel Lane - Shadwell (now Tower Hamlet.) There by at least 1811. Since 1938 known as Garnet Street.

- King's Arms: Inn. There by at least 1811. (See: King's Arms/Shadwell, under the INNS/PUBS section.)
- St. George-in-the-East: (See under the CHURCHES section.)

New Hall - (See: Inns of Court/Lincoln's Inn/New Hall.)

New Holland - (See: Australia.)

New Kent Road - Southwark. 1751. First called Greenwich Road. Sources indicate it was called "New Kent Road" by the time of the Regency. Is now designated as the A201.

New Malden - Kingston. Farms and small holdings. Didn't develop much until the rails came in ca. 1850s-60s. Since the 1970s has been known as London's "Korea Town," with the largest/most concentrated Korean population in Europe (with, too, a sizable/20th century

Tamil population.)

New Ministry of Defence - Was formed in 1964, creating greater coordination between: the British Army, the Royal Navy, and the Royal Air Force. (See: Ministry of Defence.)

New North Road - 1812-1820. Through Islington. At the north end there was a small mews by 1829.

New Oxford Street - Plowed through the slums of St. Giles in 1839 and into the 1840s. A shop here was established in 1830, but as a dairy. (See: 55, immediately below.) Smith turned it into a sticks/canes/crops/whips shop in 1856.

- 55: James Smith and Son. Established in 1830 (but as a dairy); Smith turned this into a sticks/canes/crops/sticks/umbrellas/walking sticks/whips shop in 1857. Still run by the Smith family.

New Palace of Westminster -

- See: Houses of Parliament.
- See: Westminster.
- See: Westminster Palace.

New Palace Yard - Westminster. "New" means it dates from William Rufus' time (he reigned 1087-1100), whereas "Old" Palace Yard refers to the time of Edward the Confessor (reigned 1042-1066.) New Palace Yard is an open courtyard northwest of the Palace of Westminster. It once had a pillory standing here. Its size shrank over the years as new buildings and streets came along. Not open to the public.

New Park Street Chapel - Southwark. 1833. A Reformed Baptist chapel (although the fellowship began worshipping together in 1650.) When this was outgrown, the chapel moved to a site built on the Elephant and Castle Inn property, and was newly named the Metropolitan Tabernacle; burned in 1898. Rebuilt, but destroyed in WWII. Opened again in 1959.

New Pye Street - Westminster. (See: Old Pye Street.)

New Regency Street - (See: Regent Street/Quadrant.)

New River Canal - Forty miles/64 km long. Built by Sir Hugh Myddleston in 1613. It ran between Canonbury Road and St. Paul's Road, bringing fresh water to Clerkenwell, from Hertfordshire. Built to supply London with water from Hertfordshire.

- See: Islington/New River Canal.
- See: New River Company.
- See: rivers and brooks of London/New River Canal.

New River Company - This company, via the New River Canal, supplied water (from Hertfordshire, 40 miles/64 km into London at Islington,) since the 17th C. via the New River. (See: New River Canal.)

- New River Pumping Station: 1854-6.

New Road - Laid out in 1756, opened in 1761. From Paddington to Islington. Since 1857, known as Marylebone, Euston, Pentonville, and the City Road(s.) Built so that drovers taking their cattle to Smithfield could bypass central London and particularly Oxford Street and Holborn. (See: Pentonville Road.)

- St. Pancras New Church: 1820s, Upper Woburn Place. (See under the CHURCHES section.)

New Scotland Yard - "Old" Scotland Yard moved to 6 Derby Gate ca. 1887 in what is now the Norman Shaw Building; this location is described as "nothing more than two buildings connected by an arch," although LONDON, FROM THE EARLIEST TIMES TO THE PRESENT DAY says it has (at least two) pointed roofs. Since 1967, the New Scotland Yard relocated to 10 Broadway, off Victoria Street. (See: Whitehall/4 Whitehall Place, for previous Scotland Yard locale/information.)

New South Wales - (See: Australia.)

New Spring Gardens -

- See: Spring Gardens.
- See: Vauxhall Gardens.

New Square - Lawyers here. A completely 17th C. square, from 1697; New Square and its cloistered churchyard look much today as they did in the 1690s. (See: Inns of Court/Lincoln's Inn/New Square.)

- Wildy & Sons: Established 1830, bookstore (of legal, as in lawyerly, books.)

New Zealand - Was first explored by the British in 1768-71 while Captain James Cook ventured around Australia and New Zealand. (See: Australia.) Adopted the statute/became members of the British Commonwealth in 1947.

New Zealand House - Haymarket. Built ca. 1958-62. Built on the site of the Carlton Hotel.

Newbury Park - Redbridge. Held by Barking Abbey until the Dissolution of the Monasteries. Henry VIII granted the holding to Sir Richard Gresham (mercer/Lord Mayor of London/father of Thomas.) Was an agricultural area into the late 19th century.

Newcastle House - Inns of Court/Lincoln's Inn Fields. Built in 1641-42 for the Earl of Carlisle. Bought in 1672 by the 1st Marquess of Powis and renamed Powis House; burned down in 1684. Powis lost the house, but it went back to the Powis family in 1705, who sold it to John Holles; John Vanbrugh made alterations, and it was then called Newcastle House. The house was divided in half, one half bought by James Farrar (a solicitor); the solicitors Farrar & Co. yet occupy the house, purchasing the other half in the 20th century.

In 1825 the other half became occupied by the Society for the Promotion of Christian Knowledge, which was established in 1699 by Thomas Bray. (See under S.)

Although the reunited halves had alterations in the 1930s, Newcastle House retains much of its 17-18th century appearance.

Not to be confused with another Newcastle House, 17th century, in Clerkenwell.

Newell Street -

- See: Limehouse/Newell Street.
- See: Wapping/Newell Street.

Newgate Market - (AKA ca. 1860 as: Metropolitan Meat-Market.) Copenhagen Fields. Following an Act of Parliament in 1852 (and due to people no longer liking having live animals/butchery and the attendant filth at Smithfield Market,) this market opened in 1855. Buildings went up in 1860, Newgate Market was abolished, and in its place came the Metropolitan Meat Market.

- See: Islington/Copenhagen Fields.
- See: Metropolitan Cattle Market.
- See: Paternoster Row/Newgate Market.

Newgate Prison - (AKA: Newgate Gaol. AKA simply as: Newgate.) Newgate Street. Its earliest existence is murky, but at least dates from 1188, under Henry II's reign. Suffered serious damage in the 1381 Wat Tyler riots. Enlarged and refurbished in 1423. It burned in 1672; rebuilt in 1770-78. In the 18th and 19th centuries it was the primary place of imprisonment for ***serious crimes* in London**; housed all manner of prisoners: debtors, famous highwaymen, murderers, and political prisoners. It was damaged in the 1780 Gordon Riots (and most of the inmates released by the mob); was rather grandly rebuilt in 1782 by George Dance.

The exterior had this appearance: high walls, big doorways, and blocked in spaces where windows ought to have been. Inside, it was described as "smelly, (with) no drains, no windows, no air."

The prisoners ate at rough tables. They could buy beer.

There was an infirmary upstairs for sick prisoners, but it was the (male) gaolers who looked after sick prisoners (both male and female), there was no doctor.

Executions were no longer carried out at Tyburn after 1783, so much of the practice moved here, outside the prison, on the street Old Bailey. Huge crowds of 30,000 and up would gather to watch, as late as Charles Dickens' time. Regency bucks were known to attend hangings here. Up to twenty convicts could be hanged at one "drop." On the Sunday before an execution, visitors could pay a shilling to sit in the gallery of Newgate Prison Chapel, to witness the "execution service" held for the condemned. The condemned sat in a large railed-off area called the "condemned pew," with a coffin sitting on a table before the prisoner(s); this coffin-displaying practice was discontinued in 1817. Other prisoners were allowed to crowd into the chapel, the usual "sport" being to jeer at the prisoner(s) soon to die.

The cells for prisoners condemned to death were beneath Newgate; 9 feet x 6 feet, with a vaulted stone roof. These cells had a small window high up in the wall, barred with double grates.

Contained a place called the Press Yard, where a prisoner's chains were removed prior to execution.

The last public beheadings here were in 1820, this being the five convicted Cato Street conspirators. (They were beheaded by use of a surgeon's knife.) After public executions were abolished in 1868, they were carried out *inside* the prison, in a shed on the right of the exercise yard, with only invited dignitaries and/or reporters allowed, the completion of which was announced by a black flag.

Prisoners slept on bare boards on the floor, covered with "old, old straw." No sheets or blankets (unless friends provided them.)

The prison had a tiny shop (there by at least ca. 1817) from which prisoners could buy drink, food, and straw.

Until 1714, a prisoner could keep pigs inside the walls.

Newgate was also a holding ground for those prisoners intended for Transportation.

The prison's neighbors consisted of coffee-houses and gin-palaces. Too, the Old Bailey was next door. (You may care to see: Old Bailey, under O.)

The lead man of the prison was known as the Governor (i.e. what Americans call the Warden.)

Demolished for good in 1902. Replaced by today's Old Bailey (also known as the Central Criminal Court, 1904-7.)

Nicknames for Newgate were: the pitcher, the stone pitcher, the start, the stone jug.

Newgate Street - North of St. Paul's Cathedral. Named for the nearby Newgate, one of the seven ancient gates in the old London Wall. (See: gates.) Today it is part of the A40.

- St. Sepulchre's Church, under the CHURCHES section.

Newington - Southwark. "Newington" means: new farmstead. Dates from the 11th century. (See: Elephant and Castle.)

Newington Butts - Southwark. Its name is believed to have derived from "archery butts," i. e. an archery practice ground. Was a rural hamlet during the Regency, having been known in the 16th centuries for hosting plays (outside the City, which forbade them.)

- St. Mary: Origins date back to the Saxons. Last version of this church was built in 1792, but moved to Kennington Park Road in 1876. (Near St. George's Circus.) The old churchyard is now a childrens' playground, since 2008.

Newington Gardens - (See: Horsemonger Lane Gaol.)

Newington Green - Islington. 1650s. Pilasters by Inigo Jones. (See: Islington/Newington Green.)

Newlands - Barnet. (See: Edgware/Newlands.)

Newlands - Southwark. Nunhead area. Late Victorian, never did well until 1884 when it was designed as a larger development called Waverly Park estate.

Newman Street - 1750-70. Home to artists. North off Oxford Street.

- 14: Benjamin West (painter) kept a house and studio here, from 1775-1820 (when he died.) The house and studio are now gone.

Newmarket - Sixty-two miles/100 km from London, in the county of Suffolk, east of London.

Newmarket was an ancient market town, but here I write of it as a thoroughbred racecourse. There was racing here since 1174, but as a racecourse it was founded in 1634 by Charles I. Too, it is/was the famous place from whence horseflesh was viewed/sold.

- Jockey Club: Founded at Newmarket in 1752; to which gentlemen belonged as race-horse owners and as members. Attached to the Jockey Club was the Coffee Room, where young dandies liked to become members, at least as late as 1817. (See: Jockey Club, under the CLUBS section.)
- Tattersall's: Also famous for viewing/selling horseflesh. Moved here in 1939. (See under T.)

Newport Market - Near Leicester Square. A country market. Takes its name from Mountjoy Blount, Earl of Newport, who lived here for 30 years in the 17th C., in Newport House. The house and estate were sold, and in 1686 streets were laid out and a license for a market obtained. It was held on Tuesdays, Thursdays, and Saturdays weekly, hosting all manner of merchandise, including meat, with the sole exclusion to the market being live animals. When the Curzon family gave up their interest in the market (and area) in 1828, the market was rebuilt ca. 1830; it did not equal its past. By the 1870s the area was slums. The Metropolitan Board of Works bought it, with an attempt at restoring the Market in 1872, but it failed. The market was swept away in 1882 by the construction of Shaftesbury Avenue.

news sheets - (See: newspapers/new sheets.)

newspapers/news sheets - (Both terms were used during the Regency era, with "news sheets" being more common.) During the French Revolution, London had 145 daily news sheets. During George III's time the number rose from 35 to 150; by the time of his death Britain overall had over 300 newspapers. The first so-called London penny paper was founded in 1855, *The Daily Telegraph.*

- See: City Press, the - 1857.
- See: Daily Courant, the - (See: Ludgate Circus/Daily Courant, 1702.)

- See: Daily Telegraph - In the paragraph immediately above.
- See: Fleet Street/127 - The Morning Advertiser, 1825.
- See: Fleet Street/Printing House Square/Times, the, under F - 1785.
- See: Globe, the - Under: Strand, below.
- See: Lloyd's of London/Lloyd's List.
- See: Morning Post, the - 1772.
- See: Pall Mall Gazette, the - 1865 evening newspaper.
- See: Philosophical Transactions - Scientific publication, since 1645.
- See: Political Register, the - 1802-37, William Corbett's Tory report.
- See: Stamp Office - Where the news sheet tax was paid.
- See: Strand, the - For *The Globe* (1890,) and *The Morning Advertiser* (1794, which was England's 2nd most popular news sheet by the middle of the 19th century.)
- See: Sunday Times, the - 1822.
- See: W. H. Smith Company, under W. - A distributor of news sheets.
- You may care to see: journals.
- You may care to see: magazines.

Newyears Green - (Also seen as: New Years Green.) Hillingdon. Dates from at least 1754. Enclosure of the fields was in 1813. Unfortunately in modern times Newyears Green Lane hosts a waste dump, which has led to illicit dumping in the wider area, so that even though there is a Wildlife Trust here the area is currently less than savory.

nightmen - Men who removed buckets of nightsoil (human waste,) usually in cities, where there was less room to dig waste pits. (See: sanitation.)

nightstand - NOT a table next to the bed on which to place a ewer or a candlestick. In the Regency, a nightstand was a piece of furniture meant to hold a chamberpot. You might take the chamberpot out of it for use, or it might have a covered hole atop it, which one opened and then used rather like a modern (but obviously unflushable) toilet.

Nine Elms - Wandsworth. In the early 19th C. there were market-gardens here, supplying London with vegetables, one of their crops being asparagus. Site of the New Covent Garden Market, 1974. (See: Covent Garden/Market, the.)

nine-nine-nine - Dialed on a phone as: 999. First seen in 1937. This is the UK's equivalence to America's 911, an emergency services phone number. (Note: the telephone was first seen in the UK in 1876, at Glasgow's British Association for the Advancement of Science fair, to no one less than Queen Victoria, among many others. Telephones began to be installed in London in 1878.)

nine-pins - A game. (See: bowling green.)

Noah's Ark - Toy, game, and sports shop, established by John Hamley in 1760 in High Holborn. In 1881, it was then known as Hamley Brothers, and moved to 188 Regent Street. Royal Warrant in 1938. Is currently still known as Hamley's; the present store opened in 1906. (This Noah's Ark is not to be confused with the rough area: Holy Land/Noah's Ark.)

Noak Hill - Havering. A village truly on a hill. First recorded in 1490, but known to pre-date that record. An agricultural manor.

- Angel, the: Public house. Existed prior to 1824, about which time the inn was converted into two cottages (that still exist.)
- Bear Inn: Pub, on the edge of Harold Hill, first called Goat House. The name changed to Bear Inn in 1715. Hosted a rather large menagerie in the 1970s.
- Noak Hill Common: Enclosed in 1814.
- St. Thomas's Church: 1842. Chapel of ease.

Noble Street - The City. Parts of ancient Roman city wall remain here.

- Coachmakers' and Coach Harness Makers' Hall: (See under C.)
- Haberdashers' Hall: On Gresham Street, where it corners with Noble Street. (See under H.)

Nonconformists - In England this term by and large meant: the Baptists, Presbyterians, Quakers, the Separatists, and other groups religiously in the minority, after a series of laws passed (after 1660) disallowing their ability to remain within the Anglican church. There were no Nonconforming chapels in London prior to the 17th century - although nonconformist groups did have secret gatherings.

- ➢ See: Oundle.
- ➢ See: Stoke Newington.

Nonsuch House - Not to be confused with Nonsuch Palace. Built in Holland, and brought to London in total, brick by brick; built without mortar or iron, held together only by wooden dowels and wedges. Its expanse went clear across London Bridge, having an archway for traffic. Gone from London Bridge ca. 1760. (See: London Bridge, in the BRIDGES section.)

Nonsuch Palace - Built near Ewell, Surrey, for Henry VIII. Henry bought the entire manors of Cheam and Cuddington in order to build this palace.

- ➢ See: Cheam.
- ➢ See: Cuddington.
- ➢ See: Lower Cheam.

Built to be a hunting lodge, its grandeur said otherwise.

It was almost complete when Henry died in 1547.

Stayed with the Crown until Charles II gave it to his mistress, Barbara Villiers; it burned in the Great Fire of 1666, after which Mistress Villiers demolished it and sold off its materials in 1684.

Destroyed in the Great Fire of 1666. Its stones were then used by Lord Berkeley to build a mansion in Epsom. The palace is now utterly gone.

Nonsuch Park - West of Cheam. Connected to Nonsuch Palace. The park still exists.

Norbiton - Kingston. Recorded by at least 1205. Became a parish in 1842.

- Norbiton Common: Now a rarely used term for the southern section of Norbiton. In 1697 seven acres were selected as a place for the poor to work at cultivating flax. The entire common (320 acres) was enclosed in 1808, quickly springing up new farms. Developed after the 1850s.
- Norbiton Hall: Mid 18th century. Home of Sir John Phillips. Rebuilt in the 1930s as a mansion block.

Norbury - Croydon. The manor belonged to the Carews of Beddington from 1385, for almost five centuries.

- horse races: Here from 1868 to ca. 1880.
- Norbury Hall: 1802, possibly (but not likely) built by John Nash. Gray brick. Now a retirement home; its grounds are now playing fields.
- Norbury Park: After 1935.
- Northbury: The manor house. Here since 1359.
- Thornton Heath: The common.

Norfolk House - 31 St. James's Square. George III was born here in 1738, in the older house in the back. The "newer" house was built in 1748-52 for the 9th Duke of Norfolk. There was a 1756 housewarming given by the Duchess. One source says it was pulled down in 1935, another says 1938. (See: St. James's Square/31.)

Norfolk Street - Now known as Dunraven Street, but not before 1840. (See: Dunraven Street.)

Norland Square - Kensington. 1845.

Norman Shaw Building -

- See: New Scotland Yard.
- See: Whitehall/4.

North Acton - Ealing. (See: Acton/North Acton.)

North Audley Street - Mayfair. Building began ca. 1727. By the 1790s it was mostly peopled by tradesmen, yet in the early 19th C. it still held some social cachet as a place of residence.

North Cheam - Sutton. (See: Cheam/North Cheam.)

North Circular Road - (Now known as the A406.) Almost 26 miles/42 km long. Completed in 1933.

North Cray - Bexley. The manor was owned by Sir John de Rokesle in the 12th century; there was a church here at that time. Thomas de Poynings got the manor when he married Agnes de

Rokesle in the 14th century. United with the parish of Ruxley in 1557. Became popular for gentlemen's retreats in the mid 18th century. Farming village.

- Loring Hall: (See: Woollet Hall, below.)
- North Cray Place: Grand house, mid 18th century. Pulled down. Replaced by North Cray estate.
- Vale Mascal: Grand house, mid 18th century. Had a Gothic bath house (survives,) possibly by Capability Brown.
- Woollet Hall: 1760, for Viscount Castlereagh (Foreign Secretary, 1812-22, who was highly unpopular.) He committed suicide here in 1822. Now called Loring Hall, it became a private nursing home.

North Dulwich - Southwark. (See: Dulwich/North Dulwich.)

North Ealing - (See under: Ealing/North Ealing.)

North End - Bexley. North end of Crayford. First seen in records from the 1760s. Brickworks and quarries here from the later 19th century.

North End - Camden. Part of Hampstead Heath, at where North End Way and Spaniards Road meet. Best known for "its triangle of pubs." (See entries, below.) William Pitt the Elder (Earl of Chatham, and statesman) lived in North End in 1766-67.

- Collins' Farm: John Linnell (artist) brought his family here to live in the 1820s; he did a painting of the Collins' Farm landscape in 1831. Now called Wylde's Farm.
- Old Bull and Bush, the: Gainsborough, Hogarth, and Reynolds (famous artists) all drank here. (See under the INNS/PUBS section.)
- Spaniards Inn: 17th C., though now much altered. (See under the INNS/PUBS section.)

North End - Hammersmith & Fulham. (A hamlet between Walham Green and Hammersmith, at the north end of Fulham.) Was used for archery practice from the Middle Ages to the early 17th century. A village here by 1745, on either side of North End Lane (now Road.) Expanded rapidly after 1814; before then it was market-gardens and gardeners' cottages, (although it should be noted the gardens and cottages remained until deep into the 19th century.) It later developed (ca. 1880) into West Kensington. (See: Kensington/West Kensington.)

- St. Mary's Church: Built ca. 1814, but took on the St. Mary's name in 1835.

North Hyde - Hounslow. Dates from the 13th century. 100 feet above sea level. The lords of the manor, the Bulstrode family, owned North Hyde in the 18th century. Eight houses here in 1794. A barracks and a powder magazine were here shortly after 1801. (See: hide.)

North Kensington - Kensington & Chelsea. (See: Kensington/North Kensington.)

North Lambeth - Lambeth. CHAMBERS LONDON GAZATTEER states: "One of the most imprecisely defined districts in London. 'The history of this district was for many hundred years the history of Lambeth Palace,' wrote S. O. Ambler in 1923, when things had already become less clear-cut. Some authorities now consider North Lambeth to consist of Vauxhall, Waterloo and South Bank areas, but each of these has a distinct identity in its own right and the term 'North Lambeth' is only useful when it is necessary to consider the borough's riverside parts collectively." (See: Lambeth Palace.)

North Middlesex Hospital - (See: Silver Street, Enfield/workhouse.)

North Ockendon - Havering. Farms and laborers' cottages. Became part of Hornchurch in 1935.

- bakehouse, and forge: Ockendon Road. These buildings yet exist from the 17th century.
- St. Mary Magdalene: Dates from 1175. Flint-faced. It has elements yet from the 13th, 14th, and 15th centuries.

North Row - Near the junction of Oxford Street and Park Lane.

North Villa - (See: Regent's Park/"Area in"/North Villa.)

Northampton Square - Built ca. 1830.

- Northampton House: Originally a home for the Earls of Northampton, and before 1802 it was a private asylum. After 1802 it became a private residence. (Obviously, the house pre-dated the square.)

Northolt - Ealing/Hillingdon. Was originally Northall (counterpart of Southall.) Since the 8th century. Called "Northolt" since ca. 1700; pasture and hay fields, providing for the horses of London. Didn't change much for two more centuries.

- manor house, the: 13th century. Pulled down three times, and rebuilt twice in the 14th C., when it gained a moat; then went to ruin.
- Northolt Park: Ealing/Harrow. Northern part of Northolt, built post-WWII.
- St. Mary's Church: 13th century.

Northumberland Avenue - 1874. Northumberland House was demolished to make way for this street. (See: Northumberland House.)

Northumberland House - Charing Cross/the Strand. By Adam; London residence for his patron, the 1st Duke of Northumberland (a Percy,) ca. 1773. The original house dated from 1605, at which time it was known as Northampton House. Demolished in 1874 to make Northumberland Avenue and the Thames Embankment. (Until this time the Percy Lion, with an outstretched tail, adorned Northumberland House, but at the house's demolition, the lion was moved to Syon House.)

Northwood - Hillingdon. The manor had a grange since 1248 (possibly on the present Grange's site.) Wooded. Very rural until the late 19th C.; supplied firewood to London as late as 1870.

- Holy Trinity Church: 1854.

Norwich - (Pronounced NOR-itch.) Located in the county of Norfolk. "Wic" is an ancient word that means a port, and Norwich was an inland port. Dates from at least the 10th century. At that time, it would have looked like a village to modern eyes, but was considered to be a busy and fairly important town. Its population in the year 1500 was around 10,000 persons. A 1579 plague killed approximately 1/3 of the people living here. In 1565 silkweavers fled to here from persecution in (what is now) Belgium and Holland (and brought their pet birds, canaries, with them. By the 18th C. Norwich was famous for its canaries.) Some weaving of silk continued here until deep into the 18th century. Otherwise, in the 18th century Norwich's main industries were wool and leatherworking. Norwich's wall gates were taken down in 1791-1801, to improve traffic. The population in 1801 had grown to 36,000, but now it was falling behind other towns as its population began to expand more slowly than did Midlands and northern towns.

- Gurney Court: In Magdalene Street. Elizabeth Fry (prison reformer) was born here in 1780.

Norwood - Croydon/Lambeth. As its name indicates, until the 17th C. this area was covered by the Great North Wood. There were large areas of heathland, however, by the mid 18th C. due to deforestation. Mostly a Victorian development.

- West Norwood: Despite the "west" this is actually South Norwood. Had been called Lower Norwood until early 19th C. development.
    - Norwood House of Industry: Elder Road. A workhouse school. 1810. Now mostly demolished.
    - St. Luke's: 1825.

Norwood Green - Ealing. First mentioned in the year 832, when it was willed to the Archbishop of Canterbury.

- Norwood Hall: 1803, by Sir John Soane. Extended in the late 19th century.
- St. Mary's Church: Norman. Rebuilt in the 14th century. Brick tower dates from the late 19th century.

notary public - (See: Scrivener's Company.)

Notting Dale - How "Notting Hill" was known during the Regency. (See: Kensington/Notting Hill.)

Notting Hill -

- ➢ See: Kensington/Notting Hill.
- ➢ See: Ladbroke Grove.
- ➢ See: Portobello Road.

- Hippodrome, the: Horse racing. 1837-41. (See under H.)

Notting Hill Gate - First formed a junction here with Portobello Lane (now Pembridge Road.) Tolls gathered here until 1864. Streams of vehicles went through here.

Notting Hill Square - Former name of Campden Hill Square, Kensington. (See: Kensington/Campden Hill Square.)

Nottingham House - (See: Kensington Palace, in the first paragraph.)

novels - That is, fiction for the sake of storytelling (rather than to provide instruction or moral lessons) were a fairly new art form by the late 18th-early 19th centuries, following the relaxation of ca. 1700AD governmental controls. During the Regency, novels were still sometimes considered scandalous and/or wasteful of one's time and consideration, especially those of Gothic style storylines. Still, note that Jane Austen's entire family were avid readers of novels.

- See: booksellers/bookshops.
- See: Lane's - Publisher of the Minerva Press.

Nunhead Cemetery - Southwark. 1840.

nursery-gardens - (AKA: nurseries.) Nursery-gardens propagate young plants; orchards tend maturing plants. "Nurseries" is often seen used interchangeably with "market-gardens," (the former perhaps being more 20th C., the latter being older usage.)

- See: Dalston.
- See: King's Road.
- See: market-gardens.
- See: orchards.
- See: Stockwell.

nursing - (Medical.) During the Regency era, virtually all nurses would have been men, usually having at one point or another been associated with military service. Florence Nightingale founded the first school for (medical) nursing in 1859, in St. Thomas' Hospital. Not only did she introduce women into nursing, but she is also credited with promoting much more hygienic practices.

- See: Southwark/St. Thomas's Hospital - Note on Florence Nightingale.
- You may care to see: childbirth - Regarding midwives.
- You may care to see: wetnurse.

Oakeley Square - Chelsea. (See: Chelsea/Carlyle Square.)

Oatlands Park - Near Weybridge, in the county of Surrey. Built ca. 1538 following the Dissolution of the Monasteries. Was a royal palace (Oatlands Palace) for Anne of Cleves, built for her by Henry VIII. Near Weybridge, country home of the Duke (Frederick, son of George III) and Duchess of York (Frederica Charlotte Ulrich, daughter of Frederick II of Prussia). She was plain, loved animals, and turned her home into a kind of menagerie. She was much adored in the district, being of "kindly disposition." The house was described as a "little castle." Leased in 1790 by Prince Frederick (2nd son of George III/Duke of York.) The mansion burned down in 1794. Rebuilt in the Gothic style. The Duchess of York died in 1824, and at the Duke's death in 1827 the house was sold. Remodeled in 1830.

Became a hotel in 1856, the South Western, later called Oatlands Park Hotel.

Used as a hospital during WWI, but now yet stands again as the Oatlands Park Hotel.

The garden (which became the park) was described as beautiful.

oats - This grain is/was plentiful in Britain. It's not lumped in with other grains under the misleading (to Americans) term of "corn." Example (speaking of three grains, the first two being wheat and barley): "I'm taking my corn to market, and my oats as well." (You may care to see: corn, under C.)

observatories - As in, used for astronomy.

- See: Greenwich Observatory.
- See: Kew Observatory.

of age - During the Regency era, being of age meant one had obtained the age of 21. For both men and women. (You may care to see: age of consent.)

oils - Many households made their own flavored/scented oils, be they scented with savory herbs, lavender, rose, etc.

- See: food/oils.
- See: Mitcham - For a commercial supplier of oils.

Old Admiralty - (See: Admiralty.)

Old Bailey - (AKA: Sessions House. AKA - and originally built as - the Justice Hall. Later, AKA: the Central Criminal Courts, starting in 1834.) Newgate Street, the City. It is London's most important Crown court. Deals with criminal (as opposed to civil) cases from London, and major crimes from the entire country.

(See: City, the - For notes on how the ancient part of London, the City, has its own systems of justice, including the Old Bailey, as opposed to answering to Westminster.)

There had been a medieval gatehouse (a "bailey") here (1539; it had been next to/a part of Newgate Prison, used for housing prisoners, specifically murderers and thieves. Burned in the Great Fire of 1666. Rebuilt in 1674. The court had no roof, a safeguard against disease; open to the weather until 1734. This is a case where the building took its name from the street on which it was built: Bailey. (See: Newgate Prison, note under.) Rebuilt in 1774.

Newgate Prison, which resided next door, burned in 1780.

As stated above, in 1834 it became known as the Central Criminal Court; it was established by legislation in order to adjudicate for all Greater London area communities. This new court sat in the former Sessions House, just south of the Newgate Prison on Old Bailey Street, hence both the courts and the prison took on the "Old Bailey" label.

Newgate was finally demolished in 1902.

The Sessions House reopened at the site of said former Newgate Prison in 1907; its present frontage dates from 1902-7, by Edward W. Mountford. Atop it stands a gilded statue holding scales, symbolizing Justice; the statue stands atop the famous copper dome. (It should be noted that this "Justice" is not blindfolded, as is often misspoke. She holds the scales of justice, a sword, and some say a stern expression.) Inscribed above the main entrance is the motto: "Defend the children of the poor and punish the wrongdoer."

Almost all the country's serious criminal cases have been tried here since 1834. (Criminal cases are tried here; important civil cases are tried at the Royal Courts of Justice.)

- 18: Magpie and Stump, pub. Served "execution breakfasts" when Old Bailey took over the execution duties from Tyburn in 1783. These lasted until 1868, when public executions were abolished. (See: Magpie and Stump, under the INNS/PUBS section.)

Old Battersea House - Battersea. 1699, possibly by Wren. Was known as Terrace House until 1931, when its new owner (author Wilhelmina Stirling) named it Old Battersea House.

Old Bexley - (See: Bexley/Old Bexley.)

Old Bond Street - Mayfair. (See: Bond Street/Old Bond Street.)

Old Brentford - (See: Brentford/Old Brentford.)

Old Broad Street - (AKA: Broad Street.) It was known as "Old" by the time of the Regency. Near the Bank of England. (See: Broad Street.)

- 19: City of London Club. 1834. Gentleman's cub. (See: City of London, under the CLUBS section.)
- Excise Office: (See under E.)
- Stock Exchange: (See under S.)

Old Burlington Street - Ca. 1730 (or earlier.) Described as "sensible and staid."

- 4: Poole & Cooling, tailors. (See: Savile Row/15.)
- 31 & 32: Two Anglo-Palladian form houses, 1718-23.

Old Charing Cross Hospital - Agar Street. 1834, by Decimus Burton. No longer a hospital.

Old Church Street - Chelsea.

- 46: Old Dairy, the. Built in 1796; supplied by cows that grazed in surrounding fields. (See: Chelsea/Old Church Street.)

old clothes - To buy (or sell.)

- See: Monmouth Street.
- See: Rag Fair.

Old Compton Street - Westminster. (See: Soho/Old Compton Street.)

Old Coulsdon - Croydon. (Pronounced: cools-den.) The (Coulsdon) manor was held since before Domesday book, by the Abbey of St. Peter, Chertsey, until the Dissolution.

The manor went to Thomas Byron in 1782, remaining with the Byron family until approximately the 1920s. In the 19th C. the village of Coulsdon was a few houses around a village green, in what is now called Old Coulsdon; in the 1820s it was a fairly busy coaching road. The "old" was added when a new settlement sprang up around Coulsdon South and Smitham rail stations (ca. 1841.)

- Coulsdon Court: Built for the Byrons, 1850s.
- St. John the Evangelist: 12th century. Tower dates from the 15th century.

Old Curiosity Shop - 13 Portsmouth Street (southwest corner of Lincoln's Inn Fields.) Claims to be (but was not) the shop immortalized by Dickens, as it took on the name 20 years after the book came out; the fictional home of Little Nell was more likely modeled from a shop at the south end of Charing Cross Road. However, the building does date from 1567.

Old Deanery, the - Deans Court. Wren, 1670. Began as the home of the Dean of St. Paul's. Restored in 1983 (as offices.)

Old Ford - Tower Hamlets (on the far north of Bow.) Dates from at least 1268. Was an important crossing point of the River Lea on the primary road from London into Essex during medieval times. Growth stemmed from the arrival of the railroads.

Old Gravel Lane - (Now called Wapping Lane, or Wapping High Street.) On Dec. 19th, 1811: The landlord, his wife, and a female servant, of the pub *King's Arms* were murdered in the rooms on this street.

- See: Ratcliffe Highway - For more information on the 1811 murders.
- See: Wapping/Wapping High Street.

Old Hall - (See: **Highgate Hill**/South Grove/17.)

Old Hall - (See: Inns of Court/**Lincoln's Inn**/Old Hall.)

Old Horse Guards - (See: Royal Guards.)

Old Isleworth - Hounslow. A "solid" 17th C. village, of which nothing remains after the rails came in. (You may care to see: Isleworth.)

- All Saints: Very ancient. Rebuilt in 1707, and in 1970. (See under the CHURCHES section.)
- Church Street: 18-19th C. stuccoed terrace houses.
- London Apprentice public house: 1731. Purportedly named for the apprentice liverymen who rowed here from London on days off.
- Lower Square: 18-19th C. stuccoed terrace houses.

Old Jamaica Inn - London's 1st Coffee House, St. Michael's Alley, off Cornhill. Opened in 1688. (See: Jamaica Inn, under the INNS/PUBS section.)

Old Jewry - Cheapside. Runs between Poultry Street and Gresham Street, dividing Cheapside from the Poultry. William the Conqueror, in 1170, had invited Jews from Rouen to settle here. Named thus from 1290; it was eventually a medieval Jewish ghetto. A one-way street. Still exists, but now is mostly financial offices.

Old Kent Road - Southwark, 1789. Known as: Kent Street Road at first, and was thus called in an 1807 reference. Runs from east Newington to New Cross Gate, largely following the ancient route to Canterbury.

- 220-250: These houses yet survive (much altered.)
- 320: Now known as the Thomas-á-Becket, to medieval travelers it was known as "Thomas-à-Watering." A pub, long since renowned for its boxing; it contains an unofficial museum, and a later gym above the pub. (See under the INNS/PUBS section.)
- Deaf and Dumb Asylum: For deaf and mute children (both male and female.) The Duke of Gloucester laid the foundation stone in 1807. The building is "large and plain." It was first established in 1792 in Fort Place, Bermondsey. It was the first school for deaf and mute children in England.
- South Metropolitan Gasworks: 1840s.

Old London - Nickname for the "actual, ancient" part of London. (See: City, the - Note under.)

old maid - Unflattering term for an unmarried woman, particularly if older. Was a term long in use by the time of the Regency. (See: spinster.)

Old Malden - Kingston. An alternate name for Malden Manor (the latter a name brought along by the establishment of a local rail station); Old Malden was mostly agricultural until industry came in ca. the 1850s.

- manor house, the: 1620s. Enlarged in the 18th century. Became the University of Oxford's Merton College. (See: Oxford College/Merton College.)
- St. John the Baptist: Mid 11th century.

Old Palace Yard - By St. Margaret's, Westminster. Had been the courtyard of the old Westminster Palace in the time of Edward the Confessor. (Described as the large paved area between the Palace of Westminster and Westminster Abbey.) Sir Walter Raleigh was beheaded here in 1618. The statue of Richard the Lionheart was placed here in 1860. (See: New Palace Yard.)

- 7: 18th C. building, by Vardy or Ware. Palladian style. The last remaining house in this yard.
- Jewel Tower: 14th century. Was a part of the Palace of Westminster, and was used for storing the royal jewels until Henry VIII died. In 1869-1938, this became the Weights and Measures Office. Now a museum. (See: Westminster Palace/Jewel Tower.)

Old Public Offices - Downing Street and King Charles Street. For four departments of State. 1862-74.

Old Pye Street - Westminster. Parts of this old street (and the equally old New Pye Street, and both of which had fallen into slums) were swallowed up in 1845 when the new Victoria Street ran through here. (See: Victoria Street.)

Old Quebec Street - (See: Quebec Street.)

Old Regent Street - (See: Regent Street.)

Old Royal Observatory - Greenwich. Designed by Wren, for Charles II's interest in astronomy. Through it passes the *prime meridian* of the world - AKA: Greenwich Mean Time, term dates from 1884. (See: Greenwich Observatory.)

Old Scotland Yard - (See: Whitehall/4/Scotland Yard.)

Old Seacoal Lane - (See: Seacoal Lane.)

Old Southall - (See: Southall/Southall Green.)

Old Street - **Finsbury**. An old name for Old Street was: St. Luke's (street.) CHAMBERS LONDON GAZETTEER states: "From medieval times until the slum clearance programme of the 1870s, its position on the edge of the City of London made St. Luke's a haven for all kinds of prohibited activities, from astrology and wizardry to bearbaiting and prostitution. Thieves and pickpockets could make regular forays into the City and then lose any pursuer in the maze of courts and alleyways around Whitecross Street... The reputation of St. Luke's as a 'rookery'... reached a peak in the first half of the 19th century. 'Flash houses'...were more numerous here than anywhere else in London." By 1900 this district had been cleared of its slums and had sprouted workshops, warehouses, and tenement blocks for workers. (Although much that had been disreputable simply moved east on Old Street, so the area remained rough into the 1930s.)

- St. Luke's Church: Completed in 1733, attributed to Nicholas Hawksmoor and

John James. Its tower is a fluted obelisk topped by a gold dragon (that some Cockneys will tell you was a plague flea.) Closed in 1959. (See: St. Luke, Finsbury, under the CHURCHES section.)

- St. Luke's Hospital: In the 16th C. this area's marshes were drained, and a hospital (not yet St. Luke's) for plague victims was built; stood until 1736.

  St. Luke's was founded in 1751, the only other insane asylum in London other than Bedlam; it was Britain's first psychiatric teaching hospital. For those who could not afford private treatment.

  Was only easily accessible to medical persons, so the public weren't allowed in for viewings as at Bedlam. In the early 19th C., its head, for 48 years, was Thomas Dunston; his preferred punishment for offences was to repeatedly cast a patient head first into a cold water tank, almost to the point of drowning.

  Was first in Windmill Street, but in 1786 moved to Old Street. The building is described as gloomy, three-storied, with an additional basement story; women were housed in the western portion, men in the eastern. Housed approximately 300.

  Moved in 1916 to Muswell Hill, then being known as St. Luke's Woodside. In 1948 annexed to Middlesex Hospital. Survived until 1960, lastly as the Bank of England's printing works.
- St. Luke's School: Founded in 1698, primary school. The building still exists.

Old Street - Islington/Hackney. Ancient; connected Clerkenwell and Shoreditch, bisected by City Road. Developed in the 17th C. when it became a resort area (St. Agnes Well.)

- Goat Brewhouse: 1742. Near Whitecross Street. Samuel Whitbread made porter here. Soon moved to Chiswell Street; there 250 years.

Old Town - A terrace in Clapham. (See: Clapham/Old Town.)

Old Treasury Building - (See: Whitehall/Treasury.)

Oliver's Island - Hounslow. A quite small island in the Thames, near Strand on the Green. Some say it was named for Oliver Cromwell, but records don't support this. Originally called Strand Ayt, until approximately 100 years after the Civil War. There was a fee assessed here (rather like a tollbooth) from the late 18th C., the levied charges going to navigation improvements on the river; it was wooden and somewhat castle-like; a barge collected the tolls.

Oliver's Mount - (See: Grosvenor Square - Note under.)

Olympia Exhibition Hall - Built 1884, being at first called the National Agriculture Hall.

Olympic Pavilion - Opened 1806. This was somewhat comparable to Astley's Amphitheatre. (See: Wych Street/Olympic Pavilion.)

omnibus - A coach used for public transport; could hold about 20 passengers. Invented in France. First one in London was in 1829; it ran from Paddington to Bank, with a shilling fare. Usually pulled by 3 horses abreast. Was widely used by the populace. At the time, often called the horse-bus. Its heyday was in the 1850-60s.

Onslow Gardens - Built ca. 1846.

Onslow Square - South Kensington. Built in 1846. Named for its landlord, the Earl of Onslow.

- 36: William Thackeray (author) lived here from 1854-62.

operating theater - That is, a room in which surgeries could be observed. The oldest one in Britain dates from 1822, located in the roof garret of the church of St. Thomas (which has been attached to St. Thomas's Hospital.) Note: anesthesia began being used in 1846, both here and universally. The St. Thomas operating theatre is now a museum, called the Old Operating Theatre & Herb Garret.

- See: anesthesia.
- See: Southwark/St. Thomas's Hospital.

opium -

- See: Figge's Marsh/Pound Farm.
- See: laudanum.
- You may care to see: Tavistock Street/36.

opticians - Could sell: spectacles, double spectacles (a type of early bifocal,) quizzing glasses (was a solitary lens, held in one hand by a handle, often used at the theatre,) magnifying glasses, mirrors (including professional needs, such as tooth mirrors for dentists,) opera glasses, telescopes, and (post-Regency) microscopes.

- See: spectacles - Includes note on tinted lenses.
- See: Spitalfields/John Dolland.

orangery - A forcing garden (hot house) for growing oranges. Usually to be found on large estates, to provide fruit in the winter months. Some were heated by fireplaces, some by rather ingeniously piped hot air brought from the kitchens.

- See: Chelsea Physic Garden.
- See: Orangery, the.
- See: pinery.

Orangery, the - Parts of it date from the 1630s, at which time it was part of the Holland House expanse. Now a restaurant. (See: Kensington Palace/Orangery, the.)

Oratory, the - Brompton. (See: Brompton Oratory, under the CHURCHES section.)

Orchard Court - Portman Square. 1929.

Orchard Street - Westminster. Off Portman Square. Existed by at least 1787. (See: Portman Square/Orchard Street.)

orchards - During Georgian and Regency times, there were many orchards surrounding London; plentiful well into the 19th century. They are different from a nursery-garden in that the latter propagates young plants, but an orchard has older plants.

- See: Ealing.
- See: food - The various fruits listed there.
- See: fruits.
- See: market-gardens.
- See: nursery-gardens.
- See: Putney.
- See: Tubbenden.

Order of Bards, Ovates and Druids, the - 1964. (Though they claim to have revived an ancient term.) An ovate was a Celtic priest or natural philosopher.

Order of the Bath, (the Most Honourable) - Order of Chivalry. Founded on 10/12/1399 by Henry IV - although this 14th C. version never existed as an Order with knights as a military order with statutes and numbers refurbished when vacancies happened.

The Order of the Bath as we know it today originated under George I on 5/18/1725. Took its name from the elaborate medieval ceremony for appointing a knight, one part of which was ceremonial bathing/purification. It's made up of the monarch, the Great Master (often the heir to the throne,) and since 1815 three manner of members (who belong to either the Civil or the Military divisions):

- Knight (or Dame) Grand Cross
- Knight (or Dame) Commander
- Companion

Before 1815, there was only one class of member: Knight Companion (which exists no longer.) Are usually senior civil servants or military officers. Persons not subjects of the monarch (or foreign nationals) may be Honorary Members.

<u>The seniority of the British Orders of Chivalry</u>:

1. The Most Noble Order of the Garter.
2. The Most Ancient and Most Noble Order of the Thistle.
3. The Most Illustrious Order of St. Patrick (dormant.)
4. The Most Honourable Order of the Bath.

- See: INTRO-REIGNS section/British Kings & Queens and their Reigns/Henry IV.

Order of the Garter, (the Most Noble) - An order of chivalry, founded by Edward III in 1348. Made up of the King and the Prince of Wales, with each having 12 companions (for a finite total of 26, with 24 Knight Companions.) Some accounts say the name derived from the king's mistress (Joan of Kent, Countess of Salisbury) having dropped her garter, the king retrieving it to his own knee, and saying (in Middle French): "may evil come to the one who has impure thoughts", or more literally: "Shame on him who thinks ill of it." (Although it should be noted that in the 14th C. a garter was primarily a garment used by males, so this tale is probably apocryphal.) Women could be appointed to the Order (as far back as the 14th C.,) but were not made companions. It is prestigious to be named to this Order, and appointments to it are solely at the monarch's discretion. By being appointed, one is created a Knight or a Lady.

- See: INTRO-REIGNS section/British Kings & Queens and their Reigns/Edward III.
- See: Order of the Bath - For the order of seniority among the Orders of Chivalry.

Order of St. Patrick, (the Most Illustrious) - Dormant. Order of Chivalry. Associated with Ireland. Created by George III in 1783. Lasted until 1922, when most of Ireland became independent as the Irish Free State. No knight of the Order of St. Patrick has been created since 1936, even though the order is technically still in existence (but gone dormant,) and in 1974 the final surviving knight died.

Order of the Thistle, (the Most Ancient and Most Noble) - Purportedly the second oldest order in Britain, it is claimed it was created by King James V of Scotland (AKA: James I of England and Ireland) in 1540. Made up of the monarch himself and 12 Knights, as selected by the king. It is the oldest order of chivalry connected with Scotland. (Re)founded in 1687, by James VII of Scotland (James II of England and Ireland,) who claimed he was reviving an older Order. Made up of the monarch and sixteen knights and/or ladies. The appointments are made solely by the monarch's discretion. Its motto (from the Latin) translate as: "No one cuts* me with impunity." *Meaning: assails/attacks. (See: Order of the Bath - For the order of seniority among the Orders of Chivalry.)

Ordnance Regiment -

- See: Royal Fusiliers.
- See: Tower of London/"Other Places & Things"/Waterloo Barracks.

Orleans House - (See: Twickenham/Orleans House.)

Orme Square - Built ca. 1815. (See: Bayswater/Orme Square.)

Ormand Road - (See: Richmond/Ormand Road.)

Ormonde Lodge - (See: Richmond Lodge.)

orphanages - In the 19th C. one could be deemed as an orphan due to losing one's parents, but also through being squeezed out of family life by abandonment or overcrowding. Orphanages were often crowded and unsanitary. The government provided no support; funds had to be raised through charitable contributions.

- See: asylum - For the word's meaning at the time of the Regency.
- See: Foundling Hospital.
- See: Lambeth Asylum - For girls.
- See: London Orphan Asylum.

Orpington - Bromley. Dates from at least 1032. Did not develop much until the rails came in/the 1860s.

- All Saints: Saxon origins. Yet has a sundial with runes. Remodeled in 1200. Priory nearby from 1270.

Osborne House - Isle of Wight. Designed by Prince Albert, finished in 1851. Queen Victoria died here in 1901. Gifted to the nation in 1902 by Edward VII.

Osidge - (Rhymes with: sausage.) Barnet. Dates from at least 1176. The land was sold after the Dissolution, with the condition that the land would provide faggots (wood) for the burning of heretics; ca. this time a manor house was built (called Osidge); the house was rebuilt in 1808.

osiers - (Also often seen as: osier beds, the latter being where they are grown.) Any of several types of willow good for basket-weaving purposes. Were used frequently in the 17-19th centuries as a way to earn money for smallholders.

- See: Platt's Eyot.
- See: Seething Wells.

Osnaburgh Street - Regent's Park, Fitzrovia. Named for Prince Frederick, Duke of York and Albany, and Prince-Bishopric of Osnabrück (brother of George IV.) There by at least 1831.

- St. Saviour's Hospital: Built in 1850-2, Victorian-Gothic style. Renamed to St. Saviour's Cancer Hospital in 1872. Renamed in 1892 to St. Saviour's Hospital for Invalid Ladies, but in 1893 this was changed to St. Saviour's Hospital for Ladies of Limited Means. By 1929 was known simply as St. Saviour's Hospital. Closed in 1962.

Osterley - Hounslow/Ealing. First recorded in 1274.

- Osterley Park House: (See at its own listing.)
- St. Francis's Church: Great West Road. 1935.

Osterley Park House - Isleworth. (Rarely also seen simply as Osterley House.) Approximately 500 acres in a 6 mile/10 km circumference park. Originally dates from 1562 for Sir Thomas Gresham (founder of the Royal Exchange.) Gresham replaced the former farmhouse with a "faire and stately brick house." Bought in 1713 by Sir Francis Child (grandfather of Lady Sally Jersey,) the former's grandson having it completely remodeled in 1761-80 by Robert Adam; red brick with stone dressings; a double colonnaded portico of Portland stone. It ceased to serve as a home ca. the beginning of the 19th century. At some time it passed to the Earls of Jersey, who opened it to the public as a park in 1939 (and in 1949 gave it to the National Trust.)

Oundle - A town that dates from the 8th century, property owned by Peterborough Abbey. There was a parish church here from the 13th century. Before the Reformation, there was already a guild grammar school here; governed by the Grocers' Company, for members' sons and for the poor. Oundle did not develop much in the 19th century. Throughout the 19th century, Oundle had a strong nonconformists tradition. (See: Nonconformists.)

Outer Circle - (See: Regent's Park/Outer Circle.)

Oval, the - (See: Kennington/Oval Cricket Ground.)

Ovington Square - Knightsbridge. After 1846.

Ovington Street - Belgravia, near Chelsea and South Kensington. Ca. 1840. Long and straight.

oxen - (See: Smithfield Market.)

Oxford - Not in London; is in Oxfordshire. (See: Oxford College.)

Oxford College - (Also called: Oxford University.) To speak of the city of Oxford, one must invariably also speak of Oxford College (which is actually a collection of colleges; is now forty independent colleges strong, scattered throughout the city.) Oxford is 56 miles/90 km from London, in Oxfordshire.

The college (as a whole) was founded in the 13th C., some sources say the 11th century. Anyway, it is the oldest university in England.

In the 13th C. Oxford's city wall was rebuilt/repaired over an older wall, encompassing 115 acres; its circumference was approximately two miles/3.2 km. The wall had four entrances/gates (with four smaller gates as well.) The wall yet exists.

Oxford was considered a town until it became the See of Oxford in 1542.

Only Anglicans were admitted to the colleges (until 1866.) Women were not admitted until well into the second half of the 19th century.

It has three terms, each only 8 weeks long: Michaelmas (Oct-Dec,) Hilary (Jan-Mar,) and Trinity (Apr-Jun.)

Some of what makes up the surrounds of Oxford (both the colleges and the town itself) include:

- All Souls College: A graduate college. Founded in 1438.
- Balliol College: 1263. Pink and yellow neo-gothic buildings.
- Bodleian Library: Cattle Street. Has over six million books and 50,000 manuscripts. Its first wing was endowed in 1602 by Sir Thomas Bodley (the wing had housed a university library since 1488.)
- Brasenose College: Founded in 1509.

- Christ Church College: First a convent, in 730AD. Founded as a college in 1525 (or 1546.) Dwarfs the other colleges. Called "The House." Oxford's "grandest" quad, with the "most patrician" students. Christ Church's chapel is also Oxford's cathedral (the smallest cathedral in all of England.)
- Corpus Christi College: Founded in 1517.
- Exeter College: Founded in 1314.
- Green College: Founded in 1979.
- Harris Manchester College: Founded in 1786.
- Hertford College: Founded in 1282.
- Isis, the: In Oxford the Thames river is known as the Isis.
- Jericho: Victorian. (See under J.)
- Jesus College: Founded in 1571.
- Keble College: Founded in 1870.
- Kellogg College: Founded in 1990.
- Lady Margaret Hall: The oldest women's college in Oxford. Founded in 1878.
- Linacre College: Founded in 1962.
- Lincoln College: Founded ca. 1427-29.
- Magdalen College: (Pronounced MAUD-lin.) Founded in 1458. Often considered Oxford's prettiest college.
- Manchester College: Founded in 1886.
- Mansfield College: 1838, as Spring Hill College. Named Mansfield College in 1886.
- Merton College: Off Merton Street. Founded in 1264. Its library dates from the 14th century. (See: Old Malden/manor house, at its own listing.)
- New College: New College Lane. Founded in 1379.
- Nuffield College: Founded in 1937.
- Oriel College: Wedged between High Street and Merton Street. Founded in 1326.
- Pembroke College: Founded in 1624.
- Queen's College: Founded in 1340-1. Rebuilt in the 17th and 18th centuries.
- Regent's Park College: Established in 1810, incorporating an education society founded in 1752. Moved to Pusey Street in 1927.
- St. Anne's College: 1878.
- St. Anthony's College: 1950.
- St. Catherine's College: Manor Road. Built 1960-64, founded in 1963.
- St. Cross College: 1965.
- St. Edmund Hall: Founded in 1226.

- St. Hilda's College: 1893.
- St. Hugh's College: 1886.
- St. John's College: Founded in 1555.
- St. Peter's College: 1929.
- Somerville College: Woodstock Road. Founded 1879. Oxford's most famous women's college. (The oldest is Lady Margaret Hall.)
- Spring Hill College: (See: Mansfield College, above.)
- Trinity College: Broad Street. Founded ca. 1555.
- University College: High Street. Founded in 1249. Described as "black-sooted."
- Wadham College: Founded in 1610.
- Wolfson College: 1966.
- Worchester College: Beaumont Street. Has the derisive nickname of "Botany Bay." Founded 1714.

Oxford and Cambridge Boat Race - On the Thames, from Putney to Mortlake. Held since 1829. Is rowed in March. Was often very cold.

Oxford Circus - Westminster. At the junction of Oxford Street and Regent Street.

Was first called Regent's Circus North (as part of Nash's building of Regent Street.)

It had a southern counterpart, from 1880, called Piccadilly Circus, and which was grander than Oxford Circus. Oxford Circus never had Piccadilly Circus's circular arrangement (but rather just a rounding out of the street's corners.) Oxford Circus's Corinthian arcades were probably added by John Nash, whereas the other building in the area was by a local builder, Samuel Baxter.

The 0xford Circus name supplanted the Regent's Circus North one in the 1890s (at which time it was also becoming notorious for its traffic congestion.) Sir Henry Tanner rebuilt the street in the 1920s. (See: Piccadilly Circus.)

Oxford Market - On the corner of Great Titchfield Street and Market Place. Built to supply the burgeoning district of Cavendish Square, 1721. The market was designed by Gibbs was demolished in 1800. It was originally built of wood; rebuilt in 1815. By 1820 it had become a bit of a gathering spot for radical activity. Square arcaded building, steep roof with a weather vane. Sold at auction in 1876, demolished in 1880. It is also unclear exactly what sort of market this was, other than it is stated to have been a "classic market."

Oxford Square - Post-1840. (See: Hyde Park Square - Note under.)

Oxford Street - Mayfair; Marylebone; Soho; Westminster. Goes about 1 mile/1.6 km from Marble Arch to Tottenham Court Road.

Was Tyburn Road (AKA: Tyburn Turnpike) until around 1783, when the last public hangings here were put to an end; and then was known for a while as Oxford Road, but by the mid to late 18th C. it was being called Oxford Street. A long commercial street of drapers, shoemakers, furniture shops. In 1800, there were 150 shops on this street. Shops might stay open until 10:00pm on some nights. The last private homes were gone by the 1930s.

- 54: Dickins & Smith (later Dickins & Jones.) Drapers, established 1790. In 1835 moved to Regent Street. In THE MEMOIRS OF HARRIETTE WILSON she refers to: "Smith, the haberdasher of Oxford-Street" (circa 1813) and that he "sold such good gloves and ribbons." Smith was rather deaf.
- 400: Selfridge's. Department store. 1908.
- New Bond Street: This street reached Oxford Street in the 1720s. (See: Bond Street/New Bond Street, under B.)

oysters -

> ➢ See: fish/oysters.
> ➢ See: Mile End Road.

-P-

Paddington - Westminster. Dates from at least 998. The manor of Paddington was owned by the Bishop(s) of London, even into the Regency. A lot of the surrounding land was owned by the Abbot(s) of Westminster.

The original village of Paddington lay between Edgeware and Harrow Road. In the 18th C. the area gained its predictable share of gentlemen's homes, plus the area was the lesser for also having gravel extraction here. In 1820, Paddington still contained many rural spots, being an agricultural district, and also an area for brick and tile manufactories. It was connected to London, but it maintained an isolated feel. Public conveyance to the City was provided by one Mr. Miles, who supplied pair-horse coaches. The trip took three hours. The charge for an outside passenger was two shillings, three for inside.

- Bayswater Road: (Past Tyburn Gate.) Scarcely populated road in the early 19th C., with only a house every mile or so, until one arrived at Craven Hill. Runs two miles/3.2 km straight (one of London's straightest streets.)
- Burial-ground: 1763. Just beyond Stanhope Place. Approximately one acre.
- Carnaby Market: In 1665 there was a pesthouse here (first one in London, during

the Great Plague, built for plague victims.) On a portion of the estate of Lord Craven, Karnaby House, built in 1683; the street being laid out approximately 1685-86. By 1690 was covered with small homes. There was a market here ca. 1720 for fish, meat, and vegetables, then called Lowndes Market. But the present market dates from 1823. Cholera broke out here in 1854. The modern market was known as representing the "free spirit" of the 1960s, and is yet known for its stylish/hip clothing stores.

- Connaught Place: (See under C.)
- Connaught Square: (See under C.)
- Connaught Terrace: A Building Act in 1816 caused the journeymen who resided here to vacate, so that Connaught Terrace could be built.
- Craven Hill: (East of what became Craven Gardens.) Pleasant hamlet, there since at least 1665.
- Edgeware Road: As early as 1783 (probably earlier) connected Paddington to London. (Edgeware Road, north of the New Road, is now called Marylebone Road.)
- Grand Junction Canal:
    - See: Paddington Canal, below.
    - See under G.
- Grand Junction Street: Circa 1828. Now called Sussex Gardens.
- Holy Trinity: 1845. Bishop's Road.
- Lancaster Gate (street): 1866. During the Regency this area was open land.
- Paddington Canal: Paddington Canal joins Grand Junction Canal at Bull Bridge, near Northwood, Middlesex (but Paddington Canal has long since been absorbed into the Grand Union canal system.) Opened for passenger barge traffic in 1801, linking London (at Paddington Basin) and Uxbridge. As time passed (post-Regency,) human filth and waste were such a problem that the phrase "stinking Paddington" came into use.
- Paddington Church: The actress Sarah Siddons was buried here in 1831.
- Paddington Green: (See at its own listing.)
- Praed Street: Built in the 19th C. ca. 1828.
- St. James: 1843.
- St. Mary: Rebuilt 1788-91 (near the site of the earlier version.) Doric-style portico. The statue of Sarah Siddons (on the green) was added in 1897. (See: St. Mary, Paddington Green, under the CHURCHES section.)
- St. Mary's Hospital: Established 1843, opened 1851.

- Shakespearean, the: Public house. On the corner of Carnaby Street and Foubert's Place, since 1735; still stands.
- Sussex Gardens: Built ca. 1828. First known as Grand Junction Road. Continuation of Marylebone Road. (See: Grand Junction Road, above.)
- Swimming Baths: 1874.
- Tyburnia: (That area just beyond the Tyburn Gate.) Its name of "Tyburnia" was never popular (no doubt because of the association with the hangings at Tyburn,) and so this area became more generally known as Hyde Park (not to be confused with the nearby park.) Most of this district's roads were built post-Regency, in the time of William IV. All were completed by 1849.

Paddington Green - Westminster. Began to grow in the 16th century. Had a "refined air" until the 19th C., when urbanization crept in. London's first horse-drawn bus service began here, in 1829; run by one Edward Shillibeer; ran between Paddington Green and the Bank, via the New Road.

- Paddington Green Children's Hospital: 1883. Now part of St. Mary's Hospital.
- St. Mary: 17th century. Rebuilt 1791. (See: St. Mary, Paddington Green, under the CHURCHES section.)
- White Lion pub: From 1524. Edgware Road, opposite the end of what is now called Bell Street. Rebuilt twice. In the 1860s became the Metropolitan Music Hall. Demolished in 1962 and replaced by a police station.

Painter-Stainers' Hall - (For the Worshipful Company of Painter-Stainers.) 199 Little Trinity Lane. Painters of metals and woods. AN ENCYCLOPAEDIA OF LONDON states: "It is believed that the art of the Stainer was that of producing, on plain woven fabrics, both coloured and figure subjects in imitation of tapestry; and probably actual painting on canvas were included as stained cloth. Painting meant primarily painting on wood..." Existed as early as 1283. The Painters and Stainers united in 1500. Incorporated in 1581. Hall here since the 16th century. The last Hall was constructed in 1670, and extensively repaired in 1776-7.

In 1769 they set up a labor exchange at: 2 Ironmonger Lane for those engaged in house painting. A new wing was added in 1880.

Totally destroyed by WWII bombs, and largely rebuilt. Livery company. 28th in the order of precedence.

paintings - (See: art/artists.)

palace - (See: palaces. Note the s.)

Palace of Westminster - (See: Westminster Palace.)

Palace Yard - Westminster.

- See: Westminster Abbey.
- See: Westminster Palace.

palaces - In the past, the term *palace* was applied to the homes of royalty, of course, but also English Archbishop(s,) such as: Hampton Court Palace, or: Lambeth Palace. Otherwise such buildings were primarily the privilege of royalty (the latter of which were also known to confiscate previously non-royal palace homes, or accept them as "gifts," as happened with Hampton Court Palace.) As the 17th C. was left behind, the practice of calling non-royal but grand homes "palaces" became increasingly a continental practice only, and the grand homes in the UK were simply called a house, (such as Burlington House, Devonshire House, Hertford House.)

For London's royal palaces, see:

- Bridewell Palace - Had been a royal palace, but became Bridewell Prison ca. 1618.
- Buckingham House - Later: Palace.
- Carlton House - George IV wanted this house to become a palace, but in 1820 he decided it was shabby and withdrew from further building of the site.
- Hampton Court Palace - Belonged to Cardinal Wolsey/Archbishop of York, until he gave it to Henry VIII.
- Kensington Palace.
- Kew Palace.
- St. James's Palace - Ambassadors are still accredited to here; it is yet the official seat of the monarchy (even though the royal family now resides at Buckingham Palace.)
- Tower of London - In truth it remains a palace, despite having served so many additional purposes, plus having no monarch reside here since Henry VIII.
- Westminster Palace - Long since burned down.
- Whitehall, Royal Palace of.

paleontology - The study of fossil animals and plants. Not truly an area of study during the Regency, although people certainly collected fossils. (Paleontology began to develop as a field of study in the 1840s.) The fossils were thought to be antediluvian (from before Noah's Ark and the Flood,) supposed to be examples of ancient animals that perished from not gaining the safety of the Ark. This belief wouldn't have been held by everyone-among those with higher education it was known there had been prehistory events, but scientific minds hadn't yet established clear concepts. It wouldn't be until Darwin's Theory of Evolution

(1858) and the idea of natural selection that people began to classify which animals had gone extinct.

Richard Owen (biologist, b.1804-d.1892) coined the word "dinosaur,"(1842,) from the Latin for "terrible lizard." Certainly, before the term was created, people would have stumbled across dinosaur fossils; they just wouldn't have known what to call them.

- You may care to see: Linnean Society - For scientists of the Regency.
- You may care to see: Surrey Institution - A membership for persons interested in the sciences.

Pall Mall - In Mayfair and St. James's, Westminster. (The "Pall" is now usually pronounced as though in "pallet" or "mallet" - so: pal mal, not: poll moll.) Named for the 17th C. game *pallemaille* (a sort of cross between croquet and polo.)

Was built as a royal road, to lead to Buckingham Palace.

In the 18th C. this became a street for being seen and for meetings, with many coffee-houses and chocolate-houses used for conducting business. It was where foreign visitors often stayed, due to its vicinity to St. James's Palace and governmental buildings. The 19th C. brought in gentlemen's clubs (as you'll find at individual listings below in this entry.) Pall Mall was described as "straight, gloomy, and reserved."

Shopping for both men and women (as opposed to Bond Street, which was a "males only" shopping district after the morning hours; a female walking in Bond Street in the evening was considered likely to be of low quality.)

Experimental gas lighting here in 1807, the first street in London to have it. (See: gas lighting.)

- 52: The British Institution. (See under B.)
- 70: Guards' Club, from 1848. (See: Guards' Club, under the CLUBS section.)
- 71: Oxford and Cambridge Club: Founded in 1830, but the building was not built on this site until 1837. (See under the CLUBS section.)
- 79: Today's building stands on the site of Nell Gwyn's house (mistress of Charles II.) All Pall Mall property yet belongs to the Crown, except number 79, because Nell Gwyn would not live in a home she could not own, and so Charles II gave the rights to the property to her.
- 80-82: (See: Schomberg House, below.)
- 89: (See: Schomberg House, below.)
- 100: Home of John Julius Angerstein (businessman/Lloyd's underwriter,) ca. 1824. Where the National Gallery's collection began/resided until 1838. Until WWII, this was the site of: Carlton Club.
    - See: Carlton Club, under the CLUBS section.

> ➢ See: National Gallery, below.
> ➢ See: National Gallery, under N.

- 104: Reform Club. 1836. (See under the CLUBS section.)
- 106: Travellers Club. 1832, by Charles Barry. (See under the CLUBS section.)
- 107: Athenaeum Club. Established in 1823 or 24. Built on the site of Carlton House. (See under the CLUBS section.)
- 116: United Services Club, 1827, by Nash; here until 1974. (Now is the Institute of Directors.) Corner of what is now Waterloo Place and Pall Mall East. (See under the CLUBS section.)
- 125: Christie's Auction House. 1770 (second source said 1808) to 1823, when it moved to 8 King Street. (See under C.)
- Carlton House: (See under C.)
- Christie's Auction House (See under C.)
- Clarence House: 1825-7. (See under C.)
- Marlborough House: (Adjacent to St. James's Palace; it is, in fact, actually a part of St. James's Palace, as are also Clarence House and Lancaster House.) 1709, Sir Christopher Wren, for the 1st Duke and Duchess of Marlborough, finished 1711. The duchess had objected to the military appearance of their Blenheim Palace in Oxfordshire, and commissioned Wren to build this abode; the design was described by the duchess as "strong, plain, and convenient" (just as she'd ordered it to be.) She lived here until she died in 1744.

  Became State property in 1817, for Princess Charlotte and Prince Leopold. In the 1860s, extensive remodeling obscured the house's original simplicity. The balustrade, north range, porch, and upper stories were added in 1863. Since 1961 has housed the Commonwealth Secretariat (AKA: the Commonwealth Conference Centre.) Provides, among other things, guest quarters for Commonwealth dignitaries who are visiting London. The Queen's Chapel adjoins Marlborough House. (See: Queen's Chapel, below.)
- National Gallery, 1824-32. Site of John Angerstein's mansion. When Angerstein died, George IV encouraged the government to buy up his art collection. Present "home" was constructed in 1832-38. (See: 100, above.)
- Queen's Chapel: Part of St. James's Palace. Marlborough Road, south of Pall Mall. Adjoins on to Marlborough House, behind which it is obscured from sight. Built by Inigo Jones, 1627, for Charles I's planned marriage to the Spanish Infanta, although Charles ended up marrying Henrietta Maria instead. Is a part of St. James's Palace, although separated from St. James's Palace by

Marlborough Gate, (which was also by Inigo Jones.) The exterior is "quite plain," Palladian. The interior has retained its 17th C. appearance. Restored after WWII damage. Originally was Roman Catholic, now an Anglican church.

  - See: Queen's Chapel, St. James's Palace, under the CHURCHES section.
  - See: St. James's Palace/Queen's Chapel.

- Schomberg House: 80-82 Pall Mall. (Its present address is: 89 Pall Mall.) Since 1698. Queen Anne architecture; tall Dutch windows.

Thomas Gainsborough (artist) lived here from 1774-88.

Schomberg House backed upon Marlborough House. There was a party-wall with a communicating door. Enjoyed royal patronage.

During the Napoleonic Wars, when it was so difficult to come by building products, business fell off. They took in partners Ashby & James (and added their names to the place's title,) but the decline in business continued. In 1820, Harding & Howell split off, setting up another shop at Numbers 5, 7 & 9 Regent Street, which became highly fashionable. (See: Harding, Howell & Co., immediately below.) The old firm stayed on at Schomberg House as Harding, Ashby, Allsop & Co. into the 1830s (at which time it was one of the last shops, becoming surrounded by gentlemen's clubs.)

The interior was gutted following WWII, to be refilled with new offices. Since 1908-11, Schomberg House was incorporated into a rebuild, which houses the Royal Automobile Club.

  - Harding, Howell, & Co.: A fine draper's shop, from 1796-1820, (Dee Hendrickson's REGENCY REFERENCE says until 1829.)

    It is referred to as "London's first department store" (although the term itself is 20th century.) Sold: clocks, fans, furs, haberdashery, hats, jewelry.

    Harding, Howell & Co. acquired all the three "apartments" available on the street level, converting them into five shops separated by glazed mahogany partitions. At the entrance was the shop for furs and fans, then next a haberdashery for "silks, muslins, lace, gloves, etc." To the right: jewelry, ormolu, clocks. Left, perfumery and items for the toilette. Another for millinery and dresses, and all feminine clothing items. Ground floor of the west wing held furniture; east wing, articles of foreign manufacture.

    Up the staircase was a breakfast room; the whole rest of this floor was given over to displaying fabrics (their specialty.) Floor above contained the work-rooms.

- War Office, the: Here from the 2nd half of the 19th century. (See under W.)

Pall Mall East - Not a charming area during the Regency. Became Trafalgar Square in Victoria's time. (See: Trafalgar Square.)

- Charles Knight: "A publisher worthy of all praise," began a bookselling business on this street in 1822. In 1832 he produced the *Penny Magazine.*

Pall Mall Gazette - 1865, evening newspaper.

Palmer's Green - Enfield. While it currently dates from Edwardian times, there was a Palmers Field here in 1204, plus in 1325 a road called Palmers Green. Still, there was no real settlement here until the late 16th century, at which time there were four houses. Palmer's Green had 54 homes by 1801. Today has the nickname "Little Cyprus."

Palmer's Village - 2-3 acres, a village green with a maypole, near Buckingham Gate. (Now covered by Victoria Street, since 1851.) By 1857, this area was tenements.

- Prince of Orange Inn: From ca. 1817 or earlier.

Pancras Road - (See: St. Pancras, under S.)

panorama - A panorama was a picture/pictures that surrounded the viewer. Some of them were designed to move so that one long scene unfolded before the viewer's eyes. They could be large (as in a round room with pictures surrounding the viewer,) or small enough to be portable. (See: Leicester Square/Barker Panorama.)

Pantheon, the - (From 1833, AKA: Pantheon Bazaar.) South side of Oxford Street. Built 1770-71; opened in 1772. Thomas Gainsborough (painter) lived here at one time. Burned down in a fire in 1792. Was rebuilt, but by this time had lost its luster (as soon as the 1780s.)

In 1789 it was converted to an Opera House, being renamed the King's Theatre, Pantheon. Burned in 1792 (after completing only one full season); it was gutted, but the lovely facade remained. Reopened for "public entertainment" in 1795, being then mostly used for exhibitions and masquerades. Described as "but a fancy, large room for balls, music, masquerades, etc.," and also as a "winter Ranelagh." Sold and used as a theatre again in 1812; closed in 1814.

Empty until it was rebuilt as the Pantheon Bazaar (a shopping bazaar) in 1833-54. Demolished for good in 1937-38.

Panton Street - Named for Col. Thomas Panton, a reformed gambler and property developer (d. 1685.)

- Stone's Chop House: 1770. A chop house was a place to dine. Destroyed in an air raid in 1941.

- Tom Cribb, the: Pub. Bought in 1811 by the Regency (ex)prize-fighter Tom Cribb. (See under the INNS/PUBS section.)

pants - Men did not wear a garment called pants during the Regency era. "Pants" was a later abbreviation of: pantaloons.

Men wore: breeches (sometimes called culottes, an older term); pantaloons (longer than breeches); and late in the Regency era: trousers (full length to the ankle) - although full-length trousers were at the time mostly worn by the working classes such as laborers and sailors (whose legs needed protection.) Men also wore: buckskins (which were leather breeches.) All were worn with either stockings and shoes, or tucked into boots.

Women did not wear any sort of breeches or trousers.

> See: fabrics.
> See: men's apparel.
> You may care to see: hose.
> You may care to see: undergarments.

paper - The types of paper available to Regency era people were:

- parchment - Specially prepared animal skin, usually of calves, fawns, goats, or sheep, it could be scraped down and reused until it became too thin.
- foolscap - It had this name because by the 18th C. there was commonly a watermark of a fool's cap on it. In modern usage "foolscap" or "foolscap folio" refers to the standardized size of the paper (13¼x 16½ inches,) used before A4 (8.27 x 11.69 inches, from the year 1922) became the standard. Was popular with Regency letter writers because it wasn't as large as some other papers, and was easy to fold and seal for writing out the recipient's direction (meaning, in America, the recipient's address.)
- vellum - Finer, higher quality parchment made from the skins of young calves or lambs, and which was used by wealthier people and for official documents.
- shredded rags - Most paper was made of shredded linen and rags, and produced by hand, cast in flat molds.

Short of a few experiments with vegetable matter papers (which were usually off-white and not first quality) there was no wood pulp paper yet.

Sold by the page or in a quire (a bundle of 24 sheets, which was 1/20th of a ream.) Circa 1775, two quires cost approximately a pricey two weeks' worth of a housemaid's wages. Due to the price, paper was often reused, such as on the back, or scraped clean if it was parchment, or by tearing off the used parts. There was also the practice of cross-writing, where you'd fill up a page, then turn it 90 degrees and write cross-wise over the already written lines, particularly for the post, because you tried to keep a letter less expensive for the *recipient*, who had to pay to receive it.

- See: ink.
- See: post, the.
- You may care to see: quill.

parachute - 1802, first parachute jump in England. (See: Lord's Cricket Ground - Note under.)

Paragon, the - Semi-detached housing. (See under: Blackheath/Paragon.)

parasol - (See: umbrella.)

parchment - (See: paper.)

Parish Clerks' Hall - (For the Worshipful Company of Parish Clerks.) The Parish Clerks were granted their Royal Charter in 1442 (which was superseded by a 1449 one.) First housed in Bishopsgate. Moved in 1562 to Brode Lane (later Queen Street,) Vintry. Burned in the Great Fire of 1666. A new hall was built in 1671, west of Wood Street and south of Silver Street, off Falcon Street, Aldersgate. The Parish Clerks were, at first, a sort of lesser clergy, not constrained by the rule of celibacy. The Hall was damaged in 1765 by fire, with subsequent repairs and enlargements. Its entrance moved in 1848 from Wood Street to Silver Street. Totally destroyed by WWII bombs, and not rebuilt. The Company does not have livery, nor does it number in precedence.

Park Crescent - Regent's Park, Marylebone; northern end of Portland Place, by Nash, begun 1812. The builder was bankrupted, so that work was not finished until 1818. Terraces were begun in 1820. The crescent served as the northern end of Nash's planned route from St. James's to Regent's Park and was meant to be a circus (not the semi-circle we know now); it was intended that there would be a matching arc, situated in the park, that along with Park Crescent would all become known as Regent's Circus, but the second arc was never built. Large houses overlooking the park.

Park Crescent, and other parts of Nash's surrounding terraces, had to be restored after WWII damage.

(Beyond the following list, more terraces were added as the years advanced beyond the Regency era.)

- Cambridge Terrace:
    - See: Regent's Park/Cambridge Terrace.
    - See under C.
- Chester Terrace: (Park Crescent's eastern border.) 1824-5. 313 yards long; 52 Corinthian columns. Built by James Burton, to designs by John Nash; described as "taut and crisp." Presently serves as homes for the wealthy.
- Clarence Terrace: Designed by Decimus Burton, ca. 1830. (Second source says dates from 1823; third source says it was built 1821-3.) The smallest of the Park

Crescent terraces.

- Cornwall Terrace: Named for the Duke of Cornwall (an early title of George IV's.) First terrace of Park Crescent, 1821. Designed by Decimus Burton, who took over the Regent's Park project when John Nash was dismissed following George IV's death in 1830.) Was made up of 19 houses.
- Cumberland Terrace: Designed by John Nash, 1826-7, built by William Mountford Nurse (with a resident architect, James Thomson.) Named for Ernst (George IV's brother,) Duke of Cumberland. Some call Cumberland Terrace the "most splendid" of all the Park Crescent structures. It consists of three main blocks connected by decorative arches.
  - See: Cumberland Terrace, under C.
  - See: Regent's Park/"The Homes"/Cumberland Terrace.
- Hanover Terrace: The second terrace constructed as part of Park Crescent, 1822-3, also by John Nash. Twenty houses, that were arranged in the front so that they were a "single group" with a roofed gallery along the ground floor that ran continuously. James Elmes (architect/author) described the terrace in 1828: "It has a center and two wing buildings, of the Doric order, the acroteria of which surmounted by statues and other sculptural ornaments in terra cotta. The center building is crowned by a well-proportioned pediment, the tympanum of which is embellished - with statues and figures in a wretched style of art, which the architect would do well to remove... The stories of the mansions are lofty, and elegantly finished, and the domestic arrangements of the various rooms convenient, and laid out in a masterly style."
- Holy Trinity Church: Park Square. Built by Sir John Soane. (See under the CHURCHES section.)
- Inner Circle: Also contained homes, notably one of which was one of the homes for Mrs. Fitzherbert, Prinny's mistress/disallowed wife. (See: Regent's Park/Inner Circle.)
- Park Square: Was formed (in place of Nash's once intended Circus, Regent's Park) in 1823-25. It had a central square with two facing terraces (those terraces being: Park Square East, and Park Square West. (See at their own listings.) Large, elegant terrace houses. One of the larger private squares in London. Is just north of Park Crescent (with an underpass under Marylebone Road, that connects it to Park Crescent.) The dominating plane trees were planted here in 1817. (See: Park Square, at its own listing.)
- Sussex Place: 1822. On the outskirts of the park. 26 houses, named for Augustus,

Duke of Sussex (George IV's younger brother.) Overlooks the boating lake.

- Ulster Terrace: Built ca. 1824-27. (See under U.)
- York Terrace (east and west,) 1822. (See under Y.)

Park Lane - Mayfair, Westminster. Henry VIII enclosed Hyde Park, resulting in Park Lane's existence. Remained a mere track known as Tyburn Lane, but by 1746 had this new name. In the Regency it would have been a narrow road running between a sweep of grand houses and a green stretch. By the 18th C. (and onward) it housed the wealthy, including the Grosvenor family (later the dukes of Westminster) from 1806. By the 1820s this area was quite built up with "very fine houses." Runs from north to south, around the edge of Hyde Park.

- 132: (See: Dunraven Street/22.)
- Aldford House: 1897.
- Dorchester House: (See under D.)
- Grosvenor House Hotel: 1929. (See: Grosvenor House, under G.)
- Londonderry House: 1850. (See under L.)
- Park Lane Hotel: 1927. Now is the Sheraton Park Lane. The first British hotel with a bathroom for each bedroom.

Park Place - Very well preserved 18th C. cul-de-sac, off of St. James's Street.

- 12: William Pitt the Younger (Tory/Prime Minister) lived here for a short while ca. 1801.

Park Royal - Brent/Ealing. Had been a village called Twyford, but in the very early 20th C. developers called it Park Royal due to exhibitions of the Royal Agricultural Society here. Park Royal is not to be confused with London's royal parks, of course. (See: Twyford.)

- West Twyford: (Also sometimes called: Twyford Abbey.) An old name, still seen on some road signs; is the most western part of Park Royal. By ca. 1931 had blended into Acton's sprawl.

Park Square - (AKA: Park Square Gardens.) Regent's Park. The Plane trees here were planted in 1817. Large, stuccoed, stylish terraced houses, 1823-24, by John Nash. One of London's largest private squares. Built on land that belonged to the Crown. This land had been meant to be the north part of Nash's Circus, but finances canceled its building; it became instead Park Square, 1823-24. The east street of the square is called: Park Square East. The west street of the square is called: Park Square West. If you cross over Marylebone Road (its southern border,) you are immediately in: Park Crescent.

- ➢ See: Park Crescent/Park Square.
- ➢ See: Park Square East.
- ➢ See: Park Square West.

- Diorama, a: (Of revolving architectural displays) was here in 1823.

Park Square East - Built in 1823-25. Mirror image to Park Square West. Stucco. Slate roofs.

Park Square West - Built in 1823-25. Mirror image to Park Square East. Stucco. Slate roofs.

Park Street - Mayfair. Building began here in the 1720s, completed in the 1770s. One of the places where Mrs. Fitzherbert lived (up to her secret marriage to Prinny, 1784.)

- 70 to 78: The only original/18th C. homes still on this street.

Park, the - A common way to refer to Hyde Park. (See: Hyde Park.)

Park Village - (See: Park Village East & Park Village West.)

Park Village East & Park Village West - Camden Town. The two streets are also collectively known as Park Village. A continuation of Nash's (never fully realized) plans for Regent's Park. 1824-28 stucco villas, a long row of "attractive and sophisticated cottages" also described as "delightful." Off Albany Street, Park Village West survives intact, with copious trees. Park Village East more meanders (being less of a crescent, having been disrupted when rails came in ca. 1845) and extends Prince Albert Road. The two villages combined Gothic, Italianate, and Tudor styles.

- 12: Dr. Johnson (lexicographer) lived here. Described as the most impressive of the villages' villas.

Parkinson's Disease - During the Regency this disorder would have been called "Shaking Palsy." It took its later name from James Parkinson (of Hoxton Square, Hoxton,) who wrote his *Essay on Shaking Palsy* in 1815.

parks - Numerous London parks were not open to the public during the Regency era.

- See: Battersea Park.
- See: Bushy Park.
- See: Greenwich Park - Oldest royal park in London.
- See: Green Park.
- See: Hyde Park.
- See: Kensington Gardens.
- See: Peak District - 1951, first *national* English park.
- See: Regent's Park.
- See: Richmond Park - London's wildest park.
- See: royal parks.
- See: St. James's Park.
- You may care to see: forests.

Parliament - The book PARLIAMENT HOUSE states: "...Parliament really means a meeting together of the King, and the three Estates of the realm - the clergy, the Lords and the Commons - in one great Council." Parliament only really started meeting regularly (when called by the King) ca. 1295, under Edward I.

The English Parliament divided into its two houses (the Lords and the Commons) in 1332.

ROYAL BRITAIN informs us: "A 'Grand Remonstrance' passed by MPs on 22 November 1641, presented a long list of the King's failings in government - and for the first time made it clear that parliament could remove a king who was guilty of abuses of power... Within 50 years came the establishment, in 1688, of the constitutional monarchy in which the king and queen were subject to the will of MPs." (See: Great Britain - The note on becoming a Constitutional Monarchy.)

To this day, the monarch must give her/his assent for an Act of Parliament to pass into law, which has never been refused since 1708.

The ("modern") Lords' Chamber was completed in 1847, the Commons Chamber in 1852.

Parliament is in session Monday through Thursday.

To this day, people say "Westminster" to mean either Parliament or the government in general.

- See: Lower House.
- See: St. Stephen's Chapel.
- See: Season, the - For when Parliament sat during the Regency era.
- See: Upper House.
- See: Westminster Palace.

Parliament Chamber, the - (See: Upper House.)

Parliament Hill - (See: Hampstead Heath/Parliament Hill.)

Parliament Square - At the northwest end of what had been the Palace of Westminster. Laid out in the 1840s-50s; completed in 1868. Today's garden space had been a block of narrows streets and houses during the Regency.

- See: Houses of Parliament.
- See: Westminster/Parliament Square.

Parliament Street - Whitehall. A continuation of Whitehall since the early 18th century (now much widened.)

Parliamentary Council - 1833. (See: Whitehall/36.)

Parson - (See: Church of England/Parson.)

Parsons Green - Hammersmith & Fulham. A rectory stood on the green's western edge by at least 1391. A big pond dating from 1559 was at its southeast corner. In August every year (since the mid 17th C. to 1823, when it was suppressed) there was a pleasure fair here. Was sparsely populated until ca. 1840s.

- Parsons Grove: A clump of trees on the green's west side, since 1424.
- St. Dionis' Church: 14th century. The district takes its "Parsons" name from the rectory here.

passing on the right - That is, why the British drive on the left side of the road. (See: London Bridge, in the BRIDGES section - The note under.)

pastries -

> ➢ See: confectioner.
> ➢ See: food - Various listings there.
> ➢ See: Gunter's.
> ➢ See: Herbert & Jones.
> ➢ See: Soho/Gerrard Street.

Paternoster Row - For centuries, this street was a haven of booksellers. WWII damage all but wiped out this street, claiming an estimated 5,000,000 books as part of the damage.

> ➢ See: Little Britain - Note under.
> ➢ See: St. Paul's Churchyard.

- Chapter Coffee-house: In Chapter-house Court. A club for literary encouragers. (See under the CLUBS section.)
- Newgate Market: There until 1867, when it was abolished. Occupied the area now known as Paternoster Square. Was a carcass and butchers' meat market, used largely by West End butchers (to obtain carcasses.) Had a market-house, a clock, and a bell turret at its center. (See under N.)

Paternoster Square - Just to the north of St. Paul's. Where this district was pulverized by WWII bombs, the City built this square. (See: Paternoster Row/Newgate Market.)

- 10: The Stock Exchange moved here in 2004. (See under S.)

patron saints - Of England: St. George. Of London: Thomas á Becket.

Pattenmakers' Company - (AKA: the Worshipful Company of Pattenmakers.) A patten was a kind of overshoe meant to lift one's feet out of the rain or mud of the road; picture a clog-like shoe with either a thick wooden sole, or it could be iron-shod, almost like primitive carriage springs, except without the give.) Keep in mind that in medieval times most roads were made of dirt (or, most of the time, mud.) The Pattenmakers (whose product tended to be the iron-shod type) and the Galochemakers (whose product tended to be wooden clogs) were separate misteries in the 14th century. (See: mystery.) Both became affiliated with the Pouchmakers (probably because pattens/galoches required leather ties,) but then the Pouchmakers merged with the Leathersellers.

The Pattenmakers obtained their Charter in 1670. Granted livery in 1717. Never had a hall. 70th in the order of precedence. Pattens were still used during the Regency, but there was a fading need and fading popularity.

They now have a hand in designing and fabricating orthopedic shoes. (See: halls/"no hall"/Pattenmakers' Company.)

Paul's Cross - Located at the northeast corner of Old St. Paul's. (See: St. Paul's Cathedral, under the CHURCHES section.) Paul's Cross was a covered outdoor pulpit, used for sermons and proclamations regarding news of the day in Tudor and early Stuart times. Referred to in a 1547 primary source. According to PILGRIMS' LONDON: "It seems to have been open to use by any of the clergy who wanted to hold forth on some issue of general interest, much like Speaker's Corner in Hyde Park today... But unpopular speakers took considerable risk of life and limb..." because in the far past there was no such thing as police protection should the listening crown turn ugly. Destroyed in 1643 by Puritans (the cross and the pulpit.) Old St. Paul's is entirely gone (replaced by the present St. Paul's Cathedral) but the outline of Paul's Cross is still visible at the same site.

Paul's Walk - Nickname for the nave in St. Paul's Cathedral. Until the Royal Exchange was built in 1566, Paul's Walk was a bit of a banking center for merchants; yes, in the cathedral.

Pavilion, the - Hans Town mansion, 21 acres. Land bought in 1797 by Henry Holland, but the mansion was slowly built. Three sides of a quadrangle, open to the north, with handsome iron gates. Portico of four Doric columns. Extensive lawn, sheet of water next to it. Ice-house. Has imitation ruins (a folly) of an "ancient priory." Pulled down in 1879. The area is now occupied by Cadogen Square, Pont Street, and more neighboring streets.

Paviors' Company - (AKA: the Worshipful Company of Paviors.) Road engineering. Records on Paviors date back to 1276. Ordinances in 1476. Attempted to obtain a Charter in 1673, but the Court of Aldermen opposed it. To this day the Paviors have remained unincorporated. Livery Company, since 1479. Never had a hall. 56th in the order of precedence.

pawnbrokers -

- See: Gracechurch Street.
- See: Swallow Street.

Paxton and Whitfield - 93 Jermyn Street, St. James's. Cheeses. Established ca. 1740; located here since 1797; still here. (The house itself was built in 1674.) It would have been called something else in the Regency, for Mr. Paxton and Mr. Whitfield took over the business under their names ca. 1845. LONDON-THE SECRETS AND THE SPLENDOURS describes the shop as: "...a narrow, dark shop, with a discreet black-painted facade and a large window..." (See: Jermyn Street/93.)

PC - Abbreviation for: Police Constable. Before the formation of the Metropolitan Police (1829,) PC was not used as much, you would be more likely to just hear "constable."

- See: constable.

- See: Watchmen.

Peabody Square - Shadwell. 1867, built on the site of the old Magdalen Hospital. (See: Magdalen House.)

Peacock House - Nickname for Debenham House, 1905-07. (See: Holland Park/Debenham House.)

Peak District (national park) - Brushfield, Buxton, southern end of the Pennines (not London.) Britain's first ever *national* park (as opposed to a city park or a royal park.) Since 1951.

Pearly Kings and Queens - The tradition of decorating clothing with a multitude of buttons was begun by one Henry Croft, 1875.

- See: St. Martin-in-the-Fields, under the CHURCHES section.
- You may care to see: Morris dancer.
- You may care to see: mummers.

Peckham - Southwark. Named for the River Peck. Started out as a royal hunting ground. Evolved into a small village that grew crops for London. The population grew rapidly between 1820-40. An annual fair was held here from the time of King John every August 21-22-23, until 1827.

- North Peckham: 1970s.
- Peckham Rye Common: (Also seen simply as: Peckham Rye.) "Rye" implies a common or untilled ground. This one has been used as a recreation ground for centuries, at least as far back as the 14th century. Sixty-four acres. In the 2nd half of the 18th C. the green was surrounded by market gardens. Extended (by 49 more acres) in 1890 when Homestall Park was adjoined; in 1892 took on the name of Peckham Rye Park.
- Queen's Road: (See: Queen's Road, Peckham, under Q.)
- Rye Lane: An old road, truly Cockney.

Pelham Crescent - Chelsea, South Kensington. "Regency" (in style, though not in age) town houses, by George Basevi, ca. 1840.

- Pelham Place: George Basevi, ca. 1840. Runs northward out of Pelham Crescent's center.

pell mell - 17th C. game. Seen spelled a variety of ways, such as *pallemaille.* The game's popularity did not last into the Regency. (See: Pall Mall - For the street named for the game.)

Pembroke House - Whitehall (amid Whitehall Palace ruins.) Built in 1723-24. Was the London residence for the Earl(s) of Pembroke. Pulled down in 1938 to build the new Ministry of Defence. (See: Ministry of Defence.)

pencils - Invented by a Frenchman in the late 18th century (the graphite being mislabeled as lead, as it was first thought to be.) They were expensive: sixpence each in 1800. Most (younger) schooling would have been conducted with a slate and chalk (rather than paper and pencil, or quill.)

Before the invention of the pencil, pens and ink had been available for centuries. Ink could be homemade.

- You may care to see: ink.
- You may care to see: paper.
- You may care to see: quill.

Penge - (Pronounced: penj.) Bromley. One of London's few Celtic place names. Was a haunt for gypsies until the early 19th C., until the common's enclosure in 1827. Growth really came along once the nearby Crystal Palace (built in 1851) relocated here.

- St. John the Evangelist: 1850.

penicillin - Discovered in 1928 by Alexander Fleming at St. Mary's Hospital/Paddington. Limited at first, but mass-produced by the 1940s.

- See: antibiotics.
- See: germs.

Penny Post - (See: Post, the.)

pens - For writing. (See: quill.)

Pentland House - (See: Lee/Pentland House.)

Pentonville - Islington. Built in the mid 18th century. Contains yet some of the original houses.

- Pentonville Prison: 1840-42. (AKA: the Model Prison.) Caledonian Road, in the Barnsbury area of Islington. Built in a radial design. Is one of London's busiest local prisons. (See: Model Prison.)
- St. James's Church: 1787. Palladian. Turned into flats and offices in 1990, but with much the same look. (See under the CHURCHES section.)
- White Conduit House: Pleasure-gardens and tea-rooms, 1730; remained here for nearly a century. Thomas Lord (later of Lord's Cricket Ground fame) ran a cricket pitch here.

Pentonville Prison - (See: Pentonville/Pentonville Prison.)

Pentonville Road - Runs east from Kings Cross to City Road. Built in the mid 18th century, named for the new nearby town of Pentonville; was part of the New Road, which was intended to help bypass coach traffic and cattle drovers. (See: New Road.)

Pepperers, the - (See: Grocers' Company.)

Percy Street - Off Tottenham Court Road, ca. 1764.

perfumes -

- See: Jermyn Street/89.
- See: Bond Street/Old Bond Street/33.
- See: St. James's Street/29.

- See: Soho/Atkinson.

Perivale - Ealing. Was originally called Greenford Parva, or Little Greenford, and Perivale may be a corruption of "Parva," or the name may come from "Pear Vale." Dates from the Middle Ages. Has affiliations with the Mercers' Company. Until the 20th C., was described as "very quiet." Population in 1911 was under 100.

- St. Mary the Virgin: (See under the CHURCHES section.)

Perry Hill - Lewisham. May date back to the 6th C.; certainly on record by 1473. Perrystreete became Perry Street Hill, which evolved into Perry Hill.

- Perry Hill Farm: Once known as Clowders. Affiliated with the Leathersellers' Company. Now gone.

Perry Oaks - (See: Heathrow.)

Perry Vale - Lewisham. Marshy. Not much settled until the later 18th century, at which time it still showed on maps as "Perrys Low." Changed to "Perry Slough" in 1802; the date when "Perry Vale" appeared on maps in unclear. The "perry" part indicates pears/orchards were grown here. Now hosts a large number of modern houses.

Pest Houses, the - (AKA: Five Chimneys.) Vauxhall Bridge Road. Homes built for poor people struck by the pestilence, 1644 (before the 1665 Great Plague.) In the early 18th C. it became almshouses.

There would have been many pest-houses during the Great Plague of 1665. Pest-houses were used (often) for a forcible quarantine. (See: Great Plague of 1665, under G.)

Peter Pan statue - 1912. (See: Kensington Palace/Peter Pan statue.)

Peter's Lane - During the Regency, this street was known as: Cowcross Street. (See under C.)

Petersham - Richmond. Belonged to St. Peter's Abbey, Chertsey, 7th century. In the Middle Ages this was a sanctuary place. (See: sanctuary, under S.) In the 15th C. the village was handed over to the Crown. Its sanctuary legacy made it a refuge for the London rich, so it has yet many fine Stuart and Georgian homes/mansions, mostly surrounded by green space.

- Gordon House: The eccentric Duchess of Queensberry lived here in the 18th century. In 1971 it became the German School.
- Ham House: (See under H.)
- Petersham Common, Petersham Meadows, and Petersham Park: These are all extensions of Richmond Park. Petersham Common yet contains a beautiful, secluded wood.
- St. Peter's Church: 1266. Thoroughly rebuilt in 1505. Tower added in the 17th century. Pew boxes added in the Georgian era.

Petticoat Lane - Aldgate, the City, at the corner of Bishopgate and Middlesex Street. In 1373 this street was known as Berwardes Lane. By 1500 it was Hog (or Hogs) Lane, and was lined with elms. Known as Petticoat Lane by 1603, at which time "petticoat" meant a wider variety of skirts rather than just the kind of slip or underwear we might think of now. Also at this time the area had become commercial in nature, selling bric-à-brac, used clothes, and such. Hosted an 18th C. market, held on Sundays. Continued to remain a center for secondhand trading, up to the present Sunday market. Known as Petticoat Lane until prudish Queen Victoria had it changed to Middlesex Street in 1846; a second source said 1830. Despite the official name change, the street is still known as (and generally called) Petticoat Lane. (See: Spitalfields/Petticoat Lane.)

Petty France - The City; area near St. James's Park, built 1737. Name derives from Huguenot immigrants who settled here. (See: Spitalfields.)

- 102: Home Office. British intelligence. (See: Home Office.)
- New Broad Street: In the past, was marshy land outside the City wall. Not much developed until there came in late Victorian masonry-faced buildings. No through traffic.

pewter - (See: Shoreditch/Cheshire Street.)

pewterers -

- See: Englefields.
- See: Pewterers' Hall.
- See: Shoreditch/Cheshire Street/Engelfields.
- See: Wapping.

Pewterers' Hall - (For the Worshipful Company of Pewterers.) First record dates from 1348. Charter granted in 1473. Was a going concern until the rise of designs in silver in the 18th C., when this craft knew a severe drop off. Its first Hall burned in the Great Fire of 1666; the second in 1840 (this had been at Lime Street); but with its third Hall in 1961 it moved to Oat Lane, near London Wall. Livery Company. 16th in the order of precedence.

pheasant-shooting - (See: Selsdon.) Of course, many country estates could provide for this sport.

Philanthropic Society, the - Charity, founded in 1788. This society was founded to care for deserted and vagrant children (boys,) specifically those who were the children of convicted felons or were themselves delinquent. Incorporated by Parliament in 1806. Moved to a new building off London Road, Southwark.

Philharmonic Society of London, the - Established in 1813 to promote instrumental music in London. Now a membership society/charity. At 48 Great Marlborough Street. Later added "Royal" before its name. Closed in 1830. (See: Argyll Rooms.)

Phillips - Auctioneers. Established by a former head clerk from Christie's in 1796. Napoleon and Brummell were patrons. At 101 New Bond Street. Bought out in 1999.

Philosophical Transactions - After 1695. A scientific publication. This publication still exists. (See:

Royal Society.)

photography - There are no Regency era photographs; earliest versions date from 1826. The first photo-image of a *human* dates from 1838, by Daguerre, who invented the daguerreotype process of photography. (You may care to see: art/artists.)

Physic Garden - (See: Chelsea Physic Garden.)

physicians -

- See: doctors/physicians.
- See: Royal College of Physicians.

Picardy - Bexley. 17th century. Now called Lower Belvedere.

- Heron Hill: Picardy's grandest house. Sold in 1884, developed as housing.
  - Ye Olde Leather Bottle: Heron Hill public house. Supposedly dates from 1643 (at that time called just The Bottle.) Rebuilt in the late 18th century. Yet survives.

Piccadilly - St. James's and Mayfair districts, Westminster. Technically, the south side of Piccadilly (Street) is in St. James's, whereas the north side is in Mayfair. Piccadilly's name dates from the 17th C., presumed to be derived from "Pickadills," the Elizabethan throat ruffs that had made the fortune of one of this area's early residents.

The area was laid out in the 18th century. (See: Piccadilly Hall, at its own listing - The note under.) Piccadilly is largely described as being bounded by Oxford, Park Lane, Piccadilly, and Regent Streets. While this part of the 18th C. street located in London was "smart," where it led out of town it became a mere "rough road."

At the time of the Regency it had almost a "village air," even though it had been a thriving shopping area since the 18th century (at which time it was made up mostly of bookshops.) The street itself is a broad avenue. "Fashionable gentlemen seldom ventured far east of Piccadilly" was a Regency sentiment.

Near Piccadilly were a number of shops (to accommodate the many travelers who stayed at the inns nearby) for exchanging money: Napoleons, Louis d'ors, light guineas (chipped or mutilated coins,) any kind of gold.

- 10: Swan & Edgars: (Next to the Bull and Mouth.) Was established in 1812. (Swan died in 1821, without issue.) Haberdashery. (See: 40, below - Note at.)
- 14: Thomas Hawke: Tailor, established here by the 1790s.
- 19: Cordings: 1839. Raincoats, tweeds, waterproof boots, woolens.
- 22: This building was described as a hall. The Athenian Lyceum (a debating society) was granted a license to hold meetings here in 1807. Closed in 1809, the society then disbanding. The hall became a museum, housing William Bullock's art, armoury, and natural history collections (which had previously been housed

in Liverpool.) The collection moved to the Egyptian Hall in 1812, and ended being sold at auction in 1819. (See: Egyptian Hall, below.) The property's lease (from the crown) ended in 1817, and the hall was pulled down to make way for Regent Street.

- 23 Piccadilly East: (See: 103, below.)
- 40: The Bull and Mouth: Coaching inn. (Brighton to London run.) Had a life-sized statue of a bull over an equally large "moon-shaped, smiling" face. Located where Swan & Edgar is now. (See: 10, above.)
- 46: Albany. Gentlemen's apartments. It is considered mildly ignorant to refer to this building as "the" Albany. (See: Albany, below.)
- 49: Naval and Military Club: (AKA: The In and Out, because of its driveway signs.) Dates from 1862. Prior to being the Naval, it was Cambridge House. Lord Palmerston lived here from 1857 to his death.
    - See: Cambridge House, under C.
    - See under the CLUBS section.
- 78: Devonshire House: 1740. (See under D.)
- 80: Formed one house along with number 79 (ca. 1740.) Is said to have been the first stuccoed house in London.
- 81: Watier's Club: Opened in 1805. Watier had been a cook to the Prince Regent, who asked him to establish this club. Because Watier had been a cook, some wags occasionally refer to this club as "Waiter's," a misnomer you see regularly in research sources. Macao was the preferred card game played here. Closed in 1819.
    - See under W.
    - See: Watier's Club, under the CLUBS section.
- 102: Sir Thomas Lawrence, the painter, lived here from 1796-8. This property later became the Junior Constitutional Club, 1887. (See: Junior Constitutional Club, under the CLUBS section.)
- 103: Sir William and Lady Hamilton lived here (at least prior to Lord Nelson's death, as he had visited them here.) Sir William, while holding Nelson's hand, died here in 1803; (at that time this house was numbered "23 Piccadilly East.")
- 105: Pulteney's Hotel: (Also seen as: Pulteney Hotel.) On the corner of Piccadilly and Brick Street. Built ca. 1780 by Novosielski, for the Earl of Barrymore, who died before the home could even house his furniture.

    Sir Robert Smirke added the Grecian-Doric porch.

    The building burned, then reopened as the Pulteney Hotel. "Across the way" from Watier's Club; it also overlooked Green Park. The Czar of Russia stayed at the Pulteney in 1814. It had a French chef.

ROMANTIC LONDON states: "In 1823 the house was still the 'Pulteney Hotel'; but in 1829 it was in the possession of the Marquis of Hertford. In 1851 the old building was partially pulled down, and rebuilt with Portland stone. The character of the front was retained but much improved, and raised some fourteen feet, and the interior was entirely re-arranged."

Sir Julian Goldsmid, Bart., bought the house following the fourth Marquis' death. When Sir Julian died, the Isthmian Club bought the house.

The house stood empty a while, then became the Green Park Hotel. Has housed the Wallace Collection since 1900. (See: Hertford House.)

- 106: Coventry House. The Coventry family lived here from 1764 to early in the 19th century. In 1859 it became the St. James' Club (this club specifically spells St. James' with just one "s," and is not to be confused with: St. James's Club.)
- 107: Marshall Blücher (Russian field marshal/led troops against Napoleon in 1813 and 1815) lived here briefly in 1814. In 1885 the house became the Savile Club.
- 116: Originally built for Mr. Henry Thomas Hope (British MP/patron of the arts,) 1848-9. Sold to the Junior Athenaeum in 1868.
- 127: The Cavalry Club, 1890.
- 138: The fourth Duke of Queensberry (described as "an old sybarite") lived here until his death in 1810; he was often seen sitting in the bow window (which in the late 19th C. was fronted anew in stone, as was number 139,) and was known to call out crude comments or suggestive invitations to passing females.
- 139: Lord Byron (poet) once lived here (it was known then as 13 Piccadilly Terrace, 1816.) Its frontage was resurfaced in the late 19th century, as was number 138. (See: Piccadilly Terrace, at its own listing.)
- 144: Built in 1795, designed by the Adam brothers; its first occupant was Sir Drummond Smith (Baronet,) who died in 1816. The property's Crown Lease was then bought by Thomas Wentworth Beaumont (politician/soldier.) Before he went to live at 40 Piccadilly in 1857, Lord Palmerston (was the Prime Minister twice) lived here for a year.
- 149: Apsley House: (See under A.)
- 181: Fortnum & Mason: Grocers. (See: Fortnum & Mason, below.)
- 185: Swaine Adeney Brigg & Sons: (AKA: Swaine and Adeney. Was known as: Swaine & Co. from 1798 to 1825, then Swaine & Isaac until 1848.) Whip, glove,

and umbrella-makers. Here since 1760, as a whip-making business under a John Ross; there was a fire in 1769, and Ross moved to 238 Piccadilly. He sold to James Swaine, whip-maker, in 1798. Royal Warrant granted by George III, for carriage riding whips. Moved to 224 (a few doors to the west) in 1822; then to 185 in 1835. Now also makes bridle-leather luggage.

- 187-8: Hatchard's: Lending library, established in 1797 by John Hatchard, five doors down from its present location at 173; in 1801 was at 187-8. The Duke of Wellington was a loyal customer. Rebuilt in 1910; described as "atmospheric." One went there for books, coffee, and conversation. Has three floors now, at least two in the time of the Regency.
    - Royal Horticultural Society: Met here at Hatchard's, from 1805. (See under R.)
    - Royal Society for Literature: First met here, starting in 1820. (See under R.)
- 197: St. James's, Piccadilly. (See under the CHURCHES section.)
- Albany: 46 Piccadilly. On the north side of Piccadilly there is a small courtyard (Albany Courtyard.) It consists of a long double row of chambers running from Piccadilly to Burlington Gardens; this is the entrance to Albany, during the Regency an exclusive set of bachelor gentleman's rooms. (See: flat, a - For an explanation of how to call bachelor rooms.)

    Built in 1754-8, and improved by Henry Holland in 1787, being at that time called Melbourne House, a residence for Viscount Melbourne (the Melbournes had spent an exorbitant £100,000 on this residence.) According to two sources it was at about this time that it became home to Frederick, Duke of York and Albany (George III's 2nd son) and his new bride Princess Frederica of Prussia.

    Subsequently became Dover House, and (later yet) the Scottish Office. (See: Dover House, under D.)

    Extended in 1802 (2nd source said 1803,) when the gardens were built over, and it was converted into 69 sets of chambers for bachelors' apartments. Lord Byron (poet) lived there (among other equally famous names, at this time the residence now being called Albany.) Always was a fashionable address. Remodeled in 1812.

    Jane Austen's brother ran a bank in its courtyard.

    Some claim geographically speaking, that the front door is in St. James's, the back doorstep in Soho.

(**NOTE: It is NOT referred to as the Albany, just Albany.** Using "the" indicates a mild ignorance.)

Married men were admitted after 1878 (as opposed to bachelors.) Women were admitted after WWII.

- 203: Simpson's bookstore. 1936, modernist design. Now home to Waterstone's (bookstore.)
- 213: 1894, the first Joe Lyons teashop opened here.
- (Mr.) Bullock's Museum: Quoting from REGENCY ENGLAND: "...an enthralling jumble of weapons and armour, stuffed animals, curiosities, and antiquities."
- Burlington Arcade: (Corridor off Piccadilly.) Opened 3/20/1819. Built for Lord Cavendish, to keep people from throwing garbage over the wall into his garden. 41 shops within.
- Burlington House: (See under B.)
- Egyptian Hall: First opened in 1800 in Liverpool by one William Bullock. Was a museum of arms, armor, and curiosities Captain Cook had brought back from the South Seas. In 1809, moved to London, housed at 22 Piccadilly. (See: 22, above.) The Egyptian Hall moved here in 1812, into this building designed by Peter Frederick Robinson (architect.) There were two statues above the door, at their feet the word "Exhibition" as part of the stone.

  The hall was destroyed and replaced by Egyptian House (an office block) on this site in 1905.

  Not to be confused with the Egyptian Gallery in the British Museum. Nor the Egyptian Hall in the Mansion House.

  (See: 22, above - The note at.)
- Eros, statue of: 1892-3, by Alfred Gilbert. "Eros" is the common interpretation of this statue, but it is actually meant as the Angel of Christian Charity, a memorial to Lord Shaftesbury for his philanthropy. (AKA: the Shaftesbury Memorial fountain and statue.) The first public monument made of aluminum. The statue was moved and/or neglected in a county hall room from the 1820s to well into the 20th C. before being restored to Piccadilly Circus; its bow is supposed to be facing northeast, but is now erroneously facing southwest since being restored to the Circus.
- Fortnum & Mason: 181 Piccadilly. Grocers; catered to aristocratic clients, utilized by the Royal family (as well as the public.) Still there. Founded in 1707 by one of Queen Anne's footmen, William Fortnum (and his grocer friend, Hugh

Mason) at a site very near the present one. Royal Warrant issued in 1836. Plate glass windows lit by gas in 1840. Rebuilt in 1927-8. They built Mason's Yard, behind the shop, to handle deliveries. The clock, with bowing and 18th-century-clothed Mr. Fortnum and Mr. Mason figures, was put here in 1964.

- Hatchard's: Bookstore. (See: 187, above.)
- Inns (of Piccadilly): (See: all of the below, under the INNS/PUBS section.)
  - Bull and Mouth
  - Lemon Tree
  - Spread Eagle
  - Three Kings
  - White Bear
  - White Horse
- Melbourne House: (See: Albany, above.)
- Pulteney's Hotel: (See: 105, above.)
- Ridgeway's Bookshop: Patronized by Lord Byron (poet.) Owned by James Ridgeway, who was known as a radical pamphlet- and bookseller.
- Ritz Hotel: Opened in 1906.
- Royal Academy of Arts: Founded in 1768, to teach fine arts. Famous annual summer exhibition for over 200 years. (See under R.)
- St. James's Church: At 197 Piccadilly. 1684, Wren. (See: St. James's, Piccadilly, under the CHURCHES section.)
- St. James' Club: 106 Piccadilly. Is specifically spelled with only one "s." Not to be confused with St. James's Club/men's club (See under the CLUBS section.)
- Savile Row: (See under S.)

Piccadilly Arcade - 1910. An extension off Burlington Arcade.

Piccadilly Circus - Regent Street, Westminster. Built by John Nash in 1819 as Regent's Circus South. In 1880, when it was updated at the same time as Charing Cross Road and Shaftesbury Avenue, the Circus ceased to be a circle, but by then the name of Piccadilly Circus had stuck; the circus is now a triangular shape.

In the last century, an 1893 statue of Eros (isn't really of Eros, is "the Angel of Christian Charity," but everyone mistakes it for Eros) was moved from here, but later returned. (See: Piccadilly/Eros.)

Piccadilly has always served as a meeting place, be it persons of the *bon monde* or those of various subcultures. (See: Oxford Circus.)

- County Fire Office: 1819-20. (See under C.)

- Criterion Theatre: 1874.

Piccadilly East - How Piccadilly was called, circa 1803, at least in part. (See: Piccadilly/103.)

Piccadilly Hall - (Also originally seen written as: Pickadill Hall.) Built in 1611, after the plot of land was sold to one Robert Baker (a tailor,) who had the hall built for him. Because of this house here (named for the piccadills, Elizabethan ruffled neck collars, that made the fortune of Baker,) there sprang up the westward-stretching road known as Piccadilly, the latter so named circa 1627. Piccadilly Hall was gone by the time of the Regency.

Piccadilly Terrace - Lord Byron (poet) had a home here at number 13. His rent was £700 per year. He lived here while estranged from his wife (1816.) Remodeled in 1889 and during WWI. (See: Piccadilly/139.)

Pickering Place - An alley between St. James's Street and Pall Mall; off St. James's Street, through an archway north of Berry Brothers & Rudd. (See: St. James's Street/3.) Pickering Place was built in 1731. According to MYSTERY READER'S WALKING GUIDE, LONDON: "To get a closer look wait until you reach the bottom of St. James's Street, cross, and then walk back. Walk through the archway into the courtyard. You have to keep your eyes peeled to spot the entrance, and if the gate is closed, you will only know that you are at Pickering Place by the number 3. The alleyway retains its eighteenth-century timber wainscoting, on which a plaque notes that the diplomatic office of 'The Republic of Texas Legation 1842' was located here." In this small square, the last English duel was fought. (See: St. James's/Pickering Place.)

Pickett Street - New name given to this street when Butcher's Row was pulled down in 1790-1815. Later was the east side of the Strand.

pickles - What Americans think of as pickles would have been more likely known to Regency folk as "pickled cucumbers." Many kinds of food were pickled.

- See: food - Notes about pickling.
- See: food/pickles.
- See: Mackey & Co.

picnic - The term was in use by the Regency. It was a bit more of a formal event than a modern picnic (at least for the upper classes,) having serving attendants and quite possibly tables and chair *al fresco*.

pictures - As in paintings. Photography had yet to be invented at the time of the Regency.

- See: art/artists.
- You may care to see: photography.

Pidcock's Menagerie - (See: Exeter Exchange.)

Pie Corner - Smithfield, nearly opposite Giltspur Street and St. Bartholomew's Hospital. Where the Great Fire of 1666 came to a halt, it started in Pudding Lane. (See: Great Fire of 1666, under G.)

- Fortune of War Tavern: On the junction of Cock Lane. This is where Resurrectionists (body-snatchers) brought the stolen bodies of executed criminals, taken from Newgate Prison or stolen from St. Sepulchre's churchyard. The tavern is now gone. (See: Cock Lane/Fortune of War tavern.)

pies -

- See: food/pies.
- See: pastries.

pigs -

- See: food/pork.
- See: pork.

pillar boxes - (See: post boxes.)

pillory - A pillory could be erected anywhere, but it was "best placed" in a public spot with plenty of elbow room for the attendant spectator crowds, such as at Charing Cross. It was a wooden structure, usually with holes for the head and hands to pass through and be fixed in place. The thought behind the structure was to be uncomfortable and to expose the punished person to public abuse, not least because one had to stand a long time. There were also versions where one was held by the legs in a sitting position; sometimes one was also made to sit on a wooden triangle, to increase the discomfort. Can also be called: the stocks. By 1816, the pillory was only used to punish perjury and subornation (bribery,) and the practice was abandoned altogether by 1830. Not a likely punishment at the time of the Regency.

Pillory Lane - Slum. (See: St. Katherine's, Tower Hamlets.)

pilots - As in, those who piloted ships (navigators.)

- See: Trinity House.
- You may care to see: naval matters.

Pimlico - Westminster. Supposedly named for a publican or his "long forgotten drink," a 17th C. ale called "Ben Pimlico's Nut Browne"; or it may refer to a place in Honduras from where mahogany was delivered. Either way it should be noted that a 1628 document refers to the area as "Pimplico" (with the extra p.)

The area of Pimlico was not developed until the 1840s. Before then it was a place for unloading ships of coal and timber. There are records of occupation dating back to 1626, but until the more formal development in the 1840s it was mostly market-gardens belonging to the Grosvenor family. In fact, it used to be further north, until the evolution of Buckingham House morphing into Buckingham Palace (1825,) forced the area then called Pimlico into an area called South Belgravia, which was developed by Thomas Cubitt (the area now covered by Dolphin Square.)

During the Regency this area was little more than swamps, near Five Fields, consisting of some market-gardens, wastelands, a few scattered huts, and some houses near the river.

- See: Five Fields.
- See: Tothill Fields.

Its present borders are, to the east: Vauxhall Bridge Road. To the west: Chelsea Bridge Road. To the north: Ebury Street.

- Ebury Street: (See under E.)
- Eccleston Square: (See under E.)
- Jew's Row: (See: Chelsea/Jew's Row.)

Pimlico Road - Was called Grosvenor Road throughout the 19th century. (See: Grosvenor Road.)

pineapple - Was the medieval sign for a confectioner's shop. (Also symbolized hospitality.) Even into Victorian times, having pineapple on your table was a symbol of wealth, because they were rare. (See: pinery.)

pinery - A forcing garden (hot house) for growing pineapples. Usually only seen on grand estates.

pink - (AKA: hunting pink. Plural: pinks.) As in the red coat worn during foxhunts. From every source I have seen, it appears that hunting pink coats came along later in the 19th century, post-Regency. (See: Mason's Yard/Maxwell, Henry.)

Pinner - Harrow. Old village whose name is taken from a stream called the Pinn. It dates back to at least the 1230s, but the town's current aspect is 20th century. According to CHAMBERS LONDON GAZETTEER: "During the early 19th century, in the first significant shift in Pinner's character since medieval times, large farms supplanted Pinner's many smallholdings, making it a place of fewer farmers and more agricultural labourers, whose numbers then declined as dairy farming began to replace crop-growing."

- Commercial Traveller's School: 1855.
- Pinner Park: Ancient 250-acre deer reserve for the lord of Harrow Manor.
- Queen's Head Inn: 1705. Still there. (See under the INNS/PUBS section.)
- St. John-the-Baptist: Parish church. Perpendicular tower. Some parts date from the 13th century. Restored in 1879-80. This saint's feast day has been celebrated here (and still is) with a midsummer fair in June since 1336.

Pinner Green - Harrow. A quiet northern corner of Pinner. Despite the inference of its name, Pinner Green was a separate hamlet from Pinner in the Middle Ages. In 1565 a windmill was here. In the 18th C. some cottages arrived. In 1809, a toll-bar.

- Bell Inn: 1751.
- Pinner Cricket Club: Began playing on the green in 1892.

pint - In both the imperial (modern British) and American systems, a pint is generally acknowledged as being 1/8th of a gallon (2 cups, American,) although the British imperial size is about 20% larger. America still uses the old English measures, while Britain went to the imperial method of measuring. Pints around the "metric" (rest of the) world can differ in size.

- See: measurements.
- See: Turners' Company - Who established the pint size.

pipe makers -

- See: Carnaby Street/45/Inderwick's.
- See: Elephant and Castle.
- See: tobacco.

pipes -

- For the moving of water - (See: Lamb's Conduit Street.)
- For smoking - (See: pipe makers.)

Piss Pot Hall - (See: Hackney/Lower Clapton/Piss Pot Hall.)

Pitshanger Manor - Ealing. 1803, Sir John Soane (architect) designed this manor as his country home, on the site of an earlier one. Found in Pitshanger Village; the manor once covered land from Hanger Hill to Mattock Lane.

Placentia - Ancient palace, long gone by the time of the Regency.

- See: Greenwich/Bella Court.
- See: Greenwich/Royal Naval Hospital.
- See: Greenwich Hospital.

Plaisterers' Company - (AKA: the Worshipful Company of Plaisterers.) Mentioned as early as the 14th century. Royal Charter in 1501; had a later Charter in 1679. "Plaisterer" is the ancient spelling of "plasterer"; they did plaster work. Their first Hall was on the corner of Addle Street and Philip Lane, but it was destroyed in the Great Fire of 1666. Second Hall, 1669, built by Wren; but it burned also, in 1882. Has a new Hall, from 1972, at One London Wall, built to resemble the work of Robert Adam; described as one of London's "finest and largest" Halls in London. Livery Company. 46th in the order of precedence.

Plaistow - (Pronounced: "playstow.") Bromley. Dates from at least 1278; name implies it was a place where persons gathered to play games. The estate was sold in 1777 to a rich Swiss banker, Peter Thellusson, at which time he built Plaistow Lodge. CHAMBERS LONDON GAZETTEER notes: "Thellusson died in 1797 after writing the most complex will in English history, which forced an immediate change in testamentary law and provided inspiration for Dickens' novel *Bleak House.*" Was entirely rural until 1875.

(There is also a Plaistow in Newham, now usually given the Cockney pronunciation

"Plar-stow", on the southeast side of West Ham. Genteel merchants and notable citizens used it as a pleasure retreat in the 18th C., but the rails drove out the gentry ca. the 1840s.)

plane trees - (AKA: London plane, the.) London is graced with many plane trees. They have a distinctive peeling bark, which gives the trunks a rather impressionistic arty look. (See: trees/plane.)

planets - In our solar system. Regency era persons could be familiar with six of the nine planets - a seventh being, obviously, Earth. (The six they might know about are marked with a checkmark: √.) Here is a list, in order from the sun:

- √ Mercury - Date of discovery is unsure, but it was seen through a telescope, in 1610, by Galileo. Visible to the naked eye.
- √ Venus - Discovered in 1610. Visible to the naked eye.
- Earth
- √ Mars - Discovered in 1659. Visible to the naked eye.
- √ Jupiter - Discovered in 1610. Visible to the naked eye.
- √ Saturn - Discovered in 1610. Visible to the naked eye.
- √ Uranus - Discovered in 1781, by William Herschel. He called it Georgium Sidus (Georgian Planet,) in honor of King George III; Astronomer Johann Bode renamed it later as Uranus, in keeping with the mythology-driven names of other planets. This new name was generally accepted by the mid 19th century. Some persons with particularly sharp vision are able to see it with the naked eye, given the right conditions.
- Neptune - Discovered in 1846.
- Pluto - Discovered in 1936. In 1992 its status as a planet was questioned. The term "planet" was reassessed in 2006; this led to Pluto being reclassified as a dwarf planet, no longer considered to be the ninth planet from our sun. Pluto's status was re-examined in 2018; keeping a rather long explanation short: it's not a planet in the same way others in our solar system are, being outside the Kuiper Belt. In other words, the debate runs on.

plants - In England during the Regency. (This list is not all-inclusive):

barley

blackberries

corn - (See: food/corn.)

crabapple - Can be grown into either a bush or a tree.

dandelion - Until the 15th century it was called: lion's tooth.

deadly nightshade

elderberry

gooseberry - In Britain, also called: goosegog.

grass

hawthorn

hay

herbs - (See: food - For many listings.)

holly

honeysuckle

ivy

japonica

laurel

lilac

mandrake

oats

osiers - (See under O.)

privet (hedge)

snowberry

strawberries

- See: flowers.
- See: food - For many plant listings.
- See: hedgerows.
- See: trees.

Plashet - Newham.

- Katherine Road: Named for Elizabeth Fry's daughter. Elizabeth Fry went into the prisons, was horrified, and became an advocate for prison reform. (See: Plashet House, below.)
- Plashet Cottage: Elizabeth Fry's daughter lived here. (See: Plashet House, below.) Pulled down in the 1880s.
- Plashet House: From 1809-29 was the home of Elizabeth Fry. Demolished in the 1880s.
- Plashet Zoo: 1964.

Platt's Eyot - Richmond. (See: ait.) One of the largest small islands, and the most western, in the Thames. Now called Port Hampton Business Island (it has private owners.) Known for its osiers, willows for basketweaving, until the 1880s. (See: osiers.) Owes its current hilly topography to late 19th C. excavation soil that was dumped here.

Playhouse Yard - Off Blackfriars Lane. There had been an Elizabethan playhouse here, built by Richard Burbage, Blackfriars Playhouse. Shakespeare performed here. (See: Blackfriars

Lane/Playhouse Yard.)

playing cards - Were popular during the Regency era. Unlike prior eras, most Regency folk saw nothing wrong with playing cards, which had once been viewed by some as being temptations/tools of the devil.

- See: activities/entertainment/sports - playing cards, under A.
- See: INTRO-REIGNS section/British Kings & Queens and their Reigns/Henry VII - For invention of.
- See: Makers of Playing Cards.

pleasure boating - Of course boating happened on the Thames, and in those parks with bodies of water that were suitable, plus generally anywhere where water was conducive to a leisurely row.

- See: Alperton.
- You may care to see: boating, under B.

pleasure gardens - (Also seen as: pleasure-gardens.) Basically, gardens for strolling, listening to music, seeing fireworks, etc. One paid a fee to enjoy one of these formal garden's offerings. Some had booths; some provided food and/or drink. Sometimes their reputations were dicey, especially after dark.

- See: Bagnigge Wells.
- See: Cremorne - Mid 19th century.
- See: Islington/Sadler's Wells.
- See: Ranelagh Gardens.
- See: St. George's Fields Circus - (AKA: Royal Circus.)
- See: Vauxhall Gardens.

Plough Court - (See: Lombard Street/Plough Court.)

Plough Lane - (See: Campden Hill Road.)

Plow'd Garlic Hill - (See: Telegraph Hill.)

Plumbers' Company - (AKA: the Worshipful Company of Plumbers.) Had Ordinances granted in 1365, 1488, and 1520. Charter in 1611. AN ENCYCLOPAEDIA OF LONDON says: "Although it no longer controls the trade it strongly supports technical training and is still the registration authority for qualified plumbers." Livery Company. 31st in the order of precedence. Doesn't have a hall of their own.

Plumstead - Greenwich. East of Woolwich. Thousands of acres of marshes. Dates from at least the year 970. Called an "insignificant" rural area into the mid 19th century.

- Plumstead Common: A "chain" of open spaces. In the 18th C. there was a parish workhouse here, and from 1764 a windmill. Began to be developed in the 1840s. CHAMBERS LONDON GAZETTEER says: "Plumstead Common has some of the most varied terrain of London's open spaces, including wooded ravines, ponds, pudding-stone* boulders, and an ancient burial mound on Winn's Common." (*Puddingstone is: a conglomerate rock with dark-colored rounded pebbles in it, which contrast with finer grains, making it look like raisins in a Christmas pudding.)

- St. Nicholas: 12th C. origins. Had a 1660s tower, which didn't match style with the church itself. (See under the CHURCHES section.)
- Severndroog Castle: 1784. The land had a triangular shape. (See: Shooter's Hill/Castle Wood.)

Pluto - (See: planets/Pluto.)

poaching - Contrary to our expectations of the harshness of 18-19th century laws (there were some 200 crimes that could result in punishment by death,) small-creature poaching was not a felony. It was punished by a fine or (if the offender couldn't pay) corporal punishment (as in a caning or the stocks.) Note, though, that since most deer were raised in deer parks (which were private property, if not outright royal,) taking a deer was a felony punishable by death. (See: Verderers - Forest guardians.)

Poland Street - (See: Soho/Poland Street.)

police - The English populace did not like the idea of a standing police force. Long after it was clear the country needed some manner of law enforcers, a formed constabulary was resisted.

First allowed were: watchmen (also called: Charlies, because they came about in the time of Charles II.) Charlies/watchmen acted on the orders of the (unpaid) local magistrate. (See: justice of the peace.) They carried a bell (for ringing out the hour, which was generally appreciated,) and a staff or possibly a cudgel. These watchmen were mostly old men, sometimes drunk, sometimes given over to accepting bribes - although sometimes they did their best for their magistrates, not wishing to have a worse reputation than their fellow parishes. Although one older man was often ineffective in preventing crime or apprehending offenders in any one district, they were seen as at least providing one layer of mild protection that had not previously been afforded the populace. In the 17th C., affluent young men liked to "box the watch," by trapping a watchman in his wooden shelter box, that gave him some shelter when he wasn't walking the streets of his area and ringing the hour. (See: Charlies.)

In 1749 Henry Fielding (novelist) was appointed as the salaried Chief Magistrate of Westminster. He conducted studies, trying to determine why crime was increasing. He and his brother, John, worked out of Bow Street, which eventually led to establishing his private police force for hire: the Bow Street Runners. (See under B.)

Technically, the first (formal/paid) police force in London was the Thames River

Police, founded in 1798, operating by 1801, but they were restricted to policing only the docks. (See: Thames River, The/the paragraph: River Police Force.)

By the time of the Georgian and Regency eras, multiple attempts to pass legislation for a police force still failed, but the need became increasing obvious. The term "police" was used, but those who patrolled Regency streets were called: a constable (rather than a policeman.) A constable was an officer of the parish. They might still be referred to as the Watch by older folk, but that term was fading - finally making way for the new and much-needed Metropolitan Police in 1829.

- See: Church of England/Beadle - Church warden.
- See: Bow Street.
- See: Bow Street Runners.
- See: City of London Police Force - Not to be confused with the Metropolitan Police Force.
- See: constable.
- See: copper - A nickname for constables.
- See: Great Scotland Yard.
- See: Jewry Street/26 - Headquarters of the City of London Police Force.
- See: justices of the peace - For outside London.
- See: Marylebone Watch House.
- See: Metropolitan Police.
- See: punishments.
- See: Thames, the - There, see: River Police Force, technically the first police force in London.
- See: thief-takers.
- See: Wapping - Marine police.
- See: Watch House.
- See: Watermen.

police boxes - Blue, contained a phone accessed by an outside little door, with a flashing light on top (to signal a constable to call in to the local police station.) They were used by 1920-60s constables to be in contact with colleagues. Replaced by: portable radios. Very few are yet to be seen on London streets; there remains one on the west side of Piccadilly Circus, dating from 1935. They were almost always blue, with the notable exception of police boxes in Glasgow, Scotland, where until the 1960s they were red. (Yes, the police boxes were like the famous one, the *TARDIS*, on the television program *Doctor Who*.)

Political Register, the - Begun in 1802, a weekly Tory report, by the political commentator and member of Parliament, William Cobbett (whose views earned him the nickname "The Poor Man's Friend.") Cobbett was imprisoned ca. 1815 (and in 1817 went to America for some years.) The report ceased in 1836, a year following Cobbett's death.

polo - Mounted on horseback team sport. Its nickname: The Sport of Kings. First seen in the 6th century. British officers who'd seen it in India, 1860-ish, brought the game to England. A polo pitch is roughly the size of nine American football fields. (See: Hurlingham Club, under H.)

Polytechnic Institute - Founded in 1838 in Regent Street, responding to the growing Industrial Revolution. Became the Royal Polytechnic Institute, then the London Polytechnic, whose degrees were validated by the University of London. Is now the University of Westminster, since 1992.

Pond Square - (See: Highgate Hill/Pond Square.)

Pond Street - Hampstead. From at least 1752.

Ponder's End - Enfield. From at least the late 16th century. A flour mill built in the late 18th C. still stands. Factories flourished from the 1840s on.

- Grout and Baylis: Crape (black gauze) mill, 1809.

pool - As in the game with a cue ball and table pockets. In England it is known as: snooker. (See under S.) Dates from the second half of the 19th century. (You may care to see: billiards.)

Pool of London - A way of referring to the body of water just under the old London Bridge. CHAMBERS LONDON GAZETTEER writes: "...London's pool is 'the part of the Thames between London Bridge and Cuckold's Point,' which is located at the north-eastern tip of the Rotherhithe peninsula. However, this definition includes the Lower Pool, which is the stretch between Wapping and Limehouse." In 1934 1,500 tons of sand was dumped here to form a bathing beach.

Pope's Head Alley - Dates from at least 1677. (See: Lloyd's of London - Middle area paragraph.)

Poor Laws - (See: workhouses.)

poor, the -

- See: almhouses.
- See: East End.
- See: orphanages.
- See: rookeries.
- See: St. Giles.
- See: Seven Dials.

Poplar - East End. At least since the 17th C., at which time it provided homes for dock workers. When the West India Docks came along in 1802, they stimulated rapid growth here. Poplar Fields became known as Poplar New Town in the 1830s. Poplar became a borough in 1900.

Near Stepney. In 1841 had 30,000 residents; during Victoria's reign this area turned into a slum.

- Poplar Hospital: 1835.

porcelain - As in tableware/decorative pieces.

> See: Bow.
> See: china.
> See: earthenware shops.
> See: Limehouse/Limehouse ware.
> See: Worchestershire/Worchester Royal Porcelain Co., under the BRITISH COUNTIES section.

pork - Readily available in London...to those who could afford it.

> See: butchers.
> See: food/pork.
> See: St. James's Market/Wall's Meat Co.

Port of London Authority - Tower Hill. Established in 1908 to bring order out of the busy Thames River chaos. (See: docks - Note under the opening section.)

porter - Porter was a heavily roasted brown malt mashed over and over again. Hops are boiled with the malt before fermentation. Strong, with a bitter edge. Would keep for a year. (See: Chiswell Street/Whitbread's Brewery.)

Portland Place - Marylebone. Adam Brothers, 1773. A second source said it was laid out in 1776-80. Its northern end is the Park Crescent. Street was incorporated into Nash's plans for Regent's Park. Is 125 feet wide. (See: Marylebone/Portland Place.)

- 19: (Originally was number 65.) Built by Joseph Rose (a plasterer for the Adam brothers.)
- 41: General Thomas Gage (commander in chief of British forces/Battle of Bunker Hill/USA) lived here 1775-87.
- 46-48: By John Adam, 1774.
- 98: This location became the U. S. Embassy in 1863-66. (See: United States Embassy, under U - For other locations.)
- Broadcasting House: Since 1931, the home of BBC radio.
- Langham Hotel: Victorian. (See under L.)
- Statue of Sir George Stuart White (Victoria Cross-awarded Field Marshal,) in the middle of this broad street, dates from after 1879.

Portland Road - Notting Hill, North of Cavendish Square. 1850s. Portland "Road" and Portland "Place" run parallel to one another.

Portland Town - The previous name for High Street, St. John's Wood. (See: St. John's Wood.)

Portman Square - Marylebone. Begun in 1761 (or 64,) completed in 1784-5. Built on land owned by the Portman family. Fashionable address still in the Regency era.

- Courtauld Institute: 20th C. organization. Moved from Portman Square in 1990 to Somerset House.
    - See: Courtauld Institute, under C.
    - See: 20 Portman Square, below.
- Gloucester Place: Well-constructed private homes. (See under G.)
- Hindostanee Coffee House: 1809. A curry house. Owned by Dean Mahomed. Closed in 1812.
    - You may care to see: curry.
    - You may care to see: food/curry.
- Orchard Square: 1929.
- Orchard Street: Described as "fine." Existed by at least 1787.
- 20 Portman Square: Home House. Robert Adam (and his brothers,) built here for the patron, the Countess of Home, in 1773-7. Described as Adam's finest town house design; also described as sumptuous. The building was restored by Samuel Courtauld, who left the house and his impressionistic and post-impressionistic paintings collection to the University of London; although the University owned the collection, it remained here (in the house that was gifted for the very purpose of holding the collection for the University) until the collection moved to Woburn Square, in the Courtauld Institute Gallery, ca. 1940. There until 1990, when it moved to Somerset House.
- 14 York Place, Portman Square: (Now 120 Baker Street.) Pitt the Younger lived here from autumn 1802-May 1804. Built ca. 1790. This house was part of the Portman Estate which was rapidly growing during the late 18th century. Baker Street's name is derived from Sir Edward Baker, who helped Portman develop the estate. Pitt's eccentric niece, Hester Stanhope, lived here with him.
- Upper Berkeley Street: Georgian street. Now contains many hotels.

Portobello Road - (AKA: Portobello Road Market.) Notting Hill, Kensington/Chelsea. While it existed as a simple track in the Regency era, this is mostly a post-Regency road; known for its fortunetellers, side-shows, horse traders, and charlatans since Victorian times. Named after Puerto Bello (also seen as: Porto Bella) in the Caribbean. On the site of an 18th C. farm. Now known on Saturdays as a busy antiques market, here since the 20th century.

portraits - (See: art/artists.)

Portsmouth Street - Southeast corner of Lincoln's Inn Fields. Contains an antique shop (at number 13) that calls itself "The Olde Curiosity Shop," supposedly the one in Charles

Dickens' tale, but often refuted as such. (See under O.) At any rate, the timber-framed shop does date from 1567. The street existed by at least the 17th century. (See: Inns of Court/Lincoln's Inn Fields/Portsmouth Street.)

Portugal Street - North of St. James's Park, Holborn. Named for Catherine of Braganza, Portugal, wife of Charles II.

post - (See: post, the.)

post boxes - (AKA: pillar boxes.) Postal boxes, found on many street corners. First appeared in 1855, green. Between 1866-79 their color was standardized to the familiar red. (See: post, the.)

Post Office, the -

- See: General Post Office.
- See: post, the.

Post Office Tower - 1964. (Now the London Telecom Tower.)

post, the - (Also called the Royal Mail. The building is now also referred to as GPO, short for General Post Office.)

The Royal Mail dates from 1516. The post delivery system was first opened to the public in 1635 by Charles I.

The Royal Mail coaches did not pay tolls at turnpikes.

The post had first been at the Windmill in Old Jewry, then at the Black Swan in Bishopgate. After the Great Fire of 1666 it was at Covent Garden, but in 1678 it moved to Lombard Street.

The mail coach system (as opposed to mounted postboys) was established in 1784.

In 1805 it no longer cost one penny; it now cost two pence to send your letter. In 1812 the cost of sending a letter 15 miles or less rose to four pence, and up to 17 pence for 700 miles. In 1812 the price was up again, four pence to send a letter 15 miles or less. (These prices are based on a single sheet, folded and sealed with a wafer; envelopes weren't used until the 1840s.)

In 1829, the GPO's first purpose-built building was constructed on the site once occupied by the ancient church St. Martin's-le-Grand, Cheapside (and 130 houses had to be demolished to make way for this new home for the post as well.)

In 1839, adhesive stamps (that required moistening to stick) were first used, in America. Invented in 1838 by James Chalmers (Scottish inventor.)

The post might be delivered several times per day (as opposed to the modern practice of once per day.)

The first of the famous pillar boxes (post boxes to be found on street corners, etc.) appeared in 1855. (See: post boxes.)

The final mail coach run was in the year 1874.

IMPORTANT NOTES: Until 1840 and the introduction of the penny-post (and therefore pre-payment with postage stamps) it was the recipient who paid the fee, rather than the sender, so keeping one's missives short (enough to be but one folded page) was considered good manners. In order to make the most of that one page, there was the practice of cross-writing: filling a page with script, then turning it to write across the already written lines at a 90 degree angle.

There were no envelopes (until ca. 1840,) the letter (of one sheet or sometimes more) being folded into its own envelope-like shape, the direction (that is, the address) written on the side without folds, then flipped over and sealed with red wax (or black, if there'd been a death in the family.) Not everyone always used wax; there were also wafers (primarily made from wheat) that were wetted and stuck on to hold the letter closed.

Postcards were allowed in the Royal Mail in 1894.

(See: General Post Office.)

Postman's Park - 1880. (See: St. Botolph-without-Aldersgate/Postman's Park, under the CHURCHES section.)

Pot Kilns - Havering. A tiny hamlet, often unmarked on maps. Was the center of the Upminster brickfields from 1708; the first brick kiln here in 1774. Also here: tiles, and pots (chimney, flower, and kale pots - the latter used to make broth and/or pottage.)

potatoes -

- See: food/potatoes.
- See: vegetables/potatoes.

Potteries, The - (See: Kensington/Potteries.)

pottery -

- See: Cheam.
- See: Devon, under the BRITISH COUNTIES section.
- See: Lambeth/potters.

Poulters' Company - (AKA: the Worshipful Company of Poulters.) This Company formed as early as 1299, with Ordinances that existed before 1370. AN ENCYCLOPAEDIA OF LONDON states: "The Lord Poulter was a seller of table-birds, rabbits, butter and eggs." In 1368 the Poulters were given the power to oversee the sale of pigeons, poultry, rabbits, small game, and swans. Supposedly in 1504 Henry VII granted a Charter, but it ceased to exist, leaving the earliest recorded Charter for this company dating from 1665. Their first Hall was in Butcher Hall Lane, 1630; it burned in the Great Fire of 1666. They no longer have a Hall. Livery Company. 34th in the order of precedence.

poultry - As in birds (not the street.)

- See: butchers.
- See: food - Various listings there, such as: chicken, goose, turkey, etc.
- See: Leadenhall Market.

Poultry Street - The City. (Not to be confused with The Poultry.)

- Poultry Street Chapel: 1819. (See: City Temple, under C.)

Poultry, The - Eastern end of Cheapside (between Bucklersbury and the Mansion House.) Named for the product once sold there; poulters (those who dealt with poultry) here before the Great Fire of 1666.

pound, the (£) - (See: money/pound.)

pounds - As in weight.

- See: stone - 14 pounds.
- You may care to see: measurements.

Poverest - Bromley. Roman remains have been unearthed here. Remained "wholly agricultural" throughout most of the 19th century.

Powell, James & Sons - Decorative glass. (See: Whitefriars Glass.)

Powis House - Belonged to the 3rd Viscount Dungannon. Dungannon agreed to have the house pulled down, and Trevor Square, Knightsbridge, was built over the site in the 1820s.

pox, the - There were different forms of pox, but primarily known in the Regency was: smallpox. (See under S.)

precedence - Formal order of status.

The term "Prime Minister" wasn't used in any precedence listing until 1905.

- See: halls.
- See: Lord Mayor.
- See: Prime Minister.

Pre-Raphaelite Brotherhood - Founded by artists in 1844, to resist "contemporary art tastes."

Presbyterians - This religion was represented in London by at least the early 17th century.

- See: King's Weigh House Chapel.
- See: St. John, Clerkenwell, under the CHURCHES section.
- See: St. Paul Presbyterian Church, under the CHURCHES section - 1859.

Prescott Street - Whitechapel. At least by 1708. Named for a builder named Prescott. Renamed as Great Prescott Street by 1799.

presentation at court (of young women, to the Queen) - Took place at St. James's Palace. One was required to wear court dress (essentially old-fashioned Georgian styles.)

- See: Queen's drawing-room.
- See: levee - Presentation of young men to the king.

preserves - (As in preserving food.)

- See: food - Notes on preserving food.
- See: MacKey & Co.

press-ganging - (See: impressment.)

prime meridian, the - The earth's chosen meridian, assigned as the zero of longitude.

- See: Greenwich.
- See: Greenwich Observatory.

Prime Ministers (a partial list of) - Ca. 1713 the term "Prime Minister" appears as an unofficial title for the leader of the government (who was, with two exceptions, the head of the Treasury.) In fact, at that time more than one man could be called a Prime Minister, meaning he was one of the chief ministers in the government.

Since the Prime Minister title/office wasn't officially bestowed, there was no "first" PM, although historians generally grant that designation to Sir Robert Walpole, 1st Lord of the Treasury, 1721.

During the Georgian/Regency eras, this leader would have been referred to by whatever his official designation was (as mentioned, usually the head of the Treasury.)

The title of Prime Minister (AKA: the PM) did not come into common use (as we think of it now) until the 20th century. In fact, until it was finally mentioned in the list of Precedence in 1905, most men (who held this power) called the term Prime Minister "odious," or "an affront to the king," or "an office unknown to the Constitution."

- See: Constitution.
- See: precedence.

All the same, before that mention in 1905, the title of Prime Minister had already long since begun its rise to be the most powerful governmental position (including that of the monarch) - despite no legal documents that described its powers or acknowledged its existence.

Georgian/Regency "Prime Ministers" (again, a term used later):

1770-1782: Frederick, Lord North. Tory. Resigned following American independence.

1782-1783: William Petty, Earl of Shelburne. Whig.

1783: William Bentinck, Duke of Portland. Whig.

1783-1801: William Pitt the Younger. Tory; he called himself an "independent whig," although it has to be noted he was responsible for what is called "new Toryism." He was the youngest PM ever, in office at age 24. Resigned once he and the king fell out over Pitt's support of Catholic emancipation.

1801-4: Henry Addington. Tory. Resigned in 1804. Later was raised to be the first

Viscount Sidmouth.

1804-06: William Pitt the Younger. 2nd term, still Tory. He died in 1806.

1806-07: The 1st Baron Grenville (William Grenville.) Whig.

1807-09: The 3rd Duke of Portland (William Cavendish-Bentinck.) Whig.

1809-12: Spencer Perceval. Tory. He was the first PM to be assassinated (in the lobby of the House of Commons, shot by a man with a grievance against the government, 5/11/1812.)

1812-27: The 2nd Earl of Liverpool (Robert Banks Jenkinson.) In April/1827 he asked the king to find a successor, because he had suffered a severe cerebral hemorrhage; he died the next year. The king selected George Canning (who had been the Earl of Liverpool's right-hand man,) but Canning's health was frail and he died in Aug/1827, becoming the PM with the shortest term in office: 119 days.

Primrose Hill - Camden. (See: Regent's Park/Primrose Hill - The former of which it is, strictly speaking, a part.) Primrose Hill was cleared of its trees and became open meadowland in the 17th century. Wild animals, footpads. Used by duelists. Its summit is 206 feet high.

- St. Marks Church: 1851.

Prince Henry's Room -

- See: Fleet Street/17.
- See: Inns of Court/Temple (1st listing)/Inner Temple/Inner Temple Gateway/Prince Henry's Room.

Prince Regent Lane - Newham. Started as Trinity Marsh Lane. Existed in the Middle Ages. In the 19th and early 20th centuries was known as Prince Regent's Lane, but then dropped the "s."

Prince's Gate - Kensington Road. Opposite Rutland Gate, Knightsbridge. 1848.

- 14: Built in 1849.

Princes Street - Drury Lane, the City. Near the Bank of England. There by at least 1734.

Princes Street - Hanover Square. Existed by at least 1813.

Prinny - Nickname for the Prince Regent from 1811-1820. He served as Regent during his father's illness/madness, becoming George IV when his father, George III, died in 1820.

This nickname would not have been used in his presence, nor in print. To say this to his face (or to print it) resulted in his public disfavor and even imprisonment.

As a younger man, Prinny (George Augustus Frederick) was disapproved of by his father, George III. The king thought his son to be a bit of a wastrel, more interested in entertaining, gambling, and generally preferring flamboyance over serious concerns.

Regardless, and though thought at the time to be a profligate spender, many truly elegant and iconic features of London (and Bath, and Brighton) are due to George IV's interest in architecture and civic aggrandizement.

By the time he was 35, Prinny weighed in at 17-1/2 stones (245 lbs.) His marriage to Princess Caroline of Brunswick in 1795 was a disaster; they separated households within a year, having one female child. He was somewhat popular with the populace until his marriage fell apart; he never regained the people's esteem for long after that. George IV died in 1830. His only child, Princess Charlotte Augusta of Wales, died in childbirth at age 21, 1817. William IV (Prinny's brother) reigned from 1830-1837. (See: INTRO-REIGNS section, British Kings & Queens and their Reigns/George IV.)

printing, as in books - (See: publishers.)

printing, as in news sheets -

- See: newspapers.
- See: Times, the - For first commercial rotary printing press, 1815.

Printing House Square - East of Fleet Street. Took its name from housing the King's Printer (called the Queen's Printer while a female reigns,) having the exclusive right to print the King James Bible and the Book of Common Prayer. Home to the *Times* (since 1785, name changed from *The Daily Universal Register* to the *Times* in 1788); the *Times* stopped printing here in 1974, moving to Gray's Inn Road, and then to Wapping. This area is now completely redeveloped.

prints - As in printed pictures.

- See: art/artists.
- See: publishers.

priory - That which is under the rule of a prior, not an abbot (or abbess.)

Priory Church of St. John - St. John's Square. (See under the CHURCHES section.)

Priory Walk - Between South Kensington and Fulham. A stuccoed terrace with colorfully painted frontages, mid Victorian build.

prisons - Most 18-19th C. persons would have written "gaol" (pronounced the same as: jail) rather than "prison," although the later was in use.

Gaols/prisons were generally fortified buildings manned by well-armed warders. In London's early days, and probably due to their stout builds, often City gates (Ludgate, Newgate, etc.) were used as prisons.

The general idea was that gaols were a holding place prior to the prisoner's time in court; the concept of a prison as a place to work toward prisoner reform only grew as the 19th C. advanced. In fact, even the idea of the prison itself being a punishment (rather than just a temporary holding place) first appeared ca. 1773, with a penitentiary being the first purpose-built building for keeping prisoners for longer terms/punishment, but the penitentiary idea of imprisonment was scant in the early 19th century, let alone the concept of reforming inmates. (See: punishments - Notes at the end, for more on the purposes of imprisonment.)

Prisoners could buy privileges, such as a cell to themselves, food, beds, books, etc. (usually brought in by friends or family,) and discipline was usually set by the prisoners themselves (rather than the warders.)

Most prisons consisted of large rooms, in which the prisoners lived communally, regardless of age, gender, or the nature of their crime. The separation of genders was just beginning to be seriously called for ca. 1817, and was not all that quickly adopted as a practice.

"Bridewells" were local houses of corrections for petty offenders, run by local magistrates. Bridewell Prison (began in the 17th century) evolved into use in the 17-19th centuries as a term for imprisonment in general, such as in: "If that lad doesn't mind his ways, he'll end up in Bridewell," meaning "gaol" but not necessarily that specific one. (See: Bridewell Prison.)

In Debtor's Prison, you stayed until you paid off your debts (or were "ransomed" by friends.) *A peer of the realm (a lord) could not be placed in Debtor's Prison.* Imprisonment for debt was abolished in 1860.

Private prisons (those run by a private individual or organization rather than the State) were more likely to be seen out in the countryside, as opposed to the London gaols, which were the responsibility of the Crown.

A Quakeress named Elizabeth Fry, appalled by the conditions in which women prisoners were kept, campaigned for the 1823 Gaols Act. It led to chaplain visits, paid gaolers (who then tended less to seek bribes,) and women warders in charge of female prisoners.

In 1877, all prisons came under the aegis of the prisoner commissioners/Home Secretary, thereby centralizing the running of prisons.

- See: Bloody Code.
- See: Bow Street.
- See: Bridewell - For criminals and heretics.
- See: Brixton.
- See: Clerkenwell Green.
- See: Clink, the - For holding convicted persons of religious misdemeanors, and Nonconformists. First prison to hold women prisoners.
- See: Coldbath Fields.

- See: compters - Prisons directly under the sheriffs.
- See: debtor's prison.
- See: dueling spots.
- See: Fleet Prison - Bankrupts' and debtors' prison.
- See: gaol.
- See: Horsemonger Lane Gaol.
- See: House of Detention.
- See: justices of the peace - For outside London.
- See: King's Bench - (See: Southwark, below.)
- See: Ludgate.
- See: Marshalsea.
- See: Metropolitan Police.
- See: Millbank - Prisoners intended for Australian transport were sent here.
- See: model prison - For the new concept of reforming prisoners.
- See: Newgate - The principle prison for holding those accused of serious crimes.
- See: Pentonville/Pentonville Prison - 1840-42.
- See: poaching.
- See: police.
- See: punishments.
- See: Queen's Bench Prison.
- See: rough places.
- See: Southwark/Borough High Street/King's Bench.
- See: Tothill Fields Prison.
- See: Tower of London.
- See: Tun, the.
- See: Watch, the.

private schools - Largely equals what an American would call a public school. That is, schooling that the student does not pay for, but rather is paid for by concerned citizens*. For instance: Blewcoat School. (*In the 19th century, except for the rare occasion when a royal person decided to sponsor a charity school that interested him/her, the State did not pay for schooling/building schools.)

- See: education.
- See: public schools - For the converse.

privateer - A licensed (by the Crown) British not-quite-pirate (my words,) who was permitted (even encouraged) to prey on French and Spanish ships. Could be an ex-Navy individual. The term was for the rights granted the person, but could also be shorthand for his ship.

Privy Council - The Queen's (or King's) private council.

- See: Cabinet - Note under.
- See: Whitehall/Privy Council.

Proclamation Society - (AKA: the Society for the Reformation of Manners.) Founded ca. 1787. Its main supporter was the reformer William Wilberforce. There had been (since at least the 1690s) foundations promoting manners and public decency, and this was a new version thereof, except it aimed to reform from the top down, with "higher society" setting examples for the lower classes. Relaunched in 1802 as the Society for the Suppression of Vice; a primary aim was to suppress "low and vicious periodicals." It lasted until 1885.

prostitution - AKA: the Cyprian Game. For prostitutes some nicknames were: Cyprian; the demimonde; doxy; French girls*; nymph; pocket venus. Prostitution was not illegal during the Regency. One survey (perhaps not wholly accurate) ca. 1800 believed London hosted 50,000 prostitutes, 20,000 of which were females forced out of menial service and/or "seduced early in life." By 1862, the number had grown to 80,000. Many mistresses started as prostitutes. Some places where it was practiced/for info on:

*During the Regency era, Britain was often at war with France, so it's not surprising that many things considered to be risqué or scandalous were attached to the term "French": a French girl (a prostitute, not necessarily French at all); French kiss (a kiss that includes use of the tongue); French letter (a condom.)

- See: Asylum for Female Orphans.
- See: Berkeley Row.
- See: Covent Garden.
- See: Magdalen House - A charitable house of instruction, intended to help young women cease the trade of prostitution.
- See: Queen Street.
- See: Ratcliffe Highway.
- See: Soho.

protected London properties - Buildings, properties, and landmarks that cannot be pulled down, usually owing to historical significance. (See: National Trust.)

Protestants - As in religious groups, in England.

- See: Austin Friars - Dutch Protestants.
- See: Huguenots - French Protestants.
- See: Mill Hill - Note under, regarding a Protestant dissenters'

grammar school.

- See: St. Clement's Eastcheap, under the CHURCHES section - French Protestants.
- See: St. Etheldreda's Chapel, under the CHURCHES section.
- See: St. Mary Axe, under the CHURCHES section - Spanish Protestants.
- See: Southwark Cathedral.

pruning shears - 1815. (See: gardens.)

Public Record Office - Is the British national repository for archives. The Crown kept its public records in Wakefield Tower until 1856. (See: Tower of London/"The Towers"/Wakefield Tower.) The Public Record Office was founded in 1838, thereby establishing a way of gathering documents that were otherwise spread over many places throughout the kingdom (such as courts, churches, baptismal registers, etc.)

A new Public Record Office was built in 1896 on Chancery Lane. (See: Chancery Lane.) A new Public Record Office was built in Kew, Richmond in 2003, combining with the Historical Manuscripts Commission, forming the *National Archives*, (with the Public Record Office still existing as a legal entity, as legislation has not been changed.) Now often called by its initials, called "*the* PRO," referring to the old building that yet stands on Chancery Lane.

public schools - Largely equals what an American would call a private school. That is, a school that must be paid for by a parent or a patron. Some examples: Canterbury; Eton; King's School; Winchester.

- See: Charterhouse - There was a charity school for boys there.
- See: colleges/universities.
- See: education.

publishers - Of novels, poetry, bibles, newspapers, scandal sheets, etc. William Caxton established the first English printing press in 1476, near Westminster Abbey.

- See: Albemarle Street/50/John Murray.
- See: Barker & Howard.
- See: British & Foreign Bible Society.
- See: Fleet Street.
- See: Printing House Square - On publishing the King James Bible and the Book of Common Prayer.
- See: St. Paul's Churchyard/Paternoster Row - Longman's.
- You may care to see: booksellers/bookshops.

pubs - (A commonly used nickname for: public houses. Term was used in the 19th century.) Most were affiliated with a particular brewery, and therefore could only sell that brewery's products.

- See: inns, under I.
- See: the INNS/PUBS section - Notes under.

Pudding Lane - Purportedly where the Great Fire of 1666 began. (Near the Monument, later constructed to commemorate this fact, just north of Billingsgate.) The lane was named for offal, that is "puddinges and the other filth of Beastes," not for a kind of dessert. (You may care to see: Great Fire of 1666.)

puddings - (See: food/puddings.)

pugilism - (See: boxing.)

Pulteney's Hotel - (See: Piccadilly/105.)

Puma Court - (See: Red Lion Court.)

Punch and Judy puppets - While these long-famous puppets might yet be found at fairs and such during the Regency era, their true heyday was already past. (See: Covent Garden - The note a couple of paragraphs down.)

punishments - Throughout London's existence, and up to the 19th century, there were many ways to be punished depending on the century and the law. Warning: the following list is grisly. (And it is not all-inclusive.) Punishments over time included:

banishment - An ancient punishment, a bit different from transportation.

beheading - Considered to be "more humane" than hanging. (See: Tower of London/"Other Places & Things"/Tower Green - For important/royal beheadings.)

being boiled

branding - Sometimes on the thumb for theft.

burned at the stake - Until 1753 a woman found guilty of killing her husband could be burned at the stake. (See: strangulation, below - The note under.)

caning - Being whipped with a thin cane.

drawn and quartered - (See: drawn and quartered, under D.)

fines - Very common, up to and including the Regency era.

gibbeting - Placed inside an iron man-shaped cage, usually done after the prisoner was dead, to serve as a deterrent.

hanging - (See: hangings, under H.)

imprisonment - Keep in mind that gaol was usually used just to hold a criminal until they could be brought to court; imprisonment for its own sake/as punishment was a later concept.

mutilations - Such as an ear cut half or fully off.

outlawry - Removing the accused from the protection of the law.

pillory - Uncomfortable and meant to humiliate. Can also be called: stocks.

pressing - Under a board covered with heavy stones, abolished in 1772.

removal of a body part - Such as a hand for thievery. (See: mutilation, above.)

stocks, time in the - (See: pillory, above.)

strangulation - Sometimes was done before the fire was lit to spare the prisoner from feeling being burned at the stake.

torture - Punishment by torture was never made legal in England, although the king or his council could authorize it.

transportation - Being sent to another country, usually for 7 years' time. (See under T.)

whippings.

Many of these punishments were no longer practiced by the time of the Regency; the Regency era mostly stuck to: death, deportment, fines as their forms of punishment.

At the time of the Regency, there were some 200 crimes that could result in the death penalty. Among the 200: impersonating an army veteran, murder (dueling, although illegal, was not considered murder until the 1840s,) sodomy, stealing a sheep, stealing something from a shop worth more than five shillings, treason. Despite these things being the official law, it is important to note that (before, and into the 19th century) most convictions did not result in death, nor even in imprisonment; prison was for holding suspects until trial, or until they were put to death (once convicted,) or until they could be transported; also used for debtors. (See: prisons - For more on Debtor's Prison.) It was too expensive to build gaols/hold prisoners, so punishment was usually swift, such as a fine or being placed in the stocks. In 1808, pickpocketing ceased to be punishable by death (but rather by imprisonment or transportation); this was to encourage prosecution of pickpocketing, which was more likely if the punishment for it was not so severe.

The notion of trying for reform of prisoners did not come along until the 18-19th centuries, and was slow to be implemented. (See: prisons - Note at.)

- See: Bloody Code.
- See: cheats.
- See: hangings.
- See: hulks - Ships/floating prisons.
- See: Jack Ketch - Executioner.
- See: Old Street, Finsbury.
- See: poaching.
- See: police.

➢ See: prisons.

Putney - Wandsworth. Across the Thames from Fulham. Dates back to Domesday Book. Had a busy ferry trade until Putney Bridge came in in 1729. Was known for boating and recreation; some commerce. Gentlemen's homes from the early 19th century. Market-gardens and orchards disappeared as the 1840s advanced. Now Victorian and Edwardian homes, and many boat houses.

- Putney Bridge: Built 1727-9. The Boat Race, first held in 1829, starts from here and goes 4-1/2 miles/7.2 km to Mortlake; between the Cambridge and Oxford teams. (See under the BRIDGES section.)
- St. Mary: Parish church. Present church dates from the 15th century. 14th C. tower, restored during the church rebuild of 1836-37.

Putney Heath - Wandsworth. No more than a small village until ca. 1890. Used by 18-19th C. duelists.

- Bowling Green House: The mansion villa where William Pitt the Younger (twice a Prime Minister) died on 1/23/1806.
- Wildcroft: Home of David Hartley (scientist); he incorporated experimental fire reduction/prevention techniques.

Putney Vale - Wandsworth. A rather small locality.

- Bald Faced Stag: A 1650 public house first known as the Halfway House. Notorious highwayman Jerry Abershaw was based here ca. 1790-95 (1795 being when he was hanged.)
- Putney Vale Cemetery: 1891.

-Q-

Quadrant, The - (See: Regent's Street/Quadrant.)

Quakers - More formally called: the Society of Friends. (See under S.) The nickname "Quakers" either comes from the founder, George Fox, telling a magistrate to quake at the name of God, or from the physical shaking that purportedly accompanied religious worship.

➢ See: Bunhill Row/Friends Burial Ground.

➢ See: Jordan's Meeting House and Burial Ground.

➢ See: Mill Hill.

- See: Spanish and Portuguese Synagogue.
- See: Upton, Newham.

Quarter Days - (See: rent.)

Quarter Sessions - Held in each county, four times per year, these were court sessions to judge serious offenses. These were rather major gatherings of important county leaders, also allowing them to conduct non-judicial business. (See: justices of the peace.)

Quarterly Review - 1809, literary and political periodical, from the publishing house John Murray. (See under J.) Ceased publication in 1967.

quay - Note, this word is pronounced: key. (See: docks, for examples of quays around London. There were many.)

Quebec Street - (AKA: Old Quebec Street.) Near Portman Square, off Oxford Street. Its name derives from General Wolfe's 1759 capture of Quebec (of what would become Canada,) and this street was built around that same time.

Queen Anne Street - (See: Marylebone/Queen Anne Street.)

Queen Anne's Gate - Westminster, overlooking St. James's Park. Back of Birdcage Walk. Leads from Queen Street to Dartmouth Street. Became Queen Anne's Gate in 1874 when Park Street and Queen Square were renumbered and renamed as Queen Anne's Gate. (See: Queen Square.)

- 40-44: National Trust, the. Founded in 1895. (See: National Trust, under N.)

Queen Elizabeth Gate - 1993. Named for the Queen Mum (Elizabeth II's mother, also named Elizabeth.) Behind Apsley House, the beginning of Hyde Park proper.

Queen Mary's Terrace, remains of - (See: Ministry of Defence.)

Queen Square - Bloomsbury, off Great Ormond Street. Built in 1716-25. King George III was treated for mental illness in a home here near the end of his reign. Became Queen Anne's Gate in 1874. The statue here was mistakenly thought to be of Queen Anne, but is now thought to be of Queen Charlotte, George III's wife. (See: Queen Anne's Gate.) Many of its current buildings are yet linked to medicine, in particular neurology.

Queen Street - Brompton. Early name of Hans Road, ca. 1770, so known until ca. 1794.

Queen Street - Lincoln's Inn Fields, West End. (See: Great Queen Street.)

Queen Street - Regent's Street, off. Built ca. 1670 (after the Great Fire of 1666) to connect Guildhall with the Thames. Coach-builders had workshops here. Had French girls (prostitutes) living here; despite these "upper rooms," the Beadles kept strict rules.

Queen Victoria Street - 1860-70s. (See: New Earl Street.)

Queenhithe - (Also sometimes seen as: Queenhythe.) A shipping dock, upstream along the Thames (upriver of the other major docks, that is.) Although one of London's main harbors, it was for small boats and barges only. One of the four original City deep-water harbors.

Dates from the 9th century. So called because the custom duties collected here were all paid to the Queen.

Queen's Bench Prison - Borough High Street, Southwark. There was also a (separate) King's Bench in *Westminster* - although it should be noted that in the 16th century this separate (Queen's Bench) Southwark location was listed as King's Bench (as the monarch at the time was male.)

The prison moved in 1755-58 to a new nearby site. Burned in the Gordon Riots in 1780, but was soon rebuilt. In 1840 it was amalgamated with two other prisons at its original site and renamed Queen's Bench Prison (as a Debtor's prison; with Queen Victoria on the throne) taking in many of the Marshalsea and Fleet Prison debtors.

Imprisoning persons for debt was abolished in 1860.

Renamed Southwark Convict Prison in 1872. Demolished in 1880.

Queen's Chapel - (AKA: The Queen's Chapel at St. James's Palace.) Pall Mall. Adjoins on to Marlborough House.

- See: Pall Mall/Marlborough House.
- See: Pall Mall/Queen's Chapel.
- See: Queen's Chapel, St. James's Palace, under the CHURCHES section.
- See: St. James's Palace/Queen's Chapel.

Queen's Chapel of the Savoy - Savoy Hill, off the Strand, Westminster. The savoy was a mansion owned in the 13th century (and onward) by the earls of Richmond. The chapel was built ca. 1516 (a second source says 1505,) in the Perpendicular style. It was first a part of the Hospital of St. John. The present south front and the bell turret were rebuilt in ca. 1820 by Sir Robert Smirke. After a fire in 1864, the interior was rebuilt by Robert's brother, Sydney Smirke. PILGRIMS' LONDON states: "This" (chapel) "is associated with the queen" (Elizabeth II) "through her right to the Duchy of Lancaster and is also the Chapel of the Royal Victorian Order" (i.e., it literally belongs to the queen, not the London diocese.)

Queen's College - Founded in 1848. (See: Harley Street/43-49.)

Queen's drawing-rooms - Young ladies making their debuts into society must first meet the queen, wearing prescribed, formal dress (basically Georgian styles.) This took place at St. James's Palace. (The word "debutante" dates from 1801, but I have never seen it used in primary Regency sources.)

- See: drawing room.
- See: levee - For men/meeting the king.
- See: presentation at court.

Queen's Gallery - Buckingham Gate, Buckingham Palace Road, on Buckingham Palace grounds.

1830, by John Nash. Built first as a conservatory, it became a chapel. In 1962 it was designated by Queen Elizabeth II as an art gallery.

Queen's Gate - Kensington and Chelsea, with part of the road being in Westminster. Dates from ca. 1855, its name at that time was Prince Albert Road (or Albert's Road.) Prior to that was Brompton Park. (See under B.) The name changed to Queen's Gate in 1859. It runs south from Kensington Gardens Queen's Gate, meets Kensington Road, and goes on to Old Brompton Road.

Queen's Hall - Langham Place. 1893.

Queen's House - There have been many Queen's House(s) in London's history; if a queen lived there, this was often its informal name. (Whereas when a king lived somewhere, a house usually took on the title of "palace," so the phrase "the King's House" is far less seen in historical listings.) The following are the most famous Queen's House(s.)

Queen's House - How **Buckingham House** was called in the early part of the Regency, because Prinny's mother, the Queen, lived here, until Nash turned it into a royal residence/palace for Prinny (then George IV) in the 1820s. (See: Buckingham House.)

Queen's House - Greenwich. 1616-37, by Inigo Jones (the construction of which garnered Jones his first acclaim.) Designed for the wife of James I, Anne of Denmark; finished for the wife of Charles I, Queen Henrietta Maria. First London house built in the Palladian style. Stands, set back, between the two halves of the Royal Naval College. The two wings were added in 1809; linked to Colonnades that date from 1807. Its shape is a double cube (another source describes it as being shaped like an "H," a white double pavilion.) There is a Venetian window above the altar (the first of its kind in England.) Restored (faithfully) from 1984-90. (See: Greenwich/Queen's House.)

- National Maritime Museum: Is the Queen's House west addition, since 1937.

Queen's House - Tower Green. (See: Tower of London/"Other Places & Things"/Queen's House.)

Queen's Park - Brent/Westminster; two locales, on either side of the Bakerloo/Silverlink railway line. The northern portion is usually spelled without an apostrophe. Late 19th century.

Queen's Road - Kensington. The Regency name for Kensington Palace Gardens (street) was: Black Lion Lane. ROMANTIC LONDON states (of the later queen): "...Princess Victoria used often to drive out from Kensington Palace along what is now Queen's Road, but what was then called Black Lion Lane." (See: Queensway.)

Queen's Road - Peckham. Southwark. Was market-gardens until it began to develop in the 1840s.

Queen's Row - Former name for a portion of Brompton Road. Built ca. 1770. Had raised pavements with steps in front.

Queen's Square - (See: Queen Square - Note the lack of an "'s.")

Queen's Square Place, Westminster - Jeremy Bentham (social reformer/writer) lived on this street. Died in 1832, age of 85. William Hazlitt (essayist/philosopher, died in 1830) lived next door.

Queen's Walk - Runs along Green Park's eastern edge. 1730s. (See: Green Park/Queen's Walk.)

Queen's Wood - Haringey, abutting on Highgate Wood. Ancient woodland, originally part of the old Forest of Middlesex. 52 acres. Was once called Churchyard Bottom Wood; renamed to Queen's Wood in 1898 (named for Queen Victoria.) Is a Nature Conservancy. (See: forests - Note at.)

Queensberry House - 1720s, for the Duke and Duchess of Queensberry. Now much altered and home to the Royal Bank of Scotland, 1855. Not to be confused with modern flats of the same name near Richmond Green.

- See: Uxbridge House.
- You may care to see: boxing - For the 1867 reference to the Marquess of Queensberry of boxing fame.

Queensbury - Harrow/Brent. A suburban development that grew between WWI and WWII.

Queenstown Road - Wandsworth. Largely dates from the 1860s.

Queensway - Westminster. Formerly was: Black Lion Lane, running from Kensington to Westbourne Green. (Black Lion Gate remains at Kensington Gardens' northwest corner.) Once Victoria had her coronation (1838,) it was renamed: Queen's Road. Changed to "Queensway" a hundred years after that (because there were too many Queen's Roads.)

quill - (AKA: quill pen.) The writing implement used during the Regency era. Literally a quill, a molted flight feather from a bird. The best feathers came from geese, swans, or turkeys. The quills were cured first, so the point one cut into the end would last longer. A quill had to be repeatedly dipped into the ink source, having no reservoir for ink (beyond the little that might cling in the feather's hollow shaft.) Gentlemen might carry a pen knife, for (repeatedly) sharpening/trimming one's quill to a new point (making an oval hole, called the nib.) Steel pens came along with the 1827 invention of the fountain pen, in France, by a Romanian inventor named Petrache Poenaru.

- See: ink.
- See: paper.
- See: pencil.

quilt - The term "quilt" is seen in England by at least 1373. Quilting was considered a normal part of an Englishwoman's sewing skills; but before 1700 quilting wasn't about piecing different fabrics together, but more about using stitches to outline or accentuate crewel work. You'd have two whole pieces of fabric with batting between, and the stitching made patterns (and created "pockets" that helped hold in body heat); these patterns could be elaborate.

Mosaic quilts (pieces of disparate fabrics,) and appliquéd quilts came along in the 18-19th centuries. The mosaic was often the same repeating pattern, such as a diamond, often with many pieces. The appliqué was done by cutting pattern motifs out of chintz (which came from India, and was expensive,) the motif pieces then being stitched onto less expensive English cloths; these were considered "best" and kept for special guests or occasions. Quilts would have been far less common than counterpanes (what Americans call bedspreads,) because a quilt's creation was "useless leisure-time activity," and only the ladies of great houses had anywhere near that amount of leisure time.

Regency ladies would not have called their quilt either a patchwork quilt, nor a crazy quilt.

(You may care to see: blankets.)

Quit Rent - Yearly ceremony. (See: Royal Courts of Justice - Note at.)

-R-

races -

- See: activities/entertainment/sports, under A - Various listings.
- See: Ascot - Horse race, inaugurated in 1711 by Queen Anne.
- See: Brighton, under the BRITISH COUNTIES section.
- See: Epsom - The Derby was first run here in May/1780; is now held in June.
- See: Grand National - 1837.
- See: Lewes.
- See: Newmarket.

rag and bone man - One who gathered clothes too ragged to be remade, and bones. The former was used to make paper, the latter was burned and sold as ashes.

Rag Fair - Houndsditch. In a triangular area bounded by Houndsditch, Leadenhall Street, and St. Mary Axe. This area had old clothes sold here since the early 16th century, but by the 17th century it had evolved into a definite Sunday market with stalls for old or second-hand clothes and textiles. Was a place unlikely to be frequented by "genteel folk"; was in fact a necessary industry to provide clothing for those of the lower echelons. In the 19th C. there was a fair amount of pickpockets/assaults here. All evidence indicates this fair disappeared in the later 19th century.

It should be noted, anyplace that set up the trade of used/old clothes might be called a rag fair. There was more than one in London (and in other English towns,) but most people mean this one when they speak of Rag Fair.

railways - The earliest railway in London was built in 1836. Ran to Greenwich. The London to Deptford Railway opened in 12/14/1837, mounted on a twin-track viaduct; a 14 minute trip.

The first *railway station* was opened in 1841 at Fenchurch Street, terminus for the London-to-Blackwall run.

Much of the UK was truly revolutionized/urbanized by the arrival of the rails. Nationalized in 1948 as British Railways; changed to British Rail in 1965.

Rainham - Havering. Evidence of ancient residents here, even before the Saxons. Had a medieval wharf, which was improved in the late 1710s. Market gardens.

- Rainham Hall: Ca. 1728. Now a National Trust property.
- Rainham Marshes: Middle Ages monks of Lesnes Abbey grazed sheep here.
    - Three Crowns Inn: Purportedly first here as early as 1550. Rebuilt in the early 19th century. Mostly pulled down in the 1970s.
    - St. Helen and St. Giles Church: Ca. 1179. Remains, largely unchanged. (See under the CHURCHES section.)

Randolph Crescent - Westminster (in what has been known since the mid 20th C. as Little Venice.) 1875.

Ranelagh Gardens - (AKA: Ranelagh Pleasure Gardens.) Opened in 1742. Did a good job of "keeping out persons not of the privileged class," right up to the time of the Napoleonic wars. Closed in 1805 for lack of funds. (A second source said the concerts ended in 1803.) When it opened, it cost half a crown (2 shillings, 6 pence) as an entry fee, which included coffee and punch. Some of its pleasures were: dancing, promenading, refreshments, tableaux - and, perhaps most famously, discreet corners for wooing. The gardens were rebuilt in 1860. Is now the site of the annual Chelsea Flower Show, which dates from 1913; its grounds survive as the gardens to Chelsea Royal Hospital.

> ➢ See: Chelsea/Ranelagh Gardens.
> ➢ See: Royal Hospital/Chelsea.

- Rotunda, the: The orchestra was at the center, with tiered boxes around. Described (perhaps hyperbolically) as having hundreds of lamps. Had "handsome, painted boxes" (for the taking of refreshments.)

Ranger's Lodge - (See: Hyde Park/Ranger's Lodge.)

Ratcliffe Highway - (Also sometimes seen spelled as Ratcliff.) Came into being during Tudor times. The area once known as Ratcliffe has been swallowed up into Limehouse now; now known as the Highway. (See: St. George's Street.)

Long known as a rough place, with occasional throat-cuttings. Hosted petty thieves, prostitutes, slip-shops, taverns, and sailors come ashore. There were some famous murders here in 1811, two whole households were slain. (See: Old Gravel Lane.)

- 29 Ratcliffe Highway: In 1811, was a hosiery owned by one Mr. Marr. (Mr. Marr lived somewhere on this street. He, his wife, his baby, and his 13-year-old apprentice were murdered in the shop in 1811 (their heads battered and their throats cut,) apparently following a robbery.
- 30 Ratcliffe Highway: Bow-window frontage.

Rathbone Place - Leads from Oxford Street to Charlotte Street, in what used to be St. Pancras, but is now Marylebone. Dates from ca. 1718; was originally called Glanville Street, then Upper Rathbone Place (until approximately 1900,) then Rathbone Street. Is now mostly offices and retail spaces.

- 12: William Hazlitt (critic/essayist) lived here from 1802-05.
- 34: Temple of Fancy. Stationers/booksellers. Also sold toys.
- 50: John Constable (painter) lived here ca. 1802-05.
- Heal and Son: Bedding shop established in 1810 by John Harris Heal. There until 1840, when it moved (as Heal and Son) to its present site in Tottenham Court Road.
- Red Lion Square: North of Lincoln's Inn. Built 1698. A place for executions and duels.
    - 23: Jonas Hanway lived here. By the time he died in 1786 his introduction of the umbrella had been accepted by other Londoners.

Rawstorne Street - (See: Montpelier Place.)

Raymer's Lane - Harrow. Here since medieval times (with its early name being Bourne Lane.) Small holders worked local farmland here in the early 19th century.

Raynes Park - Merton. 1867. (See: West Barnes.)

Reading Room, the - (See: Bloomsbury Square/British Museum/Reading Room.)

Rector - (See: Church of England/Rector.)

red coats - The famous British red coats (uniforms) came into being first ca. 1704-14.

- See: Royal Guards.
- You may care to see: military uniforms.

There is also the red coat that foxhunters wear, called: pink, or hunting pink. (See: Mason's Yard/Maxwell, Henry.)

Red Lion Court - Off Commercial Street. Dates from the 17th century. Highwayman Dick Turpin accidentally killed Tom King (a comrade in thievery) here in the 18th century. The court is described as wide. Is now known as Puma Court, which name it took on in the Georgian era.

Red Lion Square - South of Theobald's Road. Built 1698. (See: Upper Rathbone Place/Red Lion Square.)

- Church of St. John: 1874-8.

Red Lion Street - (See: Britton Street.)

Redbridge - In north Ilford. (Historically Ilford was called Great Ilford, to distinguish it from Little Ilford, which was in the nearby borough of Newham.) It is mostly in the borough of Redbridge, but part is also in Newham. In the 16th C. there was a crossing here known as Hockley's Bridge. In 1642 a red brick bridge took its place, standing for two centuries, and giving the area its name; which was replaced by an iron bridge. In the early 19th century Redbridge was rural.

Redcliffe Gardens, and **Redcliffe Square** - Chelsea. Houses, 1869-72. Redcliffe Gardens, a significant road, runs northwest to southeast, through Redcliffe Square.

Reform Club, the - 1834. (See under the CLUBS section.)

regattas - Boat races; term was in use during Georgian/Regency times.

Reformed Baptists - (See: Baptists.)

Regent Park - (See: Regent's Park.)

Regent Street - (Infrequently seen written as: Regent's Street.) Westminster. Conceived "Royal Mile" by John Nash, to connect Carlton House (which never did end up being made over into a palace) to Regent's Park, taking up what had previously mostly been Swallow Street. Runs from the Athenaeum, Pall Mall, to north of Oxford Circus. Ends at All Souls Church, Langham Place.

Some 700 shops were pulled down to form the new street. Built between 1817-1823. (A second source says it was commenced in 1814, and built between 1816-20. Yet another says the street was commenced in 1812. A fourth source says 1813-23.)

The new Regent Street followed the old course of Swallow Street, from Piccadilly to Portland Place.

In the late 1820s George IV decided against the planned palace here (Carlton House,) going to Buckingham House (later Palace) instead. This resulted in Regent Street ending not at a palace but a flight of stairs only (which led down into St. James's Park); the Duke of York's Column went here in 1835.

- See: Duke of York Column.
- See: Duke of York Steps.

The east side of the street was favored for shopping; was described as "new and extremely fashionable" in 1822. White-stucco or stone frontages. Beadles were on duty until the shops closed at eight at night; bell rung at closing time, and the gates locked. (See: Beadles - For a description of such.)

Over a hundred years later, George V had the street made over into New Regency Street, 1927.

Rebuilt twice between 1905-1930, being at this time "seriously altered" away from Nash's Quadrant design, by Norman Shaw in 1905-8, and Sir Reginald Blomfield, in 1920-30.

- 5, 7 & 9: In 1820, was the new shop for Harding & Howell (who had split off from Schomberg House.) Drapers. Became highly fashionable. (See: Pall Mall/Schomberg House.)
- 14-16: A princely townhouse was built here by John Nash, 1819, for himself and a male relative.
- 68: Café Royal: Opened in 1865.
- 112: Garrard. Jewelry. (See under G.)
- 188-196: Hamley's. Was established as a toy store in 1760. Still here. (See: Noah's Ark.)
- 191: Rudolf Ackermann. He was the son of the senior Rudolf Ackermann. (See: Strand/96, under S, for the former.) Was one of the first lessees on Regent Street, opening a print shop independent of his father's, 1826.
- 214-220: Liberty. 1875. (Named for the proprietor, Arthur Liberty.) Oriental fabrics, ornaments, and crafted goods. Is a mock-Tudor building.
- 246: Argyle Rooms: Also seen spelled as: Argyll Rooms. (See under A, spelled as: Argyle.)
- All Souls Church: Survives from Nash's original lay out of the street. (See: All Souls, under the CHURCHES section.)
- Argyll Rooms: 246 Regent Street. (See under A, at the spelling: Argyle.)
- Café Royal: 1865.
- Carlton House: (See under C.)
- County Fire Office: (See: Lower Regent Street/County Fire Office, below.)
- Hamley's Toys: (See: 188-196, above.)
- Liberty's: (See: 214-220, above.)
- Lower Regent Street: West End shopping. Built under John Nash and Burton, completed 1825.
    - County Fire Office, the: 1819-20. Its design was influenced by Somerset House. (See: County Fire Office, under C.)

- Piccadilly Circus: (See under P.)
- Polytechnic, the: 1838, at the north end of Regent Street. Later called Regent Street Polytechnic, the nucleus of the University of Westminster.
- Regent's Circus North: (See: Oxford Circus.)
- Regent's Circus North: (See: Piccadilly Cicrus.)
- Quadrant, The: (Reminiscent of the semi-circle circus in Bath, because it was designed by the same man); Nash, 1819-20.

  On 7/15/1816, due to a lack of finances (the Napoleonic Wars had drained the country's coffers) an order was issued to stop the building of Regent Street north of Piccadilly Circus to Carlton House; the Quadrant was finally completed in 1820. Five stories high, faced with stucco. Nash's colonnade (270 feet long) was made up of cast-iron columns that were 16 feet, 2 inches tall, forming a covered promenade. Nash's colonnade was removed in 1848, and the whole Quadrant was seriously altered in 1905, leaving no signs of Nash's work. (See: Air Street.)
- Thomas Reid: Opened a bakery on the west side of this street in 1823.
- Verrey's restaurant: Established here in 1826.

Regent Street Quadrant - (See: Regent Street/Quadrant.)

Regent's Canal - (Its proper name is: the North Metropolitan Canal, but that title is seldom if ever used.) Built from 1812 to its opening in 1820. Links with the Grand Junction Canal at Paddington (the industrial center of the Midlands) and with the Thames at Regent's Canal Dock at Limehouse. Twelve locks, forty bridges. The Canal provided relief for the roads, which had before then been the only source for moving heavy products through London.

Regent's Circus North - Name of Oxford Circus until the 1890s.

- See: Oxford Circus.
- See: Piccadilly Circus.

Regent's Circus South - Name of Piccadilly Circus until 1880.

- See: Oxford Circus.
- See: Piccadilly Circus.

Regent's Park - (Official name: The Regent's Park.) Westminster/Camden. Was formerly Marylebone Park, a royal hunting ground leased to the dukes of Portland. Full of lakes, open spots, and promenades. (See: ***THE PARK***, below.)

***

(***THE HOMES/THE TERRACES***:) Cream-colored terraced houses, palace-like. Built on three sides of the park. Built between 1811-38. Eight of the 56 villas Nash imagined ended up being built.

On the east side of the park resided Cambridge, Chester, and Cumberland Terraces. On the west: Cornwall, Hanover, and Sussex Place Terraces (although Sussex Place was not called "Terrace," just "Sussex Place.")

- Cambridge Terrace: On the southeast side of Regent's Park. Built in 1825, designed by John Nash. Described as a "short line of houses."
- Chester Terrace: The terrace is 325 yards long, a long row of Corinthian columns. (See: Park Crescent/Chester Terrace.)
- Cornwall Terrace: Built 1820-1. (See: Park Crescent/Cornwall Terrace.)
- Cumberland Terrace: Designed by John Nash, 1827-8 (a second source said building began in 1825; a third said 1826.) 276 yard long facade with Ionic columns. Rather palatial in its appearance. (See: Park Crescent/Cumberland Terrace.)
- Gloucester Terrace: (See under G.)
- Hanover Terrace: (See: Park Crescent/Hanover Terrace.)
- Sussex Place: (See: Park Crescent/Sussex Place.)

Many of the seven above are also listed under "The Park," below.

***

(***THE PARK***:) Was first monastic lands, then a hunting ground for Henry VIII. Subsequently leased to the dukes of Portland. Had been Marylebone Park, until the Portland lease ended and the land reverted to the crown in 1811, when Nash said it should be made into a regent's park. 500 acres. Enclosed in 1812. Nash's assistants were Decimus Burton and James Burton. Work continued from 1812-27. 410 acres.

Open to the public in 1838. Prior to this time only a privileged few were granted tickets of admission, these being issued by the Royal Household.

The following listings are in/near Regent's Park:

- Abbey Lodge: (See: Abbey Lodge, under A, the first listing.)
- Aquarium, the: (See: Zoological Gardens/1853, below.)
- Broad Walk, the: Lined with chestnut trees.
- Colosseum: Southeast corner of the park. Opened in 1826. A huge rotunda designed by Decimus Burton, opened as an entertainment center. Circular building with a massive portico. Used for exhibitions and panoramas. Pulled down in 1875.
- Doric Villa: (See under D.)
- Gates (of Regent's Park,) the:
    - Gloucester Gate: The east gate. (See, below.)
    - Hanover Gate: The West gate. (See: Abbey Lodge, under A, the *Hanover*

Gate one.)

- Macclesfield Bridge: The north gate.
- York Gate: The south gate. (See under Y.)

- Gloucester Gate: The eastern gate/entrance of Regent's Park. 1826. (See under G.)
- Gloucester Terrace: Built mostly between 1843-52, builder was William Kingdom. (See under G.)
- Hanover Gate: Northwest side of the park, 1825, by John Nash (architect.) Baroque octagon. (See under H.)
- Holme, The: (Also known simply as: Holme.) James Burton's residence, built by him and designed by his son, Decimus, in 1818-19. James lived here until 1834. Stucco villa.
- Inner Circle: Mrs. Fitzherbert (mistress of Prinny) had a residence here. The Inner Circle contains Queen Mary's Garden, and its roses, the garden and roses dating from 1932. 1 km long. (See: St. John's Lodge, below.)
- Kent Terrace: It is considered part of the Regent's Park development by Nash, but it faces toward Park Road, away from the park. (See under K.)
- Lake, The: (AKA: the Boating lake.) In the western part of the park. The lake's depth was reduced to only four feet in 1867, as a response to its ice breaking, 1/15/1867, and 40 (out of the 200 who were plunged) died here.
- Liberty's Department Store: 1924.
- London Zoo: (See: Zoological Society, below.)
- Macclesfield Bridge: (See under the BRIDGES section.)
- North Villa: On the east side of the park. Built in 1827 for one Thomas Lennard, by Charles Robert Cockerell and Decimus Burton. At first called Albany Cottage, even though it was hardly cottage-sized; the name changed to North Villa in the mid 1830s.
- Outer Circle: Carriage drive, 2-3/4 miles/4.4 km around. Now a road. It encloses the Inner Circle, and largely encompasses the park's borders. It is lined by a "spectacular" row of Georgian houses (now in large part offices.)
- Park Crescent: (See under P.)
- Park Square East: 1823-5, grand, Ionic. (See: Park Square, under P.)
- Park Square West: Also 1823-5, grand, Ionic. (See: Park Square, under P.)
- Primrose Hill: North side of the park. 60 (or 62) acres, rises to 203 (or 206) feet in height. Probably got its name in the 15th C. from an abundance of the primrose flower growing here. Obtained for public use in 1853 (a second source

said 1841) from Eton College. Used by duelists well into the 19th C., because its summit was at least one mile/1.6 km clear of any housing. Hosts clusters of chestnut and plane trees. Great locale from which to look down over London.

- Queen Mary's Gardens: 1930s.
- St. Andrew's Place: (See under S.)
- St. Dunstan's Lodge: (See under S.)
- St. John's Lodge: On the southwest side of the park, on the Inner Circle. Villa; the second in Regent's Park to be occupied. Built in 1817-18 for Charles Augustus Tulk (magistrate/opponent of capital punishment,) by the architect John Raffield. Tulk moved out in 1821; empty until 1826 when John Maberly (MP/businessman) moved in.
- St. Katherine's Hospital: Moved to Regent's Park in 1825. (See under S.)
- Sussex Place: One of the original Nash terraces, built 1822. Corinthian columns and domed towers. Built to showcase Regent's Park. (See: Park Crescent/Sussex Place.)
- Winfield House:
    - ➢ See: St. Dunstan's Lodge.
    - ➢ See: Winfield House, under W.
- York Terrace: John Nash, 1822.
    - ➢ See: Park Crescent/York Terrace.
    - ➢ See: York Terrace, under Y.
- Zoological Society: (AKA: London Zoo. AKA: the Zoological Society of London. Its official name is: the Gardens of the Zoological Society of London.) Housed in the Zoological Gardens, in Regent's Park. Founded in 1826, laid out by Decimus Burton, and opened in 1828, incorporated in 1829 by Royal Charter. 36 acres.

  In 1834 William IV gave the animals from the Tower's Royal Menagerie (plus those at Windsor Great Park) to the London Zoo/Zoological Society.

  Open to the *public* for the first time in 1847.

  Still here.

    - o 1835: First chimpanzee.
    - o 1836: Four giraffes.
    - o 1840: A lioness, who promptly tripped and died, leaving her mate behind to pine.
    - o 1843: Opened the first Reptile House in the world.
    - o 1853: Aquarium. The world's first public aquarium. Not to be confused with the Royal Aquarium, on Tothill Street, Westminster. (See: Royal

Aquarium, for the latter.)

- 1913: The Mappin Terraces were added (these being a kind of "natural terrain" in which to house the animals, as opposed to cages.) Also described as a reinforced concrete amphitheater where the bears and other animals roam free of bars.
- 1934: The penguin enclosure opened.
- 1962-5: The elephant and rhinoceros houses were added.
- 1967: Giant aviary (designed by Princess Margaret's then-husband, Lord Snowden.)
- 1976: The Lion Terraces were built.

Regent's Park College - 1853. A Baptist school for training ministers. (See: Holford House.)

Regent's Park Zoo - Officially is the: Gardens of the Zoological Society of London. More familiarly called: the London Zoo. (See: Regent's Park/Zoological Society.)

Regent's Street - (See: Regent Street.)

relation vs. relative - During the Regency era, English persons were far more likely to speak of one's relations, rather than relatives. (Example: "Has she no relations with which she might reside?")

religion - The official church in England was/is the Church of England (the Anglicans.) During the Regency era, dissenting from the official church was a "stopper" for many ambitions, such as in the fields of politics, schooling, etc. Being of a dissenting faith was often a societal setback.

- See: Bunhill Fields.
- See: Catholics.
- See: Church of England.
- See: Clapham Sect, the.
- See: dissenters.
- See: Dissolution.
- See: Jews - Several references under J.
- See: Methodists.
- See: mosque.
- See: Presbyterians.
- See: Protestants.
- See: Quakers.
- See: Sikhs - 20th century.
- See: synagogues.

- See the entire CHURCHES section.

rent - As in paying rent. From medieval times, four holy days were handy ways of marking the deadline for the "paying of the rents" (as well as hiring servants, the start of school terms, and other regulated tasks.) Those quarterly dates being:

- *Lady Day* - March 25th.
- *Midsummer* - June 24th.
- *Michaelmas* - September 29th.
- *Christmas* - December 25th.

  - You may care to see: house, a - For an expectation of how much rent might be.
  - You may care to see: Royal Courts of Justice - For the note on the yearly Quit Rent event.
  - You may care to see: year, beginning of.

restaurant - A term not much used in the Regency (it is more Victorian/ Edwardian.) During the Regency most dining took place at home, at friends' homes, or in pubs or inns. Going back some 500-600 years, a restaurant-like place might be referred to as an "eating house." In the Regency, people would have called it a chophouse. Too, keep in mind places that prepared food for sale did not have menus; you either brought your own cut of meat to be cooked, or you ate what the chef prepared.

- See: chophouse.
- See: cookshops.
- See: Claridge's.
- See: inns, under I - For more information on how inns served their communities in a traveler's-restaurant-sort-of-way.
- See: the INNS/PUBS section - The notes at the start of.
- See: Rule's.

resurrectionists - A name for those who illegally dug up the recently deceased, selling the bodies for medical study.

- See: body-snatching.
- See: hospitals - For further notes on dissection.
- See: St. Sepulchre, under the CHURCHES section - For a legal method of acquiring bodies for medical study.

Richmond - (AKA: the London borough of Richmond-upon-Thames.) Surrey. In Edward III's time this area held the palace of Shene; rebuilt after a 1499 fire, then becoming Henry VII's favorite palace and renamed after his earldom in Richmond; that is, the palace was then named Richmond Palace, and its attendant village called Richmond-upon-Thames. From early on, in common parlance, the area was often referred to simple as Richmond. The rich often vacated to here during times of plague. 18th C. houses still survive here. Narrow streets. Queen Victoria was the monarch who opened the palace to the public. (See: Richmond Park.)

- Ham House: Built on the Thames (across from Twickenham,) 1610. Home of the Earls of Dysart. Now restored to its 17th century form, and administered by the Victoria and Albert Museum. (See: Ham House, under H.)
- Hampton Court: (See: Hampton Court Palace, under H.)
- Maids of Honour Row: Street built in 1724; a terrace of four red brick houses, built for the attendants of the future George II's wife, Caroline. Still there. (See: Richmond Green/Maids of Honour Row, at its own listing.)
- Marble Hill House: 18th C., Palladian. Still there. Beautifully landscaped grounds. (See: Marble Hill House, under M.)
- Ormond Road: Until at least 1841 was known as Ormond Row; name had changed to Ormond Road no later than 1942. Hosts a terrace of 18th C. houses.
- Richmond Green: (See at its own listing.)
- Richmond Lock: 1894.
- Richmond Lodge: (See at its own listing.)
- Richmond Theatre: 1899. In EYEWITNESS TRAVEL GUIDES: LONDON, it states: "Edmund Kean was closely associated with the previous theatre on this spot…"; the name then was: the Theatre Royal and Opera House. Not to be confused with London theatres of similar names. (See: Theatre Royal, under the THEATRES section, for a note on how often this title is applied to various theatres.) Refurbished in 1991.
- Richmond Town Hall: 1893.
- Roebuck, the: 130 Richmond Hill. A 1738 pub. Still there. (See under the INNS/PUBS section.)
- St. Mary Magdalen: Richmond parish church. At the back of the opposite side of George Street. Rebuilt in the 18th C., except the stone tower.
- Sandycombe Lodge: (See under S.)
- Three Pigeons, the: 87 Petersham Street. A 1735 pub. Still there.

Richmond Gate - Designed by Capability Brown in 1798. Located in the northwest corner of Richmond Park.

Richmond Green - Twenty acres; called "enormous" (as city greens go.) 18th C. homes still here.

- Asgill House: Ca. 1765, by Sir Robert Taylor. Off the northwest corner of Richmond Green. Described as a "jewel of a villa."

- Maids of Honour Row: (Sometimes seen as: Maid of Honour Row.) Built in George I's time. Aristocratic locale. Home of the Maid of Honour cheese-cakes, supposedly invented by a Lady-in-Waiting. (See: Richmond/Maids of Honour Row.)
- Wick House: (See under W.)

Richmond Hill - Richmond, Surrey. In the 16-17th centuries, it hosted idyllic country mansions for the wealthy. In the late 18-19th centuries, because of its views, grand houses climbed the hill, tastefully spaced; among them: Ancaster House (1873,) Downe House (1780,) and Wick House (for Sir Joshua Reynolds, in 1772.) Richmond Hill, now: "suburban sprawl," more or less attached to London.

  - See: Ancaster House.
  - See: Downe House.
  - See: Wick House.

- 130 Richmond Hill: The Roebuck. A 1738 pub. Still there.
- The Star and Garter Hotel: A house-hotel, added to in 1780 and 1808. The owner failed at his trade however, ending by dying in debtor's prison. New management of the hotel came in ca. 1810, with exorbitant prices that only served to keep visitors away. Rebuilt in 1864, it burned in 1870. It became fashionable again, however, in the 1870-80s. Closed prior to 1914. Demolished 1919. In 1924 the Star and Garter Home for Disabled Soldiers and Sailors was built here.

Richmond House - (See: Richmond Terrace.)

Richmond Lodge - In the Kew Gardens park, north of Richmond Palace. Was formerly known as the Keeper's Lodge (at least prior to 1762. Also had been known as Ormonde Lodge.) Prinny lived here as a child, until 1771, when the family moved to the White House at Kew. Pulled down. (See: Kew Gardens/Richmond Lodge.)

Richmond Palace - (See: Richmond Park.)

Richmond Park - Richmond, Surrey. In the 12th C., this area was originally called Sheen (or Shene) Chase. When it burned in 1499, Henry VII replanted and named it for his earldom in Yorkshire (Richmond); Richmond Palace was built here in 1500.

Henry VIII put an 8 mile/13 km walk around the park.

Elizabeth I died at the palace here, 3/24/1603.

Enclosed with brick walls for hunting grounds in 1637 by Charles I. This was an unpopular move, even though locals continued to be allowed to walk and gather firewood here (a right that yet exists.)

The palace was demolished under Cromwell. In 1649 the park was granted to the

City, but returned to the Crown following the Restoration.

Charles II reopened the park to the public, although it appears it wasn't permanently left open until Edward VII's time in 1904.

It is the largest and wildest city park in London (and in Europe; "unimproved" and unenclosed.) Has long walks. Today there only remains Henry VII's gate (with his arms) and the now restored buildings of the Wardrobe. (See: Royal Wardrobe.)

From 1819 onward the woods here hosted beech, chestnuts, elm, hornbeam, larch, lime, and sycamore trees, and there are still hundreds of ancient oaks. Red deer and fallow deer live here yet. There remain 18th C. homes around Richmond Green. Borders right on Wimbledon Common, and Putney Heath.

Petersham Common, Meadow, and Park are all extensions of Richmond Park. (See: Petersham.)

- Mortlake: (See under M.)
- Pen Ponds: 18 acres. Fish. Waterfowl. Formed in the time of George II.
- Royal College of Physicians: Near Warwick Lane. Institution granted in 1518 by Henry VIII. Present building (now much modified) dates from 1827, by Sir Robert Smirke. Modified in 1964 by Sir Denys Lasdun. The building in Warwick Lane remains, but the college has since moved to Regent's Park. (See: Royal College of Physicians, at its own listing.)
- White Lodge, the: Built in 1727 in the Palladian style, as a royal hunting lodge for George II. His daughter, Princess Amelia, came here in 1751. Once home to Queen Mary; is where the future Edward VIII was born (1894.) Since 1955 has housed the Royal Ballet School; a second source said since 1926.

Richmond Road - (See: Twickenham/Richmond Road.)

Richmond Terrace - 1825, by architect Thomas Chawner. Had been a terrace of eight houses, built over the burned (in 1791) Richmond House. Now offices.

Richmond-upon-Thames - (See: Richmond.)

Riding House Street - Westminster. Connects the top of Regent Street with Great Portland Street. Was originally Riding House Lane. Derived its name from a barracks and riding house (a riding academy) of the First Troop of Horse Grenadier Guards, nearby from 1726-88.

Riddlesdown - Croydon. May date back to the 7th C.; first mentioned in writing in 1277. Chalky soil. In the late 18th C. there was a lime quarry here, stood for some 200 years. In 1883 the Corporation of London acquired most of Riddlesdown, preserving it as open space.

Ridgeway's Bookshop - Piccadilly. Patronized by the poet Lord Byron. (See: Piccadilly/Ridgeway's Bookshop.)

Ring, The - 1910.

- See: Blackfriars Road/Ring.
- See: Surrey Chapel, under the CHURCHES section.

Rippleside Road - Between Barking and Dagenham. "Ripple," from the Old English, meant a strip of land. There was a Ripple Street here from the 16th century. The name changed to Ripple Side. In the current day it is now Ripple Road, which it was called from at least 1922.

- Eastbury Manor House: Tudor-style brick mansion, reportedly built in 1572. Three sides of a quadrangle, which includes (from THE FACE OF LONDON): "...an octagonal tower and a tall stack of weirdly-decorated chimneys..." Now a museum.

Ritz Hotel - Piccadilly. 1906.

River Fleet, the - Flowed from the Thames at Blackfriars, through Holborn and St. Pancras, and to Parliament Hill on Hampstead Heath. Has been culverted over, and so can no longer be viewed, but yet flows under Farringdon Road. (See: Fleet River, under F.)

river races -

- See: activities/entertainment/sports, various "boating" listings, under A.
- See: Doggett's Coat and Badge race - On the Thames.

rivers (and brooks) of London - Most were eventually covered over, due to either pollution or local building; although they can't be seen, many yet flow underground.

- Black Ditch, the: This was ever its name. It rose in Whitechapel. Now covered over.
- Brent, the:
  - See: Brentford.
  - See: canals - Notes under.
  - Wilsdon/Welsh Harp.
- Counter's Creek: It rose near Kensal Green cemetery.
- Effra, the: Came from Norwood in South London. Now largely unseen.
- Fleet, the: "Fleet" is Anglo-Saxon for estuary.
  - See: Fleet River.
  - See: River Fleet, the.
- Hackney Brook: In east London, also the north border of Abney Park cemetery.
- Lea, the: (Also seen sometimes as: Lee.) Starts in the Chiltern Hills, down to east London, meeting the Thames. One of the larger rivers in the London area. (See: canals, notes under.)

- New River: (See: Islington/New River Canal.)
- Stamford Brook: Rises at Wormwood Scrubs, East Acton. Goes into the Thames at Hammersmith.
- Thames, the: London's most important river. (See under T.)
- Tyburn, the: (See: Tyburn River, under T.)
- Walbrook, the - (See under W.)
- Wandle, the: (See: Carshalton/Wandle.)
- Westbourne, the: Came from Hampstead. In the 18-19th centuries it flowed through desolate fields and swamps. Now covered over, and known as the Ranelagh Sewer. (See: Westbourne, under W.)

Riverside - On the north side of the Thames, East London. Part of the 21st century development called Thames Gateway, 2004-2013. Runs from Beckton in Newham, to Wennington in Havering.

robe-makers - (See: Ede & Ravencroft.)

Robert Street - (See: Adelphi/Robert Street.)

Roe Green - Brent. Corruption of "Row Green" ("wro" means a nook or corner.) A moderate size hamlet grew up here in the 18-19th centuries.

- Kingbury Manor: Roe Green Park. 1899.

Roehampton - Wandsworth. Was known in the 14th C. as East Hampton, then Rokehampton. Throughout the 19th C. "handsome" villas could be found in the vales and hills.

- Roehampton House: Roehampton Lane. Built in 1710-12, by Thomas Archer, for Thomas Cary (import/export merchant.) North and south wings were added in 1910-13. Queen Mary's Hospital (founded in 1915) was here from 1915-83.

rollerskates - First demonstrated in 1760 at a Soho Square masquerade party; demonstrated by a clockmaker/instrument maker, John Joseph Merlin. They were boots with wheels fitted on. However, rollerskates remained rare well into the 19th century.

Roman Bath - Discovered near Somerset House, at what is now designated as 162A Strand Lane. Not Roman, it's actually a 17th C. cistern that had been used to supply the fountains in Somerset House gardens. Fifteen foot long tub, with a natural spring. Rediscovered in the 1830s, at which time it was falsely dubbed Roman. (See: Strand Lane/162A.)

Roman Doric Column - (See: Monument, the.)

Roman Road - Tower Hamlets. So called because of some evidence of Romans here in ancient times, although it probably was a little used path. Starting in 1790 it was called Green Street (before that, part of it was called Driftway.) A market here in 1843. The present name dates from the mid 19th C., a marketing ploy. Widened in the mid 1870s. Surroundings rebuilt in the mid 20th C., the market moving off-road in 1959 (although stall owners were reluctant to move, with many lingering on Roman Road.)

Romford - Havering. Ancient cattle and corn market-town, first recorded in the 12th century. Market charter dates back to 1250, held on Whitsun (medieval, seventh Sunday after Easter.) In the 15th C. the market here was known for selling leather goods (made at nearby Hornchurch; particularly known for its leather breeches.) By the 17th C. it was a quite large agricultural market, including livestock and tools. It was also a coaching halt on the London-to-Colchester road, so had many inns. Breweries began to spring up here ca. 1800. In modern terms, has been known as a shopping center since the 1920s.

- Raphael Park: 1904.
- St. Edward the Confessor: Parish Church, on this site since 1410. Built anew in 1849.

Romney House - 1797. (See: Hampstead/Romney House.)

rookeries - Term for seedy areas, such as east of Charing Cross or in St. Giles. Foul alleys. Havens for criminals. The poorest of the poor lived in the rookeries, as did "every kind of misfit and villain." St. Giles was so notorious, even the Watch (police) seldom ventured there. (Of course, rookery is also the word for a place where crows nest.)

- ➢ See: rough places.
- ➢ See: St. Giles.

Rookery, the (hotel) - (See: Cowcross Street/Peter's Lane.)

Rookery, the (park) - Streatham, 1913.

rose - The national flower of England. (You may care to see: flowers.)

Rose Street - Given its name to conjure thoughts of England (the Rose being the national flower of England.) Built in 1770-81, "not grand" (but more than serviceable.) By 1820 its ground floors were becoming a shopping venue. Street changed drastically in a 1972 standardized rebuild. Open to pedestrians only from the 1980s.

- 33: Lamb and Flag. Pub. (See: Lamb and Flag, under the INNS/PUBS section.)

Rosebery Avenue - Camden and Islington. Constructed in the 1890s. Links Clerkenwell Road with Islington.

Rosehill - Sutton. There is some debate as to whether it is two words. The tendency leans toward calling the locality Rosehill, and the road (connecting Rosehill with Angel Hill and Sutton High Street) as Rose Hill.

- Rosehill Farm: From at least the mid 18th century. Later called Rosehill House.

Rosslyn Hill - Hampstead. Road, a continuation of (Hampstead) High Street, from at least the 1750s. Was a bit steep.

Rotherhithe (docks) - Southwark. A port. A broad peninsula into the Thames. Between Bermondsey and Deptford. Known as Redriffe ca. the 1650s. The Mayflower launched from here toward the "new world" in 1620. 754 acres; is now chiefly the Surrey Commercial Docks.

There are no bridges here. The world's first under-river passage was built here in 1843, called the Thames tunnel; passage from Rotherhithe to Wapping (not to be confused with 1994's Channel Tunnel, familiarly known as the Chunnel.)

- See: docks/Howland Great Wet Dock.
- See: docks/Surrey Commercial Docks.

Rotherhithe (street) - One of London's longest roads. In 1765 was ruined by fire. Rebuilt. Near the docks. The population here ca. 1801 was a bit over 10,000; it was nearly 38,500 by 1901.

- St. Mary's: May have Saxon origins. Now "plain, Georgian." (See under the CHURCHES section.)

Rothschild's Bank - (See: New Court/Rothschild's Bank.)

Rotten Row - (See: Hyde Park/Rotten Row.)

Rotunda Museum - (See: Greenwich/Rotunda Museum.)

rough places (and rough activities, and rough people, and rough things) - Dangerous places/havens for criminals/dueling spots. Unfortunately, also where the poor and immigrants often lived.

- See: cheats.
- See: Clerkenwell Green.
- See: cock and hen club.
- See: Field Lane.
- See: Finchley.
- See: Five Fields.
- See: flash-house.
- See: Fleet Ditch.
- See: Hackney/London Fields.
- See: Hay Hill.
- See: Highgate Hill/Flask Tavern.
- See: Holy Land.
- See: Jacob's Island.
- See: Lambeth - For the clandestine disposal of corpses.
- See: Monmouth Street.
- See: Pie Corner/Fortune of War Tavern.
- See: poaching.
- See: Ratcliffe Highway.
- See: Red Lion Court.
- See: rookeries.

- See: St. Giles - Infamous slum area.
- See: Seven Dials.
- See: smugglers.
- See: Snow Hill.
- See: Swallow Street.
- See: Tiger's Head, under the INNS/Pubs section - For smuggling.
- See: Wapping.
- See: Wentworth Street.

roundabout (as in: first traffic circle) - 1926, in Parliament Square.

rounders - A game invented by the British, somewhat like baseball, but with which it is not to be confused. Also mustn't be confused with the game cricket.

Roxeth - (AKA: South Harrow.) Existed from at least the year 845. A manor by 1514. Developed in the 1840s, and while it always remained a separate locality, it was kind of swallowed up and became seen as more "Harrow" than "Roxeth"; in the 21st century "Roxeth" as an identifier is resuming in popularity.

Royal Academy of Art - (Most often simply referred to as: the Royal Academy.) *Not to be confused with: the Royal Society of Arts, nor with the: Royal College of Arts.*

Now at Burlington House, Piccadilly (across from 185); was in Somerset House from 1780-1836.

- See: Burlington House/Royal Academy of Art.
- See: Linnean Society.
- See: Somerset House/Royal Academy of Art.

Institute of painting founded by George III as an art school and a forum for annual exhibits of work by contemporary artists, opened in 1768. The painter Joshua Reynolds was this society's first president, who suggested getting painters to provide a work for display and sale, so the charitable funds raised could help support Capt. Coram's *Foundling Hospital.* (See under F.)

The first Royal Academy Exhibition was held in 1769. The hospital was a fashionable charity interest from the start. From under George III's interested eye, this charitable act/display grew into the Royal Academy of Arts shows; from 1787 to the present day the Academy has held an annual (and famous) summer exhibition.

In the Great Room, members' paintings were (according to LONDON STEP BY STEP): "hung 'above the line' (the cornice) as part of the summer exhibitions held in the room 1780-1836."

Point to remember: at the time of the Academy's founding, there were (increasingly) galleries for the selling of art - but there were no other forums for publicly displaying art (until this time, art being only solicited for/displayed in private homes and/or in the form of public statues.) In other words, museums or galleries that displayed art (that had not been pre-solicited) were a fairly new concept. (See: museums - Which in the 18th C. were often in pubs and mostly displayed things such as sporting memorabilia, more for drawing in the populace than being for sale.)

The Academy was very much a teaching place (as well as for selling and promoting art,) with professors, students (first enrolling in 1769,) and models of the various styles (casts, statues, etc.) Inclusion as an artist was via election, fundamentally giving the organization a club-like feel, not least because those elected in tended toward exclusivity and conservatism of artistic style. Ca. 1772 there were 40 or so artists as members.

The works of only two women were included prior to the 20th century; in fact, women could not study here until the late Victorian era. Certainly, women did paint as a leisure pastime, it's just that very few were granted any professional situations until well past the Regency era.

The academy concerns itself with the fine arts; whereas the Royal Society of Arts gets into, as they always did, more broad matters. Since the Royal Academy of Arts' aim was to promote visual artists as being more than "mere craftsmen," ironically they excluded engravers until 1857 - because engravers were "concerned with manual reproduction" rather than "creative art."

- See: Royal Society of Arts - For contrast.
- See: Somerset House/Royal Academy of Art.

Was first housed in Pall Mall, 1768-71. From 1770-1836 was housed in Somerset House. Then moved to Trafalgar Square in 1837-68 (where it shared space with the National Gallery); was then in Burlington House, Piccadilly, from 1868 onward; which cramped space prompted the Academy to purchase the Museum of Mankind locale, which was behind the Academy. (See: Museum of Mankind.)

Royal Academy of Music - Founded in 1822; Fanny Dickens (sister of Charles) attended that year. First at Tenterden Street, Hanover Square. Royal Charter granted in 1830. Its original rooms were described as "dyull and heavy." The Academy moved in 1911 to Marylebone Road. Present building from 1911, in a red brick English Baroque style.

Royal Air Force - Formed in 1918 by joining the Royal Flying Corps and the Royal Naval Air Service. (Until 1918, what air force there was had been part of the Royal Navy.)

Royal Albert Hall - Founded by Queen Victoria in 1871.

Royal Aquarium, the - On Tothill Street, to the west of Westminster Abbey. Opened in 1876; ran until it was demolished in 1903. Had sea creature tanks, an art gallery, a skating rink, and a theatre. Methodist Central Hall is now located here. Not to be confused with the

Aquarium of Regent's Park. (See: Regent's Park/Aquarium, for the latter.)

Royal Arcade - (See: Bond Street/Old Bond Street/Royal Arcade.)

Royal Armoury - (See: Tower of London/"Other Places & Things"/Royal Armoury.)

Royal Army Medical College - Built ca. 1872-1902 on the site of the Millbank Prison. (See: Millbank Prison.)

Royal Arsenal - 1805. Built on the site of an ordnance depot in Woolwich. Stopped manufacture in 1967, and closed completely in 1994. (See: Woolwich/Royal Laboratory.)

Royal Artillery Monument - Hyde Park Corner, 1920, dedicated to WWI casualties.

Royal Assent - To this day, the monarch must give her/his assent for an Act of Parliament to pass into law, which has never been refused since 1708.

Royal Astrological Society - Founded in 1831 as the Astronomical Society of London. Also achieved its Royal Charter in 1831, at which time its name changed to the Royal Astronomical Society.

- See: Kensington/Campden Hill Road - For note on James South, co-founder of the Royal Astrological Society.
- See: Linnean Society - For sharing space at Burlington House with.

Royal Avenue - Chelsea. The only part of the route meant by William III to connect the Royal Hospital and Kensington Palace that ended up being built, by Wren. This is a square off of King's Road. Has plane trees, gravel down the center, and was laid out (originally) in the late 17th century. Described as "elegant," lined with lime trees and attractive homes.

Royal Bank of Scotland - 1 Fleet Street. It was established in 1727 (as a rival to the Bank of Scotland. (See: Fleet Street/1.)

Royal Blackheath Golf Club - 1766. (See: Blackheath/Royal Blackheath Golf Club.)

Royal Botanical Gardens - (See: Kew Gardens.)

Royal Botanical Society of London - 1839. (See: Kew Gardens/Royal Botanical Society of London.)

Royal Brompton Hospital - 1840s. (See: Fulham Road/Royal Brompton Hospital.)

Royal Caledonian Asylum - Copenhagen Fields (later Caledonian Road.) Founded in 1815, moved to the Fields in 1827. CHAMBERS LONDON GAZATTEER tells us it was for the: "children of soldiers, sailors, and mariners, natives of Scotland, who have died or been disabled in the service of their country; and the children of indigent Scotch parents residing in London, not entitled to parochial relief."

royal chapels - (See: Chapel Royal.)

Royal Circus - (AKA: St. George's Fields Circus. AKA: Royal Circus and Equestrian Philharmonic Academy, but it was more widely known as "Hughes," for its owner Charles Hughes.) Near Blackfriars Bridge. Opened in 1782. Burned in 1799; again in 1803. Rebuilt by 1806, designed by Rudolph Cabanel.

In 1809, it was made over by one Mr. Elliston into a theatre for plays, and called the Surrey Theatre. In 1814, when Elliston left, it again became a circus building, until 1827 (when it was again the Surrey Theatre under Elliston.) Burned in 1865; rebuilt. (See: Surrey Theatre, under the THEATRES section.)

Royal Cockpit - Built in the 18th century. On Cockpit Steps, Westminster, until 1816, when it was demolished. Left behind was a set of narrow stone steps leading down from Queen Anne's Gate to Birdcage Walk. (See: Two Chairmen, under the INNS/PUBS section - The note there.) Acts of Parliament passed in 1849 and 1911 finally put paid to the practice of cockfighting in the UK.

Royal College of Arms -

- See: College of Arms.
- See: Herald's College.

Royal College of Arts - Kensington Gore. Founded 1837, as the Government School of Design, in Somerset House (at that time was also called: the Metropolitan School of Design.) Expanded and moved in 1853, to Marlborough House. Had various names in 1857 and 1863, and moved to South Kensington. In 1896, it became the Royal College of Art. Public research university. Took on the Royal College of Arts name in 1896 or 97. (Not to be confused with the Royal Academy of Arts.)

Royal College of Music - Prince Consort Road, South Kensington. Established 1882; opened 1894.

Royal College of Organists - (Also called: RCO.) 1864, founded as The College of Organists. Now is west of Albert Hall. Was in Kensington Gore from 1903-91. Royal Charter in 1893. To promote choral music and organ playing.

Royal College of Physicians - (AKA simply as the: College of Physicians.) Founded in 1518 by Thomas Linacre, Henry VII's and Henry VIII's royal physician. The body of physicians first gathered in Linacre's home, in Knightrider Street, then in an Amen Corner house, destroyed in 1666. Then the college was located in Warwick Lane (the house was built in 1674-89,) where the college stayed until it moved in 1825 to Trafalgar Square. This building is now partly inhabited by Canada House; the site also houses the 1887 version of the Cutlers Hall. Moved in 1964 to St. Andrew's Place, Regent's Park.

Physicians (as opposed to surgeons) joined the Royal College of Physicians, whereas surgeons were overseen by the Royal College of Surgeons.

- See: doctors/physician.
- See: doctors/surgeon.

Royal College of St. Peter at Westminster - (See: Westminster School.)

Royal College of Science - South Kensington. 1872. A constituent college of Imperial College London, 1907; was wholly absorbed into Imperial in 2002.

Royal College of Surgeons - South side of Lincoln's Inn Fields, still located there although the present building dates from 1835-6, by Sir Charles Barry. Has an 1806 facade (by Nash); was enlarged in 1888.

Was founded in 1800, following their prior affiliation with the Barber-Surgeons Company. (See: Barbers' Hall.) Is approached via a gateway from Lincoln's Inn Fields. The 1620 chapel was designed by Inigo Jones.

Surgeons (as opposed to physicians) were overseen by the Royal College of Surgeons, whereas physicians joined the Royal College of Physicians. (See: Inns of Court/Lincoln's Inn Fields/Royal College of Surgeons.)

Royal Courts of Justice - It hosts the Law Courts (the Court of Appeal,) and the High Court of Justice of England and Wales. It deals primarily with civil litigation; important civil cases are tried here; (criminal ones at the Old Bailey.)

The initial building dated from the 13th century; first located at Westminster.

In 1882, moved into the north side of the Strand, where the Strand and Fleet Street meet, near the Inns of Court. (See: Clement's Inn.)

By George Edmund Street (architect,) 1874-82, in Gothic Revival style. According to LONDON by Knopf Guides: "Its facade of brick skirts Bell Yard as far as the corner of Carey Street, where it ends in a graceful tower of brick checkerwork." Has a turreted fairytale appearance (seen from Fleet Street,) made to look as if it dates from the 13th century.

Has a hall, 238 feet long by 80 feet high. Has a ribbed, vaulted ceiling. Again from LONDON by Knopf Guides: "A warren of corridors and staircases lead from it to the hundreds of offices that are all part of the thirty-five courts of the Supreme Court of Justice." A second source said there are fifty courts. Some of the courts here are: admiralty, appeals, chancery, divorce, probate, and the Queen's Bench.

Quit Rent: Since the 13th C., there is a yearly ceremony here: the Quit Rent, which is a token lease paid for use of a forge that is where Australian House is now (on the Strand.) The yearly fee: six horseshoes and sixty-one nails.

- See: Courts of Common Law and Equity - For contrast to the RCJ.
- See: Westminster Hall/Royal Courts of Justice.

Royal Crescent - Holland Park, Kensington. Designed in 1839. Two curved quadrant terraces, made into a crescent shape.

Royal Docks - (See: docks/Royal Docks.)

Royal Doulton - The "royal" was granted in 1901.

- See: Doulton Fine China.
- See: Lambeth/potters.
- You may care to see: china.

Royal Exchange, the - (Often referred to as the 'Change.) Not to be confused with the Stock Exchange, even though the Stock Exchange had been here until 1972, when it moved to a modern office building. Also not to be confused with the New Exchange, Covent Garden area, which was pulled down in 1737.

The Royal Exchange was rather like what American's call shopping venues/malls.

Threadneedle Street, Cornhill, the City. Stands at a right angle to the Bank of England, between Threadneedle Street and Cornhill Street.

First built in 1565-6, founded by Sir Thomas Gresham (Elizabethan entrepreneur,) who designed the building as well. The building's weathervane is an eleven foot long golden grasshopper wearing a crown (which is the crest of Sir Thomas,) atop the 180 foot tall campanile. Completed in 1568. (Spent its first year, 1567, on Cornhill, having opened with materials imported from Flanders by Flemish craftsmen.) Opened in 1569 as "a centre of commerce of all kinds" (with 100+ shops and booths, meant to supplant Bourse, Antwerp as the primary European marketplace; meant for (and used by) merchants and traders, concentrating transactions here that had previously been conducted in the streets or in crowded shops. It is the oldest mercantile institution in the City. Queen Elizabeth opened it officially in 1570, and granted it its "Royal" designation in 1571.

Until the Royal Exchange's existence, Lombard Street had been the merchants' center of finance. (See: Lombard Street.)

When Gresham's widow died, the building went to the City Corporation and the Mercers' Company.

It burned in the Great Fire of 1666. Rebuilt.

Coffee houses flourished as business centers in the courts and alleys around the Royal Exchange (perhaps in part because the Exchange was hot and stuffy and incredibly noisy.) Because the buying and selling of shares was so noisily conducted in the streets around the Royal Exchange, the dealers finally chased them off (in the 17th century.) So the dealers shifted their dealings into the coffee-houses of Change Alley - the most famous of which was Jonathan's.

The Royal Exchange was still standing in 1779 when the Royal Exchange Assurance Co. (known as the Guardian Royal Exchange since 1968) and Lloyd's (Insurance) moved in (that is, Lloyd's of London.) The Royal Exchange Assurance Co. remained here when Lloyd's moved out in 1928; Lloyd's had been here since 1774. It also briefly housed the Stock Exchange, prior to the building of the Stock Exchange's own place in 1802.

This second version of the 'Change burned in 1838, (the cause believed to be an overheated stove in Lloyd's Coffee House.) Rebuilt in 1842-4 by William Tite, from which time the present facade dates. The inner courtyard was covered in 1880 with a barrel roof. The present interior is a 1982 remodel.

Ceased to function as a trading center in 1939 (although in 1982 became the site of a Futures marketplace.) Now an elegant shopping plaza.

- See: Jonathan's.
- See: Lloyd's of London.
- See: Stock Exchange.

Royal Female Orphanage - (See: Lambeth Asylum.)

Royal Festival Hall - Southwark. The only building left from the original 1951 Festival of Britain.

Royal Free Hospital - Gray's Inn Road. 1828. Founded by William Marsden, a surgeon. Support provided by the Cordwainers' Company. Known as the "London General Institution for the Gratuitous Care of Malignant Diseases" until 1837, when the name was changed at the behest of its patroness, Queen Victoria. Present buildings date from 1897 and 1916. (Not to be confused with The Royal Hospital, Chelsea.)

Royal Fusiliers - AKA: City of London Regiment. AKA: Ordnance Regiment. (See: Tower of London/"Other Places & Things"/Waterloo Barracks.)

Royal Geographical Society - Founded in 1830. Moved to south Kensington in 1911, in the former Lowther Lodge (building dates from 1873-75,) 1 Kensington Gore.

Royal Guards, the - (AKA: the Horse Guards - meaning those regiments that are mounted. AKA: the Queen's Guard. AKA: Household Troops. Cumulatively, AKA: the Brigade of Guards. Referred to also as the: Gentlemen at Arms. Also correct to say, for instance, "the Queen's Foot Guards," "the King's Grenadiers," etc., dependent on the ruling monarch's gender, of course. As early as 1762 it was common to simply call them "the Guards.")

While not exactly interchangeable terms, it's hard to separate the terms "Royal Guards" and "Horse Guards" (or Horse Guards Parade.) Here they combine to mean two things, which are:

1. Royal Guards = The troops who guard the monarch or royal palaces, via either cavalry or infantry.
2. Horse Guard Parade = (Commonly called simply: Horse Guards.) The buildings that house:
    a) The Royal Guards (barracks.) Too, their horses and gear.
    b) Military persons and offices, such as the War Office, and the Treasury. (See both of these, below.)

To be clearer, when people speak of the Royal Guards, they mostly mean the actual persons who provide royal protection. When they speak of the Horse Guards, they mostly mean the buildings and networks that support the Royal Guards/the government/a part of Whitehall, as in a big part of the seat of government in England.

THE ROYAL GUARDS SHOULD NOT BE CONFUSED WITH:

1. Yeoman of the Guard - The monarch's personal (and now largely ceremonial) bodyguard. (See under Y.)
2. Yeoman Warders - Guards of the Tower of London. (See under Y.)

History of the Royal Guards: The Horse Guards began as the Lord Protector of the Commonwealth, Oliver Cromwell's, Life Guard. Cromwell died in September, 1658. When Charles II was restored to the crown in 1660, the Life Guards became the king's Royal Guards. (See: Life Guards, below.)

By 1661, it was recognized that the Royal Guards required housing of their own. Work began in 1663; the first buildings were completed in the summer of 1664. Red brick. Is now referred to as: the Old Horse Guards, (as opposed to the 1750-58 new Horse Guards, which was built over the Old buildings. Read on.)

Whitehall's position as the king's palace ended when Whitehall burned in 1698; the Horse Guards escaped burning; King William III and his guards moved to St. James's Palace. CHIVALRY AND COMMAND tells us: "St. James's has remained the titular residence of English sovereignty. In so doing..." (King William) "...provided Old Horse Guards with an additional role: already a Household Troops' duty barracks and an emergent War Office, from now it would also be the only official entrance through" (St. James's) "Park to the Court and Palace of St. James's, in which role it continues to the present day."

Rebuilt in 1750-58 of Portland stone, by John Vardy, to designs by William Kent after the latter died, and now called New Horse Guards. Besides being a rebuilt barrack and stables, was built as headquarters for the General Staff (there until 1876,) and used for military exercises. Elegant Palladian facades.

- Clock, the: First one lasted some 90 years; had only one hand, striking only the hour. Present clock (with two hands) dates from 1768, by Thwaites & Reed (London's oldest clockmakers.)
- Guards, the: (Listed, below.)
- Horse Guards Arch: A remnant of Whitehall Palace. Still guarded daily by two mounted sentries. As LONDON by Knopf Guides puts it: "On the Whitehall side this Palladian building forms three sides of a square, while on the other side is

Horse Guards Parade, reached by three arches at the back. Only the monarch is allowed to use the central arch." (In truth, others can use it, but must first obtain a pass. Only the monarch does not require a pass.) The courtyard with three sides (that the arch leads into) is: Horse Guards Barrack. The arch was long considered inappropriately less than sumptuous as a royal gateway. It barely allows four guards mounted abreast to ride through. (See: Horse Guards Parade, below - Note about the arches.)

- Horse Guards Barrack: (See: Horse Guards Arch, above.)
- Horse Guards Parade: Its location had originally served as the entrance to Whitehall Palace, which burned in 1698 and was abandoned. As King William III moved to St. James's Palace, this area then led to St. James's Palace. St. James's is still the titular residence of the monarchy (still receives ambassadors and such here,) and although the royals have moved to Buckingham Palace, to this day the Life Guards still guard here at St. James's Palace.

  As stated above, the first Horse Guards building was built in 1663 by Charles II. As it was increasingly used for military purposes, it became overcrowded. A new Horse Guards Parade was built in 1750-58, to (re)house barracks and stables for the Household Cavalry/Royal Guards. Palladian style, to designs by William Kent, but finished by John Vardy. U-shaped, enclosing a courtyard on the Whitehall side; here are the three arches on the St. James's Park side that give access to Horse Guards Parade. LONDON by Knopf Guides reads: (Horse Guards Parade) "...is a curious mixture of arches, pediments and eaves." (See: Parade Grounds, below - Which is part of the overall Horse Guards Parade.) Two wings were connected ca. 1755; in 1803-5 two floors were added to the wings, ending in today's appearance. As time went on, Horse Guards Parade still acted as a military center, such as to the Secretary of War/War Office, and the General Staff. During the Napoleonic Wars, Lord Wellington worked from here. This is the oldest barracks site yet in Britain.

  - Parade Grounds: Biggest clear space in London. The parade grounds were built in 1663 on the former tiltyard of Henry VIII, which had then become a cavalry stable of Whitehall Palace; all of which was incinerated in 1698 when Whitehall Palace burned down. Re-laid out when Horse Guards Parade was built in 1750-58. ROMANTIC LONDON states: "The Horse Guards' Parade seems from a very early period to have been associated with military display, a martial ceremony which was a mixture of the modern "trooping of the colours" and of mounting guard having been a familiar sight there during the eighteenth century." The yearly Trooping of the Colors (the flag is literally hoisted and ridden before the troops, harkening back to the ancient tradition of needing to physically show your troops your flag so they knew which one to rally to) is done here annually still.

- Treasury: (AKA: Old Treasury. AKA: Treasure Building. AKA: Kent's Treasury.) Designed by William Kent. Neo-classical, 1736. Backs on Dover House. (See: Treasury.)
- War Office: Responsible for the running of the Army from the 17th C. to 1964, when the responsibility transferred to the Ministry of Defence. Not actually a part of the Horse Guards, but because it is so close, it's often mistaken as such/functions hand-in-glove with the Horse Guards Parade. (See: War Office, under W.)

The Royal Guards/their Divisions:

The famous British red coats came into being in 1704-14.

The bearskin helmets came into use in 1831. The bear skins are obtained from Canada (there are no bears in Britain.) While they are often called bearskins, the actual term for these bear-skin covered hats is: a cap.

Old Guard vs. New Guard: During the changing of the guard at Buckingham Palace, these two terms simply mean those who are done with their shift, then being replaced by the following shift's guards.

All of the Royal Guards are/were soldiers in the British Army.

- <u>THE HORSE GUARDS</u>: Mounted.

  The Blues and the Royals, plus the Life Guards, are *Household Cavalry* regiments, meaning they guard the monarch and his/her household. The Household regiments are the only two royal guard units who are still cavalry (mounted units.) These two cavalry regiments were amalgamated after WWI, but were separated again after WWII.

  - **Blues and Royals**, the: (Familiarly AKA: "the Blues.") Cavalry. Blue coat; red-plumed helmet. Horse has black saddlecloth. The Blues did not become Household cavalry until 1820, after distinguishing themselves at the battle of Waterloo. Royal Horse Guards and 1st Dragoons.
  - **Life Guards**, the: (AKA: The Queen's Guards. Or: King's.) Founded by Charles II. Cavalry. Scarlet coat; white-plumed helmet; (the Trumpeteers

of the Life Guard have red plumes to go with their red coats.) Horse has a white or black saddlecloth. (See: Wormholt Common - For an exercise yard for the Life Guards.)

- THE FOOT GUARDS: All of the following Infantry regiments are, of course, on foot (not mounted.)

  Overall, they wear red tunics and the famous bearskin hats. The fur is actually bear (sent from Canada.) The 5 units' uniforms appear at first glance identical, but there are differences. All guardsmen and their officers wear the bearskin hat, since 1815 (to symbolize the victory over Napoleon, whose Imperial Guard wore their like.) The scarlet tunic had: a dark blue collar, shoulder strips pipped in white, with cuffs of dark blue and white. They also wear: dark blue trousers, with a red stripe down the sides; a white leather buff belt; gold buttons on which is the monarch's insignia.

  Their boxes (at which they stand guard when not in movement) are correctly called: vedettes.

  When the Queen is in residence, there are four regiments of Foot Guards in front of her palace, two if she's absent. Currently, in cold/wet weather, the Guard wear gray coats.

  - **Coldstream Guards**, the: The Coldstream Guard was formed after the monarchy was restored in 1660 (had started as Cromwell's Life Guards in 1650.) Named for a border village, the area from where they'd been recruited (Coldstream, Scotland.) One battalion. Their bearskins have a red plume, on the right side of the cap. A part of the Household Troop, the only Foot Guard to be so, and therefore guard the monarch's palaces.

    NOTE: In the CHELSEA BARRACKS are the headquarters for the Coldstream and the Grenadier Guards. It is a long, 5-story block (faces the parade grounds); embraces its look and purpose as a barracks.
  - **Grenardier Guards**, the: One battalion. Were first raised by Charles II, 1656, (while he was in exile.) Their purpose is: to guard the castle and Queen Elizabeth II. Also called: the First Guards. Their bearskin's plume is white, on the left side of the cap; they were granted the wearing of the bearskin following the Battle of Waterloo. (See: NOTE, above, at Coldstream Guards.)
  - **Irish Guards,** the: As their name suggests, they are Irish, recruited from Northern Ireland (and Irish neighborhoods in major British cities.) Active from 1900, founded by Queen Victoria. Battalion. Their bearskins have

St. Patrick's blue plumes, on the right side of the cap. Their buttons are arranged in groups of four, signifying they were the fourth Foot Guards regiment to be founded.

- **Scots Guards,** the: Created in 1642 by Charles I. (Also called: the Third Guard.) One battalion. Their bearskins have no plume. These guards date from a regiment raised by the Marquis of Argyll, in response to the Irish Rebellion. After the Restoration of the monarchy, the Earl of Linlithgow was commissioned to form (from the prior) the Scottish Regiment of Footguards, 1660.
- **Welsh Guards**, the: Active since 1915, by George V, who was desirous of including Wales in the components of the Foot Guards. One battalion. Their bearskin plume is white/green/white, on the left side of the cap.

Royal Horticultural Society - (At first was: the Horticultural Society of London.) Founded on 3/7/1804 by seven men who met at Hatchard's (bookstore) back room. Wanted to discuss discoveries and issue horticultural papers. Its first garden (presently there are four,) was in Kensington, 1818-22. (See: Piccadilly/187-8 - For Hatchard's.) Not to be confused with the Chelsea Physic Garden, nor the Royal Botanical Gardens.

Royal Hospital, Chelsea - (For Army soldiers.) - Royal Hospital Road, Chelsea. (AKA: Chelsea Hospital.)

Built by Wren for Charles II; begun in 1682, finally completed in 1692 (although some pensioners were admitted as early as 1689.) Charles II had the hospital built for retired and wounded soldiers. Reportedly the first hospital in London.

In 1765-82, Robert Adam altered the hospital a little.

Severe neo-classical buildings were added to the east and west in 1819-22, designed by Sir John Soane.

Rebuilt in large after severe WWII damage, is still red brick accented with white Portland stone.

The pensioners still live in the two wings. In summer, if the pensioners go out, they wear red coats and black tricorns - this uniform has looked the same since the 18th century. Otherwise their uniforms are dark blue.

History records three women were pensioners; I know one of them had disguised her gender by wearing her husband's uniform; when her sex became known (and it was learned she had served in the army) she was granted a pension and allowed to wear the blue pensioner's coat. Women pensioners were allowed officially from 2009.

Every year the bronze equestrian statue (of Charles II, their founder, dates from

1676, by Grinling Gibbons,) located in Figure Court, is decked with oak boughs in commemoration of Charles II's birthday.

Ranelagh Gardens was situated on the Royal Hospital grounds.

- See: Chelsea/Chelsea Hospital.
- See: Ranelagh Gardens, at its own listing.

Royal Hospital, Greenwich - (for sailors) - Greenwich. (See: Royal Naval College.)

Royal Hospital Road - Chelsea, (parallel with King's Road.) Has held the Royal Hospital, Chelsea, since 1692.

Royal Humane Society - In the UK, a "Humane Society" can be for the rescuing of animals, but very well might instead be an organization for preventing/rescuing of drowning persons, and granting awards for the saving of such. This society was/is the latter, founded in 1774 as, at first, the Society for the Recovery of Persons Apparently Drowned; name changed in 1776 to the Humane Society. Physician William Hawes' publication in 1773 of artificial respiration processes had prompted the founding of this organization. The "Royal" was added in 1787, following George III becoming its first patron in 1783.

- See: Hyde Park/Serpentine/Humane Society.
- See: Royal Society for the Prevention of Cruelty to Animals - For animal rescue.

Royal Institute of British Architects - Founded in 1834. Moved to current building in 1934, 66 Portland Place. Received their Royal Charter in 1837.

Royal Institution - Chemical lectures, 1799. (See: Albemarle Street/21.)

Royal Library, the - Another name for the British Museum Library. (See: British Museum Library.)

Royal Literary Fund - (A thing, not a place.) Established by the Reverend David Williams, to help "Distressed Talents." He died in 1816. The Fund was established in 1790. Royal Charter received in 1818, and permitted to add "Royal" to its name in 1845.

Royal London Hospital - (See: London Hospital.)

Royal London Militia - The barracks built in 1857, to house the Royal London Militia. (See: City Road/Finsbury Barracks.)

Royal London Ophthalmic Hospital - (See: Charterhouse Square/London Dispensary...)

Royal Mail, the - Founded by Charles I in 1635. (See: post, the.)

Royal Menagerie - Founded by Henry III, mid 13th century, when he was given three leopards by the Holy Roman Emperor, Frederick II. In 1252 the King of Norway gave him a white (probably polar) bear. In 1255 the King of France sent an elephant. Later came: an ostrich, another elephant, tigers, monkeys, and more.

The animals were fed at six in the evening.

By 1822 the collection was down to no more than some birds, an elephant, and a grizzly bear. Alfred Copps was made the new Keeper, and he added 59 species to the collection.

Housed in the Tower of London/Lion Tower until 1834, when William IV gave these animals - plus ones housed at Windsor Great Park - to the London Zoo.

In a 1930 exhumation of the Moat of the Tower of London, bones from 13-18th C. menagerie animals were uncovered, some breeds of which are now extinct, such as: Barbery Lions.

- See: Regent's Park/Zoological Society.
- See: Tower of London/"The Towers"/Lion Tower.

Royal Mews - (AKA: the Royal Stables. AKA: the King's Mews.) Buckingham Palace Road (within the grounds of Buckingham Palace, to the south.)

The mews were first erected onto/for Whitehall Palace. Was first built for falcons in 1377. (See: mews.) Horses had replaced birds here ca. 1537. CHAMBERS LONDON GAZETTEER says the Royal Mews were located at the (eventual) site of Trafalgar Square from the 14-19th centuries.

Remodeled in 1553-8.

In 1732 William Kent built the Royal Stables here, near Charing Cross, and dubbed variously as the Buckingham Palace Mews, Dunghill Mews, Great Mews, Green Mews, and King's Mews. AN ENCYCLOPEDIA OF LONDON states: "The north part" (of the mews) "was called 'Green Mews,' and that was a derivation of a street behind the National Gallery which, until it was renamed in honour of Sir Henry Irving, was Green Street." LONDON STEP BY STEP claims that Dung Hill Mews was a street *in* the Royal Mews. The surrounding district was rather slummy.

During the Regency, the Charing Cross Mews were preferred, being used in conjunction with those on Buckingham Palace Road, after George III had bought (in 1762) Buckingham House. The Royal Mews still existed, and were still used, but these others (Charing Cross Mews) were preferred by the royals at this time.

The Royal Mews stables and coach houses were rebuilt by Nash in 1825, but now situated on Buckingham Palace Road (built over the ones that were already on that site,) in the area that is now known as Trafalgar Square. LONDON by Knopf Guides states: "Nash's 1826 buildings are virtually a small village inside Buckingham Palace." The buildings formed a quadrangle.

The site was demolished in 1829-30 to build Nelson's Column and the National Gallery. Still, but to a far lesser degree, a form of the Royal Mews yet exists.

The head of the Royal Mews is the Master of the Queen's Horse, title goes back to

1391.

Royal Mile - Nickname for Regent Street. (See: Regent Street, at its own listing.)

Royal Military Academy -

- See: Royal Military College.
- See: Woolwich/Royal Laboratory.

Royal Military Asylum - Chelsea. Founded in 1801 by Royal Warrant, under Frederick, the Duke of York. Its full name was: the Royal Military Asylum for Children of Soldiers of the Regular Army. It was set up to provide a home for the children of fallen common soldiers (as opposed to officers.) Its name changed in 1892 to: the Duke of York's Royal Military School; in 1909 it was relocated to the cliffs of Dover. (See: Duke of York's Headquarters - The notes under.)

Royal Military College - (AKA: RMC.) Founded in 1801; established at Great Marlow and High Wycombe, county of Buckingham, in 1802. Moved to Sandhurst, county of Berkshire, in 1812. A British Army academy, for officer training. Reorganized at the beginning of WWII. Merged with the Royal Military Academy in 1947, now called the Royal Military Academy Sandhurst.

Royal Military School of Music - Whitton. 1857.

- See: Kneller Hall.
- See: Whitton/Kneller Hall.

Royal Mint - (AKA: Royal Mint Building.) The minting of coins began in England in the 2nd century, under Roman rule.

Was at the Tower of London from ca. 1279 to 1809 - and in the 16th C. this locale became the sole place where coins of the realm were minted/those with the monarch's head (or other kingly design) on them. (That is not to say there were no other coins, because there were: cities, or businesses, or private banks might make their own coins...but the problem came in getting the general populace to accept them. Not to mention foreign coins, which often had more acceptability than a private-business coin. For more on this subject, see: money - The paragraph on "Coinage.")

In 1710 the mint buildings formed a narrow "U" running around three sides of the Tower of London, the buildings built of mostly wood, described as "wretched."

Moved from the Tower of London in 1809 to the Royal Mint Building, built by Mr. Johnson and Robert Smirke, overlooking the Tower, in East Smithfield. Had a "mild grandeur." Largely destroyed by fire in 1815. In 1880 the buildings were reconstructed and extended.

Rebuilt again at the start of the 20th century. Little of the original buildings remained by the 1960s. Moved again in 1968 to Liantrisant, South Wales. The Tower Hill buildings were finally completely left behind in 1980. (See: Tower of London/"Other Places & Things"/Royal Mint.)

Royal Naval College - King William Walk, The College, Greenwich. Moved into the Royal Naval Hospital in 1873, coming from its original existence in Portsmouth.

Royal Naval College was built by Wren on the site of the 15th C. royal palace that had been here (Greenwich Palace.) Wren's exterior work was destroyed in 1779, but the rococo interior is still there. (Also contributing to the building were: Hawksmoor and Vanbrugh.) Rebuilt by James Stuart. During the Regency, this building operated as and was known as the Royal Naval Hospital. Was originally a home for naval pensioners. (See: Royal Hospital, Chelsea, for army pensioners.)

Nelson's funeral was held here in 1805 in the Chapel. He lay in state in the Painted Hall.

- ➢ See: Greenwich/Royal Naval Hospital - Note under.
- ➢ See: Royal Naval Hospital.

- Chapel: Wren. Rebuilt in 1779 by James "Athenian" Stuart, following a fire.
- Painted Hall: Painted by Sir James Thornhill in the Baroque style, 1708-27.
- Queen's House: (See: Queen's House, Greenwich, under Q.)

Royal Naval Female School - Dates from at least 1867. (See: St. Margarets, Richmond/St. Margarets, under S.)

Royal Naval Hospital - (AKA: the Greenwich Hospital. Also, less often, referred to as: Royal Hospital for Seamen, its prior purpose. Occupies the site where the ancient Greenwich Palace once stood. This became the Royal Naval College in 1873.

- ➢ See: Greenwich Hospital.
- ➢ See: Greenwich/Royal Naval Hospital - Note at.

Royal Navy, administrative office of - The Royal Navy began its ascension to greatness after the attempted Dutch invasion on the Thames in June, 1667.

- ➢ See: Admiralty.
- ➢ See: army - For note on why Britons preferred the navy over the army.
- ➢ See: marines.
- ➢ See: naval matters.
- ➢ See: Somerset House - Note about halfway down in the beginning part.

Royal Naval School - 1843. (See: New Cross/Royal Naval School.)

Royal Oak - Westminster. In the 1830s a railway divided Paddington in two: Bayswater to the south thrived, but Royal Oak to the north less so. There were pleasure gardens here in the

1840s. From then to 1855 the area built up a great deal.

- Royal Oak Public House: 2 Regency Street, Pimlico. 1831. Still there.

Royal Observatory - Greenwich Park, on the hill. Wren, 1675. (See: Greenwich Observatory.)

Royal Opera Arcade - Off Haymarket. Runs from Pall Mall to Charles II Street. Opened 1817 (second source said 1816-18); designed by John Nash and George Repton. First covered passage/enclosed shopping arcade in London, in the French fashion. Circular roof-lights; 17 bow-fronted shops; rather plain street entrances. (Not to be confused with the Royal Arcade which was built in the Victorian era on Bond Street/Old Bond Street.)

Royal Opera House - (See: Covent Garden Theatre Royal, under the THEATRES section.)

Royal Panopticon of Science and Art - Built on the east side of Leicester Square in the early 1850s. Opened in 1854. In 1857 became the Alhambra Music Hall.

royal parks - While London has many parks, it has eight royal ones. ((See: each at its own listing):

- Bushy Park.
- Green Park.
- Greenwich Park.
- Hyde Park.
- Kensington Gardens.
- Regent's Park.
- Richmond Park.
- St. James's Park.
- You may care to see: forests.
- You may care to see: parks.

Royal Parks Constabulary - 1872. (See: Metropolitan Police/Royal Parks Constabulary.)

royal peculiar - This terms means that the chapel or church so designated answers directly to the sovereign, not to an archbishop. In other words, the building and its clergy are affiliated directly with the monarch, and no bishop or archbishop has authority within it.

Royal Philanthropic Society - (See: Philanthropic Society.)

Royal Regiment of Artillery - (See: Woolwich/Royal Laboratory.)

Royal Regiment of Fusiliers -

- See: Tower of London/"Other Places & Things"/Great Armoury.
- See: Tower of London/"Other Places & Things"/Waterloo Barracks.

Royal Small Arms Factory - In 1816, most of the gunworks production had been transferred here from the old Lewisham Armoury. (Not to be confused with a London Small Arms Company, established 1865.)

- See: Enfield/Enfield Lock.
- See: Lewisham Armoury.

Royal Society - (See: Royal Society, the.)

Royal Society for the Arts - (See: Royal Society of Arts.)

Royal Society for the Prevention of Cruelty to Animals - Founded in 1824, at Old Slaughter's Coffee House, St. Martin's Lane, by Richard Martin (an Irish MP.) Present building dates from 1869. (Not to be confused with the Royal Humane Society, which deals with human drowning rescues, not animal rescues.)

Royal Society of Arts - (AKA: Royal Society for the Arts. Modern AKA: RSA.) 8 John Adam Street, Charing Cross. Not to be confused with the Royal Academy of Art. Not to be confused with the Royal Society of Distinguished Scientists. Founded in 1754 (being very well received by the public) as the "Society for the Encouragement of Arts, Manufactures & Commerce," but later the name was changed. It was granted its Royal Charter in 1847; the right to use "Royal" in their name was granted in 1908 by Edward VII.

This society initiated the practice of putting blue plaques on famous buildings, starting in 1867.) They have always concerned themselves with a broader spectrum, as opposed to the Royal Academy of Arts, which concentrates on the fine arts.) They held the first-ever formal art exhibition in 1760. By 1762, had grown to 2,500 members (or fellows.) Its hall was used for lectures.

Had been at Covent Garden, but since 1774, has been at John Adam Street, (which was built at the time as a portion of the ADELPHI. (See: Adelphi/6-8 John Adam Street.)

Royal Society of Chemistry - For advancing the chemical sciences. Formed in 1980 from amalgamating together: the Chemical Society (1841,) the Faraday Society (1903,) the Royal Institute of Chemistry (1877,) and the Society for Analytical Chemistry (1907.)

Royal Society of Distinguished Scientists - (See: Royal Society, the.)

Royal Society of Literature, the - Founded in 1820 by Thomas Burgess (a bishop,) having obtained the patronage of George IV, who was fond of reading. It was meant to stimulate literary talent and reward literary merit. Like the Royal Horticultural Society, first met in a back room of Hatchard's. (See: Piccadilly/187-8 - For Hatchard's.) Royal Charter granted in 1825. Alongside Trafalgar Square, they moved to a fine new house, there 1830-55 (when the building was pulled down to make way for the National Portrait Gallery.) Since, has not owned their own property. Turned out to be not so much literary as antiquarian, for some 100 years; this began to change ca. 1895, when they began to take up work for their new and/or literary merit. Women were admitted ca. 1895.

Royal Society of London for Improving Natural Knowledge - Often shortened to just the: Royal Society. (See: Royal Society, the.)

Royal Society of Medicine, the - Founded in 1805, at first as: the Medical and Chirugical Society of London. Was in Lincoln's Inn Fields until it moved to Berners Street in 1834.

Royal Charter by William IV. In 1905 moved to the corner of Wimpole Street and Henrietta Place. In 1907 a supplemental Royal Charter dubbed it the: Royal Society of Medicine. Moved into 1 Wimpole Street in 1912.

Royal Society, the - (AKA: The Royal Society of Distinguished Scientists. AKA: Royal Society of London for Improving Natural Knowledge.) Not to be confused with the "Royal Society of Arts," nor the "Royal Academy of Arts."

Scientific body founded in the 1640s, but received its royal charter from Charles II in 1662, for the pursuit of studies of science and promotion of scientific research. The oldest scientific body in the world. Originated in Oxford, and moved to establish themselves in London in 1666. Christopher Wren (architect) was their president, as later was Samuel Pepys (diarist,) and Isaac Newton (mathematician.) Located at 6 Carlton House Terrace since 1966; prior to that was in Burlington House for nearly 300 years.

Political and religious discussions were barred. The society's findings, from 1695 on, were published in *Philosophical Transactions*, a publication that yet exists.

By George II's time the society had slid into a club-like environment, with members being included on a social basis as well as a scientific one. Jonathan Swift satirized them in *Gulliver's Travels* (1726,) because by this time some experiments there had become trivial and/or unscientific.

Sir John Pringle, a physician, became president of the society in 1772, and under him the genuine exchange of scientific data and serious research was restored.

Sir Joseph Banks became president in 1778, serving for 42 (some say autocratic) years.

The Royal Society yet exists.

Royal Stables - (See: Royal Mews.)

Royal Stock Exchange - (See: Stock Exchange.)

Royal Terrace - (See: Adelphi/Royal Terrace.)

Royal Toxophile Society - Archery. (See: Toxophile Society.)

Royal Wardrobe - (AKA: the King's - or Queen's - Wardrobe.) While I will write of buildings that have housed the Royal Wardrobe, it is actually not a building, but a department of the Royal Household, and then a Department of State.

In Medieval times, those of influence might well sleep in a set of chambers made up of a bedroom attached to a secure room called a wardrobe. Hence the name.

The first Royal Wardrobe started as a large 12th C. home in Blackfriars, gifted to Edward III in 1359, after its owner died. He used it to store his State/ceremonial robes; those of the Royal Household; his treasures; others' accoutrements such as belonged to Knights of the Garter; for the garments/items of the king's ministers; cloths; hangings;

things such as beds, armour, and even ammunition (all of which had previously been stored at the Tower of London, as it would be again later.) At that time, the Royal Wardrobe also kept the Royal Household's accounts. As happens, the term Royal Wardrobe expanded to include not only the contents, but also the clerks who oversaw them; AND the fact that the Wardrobe's treasures were not infrequently used by the king as a kind of funding when he had wars to run or expenses to meet.

Ca. 1300 there were two wardrobes: the GREAT WARDROBE, a younger part of the Wardrobe, mostly clothing, furs, spices, and textiles, as opposed to the senior WARDROBE which the king used for expenditures. (Too, other palaces had smaller Privy Wardrobes, mostly personal items belonging to the king.) The PRIVY WARDROBE in the Tower of London became mostly for armor and armaments, and so was rather autonomous from the other Royal Wardrobe divisions. (SEE: TOWER OF LONDON/"OTHER PLACES & THINGS"/CROWN JEWELS.)

All of this lost its influence as the 15th C. rolled in. At the same time, the GREAT WARDROBE began to be called just "the Wardrobe," with the former's identity being mostly gone by the 16th century, being abolished formally in 1782 by the Civil List and Secret Service Money Act.

The building in Blackfriars was destroyed by the Great Fire of 1666. It was rebuilt, but not in Blackfriars; first it was in Buckingham Street, and eventually on Great Queen Street. Then, the Crown Jewels and the other contents of the Royal Wardrobe moved (back) to the Tower of London.

- See: Tower of London/"Other Places & Things"/Crown Jewels - The entire listing.
- See: Tower of London/"The Towers"/Broad Arrow Tower.
- See: Tower of London/"The Towers"/Wardrobe Tower.
- See: Wardrobe Place - Which was built where the Wardrobe *had* been in Blackfriars.

Royal Warrant - Designates royal patronage, a fact which is allowed by the Crown to be used in a store's advertising. The warrant can be withdrawn. It is considered to be a reliable warranty to the populace of top shops and prestige brands. While the process has existed for centuries, the Royal Warrant of Appointment bloomed in the Victorian era (one of the things to replace the faded away ancient Guilds/altered purpose of the Livery Companies.)

Royal Wimbledon Golf Club - (See: Wimbledon Commons/London Scottish Golf Club.)

rubber band - Invented in 1845 by Stephen Perry of Mssrs Perry and Co., London, of vulcanized rubber.

ruffians - Districts of. (See: rough places.)

rugs - In the UK, an all-over floor covering is a carpet. A smaller, movable covering is a rug. A blanket used inside a carriage is better referred to as a rug. Rugs were also used for animals (particularly to warm/protect horses.)

rugby (the game) - Legend has it the game was invented by a rector of St. Clement Danes, the Strand, ca. the 1820s; this tale is deemed unlikely. The first international rugby match was held at the Oval in 1872 (although there had been previous, non-international matches held in London before that date.) Other sources say the game was purportedly started at Rugby School in 1823 by one William Webb Ellis. The Rugby Football Union, Middlesex, was founded in 1871. (See: Kennington/Oval Cricket Ground.)

Rugby (the school) - In the county of Warwickshire. Founded in 1567. Where the game of the same name was reportedly invented.

Ruislip - (Pronounced: rye-slip.) Hillingdon. Was a rural village during the Regency era, more wilderness here than homes. Copse Wood, Mad Bess Wood, and Park Wood are residuals of the ancient 600 acre woodland here. 17th C. almshouses still exist (but not used as such now.)

- St. Martin: Ancient church. In 1870 it was partly restored, and again in 1956-7.
- South Ruislip: It's more south of Eastcore, but Ruislip residents considered it a contingent of Ruislip proper.
    - Bourne Farm: 1810s.
- West Ruislip: Developed after 1906.

Rule Britannia - Famous song. Music by Thomas Arne. Lyrics by James Thomson. Performed publicly for the first time in a masque called "Alfred" in 1740. (See: Argyll House.)

Rule's - (Also seen written as: Rules. Is now: Rule's Restaurant.) 35 Maiden Lane (Covent Garden/Strand area.) London's oldest surviving restaurant. Has been serving British traditional foods since it was established by Thomas Rule in 1798. Long used by actors and aristocrats. Dickens had a regular table here. Now has an Edwardian interior. (See: restaurant.)

Rundell & Bridge - Goldsmith/jewelers. (See: Ludgate Street/32 Ludgate Hill.)

Rupert Street - (See: Soho/Rupert Street.)

Rush Green - Barking and Dagenham/Havering. Dates from at least 1651. Small farms, well into the 19th century.

rush hour - As in traffic congestion. The term was first used in Britain in 1898. (You may care to see: traffic islands - 1860s.)

Rushey Green - Lewisham. Before the 17th C. it was also recorded as Rushet Green and Rush Green. The common land was enclosed in 1810, followed by the arrival of cottages and shops.

- Priory Farm: Late 17th century. Pulled down in 1877; its site now covered by the western end of Brownhill Road and Ringstead Road.

rushlights - (See: candles.)

Ruskin Park - Camberwell. 1907.

Russell Hill - Croydon. Rises to 360 feet above sea level. In the 19th C. the area was known as Beggar's Thorn, later as Beggar's Bush. Took on the Russell Hill name for the school's president, the first Earl Russell.

- Warehousemen, Clerks and Drapers School, the: 1886.

Russell Place - From 1867. (See: Fitzroy Square/Fitzroy Street.)

Russell Square - Bloomsbury. CHAMBERS LONDON GAZETTEER says: "The Russell family, earls of Bedford from 1550, gained possession of Bloomsbury by marriage into the Southampton family in 1669. The area remained mostly open fields until the mid 18th century." Therefore, named for the Russells, Dukes of Bedford. (There is an 1809 statue of Francis, the 5th duke, depicted leaning on a plow.) Laid out around 1801-4 by Humphry Repton - at this time the area was called Southampton Fields, and then the Long Fields. (You may care to see: Torrington Square - Also built on Long Fields, 1801.)

Once Russell Square was laid out, the original buildings around the square were built by James Burton; only a few remain. One of the largest squares in London, second only to Lincoln's Inn Fields. Became increasingly less fashionable after the 1820s. Prior to this it was solid and respectable. Was increasingly sneered at as a locale for the "nouveau riche" after the 1820s.

The square's center is still a shady retreat. (See: Russell Square Gardens, below.)

- 25-29: One of the original houses built by James Burton. Now houses the Institutes of Commonwealth Studies, 1949, and Germanic Studies, 1950 (under the University of London.)
- 67: The artist Sir Thomas Lawrence had his studio here from 1805 to until he died in 1830.
- Great Russell Street: (See under G.)
- Russell Hotel: Turn of the 20th century. Chateau-style, terracotta. Designed by the architect Charles Fitzroy Doll.
- Russell Square Gardens: Laid out anew in 2002, somewhat to its early 19th C. look (being once again railed and gated.)

Russell Street - Leads east from Covent Garden's Piazza.

- 8: James Boswell (biographer) lived here. He first met Dr. Samuel Johnson (lexicographer) locally, in 1763. (See: Davies, below.)
- 20: Charles Lamb (antiquarian/poet) lived here with his sister Mary from 1817-

1823 (having moved here from a place in the Inner Temple/Inns of Court.)

- Davies: A coffee-house, where James Boswell and Samuel Johnson first met, literally bumping into one another in 1763.
- Drury Lane Theatre: (See under the THEATRES section.)
- Rose Tavern, the: There by at least 1712, at which time it was known for its "debauchery." Gone by 1766. (See under the INNS/PUBS section.)

Russia - (This is a *very* brief description of British-Russian relations.) Formal ties between the English court and the Russian court go back to 1553, when Mary I ruled England, and Ivan the Terrible ruled Russia. There was a small but influential merchant community between the two countries from the 1720s. They were allies against Napoleon in the early 19th century. From the 19th century and on, England was often enough a land of refuge for Russian exiles and fugitives. (You may care to see: Baltic Exchange.)

Rutland Court - (See: Rutland House.)

Rutland Gate - Knightsbridge. 1838 terrace of houses.

Rutland House - Knightsbridge. Red brick mansion. Pulled down in 1833; (a large, detached house was not pulled down until 1901.) Now a series of homes, called Rutland Court.

Ruxley - Bexley/Bromley. Was called Rocheli in Domesday Book. It is thought it was deserted ca. 1557 due to plague (but people have long since returned.) Combined with St. James, North Cray in 1557.

- St. Botolph Church: Early 14th century. Yet exists, but only as a barn at Ruxley Manor.

Ryder Street - Dates back to ca. 1683. Until 1863, the west arm of Ryder Street was: Little Ryder Street. (See under L.) The east arm was Great Ryder Street. (See under G.)

Rye - Ancient word, seen in place names. Implies use as a common or untilled ground. (See: Sipson - For a place that grew the crop rye.)

-S-

Note:

St. = (As in "saint.") Alphabetical arrangement presumes the entire word is being applied.

To avoid any confusion "St." is never used in this work as an abbreviation of "street." St. is herein always an abbreviation for "Saint."

Therefore, if you are looking for, say, St. John Street, you must go, alphabetically, to s-a-i-n-t-(space)-j-o-h-n.

Sablionère, Hôtel de la - (See: Leicester Square/30.)

Sackville Street - Piccadilly, "outer march" of Savile Row. Long ago known as: Stone Conduit Close. Came to be owned by the Crown in 1536. First mentioned as Sackville Street in 1679. The Earl of Bath demolished all, and rebuilt the street in 1730; most houses completed in 1733. Remains almost wholly Georgian. Described as "confidently modest." By 1830 there were 13 tailors doing business on this street.

- 2-5: Henry Sotheran. London's oldest remaining bookshop, founded in 1761 (in York.) In London by 1815. Charles Dickens (author) shopped here.
- 16: Adeneys, tailors. In 1817, the Archbishop of Canterbury was one of their customers.
- 32: Society of Agriculture. 1798. (See at its own listing.)
- Gray's: A jeweler. Prinny shopped here, and Jane Austen wrote of it. (See: Gray's, Thomas, under G.)

Saddlers' Hall - (For the Worshipful Company of Saddlers.) Gutter Lane, Cheapside, between Foster Lane and Gutter Lane. (See: Foster Lane.) This guild has probably existed since Saxon days (certainly by the 11th century.) Royal Charter in 1363.

The Hall's location has been in Cheapside from at least the 14th century. The next hall, same locale, was in 1545; destroyed by the Great Fire of 1666. Replaced in 1670. Fire hit it again in 1815, and again in 1821 when it was utterly destroyed. Rebuilt in 1822, this was the present rendition of the Hall (excepting some rebuilding that resulted following WWII damage.) Livery Company. 25th in the order of precedence. Still has links to the business of saddlery.

(You may care to see: foxhunting - For a note on women in the hunt/the leaping horn.)

Sadler's Wells - In the current day, this area has evolved into one of London's leading areas for the performing arts, such as ballet and opera. During the 18-19th centuries, it was a pleasure garden. (See: Islington/Sadler Wells.)

- Exmouth Street: Built 1816-21. Joseph Grimaldi (the clown) lived here.
- Grimaldi, Joe: Famous clown. Performed at Sadler's Wells in the late 18th C. and early 19th C. (for almost 30 years.) The playbills would often be specific as to if it was to be a "moonlight night" because travelers had to brave the highwaymen between London and Islington.
- Musick House: 1683. Converted into a theatre in 1765, stone. In 1805, William Wordsworth wrote of seeing singers, rope-dancers, giants, dwarfs, clowns,

conjurers, posture-makers and Harlequins at the Musick House. Is now the Sadler's Wells Theatre, on Rosebury Avenue (the road being built in the 1890s) and the theatre rebuilt in 1927.

Saffron Hill - Hatton Garden. As the 19th C. advanced, and well into the Victorian era, this increasingly became a slum area.

St. Aldermanbury - (See: St. Mary Aldermanbury.)

St. Andrew's Place - (Also seen written as: St. Andrew Place.) Regent's Park area. 1823-6.

St. Augustine's Gate - (See: St. Paul's Gate.)

St. Bartholomew's Fair - (See: Bartholomew Fair.)

St. Bartholomew's Gatehouse - (Also seen as: St. Bartholomew's Gate House.) 13th C. arch, leads from Little Britain to a small burial ground. Used to lead to another church, one taken down when Henry VIII dissolved the priory in 1536. In 1595 a residence was built upon the gatehouse's space, timber, two stories. Did not burn in the Great Fire of 1666. A facade of Georgian design was built over this ca. 1702; used as a shop for the next two centuries. The original facade was revealed by 1917 bombing; restored fully in 1932.

St. Bartholomew's Hospital - (Familiarly called "St. Bart's." Formally called: the Royal Hospital of Saint Bartholomew.) West Smithfield, Spitalfields. London's oldest hospital; is the oldest hospital in England that is still on its original site. Still there, since 1123, founded by Thomas Rahere (Henry I's jester,) for the medical care of the sick poor. Only a few pieces of masonry remain from the 12th C., as stones from here were used for the 15th C. rebuild of St. Bartholomew-the-Less (church.)

Since before 1538, was a monastery (whose monks cared for the sick poor,) which was disbanded during the Dissolution; then refounded by Henry VIII in 1546.

The hospital was wholly rebuilt (and, as noted above, most of the medieval architecture lost) when the courtyard was added. (See: Courtyard, below.) Ca. 1788 the wards occupied 3 sides of a spacious quadrangle; 4 stories; "lofty"; 22 feet wide; each ward had about 15 beds. Not crowded. Quiet. Wide staircases. Each ward had a sister and a nurse. (See: nurse, under N.) Patients paid fees to be *admitted.* 428 patients. In 1800 it had 450 beds. Refaced in 1851 with Portland stone. Wholly rebuilt again in 1904-7.

Today it remains largely as it was rebuilt during the mid 18th century.

- Courtyard: Added in 1730-59 by James Gibbs, of Bath stone (which wore badly; a second source called them "Kentish clay bricks.")
- Gatehouse, the: Dates from 1702; rebuilt in 1834 by Philip Hardwick (with rooms added.)
- Henry VIII Statue: Over the "new" north gateway, was designed and constructed in 1702 by Frances Bird. Henry had refounded the hospital in 1546, after having

dissolved it in the first place, doing so just two weeks before he died. (See: West Smithfield/Henry VIII statue.)

- Lecture Theatre, the: Dates from 1795.
- Medical School: A vital part of the hospital, was added in 1662.
- Wings: The East Wing dates from 1769, the North Wing from 1732, the South Wing from 1740, and the West Wing from 1752.
  - ➢ See: Bartholomew Fair.
  - ➢ See: St. Bartholomew-the-Greater, under the CHURCHES section.
  - ➢ See: St. Bartholomew-the-Lesser - "The hospital church." (See under the CHURCHES section.)

St. Bernard's Hospital - Hanwell/Ealing. 1831, but started life as: Hanwell Lunatic Asylum. (See: Hanwell/Hanwell Lunatic Asylum.)

St. Bride's Well - A natural spring. Near St. Bride's Church. It can still be heard running, but there is no longer any access to it. There is a crypt here, inside of which is a small medieval chapel.

St. Clare - Aldgate. Convent. Suppressed ca. 1531 by Henry VIII.

St. Clare Street - (See: Church Street, Whitechapel, under C.)

St. Clement Dane's watch-houses - Night watchmen (Charlies.)

- ➢ See: police.
- ➢ See: Watch House.

St. Dunstan's Hill - The City.

- St. Dunstan's-in-the-East: (See under the CHURCHES section.)

St. Dunstan's Lodge - (AKA: Winfield House.) Situated in Regent's Park. First known as: Hertford Villa, by Decimus Burton, 1825. When its clock (that hung in front) was sold in 1830, it became known as St. Dunstan's. 12 acres. DISCOVERING AMERICAN HISTORY IN ENGLAND says: "After visiting Winfield House in 1946, Barbara Hutton" (wealthy American heiress) "decided to offer it (to) the US government to be used as the official residence of the American ambassador. For the token price of $1." It had been a white stucco (dilapidated, neo-Georgian) Regency-era villa, but in 1936 was pulled down and remade as a red brick Georgian-style house. The house was named for Ms. Hutton's grandfather. Is now Winfield House (for said grandfather,) and since 1955, the American ambassador's ***residence***, not to be confused with the Embassy. (See: Winfield House.)

St. George - Patron saint of England. (You may care to see: St. Thomas.)

St. George in the East - (The area of.) Tower Hamlets. It is actually the northern part of Wapping, but is often called by this, its old-fashioned churchy nickname (derived from its parish name, the latter having been created in 1729.) In the 18th C. it had market gardens.

In the 19th C. it had increased urbanization.

- St. George in the East church: Cannon Street Road. 1729. Designed by Nicholas Hawksmoor.

St. George's Circus - (AKA: Royal Circus.) St. George's Fields, Lambeth, Southwark.

Not to be confused with: St. George's Fields Circus - Which was a circus, not this traffic junction.

Southwark. 1771. Built to commemorate the completion/junction of new roads through St. George's Fields; it was the first traffic junction purposefully built in London, at first with an obelisk that had four oil lamps affixed to it (the obelisk was relocated in 1905 to Geraldine Mary Harmsworth Park.) The obelisk had been built to commemorate one Brass Crosby (Lord Mayor of London, 1770/objector to impressment.) The obelisk returned to its St. George's Circus location in the 1990s, now minus the oil lamps.

The 1812 Act for Improving St. George's Field required all new building around the Circus to have concave fronts.

The roads meeting at this junction: Blackfriars Road, Borough Road, Lambeth Road, London Road, Waterloo Road, and Westminster Bridge Road. (See: Royal Circus.)

St. George's Fields Circus - Another name for the Royal Circus. (See under R.) In 1782, an "equestrian and philharmonic society" erected here. Burned in 1803; replaced by the Surrey Theatre in 1809. (See: Surrey Theatre, under the THEATRES section.)

St. George's Fields - Lambeth, Southwark. (AKA: Southwark Fields, until the late 15th century.) Triangular marshy area, between Blackfriars Road and Westminster Bridge Road. (Near St. George-the-Martyr church.) There were 'no popery' riots staged here in 1780, more commonly called the Gordon Riots. (See: Lambeth/St. George's Fields.)

- Bethlehem Hospital: (Better known as Bedlam, the lunatic asylum) moved here from Moorfields in 1811. (See: Bedlam.)
- Magdalen House: Home for young and penitent female prostitutes. (See under M.)
- St. George's Cathedral: Roman Catholic, built 1840-8. (See: St. George's, Southwark, under the CHURCHES section.)
- St. George's Circus: (See at its own listing.)

St. George's Fields - Westminster, north of Bayswater Road. This is a modern term for this area, little seen on London atlases. (Not to be confused with St. George's Fields, Lambeth, Southwark.) Before being dubbed St. George's Fields, was a burial ground from 1763. The land was owned by St. George's in Hanover Square, which sold it in 1967 to developers.

St. George's Hospital - Hyde Park Corner, Knightsbridge. Site selected in 1733. Opened before 1746. Was converted from Lanesborough House. (See: Lanesborough, the hotel, under L.)

For: the "sick and lame." In 1788 hosted approximately 150 patients, with wards for men, and wards for women. Had a "good garden." First housed at a corner of Hyde Park, so patients would benefit from fresh air. Rebuilt at the same location in 1827. Had sixty beds until it was rebuilt in 1835 by William Wilkins. It did not have an on-site medical school, as the hospital refused the teaching of anatomy, so a medical school sprang up adjoining the hospital, called: "the School of Anatomy and Medicine adjoining St. George's Hospital," founded in 1830 and located at 1 Grosvenor Place. In about 1988, this site became The Lanesborough (hotel,) taking its name from the old designation.

St. George's Place - Knightsbridge. Six houses, replaced in 1863 by the Alexandra Hotel.

St. George's Square - (AKA: George Square.) Pimlico. Long and narrow, not "square" in reality. Leads to Grosvenor Road and the Thames. Started in 1835.

- St. Saviour's: Lupus Street. Dates from 1864 (See: St. Saviour's, Pimlico, under the CHURCHES section.)

St. George's Street - (Now St. George's Highway.) Had been Ratcliffe Highway. The Highway burned (as did the neighboring hamlet of Ratcliff) in 1794. Also had a series of murders in this street in 1811. (See: Ratcliffe Highway - For more on the murders.)

- 29: Lace shop. The owner was one of the murdered on Dec. 7, 1811 (as was his wife, a shop-boy, and an infant.)

St. Giles - Camden. (East end, not far from Charing Cross; northwest corner of Covent Gardens; where New Oxford Street is now.) Existed by at least 1101. Rookery/poor district of London. During the Regency and Charles Dickens' time, the residents were predominantly Irish. Mostly pulled down by 1849, but during the Regency it was a terrible slum.

This infamous rookery is now also covered over in part by the 20th century block called Centre Point. (See under C.)

The name is so tainted that the area is seldom called St. Giles in modern usage despite still being its official name.

- See: Carrier Street.
- See: Church Lane.
- See: Holy Land.
- See: St. Giles-in-the-Fields, under the CHURCHES section.

St. Giles Circus - 20th C. name for the open space made by the junction of Oxford Street, Tottenham Court Road, New Oxford Street, High Street, St. Giles, and Charing Cross Road.

St. Giles-Cripplegate - A church. John Milton (17th century Commonwealth poet/author of *Paradise Lost*) is buried here. (See under the CHURCHES section.)

St. Helen's Place - Bishopgate.

- 5-7: Leathersellers' Hall: Here since 1543. (See under L.)

St. James's - (The district of.)

Piccadilly, Westminster. Was originally a swamp. There was a St. James's Hospital here, ca. 1117, for "leprous maidens" (AKA: St. James-the-Less Hospital.) By the 15th C. it had converted to a convent. Whitehall Palace burned in 1512, prompting the new king Henry VIII to drain the marshlands and build St. James's palace over the old hospital's site, 1531. (He'd first intended St. James's to be a smaller retreat from the royal court at Whitehall, but when the latter burned he turned to St. James's as his new palace.)

> ➢ See: St. James's Palace.
>
> ➢ See: St. James's Street.

Henry Jermyn, Earl of St. Albans, developed this area (having been granted the land by Charles II.) At the bottom of the street stands Henry VIII's gatehouse, which leads to St. James's Palace.

In the 18th C. the elegant homes here were joined by government offices and foreign embassies, along with coffee-houses (used as places of business,) men's shops, and of course the men's clubs (such as Boodle's, Brooks's, and White's - See under the CLUBS section.) Note: the gentlemen's clubs have no nameplates, rather a case of "if you have to ask, you don't belong." During fashion dictator Beau Brummell's time, many bachelors had apartments in the St. James's district. (See: Piccadilly/Albany, for instance.)

Remodeled by Nash in 1829 for George IV.

There were no shops in St. James's intended for women's purchases (men's only) - i.e. while a woman could make a purchase here, it would be a man's product. To this day, Jermyn Street is a bastion of men's shops.

- Albany: Gentlemen's quarters.
  - ➢ See: Piccadilly/Albany.
  - ➢ See under A.
- Almack's: (See: King Street/26-28, below.)
- Athenaeum, the: by Nash, 1824. (See: Waterloo Place/116, below.)
- Birdcage Walk: Near St. James's Palace. (See under B.)
- Boodle's: Gentlemen's club. (See under the CLUBS section.)
- Brooks's: Gentlemen's club. (See under the CLUBS section.)
- Buckingham House: (Was not known as "palace" during the Regency.) Was in St. James's Square. (See under B - Much more.)
- Bury Street: Where (fashion icon) Beau Brummell's father rented rooms to the Quality. (See under B.)
  - Wilton's: Founded in 1742. Fish and oysters. (See: Bury Street/Wilton's.)

- Carlton Gardens: Built by John Nash. (See under C.)
- Carlton House Terrace: By John Nash, in the late 1820s. (See under C.)
- Downing Street: Is the residence of the Prime Minister. Is to Britain what 1600 Pennsylvania Avenue, Washington D.C. is to America. (See under D.)
- Floris: Perfumes. (See: Jermyn Street/89.)
- Jermyn Street: (See: St. James's Square/Jermyn Street.) Elegant men's shops.
- Kent & Sons: Established 1777 by William Kent; the Kent family were owners until 1932. Brush-makers. By the 1820s they were making toothbrushes, with the warrant of service to George IV. The handles were mostly made from the leg bones of bullocks. In 1897-1940, they were located at 75 Farringdon Road. Moved to Apsley, Hertfordshire in 1984. (You may care to see: toothbrushes.)
- King Street: (Also seen as: King's Street.) 1682.
    - 26-28 King Street: Almack's. Exclusive club for both sexes, where those of the highest *ton* gathered, invited by the Patronesses by virtue of vouchers. No strong drink allowed. If you came late, or wore the wrong clothes, you might be turned away - even the Duke of Wellington was turned away once for wearing trousers instead of the required breeches. Held only on Wednesday nights.

      The famous *Tom and Jerry* poem by Cruikshank reads:

      "*If once to Almack's you belong,*
      Like Monarchs, you can do no wrong;
      But Banished thence on Wednesday night,
      By Jove, you can do nothing right."

      (See: Almack's, under A, where there is far more information.)
- Mayfair: Has long been one of London's most exclusive places of residence. (See under M.)
- Pall Mall: An area of gentlemen's clubs. (See under P.)
- Paxton & Whitfield: Cheeses, under this name since ca. 1845. (See under P.)
- Pickering Place: In LONDON-THE SECRETS AND THE SPLENDOUR it states: "...in 1698, the Widow Bourne opened a grocer's" (in St. James's Street) "where, among other goods, she sold coffee - you can see the sign hanging outside 3 St. James's Street today. Her daughter married a painter-stainer called William Pickering, after whom Pickering Place (to the rear of number 3) was named. It's a delightful little square, the smallest in London." (See under P.)
- St. James's Market: (See at its own listing.)
- St. James's Palace: (See at its own listing.)

- St. James's Park: (See at its own listing.)
- St. James's, Piccadilly: Wren church, completed in 1684. (See under the CHURCHES section.)
- St. James's Street: (See at its own listing.)
- Savile Row: Men's tailoring.
    - ➢ See: St. James's Street - For men's outfitting.
    - ➢ See: Savile Row, under S.
- Spencer House: (See: St. James's Place/Spencer House.)
- Waterloo Place: Built in the late 1820s. By John Nash; part of his triumphal connection of Regent's Park and Pall Mall.
    - o 116: The Athenaeum. Decimus Burton, 1830, men's club. (See under the CLUBS section.)
- Wedgwood and Byerley's shop: Wedgwood dishes there by at least 1809.
    - ➢ See: St. James's Square/York Place.
    - ➢ See: Soho/Wedgwood.
- Westminster Palace: (See under W.)
- White's: Gentlemen's club. Founded by an Italian named Francis White, in 1693. Still there. (See: White's, under the CLUBS section.)
- Whitehall: District of civic duty. (See under W.)
- Whitehall Palace: Burned in 1698, but Inigo Jones' Banqueting Hall still exists. (See: Whitehall Palace, under W.)
- Wilton's: Restaurant, founded in 1742 selling fish and oysters. (See: Bury Street/Wilton's, above.)
- York Street: Shopping. (See: St. James's Square/York Street, at its own listing, under S.)

St. James's Market - Where the servants shopped for their masters, for meat, fish, vegetables, etc. Demolished in 1816, to make way for the new Regent's Street. A new market was put here between the new street and the Haymarket (ironmongers, grocers, chemists, and also tradesmen's homes.)

- The Wall's Meat Co.: Edmund Cotterill established a pork-butcher shop in 1786. In 1790, Richard Wall was apprenticed; became the sole proprietor in 1807. Supplied pork to Carlton House (and continued to supply after the prince became George IV.) Demolished in 1816 (along with the rest of the market;) moved to a market near Haymarket. Now in Banbury, Oxfordshire.

St. James's Market (street) - 1922, to connect Haymarket and Market Street.

St. James's Palace - Stable Yard, off Cleveland Row, Pall Mall. Was originally a swamp; then St. James's Leper Hospital for Women; there was a St. James's Hospital here, ca. 1117, for "leprous maidens," (AKA: St. James-the-Less Hospital, suppressed ca. 1531.)

Because Whitehall Palace burned for the first time in 1512, (and after Henry VIII suppressed the hospital ca. 1531,) Henry acquired the old hospital/convent, drained the surrounding marshland, and hired John Morton to build a palace here, said was to be a manor house of brick for Anne Boleyn, built 1532-40. The deer park yet remains (although now a lesser area,) now being occupied by Green Park, Hyde Park, and St. James's Park. Not much else from the Tudor era remains, except the brick gatehouse from when the palace was grouped around four courts (only two now remain); the court yards are described in NAIRN'S LONDON as: "ordinary, deliberately casual."

Was not an official royal residence until 1698 (following the second burning of Whitehall Palace.) It remained the (main) royal residence from 1698 to 1837 (at which time Queen Victoria moved her court to Buckingham Palace.)

St. James's Palace was refurbished by Queen Anne (prior to 1712.) George IV was born here in 1762. Described as a "rambling dark red brick building." Burned in part in 1809; the state apartments survived.

Called "the Court of St. James," to which ambassadors are still accredited, despite the fact the Royal Family now resides at Buckingham Palace. That is, St. James's Palace is still the Court's Official Residence, but now not used as such.

This is where young Regency women were "presented at court."

- Accession Council, the: Is still held at St. James's. A ceremonial body. Gathers when the ruler dies, and formally proclaims the accession of the successor to the monarchy. (The fact that the successor automatically ascends dates from 1701's Act of Settlement; the proclamation is ceremonial.)
- Aviary: Put in by Charles II. It evolved into Birdcage Walk. (See: Birdcage Walk, under B.)
- Chapel Royal: Ambassador's Court. Built for Henry VIII ca. 1532. This, and the Gatehouse, are the only items still standing from Tudor times. Extended in 1836 by Robert Smirke, and most of the present interior is from then. A chapel royal does not answer to an archbishop, but rather directly to the sovereign. There are five in London. (See: Chapel Royal, under C.) George IV was married to Queen Caroline of Brunswick here, 4/8/1795. (Not to be confused with the Queen's Chapel; this Chapel Royal is built inside the palace; the Queen's Chapel is outside the palace.)
- Clarence House: West of the Queen's Chapel. By John Nash, completed in 1827.

Was the home of the Queen Mother, Elizabeth II's mother, who was also named Elizabeth. See: Clarence House, under C.)

- Clock Tower: Remains from Tudor times.
- Friary Court: (See under F.)
- Gatehouse: Tudor. Main entrance to the palace. Fortified. Opens into Colour Court. (This, and the Chapel Royal, are the only things still standing from Tudor times.)
- Gentlemen at Arms: The sovereign's personal bodyguard.
    - ➢ See: Royal Guards.
    - ➢ See: Yeoman of the Guard.
- Horse Guards Barracks:
    - ➢ See: Royal Guards/Horse Guards Arch.
    - ➢ See: Royal Guards/Horse Guards Parade.
- Horse Guards Parade: (See: Royal Guards/Horse Guards Parade.)
- Lord Chamberlain, the: Is housed here, along with other court officials.
- Queen's Chapel: 1632-35, of Portland stone; Inigo Jones was ordered to build a chapel for Charles I's intended bride, the Infanta of Spain; she was a Catholic, who would not be able to hear mass in a Chapel Royal. The Queen's Chapel is not to be confused with the Chapel Royal. (See, above.)
    - ➢ See: Chapel Royal, above.
    - ➢ See: Pall Mall/Queen's Chapel - More at.
    - ➢ See: Queen's Chapel, St. James's Palace, under the CHURCHES section.
    - ➢ See under Q.
- State Apartments: Were rebuilt in 1703, by Wren for Queen Anne. (See: Friary Court, under F - Note at.) In 1809 a major fire, again, led to refurbishment of the State Apartments. The apartments link with Clarence House.
- Yeomen of the Guard:
    - ➢ See: Gentlemen at Arms, above.
    - ➢ See: Yeomen of the Guard, under Y.

St. James's Parish Workhouse - Soho. 1727. With 750 people, was overcrowded in the year 1800. Men and women were in separate areas. Everyone worked at odd jobs (if they could) such as needlework, slop-work, spinning yarn, etc. It was a dreaded place to end up (as were workhouses in general.) Children under two were fostered out; those over the age of two were boarded and given an education at the parish school. (See: workhouses.)

St. James's Park - The smallest Royal park in London. Takes its name from a leper hospital founded in 1117 by Queen Matilda. Enclosed in the 16th C. (ca. 1532) by Henry VIII when he seized the property from Westminster Abbey. In 1536 Henry VIII decided to make the area into a park, and so had the marsh drained and deer brought in (not so much for hunting, surprisingly, but for decoration.)

Charles I had ceremonial walks laid out.

It fell into a disused/neglected state until Charles II took an interest in it, after the Restoration, when it all was redesigned in the severe French style/pleasure walks, and Charles II then went on to open it to the public in 1662, or at least as stated in MYSTERY READER'S WALKING GUIDE - LONDON: "Charles II let the Londoners in to see him feeding the birds."

Remodeled again in 1828-29 by Nash, to look much as it does today; he turned the "blah" canal into a curving, graceful lake.

Since the 18th C., lawn chairs could be had for a fee.

During the Regency: had the French garden look given it by Charles II.

Nash's late 1828-29 remodel gave it the look it basically has today, with conifers, cypresses, fig trees, mulberry trees, plane-trees, and weeping willows, plus beautiful flower beds. There are large shrubs and winding footpaths. Today is 93 acres. Admission required a payment; ROMANTIC LONDON states: "St. James's Park up to a comparatively recent period was not open to members of the public unless they had business there or were furnished with a pass."

In 1762 there was a cockpit in the park, a circular room surrounded by rows of seats. Cockfighting was outlawed in 1849.

The Russian Ambassador gave Charles II pelicans, whose descendants are still fed by park attendants.

The gates were locked at night, although (in the 18th C.) some 6500 people had keys (allowing for prostitution to flourish here at night.)

The park was the primary London venue for licensed milk sellers (and their cows) from the 17th C. through the mid 19th century.

- Birdcage Walk: Runs on the south side of the park.
    - See: St. James's/Aviary.
    - See under B.
- Buckingham House: Later Palace, which structure was begun in 1825. (See under B.)
- Chain Bridge, the: Was built in 1857. Is now concrete.
- Chinese Bridge, the: Over the canal, was built in 1814, and destroyed a few years

later. The canal was then made into a lake. (See: "Remodeled again..." paragraph, above.)

- Horse Guards: In 1922 Mrs. Orford lost her privileges to run a bun and sweet shop that the Orford family had owned and run for some 300 years on this spot near the park entrance and situated near to the Horse Guards. (See under H.)
- Lake, the: 1828. Designed by Nash; serpentine in shape (although not to be confused with the Serpentine in Hyde Park,) replacing a former canal. No swimming or boating is allowed. There yet remain here pelican descendants, a gift made by a 1664 Russian ambassador to King Charles II.
- Marlborough Gate: 1828. (See under M.)
- Rosamond's Pool: Left intact during the park revamping by Charles II. Filled in, in 1770.
- Rotunda, the: Built in 1814 by John Nash, for an exhibition in the park. It moved to Woolwich, where it became the first military museum.
- Royal Mews: (See under R.)

St. James's Place - (Please note this is "Place," not "Palace.")

- 22: The banker Samuel Rogers lived here from 1800-1855. (Dismal flats occupy the space today.)
- 27: (See: Spencer House, below.)
- 35: (Now the Dukes Hotel.) During the Regency, was a private home, one that had been there since Charles II, to 1895.
- Spencer House: 27 St. James's Place. Located between St. James's Place and Catherine Wheel Yard. Built in the last half of the 18th C. for the first Earl Spencer (an ancestor of Princess Diana, nee: Diana Spencer; died August/1997,) 1756-1766. Palladian palazzo mansion, as designed by John Vardy. In 1985 was purchased by the J. Rothschild Administration. Its splendid garden and terrace overlook Green Park.

St. James's Royal Hotel - 76 Jermyn Street, Pall Mall. Here by at least 1820. In 1860 became the London and Provincial Turkish Bath Company.

St. James's Square - Laid out in 1676 (second source said 1665; a third and fourth source said 1673; a fifth source said the square was completed in 1675; a sixth said it was *begun* in 1660) for Lord St. Albans (the Earl and diplomat Henry Jermyn,) on land leased from the crown. (St. Albans was a favorite of Charles II.) A central garden, with trees, lawns, paths, with the aristocratic town houses situated across the streets around the garden square. Still has the lovely green garden at its center, but none of the original homes still exist. Enclosed by Jermyn Street, the Haymarket, Pall Mall, and St. James's Street.

- 4: Nancy Landhorne Astor, the first female MP to sit in the House of Commons, lived here ca. 1919. Probably built by Edward Shepherd, after 1725. Has 77 rooms, servants' quarters, and a private courtyard garden.
- 7: Lady Francis lived here. Caroline, Prinny's wife, stayed at this home during the trial of 1820. Is now the Royal Fine Arts Commission's Office.
- 8: Was at some point Lord Castlereagh's home (around the time of Waterloo.)
- 9, 10, 11: Built in 1736, Chatham House (this name came later.) On the north side of the Square. Has been a home to William Pitt the Elder (Prime Minister); the Earl of Derby (three-time PM); and Mr. Gladstone (four-time PM.) Now the Royal Institute for International Affairs. Designed by Henry Flitcroft.
- 14: London Library, the.
    - ➢ See, below.
    - ➢ See: London Library, under L.
- 15: Late 18th C. home. (See: Lichfield House.)
- 16: The home of one Mrs. Edmund Boehm (society matron.) Prinny was dining at a banquet here with his foreign secretary (Lord Castlereagh) and others when news of Wellington's victory at Waterloo was delivered by one battered and bloodstained Major Percy. Percy bore the Eagle and tattered colors of France with him. The ladies were removed from the gathering, Wellington's victory message was read aloud to a silent room, and then the list of the wounded and the dead. Major Percy was on the spot made Colonel Percy by the Prince Regent; and in tears, Prinny said, "It is a glorious victory, but…I have lost many friends." This is now the address of the East India Club. (See under the CLUBS section.)
- 20: In 1772-4, the patron who commissioned Adam to design this home was Sir Watkin Williams-Wynn. Known as Chandos House, on Chandos Street, in St. James's Square. Adam interior remains. (See under C.)
- 21: Elizabeth Bowes-Lyon (Queen Elizabeth II's mother, much beloved by the nation and dubbed "the queen mum") was born here on 8/4/1900.
- 31: Norfolk House. George William Frederick (later George III) was born here on 6/4/1738 (in the older house in the back, not the "newer" one, built in 1752.) The prince returned here, having been evicted from St. James Palace by his father (George II,) who called him "the greatest ass and greatest liar"; the prince having rented space from the Duke of Norfolk. (See: Norfolk House, under N.)
- 33: James Fenimore Cooper (American author) lived here for a few months in

1828.

- Buckingham House. (See under B.)
- Chandos House: (See 20, above.)
- Chatham House: (See 9, 10, 11, above.)
- Jermyn Street: Built ca. 1680. One end runs through Haymarket, the other St. James's. (See under J.)
- Lichfield House: (See: 15, above.)
- London Library, the: 14 St. James's Square. 1841. (See under L.)
- Royal Opera Arcade: (See under R.)
- St. James's, Piccadilly: (See under the CHURCHES section.)
- Union Club, the: (See under the CLUBS section.)
- Winchester House/Palace: (See under W.)
- York Street: Wedgwood (plate designer) moved here (from Soho) in 1809 or so, after being featured in Ackermann's Repository of Arts. (Wedgwood's business had been founded in 1759.) Is now renamed Duke of York Street. (See: Wedgewood dishes, under W.)
    - See: York Street, under Y.
    - See: Soho/Wedgwood.

St. James's Street - Westminster. Outfitters for gentlemen. Built in 1670. Leads from Piccadilly to Pall Mall.

This was a man's street. It was a bastion of men's clubs, bachelor apartments, shops for men, and a lounging spot for beaus and dandies. Women could, in the mornings, shop here with a maid, friend, or male along (there were some products for women, such as women's riding hats); but any evening appearance was "not done." A woman appearing past the morning hours would be likely deemed "fast" (if not outright a prostitute.) To be clear, the businesses here were aimed toward supplying male needs.

- 2: In 1807 James Swallow, hatter, opened here.
- 3: Berry Bros. & Rudd, wine and spirits merchants. (AKA: Berry Bros.) Founded in the 1680s elsewhere, but moved to St. James's Street in 1730 - possibly at 3, but the number 3 property was not bought by James Berry until ca. 1801. Ca. 1789 the business was known as the Old Coffee Mill; presumably the name changed to "Berry's" ca. the 1801-ish purchase of the property at 3. They went right on selling tea and coffee in addition to wine, until ca. 1850 when they chose to concentrate on wine only.

  Beau Brummell (fashion icon) was often weighed here on the Great Scales (as were customers since 1765,) one of the nine leather-bound records noting if he was wearing boots, half-boots, great coat, etc.; the scales are still there. Still has its fine (if austere) paneled interior, and lovely but strangely shaped black windows.

Berry Bros.' claret bottles have had distinctive black-n-white labels for the past 200 years. Known for its clarets and whisky.

NOTE (about sign hanging outside 3 St. James's Street): LONDON-THE SECRETS AND THE SPLENDOUR states: "...in 1698, the Widow Bourne opened a grocer's where, among other goods, she sold coffee - you can see the sign hanging outside 3 St. James's Street today." (See: Pickering Place, as this sign is a marker for that little square.)

- 6: James Lock. (AKA: James Lock & Co. AKA: Lock & Co. AKA simply: Lock's.) Hatters. Still making men's hats, for over 300 years; it is London's oldest shop. (They also made: ladies' riding hats, and servants' livery hats, etc.) The business was founded in 1676 by Robert Davis as a hatter's shop. Following his death, his son Charles (in 1747) hired James Lock as an apprentice. In 1757, Lock married the master's daughter, Mary. He inherited the business in 1759, and moved the business to this location at number 6 in 1765. On the southeast end of St. James's Street.

  The interior is black wood paneled walls, and unusual "coffin" staircase (from 1690, it's believed,) and elegant white hat boxes stacked abundantly. Overall, it looks much as it would have in the 17th century.

  In 1850 invented the bowler hat, although Lock's called it a Coke (was invented for one Mr. William Coke,) as Lock's still call the hat to this day. (See: Lock's, under L.)
- 8: Lord Byron (poet) lived here from 1808-1814. A Mr. Dolman's business, that of hatter and hosier, was at this address at the same time. (In 1960 a house was built over this site, called Byron House.)
- 9: Lobbs. Been making shoes and boots for the gentry since 1780. Here since the 1850s. LONDON-THE SECRETS AND THE SPLENDOUR states: "The business was established in Victorian times by John Lobb, ironically a lame Cornish farm boy who became bootmaker to Edward, Prince of Wales." STYLE CITY LONDON states: "A Cornish farmboy who learned the bootmaking craft, John Lobb received a royal warrant from...Edward VII..." (the king b.1841-d.1910,) "...Still specialize in and have become almost synonymous with the art of hand-made shoe(s)." To this day, is yet mostly shoes and boots for men (although they do now also provide for women.)

- 18: James J. Fox, cigar merchants, established 1881. (The building dates from 1787.)
- 19: Robert Lewis, smoking supplies since 1787. Christopher Lewis set up a tobacco shop here in 1787; his company, called Robert Lewis, first sold Havana cigars here by 1830. Joined with James John Fox (to become the store J. J. Fox & Robert Lewis) post-1870s.
- 23-27: "The Economist" building, dates from 1964, by Alison and Peter Smithson. (See: 28, below - Which is in the angle of the Economists' L-shaped area.)
- 28: Boodle's, gentlemen's club. (See under the CLUBS section.)
- 29: Harris & Co., chemists. (Most likely called itself an apothecary during the Regency.) Established here in St. James's Street in 1790. Royal Warrant in 1938. Perfumes, hair tonics, and other creams and toiletries. During the Regency this street provided shopping for <u>men</u>, so they could purchase perfume here for their ladies. Upstairs lived the caricaturist, Gillray, who threw himself out the window in 1815, dying as a result. (You may care to see: chemist.)
- 37: White's: Gentlemen's Club. Plainish facade. Some sources give the address as: 38. The bow window was added in 1811. Conservative in design and political leanings. (See under the CLUBS section.)
- 49: The Guards' Club: Gentlemen's club, from 1810-26, and again in 1827-48. (See: Guards' Club, under the CLUBS section.)
- 60: Brooks's: Gentlemen's club.
    - See: Brooks's, under the CLUBS section.
    - See: Club, the, under the CLUBS section.
- 69: Carlton, the. Modern. (See: Thatched House Tavern, under the INNS/PUBS section.)
- Boodle's: Gentlemen's club. 28 St. James's Street.
    - See: 28, above.
    - See under the CLUBS section.
- Brooks's: Gentlemen's club.
    - See: 60, above.
    - See under the CLUBS section.
- Cocoa-Tree Club: Lord Byron (poet) was a member here. (See under the CLUBS section.)
- Harris, D. R.: Apothecary. (See: 29, above.)
- Haymarket: (See under H.)

- Hoby's: Corner of St. James's Street and Piccadilly. Royal bootmaker. (See under H.)
- Humphrey, Mrs.: Somewhere on St. James's Street was a shop run by Mrs. Humphrey, who sold caricatures, among them those of Gillray. Gillray's caricatures sometimes would spear the very sort of gentleman who frequented her shop. Among them: Prinny, who had at least one caricature featured here, ca. 1789. (You may care to see: 29, above - Note at.)
- Justerini and Brooks: Wine merchants, established ca. 1790.
- Lobb's: Shoes and boots. (See: 9, above.)
- Lock's: Hats. (See: 6, above.)
- Pickering Place: (See under P.)
- St. James's Palace: (See at its own listing.)
- Thatched House Tavern: There by at least 1815. Was "kept" (owned/managed) by Almack, as in Almack's Assembly Rooms.
    - See: 69, above.
    - See under the INNS/PUBS section.
- White's: Gentlemen's club.
    - See: 37, above.
    - See under the CLUBS section.

St. John Street - Westminster. Ancient, dates from at least 1170. Called by some version of this name from the 15th century; it actually only meant the lower half of the street*, the upper half being known variously as: Chester Road, Islington Road, and (a bit oddly) as St. John Street Road - until 1905, then being known anew as part of St. John Street. (*This lower half had two names, too. It was St. John Street, Smithfield, and St. John Street, Clerkenwell - until 1866 when it all fell under the "St. John Street" name.)

St. Johns - Lewisham. The southernmost section of Deptford.

- Stone House: 1773. One of St. Johns' first significant structures. It gained the nickname "Comical House" because the architect George Gibson (who designed it for himself)) chose an overly ornate church-like design. Recently restored.

St. John's Gate - St. John's Lane, Clerkenwell. The gate was Tudor; built in 1504 (replacing an earlier structure) by Prior Docwra; parts of a 12th C. church and the 1504 Gatehouse are all that remain of the Priory of the Order of St. John, established here in 1110 (a second source said 1140); the 12th C. priory was one of the first hospitals in Europe. In 1731-54 the offices for *Gentleman's Magazine* were here. Reestablished as a priory in 1831, at which time it took on the ambulance and nursing efforts it yet does now (a museum here commemorates the volunteer St. John Ambulance Brigade.) It is also now part of a museum.

St. John's Lane - South of Clerkenwell Road, laid out in the 12th century, but is otherwise undistinguished.

- Gateway of the Knights of St. John. Gothic, 1504. AKA: St. John's Gate. AKA: Prior Docwra's Great Gate. (See: St. John's Gate, at its own listing.)

St. John's Lodge - Regent's Park. 18th C. villa. (See: Regent's Park/St. John's Lodge.)

St. John's Square - Dates from the 12th century. Its prior name was: St. John's Court. (AKA just: St. John's.) The term "St. John's Square" was seen by 1712, and used commonly by the mid 18th century.

- St. John's Church (or Priory): (See: St. John, Clerkenwell, under the CHURCHES section.)

St. John's Wood - A wooded area that once belonged to the Knights of St. John of Jerusalem (or, more technically, the Order of the Hospital of St. John of Jerusalem.) CHAMBERS LONDON GAZETTEER says: "Henry Samuel Eyre, a London wine merchant, purchased the estate from the Earl of Chesterfield in 1732. St. John's Wood did not evolve in the same way as many other smart parts of London. Its low-lying situation, poorly served by roads, did not attract gentlemen's seats and yet the Eyre family were keen to profit from its development, unlike more protective and resistant landowners elsewhere. In 1794 they commissioned a plan that would have seen St. John's Wood laid out in the same style as the spa town of Bath, but this was stymied by recession during the Napoleonic Wars. To the south of the Eyre estate, the area around St. John's Wood High Street was built up as Portland Town in the early 19th century, with housing for the working classes." In 1814, became the home for Lord's Cricket Ground, when the latter moved here from Dorset Square. (See: Lord's Cricket Ground.)

- St. John's Wood Barracks: Built in 1832, more formally known as the Riding Department of His Majesty's Ordnance. The King's Troop, Royal Horse Artillery was formed in the 20th C.; it has been housed here since 1946.
- St. John's Church: The land was bought in 1808. Church built in 1814.

St. Joseph's Hospital - After 1866. (See: Highwood/Holcombe House.)

St. Katharine's Dock - Begun in 1825, completed in 1828, on the site of the St. Katherine's Hospital, very near the Tower of London. Closed in 1968, now a successful development. (See: docks/St. Katharine's Dock.)

St. Katherine's Dock - (See: St. Katharine's Dock, spelled with two a's.)

St. Katherine's - Tower Hamlets; between Wapping and the Tower. (Also seen as: St. Katharine's, with two a's.) Dock. In the general area where St. Katherine's Hospital stood. The Katherine Docks Act of 1825 displaced some 11,000 persons and the slums in which they lived with names such as Cat's Hole, Dark Entry, and Pillory Lane.

- See: docks/St. Katharine's Dock - Note it is spelled with two a's.
- See: St. Katherine's Hospital - One a.

St. Katherine's Hospital - (Also seen spelled: St. Katharine. AKA: Royal Hospital of St. Katharine's by the Tower.) Used to be situated by the Tower, but is now opposite the northeast entrance to Regent's Park after it moved in 1825 due to the construction of St. Katharine's Dock. Founded in 1148 by Matilda (wife of King Stephen.) Neo-Gothic buildings there now. Incorporates what had been the charitable foundation of St. Katharine (now the Danish church in London, since 1949) and houses by Ambrose Poynter built in 1826. It was never a medical hospital, but rather a charitable institution for the "maintenance of poor persons," leaning more toward a church and charity than a hospital. Its chapel was demolished in 1827.

St. Luke's Hospital - Insane Asylum. (See: Old Street, Finsbury.)

St. Luke's - Islington. A little used name for Old Street's western part.

- See: See: St. Luke's Hospital, above.
- See: Old Street, Finsbury.

St. Margarets - Richmond. Was the northern part of Twickenham Park from the 16th century. Is now popular with the professional classes.

- Gordon House: 1867. For the Earl of Kilmorey. Became part of the Royal Naval Female School. (See: St. Margarets, below, in this entry.)
- St. Margarets: A ca. 1830 house built for the Marquis of Ailsa on the 17th C. site of a home once belonging to Richard Sheridan (dramatist.) Pulled down in the 1850s. The Earl of Kilmorey built a new house, but never lived in it here; in 1856 it became home to the Royal Naval Female School.

St. Margaret's - Westminster. (See under the CHURCHES section.)

St. Martin-in-the-Fields - (See under the CHURCHES section.)

St. Martin le Grand - The street, as opposed to the church. (See: St. Martin le Grand, under the CHURCHES section.) This street was named for the church. The area was renowned in the 15th C. for lacemaking. Venue of shoemakers.

St. Martin's Lane - Westminster; Covent Gardens' western border street. (Also the eastern border of Soho.) The buildings of this street were pulled down to make way for Trafalgar Square, post-Regency. But it does still host some 18th and 19th C. buildings. Is now the site (or near to) many theatres. This was the road one took between Covent Garden and the Strand, until Charing Cross Road was built in 1887. (See: Charing Cross Road.)

- 60-62: The first workshop of Chippendale, the furniture-maker. Here in the 18th century, stayed for six decades. (See: Goodwin's Court.)

- 96: Stood until 1828, belonging to a Mr. Powell, a "colour-man." The house is described as "wonderful" and "curious." It had a picturesque Queen Anne front door-frame with spread eagle and carved flora. A room inside the house was used by Hogarth in his *Marriage à la Mode* series (the picture being the one with a quack/doctor in it.)
- Aldridge's Repository: (See: Horse and Carriage Repository.)
- Cecil Court: (See under C.)
- Goodwin's Court: (See under G.)
- Scotch Arms: "Near St. Martin's Lane and Charing Cross" was a tailors' club. (A club for tailors, not unlike clubs for gentlemen.) Existed here in 1812 (based at the Scotch Arms.)
- Seven Dials: Notorious rookery. (See at its own listing.)

St. Martin's Parochial Building - Near St. Martin-in-the-Fields; on St. Martin's Lane corner. Three late Regency buildings by Nash are here, left from Nash's (partially realized) West Strand Improvements scheme: 1) The vicarage (is 3 stories tall,) 2) St. Martin's Vestry Hall, and 3) St. Martin's National School, dating from 1830.

St. Mary Aldermanbury - (See under the CHURCHES section.)

St. Mary-at-Hill - Lovat Lane, Eastcheap. Wren church. On street of same name. (See under the CHURCHES section.)

St. Mary Bethlehem, hospital of - (See: Bedlam.)

St. Mary Cray - Bromley. There is no apostrophe in its name (as in "St. Mary's Cray,") although the nearby St. Paul's Cray leads some to make the mistake of adding one. This area dates from at least 1032, when King Canute granted land to the priors of Christ Church, Canterbury. This area was once known as South Cray, but the church's building soon changed the district's name. (See, below.) In the late 18th C. it was written of as a "populous, handsome village." Industrial growth began ca. 1926. Only a few early 18th C. houses and Victorian terraces survive on the High Street.

- St. Mary's Church: Early 13th century. Late 19th century "restorations" mostly hide its medieval beginnings.

St. Mary Spital - North of Bishopsgate. (See under the CHURCHES section.)

St. Mary's Axe - Houndsditch. Gone by the Regency era. (See under the CHURCHES section.)

St. Mary's Hospital - Paddington. Established 1843, opened 1851.

St. Michael's Alley - Cornhill. Hosted the first coffee-house in London, 1652. (See: Cornhill/St. Michael's Alley.)

- Jamaica Inn, the: (See under the INNS/PUBS section.)
- St. Michael's Cornhill: (See under the CHURCHES section.)

St. Nicholas Shambles - A parish, east end of Newgate Street, and in the neighborhood of Eastcheap. (See: Butcher's Hall.)

St. Pancras - Camden. Medieval. Until 1760 this area was a spa (recreation site.) Much of what had been known as St. Pancras is now designated by other place names such as Kings Cross and Somers Town.

- St. Pancras Church: Pancras Road. Believed to have been rebuilt ca. 1350, and possibly had 7th C. origins.
  - See: St. Pancras-by-the-Inwood, under the CHURCHES section.
  - See: St. Pancras Old Church, under the CHURCHES section.

St. Pancras Churchyard - Until ca. 1839. (See: Highgate Cemetery.)

St. Pancras Station - Railway station, 1868.

St. Paul's Cathedral - Ludgate Hill, the City. St. Paul was (and remains) London's patron saint (as opposed to St. George, the patron saint of England.)

There was a cathedral on this site since approximately 604-10, built by Ethelbert, king of Kent. (He was the first Christian English monarch.) Rebuilt in stone in 675-85; destroyed by Vikings in 961. A third version was lost to fire in 1087. The fourth, Norman, version stood for almost six centuries, but was lost to the Great Fire of 1666. (The statue of St. Paul's one-time dean, John Donne, survived the Great Fire. Donne wears a shroud and stands on a funerary urn, which yet bears scorch marks.) The fifth design was authorized in 1675; built in layers, so the first ceremony to be held here (the first service after the Great Fire of 1666, held on 12/2/1697) had to wait until 1697 (as the building continued; today's church is that fifth version.)

The outdoor statue of Queen Anne is late 19th C., a copy of the 1712 original that marked the cathedral's completion.

Neo-classical, with much Baroque detailing (English Renaissance architecture,) by Wren, 35 years in the making, completed in 1710. The dome is actually two domes, with a brick cone between them, built to support the whole.

The hour bell (called "Great Tom," is one of three bells) still rings for apprentices at the end of their lunch break.

The Duke of Wellington's memorial monument was admitted inside the church in 1912. (Prior to that there was an objection to having an image of a horse in a church.)

NAIRN'S LONDON gives us this summary: "Wren might have chosen grandeur, or drama or *terribiltia* or excitement. Instead, there is overwhelming compassion, the common touch ennobled. No wonder that cockneys love it, and see it as a badge as well as a symbol."

(SEE: ST. PAUL'S CATHEDRAL, IN THE **CHURCHES** SECTION.)

- Chapter-house, the: On the north side of the cathedral. First built in 1332. Re-erected in 1712. Gutted by WWII damage in 1940, rebuilt.

- Grub Street: North of St. Paul's. (See under G.)

St. Paul's Churchyard - Heart of the drapery trade; and booksellers (from the 16th century.) The author Thomas Malory set this as the site of Arthur's sword-in-the-stone fictional miracle, as written by him in *Morte d'Arthur.* Was sometimes the site of executions, at least up to the 17th century.

- Paternoster Row: Longmans (the publishers) has been here since 1724.
- Queen Anne statue: Dates from 1886.
- St. Paul's Cross: (AKA: Pol's Stump.) A wooden pulpit was used for proclamations, until it was torn down by Cromwell's men. The papal announcement that condemned Martin Luther was read aloud here. A memorial to the cross' one-time existence here was not placed until 1910.
- St. Paul's School: (See at its own listing.)

St. Paul's - Covent Garden.

> - See: Covent Garden/St. Paul's.
> - See under the CHURCHES section.

St. Paul's Cray - Bromley. CHAMBERS LONDON GAZETTEER notes: "St. Paulinus was buried at Rochester in 644 and the original village church dedicated to him may date from shortly after that time. The village was simply called Craie in Domesday Book and became Craye Paulin after the church was rebuilt around 1200." St. Paul's Cray remained agricultural in nature halfway into the 20th century.

- St. Barnabas's Church: 1964.
- St. Paul's Church: Ancient. Declared redundant (to St. Barnabas) in 1977. Is now offices.

St. Paul's Gate - (Was also sometimes called: St. Augustine's Gate.) Southeast corner of Watling Street. Burned in the Great Fire of 1666; not rebuilt.

St. Paul's School - St. Paul's Churchyard. (That is, literally in the churchyard of St. Paul's Cathedral.) Founded in 1509, replacing a 12th C. school attached to St. Paul's Cathedral. Completed in 1512; a single story school, with four rooms: an entrance hall, a chapel, and two schoolrooms. Some boys boarded in dormitories situated in the four-story houses flanking either side of the school (one house was for the high master, and the other for the second master.) Destroyed in the Great Fire of 1666. Rebuilt. Rebuilt again and enlarged in 1822. Removed in 1884 to Hammersmith Road. (See: Fulham/St. Paul's School.)

St. Peter's Square - Hammersmith, 1839.

St. Petersburg Place - Bayswater. Built ca. 1815; first called Petersburg Place (without the "St.",) probably in honor of Tsar Alexander I's 1814 visit to London. Was called St.

Petersburg Place by at least 1842.

St. Stephen's Chapel - (AKA: St. Stephen's Crypt.) The home of the Commons until 1834, when it burned. Rebuilt as St. Stephen's Hall in the late 19th century.

> ➢ See: House of Commons.
> ➢ See: Lower House.
> ➢ See: Westminster Palace.

St. Stephen's Crypt - (See: St. Stephen's Chapel.)

St. Stephen's Porch - The public entrance to the Houses of Parliament. (See: Houses of Parliament/St. Stephen's Porch.)

St. Swithin's Lane - Near St. Swithin's Church, Candlewick Street.

- New Court: (See under N.)
- Salters' Hall: (For the Worshipful Company of Salters.) Originated as: the Guild of Corpus Christi.

  The Salters did not produce salt, they salted provisions.

  Royal Charter in 1394. The first Hall was in Bread Street, and was probably built in the mid 15th century. On this site since 1641. The third Hall was destroyed in the Great Fire of 1666. The fourth version stood until it was demolished in 1821, had been in St. Swithin's Lane; it was smallish, brick, with an entrance opening in an arcade of three arches.

  Today's Hall is at Fore Street, 1976. Livery Company. 9th in the order of precedence.

St. Thomas - (Thomas á Becket, Archbishop of Salisbury.) Murdered in 1170, during Henry II's reign. Patron saint of London.

> ➢ See: The INTRO-REIGNS section/British Kings & Queens and Their Reigns/Henry II.
> ➢ You may care to see: St. George.

St. Thomas's Gate - (See: Tower of London/"Other Places & Things"/Traitor's Gate.)

St. Thomas's Hospital - (See: Southwark/St. Thomas's Hospital.)

Salisbury Court - Off Fleet Street. Was the medieval London home (and episcopal court) of the Bishop of Salisbury; he had an inn above for visitors. Samuel Pepys (diarist) was born here in 1633. There was a theatre that stood 1629-66 on the court's south side, it burned in the Great Fire of 1666; the theatre was repaired and became Dorset House during Elizabeth I's time. Dorset House was the beginning of what became Salisbury Square. (See: Edmonton/Salisbury House - The note at.)

Salisbury House - (See: Edmonton/Salisbury House.)

Salisbury Square - The City. Largely on the land that had been occupied by Salisbury Court.

- See: Fleet Street/Salisbury Court/Salisbury Square.
- See: Salisbury Court.

Salisbury Street - Rebuilt in 1783, by architect James Paine. (See: Edmonton/Salisbury House - The note at.)

salt -

- See: food/salt.
- See: St. Swithin's Lane/Salters' Hall - The Salters didn't produce the salt, they used it to salt provisions.

Salt Hill - A place outside London, in Slough, Berkshire, at which coachmen (of the stages or mails) took their dinner. Before 1974 Slough was part of Buckinghamshire.

Salters' Hall - (See: St. Swithin's Lane/Salters' Hall.)

Salvation Army, the - Started in London's East End, in 1865. First called: the East London Mission. Name changed to Salvation Army in 1878.

sanctuary - In early times some churches were granted this status. The crown could not arrest someone who had attained (that is, physically gone into) a place of sanctuary. The practice was abolished in 1623.

- See: St. Martin-le-Grand, under the CHURCHES section.
- See: sanctuary, under the CHURCHES section.
- See: Sanctuary, the, below.
- You may care to see: liberties.

Sanctuary, the - Dean's Yard.

A sanctuary was a medieval safe place for escapees from the law, with the exception of Jews and traitors (who were not allowed to enter.)

An independent building very near Westminster Palace and Westminster Abbey, a cruciform stronghold dating from Edward the Confessor; two stories high. It was so solid, it was difficult to demolish in 1750. (See: Westminster Palace/Sanctuary.)

There were four or five sanctuaries in the City during medieval times. However, the right of sanctuary was abolished in 1623.

- See: St. Martin-le-Grand, under the CHURCHES section.
- See: sanctuary.
- See: Ye Olde Mitre Tavern, under the INNS/PUBS section.

Sanderstead - Croydon, Surrey. Dates from at least 880, belonging to the Bishop(s) of Winchester. Had no public house (as they were forbidden by the manor family.)

- All Saints' Church: 1230. The unusually shaped tower dates from 1310. Yet exists.
- Sanderstead Court: 1676. Refurbished in the 18th century. In the early 20th C.

became Selsdon Court (Hotel.)

sandwich - Edward Gibbon wrote in his diary, dated Nov. 24, 1762: "...in the middle of a coffee-room, upon a bit of cold meat, or a sandwich..." (showing that the term was in usage by at least 1762.) Tradition has it the 4th Earl of Sandwich (b.1718-d.1792) invented this casual style of dining when he didn't want to leave the gaming table for food, but this tale is now largely held to be apocryphal. (See: Beefsteak, under the CLUBS section.)

Sandwich Islands - (See: Hawaii.)

Sandringham - In the county of Norfolk. Royal castle (a home Queen Elizabeth II is said to like best.) Eight miles/12.9 km northeast of King's Lynn. Is a 19th C. building, mock Tudor. Purchased in 1861 for Edward, Prince of Wales. It has 200+ rooms. The *park* is 300 acres (open now to the public, since 1908; with the museum being opened to the public in 1930; the house in 1977, the year of the queen's Silver Jubilee. The entire property still belongs, however, to Queen Elizabeth II, and the entire estate amounts to some 7,000 acres.

Sands End - Hammersmith and Fulham. (See: Fulham/meadows.)

Sandycombe Lodge - 40 Sandycoombe Road, Twickenham, Richmond-upon-Thames. (The lodge and the road are spelled differently.) J. M. W. Turner (artist) built this house for himself in 1813, as a summer retreat, in "picturesque-cottage style."

sanitation - Unfortunately, during the Regency it was still entirely common to dump the contents of one's chamberpot out of the window. Many streets had a ditch where raw sewage openly ran, to be washed away (or at least downstream) by the rain.

- See: cesspits.
- See: Chelsea Waterworks Company - 1723.
- See: General Board of Health - 1848.
- See: medicine - For the concept of germs.
- See: nightmen - Those who removed human waste.
- See: sewers.
- See: waste pits.
- See: water.

Sarjeant's Inn - (See: Serjeant's Inn. Note it is spelled with two e's.)

Saturn - (See: planets/Saturn.)

Savile House - (See: Leicester Square/Savile House.)

Savile Row - Piccadilly, St. James's, Mayfair. Street rebuilt from 1730. Runs parallel to Regent Street, south of Conduit Street. (Savile was the Earl of Burlington's wife's maiden name.) Gentlemen's tailors, the first being established in Savile Row in 1806. By 1838 was "teeming" with tailors. To this day "Savile Row" stands for the best in men's suits. Savile Row was also an address for prominent doctors; (in the 1840s a lot of the doctors defected to Harley Street.)

- 1: Gieves and Hawkes. First known as: Hawkes & Co. Tailors; the oldest tailor shop in Savile Row*. Established in 1732 (a second source said 1785,) on the site of a previous house. From 1811-16, Lord George Cavendish lived here rather than at Burlington House. (*While Gieves & Hawkes is the *oldest* tailor business on Savile Row, they didn't move *here* until 1912; and Gieves and Hawkes' names were not united until the 1970s.)
- 3: Housed the Albany Club; also Lord Nelson and Lady Hamilton. Much later, it was home to the Beatles (musical group's) Apple Corporation.
- 11: Henry Maxwell & Co.: Founded in 1750. Maxwell started with making spurs on the forge in his Soho backyard from 1756. Royal Warrant from George IV. Also made clothing, including: pink (the red coat worn by foxhunters.) Moved to Savile Row in the early 20th century. Today are shoe and bootmakers, and Maxwell's spur collection is kept at 83 Jermyn Street.
- 14: The Restoration playwright Richard Brinsley Sheridan died here on 7/7/1816. (May have also at one time lived at number 17.)
- 15: Henry Poole & Co. Tailor. In 1806 James Poole set up a draper's shop, Everett Street, Brunswick Square. By the time Waterloo occurred, Poole was providing military tunics. He opened a shop in 1822 at 181 Regent Street; then had a headquarter at 4 Old Burlington Street (at which time the shop was known as: Poole and Cooling.) James died in 1846; his son, Henry, took over the business, at which time he enlarged their shop and gave it a new entrance on Savile Road, as opposed to the old entry at the 4 Old Burlington Street address. (See: Old Burlington Street/4.)
- 17: Richard Brinsley Sheridan (playwright,) in debt, died here on 7/7/1816.

Savoy Chapel - Savoy Hill, the Strand. Gothic. Residual of the 1268 Savoy Palace that was once here. In 1505 it was rebuilt as a chapel for the charity hospital that had been established on the old Savoy Palace site. In 1670 it partly burnt. Most of the present building dates from 1864; Perpendicular. Now a private chapel for the Queen, the Chapel of the Royal Victorian Order.

Savoy Court - The only highway where driving on the right is permitted in England, and this by Act of Parliament. It is a private road, not a public one. Done to allow carriages to more easily pull before the Savoy Theatre, opened in 1889.

Savoy Hotel, the - The Strand. For six centuries a building called the Savoy (and/or Savoy Palace) has stood here, raised first in the 14th C. by the first Duke of Lancaster. Burned in the Peasants' Revolt of 1381. Was a palace for Peter of Savoy. In 1505 it was rebuilt as a hospital for the poor. It opened in 1889 as the Savoy Theatre and Hotel. (See: Savoy Court - Note at.)

Savoy Palace - (See: Savoy Hotel.)

Scarborough Fair - Was an actual fair in the county of Yorkshire, closed by 1788. (See: fairs, the note there.)

Schomberg House - (See: Pall Mall/Schomberg House.)

school terms - (See: rents.)

schools -

- See: Blewcoat School.
- See: Bluecoat School - AKA: Christ's Hospital.
- See: Cambridge.
- See: charity schools.
- See: colleges/universities.
- SEE: EDUCATION.
- See: Eton.
- See: Grammar School - In Guildford borough.
- See: Great Windmill Street School.
- See: Greycoat School.
- See: Harrow.
- See: Highgate School.
- See: Holborn Charity School.
- See: rents - For school terms.
- See: St. Paul's School.
- See: Sir John Cass's Foundation School.
- See: Sunday schools.
- See: Westminster School.

Schweppes Mineral Waters - The world's first carbonated beverage (mineral water.) Schweppes first sold his soda water through apothecaries. Began in Geneva, Switzerland in 1783, by Jacob Schweppe (with partners Jacques and Nicholas Paul.) Business dissolved in just a few years, and Schweppes took the idea to London in 1792, first in Drury Lane, then establishing a business at 11 Margaret Street, Cavendish Square in 1795; he retired in 1798, and the business remained (under other owners, but the Schweppes name) here until 1831. Then moved to 51 Berners Street. Present address is: Schweppes House, 1/4 Connaught Place.

science - The term "biology" was coined in 1802 by Gottfried Treviranus (German naturalist/physician.) The microscope was invented in 1826.

- See: Royal Society, the.
- See: Surrey Institution.

Science Museum - Exhibition Road, South Kensington. Founded in 1847, opened in 1857. Altered and changed in 1909.

Scientific Instrument Makers' Company - (AKA: the Worshipful Company of Scientific Instrument Makers.) Began in 1956. Granted Livery in 1964. Shares a Hall with the Glaziers, and with the Launderers. Livery Company. 84th in the order of precedence. (See: Glaziers' Company - For more on their Hall.)

Scotch Arms, the - (See: St. Martin's Lane/Scotch Arms.)

Scotch House - Knightsbridge, 1830. Shopping.

Scotland - (See - admittedly erroneously - under the BRITISH COUNTIES section.)

Scotland Yard -

- See: Great Scotland Yard.
- See: Whitehall/4 Whitehall Place.

Scottish Office, the -

- See: Dover House.
- See: Piccadilly/Albany.

Scriveners' Company - (AKA: the Worshipful Company of Scriveners. In medieval times, AKA: the Mysterie of the Writers of the Court Letter. After its Charter, AKA: Master Wardens and Assistants of the Company of Scrivenors {sic} of the Cittie {sic} of London.) The City. Belonged to the Text-writers (who had a second branch that developed into the Stationers.) The scriveners drafted legal forms, being lawyers up to the point of drafting wills and legal deeds. First ordinances granted in 1373. Royal Charter in 1617. Holds yearly exams; requires any notary public in the City (or within a 3-mile/4.8 km radius thereof) to belong to this company prior to practicing their employment. Livery Company. Their Hall burned down in the Great Fire of 1666; rebuilt. Sold their Hall to the Coachmakers in 1703. Destroyed in WWII bombing. They have no Hall now (but the site is at Noble Street, near Guildhall.) 44th in the order of precedence.

scurvy - James Lind (Scottish doctor) discovered the use of citrus in the diet to combat scurvy ca. 1747, but it took approximately 50 more years for the practice of consuming Vitamin C to spread and be a firmly rooted naval practice. It is the source of the pejorative "Limeys" for British sailors, which Americans started using in the 19th century because the British sailors drank the juice of limes to stave off the disease. Another dish used to prevent scurvy was: pickled cabbage (which was easy to keep on ships.)

Seacoal Lane - (Also seen written as: Old Seacoal Lane.) Off Farringdon Street. Where coals were landed upon coming into London. The Fleet Prison once stood here. (See: Fleet Prison.)

season, the - The time of the year when the gentry and the aristocracy resided in London, throwing fêtes and soirees, and launching marriageable daughters. Letters from the late 18th C. say London emptied in August, only to refill in February; others say housing was most expensive from Christmas to June due to parliament and families being in town. I've read it ran from November to May.

Some of the discrepancy may come from the difference between 18th C. practices and 19th C. ones; as the roads were somewhat better in the 19th C. that may have played a part. Too, some relate the highest number of season attendees coming to town after Easter - which is not held on the same day every year. This holds some water, because calendars show the theatre seasons tending to start after Easter, around May 1st. Regardless of its actual span, people seemed to want to avoid winter travel and so settled into London before the mud and ice came. Or after it melted. Most sources say the season was over when London got too warm (and therefore smelly.)

As to the little season: current opinion states that it never existed. Some say it was an invention of the author Georgette Heyer. (You may care to see: delope.) If the little season existed, it was supposedly in the autumn, September to November. It would have been for those people who came back to town early, providing entertainment for one another. I've never found reference to it in any resource (other than denials it existed.)

secretary - During the Regency era, if one had a secretary (to help conduct business, execute your office of duty, etc.,) that person would be male.

sedan chairs - A covered seat mounted on two poles, carried by one man fore, one man aft, to transport paying customers (if the chair was not privately owned.) No wheels. Introduced into London by 1634. Little used by the time of the Regency, and usually then only in towns like Bath (which was hilly) and only by the infirm. By ca. 1795 London streets were simply too crowded with wheeled conveyances to allow this form of travel anymore. (You may care to see: Bath Chair.)

seeds - While one could purchase seeds commercially during the Regency, there was a solid interest in matters horticultural and in amateur botany, so the exchanging of seeds (and cuttings, and plants) among interested friends would have naturally occurred as well.

- See: Corn Exchange.
- See: Devon/House of Sutton, under the BRITISH COUNTIES section.
- You may care to see: botanical gardens.
- You may care to see: grains.

Seething Lane - By Tower Hill. Samuel Pepys (diarist) lived here in the 1660s.

- St. Olave's: (See: St. Olave's - Hart Street, under the CHURCHES section.)

Seething Wells - Kingston-upon-Thames. The bubbling spring here was described in the 18th C. as "cold in summer and warm in winter." The osier beds (pliable willows good for basketweaving) and a wharf were here by the early 19th century. (See: Surbiton.)

Selfridge's - 400 Oxford Street. Famous department store, known for having "everything." 1908. Founder Henry Gordon Selfridge was an American.

Selhurst - Croydon. Dates from at least 1225.

- Selhurst Farm: Dates from the early 19th century. Later called Heaver's Farm.
- Selhurst Park: A gated estate from the 1850s.

Selsdon - Croydon. Much of this area is high (as London measures,) with some areas at 500+ feet above sea level. The church used to own this roughly square mile farmland; the woodland was used for pheasant shooting in the 19th century.

semaphore - Invented in 1794, first in France. Used by the Royal Navy. (See: Telegraph Hill - Final note, on semaphore signals.)

sepsis - Infection. After childbirth, it was not uncommon for women to die of it. This childbirth sepsis was usually called "puerperal fever."

Sergeants' Inn - (See: Serjeants' Inn.)

Serjeants' Inn - (Also sometimes seen spelled as: Sergeants' Inn.) Chancery Lane. South side of Fleet Street; reached through an archway. From 1443. An Inn of Chancery; one of two inns/of the Serjeants-at-Law in London (the other being: Chancery Lane.) There were two Serjeants' Inns by 1500, but the Fleet Street one did not get a renewed lease, so the two combined in 1730. The last one (the Chancery Lane one) sold in 1877 (although the society wasn't dissolved officially); the last member died in 1921. Chancery Lane held 18th C. homes, completely lost to WWII bombing.

Serpentine, the - Hyde Park, river. (See: Hyde Park/Serpentine.)

servants' registry - Where one went (or sent one's male secretary, or butler) to hire new servants in London. There were actually quite a few registries, with one being located in the Strand, but very little information on these Regency era businesses have survived for researchers to find. (See: Strand/servants' registry.)

serviettes - This term is Victorian. Regency folk called them napkins, as in a cloth for wiping your fingers while dining. (See: clouts - For diapers.)

Sessions House - Clerkenwell.

- See: Clerkenwell Green/Middlesex Session House.
- See: Old Bailey.

Seven Dials - Poor, criminal district. East end, near what became Charing Cross; north section of St. Martin's Lane, Covent Garden. Named for a pillar put up in the 17th C. (when this area was first developed,) topped with six blue-faced sun dials. The architect had been approved to build six streets and a church, but he cheated, building a seventh street and no church, hence the sun dials numbering only six despite there being seven dials/streets.

Even constables were afraid to venture into Seven Dials, especially after dark.

The following list is of some of the Seven Dials area streets, how the streets were first called → what they were called in the 18-19th centuries → and what they are called today:

- Castle Street → Castle Street → Shelton Street (this latter from 1938.)
- Church Street → Queen Street → Short's Gardens (from 1906.)
- Earle Street → Earle Street (Great, and Little) → Earlham Street (from 1938.)
- King Street → King Street → Neal Street (from 1877.)
- Little Monmouth Street → White Lion Street (Great, and Little) → Mercer Street (from 1938.)
- Monmouth Street → Dudley Street (1845-1886, described then as squalid) → Shaftesbury Avenue (from 1886.) (See: Monmouth Street, under M.)
- St. Andrew's Street (Great, and Little) → St. Andrew's Street (Great, and Little) → Monmouth Street (from 1938.)
- King's Head Court → Neal's Yard → Neal's Yard.

The pillar was torn down in 1773, because it was rumored that treasure was buried beneath it. In 1822 the pillar was re-erected, in Weybridge, Surrey. A copy was re-established at the original location in 1989.

(See: Holy Land - Which neighbors onto Seven Dials.)

Seven Sisters - Haringey. Supposedly named for trees planted by seven sisters before they went their individual ways; all the same, seven elms (surrounding a walnut tree) did exist here in the 17-18th centuries. The walnut died in 1790, but the seven elms lasted, giving the new turnpike road its name. (The elms were taken down ca. 1840.) Current architecture is described as "uninspired."

- Seven Sisters Road: 1832.

Seveney Street - Islington. Also known as Essex Street. (See: Islington/Lower Street.)

Severndroog Castle - (See: Shooter's Hill/Castle Wood.)

sewers - Up to the early 19th C. most of London was yet dependent on cesspits (and dumping waste into the Thames, or simply dumping chamber pots out of one's window and into the street.) In 1849 the polluted Thames River was identified as the source of many cholera outbreaks, but even so up to 1866 many people believed cholera was caused by "bad air." A massive city-wide system did not come into being until 1859.

- ➢ See: Commission of Sewers.
- ➢ See: nightmen.

- See: sanitation.

sewing - If you were more privileged, you wouldn't sew your own clothes (nor repair them.) Servants, or hired help (such as tailors, milliners, or modistes,) did the work. There were very little ready-made clothes (and the few there were, were expected to be fitted to the buyer.) As garments aged they were often remade for one's self, one's family, and/or the servants. Refined ladies did stitch, of course, but those would have mostly been decorative pieces.

sewing machines - Invented in 1790 by Thomas Saint (cabinet-maker,) although it was first intended just to sew on leather or canvas. It was decades before sewing machines overtook hand-sewing. Virtually every Regency era garment would have been hand-sewn. (You may care to see: activities/entertainments/sports - stitchery, under A.)

Seymour Place - Marylebone. Begun in 1813, completed in 1831.

Shad Thames - Southwark. The name is a corruption of "St. John at Thames." Shad Thames' medieval name was: Horselydown. The parish church of Horselydown, built in 1728, was dedicated to St. John. (See: St. John - Bermondsey, under the CHURCHES section.) Now a largely mid 19th C. industrial area near the Docklands.

Shadwell - Now: Tower Hamlets (since 1965.) District just east of the Tower of London. There had been a Roman quarry here, later used as a cemetery. Maritime industry came here in the 1630s. Had a chapel in 1656; became a parish in 1669. Slums were here by the 1830-40s.

- Prospect of Whitby: Pub. (See under the INNS/PUBS section.)
- St. Paul's Church: By at least 1720. (See: St. Paul - Shadwell, under the CHURCHES section.)
- Shakespeare's Walk: Jane Randolph was born here in 1720; she went on to marry Thomas Jefferson (American president.)

Shaft Alley - (Also seen as: Shafts Court.) The City. Ancient. Near Leadenhall Street's northwest corner and St. Mary Axe Street. The street's name came from a one-time maypole (shaft) here. By at least 1800 it was known as: Sharp's Alley; known for being dirty/for having knackers here.

- St. Andrew Undershaft: (See under the CHURCHES section.)

Shaftesbury Avenue - Westminster. Named thus after the Regency, when the street was constructed over other older streets, 1885-86. Formerly was King Street and Dudley Street (which latter was, during the Regency era, formerly known as Monmouth Street); the only truly utterly "new" part of Shaftesbury is between Piccadilly Circus and Rupert Street. Construction of this street pulled down a lot of old slums/rookeries. (It was named for Lord Shaftesbury, whose life's work was to help the very kind of people who were dispossessed by this road's construction.) Modern nickname: Theatreland. The theatres came in beginning in

1888.

Shaftesbury House - (See: Chelsea/Shaftesbury House.)

Shaftesbury Terrace - Regency name for what was later Victoria Street (1845,) running between Vauxhall Bridge Road and Grosvenor Gardens. (See: Victoria Street.)

shambles - Is an ancient name for a butcher's quarters or shop. Now rarely seen except in old place names.

Sharp's Alley - (See: Shaft Alley.)

shearmen - Those who sheared the nap from cloth - *not*, as might be assumed, those who sheared sheep. (See: Mincing Lane/Clothworkers' Hall.)

sheep - Sheep were long vital in the UK, a source of food and (perhaps even more importantly for the nation,) as wool, one of the backbones of the British economy.

- ➢ See: food/lamb.
- ➢ See: food/mutton.
- ➢ See: staplers.
- ➢ See: wool - Several listings at.

sheets - Jane Austen has a character in *Emma* (Mrs. Elton) who speaks of taking her own clean sheets with her whenever she travels (via inns.) The term "sheets" is in use by at least 1789. They could also be called: linens - a term which includes tablecloths, Holland cloths, napkins, etc.

- ➢ You may care to see: blankets.
- ➢ You may care to see: towels.

Shepherd's Bush - Hammersmith and Fulham. Named for the shepherds who rested their sheep here on the way to London markets. Dates back to at least 1635. Until 1860 it was just a rustic hamlet.

- Shepherd's Bush Green: Triangular open space. In 1872, was acquired for public use.
- St. Stephen's: Consecrated in 1850.

Shepherd's Market - Built for Edward Shepherd, mid 18th century. (See: Mayfair/Shepherd's Market.)

sheriff - Name derives from "shire reeve." London was granted the right to elect its own Sheriff in 1199. This was a significant concession by the Crown because up to this point a king's sheriff was to act as the king's agent on the spot; now the sheriff acted for London. (You may care to see: Lord Mayor.)

Ship Court - Near Old Bailey, the City. William Hogarth (painter, b.1697-d.1764) was born here. A Ship Tavern used to stand here from 1654.

shipbuilding -

- See: Deptford.
- See: Limehouse.
- See: ships/shipping.
- See: Shipwrights' Company.

ships/shipping -

- See: Deptford.
- See: docks.
- See: naval matters.
- See: shipbuilding.
- See: Shipwrights' Company.
- See: Thames, the.

Shipwrights' Company - (AKA: the Worshipful Company of Shipwrights.) Ancient fellowship. Those skilled in ship-building and repair. AN ENCYCLOPEDIA OF LONDON says: "During the 16th century there was conflict between the shipwrights of the City and those of 'Redrith' (i.e. Rotherhithe,) the latter being granted a royal charter in 1605 and another in 1612. Despite these charters, the City body successfully maintained its independence and the struggle went on." The Shipwrights' Company formed in 1782. Livery Company. Does not have its own Hall, sharing the Ironmongers' Company's Hall, Shaftesbury Place. 59th in the order of precedence.

Shirley - Croydon. Dates from 1314. Situated beside a common on the old road between Croydon and West Wickam, it was a 17th C. hamlet. Much of Shirley dates from the 1930s.

- St. John's Church: Built by George Gilbert Scott in 1856, replacing an 1835 chapel.
- Shirley House: Built in 1721. Became the Shirley Park Hotel in 1912. On its site Trinity School came in, in 1965.
- Upper Shirley: (See under U.)

Shirley Oaks - Croydon, northern. In the Middle Ages this area belonged to the archbishops of Canterbury.

- Oak Farm: Here by at least 1800.

shirt-makers - Men's. A Regency man's shirt was much like a nightshirt, only shorter. Often was white. Pulled on over the head, fastening with buttons or ties. They tended to be a bit billowy. It was uncommon to have a "sham shirt" (also called a dicky,) a false front to save one from having to change to a whole new clean shirt, but they did exist.

- See: Jermyn Street.
- See: tailors.
- You may care to see: fabrics/lawn - Often men's shirts were made of

lawn.

shoe black - (Also seen as: shoeblack.) One who shines the shoes or boots of those passing by, for money. Usually a boy (as opposed to an adult.) Term first seen in 1745. (In America: shoeshine boy.)

Shoe Lane - A street near the Inns of Court, off Fleet Street, the City. Early on it was known as Show Well, but by the time of the Restoration (16th C.) was known as Shoe Lane.

- Cogers: Debating society. 10 Shoe Lane. (See under C.)
- Gunpowder Alley: An offshoot of Shoe Lane. Dates back to at least the 17th century.

shoemakers - Boots and shoes could be made by two different purveyors - or, just as often, one merchant produced both.

- ➢ See: cobblers.
- ➢ See: Cockspur Street/Edward Rymer - Bootmaker.
- ➢ See: Cordwainers' Hall.
- ➢ See: Hornchurch.
- ➢ See: Oxford Street.
- ➢ See: St. James's Street/9/Lobbs.
- ➢ See: St. Martin-le-Grand.
- ➢ See: Shoemaker Row.

Shoemaker Row - Also seen as: Shoemakers' Row. (See: Carter Lane.)

shoeshiners - (See: shoe black.)

Shooters Hill - Greenwich. An ancient woodland. Dates from at least 1226. The road (bearing the same name) was part of Watling Street (and is currently part of the A207.) Summit: 432 feet. A village grew up here in the mid 19th C. on the hillside.

- Castle Wood: The eccentric Lady James of Eltham built the "Gothic folly" Severndroog Castle on the land of Castle Wood, in memory of her husband (Sir William James) in 1784. In his military service he had captured a fortress of that (anglicized) name on India's Malabar Coast.

shopping - Regency era shops were not required to set any specific hours, could open and close when they liked.

- ➢ See: Bond Street.
- ➢ See: Burlington Arcade.
- ➢ See: Cheapside.
- ➢ See: Covent Garden.
- ➢ See: Jermyn Street.
- ➢ See: markets.

- See: Pall Mall.
- See: Royal Exchange.
- See: Royal Opera Arcade: 1817 - First covered shopping venue in London.
- See: St. James's Street.
- See: various listings - Such as: drapers, hatters, shirt-makers, tailors, etc.

Shoreditch - Hackney. The medieval part of Shoreditch had stood in what is now South Shoreditch. (See, below.) The 16th C. brought "significant" building; in Tudor times this area was known for its silk industry (by Flemish immigrants.) There were some 10,000 residents here by 1750; 100,000 by 1850, by which time there was significant industry and slums here.

- Cheshire Street: Has had various names, including: Hare Street; now is (on Sundays) part of Brick Lane Market.
  - Englefields Ltd.: The oldest pewter cast manufacturer in London. Some of their molds date back 300 years.
- Columbia Market: 1869.
- Curtain Road: (See under C.)
- Shoreditch High Street:
  - Christ Church, Spitalfields: (See under the CHURCHES section.)
  - St. Leonard's Church: (See under the CHURCHES section.)
- South Shoreditch: CHAMBERS LONDON GAZETTEER notes: "More of an administrative term than a recognized locality, South Shoreditch represents roughly the part of the borough of Hackney that lies south of Old Street." The site of beer gardens, nurseries, and theatres since Elizabethan times. In the 19th C. was known for furniture-making and printing.

Shortlands - Bromley. Had been called Clay Hill (not to be confused with the Clay Hill in Enfield.) CHAMBERS LONDON GAZETTEER tells us: "The medieval field pattern here consisted of sets of long and short fields, called Longelonds and Shortelonds, and the latter gave their name to a house built at the beginning of the 18th century."

- St. Mary's Church: After 1865.

Short's Garden - Close to Covent Garden. In 1816 described as overcrowded and "wretched."

showers - A way of bathing. Largely a post-Regency concept. (See: bathroom.)

Shri Swaminarayan Mandir - Neasden, northwest London. The first Hindu temple of its kind to be built in Europe, 1995.

Sidcup - Bexley. First recorded in 1254, although there was no hamlet here until 1675.

- Sidcup House: 1717.
- Sidcup Place: 1743. Reportedly started as a star-shaped fort but, if so, was soon converted into a house. Much extended.
    - Church of St. John the Evangelist: 1844.

signs, hanging - In the medieval era (when most people couldn't read) businesses had hanging signs decorated with recognizable symbols. To this day, some hanging signs can yet be seen in London. Some examples:

- barber: Red and white pole. (Said to represent the white cloths and bits of blood that came in when nicked.)
- confectioner: A pineapple.
- mercers: A golden ball.
- snuff: A Highlander statue standing before the shop. (Although a Highlander on a hanging sign would have worked, too.)

Sikhs - Did not have a sizable presence in London until the 20th century. (See: Sri Guru Singh Sabha Gurdwara.)

silhouettes - The art of tracing a shadow, and then cutting out its edges to make a paper portrait. (See: Strand/Mr. Meirs.)

silkweaving -

- ➢ See: fabrics/silk.
- ➢ See: Hoxton.
- ➢ See: Huguenots.
- ➢ See: Shoreditch.
- ➢ See: Spitalfields.
- ➢ See: weavers.

Silver Street - **Enfield**, southwest Edmonton. Not to be confused with the Silver Street in Kensington.

- Millfield House: 1792. Now an arts center/the Millfield Theatre.
- White Lodge: 16th C. clapboard building with a 19th century exterior. Walled garden. Icehouse. Now a medical practice.
- workhouse, a: 1842. Later became the North Middlesex Hospital.

Silver Street - **Kensington**. Not to be confused with Silver Street in Enfield. (See: Kensington/Silver Street.)

silverplating - By electrical deposition, invented in 1840.

silversmiths - Their premises were often very well outfitted, meant to reflect the expensive nature of their product.

- ➢ See: Bond Street/New Bond Street/165-169.

➢ See: Gracechurch Street.

Simpson's-in-the-Strand - Restaurant.

➢ See: Simpson's Tavern.

➢ See: Strand/Simpson's Restaurant.

Simpson's Tavern - (AKA: Simpson's-in-the-Strand.) 100 Strand. Founded on this site in 1828, but before then opened as the Grand Divan Cigar ("a home for chess") in 1818 by a Mr. Reiss. Reiss was joined by Mr. Simpson "some thirty years later" as Simpson's Divan and Tavern. It was taken down in 1900 (when the Strand was widened,) but reopened in 1904; having an interior much like it had in 1848. Still has a "males only" feel to it at lunchtime, and as of 1995 ladies were admitted to its paneled ground floor restaurant only on Saturdays. (The upstairs restaurant is open to ladies without restrictions.) Described as having a "low front."

Single Street - Bromley. A hamlet on a street of the same name. The present name of Single Street dates from 1871 (had been Berry's Green, which still exists, now described as a wooded rural hamlet area with scattered farmland.)

- Berterye, manor of: ("Berterye" is seen spelled many ways, including "Betlrede.") From 1145. It gave its name to Berry's Green.

Sion College - (Not to be confused with Syon House.) Originally on London Wall. College, guild of clergy (incumbents of City parishes,) and almshouses. Royal Charter in 1630. Damaged in the Great Fire of 1666. The almshouses closed in 1884, the almspeople becoming pensioners. Present building dates from 1886, on Victoria Embankment (and this building sold in 1996, and was converted into offices.)

Sion Row - (See: Twickenham/Sion Row.)

Sipson - Hounslow, on Sipson Road. Dates from at least 1214 (with Bronze Age residents proved by excavations.) By the 16th C. wheat and rye were being grown here. In the late 18th C. the common was enclosed, but Sipson remained very undeveloped until after 1836.

Sir John Cass's Foundation School - Aldgate (on the corner of Houndsditch.) In 1719 Sir John set up, for 50 boys and 40 girls, a school in St. Botolph-without-Aldgate's churchyard. He died in 1718. Refounded in 1748. Moved in 1869 to Duke's Place.

Sir John Soane's Museum - 1837. (See: Inns of Court/Lincoln's Inn Fields/Soane Museum.)

Sise Lane - The City. "Sise" is an abbreviation of St. Benet Sherehog. Known as Sise Lane by at least 1762.

sixes and sevens, at - The phrase purportedly comes from the ancient yearly precedence change between the Skinners' Company and the Merchant-Taylors' Company; their precedence changes from sixth to seventh (and vice versa) yearly. The phrase means being confused, disarrayed. (See: halls - For the note on the yearly precedence change.)

skating -

- See: iceskating.
- See: rollerskates.

Skinner Street - Snow Hill. 1802, precursor road to the Holborn Viaduct (the latter being built in 1869.)

- 42: John Wallis, London "Instructive Toy Warehouse."

skinners - Worked with pelts, as opposed to hides, the latter of which were the province of the Tanners. (Informational note: Wool was handled by the Woolmongers. Leatherworkers handled leather.)

- See: Skinners' Hall - For distinction of Skinners vs. Tanners.
- See: Walbrook Street.

Skinners' Hall - (For the Worshipful Company of Skinners. AKA: the Skinners' Company.) Dowgate Hill, the City. Located on or near the site of the first Hall, here in the 13th century. Royal Charter in 1327. This Company traded in furred pelts (as opposed to the Leathersellers, or the Tanners - the latter of which tanned animal pelts, removing the fur and curing the hide.)

Has frontages on College Street and on Dowgate Hill. According to THE LOST TREASURES OF LONDON: (The present Hall) "...dates from 1668-9, having been rebuilt after the Great Fire." The prior hall was called Copped Hall. A new frontage was added in 1791 by William Jupp; it is Ionic in character, with the Company's Arms on the pediment. The fittings and decorations were completely altered in 1847-8. NAIRN'S LONDON STATES: "At the end of it is a tiny arcaded courtyard with Skinners' Hall proper, a seventeenth-century building, on the other side."

Sixth in the order of precedence - but the Skinners and the Merchant-Taylors disputed their order of precedence, so in 1484 the Lord Mayor declared they would change 6th and 7th positions on a yearly basis, which they do yet to this day. It is one of the Great Twelve companies of London. Livery Company.

skittles - (Also called: ninepins.) A game like bowling, played with nine pins, outside, on a skittle alley (length of grass.) Had its heyday by the Georgian era, but was still sometimes played during the Regency.

Slade Green - Bexley. Called "Hov" in Domesday Book; then became known as the manor of Howbury. By the 16th C. it took on the Slade Green name. Not much developed until the late 19th century.

slaughter - Of animals. (See: knackers.)

slaves - Slavery had no legal foundation in England.

It was fundamentally Sir Francis Drake who began the English slave trade ca. 1563 by abducting West Africans for sale.

By 1772 there was a growing segment in the UK that looked poorly upon slavery. Parliament passed a law in 1807 making it illegal for any *British citizen* to transport slaves. The Act did not end slave trading (as captains would smuggle slaves and, horrifically, throw the captives overboard if their ships were caught and about to be boarded,) at least until slave trading was abolished in all *British colonies* as well; this Slavery Abolition Act of 1833 finally ended British slaving, granting freedom to all British Empire slaves.

- ➢ See: Society for the Abolition of the Slave Trade.
- ➢ You may care to see: bondsman, being a.

Sloane Gardens - During the Regency this was known as George Street. (See under G.)

Sloane Square - Belgravia, Kensington, Chelsea. Laid out in the 1780s. Named for Sir Hans Sloane, and built as part of the Hans Town development. CHAMBERS LONDON GAZETTEER explains: "The square functioned as a service provider for the new district" (Hans Town) "with stables, sheds, workshops, bakehouses and some accommodation for staff." At that time it was small and pleasant. An open square where boys sometimes played cricket. AN ENCYCLOPAEDIA OF LONDON states: "In the early years of the 19th century, Sloane Square was merely an open space, enclosed with wooden posts connected with iron chains." Has a vaguely Parisian air.

- Bloody Bridge: Used to be at the northeast corner of the square. 12-14 feet wide. Had walls of "sufficient height" to prevent crossers from falling into the Westbourne, which flowed beneath it.
  - ➢ See: Hyde Park/Serpentine.
  - ➢ See: Westbourne, under W.

  The bridge dated from the time of Charles II. The name probably derived from it being a place for robberies and murders. Also a place used by duelists. Late in its life it became known as Grosvenor Bridge. Now gone.
- Holbein Place. (See under H.)
- Royal Court Theatre: 1887-88 (replacing a former Court Theatre.) Now considered England's foremost home for new playwrights.
- Venus Fountain: 1953.

Sloane Street - Knightsbridge and Chelsea, 1780. Built by Henry Holland, on land leased from Lord Cadogen. This street was named for Sir Hans Sloane.

- 187-201: Georgian houses. This street is now known for its classy shops.

slum - A word coined by the Georgians, but it didn't come into common use until ca. 1850. Regency era folk would have used: rookery. (See: rookeries.)

small beer - A weak version of the beverage, only about 2% alcohol.

- See: beer.
- See: food/beer.
- See: water - For why so many drank beer.

Smallbury Green - Hounslow. Southeast of Osterley. Until the late 19th C. this was the area's name, but it is now called Spring Grove, which is the northwest corner of Isleworth.

smallpox - Affected all classes. Mortality rate was up to 60%. Left scars and sometimes blindness. Inoculation against it began in 1721, when a small cut would be touched with an infected victim's pus; 2% of those thus inoculated died.

Inoculation was controversial and not widespread; smallpox still ran rampant among the poor for decades. A more effective vaccination was invented in 1772, gaining much wider use by 1800-10; Parliament voted in funds for smallpox vaccinations in 1802.

Smeatonian Society of Civil Engineers - (See: Society of Civil Engineers.)

Smith, Dickins & - Oxford Street haberdasher, ca. 1813. (See: Oxford Street/54.)

Smith, James (& Son) - (See: New Oxford Street/55.)

Smith Square - (See: Westminster/Smith Square.)

Smith, W. H. Company - News sheets distributor. (See: W. H. Smith Company, under W.)

Smitham Bottom - (Rhymes with "with-'em.") In the 18th C. was a "desolate area, a place for gypsies and highwaymen."

- Red Lion Inn: By at least 1735. (Not to be confused with the Red Lion Inn on Hillingdon Heath, nor the Red Lion Tavern on Chick Lane.)

Smithfield - "Smithfield" derives from "smooth field." In the 3-4th centuries the Romans used these fields as a cemetery. Later used for executions for some 400 years, but into the 17-18th centuries did so only sporadically, including Protestant martyrs, witches, and Scottish rebels. In medieval times there was a horse market here every Friday. Smithfield is the only existing wholesale market in central London. (Not to be confused with: East Smithfield, close to the Tower of London - executions were also held there, but at a more minor level.) Cattle were for sale here every Friday from the 12th C. on. (See: Smithfield Market.)

- Giltspur Street: Knights had once jousted here. (See under G.)
- St. Bartholomew the Great: (See under the CHURCHES section.)
- St. Bartholomew's Hospital: (See under S.)
- Saracen's Head: Cock Lane. Inn. (See: Saracen's Head - Aldgate, under the INNS/PUBS section.)
- Smithfield Market: (See at its own listing.)

Smithfield Market - The City. Covers 10 acres; is an open square. Ancient meat market, dating back to 1123. Site of the medieval St. Bartholomew's Fair, held here every August, from 1133; a large cloth market rather like a carnival, including foreign goods, dancing bears, wrestling matches, etc. Lasted for up to 14 days. Suppressed in 1855.

From 1305, oxen were sold here. Also: cows and geese.

The gallows here were removed ca. 1413, moving to Tyburn.

CHAMBERS LONDON GAZETTEER says: "...the Corporation of London gained the right to collect market tolls from 1400, although it was not until 1638 that a formal charter was granted."

Legally sanctioned in the 17th C., when it was taken over by the City, being then reorganized as a live cattle market ("cattle" meaning bovines and horses.) It was paved and enclosed by railings in 1615. Live cattle (as opposed to butchered meat) and sheep were sold here until the mid 19th century. Because there was no refrigeration, cattle were driven to market, congesting traffic, and were slaughtered on site. (Switched to being a market for butchered meat in 1868.)

Became very crowded, but resisted being moved until the Smithfield Market Removal Act of 1852 forced it to shift in 1855 to the Caledonian Market in Copenhagen Fields, Islington, (where it exists today.) As stated above, had been the site of the Bartholomew Fair, alternately sometimes called Cloth Fair (but not to be confused with Cloth Fair - Spitalfields); from 1133. (See: Bartholomew Fair, under B.) Had been held annually in August (for up to 14 days,) until it was suppressed in 1855, at the same time as the move to Islington. (See: Newgate Market - For more on this move.)

The present market buildings are Victorian, 1866-8, by Sir Horace Jones (at which time it took on the formal title of "London Central Meat Market," but is otherwise known as the Metropolitan Meat-Market, which evolved out of Newgate Market.)

A Poultry Market opened here in 1875. It burned in 1958; rebuilt in 1962.

The General Market was built in 1883. The Annexe Market in 1888.

An ancient gateway still stood in 1901, just opposite the fair-ground, the remnants of an entrance to the Priory of St. Bartholomew. The long glass-and-iron buildings date from 1868.

smithies - Most communities (of more than a few houses) would host a smithy, the place where a blacksmith had his forge.

- See: Finchley.
- You may care to see: Blacksmiths' Company.

smoking - Tobacco. In the Georgian era, some women smoked, but except for the aged, most Regency women did not; it was considered unladylike. (However, in the 19th C. snuff was yet enjoyed by women, of all social strata.)

- See: Elephant and Castle - For clay pipes.
- See: pipe makers.

- See: snuff.
- See: tobacco.

smugglers - Despite the penalties if caught (transportation or death,) smuggling was widespread into (and past) the Regency era. This was not least because England is an island, and was always at war with someone, particularly France, and there was profit to be made on restricted or blockaded items such as lace, silk, sugar, wine, etc. (See: Tiger's Head, under the INNS/PUBS section.)

Snaresbrook - Redbridge. First seen in 1599. Was a 17th C. coaching halt on the way to Epping.

snooker - In America it's called: pool (as in the game with a cue ball and table pockets.) Originated in the second half of the 19th C. by British Army officers.

Snow Hill - The City. Narrow, steep thoroughfare; ruffian's hang out. (It was said the 18th C. ruffians amused themselves sometimes by putting women in barrels and sending them rolling down the hill.)

- Saracen's Head, the: (See: Saracen's Head - Aldgate, under the INNS/PUBS section.)

snuff - Tobacco in powder form, inhaled. Tobacco first came to England ca. 1560 as snuff, later as rolled and smoked. (This is the reverse of how most of Europe started with tobacco products.) *Smoking* was wildly popular in the 17th C. with both men and women, but by 1773 Samuel Johnson writes how unfashionable smoking (as opposed to taking snuff) had become. (It would have been considered highly shocking to see a 19th C. woman smoking; however, snuff was acceptable, right up to duchesses.) However, increasingly in the 18th C. the practice of taking snuff was mostly practiced just by fashionable young men although some women continued to buy, use, and enjoy snuff clear up to Victoria's time - when smoking again tended to displace snuff.

Chewing tobacco was generally left to rough sorts, such as Mariners and manual workers.

Snuff could be scented ("perfumed") for varying tastes - for instance: lavender.

Snuff sellers (before and during the Regency) tended to put a carved figure of a Highlander in front of their shops, because of the accepted characterization that the Scottish were enamored of tobacco, especially in snuff form. (Whereas an American Native figure tended to indicate a shop where rolled tobacco was sold - of course, a shop could and often did sell both.)

- See: Coventry Street/David Wishart.
- See: Minories/James Taddy.
- See: tobacco.

Soane Museum - Founded after Soane's death in 1837. (See: Inns of Court/Lincoln's Inn

Fields/Soane Museum.)

soap - Records of soap manufacture date back to Charles I. Sold in pieces cut off a long bar. This practice was in place until around the 1880s. Plus, many households made their own.

- See: Yardley soaps.
- You may care to see: bathroom.

soccer - The first soccer (what is known in Britain as football) cup final was held at the Oval (a Kennington cricket ground) in 1871. There were no formal rules until 1861 - and those do not much match today's handless rules. (See: football.)

Society for the Abolition of the Slave Trade - (AKA: Society for Effecting the Abolition of the Slave Trade.) 1787. William Wilberforce (social reformer/MP,) was one of twelve men who met at a London printing shop to form this organization. They achieved their goal (the formal end of slavery) in 1807. They were superseded by the Anti-Slavery Society in 1823.

- See: Anti-Slavery Society.
- See: slaves.

Society for Superseding the Necessity of Climbing Boys - Formed in 1803. One of their first actions was to offer an award for a chimney-sweeping device. The society lasted until at least 1832. (See: chimney-sweeps.)

Society for the Promotion of Christian Knowledge, the - Began in 1699 by Thomas Bray. Established charity schools for the poor.

- See: Newcastle House.
- See: Society for the Propagation of the Gospel in Foreign Parts.

Society for the Propagation of the Gospel in Foreign Parts, the - An offshoot of the Society for the Promotion of Christian Knowledge. Established in 1701, an offshoot that exclusively took over the societies' efforts outside Britain (primarily North America and the West Indies.)

Society for the Relief of the Infant Poor in London, the - Charity, founded 1769.

Society for the Suppression of Vice, the - 1802. (See: Proclamation Society.)

Society of Agriculture - Founded in 1793 by Sir John Sinclair (Scottish politician.) From 1798, the Society was situated at 32 Sackville Street. Closed in 1822. The Royal Agricultural Society of England - a kind of successor - was founded in 1838, located elsewhere. (You may care to see: statistics, a word John Sinclair was the first to use, 1784.)

Society of Antiquaries - Founded in 1572 by Archbishop Parker; the members assembled in a private home for their first 20 years. King James I dissolved the Society in 1604, offended by some of their proceedings. Was somehow resurrected by at least 1659, with public meetings being resumed in 1707. It gained its Royal Charter in 1751, in which they were charged with "the encouragement, advancement and furtherance of the study and knowledge of the antiquities and history of this other countries." In 1776 George III ordered their inclusion in Somerset House, and they took residence there in 1781. Moved in 1866 to Burlington House, where it remains. Governed by a twenty man council and a president; membership was limited to a total of 1,000 (this is no longer true); membership by election. (See: Somerset House/Society of Arts.)

Society of Apothecaries, the - Established 1617. Based in London. An Act of Parliament in 1815 gave the Apothecaries the right to set examinations of those desiring to run a pharmacy. (See: doctors/apothecary.)

Society of Arts - (See: Royal Society of Arts.)

Society of Artists - (AKA: Society of Artists of Great Britain.) Established in May/1761, a brotherhood of artists, in order to display the work of living members. Many of the foremost members absconded in 1768, in part leading to the formation of the Royal Academy of Arts. (See under R.) The Society of Artists ended in 1791, following a decline.

Society of Civil Engineers - Founded in 1771, by John Smeaton (civil and mechanical engineer/physicist, d.1792.) After Smeaton's death the society was renamed: Smeatonian Society of Civil Engineers. Whereas the Institute of Civil Engineers is the first *professional* body of civil engineers, the Society of Civil Engineers is the *oldest* (but not, at least originally, made up of all professionals. Yet exists. (See: Institute of Civil Engineers.)

Society of Cogers - (See: Cogers.)

Society of Friends - (AKA: Quakers.) Not to be confused with "Society of the Friends of the People."

- See: Bunhill Row/Friends Burial Ground.
- See: Quakers, under Q.

Society of Jesus, the - Also more familiarly known as Jesuits. Catholic. Founded in 1540.

Society of Painters in Oil and Water-Colours - (See: Society of Painters in Water-Colours.)

Society of Painters in Watercolours - Spring Gardens. (Not to be confused with the Royal Society of Arts.) Founded in 1804; members exhibited and sold their watercolours at an annual exhibition. In 1881, "Royal" was added to the society's name. Originally located at 16 Old Bond Street; moved in 1809 to Spring Gardens, where it stayed until 1820. (See: Cox's Museum.)

In 1813 oils were first added to the exhibition, so that from 1813-1820 it was known as the Society of Painters in Oil and Watercolours. Reverted back to watercolours in 1820, and resumed its original name, now at the Egyptian Gallery. Moved to Pall Mall East in 1822; in the 1930s to Conduit Street.

Society of Supporters of the Bill of Rights - Founded in 1769; folded ca. 1774.

Society of the Friends of the People - Founded in 1792; dissolved ca. 1793. Had sought greater representation in Parliament of the masses. (Not to be confused with "Society of Friends"/Quakers.)

Soho - Fitzrovia, Westminster. Where an area once known as Kempsfield had been. Known briefly as King's Square. But called Soho as early as 1641.

Western border: St. Martin's Lane. Northern border: King's Highway to Oxford. (A second source says the area's borders are: Charing Cross Road, Coventry Street, Oxford Street, and Regent Street.)

In medieval times, this was verdant farmland that belonged to the Convent of Abingdon and the Hospital of Burton St. Lazar. Then Henry VIII seized the land and made it into a royal park (suitable as a hunting ground; "So-ho" was a yell used to call off the hounds during a hunt.) Attached to the palace of Whitehall.

Began to really develop in the mid 17th C., when French Huguenots took up residence; by 1740 this area was primarily dominated by these French traders. (Soho is a district that has attracted foreign communities for the last 300 years.)

- ➢ See: Leicester Square.
- ➢ See: Soho Square.

In the 18-19th centuries this area was known for its theatres, few of which still remain. Also in Georgian and Regency times, prominent prostitutes' homes/businesses were located here. Became infamous as a red-light district following WWII. The prostitutes weren't forced out until 1959 legislation came along, and peep shows and porn shops yet thrived here until a 1986 crackdown forced them out.

- Atkinson, the perfumer. (Here until 1832, when he moved to Old Bond Street.) Had a life-size stuffed bear out front to advertise his specialty of bear grease for "men's luxuriant hair."
- Berwick Street: (See under B.)
- Broad Street: In 1757 William Blake (poet) was born here. Is now called Broadwick Street.
- Carnaby Street: Famous clothing street. (See under C.)
- Charlotte Street: (See under C.)
- Church Street: French and Swiss watchmakers, and jewelers.
- Dean Street: (See under D.)
    - 21: In 1763, in his first visit to London, seven-year-old Mozart (and his four-year-old sister) performed here. It was then known as Caldwell's Assembly Rooms; it is now the Ben Uri Art Gallery. (See: Soho Square/Frith Street - For more on Mozart.)
- Frith Street: (See: Soho Square/Frith Street.)

- Gerrard Street: Pastry cooks. (See under G.)
- Golden Square: (See under G.)
- Great Windmill Street School: Survived until the 1830s. Surgical teachings and dissection. Was another name for the Hunterian Medical School. (See under H.)
- Greek Street: So named for a group of poor people who settled here after fleeing the Turks in 1675. Leads north to Soho Square.
    - House of St. Barnabas: At the top of Greek Street. Built in 1740, described as "handsome." Established as a refuge for homeless women in 1846.
- Leicester Square: (See under L.)
- Meard Street: 1722-32. Serves as a short link between Wardour and Dean Streets. Early Georgian.
- Middlesex Hospital: (See under M.)
- Old Compton Street: Westminster. Soho's High Street. Is broad. Until the late 17th C. this was hunting ground. Named for its landowner, Spencer Compton, Earl of Northampton (d.1643.) By the end of the 18th C. almost all of the houses had a tavern or shop on their ground floors. Huguenots lived here; the street was known for hosting (largely French) foreigners. (See: Compton Street.)
- Oxford Street: (See under O.)
- Poland Street: Runs from Broadwick Street to Oxford Street.
    - 15: In 1811, Percy Bysshe Shelley (poet) lived here after being sent down (sent home in disgrace) from Oxford.
    - 50: (Author) Madame D'Arblay (AKA: Fanny Burney's) childhood home was here, 1760-1770.
- Rupert Street: Built ca. 1677, named for Prince Rupert. Described as handsome and well-built, at least until there was a lot of rebuilding in the 1720-30s. It got a footway extension in 1873-74, connecting it to Brewer Street. Much of the street now dates from the 1880s.
- St. Anne's: Wardour Street. Built in 1686, designer uncertain (but presumed to be one of Wren's many masons working for him in the post-Great Fire City.) It was a bit of a revival of one of the earliest forms of church architecture, being a plain galleried design with an apse flanked by square chambers. The tower was added in 1802-6. Hazlitt is buried here, died 1830. Also buried here is Theodore, King of Corsica, died 1736. (Theodore relinquished his kingdom, due to huge debts, "for the use of his creditors.") Only the church tower now remains following a 1940s bombing.

- St. Martin's Lane: Western border of Soho, beyond which is Covent Garden.
- St. Patrick's: Catholic, built for the Irish community here in the 18th century. (See: St. Patrick's - Soho, under the CHURCHES section.)
- Soho Square: (See at its own listing.)
- Wardour Street: Secondhand bookstalls. (Now big in the film industry.)
    - St. Anne's: (See, above.)
- Wedgwood: Dishes manufacturer. (His blue wares became famous.) Moved from Soho to York Street, St. James's Square after he was featured in an 1809 Ackermann's *Repository of Art.*
        - ➢ See: St. James's Square/York Street.
        - ➢ See: Wedgwood dishes, under W.

Soho Bazaar - Soho Square. Opened in 1816. Shops, such as jewelry, lace, millinery. It benefitted the widows and daughters of men killed in the Napoleonic Wars; stalls selling merchandise were rented rather cheaply, as financed by one benevolent Mr. John Trotter. "A plain and modest style of dress on the part of the young females who serve at the stalls is invariably insisted on, a matron being at hand to superintend the whole."

Soho Square - Fitzrovia, Westminster. One of the earlier London squares, laid out in 1677 on land formerly known as Soho Fields. It was originally (in the 17th C.) called King's Square (after Gregory King, a land developer, engraver, and herald,) then Monmouth Square. For most of the 18th C. it was a very fashionable residence. But when Mayfair came into being (later 18th C.,) the fashionables tended to move there, leaving Soho to (in the parlance of the day) "Greeks, Ishmaelites, cats, Italians, tomatoes, restaurants, organs" - in other words, a then looked-down-upon foreign influence, as well as doctors and lawyers. It is currently one of the few remaining green spots in Soho.

The 19th C. statue of Charles II (in the square's green center) was removed in the 1870s, but returned in 1938.

- 32: Joseph Banks went with Captain James Cook on the 1768-71 exploration of Australia and New Zealand. Banks became a famous and influential botanist. Lived here sometime after 1771.
- Frith Street: Named for Richard Frith, a land developer who was bankrupted before he could profit from the investment here, 1678. Built up in 1718. Was increasingly developed in the 18th century. By the mid 19th C. contained many shopfronts: tailors, dressmakers, goldsmiths, jewelers, watchmakers. Completely remodeled in 2001. Presently holds a lush hotel.
    - 6: Built in 1718. William Hazlitt (essayist) died here in 1830. Now called

Hazlitt's (hotel,) 1718.

   - 20: Mozart composed here, 1764-5, on his second visit to London, at the age of 8. (Not an elegant address, but described as "serviceable.")
   - 54: (Is now 61.) Built in the late 17th C. by Richard Campion (carpenter.) Four stories and a basement; front is stuccoed and three windows wide. Dr. John Snow (of the famous Snow's 1859 Map of London) rented here beginning in 1838. There is some confusion on maps of this time, but in 1819 this address of 54 was located in the middle of the first block south of Soho Square, but north of the Greek Street (later Bateman Street) intersection.
- Hospital for Women: First general hospital for women in London. Begun in 1843. Moved to 30 Soho Square in 1852. Number 29 was acquired and added in 1865.
- Linnean Society: (See under L.)
- Soho Bazaar: (See at its own listing.)

solicitors -

> ➢ See: lawyer/attorney/solicitor.
> ➢ See: Inns of Court - Many notes at.

Solicitors of the City of London Company - (AKA: the City of London Solicitors Company.) This Company's members must practice (or have practiced) within a one mile/1.6 km radius of the Bank of England. Founded in 1908, and registered in 1909. Livery granted in 1944, by the Court of Aldermen. Royal Charter in 1957. Has no hall. Its offices are at 4 College Hill, London. Its guild church is St. Mary Abchurch. 79th in the order of precedence.

Somers Town - Camden. (Pronounced: Summers Town.) Built ca. 1790. Intended to be a pleasant suburb of London, only one 15-sided block was raised before the building schemes of Lord Somers petered out. French émigrés, escaping the Revolution, fled here, so Somers Town flourished all the same (resulting in a French church and four charity schools for the émigrés' children.) In 1823, more émigrés arrived (this time fleeing the revolt in Spain. By 1840 it was considered a disordered, filthy area.

- Duke's Row: (Also seen as: Duke's Road.) Existed by the time of the Regency.
- 29 Johnson Street: This street is now called Cranleigh Street. A youthful Charles Dickens lived in a home here when it was newly built in 1824.

Somerset House - Lancaster Place, the Strand (just east of Waterloo Bridge.) During the Renaissance it was a palace for Edward Seymour, Duke of Somerset (Henry VIII's son's regent in 1547.) The duke died before the house was finished, and the property passed to the Crown.

In 1603 it was called Denmark House, while Anne of Denmark (wife of James I of

England) lived here. So known into the early 18th century.

Starting in 1642, the building was the administrative center for the Royal Navy.

The 1547 building was demolished in 1775. It had been falling into ruins, so it was redesigned by Sir William Chambers (and by Wyatt, following Chambers' death) as one of the first buildings specifically built to house offices, between 1776-86, in the classical style; built around a quadrangle court. Completed in 1800-09.

During the Regency this building was officially designated as the Queen's dower house (this being Queen Charlotte, Prinny's mother,) but shortly thereafter she was installed in Buckingham House, to serve as her dower house instead.

The eastern wing was added in 1824 (a second source says it was added in 1829-34; a third said 1835,) by Robert Smirke. King's College is now located here. (See: King's College, below.)

The western wing (facing Waterloo Bridge) was added in 1852-6, by Sir James Pennethorne; known as: the New wing.

The southern facade's arches were water gates until the Victorian Embankment took place.

Somerset House yet remains an office complex.

- Courtauld Institute of Art, the: (Of London University.) Founded in 1931. Was at 20 Portman Square ca. 1940-90. Situated in the north wing of Somerset House since 1990. Was granted a 100 year lease in 1987, to use Somerset House as its headquarters (limiting the number of government offices remaining to this day.)
    - ➢ See: Courtauld Institute, under C.
    - ➢ See: Portman Square/20.
    - ➢ See: Royal Academy of Arts, below - The note under.
- Fine Rooms: (See: Royal Academy of Arts, below.)
- General Register of Births, Deaths, and Marriages: (See: Royal Academy of Arts, below.)
- King's College: East wing of Somerset House, completing the river front of the Somerset House complex. Founded in 1828 by the Duke of Wellington. Designed by Robert Smirke, opened in 1834. It has been affiliated with the University of London since 1908. (See under K.)
- Public Records: Were often housed here, most notably ca. 1775-1800. Was the central record office for births, marriages, and deaths. In truth, such records weren't only here, but (until the Public Records Office began in 1838) were scattered throughout the kingdom, in churches, courts, etc.
    - ➢ See: General Register of Births, Death and Marriages.

   - See: Public Records Office, under P - 1838; until this, official records were not required to be gathered in one place.
- Roman Bath: Next door, a purported Roman bath was discovered. Unromantically it is really the remains of a cistern that fed the garden fountains of Somerset House. (See: Strand Lane/162A.)
- Royal Academy of Arts: Housed here from 1780-1836. (See under R.) After the Royal Academy of Arts moved out in 1836, these became the offices for: the General Register of Births, Deaths, and Marriages, until 1973. The Academy was housed in the: Fine Rooms, built specifically to house it (and the Society of Antiquaries,) and which now house the Courtauld Institute of Art. (See, above.)
- Royal Society, the - and the Society of Antiquaries: Both are/were housed here.
   - See: Royal Academy of Arts, above - Note at.
   - See: Society of Antiquaries, at its own listing.
- Society of Antiquaries: (See at its own listing.)
- Stamp Office, the: Moved here in the 1770s, from Lincoln's Inn. (See: Stamp Office, at its own listing.)
- Statue of King George III, the: Stands in the center of the courtyard. Constructed by John Bacon in 1778. The king is represented holding a ship's rudder.
- University of London:
   - See: Burlington House.
   - See: University of London - At its own listing.

Somerset Street - Mrs. Dorothy Jordan, the actress (and mistress of Prinny's brother William, Duke of Clarence) lived here ca. 1792.

songs -

   - See: ballad-seller.
   - See: God Save the Queen.
   - See: music.
   - See: Rule Britannia.
   - See: The THEATRES section.
   - You may care to see: instruments, musical.

Soper's Lane - (AKA: Soper Lane.) The City. This was a 14th C. name for Queen Street. Home to soap-makers and shoemakers. Was highly damaged in the Great Fire of 1666. Soon rebuilt, at which time it was named Queen Street in honor of Catherine of Braganza. Probably gone by the time of the Regency; utterly gone now.

Sotheby's Auction House - 1744. For their first 100 years Sotheby's were the auctioneers for all the great libraries selling their books. Despite that, did not really become preeminent until the 20th century.

Were in Wellington Street until 1907. Since 1907, Sotheby's is now at 34-35 New Bond Street (which from 1869-92 had been a gallery for the painter Gustave Doré.)

Sotheran, Henry - Bookshop, 1761. (See: Sackville Street/2-5.)

South Acton - (See: Acton/South Acton.)

South Africa House - Trafalgar Square. Built 1935, on the site of Morley's Hotel (there until 1831.) Trafalgar Square. Was the South Africa embassy until 1994, when South Africa had its first democratic election (and joined the Commonwealth.)

South Audley Street - Mayfair. Alderman Wood (a City alderman who rode with Queen Caroline - George IV's estranged wife - when she returned in triumph to England in 1820, and from whose balcony she bowed to the crowds) lived here.

- Audley Chapel: This is the same thing as the Grosvenor Chapel. (See: Grosvenor Chapel, under the CHURCHES section.)
- Chesterfield House: By Isaac Ware, 1747-52, for the 4th Earl of Chesterfield. At the top of Stanhope Gate. Taken down in 1937. Is now flats.
- Grosvenor Chapel: 1730. (See under the CHURCHES section.)

South Bank - From Battersea to Southwark and Greenwich. Literally, the land on the south bank of the Thames, runs right alongside to Southwark; the two are often tangled in descriptions, although the South Bank designation is more modern. (See: Southwark.) These days, when people speak of South Bank they mean the cultural quarter (opposite the Victoria Embankment) that attracts a yearly six million visitors, including an aquarium, the Royal Festival Hall (1951,) restaurants, theatres, the London Eye, and more (all of which date from the 20th century.)

- County Hall: (See under C.)

South Barnet - Barnet. A little used name for the far southeast corner of Barnet. Other (older) names: Sans Barnet, Sarnes Barnet, Sarnets Barnet. (Current residents might tell you they live in East Barnet or Brunswick Park.) The Bishop of London gave this area to the knights of the Order of the Hospital of St. John of Jerusalem (the Knights Hospitaller) in the 12th century (but they were suppressed in the 16th century.

South Bromley - (See: Bromley-by-the-Bow/South Bromley.)

South Chingford - Waltham Forest. Existing alone here in the mid 19th century were: the Hall, Chingford Mill, a ferry house, and three farms.

- Chingford Hall: A hall has stood here for over 1,000 years; the present one from about 1840, offices since WWII.

South Croydon - Croydon. Had been the medieval manor of Haling Park, 400 acres, 1592. Is now a higher-end community.

- Blunt House: 1759. Parkland setting. Sold in 1850 for building up the area.
- Croydon cattle market: Drovers Road. Established in 1848.
- St. Peter's Church: 1851. Burned 1864, rebuilt 1865.

South Ealing - Ealing. Distinct from Ealing proper. CHAMBERS LONDON GAZETTEER explains: "South Ealing is centred on the twin hubs, one ancient and one modern, of its church and Tube station. In the Middle Ages, St. Mary's Church was at the heart of Ealing itself and this area was known as 'the town,' as opposed to 'the village' of Little Ealing, which lay further south." (See: Little Ealing.)

South End - Camden. Elizabethan hamlet. Is now the southeast corner of Hampstead. (Not to be confused with Southend, Lewisham.)

South Harrow - Harrow. (See: Roxeth.)

South Kensington - Located south of Kensington Village. Mostly built 1862-77. Some houses were added in 1856, but it was mostly dairy farms, market-gardens, orchards, and mews before then.

- Alexander Square: 1827-30.
- Gore House: (See under G.)
- Little Paris: (AKA: Petite Paris.) While Frenchmen have gathered here for years (if not centuries,) this nickname for a part of South Kensington is a post-Regency term.
- Science Museum: 1847. (See at its own listing.)
- South Kensington Museum: Cromwell Road. Built ca. 1850. Original name of the Victoria and Albert Museum.

South Kenton - Brent. 1927. Distinct from Kenton.

South Lambeth - Lambeth. CHAMBERS LONDON GAZETTEER tells us: "...an extensive manor in the Middle Ages, stretching almost as far as Mitcham. The manor was probably in the possession of the Crown for much of its existence, until it was absorbed within Vauxhall at the end of the 13th century." Separated from Lambeth proper by Kennington. Became more of a residential area after Vauxhall Bridge connected South Lambeth and Westminster in 1816.

- Beaufoy vinegar distillery: Moved here in 1810. Some parts still survive.

South Moulton Street - Mayfair. Runs from Oxford Street to Brook Street. Built in the mid 18th century. Widely rebuilt ca. 1900.

- 17: William Blake (poet) lived here in 1803.

South Quay - Tower Hamlets. Completed in 1987, a development on the south side of the former West India Docks. (See: docks/West India Docks/South-West India Dock.)

South Ruislip - Hillingdon. (See: Ruislip/South Ruislip.)

South Sea Company - Founded in 1711. CASSELL'S EIGHTEENTH CENTURY BRITAIN states: "This was launched in order to consolidate £9 million of national debt that was not secured against the proceeds of taxation; this unfunded debt was changed into South Sea stock. The company was thus from the start primarily a financial corporation, and was only marginally concerned with trading activities"; it was a monopoly for trade with South America.

Essentially, the South Sea Bubble (1720) was promises of exaggerated profits for investors, leading to a ruinous collapse for investors and merchants. (The term "South Sea Bubble" to this day yet implies incredible promises that end in financial disaster.) When the Bubble burst, it led to the rise of the Bank of England (as it took charge of the national economy, ca. 1720.) Closed utterly in 1853.

South Sea House - 37 Threadneedle Street, 1720-7; built for the South Sea Company. Destroyed by fire in 1826. Large, plain, three-story, handsome, brick, ornamented with Portland stone. The Broad Street frontage, in 1832-33, became the City of London Club.

The Threadneedle frontage became the British Linen Bank, whose beginnings come out of the Scottish linen industry - begun in 1727, and brought to England in the 1740s; Charter in 1746. First called the British Linen Company; "Bank" was only achieved in 1906 (despite long serving as a center for finances.)

The South Sea Company closed completely in 1853, and by 1854 the property was occupied by the Baltic Exchange. (See under B.) The site is now partially covered by Lloyds Bank. (See: South Sea Company.)

South Shoreditch - (See: Shoreditch/South Shoreditch.)

South Tottenham - (See: Tottenham/South Tottenham.)

South Twickenham - Richmond. Southeast "quiet corner" of Twickenham.

- Cross Deep: Road, from at least 1719. Had some imposing mansions.

South Woodford - Redbridge. A separate community from Woodford.

- St. Mary's Church: By at least the 18th century.

Southall - Ealing. (Pronounced: South-all.) Dates from at least 1198. A market was granted in 1698 by a charter given by William III, market day being Wednesday. The brickfields came along in the second half of the 19th C. (before then had been quite rural.) Very crowded by the 1940s. Its current high Asian/Indian population dates from the 1950s.

- Havelock Road: Named for Sir Henry Havelock (British general in the 1830-40s' Afghan and Sikh wars.)
- Southall Green: Ancient. Sometimes referred to as Old Southall. Flanks what is now called King Street. Its manor house dates from at least 1587, and although

it's been rebuilt and altered, it remains the most authentic building of its kind in London. The green had 33 houses here at the end of the 18th century.

Southampton Fields - (See: Russell Square.)

Southampton House - Occupied the north side of Bloomsbury Square until the house was pulled down in 1800.

Southampton Place - (See: Camden/Camden High Street.)

Southampton Square - (See: Bloomsbury Square.)

Southampton Street - Used to be in Bloomsbury, but is now considered to be in Westminster.

- 27: Garrick lived here, 1750-1772. Now called Garrick House.
- Gallery of Arts: In 1780 John Bell became a distributor of French books in London. His place of business was called the British Library (by him); not to be confused with the later British Library associated with the British Museum. His business was otherwise called: Bell's Library. In 1805, he opened The Gallery of Arts. He held exhibitions there, and sold books and prints. In 1806 he began putting out a monthly magazine (like Ackermann's, and nicely done as well); this magazine was mostly concerned with dress fashions and society gossip; it was known as La Belle Assemblée, and was produced 1805-1837. (See: La Belle Assemblée, under L.)

Southborough - Kingston. Growth from the 1860s.

- Southborough Lodge: 1808. On Surbiton Common.

Southbury - Enfield. Southbury field shows in records of 1572. 237 acres.

- Southbury Road: 1803. First known as Nags Head Road, took on the Southbury Road name later into the 19th century.

Southend - Lewisham. Lewisham proper is 2-1/2 miles (4 km) to the north, granting this area its southern 16th C. name. In the 18th C. there was a cutlery manufacturer here, on the River Ravensbourne, producing some of England's best. It took on the name Upper Mill, then grinding corn and cutting wood, and in the late 19th C., providing electricity. Some of Lewisham's wealthiest lived here. (Not to be confused with South End, Camden.)

Southgate - North London. Existed by at least 1784.

Southwark - (Pronounced Suth-ick.) Literally the south bank of the Thames.

- See: Bankside, below.
- See: South Bank - The notes at.

Also, ofttimes referred to as 'The Borough' (and the area still clustered at the south end of London Bridge is yet called this, although Southwark has grown far beyond its original edges.)

Originally the site of a Roman garrison.

Later, was part of the See (that is, the jurisdiction of) of the Bishop of Winchester.

A quick glance at the street's residences (below) will quickly show this was an area where trade, prisons (for which the area was known, particularly in the medieval era,) and breweries happily co-existed. There was a fruit and vegetable market thriving here since before 1276. Southwark Fair was banned in 1763. Theatres thrived here, too, in medieval times because Southwark wasn't quite completely "linked" to London; there were pockets of land that had once been church property, controlled by the Bishop of Winchester - they remained self-governing (and were called: liberties,) and so some of the medieval London strictures against theatres were circumvented. (See: liberties.)

The Borough came to contain many galleried old inns, such as the White Hart, and the George. (See, both, below.)

The Festival of Britain, a fair, was held here beginning in 1951 (the 100th anniversary of Queen Victoria's Great Exhibition.)

- 49-50: There was a tavern here called Cardinal's Cap by at least 1613. Appears to have ceased to be a tavern prior to 1830.
- Anchor Pub: 1 Bankside. Built in 1770-1775, partly on the site of the Globe, Shakespeare's theatre. The pub remains to this day. Doctor Johnson drank here. Riverside, with fine views.
- Bankside: Term applied to the Southwark waterfront both west and east of Southwark Bridge, on the south side of the Thames, and also loosely applied to the main street running nearby. The longest walk in London, described as a "long and straggling riverside thoroughfare." Bankside fell outside the City and therefore its laws, so this area was rowdier, with theatres and bawdy houses, and all manner of entertainments banned to its north. This is where Shakespeare's Globe Theatre stood, destroyed by a second fire in 1613 (and its very likeness rebuilt, but not until the modern time of 1996.) Although Bankside and Southwark are often linked together, Bankside has status distinct from the Borough of Southwark.
- Borough: Name derives from "burgh," signifying the presence of defense (for the then nearby London Bridge.) Most of the Borough burned in 1676 (the so-called Little Fire of London.) NOTE: The Borough and Southwark lie along each other, and are separate, but are often spoken of as being a bit of a common entity.
- Borough High Street: Parts of this street still retain their medieval form. In the southern part of this street resided the Horsemonger Gaol, small. Borough High Street is the main road south out of London. In the Regency, it was dotted with a collection of coaching inns.

- 77: George Inn, the. 1676 rebuild; the only example of a traditional galleried coaching inn left in London (now a pub.) Is a rare example of a medieval pub. Open galleries overlooked the cobbled city road. East of the high street. The north and east wings were demolished in 1889. (See: George Inn, under the INNS/PUBS section.)
- Borough Market: There was a market here since 1276. This fruit and vegetable market was on Borough High Street until moved to its present location in 1756. The buildings, south of the Cathedral, date from 1851. (See: Borough Market, under B.)
- Horsemonger Gaol: (AKA: Horsemonger Lane Gaol.) On the southern part of the street. Small. Leigh Hunt was imprisoned here for calling Prinny "a fat Adonis of fifty." (See under H.)
- King's Bench Prison: Established in the 14th C. at Westminster Hall. Was attached to the Court of King's Bench, Westminster Hall, to hold those awaiting trial and as a debtor's prison. Its name derives from the gaols being attached to the court of King's Bench, which moved from town to town around the country, arriving quarterly.

  After Westminster, its housing was at the east side of Borough High Street.

  In the 16th C., when Elizabeth reigned, this was known as Queen's Bench Prison.

  During the Commonwealth (1649-1660) it was temporarily called: the Upper Bench (since there was no king.)

  First demolished in 1754; rebuilt and moved in 1758 farther westward, to what is now known as Scovell Road, St. George's Fields. Largely destroyed in the 1780 Gordon Riots. Restored. Demolished in 1880, and now covered over by the Scovell Estate. Also, its name changed again in 1842 to Queen's Bench, taking in many of the Marshalsea and Fleet Prison debtors. (See: Queen's Bench, under Q.)
- Marshalsea Prison: (See, below.)
- Queen's Bench Prison: (See under Q.)
- St. George-the-Martyr Church: 1733-36, rebuilt on the site of an earlier church. By John Price. (See under the CHURCHES section.)
- Southwark Cathedral:
  - See: below.
  - See: St. Mary Overie, under the CHURCHES section.

  - ➢ See: Southwark Cathedral, under the CHURCHES section.
- o Talbot Inn: (Renamed after the Great Fire of 1666; had been the Tabard Inn.) Demolished by fire in 1873. In Talbot Yard.
- o White Hart Inn: 22 Great Suffolk Street. 18th C. pub. It yet exists, although now wearing modern "clothes."

(Resuming "Southwark" alpha listings:)

- Brewery: Of Messrs Barclay, Perkins. Left to these two gentlemen by the previous owner when he died in 1781. Greatly damaged in 1852, but rebuilt.
- Cardinal's Cap Alley: Tiny, in the medieval period was famous for its brothels. NAIRN'S LONDON calls it: "...stock-brick walls between a big tree and a back garden, leading from public to private world."
- Christ Church Tower: 1876. Kennington Road.
- Clapham: (See under C.)
- Clink Prison:
  - ➢ See: Southwark/Liberty of the Clink, below.
  - ➢ See under C.
- Clink Street: (See under C.)
- County Hall: (South Bank Centre.) 1933. (See under C - For pre-1933 information.)
- Cross Street: STYLE CITY LONDON describes this street as "a small lane lined with Georgian townhouses between Essex Road and Upper Street." Later in the 19th C. was rebuilt as a terrace of cottages called Meymott Street.
- George Inn: (See: Borough High Street/77, above.)
- Guy's Hospital: In St. Thomas's Street, east side of Borough High Street, (across the street from St. Thomas's Hospital, of which Guy had been a great supporter; when St. Thomas's became severely overcrowded, Guy opted to open a new hospital.) Charity hospital. From 1725 (although, five different sources give these five different founding dates: 1721; 1721-24; 1724; 1725; 1726.) The facade dates from 1773. Established by Thomas Guy, who had made a fortune in the "South Sea Bubble" (getting out before the "Bubble" burst in 1720.) Rebuilt in 1778. Ca. 1778 some of the older wards were described as "too low" (some only 9-1/2 feet high.) 304 patients. A dental surgeon joined the staff in 1799, bringing Guy's Hospital a flare of fame for such an innovation. John Keats (poet) began his study of medicine here in 1815. The east and west wings were added in 1852. The "world's tallest hospital tower" was added in 1974.

- Guys Hospital Chapel: NAIRN'S LONDON provides this description: "...a pretty eighteenth-century building, which is a pleasant enough surprise; but what is worth a special visit, even in London, is John Bacon's monument to Thomas Guy, set up in 1779. The figure of Guy leading a sick man into his hospital is all compassion without the least taint of moralizing or the horrible smugness of Victorian charity."

- Hay's Wharf: 1857. (See under H.)
- Hop Exchange: Buildings date from 1866-67.
- Hopton's Almshouses: Holland Street (turns off Southwark Street.) Built ca. 1740, in compliance with one Charles Hopton's will. (See: Hopton Street, under H.)
- Horsemonger Gaol:
    - See: Borough High Street/Horsemonger Gaol, above.
    - See: Horsemonger Lane Gaol, under H.
- Jacob's Island: In the 1840s was a slummy east Southwark area. On the edge of the Thames River. "Beyond Dockhead," as author Charles Dickens put it. (See under J.)
- Kennington: Elegant 18th C. terraces; became truly respectable by the 1820s.
    - Christ Church Tower: 1876.
- King's Bench (prison): (See: Borough High Street/King's Bench Prison, above.)
- Liberty of the Clink, the: LET'S GO, THE BUDGET GUIDE TO LONDON, 1995 states: "The Bishop of Winchester's Court had jurisdiction over these 70 acres of Bankside land, which for several hundred years made up London's red-light district. 'The Clink' was the Bishop's private prison for London's criminals."
    - See: Clink, under C.
    - See: liberties.
- Marshalsea, the (prison): Borough High Street, Southwark. From 1377 to 1842, was primarily a prison for political prisoners (traitors, felons, pirates,) and later for debtors. Was attacked in the 1381 Wat Tyler riot, as well as the 1450 Jack Cade riot. Massive breakout in 1504, due to its atrocious conditions. Moved in 1811 farther south down Borough High Street (as was known to Charles Dickens, because his father was imprisoned here in 1824.) Today its location would have been beside the John Harvard Library, close to the Local Studies Library. Shut down in 1842. Demolished in 1849; all that remains now is a wall containing the entrance arch, in a bit of garden. (See: Marshalsea Prison, under M - The note

at.)

- National Theatre: (See: Royal National Theatre, below.)
- Old Kent Road: 1789. (See under O.)
- Royal Festival Hall: 1951.
- Royal National Theatre: 1978, opened by Sir Laurence Olivier.
- St. George the Martyr:
    - See: Southwark/Borough High Street/St. George the Martyr Church, above.
    - See: St. George the Martyr, under the CHURCHES section.
- St. Mary Overie (or "over the water"): Since 1106. Contains the effigy of the 14th C. writer, John Gower. (See under the CHURCHES section.)
- St. Thomas Street: In 1815, while living here, John Keats (poet) called it "a beastly place in dirt, turnings and windings."
    - St. Thomas's Old Operating Theatre: 9A St. Thomas Street. A 19th C. surgical hospital, (re)discovered in 1956, the only known example of an operating theatre from the pre-Victorian part of the 19th century.
- St. Thomas's Hospital: This charity hospital originated in the Priory of St. Mary Overy (also spelled Overie,) being founded in 1106. It took on the name of "St. Thomas the Martyr" to honor Archbishop Thomas à Becket in the late 12th century. It stood where Southwark Cathedral is, since 1228.

  In the 13th C., the hospital moved to Borough High Street, Southwark.

  It was closed in 1540, by Henry VIII; reopened in 1551 by Edward VI, then being called "St. Thomas the Apostle," and being administered by the Crown as a Royal Hospital. The City bought it from the Crown in 1553; being then a municipal hospital until 1703, when Queen Anne's personal physician was appointed as director, and the hospital came back to the Crown. Remained a royal hospital into the 19th century.

  Some of the wards (ca. 1788) were only 18 feet wide. 440 patients.

  The front was remodeled (looking "more open") in 1842.

  The Charing Cross Railway came through in 1859, so the hospital moved again, to Lambeth Palace Road in 1871, and these Southwark buildings were dismantled. The hospital founded by Sir Thomas Guy remained when St. Thomas's moved out. (See: Guy's Hospital, above.)

  Florence Nightingale founded the first nursing school in St. Thomas's Hospital, in 1859.

  (See: operating theatre.)

- South Belgravia: 1830-40s.
- Southwark Cathedral: Not Catholic until 1905 (at which time it also took on Cathedral status.) There was a church first here by 607. Some parts date back to the 12th C.; it is London's second oldest church after Westminster Abbey. Its official name is St. Saviour's, dating from when it became the parish church following the Reformation. The east end and tower were remodeled in 1818. Had a 19th C. raised bridge approach. Partially rebuilt in 1890.
    - See: St. Mary Overie, under the CHURCHES section.
    - See: St. Thomas's Hospital, above.
- Southwark Gate: Demolished in 1760.
- Southwark Town Hall: 1793. Demolished 1859.
- Trinity Square: AKA: Trinity Church Square. (See: Trinity Square, under T.)
- White Hart Inn: Shakespeare wrote of it, and it was still there in Dickens' time. (See: White Hart Inn - Southwark, under the INNS/PUBS section.)

Southwark Bridge Company - 1814-19. (See: Southwark Bridge, under the BRIDGES section.)

Southwark Park - 1869.

Sovereign's Bodyguard, the - (See: Yeomen of the Guard.)

spa - Spas could range from a simple flowing well that one walked to visit, to a set of formal rooms with a pump at its core. Spas were popular in the 18-19th centuries, especially those that combined the lure of "medicinal waters" with aspects of leisure. On the one hand, the point was to drink the supposedly recuperative waters that came from natural wells or springs, but the other advantage was that it made for a meeting place, where there might even be assemblies and dances. Many districts hosted a well or spa of some sort. Examples: Bath/Lower Rooms, and Upper Rooms; Cheltenham; Tunbridge Wells.

Spa Fields - Clerkenwell. Open fields, laid out with walks. Scene of a riot in the winter of 1816.

Spa Fields Chapel - Clerkenwell. The property hosted an "amusement palace," until it was bought in 1777 by the Countess of Huntingdon and rebuilt for Calvinistic Methodists at her commission. It was round.

Spaniard's Inn - (See: Hampstead Heath/Spaniard's Inn.)

Spanish and Portuguese Jews' Synagogue - Also seen written just as: Spanish and Portuguese Synagogue. AKA: Bevis Marks Synagogue (in the district of Bevis Marks, Houndsditch, the City.) 1700-01, by Joseph Avis, a Quaker who purportedly refused to profit from building a House of God, so he gave his fee back to the congregation. Plain style. Set back in a secluded courtyard. Still exists.

sparkling wine -

- See: champagne.
- See: food/drinks/champagne.

Speaker's Corner - Northeast corner of Hyde Park, across from where the Marble Arch eventually settled. In 1872, Hyde Park was officially granted the right to host public meetings, and thus began Speaker's Corner. An 1855 protest against the Sunday Trading Bill had marked the beginning of this location as a public forum for dissatisfaction, and a series of riots in 1866 soon led (1872) to the government establishing this location as being available, by law, for free speech usage, specifically on Sundays. (See: Hyde Park/Speaker's Corner.)

special licenses - In order to marry quickly, without posting the banns for three Sundays in a row as otherwise required.

- See: Doctor's Common.
- See: marriage.

Spectacle Makers' Company - (AKA: the Worshipful Company of Spectaclemakers. Also seen as: Spectacle-makers.) Formed in 1563; Charter in 1629. Always dealt in optical equipment as well as spectacles. Livery Company, granted in 1809. Has no hall of their own, housed in the Apothecaries' Hall, Black Friars. 60th in the order of precedence. Was undermined by advances in the Industrial Revolution.

spectacles - Regency persons would never have called them "glasses." Sunglasses (would have been called: tinted lenses, or tinted spectacles) were introduced to London in the 1750s, but were used for correcting certain vision issues rather than for shielding the eyes from sun-glare.

- See: opticians.
- See: Spectacle-makers' Company.
- See: Spitalfields/John Dolland.

Spencer House - (See: St. James's Place/Spencer House.)

spices - Many spices were imported to London.

- See: food - Look for various spices in the alpha list.
- See: Mincing Lane.

Spinning Jenny, the - A weaving loom. Invented in 1764, it revolutionized the production of cloth; many homes had one.

- See: textiles.
- You may care to see: fabrics.

spinster - Originally was: spinner, a term for a female spinner of cloth (done by hand.) By the end of the 17th C. "spinster" had also come to mean an unmarried woman. (See: old maid.)

spital - A shortened version of "hospital." Seen in place names. Example: Spitalfields.

Spital Square - Name derives from the nearby St. Mary Spital (hospital) and Spitalfields (market.) Mostly a residential area. Weavers here, the homes of either master weavers or silk merchants. Eastern arm of the square was built ca. 1733. (See: Bishopsgate/Spital Square.)

Spitalfields - Commercial Street. North of Whitechapel. Derived its name from the 1197 St. Mary Spital ("spital" being a corruption of hospital,) a medieval priory and hospital, closed in 1538. There was a market here by at least the 13th C., and Spitalfields Market (fruits and vegetables earlier, belatedly becoming a textile market,) officially dates from the 1680s. There until 1991, when it moved to the eastern suburbs (north of Ruckholt Road, Temple Mills.)

Began to develop as a district in the 17th C., when it was an area of Huguenot silkweavers. In the early 18th C. it was a bit of a "new town," an area of residential growth just beyond the city. It declined as the East End arose; by 1750, this area was densely populated; ca. 1790 it took on the nickname Petty France. The Huguenots' homes on these streets were/are attractive and pleasant, those falling into disrepair doing so only after 1880, at which time Jewish workers moved in and area had the nickname Little Jerusalem. Georgian and Victorian facades yet exist here. The market was redesigned in 1887 in the Arts & Crafts style; moved in 1991 to Leyton, east London.

- Artillery Lane: Spitalfields was once the site of archery and gunnery practice.
    - 56: Georgian shopfront.
- Christ Church, Spitalfields: 1725-29. (See under the CHURCHES section.)
- Church Street: Where local carriages were housed.
- Elder Street: Was a residential street for Huguenot families/ weaving businesses, starting in the 17th century.
- Folgate Street: (See under F.)
- Fournier Street: (See under F.)
- Fruit and Wool Exhange: Brushfield Street. 20th century. (See: Wool Exchange, under W.)
- John Dolland: Had a spectacles shop here from 1750. In 1761 he became the king's optician. His business evolved into Dolland & Aitchinson, a chain of retail opticians, which in 2009 combined with Boots opticians (being fully absorbed in 2015.) The area went on to become known for its opticians. (You may care to see: spectacles.)
- Little Jerusalem: After 1880. (See under L.)
- Petticoat Lane: (Now Middlesex Street, so renamed by Queen Victoria, whose sensibilities were offended by the prior name.) Old clothes, wigs, shoes, etc.,

primarily cast-offs. (See: Petticoat Lane, under P.)

- Spitalfields Market: Commercial Street. Founded in 1682, under Charles II's authority. Fruit and vegetable market. Last set of market buildings dated from the turn of the 19th C., (and are now occupied by stalls.) Moved away from here in the 1980s.
- Whitechapel High Street: (See under W.)
- Wilkes Street: Dates from at least the 1750s.

Spode China - Bone china. (See: Staffordshire, under the BRITISH COUNTIES section.)

Sporting Magazine, The - Published from 1792-1870. Covered many sporting items, including the formation of driving clubs.

sports - Of the Regency era.

- ➢ See: activities/entertainment/sports, under A - Various listings.
- ➢ See: various sports by name - Such as: archery, cricket, football, tennis.

sports equipment - (See: Noah's Ark.)

Spring Gardens - St. James's. Had been a pleasure garden, for which the street is named. Had been rather like Vauxhall, which it became in 1785. (See: Vauxhall Gardens.) As a street, Jane Austen (author) walked here.

- Buckingham Court: Built by at least 1718.
- Old Admiralty, the: (See: Admiralty, under A.)
- Society of Painters in Water-Colours: Here in 1809. (See under S.)

Spring Grove -

- ➢ See: Isleworth/Spring Grove.
- ➢ See: Smallbury Green.

Springfield Park - Hackney. Much of the land around here ca. 1664 belonged to the Webbe family, along with Spring Hill Farm. The county bought the land in 1902.

- Springfield House: Also called the White Lodge due to its stuccoed exterior. Had a frontage with five bay windows. 1820s.

spurmaker -

- ➢ See: halls/"No Hall"/Spurriers.
- ➢ See: Savile Row/11.
- ➢ See: spurriers.
- ➢ You may care to see: halls/"No Hall"/Loriners.

spurriers - A spurrier is someone who makes spurs. Women seldom wore spurs, because they tangled with their skirts. The Spurriers were part of the Blacksmiths' Company, probably into the early 19th C.; but now is much more a surname than a profession.

- ➢ See: Blacksmiths' Company.
- ➢ See: halls/"No Hall"/Spurriers.

spying/British spies -

- ➢ See: Home Department - Internal.
- ➢ See: Home Office - External.

Square Mile, the - Another way of referring to the City. (See: City, the, under C.)

squares - That is, blocks of housing. Usually had a private park at the center, surrounded on 3-4 sides of (often) like-styled homes, usually fairly gracious. The first square built in London was: Bloomsbury, 1660s. The largest square in London is: Lincoln's Inn Fields. The idea of squares took on desirability in the Georgian era, continuing on well past the Regency era.

Sri Guru Singh Sabha Gurdwara - Havelock Road, Southall. Is the largest Sikh temple outside of India. Modern. (See: Sikhs.)

Stable Yard Road - Buckingham Street, near St. James's Palace. Green Park.

- Clarence House: 1827. (See under C.)
- Lancaster House: (See: York House, below.) Is actually a part of St. James's Palace, as are Clarence House and Marlborough House. Is currently Prince Charles and his wife Camilla's residence.
- York House: (Not to be confused with York House, Pall Mall.) Stable Yard Road and Queen's Walk. Originally was a 13th C. town house, enlarged by Cardinal Wolsey into a palatial mansion. It went to the Crown in 1529 at Cardinal Wolsey's fall, becoming York Palace, and then Henry VIII renamed it Whitehall Palace. (See under W.) Rebuilt by Inigo Jones, and Jones' son-in-law, John Webb, mid 1600's. Wren added to it in 1685. Damaged in 1691 by fire; burned entirely in 1698 (leaving only the Banqueting House) and was not rebuilt (and never again used as Westminster Palace.)

  Could enter via the Watergate on the Thames (now the only remnant of York House yet remaining.)

  Then, a York House was rebuilt totally anew by Benjamin Wyatt for the Duke of York, son of George III, 1825-27 (although the Duke died before the building was completed.) It was then sold to the Marquess of Stafford, at which time it was called Stafford House; expanded in 1833; completed in 1840 by Robert Smirke. Interior was designed by Charles Barry. Later known as Lancaster House (1912.)

  From 1913-46, it housed the London Museum. It is now a conference center.

stables - In Regency England, a stable was more likely to be found out in the country; whereas a mews would be the term of use in any town of size.

- See: mews.
- See: Royal Mews.

Stafford House - (See: Stable Yard Road/York House.)

Stafford Row - Used to be where Bressenden Place met Buckingham Palace Road.

- 5: Ann Radcliffe, Gothic author whose works were popular with Regency misses (and gentlemen, for that matter,) lived here.

Stamford Bridge - Hammersmith and Fulham. There had been a bridge at the "sandy ford" here, (but by 1839 it was a railway station.)

- Stamford Bridge Stadium: 1877. Home of the Chelsea Football Club from 1906.

Stamford Hill - Hackney/Haringey. Was "Sandford Hill" in the 13th century. In the 18th-early 19th centuries, rich merchants built homes here. Hasidic Jews, escaping crowded East End tenements, came here in the late 19th century. Developed rapidly after the rails came in 1872. This area continued to attract Hasidic Jews, and is now (outside of New York and Israel) the most orthodox Jewish location.

Stamford Street - Lambeth and Southwark. Built at the beginning of the 19th century. Off Blackfriars Road. Roughly over where a prior road, Holland's Leaguer, had been; the latter of which was home to an infamous brothel portrayed in a 17th C. comedy.

Stamp Office, the - Moved from Lincoln's Inn to Somerset House in the 1770s. (The newspapers had to all be taken here and stamped before distribution, and also to pay a tax.) According to A PORTRAIT OF GEORGIAN LONDON: "Stamp Duty, which is imposed on certain legal documents, is Britain's oldest Inland Revenue tax, dating back to 1694." It was also intentionally designed to help control the press, with the high tax forcing several news sheets to fold, until its repeal in 1855. (The 1765 tax England imposed on its American colonies - a stamp tax repealed one year later - was one of the resentments that led to the American Revolutionary War of 1776.)

Adhesive postage stamps were invented in 1838 by James Chalmers (Scottish inventor.)

Standard, the - Cheapside, near Honey Lane. A conduit, which is a leaden cistern cased in stone. Dates from ca. 1337. Also used as a place of execution. It was not rebuilt after the Great Fire of 1666.

Stanmore - Harrow. Recorded as "Stanmere" in Domesday Book. Known as Great Stanmore; was heathland; name evolved to Stanmore Common. This old settlement was abandoned, probably due to plague, and a new one built no later than 1632.

- Stanmore Old Church: Its 1631 remains are behind a Victorian version.

Stanmore Park - Harrow. A mansion on 56 acres, built in the 1720s, possibly over the site of an older moated home. Became a boys' school in the 1880s, until 1938 at which time it was pulled down and RAF Stanmore Park air base came in here; closed in 1997. Now a housing development.

Staple Inn - Dates from 1586. (See: Inns of Court/Staple Inn.)

staplers - Those who deal in wool, a product considered a British "staple," supposedly hence the name. That is one explanation of where the term "staple" comes from, but other sources claim that, until the reign of Edward III/14th C., wool could only be exported from designated (staple) ports.

- See: Inns of Court/Staple Inn.
- See: Wool Merchants.

Star and Garter Home for Disabled Soldiers and Sailors - 1924.

Star Chamber - Used to be part of Westminster. Gone by approximately 1640-41, dissolved. LONDON THROUGH THE AGES states: "...an infamous branch of the judiciary answerable only to the king and possessing tremendous powers; it was not answerable to Common Law, dispensed with juries, could examine witnesses and proceed on mere rumour, and could inflict torture and any penalty short of death."

Starch Green - Hammersmith and Fulham. Takes its name from 18-19th century laundries here. Now a little used local name.

State Paper Office, the - 1829-31 (second source says 1833.) Built where the Foreign and India Office now are.

Stationers' Hall - (For the Worshipful Company of Stationers' and Newspaper Makers'; usually known as the Stationers' Company, as they were called until 1937.) Stationers' Hall Court; Ave Maria Lane, near to St. Paul's Churchyard.

Supposedly the term "stationer" referred to the fact a bookseller was not itinerant (as most were,) but had a fixed place of business. Although it might well have derived from the term "stationarii" - keepers of standard texts at universities.

Has existed for 600+ years. The Stationers were established as a Brotherhood in 1403, receiving their Royal Charter in 1557 (mostly out of the government's desire to control heretical publications.) They largely set the print standards until the Statute of Anne, 1710 (also called the Copyright Act of 1710; repealed and replaced by the Copyright Act of 1842.)

When printing came to England in the late 15th C., the Stationers were forward-looking enough to embrace the new technology.

The Ave Maria Lane hall was built in 1670-4 after a predecessor burned in the Great Fire of 1666; facade was resurfaced in Portland Stone in 1800 by McIntyre. The beautiful north windows date from 1894.

Once was the home of the book publishing monopoly. All books to be published were registered here until 1911.

Livery Company, for the Communications and Content Industries. 47th in the order of precedence.

statistics - A word first used by Sir John Sinclair, a Scottish politician, in his groundbreaking work *Statistical Account of Scotland*, 1784.

steam engine - Invented in 1769, which in part led to the Industrial Revolution with its huge changes to farming techniques, transportation, and urbanization of society. Its invention is credited to either James Watt or George Stephenson, but they were improving on earlier designs. The steam boat was invented in 1785 by William Symington. The steam locomotive was invented in 1802 by Richard Trevithick. (See: docks/Victoria Docks - The first dock to open to steamships.)

Steelyard, the - North bank of the Thames, ward of Dowgate, the City. Rich medieval German merchants were allowed to build a mansion for themselves, which came to be known as the Steelyard. A separate, walled community. Due to competition, they were expelled from London in Tudor times. Its privileges were suspended in 1598 by Elizabeth I; its building mostly destroyed by the Great Fire of 1666.

steeplechases - Horse race, over obstacles. (See: activities/entertainments/sports - steeplechasing, under A.)

Stepney - East End. From Aldgate to Bow, Hackney to the Thames. Dates from at least the 11th C., the principal owner at that time being the Bishop of London. As the Royal Navy grew, the area hosted retired naval officers and seamen. Was absorbed into greater London as the 19th C. advanced, and became filled with shops. Orchards, hamlets, and market-gardens in Georgian times. Had become a slum by Victorian times. A Jewish population moved in at the end of the 19th century.

- Mile End Road.
- St. George-in-the-East: (See under the CHURCHES section.)
- St. Mary's-Bow Road. (See: St. Mary-Bow, in the CHURCHES section.) Not to be confused with St. Mary-le-Bow.
- Trinity House: (See under T.)

Stepney Fields - Rapidly developed after 1800, when Commercial Street was built over it. (See: Commercial Street.)

Stepney Green - Georgian; previously had been called Mile End Green, the latter of which existed prior to 1381.

Stepney Marsh - (See: Isle of Dogs.)

stethoscope - The first version, a wood-turned cylinder, was invented in 1816, in France, by Rene

Theophile Hyacinthe Laennec (pupil to Napoleon's personal physician.) A stethoscope with ear pieces was invented in 1828.

still-room - In private homes, where cordials and other alcoholic drinks, herbal remedies, tonics, essences (perfumes,) and household cosmetics were made. Usually the domain and tasks of females.

- See: food/camomile.
- See: food/feverfew.
- See: food/hyssop.
- See: food/lavender.
- See: food/southernwood.
- See: food/wormwood.

Stinking Lane - (AKA: On a 1699 map it was: Chick Lane, as it still was in a 1777 court record.) Near Newgate Street. Was given the Stinking Lane name due to the refuse/filth that accumulated here from nearby Newgate and Smithfield Markets. In the 17-18th centuries old clothes were sold on this street. It was a rough area overall, with drunks, pickpockets, and prostitutes. During the Regency, it was called: West Lane. Now: King Edward Street, since 1843. (See: Chick Lane.)

Stock Exchange - (AKA: London Stock Exchange.) Not to be confused with the Royal Stock Exchange, which housed the Stock Exchange until 1972. (See: Royal Stock Exchange, under R.) Also not to be confused with the Stocks Market (note that the latter is "Market" - not Exchange - and that the "Stocks" is plural.)

Located at Old Broad Street. Ian Nairn (in 1966, so before they moved in 1972) in NAIRN'S LONDON described finding its location: "Go...to Bartholomew Lane, a quiet street at the back of the Bank of England. A quiet cul-de-sac opens off it - Chapel Court. And at the end is a demure stuccoed front, one bay wide, which is the main entrance to...the Stock Exchange... The public gallery has an unprepossessing entrance in Threadneedle Street, apparently unrelated, which seems to be just a set of office stairs."

Renamed in 1773 from Jonathan's (coffee house) to the Stock Exchange, and moved to Sweeting Alley (in Threadneedle Street.) In 1773, this took over (from the Royal Exchange) dealings in stocks and shares (because the Royal Exchange was so overcrowded.) It belongs to its members, being (as said in A PORTRAIT OF GEORGIAN LONDON): "...one of the most distinguished worker's cooperatives in the country." Its constitution was drawn up formally in 1812.

A larger building was acquired in Capel Court, Threadneedle Street, built 1801-24. It was a triangular site fitted in-between Threadneedle Street, Throgmorton Street, and Old Broad Street. Enlarged in 1853-4, by Thomas Allason; and by J. J. Cole in 1882.

Site demolished ca. 1966-9. Moved to Old Broad Street from 1966-73. Relocated in 2003 at 10 Paternoster Square.

(See: Jonathan's Coffee House - For the Stock Exchange's foundations.)

stockings - Worn by both men and women. Also called: hose. Stockings were fastened beneath the knee, using a ribbon or cord garter. Made of: cotton, silk, wool, or worsted (woven wool.)

- See: Framework Knitters' Company.
- See: pants - Note at, for men.

Stockley Park - Hillingdon. A 20th C. business park and public park; one of the few London parks established in the 20th century.

Stocks Market - (Infrequently seen as: Stock Market.) The City. In the Regency (until 1826) it was referred to as "Fleet Market."

Americans might immediately think of trading stocks, as on Wall Street/USA, but this was a market that sold products. (In the UK, a stockist is an old-fashioned way of referring to a retailer, or a dealer, often in a particular brand.)

Not to be confused with the Stock Exchange.

- See: Fleet Market, under F.
- See: Fleet Market reference, below, in this entry.

Was the earliest fully recorded market building in Britain, 13th century. For butchers and fishmongers; built because the Mayor (ca. 1274) made an attempt to move the market from Cheapside in preparation of a royal visit to the City. Originally called the Hales (another word for stocks.)

Rebuilt several times, being in the 17th C. a "stone house" divided into sections for fish and meat. The Great Fire of 1666 destroyed it; rebuilt on the site of St. Mary's, Woolchurch. Near its demise, mostly sold just herbs.

Torn down in 1737, for construction of the Mansion House. (See: Mansion House.) The market moved and was given its old name: Fleet Market. Designed by George Dance, Sr., built on a new bridge over the Fleet river. It was two rows of single-story shops, with a covered walkway with skylights. Cleared again in 1826 for Farringdon Street (the latter completed in 1830.)

Stockwell - Lambeth. First recorded in 1197. CHAMBERS LONDON GAZETTEER says: "After its release by the Crown in 1598, the manor was held by the viscounts Montagu in the 17th century, the Chute family in the 18th and the Thornycrofts in the 19th." The manor house was pulled down in 1755; a new one didn't even last a century. In the 19th century the area of Stockwell was mostly nurseries. Developed in the 19th C. after the coming of the rails.

Stoke Newington - Hackney. A pleasant, populated village between Hackney and Islington, of elegant 18th C. houses. "Stoke" denotes a town built where woods once stood, in this case a portion of the great Middlesex forest. By long tradition this is an area attractive to nonconformists or outsiders. In 1835 the village was fundamentally situated along one long road, and its population was 3,500; it was rural. Daniel Defoe (author) once lived here ca. 1684.

- Abney Street Cemetery: Built ca. 1840. Built on the grounds of the mansion (pulled down in 1845) of one Sir Thomas Abney, a well-known nonconformist, and a member of the Fishmongers' Company, and Lord Mayor of London in 1700.
- Church Street:
    - St. Mary: 1858, by Sir G. Gilbert Scott. This St. Mary's is just opposite another St. Mary's dating from the 16th C. and situated on the north side of the street. This latter St. Mary's would have been the village church in the Regency. (See: St. Mary, Newington Butts, under the CHURCHES section.)
- Clissold Park: 1889 (or 1899.) In what is now part of this park, stands an 18th C. porticoed mansion.
- Mermaid Tavern: Near the junction of Mare Street and Amhurst Road. Pulled down in 1844, except that the assembly room was preserved.
- Springfield Park: 1905.

stone - British measure of weight, equal to 14 pounds in America.

Stone Buildings, the - (See: Inns of Court/Lincoln's Inn Fields/Stone Buildings.)

Stone Conduit Close - (See: Sackville Street.)

Stone of Scone - AKA: Stone of Destiny. (See: Westminster Abbey/Stone of Scone.)

Stone's Chop House - (See: Panton Street/Stone's Chop House.)

Store Street - (See: Bloomsbury/Store Street.)

stories - As in the number of stories/floors in a home or business, is different between the UK and America. (See: floors.)

Strand - (AKA: the Strand.) Strand means: bank or shore. Westminster. Street closest to the Thames (until the Victoria Embankment, 1864-70, pushed it inland a bit.) Dates from 1185. Temple Bar marks where Fleet Street and the Strand meet. Centuries ago it was first known as "Stronde," the name meaning "bank" or "shore." According to CHAMBERS LONDON GAZETTEER: "Many maps still give the Strand as the name of the district that everyone else knows as Covent Garden." The great Tudor houses along here were pulled down in the 17th C., being replaced by residential streets; ca. 1634 there were builders of Hackney coaches here. By the late 19th C. this was decidedly a theatre district. The area includes the shopping area known as New Exchange.

The West Strand Improvements were planned by Nash, but carried out by Herbert ca. 1830.

- 96 (extended to 101): Ackermann's Repository of Arts, established in 1771. Was a print shop. The fashionable came here to view his prints. Once a week Mr. Hatcher gave evening receptions. From 1809 (his shop was lighted by gas from 1810, being the first shop in London solely lit by gas) through 1829, he published a monthly periodical (with the same name as the shop) which was beautifully detailed. It modeled examples of carriages, dress, furnishings and furniture, and numerous items that reflected elegant living.
- 100: (See: Simpson's Restaurant, below.)
- 132: In 1740 this was a booksellers' establishment. (See: circulating libraries, under C - Note at.)
- 178: Edmund Lloyd, Patent Stove Grate Manufacturer and Furnishing Ironmonger. Here by at least January/1816.
- 186: W. H. Smith, news vendor/distributor (See under W.)
- 188-191: Crown & Anchor Hotel. Dr. Johnson supped here with Boswell.
- 213: George Public House. (See: George, under the INNS/PUBS section.)
- 216: Twinings teas. Has been selling tea here from 1706. (Second and third sources say Thomas Twining opened his shop as "Tom's Coffee House" in 1706, and despite the "coffee" in its name, it also sold tea from early on, certainly as tea-drinking grew increasingly popular in England.) The slender, neo-classical porticoed doorway has a Chinese Mandarin reclining on either side, above the door, reflecting a time when all tea came from China. The doorway dates from 1787, when the shop was known as the Golden Lion (or Lyon); opened in 1707. The lion was the identification mark for their business. The name changed to Twinings around 1741, when Thomas Twining's son, Daniel, was selling tea here. Jane Austen bought tea from Twinings here in 1811. In 1837 Queen Victoria granted Twinings its first Royal Warrant. Declared the "narrowest shop in London," it is also the oldest business in Britain to still be in its original location.
- 222-225: Lloyds Bank. Started in 1765 in Birmingham as Taylors & Lloyds. (Founders: John Taylor, Sampson Lloyd, and their two sons.) It was a town bank, its clients largely from manufacturing and mercantile concerns. The Taylor family bowed out in 1852, and it became Lloyds & Co; and in 1865 became Lloyds Banking Company Ltd. Circa 1884 spread to London. Celebrated its 250th anniversary in 2015. (Not to be confused with Lloyd's of London.)

- 229-230: Wig and Pen Club, the. The only building on the Strand to survive the Great Fire of 1666. (See: Wig and Pen Club, under the CLUBS section.)
- 440: Coutts & Co. Bankers to the Royals. (See under C.)
- Adelphi Theatre: (See under the THEATRES section.)
- Burgess, John, & Sons Warehouse: "Italian warehousemen to Her Royal Highness the Duchess of Gloucester," established 1760. Now situated in Shaftesbury Road. Pastes, horseradish, delicacies; their anchovies made them famous.
- Coal Hole, the: Pub. (See under the INNS/PUBS section.)
- Crown and Anchor: There by at least 1811. Still exists. (See: Crown and Anchor, under the INNS/PUBS section.)
- *Globe, The*: Newspaper. Established here in 1803. (In 1921, it was absorbed by the Pall Mall Gazette, and then this was absorbed by the Evening Standard in 1923.)
- King's College: (See under K.)
- Law Courts: Same as: Royal Courts of Justice, below.
    - See: Courts of Common Law and Equity/Chancery Court - Note at.
    - See: Law Courts, under L.
- Madame Tussaud: Opened her waxworks here, perhaps as early as 1802. In 1835 she moved to Baker Street. (See: Baker Street/Madam Tussaud's.)
- Mr. Meirs in the Strand: Made silhouettes of Regency folk. (See: silhouettes.)
- *Morning Advertiser, the*: 1794, newspaper published by the London Society of Licensed Victuallers. (In 1794, it was first called The Publican's Morning Advertiser.) Here in the Strand for 30 years until 1825, when they moved to 127 Fleet Street. It reported on trade issues, without a dedicated political slant. Was very popular by the middle of the 19th century. The UK's oldest continuous newspaper. (You may care to see: London Society of Licensed Victuallers.)
- Royal Courts of Justice:
    - See: Law Courts.
    - See under R.
- St. Clement Danes: Wren, begun in 1679. Now on a traffic island in the Strand. (See under the CHURCHES section.)
- Savoy (hotel): 1889. (See at its own listing.)
- servants' registry: There was one on the Strand during the Regency, but I've been unable to locate its name or a fuller address. A servants' registry was where one went (or sent one's secretary) to hire new servants. You or your secretary would hire a butler and/or a housekeeper, who would go on to hire the other

needed servants. Of course, servants could also be recommended by family or good friends. If trusted, servants could recommend their own relatives for positions. (Too, servants might also travel with their employers between a town and a country home.)

- Simpson's Restaurant: 100 Strand. (Also called: Simpson's-in-the-Strand.) Earliest restaurant (as in the modern sense,) opened 1828, first as a "cigar divan." Rebuilt 1848, and the present building in 1904. (See under S.)
- Somerset House: (See under S.)
- Temple Bar Monument: (See under T.)

Strand Lane - This street dates from at least the Georgian period.

- 162A: The Roman Bath. So called from the 1830s. Actually, it's not a Roman bath at all, but the remains of a 1612 cistern that used to serve the fountains of the gardens of Somerset House. It was used anew in the 1770s as a cold water plunge bath, attached to 33 Surrey Street. Still, the idea they were of Roman origin lingers.
  - ➢ See: Somerset House/Roman Bath.
  - ➢ See: Roman Bath, under R.

Strand Magazine, the - Founded in 1890; survived to 1950. Monthly. Short fiction and general interest articles.

Strand-on-the-Green - Hounslow. Centuries-old waterside hamlet between Chiswick and Kew Bridge. Cistercian monks, 1135, established Langthorne Abbey here; it grew into one of England's wealthiest religious houses. From the 13-17th centuries it was just a "strand" (bank or shore.) The 18th C. brought wealthy residents and their mansions; otherwise was fishing, orchards, and market gardens.

Strand Palace Hotel - (See: Exeter Hall.)

Stratford - Newham. 1820, a straggling village, known for animal slaughter, river mills, and baked bread.

Stratford Place - 1775 cul-de-sac (just off Oxford Street, Marylebone,) built on the site of the Lord Mayor's Banqueting House.

- 7: Martin Van Buren (later American president,) lived here prior to 1832 as a minister to Great Britain.

Stratherne Villa - (See: Gloucester House.)

Stratton Street - Piccadilly. Built in 1693.

strawberries -

- ➢ See: food/strawberries.

- See: fruit/strawberries.
- See: Whitton.

Strawberry Hill - Twickenham estate, overlooking the Thames, Richmond. (Later the name of a suburb that grew up in this vicinity.) In 1698 the Earl of Bradford's coachman built (or bought) a cottage here. Became Horace Walpole's villa, then looking like a gothic/rococo castle, 1747; Walpole named it Strawberry Hill (which fruit grew in the area; there was no real hill.) The mansion was further developed from 1753-76, becoming the exotic building (which inspired the *Beatles* song) still existing. Now houses St. Mary's College. The towers were added in Victorian days. Reopened to the public in 2010.

Streatham - (Pronounced: Stret-tem.) Lambeth. Had chalybeate springs, discovered ca. 1659, attractive to Londoners who wished to take the waters.

- Rookery, the: Park. 1913. (See: Streatham Common/Well House, below.)
- St. Leonard's: Parish church, 1291; rebuilt in the 14th century; thoroughly rebuilt in 1830.
- Streatham Common: A public open area since 1884.
    - Streatham Wells: Unearthed in 1659. A new well was dug on Valley Road in the 1790s when this one became contaminated.
    - Well House: 1783. Later called the Rookery.
- Streatham Hill Theatre: 1929.
- Thrale Place: "Thrale Place" appears to have been the name of a particular house, and therefore lent its name to the nearest street. (See: Streatham Park.)

Streatham Park - The Thrale family's country retreat. (Ralph Thrale was a 1730s Southwark brewer.) Pulled down in 1884.

Streatham Vale - Until 1860 not much here but fields and tracks used by gypsies.

- Grey Hound Inn, the: Ca. 1730, used by gypsies.

street lighting -

- See: gas lighting.
- See: Hyde Park/Rotten Row.
- You may care to see: lamps.

stucco - Was an exterior texture seen/put on homes in Georgian/Regency London, beginning from ca. 1740. (See: Piccadilly/80.)

Stukeley Street - (See: Coal Yard.)

Stultz's - Tailor. (See: Clifford Street/10.)

subscription libraries - A reading society; mostly used by the middle classes. Universal free libraries came into being ca. 1850; until then the only subscription library free to the public was Chetham's in Manchester, and it still occupies its original 15th C. buildings. (See: libraries.)

Sudbury - Brent. 13th century. Sudbury Court was the main Middlesex residence of the archbishops of Canterbury up to almost the 15th century. Squatters lived here until 1759 houses came in. Enclosed in 1817. Now known for its Indian population.

Sudbury Common - The name of the land between the foot of Harrow Hill and Sudbury until 1803.

Suffield Hatch - Waltham Forest. 13th century. South Field, a 1758 farm, gave its (corrupted) name to this area (and was gone by 1880.)

Suffolk Street - Dates from 1664. Trafalgar Square area. The fine houses here are from ca. 1825.

suffrage, women's - 1918. In the 18-19th centuries, a woman was yet considered chattel - that is, the property of her husband.

- See: National Union of Women's Suffrage Societies.
- See: votes, for women.
- See: Women's Rights.
- You may care to see: marriage.

sugar - Little seen in Europe until deep into the 16th C., coming from India and America. The more money you had, the more likely you were to have sugar at hand. The poor were more likely to have honey, when they could harvest or afford it. (Indeed, everyone used honey.)

- See: docks/West India Dock.
- See: East End.
- See: food/sugar.

suicides - The custom of burying suicide victims at crossroads (with a stake driven through the body in hopes of securing the "lost soul from wandering aimlessly") was abolished on 7/8/1823 by Act of Parliament. George IV pushed this act through, having become annoyed at the proximity of suicide burials very near Buckingham House. Suicide was illegal, considered by the Church to be blasphemy, and also because it denied the Crown a subject. If found sane (not a legal defense,) the suicide forfeited his property, so a suicide was usually found not to be in his right mind, so his family did not suffer loss of property. (The act could also be called: self-murdering.)

Summerstown - Wandsworth. Mills here from the Middle Ages on; the district's industry was definitely based around mills and weaving in the 18-19th centuries.

Sunday Times - Newspaper. Founded in 1822. Although established separately, has been affiliated with The Times since 1966. Still exists.

Sunday schools - For poor, working children. So called because the children attended on their one day off from the work week. Spread rapidly ca. 1735 as a concept for educating the "lower orders" in both academics and religion. Spread even more as industrialization expanded; as the late 19th C. advanced, these Sunday schools were more about religious indoctrination and less about academics, because it was felt too much literacy led to dissention and dissatisfaction among the lower orders.

Sunderland House - 38 Curzon Street; corner of Curzon Street and Shepherd's Market. Built in 1901 by the Duke of Marlborough (who lived here until his 1906 divorce.) Now called Lombard House.

Sundridge - Bromley. The district existed from the year 987, first known as Sundresse. In the 17th C. wealthy Londoners built here.

sunglasses - (See: spectacles.)

supper - (See: meals.)

Surbiton - Kingston. Existed by at least 1648. About 40 houses here in the early 19th century. Before it became Surbiton, it was known as Seething Wells. Now a 20th C. borough.

- Surbiton Place: Dates from the mid 18th century.

Surgeons' Hall - (See: Barbers' Hall.)

surgical training - Gloves were not used during medical care/surgeries until ca. 1900. For that matter, the simple washing of hands was only slowly being accepted as the 19th C. marched on; they did not understand the nature of germs.

- See: doctors.
- See: hospitals.
- See: Hunterian Medical School.
- See: resurrectionists - Those who steal dead bodies from graveyards.
- See: Soho/Great Windmill Street School.

Surrey Chapel - (See under the CHURCHES section.)

Surrey Commercial Dock - (See: docks/Surrey Commercial Dock.)

Surrey County Cricket Club - Opened 1846. (See: Kennington/Oval Cricket Ground.)

Surrey County Gaol - (See: Horsemonger Lane/Horsemonger Lane Gaol.)

Surrey Institution - (Not to be confused with the Royal Institution.) Surrey. The building dates from 1788-9. The Institution was founded in 1808 by subscribers. Lectures, chemical laboratory, library, and reading rooms. Closed in 1823. United Africa House was built on the site, 1959.

Surrey Iron Railway - 1801. Horse-drawn. Ceased to be in the 1840s. (See: Mitcham/Surrey Iron Railway.)

Surrey Quays - (See: docks/Surrey Commercial Docks.)

Surrey Square - (See: Walworth/Surrey Square.)

Surrey Theatre - (See under the THEATRES section.)

Surrey Zoological Gardens - The animals from Cross's Menagerie came here ca. 1829; and this zoo opened in 1831. Closed in 1877. 13 acres, east of Vauxhall Gardens. (See: Cross's

Menagerie.)

Sussex Gardens - (AKA: Grand Junction Road, Paddington.) 1828.

Sussex Place - (See: Park Crescent/Sussex Place.)

Sussex Square - Post-1840. (See: Hyde Park Square - Note under.)

Sutton - First recorded in Domesday Book; although it might not have been much of a settlement into medieval times. In the 18th C. was little more than some houses along the High Street. Grew when the road to Brighton got busier, and more so when the rails came ca. 1847.

- St. Nicholas: Medieval parish church. Pulled down/replaced in 1864.
- Sutton Common: Club-shaped length of farmland north of Sutton village. Enclosed in 1809. Mansions came late in the 19th century.
- West Sutton: Developed after the 1860s.

Sutton Cricket Club - 1858. (See: Lower Cheam/Sutton Cricket Club.)

Sutton House - Homerton High Street, Hackney. Tudor, 1535, for Ralph Sadleir, originally called Bryck Place. The front was altered in the 18th century. Red brick. In the early 19th C. it was a boys' school (through at least 1818.) In the later 19th C. it became a girls' school. There was a succession of multiple residents/schools. Still standing.

- See: Hackney/Sutton Place.
- See: Homerton/Sutton House.

Sutton Place - (See: Hackney/Sutton Place.)

Sutton's Hospital in Charterhouse - Charterhouse Square. (See: Charterhouse.)

Swaine Adeney Brigg & Sons - Whip-makers, gloves, umbrellas, leather items. (See: Piccadilly/185.)

Swallow Street - How the road was called until it became Regent Street. Act was passed in 1813, but not called Regent Street until 1823.

Swallow Street was not a particularly nice street, with pawnbrokers and dram-shops; said to be frequented by highwaymen. The street was long, irregular, and dingy. Still, there were rules, which stated that no butchers, green grocers, other domestic trade, or pubs were allowed. Shops were at ground level, with the shopkeepers' residences on the next level up, and visitors' or rich bachelors' rooms one more level up yet. A short stretch of Swallow Street is still there, from Piccadilly to the south side of the Quadrant.

Swan & Edgars - Haberdashery. (See: Piccadilly/10.)

Swan Alley - Dense number of houses. Removed in 1835-40 to make Moorgate.

Swan and Hoop Inn - (See: Cornhill/Swan and Hoop Inn.)

Swan House - Chelsea Embankment. 1875, by Norman Shaw. (See: Chelsea/Old Swan House.)

swan upping, the ceremony of - Was a grand celebration by the 18th century, where before it had been a simple yearly check on the king's swan population at Henley-on-Thames. (See: Swan with Two Necks, under the INNS/PUBS section.)

Swan Walk - Chelsea. 18th C. houses remain. Near Chelsea Physic Garden. There used to be an Old Swan Inn here, lending its name to the street.

Sweeting Lane - At some point became Freeman's Place; today known as Royal Exchange Buildings (Street,) so named for buildings erected here in 1906. Near the east side of the Royal Exchange.

Sweetings - 39 Queen Victoria Street. 1906. London's oldest fish restaurant, being first established in 1830 in Islington. Present "atmosphere" is Edwardian.

swing - An ancient bit of fun, such as children play on. Usually a wooden seat suspended from a tree by rope. Period drawings liked to show swings being ridden by young lovers.

sword-maker -

- See: Wilkinson.
- You may care to see: weapons.

Sydenham - Lewisham/Bromley. Dates back to at least 1206; was spelled as some version of "Chipeham" until the late 17th C. when the "p" became a "d."

- Sydenham Green: 17th century. Now called Bell Green. Up to the early 19th C. was common land. CHAMBERS LONDON GAZETTEER states: "...occupied by a handful of elegant properties, but enclosure in 1810 changed its character forever. Bell Green was divided into smallholdings, most of which were accompanied by rude cottages, and it became a village of humble farmers divided by a maze of paths."
- Upper Sydenham: (See under U.)

Sydney Street - (Sometimes seen spelled as: Sidney Street.) Chelsea. Dates from 1851.

synagogue - The first synagogue in London (following Jewish resettlement in 1656, during Oliver Cromwell's time) was in Creechurch Lane, Leadenhall. (See: Spanish and Portuguese Jews' Synagogue.)

- Bevis Marks Synagogue: (See under B.)
- Duke's Place (Synagogue): Houndsditch. 1722. Enlarged in 1765. Pulled down in 1788. The rebuild of 1790 is described in a contemporary piece as: "Fashionable for bar-mitzvahs and weddings." Destroyed in WWII (the Great Synagogue then moving to Adler House, Tavistock Square.)

Syon House - Located on Syon Park, Brentford, Middlesex. (Not to be confused with Sion House.) LET'S GO, THE BUDGET GUIDE TO LONDON says: "...just across the Thames from Kew in Brentford (walk across Kew Bridge and left along London Road..." Named in honor of Mt. Zion.

The home of the Percys, Earls and Dukes of Northumberland, still in its hereditary line of ownership for the past 400+ years (since 1594.) The "Syon" name is taken from a convent that was moved here in 1432 (had previously been founded in 1414 in Twickenham by Henry V; was suppressed and forfeited to the Crown in Henry VIII's time. The Tudor shell of the present house dates from 1547, but was forfeited again, being granted by Elizabeth I to Henry Percy, 9th Duke of Northumberland, in 1603.) Ca. 1761 Adam did some of his best designing here. Rebuild ongoing in the 1820s. Percys still live there, and the place still looks rather like a royal palace; it is described as "sumptuous" and "secluded." Grounds by Capability Brown, 18th century. The Conservatory dates from 1827. Remodeled interiors by Robert Adam, 1778 (second and third sources say Adam was commissioned in 1761 to improve the house.) The Tudor exterior facade was retained. That third source said Adam did the interior in 1766. Conservatory dates from 1827-30. Became a garden center in 1965. (See: Syon Park.)

Syon Park - Hounslow. Part of the Syon House estate. Famous battles took place here in 1016 and in 1642. (See: Syon House.)

- Great Conservatory, the: 1820s, its construction pioneering the use of glass and metal.

syphilis - Venereal disease, common enough during the Regency era. (See: Lock Hospital.)

-T-

Tabard Street - (See: Kent Street - Tabard Street.)

table tennis - Invented and introduced to London ca. the 1880s.

tailors - For men:

- See: Aldgate.
- See: Bond Street/Old Bond Street/Weston.
- See: Bury Street/30.
- See: Clifford Street/10/Stultz.
- See: Conduit Street/52.
- See: Conduit Street/Meyer.
- See: Ede & Ravenscroft.
- See: Grosvenor Street/Milne - One of Lord Byron's tailors.
- See: Hanover Street/19.
- See: Henry Poole & Co.

- See: Jermyn Street.
- See: Maddox Street.
- See: Old Burlington Street/4/Poole & Cooling.
- See: Piccadilly/14/Thomas Hawke.
- See: Sackville Street/16.
- See: St. James's/Savile Row.
- See: Savile Row/1.
- See: Savile Row/11.
- See: Savile Row/15.
- See: Weston - (See: Bond Street, above.)

For women's clothing:

- See: dressmakers.
- See: milliners.
- See: modiste.
- You may care to see: dresses, women's.

Tailors Asylum - (AKA: Tailors Benevolent Institution for the Relief of Aged and Infirm.) Kentish Town, St. Pancras. 1837. Was for aged/infirm journeyman-tailors and their wives.

Talbot Yard - (See: Southwark/Borough Market/Talbot Inn.)

Tallow Chandlers' Hall - (For the Worshipful Company of Tallow Chandlers.) Incorporated in 1462. The original hall was probably in Bishopsgate.

They made candles from tallow, which was less expensive than beeswax; the common man was far more likely to burn tallow candles, with beeswax candles being reserved for churches, nobility, or royalty. (See: candles.)

Royal Charter in 1462. On the west side of Dowgate since 1476. In 1577 they were noted as "viewers" (able to inspect and seize bad product) of: butter, hops, oil, soap, and vinegar (as well as tallow/tallow candles.) Rebuilt by Wren (although other sources say not Wren, but rather the company's Capt. John Caines, he being inspired by Wren) after the Great Fire of 1666. Exterior completed in 1672, interior completed in 1676. Largely altered in 1881. New entrance in 1905. Reception Room: built in 1671-87.

Livery Company. 21st in the order of precedence. Their business was lost after the advent of electric lighting, but the Company continues on as a charitable organization. (See: Wax Chandlers Hall - For beeswax, as opposed to tallow.)

tanners - Those who tan hides. Had premises near Fleet Street. (Note: Leatherworkers worked tanned leather; Skinners worked with pelts; Woolmongers with sheep's wool.) There was no tanners' guild in London; the closest to it would have been the Curriers, who were curers of leather. (See under C.) Tanning a hide would have been a fairly well understood process by the populace, at least in the country, with small animals that weren't severely punished under poaching laws (unlike deer, which were illegal to take except by the landowner.)

- See: Hornchurch.
- See: Leathersellers Hall.

Tate Gallery - (Its actual name: the National Gallery of British Art.) Not to be confused with the National Gallery in Trafalgar Square. 1897. Art museum, built on the 18-acre site of the Millbank Prison. Named for Sir Henry Tate, a sugar refiner who gave to the nation the founding 65 paintings of this gallery, and much of the founding money.

Tattersall's - (AKA: Tattersall's Horse Repository.) At the southeast corner of St. George's Hospital. Founded in 1766. Moved in 1865 to Knightsbridge Green. Moved to Newmarket in 1939.

Established in 1773 (a second source said 1766) by Richard Tattersall. Foremost auctioneer of Bloodstock (horses.) Also auctioned carriages, harnesses, hounds, and other equestrian items.

Sales were open on Mondays and Thursdays in the winter; Mondays only in the summer. Men went there for fashionable lounging and bet-laying in the provided room (for a guinea fee) on days that the sales were not on. Bets were often settled (paid up) at Tattersall's "as it is not the custom for the men of the Ton to pay at the spot. They pay up at Tattersall's."

One hundred-twenty horses - not to mention a collection of coaches and hounds in kennels (the kennels were described as "commodious") - could be accommodated here. An average of one hundred horses "passed under the hammer" (were auctioned) here weekly. The average cost of a horse bought here was 40 to 200 pounds (for saddle-horses,) and a pair of coach horses brought 150-400 pounds. "Excellent" hunters would run you 350 pounds; race horses upward to 1,500 pounds. Car or agricultural horses were seldom sold here.)

Horses from Tattersall's were sometimes sold at an off-site, like at race courses, or a gathering at Newmarket.

The stables have been described as having a Grecian style. There was a covered area, underneath which the horses were walked before interested persons.

taverns - Although they certainly continued to exist, some sources claim that the taverns became unfashionable in the early 19th century, so men joined clubs such as Boodle's, White's, etc. (See under the CLUBS section.) Not to be misunderstood: taverns were still "appreciated" but perhaps more so by the lower classes than the upper echelons - which is not to say that those of the *ton* never went to taverns or pubs, just that the camaraderie that used to be shared in the taverns and coffee-houses shifted to the private clubs. (See: the INNS/PUBS section - For comparison.)

Tavistock Square - Bloomsbury, one block east of Gordon Square. Built by Thomas Cubitt, 1824. The Regency houses on the west side are still intact.

Tavistock Street - Covent Garden. Built ca. 1707.

- 36: Thomas de Quincey wrote his "Confessions of An Opium-Eater," 1821, while living here.

taxes - During the Regency, there were many kinds of taxes, such as on chocolate, hats, windows, and wine.

- ➢ See: candles.
- ➢ See: Excise Office - Duties on ale, beer, candles, chocolate, coffee, hops, liquors, malt, paper, soap, starch, tea, vellum, and more.
- ➢ See: glass windows.
- ➢ See: hats.
- ➢ See: Stamp Office - News sheets.

taxies - (Motorized.) Invented in 1891, first formally called taximeters. (You may care to see: hackney cabs, for the Regency era, non-motorized version of a "taxi.")

tea - Tea was introduced into England ca. the 1660s; supposedly Queen Catherine from Braganza, Portugal (wife to Charles II) introduced the drink. It was first sold from Garraway's Coffee House.

The idea of ***afternoon tea*** was introduced to Britain by Anna, Duchess of Bedford, ca. 1840.

Tea bags were invented in 1908 (by an American.)

"Tea" (as a structured afternoon meal) wasn't a Regency era practice. (See: meals.)

- ➢ See: coffee-houses.
- ➢ See: Garraway's Coffee House.
- ➢ See: Strand/216/Twinings Tea.
- ➢ See: Tetley Tea - The brand name "Tetley Tea" dates from 1837.

tea gardens - Frequented, as Jane Austen put it, "by the middling classes, especially on a Sunday." They weren't quite pleasure grounds, but were pretty much what their name implies: a garden space where one consumed tea (and edibles.)

Teddington - Richmond. Once Victorian, it is now a 20th C. suburb, but having existed from ancient times, variously known as Tudddington and Totington (purportedly a corruption of Tide-End-Town,) being the highest point of the Thames affected by tide. Once belonged to Westminster Abbey, ca. 1197.

- St. Mary's Church: (AKA: St. Mary Teddington. AKA, modern: St. Mary with St. Alban; St. Alban's is now an arts center.) Ferry Road. 16th century. Parish church. Yet exists.

- South Teddington: No buildings here at all until 1851.
- Teddington Lock: 1811. Rebuilt with a side-lock in 1857.

teenagers - This is a 20th C. concept. Prior to that, unless you were privileged, you were either a child or you were old enough to work. You worked or married as soon as best served your circumstances/family, or you joined the military (as young as 12, or even younger,) or began a (usually) seven year apprenticeship (boys,) or went into service (girls.) Even among those with wealth, a 12-17 year old was expected to be educated (boys,) or trained how to manage a household (girls,) and meet societal expectations (both genders.)

telegraph - Invented in the 1830-40s by (American) Samuel Morse (and other inventors.) First telegraph sent via the use of Morse Code in 1844, from Washington, D.C. to Baltimore, Maryland, USA. There was a telegraph line laid across the Atlantic Ocean in 1866, connecting the U.S. and Europe for telegraph messages.

Telegraph Hill - Lewisham. Named for the semaphore* signal tower, 1795, at the 150 foot tall top of the hill; was one of the stations that transmitted the Waterloo victory to London; pulled down in 1823. (Note that this was transmitted by semaphore, not telegraph, which had yet to be invented.) Prior to the building of the signaling station, the area had been called Plow'd Garlic Hill. The Worshipful Company of Haberdashers had extensive holdings in Hatcham, including here; they added houses here ca. 1859.

(*Semaphore is a system of communication via visual signals, using towers that have pivoting shutters; semaphore can also be achieved by the use of humans manipulating signal flags. Was used from the 18th to the 20th century, especially between naval ships.)

telephone - The first telephone call occurred in London in 1876, by Alexander Graham Bell, who called Ravenscourt Park, where resided the owner of Brown's Hotel, from whence the call was made. (See: nine-nine-nine, under N, for more details on the telephone.)

Temple & Crook - Belgravia/Mayfair. Founded in 1810. Household utensils and equipment. Royal Warrant in 1922.

Temple Bar - (AKA: Temple Gate.) Marked the junction of Fleet Street and the Strand. Stood in the middle of the street, on the medieval royal roadway from the Tower of London to the Palace of Westminster. Dates from 1191, originally nothing more than two posts with a chain between them, barring entrance into Fleet Street. In 1351 a large gateway (with a jailhouse in its upper story) was built on the site.

Wren's three-arched gateway stood here from 1672-1878; taken down because it blocked traffic, and was moved to Theobold's Park, even though it was looking rather dilapidated by then. (See: Theobald's Park.)

The memorial topped by the Griffin (which is actually a dragon; the London

Dragon) on the site of Temple Bar dates from 1880, by H. Jones. It can be called: Temple Bar Marker. It also holds a statue of Queen Victoria.

- See: Fleet Street.
- See: gates.
- See: Inns of Court/Temple (Overall)/Middle Temple/Temple Bar.

Traditionally, the Monarch must get permission from the Lord Mayor before passing through here on into the City, as this is the western boundary of the City of London. (Aldgate being the eastern boundary.)

Temple Bar stood where the Griffin (which is actually a dragon) now stands, marking (as it always did) the division of the City and Westminster.

Miscreants' dismembered body parts were tumbled here on display, right up to 1772, and murderers were sometimes hanged here (at least up to the 18th century.)

In 2003 Temple Bar was re-erected near St. Paul's Cathedral's northwest tower. Portland Stone.

Temple Church - (See: Inns of Court/Temple (2nd entry)/Temple Church.) Dates from 1240. (Not to be confused with City Temple, the latter being built in 1874.)

Temple Fortune - Barnet. Separated from Hendon by the River Brent. Dates from Saxon times, being affiliated with the Knights Templar from 1243, but not noted by its present name until 1754 (when there was but one farmhouse on the green here.) Isolated until the 1820s.

Temple Mills - Waltham Forest. The Knights Templar were granted land here in 1185. Once the Knights were dissolved, the land passed through a collection of owners, bringing in agriculture and mills, the latter lasting until the later 19th century.

- White Hart Tavern: Early 18th century.

Temple of Fancy - Book, watercolor, and toy sellers. (See: Upper Rathbone Place/34.)

Temple of Mithras - Queen Victoria Street. Roman ruins dating from the 2nd century, discovered in 1954.

Temple, the -

- See: Inns of Court/Temple (1st entry, "Overall.")
- See: Inns of Court/Temple (2nd entry, "The Area of.")

tennis - Played in England at least since the 15th century. Henry VIII enjoyed tennis, and was considered to be fairly proficient at the game. It was first played with wooden bats, but rackets strung with sheep's gut replaced the bats ca. 1500. During the Regency the original form of the game (more like Squash) was yet played: with a hard ball, a large court with four walls "...round three of which ran a penthouse in imitation of the cloisters in which the game was no doubt original played" (the quote being taken from *The Rise & Fall of a Regency Dandy*.)

It was played indoors until mid Victorian times (when an outdoor version became popular,) known as: lawn tennis. (See: Lord's Cricket Ground - Note under, regarding the formation of lawn tennis rules.)

The modern game was refined in 1873 by one Major Walter Clopton Wingfield.

The All-England Club was founded in 1868 (but at first for the play of croquet.)

The All-England Club tennis courts were built in 1875. The first Wimbledon tennis championship was held in 1877.

- See: Hampton Court Palace/Indoor Tennis Courts.
- See: Wimbledon/All England Lawn Tennis.

Tenterden Road - Hanover Square. Existed by at least 1822.

- Royal Academy of Music: (See under R.)

Terrace House - (See: Old Battersea House.)

Tessier's - Silver- and Goldsmiths. 26 New Bond Street. Established in 1851.

Tetley Tea - Huddersfield, 1837. Joseph and Edward Tetley opened shop with the name "Tetley Brothers-Dealers in Tea" after having sold their tea previously from horseback. (See: tea.)

textiles - The primary English cloths manufactured in the 18th C. were wool and worsted, their dominance lasting into the early 19th century. During the time of the Napoleonic wars, however, cotton rose and dominated because of the spread of the use of spinning jennies (allowing ease in home spinning.) Too, Edmund Cartwright's power loom led to manufacturing factories, providing not only cotton cloth but employment opportunities. By the early 19th C. some 100,000 Britons were employed in cloth manufacture.

- See: cloth.
- See: drapers.
- SEE: FABRICS.
- See: Scotland/Whytock, under the BRITISH COUNTIES section.
- See: Spinning Jenny.

Thames Barrier - (See: Thames Flood Barrier.)

Thames Conservancy Board - Dates from 1857.

Thames Embankment - 1864. (See: Embankment.)

Thames Flood Barrier - (AKA: Thames Barrier.) Runs from Newham to Greenwich. 1975-83. This improvement was built to prevent flooding, and did away with the high tides of yore.

Thames River Police, the - Created in 1798 by dockland merchants. (See: "River Police Force" paragraph, under: Thames, the.)

Thames River, the - (Pronounced "temms," rhymes with stems.) AKA simply as: the Thames.

"Thames" is perhaps a corruption of the Latin word Tamesis. "Thames" is the second-oldest place name in Britain (Kent being the first,) and other sources think it was perhaps derived from a Celtic root word "teme, " meaning river or dark river.

Keep in mind that the Thames is tidal (having an ebb and flow affected by the phase of the moon.) Parts of it are fresh water, parts are seawater. It shifts approximately every six hours. It usually runs at 6-7 knots.

Was often packed with ocean-going sailing ships: huge East Indiamen, tea clippers, galliots, whalers, schooners, and hundreds of smaller vessels. It was a very busy port during the Regency era, often so congested with ships waiting on the tide that it might be two weeks before the vessel could unload.

In Oxford, the Thames is known as the Isis.

RIVER POLICE FORCE, the: (Later AKA: Wapping Police Force.) Founded in 1798, set up by the West India Company and active by 1801. Its headquarter was at Wapping. It consisted of some 60 constables who guarded/boarded the ships. Technically it was London's first police force, but this group worked only the docks. (See: Watchmen.) Was in response to unscrupulous fees and outright theft, which had spiraled out of control. This force became part of the Metropolitan Police after most of the docks had been rebuilt (post-Regency) and the corrupted Legal Quays system done away with.

The Thames is 215 miles/346 km long, the longest river in England (while the Severn, at 220 miles/354 km, is the longest in Britain.)

Some fish that could be had from the sea-salty part of the Thames: barbel, carp, dace, eel, flounder, herring, pike, salmon (extinct in the Thames since 1860,) and trout. Some fish that can be had from the fresh water (non-tidal) canals farther up the Thames: bleak, bream, roach. Currently, the Thames hosts 80 species of fish.

- See: Doggett's Coat and Badge Race.
- See: drinking water.
- See: fish.
- See: Frost Fair.
- See: iceskating.
- See: Port of London Authority - 1908.
- See: Wapping/Wapping Police Station.
- See: water - Why you didn't drink from the Thames.

Thames Street - So called until 1799.

- See: Lower Thames Street.
- See: Upper Thames Street.

Thames Tunnel - The first underwater tunnel in the world; ran from Wapping to Rotherhithe. Was begun in Jan. of 1825, but work delayed until 1832. Work was finally completed (for foot passengers) on 3/25/1843. Converted to a train tunnel in the 1860s. Not to be confused with the late 20th century "Chunnel." (See: Channel Tunnel, for the latter.)

thatched roof buildings - Thatching is building a roof with dry vegetation, such as rushes, straw, or the like. It was usually rather thick, the layered vegetation serving to shed water away from reaching the inside-most layers and providing insulation. Thatched roofs were not allowed in London since the Great Fire of 1666. (See: Globe Theatre, under the THEATRES section, for the one exception.)

Theatreland - Touristy nickname for the gathering of theatres/playhouses in the West End. The term has been in use for approximately 100 years.

theatres - (See the THEATRES section.)

Theatres were banned from the City in 1574; they fled to Southbank (because it was outside the reach of the City laws.) Not permitted again until after the Restoration. LONDON REDISCOVERED states: "...Henry Fielding's crude satires at Nash's Haymarket Theatre caused the Lord Chamberlain to reintroduce powers of censorship in 1737 which were lifted only in 1968."

Still, for all that theatre was yet fairly tightly controlled in the 18th C., the 1788 Enabling Act made it much easier to license a theatre and mount shows which would once have been quashed. Theatre was flourishing by 1800.

You could own or rent a box, of course, but you could not reserve a seat in the gallery or pit; the space was yours by dint of physically occupying it as the program began. Queuing was not practiced, so there were often scuffles over seating. Patron boxes were no longer permitted on the stages themselves after 1763, due to theatrical reforms by the renowned actor David Garrick.

For amateur theatrics, see: Sans Souci. (Under the separate THEATRES section.) Although, of course, amateur theatrics might be found anywhere from cottages to castles.

Theobald's, Palace of - (Is pronounced: Tibbald's.) About 1-½ miles/2.4 km from Theobald's Park. Pulled down in 1762. The Theobald's Park (mansion) was built in its place.

Theobald's Park - Mansion, 1765-70. Two hundred acre grounds. The Old Temple Bar, removed from Fleet Street, was placed in 1888 at one of the park's entrances. (See: Temple Bar.)

Theobold's Road - Holborn. Named for Theobald's Palace. Dates from at least 1603. (See: Inns of Court/Gray's Inn/Raymond Buildings.)

Theory of Evolution - Charles Darwin, 1858. (See: Linnean Society.)

Theosophical Society - Founded ca. 1887. Proponents of women's rights.

thief-takers - Nickname for the Bow Street Runners (or any of the various law enforcement agencies) prior to the formation of the Metropolitan Police.

- See: Bow Street/4.
- See: Metropolitan Police.

Thomas Coram Foundation for Children - (See: Foundling Hospital.)

Thorney Island - (See: Island of Thorney.)

Thornhill Road - Islington. Road built ca. the 1820-30s.

- 10: The Albion, a pub now, formerly a coaching inn. (See: Albion, the, under A.)

Thornhill Square - Mid 19th century. (See: Islington/Thornhill Square.)

Thornton Heath - Croydon. Originally was 36 acres of common land, with a pond for watering cattle (and used by Charcoal burners as a water source, resulting in the name of Colliers Water Lane.) There was a gallows here from at least 1722.

- Wheatsheaf Coaching Inn: 757-759 London Road. Late 18th century. Supposedly haunted. The building yet exists, but the pub is closed.

Threadneedle Street - The Bank of England's governor had a mansion on the street by 1724.

- 5: Threadneedles (luxury hotel.) Is directly behind the Bank of England in the City's Square Mile. Is itself located in a banking hall built in 1856.
- 30: Merchant Taylor's Hall. Since the 14th century. Post-1666 interior, stood until the Blitz of WWII. (See: Merchant Taylors' Hall.)
- 33: South Sea House. (See under S.)
- Baltic Exchange: (See under B.)
- Bank of England: The "old lady of Threadneedle Street." (See under B.)

Three Mills - Newham. A trading site for some 900 years, with tidal mills here during the Middle Ages. The name has been in use since the 16th century.

- House Mill: 1776. Largest watermill in Britain, once providing much of London's flour (and gin.) Ruined by WWII bombing, but restored for tourism.

Throgmorton Avenue - Built ca. 1876. South side of London Wall. The complete length of this street is co-owned by the Carpenters' Company and the Drapers' Company.

- Carpenters' Hall: They had a book of ordinances lodged at Guildhall by 1333. Incorporated in 1344. First here in 1428-9. Even in such early days, the Carpenters were more of a "friendly society" than a hard & fast guild. The society waned following the Great Fire of 1666 (although this building did not burn in that fire,) because fire-resistant materials were then required in city building; by 1739 they had surrendered all control of the craft, including the binding of apprentices. Pulled down in 1876 to make way for Throgmorton Avenue; a new hall was built in 1880 on the south side of London Wall/NE corner of Throgmorton Avenue, using some features from the old Hall. (See under C.)
- Drapers' Hall: (See under D.)

Throgmorton Street - The City. Since 1801, home to the Stock Exchange. Narrow street, with little traffic, used mostly by those concerned with the Exchange.

- See: Jonathan's Coffee House.
- See: Stock Exchange.

tile-making -

- See: Barnet/Child's Hill.
- See: Tylers and Bricklayers' Company.

Tilney Street - Park Lane, Mayfair. Street dates from at least 1740. Mrs. Fitzherbert (George IV's mistress/disallowed wife) lived here following her reunion with Prinny in 1800.

timber - Providing wood for London was a common source of income for communities that yet had woods.

- See: docks/Butler's Wharf.
- See: Kidbrooke.
- See: wood.

Times, the - News sheet. 1785. First known as The Daily Universal Register. Called "The Times" since 1788. Obtained the first commercial rotary printing press in 1812; it could print 1,400 one-sided sheets in an hour. (See: Fleet Street/Printing House Square.)

Tin Plate Workers' Company - (AKA: the Worshipful Company of Tin Plate Workers. Also seen spelled as: Tin-plate Workers.) First was part of the Wire Workers' (or Wire Drawers') Company, which had existed from 1469. Then tin craftsmen were part of the Ironmongers' Company; (whereas wire workers were part of the Girdlers' Company, making wire things like cages, fishhooks, traps.) The two groups of craftsmen united, becoming the Tin Plate Workers, with their Royal Charter in 1670. Livery Company. It has no hall. 67th in the order of precedence.

tinderboxes - If you couldn't borrow a flame from another candle or fire on the grate (often via a spill or taper,) one could use a tinderbox to make a spark. Made of wood or metal, one of these boxes contained a flint, a firesteel to strike it against, and something combustible (cloth fibers, lichen, bits of bark, etc.) Once a spark was achieved and caught by the fibers, it was often then that one used a match (which at the time of the Regency was a bit of card, rope, or wood dipped in sulfur, not the striking matches later developed) to transfer the flame to whatever required lighting.

- See: candles.
- See: matches.
- You may care to see: lamps.

tobacco - Sir Walter Scott (novelist) brought the first cargo of tobacco to England in 1573. Within 30 years it was a popular product.

By the 1800s there were 200 pipe makers in London. (They would have been members of the Tobacco Pipe Makers.)

Many tobacconists had a life-size carved wooden Scotsman outside their store, brightly painted, a symbol for tobacco which seems to have originated in the 18th C. to distinguish the fact that the shop sold Scots snuff as opposed to Bristol snuff. Tobacco was often smoked in pipes.

Nineteenth century women did not smoke tobacco, except rarely; it would have been considered highly shocking. However, they did sometimes use snuff - even duchesses.

Chewing tobacco was generally left to rough sorts, such as Mariners and manual workers.

- See: Carnaby Street/45/Inderwick's - Pipe makers.
- See: Coventry Street/David Wishart.
- See: docks/London Docks/Queen's Warehouse.
- See: docks/Tobacco Docks.
- See: Elephant and Castle - For clay pipes.
- See: Fribourg & Treyer's - For cigars.
- See: Minories, The/James Taddy & Co.
- See: St. James's Street/19 - Smoking supplies and cigars.
- See: snuff.
- See: Tobacco Pipe Makers and Tobacco Blenders' Company.
- See: Wilton Place.

Tobacco Dock - 1813. (See: docks/Tobacco Dock.)

Tobacco Pipe Makers and Tobacco Blenders' Company - (AKA: the Worshipful Company of Tobacco Pipe Makers and Tobacco Blenders.) Incorporated as a trade association in 1619, making clay pipes. Existed into the 19th century. This Company dissolved twice, (the second closing being in 1868,) and so is now listed as a modern Company, with a 1954 revival, gaining Livery in 1961. Still involved in the trade. Has no hall. 82nd in the order of precedence. (See: Elephant and Castle, for clay pipes.)

Tokyngton - Brent. (Pronounced: Toke-ing-ton.) Dates from at least 1171. Was economically fairly important during the Middle Ages. Its chapel survived to the 18th century. In the mid 19th C. was on-and-off known as Oakington Park; then known as Sherrin's Farm, with the Tokyngton name coming back in ca. the 1910s.

tollgates - Not too many tollgates existed until the 17th C., but then increasingly into the 18th & 19th centuries. Might or might not actually possess a gate across the road, it was nonetheless a road block where one paid a fee (toll) in order to pass through. During the Regency, virtually all major roads out of London had tollgates. They were abolished in 1864. (See: turnpike.)

Tollington - Islington. Ancient, dating from ca. 1000; by the 14th C. was replaced in name by "Holloway." (See under H.)

- Devil's House: Pub, stood until at least 1811 (under a less sinister name by the 19th century.)
- Tollington Lane: Nicknamed Devil's Lane, for a 17th C. highwayman.
- Tollington Park estate: 1840s.

Tolworth - Kingston. Dates from at least the time of Domesday Book. The name "Tolworth" wasn't fixed until the late 19th C., having evolved from various spellings such as "Taleorde." CHAMBERS LONDON GAZETTEER states: "The manor was given to Henry, Earl of Westmoreland by Elizabeth I, and was bought by Nathaniel Polhill, MP for Southwark, in 1781. For most of the 19th century the earls of Egmont were Tolworth's principal landowners."

- St. Matthew's: 1875.

Tooley Street - Bermondsey. This street dates back to the Danes' King Cnut, 11th century. ("Tooley" is an ancient corruption of "St. Olaf's.") Rich merchants lived here in the 13-14th century. Warehouses.

- Dean Street: Just off Tooley Street. (See under D.)
- London Dungeon: 1974. Modern. Macabre entertainment venue.
- St. Olave's: (See under the CHURCHES section.)
- St. Olave's Grammar School: Founded in 1560 for boys. Girls since 1998.

toothbrushes - Toothbrushes, as we think of them today (nylon handle and bristles,) were invented in 1938. However, toothbrush forms date back to 3000BC, these ancient ones usually in the form of a frayed twig. The first bristled toothbrushes came from China in 1498, hog's hair on a bamboo or bone handle. Ca. 1780 the first mass-produced toothbrush in England was produced by William Addis.

Toothpastes were unlike those of today. Regency era people might have just brushed with water, or used salt, mint, chalk, or ground charcoal.

- ➢ See: dentists.
- ➢ See: doctors/barbers - Barbers often provided dental care.
- ➢ See: St. James/Kent & Sons.

Tooting - Wandsworth. CHAMBERS LONDON GAZETTEER explains: "The manors of Tooting (subsequently Totting Graveney) and Totting Bec were in existence by the time of Domesday Book and each became the centre of a farming village over the course of the Middle Ages." In the 18th C. country homes came in.

Tooting Bec Common - Wandsworth. Tooting Bec is also known as Upper Tooting, interchangeably. The manor passed through monastic (a dependency to the Abbey of Notre

Dame du Bec in Normandy) and public hands, eventually coming to the Duke of Bedford. Acquired for the public (along with Tooting Graveney Common) for a total of 218 acres in 1873-75.

Tooting Graveney - Wandsworth/Merton. Chertsey Abbey owned the manor; leased in the 12-13th centuries to the Graveney (also seen as Gravenel) family.

- St. Nicholas Church: Medieval. Round tower. Pulled down in the 1830s, and replaced.
- Totting Lodge: 1803; renamed to: Manor House, in 1811.

Tories - One of two 18-19th C. political parties in England. Began as a loosely associated group that supported Catholic James for king (following his brother, James II's, death,) at which time they were called the Abhorrers, because they abhorred the Exclusion Bill, (which disallowed a Catholic's claim to the throne.) Evolved into the Tories, who supported: the Church of England/High Church Anglicans, and the gentry. (As opposed to: the Whigs, who supported the great aristocratic families, and the royal family.)

By the later 18th C. (1784) the Tories had coalesced as a political movement under the leadership of William Pitt the Younger. The name Tory derived, unflatteringly, from an Irish expression that meant bandit. Now associated with the Conservative Party. Roughly summarizing: Tories equal Conservatives; Whigs equal aristocratic Liberals. (See: Whigs.)

Torrington Square - Bloomsbury. Laid out in 1800 on land previously called Long Fields. (See: Long Fields.)

Tothill Fields - In medieval times was a vast, marshy area. "Tothill" was the name of an artificial, ancient mound on the Island of Thorney, long since gone, with only the Tothill name remaining to remind us of its existence. The hill seems to have been gone by the time of the Regency, although was noted on a map dated 1746. Post-Regency, it became the areas of Victoria and Pimlico.

- See: Five Fields.
- See: Pimlico.

Tothill Fields Prison - (Also known simply as: Tothill Prison.) Built in 1616, a "bridewell" for able-bodied prisoners, who were put to work. (See: Bridewell Prison.) Somewhere between 1767-early 19th C. it became a prison for women, and boys under age 17. Closed in 1877. Eventually became the site of Westminster Cathedral. (See under W - Do not confuse with Westminster Abbey.)

Tottenham - Haringey. First recorded in Domesday Book. Received its Charter of Incorporation in 1934. Edmonton is two miles/3.2 km north of Tottenham, although connected to it by a series of streets. Wealthy merchants here from the 12th century. Growth came in the late 18th C.; did not become urban until after the rails came in/1840s.

- All Hallows: Ancient. Gothic. On three sides of it flows the Mosel, a rivulet.
- Bruce Castle: Lordship Lane. Originally called Tottenhall manor house, soon corrupted to Tottenham. Mansion of Robert Bruce, father to the 14th century Scottish king (of the same name.) Rebuilt in the later 17th, and the 18th, and the 19th centuries. In 1827 it was made into a boys' school, Hill School. Now a museum and park.
- High Cross, the: Ancient. Was first a column of wood, but replaced in the 17th C. with a brick octagonal column. In 1809 it was given a coating of stucco.
- High Road: Had six inns here in the 15th century. Almhouses (for 8 people) were built here in 1596.
- South Tottenham: Was mostly undeveloped until the mid 19th C.; today described as "somewhat shabby."

Tottenham Court Road - Camden. Near Montagu House (the British Museum,) Bloomsbury. There was a mansion, Tottenham Court, here once, centuries ago. The street was built mostly from 1770-1800. At least by the 1820s there were some confectioners along here. Known for furniture production from the late 18th C.; especially known for its cabinets. Still known today for furniture (and now electronics.) According to THE ROUGH GUIDE TO LONDON, this street makes "a strong challenge for London's least prepossessing street."

- Whitfield's Tabernacle: (Also rarely seen spelled as Whitefields Tabernacle.) George Whitfield, a Methodist student of John Wesley (founder of the Methodists) had a church in this road, from which he gave charismatic preaching.

Tottenham Hale - Haringey. There were residents in "the Hale" from the 13th C., but *Tottenham* Hale is not mentioned until 1754. A satellite of Tottenham. 600 residents in 1840. Grew to connect with Tottenham in the 1860s. Factories are from the 20th century.

Tottenham Lane - Haringey. Former name of Turnpike Lane (and it's still known by this name to the southwest.) Turnpike gate here from 1765; gone by 1872's abolishment of turnpikes.

Tottenham Wood - (See: forests/Bluebell Wood.)

Totteridege - Barnet. CHAMBERS LONDON GAZETTEER calls it: "An unaffordably lovely ribbon village strung along the road from Whetstone to Highwood Hill and set amidst farmland, parks, and golf courses." 400 feet above sea level.

- Orange Tree, the: Became a public house in 1755. Still exists (although much altered.)
- St. Etheldreda: From at least 1250. Rebuilt in 1790, being then called St. Andrew's. The churchyard holds a 1,000 year old yew.
- Totteridge Park: Mansion. 1750. Refurbished in the early 20th century.

towels - In Middle English (11-15th centuries) we find the word "toaille," from the German. All the same, the invention of the bathing towel is credited to 17th C. Turkey, and the world's reception of Turkish baths. These first towels were a flat, woven bit of cotton or linen, rather narrow. Loops that stuck up from the fabric began to appear by the 18th century, borrowing the idea from carpets.

Regency era people would have used whatever they had available for drying themselves, probably a length of cotton or linen, but the 19th C. had to advance before the looped-style cloths became more prevalent/affordable (and wider, to better fit the body.) Once the production of cloth became industrialized (1840s and on,) shops began to regularly stock pre-made towels for the general population. (You may care to see: bathroom.)

Tower Bridge - 1886-94. (See under the BRIDGES section.)

Tower Green - Green space within the Tower of London.

- ➢ See: Tower of London/Queen's House.
- ➢ See: Tower of London/Tower Green.

Tower Hamlets - Victorian. Named "Tower Hamlets" in 1965.

- ➢ See: Bethnal Green.
- ➢ See: Shadwell.

- Tower Hamlets Cemetery: 1841.

Tower Hill - Stepney. Situated outside the Tower of London's walls. Last public execution by axe on Tower Hill was in 1747, that being of the Jacobite Lord Lovat, at age 80. (Between 1347-1747, 125 eminent persons were executed here, as opposed to the privileged 10 executed *within* the Tower of London.)

There are no records of females being beheaded here on Tower Hill (but rather at the scaffold in the Tower of London itself, to avoid rioting.)

- All Hallows: At least since 1666.
- Crescent, the: 18th C. houses.
- Mint, the: At the northeast corner of the Tower of London. Designed by John Johnson; completed by Robert Smirke.
  - ➢ See: Mint, the, under M.
  - ➢ See: Royal Mint.
  - ➢ See: Tower of London/"Other Places & Things"/Royal Mint.)
- Seething Lane. (See under S.)
- Tower of London: (See: Tower of London, the, at its own listing.)
- Trinity House: (See at its own listing.)

Tower of London, the - The City. On Tower Hill.

(Also commonly referred to simply as: the Tower. Its full official title is: Her

Majesty's Fortress and Palace, the Tower of London. Can also be referred to as: Tower Keep, since that was its original purpose. AKA: The Norman Keep.)

Despite its name, the Tower of London is actually a *series* of towers - having started with the original one, the White Tower. When people speak of "the Tower," they often are thinking of the White Tower, due to its visual prominence, but the truth is the title "Tower of London" encompasses all the towers and their enclosed environs. It is, in essence, a little city of its own.

Built in the southeast corner of London's Roman city walls, the White Tower has been an observation post, a stronghold, storehouses, and more. The White Tower was built for William the Conqueror ca. 1078, built of earth and timber. It was intended to dominate the area (and intimidate the people.) It stood alone for 100+ years. Because it stood alone at first, this is why the whole lot are still called the "Tower" of London (rather than, say, the "Castle of London," which it more resembles today.) It is the second largest Norman era keep in England (the first being Colchester.)

The broader Tower of London (beyond just the White Tower) covers eighteen acres, and currently has 21 towers standing, and two bastions. The bastions are Legge's Mount (northwest corner of the Outer Wall,) and Brass Mount (northeast corner.) The Tower(s) of London are contained within two concentric walls.

Henry III continued building in the early 13th C., and in the late 13th C. building was largely (for the time) completed by Edward I. Edward I also built a moat, 1272-1307.

As early as Elizabeth I's time (late 16th C.) there were tourists here, paying a fee to visit the sites.

The Tower of London has served many purposes: an arsenal, a fortress, home to the royal mint, a menagerie, a prison, a royal palace, storehouses, a place of execution (but only for a select few who drew royal censure and special treatment, "regular" (non-privileged) offenders were held elsewhere and/or executed on Tower Hill.) It was also a treasury to hold the Crown Jewels. While it is and has been all the above, it has long operated like its own village, complete with apartments, a doctor, innkeepers, a church, and families with children.

It was never particularly popular as a royal residence (other palaces were more opulent or comfortable); not used as a royal home after ca. 1533; Henry VIII was the last monarch to use the Tower as a royal residence.

Its walls run to 10 feet deep.

Windows and turrets were added centuries later by Christopher Wren, in the 1690s (mostly where arrow slits had been.)

Prisoners were often kept in upper rooms. It is thought some 130 persons were beheaded at the Tower of London or at nearby Tower Hill, between 1388-1747. (Over the years, at least 40 prisoners managed to escape.) Only traitors and noble persons ranked imprisonment here. (See: Tower Green, below in this entry.) It was considered a privilege to be allowed to be beheaded in private.

It has always been guarded by the colorful guards known as Yeoman Warders, still today dressed in Tudor garb, there being 41 of the Yeoman Warders. Their nickname is "Beefeaters," which probably represented the fact that of old they were considered important enough soldiers as to be guaranteed meat as part of their compensation/assignment. But don't call them that; it will not be appreciated.

People (visitors/sightseers) were so interested in the Tower, it early became the first London tour site to have its own comprehensive guidebook: "An Historical Description of the Tower of London and Its Curiosities," 1750. It still held prisoners despite the sightseers. The Tower was open to the general public in 1875.

The two following lists might not prove all-inclusive; they are intended as a launch for one's own research.

<u>OTHER PLACES AND THINGS</u>: BESIDES THE TOWERS (WHICH ARE IN THEIR OWN LIST, BELOW) THIS IS A LIST OF OTHER PLACES AND THINGS IN THE TOWER OF LONDON:

- Beefeaters:
    - See: Beefeaters, under B.
    - See: Yeoman Warders, below.
- Ceremony of the Keys: (A service, not a location.) Going back at least seven centuries, this ritual takes place nightly, wherein several Tower gates are locked by the Chief Yeoman Warder (and one escort.) At the Bloody Tower's entrance a sentry asks, "Who comes there?" The Chief Warden answers and the ceremony is at an end.
- Constable of the Tower: (A person, not a location.) The head man, overseer of the Yeoman Warders. From 1806-1826 the man in this position was General Francis, Earl of Moira and Marquis of Hastings. From 1826-1852 it was Field-Marshal Arthur, Duke of Wellington.
- CROWN JEWELS: When people speak of the crown jewels, they mostly mean the (140 or so pieces of) coronation regalia, and that's primarily what's on display when one tours the Tower of London. However, there are many items

besides coronation crowns and scepters: there are also bracelets, orbs, rings, robes, silver plate, spurs, swords, trumpets, and many more royal accoutrements. Over the years, sometimes all these things were stored together, sometimes much of the regalia (after all, robes and sashes require repair) were maintained at the Royal Wardrobe - but, at any rate, there have been jewels displayed at the Tower of London since 1670. (See: Royal Wardrobe, under R.) *Read on for more Crown Jewel details.*

Edward the Confessor (born in approximately the year 1003, died in 1066) was the first to gather royal regalia/jewels.

The jeweled royal collections have been in the Tower of London pretty much continuously - with exceptions noted below - since 1303. (They have moved a half dozen or so times, with the place they are kept always being deemed: the Jewel House.)

There have been two sets of crown jewels -

THE FIRST SET OF CROWN JEWELS:

Henry III (ruled England from 1216-1272) made the collection of royal jewels and regalia more formal (since Edward the Confessor's time.)

In Edward I's time (ruled from 1272-1307,) there is a record of a theft at Westminster of some of the valuable plate and jewels. So Edward I ordered the remainder of the royal jewels and regalia to be stored at the Tower of London, in the Wardrobe Tower, 1303.

In 1366, Edward III (ruled from 1327-1377) built a Jewel House to house the treasure. (See: Jewel House, Westminster, at its own listing under J - For this non-Tower-of-London Jewel House.)

When King Charles I was deposed, beheaded, and the monarchy abolished (in 1649,) this founding collection of crown jewels was seized and largely melted down for the benefit of the new (and relatively short-lived) Commonwealth.

THE SECOND SET OF CROWN JEWELS:

Charles II, upon reclaiming the throne from the Commonwealth (in 1660,) had a new set of crown jewels begun. These are the base of the present crown jewels. (Of course, the royal collections are being added to all the time, by gifts from foreign potentates, marriage gifts, etc.)

THE MARTIN TOWER, in the Tower of London, was next to host the jewels. The practice of *displaying* the crown jewels dates from Charles II's time (ruled England from 1660-1685.) The tower was opened to the public (so they could view the jewels) in 1670. (Wasn't open to just anyone of the public, you had to get permission to enter the Tower of London.)

The crown jewels were kept here for centuries, in an old smoky cupboard in one of the ground floor vaults, dimly lit by two tallow candles. They were shown to visitors by "an ancient harridan of the most ungainly appearance." The jewels were behind bars, but, shockingly, guests were allowed to reach through the bars and touch them.

One Colonel Blood stole some three pieces of the jewels from here in 1671. He was caught, and - oddly enough - pardoned by Charles II, creating rumors of collusion as the King had been in need of funds.

In 1841 the Grand Storehouse (adjacent to the Jewel House) burned, but the jewels were kept safe.

The crown jewels were in Martin Tower until 1869, then moved to Wakefield Tower. HIS MAJESTY'S TOWER OF LONDON states: "In 1870 the Crown Jewels and Royal Regalia were transferred from the Jewel House near the Martin Tower to the Wakefield Tower, where they remained till World War 2 when they were removed to a place of greater safety. They were returned in 1947." (The Crown Jewels and the contents of the one-time Royal Wardrobe had been stored in the basement of Windsor Castle during the war.) They continued in Wakefield Tower until 1967, when they moved to Waterloo Barracks.

Today's Jewel House (in the Waterloo Barracks, ground floor) dates from 1994.

- Residence of the Keeper of the Jewel House: (See below in: "The Towers"/St. Thomas's Tower.)

(Tower of London "Other Places" listing, cont'd):

- Dungeons, the: In the White Tower. Descended to via the spiral stairway. The present dungeons, despite expectations, are well lighted and clean. The brick walls and arches were added in 1730. Torture was traditionally carried out in the eastern dungeon. (Punishment by torture was never made legal in England, although the king or his council could authorize it.) Few records have been found recording the torture of women. The eastern dungeon's south end contains "Little Ease." (See below in: "The Towers"/White Tower/Chapel of St. John-the-Evangelist - Paragraph about Little Ease.)

The western dungeon contains the forty foot deep well meant to provide water during a time of siege.

- Elizabeth's Walk: (See below in: "The Towers"/Bell Tower.)
- Fusiliers' Museum: (See: Great Armoury, below.)
- Gates: The present railings and gates date from 4/28/1939, replacing old wooden palisades.
    1. Bulwark Gate: (AKA: Quizzing Gate.) This gate, in the oldest plans of the Tower, is shown fifty yards or so up the Hill from the existing west entrance. Tower prisoners were handed over here to the Sheriffs of London.
    2. Gateway to the Outer Ward: (See below in: "The Towers"/Byward Tower.)
    3. Lion Gate: Completely gone now. A medieval causeway was unearthed in 1936, with drawbridge pit; at the north end of the causeway had stood Lion Gate.
    4. Wardyng Gate: An old name for the Gateway to the Outer Ward. (See below in: "The Towers"/Byward Tower.)
- Grand Storehouse, the: (AKA: the Small Armoury.) Not to be confused with the Great Armoury.

    The Small Armoury opened in 1696, on the upper floor (of its present site.) Built by Wren. Destroyed by fire in 1841. Rebuilt by Salvin in 1845, now known as WATERLOO BARRACKS.

    - ➢ See: Officers' Mess, below.
    - ➢ See: Waterloo Barracks, below.
    - The Heralds' Museum: Housed and explained British heraldry's history. From the 1980s. Closed now.
- Great Armoury, the: (AKA: the Grand Armoury.) Not to be confused with the Small Armoury. (See: Grand Storehouse, above in this entry.)

    A "new" building added to the Tower by Wren in 1680; half an H-shaped building. Was formerly called the Horse Armoury; (it would have still been known as the Horse Armoury during the Regency era.) In the mid 19th C. was used as the Officers' Mess. (Is now the New Armouries and Royal Fusiliers' Museum, not long after and since the mid 19th century.) Burned in 1841.
- Heralds' Museum: (See: Grand Storehouse, above.)
- Hospital Block, the: A block of buildings built in the 18th century. Used during the Crimean War (1850s) to house war invalids.

- Jewel House: (See: Crown Jewels, above.)
- King's House, the: (See: Queen's House, below.)
- Liberty, the: (AKA: the Tower Liberty.) A strip of ground between the Tower and the City. Includes Tower Hill and formerly East Smithfield. Guarded by the Crown, and a thorn in the side of the City because they had no authority over those who lived there. Had its own local court into the 19th century (mostly Tower officials.) The Liberty was dissolved in 1894.
- Lieutenants' Lodgings: (See: Queen's House, below.)
- Main Guard, the: Formed in 1846, surrounding an earlier storehouse's shell. Pulled down in 1898 for another guard house. (Sometimes called: Queen Victoria's Canteen.)
- Medieval Palace, the: (See below in: "The Towers"/Lanthorn Tower - Look at "collectively.")
- Menagerie:
    - See: Royal Menagerie, below.
    - See below in: "The Towers"/Lion Tower.
- Moat, the: Built by Edward I. Surrounding the structure, is 120 feet wide. Was dug in the late 13th-early 14th centuries. It was water-filled until 1843 by very smelly Thames River water. It was the Duke of Wellington who, as Constable of the Tower, and due to typhoid outbreaks, finally persuaded Queen Victoria to allow crews to clean out piled up silt so the stagnant waters could be washed away by the tide of the Thames. During WWII the moat was planted with a (temporary) vegetable garden to support the war effort. It is now filled with grass; occupied by a tennis court and a bowling green for residents of the Tower's entertainment.
- New Horse Armoury: Built in 1825, on the south side of the White Tower. Pulled down in 1883.
- Officers' Mess, the: Built by the architect Salvin ca. 1845, similar in style to the Waterloo Barracks, which he also built. (See: Grand Storehouse, above.)
- Ordnance Office: Built over two phases in 1777 and 1792. In 1853-6 it was given an upper floor and used as a storehouse.
- Oriental Armoury, the: Housing weapons from Asia, was moved to Fort Nelson, Fareham, Hampshire.
- Police: The Tower of London got its own first police force (Metropolitan force) in 1846: a serjeant and 13 constables. Replaced with Warders in 1924.
- Queen's House: Stands on Tower Green. Older references refer to this as the

"King's House," but since the current monarch is female (Queen Elizabeth II,) it is called the Queen's House. (But, see: the "Lieutenants' Lodging" paragraph, just below.)

The Queen's House is attached to the Bell Tower, Inner Wall, from 1540; southwest corner of Tower Green. L-shaped building.

Was used from its conception in 1530 to the late 17th C. as the LIEUTENANTS' LODGING, as it was then known (referring to the Lieutenants of the Tower.) Is now the Governor of the Tower of London's residence. Has rather a bit of a country cottage-type facade. (Renamed as the King's House in 1880.) Just to be clear, this building was the Lieutenants' Lodging for centuries; not called the King's (or Queen's) House until 1880.

Because the entire Tower was considered impregnable, prisoners were kept here (a sort of kindness, as it was more comfortable than some of the towers.) Most notably Henry VIII's 2nd and 5th wives are presumed to have been held here (Anne Boleyn, 1536; and Catherine Howard, 1542) and the nine-days-only monarch, Lady Jane Grey, in 1554. Sir Thomas More was kept here as a prisoner (1535); he had servants and comforts (until they were later punitively removed.)

On the ground floor of the Queen's House resides the Constable's Office; the Resident Governor (and his family) reside in the remainder of the house.

The Lieutenant of the Tower for the years 1763-1810 was Lieutenant-General Vernon. From 1810-1831 it was Colonel George, Earl of Munster. The Deputy-Lieutenant for the Tower from 1794-1826 was Colonel John Yorke. From 1826-1839 it was Colonel Francis Doyle. The Major of the Tower from 1793-1812 was Colonel Matthew Smith. From 1812-1816 it was Lieutenant-Colonel MacLean. From 1816-1857 it was Major (later Colonel) J. H. Ebington.

- Raleigh's Walk: (See below in: "The Towers"/Bloody Tower.)
- Ravens, the: (Birds, not a location.) Supposedly beginning ca. 1078, the refuse thrown from the White Tower (then the only building of any size on Tower Hill) attracted scavenging ravens. As building in the area increased, the ravens became more scarce.

During Charles II's reign the legend somehow began that if the ravens ceased to reside in the Tower, the White Tower would crumble and the British empire with it; so the ravens' wings were clipped from then on, to assure the legend never had a chance to come true.

All the ravens died from bombing during WWII, being afterwards restored. Nowadays the ravens have just one wing clipped, and are kept in the White Tower. There are six, plus a seventh, a spare.

- Royal Apartments, the: South of the White Tower. Cromwell had these demolished, never to be rebuilt (since the Tower ceased to be a royal residence during the Commonwealth.) HIS MAJESTY'S TOWER OF LONDON states: "...a fragment of the Wardrobe Tower, all that has been left by Oliver Cromwell of the Royal Apartments which were situated in this area..." (in the) "...12th century."
- Royal Armoury: (Also seen as: Royal Amouries, now due to the collection of arms and armour that is split between three locations, since 1983.) White Tower. Founded by Henry VIII; Charles I built it up. Was open to the public in 1670. Arms ceased to be manufactured here in 1810-15.
    - ➢ See: Oriental Armoury, above.
    - ➢ See below in: "The Towers"/Middle Tower.
  - CROWN JEWELS: (See above in: "Other Places & Things"/Crown Jewels.)
- Royal Menagerie: The tower housed the Royal Menagerie in and around the Lion Tower until 1834 (since the 12th century.) Visitors have toured the Tower since at least the 16th century. In 1834, the animals were moved to the new Regent's Park Zoo.
    - ➢ See below in: "The Towers"/Lion Tower, below.
    - ➢ See: Royal Menagerie, under R.
- Royal Mint, the: For the minting of coins of the realm. Was housed at the Tower from 1300-1809. Was moved out of the Tower area to a fine building overlooking the Tower. Moved again, to Wales, in 1970s. (See: Royal Mint, under R.)
- Royal Observatory, the: Was in the Tower until 1675, when it moved to the Wren-designed Flamsteed House, Greenwich.
    - ➢ See below in: "The Towers"/White Tower - For a note on an observatory before this Greenwich one was built.
    - ➢ You may care to see: Greenwich Observatory.
- Royal Regiment of Fusiliers: Founded by James II in 1685, to protect the Tower's royal guns. (See: Waterloo barracks, below.)
- St. John-the-Evangelist, the Chapel of: (See below in: "The Towers"/White Tower/Chapel of St. John-the-Evangelist.)
- St. Peter ad Vincula: (AKA: The Chapel Royal of St. Peter ad Vincula; ad Vincula means "in chains.") 12th century, added to the Tower by Henry I.

Repaired by Edward III. Fire in 1512; restored by Henry VIII in 1520, being the 3rd chapel on the site. Famous burials here, including Anne Boleyn. Became a Chapel Royal in 1966. (See: Chapel Royal, under C.) Rather than being below the building, the CRYPT of St. Peter is to the north; quite possibly an earlier version of the chapel had been built directly above the crypt. The chapel never has had stained glass windows; is rather plain. (See below in: "The Towers"/White Tower/St. Peter ad Vincula.)

- Small Armoury, the: (See: Grand Storehouse, above.)
- Tower Bridge: (See under the BRIDGES section.)
- Tower Green: Now a green patch (lawn.) In medieval times this area was actually a garden. Princess Elizabeth (later Queen) was allowed to exercise here. From her time until the 20th C. (when the lawn went in) the area had been covered with cobbles.

  Next to the chapel of St. Peter ad Vincula (to the north) and the Queen's House (to the south.) Only ten people have been executed here. (The usual place for "normal" (common folk) executions was: Tower Hill. See at its own listing.) The people executed here at Tower Green were:

  - Farquhar Shaw and his two cousins, Samuel and Malcolm Macpherson, were shot here at dawn, 1743.
  - Anne Boleyn (1536, 2nd wife of Henry VIII. Beheaded.)
  - Margaret Pole, Countess of Salisbury (1541.)
  - Jane Boleyn, Viscountess Rochford (1542, Anne Boleyn's sister-in-law.)
  - Catherine Howard (1542, 5th wife of Henry VIII. Beheaded.)
  - Lady Jane Grey (1554.)
  - Robert Devereux, the 2nd Earl of Essex. (He was held in a tower on the northwest corner of the Tower of London for two weeks before his execution on 25 February 1601. This tower was named Devereux Tower in his memory. (See below in: "The Towers"/Devereux Tower.)
  - Josef Jakobs was the last man executed here, in 1941, by firing squad. He was a WWII spy.

(William, Lord Hastings was executed nearby, in 1483, so some people count his execution as an eleventh here. He was done away with quickly - Richard III had declared he would not eat until Hastings was dead - so there was no time to erect the official scaffold.)

(Tower Green, continued):

There are several 1540s timbered buildings here, including the Queen's House. (See, above.)

The lead fountain dates from 1913.

The private scaffold was located north of the lead fountain, across a roadway. When in use for an execution, there would have been a five foot high dais, draped in black. The dais had wooden steps leading up to it, and a rail around it. Straw would have covered its top.

- 1: Home to the Tower Chaplain since at least 1616.
- 2: Built in 1735 for the clerk of the Office of Ordnance, but eventually housed the Tower medical officer/doctor.
- 4 & 5 Tower Green: Next to Beauchamp Tower; beside the Inner Ballium Wall. Rebuilt in the late 17th century. Yeoman Warders and their families reside here (as they do in houses on the south side of the Green.) The present buildings purportedly replaced others blown down by a storm in 1703. Supposedly were originally wooden. Number 5 is traditionally the home of the Yeoman Gaoler (since at least 1554.)

- Tower Hill: Where the Tower of London sits. (See under its own listing.)
- Tower Subway: 1870. Tunnel under the Thames.
- Towers, the: (See at its own section entitled "The Towers," below.)
- Tower Wharf, the: Outside the Tower of London. First mentioned in 1228. Open to the public in 1893. Now used as a park. There are 62 guns (cannon) here, fired off on special occasions. No record has been unearthed to explain the count of 62 (although theories abound.)
- Traitor's Gate: So called because prisoners were delivered to the Tower by way of this water-gate. Built in 1242. Originally called the Water Gate. In Tudor times, it was known as St. Thomas's Gate. (Henry VIII, in a public relations move, named it for Thomas à Becket.) The Thames (except at low tide) flowed right through this gateway, to the steps of the Bloody Tower Archway. Was the main river entry to the Tower (after the outer walls were built around the White Tower and the Thames was pushed back.) Since this was the gate by which prisoners/traitors were delivered into Tower imprisonment, it took on the name of Traitor's Gate. In the 18th C. it was used as the Tower Infirmary. The portcullis is now gone. The entrance to the tunnel was bricked up ca. 1843. Upon the gate rises St. Thomas's Tower. (Not to be confused with York Water Gate.)
- Wall Walk: (AKA - Elizabeth's Walk.) There is also a wall walk each on the east

and the north sides, but most people mean the one used by Elizabeth I, a rampart attached to the Bell Tower. Its construction currently dates from the 19th century. (See below in: "The Towers"/Bell Tower.)

- Water Lane: The area (road) between the outer and inner walls of the Tower keep.
- Waterloo Barracks: This site had originally been the Grand Storehouse, built in 1694. Destroyed by fire in 1841. Rebuilt in 1845 by Salvin, as the Waterloo Barracks. At this time the Tower had its largest ever garrison of soldiers (could accommodate 1,000 men.)

  Was used until 1947 by units of guards for the Tower. HIS MAJESTY'S TOWER OF LONDON (copyright from 1951) states: "In April 1949 the Regimental Depot, or home, of the Royal Fusiliers (City of London Regiment) occupied Waterloo Barracks. This move was a return of that famous regiment to its birthplace, for under authority of the Royal Warrant dated June 11, 1685, the Royal Regiment of Fusiliers, or Ordnance Regiment, was raised in the Tower of London by George Legge, first Lord Dartmouth... For four years after its formation the regiment remained in the Tower and except for short spells of temporary duty in 1882 and 1935, battalions of the regiment have ever been stationed in the tower throughout its 264 years of service."

  - See: crown jewels, above.
  - See: Waterloo Barracks, under W.

- Yeoman Warders: (AKA: Beefeaters. See under B. They supposedly earned this nickname due to receiving weekly portions of beef as part of their recompense. But don't call them by this, it won't be appreciated.)

  Have been here at the Tower since the 14th century. Not to be confused with the Yeomen of the Guard, the monarch's Bodyguard at St. James's Palace (except that the Yeomen Warders <u>are</u> also members of the Yeomen of the Guard, Extraordinary.)

  At first, the Yeoman Warders acted as more of a society than a military force. Their duties have included: attending the gates, guarding prisoners, manning the night watch, and (more "recently") showing visitors around the Tower (which they've done since at least Elizabeth I's time.)

  To qualify to serve as a Yeoman Warder, a candidate must have a minimum of 22 years honorable service in the armed forces. Undress uniforms are blue; HIS MAJESTY'S TOWER OF LONDON states: "In 1858 Her Majesty Queen Victoria approved of the Yeomen Warders wearing blue undress uniform and this is the dress in which the public usually see them." Their dress (State) uniforms are the famous red-n-gold design, authorized by young Edward VI in 1552; the attire is that of Henry VII's Bodyguard. Their traditional weapon is a partisan, a kind of long spear.

THE TOWERS:

The Beauchamp Tower: (Pronounced: Bee-chum.) Named for its most famous (14th C.) prisoner: Thomas Beauchamp, the Earl of Warwick. This tower is best known for the stones (virtually all) containing scratched messages left by prisoners. It wasn't purpose-built as a gaol; prisoners were squeezed in where space provided. It currently houses items which are found during excavations. Much repaired. Restored in 1852-3 by Anthony Salvin.

The Bell Tower: On the Inner Ward, southwest corner. Ca. 1200. The second oldest tower here (after the White Tower.) Two stories; the two stories exist as two separate chambers, both of which must be entered via using the Queen's House (too, the upper room - "strong-room" - can also be reached via a battlement from the Beauchamp Tower.) The Bell Tower is the only part of this curtain wall that still exists. The King's House was connected to the Bell Tower in the 16th century; at this time this tower sometimes took on the role of housing important prisoners. (See: Queen's House, above - For the King's House.) Called the Bell Tower because curfew is still rung from here every evening (since the 1190s;) the present bell dates from 1651. Elizabeth I (while a princess) was imprisoned here. She was allowed to walk on the attached ramparts (with five others in attendance,) and to this day this rampart is called ELIZABETH'S WALK (or WALL WALK,) and is currently of 19th C. construction.

The Bloody Tower: (AKA: The Garden Tower.) Entrance to the Inner Ward. Adjoins on to Wakefield Tower. 1225. Began life as an arched opening in the inner wall (by Traitor's Gate.) You went through the arch, up steps, and then you were in the Bloody Tower. This is the only rectangular tower here at the Tower of London.

Originally called the Garden Tower (due to the nearby officers' garden,) until the Young Princes went missing in 1483 - although it should be noted that the "Bloody Tower" title was not recorded prior to 1579; HIS MAJESTY'S TOWER OF LONDON says that the name changed to "Bloody" in 1597. (Two children's bodies were found under a staircase in 1674, and some modern genetic evidence recently processed arguably indicates these were indeed the two murdered little princes.)

The Thames flowed right up to the BLOODY TOWER ARCHWAY steps, via Traitor's Gate. The southern part of the archway was built by Henry III in the 13th C.; the northern by Richard III in the 15th century.

Connected to the Bloody Tower is a rampart called RALEIGH'S WALK, named for Sir Walter Raleigh, who exercised here while imprisoned (late 16th century.)

The practice of torture was discontinued here in the 17th century.

The plane trees here are approximately 150 years old.

(See the Bloody Tower's Ceremony of the Keys, above in: "Other Places & Things"/Ceremony of the Keys.)

The Bowyer Tower: Inner Wall, on the North Wall Walk. 13th century. Where, traditionally, Edward IV imprisoned the Duke of Clarence ca. 1477, and where the Duke was reputedly drowned in a butt of Malmsey (Madeira wine) in 1478 (at least according to Shakespeare.) It is believed it is called the Bowyer Tower because bows (as in weaponry) were made there. Used now for administrative purposes.

The Brick Tower: Inner Wall. Built ca. 1300. Named for what it was made of. In the 16th century it housed the Master of Ordnance. Used now primarily for administrative purposes.

The Broad Arrow Tower: Inner Ward. Named for the symbol stamped on royal goods, to show regal ownership. Was linked to the Royal Wardrobe from the 14th century, the items here being royal robes and furnishings. Prisoners were here in the 16th and 17th centuries.

(See: Wardrobe Tower, below.)

The Byward Tower: (AKA: Gateway to the Outer Ward. At first was known as the Wardyng Gate.) 1238-72. Its name comes from the fact it stood by the ward (outer area) of the Tower. Demolished ca. the 1670s. The gate was given greater height in the late 18th-early 19th centuries. Its gate still exists. Has one arch now, in place of the three it had in 1597. The causeway that leads to it dates primarily from the 18th century.

The two-story postern on the southeast side was built in the 14th century (extended in the 16th century.) It is the residence of the Chief Warder (once known as the Yeoman Porter,) the chief custodian of the Tower Keys.

In 1957, medieval paintings, largely of gold and green, were uncovered here.

Now the main entrance for visitors. To enter after dark, one must know the password; the password has been changed daily since 1327.

The Constable Tower: Inner Ward. Named for the Constables (those leaders of the Tower guards under the command of the Sovereign, who had direct control of the Tower of London) who resided here, until the reign of Queen Elizabeth I. (She had been imprisoned here once, and hated the Tower, and so refused to live in it.) Reconstructed 1849-50.

The Coldharbour Tower: The second strongest part of the Tower of London (after the White Tower,) the Coldharbour Gate was demolished in 1675, with only a few rocky ruins left today.

The Cradle Tower: Outer Wall. One of six towers that faces to the south. Built in 1348-55, a private water gate for Edward III. HIS MAJESTY'S TOWER OF LONDON states: "...so named because of a subsidiary entrance through it from the Moat into the fortress. This entrance was used when Traitor's Gate was out of action, and also as a water gate to the Royal apartments standing" (once) "immediately north." Often used as a prison, for lesser important personages. The upper floor was removed in 1776; restored in 1879.

The Develin Tower: Outer Wall. Not open for public display.

The Devereux Tower: Inner Wall. 13th century. Robert Devereux, a favorite courtier to Elizabeth I, was imprisoned here, and it was named for him after his execution. The Armouries and the Mint once stood against the outer wall behind this tower.

(See above in: "Other Places & Things"/Tower Green/Robert Devereux.)

The Flint Tower: Inner Wall. Built ca. 1300. Named for the flint stone used to build it; Norman style. Used now for administrative purposes.

The Garden Tower: Better known as the Bloody Tower. (See, above.)

The Jewel House: (See above in: "Other Places & Things"/Crown Jewels.)

The Lanthorn Tower: Inner Wall. Built ca. 1238-72. It got its name from the fact that a lantern was shone at its summit - recall that the Thames lapped right up to the Inner Wall in ancient days, so this lantern was to help guide ships on the river. Meant as a defense, yes, but also a comfortable/pleasant set of apartments for the king/queen. Largely destroyed by fire in 1774; rebuilt to the 13th C. style a little to the north in 1883, to make it more Victorian-tourist-worthy. (See: Wakefield Tower, below - Note at.)

Collectively the Lanthorn, St. Thomas's, and Wakefield Towers are known as 'the Medieval Palace' (besides the White Tower, being the most ancient parts of the Tower of London.)

(See: Wakefield Tower, below - For a note on a Queen Victoria rebuild of Lanthorn Tower.)

The Lion Tower: Demolished. Faced the Middle Tower from the west. Had been almost completely surrounded by water, originally as a barbican. The Royal Menagerie was housed in and near this tower, hence how it got its name. HIS MAJESTY'S TOWER OF LONDON states: "...on the site of the modern Tower Restaurant stood the Lion Tower, semi-circular in shape, in which the royal animals were housed. It was built by Edward I and from the fourteenth century to 1834 the Royal Menagerie was lodged within or near it."

- See: Royal Menagerie, under R.
- See above in: "Other Places & Things"/Royal Menagerie.

The Martin Tower: Inner Ward. Built in approximately the mid 13th century. Was significantly rebuilt, this time in brick, in the 17th century. Following the Commonwealth period, the Crown Jewels were stored here in a large, vaulted ground floor room, 1669-1869. During this time Martin Tower was known as the Jewel Tower.

Colonel Blood stole the jewels from here in 1671. (He was caught, and - oddly enough - pardoned by Charles II, creating rumors of collusion as the King had been in need of funds.)

The crown jewels were here until 1869, then moved to Wakefield Tower. (See, below.) HIS MAJESTY'S TOWER OF LONDON states: "In 1870 the Crown Jewels and Royal Regalia were transferred from the Jewel House near the Martin Tower to the Wakefield Tower, where they remained till World War 2 when they were removed to a place of greater safety. They were returned in 1947."

From the 18th C. instruments of torture were displayed here, including a block and axe. A 20th C. rebuild/partial restoration was done to create a 17th C. appearance.

Is now the Tower Shop (built over the prior Martin Tower.)

The Middle Tower: 1280, as a fortified gatehouse; this tower was surrounded by moat water, and was reached via a drawbridge. Stands "in the middle" between Byward Tower and Lion Tower. There was a 1717 partial rebuild. Now the Tower of London's main entrance; over the arch is carved "George I 1717" and his coat of arms. Now used as the Royal Armoury's offices.

The Records Tower: (See: Wakefield Tower, below.)

The St. Thomas's Tower: 1276. Located over Traitor's Gate, in the outer wall; linked to the upper story of Wakefield Tower. Built by Edward I. Partially rebuilt in the 19th century. Named for St. Thomas à Becket (he was Constable of the Tower for one year.) It was built because the king felt he had weakened his fortress by cutting out the Water Gate, later called Traitor's Gate. (See above in: "Other Places & Things"/Traitor's Gate.) So the king put this guardhouse over the gate as reinforcement. It is the residence of: the Keeper of the Jewel House.

The Salt Tower: (AKA: Julius Caesar's Tower, seemingly because it was near the Roman City Wall.) Inner Ward. One of the oldest towers, built ca. 1230-40. Much repaired, the most recent being in 1858. Three stories. Used as a prison, particularly for Jesuits. Has 76 inscriptions from prisoners on its walls, some of them rather elaborate. Sometimes served as a storehouse.

The Wakefield Tower: Was originally called Blundeville Tower, after the then Constable of the Tower, John de Blundeville. Was also once called: the Hall Tower; and Records Tower - See below in this entry.)

Its lasting name comes from William de Wakefield, King's Clerk and the holder of the custody of the Exchanges in the Tower in 1334.

Henry VI was by tradition found murdered here in 1471.

Inner wall; adjoins on to the Bloody Tower. Built 1221 or 1225 or 35. It is the only surviving part of Henry III's palace here, the rest falling to such ruin it was pulled down in the 17th century. It was the largest tower here except for the White Tower.

The Oratory remains. The upper floor is reached via a 19th C. link building built by architect Anthony Salvin.

State documents were stored here 1360-1869, at which time it was called the

RECORDS TOWER. (See: Public Records Office, under P - To understand the scattered nature of records such as baptisms, court events, family matters, etc.)

The Crown Jewels were kept here from 1869-1967, then they moved to the Waterloo Barracks. (See above in: "Other Places & Things"/Crown Jewels.)

There was a 13th C. wall that connected this tower to Lanthorn Tower. Charles II had the wall taken down & replaced with a shed for storing ordnance. Queen Victoria ordered the shed (and Lanthorn Tower) removed and the two then restored in the 13th C. style (to make it more worthy for Victorian tourists.) Salvin/expert at restoring medieval buildings, was the architect; he built a wall almost exactly over the old wall and the tower several feet to the north of the old tower.

The Wardrobe Tower: 12th C. tower (built near the remnants of a Roman wall and bastion.) When the Crown Jewels were first brought from Westminster Abbey in 1303, they stayed here. (See above in: "Other Places & Things"/Crown Jewels.)

This tower was built over the site of the Royal Apartments (see above, in this entry.) It is mostly a ruin now, with only walls of a circular tower, modestly sized.

- See: Broad Arrow Tower, above.
- See: Royal Wardrobe, under R.

The Well Tower: Outer Wall. Built by Edward I, 1275-79. Had two shafts down to an underground well. Built to protect the river frontage. Not open for public display.

The White Tower: (AKA: the Norman Keep.) <u>It is called the White Tower because Henry III had it whitewashed in 1240.</u> This is the most identifiable tower of the whole structure, the central tower with four turrets so often photographed by tourists and travel guides. (See: notes above - At the very beginning of this Tower of London entry, regarding what constitutes the "Tower of London.")

Of the White Tower's turrets, three are rectangular and the one in the northeast corner is circular (this last being where the first royal observatory was placed - read lower in this same entry for more on this.) Each turret is surmounted by a "magnificent" weathervane topped by a Royal Crown. The northeast turret (Flamsteed's Tower/one-time observatory) was refitted as a clock tower in 1853-4; the clock was removed in 1913.

The White Tower was built by William I (AKA: William the Conqueror); designed by Gundulf (Bishop of Rochester) 1078-98, built over the site of an earlier wooden keep version. It is a kind of keep only found in England (and only in the early

Norman period,) called a hall keep.

An encircling wall was built in 1097.

Henry III added a great hall and royal apartments, in 1241, and had the whole whitewashed, hence the name "the White Tower" (even though it is more of a yellowy-gray these days.) Walls are 90 feet high and 15 feet thick in places. It is not quite a square, because the west side measures 107 feet, and the south 118 feet. Kentish ragstone, with Caen stones brought from Normandy to strengthen it. The four onion-shaped cupolas on the turrets were first conical, probably remaining so into the 16th century. The original door was 15 feet above ground level, so it couldn't be easily burned during invasions. Wren added doors ca. very early 18th century. Has a staircase in the northeast corner, built in a clockwise spiral for ease of defending the stairs by right-handed swordsmen. Wren also enlarged the Norman windows. All the walls and most of the windows were refaced/altered by Wren, too, (but you can still see four of the original small windows on the upper story's side.) The whole structure was restored early in the 18th C., and several more times in the 19th century.

Was where ancient sovereigns spent the night before their coronation.

This tower was largely occupied by the Board of Ordnance from Charles II's time, until 1881, when the stores were moved to Woolwich.

The flagpole was added to this tower in 1890. The White Tower is a Royal Palace, so the Union flag is flown from 9:00am to Retreat.

The ROYAL ASTRONOMER of 1675 first worked from the top of this building, but shortly moved into the newly built ROYAL OBSERVATORY, Greenwich. (See: Greenwich Observatory.)

The White Tower had its own well in the WESTERN DUNGEON (a valuable asset inside a fortress, so as to provide water during a siege.)

The roof is covered with lead and is flat.

The White Tower was restored in 1863.

Arms and Armour are now displayed here.

- Chapel of St. John-the-Evangelist, the: (AKA: St. John's Chapel. AKA: St. John's Chapel in the White Tower.) Chapel Royal. (See: Chapel Royal, under C.) On the ground floor. Norman; dates from 1080. Was once gorgeously adorned, but was reduced to a significantly plain look ("stark and pristine beauty") by the Reformation. The only chapel in the world with an "aisled nave and encircling ambulatory" (an ambulatory being a place where women were permitted to attend the chapel services, which were otherwise males-only.) Was once the chapel of the Knights of the Bath, ca. 1399.

HIS MAJESTY'S TOWER OF LONDON states: "Records show that it" (the chapel) "was built between 1080-88 and was never subjected to the ravages of the elements. Henry III ordered it to be painted in high colors and furnished with arras and tapestries, and only in the nineteenth century was it thoroughly scoured and cleaned. Thus visitors can be certain that they are regarding genuine Norman architecture which has been little, if at all, repaired."

Despite restoring the monarchy, Charles II had the chapel dismantled; the chapel became a repository for state papers until 1858. Queen Victoria ordered it converted back to a chapel.

The twelve apostles are represented on the circular pillars.

Restored in 1864.

The tiles on the floor are modern.

The stained glass went into widened windows, by Wren, in the very early 18th century.

This chapel was used in olden days by nobility and royals, whereas Yeomen of the Tower and prisoners would have used the Chapel of St. Peter ad Vincula. (See, below.)

Beneath the chapel is a cell called "Little Ease"; it is at the south end of the EASTERN DUNGEON. It is only four feet by four feet (and 9-10 feet in height,) enclosed by oaken doors. Guy Fawkes (Gunpowder Plot planner) was tied here to a ring in the floor while he awaited his trial.

- Chapel of St. Peter ad Vincula: Is attached to (but free-standing from) the White Tower. Added by Henry I. Rebuilt by Henry VIII in 1520, being the third chapel on this site.

  This chapel was used in olden days by Yeomen of the Tower and prisoners, whereas nobility and royals would have used the Chapel of St. John-the-Evangelist. (See, above.)

  In 1666's Great Fire, all the organs in the City were destroyed. In 1676 Father Bernhardt Schmit, a famous organ-maker, built an organ that is now in St. Peter ad Vincula, (the organ was originally at the Palace of Whitehall, but here for a long time since Whitehall was destroyed in the late 17th century.)

  This chapel is still used by about 150 worshippers.

  (See above in: "Other Places & Things"/St. Peter ad Vincula.)

Tower Street - Edward Lloyd (who lent his name to Lloyd's of London) owned a modest coffee-house here until his death in 1712. In 1770, those interested in Marine Insurance bought

"Lloyd's List," a news sheet. (See: Lloyd's of London/Lloyd's List.) In that same year Lloyd's business moved to a new coffee-house in Pope's Head Alley. Four years later, moved again to the second Royal Exchange, an association which lasted until 1928 when it moved to its own premises in Leadenhall and Lime Streets.

- See: Jonathan's - More information at.
- See: Lloyd's of London - More information at.

Tower, the - (See: Tower of London, the.)

Tower Wharf, the - (See: Tower of London/"Other Places & Things"/Tower Wharf.)

Toxophilite Society, the - Toxophilite means: "Lover of the Bow." This Society was founded in 1781 at Leicester House, Leicester Square, to promote a resurgence of interest in archery. The Prince of Wales, George Augustus (later to be George IV,) and aware that when he was in Scotland he was protected by the Royal Company of Archers, became a patron of the sport/the Society in 1787, giving out several prizes. In 1791 it had 170 members, but the Napoleonic wars dragged the membership all the way down to 16; still, the Society survived. They had no regular place to shoot, going where they were invited. In 1834 they had earthen butts they used in Regent's Park; the Park added a club house in ca. 1847; the Society's presence there was regularized by "common usage" in 1996. Women were admitted in 1919, but weren't recognized as full members until 1939. The name changed in 1861 to: Grand National Archery Society. To this day, British royals still remain as patrons.

toy store -

- See: Noah's Ark.
- See: Rathbone Place/34/Temple of Fancy.
- See: Regent Street/Hamley's.
- See: Skinner Street/42.

Toye, Kenning & Spencer - Founded in 1801. Insignia and embroidery, fancy miniature enameled boxes - everything for a uniform except the garment.

toys - (See: games, children's.)

Trafalgar Square - Westminster. Tradition (and logic) has it that King William IV named this square after the famous battle. It was conceived in 1820 by Nash; formation began in 1824 (without Nash.) Construction began in 1829, but the main construction dates ran from 1836-41, including leveling (of several hundred houses) and paving the area (ca. 1840, at which time the north terrace was added below the National Gallery.) The Royal Mews had previously been here, wiped out by the construction. In the Regency, it was "Pall Mall East" that ran through this area.

- See: Charing Cross.
- See: Chelsea Square - The note at. (Also a "Trafalgar Square," but

not this Westminster one.)

- See: Royal Mews.

Unlike many of London's squares, this one has been open to the general public since it was first built.

- Admiralty Arch: (See under A.)
- Canada House: 1824-7, by Smirke. (See under C.) East side of the square.
- Chandos, the: Pub. 1647. (See under the INNS/PUBS section.)
- Charles I Monument: 1633, by Le Sueur. Equestrian statue, considered by some to be London's finest. Looks toward the Banqueting House/Whitehall (ironically from where Charles I stepped for his execution in 1649.) The statue was originally commissioned by Lord Weston for his Roehampton garden, but the 1642 Civil War got in the way. The statue went temporarily to St. Paul, Covent Garden, then went missing. It was reported to have been melted down, but this was only a ruse to keep it hidden and safe. It was rediscovered in a brazier's shop in 1660, at which time Charles II bought it and had it placed here (in what would become Trafalgar Square) in 1675. It is the tradition that all distances from London are measured from this site. The plaque on the base was added after WWII.
- Fountains: Added in 1939.
- George IV Monument: 1841, by Sir Francis Legatt Chantrey (sculptor.) Equestrian statue. Erected here in 1842. (George IV had himself commissioned this statue, having meant it for the top of Marble Arch.) He is shown in Roman toga.
- Lions, the: At the base of the Nelson Column. Added in 1867-68.
- National Gallery, the: 1838. (See under N.)
- Nelson Column, the: (AKA: Nelson's Column. AKA: Nelson Monument.) 1843. Was to commemorate the naval hero, but the statue of Nelson was not put atop the column until 1854. On the north side of the square. Designed by Edward Baily. 184 feet high. One quarter of the cost was provided by the Russian Tsar. (See: Lions, above.)
- Royal Mews: Here from the 14-19th centuries. (See under R.)
- St. Martin-in-the-Fields: Pall Mall East. (See under the CHURCHES section.)
- South Africa House: 1935, on the site of Morley's Hotel (1831.)

traffic islands - First in Britain in the 1860s. (You may care to see: rush hour.)

traffic lights/signals - First in London in 1868, outside the Houses of Parliament, although it was a bit of a fail, and traffic lights weren't much seen until the 1920s. In 1926 there were tricolored, manually operated traffic lights in Piccadilly. (You may care to see: driving tests.)

Traitor's Gate - Associated with Tower Hill executions. In Tudor times it was known as St. Thomas's Gate. (See: Tower of London/"Other Places & Things"/Traitor's Gate.)

Traitor's Hill - (See: Hampstead Heath/Parliament Hill.)

trams - Public transportation, ran on rails, pulled by horses. The first came to London in 1861. First electric ones began running in 1901. The last one running in London closed in 1952.

transportation - (As in a punishment, not locomotion.) Transportation meant banishment from England. The public's growing revulsion with public executions led to the Transportation Act of 1718. The convicted were transported to: America (until the country's independence from Britain in 1776); Australia (then known as: New South Wales, its penal colony established in 1788); and the West Indies. The usual length of the sentence was seven years. The practice ended in 1868.

- See: Australia.
- See: Bloody Code.
- See: hulks.
- See: punishments.

transportation - During the Regency era. (As in locomotion/getting around.)

- See: coach.
- See: hackney coach.
- See: horses.
- See: sedan chair.
- See: Watermen.

Traveller's Club - 106 Pall Mall. 1829-33 (Second source says 1830-32.) Designed by Barry. Looks like an Italian palazzo. For gentlemen who had lived or traveled abroad. (See under the CLUBS section.)

Treasury, the - (AKA: Treasury Building. AKA: Treasury Main Building. AKA: Old Treasury. AKA: Kent's Treasury. More modern nicknames: 1. The Government Office, and 2.GOGGS, short for: Government Offices Great George Street.) It is the government department for managing economic/public finance policy.

(For the: *First Lord of the Treasury*, see: Downing Street/10.)

Westminster. The 1 Horse Guards Road side of the building, facing St. James's Park, was the side of the structure that was most associated with the Treasury for a long time; its building dates from 1733-36, by William Kent. Significantly enlarged by Sir John Soane in 1824-7, adding new rooms for the Board of Trade, and the Privy Council.

The present facade dates from 1846-47, by Sir Charles Barry (who again enlarged it, but retained Soane's column and frieze.)

The beginnings: the very beginnings of a Treasury in England date back to someone who was known as Henry the Treasurer, a Winchester servant under William I; the royal treasure/treasury was first at Winchester.

Under Henry I (12th C.) the Treasury became its own thing, separating from the Royal Household. While this was still the king's treasure, it now had oversight and management, via a Lord Treasurer.

THE EXCHEQUER: This 12th century "first version of the Treasury" (my words) took its name from a literal checkered cloth, on which was worked out the auditing by the Barons of the upper Exchequer and the City accountants; the sums of money paid were laid out on the cloth, plain to see, the sums then committed to recording on parchment rolls. The name "Exchequer" is used far less these days, but it still means the money due to/managed by the government.

After the Norman Conquest the Treasury moved to Whitehall Palace.

In Tudor times, the Lord Treasurer became an officer of the State, almost as important as the Lord Chancellor.

In 1660 the Treasury was at the Exchequer Receipt Office, Westminster Cloisters. Then it moved to 70 Whitehall (had been Henry VIII's cockpit.) Whitehall Palace burned in 1698. The only part that remains is the Banqueting House (of 1622,) and Cardinal Wolsey's wine cellar (now under the Ministry of Defence's building.)

George Downing was appointed in 1667 by Charles II to reform the Treasury and the collection of taxes. "Downing Street," the Prime Minister's home and offices, got its name from this gentleman, the builder of Downing Street. (See: Downing Street.)

A whole new Treasury, by Kent, was built and ready in 1734, on Horse Guards, moving from Whitehall. (This is when it took on the 1 Horse Guard Road address.) This building (and an expansion into a new building by architect John Soane) remained there, but had severe damage by WWII bombs in 1940.

Following that damage, the Treasury slid over into the GOGGS (Government Offices Great George Street) location, which gives the address of: Great George Street (but the west side of which is still the 1 Horse Guards Road address.)

- See: Board of Trade.
- See: Cock Pit, the.
- See: Royal Guards/Treasury.

trees - Of Regency era England. (Not an all-inclusive list.)

acacia

apple

ash

beech

cherry

chestnut

copperbeech

crabapple - Can be grown as either a bush or a tree.

damsons

elder

elm

greengages

hawthorn

hornbeam

horse-chestnut

laburnum

larch

lemon - Would be grown in a greenhouse.

lime - Large and deciduous trees, not the citrus kind - Although see: "Trees grown...," below.

may (tree)

medlar - Apple-like, native to Asia.

mountain ash - In Scotland called: rowan.

mulberry

oak

pear

plane - Also called: London plane. Related to the American sycamore. (See under P.)

plum

poplars

quince

silver birch

sycamore

thorn

willow

yew.

Trees grown in Regency hothouses: lemon, lime (the citrus kind,) oranges, pineapples.

- You may care to see: fruit.
- You may care to see: plants.

Trevor Square - Knightsbridge. Takes its name from Sir John Trevor, whose 1818 house was built here. Designed in the 1810s, with the houses being built in the 1820s.

- Powis House: (See under P.)

Trinity Almshouses - Tower Hill, Stepney, on what is called Mile End Waste, an extensive open space on Mile End Road. The Almhouses were built in 1695, for retired sea captains and their widows.

Trinity Church Square - (AKA: Trinity Square.) Kennington, Southwark. 1823-24. NAIRN'S LONDON notes: "One of the best squares in London, and all the better for being early Victorian rather than Georgian." (See: Kennington/Trinity Square.)

- Church of the Holy Trinity: 1822.
- Statue of Alfred the Great: Dates from ca. 1395.
- Trinity House: (See at its own listing.)

Trinity College - Cambridge. Founded by Henry VIII in 1546. (See: Cambridge/Trinity College.)

Trinity Hospital - Greenwich. Almshouses. Founded in 1613 by Henry Howard, the Earl of Northampton. In 1812 was rebuilt, in the Gothic style.

Trinity House - (AKA: the Corporation of Trinity House.) Trinity Square, Tower Hill, Stepney. Charter granted by Henry VIII in 1514, but the organization pre-dates the charter. It was formed for the "relief, increase, and augmentation of the Shipping of this realm of England," to build British lighthouses; buoys; beacons; other nautical markers; and has served as Britain's chief pilotage (that is, licensing of nautical pilots) authority. Also provides for the welfare of sailors. Controls lighthouses in England and Wales.

Moved to its present locale/designed in 1793-5 by Samuel Wyatt. Fronted with stone. There was a complete interior remodel in the 20th C. following WWII damage.

Trinity Marsh Lane - (See: Prince Regent Lane.)

Trinity Square - (See: Trinity Church Square.)

Truefitt & Hill - Gentlemen's hairdressers. (See: Bond Street/Old Bond Street/23.)

Trumper, Geo F. - Gentlemen's fashion, since 1875. (See: Curzon Street/9.)

Tubbenden - Bromley. Not seen on most maps, but it dates from 1240. Was considered an outlying district of Farnborough. Had many orchards, up to the 20th century.

Tube, the - (More properly known as: the London Underground.) Subway. 1863, at that time ran on steam. The first electric train of the Tube ran in 1890. (See: Metropolitan Underground Railway.)

The famous diagrammatical Tube map was designed in 1931. Although amended over time, it remains much the same as that original.

tuberculosis -

- See: consumption

- See: diseases/consumption.

Tudor Street - The City. In the 17th C., King Tudor Street was expanded, creating Tudor Street. (See: Whitefriars Glass.)

Tufnell Park - Islington and Camden. Had been part of the manor of Barnsbury. William Tufnell inherited the manor in 1754. Serious building here in 1845.

Tufton Street - Westminster. There was a cockfighting pit here in approximately 1821; it was probably the last existing cockpit in London.

Tulse Hill - Lambeth. The three estates of Bodley, Scarlettes, and Upgrove were here by 1352. Henry VIII seized the property (from the ownership by the Hospital of St. Thomas the Martyr.)

- Brockalle House: 1563. By 1656 the Tulse family owned it. In 1807 the estate was divided in two; shortly pulled down.
- Brockwell Hall: 1813.

Tun, The - A Cornhill prison, so named because it was shaped like a barrel of wine (a tun.) Affiliated with the Watch. (See under W.) Became a general term for imprisonment: "I'm going home before I'm tossed in the tun." Described as a small lock-up, the like of which were also referred to as compters.

- See: compters.
- You may care to see: measurements/tun.

Tunbridge Ware - Tunbridge Ware is intricately inlaid woodwork, usually in the form of boxes. Characteristic of 18-19th century work that came out of Tonbridge (note spelling; Kent market town) and Royal Tunbridge Wells, Kent (spa town.)

tunnels - While we mostly think of the 20-21st centuries as having the technology to allow for safe tunnel construction, there did exist some early ones:

- See: Adelphi/Lower Robert Street.
- See: City, The/St. Sepulchre's.
- See: Hampton/Hampton House.
- See: Islington/Islington Tunnel.
- See: Lindsey Row/4.
- See: Maida Hill/Maida Hill Tunnel.
- See: Thames Tunnel - 1832. Underwater.
- See: Underground Tunnel - (AKA: the Tube.) 1863.
- You may care to See: Channel Tunnel - 1994. Familiarly known as the Chunnel, underwater tunnel connecting England and France.

Tunworth - (See: Kingsbury.)

turkey - William Strickland (d.1598) is credited with introducing the turkey to England. There is a turkey in his coat of arms, the earliest depiction of the fowl in England. (See: food/turkey.)

Turkey Street - Enfield. Links Bulls Cross with Enfield Wash. The street existed by 1427; ten houses here in 1572. Probably started as "Tuckey," but corrupted to "Turkey" in the 19th century.

Turnbull and Asser - 71-72 Jermyn Street. Shirtmakers. Founded in 1885, but in Jermyn Street in 1903. Royal Warrant awarded by Prince Charles in 1980, the first one he granted.

Turners' Company - (AKA: the Worshipful Company of Turners.) As in turning-lathes. Was a Guild by the 12th century. The Turners established the size of an English pint, because they were sworn to make no measures other than a gallon; potells (two quarts); quarts, and pints. (Before then, there had been "about a pint", called chopyns, and about half a pint, called gylles, which under their oath became unacceptable.) Royal Charter in 1604. The Turners was the first company to pay attention to technical education, in the 19th century. Livery Company. Has no hall. 51st in the order of precedence. (See: Furniture-makers' Company, information at.)

Turnham Green - Hounslow. Existed at least by the mid 17th century. The lord mayor was accosted at pistol point by a bold daylight robber here in 1776. By the mid 19th C. was the "commercial center" of Chiswick. In 1642 almost 1,000 men died here in the Battle of Turnham Green. In the 18th C. grew into a coaching halt on the way to Bath.

turnpike - While it might physically resemble a gate across the road, a turnpike could also be less formal in its construction/presentation. One also tends to associate "turnpike" with country lanes (since turnpikes were not built into city walls.) The turnpike at Durdham Down, Clifton, Bristol is undoubtedly more handsome than the majority of turnpikes (which might be no more than a gate across the road, although they could be large enough that they were later converted into homes.) A turnpike was where one paid the fee for use of the road; the amount paid depended on the manner/size of your vehicle.

The turnpikes came into being around 1673 to help mend roads (that were too often made almost impassable, particularly in winter.) They provided funds that local taxes were not sufficient to cover.

The collecting of tolls at turnpikes existed well into the Regency era. Turnpikes were abolished ca. 1866; with the Turnpike Trust shutting down in 1870.

The Royal Mail coaches did not pay tolls at tollgates or turnpikes.

- See: milestones.
- See: tollgates.

Turnpike Lane - Haringey. (See: Tottenham Lane.)

Tussaud's - (See: Baker Street/Madam Tussaud's Waxworks.)

Twickenham - Richmond; located just across Richmond Bridge. Ancient. The street patterns largely date from ca. 1635. Contains some fine examples of 17th C. houses. In the 18th C. it was a countrified village desired by those of fashion/wealth (and also attracted painters and writers.)

- Hampton Court: (See under H.)
- Montpelier Row: Ca. 1720, gracious terraces.
- Orleans House: Orleans Road. 1720, by James Gibb. Only the Octagon Room remains of the house today. Named for Louis Philippe, exiled Duc d'Orleans, who lived here 1800-1817.
- Richmond Road:
    - Marble Hill House: Palladian. 1724-29, for George II's mistress, Henrietta Howard, Countess of Suffolk. She lived here until her death in 1767. (See under M.)
- St. Mary: Twickenham parish church. A church probably stood here in the late 11th century. Rebuilt in the early 18th C.; restored several times since. Alexander Pope (poet) is buried here (he'd had a villa here.)
- Sion Row: Ca. 1720, gracious terraces.
- South Twickenham: (See under S.)
- Twickenham Bridge: A footbridge was here in 1894, the concrete one in 1933.

Twinings - Tea sellers. (See: Strand/216.)

Twyford - Not in London, is in Berkshire. Means: "double ford," because this city had two fords over the River Loddon. Dates from at least the year 871. Was agricultural until rails came in 1838. (See: Park Royal.)

Tyburn - (Hosted: Tyburn Tree, AKA: Tyburn Gallows.) Near Mayfair, where Marble Arch now stands, Hay Hill. (See under H.) Executions seem to have begun here ca. 1196. Over the centuries it claimed tens of thousands of condemned prisoners, of every manner of offense. (See: Hay Hill - Note that explains Tyburn's name.)

Executions were held once a month, usually the first Monday, and were well-attended by the public, complete with hawkers and vendors. Until they ceased altogether, executions (with the exception of those held at the Tower of London) were always public spectacles. There had been a large permanent stand (for viewing the hangings) known as "Mother Proctor's Pews."

There used to be a three-legged gallows (of 1571) here, which could hang 24 persons at once, 8 per beam. It was replaced by a movable gallows in 1759, and the last hanging here was in 1783, but the old three-legged "tree" wasn't actually removed until 1825.

After 1783, hangings moved to just outside Newgate Prison, (where the crowds, upwards of 30,000, were easier to control.)

The gallows had stood at the junction of Edgware Road and Oxford Road for nearly 500 years.

Tyburn was also the name of a winding stream.

- See: Old Bailey.
- See: Tyburn River.

Tyburn Gate - Stood until 1829. Connaught Place was built over the site.

Tyburn River, the - In ancient times the name was Tye Bourne (meaning Tye River,) but corruption of the name had made it "Tyburn" long before the Regency. Had two tributaries to the Thames, between which was the "Island" of Thorney - was once an island, but has not been so for many a century. This is where Westminster now stands. The river flows underneath Buckingham Palace to Regent's Park; Primrose Hill; Haverstock Hill; and to Belsize Park. It is now culverted over and so cannot be seen.

Tyburn Turnpike - (AKA: Tyburn Road.) Former name of Oxford Street.

- See: Oxford Street.
- See: Tyburn.

Tyburnia - (See: Paddington/Tyburnia.)

Tylers and Bricklayers' Company - (AKA: the Worshipful Company of Tylers and Bricklayers.) Bricklayers were layers of brick; Tylers were layers of roof and floor tiles. Guild formed in 1416. Royal Charter in 1568. Their control over the craft began to decline in the 17th C., resulting from a lot of foreign labor in London following the Great Fire of 1666, never to be fully recovered. Used to have a hall at 52 Leadenhall Street, which burned in the Great Fire. A new Hall lasted until 1883. Livery Company. 37th in the order of precedence.

typewriters - Invented in the 1860s. (You may care to see: ink.)

typhus - Usually called gaol fever, often spread by lice. (See: diseases/gaol fever.)

-U-

Uganda House - Trafalgar Square. 1915.

Ulster Terrace - Near Park Crescent, Regent's Park, Westminster. Built by John Nash, ca. 1824-27. Named for George IV's brother, Prince Frederick, who besides being the Duke of York and Albany, was the Earl of Ulster. (See: Park Crescent/Ulster Terrace.)

umbrella - Umbrellas were invented in 1786, and were finally a popular item by the time of the

Regency. It was held in the center of its post, the end being straight and usually pointy. They were made of split cane or whalebone, with oiled fabric, and could be quite heavy. (See: Piccadilly/185/Swaine Adney Briggs & Son.) A second source said umbrellas were introduced in the 1750s to England by Jonas Hanway, merchant and travel writer. (See: Upper Rathbone Place/Red Lion Square/23.)

Parasols, on the other hand, had been around for ages, and could be made of silk. Parasols were decorative, without waterproof abilities.

undergarments - That is, underwear. In a time when there was not so much bathing or clothes-washing, your undergarments were as much about protecting your outer clothes from *you*, as the other way around. It was easier to change out/launder underclothing than an entire ensemble.

(The following lists are not all-inclusive.)

Men's undergarments: comprised of a shirt (specific to being under one's regular shirt, and which had voluminous sleeves, ornate cuffs, and was longer in the back than in the front) and drawers (the latter being a lining for under one's breeches or pantaloons; drawers were not worn by everyone, some men wore none. Men wore stockings. (See: stockings, under S.)

Women: Wore a shift (or a chemise,) a simple sleeveless linen garment reaching to below the knees. It slipped over the head, secured at the waist by a drawstring or buttons. Over this went stays (shaped with whalebone or cane sewn in) or a corset; both laced, and stays were usually laced at the front and often had shoulder straps. Over this went a petticoat (from the waist to the ankles; in the Georgian period it was often revealed through a split in the outer gown's skirt, intended to be seen - but far less so by the Regency era, except for court dress.) Lastly, one donned the actual dress. The thinner fabrics of the Regency's round gowns led to stays being abandoned, and corsets made shorter to accommodate the empire-style dresses. Women wore stockings, to the knee. (See: stockings, under S.) They adopted drawers (like bloomers) once Princess Charlotte (George IV's daughter) was seen wearing them ca. 1817.

(You may care to see: dresses, women's.)

Underground, The - Also known by the nickname: the Tube. Subway. 1863.

- See: Tube, the.
- You may care to see: Thames Tunnel - To show the Tube was not London's first underground transport tunnel.
- You may care to see: tunnels.

Underhill - Barnet. It lies "under" (at the foot of) Barnet Hill. Pretty rural until the 1860s rails came in.

- Red Lion Inn: Built in the mid 18th century. Rebuilt in the 1930s.

underwater tunnel - (See: Thames Tunnel.)

underwear - (See: undergarments.)

uniforms, military -

- See: military regalia.
- See: red coats.
- See: Toye, Spencer & Kenning.

Unilever House - Built in 1930, replacing an 1875 hotel called De Keyser's, which closed in 1927. (See: Bridewell Prison.)

union - As in a professional affiliation of workers. Used in this sense, "union" was a word just starting to be heard in the early 19th C. in the UK, but didn't really become a concrete concept/movement until closer to the 1860s (as the Industrial Revolution aged.)

The National Association of United Trades for the Protection of Labour was founded in 1845, but had a rather small profile until around 1860 (the year the London Trades Council was founded.)

Prior to the rising of unions, the Guilds served something of the same purpose, but were more about training and regulation of a craft than defending workers' rights.

- See: friendly societies.
- See: International Working Men's Association - 1864.
- See: Islington/Copenhagen Fields - 1834.
- See: London Trades Council - 1860.

Union Jack, the - (See: flag, British.)

United Africa House - (AKA: UAC House.) Formed in 1929 for trade from West Africa. Built ca. 1959. Built on the site of the Surrey Institution.

United Kingdom - This title did not come into use until 1801.

- See: flag, British.
- See: Great Britain - (1604.)
- See: INTRO-REIGNS section/British Kings & Queens and their Reigns/Henry III.
- See: INTRO-REIGNS section/British Kings & Queens and their Reigns/Edward I.

United Nations, the - (AKA: the UN.) Founded in 1945. The first meeting of the United Nations was hosted in the Methodist Central Hall, London, in 1912. The UN is now housed in New York, USA, since 1951.

United Service Club - Gentlemen's club. 1827.

- See: Institute of Directors.

- ➢ See: Pall Mall/116.
- ➢ See: United Service Club, under the CLUBS section.

United Services Museum - 1895. (See: Whitehall, Royal Palace of/Banqueting House.)

United Society of Master Chimney-sweepers - First met 5/01/1826 at the Eyre Arms Tavern, St. John's Wood. They formed this union in hopes of making their manner of chimney-sweeping (by using climbing boys) seem less horrific/abusive. The use of climbing boys was not effectively banned until 1875.

- ➢ See: chimney-sweeps.
- ➢ See: climbing boys.

United States Embassy - 24 Grosvenor Square. 1959. (NOT TO BE CONFUSED with the modern *residences* of U. S. Ambassador(s) at Winfield House.)

After American independence in 1776 (the Revolutionary War ending in 1783,) diplomatic relations between America and England were set up in 1785. (John Adams, later American president, was the first U.S. Ambassador to England, in 1785.)

The accords were shattered, and the War of 1812 then played out, with diplomatic relations between the two countries being restored/reenacted in 1815.

- The US Legislation was first at: Great Cumberland Place (ca. 1792-1863.)
- In 1863-66, was at: 98 Portland Place, Piccadilly.
- In 1883-1893, at: 123 Victoria Street, Westminster. They were upgraded from a legislation to an embassy in 1893; remaining at 123 Victoria Street until 1912.
- In 1912-1938, at: 4 Grosvenor Gardens.
- In 1938-2018, at: London Chancery Building, 1 Grosvenor Square, Westminster. (AKA: Macdonald House.)
- A new site was purchased in 2008 at: 33 Nine Elms Lane, construction started in 2013, fully opened on Jan. 16, 2018.

United States Legislation - (See: United States Embassy.)

United University Club, the - (See: University Club.)

universities -

- ➢ See: colleges/universities.
- ➢ See: education.
- ➢ See: private schools.

University Club, the - 1822-6. Designed by Wilkins and J. P. Gandy-Deering. (See: United University Club, under the CLUBS section.)

University College - (AKA: University College London.) Near the top of Gower Street, off Malet Street. Founded in 1826, foundation stone laid in 1827; by William Wilkins. Neo-classical. Opened in 1828. (See: University of London, of which this is one of its colleges.)

Unlike Cambridge and Oxford (which only admitted Anglicans,) students of all faiths (or none) were admitted here. This, therefore, became known as the "Godless College." LET'S GO-BUDGET GUIDE TO LONDON, 1995 states: "University College was chartered (along with King's College in The Strand) as the University of London in 1836, making London the last major European capital to acquire a university." It became, in 1878, the first (anyway the first in England) to admit women to its degree courses. Incorporated with the University of London in 1907, the latter being its oldest and largest college.

University College Hospital - Gower Street, 1833. Rebuilt (flamboyantly) in 1906. Now known as the Cruciform, since 1996.

University of London - (AKA: London University.) Malet Street, Bloomsbury. Partly founded in 1826 (in part to establish a center of higher learning not connected to the Anglican church,) from which it now became possible to earn medical degrees (MB and MD.) This first building opened in 1826, in Gower Street, Bloomsbury. It began with University College. The University of London was created as such in 1836 by Parliament, the "umbrella" title for a number of colleges (scattered around London) under it. Now is host to fifty semi-autonomous schools, colleges, and hospitals, situated over a 40 mile/64 km area, and is the largest university in Britain.

- ➢ See: Burlington House.
- ➢ See: Gower Street.
- ➢ See: Malet Street.

They were the first to use ether during surgeries, 1846.

The university opened its examinations to women in 1878.

- Imperial College: (See under I.)
- Senate House: 1930s, by Charles Holden. This is the college's administrative center, with a library described as "priceless."

University of Westminster - Established in 1838. (See: Regent Street/ Polytechnic.)

Upholders' Company - (AKA: the Worshipful Company of Upholders.) Originally called the fripperies - those that repaired old clothes - from the 14th century. By 1502 were recorded as the Upholders. Charter in 1626. "Upholder" is an old word for upholsterer. Livery Company. No hall. 49th in the order of precedence. Upholsterers might also sell wallpapers. Had a Hall in 1646, a property called Wingfield House (or Wingfield Place,) in the ward of Castel Baynard. It burned in the Great Fire of 1666; never replaced; the Upholders have no Hall. (See: upholsterers.)

upholsterers - The older name for those who upholster (inspect and repair furniture) was: upholders.

- ➢ See: halls/"No Hall"/Upholders' Company.

- See: Upholders' Company.

Upminster - Havering. East of Hornchurch. Had a parish church from the 7th century on.

- Gaynes manor house: Rebuilt in the late 18th C., Palladian, for Sir James.
- St. Laurence Church: Early 13th C.; its original tower still stands.
- Upminster Bridge: (See under the BRIDGES section.)
- Upminster Mill: 1799. Octagonal. North of the main Hornchurch Road.

Upney - Barking and Dagenham. CHAMBERS LONDON ENCYCLOPEDIA states: "A former village, now absorbed within eastern Barking. Upney is something of a rarity in the geography of London: a place that has lost its identity despite having a (rail) station that bears its name..." Was mostly built up between the world wars.

- Eastbury House: Built during Queen Elizabeth I's era. Yet exists; a National Trust property.

Upper Berkeley Street - (See: Portman Square/Upper Berkeley Street.)

Upper Clapton - (See: Clapton/Upper Clapton.)

Upper Edmonton - Enfield. Centered on Angel Road, Fore Street, and Silver Street; now densely populated. The 19th C. brought industry here, especially along the River Lea.

- Bell, the: Inn; so popular that several inns claimed the name, leading to an Old Bell and an Oldest Bell.

Upper Grosvenor Street - Mayfair.

- 16: Sir Robert Peel (founder of the Metropolitan Police) lived here.

Upper Harley Street - 1920s. (See: Brunswick Place.)

Upper Holloway - Islington. Between Camden Road and Archway. 17th C. inns. Not very residential until the 1840s. (See: Holloway.)

Upper House - (AKA: The House of Lords.) Parliament split into two distinct houses in the 14th century. The Lords was housed in the White Chamber in the southern end of the building of Westminster; this was the building Guy Fawkes (17th C. revolutionary) meant to blow up.

It had two stories, and (until 1801) the Lords met on the upper one. It was in the White Chamber from the 16th C. until 1801, when it moved to a hall once used by the Court of Requests.

The devastating fire of 1834 necessitated the building of new quarters, the magnificent and Gothic building at which Parliament still sits. The Lords first sat in the new Parliament building in 1847.

The members of the House of Lords are not elected, being the Lords Spiritual (Archbishop of Canterbury, etc., 26 Archbishops in all,) and the Lords Temporal (English peers and 16 representative Scottish peers,) and the Lords of Appeal, also known as the Law Lords, who form their highest court.) The Head of the Judiciary is the Lord Chancellor, who presides over the House. He sits on the Woolsack, situated before the Throne. (The Throne is for the monarch, who is not allowed in the House of Commons and must open Parliament from the House of Lords.)

Their main purpose is to provide a forum to more fully discuss Bills in detail and to work on any revisions.

- See: Cabinet, the.
- See: Houses of Parliament.
- See: Lower House.
- See: Westminster.

Upper Rathbone Place - Leads from Oxford Street to Charlotte Street, in what used to be St. Pancras, but is now Marylebone. Dates from ca. 1718; was originally called Glanville Street, then Upper Rathbone Place (until approximately 1900,) and now Rathbone Street. Is now mostly offices and retail spaces.

- 12: William Hazlitt (critic/essayist) lived here from 1802-05.
- 34: Temple of Fancy. Stationers/booksellers. Also sold toys.
- 50: John Constable (painter) lived here ca. 1802-05.
- Heal and Son: Bedding shop established in 1810 by John Harris Heal. There until 1840, when it moved (as Heal and Son) to its present site in Tottenham Court Road.
- Red Lion Square: North of Lincoln's Inn. Built 1698. A place for executions and duels.
    - 23: Jonas Hanway lived here. By the time he died in 1786 his introduction of the umbrella had been accepted by other Londoners.

Upper Shirley - Croydon. Southern portion of Shirley. (See: Shirley, under S.)

- Badger's Hole: An enclave dating from the mid 18th C., on squatters' land. By the 19th C. had evolved into Upper Shirely, a hamlet.
- post mill, a: 1810. Burned; present tower mill dates from 1854.

Upper Street - (See: Islington/Upper Street.)

Upper Sydenham - Lewisham. The industry of forestry was important here in Elizabethan times (also providing charcoal and shipbuilding wood.) Alas, the forest was nearly gone by the end of the 18th C., and dairy farming took over. Stayed mostly rural until after the 1850s. (See: Sydendam.)

Upper Thames Street - Geoffrey Chaucer was born here ca. 1340...but the name of the street was different then. (See: Lower Thames Street.)

- Vintners' Hall: (See under V.)

Upper Wimpole Street - 1778. (See: Wimpole Street/Upper Wimpole Street.)

Upper Woodcote - Croydon. Was 800 acres of the Beddington family estate until 1859; since known for its trees/horticulture. (See: Woodcote.)

Upton - **Bexley**. Isolated. Heathland hamlet.

- Red House: Ca. 1858.
- Wye Lodge: Lion Road. 17th C. farm building. Now much altered and has a different name.

Upton - **Newham**. A community of Quakers were here in the late 18th C. and on. An attractive hamlet until ca. 1876, when it began to grow rapidly.

- Spotted Dog, the: Upton Lane. 16th C. beginnings. Newham's oldest building.

Upton Park - Newham. Late Victorian development.

Uranus - (See: planets/Uranus.)

U. S. Embassy - (See: United States Embassy.)

utensils - (See: household utensils.)

Uxbridge - Hillingdon. Probably dates from the 7th C., but there's no written record until the mid 12th. Was granted a weekly market in 1294, along with a yearly fair. Located near the River Colne, and the Grand Junction Canal, via which flour was sent from Uxbridge into London. (Uxbridge provided most of London's flour for some 200 years.) Was a flourishing coaching halt in the 18th century. The late 18th to early 19th C. canals confirmed it as a thriving market town, although it must be noted that in the early 19th century Uxbridge had an unsavory reputation for assaults/theft.

- Market-house, the: Present version dates from 1789, replacing a 1561 version. Covered. Supported on columns.
- St. Margaret's: In the early 13th C. was a Chapel of Ease. Parish church, ca. 1448. Perpendicular style. Restored 1872. Is hidden behind the market-house.
- Treaty House: A 17th C. mansion (rebuilt/reduced from the original.) Is now a pub named the Crown and Treaty.
- Uxbridge Cricket Club: (See: Uxbridge Moor, at its own listing.)
- Uxbridge Moor: (See at its own listing.)

Uxbridge House - 1792 town house for the Marquis of Anglesey. Built on the 1720s site of Queensbury House. In 1855, it was given over to a bank, and now houses the Bank of Scotland. (See: Queensbury House.)

Uxbridge Moor - Hillingdon. Industrial area. CHAMBERS LONDON GAZETTEER explains: "The Grand Junction (now Grand Union) Canal was dug through the moor in 1794, connecting Uxbridge with the Thames at Brentford. By 1800 the link to Birmingham was complete. Wharves and warehouses were constructed along the canal and coal for the surrounding district was offloaded here, while corn was taken abroad." Grew into a thriving commercial zone: oil mills and mustard mills were here; also glassworks, and gas works. Now: business parks and industrial works. Cricket played here, with the Uxbridge cricket club being here from 1789 (moved in the 1820s to Uxbridge Common.)

- St. John's on the Moor: Church. 1838.

-V-

Vale of Health - Camden. Tiny hamlet in Hampstead Heath, formerly a swamp, when it was known as New Spring Garden.

- See: Hampstead/Well Walk.
- See: Hampstead Heath/Vale of Health.

Valence - Barking. The (later) Earl of Pembroke received the estate in 1309 upon the death of his sister. In 1806 the estate was broken up, but building here was slow for years after.

- Valence House: Probably first built in the 14th C. Enlarged. Reduced. Enlarged again. (And subsequently remodeled over the centuries, with the present house dating primarily from the late 17th C.) The London County Council bought the house in 1901, selling it to Dagenham Council in 1926.

Valentines Park - Redbridge, Ilford. 1899. Edwardian. There was some housing here in prior years.

valet - Personal male assistant, particularly in dressing and the care of clothes. The British pronounce it so that it rhymes with "pallet" (VAL-it; not the French "vuh-lay.")

Vanbrugh Castle - (See: Greenwich/Maze Hill/Vanbrugh Castle.)

Vauxhall - (See: Vauxhall Gardens.)

Vauxhall Bridge Road - Ca. 1816 (being built at about the time the bridge was put in, the latter from 1811-16.)

Vauxhall Gardens - (AKA: Vauxhall Pleasure Gardens, and frequently also just as: Vauxhall.) Pronounced: Voxhall -or- Voxall. On the Thames, at Lambeth. CHAMBERS LONDON GAZETTEER states: "The Gascon mercenary Falkes de Bréauté gained possession of the manor in 1233 through his marriage to wealthy widow Margaret de Redvers and built Falkes' Hall, later called Fox Hall. Jane Vaux, possibly a descendant of Falkes de Bréauté, owned a house here in 1615 with eleven acres of grounds called the Spring Gardens, which were opened as a pleasure park in 1660."

Other sources go on to say: Laid out in 1661. Known as New Spring Gardens when it re-opened as an extended, revamped pleasure garden in 1732; had two-story supper boxes, to go with several new walks and avenues planted with trees, statues, gravel walks, and buildings. After 1750, you got there by boat or via Westminster Bridge.

In 1785 the name changed from New Spring Gardens to Vauxhall Gardens.

The promenades were used for strolling; secluded walks (from whence a lot of its often dicey reputation sprang); hundreds of decorated alcoves for dining (ditto); a bandstand; and a music room for recitals.

Opened on or around June 4th every year (King George III's birthday) in the early 19th C.

Masquerade nights were more expensive than ordinary nights. Vauxhall was often visited by Prinny. Gardens were illuminated by 1,000 lamps. Admissions were for Mondays, Wednesdays, and Fridays, for a fee (I saw a listing of 3 shillings, sixpence; another source listed the fee as being "around two shillings.") Attendees admired fountains, the cascades, and Roubiliac's fine statue of Mr. Handel (musician,) or listened to the musicians playing in the orchestra pavilion, before supping on Arrack punch (the famous Vauxhall punch,) custards and syllabubs in one of the small supper boxes arranged in the leafy dining arbors. Young ladies "squealed and squawked when they ventured alone into the Dark Walk," a somewhat isolated set of walks for strolling, where daring and impudent young gentlemen might be hovering about, waiting to pursue a dalliance. (See: food/Arrack punch - For a definition.)

ENGLAND IN 1815 AS SEEN BY A YOUNG BOSTON MERCHANT says: "At 11:00 the nobility and fashionables began to enter, when there was a grand display of dress, for most all who are here appear in full dress... At two o'clock the party to which I belonged left the garden, as the dances had begun, this being the signal for the departure of respectable ladies."

Vauxhall was done away with in 1859. Despite the closing of Vauxhall, the 18th C. proprietor left his legacy by leaving behind streets named Johnathan Street and Tyers Street. Today there stands a pretty little park called Vauxhall Park. A small remnant called Spring Gardens still exists.

Beginning in the 18th C., when it was time for the fireworks a bell would ring.

People could own private boxes.

Madam Squi (a wirewalker) performed here in 1816. There were also sword-swallowers and equestrian acts. Music was played from 6:00-9:00 pm. Gas light was brought in, in 1846.

While Vauxhall was primarily a "middle class" (See under M) entertainment, it attracted a wide range of London sorts, from royalty down to pickpockets and prostitutes. A lady would never go to Vauxhall *unescorted*, especially at night.

Vauxhall Park - 1890. A little south of where Vauxhall Pleasure Gardens had been.

vegetables - Mostly unable to grow their own vegetables (due to lack of space,) however Londoners had access to many street markets and costermongers. The variety of produce would be much greater in the summer, although there were some winter crops (and preserved foods were to be had, such as pickled vegetables.) Some of the following are actually fruit but are included here due to how they're primarily used.

Salads of the time were usually mostly made up of lettuce and cucumbers. While not wildly popular, salads were usually to be found on an evening table at a grand supper.

Most vegetables were served both hot or cold.

ALSO SEE EACH LISTING UNDER "FOOD" IN THE F SECTION, as there may be additional information there.

This list is not all-inclusive.

These vegetables (including some herbs) could be had during the Regency:

asparagus

beets - Also seen as: beet-roots.

broccoli

cabbage

capers

cardoons

carrots

cauliflower

cayenne - Sometimes seen spelled as: chyan.

celery

chervil

chives

cresses

cucumbers

endive

French beans - What Americans call: stringbeans.

garlic

green onions - Or: scallions. I've seen Regency era receipts using either term.

kale

kidney beans

lettuce

marrow - Squash-like.

mint

mushrooms

onions

parsley

parsnips

peas

potatoes - Came to Britain ca. 1580; were widely consumed, especially as the 19th century went on, but for some reason during the Regency they were seldom grown in private gardens. All the same, they are seen in numerous receipts.

pumpkins

radishes

rhubarb

saffron - Imported.

savoy

scallions - Or: green onions. (See, above.)

skirrets - Carrot-like.

sorrel

spinach

tomatoes - Few people grew them, due to the incorrect belief they were poisonous; when used, they were invariably cooked.

truffles

turnips

- See: Covent Gardens.
- See: food - Various listings there.
- See: fruit.
- See: Nine Elms.
- See: Walworth.

Vegetarian Society, the - Formed in 1847 in Ramsgate, Kent. The writer Percy Bysshe Sherry, b. 1792-d.1822) was a fervent vegetarian, and published works on the subject.

vellum - (See: paper.)

venereal disease - A known problem during the Regency.

- See: condoms.
- See: diseases/gonorrhoea.
- See: diseases/syphilis.
- See: Grosvenor Place/Lock Hospital.

Venus - (See: planets/Venus.)

Verderers - (Also called: Foresters.) British officials who deal with *common* land that is found on Crown property that once was royal hunting grounds. Existed from the 13th century, in order to enact forest law on the king's behalf. Dealt with crimes such as: poaching of venison, and illegal woodcutting. Mostly dealt in fines. Also provided administration of the forest. Serious crimes were sent to higher courts. The Verderers regained importance in the 17-18th centuries, due to wanting to protect the planting of oaks (for shipbuilding.) Verderers can yet be found in Epping Forest, the Forest of Dean, and New Forest.

- Verderers Court: Reconstituted in 1877, as the custodians of Commoners, common rights, and the Forest topography.
    - See: Chigwell Road/King's Head Inn.
    - See: poaching.

Vere Street - Marylebone, off Oxford Street (a continuance of Welbeck Street.) The Oxford family lived nearby, and Vere was one of the family names. Here by at least 1770.

Verrers - "Verrers" derives from a French term for applying design and gilding to the rear side of a mirror's finish. (See: Glaziers' Company.)

Verrey's - Restaurant, Regent Street, established 1826. (See: Regent Street/Verry's Restaurant.)

veterinaries -

- See: doctors/Barber.
- See: London School of Veterinary Surgery.

Vicar - (See: Church of England/Vicar.)

Victoria - Westminster. A railway terminus, although the name began to be used in this area a year after Victoria's accession to the throne in 1837.

Victoria and Albert Museum - Cromwell Gardens, South Kensington. Tentative buildings were first erected in 1857, constructed on the site of the Hale House estate. It was first known as the South Kensington Museum. In 1899, the museum finally went full-forward in Cromwell Road.

- See: Broom Farm.
- See: South Kensington/South Kensington Museum.

Victoria Dock - Informal name for the Royal Victoria Dock. 1855. (See: docks/Royal Victoria Dock.)

Victoria Embankment - Victorian. (See: Embankment.)

Victoria Gate - 1854. Entrance to the road between Hyde Park and Kensington Gardens, which led to Exhibition Road.

Victoria Memorial - 1911. At one end of the Mall (the other end of the Mall is the Admiralty Arch, 1910.)

Victoria Park - Bethnal Green. 1845.

Victoria Square - 1838. Just south of where the Royal Mews were.

Victoria Street - Built in 1845, opened in 1851. During the Regency, it was the site of a miserable slum called "Devil's Acre," Westminster (in the areas of Orchard, Pye, St. Anne streets, and Shaftesbury Terrace,) a nickname used by Charles Dickens (author,) having by his time changed from an acceptable street to a depressed and undesirable locale.

Victoria Tower - 1860. A 336 foot square tower attached to the Palace of Westminster. Every Act of Parliament ever passed is housed (some would say stuffed in) here. This tower is to the south, opposite the Clock Tower/Big Ben on the north.

Note: the Clock Tower, opposite the Victoria Tower, is now called: Elizabeth Tower, a 20th century term to commemorate Queen Elizabeth II's long reign. (See: Clock Tower.)

Victuallers -

- See: Licensed Victuallers Asylum.
- See: London Society of Licensed Victuallers.

Villiers Street - Off the Strand, near what would become Charing Cross.

- 47: Gordon's Wine Cellar. London's oldest wine bar; 300 years old. (See: Gordon's Wine Cellar, under G.)

Vine Street - In 1675 it was called Little Swallow Street.

(Re)laid out in 1686; named for an 18th C. pub that had stood here, called The Vine. The pub itself might have taken its name from nearby Roman ruins of an actual vineyard. Certainly by at least 1720 it was called Vine Street. Accessed into the St. Giles rookery. Later known as Grapes Street. This street was gone by 1920, taken down when the Regent Street Quadrant was rebuilt.

vinegar - (See: food/vinegars.)

Vintners' Hall - (For the Worshipful Company of Vintners.) The Vintry, Upper Thames Street. "Vintners" is thought to derive from "wine-tonners", those who produced the wine (as opposed to Taverners, who sold it to the public.) Has medieval, if not Saxon, origins. Royal Charter in 1363.

AN ENCYCLOPAEDIA OF LONDON states: "There was a thoroughfare called Stody's Lane, where now is that part of Queen Street which forms the north approach to Southwark Bridge. Land abutting on this lane came to the Company through one of the craft, Sir John Stody, who bequeathed it in 1357. Here was the first hall - perhaps merely an old house used as a hall. In 1446 Guy Shuldham devised to the Company adjacent lands... The Company there built...a new hall, between Thames Street and the river."

The Hall burned in the Great Fire of 1666; rebuilt in 1671, of brick. It is one of the few Company Halls to have survived WWII damage intact. At the entrance there is a carved swan - because the Vintners' share with the Dyers' Company a charge to care for the

Queen's cygnets. (See: swan upping.) Livery Company. 11th in the order of precedence; one of the Great Twelve companies of London. (See: Free Vintner.)

Vintry, the - It is one of the wards of the City. (See: wards, under W.)

- The Worshipful Company of Vintners. (See: Vintners' Hall.)

votes, for women -

- See: Lower House - For women getting an equal vote in Parliament.
- See: suffrage, women's.
- See: National Union of Women's Suffrage Societies.

-W-

W. H. Smith Company - Currently at: 186 Strand. Established in 1792, then in Little Grosvenor Street. Moved near the Stamp Office at Somerset House in 1820. William Henry, and brother Henry Edward, took over their father's news sheet operation (as vendors thereof) in 1816. Became W. H. Smith & Son in 1846. Its circulating library ran from 1860-1961. Distributed news sheets outside the capital. Was responsible for creating the ISBN (International Standard Book Number) system, 1965.

Waddon - Croydon (on its western side.) Dates from at least the 12th century. Hosted the Waddon Court estate through the Middle Ages; known at that time for its mills. Industrialized from 1867, and now known for its business and retail parks.

wagering - Although the word "bet" was used during the Regency era, "wager" was a more common Regency term. (Just as "gaming" was more used than "gambling.") There was a lot of wagering to be found at the gentlemen's clubs. (See: the CLUBS section.)

Walbrook River, the - London. Importantly, the Walbrook provided ***fresh*** water to London. Runs through the City from the Thames to Shoreditch. Has been culverted over, so is no longer viewable; now called the London Bridge Sewer.

Walbrook Street - The City. Skinners (as in those who work with animal pelts) has premises here. (See: Skinners' Hall.)

Waldorf Hotel - The Aldwych. 1906-8 hotel.

Walford - Fictional borough featured in the BBC TV program *EastEnders.*

Walham Green - (See: Kensington/Walham Green.)

Wall End - Newham. Also seen spelled as Wallend - although neither use is heard much anymore; it's a part of Newham, between Barking and East Ham. Dates from the Middle Ages, a fairly isolated hamlet. Little occupied until the mid 19th century.

wallpaper - First introduced to England as "paper tapestry" (from China) in 1590. Increasingly popular from the end of the 18th century. One could have the paper hung for hire, or do it one's self. (See: Upholders' Company.)

walls, of London - (See: gates.)

Walnut Tree House - (See: Leyton/Walnut Tree House.)

Waltham Abbey - Near Epping Forest. The Abbey is more formally known as Waltham Holy Cross. Norman church, built 1057. Enlarged in the 14-15th century. Purchased in 1795 by the government for the purpose of making gunpowder there. The nave ceiling dates from 1860.

Waltham Forest -

- See: forests.
- See: Lloyd Park.

Walthamstow - Waltham Forest. (Pronounced: wall-them-stoh.) Although a fair distance from London, this village developed fairly early. First known just as Waltham. Was a gathering of hamlets in the 18th C., providing country retreats for the wealthy. Terraced houses came in after its enclosure in 1850. Has access to Epping Forest.

- Upper Walthamstow: Eastern part, north of Whipps Cross. Muddy dairy land until after 1848.
- Walthamstow Marshes: Southwest corner of Walthamstow Wetlands, from the Middles Ages (at which time it was rather perilous to cross.) Drainage began in the 16th century. About 100 acres of open space yet survive/are protected.
- Walthamstow Village: Upper Walthamstow. Also called: Church End. Dates from the time of Domesday Book. Built up after 1850.
    - Chestnuts, the: Hoe Street. House here since at least 1600. Present one dates from 1745-47.
    - Orford House: 73 Orford Road. Built ca. 1802. Now (since 1921) a private members club, and public events venue.
    - St. Mary's: 8 Church End. 1145AD origin. The Norman parts are all gone now, except some pillar bases. Still a functioning church.
    - Squire's Almhouses: 1795.
    - Vestry House: 1730; started out as the parish workhouse. Now a museum/archive.
    - White House: Dates from the 15th century. Later called Ancient House. Nicely restored in 1934.

waltz, the - A type of dance. (See: Almack's Assembly Rooms/The Waltz at Almack's.)

Walworth - In the parish of Newington Butts/Southwark. Rural; known for its abundant fruits and vegetables. One of London's favorite cricket grounds was on Walworth Common in the early 18th century. In 1820 it was inhabited by "employed and content citizens."

- Liverpool Grove: Had been Liverpool Street; laid out as Liverpool Grove in 1827.
  - St. Peter's: 1825, by Sir John Soane.
- Surrey Square: 1793-94, by architect Michael Searles. Still holds pleasant Georgian buildings.

Wandsworth - Named for the river Wandle; a corruption of the original name of Wandlesworth. In the Middle Ages was mostly farming and market gardening. The 16th C. brought in breweries. At the end of the 18th C. this district was inhabited by Huguenot refugees. Dutch metal workers followed, bringing in smelting and specializing in cookware. Since the 18th C. this area has been one for the dyeing of cloth.

- All Saints: Parish church. Existed by 1234. Rebuild, late 18th century.
- Alton Estate: 20th century.
- East Hill: Burial ground for Huguenots.
- Queenstown Road: (See under Q.)
- Wandsworth Common: Here since Domesday Book. Had two halves, known as Battersea West Heath, and Wandsworth East Heath; being collectively known as Wandsworth Common by the mid 18th century.
- Wandsworth Prison: 1851.
- West Hill: Wandsworth's western slope. Not much developed until villas came in in the mid 19th century.

Wandsworth Road - Lambeth. Ancient route. Runs from Vauxhall toward Clapham Junction. Until the late 18th C. was farms and market gardens. Developed quickly in the 1850-70s.

- Nag's Head public house: Prior to 1820.
- Plogh brewery, the: 1820.

Wanstead - Redbridge. Dates from at least the year 824. The mid 18th C. brought in wealthy landowners. There were 120 houses here in 1790.

- St. Mary the Virgin: (See: St. Mary-the-Virgin, Wanstead, in the CHURCHES section.)

Wanstead Flats - Redbridge. One of the largest bits of common land in east London (but rather featureless.) Welsh, Scots, and northern English men had a cattle market here from the late 18th C., from the end of February through the start of May. Between Epping Forest and the City of London Cemetery, Essex.

- Wanstead House: 1715. Two stories. Portland stone. Palatial. The portico had six Corinthian columns. Pulled down in 1820.

- Wanstead Park: Laid out in the 17th century. Purchased by the Corporation of London in 1881. Its waterways are fed by the River Roding.

Wapping - Tower Hamlets. Came into being in Tudor times, known then as Wapping-on-the-Woze ("Woze" indicating mud.) Dangerous district, even in daylight. South of Whitechapel. There was a wharf here by 1395. Boat-building and taverns, and pewter-casting. The marsh was drained ca. 1540. Didn't really get cleaned up until 1926 slum clearances came along.

- Ivory House warehouses: 1854. St. Katharine's Docks (see under: docks/St. Katharine's Dock/Ivory House.)
- London Docks, the: Built 1800-1820. (See "Docks.") When the 19th C. docks came in, their forty foot high walls more or less cut Wapping off from London proper, and hence the rise in the unsavory element here. Specialized in brandy, rice, tobacco, and wine. When the docks later failed, the district improved.
- Newell Street: (See: Limehouse/Newell Street.)
- Prospect of Whitby: 57 Wapping Wall. (See under the INNS/PUBS section.)
- St. Anne's: Built by Hawksmoor. (See: St. Anne's - Limehouse, under the CHURCHES section.)
- St. George's-in-the-East: North part of Wapping.
    - See under S.
    - See under the CHURCHES section.
- Wapping High Street: 18th C. houses and warehouses still stand here. Had been called Old Gravel Lane, until at least 1832.
- Wapping Police Station: (AKA: the Metropolitan Special Constabulary.) Home of the marine police, founded in 1798 (a second source said 1801); the world's oldest *uniformed* police force. At first was not part of the soon-to-be Metropolitan Police, not until well into the 19th century. (See note under: Thames River - Paragraph/"River Police Force.")

War Cabinet, the - 1938. (See: Cabinet War Rooms.)

War of 1812, the - (See: America.)

War Office, the - Was responsible for administering the Army from the 17th century, ca. 1684 to 1964, (at which time the responsibility transferred to the Ministry of Defence.) The War Office settled into the Horse Guards in 1722 - although it was never really connected to/a part of the Horse Guards; stayed there until 1858. Then moved to Cumberland House, Pall Mall for the rest of the 19th C.; then to the building now known as the Old War Office Building, at the junction of Horse Guards Avenue and Whitehall. (See: Royal Guards/War Office.)

Wardour Street - Soho. An older street had been here, but in 1686 it was rebuilt and renamed as

Wardour Street. Affiliated with the British movie film industry since the 1920s.

- 106: Thomas Sheraton, the cabinetmaker, had a business here ca. 1795-1800.

Wardrobe, Great, the -

> ➢ See: Richmond Park - About halfway down the entry.
> ➢ See: Royal Wardrobe.
> ➢ See: Tower of London/"Other Places & Things"/Crown Jewels.
> ➢ See: Tower of London/"The Towers"/Wardrobe Tower.

Wardrobe Place - The City. Once the site of the Royal (or Great) Wardrobe, where robes of state were kept.

- 3-5: Were built in 1710.

> ➢ See: Richmond Park.
> ➢ See: Royal Wardrobe.

Ward's Fields - (See: Bryanston Square.)

Warrington Crescent - Maida Vale, Paddington. 1850s.

wards - Meaning the wards (that is, the divisions) that make up the City. There are 25 wards (some sources say 27); in Tudor times there were 26. These wards allowed areas within the City to basically have control over their own local governing. Each ward elected their own alderman.

> ➢ See: Aldermen.
> ➢ See: City, the - To understand the importance of this ancient core of London.
> ➢ See: Wards Without.

Please see each of these at their own listings:

Aldersgate

Aldgate

Billingsgate

Bishopgate Within

Bishopgate Without

Bread Street

Bridge Within

Bridge Without - It is the Borough of Southwark (its ward - Bridge Without - being formed in 1554.)

Broad Street

Candlewick

Castle Baynard

Cheap

Coleman Street

Cordwainer

Cornhill

Cripplegate Within

Cripplegate Without

Dowgate - (See: Dowgate Hill.)

Farringdon Within

Farringdon Without

Langbourne - The "bourne" does not refer to a stream (as it usually would,) the name is a corruption of the Langobards (Lombards) who settled in this area.

Lime Street

Portsoken

Queenhithe

Tower

Vintry

Walbrook.

wards - Meaning those underage persons under another's protection. While a street orphan might be placed in an orphanage, school, or workhouse, many 19th C. orphans never came under official notice, living as street urchins.

Those orphans with titles and/or money were far more likely to come under the state's power. Or a dying father might have requested a friend or relation take in his child, or someone could volunteer to do so, etc. The point being, if an orphan had a title or money/the potential for money, he/she was far more likely to be named as someone's ward.

Wards Without - LONDON, FROM THE EARLIEST TIMES TO THE PRESENT DAY notes: "There had always been more squalid tenement buildings and more poverty and crime in the outer suburbs than within the City boundaries because they were not governed by the Lord Mayor...few of the suburbs outside the walls of the City had been made into wards (known as Wards Without.) ...In 1636 (Charles I) created an entirely new Corporation to govern these areas, and divided them into four large wards." Due to the Lord Mayor's jealousy and to civil war, the Corporation was swiftly suppressed, leaving no proper "wards without" governance until Queen Victoria's reign.

Warren Street - Camden. (Now north Fitzrovia.) Laid out in 1799 by Charles Fitzroy, 1st Baron Southampton, on what is now Euston Road; named for Fitzroy's wife, Anne Warren. Known for its artists, engravers in particular. Retains its Georgian appearance.

Warwick Avenue - Maida Vale, Westminster. (Pronounced: Wor-ick.) Stuccoed houses. First called Green Lane. Name changed to Warwick Road in 1827 (later Warwick Avenue.) The large homes here came along in the 1840s.

- St. Saviour's: 1856.

Warwick House - Built ca. 1663. Alternate home of Princess Charlotte, when not at Windsor, adjacent to her father (Prinny's) Carlton House palace in Pall Mall.

Warwick Lane - City. (See: Ave Maria Lane, which is the southern extension of Warwick Lane.)

- Cutlers' Hall: Here since 1887. (See under C.)
- Royal College of Physicians: (See under R.)

Warwick Street - Now called Warwick House Street, it is the remaining part of the old Warwick Street that was closed in 1661, as Pall Mall was developed.

wassail - A drink made of liquors, fruit, and spices, usually rather strong. The word means "your health." To go wassailing is to walk from house to house seeking at each a serving of wassail; the ceremonial cup or bowl was passed around; the process might include singing of carols. Some places include in their wassailing (to this day) going to the orchard, and dousing the trees with wassail in order to ask for abundant crops; a gun is often fired to wake the orchard and/or chase away evil spirits. Usually held on Twelfth Night (Epiphany.)

waste, human - Keep in mind that much filth was often dumped out one's window, well into the 19th century.

- ➢ See: sanitation.
- ➢ See: sewers.

Waste Market - Whitechapel. "Waste" describes where the market was held: on the waste in Whitechapel. (AKA: Whitechapel Market.) Dates from the mid 19th century; with more controls (to eliminate too many nuisance traders) coming along in 1904. Living up to its name, in 2008 Waste Market was the first market in the UK to recycle all the waste it generates.

waste pits - Dug in order to bury human waste. An ancient practice.

- ➢ See: nightmen.
- ➢ See: sanitation.
- ➢ You may care to see: sewers.

Watch, The - (AKA: Watchmen. They date from 1416, at least formally.) At first they were townsmen who served terms, walking the night streets and calling out the hours, but so many of those townsmen paid others to take their turn, that eventually the position of Watchman became a paid position. Charlies (or the Watch) were the older form of policing in London - and existed into the early 19th C., although their presence on London streets was significantly waning by then, as they had very little actual authority beyond carrying a cudgel and calling out the hours.

- ➢ See: Charlies.

- See: curfew.
- See: Metropolitan Police.

watches - There were pocket watches, sometimes worn on a chain, sometimes stashed in one's waistcoat pocket. There were also watches that women could pin to their clothing. The wristwatch wasn't invented until 1868.

- See: Soho/Church Street.
- You may care to see: clocks.

Watchhouses - (Also seen as: watch-houses.)

- See: Charlies.
- See: Marylebone Watch House.
- See: St. Bartholomew-the-Great, under the CHURCHES section.
- See: St. Clement-Danes watch-houses.

Watchmen - (See: Watch, The.)

water - Not to cast aspersions, but I'm not sure I'd care for a glass of water to drink from the *modern* Thames River. Centuries-old London already knew better; the river was undeniably polluted in the 18-19th centuries. Most Londoners' diet included small beer (weaker than today's, with only about 2% alcohol) in order to avoid directly drinking Thames (or other City) water; the brewing process made the source liquid consumable. Even young children were given small beer, especially if they were laborers. The consumption of small beer lasted well past the Regency era. Direct water consumption from a source only happened outside City limits...

...Or from wells, or sometimes natural springs, around which often sprang up spas, a destination where one drank "the waters" for one's supposed health. Indeed, the city of Bath came to prominence not least because of its famous spa waters - also known of and utilized by the ancient Romans. Note that reaching a spa, at least from London, usually involved a fair investment of travel time.

- See: beer.
- See: Chelsea Waterworks Company.
- See: drinking water.
- See: forcier - A water pump.
- See: General Board of Health - 1848.
- See: Metropolitan Drinking Fountain - For watering horses, 1859.
- See: milk - For an alternative to drinking water.
- See: spa.
- See: Thames, the.
- See: the INNS/PUBS section - The notes at the start.

➢ See: Walbrook River.

Water Gate - (AKA: York Water Gate. Not to be confused with Water Gate, an early name for Traitor's Gate at the Tower of London.) At the bottom of Buckingham Street. A huge arch. Marked the entrance to the Villiers Palace (from the Thames.)

➢ See: Stable Yard Road/York House.

➢ See: York Water Gate.

Water Lane - Constructed in 1275-85, land reclaimed from the River Thames, so Edward I could create the Outer Ward of the Tower of London. By at least 1649 known as Tower Street. Now known as Great Tower Street. (See under G.)

Waterloo - Lambeth. Developed as a district post-Regency, especially after the 1840s rails came in.

Waterloo Barracks - Tower of London. (Not to be confused with Wellington Barracks.)

Also alternatively known as the Jewel House, since the Crown Jewels were moved in here in 1994 (where they remain.)

➢ See: Tower of London/"Other Places & Things"/Crown Jewels.

➢ See: Tower of London/"Other Places & Things"/Waterloo Barracks.

Waterloo Place - Piccadilly. Built by John Nash, 1816, as part of the proposed Regent Street. Construction was meant to be the southern end of the sweep from Carlton House Terrace to Regent's Park. Prior to 1816 it had been a series of small streets and alleys.

- 107 Pall Mall (right at the corner of Waterloo Place): The Athenaeum. The gentlemen's club, 1824. (See: Athenaeum, under the CLUBS section.)
- Duke of York Column: 1834. Pink granite.

Waterloo Road - Lambeth and Southwark. Built ca. 1816.

- St. John's Waterloo Church, 1824. Largely destroyed in WWII, but restored in 1951.

Waterlow Park - 1889. (See: Highgate Hill/Lauderdale House.)

watermen - Those men who ferried customers across the rivers (most importantly the Thames) for a living. Before coaches became popular in the early 17th C. people mostly traveled by water (or by walking.) Watermen existed by at least King John's time (12-13th C.)

The watermen produced the first on-the-water police force in July, 1798 - separate from the Watchmen on land. (See: Thames River - Paragraph on "River Police Force.")

➢ See: Watermen's and Lightermen's Hall.

➢ You may care to see: bargemen.

Watermen's and Lightermen's Hall - (For the Company of Watermen and Lightermen. Note that it is not the "Worshipful Company of..."; this City Guild has *not* been given a Grant of Livery.) The company licensed Thames Watermen (a task now done by the Maritime and

Coastguard Agency.)

Watermen: took paying customers across the Thames (and other estuaries around London,) in a time when there were few bridges. (See: the BRIDGES section - The note at the start.)

Lightermen: Port of London men who transported goods between quays and ships, using flat-bottomed barges called lighters. The Lightermen were joined with the Watermen in 1700. (See: Lightermen, under L.)

The Hall had been in the neighborhood of Upper Thames Street; this burned in the Great Fire of 1666. Rebuilt in 1719-22. Located now at: 18 St. Mary-at-Hill, Lower Thames Street, Eastcheap; present site purchased in 1776; moved in in 1780.

The Watermen's and Lightermen's Company was formed in 1514 under Henry VIII. The Company does not have livery (and never did,) nor ever a charter. Nor does it number in precedence (among the other Companies.) AN ENCYCLOPAEDIA OF LONDON states: "Its constitution has always been settled by statute."

Watier's Club - (Also early on occasionally seen spelled as "Waiter's Club.") 81 Piccadilly. Begun in 1805. Closed 1819. (See under the CLUBS section.)

Watling - Barnet. There was a farm here from 1321, and it existed until it was demolished in 1927. Named after the nearby Watling Street. Grew up as a district from ca. 1927.

Watling Street - Ancient. First called by this name in 1230, although it is thought a road existed here back into Roman times; ancient Dover Road was the first bit of what would become Watling Street.

- See: Dover Road.
- See: Edgware.

Waverly Park - (See: Newlands - Southwark, under N.)

Wax Chandlers' Hall - (Also seen as: Waxchandlers.) For the Worshipful Company of Wax Chandlers. Wood Street, Cheapside. Beeswax, as opposed to tallow. Beeswax candles were more expensive than were ones made of tallow; more likely to be seen in churches, or the homes of nobility or royalty. 6 Gresham Street; here since 1501, although the guild formed prior to 1330. Its hall has always been located here. Royal Charter in 1484. Rebuilt following the Great Fire of 1666. Demolished in 1852, with a small Hall by C. Fowler replacing it. Their sixth and current Hall dates from 1954, following WWII damage. Livery Company. 20th in the order of precedence. Currently one of the City's smallest counts of guild members, about 120. Now includes beekeeping and honey production.

- See: candles.
- You may care to see: Tallow Chandlers' Hall.

weald - Seen in place names, it is a Saxon word for a wood.

weapons - Gunshot was never manufactured within the City (the Square Mile,) due to its explosion nature.

In 1807, the scent-bottle lock (which came to be known as the percussive cap) was invented by Alexander John Forsyth (Scottish Presbyterian clergyman); this made it simpler to load pistols/rifles. Regency men liked the new ignition device, and had their flintlocks converted to use them. The tube (or pill) lock was invented in 1814, by Joseph Manton (gunsmith,) a more reliable form (single-use pills or pellets) of ignition; also adopted by many Regency gentlemen.

- See: Enfield/Enfield Lock - Made muskets, which started Enfield's connection with gun-making.
- See: Gunmakers' Company.
- See: gunpowder.
- See: Hurlingham Club - 1867 gentleman's shooting club.
- See: knives.
- See: Manton's - Shooting gallery.
- See: Tower, the/White Tower.
- See: Wilkinson - Sword-makers.
- See: Woolwich/Royal Laboratory - For manufacturing explosives, fuses, and shot for military use.

weavers - Those who wove cloth for a living.

- See: fabric/cotton - Power looms vs. handlooms.
- See: fabric/silk - Jacquard loom.
- See: Edmonton.
- See: silkweavers.
- See: Summerstown.
- See: Weavers' Company.

Weavers' Company - (AKA: the Worshipful Company of Weavers.) Possibly the oldest London guild, certainly the first to have a Royal Charter granted (by Henry II,) ca. 1155. Its final Hall stood in Basinghall Street, and was demolished in 1856. Livery Company. 42nd in the order of precedence.

Webb, William - Robemaker. (See: Ede & Ravenscroft.)

Webber Street - (See: Higgler's Lane.)

weddings - Popular/fashionable churches for weddings:

- St. George's, Hanover Square.
- St. Margaret's, Westminster.

There were more. On the whole, people married at one's parish church. Weddings tended to be private affairs, sparsely attended (with the exception of some royal weddings); the lavish type of wedding for non-royals did not come along until into the Victorian era. (See: marriage.)

Wedgwood dishes -

- See: St. James's Square/York Street.
- See: Soho/Wedgwood.

Weights and Measures Office - 1869-1938. (See: Westminster Palace/Jewel Tower.)

Welbeck Street - Marylebone. Historically linked with the medical profession, starting from 1799. (See: Vere Street.)

Well Hall - Greenwich. There was a building recorded as being here as early as the 13th C.; and a Tudor building of this name was here by the 16th century. Sir Gregory Page obtained the property in the 1730s, demolishing all but the inner moat and the barn (the latter of which is currently a pub.)

- Well Hall Road: 1910. Had been Woolwich Lane (and is now the A205.)

Well Street - West End. Maudslay, Sons & Field, mechanical engineers. Established in 1795.

Well Walk - Hampstead.

- 6: John Constable (artist) lived here in the 1820s. (Now known as number 40.)

Welling - Bexley. In 1362 was known as "Wellyngs." Turned into a coaching halt on the way to Dover. Rural/market gardens until the 1920s.

Wellington Arch - (See: Hyde Park Corner/Wellington Arch.)

Wellington Barracks - (Not to be confused with Waterloo Barracks in the Tower of London.) 1834-59. Birdcage Walk. According to LONDON STEP BY STEP, Wellington Barracks is built on the site of the Great Storehouse, which burned down in 1841. Now contains the Guards' Museum.

- Guards' Chapel of Wellington Barracks: Built in 1839-40 to resemble a Grecian temple. The interior was drab enough that the chapel was closed in 1877 until funds could be raised to refurbish it. Seriously damaged by bombing in 1944; rebuilt in 1961-3.

Wellington boots - (AKA: Wellies.) Not until 1856. Named for the Duke, who wore a leather version that had been adapted from Hessian boots. Always meant to be "practical wear," they are now waterproof rubber boots.

Wellington Museum - (See: Aspley House.)

Wellington Street - Covent Garden. Laid out in 1817; known as Charles Street until 1846. (See: Charles Street.) The northern portion of the road took several more years to be completed. The auction house Sotheby's was here. (See: Bond Street/New Bond Street/34-35/Sotheby's.)

Welsh Office - (See: Gwydyr House.)

Wembley - Brent. While this tiny hamlet existed from 825, it never grew much (possibly because much of the area is common land.) In 1805 there were three farmhouses, one inn, two mansions, and some 20 other houses here. The old village basically dissolved with the coming of the rails and the 20th century.

- Wembley Hill Estate: 1899.

Wembley Park, and **Wembley Stadium** - Brent. 1922-4. Started life as a country estate and mansion. Sold in 1881, turned into Wembley Park. The first Football (soccer) Association Cup was played for here in April, 1923. (See: tennis.)

Wennington - Havering. Described as "remote and dispersed." Dates from the 10th century. From 1066 (and possibly earlier) the manor was held by Westminster Abbey. Marshy, with areas being drained/reclaimed over the centuries.

- Church of St. Mary and St. Peter: Dates from approximately 1198. Much of it yet dates from the 14th century.

Wentworth Place - Hampstead. Now known as Keat's Grove, (and it hosts the home of the poet, Keats' House.) John Keats moved here in 1818-20. Now one building, at the time it was a pair of semi-detached houses, built in 1815 on the edge of the Heath. Living in the other part of the building was Fanny Brawne, who became betrothed to Keats. He contracted consumption and died of it, several years later, never having married Fanny. (You may care to see: Kentish Town/2 Wesleyan Place - For where Keats lived in the summers.)

Wesleyan Place - (See: Kentish Town/2 Wesleyan Place.)

West Acton - Ealing. In 1786 there was virtually no habitation here. Even by 1876 this area had avoided the slums to be found elsewhere in Acton.

West Barnes - Merton. Its history is well tangled with Raynes Park, which consumes most of West Barnes. Parts of the area were owned by the Merton Priory in the 14-15th centuries. West Barnes farm ran from Merton Common to the Beverly Brook. The farm was given up when the Dissolution came. Divided between two brothers in the early 17th C., becoming Moat Farm (survived into the 1920s) and Park House Farm. The latter was acquired in 1867 and became Raynes Park. (See under R.)

West Brompton - Kensington & Chelsea. Until the late 18th C. was fields and market gardens. The Gunter family (the confectioners - See under G) bought much of this area in 1801; through the century they and their lessees built thousands of houses. Now virtually squeezed out by the spreading of Chelsea, Earls Court, and Fulham. (See: West Brompton Cemetery.)

West Brompton Cemetery - Forty acres. Founded in 1837; consecrated in 1840. At first was called the West of London and Westminster Cemetery. Soon was more commonly referred to simply as "Brompton Cemetery." (See under B.)

West Drayton - Hillingdon. Known by this name by the 15th century. In 1547 Henry VIII gave the manor to Sir William Paget (statesman/accountant); his line held it into the 18th C.; only the brick wall and gatehouse of the manor house survived from its 18th C. demolition. Was a small agricultural area until ca. 1838, when rails and brickmaking came to the district.

- St. Martin's church: 12th C. origins, yet exists.

West Dulwich - Lambeth/Southwark. Dates from at least 1344. Grew up in Victorian and Edwardian times; did not have the West Dulwich name until 1926. (You may care to see: Dulwich.)

West Ealing -

- See: Ealing/Northfields.
- See: Ealing Dean.

West End - Hillingdon. An almost forgotten name now (as it is swallowed up by airport extensions.)

- Elder Farmhouse: 17th C., brick frontage from 1752.
- Pheasant Public House: West End Lane. Ca. 1800.

West End, the - Westminster. This is <u>the West End</u> most people refer to, as in a posh place to live, shop, and be entertained. It has no clearly defined boundaries; it includes Bond Street, Oxford Street, Piccadilly Circus, and Regent Street, plus Covent Garden, Leicester Square, and Shaftesbury Avenue - in other words, the *tony* Mayfair, shopping, and theatre areas.

After the Great Fire of 1666 more homes were built here, by those who were no longer as interested in residing in the (crowded) City. "West End" is now a term that generally implies more privileged homes/persons; the term was in use as such by the early 19th century. In a more modern sense, it's also fairly synonymous with references to attending the theatre. As noted, it takes in the areas of: (for theaters) Leicester Square, Piccadilly Circus, and Shaftesbury Avenue, and (for shopping) Oxford Street, and Regent Street.

In Georgian times this was the center of furniture-making. (See: Leicester Square.)

CHAMBERS LONDON GAZETTEER explains: "...the West End is a comparable newcomer to the capital's social scene. When the City of London first took shape, its prime entertainment zone was...at Southwark. With the shift of government and ecclesiastical influence to Westminster, development...did not at first reach this far inland... Early in the 19th century shops in the West End began to cater for the many rather than the privileged few, and music halls and other places of entertainment were built." When the rails came in the 19th C., they cemented the West End's status as a place for entertainment.

(See: East End - The West End's antithesis.)

West Finchley - Barnet. Less distinct or historic than Finchley proper.

- Lovers (or Love) Walk: 1800; still exists.
- Nether Street: Brick houses and cottages were here since the Middle Ages; though to its west the area was heavily wooded into the 18th century. In the next century it went from elms to hay fields.

West Ham - Newham. First mentioned in the 12th century. Belonged to the Abbey of Stratford, 1135-1538. After the Dissolution this area suffered. Recovery came in the 17th C., bringing in leather and weaving business, followed by rural homes for City businessmen. In 1762 there were 455 mansions and 245 cottages here. The 1840s brought in chemical works, distilleries, and textile factories.

- West Ham Park: 1874.

West Hampstead - Camden. Throughout the medieval period this subsection of Hampstead barely qualified as a hamlet, growth beginning in the 17th century. There was only one inn and two beer-shops here by 1851. Built up ca. 1890-1905.

- West End Lane: Rain frequently made this road "impassably muddy."

West Heath - Bexley. Little developed before Victorian times.

West Heath - Camden. Extension of Hampstead Heath. From the 1730s there were horse races here. Not much developed until the later 19th century.

West Hendon - Barnet. Was long ago part of Tunworth (now Kingsbury) but came under Westminster Abbey control; under the parish/manor of Hendon by the 10th century. No real settlement here until the late 1860s.

- Welsh Harp reservoir: 1830s.

West India Docks - (In the Isle of Dogs.) Begun in 1800, opened in 1802. (See under: docks/West India Docks.)

West Kensington - Built ca. 1880. Not really in the Borough of Kensington; is actually in Hammersmith.

- See: Fulham/North End.
- See: Hammersmith/West Kensington.

West Kilburn - Westminster. Hard to define district, north of Harrow Road and west of Maida Vale.

- Queen's Park: An estate built after 1873.
- St. Peter's Park: Mid 1860s; the far eastern side of West Kilburn. Now sometimes called Maida Hill.

West Lane - West Smithfield. (See: Chick Lane.)

West London Infirmary and Dispensary - 1818. (See: Charing Cross Hospital.)

West Norwood - (See: Norwood/West Norwood.)

West of London and Westminster Cemetery - (See: West Brompton Cemetery.)

West Ruislip - (See: Ruislip/West Ruislip.)

West Smithfield - (See: Smithfield.)

- Henry VIII statue, on top of the Henry VIII Gateway. It is the only statue of Henry VIII in all London. It commemorates his giving of St. Bartholomew Hospital to the City. (This is the same statue mentioned at the entry: St. Bartholomew's Hospital/Henry VIII statue.)

West Strand Improvements - Built ca. 1830.

West Sutton - (See: Sutton/West Sutton.)

West Twyford - Ealing/Brent. (See: Park Royal/West Twyford.)

West Wickham - Bromley. Ancient. The "west" was added in the 13th century. In the late 16th century Samuel Lennard got Wickham Court; his descending family held the estate for nearly four centuries. A wealthy locale.

- Wickham Court: Remodeled in the 19th C. with a "castle-like" appearance.

Westbourne - The stream. Flowed from Hampstead into Hyde Park. Long covered over; now known as the Ranelagh Sewer.

  - See: Hyde Park/Serpentine.
  - See: Sloane Square/Bloody Bridge.

Westbourne Green - Westminster. Hard to say these days, but most sources believe this area lies midway between Bayswater and Maida Vale, north of the Westway (A40.) In the 17th C. there were just a few houses in this popular beauty space. Westbourne Green was the forebear, with Westbourne Grove and Westbourne Park growing into it until 18th C. developers came in; didn't really develop much until ca. 1801-1820s.

Westbourne Grove - Westminster. (See: Westbourne Green.) An 1830s single street, with offshoots. Was Bayswaters' commercial center in the later 19th century.

Westbourne Park - Westminster/Kensington/Chelsea. (See: Westbourne Green.)

- Westbourne Place: 1640s mansion. Turned into Westbourne Park after a demolition in the 1850s and a rebuild of two villas now called Westbourne Park Road, and Westbourne Park Villas, in the 1860s. For a while called Westbournia.

Westbourne Terrace - 1847-52. Until 1840, cricket was played on this site.

Westcheap - (See: Cheapside.)

Westcombe - Greenwich. Westcombe was separate from Combe since before Norman times, by Westcombe Hill. The Crown owned it, but then it came into the hands of Gregory Ballard, Richard II's butler. Remained farmlands through the Middle Ages. In the 18th C. two properties dominated the area:

- Westcombe Park: 1720s. 50 acre garden, attached to Westcombe House, pulled down ca. 1850s. In 1876 middle classes built here.
- Woodlands: 1774. For the merchant John Julius Angerstein (first chairman of Lloyd's of London,) died 1823. (There is also a town called Woodlands/Hounslow - See at its own listing.)

Western Exchange, the - (See: Bond Street/Old Bond Street/Western Exchange.)

Western Literary and Scientific Institute - (See: Leicester Square/Western Literary and Scientific Institute.)

Westminster -

(NOTE: It is easy to get confused between: Westminster (the area of,) Westminster Abbey, Westminster Cathedral, Westminster Hall, and Westminster Palace, etc., although they are all separate things. If something seems "off," try doublechecking which entry you mean to be reading. Or even if perhaps you really are looking for a ***Whitehall*** *entry.)*

"Westminster" means two things: 1. The district which encompasses the seat of government; and 2. Westminster Palace, the original, ancient building/king's seat from which the governmental district derived its name. (See: Westminster Palace - At its own listing.)

WESTMINSTER VS. WHITEHALL: In reading many sources, one finds the statement "it is the seat of government" gets applied to *both* Westminster and Whitehall.

Here's the explanation: Whitehall, like Westminster, was a royal palace. When Whitehall Palace burned in 1698, much of the government/royal business moved to Westminster Palace, (and the royal residence became St. James's Palace, which it still officially remains.) Whitehall was never rebuilt as a *palace.* In terms of representing "the government" (area,) Westminster overtook Whitehall at that time.

The two are also physical neighbors, one blending into the other, or across the street, or attached to one another - allowing for the flow and function of both. Both Westminster and Whitehall are still very much governmental areas, with Whitehall hosting Downing Street, the Horse Guards, Scotland Yard, and more; and Westminster hosting Big Ben in its Elizabeth Tower, Civil Service offices, the Houses of Parliament, the Treasury, and more. So it's fair to say either is the "seat of government," although the whole truth is together they both are.

Westminster stands on the Island of Thorney. (See: Island of Thorney, under I - For more of an explanation of the name "Westminster"); the name derives from the fact this area (this minster) was west of the City - as opposed to St. Paul's Cathedral, which was east. (You may care to see: minster, under M.)

Cnut, the Danish king, had a palace here in the 11th C., and Kings of England were based here since Edward the Confessor had the Abbey rebuilt next to Westminster Palace, in 1042. They stayed until 1512, when Henry VIII moved out of Westminster Palace to Whitehall Palace. Council meetings and parliamentary gatherings (i.e. Parliament itself) were held here since 1265-1834, when it burned.

In medieval times Westminster was a distance away from London (which city had yet to grow large enough to encompass the area of Westminster.) So at that time the seat of government (the king) really was separated from London - and so the distinction between the Capital City vs. the seat of the monarchy/government remains to this day, even though Westminster is now engulfed by larger London.

During the reigns of Henry III/Edward I, four <u>women</u> were summoned to (served in) Parliament, being landowners: the Abbess of Barking, the Abbess of St. Mary's of Winchester, the Abbess of Shaftesbury, and the Abbess of Wilton. There is no record of their gender being an issue or contention. (Keep in mind that during/around the 13-15th centuries, while the world was a patriarchal place, women sometimes found themselves in positions of power. Men went off to war or crusades, and often wives held the castle until they returned. Abbesses managed a lot of land and power via the church. So this was a time when a woman could yield a large amount of influence, despite the usual gender roles.)

In the midst of its eminence, Westminster still managed to house some of the worst slums. Damp and unhealthy terrain. One of the slum areas in the 19th century became known as "the Devil's Acre," in the area of Orchard, Pye and St. Anne streets. (See: Victoria Street.)

- Cannon Row: There at least by the 1670s. (See under C.)
- Carlton House Terrace: 1827. (See under C.)
- Court of Chancery, the: Built by John Soane, 1822-5. Demolished in 1883. (See under: Courts of Common Law.)
- Court of King's Bench, the: Built by John Soane, 1822-5. (See: Courts of Common Law/Court of King's Bench.)
- Dean's Yard: 14th C. or earlier. Secluded, grassy square. Private property, belonging to the Dean and Chapter of Westminster. Is the entrance to Westminster School, at Ashburnham House. (See under A.) Near Little Dean's Yard. (See: Dean's Yard, under D.)
- Exchequer, the: (AKA: Her Majesty's Exchequer.) Ancient. The name derives

from the checkered cloth that was used - it had alternating squares of color to make it easier to maintain separated piles of money by accountants. (See: Treasury, under T.)

- Houses of Parliament: 1834, completed in 1870. Before fire in 1834, the two houses of Parliament were in Westminster Palace (of which only the Banqueting Hall remained after the fire.)
    - ➢ See: Houses of Parliament.
    - ➢ See: Lower House.
    - ➢ See: Upper House.
    - ➢ See: Westminster Palace.
- Jewel House: A separate, small stone building built by Edward III to house his treasure/crown jewels.

  Although briefly used to house the crown jewels, do not confuse this small building with the much longer-term/utilized Jewel House(s) in the Tower of London. (See: Tower of London/Crown Jewels - For the latter/the place where the crown jewels have long been displayed.)
- Little Dean's Yard: Behind this is the reputedly oldest garden in London, about 1,000 years old. The arch dates from 1734 and is deemed "solid and appropriate."
    - o Westminster School. (See at its own listing.)
- Maida Vale: (See under M.)
- Old Compton Street: (See: Soho/Old Compton Street.)
- Parliament Square: At the northwest end of what had been the Palace of Westminster. (See under P.)
- Queen Anne's Gate (Street): 1770s. (See under Q.)
- St. John's, Smith Square: 18th century. (See under the CHURCHES section.)
- St. Margaret: Largely 16th century. Sir Walter Raleigh may be buried here in the chancel. The House of Commons' church since 1614. (See under the CHURCHES section.)
- St. Martin-in-the-Field: (See under the CHURCHES section.)
- St. Stephen's - Westminster chapel. First built supposedly in 1141. Became the home to the House of Commons until the new Parliament building in 1834.
    - ➢ See: Lower House.
    - ➢ See: St. Stephen's Undercroft, under the CHURCHES section.
    - ➢ See: Westminster Hall.
    - ➢ See: Westminster Palace.

- St. Stephen's Porch: The public entrance to the new (1834) Houses of Parliament.
- Smith Square: Smith Square contains Barton Street, Cowley Street, and Lord North Street - all early 18th C. streets, "beautiful."
    - Barton Street. (See under B.)
    - Cowley Street. (See under C.)
    - Lord North Street: 1720-25. (See under L.)
    - St. John's Church: Built here in the 18th century. (See: St. John - Smith Square, under the CHURCHES section.)
- Star Chamber: (See under S.)
- Thorney Island: The beginning place of Westminster. (See: Island of Thorney.)
- Treasury, the: (See under T.)
- Tufton Street: (See under T.)
- Victoria Tower: 1860. (See under V.)
- West Kilburn: 1860s. (See at its own listing.)
- Westminster Abbey: (See at its own listing.)
- Westminster Hall: (See at its own listing.)
- Westminster Palace: (See at its own listing.)
- Westminster School: (See at its own listing.)

Westminster Abbey - Broad Sanctuary, Parliament Square. Officially known as "the Collegiate Church of St. Peter at Westminster." Does not hold cathedral status.

Not to be confused with Westminster Cathedral.

It is Britain's official church.

Where the kings (and queens) of England have been crowned ever since William the Conqueror.

The earliest church in England, possibly dating from as early as the year 605, although no records of it date from before ca. 970 exist. It started as a monastery, dedicated to St. Peter, and was "insignificant." Rebuilt by Edward the Confessor in "much grand style," the Abbey was consecrated in December, 1065.

In 1245, the "new Abbey" was begun (rebuilt) under Henry III, now in the Gothic style.

The present day chapter house, choir, transepts, parts of the cloisters, and one bay of the nave date from the 1245-69 rebuild. Other parts of the cloisters date from the 13th and 14th centuries. The beautiful Henry VII Chapel was added in 1503-12. The west front and west twin towers were added by Hawksmoor in 1734 (with the lower portions having first been restored by Wren after the Great Fire); completed in 1745. The present north entrance carvings are Victorian.

Technically, it ceased to be Westminster Abbey after 1540, when the monastery was dissolved by Henry VIII (then being dubbed the Collegiate Church of St. Peter at Westminster in 1560, by Elizabeth I,) but the old name remains. Because the dean answers directly to the sovereign, the Abbey is therefore a "royal peculiar," (since 1560.)

St. Edward's Chapel contains the Coronation chair, and the tombs of numerous monarchs; eighteen in fact, including Elizabeth I. There are more intriguing BURIALS/MEMORIALS in the Abbey:

- Geoffrey Chaucer is buried here (not for his writings, but because he was the king's Clerk of the Works - the funerary monument to him was added in Tudor times; his burial here was the beginning of Poets' Corner.
- Ben Jonson (buried, by his own suggestion, standing up, so he would not take up too much room, his name was misspelled on his tomb.)
- Samuel Johnson (lexicographer/author of the first English dictionary.)
- Milton has a memorial here (but is actually buried at St. Giles, Cripplegate.)
- Aphra Behn rests here (the first professional female writer in England, 17th century.)
- Shakespeare was not interred in Poet's Corner (in the south transept) until 1740.
- Robert Burns wasn't brought to Poet's Corner either until 1885.
- William Blake, too, wasn't here until so late as 1957.
- In fact, today we see some 5,000 graves and memorials within the abbey (in part because, to raise funds, the church would allow those who could afford the fee to be buried here.)

- Deanery Courtyard: (See under D.)
- Jerusalem Chamber: (See under J.)
- Poet's Corner: In 1400 Geoffrey Chaucer was buried in Westminster Abbey. Edmund Spenser was buried near Chaucer in 1599, and the idea of a "Poet's Corner" was born. (See: list of BURIALS/MEMORIALS, above.)
- Stone of Scone: (AKA: the Kingstone. AKA: the Coronation Stone.) The kings of England having previously been crowned upon the Kingstone at Kingston-upon-Thames, after the late 13th C., were then crowned in Westminster Abbey, upon the Stone of Scone (or Stone of Destiny.) It was brought/confiscated from Scone, Perthshire, Scotland by Edward I (in Scotland it had been used in the

Coronation of 34 Scottish kings, dating from 850 AD.) In 1301, Edward had an oak throne built to house the sandstone Stone. It now resides in the Edward the Confessor shrine in the Abbey, behind the high altar.

- ➢ See: Kingston-upon-Thames/Kingstone.
- ➢ See: the INTRO-REIGNS section/British Kings and Queens & Their Reigns/Edward I.

- Waterford Crystal Chandeliers, the: Date from 1965.
- West Towers, the: Added in 1735-45.
- Westminster School: Located behind Westminster Abbey. (See at its own listing.)

Westminster Bank - (AKA: National Westminster Bank, since 1968.) Began in 1834 as London County and Westminster Bank.

In 1833, the National Provincial Bank was founded; it merged with Westminster Bank in 1968, the two becoming: the National Westminster Bank. Has been part of the Royal Bank of Scotland Group since 2000; the Group's core domestic business is now a subsidiary of NatWest Holdings. At 250 Bishopsgate.

Westminster Bridge - 1750. (See under the BRIDGES section.)

Westminster Bridge Road - Lambeth and Southwark. Land for this road was purchased in 1740-46, and was built soon thereafter.

- Astley's Amphitheatre: (See under A.)

Westminster Cathedral - *Not to be confused with Westminster Abbey, nor with Hampshire's Winchester Cathedral.*

On the far west side of Westminster, off Francis Street. Erected in 1618 on the site of an old prison (which in 1836 was rebuilt and called Tothill Prison.) Jane Austen (author) died on July 18th, 1817, and was buried at the cathedral.

The 1836 building was expanded in 1850, via the purchase of Elliott's Lawn, expensive adjoining property.

The land was bought by the Catholic Church in 1867, but it was years until the Cathedral's design was set. The foundation stone was laid in 1895. Finished in 1903, to designs by John Francis Bentley (ecclesiastical architect,) Italian-Byzantine style. It is England's principal Roman Catholic cathedral; seat of the Cardinal Archbishop of Westminster. (See: Westminster Cathedral, under the CHURCHES section.)

Westminster Hall - Off New Palace Yard. At: 3 St. Margaret St., Westminster. The oldest surviving governmental building in Britain (in its original form since it was founded, to now.) Built in 1097-9, by William II (William Rufus,) as a part of Westminster Palace.

Measures 67 feet x 240 feet (20 meters x 73 meters; floor area: 17,000 square feet (1,547 square meters.) The walls were six feet thick (2 meters); today being heightened and refaced.

Prior to their coronation, the king or queen would be acclaimed by their lords here, and coronation breakfasts or banquets held here.

In 1394-1401, Richard II had it rebuilt by Henry Yevele, who added the 600 ton hammer-beam roof's massive buttresses. (This version was heavily restored in 1820.) Richard II also commissioned other trappings, including 26 carved angels on the roof, and niches filled with images of past kings (and including Richard II.)

In the 19th and 20th centuries, repairs were done, including stairs to the new St. Stephen's Hall by Charles Barry in 1850; restored flying buttresses in 1883 by J. L. Pearson; 1913-24 repairs to the roof; and post-WWII repairs.

Courts of Law were held here, (until 1820, when they moved to nearby buildings.) Over some 600 years, the following courts were located here:

- Common Law Courts: (AKA: Courts of Common Law and Equity. AKA: Courts of Law. AKA: Law Courts, the.) In the 13th C. was at the opposite end of the Hall from the Royal Courts of Justice. Moved in 1741 to a new building of its own immediately outside the Hall. When the area had to be cleared for George IV's coronation in 1820, the courts were built anew along the Hall's western wall; designed by Sir John Soane, opened in 1826. Were outgrown in some 40-odd years, leading to their removal in 1882 to the Strand. (See: Courts of Common Law and Equity, under C.)
- Court of Chancery: In Westminster Hall from 1835-58. (See: Courts of Common Law and Equity/Court of Chancery, under C.)
- Court of Common Pleas: Civil cases, between Subject and Subject. (See: Courts of Common Law and Equity/Court of Common Pleas, under C.)
- Court of Exchequer: (See: Courts of Common Law and Equity/Court of Exchequer, under C.)
- Court of King's Bench: (See: Courts of Common Law ad Equity/Court of King's Bench, under C.)
- Courts of Requests: The House of Lords moved here in 1801.
    - See: Courts of Common Law and Equity/Courts of Requests, under C.
    - See: Upper House.
- House of Commons:
    - See: Houses of Parliament.

   - See: Lower House.
   - See: Upper House.
- House of Lords:
   - See: Lower House.
   - See: Upper House.
- Law Courts:
   - See: Common Law Courts, above.
   - See: Royal Courts of Justice, below.
- Royal Courts of Justice: From the 13th C. to the mid 19th C. this was home to the first English law courts - the Royal Courts of Justice (See under R,) also known as the Law Courts - and remained so until their removal to a Gothic building in the Strand 1882. (The law courts survived the 1834 fire.) In the 17th C. the COURTS OF CHANCERY and the KING'S BENCH were at one end of the hall (at the other end was the Court of Common Pleas.) High Treason trials were held here until 1825. When the area had to be cleared for George IV's coronation in 1820, the courts were built anew along the Hall's western wall, designed by Sir John Soane, opened in 1826. Outgrown in some 40-odd years, leading to their removal in 1882 to the Strand.
- St. Stephen's Cloisters: Rebuilt in 1526-9 by John Chambers.
- St. Stephen's Crypt: Purportedly first build in 1141. Was home to the House of Commons; was one of only two buildings to survive the 1834 fire at Westminster Palace (along with the Royal Courts of Justice.) Restored as St. Stephen's Hall in the late 19th century.
   - See: Courts of Common Law and Equity.
   - See: St. Stephen's Crypt, under the CHURCHES section.
   - See: Westminster/St. Stephen's Crypt.

Westminster Hospital - Dean Ryle Street, Horseferry Road. Founded in 1720. Built in 1729. Remodeled in 1832.

- Westminster Medical Society: Were discussions, held at Westminster Hospital. Existed by at least 1838.

Westminster Medical Society - (See: Westminster Hospital/Westminster Medical Society.)

Westminster Palace - (AKA: the Palace of Westminster.) Isle of Thorney, alongside the Thames, east of Westminster Abbey. Also once known as "the House of Parliament," because the Upper and Lower Houses resided here until a devastating fire in 1834.

   - See: Houses of Parliament.

> ➢ See the paragraph below that begins: "From 1532..."

Westminster Palace was the original "seat of government," is now also the all-encompassing name for the district in which governmental concerns are carried out.

CHAMBERS LONDON GAZETTEER explains: "From 785 it was the site of a monastic foundation which Edward the Confessor re-endowed and to which he added a large, stone abbey church, consecrated in 1065; this was referred to as the 'west minster' to distinguish it from the 'east minster,' St. Paul's Cathedral in the City of London."

Built in 1042 for Edward the Confessor; starting life known as *Westminster Hall.* (See at its own listing.) Was a "palace," despite being only one room with one solar (private chamber) to which the king could retire - being designated a "palace" because the king lived and worked here. As halls/rooms/solars/courtyards were added, the hall took on more of the look we modern viewers consider to be a palace - that is, multiple rooms for multiple purposes. The "Palace of Westminster" is *still* the official name for the Houses of Parliament (reflecting its origin as a royal residence,) although the two are located now in different places.

From 1532 (when there was a fire, which caused the king to move elsewhere - and royalty never again resided here,) this then served as the home of the House of Commons (St. Stephen's Chapel,) and home of the House of Lords (White Chamber,) until Oct. 16/1834, when all was burned to the ground except for Westminster Hall, St. Stephen's crypt, and the Jewel Tower. (See: Jewel House/Westminster, not to be confused with: Tower of London/Crown Jewels.)

The seat of government (Houses of Parliament) then moved to Parliament Square (which is still referred to as "Westminster," in whose general area it is situated,) the first stone of which was laid in 1840. The public entrance chiefly used is through Palace Yard and Westminster Hall. The new House of Lords dates from 1847. It is the highest court of appeal in the United Kingdom. Reporters were banned from the chamber until 1803. In 1828, the historian Lord Macauley described the reporters allowed in the gallery as "the fourth estate of the realm," (hence the phrase.) The new House of Commons followed in 1847.

Parliament is in session Monday through Thursday.

- Abbey Garden: 900 years old, claiming to be the oldest cultivated garden in London.
- Clock Tower, the: (Note: BIG BEN is actually the name of one of the bells, not the clock, nor the tower.) The Clock Tower was built in 1834 - and is now known as: the Elizabeth Tower - since the 20th century. (See: Big Ben.)
- Jewel Tower: Old Palace Yard & Abingdon Street. (It is close to, but southwest

of, the palace; located a few hundred yards from Westminster Hall.) Built 1366-7, by Yvele for Edward III, to house his personal treasure of jewels and silver. (The crown jewels, for most of their history, have been held at the Tower of London, rather than here.) Three story tower. Until 1547 this remained part of the Royal Wardrobe. Also served as Parliamentary offices until 1621. Was a governmental records storehouse (held the archives for the House of Lords) from 1621-1864, having survived the fire of 1834. Remodeled in 1719 (from which time all the windows and doorways date.)

It was the OFFICE OF WEIGHTS AND MEASURES administration from 1869-1938, at which date it became a National monument. After WWII it was opened to the public (after restoration.)

The tower is still mostly in its original condition (the medieval decoration on the Kentish ragstone outer walls was removed in 1719 however.)

- Sanctuary: Opposite Dean's Yard. (See under S.)
- St. Stephen's: (See under: Westminster Hall/St. Stephen's Crypt.)

Westminster Palace Hotel - On a triangular site, junction of Tufton Street and Victoria Street. Built in 1860, first hotel with hydraulic lifts. Now demolished.

Westminster School - Ashburnham House. (See under A.) Little Dean's Yard. (More officially known as: the Royal College of St. Peter at Westminster.) Located on the south side of Westminster Abbey. Originally a dormitory of the Abbey Benedictine monks (1179,) first founded as a royal college by Henry VIII in the 1540s following the Dissolution of the Monasteries; in 1560 Elizabeth I granted the school an endowment for "Queens Scholars," (and this is taken as the official founding date for the school.) LET'S GO-BUDGET GUIDE TO LONDON confirms that it was officially founded by Elizabeth I in 1560 following the Dissolution; at which time this was the King's Grammar School. Still occupies one side of Dean's Yard, in Little Dean's Yard. (Dean's Yard and Little Dean's Yard are the school's two courtyards - the latter being the prettier.)

Teaching took place here from 1591-1884 (and sources imply all schooling was fundamentally in this one building, there were no individual classrooms.)

- The Abbot of Westminster's Hall/of his palace became the dining hall for Westminster School.
- Great Hall: Little Dean's Yard. Built ca. 1070. The stone archway (1734) has graffiti of an elegant nature carved into it, having been paid for by schoolboys who wished their names carved here by abbey masons.

Weston - John Weston, coat-maker/tailor. (See: Bond Street/Old Bond Street/Weston.)

wet nurse - A woman who had had a child and was still producing milk, hired to feed a child whose own mother could or would not. The wet nurse would need to live with or near the child, who would require multiple nursings per day. (You may care to see: baby bottles.)

wheat - The grain.

- See: Heston.
- See: Sipson.
- You may care to see: corn - For a description of what Britons call grains.

Wheelwrights' Company - (AKA: the Worshipful Company of Wheelwrights.) When Wheelwrights and Coachmakers petitioned for a charter in 1630, it was granted to the Wheelwrights in 1670 (with the Coachmakers getting a separate incorporation in 1677.) Livery Company, granted in 1763. Has no hall. 68th in the order of precedence. (You may care to see: Coachmakers' Company - With whom the Wheelwrights were affiliated until they both became incorporated Guilds.)

Whetstone - Barnet. In the late 14th C. it was referred to as "Weston." Described as a "ribbon village on the Great North Road," lined with houses and inns by the late 17th century. Industry was wood-related or traveler services; toll here from 1825-1862.

Whigs, the - One of the two 18-19th C. political parties of England. Ca. 1680 they were first known as the Petitioners, for supporting the Exclusion Bill, not wanting the Catholic James (Mary II's father, Duke of York) to inherit the throne of his brother, James II. The Whig name came from the Scottish "Whiggamore" (militant Presbyterians seen as rebels by those who supported the Stuarts ca. the 1680s.) These "militant origins" led to this party being associated with republicanism (as in, supporting the Republic/the people.) They supported the aristocratic families, Low Church, dissenters, and (later) the Hanoverian succession, wealthy merchants, property owners, and industrial interests. In the early 19th C. the Whigs also came to stand for supporting parliament (over the royal family,) free trade, Catholic emancipation, and the abolishment of slavery. Roughly speaking, Tories equal Conservatives; Whigs equal aristocratic Liberals. Were superseded by the Liberal party ca. 1868. (See: Tories.)

whip-maker - (See: Piccadilly/185/Swain Adeney Briggs& Son.)

Whipps Cross - Waltham Forest. The name probably corrupted from Phippe's Cross (from a 14th C. resident.) Developed after the 1850s.

- Forest House: 1683, for a Huguenot banker. Stood almost 300 years.
- Whipps Cross Road: Hosts some surviving Georgian homes from ca. 1767.

whisky - (AKA: Scotch whisky. And: Scotch.) Dates back before 1500 (possibly as far back as 500AD,) product of Scotland. Note its spelling, without an "e"; the Irish or American version is: whiskey.

Whitbread's Brewery - Bought by Samuel Whitbread (the elder, brewer/MP/d.1796) in 1750. George III and Queen Charlotte visited the brewery in 1787. Not used as a brewery since 1976. (See: Chiswell Street/Whitbread's brewery.)

Whitcomb Street - (See: Leicester Square/Whitcomb Street.)

White - (Looking for White's, as in the gentlemen's club? See below, right under "Whiteley's.")

White Conduit Fields - (See: Islington/White Conduit Fields.)

White Conduit House - (See under: Pentonville/White Conduit House.)

White Hart Lane - Haringey. Described as a long and winding road between the High Roads of Tottenham and Wood Green. Existed by 1619, at which time the western part was called Apeland Street. Fine 17-18th century homes lined the lane, but the area was largely undeveloped until ca. 1810.

White Horse Street - Originally a lane leading into Shepherd's Market. Near Piccadilly. Named for the White Horse Inn. (See: White Horse Inn, under the INNS/PUBS section.)

White House - Gilwell Park/Epping Forest/Essex. Henry VIII had a hunting lodge here for Edward (his doomed son); Henry later gave it to Sir Edward Denny of Waltham Abbey. Renamed the White House when it was rebuilt in the late 18th century. The owner went bankrupt in 1812, so the Crown seized the property, selling it at auction. Is now affiliated with Lord Baden-Powell's Scout program (in America, called the Boy Scouts.)

White House - Richmond. George III's residence from 1771, demolished in 1802. At the age of eleven, Prinny was housed (along with his brother Frederick) in the nearby Dutch House, due to overcrowding at the White House. (See: Kew Palace.)

White Lion Street - Shoreditch. Called White Lion Street from at least 1724 until 1938. (See: Folgate Street.)

White Lodge, the - (See: Richmond Park/White Lodge.) Not to be confused with another White Lodge. (To see the other: Silver Street - Enfield/White Lodge.)

Whitechapel - East of Aldgate, East End, Tower Hamlets/formerly Bethnal Green. It was the most important entry into the City. The heart of the East End. (See under E.) Takes its name from the white stone walls of St. Mary Matfelon.

- See: St. Mary Matfelon, under the CHURCHES section.
- See: Whitechapel High Street/St. Mary Matfelon.

One source says Whitechapel has always been a district for the poor, and for criminal activity. Another source said that, yes, it was a poor district, but that "most residents were 'quietly respectable.'" The late 15th C. brought in brick- and tile-making, lime-burning, and woodworking. Spanish and Portuguese immigrants here by the late 17th C., giving it the eventual nickname as "the Jewish East End." German immigrants followed, as did brewing, clothing, engineering, and sugar refining. Was one of London's three large hay markets (the others being Haymarket and Smithfield); the hay came into the city on Tues/Thurs/Sat (out of Essex, Hertfordshire, and Suffolk) at 7:00am until about luncheon. Where the most unsavory second-hand clothes went to market. Called, with dark humor, Rosemary Lane, because of the stench of musty rags and old burnt shoes. It closed in 1927.

During Victoria's reign Whitechapel was the location of Jack the Ripper's six grisly murders ca. 1888.

- Brick Lane: From ca. 1671 (or earlier.) It got its name from being the route taken by carts from nearby brick kilns. Now a market for second-hand stuff, bric-a-brac, etc.
- George Yard: (See: Gunthorpe Street, under G.)
- London Hospital:
  - See below under: Whitechapel Road/London Hospital.
  - See under L.
- Petticoat Lane: (See under P.)
- St. Mary Matfelon:
  - See: Whitechapel High Street/St. Mary Matfelon - At its own listing.
  - See under the CHURCHES section.
- Whitechapel Foundry: AKA: Bell Foundry. (See: Whitechapel Road/32-4.)
- Whitechapel High Street: (See at its own listing.)
- Whitechapel Market: (See: Waste Market.)
- Whitechapel Road: (See at its own listing.)

Whitechapel High Street - Whitechapel, East End. "Pestered with cottages." Connects Aldgate High Street with Whitechapel Road. Was the Roman road from London to Colchester. According to LONDON by Knopf Guides: "From Aldgate, Whitechapel High Street was once the departure point for the main road to the fields of Essex. Its former traffic of wagons and ox-carts explains the unusual width of Whitechapel Road and Mile End Road: the houses that line these highways were built at a safe distance from the mud and cow dung in the center. Behind these busy main roads, Whitechapel is actually filled with a fascinating maze of alleyways, courtyards and narrow, winding, sunless streets." (See: Whitechapel Road.)

- St. Mary Matfelon Church: A church has probably stood here since the 13th century. Became the Whitechapel parish church in 1338. Was rebuilt at least twice since; the present building went up in 1882. (See under the CHURCHES section.)

Whitechapel Road - Whitechapel, East End. Connects Aldgate (as Whitechapel High Street) to

Mile End Road. Built up by the 19th century. For centuries the center median of this road was used as a hay-market. (See: markets/Whitechapel Road Market.)

- 32-4: Whitechapel Bell Foundry. The foundry existed from 1420 (in Houndsditch; moved to Whitechapel in 1583; a second source said the move was in 1738,) but this particular manufacturer dates from 1738, when a foundry was established in the 17th century. Was famous for the huge bells it produced: Big Ben (the Elizabeth Tower's biggest bell,) and the Liberty Bell (the foundry received the order for the latter on Nov. 1st, 1751, for the Philadelphia State House, America.) Existed until at least 1962.
- London Hospital: Founded in 1740. (See under L.)
- Whitechapel Market:
    - ➢ See: markets/Whitechapel Road Market.
    - ➢ See: Waste Market.

Whitefield's Tabernacle - Alternate spelling. (See: Whitfield's Tabernacle.)

Whitefriars - Monastery for Carmelite monks, founded in 1241. Near the Blackfriars' monastery; stood in what is now Printing House Square. Gone by the time of the Regency. Seen in place names. The monks wore brown habits, but over them they wore distinctive white mantels, and hence the name. Offered hospitality to travelers and aid to the poor.

Whitefriar's Crypt - 65 Fleet Street. 14th C., but not excavated until 1927. Whitefriars is another name for Carmelites.

Whitefriar's Gateway - (AKA: Whitefriar's Gate.) 1676. Still standing. Near the Inns of Court.

Whitefriars Glass - (AKA: James Powell & Sons. AKA: the Old Glass House.) Glass-makers. 1740, in Tudor Street, the City. (Although they did first open in a small place off Fleet Street in 1720.) Renowned for the beauty of their glass colors (and its decorative designs for vases, bowls, etc.) Owned by James Powell, who bought the factory (that made the glass) in 1834. In Tudor Street until they moved to Harrow in 1922. Closed in 1980. (See: Tudor Street.)

Whitehall - Westminster. Occupied since at least the 9th C., (but probably since prehistoric times.) As a street, follows an earlier street called King Street; was long since called "Whitehall" by the time of the Regency. One kilometer long, connects Trafalgar Square (the street being known as Hog Lane in the Regency) and the post-Regency Parliament Square. Home of the Civil Service. At one time Whitehall would have specifically meant "the Royal Palace of Whitehall," but the term is now used to represent government in London, rather than just the one building.

- ➢ See: Westminster - The "WESTMINSTER VS. WHITEHALL" entry.
- ➢ See: York Place - For foundation of Whitehall.

- See: Whitehall, Royal Palace of.

- 4 Whitehall Place: SCOTLAND YARD, 1829. (AKA: Great Scotland Yard. AKA: the Metropolitan Police, after that force was founded in 1829.) Building by Norman Shaw, 1888 and 1912. The Metropolitan Police (force) was housed here until 1891 when it moved to Derby Street (New Scotland Yard; New Scotland Yard moved to 10 Broadway in 1967.) Scottish kings and ambassadors were once housed here in this street (hence the "Scotland" part of the name.)

  (See: Great Scotland Yard.)

  The City objected to the 1829 Police Force Proposal, and so to this day the roughly square mile of the City has its own police force. They wear red and white checked caps, and epaulettes. (See: City of London Police Force.)
- 36 Whitehall: Parliamentary Counsel. (AKA: Office of the Parliamentary Counsel.) Government lawyers who specialize in drafting bills/legislation. 1833. Until this office was developed, bills were drawn up by barristers, MPs, or judicial members. Rusticated stonework on the ground floor. North bay added in 1806.
- 65 Whitehall: (See: Gwydry House, below.)
- Admiralty: 1725, by Ripley; replacing a 1695 building. Stone screen by Robert Nash, 1761, but altered in 1827. Much remains as it was in Admiral Nelson's time. The Lords of the Admiralty lived here. (See under A.)
- Admiralty House: (Same as "Admiralty." See immediately above.)
- Banqueting House, the: (See under: Whitehall, Royal Palace of - At its own listing.)
- Cabinet Office: 1845, by Charles Barry. (See under C.)
- Clarence, the: Pub, 18th century. (See under the INNS/PUBS section.)
- Dover House: (See under D.)
- Downing Street: (See under D.)
- Foreign Office, the: (AKA: Foreign and Commonwealth Office.) Victorian interiors, 1860-70s. (See: Foreign Office, under F.)
- Gwydry House: 65 Whitehall. 1772. (See under G.)
- Horse Guards, the: (See: Royal Guards.)
- Kent's Treasury: (See: Treasury, below.)
- Old Admiralty: Same as "Admiralty." (See, above.)
- Privy Council Chamber: Hosts the Privy Council of England, AKA: Her (or His) Majesty's Most Honourable Privy Council. By John Soane, 1824-6. The monarch's private council, advisers to the monarch of the Kingdom of England.

Typical among this body of advisers: diplomats, judges, leading churchmen, military leaders, senior members of the House of Lords, or those of the House of Commons. "Privy" does not derive from anything to do with toilets, but comes from an ancient term meaning "of one's own."

- Scotland Yard: (See: 4, above.)
- Statue of Charles I: Equestrian. At the north end of Whitehall. Cast in 1633, and erected here in 1676. (In 1655 Cromwell's men found where Royalists had hidden this statue in the crypt of St. Paul's, Covent Garden. It was to be melted down, but a brass-worker named John Rivett instead kept it intact, melting down other bits of brass instead, and returning it later to a pleased Charles II following the Restoration. On the anniversary of Charles I's death each year, a wreath is laid here. (Cromwell's statue stands at the other end of Whitehall, being described as "brooding.")
- St. Margaret's: (See under the CHURCHES section.)
- Treasury, the: (AKA: Kent's Treasury. AKA: the Old Treasury. Sometimes AKA: the Exchequer - For more on this, SEE: TREASURY, under T.)

Whitehall Court - 1884 apartment building.

Whitehall Place - (See: Whitehall/4.)

Whitehall, Royal Palace of - Westminster (on the east side of Whitehall, opposite the Horse Guards.) Built in 1245, this was a York Place residence for the Archbishops of York, which Cardinal Wolsey remodeled and enlarged in 1514. (See: York Place.)

Henry VIII confiscated this property in 1529; made it his palace in 1532, at which time he renamed it Whitehall. He rebuilt and extended the residence. Burned down in 1698 (at which time St. James's Palace became the official royal residence, being then the principle residence for the Tudor and Stuart monarchs.) Not rebuilt. (See: Banqueting House, below.)

- Banqueting House: (AKA: Banqueting Hall.) THIS IS THE ONLY *BUILDING** OF WHITEHALL PALACE THAT IS YET STANDING. Corner of Horse Guards Avenue and Whitehall. Opposite the Horse Guards, and in similar Renaissance style. (*There is, however, also remaining the 16th C. tennis courts, remains can be seen just before 10 Downing Street; a terrace, Queen Mary's Terrace, by Wren in 1691; and a 16th C. wine cellar.)

  Elizabeth I was the first to build a banqueting hall here, in 1581. Originally built of Oxford and Northamptonshire stone, but it did not weather well. Rebuilt in 1605; destroyed by fire in 1619. Rebuilt again, this time in the

Palladian style (the first English building to be built in this classical style,) by Inigo Jones 1619-22. As said, it is the only part of the palace that now survives, having escaped a 1698 fire. When the palace did burn, the Royal Court moved to St. James's Palace (which, to this day, is now the official seat of the monarchy.) The fire was supposedly due to a Dutch maid who hung laundry too close to a fire in hopes of drying the cloth faster.

From 1724-1890, it served as a Chapel Royal; George I converted it, although it was never consecrated. It was refaced in 1829-30 in Portland stone, by Soane. Queen Victoria gave it to the United Service Institution for its museum, 1895-1962. Now restored to a banqueting hall.

There was a refacing in 1829-30, of Portland stone. A north entrance and staircase were added in 1809 by Wyatt.

Has a 1635 Rubens ceiling, which depicts a "glorious" representation of James I as peacemaker and faithful defender of his people (as ordered created by his son, Charles I.)

A bust of Charles I was added in 1798 over the staircase entrance (this was the site of the window through which he stepped to meet his execution, on Jan. 30th, 1649.)

- Horse Guards: Was built on the site of Whitehall Palace. (See: Royal Guards.)
- Treasury: (See under T.)
- York House: Ca. 1240 the Archbishop of York, Walter de Grey, bought property here, calling it York Place. Henry VIII rebuilt/extended the house, then being called Whitehall Palace (AKA: the Palace of Whitehall.) This location was later known as York House.
    - See: Stable Yard Road/York House.
    - See: Whitehall.
    - See: York House.
    - See: York Place
    - You may care to see: Royal Mews.

Whitehall Theatre - 1930. Built on the site of Ye Old Ship Tavern. (See under the INNS/PUBS section.)

Whiteley's - Bayswater. A store. Victorian, 1889.

White's - Gentlemen's club. 37 St. James's Street. Dates from 1736. Previously was White's Chocolate House. Plainish facade. (See under the INNS/PUBS section.)

Whitestone Pond - Hampstead. Highest point in north London. Derived its name from the white milestone nearby. (See: Hampstead/Whitestone Pond.)

whitewash - Lime and chalk mixed with additives, used for both interior and exterior walls. Could be white, or colored by animal blood or vegetable dye, pink being not uncommon. Took several days to dry. Common in the Regency.

Whitewebbs - Enfield. (Also seen as: White Webbs.) There was a mansion of this name, here from the mid 16th century. Granted to Robert Huicke (physician to Henry VIII and Elizabeth I) in 1570. Purportedly the Gunpowder Plot was hatched here in 1605 (a claim also made by the Eastbury Manor House in Upney.) Pulled down; a new one was built in 1791; this Whitewebbs was redone in 1881 in a French chateau style. Now a golf club and public park, since ca. 1931.

Whitfield's Tabernacle - (Also seen as: Whitefield's Tabernacle.) "An institutional church of the Congregational body" (as listed in THE FACE OF LONDON.) In other words: it was a chapel built specifically for the Reverend George Whitfield and his Nonconforming followers. PILGRIMS' LONDON says: "George Whitefield's first chapel..." (which he called a 'tabernacle')"...was constructed in 1741 in the Moorfields... In 1756 he put up a plain brick building on Tottenham Court Road, which was known as 'Whitefield's Tabernacle' for nearly two centuries." Rebuilt in 1903 as an ornate red brick building. It is now gone.

whitsun - (AKA: Pentecost. AKA: Whitsunday.) Medieval. It was the seventh Sunday after Easter, to celebrate the descent of the Holy Ghost upon the disciples.

Whittington Hospital - Founded in 1822. (For more on Dick Whittington, see: Highgate Hill/statue of...)

Whittlesey Street - South Bank. 1820-30. "True cockney" in flavor.

Whitton - Richmond-upon-Thames/Hounslow. An 11th C. heath-side hamlet. Had strawberry fields well into the 20th century. Didn't have a High Street until the late 1930s, Percy Road having previously served the purpose.

- Kneller Hall: First built in 1646-64. Named for the portrait painter Godfrey Kneller (founder of the English Academy of Painting.) Pulled down in 1847, rebuilt with the current building, the Royal Military School of Music, 1857, training musicians for the army. (See under K.)
- Whitton Place: Built in 1725 by the Earl of Islay (later the Duke of Argyll.) Very grand.

W. H. Smith Company - (See: at the top of this "W" listing.)

wick - An ancient word (also: wic -or- wich) meaning a harbor/port/trading place. Seen attached to communities near water. Examples: Dulwich, Norwich, Warwick.

Wick House - 144 Richmond Hill, Richmond, Surrey. Built in 1772 for Sir Joshua Reynolds (painter,) built by Sir William Chambers. Reynolds lived here until his death in 1792. Near the corner of Nightingale Lane and Richmond Hill.

Widmore - Bromley. Dates from at least 1226. Was a sleepy hamlet into the 19th C., with a brickworks; grew after the 1850s.

Wig and Pen Club - 229-230 Strand. Gentlemans' Club. (See under the CLUBS section.)

wig-makers -

- See: Bond Street/Old Bond Street/23/Truefitt.
- See: Chancery Lane - For lawyers' wigs.
- See: Ede & Ravenscroft - For lawyers' robes.
- SEE: WIGS.

Wigmore Street - Leading off Cavendish Square.

- Christian's: Drapers. Jane Austen shopped here.
- Wigmore Hall: 36 Wigmore Street. Opened in 1901 (as Bechstein Hall, named for a famous piano manufacturer.) Became Wigmore Hall in 1917.

wigs - (Worn on the head. Not the buns.) Wigs, so popular in the late 18th C., had become largely unfashionable for the general populace by the time of the Regency (although they were often still worn by servants in livery, and were required for lawyers in court. Some older persons still wore them.)

- See: Chancery Lane - For lawyers' wigs.
- See: Courts of Common Law and Equity/Court of King's Bench - For: wigs in court, starting in the 17th century.
- See: Ede & Ravenscroft.
- See: wig-makers.
- You may care to see: "hair" items listed at H - As haircutters would also be capable of providing care for wigs.

Wiley's Legal Bookstore - Inns of Court. Founded here in 1830.

Wilkinson - Ludgate Street. Sword manufacturers. Founded in 1772 by Henry Nock, gunmaker to George III. (James Wilkinson was Nock's apprentice.) Wilkinson inherited the business in 1805 as Wilkinson & Sons, making military and sporting arms and swords. Royal Warrant since Queen Victoria's time.

Willesden - (See: Wilsdon.) Brent. Existed from at least 1086. Stayed rural until some development ca. 1820. When the rails came in the 1850s this area became more working-class. Willesden's Charter of Incorporation was received in 1933.

William Green's Pistol Repository and Shooting Gallery - 1836. (See: Leicester Square/Savile House/William Green's....)

William Kent House - 20th C. name.

- See: Arlington Street/22.
- See: Wimbourne House.

Wilsdon - The name of this district, which after ca. 1860 became known as Willesden. Five miles/8 km from Oxford Street. A village, favored for walks. Not developed until well into Queen Victoria's reign. Streets are largely tree-lined, pleasant.

- Gladstone Park: 1901.
- St. Mary: Ancient. Partly rebuilt in 1827. Battlemented tower; ancient roof.
- Welsh Harp: (AKA: the Brent Reservoir.) A lake formed in 1838 when the bed of the River Brent was enlarged.

Wilton Crescent - Belgravia. Built by Seth Smith, 1827.

Wilton Place - Belgravia. 1827. Previously was a cow-yard, entered by a narrow passage from Knightsbridge. The west corner of Wilton Place had a tobacconist's shop, run by a Mrs. McDowell, doing business here for many years until her house was pulled down in 1841.

- St. Paul: 1840-43, Thomas Cundy Jr. (See under the CHURCHES section.)

Wilton Royal - Carpets. (See: Wiltshire/Wilton Royal Carpets, under the BRITISH COUNTIES section.)

Wilton's - Fish and fresh oysters. (See: Bury Street/Wilton's.)

Wimbledon, the borough of - Merton. Purportedly in 598 this was the site of a battle between the king of Wessex and the king of Kent. For centuries Wimbledon was part of the Mortlake manor, belonging to the archbishops of Canterbury. Received its Charter of Incorporation in 1905. In 1881, it had only 15,950 inhabitants. Of course, in modern times "Wimbledon" is synonymous with tennis.

- All England Lawn Tennis and Croquet Club: Founded in 1868. Moved from Worpole Road into Church Road in 1922. The famous tennis matches are held every June-July. Officially known as: the Lawn Tennis Championships of the All-England Club.
  - See: tennis.
  - See: Wimbledon Park.
- St. Mary: Parish church. Founded in the 14th century. Rebuilt in 1786, and in 1843.
- South Wimbledon: Mostly undeveloped until the 1850s. (See: Merton.)

Wimbledon Chase - Merton. Fields where stag hunts were held in the 19th century. Now a small conservation area.

- Richmond Avenue: Early 20th century.
- Quintin Avenue: Early 20th century.

Wimbledon Commons - Merton. 1,200 acres, London's largest common. Near Richmond. Described as a wild, natural, open space. There are the remains of a Celtic earthenwork on the Commons, called Caesar's Camp. (See, below.) There were some cottages and farms here ca. the 13th C.; the area provided grazing, hunting grounds, water, and wood. Called by this name by at least 1789 (at which time a duel was fought here, the Duke of Richmond vs. a colonel); in the 18th C. it was known as a dueling spot. In 1817 a corn mill was built here. Secured for the public in 1871.

- Caesar's Camp: Popular, if inaccurate, nickname for Bensbury Camp, a hill-fort that might date from the 7th century. Probably not Roman, but Celtic.
- Chester House: (See at C.)
- London Scottish Golf Club: 1864. (Later, the Royal Wimbledon Golf Club.) Players must wear a red coat or sweater (originally a coat) while on the course.
- tennis: The first Wimbledon tennis championship was held in 1877, men's singles only. (See: Wimbledon/All England Lawn Tennis, above.)

Wimbledon Park - Merton/Wandsworth. Sir Thomas Cecil built a mansion (1st of 4 local ones) here in 1588. Had: a deer park, and 20 acres of gardens. In the early 18th C. it sold to the Spencer family, at which time the manor was expanded/doubled to 1,200 acres; landscaped in 1765 by Capability Brown (adding a 30 acre lake made out of a bog.) Sold to John Augustus Beaumont (insurance magnate) in 1845; he sold some land so others could built grand homes. In 1889 land was leased to cricket, golf, and tennis clubs. Went to the council for public use in 1914.

- ➢ See: Wimbledon.
- ➢ See: Winbledon Commons.

Wimbourne House - St. James's, Westminster. (AKA: the William Kent House. AKA: Wimborne House, lacking the u.) Palladian style. 1743-54, finished after William Kent (architect's) death. (See: Arlington Street/22.)

Wimpole Street - West of Harley Street, Westminster. Named after Wimpole Hall (Cambridgeshire,) which belonged to the Harley family (and who developed the Cavendish estate,) 1724. Only seven houses here ca. 1800. Then, in came substantial (if uninspiring) terrace homes. Fashionable residential address by the very late Regency era. Circa Victorian times this street became known for the many doctors residing here. Tennyson called it a "long, unlovely street." Now known for dentistry.

- 27A: The *fictional* address of Henry Higgins, from George Bernard Shaw's play *Pygmalion* (later made for film as the musical *My Fair Lady.*)
- Upper Wimpole Street: 1778, when Marylebone Gardens were enclosed.

Winchester Cathedral - *Not to be confused with Westminster Cathedral.* Winchester Cathedral is in Winchester, in the county of Hampshire.

Winchester College - School for boys. Founded in 1382 by the Bishop of Winchester; first scholars there in 1394.

Winchester House - (AKA: Winchester Palace.) Situated on the southwest corner of St. James's Square. Palace home of the Bishops of Winchester from the 12th C. to 1626. "The Clink" was a prison attached to the palace (being the first in which women were regularly confined, and also intended for confining Royalists.) Only the 14th C. rose window (stands a few steps to the east) remains of Winchester House, having been revealed when a fire broke out in 1814. (See: Clink Prison.)

Winchester Square - Bankside, Southwark. NAIRN'S LONDON calls it: "...a near-mystical re-use of the exact shape of the medieval courtyard of Winchester House." (See: Winchester House.) The square dates to the 19th century.

Winchmore Hill - Enfield. Dates from at least 1319. A village green. Separated from Southgate by the Grovelands estate since the 15th century. Woody. Described in 1801 as a "thriving settlement." By 1882 had about 500 houses.

- St. Paul's Church: 1827; remodeled after an 1844 fire.

Windmill Lane - Camberwell. Was a poorer district. Still known as Windmill Lane in 1878. Now known as Bethwin Road, from ca. 1881.

windows - Glass windows came into general use in London in Tudor times (16th century.) Of course, even into the Regency era the ability to afford glass windows was contingent on one's income. (See: glass windows, under G.)

Windsor - (The castle - although the surrounding community is also called Windsor.) Located in Berkshire; Windsor Castle is situated in the town of Windsor, 21 miles/34 km east of London. It was built across the side of a hill.

Windsor is an ancient borough. Founded by William the Conqueror, it was erected in 1078-80 as a defensive citadel on the Thames; built of earth and timber.

Windsor received its Charter from Edward I (13th century.) It was then called New Windsor, so as not to be confused with Old Windsor, a village along the Staines Road.

Rebuilt by Henry I in stone; and rebuilt by Henry II. Again by Edward III after 1350. Then again in the 17th century. And yet again under George IV (who gave it its castellated casing via architect Jeffrey Wyatville, in the 1820s.)

This is where Princess Charlotte (daughter of Prinny, the latter of who would later be George IV,) spent much of her youth. (See: Warwick House.) Prinny had lived here at Windsor as a young man himself.

It was damaged by fire in 1992 (six rooms and three towers); they are being restored. (See: Great Hall, below.)

Eton College is right across the Thames from the Castle. The bridge over the Thames (from Windsor to Eton) dates from 1822. (See: Windsor Bridge, under the BRIDGES section.)

- Ascot Heath: (See: Ascot, under A.)
- Great Hall, the: Burned in 1992 (although a human chain, involving Prince Andrew, was instigated and managed to save most of the treasures and art.)
- Great Windsor Park: (AKA: Windsor Great Park. AKA: Great Park. AKA: the Home Park.) 4,800 acres. (See: Windsor Great Park - At its own listing.)
  - Royal Lodge: In the Great Park. A thatched cottage built by Nash, ca. 1815. Was once a favorite residence of George IV. I think the name "Royal Lodge" was attached to it after George IV's time, however.
  - Virginia Water: Large lake at the south end of the park. Formed in 1746 by the Duke of Cumberland. Over two miles/3.2 km long.
- Guildhall: High Street. Wren, 1686.
- Home Park, the: (See: Great Windsor Park, above.)
- Royal Lodge: (See: Great Windsor Park/Royal Lodge, above.)
- St. George's Chapel: (See: St. George's Chapel-Windsor, in CHURCHES section.)
- St. John-the-Baptist: Rebuilt in 1822.
- Snow Hill: The equestrian statue here of George III dates from 1831.
- Theatre Royal: 32 Thames Street, Windsor (after 1815.) Purportedly grew from a 1706 booth. By 1778-93 performances were taking place in a little barn about one mile/1.6 km outside town, on Peascod Street. An actual theater came along in 1793, on the High Street. George III, while in residence at Windsor Castle, liked to come to performances here. Only open for six weeks in summer. This sold in 1805, upsetting Windsor citizens, who raised the £6,000 needed to build a new theatre. Opened in 1815 on the site of the present theatre.

Windsor Great Park - (AKA: Great Park, as Great Windsor Park, and as Home Park.)

- Copper Horse, the: The name given to the equestrian statue of George III, dates from 1821, by Westmacott. At the north end of the Long Walk. Commissioned by George IV. Erected in 1831. Is, as one might guess, made of copper.
- Frogmore House: Also simply called: Frogmore. (See under F.)
- Leptis Magna: Ruins/columns on the Ascot side of Virginia Water. Presented to Prinny in 1816. They were actual ruins from Leptis Magna/Libya. They had originally been intended for the British Museum, but Prinny asked for them, and so got them, putting them here.
- Long Walk, the: Laid out by Charles II. Is three miles/4.8 km long, connecting the castle to Windsor Great Park.

- Royal Lodge: Prinny had Nash rebuild a mid 17th C. thatched cottage here (called Lower Lodge,) ca. 1815, which Prinny greatly enjoyed; it was at that time called the Prince Regent's Cottage. When he ascended to the throne (1820) it was called King's Cottage. It took on the Royal Lodge name in the late 1820s.
- Virginia Water: William, Duke of Cumberland (and 2nd son of George II) created the Virginia Water (a lake) here, in the 1750s.

wine merchants - Wine was little drunk by the lower orders, due to expensive taxes.

- See: Berry Bros & Rudd.
- See: Christopher & Company.
- See: St. James's Street/3.
- See: St. James's Street/Justerini.
- See: Villiers Street/47.
- You may care to see: food/drinks/wine.
- You may care to see: liquors.

Wine Office Court - 17th C. street near Fleet Street/the City. It is said the name most likely derives from buildings here that granted licenses to sell wine.

- Ye Olde Cheshire Cheese: 17th C. pub.
    - See: Fleet Street/Ye Olde Cheshire Cheese.
    - See: Ye Olde Cheshire Cheese, under the INNS/PUBS section.

Winfield House - Outer Circle, Regent's Park. Dates from 1825. Was St. Dunstan's Lodge. (See: St. Dunstan's Lodge.)

Wire Workers' (or Wire Drawers') Company - (See: Tin Plate Workers' Company.)

Woburn Walk - Bloomsbury. Built in 1822-5 by Thomas Cubitt to provide a shopping terrace around Bloomsbury (the first in London intended for pedestrian traffic only.) Bow-fronted shops. A high pavement on the east side protected the shops from having mud flung on them by carriages.

women's dresses - (See: dresses, women's.)

Women's Rights - During the Regency era women were yet considered their husband's chattel. The upside: her husband was responsible for her debts; he was also responsible for any children born to the marriage (regardless of whether he suspected he was not the actual father.) The big downside: the wife had to comply with his will; what was hers at the time of her marriage (a dowry, an income from property) became her husband's; even her children belonged to her husband, not to her; (children of a wife were his; children from his mistress were the responsibility of the latter.) It was still legal for a man to beat his wife (so long as the stick was an inch wide or less.)

Mary Wollstonecraft's *A Vindication of the Rights of Women* was published in 1792, now considered one of the founding works of feminist philosophy.

- See: businesses, owned by women.
- See: marriage.
- See: of age.
- See: suffrage, women's.
- See: Theosophical Society - 1887.
- See: votes, for women.

wood - (See: woods. Note the s.)

wood - Wood/lumber/timber.

- See: Cheapside/Wood Street.
- See: coal - For an alternative fuel.
- See: Kidbrooke.
- See: Northwood.
- See: timber.
- See: Wood Street.

Wood End - Ealing. Northeastern section of Northolt, but mostly considered to be the northern edge of Greenford. From the 13th century. Hamlet, with woodlands deep into the 18th century.

Wood End - Hillingdon. North-central section of Hayes. Dates from at least the early 16th C., but probably earlier. Largely agricultural until late in the 19th century.

- Wood End house: 17th century.

Wood Green - Haringey. In 1502 was a clearing off Tottenham Wood. A mere hamlet until the mid 19th century. Now a shopping center.

- St. Michael's Church: 1844.

Wood Street - In Cheapside. Indeed, wood was sold here.

- Haberdashers' Hall: Rebuilt in 1862-4.
- St. Alban's Church: (See under the CHURCHES section.)
- Waxchandlers' Hall: (Opposite the Haberdashers' Hall.) Site owned by the Waxchandlers' Company since 1493. Rebuilt following the Great Fire of 1666. Demolished in 1852, with a small hall by C. Fowler then being built.

Woodberry Down - Hackney. Until the 1820s was dairy farmlands. Prone to flooding. By the early 20th C. had become a posh area.

Woodcote - Croydon/Sutton. CHAMBERS LONDON ENCYCLOPAEDIA says: "Originally an extensive estate stretching from present-day Clock House in the south to Wallington in the north. Most street atlases now identify Woodcote as the locality on the western side of Purley..." Dates from 1200. The estate was known variously as Woodcote, Woodcote Lodge, and Woodcote Hall.

- Upper Woodcote: (See under U.)
- Woodcote Hall: Mansion. Earliest parts date from the 1820s.

Woodford - Redbridge. For centuries was just a collection of hamlets in cleared forest areas. Wealthy home owners built here during the Restoration. Deforested in the early 19th C., at which time there were so many grand houses that they were squeezing out agriculture here. CHAMBERS LONDON GAZETTEER claims Woodford is: "The geographical and social high point of east London, situated to the north-east of Walthamstow, from which it is separated by a sliver of Epping Forest."

- South Woodford: Separate from Woodford. (See under S.)
- Woodford Bridge: CHAMBERS LONDON GAZETTEER explains: "Before the first bridge was built in the 13th century, there was a woodland ford across the River Roding on the road to Albridge... Complaints were made about the state of the horse bridge in 1404 but it was not until 1573 that it was replaced by a wooden cart bridge." Stone bridge in 1768, but flooded out in 1771; replaced, the new bridge standing for some two centuries. Woodford Bridge, a housing district, had 1,188 residents by 1871.
- Woodford Green: West-central part of Woodford, for centuries its most stylish hamlet. Purportedly has the oldest village cricket green yet is use.
    - Highams: Mansion. 1768. Later called Highams Park.
    - Hurst House: 1714. "Grand," built for a prominent brewer. Is yet a private home.
- Woodford Wells: Northernmost hamlets. Dates from at least 1285. Never was a success as a spa. Remote; didn't develop until the 1850s.

Woodgrange Park - Newham. Dates from at least 1198, possessed by Stratford Abbey. Agricultural up to the 1850s.

Woodlands - Hounslow. From at least 1485. Was known as Hounslow Fields until the early 19th century. Market gardens. Enclosed in 1818.

(Woodlands is also the name of a house is Westcombe. See: Westcombe/Woodlands.)

Woodmongers - (AKA: The Worshipful Company of the Woodmongers and the Coal Trade of London. Sometimes called: the Fuellers; not to be confused with Fullers.) Their heyday was in the 17th century. Defunct in 1746. Not to be confused with Woolmongers. (See: Carmen, with which the Woodmongers once combined.)

woods - This is not to reflect a judgment on whether an area was a forest or woods; it is to gather the listings in one place.

- See: forests.
- You may care to see: Verderers - For those who monitored wood-cutting.
- You may care to see: wood - For places that sold wood.

Woodside - Croydon. Dates from at least 1332. Difficult-to-plough farmland, mostly used for grazing. Was a hamlet in the early 19th century.

- Ashburton Park: 1788.

Woodside Park - Barnet. The Peacocks (family) of Redbourn had land here from the 16th C.; descendants sold to Sir John Lade, who built the Frith manor house, 1790. Poor soil, mostly used for haymaking, so little populated.

- Woodside House: Whetstone. Ca. 1840, for Joseph Baxendale.

wool - For centuries, wool was England/Britain's most important product/export.

- See: Basinghall Street.
- See: staplers.
- See: the "wool" listings, below.

Wool Exchange - 1874. 25-29 Coleman Street. In the 20th C., the wool sales moved to the new Fruit and Wool Exchange, Brushfield Street, Spitalfields.

Wool Merchants -

- See: Inns of Chancery/Staple Inn.
- See: Leadenhall Street.
- See: Wool Staplers.
- See: Woolmens' Company.

Wool Staplers - (Also seen as: Wool-staplers. AKA: the Company of Merchants of the Staple of England, the Merchants of the Staple. AKA: the Merchant Staplers. Note: that they never were the "Worshipful Company of...," in other words, never a Livery Company.) Existed since perhaps 1282, they achieved their Royal Charter in 1319. Dealt in lead, skins, tin, and wool. Existed in the Medieval era. The "Staple" was a Crown-required designated market (and may have gotten its name from wool being one of England's staple crops.) Had total control over export of the above items. First at Antwerp, then Bruges, then Calais, then came to Westminster - moved in 1378 to Staple Inn, Holborn (temporarily, then moving back to Westminster.) When production of wool increased, it reduced the Staple's complete control of the product. The Merchant Staplers limped on, but only in local marketplaces.

- See: Inns of Chancery/Staple Inn.
- See: Leadenhall Street.
- See: Woolmens' Company - Noting the Woolmen were made up of both wool merchants *and* woolpackers.

Woolmens' Company - (AKA: the Worshipful Company of Woolmen.) Dates back to 1180 (and most probably earlier, as this was when King Henry II fined them for operating without his license.) Incorporated in 1522. AN ENCYCLOPAEDIA OF LONDON says of the Woolmens' Company: "The only surviving document is a book of ordinances (1587.) Till 1779 every woolwinder required a license from the Company." Was made up of woolpackers (who wrap/pack fleeces for shipment,) and wool merchants.

For centuries, wool was a good indicator: when it thrived, so did England. And vice versa. A woolsack is the symbol of the United Kingdom's wealth.

Livery Company. Has no Hall. 43rd in the order of precedence.

- See: Wool Staplers.
- See: woolmongers.

woolmongers - Worked with sheep's wool, whereas the leatherworkers worked with leather, tanners with hides, and skinners with pelts. Woolmongers had premises near the Tower of London.

Woolwich - (Pronounced woo-lidge, or woo-litch.) Greenwich. People were here since the Iron Age. A naval town since Henry VIII's time. The dockyard closed in 1869. (See: docks.) There are still military barracks here, for in the 18-19th centuries it was often used as a parade ground. It is still a semi-rural heath.

- Dial Square: Ca. 1720; described as a "great pile of buildings." Probably built by Nicholas Hawksmoor.
- Eltham Palace: (See under E.)
- Rotunda, the: Circular building, by Nash. (See: Greenwich/Rotunda Museum.)
- Royal Artillery Barracks: (AKA: Woolwich Barracks.) Yellow brick; at least ¼ mile/0.4 km long; backdrop to the parade grounds. Designed to house 4,000 men, built ca. 1720. New barracks were built here in 1776-1802, housing the Royal Regiment of Artillery. (See, below.)
- Royal Laboratory, the: Established here in 1695, on a site then known as Woolwich Warren. The Royal Regiment of Artillery formed here in 1716. The Royal Military Academy came in 1741; both moving onto the commons in 1808. All branches of the military were taught here, learning sciences, French, Latin, drawing, fencing, and writing. It was the precursor to the Royal Arsenal (See under R); was officially established as the Royal Arsenal in 1805, manufacturing explosives, fuses, and shot. Being then used for testing and storage only, it mostly closed after WWII (combining with the Military Academy in Sandhurst in 1947.) It closed entirely in 1994.
- Royal Regiment of Artillery, and the Royal Military Academy: (See: Royal Laboratory, above.)

- Woolwich Arsenal: (See: Royal Laboratory, above.)
- Woolwich Barracks: (See: Royal Artillery Barracks, above.)
- Woolwich Commons: Approximately 159 acres. Used for artillery practice. Much of the British Army camped here before being sent to war (in order to access the Arsenal,) in the 18th and 19th centuries.

Woolwich Lane - (See: Well Hall/Well Hall Road.)

Worchester Porcelain - (See: Worcestershire/Royal Worcester Porcelain, in the BRITISH COUNTIES section.)

Worchestershire Sauce - (Pronounced "Woo-stuh-shur.") Invented in 1837. (See: Worcestershire/Lea & Perrins, in the BRITISH COUNTIES section.)

workhouses - From the 16th century, under the Poor Laws, each parish had an obligation to provide for their own poor (and the indigent, and the infirm, orphaned, old, unmarried mothers, and those mentally or physically unwell.) If an addled (or otherwise disabled) person committed a crime or offense, they were returned to the parish of their birth to be dealt with, paid for by a poor-rate tax; the parish *must* provide some shelter and food for those so designated. It might be a mere 8 x 10 foot room and one meal a day.

OLDE LONDON PUNISHMENTS says: "However, by the start of the nineteenth century the cost of poor relief was increasing; at the same time, many believed that parish relief was an easy option for those who did not want to work. In 1834 the Poor Law Amendment Act was passed, which was intended to end all...relief for the able-bodied... (It) was replaced by...the workhouse."

Each workhouse was run by a Board of Guardians, locally elected. Food was minimal, the inmates wore uniforms, and the work was hard and/or mind-numbing.

- See: poor, the - Listings under.
- See: St. James's Parish Workhouse.

working class neighborhoods - That is, streets or areas where those in the working classes (merchants, doctors, bankers, lawyers, etc.) would tend to reside/have offices. Often, one's business would be on the ground floor, and one's family would live in the rooms above.

- See: Harley Street.
- See: Keppel Street.
- See: middle class.
- See: Wimpole Street.

Working Man's College - 1854, Hampstead Road.

Wormholt Common - Hammersmith & Fulham. Later known as Wormwood Scrubs. Originally was a 200 acre wood, 60 acres of which were enclosed. In 1812, a £100 per annum rent (for a 21 year lease) procured this area for exercising the two regiments of the Life Guards.

(Copyholders were still allowed to range their cattle here, though.) In 1876, it was purchased by the government and given free to the Metropolitan Boards of Works, with the stipulation that it be preserved as a public open space, not converted into a park.

Wormwood Scrubs - Hammersmith & Fulham. In 1189 was known as Wormholt Scrubs. (See at its own listing.) Wasteland, denuded of trees, suitable only for grazing. The north part was cut off in 1801 by the building of the Grand Junction (now Grand Union) Canal.

- Wormwood Scrubs Prison: Opened in stages from 1874, taking in the prisoners when Millbank Penitentiary was pulled down in 1891.

Wormwood Street - The City. A continuation of London Wall, junctions with Bishopsgate and Camomile Street. Wormwood used to grow on the nearby London Wall. Dates back to at least before the Great Fire of 1666, in which it burned.

Worshipful Company of... - London's Livery Guilds' officials names begin with "The Worshipful Company of..." (See them under their various Company names. Example: "The Worshipful Company of Haberdashers" will be found in this work under: Haberdashers' Company.)

- See: Freemen of the City.
- See: halls.
- See: Livery Companies.
- See: mystery.
- See: Watermen's and Lightermen's Hall - For an example of a Company/Guild that does *not* have "Worshipful" as part of its proper name.

worth - An ancient word for an enclosed settlement. Used as part of place names. Examples: Hanworth, Wandsworth.

Wrythe, the - Sutton. Dates from at least 1229 (at that time recorded as "Rithe,") and went on to be misspelled as "Rye"; it did not gain the "w" until the early 19th century. Very unpopulated; two dozen homes by 1850. There was a Leicester House here, but it is not to be confused with the one in Leicester Square.

Wych Street - Ran largely where Australia House stands now/the Strand. Demolished in 1901, when Aldwych and Kingsway came through here.

- Olympic Pavilion: (AKA: Olympic Theatre; AKA: Royal Olympic Theatre.) Built in 1805, by Philip Astley, a light horseman - i.e. the proprietor of Astley's Amphitheatre. (See under A.) Opened on 9/18/1806. Burned completely in 1849. More a regular theatre, as opposed to a circus-type entertainment as was Astley's Amphitheatre. (See: Olympic, under the THEATRE section.)

Wyndham Road - Camberwell and Peckam. (See: Bowyer's Lane.)

x-rays - Discovered in 1895.

-Y-

yard - While a yard is a unit of measure (equals three feet) familiar to people of the Regency, here I speak of yard as it relates to property.

To the English, a yard is the cobbled and/or working part of a property. That is, where the horses/carriages (cars) are handled. If you mean an area with any assortment of grass/flowers/space for relaxation/enjoyment, you call that area the garden, regardless of whether it hosts any flowers or not. (See: gardens.)

Yardley Lane - Waltham Forest. Northwestern corner of Chingford, off Sewardstone Road.

- Yardley House: Country home of Sir John and Lady Harriet Silvester, ca. 1803.

Yardley Soaps - Records of soap manufacture date back to Charles I. Yardley of London (possibly under a different name) probably existed before, but the Great Fire of 1666 destroyed any record of their prior existence. Anyway, they were firmly (re)established in 1770. In 1801, Hermina Yardley married soap-heir William Cleaver, whose father had a perfumery business in London. Named for William Yardley, who purchased the business in 1823. They made: perfumes, soaps, hair pomades, and powders. Presently located at 33 Old Bond Street, from 1910. (See: Bon Street/Old Bond Street/33.)

Ye Olde Cheshire Cheese - Wine Office Court, 145 Fleet Street, the City. Opened in 1667. Samuel Johnson and Charles Dickens dined here.

- See: Fleet Street/145.
- See: Ye Olde Cheshire Cheese, under the INNS/PUBS section.

Ye Olde Mitre Tavern - (See under the INNS/PUBS section.)

year, beginning of - The calendar was adjusted in the year 1752, because of prior calculations on how the world spun had led to tiny bits of lost time, throwing the old calendar out of sync by eleven days. From medieval times until 1752, the beginning of the year (in England) was annually on Lady Day (the Feast of the Annunciation of the Blessed Virgin) on March 25th. But after the adjustment, the beginning of the year was changed to January 1st. You can find some graves where the deceased passed at just the wrong time, so that their death date shows they died both in 1751 (old calendar) and 1752 (new calendar.)

Yeoman Warders - (AKA: the Yeoman Warders of Her Majesty's Royal Palace and Fortress the Tower of London. AKA: Beefeaters.) Guards at the Tower of London.

Henry VII decided that part of his personal, dismounted bodyguard (Yeomen of the Guard,) who traveled everywhere with him, should also guard the Tower of London; this second group became the Yeoman Warders. The two units used to be united, but no longer are, being now distinct bodies; even so, the two groups still wear the same red and gold uniform, although the Yeomen of the Guard add a red cross-belt that the Yeoman Warders do not. Their red uniforms are for state occasions. The dark blue uniforms are "undress," being introduced in the 19th century. They wear the well-known flat black hats.

Again, Yeoman Warders are not to be confused with the Yeomen of the Guard - except in the fact that the Yeomen Warders and Yeomen Guards are both members of the Yeomen of the Guard, Extraordinary.

The Yeoman Warders all come from the Armed Forces (the British Army, the Royal Marines, and the Royal Air Force. Traditionally they did not draw from the Royal Navy, not until 2011, when two sailors became Yeoman Warders. To qualify, one must have 22 years of military service, must have reached the rank of warrant officer, must be 40-55 years old (at the time of appointment,) and must have gained the long service and good conduct medal.

- See: Beefeaters, under B - A nickname that the Yeoman Warders seriously dislike.
- See: Tower of London/"Other Places & Things"/Yeomen Warders.
- See: Yeomen of the Guard - For comparison.

Yeoman's Row - Just west of Beauchamp Place, on Brompton Road's south side. Still has some red brick late Georgian houses.

Yeomen of the Guard - (AKA: the Sovereign's Bodyguard.) This military corps date back to 1485, founded by Henry VII at the Battle of Bosworth, in 1485. (Like the Yeoman Warders, the Yeomen of the Guard come from service in the military.)

There were 40 Yeoman of the Guard on duty (during the day, 20 at night) in the 18th century. By 1813 their number was reduced to one daily division, which lasted until about 1837.

They are now a ceremonial position, accompanying the monarch at some State affairs, such as the Maundy service or Buckingham House garden parties, and inspecting the

Palace of Westminster cellars in remembrance of 1605's Guy Fawkes' gunpowder plot. They only muster when needed, and still wear the red and gold uniform in the Tudor style.

Not to be confused with Yeomen Warders, who serve at the Tower of London.

- See: St. James's Palace/Gentlemen at Arms.
- See: St. James's Palace/Yeomen of the Guard.
- See: Yeoman Warders - For information of the one difference in uniforms.

York Gate - Formal entrance into Regent's Park (the south gate.) The name also applies to a short street on the park's southern edge. By Nash, 1822. Named for Prinny's brother, the Duke of York. (Not to be confused with: York Water Gate.)

York House - Pall Mall. (Not to be confused with York House, Stable Yard Road. See: Stable Yard Road/York House.) Built in the 1760s. Palladian style. Bought as a personal residence in 1787 for its new owner: Prince Edward, the Duke of York. Described as small. Edward died in 1767 (just age 28.) At this time it was called York House. Prince Henry, Duke of Cumberland, moved in, and it became known as Cumberland House. In 1801 it was sold to the Union Club. Purchased in 1806 by the Board of Ordnance, yet called Cumberland House, and used thus for some 100 years. Pulled down in 1908-11, and the Royal Automobile Club is located at the site.

- See: Buckingham Street.
- See: Cumberland House.

York Palace -

- See: Whitehall, Royal Palace of/York House.
- See: York House.

- Debtor's Prison: 1705. In the castle.

York Place - This street's name was York Place until ca. 1925, when it became just another part of Baker Street. York Place ran perpendicular to York Street.

Was once the site of a famous palace. The See of York (archbishop) bought York Place in 1245, and made it into a luxurious palace for the Archbishop(s) of York. Was confiscated by Henry VIII in 1529 and called: Whitehall. (See under W.)

York Place was demolished in the 1670s; a complex of streets took its place: George Street, Villiers Street, Duke Street, Buckingham Street - all of which names were derived from the Duke of Buckingham, who wanted to be remembered by posterity. (See: Stable Yard Road.)

- 14: (York Place, Portman Square.) Pitt the Younger lived here from autumn/1802 to May/1804. (Now 120 Baker Street.)

York Street - St. James's. Was originally: Duke of York Street, through at least 1825; originally probably named for James, Duke of York, who became James II in 1685. (See: St. James's Square/York Street.)

- 19: Home (at different times) to: William Hazlitt, John Stuart Mill, and John Milton.

York Terrace - Regent's Park. 1822, by John Nash. (See: Park Crescent/York Terrace.)

York Water Gate - (Also seen written as: York Watergate. Also known simply as: Water Gate.) Not to be confused with Water Gate, an early name for Traitor's Gate at the Tower of London. Also not to be confused with the street named "York Gate.")

Located on the Embankment, near Westminster Bridge, at the bottom of Essex Street.

Built in 1626, for the Duke of Buckingham, and affixed with his motto: "Fidel Coticula Crux" ("The Cross is the Touchstone of Faith.") Built by Nicholas Stone (probably not by Inigo Jones, as is often stated.) It used to stand marking the very edge of the Thames, and, of course, the duke's residence, York House. (See: York House, under Y.) A huge arch. Since the Victoria Embankment, the gate has been left high and dry to the east of Villiers Street, in the Victoria Embankment Gardens. (See: Buckingham Street.)

Young Street - Kensington. Built in James II's time/17th century.

-Z-

Zimbabwe House - 429 Strand. Edwardian house, built 1907-08, for the British Medical Association. Has been the Zimbabwe House since 1937, (and before that was Rhodesia House.)

Zoological Society, the - Regent's Park. Founded in 1826; Gardens opened in 1828. In 1834 the Menagerie (formerly housed in the Tower of London) melded/moved into Regent's Park London Zoo. (See under R.)

zoos - The abbreviated word "zoo" was not coined until after 1831. The much more common Regency term for a collection of live animals would have been: menagerie.

- See: Cross's Menagerie - Pidcock's Menagerie.
- See: Exeter Exchange.
- See: London Zoo.
- See: Regent's Park/Zoological Gardens.
- See: Surrey Zoological Gardens.

- See: Tower of London/“Other Places & Things”/Royal Menagerie.
- See: Tower of London/“The Towers”/Lion Tower.
- See: Zoological Society, the.

Special Sections:

Bridges

British Counties

Churches

Clubs

Inns/Pubs

Theatres

Bibliography

BRIDGES:

Remarkably, until the year 1750 London Bridge was the *lone* bridge for the City of London that crossed the Thames. (Although there were a few other bridges in communities outside London proper.) With a lack of bridges, there were ferries, and many Watermen (essentially water taxis) for centuries. The Watermen's Company resisted all notions of more bridges near the City, fearing the loss of business, as indeed occurred when more bridges were finally built in the advancing 19th century.

The second City bridge over the Thames was Westminster Bridge in 1750. Maps prior to 1750 refer to "bridges," but they're really referring to piers or landing places.

Even after a bridge went in, it was often still possible to take a ferry or Waterman's craft instead. (See: ferry, under F, in the Alpha section.)

Albert Bridge - 1873. One of the loveliest bridges in London.

Battersea Bridge - Made of wood, by Henry Holland, 1771-72. Built where a ferry had been during James I's reign, which (according to AN ENCYCLOPAEDIA OF LONDON) "...was granted to the Earl of Lincoln by letters patent for £40. Built with 19 spans (of varying widths); the arches proved difficult for boats to navigate through. Lord Spencer and seventeen associates financed the bridge. In 1799 it was lighted by oil lamps, and in 1824 by gas, the pipes being brought over from Chelsea. Free of tolls in 1879. Major repairs in 1873; demolished in 1885. Present bridge dates from 1886-90, with five cast-iron arches. The only bridge between Westminster and Putney.

Blackfriars Bridge - 1760-69, Portland stone. Opened in November, 1769. Officially known as William Pitt (the Elder) Bridge, (and sometimes as the Westminster Bridge) but very soon was popularly called the Blackfriars Bridge due to its locale near that organization's locale. Designed by Robert Mylne (surveyor of St. Paul's Cathedral.) Nine elliptical arches; 995 feet long, connecting Middlesex to Surrey. Free of tolls in 1785. Despite being called "a very handsome bridge," in 1810 it was described as "decaying rapidly." Restored thoroughly in 1833. Demolished in 1860, with a temporary bridge here until 1865; the present bridge dates from November, 1869, at which time it was called the New Blackfriars Bridge; designed by

Joseph Cubitt in a style termed Venetian-Gothic, now five arches (mostly of iron) on granite piers. Widened in 1907-9 from 80 feet wide to 110 feet wide, for trams.

Bloody Bridge - (See: Five Fields/Bloody Bridge, under F in the Alpha section.)

Chelsea Bridge - 1851-8, suspension bridge; built and designed by Thomas Page. Toll until 1879. First called Victoria Bridge. Present bridge dates from 1934-7.

Clattern Bridge - Kingston. 12th C., still standing.

Deptford Bridge - 1883. (See: Deptford/Deptford Bridge.)

Fulham Bridge - (See: Putney Bridge, below.)

Grosvenor Bridge - 1860. First railway bridge built across the Thames. (See: Sloane Square/Bloody Bridge, under S in the Alpha section.)

Hammersmith Bridge - First suspension bridge in London, 1824-27. Designed by Tierney Clarke. Rebuilt 1887.

Hampton Court Bridge - Crossed the Thames from Hampton Court to Molesey. First built in 1750-53, rebuilt of timbers in 1775-8. There was an iron bridge in 1865, being pulled down in 1930. A bigger, wider bridge opened in 1933, a few yards distant from the site of the old bridge.

Hungerford Bridge - Completed in 1845; by Brunel the Younger; named for Hungerford Market. Opened as a suspension foot bridge for pedestrians. Its center span was 676 feet long. Removed ca. 1861-5 in order to build Charing Cross Station, (the removed bridge being then moved to span the River Avon near Bristol.)

Iron Bridge - Late Regency and early-Victorian nickname for Southwark Bridge. (See: Southwark Bridge, below.) The nickname came from an iron bridge being a new approach in bridge-building.

Kew Bridge - (There had been a horse-ferry here until 1759.) Was first built of wood, 1758-9, a toll-bridge. Then a stone bridge, 1784-89. Free of tolls in 1873. Rebuilt in 1903, at which time it was named for the monarch who opened it, Edward VII, although everyone still called it Kew Bridge.

Kingston Bridge – One here since medieval times. Present bridge of brick since 1825-28. Widened in 1914.

See: Hampton Wick/Kingston Bridge, under H in the Alpha section.

See: Kingston-upon-Thames/Kingston Bridge, under K in the Alpha section.

Lambeth Bridge - (The ancient way to get from Lambeth to London was by ferry.) 1862, suspension bridge, restricted to pedestrian use. Present bridge dates from 1932 (no longer just pedestrian.)

London Bridge - (AKA: Old London Bridge.) Southwark. Ancient; there may have been a bridge (not far east of any subsequent London Bridge) as early as the 2nd century. Dio Cassius (Roman statesman and historian of Greek origin) wrote of invading Germans who either swam the Thames or "got over a bridge a little way up stream.") At any rate, records speak of a woman being drowned for witchcraft at London Bridge ca. 963-84 (although keep in mind that early references to "bridges" were actually referring to piers or landing places.)

Another reminder from the start of this BRIDGES section: keep in mind the astonishing fact that for almost 1,700 years, London Bridge was the <u>only</u> (London area) bridge across the Thames.

- See: ferry, under F in the Alpha section - For other means of crossing.
- See: watermen, under W in the Alpha section - For other means of crossing.

In the year 1066, it is rumored a timber bridge stood here, with a fortified gate resembling the other gates in the wall around London.

At any rate, the first bridge we are sure of was made of stone, built 1176-1209 by Peter the Bridgemaster (also known as Peter of Colechurch.) Yes, it took 33 years to build. Peter was the chaplain of St. Mary Colechurch in the Poultry.

We know for sure that a London Bridge stood here from 1176 until 1823.

It's now thought London Bridge wasn't built so much for traffic over the water, as to be a barrier against invaders. The spans were too low for most watercraft to pass under. Too, most other rivers' bridges demanded walker and carriage tolls (at least after first completion or rebuilds,) so many people chose to pay ferry or watermen fees instead. Indeed, until the development of (and growing supply of) carriages in the 17th C., most people traveled by water (or by walking.)

The bridge was 926 feet long, 20 feet wide, and rose 30 feet above the Thames. It had a drawbridge. It had 19 pointed arches.

The practice of placing the heads of executed prisoners on spikes over the bridge seems to have started with the head of William Wallace (the Scotsman) in 1305. The last recorded spiked head was placed in 1678.

Sometime following the early 13th C. building of the bridge, houses and shops were also built atop it. PILGRIMS' LONDON states: "Over the tenth and longest pier a chapel was erected and dedicated to St. Thomas á Becket. The chapel had two levels, and the lower one was accessible by stairs from the river." Because the bridge had houses built (quite compactly) on it, and a narrow road, it naturally often was terribly congested.

DRIVING ON THE LEFT: Purportedly in medieval times a law was passed making it compulsory for drivers to pass on the right (that is, their right-hand side was the passing side,) a practice still in place on British roads. It is also claimed that drivers wanted their sword hand to be free, and since right-handedness is predominant, drivers chose to drive to the left. Either way, the Highway Bill made it law in 1835.

In 1582 waterwheels were outfitted at the two ends of the bridge, to pump drinking water up from the Thames; these were destroyed by fire in 1633. The pumping resumed in 1668-9; four waterwheels were in place by 1761; a fifth (called the Borough wheel) was added in 1767 at the southern end of the bridge.

In 1758-62 the houses and shops were removed from the bridge (after the bridge had burned in 1758,) and two central arches were removed and replaced by a single navigation span (so that larger boats could fit under it.)

LONDON THE AUTOBIOGRAPHY shows a letter by one Louis Simond, dated July 12, 1810, that states: "Nothing can well be uglier than London Bridge; every arch is of a size different from its next neighbor; there are more solid than open parts; it is in fact like a thick wall, pierced with small unequal holes here and there, through the current...rushes with great velocity, and in fact takes a leap, the difference between high and low water being upwards of 15 feet."

In 1823, an Act of Parliament was passed in order to build a new bridge; this is called New London Bridge (sometimes called Victorian London Bridge.) Was constructed upstream of the old one beginning on 3/15/1824. Completed on 8/1/1831; commissioned to John Rennie, it was completed by his son. The old bridge was used until the new one was opened. The city refused to allow waterwheels on the new bridge, so thus the pumping of water ceased.

Despite the old London Bridge being dismantled and moved (sold to an American millionaire in 1973 and reassembled brick by brick in Lake Havasu, Arizona, USA) there is a present London Bridge. It dates from 1967, a concrete version (1/3 as light as the prior version that had been sinking into the riverbed.) This new London Bridge is just to the west of where the famous old bridge stood.

- Fishmongers' Hall: Was on London Bridge's northwest corner. (See: Fishmongers' Hall, under F in the Alpha section.)
- frost fairs: (See under F, in the Alpha section.)
- St. Magnus the Martyr: Resided right next to the bridge. Its entry provided an archway through which walking persons could continue on a path that kept them from walking on the road. It stood at the bridge's end until the bridge moved in the 19th century. (See: St. Magnus the Martyr, in the CHURCHES section.)
- Nonsuch House: (Not to be confused with Nonsuch Palace.) Was built on the bridge in 1579; lavishly ornamented. Built in Holland, and brought to London in total, brick by brick; built without mortar or iron, held together only by wooden dowels and wedges. It went clear across London Bridge, having an archway for traffic. Gone from London Bridge ca. 1760.

(You may care to see: Pool of London, under P in the Alpha section.)

Macclesfield Bridge - (Nickname: Blow Up Bridge.) Serves as Regent's Park's north gate (the other gates being Gloucester Gate (east,) Hanover Gate (west,) and York Gate (south.) For some reasons, the bridge doesn't show on many period maps, but it is certain it existed by at least 1843. It got the unfortunate nickname when a barge filled with gunpowder was being towed up the Grand Junction Canal in 1874 and exploded.

Millennium Bridge - Dates from, not surprisingly, the year 2000. Near to St. Paul's. Is a foot bridge. Is featured in the film *Harry Potter and the Deathly Hallows, Part 2.*

Putney Bridge - (AKA: Fulham Bridge.) Links London over the Thames from Putney to the south and Fulham to the north. There was a temporary bridge here in 1642, built by the Earl of Essex. Medieval parish churches yet reside at either end. But until 1729, to cross here meant taking a water ferry.

The first permanent structure was built 1727-29, opened in November, 1729, timber structure, with a toll-house at both ends. Built by a carpenter, Thomas Phillips, to designs of architect Sir Jacob Acworth. Toll at first was a half-penny, and a whole penny on Sundays (the latter for a fund to provide for widows and orphans of Watermen.) Tolls discontinued in 1880. From when it began, in official records it is oft times also called Fulham Bridge. 26 spans at first (later, reduced to 23); 789 feet long x 24 feet wide. Had openings for ships to pass through, the center (and largest) one of which was called Walpole's Lock (for Sir Robert

Walpole, who worked to obtain the Act of Parliament for constructing this bridge.) Demolished soon after an 1850 ship collision. Rebuilt (on a new alignment) in 1884-6 of stone by Sir Joseph Bazalgette, of Cornish granite; widened in 1934. Not to be confused with Putney Bridge Railway Bridge, which is nearby. (See: Putney/Putney Bridge, under P, in the Alpha section.)

Queen Elizabeth II Bridge - Across the Thames at Dartford, 1991.

Regent's Bridge - (See: Vauxhall Bridge, below.)

Richmond Bridge - Leads from London, across the Thames, to Richmond-upon-Thames (the latter of which is also simply called Richmond.) Five arched spans (plus a parapet) masonry bridge in Portland stone built by James Paine in 1774-77, replacing a horse ferry that was here. Described as being very ornamental. Free of tolls in 1859. Widened in 1938-9 with efforts made to preserve its appearance.

Southwark Bridge - (Pronounced: Suth-ick.) Privately built in 1814-19; opened at midnight, by lamplight, on 3/24/1819; funded by the Southwark Bridge Company; charged a passage toll; proved financially unsuccessful. By John Rennie. Three cast iron arches supported by stone piers. Largest bridge ever constructed of this material (iron; it was first known as Iron Bridge, Dickens calls it thus in "Little Dorrit.") Central span was 240 feet long. City Corporation objected to it on grounds it would be an obstruction to river traffic. To obtain their consent, Rennie had to undertake to cross the river in three spans. Sold to the Corporation of London in 1866 (at one quarter of its original cost,) at that time becoming free of tolls. Demolished in 1913, with the present five-span steel bridge opening in 1921.

Staines Bridge - Staines. Near Windsor. Begun in 1829 under Rennie. Opened 1834.

Strand Bridge - In 1816, by Act of Parliament, its name was changed from Strand Bridge to Waterloo Bridge, to honor that battle. (See: Waterloo Bridge, below.)

Tower Bridge - Not until 1886-94. Queen Victoria commanded it be made to look old, so it would fit in with its surroundings. (Is located close to the Tower of London.)

Upminster Bridge - Upminster, Havering. Over the River Ingrebourne. Existed before 1782. Was wooden until 1891, the later version being described as "dull."

Vauxhall Bridge - 1811-16, first cast-iron bridge over the Thames in London. At first known as Regent (or Regent's) Bridge. The first stone (on the Middlesex side) was laid by Lord Dundas, as proxy for the Prince Regent. It was first called Regent Bridge, but its nearness to Vauxhall Gardens shortly led to its name change. John Rennie was hired to design it, but his designs were thought too expensive. James Walker took over, completing the bridge in 1816. Free of tolls in 1879. The second Vauxhall Bridge was built in 1895-1906, of granite and steel. No longer remains.

Victoria Bridge - 1857. Suspension bridge, built for railways. First called Victoria Bridge, but soon called Chelsea Bridge. (See: Chelsea Bridge, above.)

Victoria London Bridge - (See: London Bridge, above.)

Wandsworth Bridge - 1873. Reconstructed in 1936-40.

Waterloo Bridge - Built 1811-17, opened by the Prince Regent on the 2nd anniversary of the Battle of Waterloo, 6/18/1817. By 1816, Waterloo Bridge was the new name of the Strand Bridge (the name was changed to Waterloo by Act of Parliament in 1816, after Wellington's win at Waterloo.) John Rennie's elegant bridge of nine gracefully curved arches, with a Doric arch at each end. Built of gray Cornish granite. Was dubbed one of the glories of London. Free of tolls in 1878. Demolished in 1936; rebuilt in 1937 and opened in 1945, by Sir Giles Gilbert Scott. In the 19th C. it got the nickname "Bridge of Sighs" due to being favored by those wanting a bridge from which to leap and commit suicide.

Westminster Bridge - Lies outside the official City of London. Bridge spans the Thames from Westminster to Lambeth. Built 1738-50; opened in 1750, built by Charles Labelye, a French-Swiss engineer-architect.

It was only the second bridge over the Thames; built of masonry (and similar in appearance to London Bridge at the time.) Had 15 arches. Its piers were founded in caissons (first use of such in Britain.) The river here is 1,223 feet wide. The bridge had fifteen arches.

Twelve watchmen per night were needed to protect nighttime travelers, by rousting out the robbers who frequented the recesses on the bridge.

Had deteriorated by 1837; the foundation was revamped.

The cast-iron bridge that replaced this was built in 1854-62 by Thomas Page (and was wider than the old bridge); cast-iron bridge with 7 arches. The statue of Boadicea was added in

1902 (a second source said the 1850s.) The South Bank Lion; once stood for the Old Lion Brewery, made of Coade stone, sits on the Lambeth (south) side of the bridge since 1966.

William Pitt Bridge - Officials tried to get the public to use this name for the sometimes-called Westminster Bridge (not to be confused with the other Westminster Bridge,) but the public insisted on using the name of Blackfriars Bridge. (See: Blackfriars Bridge, above.)

Windsor Bridge - Spanning the Thames from Windsor to Eton College. 1822. 200 feet long, stone, with three arches.

Woodford Bridge - Bridge here since the 13th century. (See: Woodford/Woodford Bridge, under W in the Alpha section.)

BRITISH COUNTIES (and areas outside London):

(This is a *very* limited listing. It does not contain all the counties of England, and has only a brief listing for Scotland.)

NOTE: When looking at the distances listed below, keep in mind that a loaded coach and four could travel approximately five miles/8 km per hour, and that was if the roads and the weather were good. A lighter carriage (such as a phaeton or curricle) could manage 8-10 miles/12-16 km per hour.

(See: Royal Warrant, under R.)

Bath - The city of. To drive from Bath to London is approximately: 119 miles/192 km. In the County of Somerset, in southwest England. (Pronounced: Bawth, with a short A sound, rather rhyming with "Goth".) Bath's founding architect was John Wood (1704-54.) "Ruled" for 50 years by Richard "Beau" Nash, who came to Bath in 1705. Nash wore an immense white hat and rich embroidery on his clothes. He drove a chariot drawn by six gray horses, with laced lackeys and heralded by French horns. Said to have taught the British (at least at Bath and Tunbridge) to be more relaxed upon first meetings.

At the turn of the 19th century, it was considered *de rigeur* to be tired of Bath after a six week stay.

Low in a bowl of hills, Bath can be stifling and airless. Or rather rainy.

Bath is largely built from local, golden-hued Bath Stone, and many of them are Georgian in their architectural style.

Renowned for the foodstuffs one could acquire here.

To bathe (in seawater) in Bath: between 6 and 9 am, every morning, "the lady is brought in a close chair, dressed in her bathing clothes, to the bath; and being in the water, the woman who attends her presents her with a little floating dish like a basin, into which the lady puts a handkerchief, a snuff-box and a nosegay. She then traverses the bath...and, having amused herself thus while she thinks proper, calls for her chair and returns to her lodgings." Men and women bathed together, which Doctor Johnson called "barbaric."

The bathing was followed by a general assembly at the Pump-house, some for pleasure, some to drink the hot water, enlivened by music and conversation. Sometimes the men and ladies would withdraw to separate coffee houses.

After dinner, they met again at the Pump-house for balls or plays or visits to the gaming tables. Bath also had bowling greens, parades and promenades (there was a promenade every Wednesday at the Lower Rooms,) walks along the River Avon, and public breakfasts (held in Sydney Gardens.)

- Abbey Churchyard: The heart of the city, called the pump-yard in Austen's *Northanger Abbey.* A spacious paved area for sedan-chairs, their blue-coated attendants awaiting customers here. West front of the abbey is on the east, the Pump room on the south, the Colonnade on the west, and a row of shops on the north.
- Ainslie's Belvedere: Ca. 1790. Three stories.
- Alfred Street: 1768.
    - 8-15: 1768 terrace. Described as "fine." Number 14 is known as Alfred House.
- Argyle Street: Ca. 1789. For Sir William Pulteney, by Thomas Baldwin. At first was called: Argyle Buildings. Was meant as homes, but shops were added on in the next few decades.
- Assembly Rooms: Anyone could host an assembly room, but here we speak of the most famous (and regularly held) ones in Bath, the Lower Rooms and the Upper Rooms, otherwise known as the Assembly Rooms. (See: Lower Rooms, below. See: Upper Rooms, below.) The Lower Rooms were built in 1708 by John Wood the Senior; the Upper Rooms by John Wood the Younger in 1771. Most assembly rooms had an anteroom set aside for card playing.
- Bath street: At first called Cross Bath Street. 1791, by Thomas Baldwin. Shopping.
- Beechen Cliff: Literally a cliff, a favorite site to walk along and to view.
- Brock Street: 17-house terrace connecting the Circus to the Royal Crescent. 1763-67.
- Camden-Place: Later known as Camden Crescent. 1788, by John Eveleigh. Dignified, respectable address.
- Chapel Court:
    - 4-5: St. John's Hospital: (AKA: St. John the Baptist Hospital.) 1174, by Bishop Reginald Fitz Jocelin, for the "poor infirm." Present building dates from 1716.
- Cheap Street: Millinery or pastries were to be had here.

- Circus Terraces, the: (Often AKA: the Circus.) Built in 1766 by John Wood the Younger. At first, it was called the King's Circus. Three long, curved terraces. You could hire a room, a floor, or even an entire house here. Not to be confused with The Royal Crescent.
- Colonnades, the: At the Roman Baths. (See: Pump Room.) These are tall columns there.
- Crescent fields: The green slopes before the Royal Crescent. (See: Royal Crescent, below.)
- Cross Bath Street: (See: Bath Street, above.)
- Edgar Buildings:
    - 1-9: 1761, nine terrace houses, on raised pavement above George Street.
- Gay Street: By John Wood the Elder; completed by his son, John Wood the Younger. 1735.
- Gravel Walk: Runs behind the houses on the south side of Brock Street, connecting the Circus with the Royal Crescent.
- Great Pulteney Street: Ca. 1789. Broad and handsome pavements, over 1,000 feet long, 100 feet wide. Georgian terraces. (See: Sydney Gardens, below.)
- Green Park Buildings: Jane Austen lived here after leaving Sydney Place.
- John Wood & Son: Architects, working primarily in Bath. 1754. Among many other buildings they built the Circus (1766) and the Royal Crescent (1770.)
- King's Bath: Pump Room. The most favored of the three pumps in town. (Drinking the waters, music.) Built in 1706, and enlarged in the late 18th century (ca. 1790.)
- King's Circus: (See: Circus, above.)
- Lansdowne Hill: There by at least 1800.
- Lansdowne Crescent: On Lansdowne Hill. 1789-93.
- Laura Place: Diamond shaped square, out of which issues Great Pulteney Street.
- Lower Rooms: Assembly rooms. Date from 1708; additions in 1720 and 1749 (a second source said built in 1728.) In 1802, Tuesdays, Fancy ball. A promenade was held here on Wednesdays. On Fridays, dress balls. Beau Nash was Master of Ceremonies from 1705-61. In 1806, the Master of Ceremonies here was Mr. Le Bas. (See: Upper Rooms, below.)
- Marlborough Buildings: On the other side of the Royal Crescent, running downhill at right angles to it. Fashionable address.
- Milsom Street: Shopping, and lodging. 1762, by Thomas Lightholder. This street was mentioned several times in works by Jane Austen.

- North Parade: Built as part of a Royal Forum…that never came to be. The mid 18th C. facade remains, mostly hotels or shops now.
- North Parade Bridge: 1836, by William Tierney Clark.
- Orchard Street: (See: Theatre Royal, below.)
- Paragon, the: Early 18th century.
    - 1: Jane Austen's uncle, Leigh Perrot, lived here.
- Pelican Inn: (See: Walcot Street, below.)
- Pierrepont Street: Built as part of a Royal Forum…that never came to be. Mostly hotels or shops now, though the mid 18th C. facade remains.
- Pulteney Bridge: Robert Adam, completed in 1774. Still there, and still doing double-service as both a bridge and a shopping arcade. Very altered over time.
- Pump Room: Inscription there reads in Greek "Water is Best." (See: King's Bath, above.) Rebuilt in 1789-99. Three glasses of the water were drunk before lunch, and three more after, for the "curative" effect. There had been a Roman Bath House here in the first through fourth centuries. Georgian-Regency persons did not bathe here, instead taking "restorative drinks" from the rediscovered well of waters here. (See: King's Bath.)
- Queen Square: Spacious, open, airy, "fine Palladian" design. Built between 1729-36 by John Wood the Elder. By 1814 it was considered old-fashioned and not quite desirable. The obelisk at the square's center dates from 1738, put up by orders from Beau Nash (Master of Ceremony at the Assembly Rooms.)
- River Avon, the: There are other rivers of the same name, so this one is clarified as the Bristol Avon. "Avon" is related to the Welsh word for river.
- Roman Baths:
    - See: See King's Bath, above.
    - See: Pump Room, above.
- Royal Crescent: 1767-74. Highly fashionable residence, premier. People strolled on the front lawns, a fashionable habit on a Sunday. The green slopes before it were called the "Crescent fields," and were a fashionable walking spot. Had broad pavements, for the use of the strollers. Not to be confused with The Circus Terraces.
- St. John's Church: 1861-63. 222 foot tall spire added in 1867. Roman Catholic.
- St. Swithins, Walcot Street: 1779-90. Jane Austen's father was buried here in 1805.
- Somerset Place: Started in 1790, but architect John Eveleigh went bankrupt; his facades remain, but the rest of the building wasn't done until into the 1820s.

- South Parade: Built as part of a Royal Forum…that never came to be. The mid 18th C. facade remains, but mostly shops or hotels now.
- Sydney Gardens: (AKA: Sydney Pleasure Gardens.) At the end of Great Pulteney Street. Music, fireworks, public breakfasts (held on Mondays and Thursdays, at least once attended by Jane Austen; cakes, rolls and tea served while music was played.) Had a "moveable orchestra," two bowling greens, and a labyrinth. Surrounding it was "a ride for ladies and gentlemen on horseback."
- Sydney Place: Ca. 1795-1800.
  - 4: Built in 1792. Jane Austen lived here from 1801-5.
  - 93: Queen Charlotte lived here in 1817.
- Theatre Royal: Central, older part of town. Founded 1750, granted a royal patent in 1768 (first Royal provincial playhouse.) This was the old theatre, on Orchard Street, near the abbey. Two plays performed each evening. Its last performance was on 7/13/1805. Another, new theatre opened in October, 1805; gold and crimson interior. There were plays at this new theatre at least on Tuesdays and Saturdays, if not more often.
- Union Passage: A pedestrian-only passageway, called "an interesting alley."
- Union Street, cut through in 1806.
- Upper Rooms: Built in 1769-71. Assembly rooms. In 1802 there were two dress balls given every week, Monday at the new Rooms (Upper Rooms,) and Friday at the Lower Rooms. Two Fancy balls also, here on Thursday (Tuesday at the Lower Rooms.) Nine subscription concerts and three choral nights, in the winter on Wednesdays. In 1808, Jane Austen wrote: "ball on Monday not a very full one, not more than a thousand."
- Walcot Street: The Pelican Inn was there.
- Westgate Buildings: Austen portrays it as a "miserable home." But she also wrote it was not so "badly situated…the street is broad and has rather a good appearance."
- White Hart Inn: Directly opposite the Pump Room and the Colonnade.
- Widcombe Crescent: 1808, by Thomas Baldwin. 14 Georgian houses.

Berkshire - (Pronounced: Bark-shur.) To drive from West Berkshire to London is approximately: 50 miles/80 km A county in southeast England. Recognized as a Royal County in 1957 (by Queen Elizabeth II, and due to containing Windsor Castle.)

- Calais: Castle Street, Milliner from at least 1813. By 1820, Mr. Caleb was milliner to Victoria, the princess, and the Duchess of Gloucester. 1824, moved from Castle

Street to High Street (opposite the main gates of Windsor) with his haberdashery/silk mercer/lacemaker brother.

- Pickerings: Established 1770 at 50 High Street. Chemists. In approximately 1810, the business became Wood's (Pharmacy.) Served George III. Royal Warrant granted by Victoria. (The building remains today, described as a pretty Regency era building.)
- Windsor: The castle; the town. (See: Windsor, under W in the Alpha section.)
- Ye Olde Bell Hotel: Dates from 1135.

Birmingham - In the county of West Midlands. To drive from Birmingham to London is approximately: 129 miles/208 km Mainly known as a metal manufacturing district, especially ironwares. Circa 1780 the population was 50,000. Grew rapidly in the 19th century; called "London in miniature." The second most populated city in England, after London.

- Lunar Society: Founded 1775 for promotion of science and its application to industry. Until 1813, Called the Lunar Society because they met on the night of the full moon.
- Midlands Bank: 1836. Moved to London in 1930-6.

Brighton - Not a county, but a city in the county of Sussex. To drive from Brighton to London is approximately: 50 miles/76 km The Golden Cross was a famous and flourishing coaching inn at Charing Cross that provided fast day coaches to Brighton (12 miles/19 km per hour, reaching Brighton in 5 hours.)

It was becoming fashionable to call it "Brighton" at the turn of the century, rather than the longer "Brighthelmstone." One famous day, Prinny made it from London to Brighton (and back again to London) in 10 hours. He enjoyed the horse races held there. In 1818, a woman wrote complaining that the public coaches were bringing people to Brighton for only six shillings and this was naturally affecting what manner of person (low) was coming to Brighton.

- Brighton House: (Later known as: the Royal Pavilion; was referred to as the Pavilion, or the Marine Pavilion, by at least 1801; but note it was not the "Royal Pavilion" until ca. 1815-22.)

In 1786 this was a farmhouse, which Prinny at first rented, then bought for Mrs. Fitzherbert (his secret wife) to live in. Remodeled ca. 1787; GEORGE IV, PRINCE OF WALES states: "This first version of the Prince's Marine Pavilion was a long, low Graeco-Roman house faced with cream-coloured tiles, the centrepiece of which was a domed rotunda encircled by six Ionic columns bearing classical statues. The handsome, bow-fronted wings which flanked the rotunda to north and south were provided with those decorative ironwork balconies which were soon to become so distinctive a feature of the town." At this time Henry Holland enlarged it by adding a balancing wing, bow windows, iron balconies, and a circular saloon.

Was altered a bit in 1801 and 1803, with Edward Crace (and his son, Frederick, both interior designers) giving it a Chinese interior design. In 1803 the stables were given an East Indian design. It was decided in 1807 to remodel again, but funds were chronically short until 1815, at which time John Nash made it over into the exotic Brighton (aka: Royal) Pavilion from 1815-1822, continuing with the Indian style. The exterior today is pretty much as it was in 1822.

- Chain Pier: The first of its kind. Is built in 1823.
- famous "dippers": Martha Gunn, and Old Smoaker. (Dippers helped bathers get in and out of the seawater.)
- Golden Cross: London coaching inn. (See under the INNS/PUBS section.) Got passengers to Brighton in 5 hours.
- Marine Parade: There by at least 1801.
- Royal Pavilion: (See: Brighton House, above.)
- Royal Stables: Were (somewhat tongue-in-cheek) said to be more grand than the remodel of the Pavilion itself.
- St. Nicholas: Brighton's parish church, until 1873 when St. Peter's (built in 1827) replaced it as such.
- The Steine: This is what the primitive waterfront along the sea was called in Brighton. The Chain Pier was erected in 1822 (collapsed in 1896.)
- Theatre Royal: Opened in 1806.

Bristol - The city and county of Bristol. To drive from Bristol to London is approximately: 517 miles/832 km. Straddles the River Avon. In southwest England. In the 18th C. it was the third largest city (in population) in England, after London and Norwich; second by 1750. Manchester and Liverpool, however, passed Bristol by the early 19th century.

- Clifton Assembly Rooms: Opened in 1806.

Cambridge - The city of. To drive from Cambridge to London is approximately: 62 miles/100 km. In the east of England; it is in the ceremonial county of Cambridgeshire (formed in 1974); historically was part of Northamptonshire. Built along the River Cam. Is a university town. The university dates back to the 13th century. Now contains 31 colleges. Some of them: King's College; Pembroke College; St. John's College; Trinity College. (See: Cambridge, under C in the Alpha section.)

Canterbury - The city of. To drive from Cambridge to London is approximately: 54 miles/87 km. Is a cathedral city; in the county of Kent, in southeast England. Known as a Middle Ages pilgrimage site.

- Blackfriars: 13-14th century. Dominican Priory. (Now a Christian Science Church.)
- Canterbury Cathedral: Founded in the year 597. Secularized in 1541. (See: Canterbury, under C in the Alpha section.)

Cheltenham - A city in the county of Gloucestershire, England. To drive from Cheltenham to London is approximately: 97 miles/156 km. A Regency era resort area, with Regency era buildings still to found there.

Cheshire - (Pronounced Ches-shur.) A county in northwest England. To drive from Cheshire to London is approximately: 542 miles/871 km. Supplied cheese and salt to London.

- James North & Sons: Market Street, Hyde, Cheshire. Safety products since the 18th century.

Derbyshire - (Pronounced Dar-bee-shur.) A county in England's East Midlands. To drive from Derbyshire to London is approximately: 126 miles/204 km.

- Crown Derby (china): George III allowed Crown Derby to mark its china with a crown. ("Royal" was added to the name in 1890, by Queen Victoria's edict, hence making the name the now more familiar Royal Crown Derby. Business was established in the 1750s. (You may care to see: Doulton Fine China, under D in the Alpha section.)

Devon - Is a county in southwest England. To drive from Devon to London is approximately: 175 miles/282 km. For 200+ years, Devon has been a place for potteries, particularly in Barnstable.

- Ford Abbey: Jeremy Bentham (philosopher/radical) rented summer cottages here from 1817 onward. (See: Queen's Square Place, under Q in the Alpha section, for more on Jeremy Bentham.)
- House of Sutton, the: Established in the city of Reading in 1806. Corn merchant dealing in agricultural seeds, corn & grasses, using the penny post so customers could order. (Really took off as a seed catalog-type business after the railroads came in, but was a thriving business prior to that as well.)

Essex - Is a county in southeast England. To drive from Essex to London is approximately: 178 miles/287 km.

- Audley End: Built 1603; partially bought in 1669 by Charles II. Owing to the debt not being paid in full, after Charles II's death the property passed on to the Earl of Suffolk. Remodeled in the 18-19th centuries.
- Colchester: Has the largest Norman-era keep in England (the second is the Tower Keep, Tower of London.)

Hampshire - Is a county on the southern coast of England. To drive from Hampshire to London is approximately: 69 miles/111 km.

- Kempshott Park: Near Basingstoke. Prinny kept stag-hounds there at his hunting-box (around 1790); he referred to it as his "country house."

Hertfordshire - Is a county in southern England. To drive from Hertfordshire to London is approximately: 26 miles/42 km.

- Hatfield House: Once belonged to Elizabeth I; sold in 1607. Was home to Barbara Cartland, deceased 20th C. romance novelist.

Kent - Is a county in southeast England. To drive from Kent to London is approximately: 39 miles/63 km. The oldest surviving place name in Britain (the second oldest is: the Thames.)

- Aylesford:
  - The Friars: 13th century. Carmelite Friary. North side of the River Medway. 16th C. private house, now again a Carmelite priory/retreat.
- Margate: Sea-bathing town, mid 18th C. into the Regency.
- Tunbridge Wells: This city has been a health resort since 1606. Added "Royal" before its name after being granted the privilege in 1909 by Edward VII.

Lancashire - Is a ceremonial county (an area of England to which a Lord Lieutenant is appointed, 1997) in northwest England. To drive from Lancashire to London is approximately: 230 miles/369 km. Called "King Cotton," though even by the 1820s a good deal of spinning was still done on wooden hand-jennies, a craft often done at home. (See: spinning jennies, under S in the Alpha section.)

- Liverpool: This city historically first lay within West Derby; became a borough in 1207; then was in the borough of Lancashire. Became a city in 1880.
  - The Grand National: Horserace, from 1837. (See: Grand National, under G in the Alpha section.)

Manchester - Is in northwest England. To drive from Manchester to London is approximately: 209 miles/336 km. In the 18th C. became the nation's largest provincial town, due to it textile industry. Amazingly, did not have a member in Parliament until 1832 (probably due to Jacobite/disaffection leanings toward the Crown.)

- St. Peter's Field: Site of the "Peterloo" Massacre, Aug. 16, 1819. The first steam-loom mill was set up here in 1806.

Norfolk - Is a county in East Anglia, England. Its northern border is the North Sea. To drive from Norfolk to London is approximately: 106 miles/171 km.

- Houghton Hall: Early 18th C., Sir Robert Walpole (first Prime Minister's) home here by the 1720s. Palladian.
- Sandringham: Royal estate. (The present Queen's private home.) Occupied since Elizabethan times; a sizable Georgian mansion here, built in 1771. Purchased in 1861 for Edward, Prince of Wales (later Edward VII.)

Northamptonshire - Is a county in the East Midlands of England. (See: Cambridge, above.)

Nottingham - Is a city, in the county of Nottinghamshire, which is in the East Midlands. To drive from Nottingham to London is approximately: 128 miles/206 km.

- Trip to Jerusalem, the: Pub, founded 1189. (See under the INNS/PUBS section.)

Oxfordshire - Is a county in southeast England. To drive from Oxford (the city of) to London is approximately: 56 miles/90 km.

- Blenheim Palace: On Woodstock Manor. Baroque. Built in 1704 for the Duke of Marlborough. Designed by Sir John VanBrugh. Resembles a citadel to commemorate his greatest military victory (the Battle of Blenheim.) Had been an old royal hunting estate, given to Marlborough by Queen Anne. Capability Brown added statues to the roof and the lake mid 18th century.
- Early's of Witney: Witney Mills, Burford Rd., Witney, Oxfordshire. Blankets. In 1669, Thomas Early became (at age 14) an apprentice as a blanket-maker. Charter in 1711.
- Oxford: Medieval colleges. (See: Oxford, under O in the Alpha section.)

Scotland - (Clearly, NOT a county of England. See at its own separate entry below.)

Staffordshire - Is a county in the West Midlands of England. Landlocked. To drive from Staffordshire to London is approximately: 151 miles/242 km.

- Bass Brewing: Established in 1777 by William Bass at Burton-on-Trent. Brewers of East India Pale Ale, first produced in 1822.
- Spode: China (earthenware.) Established 1770. Josiah Spode Jr. came up with the bone ash formula which was the creation we now know as "bone china."

Suffolk - Is an ancient East Anglian county; it later merged with Mercia, and then Wessex. The North Sea lies to the east. Became the unified county of Suffolk in 1974, merging East Suffolk, Ipswich, and West Suffolk. To drive from Suffolk to London is approximately: 96 miles/154 km.

- Newmarket: Horse racing. (See: Newmarket, under N in the Alpha section.)

Sussex - Is a county in southeast England. (See: Brighton, above.)

West Midlands - In western-central England. Became a Parliamentary Borough in 1832. To drive from West Midlands to London is approximately: 106 miles/188 km.

- Birmingham: (See above, at its own listing.)
- Stevens & Williams: Stourbridge. Glassware manufacturers, established 1610 by Huguenots. Was known as Royal Brierly in 1740. Its popular cameo wares date from the 1880s. Royal Warrant from 1919.

Wiltshire - Is a county in southwest England. Landlocked. To drive from Wiltshire to London is approximately: 91 miles/147 km.

- Wilton Royal Carpets: 300+ years, 17th C. building. Royal Charter since William III, 1699. (Royal Warrant since 1908.) In the Regency, cut-pile Wilton carpeting was 4-6 shillings per yard.

Worcestershire - Is a county in southwest England. Landlocked. To drive from Worcestershire to London is approximately: 130 miles/209 km.

- Brintons: 200+ years, carpet manufacturers, Royal Warrant.
- Humphries of Kidderminster: Established 1790, Axminster carpets. Exclusive and popular.
- Lea & Perrins: Invented Worcestershire Sauce in 1837.
- Royal Worchester Porcelain Co. the: 1751, influenced by Chinese styles. 1788, George III gave permission for them to call themselves china manufacturers to Their Majesties, being then known as the Royal Porcelain Works.

Yorkshire - Is a county in northern England. It's the largest county in the United Kingdom. To drive from (north) Yorkshire to London is approximately: 198 miles/319 km.

- Castle Howard: Near Malton, vast country house, described as "one of the most striking in Britain." Started by William Talman, architect, but he was soon ousted in favor of Sir John VanBrugh and Nicholas Hawksmoor, for the third earl of Carlisle, Charles Howard; 1701-12; primarily Baroque.
- Scarborough: 1813, Lending library. (Was a reasonably fashionable seaside town; in the mid eighteenth century, a kind of genesis town for "spaws" to come.)

S C O T L A N D - Obviously, Scotland is *not* a county of England, and no such implication is intended.

United with England on 5/1/1707, thereby forming Great Britain, via the Act of Union. (See: Act of Union, under A in the Alpha section.)

In the 16th C. the bagpipes were mainly an *Irish* instrument; they were embraced by Scotland in the 18th century.

Kilts: (See: kilts, under K in the Alpha section.)

- Edinburgh: Acclaimed as "the Athens of the North" (a gathering place for intellectuals.) George IV visited Edinburgh in 1822; no British king had done so since the 1745 Jacobite Rebellion. (See: kilt, Scottish, under K in the Alpha section - George IV wearing one.)
    - Andrew Melrose & Co.: Canongate. A grocer's shop established here in 1812. (He was particularly interested in promoting teas.)
    - Balmoral: First leased to Queen Victoria in 1848. Bought by her in 1852. Royal residence. (See: INTRO-REIGNS section/British Kings & Queens and their Reigns/Victoria.)
    - Holyrood House: An abbey converted by James IV of Scotland into a royal residence. James V rebuilt it in 1543 following a fire. Charles II also rebuilt. Still a royal residence, for Elizabeth II.
    - Whytock (and Reid): Edinburgh furniture renovators. Richard Whytock was a textile manufacturer in 1807, of carpets and damasks. 1838, Royal Warrant issued. 1829-John Reid completed his apprenticeship (in Ayr.) In 1876, his sons went into business with Whytock.

  - William Crawford & Sons: Biscuit manufacturers (still.) 12 Hope Street, Edinburgh. Small shop established 1813.
- Gretna Green: (See: marriage, under M in the Alpha section.)
- Perthshire:
  - P. & J. Haggart: 32 Dunkeld Street, Aberfeldy, Perthshire. Tartan & woolen manufacturers. 1801, founded by James Haggart, from Cheviot sheep. Received its Royal Warrant in 1899.

CHURCHES (and CHAPELS):

Regency England was predominantly Anglican in faith (Church of England.) All churches in this section were Anglican during the Regency (unless otherwise noted.) They may well have begun life as Roman Catholic churches, but due to Henry VIII's founding of the Church of England in the 16th century, these churches became Anglican.

Note that Anglicans went to: church. Dissenters went to: chapel. However, there are many references to chapels in this section; most (indeed, the preponderance of the listings below called chapels) did not host Dissenters; they are usually the chapels inside of or attached to churches; they usually started life centuries ago as side chapels in Catholic churches. Once the churches were converted to Church of England, the chapels within tended to retain the names by which they had previously been called. (See: Dissolution of the Monasteries, under D.) So, just because a building or part of a building is referred to as a "chapel," that doesn't necessarily mean it's a place of worship for Dissenters. (See: Dissenters, under D in the Alpha section.) There was a selection of groups labeled as Dissenters (before and) during the Regency era, but the largest group was those who came to be known as: Methodists.

- See: Methodists, under M, in the Alpha section.
- See: religions - For a list of non-Anglican faiths in Regency London.

When an Anglican family was of rank in their community, they might well have their own (paid for) pew in church (often within short walls called a box.) Invariably these private, reserved pews faced each other across the church nave (rather than facing forward as did all the rest of the pews.) They might be immediately below the (usually elevated) pulpit, or might be up one story, looking slightly down on the pulpit.

"Peculiars" Note: There used to be thirteen churches in the City that were deemed peculiars. That is, they were exempt from the jurisdiction of the Bishop of London and the Archdeacon, being subject only to the Archbishop of Canterbury (who appointed the living - that is, the rector.) Only three remain:

1. St. Botolph's, Aldgate.
2. St. Edmund King and Martyr, Lombard Street.
3. St. Dunstan's in the West, Fleet Street.

The special ("peculiar") status of these three was revoked in 1841, leaving the above churches as peculiar in name only.

Nearly every church in London had an attached cemetery. (You may care to see: suicides, who weren't allowed a church burial.)

In the London of the Middle Ages there were some 100 churches, 88 of which burned in the Great Fire of 1666, a sad reality you will see reflected many times in this work. (You may care to see: Great Fire of 1666, under G in the Alpha section.)

ALPHA NOTE: Although you will find all the churches below listed in alphabetical order ("St." being alphabetized as "Saint,") be aware a church may be called by several names. Within old sources and materials there is an utter inconsistency in how the names and spellings are presented. This is not to be wondered at, as the churches are quite often the oldest buildings in Britain and therefore subject to creative spelling, possessions, and usage over the centuries.

I have put the churches in order according to the part of the city with which they are affiliated -or- by some other strongly identifying mark or title. Which St. Mary's are you looking for? There are over sixty listed below. It might pay to look twice, such as at: St. Mary -or- St. Mary's -or- St. Mary-le-Bow, etc.

The following list is made up of churches of particular or historical interest; there are other church listings in the Alpha sections under whatever area or borough in which they are to be found.

All Hallows Barking - (AKA: All-Hallows-by-the-Tower. AKA: All Hallows Barking-by-the-Tower. Also more rarely as: St. Mary's.) Byward Street, Great Tower Street, Tower Hill. The first church standing here was Saxon, built by Erkenwald, Bishop of London, prior to the year 675; founded by Ethelburga. A Norman church was built over the site in 1088. The present church dates from medieval times (13th & 15th centuries.) It is called "Barking" because it was once part of the Abbey of Barking, Essex. It is supposedly where Richard the Lionhearted's heart is interred. The square tower dates from 1659; Samuel Pepys (diarist) watched the Great Fire of 1666 from this tower. It is the only tower in London built by the Commonwealth's Puritans (who were far more famous for tearing things down.) The north porch (and the room over it) was added in 1883. John Quincy Adams (later an American president) married Catherine Johnson here in 1797. It is the oldest parish church in the City. Repaired after WWII damage, 1955-8, only casually resembling the medieval design.

All Hallows-Barking-by-the-Tower - (See: All Hallows Barking, above.)

All Hallows, Bread Street - Existed before 1227. Repaired in 1625. Burned in the Great Fire of 1666; rebuilt by Wren in 1680-4, at which time the parish of St. John the Evangelist, Friday Street united with All Hallows. It was pulled down in 1876-6, being then united with St. Mary-le-Bow.

All Hallows, Gospel Oak - After 1893.

All Hallows, Lombard Street - Existed by at least 1053. Rebuilt in 1494-1516. Burned in the Great Fire of 1666; rebuilt by Wren in 1694. John Wesley (founder of Methodism,) in 1735, gave his first extemporaneous sermon here. The church had a gateway at the street entrance, which was removed in 1865, and which was a mass of skulls (not real ones, but an artist's rendering.) It was referred to as "the Church Invisible" because it was so densely hemmed in by the surrounding buildings. In 1938 it was demolished; its parish being united with St. Edmund the King, Lombard Street. (See: St. Dionis Backchurch, below.)

All Hallows on the Wall - London Wall. (AKA: All Hallows, London Wall; its name was originally "-in-the-wall," being on a narrow strip of land adjoined to the old wall.) First mentioned ca. 1108. Rebuilt by Dance the Younger, 1765-7, replacing an earlier one of some six centuries that did *not* burn in the Great Fire of 1666. Much altered in 1891. Had extensive WWII damage, was abandoned for some twenty years, then rebuilt/re-consecrated in 1962; the body of the church is brick, but the tower is stone. Is the headquarters for the Council for Places of Worship (interested/active in preserving English churches.)

All Hallows Staining - (AKA: Church of All Hallows Staining.) Mark Lane. First mentioned in 1177, although possibly dates back as early as 1087 or 1136. Survived the Great Fire of 1666, but collapsed in 1671. The new church was built in 1674-5. Taken down in 1870 (except the tower) and the land was bought by the Clothworkers' Company.

All Hallows the Great Church - All Hallows Lane (off Upper Thames Street.) It is unknown when the first church was built here; a church existed here by at least 1235. Burned in the Great Fire of 1666. Rebuilt by Wren in 1683. The tower was demolished in 1876 (replaced by a belfry) and the church in 1893.

All Hallows the Less - (AKA: All Hallows-upon-the-Cellar.) All Hallows Lane, Upper Thames Street. Existed by at least 1240. This medieval church was not rebuilt after the Great Fire of 1666, although the churchyard remains.

All Hallows - Tottenham. Ancient. Gothic. The rivulet Mosel flows around three sides of the church.

All Hallows-by-the-Tower - (See: All Hallows Barking, above.)

All Saints - Blackheath. 1859.

All Saints - Chelsea. Cheyne Walk. (AKA: Chelsea Old Church.) Records go back to 1290. Restored/redesigned by Hans Holbein the Younger in 1528. (See: Chelsea/Chelsea Old Church, under C in the Alpha section.)

All Saints - Cranham. Dates back at least to 1785.

All Saints - Fulham. Ancient, with a 14th C. embattled tower. Contains a collection of 17th C. monuments. The tombs of eight former Bishops of London lie in the churchyard.

All Saints - Isleworth. West of London. Fifteenth C. tower. (See: Old Isleworth/All Saints, under O in the Alpha section.)

All Saints - Kingston-upon-Thames, Clarence Street. Some 13-15th C. parts remain. Parish church.

All Saints - Margaret Street, Fitzrovia. 1850-9, by William Butterfield, on the site of the Margaret Chapel, which PILGRIMS' LONDON describes as: "...once a nonconformist chapel of Lady Huntingdons Connexion." Also described as over-decorated.

All Saints - Tottenham parish church. Perpendicular style. Charles Lamb (18-19th C. essayist/poet) and his sister, Mary, are buried in the churchyard.

All Saints - Wandsworth. Parish church. Late 18th century.

All Saints - West Ham. Very old. Square Gothic tower.

All Souls - Langham Place, Regent's Park, Marylebone. (During the Regency, Langham Place was named Foley Street.) Built in 1822-5. This church is round. Designs by John Nash (at the time the style was ridiculed.) A circular portico nearly surrounds the tower, also circular, topped by a pointed spire (so that it was likened to a candle extinguisher); the porch and steeple are semi-detached, built out from the nave so as to appear at Regent Street's center. The interior is all cream and gold. It is the only surviving John Nash church in the City. The bust of John Nash, located in the church's porch, dates from the 1950s.

Audley Chapel - (AKA: Grosvenor Chapel.) On South Audley Street. (See: Grosvenor Chapel, below.)

Austin Friars - (See: Dutch Church of the Austin Friars, below.)

Barking Abbey - Barking. St. Erkenwold founded this abbey in the year 666 (or 674.) Burned by Vikings in 870. (See: St. Margaret's/Barking, below.)

Barking Chapel - Tower Hill. Pulled down in 1547.

Battersea Old Church - (See: St. Mary's Battersea, below.)

Bavarian Chapel - Warwick Street. 1788. Still remains. Was Roman Catholic during the Regency.

Berkeley Chapel - Charles Street, Berkeley Square. Built in approximately 1750.

Bethnal Green Church - 1825-8, by Sir John Soane. NAIRN'S LONDON says of it: "...a rough, tough little building using a post-and-lintel language outside with complete logic yet complete originality. The town is just the opposite..."

Bow Church - Bow Road. (See: St. Mary's/Bow Road.)

Bow Church - Mile End Road. (Not to be confused with St. Mary-le-Bow.) Built in the reign of Henry II, parochial in 1740. Massive square tower.

Brompton Oratory - 1853.

- See: Holy Trinity/Cottage Place/Brompton, below.
- See: St. Philip Neri.

Camden Chapel - Peckham Road, Camberwell. Built in 1797 by discontented members of the Congregation of St. Giles; licensed in 1829 as an Episcopal Chapel. Plain-looking. Byzantine-style chancel added in 1854.

Catholics - AKA: Roman Catholics. (See: Catholics, under C in the Alpha section.)

chapel of ease - Until the late 19th C., it must be noted the holdings of a church (in terms of land) could be large. Often the parish was a significant distance from the nearby towns/hamlets. Therefore there was a practice of building a local chapel as a subsidiary of the parish: a chapel of ease (so parishioners didn't have to travel so far.) Usually in time these evolved into parish chapels of their own.

Chapel of St. John - In the tower of London. (See: Tower of London/White Tower/Chapel of St. John-the-Evangelist, under T in the Alpha section.)

Chapel Royal - A chapel that answers to the sovereign, not an archbishop. (See: Chapel Royal, under C in the Alpha section.)

Chelsea Old Church - (Officially known as: All Saints, Chelsea.) Old Church Street, Chelsea. Parish church of Chelsea, here since medieval times/1290, a "charming village church." Sir Thomas More's body (or perhaps just his head) is thought to be buried here; Sir Thomas has a chapel here, and he partly designed the church. In 1532, he had the statue to himself built against the south wall of the chancel. The nave and chapel were rebuilt in 1667-74, adding a steeple with a peal of six bells. It is the only church in London to have chained books (literally connected to chains, so they can't be stolen,) gifts of Sir Hans Sloane. Partly restored in 1910. Much damaged in WWII, but well restored along its original lines.

- See: All Saints, Chelsea, above.
- See: Chelsea/Chelsea Old Church, under C in the Alpha section.

- More Chapel, the: 1527, built at Sir Thomas More's personal expense.

Christ Church - Blackfriars Road. Built 1738-41. Plain brick quadrangle. The "new" chancel dates from 1870.

Christ Church - Ealing. 1852.

Christ Church Greyfriars - By Wren. Damaged in WWII. (AKA: Christ Church, Newgate Street. See below.)

Christ Church - Lee, in Lee Park. 1855, by Sir Gilbert Scott.

Christ Church - Newgate Street. (AKA: Christ Church Greyfriars.) There was probably a church here in the 13th C., purportedly belonging to the Greyfriars. A rather magnificent new edifice was built in 1306, probably the largest church in England at the time. Burned in the Great Fire of 1666; rebuilt by Wren in 1687, the church now being only as big as the 14th C.

church's choir. Steeple completed in 1704. Since WWII bombing only the tower, steeples, and parts of the walls remain.

- See: St. Leonard, Foster Lane.
- See: St. Nicholas Shambles.

Christ Church - Oxford. Oxford's cathedral as well as one of its colleges. (See: Oxford/Christ Church, under O in the Alpha section.)

Christ Church, Spitalfields - On the corner of Commercial Street and Fournier Street, directly opposite Spitalfields Market. Built 1714-1729. A "tour-de-force" Baroque building; by Nicholas Hawksmoor; this was his largest and grandest. Victorian alterations in 1866 after an 1841 lightning strike. Magnificent portico. Now, only the outsized tower remains, with its sober spire. A charcoal tax was levied in the early 18th C., to provide funds to build 50 new churches, this being one of them. (Only 12 of the 50 were ever built. Two others were: St. Anne's, Limehouse & St. George-in-the-East.)

Christ Church - Turnham Green, main Chiswick High Road. 1843.

Christ Church - Victoria Road, Kensington. 1851.

Christ Church - Victoria Street, Westminster. 1843. On the site of a chapel that was there in Charles II's time.

Christchurch, St. Giles - Endell Street. Built 1844. Pulled down in 1930.

Church of England - (See under C, in the Alpha section.)

Church of St. John - Red Lion Square, 1874-8.

Church of St. Margaret - (See: St. Margaret Lothbury, below.)

Church of the Holy Sepulchre - (See: St. Sepulchre, below.)

City Temple - Holborn. 1874. Not to be confused with the Inns of Court's Temple Church. (See: City Temple, under C in the Alpha section.)

dissenters -

- See: dissenter, under D in the Alpha section.
- See: note at the very start of this CHURCHES section.
- See: religions - For a list of non-Anglican faiths in Regency London.

Dissolution of the Monasteries - When the Pope denied Henry VIII a divorce from his first wife, Catherine of Aragon, Henry closed the (Catholic) monasteries throughout England (late 1530s) and founded the Church of England. Some of the monasteries were converted, some went to private individuals, and too many were torn down or fell to ruin and were later demolished. You'll find many references in these pages to this tumultuous time.

- See: Dissolution of the Monasteries, under D in the Alpha section.
- See: The start of this CHURCHES section - The note at.

Dutch Church of the Austin Friars - Near London Wall. First built in 1253 as a monastery. Enlarged in 1354. Henry VIII confiscated and closed it. His son, Edward VI (died at age 15,) gifted it to Dutch refugees, who re-consecrated it in 1550. Used by the Dutch congregation, who called it "Jesus Temple," until 1940, despite a devastating fire in 1862. Destroyed by a WWII bomb. A wholly new church (half the size of the old one) was begun in 1950. (See: Austin Friars, under A in the Alpha section.)

Ely Chapel - (See: St. Etheldreda's Chapel, below.)

Foundry Chapel - (AKA: Old Foundry Chapel.) Moorfields. The first London location of John Wesley's (founder of the Methodists, b.1703-d.1791) chapel and headquarters. So named because it was in an old foundry.

Gravel Pit Chapel - (See: Hackney/Gravel Pit Chapel, under H in the Alpha section.)

Grosvenor Chapel - (AKA: Audley Chapel.) South Audley Street, Mayfair. Built in 1730. Attractive. Little.

Guards' Chapel of Wellington Barracks - 1839-40. (More information at: Wellington Barracks, under W in the Alpha section.)

Guy's Hospital Chapel - (See: Southwark/Guy's Hospital, under S in the Alpha section.)

Hackney New Church - This is the same as St. John's-Hackney.

- See: Hackney/St. John's-Hackney, under H in the Alpha section.
- See: St. John's-Hackney, below.

Hampton Church - Parish church. 1830, on the site of an older structure.

Hanover Chapel - (See: St. George's/Hanover Square, below.)

Holy Cross - Cromer Street. Joseph Peacock (architect,) 1888.

Holy Redeemer - 7 Cheyne Row, Chelsea. (AKA: Church of Our Most Holy Redeemer and St. Thomas More.) Catholic church. Opened in 1895.

Holy Redeemer - Exmouth Market, Clerkenwell. (AKA: Our Most Holy Redeemer.) Roman Catholic interior, with an Italianate campanile. Built in 1888, by John Dando Sedding (architect.)

Holy Sepulchre - This is its proper name, but it is more commonly referred to as: St. Sepulchre. (See: St. Sepulchre, below.)

Holy Trinity - Cottage Place, Brompton. Consecrated in 1829. Brompton Oratory was remodeled in 1878, by Herbert Gribble. NAIRN'S LONDON describes this version as: "Incredibly Italian, so well done that the truly Baroque stone saints in the nave (from Sienna) fit in perfectly." PILGRIMS' LONDON states: "On the right side of the Brompton Oratory is an avenue of lime trees leading back to the parish church of the district, Holy Trinity, Brompton." This latter is described as mellow, and as more utilitarian than beautiful, and it is of Gothic-revival style. Clock tower at its west end. Chancel added in 1879. This church's burial grounds were moved in 1854.

Holy Trinity - Whitechapel, on Church Street. Foundation uncertain, but it contains at least one gravestone dating back to 1596. After uniting with St. Botolph, Aldgate in 1899, this locale was used as a parish room.

Holy Trinity - Clapham, Southwark. 1774-6, built on the edge of the Common. Galleried interior. It is now the parish church. (See: Clapham/Holy Trinity, under C in the Alpha section.)

Holy Trinity - Gough Square. Southeast corner of New Street. Built in 1837, a chapel of ease to St. Bride's.

Holy Trinity - Hyde Park Corner, south end of Sloane Street, Chelsea. 1888-91, where an earlier 19th C. church had been.

Holy Trinity, Minories - First mentioned in 1657, but carvings here date back to 1620. Rebuilt in 1705-8, being then a smallish building. Was a royal peculiar until 1730. Closed in 1899, and the parish was united with St. Botolph, Aldgate. The remains were destroyed in WWII.

Holy Trinity - Paddington, Bishop's Road. (This road was later renamed Bishop's Bridge Road.) 1845.

Holy Trinity - Park Square, off Marylebone Road. Built 1824-28 by Sir John Soane. Very similar in design to St. Peter's, Walworth. The publisher known as Penguin Books began here in 1935, situated in Holy Trinity's crypt.

Holy Trinity the Less - Little Trinity Lane, **Upper Thames Street**. 1266. Rebuilt in 1607-8. Not rebuilt after the Great Fire of 1666.

Holy Trinity - Vauxhall Bridge Road (south end of.) 1851.

Independent Chapel - Kensington, 1793. Pulled down in 1929.

Jesus Temple - (See: Dutch Church of the Austin Friars.)

Jewish persons and places - (See listings under J in the Alpha section.)

Leyton Church - (See: Leyton/Leyton Church, under L in the Alpha section.)

liberty - This privilege was reserved for important people, giving them the right to hold court over their own people; they did not have to answer to the Aldermen of London. All lands belonging to the church were also liberties, and some of them had sanctuary status. That is, refuge, where neither the Watch nor the king could molest them.

- See: liberties, under L in the Alpha section.
- See: sanctuary, under S in the Alpha section.

London Oratory of St. Philip Neri - 1893. (See: St. Philip Neri, below.)

Margaret Chapel - (See: All Saints/Margaret Street.)

Marylebone New Church - 1813-17, by Thomas Hardwick, on land donated by the Duke of Portland. Purportedly the third church on the site. (See: Marylebone/Marylebone New Church, under M in the Alpha section.)

Methodists - (See under M in the Alpha section.)

Metropolitan Tabernacle - (See: New Park Street Chapel, under M in the Alpha section.)

New Church - Indeed, many churches are referred to in the local parlance as "New Church" or "Old Church," depending, of course, on whether the building is of ancient or more recent date (with "more recent" quite possibly referring, with London's long memory, to a 300+ year old building.)

New Park Street Chapel - (See: New Park Street Chapel, under N in the Alpha section.)

Old Church - (See: New Church, above.)

Old Dutch Church - (See: Dutch Church of the Austin Friars, above.)

Our Lady of Victories - Kensington High Street. 1869. Roman Catholic.

Paddington Church - Actress Sarah Siddons was buried here in 1831.

Poplar Chapel - Poplar High Street, Limehouse. 1650-54, it started life as a private chapel for the East India Company. Rebuilt 1776. Rebuilt again in the mid 19th C. in a style referred to as "medieval Victorian," in Kent stone. Later called St. Mathias; also seen spelled: St. Matthias. Closed in 1977.

- See: Limehouse/Poplar High Street/St. Matthias, under L in the Alpha section.
- See: St. Matthias, Poplar High Street, below.

Priory Church of St. John - St. John's Square, Clerkenwell. (AKA: St. John's Priory.) Original church dated from the 12th C., being at that time round; no longer round in the 14th C. rebuild. Remodeled and restored in 1956.

Queen's Chapel - Marlborough Gate, **St. James's Palace**. 1625, by Inigo Jones, for Queen Henrietta Maria, wife of Charles I. (Usually closed to the public.) This was the earliest church purpose-built for Catholic worship following the Reformation; it is now Church of England. (See: St. James's Palace/Queen's Chapel, under S in the Alpha section.)

Queen's Chapel of the Savoy - Savoy Hill, off the Strand, Westminster. 1505, in the Perpendicular style. Near Waterloo Bridge, extensively remodeled after a fire in 1864. It literally belongs to the Queen (or King,) not the London diocese. (See: Queen's Chapel of the Savoy, under Q in the Alpha section.)

Roman Catholics - (See: Catholics, under C in the Alpha section.)

Roman Catholic Chapel -

- See: St. Anselm and St. Cecelia.
- See: Sardinian Embassy Chapel.

Rotherhithe Church - (See: Rotherhithe/St. Mary, under R in the Alpha section.)

royal peculiar - This term means that the chapel or church so designated answers directly to the sovereign, not to an archbishop. In other words, the building and its clergy are affiliated directly with the monarch, and no bishop or archbishop has authority within it.

St. Alban's Church - Gray's Inn Road. 1863, by William Butterfield.

St. Alban - Wood Street, Cheapside. Dates from at least the year 930, but quite possibly back to 793 and Offa, King of Mercia. Fell into disrepair; pulled down in 1633; rebuilt in 1634 by Inigo Jones. Burned in the Great Fire of 1666. Rebuilt by Wren in 1685, described as Tudor Gothic (an unusual style for Wren.) In Victorian times it was altered, being described as being made commonplace.

- See: St. Mary, Staining, below.
- See: St. Olave, Silver Street, below.

St. Alderbury - Misused name. (See: St. Mary Aldermanbury. Note the addition of "Mary," and "man.")

St. Alfege - Greenwich. (Also spelled: St. Alphege. And: St. Alphage.) A church here since 1012. Rebuilt in 1711-14 after being destroyed by a lightning strike; by Nicholas Hawksmoor. Baroque. John James rebuilt the 17th C. west tower in 1730. Much restored after WWII damage.

St. Aloysius - Somers Town, ca. 1800. It was Roman Catholic in the Regency.

St. Alphage - London Wall. First mentioned in print as: St. Elfego, in 1108-25, but it is believed to have been erected in 1013. Dilapidated by the 16th C., it was going to be demolished, but instead the Dissolution left it as a parochial building, being then extensively rebuilt 1624-8. The upper steeple was rebuilt in 1649. Escaped the Great Fire of 1666. Repaired again in 1701, but dilapidated once more by 1774. Rebuilt and reopened in 1777. The north porch dated from 1775; it was taken down in 1913, and the new porch dated from 1914 (in a 14th C. style.) Closed in 1920, the parish being then united with St. Mary, Aldermanbury. Demolished in 1923.

St. Andrew-by-the-Wardrobe - Richmond Park (on what is now 146 Queen Victoria Street.) First mentioned in a 1244 manuscript. (The early name for this church was: St. Andrew juxta Baynard's Castle, named for a riverside fortress which once stood nearby.) Wren rebuild, 1685-93. A west gallery was added in 1774. Altered by the Victorians. Bombs in December/1940 burned it out; rebuilt 1959-61 with the plain look of Wren's design. Has a churchyard in front, landscaped and on a slope. The Royal Wardrobe had been nearby until the Great Fire of 1666.

St. Andrew - Holborn Circus, Holborn (on a triangle formed by Holborn, St. Andrew's Street, and Shoe Lane.) There had been a 13th C. stone church here, which was built over a wooden 951AD church chartered by King Edgar. Another version was built in 1485. Redesigned by

Wren in 1684-87, it had not burned in the Great Fire of 1666, but was so decrepit that Wren rebuilt it. The tower dates from the rebuild, but was resurfaced in 1704 with Portland stone. It is Wren's largest parish design. Thomas Coram, founder of the Foundling Hospital, is buried here. Bombed and gutted in 1941; reconstructed in 1961.

St. Andrew Hubbard - Love Lane. (Sometimes seen written as: St. Andrew Hubert, possibly named for a patron.) In 1202 it was referred to as: St. Andrew by Estchepe. Not rebuilt after the Great Fire of 1666 (and its foundations not being rediscovered until 1831.)

St. Andrew - Kingsbury. (See: Kingsbury/St. Andrew's, under K in the Alpha section.)

St. Andrew Undershaft - 1520-32. Leadenhall. The "Undershaft" part of the name comes from there having been a maypole that stood near to the south door. The May Day celebrations got too riotous in 1517, so the quite tall fir maypole (taller than the spire, hence the "under shaft"; dated from the 12th century) was taken down and hung along the front of houses on nearby Shaft Alley. The pole stayed for 30 years that way, until it was deemed a pagan symbol and chopped up for firewood.

Perpendicular Gothic. The latest rebuild dates from 1520-32. Has undergone much renovation/alteration over the years. Survived the Great Fire of 1666; also survived WWII bombing.

There is an effigy of John Stow, in which he holds a quill pen. John Stow was a tailor who also took it on himself to make a historical record of London, a source which modern historical writers still praise. He died in 1605, and on the anniversary of his death each year (since 1905,) the pen is replaced with a new one in his honor, placed there by the Lord Mayor. (See: St. Mary Axe, below.)

St. Andrew - Wells Street. 1846-1932. Moved, stone by stone, in 1933. (See: Kingsbury/St. Andrew's, under K in the Alpha section.)

St. Anne and St. Agnes - Gresham Street. Earliest mention was ca. 1200. Destroyed in the Great Fire of 1666; rebuilt by Wren in 1676-87. Brick; 53 feet square. The tower added ca. 1714. Rebuilt after WWII damage, with an unusual vaulted square-within-a-square plan. The two names are referring to: the oldest saint and the youngest (in terms of their personal age at time of death.) Early on it was also referred to as: St. Anne in the Willows.

Has a tree-shaded churchyard. Stucco was put over the red brick sometime in the 19th century (but the brick is now restored.)

Contains the *grounds* of St. John Zachary, which church was not rebuilt after the Great Fire of 1666; the Haberdashers' Hall was built over where the church had stood.

St. Anne - Blackfriars. Built in 1544. Not rebuilt after 1666's Great Fire.

St. Anne - Highgate, Swain's Lane. 1853.

St. Anne - Kew Palace, Kew Green. 1714.

St. Anne, Limehouse - On Commercial Road. By Hawksmoor; English Baroque, 1714-1727. Tall spire, 1686 (or possibly from an earlier version of the church.) Still has the highest church clock in England. Burned in 1850, at which time the interior was "victorianized." The organ dates from ca. 1851. Further alterations in 1891. Huge west tower, wherein rests the clock. Leafy churchyard. (See: Wapping/St. Anne's.)

St. Anne, Soho - Wardour Street. 1802-6, possibly by Wren, or by S. P. Cockerell in a Wren-like style. Square chambers flanking the sides and the barrel-like construction near the top of the tower were two of its curious features. Survived until 1940 air raids. Now only the 1685 tower remains, and the bottle-shaped steeple (by Cockerell, 1803.)

St. Anselm and St. Cecelia - (AKA: the Roman Catholic Chapel.) Lincoln's Inn Fields. In 1720-1852 it was attached to the Sardinian Embassy, being therefore known as the Sardinian Embassy Chapel. (See: Sardinian Chapel, below.)

Its name changed to St. Anselm, Duke Street (now Sardinia Street) in 1853; and in 1861 it was changed again, this time to the Church of St. Anselm and St. Cecelia.

It had one major restoration, in 1780 (following damage in the Gordon Riots.) It was taken down utterly to put in the Kingsway development. An Edwardian building of 1909 stands in Kingsway, and is named St. Anselm and St. Cecelia. It apparently was (and remained) Catholic throughout its existence.

St. Antholin - Budge Row, Round Hill. By Wren, called one of his finest. Demolished in 1875 to make way for Queen Victoria Street.

St. Antholin, Watling Street - Built ca. 1119. Named for St. Anthony the Hermit, "Antholin" being a corruption. Apparently rebuilt in 1513. Burned in the Great Fire of 1666; rebuilt in 1682-3 by Wren. Had an oval-shaped dome, and an octagonal spire described as beautiful. Pulled down in 1874 in order for Queen Victoria Street to be built.

St. Augustine - Kilburn. Built 1870-80.

St. Augustine - Corner of **Watling Street and Old Change** (near St. Paul's Cathedral's east side.) First mentioned in 1148. In 1309 it was called: St. Augustine's near St. Paul's Gate. Burned in the Great Fire of 1666; rebuilt by Wren in 1682; opened for worship in 1683. Steeple completed in 1695. Church was only 51 feet by 45 feet. Was modernized in 1878. Bombed in WWII; now only the tower remains.

St. Barnabas - 23 Addison Road, **North Kensington**. Opened 1830.

St. Barnabas - Pimlico Road, Belgravia. 1850.

St. Bartholomew by the Exchange - (Also seen written as: St.-Bartholomew-by-the-Exchange.) Built in 1226. It was called: St. Bartholomew the Less through the 14th-15th centuries (not to be confused with the church of that name in West Smithfield Square.) Rebuilt in 1438. In 1647 it was known as: St. Bartholomew near the Exchange. Burned in the Great Fire of 1666; rebuilt by Wren in 1679. Demolished in 1840-1 to make way for an expanded rebuild of the Royal Exchange.

St. Bartholomew-the-Great - Cloth Fair, West Smithfield (on the east side of Smithfield Square.) LET'S GO-THE BUDGET GUIDE TO LONDON states: "In order to reach St. Bartholomew the Great, one must enter through an exceedingly narrow Tudor house located on Little Britain"; this is one of London's rare 16th C. gatehouses, with its even rarer 16th C. timber-frame house atop.

Founded by the monk/jester/courtier of King Henry I, Thomas Rahere, in gratitude for his recovery from a fever, probably in 1103. Parts yet date from 1123. It is the City's oldest parish chapel, with the best-preserved medieval interior in London (only parts of which survive down from the 13th C.: the chancel; crossing transepts; and the Lady chapel.) It had massive Norman arches, which are yet remaining. Has a medieval font (in fact, the only one left in London.) In 1544 the priory was bought by Sir Richard Rich (staying in the family through 1862.) Escaped the Great Fire of 1666. By the 17th C. it was no longer functioning as a church, and the North Transept had become a blacksmith's business, and the Lady chapel a printing workshop; Benjamin Franklin worked here in 1725. LONDON STEP BY STEP says: "...by the 18th century it had become run down and was occupied by industrial squatters."

In LONDON by Knopf Guides: "...by the middle of the 19th century the church was no more than a ruin." Victorian restoration began in 1858. The flintwork exterior dates from 1887, by Sir Aston Webb. This is the site of the Butterworth Charity, which takes place every Good Friday, since at least 1686. Twenty-one sixpences were (and are) laid on a tomb in the churchyard, and twenty-one widows would kneel, pick one up, cross the tomb, and receive another half-crown and a bun. This ritual did not take on the "Butterworth Charity" name until 1887, when Joshua Butterworth made the perpetual endowment of it his legacy.

Just north of the church stood a watch-house (where the Charlies gathered/temporarily held prisoners,) erected in 1791. Destroyed by WWII bombing; however the church yet exists, although only a little of it remains from the 12th century.

St. Bartholomew-the-Less - West Smithfield Square. (AKA: St. Bartholomew-the-Lesser.) Founded ca. 1123; on its present site since 1184. 12th C. stones from the original St. Bartholomew's Hospital were used in the 15th C. rebuild of St. Bartholomew-the-Less' square tower, which is the chapel to St. Bartholomew's Hospital (the only survivor of the four chapels of the original priory.) PILGRIMS' LONDON says: "Although still the chapel for St. Bart's Hospital, this has been a parish church since the Dissolution (the hospital is its parish.)" The vestry dates from the 15th century. In 1547 the hospital was refounded (following the Dissolution.) At this time it became the parish church to Smithfield.

In 1789-93 the present building was designed by George Dance the Younger, replacing the decaying nave with an octagon of wood. T. Hardwick rebuilt the nave as a stone and iron replica in 1823. In 1865 Hardwick's grandson did further work on the church. Restored following WWII damage.

St. Benet Fink - Paul's Wharf, Upper Thames Street. First mentioned in 1216. Named for Robert Finke the Elder, who appears to have financed a rebuild. Burned in the Great Fire of 1666; rebuilt in 1673-76 by Wren. Dutch-looking. Pulled down in 1842-4, at which time the parish united with St. Peter le Poer.

- See: St. Peter le Poer, below.
- See: St. Peter, Paul's Wharf, below.

St. Benet Gracechurch - (Corruption of "Grass Church"; used to be a grass-market there.) First mentioned in 1053 (or at least the reference is presumed to be this church.) Burned in 1666's Great Fire; rebuilt by Wren in 1685, at which time the parish of St. Leonard, Eastcheap was united with St. Benet. Demolished 1867, at which time both parishes united with All Hallows, Lombard Street.

St. Benet, Paul's Wharf - Now known as: St. Benet Guild Welsh Church, on what is now known as Queen Victoria Street. First mentioned in 1111. Inigo Jones (the builder/architect) was buried here (and whose memorial was not replaced until 1878 even though Wren rebuilt the church following the Great Fire of 1666.) This church is believed to be the "St. Benet's" mentioned in *Twelfth Night* by Shakespeare. As noted above, it burned in 1666, and was rebuilt by Wren, in 1683, of red brick relieved by stone quoins, with stone festoons over the windows. Described as Wren's "most lovable" (and unshowy) church. The interior has only one aisle, to the north. The fittings and furnishings are almost all 17th C., and the interior is little altered. Elegant cupola. In 1879 the parish united with St. Nicholas, Cole Abbey, this space then being used for the Welsh Episcopalians (services are held in Welsh.)

St. Benet Sherehog - Perhaps named for the family Serehog, who lived nearby. Not rebuilt after being damaged in the Great Fire of 1666, although a part of the churchyard still exists on the north side of Pancras Lane. (See: Sise Lane, under S in the Alpha section.)

St. Benet's Welsh Church - AKA: the Metropolitan Welsh Church. (See: St. Benet, Paul's Wharf, above.)

St. Botolph, Aldersgate - St. Botolph was a patron saint of travelers. (See: St. Botolph-without-Aldersgate, below.)

St. Botolph, Aldgate - There had been a church here in the 14th century. Rebuilt by Dance in the 1740s. Completed (presumably a rebuild) in 1791. During the Great Plague of 1665, the churchyard was used as a plague pit. Interior has a fine barrel-vaulted roof. Situated in

Houndsditch, a district which has a church at both its ends named for St. Botolph (who was the English patron saint of travelers.)

Western end = St. Botolph Bishopgate, erected 1725 (on the site of an earlier church.)

Eastern end = The other (St. Botolph's, Aldgate,) as listed above.

It is a peculiar. (See: the "Peculiars Note" at the start of this CHURCHES section.)

(See: Holy Trinity, Minories.)

St. Botolph - Billingsgate. Built in 1181. Not rebuilt after the Great Fire of 1666; united with St. George, Botolph Lane.

St. Botolph, Bishopgate - A church here since 1212 (or earlier.) The current building was by James Gold, 1724-28. Remains a parish church. PILGRIMS' LONDON states: "The galleried interior in classical style is nicely lit by a dome and lantern installed in the nineteenth century. It possesses the original pulpit and lectern and an organ originally installed in 1764." Also described as spacious. (See note under: St. Botolph, Aldgate, above.)

St. Botolph-without-Aldersgate - Noble Street. Possibly dating from the 10th C., but anyway there was a church in existence by 1260; built to provide comfort for travelers. Rebuilt in 1627. It did not burn in the Great Fire of 1666, but was so dilapidated by 1790 that it was demolished; a new church was built on the same site. Its exterior is described as unprepossessing, although the interior is nicer, described as a lovely and virtually complete 18th C. interior. It was last rebuilt in 1788-91. East end remodeled in 1831, by N. Wright.

It now serves as the Centre for After Care of Prisoners (with public services, as in church services, being held during the week.)

- Postman's Park: The churchyard was made into Postman's Park in 1880.

St. Bride's - St. Bride's Avenue, Fleet Street. Sits over Roman building remains, and of a very early Christian church. It is believed seven different church foundations have been built here.

The name is derived from either the ancient goddess "Brighde," or from St. Bridget of Kildare, Ireland (and many claim that St. Bridget was derived from Brighde anyway.) There was some kind of church or other here since at least the 6th C.; it may well be the oldest site in London where Christianity was celebrated (this very ancient version being destroyed by the Danes in the 10th century.)

Redesigned by Wren, in the Italian style, following the Great Fire of 1666; built in 1671-74. (Two other sources said 1671-78. A fourth source gave the rebuild dates as 1680-1703. A fifth gave the dates as 1670-75.) Has Wren's tallest steeple, which was added in 1701-3, 226 feet tall, of Portland stone; often described as a "wedding cake" steeple, said to have inspired the tiered shape of bridal cakes from then on. Eight feet of the steeple was lost in a thunderstorm in 1764. Had twelve bells, renowned for their pealing.

Called the "Church of the Press" (or journalists,) and also "the printers' church," because of its proximity to Fleet Street (until recently the seat of the press in London.)

Bombed in 1940, the interior was faithfully restored. One source said that the original plans were not followed, so the church lacks a gallery, and has added stained-glass windows, but otherwise it is still basically Wren's church we see today. The present organ dates from 1957.

St. Catherine Coleman - Fenchurch Street. (See: St. Katherine Coleman.)

St. Catherine - Feltham. 1880.

St. Christopher - (AKA: St. Christopher le Stocks, although not recently. In 1348 it was referred to as: St. Christopher upon Cornhill. In 1361 it was: St. Christopher near le Stokkes.) First mentioned ca. 1282. St. Christopher was the patron saint of ferrymen. "Le Stocks" is a reference to the nearby stocks (punishment.) Burned in the Great Fire of 1666; rebuilt in 1671 by Wren. Demolished in the 1760s to build wings onto the Bank of England. The churchyard remained until 1934.

St. Clement Dane's - (Also seen written as: St. Clement Danes.) Western end of Fleet Street (now situated on an island in the Strand.) There was an earlier church of the same name here. It first had a wooden foundation, which was replaced by a stone one in 1022 (remains of which can be seen in the present tower's base.) "Danes" may be an indication of a 9th C. existence, at which time Alfred the Great allowed Danes who were married to Englishwomen to remain in the area.

Partly rebuilt in the 15th century (the lower part of the tower dates from this time, but a rebuild by Wren encased it,) and once more in 1640. It survived the Great Fire of 1666.

Wren did his rebuild in 1679-82, or at least provided plans; but the superintending architect was Edward Pierce.

The upper stage of the steeple (on the belfry; clock level) and domed vestry added in 1719-20, by James Gibb.

Supposedly the bells playing mark the hour, hence the old nursery rhyme about the "Bells of St. Clements'," although in LONDON, THE ROUGH GUIDE it states that the nursery rhyme is more likely to have originated from St. Clement's Eastcheap. The bells play every three hours, from 9:00am to 6:00pm (9:00am, noon, 3:00pm, and lastly at 6:00pm.)

From 1682 there has been a statue of Dr. Samuel Johnson (lexicographer) here. LONDON STEP BY STEP states that the monument to Dr. Johnson (outside the east apse) was by Fitzgerald, 1910.

The William Gladstone statue standing just west of the church dates from 1905.

The church was largely rebuilt in 1955-8 following WWII damage, and now contains a Royal Air Force memorial (the church is now dedicated to the RAF, since 1958.) Has a white stucco and gilt interior, contrasting nicely with the rich, dark wooden pews. Latest rebuild by W. A. S. Lloyd.

St. Clement's Eastcheap - Martin Lane, Cannon Street. (AN ENCYCLOPAEDIA OF LONDON says it is located at Clement Lane, King William Street, and goes on to explain this is the east end of what is now Cannon Street.) First mentioned in the 11th century. Burned in the Great Fire of 1666; rebuilt by Wren in 1686. United with St. Martin Orgar after 1666's Great Fire largely destroyed the latter. (See: St. Martin Orgar, above.) French Protestants met here until 1820, at which time the building was demolished (except for the tower, which was pulled down in 1851,) only to have the site marked by the construction of a new tower, now with a clock.

St. Cyprian - Clarence Gate, Glentworth Street. 1903, by Sir Ninian Comper.

St. Dionis Backchurch - Fenchurch Street. (First mentioned ca. 1198 as: St. Dionis in Lime Street; by 1241 it was: St. Dionus of Bakecherche. Sometimes it was written as: St. Dionysius'.) It is the City church dedicated to St. Denys or Dionysius, the patron saint of France. "Backchurch" was to indicate that it stood back from the street (Fenchurch Street.) Rebuilt during Henry VI's time. Burned in the Great Fire of 1666; rebuilt by Wren in 1674. The tower dates from ca. 1684. Demolished in 1878, the parish being then united with All Hallows, Lombard Street.

St. Dunstan - Feltham parish church. 1802. Plain brick, with an embattled tower and a spire.

St. Dunstan-in-the-East - Located between Great Tower Street and Lower Thames Street, St. Dunstan's Hill, Eastcheap. (Sometimes in its early life it was called "St. Dunstan by the Tower" and "St. Dunstan near Fenchurch.") A church has possibly been here since 1100; first reliable mention is in 1272. Extensive rebuild in 1633, only to burn in the Great Fire of 1666. Rebuilt by Wren, ca. 1671. The steeple was by Wren, but was not completed until 1699 (it's said the steeple was designed by Wren's daughter, Jane.) Severe decay by 1810 closed the church, but then the body of the church was rebuilt by David Laing, 1817-21 in Perpendicular Gothic; Wren's amazing spire remained. Reduced to ruins by a 1940 air raid (only the spire remained, until it was dismantled in 1950); now a pretty garden surrounding a shell.

St. Dunstan-in-the-West - (Also seen written as: St. Dunstan's-in-the-West. Also as: St. Dunstan's in the West.) 186a Fleet Street. Probably had a church here since Saxon times, somewhere around 988-1070; first record in 1185. John Donne (poet) was rector here from 1624-31. The church escaped the Great Fire of 1666.

Gog and Magog: Images of Druidic tree figures/gods, wielding hammers.) They strike the 1/4 hour on the *clock*, as referred to by Jane Austen; this clock dates from 1671. It was erected by the parishioners to honor surviving the Great Fire (due to the Dean and 40 scholars using buckets of water); the clock tower is to the side of St. Dunstan's own tower. In 1830, the

Marquis of Hertford bought this Gog and Magog clock for his Regent's Park home, but in 1935 one Viscount Rothermere bought it and returned it to the church. (See: Hertford Villa, under H in the Alpha section.)

Church was rebuilt in Victorian Neo-Gothic in 1831-3 by John Shaw the Elder, slightly to the north of the prior location, to allow for widening the street for traffic.

Remains largely medieval, with various restorations and repairs over the centuries (which observation seems to imply a long-standing octagonal shape.)

Has enormous burial grounds.

The statue of Queen Elizabeth I (which stands inside the gates and dates from 1586, the only contemporary likeness of her.) It is thought to be the oldest statue in London. For reasons unknown it was moved to the basement of a nearby pub, where it sat forgotten for many years, until rediscovered in 1839, at which time it was restored to St. Dunstan's.

There are three 16th century effigies leaning against the porch, they may be meant to represent King Lud (supposed mythical founder of London) and his sons.

This church remains a peculiar. (See the "Peculiars Note" at the beginning of this CHURCHES section.)

St. Edmund, King and Martyr - (AKA: St. Edmund, Lombard Street. Now most commonly referred to as: St. Edmund the King.) At the corner of George Yard, Lombard street. First mentioned ca. 1108. Burned in the Great Fire of 1666; rebuilt by Wren in 1690. This church remains a peculiar.

- ➢ See: All Hallows, Lombard Street, above.
- ➢ See: St. Nicholas Acons, below.
- ➢ See: the "Peculiars Note" - At the start of this CHURCHES section.

St. Edward the Confessor - Romford parish church since 1410. Built anew in 1849.

St. Ethelburga-the-Virgin - 78 Bishopgate, the City. (AKA: St. Ethelburga Bishopgate.) 13th C; another source says 15th century. Tiny; described as one of London's smallest churches. NAIRN'S LONDON calls it: "One of the sweetest things in the City; a little medieval church sitting up as pert as a sparrow... The inside is unremarkable - just a simple, villagey nave and aisle...." Missed by the Great Fire of 1666. Walls are attractively of rubble and ragstone. At its rear it has a small courtyard with a garden and a fountain.

St. Etheldreda's Chapel - (AKA: St. Etheldreda's Church. Would have been known as: Ely Chapel during the Regency.) 14 Ely Place, Holborn. Built ca. 1290; once was the chapel of the palace of the bishops of Ely. Beautiful, medieval Gothic; in the Decorated style. Dedicated to the Saxon Queen who founded Ely Abbey. It is the tradition that a 3rd C. church stood nearby. Parts date back to the middle ages. It is the lone pre-Reformation Roman Catholic worship site in London; was Catholic, then Protestant following the Reformation, then bought back by the Catholics in 1874 (from the Welsh Episcopalians,) being restored by George Gilbert Scott at that time from a near derelict condition (at which time it resumed the St. Etheldreda name.) Restored again following WWII damage. (See: Ye Olde Mitre, under the INNS/PUBS section.)

St. George - Bloomsbury Way. (This street name dates from 1910, prior to that it was called Hart Street,) Bloomsbury Square. 1716-31, to plans by Nicholas Hawksmoor. Has a 13th C. crypt. Greek cross plan. Corinthian portico. In 1800 the sanctuary was moved from the east end to the north transept, somewhat spoiling the interior. The tower is on the side of the church, the steeple of which is topped by a statue of George I in a Roman toga, the *only* statue of George I in Britain; the steeple rises in a step-like (pyramid-like) pattern, modeled on the tomb of King Mausolus of Halicarnassus. Majestic Corinthian portico. In front of the British Museum.

St. George - Botolph's Lane. (First mentioned in 1180 as: St. George's in Estchepe; by 1516 it was: St. George in Podynge (Pudding) Lane.) Repaired in 1627. Burned in the Great Fire of 1666; rebuilt by Wren in 1674. Closed in 1899, demolished in 1904. (See: St. Botolph's, Billingsgate.)

St. George - Campden Hill, Kensington. Built in 1864.

St. George Cathedral - (See: St. George, Southwark, below.)

St. George - Gravesend. Pocahontas, the Algonquin (Native American) princess, married John Rolfe, and was invited to visit the court of James I. Unfortunately she caught an infection while onboard the ship bringing her, and so was buried here at St. George. (As of 1995, there was talk of bringing her body back for burial in America, but that has not occurred, not least because they are unsure of the location of her body due to rebuilding.)

St. George - St. George Street, **Hanover Square, Mayfair**. (AKA: Hanover Chapel.) By John James, 1721-25. Baroque, with a massive Corinthian portico. Often the scene of society weddings, including during the Regency era. Still exists.

St. George (Cathedral) - **Southwark**. Off of St. George's Circus. Consecrated in 1848, Roman Catholic.

St. George the Martyr - (Not to be confused with St. George's Cathedral.) Borough High Street, Southwark. Dates from the 12th century. The parish church of Southwark. Rebuilt 1733-6 by John Price on the site of a church that was there for six centuries before. Has a "conspicuous" spire; square tower; octagonal upper story.

St. George - Wells Street, Camberwell. Built in 1824, Grecian style. Altered internally in 1908.

St. George's Chapel - Hyde Park Corner. (See: Hyde Park Corner, under H in the Alpha section.) Here since at least 1747, when a later American president, Abraham Lincoln's great-grandparents were married here. Today, the site is occupied by the Lanesborough Hotel.

St. George's Chapel - (See: **Westminster Abbey**, under W in the Alpha section.)

St. George's Chapel - Windsor Castle, Berkshire. A Royal Peculiar. (See the "Peculiars Note" at the start of this CHURCHES section.) Ten monarchs are buried here (among them are: Charles I; Edward IV; George V; Henry VI, and Henry VIII.) The chapel is closely associated with the Order of the Garter; there is an amazing wall filled with stained glass that is dedicated to the Order of the Garter. Founded in 1475 by Edward IV. Still exists, still has services.

St. George's-in-the-East - (Also seen as: St. George-in-the-East. Also as: St. George in the East.) Shadwell/Stepney, Cannon Street Road (docks area.) Built sometime ca. 1715-29. By Hawksmoor. It is now a blend of Tuscan, Baroque, Georgian and Victorian elements. There are four domed towers above the nave, referred to as turrets. Plain facade. In the 1860s it was the site of "No Popery" disruptions/riots. The interior was rebuilt in 1960-4 following 1941 WWII damage, and made modern.

St. Giles - Camberwell. There's been a parish church here since 670AD. Large and "shapeless," with a square tower surmounted by a turret. AN ENCYCLOPAEDIA OF LONDON states: "From the 17th century onwards it underwent almost continuous modification. Galleries were added, and a new south aisle was built in 1786." In 1809 coats of plaster and rough-cast were added. Enlarged in 1825. The interior was described, despite all the renovations, as having an antique appearance. Because the old parish church burned in 1842, it was rebuilt in 1844 in the Gothic style, at that time being considered one of the largest/finest parish churches.

St. Giles, Cripplegate - The City. Near Finsbury. First mentioned in 1100-35; possibly first built in 1090 (and possibly on the site of a Saxon structure.) John Milton (poet/Commonwealth civil servant) is buried here. Rebuild completed in 1550, following a 1545 fire. Did not burn in the Great Fire of 1666. Dedicated to the Hermit of the Rhone (patron saint of cripples and lepers...although "Cripplegate" may have derived from an Anglo-Saxon word that means a burrow or covered way.) Perpendicular style. The east window (described as beautiful) was installed in 1791. John Milton (17th century Commonwealth poet/author of *Paradise Lost*) is buried here.

St. Giles-in-the-Field - (Also seen written as: St. Giles's in the Fields.) 60 St. Giles High Street, Bloomsbury. Began its existence as a leprasarium; Matilda, Queen of Henry I, founded this hospital for lepers in 1101.

Henry VIII, seeing the hospital was acquiring wealth, grew avaricious; in 1539 he dissolved the hospital and claimed it for the crown.

In 1545 the site was granted to John Dudley, Viscount Lisle (later the Duke of Northumberland); he turned the site into a private home. It passed through a series of hands, with the hospital chapel becoming a parish church ca. 1550. Rebuilt in 1731-3 (the third church on the site,) of Portland stone; 160 foot high spire with a vane; by Henry Flitcroft. The Resurrection relief dates from 1687. During the Regency, would have been avoided, as the surrounding district of St. Giles was poor, dangerous, and stuffed with brothels and gin shops.

St. Giles-without-Cripplegate - A "cripple" is a covered passageway, and probably how the church took on its name. Even with that knowledge, know that this church was dedicated to the patron saint of cripples (St. Giles.)

Now inside the Barbican Centre (a huge cultural center built in 1972,) the church stands in the verdant central courtyard.

Founded in the 11th century. Last complete rebuild was ca. 1550; the tower is about 100 years older. In 1620 Oliver Cromwell (later leader of the Commonwealth) was married here. John Milton (poet/civil servant) was buried here in 1674. Did not burn in the Great Fire of 1666.

St. Gregory by St. Paul's - Built by 1070 or earlier. Burned in the Great Fire of 1666, being then not rebuilt but united with St. Mary Magdalen, Old Fish Street (which was demolished in 1886, so both parishes then united with St. Martin, Ludgate.)

St. Helen and St. Giles - Rainham parish church. From at least 1178; still much Norman construction to be seen here.

St. Helen's Bishopgate - St. Helen's Place, the City. The first church here dates from at least the year 1010, although tradition has it that Constantine (Roman emperor) built a church here in memory of his mother, St. Helena, in the 4th century. Has a curious bisected appearance (double nave) due to being used as two places of worship: one a parish church, the other as a long-gone 13th century Benedictine Convent. (One nave for parishioners, one for the sisters.) Was not destroyed in the Great Fire of 1666. The west gallery dates from 1744. Restored in the 19th century. In 1873 ,St. Martin's Outwich was united to it.

St. James - Aldgate. (See: St. James, Duke Place.)

St. James - Bermondsey. Built in 1827, designed by J. Savage.

St. James - Clerkenwell. Situated on Clerkenwell Close. Clerkenwell parish church. It is strongly supposed a church existed here by at least 1567. In Elizabethan times had been the Benedictine convent called St. Mary's. Completely rebuilt in 1791.

St. James, Duke Place, Aldgate - Built on the site of the priory of the Holy Trinity, which went to Henry VIII in the Dissolution. Henry gave the buildings to Sir Thomas Audley, who demolished the priory church and built houses here instead. Audley died in 1544, and the property went to his son-in-law, Thomas, Duke of Norfolk; at this time the road was dubbed

Duke's Place. In about 1621, the inhabitants petitioned for a place of worship; it went up in 1623, being then called Trinity Church. In 1720, its bishop referred to is as: St. James within Aldgate. Declared a parish church in Charles I's time. Escaped the Great Fire of 1666. Rebuilt in 1727. Demolished in 1874, the parish being then united with St. Katherine Cree.

St. James - Enfield Highway, Enfield. 1832.

St. James, Garlickhythe - (Or Garlickthythe, or Garlickhithe,) Garlick Hill (off of Upper Thames Street,) the City. Takes its name from the fact that garlic was once sold nearby. First mentioned in 1170 as: St. James apud Viniteriam (St. James near the Vintry.) Ca. 1204 was referred to as: St. James by the Thames; ca. 1222 also referred to as St. James apud Tamisyam (by the Thames.) Rebuilt in 1326. Burned in the Great Fire of 1666; rebuilt by Wren in 1674-83; opened to worship in 1682, completed in 1683. Wren added the spire in 1717; LET'S GO-THE BUDGET GUIDE TO LONDON said its "modest steeple" was by Hawksmoor. Classical style. It has the second highest roof in the City (St. Paul's is higher.) Because of its clerestory's clear arched windows, it is sometimes referred to as "Wren's Lantern."

St. James - Hatcham. Deptford, 1854.

St. James - Paddington, 1843. (Faces the Sussex Gardens, or as it is also known, Grand Junction Road.)

St. James - Pentonville Road. 1787, by A. H. Hurst. Yellow brick, central window. Surrounded by big trees.

St. James, Piccadilly - 197 Piccadilly, Westminster. Built for the residents of St. James's Square, and paid for by Henry Jermyn, Earl of St. Albans. Built by Wren, his own favorite. Described as elegantly built. Sources give the building date as 1674, or 1680, or 1682, or 1683, or 1684; safe to say it was built sometime between 1674-84. The organ (decorated with gilded figures) was brought here from Whitehall Palace in 1691 for James I, designed by Grinling Gibbons. Grinling Gibbons also did the woodcarvings and the marble font. Exterior: plain brick, and Portland stone. Suitable for large weddings. Restored following severe WWII damage, by Sir Albert Richardson. Has galleries and a vaulted ceiling.

St. James - St. James's Square, Kensington. 1845.

St. James - Spa Road, off Jamaica Road. 1829.

St. James-the-Less - Thorndike Street and Vauxhall Bridge Road, Pimlico. 1858-61. Slate and dusty-red brick.

St. James within Aldgate - (See: St. James/Duke Place/Aldgate, above.)

St. John-at-Hampstead - (See: St. John/Hampstead, below.)

St. John - Bermondsey. (AKA: St. John Horselydown.) Built 1732. Restored by Sir Arthur Blomfield in 1883. The tower has a fluted Ionic pillar shape. Ruined by WWII air raids. (See: Shad Thames, under S in the Alpha section.)

St. John - Bethnal Green Road. Built in 1823, by Sir John Soane. Enlarged and much altered after an 1871 fire. (See: Bethnal Green Church, above.)

St. John - Clerkenwell, in St. John's Square. (AKA: St. John's Priory. AKA: Priory Church of St. John. AKA: St. John the Baptist Church in Clerkenwell.) In 1185 the church of the Priory of St. John of Jerusalem was built here, having at that time a round nave. Damaged in the 1381 Wat Tyler rebellion; rebuilt. Rebuilt again in 1501-27, by Prior Docwra. The Duke of Somerset confiscated much of the building's stones ca. 1548 for his own Strand palace, with some repairs occurring during Queen Mary (the Catholic's) reign.

In the early 18th C. it was a Presbyterian meeting-house. Finally, in 1723, it was reborn as a parish church, again called St. John's.

United in 1931 with St. James's, Clerkenwell.

The 1504 Gateway remains. (See: St. John's Gateway, under S in the Alpha section.)

St. John - Hackney. (AKA: St. John-at-Hackney. AKA: Hackney New Church.) 1791-7. Brick, square, with a convex stone portico at each side. Seats approximately 2,000. There had been a medieval church here.

St. John - Hampstead, in Church Row. Hampstead's parish church. (AKA: St. John-at-Hampstead. AKA: St. John the Evangelist, but not until its name got this 1917 refinement.) Has 14th C. beginnings. Rebuilt in 1744-7, by Henry Flitcroft, and also John Sanderson (and others, ca. 1843.) Castellated steeple. West end modified in 1872. Brick. Near to Downshire Hill. Has a tree-shaded churchyard. Catholic. (See: Hampstead/St. John's.)

St. John - Horselydown. (AKA: St. John, Bermondsey. See, above.)

St. John - Hoxton, Shoreditch. Consecrated 1826.

St. John - Ladbroke Grove, Kensington. 1845. Built on the site of Notting Hill farmhouse.

St. John - St. John's Wood. Land bought in 1808; church built in 1814.

St. John - Smith Square, Westminster. (AKA: St. John the Evangelist, Smith Square. AKA: St. John's Chapel/Tower of London. AKA: St. John, Westminster.) Off Millbank, south end of the Victoria Tower Gardens. Built 1728-1742, by Thomas Archer. Struck by lightning in 1773. English Baroque. Charles Dickens described it as "a very hideous church with four towers at the corners, generally resembling some petrified monster, frightful and gigantic, on its back with its legs in the air." It also has the nickname "Queen Anne's footstool," and although the tale (of Queen Anne telling the architect to design the church to look like a footstool she kicked over) is probably apocryphal, the nickname persists. Destroyed by bombing in 1941, but rebuilt as a chamber music/concert hall. (See: Tower of London/White Tower/Chapel of St. John the Evangelist, under T in the Alpha section.)

St. John-the-Baptist - Croydon. Parish church of Croydon. The old church was destroyed in 1867 (but significantly older, as it yet retains medieval interior sections.)

St. John-the-Baptist - Hillingdon Heath, parish church. Gothic. Tall, massive tower. Restored in 1848. (See: Hillingdon Heath/St. John the Baptist, under H in the Alpha section.)

St. John-the-Baptist - Pinner parish church. Perpendicular tower. Some parts date from the 13th century. Rebuilt in 1879-80. (See: Pinner/St. John-the-Baptist, under P in the Alpha section.)

St. John-the-Baptist - Near **Walbrook Street**. The earliest mention of it was in 1182. Enlarged in 1412. There were apparently no monuments of importance here. United with the parish of St. Antholin after being ruined in the Great Fire of 1666. St. Antholin's was pulled down in 1874, at which time both parishes united with St. Mary Aldermanbury. This site was mostly covered over by the District Railway.

St. John-the-Baptist - In the town of **Windsor**. Rebuilt in 1822.

St. John the Evangelist - Camden, on Charlotte Street, 1846.

St. John the Evangelist - Smith Square. (See: St. John/Smith Square, above.)

St. John the Evangelist - The Tower of London.

- See: St. John/Smith Square, above.
- See: Tower of London/White Tower/Chapel of St. John the Evangelist, under T in the Alpha section.

St. John the Evangelist - Waterloo Road. Built in 1823-4.

St. John - Walham Green, North End Road, Kensington. 1827-8.

St. John - Wapping, on Scandrett Street. 1756.

St. John - Waterloo Road. (Also seen as: St. John's Waterloo.) Commissioned in 1818, built 1823-4 by Francis Bedford. Greek Revival. Has a portico and six Doric columns, supporting a pediment. For up to 2,000 people.

St. John - West Ham, 1834.

St. John - Westminster. (See: St. John's/Smith Square.)

St. John Zachary - Noble Street. Started its existence as early as 1181, being at first known as: St. John the Baptist. Before the end of the 12th century, however, it had taken on the "Zachary" name, meaning St. John, son of Zachary, i.e. John the Baptist.) Rebuilt by Nicholas Twiford in 1390. Not rebuilt after the Great Fire of 1666, but was instead united with St. Anne and St. Agnes. (See: St. Anne and St. Agnes, above.) *Haberdasher's Hall* was built over the church's site.

St. John's Chapel - Tower of London.

- See: St. John/Smith Square, above.
- See: Tower of London/White Tower/Chapel of St. John-the-Evangelist, under T in the Alpha section.

St. John's Priory - (See: St. John's/Clerkenwell.)

St. John's Wood Church - Built in 1813-14, by Thomas Hardwick, on the site of a plague pit. Episcopalian. Near the present site of Lord's Cricket Ground.

St. Joseph - Highgate Hill. Catholic. Now familiarly known as: Holy Joe's. 1858; on the site of the Old Black Dog Inn.

St. Katharine Cree - (Note it is spelled with two a's.) 86 Leadenhall Street. First referred to in 1280 as: St. Katherine de Christchurch at Alegate. "Cree" is a corruption of "Christ." Built within the churchyard of the priory of Holy Trinity. Steeple added in the 15th century. The body of the church was rebuilt in 1628-30 (the steeple being left untouched, until it was heightened in the 18th century,) and attributed to Inigo Jones. Gothic and Classical mix. Called one of the City's brightest and most attractive churches, due to its large east window; although NAIRN'S LONDON calls it "An urgent, bizarre hybrid...." One of eight churches to survive the Great Fire of 1666.

St. Katherine Coleman - First mentioned in 1301; may have been the "All Hallows Colemanch" also mentioned in the 12th century. "Coleman" may refer to a patron or builder. Escaped the Great Fire of 1666. Repaired in 1702. Demolished in 1734, but a church lacking antique or architectural merits followed, and was also called ugly. Closed in 1921; pulled down in 1925, the parish being united with St. Olave's, Hart Street.

St. Katherine Cree - (See: St. Katharine Cree, above, spelled with a second a instead of the more usual e.)

St. Katherine - Gloucester Gate (near to Regent's Park.) Designed by a pupil of Nash. Grey Gothic. Now used by London's Danish community.

St. Katherine - Hammersmith, on Queen Caroline Street. 1923.

St. Lawrence - Caterham. Ancient; restored in the 20th century.

St. Lawrence - Harrow, at Little Stanmore. Ancient. (See: Little Stanmore/St. Lawrence's, under L in the Alpha section.)

St. Lawrence Jewry - (Also seen as: St. Lawrence, Old Jewry.) At Gresham Street and King Street; in the old Jewish quarter (hence its name.) Opposite the Guildhall. Official church of the Corporation of London (the City.) Has a pew set aside for the Lord Mayor, who attends services each year on Michaelmas Day (9/29, along with his newly elected successor.) Possibly dates from Saxon times, but at least by 1136. Burned in the Great Fire of 1666; rebuilt by Wren in 1671-80. It is called one of Wren's most handsome churches.

Associated with the Girdlers. (See: Girdlers' Hall, under G in the Alpha section.)

Was well restored to Wren's design following WWII damage. Burials allowed here until 1853. Had only one aisle, on the north side, separated from the main body of the church by Corinthian columns. (See: St. Mary, Magdalene/Milk Street, below.)

St. Lawrence Pountney - According to THE ENCYCLOPAEDIA OF LONDON: "The earliest record is 'St. Laurence next to the Thames,' and it was in existence in the 11th century. The chapel of Corpus Christi and College of St. Lawrence Pountney adjoining the church were erected by John de Pountney (ca. 1334,) and this explains part of the later dedication." Following being ruined in the Great Fire of 1666 it united with St. Mary Abchurch.

St. Leonard, Eastcheap - First mentioned in 1214. Stow also referred to it as: Saint Leonard Milke Churche. Vestry rebuilt in 1584. Following being ruined in the Great Fire of 1666 it united with the parish of St. Benet, Gracechurch Street.

St. Leonard - Foster Lane. Earliest mention was in 1278 as: St. Leonard near St. Martin. Small. Repaired and enlarged in 1631. Following being ruined in the Great Fire of 1666 it was united with Christ Church, Newgate. The ground adjoining St. Botolph's, Aldersgate encloses St. Leonard's churchyard.

St. Leonard - Shoreditch, corner of Shoreditch High Street and Hackney Road. 1735-40, by George Dance the Elder. Brick edifice, Doric portico, a tall steeple. Renovated in the late 19th century by Sir Arthur Blomfield; the roof-beam was added even later. The churchyard, at least as of 1947, still hosted the old stocks and a whipping post.

St. Leonard - Streatham parish church, (near the junction of Streatham High Street and Mitcham Lane.) The first church was here probably 1291; another version from the late 15th-early 16th C., which is the time from which the existing west tower remains. Rebuilt 1830-1. (See: Streatham/St. Leonard, under S in the Alpha section.)

St. Luke - Chelsea. Sydney Street. 1820-24, by James Savage. The spire is a local landmark.

St. Luke - Finsbury parish church. 161 Old Street. Finsbury, 1733, by George Dance Sr. Repaired in 1877-8. Mostly demolished by 1959; the obelisk steeple and walls remain. (See: Old Street/St. Luke's Church, under O in the Alpha section.)

St. Luke - Greenwich, in Charlton Village. First mentioned in 1077. Rebuilt in 1629.

St. Luke - Norwood. Built post-1815, to commemorate the peace following Waterloo.

St. Magnus the Martyr - (AKA: St. Magnus Martyr.) Lower Thames Street. Named after a Norwegian earl (or jarl) of the Orkney Islands. A church has stood here since the Norman Conquest; first mentioned in 1067, a stone church was unusual at such an early date. Once stood right beside old London Bridge. Is now near Billingsgate fish market, and so is traditionally called the fishmonger's church. Wren rebuilt in 1676-90 (a second source said 1671-85,) following damage in the Great Fire of 1666. Described in NAIRN'S LONDON as having "Wren's most feminine steeples." Steeple added in 1705, and described as one of "Wren's best efforts." The interior has been remodeled twice, both times being given a baroque look.

- See: London Bridge, in the BRIDGES section.

➢ See: St. Margaret's, New Fish Street, below.

St. Margaret Barking - (See: St. Margaret's-Barking, below.)

St. Margaret - Edgware parish church. Corner of High Street and Station Road. Rebuilt 1705, and in 1845.

St. Margaret - Lee. (See: Lee/St. Margaret's, under L in the Alpha section.)

St. Margaret Lothbury - Lothbury Street (down Throgmorton Street,) Cheapside. First known church here dates from 1197. Rebuilt in 1440. Present version, 1686-1701, Wren. The sumptuous carved wood screen dates from 1689. The exterior had a degree of "Victorianism" added on.

➢ See: St. Martin Pomary, below.

➢ See: St. Mary Colechurch, below.

St. Margaret Moses - First mentioned in 1202, when it was located at "Fridai-strete." Referred to in 1299 as: St. Margaret Moysy in Frydaystrate. Named for St. Margaret of Antioch. The "Moses" seems to be for the founding priest or builder of the church. United with St. Mildred, Bread Street after being ruined in the Great Fire of 1666. By 1830, its churchyard (in Friday Street) had been paved over.

St. Margaret, New Fish Street - First mentioned in 1199 as "Sci margaret un Pont." By the 16th century. it was known as: St. Margaret, Bridge Street. The Monument now stands on this site. (See: Monument, under M in the Alpha section.) Otherwise, the church purportedly had no important monuments. United with St. Magnus the Martyr after being ruined in the Great Fire of 1666.

St. Margaret - Parliament Square. (See: St. Margaret/Westminster, below.)

St. Margaret Pattens - Rood Lane, Eastcheap. Existed by 1216. Rebuilt in 1530. Repaired in 1614-32. Burned in the Great Fire of 1666; rebuilt by Wren in 1684-7. Purportedly named for the overshoe. (See: Pattenmakers' Company, under P in the Alpha section.) The spire is 200 feet high. "Beautified" in 1855 (the term probably means too much Victorian design exuberance was applied.)

St. Margaret - Plumstead, 1858. (See: St. Nicholas/Plumstead, below.)

St. Margaret - Uxbridge parish church. In 1448 was built as a chapel-of-ease to Hillingdon. Perpendicular style; restored 1872. Is hidden behind Uxbridge's market-house.

St. Margaret - Westminster, on St. Margaret's Street. (AKA: St. Margaret's - Parliament Square.) The first church here was from the 11th or 12th centuries.

Rebuilt between 1486-1523 (the tower was added in the 18th C.,) with 18th C. and 19th C. remodeling work giving it a more Gothic Revival look. "Parliament's Church"; the parish church of the House of Commons since 1614, from which it is across the street.

The East Window, above the altar, is made of stained glass sent from Spain; it was meant to commemorate their daughter's (Catherine of Aragon) marriage to Arthur, but he died and she ended marrying his brother, Henry VIII.

There is a bust of Charles I over the entry.

Refaced in 1735 in Portland Stone. Interior significantly repaired in 1758. The apse was replaced by a square end in 1806.

Restored in 1876-8 by Sir George Gilbert Scott, at which time the galleries were removed. The west porch was added in 1876-95.

NAIRN'S LONDON describes St. Margaret's as: "...a court building by court masons, but the spatial bareness and blankness...is as strong as in merchants' churches... Yet the means for achieving this economy, in details like the mouldings of the arcades, were rich and complicated."

Fashionable place for weddings (now, and during the Regency.)

St. Margaret's-Barking - (Also seen as: St. Margaret's Church, Barking.) Norman, with Early English additions. The churchyard has an ancient gateway, which has two stories, with an embattled parapet and a turret. On the north side of the churchyard once stood (the ancient) Barking Abbey, burned in 870 by Vikings. Capt. James Cook (explorer) was married here in 1762 to Elizabeth Batts.

St. Marie de Arcubus - (See: St. Mary-le-Bow, below.)

St. Mark - Kennington. Built 1822-4, to commemorate the peace following Waterloo.

St. Mark - Mayfair, on North Audley Street. 1828.

St. Mark - Southwark, 1820s.

St. Martin-in-the-Fields - (AKA: St. Martin - Trafalgar Square.) Westminster (at Charing Cross, what would later be the east side of Trafalgar Square.) The parish church of the Admiralty. Also became the royal parish church of the sovereign (due to the fact that Buckingham Palace is within this parish.) The royal box is at gallery level, left of the altar. 1722-26, James Gibbs; the present church dates from this time, with some additions. His "masterpiece," with a stone exterior, an airy light interior, and an Italian ceiling of plasterwork (called exquisite.) Was an earlier church here, dating from 1522 (with a church first mentioned in 1222.) Rebuilt in 1544.

The font (from the earlier church) dates from 1689. Clock dates from 1758. The steeple is 185 feet tall, added in 1824. The tower was rebuilt as a replica in 1824. The 18th C. pulpit was brought in, in 1858. Nell Gwynn (king's mistress) was buried here (although the churchyard is now defunct.) LONDON by Knopf Guides states: "It rather resembles a rectangular Roman temple, with a Corinthian portico and high steeple." Has always been open to the homeless, who yet can be sometimes found sleeping among the pews.

- The Costermongers' Harvest Festival is situated here, every October; (begun in Victorian times.) This was the origin of the Pearly Kings and Queens, who wear festive "pearly" button-covered costumes. (See: Pearly Kings and Queens, under P in the Alpha section.)

St. Martin-le-Grand - Cheapside. Reportedly established in the 8th C.; certainly founded (or refounded) in 1056. Was a college of secular canons. In medieval times it was a liberty, and had special status as a sanctuary, being a refuge for debtors until ca. 1697, and the status being abolished by Act of Parliament in 1815, in order to use the site for the General Post Office; the "old" General Post Office was built on this church's site in 1825-29.

- See: liberties, under L in the Alpha section.
- See: sanctuary, under S in the Alpha section.

St. Martin Ludgate - (AKA: St. Martin's-within-Ludgate.) Ludgate Street, Ludgate Hill. First mentioned in 1174. Burned in the Great Fire of 1666; rebuilt by Wren in 1677-84. Dedicated to St. Martin of Tours. Tall spire. Purportedly there has been a church here since the 6th century. King Cadwallader was buried here. Rebuilt in 1223, and in 1437. St. Martin's is described as not being a particularly spectacular church to visit, although its dark 17th C. woodwork is of interest.

St. Martin of Tours - Bromley. (See: Chelsfield Village/St. Martin of Tours, under C in the Alpha section.)

St. Martin Orgar - Dates from the 12th century. According to AN ENCYCLOPAEDIA OF LONDON: "The church was granted by Ordgar, the deacon, to the canons of St. Paul's to hold to him at a rent." The name went through changes: St. Martin in Candelwrithtestrat in 1200-1224; St. Martin Algar in 1259; and on to: St. Martin Orgar ca. 1275. Only part of the nave and the tower survived the Great Fire of 1666, after which the parish united with St. Clement, Eastcheap.

St. Martin Outwich - At the corner of Bishopgate and Threadneedle Streets. First mentioned in 1217. Additional land came into the parish in 1230, willed to it by Matilda, wife to Martin de Ottewich. It did not burn in 1666's Great Fire. Repaired anyway in 1681. Half-ruined in 1765 by fire; demolished in 1796, and rebuilt in 1798. Demolished again in 1874, the parish then being united with St. Helen's, Bishopgate.

St. Martin Pomary - Ironmonger Lane, Cheapside. Records of a "St. Martin Pomer" date from 1250. The name reportedly stems from nearby apple trees, although it could refer to 'pomerium,' the Latin word for an open space. United with St. Olave Jewry after being ruined in the Great Fire of 1666. St. Olave Jewry was demolished in 1888, at which time both parishes were united with St. Margaret Lothbury.

St. Martin - **Ruislip** parish church. Ancient. In 1870 it was partly restored, and again in 1956-7.

St. Martin - Trafalgar Square. (See: St. Martin-in-the-Fields, above.)

St. Martin Vintry - Near Southwark Bridge. Built 1100-7. The "Vintry" probably refers to being located near a vineyard/winery. Not rebuilt after it was destroyed in the Great Fire of 1666, its parish being then united with St. Michael, Paternoster Royal. The churchyard of St. Martin Vintry remains at the corner of Queen Street and Upper Thames Street.

St. Mary Abbot's - (Also seen as: St. Mary Abbots Church.) Kensington High Street. It dates from at least the year 1111, when it added the "Abbot's" to its name, being annexed to the Abbey of Abingdon. Present building from 1872, but during the Regency the church on this site dated from 1696. Square brick tower with a clock and wooden turret, which was partially financed by George III. 278 foot spire.

St. Mary Abchurch - Abchurch Yard (off Abchurch Lane) and Candlewick (later Cannon) Street, the City. The first church was here by 1198. The name might be derived from "Upchurch" (that is, sitting on rising ground,) but one theory thinks it come from "Abbe." Rebuilt in 1681-6, by Wren, following its destruction in the Great Fire of 1666. Described as Wren's most graceful church design; simple brick outside, with a simple tower. Altar carving by Grinling Gibbons, described as having "regal unselfconsciousness." Plain brick exterior. Has not been much altered by renovators, and was repaired following WWII damage. It is 63 feet x 60 feet, making it nearly square. It is now the Guild Church of the Solicitors' Company. (See: St. Lawrence Pountney, above.)

St. Mary - Acton parish church. On the corner of High Street and King Street. Red brick. The square tower was rebuilt in 1865.

St. Mary Aldermanbury - (AKA: St. Mary Aldermary, although this is a name corruption. AKA: St. Mary the Virgin.) Cheapside, on Queen Victoria Street, at the junction of Aldermanbury and Love Lane. At about 1080 there was a Norman church here. First mentioned in records in 1181. Rebuilt in the 16th century. There is a bust of Shakespeare, surmounting a memorial to him, the likeness being approved by his widow as being well done; stands in the churchyard. He and she are buried here. Wren rebuild, 1677-82, after being destroyed in the Great Fire of 1666, of Portland stone; it was somewhat Gothic, an unusual aspect in a Wren-designed church. In 1876-7 the church was heavily restored. Damaged in WWII, leaving only the walls standing; the stones of these walls were moved in 1966 to Fulton, Missouri, USA, as a memorial to Winston Churchill (Prime Minister); however, the footprint of the old church remains yet, although the site is now a garden. (See: St. Thomas the Apostle, below.)

St. Mary Aldermary - (See: St. Mary Aldermanbury, above.)

St. Mary-at-Hill - (Also seen written as: St. Mary at Hill.) Lovat Lane, Eastcheap (near Billingsgate.) First mentioned in ca. 1190 as: St. Mary de Hull. Burned in the Great Fire of

1666. Magnificent Wren interior, shaped liked a Greek Cross, 1672-7; Wren's first church design. Victorians reworked the interior, but for once did so with little aggrandizing or altering from Wren's intentions. Damaged by fire in 1988, restored. Bombed by the IRA in 1992.

St. Mary-at-Lambeth - Lambeth, Lambeth Palace Road, South Bank. Acquired by the Archbishop(s) of Canterbury in 1197, (and associated with Lambeth Palace.) The crypt under the chapel dates from the early 13th century. The crypt was rebuilt in 1633, and again after devastating WWII damage. Tower dates from the 14th C. (and is now a museum.) Was rebuilt several times in the 14th, 15th, and 16th centuries. Adjoins the south gateway of Lambeth Palace. The churchyard houses the graves of six archbishops, and in the 17th C. took on a garden. Captain Bligh (of *Mutiny on the Bounty* fame) is also buried in the churchyard. Rebuilt in 1851-2, all but the clock tower being "Victorianized" in Kentish ragstone. The church was deconsecrated in 1972, and is now the Museum of Garden History. (See: Lambeth/St. Mary-at-Lambeth, under L in the Alpha section.)

St. Mary-at-the-Bourne - (See: St. Marylebone, below.)

St. Mary Axe - The City. Existed by 1197; referred to in 1231 as: St. Mary del Axe. The name derives from a tale of 4th C. virgins slain by an ax. Repaired (or at least a petition for repair) in 1514. In 1561 it united with St. Andrew Undershaft; according to AN ENCYCLOPAEDIA OF LONDON: "Stow (says) without quoting an authority, that the church (St. Mary Axe) was given to the Spanish Protestant refugees for worship." The pull down date is unknown, but it was long gone by the time of the Regency.

St. Mary Battersea - (See: St. Mary's Battersea, below.)

St. Mary Bothaw - Existed by 1117. In 1150 it was: St. Mary Bothage; Bothaw by 1270. Reportedly the name derives from 'boat' and 'haw,' the latter meaning a yard. United with St. Swithun's after being ruined in the Great Fire of 1666. Its site is now covered by Cannon Street Station.

St. Mary - Bow Road. (Also called: Bow Church.) Not to be confused with St. Mary-le-Bow (in Cheapside.) Established in 1311 as a chapel of ease to Stepney. Parts date from its founding and from the 15th century. Became a parish church in 1719. It is the church of the Cordwainers' Guild.

St. Mary - Cadogen Street, Chelsea. Founded in 1794. Demolished in 1877-79, when it was rebuilt anew to designs by J. F. Bentley. Roman Catholic since 1812, and during the Regency (and still.)

St. Mary, Colechurch - Existed by 1163; purportedly named for the builder, Cole. The patronage belonged to the Hospital of St. Thomas of Acon until the Dissolution, at which time it went to the Mercers' Company. Repaired in 1623. After being ruined in the Great Fire of

1666, united with St. Mildred, Poultry. When the latter was pulled down in 1872, both parishes united with St. Olave, Jewry.

St. Mary Cray - Bromley. (See: St. Mary Cray/St. Mary's Church, under S in the Alpha section.)

St. Mary - Ealing. South of the Uxbridge Road. Rebuilt 1886. The old church fell down in 1729, and a new one was erected prior to 1820. (Not to be confused with St. Mary's - West Ealing.)

St. Mary - Hampstead. 1816. The present frontage dates primarily from 1850. Was Roman Catholic during the Regency. (See: Hampstead/St. Mary's.)

St. Mary - Harmondsworth. Norman church, built somewhere in the 13-15th C.; still there (one of the few churches not "restored," read: Victorianized, in the 19th C., as so many others were.) The tower is constructed from Tudor brick.

St. Mary - Harrow-on-the-Hill. Parish church. 12-15th C., refurbished in the 19th C., post Regency.

St. Mary - Hayes parish church. 13th C. square tower made of flint and stone; 16th C. wooden roof; and a lych gate (the latter being a roofed gateway leading to a churchyard, usually where a bier was placed prior to a funeral.) Restored in 1873-4.

St. Mary - Ilford, 1831.

St. Mary - Islington. (See: Islington/Upper Street/St. Mary's, under I in the Alpha section.)

St. Mary - Lambeth Palace. (See: St. Mary-at-Lambeth, above.)

St. Mary-le-Bow - (See under the final "St. Mary" listing, below.)

St. Mary-le-Strand - (See under the final "St. Mary" listing, below.)

St. Mary - Lewisham. Parish church. The old one was pulled down in 1774, and rebuilt. Oblong, stone, plain, square tower at the west end, portico with four Corinthian columns on the south. (See: Lewisham/St. Mary's, under L in the Alpha section.)

St. Mary - Leyton. There by at least 1737. Rebuilt in 1821, except for the tower.

St. Mary Magdelan - Bermondsey. 14th century. Rebuilt 1680. Tower repaired and made more attractive (Gothic style) in 1830.

St. Mary Magdelan - Richmond parish church, located at the back of the opposite side of George Street. Rebuilt in the 18th C., except for the stone tower.

St. Mary Magdalen, Old Fish Street - On the north side of Knightrider Street at the corner of Old Change. First mentioned in 1162. Burned in the Great Fire of 1666; rebuilt by Wren in 1685. The Reverend R. H. Barnham was rector from 1824-42. In 1886 was again damaged by fire and was demolished, the parish being then united with St. Martin, Ludgate.

St. Mary Magdalene - (Note the "e" at the end of Magdalene.) **East Ham**. Norman church, ca. 1130, with an ancient graveyard. Some roof timbers dating from 1130 are still there. The apse, chancel, and nave still exist, making this one of the least modified medieval churches in London. Since 1976, a nature reserve.

St. Mary Magdalene, Milk Street - First mentioned in 1162. Following being ruined in the Great Fire of 1666, the parish united with St. Lawrence Jewry. The site was covered by Honey Lane market, the latter since also being built over.

St. Mary Matfelon - Whitechapel High Street. Built between 1250-86, among the cornfields west of Stepney, as a chapel of ease to St. Dunstan's Church. The chapel evolved into a church in 1338. Its white stone exterior gave it the nickname of Whitechapel. Damaged in a severe storm in 1362; rebuilt; and again in 1673. Rebuilt again, in 1882, after a devastating fire in 1880. Destroyed by 1940 bombing; not rebuilt.

St. Mary Moorfields - 1817, by John Newman. Was Roman Catholic, the first RC church (at the time) not to be built very simply, but instead lavishly. Demolished in 1899 (when the whole Moorfields area was rebuilt.) It was replaced by a church on Eldon Street.

St. Mary - Mortlake, in the High Street. 15th century. The building is of stone and flint.

St. Mary Mounthaw - First referred to, in 1275, as: St. Mary de Muntenhaut. It had been built as a chapel for the Mounthaunts. It had become: St. Mary de Monte, by 1298. After being ruined in the Great Fire of 1666 it united with St. Mary Somerset; when the latter was demolished in 1872, both parishes united with St. Nicholas Cole Abbey.

St. Mary - Newington Butts, Southwark. In one form or another, has existed since the 13th century. Most recent church here was built in 1792, on the grounds of what is currently called: St. Mary's Churchyard. It moved to Kennington Park Road in 1876.

St. Mary Overie - (Also seen as: St. Mary Overy. And seldom as: St. Mary-Over-the-Water, overie meaning: over the water. In 1905 AKA: Southwark Cathedral.) Southwark. Started life as the site of a Roman villa. First church here by at least the year 607. There was a 1207 fire. The choir and retrochoir date from 1213-1235, in the Early English style of Gothic. It was known as St. Mary Overie until 1540 (when its Augustinian friary was dissolved); then known as St. Saviour's (see) until 1905.

In 1905, it was designated as *Southwark Cathedral.*

Its present appearance, unfortunately, while beautiful is for the most part modern ("modern" in this case meaning the 15th C. decor has been Victorianized.

- See: St. Saviour's/Southwark Cathedral, below.
- See: Southwark/St. Thomas's Hospital, under S in the Alpha section - The note at.)
- See: Southwark Cathedral, below.

St. Mary - Paddington Green. William Hogarth (painter/social critic) was married here in 1729. Rebuilt in 1788-91 near the site of the original church. Doric-style portico. The statue of

Sarah Siddons (actress) on the green was added in 1897 (she is buried here, having lived 1755-1831.)

St. Mary - Putney parish church. 14th C. tower, restored during the church rebuild in 1836. (See: Putney/St. Mary, under P in the Alpha section.)

St. Mary, Rotherhithe - St. Marychurch Street. The present church was opened for worship in 1715. Its tower dates from ca. 1740; on the site of a medieval church. Barrel roof (resembles an inverted ship's hull.) Architect was Launcelot Dowbiggin.

St. Mary Somerset - Upper Thames Street, on the corner of Lambeth Hill. The first mention is ca. 1199. Rebuilt in the 15th century. Burned in 1666's Great Fire; rebuilt by Wren in 1695, at which time the parish of St. Mary Mounthaw was united with it. Main body demolished in 1872. The tower, standing at 120 feet tall, remains yet. A new St. Mary Somerset was built at Hoxton from the proceeds of the sale of this land. (See: St. Mary Mounthaw, above.)

St. Mary Spital - North of Bishopgate. A medieval priory, first known as Lock Spital, a hospital for lepers. Long since gone. Still, it lent its name to "Spitalfields," that area that grew over the former priory's area. First known as: St. Mary without Bishopsgate, ca. 1197.

St. Mary Staining - In 1189 it is referred to as "Ecclesia de Staningehage." Purportedly refers to the haws (yards) of the men of Staines (of the manor of Staines.) After being ruined in the Great Fire of 1666, it united with St. Alban, Wood Street.

St. Mary - Stoke Newington. First here in 1563. The box pews (described as beautiful) date from the 18th century. The 1838 rebuild was built near the original site, by Sir G. Gilbert Scott. The wooden spire was added in 1829, by Sir Charles Barry. (See: Stoke Newington/Church Street/St. Mary's, under S in the Alpha section.)

St. Mary - Teddington. 16th century. (See: Teddington/St. Mary, under T in the Alpha section.)

St. Mary the Blessed Virgin - Addington. Dates from 1080, now mainly Victorian in design.

St. Mary the Virgin - Aldermanbury, Cheapside. (See: St. Mary Aldermanbury, above.)

St. Mary the Virgin - Perivale. 13th C., stone. A wooden tower was added in the 16th century. Refurbished ca. 1850.

St. Mary the Virgin - Another name for **Temple Church**. (See: Inns of Court/Temple, the (2nd entry)/Temple Church, under I in the Alpha section.)

St. Mary the Virgin - Twickenham parish church. Existed from at least 1677. Rebuilt in the early 18th C., restored several times since. Alexander Pope (18th C. poet) is buried here.

St. Mary the Virgin - Wanstead. (Sometimes also called: Wanstead Church.) Interior described as exceptionally fine. To discourage grave robbers there is a "Watcher's Box" in the churchyard. The church was rebuilt in its present form in 1790, by Thomas Hardwick.

St. Mary Undercroft - Built beneath St. Stephen's Undercroft. It was located under the chapel where the House of Commons met from 1547-1834, the latter date being when it burned. (While it is correctly called a crypt, it is not underground. It is on the ground level, with St. Stephen's being above it and above ground by one story.) During the Regency it may have been being used as a coal cellar, but this non-religious use was put aside by a restoration rebuild by Charles Barry (post-Regency,) when it resumed its life as a chapel. Members of Parliament still use it for weddings and christenings.

- See: Houses of Parliament/St. Stephen's Undercroft, under H in the Alpha section.
- See: St. Stephen's Undercroft, below.

St. Mary - Upper Street, Islington. The old church was built in the mid 15th century. Was pulled down in 1751. Rebuilt and reopened in 1754; the rebuild is said to lack architectural distinction. The spire is built of Portland stone. The porch was added in 1903.

St. Mary - West Ealing. 1782. Rebuilt 1841. (Not to be confused with St. Mary's - Ealing.)

St. Mary - Whitechapel. 1875. (See: St. Mary Matfelon, above.)

St. Mary - Wilsdon (Willesden.) Ancient.

St. Mary - Wimbledon parish church. Founded in the 14th century. Rebuilt in 1786, and in 1843.

St. Mary without Bishopsgate - (See: St. Mary's Spital, above.)

St. Mary, Woodford - (See: South Woodford/St. Mary's Church, under S in the Alpha section.)

St. Mary, Woolchurch - (AKA: St. Mary Woolchurch Haw; "haw" is an ancient word meaning yard.) The "Woolchurch" comes from the fact, confirmed by a reference in the Liber Albus (the first publication on English common law, 1419) that the churchyard contained the beam for weighing wool. The Fleet Market was built over the site of this church, after 1666 (at which time this church burned in the Great Fire.) This parish then united with St. Mary Woolnoth.

- See: Fleet Market, under F in the Alpha section.
- See: Stock Market, under S in the Alpha section.
- See: St. Mary Woolnoth, below.

St. Mary Woolnoth - Corner of King William Street and Lombard Street, the City. There was a church here since before the time of the Normans (St. Mary, Woolchurch -or- St. Mary Woolchurch Haw,) which was rebuilt by William the Conqueror. Damaged in the Great Fire of 1666, "patched up" by Wren in 1677. Major reconstruction was needed and supplied by Nicholas Hawksmoor, 1716-27 (second source said 1714-1730.) Elegantly baroque and small; the only church Hawksmoor built within the City. It looks larger inside than it appears from the outside. Has many Corinthian columns, inside and out. Semi-circular windows. Has no spire.

John Newton (author of the hymn "Amazing Grace") was rector here from 1780 to 1807, when he died.

NAIRN'S LONDON informs us: "Outside, Hawksmoor has taken up the awkward wedge-shaped site so easily that you don't realize until afterwards just how odd the building is.... It is the mind, afterwards, which asks what on earth two small towers are doing on top of an oblong, columned temple on top of prodigious rustication."

The only *City* church not harmed in WWII.

(See: St. Mary, Woolchurch, above.)

St. Mary - Wyndham Place. By Smirke, 1820-23.

St. Marylebone Parish Church - Marylebone Road. (AKA: St. Mary-at-the-Bourne, "Marylebone" being a corruption of this. AKA: St. Mary-a-le-bourne. AKA: St. Mary's at the Bourne, or Burn.) Begun in 1813, consecrated in 1817, the present building was built by Thomas Hardwick. Ornate exterior; simple interior (due to a sudden change in its building plans.) Lord Byron (19th C. poet) was christened in this church (in a smaller version at the time) in 1778. There were three churches. The first was near Oxford Street, but was much vandalized, and abandoned. The second was on what is now Marylebone High Street. The third, as listed here, was/is sometimes called Marylebone New Church.

St. Mary-le-Bow - (Also seen as: St. Mary le Bow.) Cheapside, the City. There's been a church on this spot since at least 1091, the year its roof blew away, written of as "Ecclesiae Sanctae Mariae quae dicitur ad Arcus" (the church of St. Mary which is called 'at the Arch' or Bow.) The present building is by Wren, 1670-83, following the Great Fire of 1666. Renaissance campanile steeple, 235 feet high. It is nearly square, measuring 65 feet x 63 feet (the nave is 48.5 feet x 26.5 feet.)

Not to be confused with St. Mary/Bow Road.

Only Wren's steeple (sits forward of the main part of the church,) tower, and walls remain following WWII bombing; restored by Laurence King in 1956-64. (The porch and spire, both lovely, remain from Wren's time.)

It is said that to be a true Cockney, one must have been born within the sounds of "Bow Bells" (St. Mary-le-Bow's bells,) which tolled the curfews. They rang at 9:00pm, the curfew from the 14th C. to 1847, and again at 5:45am. The bells were smashed in WWII, and were recast but no longer ring. Even if they did, it would now be hard to meet the Cockney requirement as most of the area is now offices.

The church's interior is liberally colored in white and gold.

One source says the "le-bow" is because of the graceful bow arches on the steeple, but another says "le-bow" derived from the Norman arches in the crypt called the chapel of the Holy Spirit.

There has been an enormous copper dragon weathervane on top since 1674.

- See: All Hallows/Bread Street, above.
- See: St. Pancras, Soper Lane, below.

St. Mary-le-Strand - Covent Garden area, close to the Inns of Court/Holborn. On an island on the east end of the Strand. It used to be on the north side of the Strand, but since 1910 it was isolated when the roads were widened for traffic.

The original church, dating from at least 1147, was south of the Strand. Demolished in 1549 (its land being used for Somerset House.) In 1711 the 134 foot maypole in the Strand was moved to Wanstead Park, and St. Mary-le-Strand was rebuilt on the maypole's site. First public building by James Gibbs, 1714-1717; the church was consecrated at this new site in 1724. Conservative Baroque. Italianate exterior. Deep chancel. Has a slender steeple and an elegant portico.

As early as the 18th C., the parishioners complained of how the noise from passing road traffic could be heard within.

(See: Maypole Alley, under M in the Alpha section.)

St. Mary's Battersea - (Note the "s" on Mary.) Parish church of Battersea. A church here since the 10th century. Current building dates from 1775-6, with 17th C. stained glass. Has been called a "Georgian preaching box." Benedict Arnold (famous to Americans as a traitor) lived in London for the remaining ten years of his life. This was his parish church, where he, his wife, and daughter were buried in the crypt.

St. Mathias - Hare street. 1848. Near Bethnal Green.

St. Mathias - Poplar High Street. Also seen spelled as: St. Matthias.

- See: Limehouse/Poplar High Street/St. Matthias, under L in the Alpha section.
- See: Poplar Chapel, above.

St. Matthew - Bethnal Green, in Church Row. Built 1740 or 46. Gutted by fire in 1859; rebuilt by 1861, at which time a "peculiar upper story" was added to the tower.

St. Matthew - Brixton Hill and Effra Road. Built on authority of Parliament in thanksgiving for the victory at Waterloo. Foundation stone laid in 1822; consecrated in 1824.

St. Matthew - City road, Berkeley Crescent. 1848.

St. Matthew - Friday Street, (on the east of.) First mentioned ca. 1261. Burned in the Great Fire of 1666; rebuilt by Wren in 1685. Pulled down in 1884, the parish being then united with St. Vedast, Foster Lane. (See: St. Peter, Westcheap, below.)

St. Michael-at-Querne - (AKA: St. Michael-le-Querne. AKA: St. Michael od Bladum.) Between St. Paul's Churchyard and Cheapside; it had a right-of-way through it. First mentioned in the 12th century. After being ruined in the Great Fire of 1666, it was not rebuilt, and united with St. Vedast, Foster Lane.

St. Michael Bassishaw - Basinghall Street. First mentioned in 1187, probably having been founded in 1140. The patronage first belonged to the prior and canons of St. Bartholomew's, Smithfield, but Henry III passed it to Adam Basing, the Lord Mayor's son, in 1216. Rebuilt in the 15th century. Repaired in 1630. Burned in 1666's Great Fire; rebuilt by Wren in 1676-9. Closed in 1893. Demolished in 1897, at which time the parish was united with St. Lawrence Jewry.

St. Michael - Chester Square, Belgravia, at the corner of Elizabeth Street and Chester Row. Built in 1847.

St. Michael, Cornhill - First mentioned in 1055. A new tower or steeple was built in 1421. Burned in the Great Fire of 1666 (except the tower.) Rebuilt by Wren in 1670-2. The church was rebuilt by Hawksmoor, 1715-22, in a neo-Gothic style.

St. Michael - Crooked Lane, south side of Cannon Street. First mentioned ca. 1271 as: St. Michael Candelwestrete. In 1283 it was: St. Michael towards London Bridge. It was located very near Fishmongers' Hall (the south chapel was referred to as Fishmongers' Chapel.) Rebuilt reportedly in 1366. Burned in the Great Fire of 1666; rebuilt by Wren in 1688 (the steeple dates from 1698.) Demolished in 1830 to make way for King William Street.

St. Michael - In the Grove, on Highgate Hill. 1830. (See: Highgate Hill/St. Michael's, under H in the Alpha section.)

St. Michael le Querne - (See: St. Michael-at-Querne, above.)

St. Michael Paternoster Royal - (See: St. Michael Royal, below.)

St. Michael, Queenhithe - First mentioned in the early 12th century. Named for the nearby hithe (wharf.) Burned in the Great Fire of 1666; rebuilt by Wren in 1677. The 135 foot high tower had a gilded vane shaped like a ship in full sail "with a ball said to be capable of holding a bushel of wheat." Destroyed in 1876.

St. Michael Royal - College Hill (used to be Paternoster Lane,) Upper Thames Street. (AKA: St. Michael Paternoster Royal Church.) During the Regency, it would have been called: St. Michael Paternoster. The 'royal' is not a regal connection, but a corruption of a local street, itself named for La Reole (a wine trade area in Bordeaux.) A church was first here at least by ca. 1219. In 1409 the church was rebuilt/refounded by Dick Whittington ("four times Mayor of London Town") who had lived nearby and who is buried here. Burned in the Great Fire of 1666. Rebuilt in 1686-94 by Edward Strong, a master-mason under Wren (a second source said

1674-87.) Steeple added in 1713, with a second steeple added in 1715. Bombed in WWII; rebuilt.

St. Michael, Wood Street - First mentioned in 1170. Burned in the Great Fire of 1666; rebuilt by Wren in 1675. The 130 foot high spire was repaired in 1888, at which time the high pews were removed from the church. Demolished in 1894.

St. Mildred - Bread Street, the City. First church here was in ca. 1223-52; there is a question as to whether or not this was ever destroyed prior to its damage in the Great Fire of 1666 (it was at least repaired in 1628.) Wren built it anew in 1683. Described as handsome. Until WWII damage it had kept almost all its original woodwork and pews. The parish registers date from 1559; with an interesting entry for December 30, 1816: the marriage of Percy Shelley (poet) Mary Wollstonecraft Shelley (author.) Nothing now remains but the lower part of the tower.

St. Mildred - The Poultry. The City. First mentioned in 1175. Rebuilt in 1457. Burned in 1666's Great Fire; rebuilt in 1676 by Wren. Sold in 1871; demolished in 1872. The churchyard remained until ca. 1927.

St. Nicholas Acons - Dates from 1084. Following being ruined in the Great Fire of 1666 the parish united with St. Edmund, Lombard Street. St. Nicholas Acons' churchyard remains in Nicholas Lane.

St. Nicholas - Camden parish church. 15th C., but only the Perpendicular north part remains from that time, the remainder being mostly modern.

St. Nicholas - Chiswick parish church. Existence dates back to the 12th century (second source says 15th century.) Renovated in the later 19th century. William Hogarth (painter/social critic) was buried here.

St. Nicholas Cole Abbey - (Also seen as: St. Nicolas Cole, no h.) Distaff Lane, the City. (Now on Queen Victoria Street.) "Cole Abbey" is a corruption of "coldharbour." There was a church here by the mid 13th C.; restored in the late 14th century. Burned in the Great Fire of 1666; rebuilt by Wren in 1677. The tower was shaped like a lighthouse, because St. Nicholas is the patron saint of seamen (and also of children.) The tower (and parts of the church) was largely destroyed in WWII, but was fully restored.

- See: St. Mary, Mounthaw, above.
- See: St. Nicholas Olave, below.

St. Nicholas - Deptford Green, north end of Church Street. The west tower dates from the 15th or 16th century. Most everything else dates from 1697. (See: Deptford/St. Nicholas, under D in the Alpha section.)

St. Nicholas Olave - Bread Street, west side of. In 1242 it was "Sci Nicholai Bernard"; in 1285 "St. Nichi Olaui"; in 1303 "St. Nicholas Bernard Olof." Named for St. Olave (Olaf,) the sea-king of Norway (d. 1030); "Bernard" disappeared soon, having perhaps been the name of a benefactor. Almhouses were built in the churchyard in 1537 by the Ironmongers' Company. After being ruined in the Great Fire of 1666 the parish united with St. Nicholas Cole Abbey.

St. Nicholas - Plumstead. 17th C. square tower. In 1864 St. Margaret's (which was built in 1858) became this area's parish church instead.

St. Nicholas Shambles - 1196. The "shambles" is a reference to butchers' quarters (shambles being a very old British word for a butcher's shop or stall.) At the Dissolution the building was given to the Lord Mayor and London's citizens, the parish being then united with Christ Church, Newgate. Demolished in 1547.

St. Nicholas - Sutton parish church. Built in 1862-64. Edwin Nash. Gothic style, dressed flint and stone dressings.

St. Olave - Hart Street and Seething Lane, Tower Hill, the City. Perpendicular-Gothic. It is referred to in 1222 as: St. Olave towards the Tower. In 1368 as: St. Olave next the Friars of Holy Cross (the Crutched Friars.) There was an 11th C. version, and then a 13th C., and then one in the 15th C.; the main body of the church dates from 1450. This church was only 54 feet square, making it one of the smallest churches in the City.

In 1703 the *London Post Boy* printed that Samuel Pepys (diarist) was buried here at "Crutched Friars Church."

It is one of the few City churches to survive the Great Fire of 1666. Approached under a gateway with a decorative skull and crossbones (dates from 1658,) and spikes to deter body-snatchers.

The church was altered in 1731-2, and in 1870-1 (at which time the galleries were removed.) Inside has a friendly and intimate atmosphere. This church was the basis for Dickens's "St. Ghastly Grim" in his *The Uncommercial Traveller.* Severely damaged in WWII bombing; carefully restored.

St. Olave, Jewry - Ironmonger Lane. First mentioned in 1181. In 1320 it was referred to as: St. Olave Upwell. Burned in the Great Fire of 1666; rebuilt by Wren in 1673-6. Work done in 1880. Closed in 1888, at which time united with St. Margaret, Lothbury, (although there is still a church-like building here, now offices.)

- See: St. Martin Pomary, above.
- See: St. Mary Colechurch, above.

St. Olave, Silver Street - Kensington. 1181. Small. William Shakespeare lodged in the house here in 1604 (this information being uncovered in 1910.) After being ruined in the Great Fire of 1666 the parish united with St. Alban, Wood Street. The churchyard remains on the south side of Silver Street.

St. Olave - Tooley Street, Bermondsey. St. Olave's House was built over this site in 1831. Demolished in 1926.

St. Pancras-by-the-Inwoods - (AKA: New Church. AKA: St. Pancras New Church. AKA: St. Pancras, Euston Road.) The *new* Pancras Parish church, corner of Upper Woburn Place. Greek Revival, 1819-22, by William Inwood and his son, Henry. It seems Decimus Burton may have had a hand at it ca. 1840. The building is modeled after the Erechtheion on the Acropolis at Athens; the octagonal tower and steeple is modeled after the Tower of the Winds, also of Athens. (See: St. Pancras Old Church, below, which it replaced.)

St. Pancras - Hampstead (near to.) Dates from ca. 1180. Enlarged in 1848 and the spire was added. (This may also be the same church as referred to as St. Pancras Old Church...and everything I read causes me to change my mind back and forth as regards this question...)

St. Pancras New Church - (See: St. Pancras-by-the-Inwoods, above.)

St. Pancras Old Church - (AKA: St. Pancras Church.) On St. Pancras Road. Ancient, possibly the first church built in London. Could have 7th C. origins, probably rebuilt in the 12th C.; also ca. 1350. Across from the church was a raised, ditched, and moated enclosure called the Brille (also spelled: Brill,) from which red figure tiles and arrowheads were dug up in 1825 (suggesting Roman and possibly pre-Roman occupation of the site.)

The old church still exists; located near King's Cross Station. CHAMBERS LONDON GAZETTEER notes: "...Its parishioners migrated northwards to Kentish Town and the church was left isolated in the fields. St. Pancras Old Church survives on Pancras Road but a neo-Grecian church of the same name was built in 1822 on the corner of present-day Euston Road and Upper Woburn Place...." (See: St. Pancras-by-the-Inwoods, above.)

St. Pancras, Soper Lane - 1207. After being ruined in the Great Fire of 1666, the parish united with St. Mary-le-Bow.

St. Patrick's - Soho. Was Roman Catholic in the Regency. At least since the 18th century. Rebuilt in 1892. (See: Soho/St. Patrick's, under S in the Alpha section.)

St. Paul - Belgravia. Wilton Place. Begun in 1840, consecrated in 1843. Its grounds had previously belonged to the Foot Guard barracks and was used as an exercising ground. Described as lean on the outside, but a kind of miracle within, not least because of a huge, frilly, queenpost roof.

St. Paul, Bow Common - 1958-60. Burdett Road and St. Paul's Way, Stepney.

St. Paul Cathedral - (See: St. Paul's Cathedral, below. Note the: 's.)

St. Paul - Clapham. Original church probably dates from the 12th century. Was the old parish church in Clapham. Rebuilt in 1815. On the ridge overlooking Battersea.

St. Paul - Covent Garden, the Piazza, west side of the Covent Garden market square. (Not to be confused with St. Paul's Cathedral, Ludgate Hill, the City.)

Built by Inigo Jones, completed 1633, in the Tuscan style. Completed in 1638; Jones himself dubbed it as "the handsomest barn in England." (The king had requested it not be too fancy, nothing much above a barn.) Has a false front (called the Tuscan portico,) that actually faces away from the piazza. The entrance is through a courtyard. (The Tuscan portico was meant to be the main entrance to the church, but never was used, leaving behind a deceiving first impression that one would enter there, instead of through the courtyard as it truly does.) The interior burned and was gutted in 1795, but was rebuilt in the Inigo Jones's style by Hardwick; the stone portico and east doorcase survived the fire, and are original. Known as "the Actor's Church" due to its proximity to Drury Lane and Covent Garden theatres, and because many actors' tombstones lie in its memorial garden. (See: Covent Garden/St. Paul's, under C in the Alpha section.)

- All Souls Chapel: (AKA: Kitchener Memorial Chapel.) Was dedicated to Lord Kitchener of Khartoum, 1925.

St. Paul - Deptford Church Street, Deptford. 1712-20, by Thomas Archer. Baroque. Restored in 1856, and again in 1883; described as somber. (See: Deptford/St. Paul's, under D in the Alpha section.)

St. Paul - Fulham (known as Hammersmith after 1834.) Queen Caroline Street. Chapel of Ease. Consecrated in 1631. Restored in 1864.

St. Paul - Hounslow Heath, on the main Bath Road near the Hounslow Barracks. 1874.

St. Paul - Onslow Square, South Kensington. 1860.

St. Paul Presbyterian Church - West Ferry Road, Millwall. 1859.

St. Paul - Shadwell, 302 The Highway. (Also seen as: St. Paul's Shadwell.) Thomas Jefferson's (American president's) mother, Jane Randolph, was baptized here in 1720. Known as "the Sea Captains' Church."

St. Paul - 32a **Wilton Place**, Knightsbridge. 1843.

St. Paul's Cathedral - St. Paul's Churchyard, Ludgate Hill, the City.

(Very commonly simply called: St. Paul's; despite there being many "St. Paul" churches in London, when Londoners speak of "St. Paul's" they most often mean this grand edifice.)

St. Paul is the patron saint of London. This is the cathedral of the diocese of London.

The site has been occupied by a church since the time of King Ethelbert, with ca. the year 604's version being wooden (and centuries before that this site sported a Roman temple dedicated to Diana.) The wooden building was replaced by a stone church built for Bishop Erkenwald; was destroyed by Vikings. Rebuilt by the Saxons, 962, and this was destroyed by fire in 1087; this version's nave was used for socializing, markets, storing booksellers' wares, and even as a route to take in order to avoid rainfall when going from Cheapside to Ludgate.

Another church was built, what came to be called Old St. Paul's. (Actually, all the older versions of St. Paul's are collectively known as "Old St. Paul's," because it was such an important religious and civic center for the City.) Its spire (which, surprisingly, was some 100 feet taller than Wren's later/current spire, at 489 feet tall.) This Norman style version church took some 200 years to complete. This burned in 1561; restored by Inigo Jones in 1634-43 (in that he built a new west end.) Destroyed in the Great Fire of 1666.

The first cathedral in England following the Reformation (which ran roughly 1660-65,) the current rebuild dates from 1675-1710, by Wren, after the Great Fire of 1666, of Portland Stone. Sir Christopher Wren (St. Paul's renowned post-Great Fire architect) is buried here.

It is important to note that up to 1790 the interior lacked the plethora of memorials it now contains. The statue in the forecourt is of Queen Anne. (See: St. Paul's Cathedral, under S in the Alpha section.)

- Paul's Cross: (See under P, in the Alpha section.)
- Paul's Walk: Nickname for the nave in St. Paul's Cathedral. Until the Royal Exchange was built in 1566, Paul's Walk was a bit of a banking center for merchants; yes, in the cathedral.
- St. Paul's Churchyard: (See: St. Paul's Churchyard, under S in the Alpha section.)
- St. Paul's School: Was built in 1512, in St. Paul's Churchyard. (See: St. Paul's School, under S in the Alpha section.)

St. Peter ad Vincula - Chapel on Tower Hill, attached to the Tower of London itself. (See: Tower of London/"Other Places & Things"/St. Peter ad Vincula, under T in the Alpha section.)

St. Peter and St. Paul - Bromley parish church. Martin's Hill. Dr. Samuel Johnson's (author/lexicographer) wife is buried here.

St. Peter and St. Paul - Harlington High Street, Harlington. 80 feet high. Built on Saxon foundations dating from 1087.

St. Peter and St. Paul - Mitcham. Rebuilt in 1821, in the Perpendicular style.

St. Peter - Bethnal Green, on St. Peter's Avenue. Lewis Vulliamy (architect,) 1840.

St. Peter - Chelsea, Cranley Gardens. 1868.

St. Peter - Cornhill. (See: St. Peter-upon-Cornhill, below.)

St. Peter - De Beauvoir Town, ca. 1830.

St. Peter - Eaton Square, Belgravia. 1826. Colonnaded front.

St. Peter - Fulham (known as Hammersmith after 1834.) Built in 1829. Portico; clock-tower; and four columns.

St. Peter-in-Chepe - Cheapside. Destroyed in the Great Fire of 1666, not to be rebuilt. A plane tree marked its spot for years, well beyond the era of the Regency.

St. Peter Italian Church - (See: St. Peter's Italian Church, below. Note the: 's.)

St. Peter le Poer - First mentioned in 1181. Enlarged and repaired ca. 1615-30. Did not burn in the Great Fire of 1666, but because it was badly decayed (and obstructing traffic on Old Broad Street,) it was removed in 1788 by Act of Parliament. Rebuilt farther back, on the site of its cemetery. St. Benet Fink church was demolished in 1842, at which time both it and St. Peter le Poer united with St. Michael, Cornhill. Demolished in 1896.

St. Peter - Paul's Wharf. In 1170 it is mentioned as: St. Peter the Little; in 1267 it's called: St. Peter de la Wodewarve. After being ruined in the Great Fire of 1666 the parish was united with St. Benet, Paul's Wharf; when the latter stopped being parochial in 1879 it united with St. Nicholas Cole Abbey. The graveyard remains in Upper Thames Street.

St. Peter - Regent Street. (AKA: St. Peter's, Regent Square.) By W. and H. W. Inwood, 1822-5. Since WWII only the portico and steeple remain.

St. Peter-upon-Cornhill - Cornhill, corner of Gracechurch Street. (AKA: St. Peter, Cornhill.) Purportedly founded by King Lucius in 179AD, although this may just be folk tradition. Anyway, in 1979 the church celebrated their 1800th anniversary. Burned in the Great Fire of 1666; rebuilt by Wren in 1677-81.

St. Peter - Vere Street, off Oxford Street, Marylebone. James Gibb, 1724. Small brick church; Tuscan portico.

St. Peter - Walworth. By Soane, 1826-7. Very similar in its makeup to Holy Trinity, Marylebone.

St. Peter, Westcheap - Wood Street, on the corner of. First mentioned in 1196. It was called: St. Peter at the Cross in Chepe in 1393. Not rebuilt after the Great Fire of 1666, in which it was ruined; its parish then united with St. Matthew, Friday Street. When the latter was pulled down in 1881, it united with St. Vedast, Foster Lane.

St. Peter's Italian Church - Clerkenwell, 1863.

St. Philip Chapel - Carlton House. (See: St. Philip's Chapel, below.)

St. Philip Neri, the London Oratory of - (AKA: Brompton Oratory.) Brompton Road. PILGRIMS' LONDON states: "This is the London home of an association of secular priests founded in Rome by St. Philip Neri (1515-95.) The church popularly known as the 'Brompton Oratory' is, officially, the church of the London Oratory, the church house being next door on the west. The oratory is unique in the Roman Catholic church in that it emphasizes the aesthetic and artistic in the practice of devotional exercises." The land was purchased in 1853. Built 1880-93. Was, and remains, Catholic. Done in the Italianate Baroque style. Known for its musical services. LET'S GO-THE BUDGET GUIDE TO LONDON says: "H. Gribble built the aggressively Roman Baroque edifice in 1884." Behind the Oratory is Holy Trinity.

- See: Brompton Oratory, under B in the Alpha section.

Jane Austin Shopped Here

- ➢ See: Holy Trinity/Cottage Place/Brompton, above.

St. Philip - Stepney. (AKA: St. Philip the Apostle.) Built in 1817-21. Consecrated in 1823. In 1836 was given a district. Rebuilt in 1883. United with St. Augustine after WWII, then being called: St. Augustine with St. Philip. Is now: London Hospital's library.

St. Philip's Chapel - Carlton House built on its site, 1709.

St. Saviour - Pimlico Road (off of,) Grosvenor Road, St. George's Square, a rectangle between Grosvenor Place and Lupus Street. 1864, to designs by Thomas Cundy the Younger.

St. Saviour - (AKA: **Southwark Cathedral**, as of 1905.) South of London Bridge. Known as St. Saviour from 1540-1905. The choir and Lady Chapel date from ca. 1220. The nave was rebuilt in 1897. (See: Southwark Cathedral, below.)

St. Sepulchre's Church - (AKA: Holy Sepulchre, which is its more proper name. AKA: St. Sepulchre-without-Newgate. AKA: St. Sepulchre, Newgate. AKA: Church of the Holy Sepulchre.) Holborn Viaduct. Between Snow Hill and Giltspur Street (west end of Newgate Street.) It was first dedicated in 1137 to King Edmund of East Anglia, being called: St. Edmund without Newgate, or: St. Edmund Sepulchre, early in its existence (and was known by: St. Sepulchre by 1308); Crusaders began their journeys to the Holy Land/crusades from here, and thus it took on its name from the Holy Sepulchre in Jerusalem. A stone was brought from the Holy Sepulchre (Jerusalem) to be placed in this church.

"Without Newgate" refers to the fact it was built outside the City wall.

Was purportedly once connected to Newgate Prison by a tunnel, which (if it existed) was supposedly filled in in 1879. Its bell tolled at eight a.m. on the morning of an execution, as it is just opposite Newgate. (The bodies might be buried in the churchyard, but also were sometimes given to medical surgeons at St. Bartholomew's; the bodies of executed prisoners was the only legal way to acquire bodies. For illegal methods, see: resurrectionists, under R in the Alpha section.)

Rebuilt in the 15th C., and then restored after the Great Fire of 1666 largely destroyed it, possibly by Wren ca. 1670, although the 15th C. external walls, porch, and tower still remain. Repaired in 1738; again in 1790; the windows were altered in 1790 (but restored to the Gothic form in 1878.) The coffered ceiling dates from 1834.

Restored (but also "Victorianized") in 1875.

It is referred to as "the Musician's Church," but I believe this is a Victorian/Edwardian appellation.

Capt. John Smith (of Pocahontas/founding Jamestown, Virginia fame) is buried here.

In 1949 the churchyard was dedicated to the Royal Fusiliers.

St. Stephen - Coleman Street, Lothbury. Possibly existed by 1181; definitely by ca. 1214. Burned in the Great Fire of 1666; rebuilt by Wren in 1676. Is a plain building, without aisles,

75 feet long x 35 feet wide. The east window dated from 1843, which a 1917 bomb destroyed; replaced in 1919. The church was entirely wiped out in 1941 and the site built over.

St. Stephen - Rochester Row, South Belgravia. Near Vauxhall Bridge Road. Built in 1847-50.

St. Stephen - Shepherd Bush. Consecrated in 1850.

St. Stephen-the-Martyr - Avenue Road. 1849.

St. Stephen Walbrook - Walbrook Street (next to the Mansion,) the City. The Lord Mayor's parish church. Dates from before 1096, that version being built on the west side of the Walbrook; in medieval times there had been a brook here, which was built over (the Walbrook.)

The second church dated from 1439-1666, on the same site as the present church, which is on the east side of the stream. In the 15th C. this church's patronage was bestowed on the Grocers' Company.

Burned in the Great Fire of 1666. Wren rebuilt and did a domed interior (which is supported by Corinthian columns) in 1672-79, generally considered to be his finest (rather markedly like St. Paul's in its appearance.) To this day many consider this the most beautiful church in London. Bright, airy interior. NAIRN'S LONDON tells us: "Wren here combined four church plans in one...a domed space, a nave and aisles, an even array of columns around a central hall, and a Greek cross, all at once." Spire added in 1717, Wren. Is a relatively small church, being 75 feet high by 36 feet long. Wren's box pews were removed during Victoria's reign. Damaged by WWII bombs, but largely restored. It was restored again in the 1980s, and reopened in 1987.

St. Stephen's Chapel -

- See: St. Mary Undercroft, above.
- See: St. Stephen's Undercroft, below.

St. Stephen's Undercroft - (AKA: St. Stephen's Crypt, see note below, on this name.) Located in Westminster. First built in 1141. Rebuilt in 1292 by Edward I, in a two-storied arrangement: the lower (ground) story was dedicated to the Virgin Mary and intended for the "throngs" (the king's household;) the upper story (known in England as the first story) was for the king's use and was dedicated to St. Stephen. PARLIAMENT HOUSE states: "The former..." (the lower chapel) "...which still remains, is now called the Crypt Chapel, an unfortunate name, as it betrays total ignorance of the history of the building. It never was a crypt (which signifies a chamber below ground level,) but was simply the lower chapel, and it is always spoken of as such in the accounts of the building."

Wren refurbished it in the 18th century. In 1803 Wyatt gave it a gothic design.

After the 1834 fire (the burning down of the Parliament structures in Westminster Palace) this was remodeled and then dedicated as the Church of St. Mary Undercroft. Members of Parliament can marry or have their children christened here.

- See: St. Mary Undercroft, above.
- See: Westminster Hall/St. Stephen's, under W in the Alpha section.

St. Swithin - Cannon Street, north side of. (AKA: St. Swithun, London Stone.) First mentioned in 1272. Rebuilt ca. 1420. Burned in the Great Fire of 1666; rebuilt by Wren in 1678. South front once hosted the celebrated London Stone, placed in its present spot in the south wall in 1798; the Stone is popularly thought to be a Milliarium (an old Roman mile stone marker, marking 1,000 paces.) Had a "fine" octagonal domed roof. The church was destroyed by WWII damage in 1941; pulled down in 1962.

- See: Candlewick Street/Milliarium, under C in the Alpha section.
- See: London Stone, under L in the Alpha section.
- See: St. Mary Bothaw, above.

St. Thomas - Bermondsey. Built in 1702. In 1901 this became Southwark Cathedral's Chapter House.

St. Thomas the Apostle - First mentioned in 1170. Rebuilt in 1371. After being ruined in the Great Fire of 1666 the parish united with St. Mary Aldermanbury. (See: St. Mary Aldermanbury, above.)

St. Vedast, Foster Lane - (AKA: St. Vedast-alias-Foster.) Foster Lane, Cheapside. Earliest mention of a church here is 1170 (a second source said it is from the 13th century.) Seemingly rebuilt in 1519; at least 100 pounds was offered for that purpose by one John Throwstone. "Beautified" in 1614. Burned in the Great Fire of 1666; rebuilt in 1695-1701 by Wren. Stands in the shadow of St. Paul's Cathedral. Beautiful steeple. Smallish, measuring 69 feet x 21 feet. Its interior was utterly destroyed in WWII, and the present decorations/ furnishings were all brought from other churches.

- See: St. Matthew, Friday Street, above.
- See: St. Michael-at-Querne, above.

sanctuary - The act of seeking sanctuary from the law/Crown in a church. (See: sanctuary, under S in the Alpha section.)

Sardinian Chapel - (Also known as: Sardinian Embassy Chapel.) Near Lincoln's Inn Fields. Called the Sardinian Chapel until 1853. The church of Saints Anselm and Cecelia replaced it in 1909. (See: St. Anselm and St. Cecelia, above.)

Savoy Chapel - Not to be confused with the Queen's Chapel of the Savoy. (See: Savoy Chapel, under S in the Alpha section.)

Southwark Cathedral - Montague Close, Southwark. (Pronounced: Suth-ick.) Protestant cathedral. Largely 13th-century, but tradition says the first church here dated from the year 606. We know that at least by 1106 it had become an Augustinian priory. Medieval choir, ca. 1240. Not designated a cathedral until 1905, at which time it had reverted to the Catholics. South side of Thames, west of London Bridge. Official name: St. Saviour's. *This church was known as St. Mary Overie until 1540; then became known as St. Saviour's until 1905; when it became Southwark Cathedral.*

- See: St. Mary Overie, above.
- See: St. Saviour's, above.
- See: St. Thomas/Bermondsey, above.

Spa Fields Chapel - Calvinistic Methodist. Built before 1777. It was round. (See: Spa Fields Chapel, under S in the Alpha section.)

Spanish and Portuguese Synagogue - (See: Spanish and Portuguese Synagogue, under S in the Alpha section.)

Surrey Chapel - Blackfriars Road, Southwark. 1783, by William Thomas, for the Rev. Rowland Hill, a nonconformist (some say eccentric, b.1744-d.1833.) The congregation became noted for its singing (with an organ); some hymns were composed by (or set to popular music by) Rev. Hill himself.

The chapel was round, with a cupola on top to allow light in. THE LOST TREASURES OF LONDON states: "Its design excluded corners, where the Devil might lurk. An opening was made for the latter, long after the preacher's death, by the transformation of the chapel into a place of amusement when its use for religious purposes ceased in 1881." In 1910 this building was converted into a boxing ring (and called: The Ring.) Demolished in 1940 by WWII bombs.

Temple Church - (See: Inns of Court/Temple (2nd entry)/Temple Church, under I.)

University Church of Christ the King - Gordon Square. Dates from 1853. Associated with the now almost non-existent Catholic Apostolic Church movement.

Wanstead Church - (See: St. Mary the Virgin/Wanstead, above.)

Wesley's Chapel - 49 City Road, St. Luke's. (Also known, somewhat tongue in cheek, as the "Methodists' Cathedral," since the Methodists were not much given to pomp.) Consecrated in 1778 by John Wesley (the founder of Methodism.)

Westminster Abbey - Medieval architecture. Impressive tombs and monuments. Survived the Great Fire of 1666. Not to be confused with Westminster Cathedral. (See: Westminster Abbey, under W in the Alpha section.)

Westminster Cathedral - (AKA: Westminster Roman Catholic Cathedral.) 1894, by John Francis Bentley. Italian-Byzantine design. Red and white brick exterior. Interior contains many multi-colored marbles. Not to be confused with Westminster Abbey. (See: Westminster Cathedral, under W in the Alpha section.)

Whitfield's Tabernacle - (Also sometimes seen written as: Whitefield's Tabernacle.) 1756. (See: Whitfield's Tabernacle, under W in the Alpha section.)

Zion's Chapel - 1819. (See: Bromley/Broom Hill/Zion Chapel, under B in the Alpha section.)

CLUBS:

London has long hosted various clubs throughout its history, going back to the time of Sir Walter Raleigh (d.1618) and even further back - but here we speak of the heyday of Gentlemen's clubs to which Regency gentlemen desired to belong. They were run by managers, as opposed to a committee. Many of the clubs were not marked (i.e. they might have a street number but were not designated with a sign proclaiming the location as a club.) It was (and remains to a certain degree) that you either knew where the club was, or you didn't belong there. With a brief exception at the Athenaeum Club, until the 20th century absolutely no women were admitted. Many clubs were primarily a place for a quiet drink with like-minded fellows. Some lasted a century or two but made little impact on history - and in being for private members, left behind little description of themselves, even if they were well attended. (For instance, see: City of Lushington, below.)

There were other kinds of clubs, based on common interests and/or one's trade. For instance:

- See: All-England Club, below - Tennis.
- See: Cogers, below - Debate.
- See: St. Martin's Lane/Scotch Arms, under S - Which hosted a club for tailors.

But for the purposes of this list, the following are largely gentlemen's clubs.

Alfred, the - 23 Albemarle Street. 1808. Attracted "men of letters." Described by the Earl of Dudley as "the dullest place in existence," although the poet Byron (a member there) described it as "literary, pleasant and sober." Was a success despite any dullness, with 354 names on an 1811 waiting list. Joined with the Oriental in 1855.

All-England Club - Tennis. Not a gentlemen's club. (See: tennis, under T in the Alpha section.)

Almack's Club - Not to be confused with Almack's Assembly Rooms. (See both, under A in the Alpha section.)

American Club, the - 95 Piccadilly. For Americans. Founded in 1918. 1980s closure.

Annabel's - 44 Berkeley Square. (See: Berkeley Square/Annabel's, under B in the Alpha section.) Modern.

Arlington, the - (See: Turf Club, below.)

Army and Navy Club, the - 37 Pall Mall. 1837. Also called "The Rag," a shortening of Capt. William Duff's (of the 23rd Foot) calling it "the Rag and Famish", having found the food meager (and the "rag" being apparently a term for a brothel, a further lack of flattery.) It had a modern clubhouse (on the other side of the entrance to St. James's Square) since 1963.

Arthur's Club - (Also called just: Arthur's.) 1827. (See: Carlton Club, below.)

Arts Club, the - 40 Dover Street. 1863.

Athenaeum, the - 107 Pall Mall, St. James's. Built on the site of the demolished Carlton House (shares the site with Carlton House Terrace.) Located beside the Duke of York's Steps. Founded in 1824; erected between 1828-30 to designs by Decimus Burton, in a quasi-Grecian style, a pale stuccoed neo-classical-looking building. At first was known as "the Society," changed to "the Athenaeum" in 1830. A golden statue of Pallas Athena stands atop the portico, this statue dating from 1830 or later. Has an exterior frieze copied from the Parthenon; has a "majestic hall" that is dominated by a statue of Apollo. Candidates were expected to be established in their careers, with a select leaning toward literary members (also read: cultural elite,) but since it was deemed a fashionable club to which one would wish to belong, they had their share of "gentility-hunters" among their numbers as well. Eight of the original list of members went on to become Prime Ministers. There was at one time a sixteen year waiting list. Later in the 19th century it was noted that the food was rather sadly lacking in style and flavor, but the library was famous and called "very good." There was no bar until ca. 1970. It was not a giddy place, being far more given to quiet. When it first opened, women were invited in for a soiree on Wednesday evenings, although this practice was not a long-lived one. Its members are known for being bishops and academics. (Not to be confused with the Turf and Athenaeum Club.)

Athenian Lyceum, the - More of a debating society than a gentlemen's club. (See: Athenian Lyceum, under A in the Alpha section.)

Bath Club, the - 1894.

Beefsteak, the - (Also seen written as: Beef Steak Club.) 1735, founded by John Rich (a celebrated harlequin, a comic servant character) as "The Sublime Society of Beefsteaks." It originally resided high up in the Covent Garden theatre, in 'the thunder and lightning' room; composed of the "chief wits and great men of the nation" (quote from Chetwood, 1749, *History of the Stage.)* In 1762, by some accounts, the sandwich was supposedly invented here when the 4th Earl of Sandwich demanded beef or fowl on sliced bread so he could continue his gambling uninterrupted by a more formal meal. Perhaps not true. (See: sandwich, under S in the Alpha section.)

Moved a number of times, landing at the Lyceum Theatre.

Now at 9 Irving Street, between Charing Cross Road and Leicester Square; a first floor dining room off Leicester Square. It is a single room above a shop, (the shop being owned by the club.) It has two bedrooms used by members arriving from out of town. It has a long communal table, the members seating themselves by the order in which they arrive, with approximately 8-15 sitting down to a meal, the number of members being strictly limited to 24. George IV was obliged to put his name on a waiting list when he wished to join, waiting for a vacancy to occur; he was elected in April 1784. At the time of George IV, the members dined every Saturday at 2:00pm, November to June. They ate beefsteaks, and then toasted cheese, which was served along with port, porter, punch, and whisky toddy. They wore blue coats and buff waistcoats, and the buttons bore the motto "Beef and Liberty." They were a jolly lot, calling themselves "The Sublime Society of Beef Steaks." In 1808, the dinner meal was moved to 4:00pm; to 6:00pm in 1833; 7:00pm in 1861; and 8:00pm in 1866.

The name dates from the 18th C., at which time there were at least two other "Beefsteaks" in London (one in Ivy Lane; location of the other uncertain.)

The club dissolved in 1867 after an unsuccessful attempt to change the dining day to Friday. It was revived in 1876, at least in name and in its desire to serve "simple, plain food," and although the promise to allow it to meet again in the old room at the Lyceum fell through, the old name of "the Beefsteak" stuck. In all, it was a small club, in which the members were well known to one another and seemingly most convivial.

Note: Besides in London, over time there were quite a few "Beefsteak Clubs" around the country besides this specific one, established by various men who enjoyed dining on beef.

Boodle's - 28 St. James's Street. Established originally in 1762 by Almack (a fractured scrambling of a Scotsman's name, McCall,) in Pall Mall (that is, on the original site of White's, at which Edwin Boodle was head waiter.) The American Revolutionary war (ca. 1776) coincided with the ending of another club here, *the Savoir Vivre* and then Boodle's took over the failed venture at St. James's Street.

The subsequent building dates from 1765, designed by Holland in the Adam style. Boodle's was based in St. James's Street since 1783. Opposite of Brooks's. Has a serene air, with paintings of Grand National winners (and other countrified scenes) adorning the walls. It was intended to give country gentlemen a comfortable London base; always had more of a "country" (and relaxed) air than its peers. Was more social than some clubs, tending to be non-political.

It possesses the famous bow window facing on to St. James's Street, like White's, but added in 1824 (White's bow window was added in 1811.)

The betting book was here by at least 1814 although presumably it was on hand years before this. An 1814 edition of the betting book looks to be approximately 5 inches x 8 inches when closed. All manner of wagers, from serious to silly, were logged in the book.

Brooks's - (AKA: Brooks's Subscription House. Also as: Brooks's Club. In older works, the name is spelled: Brookes's.) Left Pall Mall in 1778. Went to: 60 St. James's Street (although it is exclusive enough that there is no actual number posted at this address.) Corner of Park Place. Opposite of Boodle's.

It took the name of Brooks's from a wine merchant who subsequently took over a failed club here. The present location was built in 1777-8 at Mr. Brooks's expense; Henry Holland designed it to resemble a small country house. Among Boodle's, Brooks's, and White's, Brooks's was perhaps the most elegant. Opened in Oct/1778. It did not prosper at first, and Mr. Brooks retired/died, ca. 1782, paupered.

In time, rich Whigs gamed there. The Great Subscription Room was where the members gathered for an active gaming evening, the preferred games being faro, hazard, macao, quinze, and whist. Gaming was not allowed in the dining room (except to decide who would pay for the meal.)

The famous *betting books* are still used (although with less flamboyant wagers than in their heyday.)

Traditionally, new members were elected by ballot between 11:00pm-1:00am. Center of left wall: fireplace with large mirror over it. A gaming table (small, four-person) on either side of fireplace. Right side: large round tables (largest seated about 10, with one flat side for dealer,) lamps on each table, and one big elegant chandelier hanging from the middle of the ceiling. Floor was black and white marble. The ceiling was painted. The walls were deliberately kept bare of pictures (in the 18th C.,) so as not to distract the gamblers. Contained no bedrooms.

Brooks's was early on non-political, but eventually William Pitt the Younger gave up Brooks's for White's (not liking the deep gaming play at the former,) and Fox and his company desisted from attending White's, those two events creating the fact that White's was the club for Tories, and Brooks's for Whigs. Since Prinny was (at least in the early days) a great devotee of Fox's, he was a member here, too.

"The Club" also meets here once per month on Tuesdays. (See: Club, the, below.)

Caledonian Club, the - 9 Halkin Street. 1891.

Calves' Head Club - Suffolk Street. Met only on Jan. 30th each year; the name derives from the food served, which in itself was a deliberately unflattering reference to the loss of Charles I's own head. Also served: a cod's head (represented Charles Stuart); a pike (representing tyranny); and a boar's head (representing the king preying on his people.) An axe on the table held the place of honor. The club had to meet secretly following the Restoration (of the monarchy.) Ended in 1734 after a riot of the populace inspired by their mocking meal.

Canning Club - 1911.

Carlton Club - 69 St. James's Street. (Prior to WWII, this club was at 100 Pall Mall.) Built in 1827, opened in 1832 as "Arthur's." Built on the site of a 1736 coffee-house of the same name.

The Carlton Club was founded by Arthur, the Duke of Wellington, for whom it was first named. A club for Conservatives (Tories); Margaret Thatcher (Prime Minister) was declared an "honourary man" in 1975 rather than change the rules to include a female Party leader. (See: White's, comment regarding Tories.)

Cavalry Club - 127 Piccadilly. 1890. The Guard's Club merged into the Cavalry Club in 1976, so it's now known as: Cavalry & Guards. A new clubhouse, in the same location, was built in 1908.

Chapter Coffee-house - (Also referred to as: the Wittinagemot of the Chapter Coffee-house.) Corner of Chapter-house Court, south side of Paternoster Row. "Men of letters, encouragers of literature" belonged to this "club." A place for pamphlets and news-sheets. Closed as a coffee-house in 1854 (being altered to a tavern.) When they spoke of a "good" book, they meant one that sold well, not necessarily one of literary value. For some years prior to 1820, it was renowned for its dullness and unappreciated quiet.

City Livery Club, the - 1914.

City of London Club, the - 19 Old Broad Street. (AKA: the City of London. AKA: the City Club.) 1832-34, by Philip Hardwick. The building is Georgian. It was nearly demolished in the 1970s, but planning permission was denied.

City of Lushington - Great Russell Street, 1760s. For "lush" read: drunkard; while this society was founded mainly for actors, it became essentially a drinking club. Lasted until ca. 1910. Boasted an eclectic, wide-ranging membership, a member of which was called a "lush."

City University Club, the - 50 Cornhill. 1895.

Clermont Club - 44 Berkeley Square. 20th C. casino, began in 1962. In 1963 the basement began hosting: Annabel's nightclub (not to be confused with an 18th C. gentlemen's club of the same Annabel's name.) Closed in 2018.

- See: Berkeley Square/44, under B in the Alpha section.
- See: Clermont Club, under C in the Alpha section.

Club, The - So exclusive (only 50 men, of the senior politician and financier stripe,) its existence was all but hidden from common knowledge until a reporter stumbled on the news in the 1990s, despite a prior 250 years of existence. Meets for dinner one Tuesday per month, at a private room at 60 St. James's Street, which is Brooks's. (See: Brooks's Club, above, note at.)

Cocoa-Tree Club, the - (Also seen as: Cocoa Tree Club.) 64 St. James's Street. Started life as a chocolate-house during Queen Anne's reign, 1669. Tory. It probably converted into a club before 1746. Lord Byron (poet) belonged. Known for its high stakes gambling. Had its own brothel up to 1840. Ceased to be in 1902 (250 of its members then being elected into the Union Club.)

Coffee Club - (See: Rota Club, below.)

Cogers - Debating society, not a gentlemen's club, per se. Be sure to pronounce it with the long "o" sound and not the frowned-upon version that has it rhyming with "dodgers." (See: Cogers, under C in the Alpha section.)

Conservative Club, the - Now at 69 St. James's Street. Opened in 1840. Was at 74 St. James's Street, 1845-1959. As the name implies, the members supported the Conservatives. Merged with the Bath Club in 1950. Dissolved in 1981. (See: Thatched House Tavern, under the INNS/PUBS section.)

Constitutional Club - 1883. (See: Junior Constitutional Club.)

Crockford's - (Also seen as: Crockfords. *Officially* was called: St. James's Club, although this was little used.) 30 Curzon Street, Mayfair. Built 1827-8, exclusively for gaming (gambling,) by William Crockford. Crockford had risen from being a fishmonger. He retired from Crockford's in 1840. It was "the queen of the gaming-clubs." As much as £20,000 pounds could be lost a night here. Played here were: Faro, Jeu d'enfer, and blind-hookey (among other games,) at night-long sessions. Hazard was officially illegal in England, but was played anyway. Ministers of the Crown, and indeed the Duke of Wellington (at one time a member of the managing committee,) were members of Crockford's. There remains a Crockford's on Curzon Street, where it is still possible to gamble, and which grew out of the old Crockford's reputation. (Not to be confused with an 1859 St. James' Club in Piccadilly, which was deliberately spelled with only one s.)

East India and Sport Club, the - (AKA: East India, the.) Presently at 16 St. James's Square. 1849. For employees, current & former, of the East India Company. In modern times it combines four clubs: East India, Devonshire, Sports (1938,) and Public School (1972) clubs.

Eccentric Club, the - (AKA: Eccentrics Society Club.) 1781. In the Covent Garden area, several addresses.) Closed in 1846. (There was a second club of this name in Leicester Square, 1858-81. And a third, at 9 Ryder Street, St. James's, 1984-86.)

Four-in-Hand Club - A driving club, founded in 1856. (See under F.)

Garrick Club, the - 15 Garrick Street. 1831. Described as a tall, dirty, gray stone building. Has ironwork trim. Inside it is flamboyant, 18th century. It is unmarked (as a club.) For aristocrats, actors, and writers. (See under G.)

Gresham Club, the **-** 15 Abchurch Lane, the City. 1843. Reopened in 1994 as the London Capital Club.

Guards' Club, the **-** In 1810-26 was at: 49 St. James's Street. In 1826-27 at: 106 Pall Mall. In 1827 they were briefly and with dissatisfaction in Jermyn Street. In 1827-48 again at: 49 St. James's Street. In 1848: 70 Pall Mall, where they stayed until the end of WWI. Now at 127 Piccadilly.

Was the first members' club in London (that is to say, the first not run as a commercial venture.) It was founded in 1810 by the Prince Regent and Wellington at 70 Pall Mall, who felt that the Guards Division (at that time meaning: the Coldstream, Grenadier, and Scots Guards; by the mid 20th C. the Welsh Guards, and the Irish Guards were allowed to join) officers returning from the war in Spain needed a club to repair to, to avoid the expensive gaming clubs and/or the often mean chop-houses or taverns. It was first housed "in a simple room" opposite Lock's (a hatter's) at the bottom of St. James's Street, in a coffee house with a sanded floor. They established a membership, then moved to the top of St. James's Street, across from White's, into a modest building. The club, too, was considered modest, but the food and wine were good; the gaming was kept to whist and was for humble stakes.

In 1919 moved to Brook Street (in the place now occupied by the Bath Club,) eventually coming to its present home in 127 Piccadilly, being merged in 1976 into the Cavalry Club. (See: Cavalry Club, above.)

Hampden Club - 1811-12. A political club. Named for John Hampden; in the time of Charles I was "the hero of the Ship Money case." ("Ship money" was a medieval tax that was levied on and off until the 17th C., mostly applying to coastal areas.) The members were well-to-do and aimed their discussions at parliamentary reforms. Became more radical (part of the Radical Movement) in 1814, now more in support of working men's rights. The fee to join was three guineas, and this high price led to this club soon folding (along with governmental pressure under the fear of such clubs fomenting radical thoughts/riots.) The founder, John Cartwright, toured the north and the Midlands, leading to the establishment of more Hampden Clubs; the first club formed outside London was in 1816, in Royton, Manchester.

Hell-fire Club - Some pundits question if such a club ever actually existed, but most state there were, over time, several gentlemen's clubs of this name. (The author of this work has personally visited the site of a Hell-fire Club in West Wycombe, Buckinghamshire, England, some 300 feet underground in a chalk cave.) It is my opinion clubs of this name, of lesser or greater debauchery, did indeed exist at various times, because there are simply too many references to it/them.

Records show a Hell-fire Club meeting in London held in May, 1746 at the George and Vulture Tavern. (See: George and Vulture Tavern, under the INNS/PUBS section.)

What is concrete enough is that some clubs of the time had bizarre ceremonies. It seems Sir Francis Dashwood, a colonel in the militia of Buckinghamshire, founded a Hell-fire Club in the late 1750s, along with a reputed twelve compatriots dubbed the "Monks of St. Francis" (or also: "Monks of Medmenham.") Legends of the sexual exploits (orgies) and weird Satanic-like ceremonies abound. It should be noted that most tales of Hell-fire club activity speak of excessive alcohol consumption, to the point one walks away with an impression that most of the time meetings might have been more drunken routs than dark and sinister bacchanals. In Dashwood's time, there are certainly accounts of "free love," and portraits of him in curious garb that strike the viewer as reflective of a Georgian gentleman not given to the usual.

Regardless, if one belonged to a Hell-fire Club, it is safe to assume one was choosing to explore drunkenness, sexual exploits, and, perhaps, a darker side of life.

Hurlingham Club, the - Shooting club. 1867. (See: Hurlingham Club, under H in the Alpha section.)

In and Out, the - (See: Naval and Military Club, below.)

Isthmian Club - Victorian. First at Walsingham House, but had to move when the site became the Ritz Hotel; circa 1896 moved to 105 Piccadilly. The club fizzled out after WWI. (See: Piccadilly/105, under P in the Alpha section.)

Jockey Club - Dates back to 1750. They met at the Star and Garter, Pall Mall. This same year, the club bought land at Newmarket on which to build a coffee room; they used the Red Lion in town for meetings until this was built.

Very soon, matters of dispute in horseracing were referred to the Jockey Club for resolution.

In 1762, nineteen members declared an intent to consistently use "colors" (silks -or- livery) on their riders, to distinguish one from another.

In modern times, racehorses' names, including spaces, are limited to eighteen characters.

These days the Jockey Club has left London and is exclusively in Newmarket.

- See: Newmarket/Jockey Club, under N in the Alpha section.
- You may care to see: jockeys, under J in the Alpha section.

Junior Athenaeum - Victorian; housed at 116 Piccadilly in 1868.

Junior Carlton Club, the - At 30 Pall Mall, 1865-1968. At 94 Pall Mall, 1968-1977. Closed/merged with the Carlton Club in 1977.

Junior Constitutional Club - 101 Piccadilly. 1887. A political club, Conservative. Over-subscription at the Constitutional Club led to forming the Junior Constitutional. Closed in 1904, becoming then the Tariff Reform United Empire Club. (See: Piccadilly/102, under P.)

Junior Naval and Military Club - 1870-79. First at 19 Dover Street, but moved to a prepared building at 66-68 Pall Mall, 1875. This move bankrupted the founder, and the club closed.

- See: Naval and Military Club, below.
- See: White Horse Inn, under the INNS/PUBS section.

Junior United Service Club - (See: United Service Club, below.)

Kit-Kat Club, the - Upper Flask Inn, Flask Walk, Hampstead. Name derived from Christopher Katt (AKA: Christopher Cat; CASSELL'S COMPANION TO EIGHTEENTH CENTURY BRITAIN says his name was Cat, and the club name derived from his tavern's specialty, mutton pies known as kit-cats.) Regardless, Cassell was a pastrycook whose home served as the club's first meeting place, 1703. Most members were Whig politicians (the Whigs had formed the club,) and the poets Keats and Shelley tipped a cup or two here as well. Was gone by 1725.

Lansdowne Club, the - 9 Fitzmaurice Place, off Berkeley Square, Mayfair. 1935. Yet exists.

Literary Club, the - (See: Turk's Head Literary Club, below.)

London Capital Club - (See: Gresham Club, above.)

Lord's - A cricket club, not a gentlemen's club. Established 1787. (See: Lord's Cricket Ground, under L in the Alpha section.)

MCC, the - (Marylebone Cricket Club) A cricket club, not a gentlemen's club. Started from a group who met at the Star and Garter Tavern in Pall Mall, and who revised the rules of cricket in 1755. They called themselves the *Je ne sais quoi* Club. In 1782 some of these members founded the White Conduit Cricket Club in Islington, where Thomas Lord took a job. In 1786, tired of making the trip to Islington, some of the leaders of Whites Cricket Club offered to finance a cricket enterprise closer to the City if Lord would find it for them. He did so, on the Portman estate, acquiring a lease for land in Dorset Fields (now Dorset Square,) Marylebone. As the 19th C. dawned, the MCC took over from the Hambledon Club the governing of the game of cricket. They moved with Lord to St. John's Wood Road in 1814. Lord was bought out by William Ward (a club member,) who then handed the reins over to one James Dark in 1835. In 1864 Dark retired, and the club bought the lease of the land, and in 1866 bought the freehold. Has a room called the Long Room, which still has very much the flavor of a clubroom. (See: Lord's Cricket Ground, under L in the Alpha section, for more.)

National Liberal Club, the - Whitehall Place. 1882. Described as "immense."

Naval and Military Club, the - 49 Piccadilly, 1865-1999. Founded in 1862. (AKA: the In and Out, because of its driveway signs.) Moved to 4 St. James's Square in the 1990s. (See: Piccadilly/49, under P in the Alpha section.)

Number Ten Club, the - 1955.

October Club, the - Made up of backbench Tory members of Parliament. Defunct ca. 1712.

Oddfellows, the - (Also seen as: Odd Fellows.) More of a fraternal society than a club, founded ca. 1745. Met at Southwark Oakley Arms, the Globe at Hatton Gardens, and the Boar's Head, Smithfield. Mostly about self-help, companionship, and a sort of Freemason's style. Also had country versions. The Oddfellows yet exist, providing charity, philanthropy, and recreation.

Oriental Club, the - (AKA simply as: the Oriental.) Stratford House, Stratford Place. 1824. A club intended for use by returning gentlemen who had served, traveled, or resided in the East (i.e. India,) and therefore mostly made up of East India Company men. Resided at first for a while in Lower Grosvenor Street, shortly thereafter moving to its present site at Stratford

House, Stratford Place, Hanover Square. Its location was deliberately chosen to be away from other gentlemen's clubs, in large part due to the many members of this club who resided in nearby Harley Street and, therefore, easy walking distance. Stratford House was built by Benjamin Wyatt, but was not a distinguished appearing building. Joined with "The Alfred" in 1855. (See: Alfred, the, above.)

Oxford and Cambridge Club, the - 1830 (but the site of 71 Pall Mall was not established until 1837.) Members must have studied at either of the named universities in order to belong.

Philosophical Club, the - 1847. (See: Rota Club, below.)

Portland, the - Began as the Stratford Club; changed to the Portland in 1825. Established the rules of the card game Bridge. Was later absorbed into the Naval and Military Club. Originally at 1 Portland Place. At 9 St. James's Square in 1909. Is now co-located with the Savile Club.

Pratt's Club - 14 Park Place. 1841. A basement club; small and exclusive. Is the personal possession of the duke(s) of Devonshire since the 1930s. Unlike most other clubs, only opens in the evening.

Press Club, the - Wine Office Court. 1882. Closed in 1986 (although still exists as a society.)

Public Schools Club, the - 1909. (See: East India and Sports Club, above.)

RAC Club, the - (AKA: Royal Automotive Club.) 89 Pall Mall. 1897.

RAF Club, the - 1917. (Originally was: the Royal Flying Corps Club.)

Rag, the - 1837. (See: Army and Navy Club, above.)

Raneleagh Club - Barn Elms, Richmond. Met here from 1894-1939. Provided sporting facilities.

Reform Club, the - 104-105 Pall Mall. 1836, by Charles Barry. Built of stone in the Italian palazzo style. Named for the Reform Bill of 1832, which sought to limit aristocratic control of the House of Commons, and "to promote the social intercourse of the Reformers of England." Traditionally, the club of wealthy radicals. In a fiction work by author Jules Verne, Phileas Fogg of "Around the World in 80 Days" sets off on his adventure from here.

Roehampton Club, the - 1901-2.

Rota Club, the - (Samuel Pepys referred to it as: Coffee Club.) Founded in 1659. New Palace Yard. Was a debating society, for the discussion of Republican ideas. It took its name from the idea they were attempting to promote: that a determined number of Parliamentary members ought to be ousted from office, replaced by "new blood," in *rotation.* The members were princes, dukes, nobility, and occasionally a "person of distinction", such as a clergyman. Not all members were of the aristocracy, and there were also guests who were engineers, mathematicians, sailors - those who could lend to the intellectual debates. Baron Munchausen (the infamous teller of tall tales/braggart) was a member, as was Benjamin Franklin, Sir Joshua Reynolds, and Boswell, among others. The president of this club is the President of the Royal Society. (See: Royal Society, under R in the Alpha section.)

Since so many wanted to join (vs. the number of openings that became vacant,) in time a new Club was formed in 1847, its constituents being distinguished Fellows of the Society; its name was: the Philosophical Club. (See, above.)

Royal Thames Yacht Club, the - 1775 is the founding date for what became the Royal Thames Yacht Club, the oldest yacht club in England (not Britain; that honor belongs to the Royal Cork Yacht Club, 1720, presumably in Ireland.) In 1775 it was known as the Cumberland Fleet, named for the Duke of Cumberland, their patron. There was no building affiliated with the club, only connecting themselves with the tea gardens opposite Vauxhall. A dinner celebrating George IV's coronation was held at the Ship Tavern in 1823, at which time the club took on the name His Majesty's Coronation Fleet, only to quarrel about the racing rules. Leading members then formed the Thames Yacht Club (seeking to affix uniform rules for the sport.) William IV became the club's patron in 1827, at which time it added the "Royal" to its name. This yacht club was the last resident of 81 Piccadilly (also leasing 80,) until the building was demolished in 1926. Now at 60 Knightsbridge. Women have belonged since 1908, but they have to be sailors themselves. (See: Watier's, below, which had also been at 81 Piccadilly.)

St. James' Club - Mid 19th century club, 1859. Specifically spelled with just one "s." Not to be confused with: St. James's Club, with "s's"; see that listing immediately below. (See: Piccadilly/106 - For the one s St. James' Club.)

St. James's Club, the - (See: Crockford's, above.)

St. Stephen's Club, the - 1870.

Savage Club, the - Started at the Crown Tavern, 1857. Was at Nell Gwynne Tavern; then at Gordon's Hotel in Covent Garden; then 8 Royal Terrace/the Adelphi; then 9 Fitzmaurice Place, Berkeley Square; and from 1936-63 at Carlton House Terrace, St. James's. Currently, as the National Liberal Club, at 1 Whitehall Place. Its purpose: "The pursuit of happiness"; Christian knowledge, fine arts, and literature. One of the founders found all the suggestions for the club's name to be pretentious, and so it was tongue-in-cheek decided to call the place "The Savage."

Savile Club, the - Founded in 1868. At 107 Piccadilly since 1885.

Travellers' Club - Pall Mall. Established in 1819. Moved to 49 Pall Mall in 1822. Moved to 106-107 Pall Mall in 1832, built by Charles Barry, inspired by the Italian mode; stucco.

Born of an idea Lord Castlereagh had in 1814, and founded in 1819 by Lord Wellington, to unite (and reunite) gentlemen who had traveled abroad, and to allow them a club to which they could bring certain distinguished foreign visitors and travelers of distinction. However, to be a member one must have traveled 500 miles (805 km) in a straight line from London, a matter of significant difficulty during the wars of the time and before railroads came along. This 500 mile stipulation caused some scandals whenever it was found a member had misrepresented the distance he had traveled. Membership in the club was much prized, and rather exclusive. Members might well stay on until dawn, hence the rule that "all candles, except those on the card-table, be put out at sunrise." Had a good library, three drawing rooms, and provided for its members a wide selection of newspapers in many languages and political flavors, card-play, meals, and billiards. Diplomats tend to be members of this club.

Turf Club, the - (AKA: Turf and Athenaeum Club, the.) First began as the Arlington Club in 1864, in Piccadilly. Established in 5 Carlton House Terrace in 1965. (Not to be confused with the Athenaeum Club in Pall Mall.)

Turk's Head Literary Club - 9 Gerrard Street, Soho. Founded in 1764 by Samuel Johnson (essayist/lexicographer) and Joshua Reynolds (portrait painter.) Members called it simply "the Club," with outsiders calling it the "Literary Club," (this would have been its more common name, as opposed to its lengthy formal name.) Was held once a week at the Turk's Head Tavern, the latter kept by one Charles Swinden. Moved in 1783 to Prince's, Sackville Street. Membership via unanimous election only, restricted to a total of 12 members, until 1773 when there were 16. In 1775, there were 21. In 1783, there were 35. Lasted until 1969.

Union Club, the - Founded in 1799, St. James's Square. Less a club, more like a respectable gaming-house until 1821; exorbitant gains and losses were had here. In 1806, it was in York House. (See under Y.) Was at one time in Trafalgar Square. Being at 86 St. James's Street, which is now Canada House, it closed in 1949. (See Canada House, under C in the Alpha section.)

United Oxford and Cambridge University Club - (See: United University Club, below.)

United Service Club, the - (AKA: United Club, the.) Later also known as "the Senior," a nickname to distinguish it from "the Junior" (the Junior United Service Club,) which was its junior by just one year.

The United Service Club was founded in 1815 when Lord Lynedoch hosted a meeting of senior army officers at Thatched House Tavern, St. James's Street, and proposed a need for a "General Military Club" in London with a house of its own. Too many officers wanted to join, however, so membership was limited to those of field rank (above the rank of Major or Commander.)

The Royal Navy Club (which had been meeting in a coffee-house) expressed an interest in joining their ranks six months later, and hence the name of the club. Parliament found the idea of such a club unsettling, but their opinion was ignored. It was Wellington's favorite club, most likely in part because its membership was almost entirely composed of distinguished veterans of the Napoleonic wars. They met first at a rented house in Albemarle Street, until in 1819 a house in Charles Street was built for the club by Robert Smirke (himself once an officer.)

The Charles Street address proved uncomfortable and too small, so it was sold to the Junior, and the house at 116 Pall Mall was built by Nash in 1828.

It has remained there in Pall Mall, with a few additions and alterations (Decimus Burton made it look more like the Athenaeum, opposite it, principally by adding a frieze, 1858.) Number 117 was acquired in 1858; numbers 118 and 119 in 1912.

The Senior and the Junior merged in 1953.

Huge rooms, scarcely heated by the fireplaces there. Since 1974, when the Senior closed its doors, it has been the Institute of Directors.

(See: Institute of Directors, under I in the Alpha section.)

United University Club, the - Founded in 1822, for those who had matriculated at Oxford or Cambridge (the first club intended for middle-class respectable professionals.) Opened in 1826. The building was in Suffolk Street, remaining there for decades, and combined the Doric and Ionic styles, giving the building a venerable air. The committee was fond of posting injunctions, restricting noise levels, numbers of newspaper to be removed from the table at once, etc.

A new wing was added in 1936, accommodations for ladies (with wives and daughters being associate members.)

After a successful vote for a merger, in March/1972 the club moved permanently into the Oxford and Cambridge Club, 71-77 Pall Mall.

University Women's Club - 20th century.

Watier's - Some references spell it as "Waiter's," but this was probably a contemporary pun, since the club was supposedly founded by a waiter...well, actually a cook.

At 81 Piccadilly. Gaming club, founded in 1805. In JANE AUSTEN'S TOWN & COUNTRY STYLE it reads: "...it supposedly found existence through a whim of the Prince, who inquired of some members of White's and Brook's who were dining with him, what sort of fare they received at their clubs? Sir Thomas Stepney replied that the food was horribly monotonous, whereupon the Prince rang for a waiter and on his appearance, asked him to take a house and organize a club. 81 Piccadilly was secured, and Waiter's club began."

Very good dinners (and very expensive) were provided here, making it a highly popular club choice. Gambling play ran very high.

Closed in 1819 (in fact, due to most of its chief members being broke.) After ca. 1824, this address was ever after a private home. Demolished in 1926.

(See: Royal Thames Yacht Club, under R in the Alpha section, the note at, which was also once affiliated with the address 81 Piccadilly.)

Wellington Club, the - 1 Grosvenor Place. Opened in 1832. Was at 116a Knightsbridge from 1932-2016 (when it closed.)

White's - 37 (or 38, see "Note," below,) St. James's Street. White's Chocolate House (also sometimes seen as: Mrs. White's Chocolate House) was founded in 1698 by Francis White, (an Italian whose birth name might well have been Francesco Bianco, 'bianco' meaning 'white.') In the 17th C., chocolate (what Americans would call hot cocoa) was an expensive drink, and therefore mostly consumed by those of the upper crust.

The business was first housed in the place where Boodle's now is (28 St. James's Street.) Four years later it moved across the street into a larger house that later became Arthur's Club.

- See: Arthur's Club, above.
- See: Carlton Club, above.

The regular elites who gathered at this coffee- and chocolate-house formed a membership they called the "Old Club," ca. 1743, which had a "Young Club," those waiting for a place in the Old Club.

A ruinous fire in 1733 forced a move to another house in St. James's Street. This place was called Gaunt's Coffee-house, "next the St. James's Coffee-house," still bearing the name of "White's."

The locale became so popular, the customers forced the owner to reorganize as a private club, somewhere around 1736.

The Betting Book (also referred to as bet-book) dates from 1743; there is still one in place, laid on a table. It was for recording private wagers.

The wagering play consisted mostly of faro and hazard, and some (technically illegal) whist. While White's was seen as not being as high-flying (accepting of huge gaming sums) as Brooks's, the play did actually often run deep; there are letters from fathers despairing that their sons may have become entangled by "the spirit of play" here and verged on penury. Fortunes were won and lost here. Professional gamblers (so long as they were free of a reputation for cheating) would seek membership here.

In 1753 the Old Club and the Young Club moved to the top of St. James's (37 St. James's Street,) and in 1781 the two clubs merged, the genesis of White's Club as we better know it today. A house was built in 1788 by James Wyatt.

Note: In 1811 the entrance was moved to a lower position than it had had (this is why some sources say the address is "37" and some say it is "38,") and current sources list the address as: 37. At that time, the old doorway was turned into the famous bow window, the latter being supported by the original entrance stairs. At this time, to afford this renovation, the subscription fee was raised to eleven guineas, and the entrance fee from ten to twenty guineas. Beau Brummell and his compatriots, when in attendance, took up places there in the bow window, other "regular" members not daring to trespass. The subscription cost had been: 11 guineas. After this 1811 renovation, it raised to 20 guineas.

White's was early on non-political, but eventually Pitt gave up Brooks's (not liking the deep play,) and Fox and his company desisted from attending White's, creating the fact that White's was the club for Tories (and Brooks's for Whigs.) Although, White's became non-political again after 1832, when the Tories headquartered out of the new Carlton Club.

Wellington was a member, as was the Prince Regent. From Walpole to Peel, every Prime Minister was a member of White's.

Like Brooks's, White's had its famous betting book, wherein all manner of wagers were recorded.

Smoking was not allowed in most rooms.

In 1814, White's had 500 members (with an even larger waiting list.)

During the Regency, one Mr. Raggert was the proprietor at White's.

Wig and Pen Club, the - 229-230 Strand. Located in two tall, narrow 1625 houses (built over Roman ruins,) the only building on the Strand to survive the Great Fire of 1666. Number 229 was built in 1625; 230 was built in the late 17th century. As the name hints, the club was for journalists and lawyers. Closed in 2003. (See: Strand/229-230, under S in the Alpha section.)

INNS and Pubs (and COACHING INNS):

The 1604 Act of Parliament recognized alehouses, inns, and taverns as places for "the receipt, relief and lodging of wayfaring people travelling from place to place…and not meant for the entertainment and harbouring of lewd and idle people to stand and consume their money in lewd and drunken manner."

Private rooms were rare and expensive, so most travelers drank, ate, and slept communally, often sleeping on the main room's floor (with tables pushed back.) The inns were a place where the post could be delivered, held, or forwarded, and business dealings were often conducted there as well (although less so as first the coffee-houses developed, and then the gentlemen's clubs.) It was only natural that these places should develop also into coach-stops as travel expanded outward from London.

Inns were woman-friendly, pubs were not.

Coaching inns (AKA: posting inns) were often bigger, busier (and sometimes fancier) versions of inns, invariably on important and busy roads. They had horses available to hire, so you might continue your journey by switching out tired horses. They were often noisy, as coaches arrived at all manner of hours. They served food and drink. Many coaching inns (and other public areas, such as markets or churchyards) had alighting stones, which were mounting blocks to aid with getting in and out of carriages.

- See: coaching halt, under C in the Alpha section.
- See: coaching inns, under C in the Alpha section.

All inns sold alcohol. By law they were required to provide food (usually at reasonable rates.)

Most coaching inns had a woman on hand who provided hot drinks for coachmen and travelers, serving from an urn or a trolley with a small heat source beneath.

Since 1393, pubs have been required to hang out a sign. To this day (and because the 14th C. populace largely couldn't read) the signs also have illustrations of their names. (You may care to see: signs, hanging, under S in the Alpha section.)

Note: It can be difficult to tell if a 200-300 year old (or more) establishment was a coaching inn, a simple inn, a pub, a tavern, or otherwise, as their ownership, their importance, and/or their provisions for the public could change. The groupings below are as they appear to have been at the time of the Regency.

- ***Special Note:*** Be sure to read the listing at: water, under W in the Alpha section - As it relates to why alcohol, beer, inns, pubs, etc. were important to every community.
- See: coaching inns, under C in the Alpha section.
- See: free house.
- See: Free Vintner.
- See: inns, under I in the Alpha section - The notes under.
- See: the PUBS section, here, below the *INNS* section.
- See: restaurant, under R in the Alpha section - To understand how inns served the purpose of.
- See: taverns, under T in the Alpha section.

INNS/COACHING INNS:

Albion, the **-** 10 Thornhill Road, Islington. A former coaching inn, Georgian. Now a pub.

Anchor Inn - (See: Anchor, the, in the PUBS section, below.)

Angel, the - 3-5 Islington High Street. Was the first overnight stay for those leaving north out of London. There may have been an inn here as early as the 13th C., with a sign showing "the Angel of the Annunciation with the Virgin Mary." For sure there was a pub called the Sheepcote here in 1614; the name "the Angel" was used in a 1638 rebuild, a coaching inn with a galleried yard. The galleried inn came down in an 1819 rebuild, replaced with a Flemish design. Was (and is) at the heart of a busy traffic junction. Rebuilt again early in the 20th century; in 1922 it became a restaurant. No longer exists. (See: Peacock, below, for another Islington inn.)

Belle Sauvage, the - Ancient coaching inn. (See: Ludgate Street/Belle Sauvage, under L in the Alpha section.)

Black Swan Inn - (See: Holborn/Black Swan Distillery, under H in the Alpha section.)

Bull and Bush - (AKA: Old Bull and Bush.) 17th C. inn, still there. (See: Hampstead/Bull and Bush, under H in the Alpha section.)

Bull and Mouth - St. Martin-le-Grand. Name was probably originally "Boulogne Mouth," purportedly a place where Henry VIII's troops met with war success one time, so this inn was supposedly named for their success there. Very busy inn, the "jumping off" point for many coaches out of London. Now the headquarters of the Post Office. Corner of Angel Street. 1830, rebuilt and renamed as The Queen's Hotel.

Claridge's - A hotel, not an inn. (See: Claridge's, under C in the Alpha section.)

Elephant and Castle - (AKA: just as the Elephant.) 119 Newington Causeway, south end of the causeway. 1765. Coaching inn at the roads coming into the City from the South, Southeast, and Southwest. Rebuilt twice, in 1819 and 1898. This pub was well known enough, that it lent its name to the entire district. Still a big, busy place for traffic. Demolished ca. 1910, and replaced by a newer tavern version, which was demolished by WWII bombs. Closed in 1959. (See: Elephant and Castle, under E in the Alpha section.)

Furnival's Inn - Holborn. Not open to the public; boarding for legal students at the Inns of Court. Stood until 1898. Was an Inn of Chancery attached to Lincoln's Inn. Entirely rebuilt in 1808. (See: Inns of Court/Lincoln's Inn/Furnival's Inn.)

George, the - (AKA: George Inn.) 77 Borough High Street, Southwark. London's only surviving galleried coaching inn (now a pub,) having stood here since medieval times. Yet overlooks a cobbled courtyard. It was destroyed by fire and rebuilt in 1676-7. (See: Southwark/Borough High Street/77, under S in the Alpha section.)

Golden Cross - (AKA: Golden Cross House.) A famous and flourishing coaching inn at Charing Cross. Owned by William Horne and his son, Benjamin Worthy Horne. Open during the Regency. Provided fast day coaches to Brighton (12 miles/19 km per hour, reaching Brighton in 5 hours.)

Half Way House - Knightsbridge inn of poor repute.

- See notes at: Knightsbridge/Rutland Gate, under K in the Alpha section - The notes at.
- See: Knightsbridge/Half Way House, under K in the Alpha section - The notes at.

Inns of Court - Not public inns at all, but rather schooling for legal minds. (See: Inns of Court, under I in the Alpha section.)

Jamaica Inn - (Sometimes called: Old Jamaica Inn.) 12 St. Michael's Alley. London's first coffee-house. Started in 1652 as "The Sign of Pasqua Rosee's Head" in St. Michael's Alley, Cornhill. THE FOOD CHRONOLOGY states (for the year 1652): "One Daniel Edwards has obtained several bags of coffee from Constantinople and set his servant, Pasqua Rosee, up in business." Merchants interested in West Indies trade met here; especially known for its trade in rum. Pulled down in 1843, but in 1869 was resurrected as a wine bar called "Jamaica Wine House," currently still there.

King's Head Inn - Chigwell Road (near Epping Forest.) Ancient hostel. The Verderer's (or Forester's) Courts were held here until 1855. Was mentioned in Charles Dickens' *Barnaby Rudge.*

Mayflower - 117 Rotherhithe Street, Southwark. Established in 1550. Is no longer an inn, but is still a pub. Named for the ship that took the Pilgrims to America, and which was moored nearby in 1620.

Old Bull and Bush - (See: Bull and Bush, above.)

Old Jamaica Inn - (See: Jamaica Inn, above.)

Peacock, the - First northerly stop from London, in Islington, for the coaches that started at the Bull and Mouth. Still there in 1821 at least.

Pear Tree Inn - Cinnamon Street, Wapping. There by at least 1811, when a supposed murderer hid here.

Prince of Orange Inn - Palmer's Village. (See: Palmer's Village/Prince of Orange Inn, under P in the Alpha section.)

Queen's Head Inn - 31 High Street, Pinner. 1705. Still here. Timber-framed building.

Red Cow Tavern - Fulham. Built over 250 years ago. Well-known coaching inn. Rebuilt 1897. Now pulled down. In Fulham, in the area that later became known, in 1834, as Hammersmith. (See: Fulham/Red Cow Tavern, under F in the Alpha section.)

Red Lion Inn - Hillingdon Heath. Charles I stopped here in 1646 while fleeing from besieged Oxford to Nottingham and the Scottish army there. Inn is still there. (See: Hillingdon Heath/Red Lion Inn, under H in the Alpha section.)

Rising Sun, the - Highwood. Turned from a 17th C. cottage to its present use as an inn in 1751.

Saracen's Head Inn - Aldgate. Historic inn, stood until the 1860s, at Snow Hill and Cock Lane. Featured by Charles Dickens in *Nicholas Nickleby.* In the 18th C., ruffians who gathered here occasionally amused themselves by putting women in barrels and rolling them down the hill.

Saracen's Head, the - 6 Friday Street, **Cheapside.** Closed 1844. (See: Friday Street/Saracen's Head Inn, under F in the Alpha section.)

Spaniard's Inn - Spaniards Road, North End, Hampstead Heath. Before becoming an inn, it was for many years supposedly used as the Spanish ambassador's (to the court of James I) residence. Purportedly established in 1585. The 18th C. highwayman Dick Turpin took refreshment here; Turpin was purportedly the inspiration for Alfred Noyes' poem *The Highwayman.* Turpin's ghost supposedly haunts here, along with the hoofbeats of his steed, Black Bess. (See: Hampstead Heath/Spaniard's Inn, under H in the Alpha section.)

Spread Eagle Inn - 84 Gracechurch Street, St. Peter Cornhill. Existed from 1637-1865. Approached through a galleried courtyard, called "quaint."

Swan and Hoop Inn - (See: Cornhill/Swan and Hoop Inn, under C in the Alpha section.)

Swan with Two Necks, the - Lad Lane (which is now part of Gresham Street.) 17th C., and still thriving in the Regency. Its sign is the crest of the Worshipful Company of Vintners and Dyers; "two necks" originally was "two nicks," because two nicks on either side of a swan's beak marked it for the Vintners; one nick marked it for the Dyers. (The swans are co-owned with the Crown.) The Swan with Two Necks was perhaps London's most important coaching inn. Up to fourteen mail coaches left here every night. It thrived until 1837 (when it took on a new business, serving the railway parcel mails.) Pulled down, but a new Swan was built in the 1850s as a railway agency. (You may care to see: swan upping, under S in the Alpha section.)

Tabard Inn - (See: Talbot Inn, below.)

Talbot Inn - Southwark. Dates from Chaucer's time (and is written of in his *Canterbury Tales.)* Renamed from "Tabard Inn" after the Little Fire of 1676. The name change is rumored to be due to a signmaker's misunderstanding, but there is also the crest of the Earls of Shrewsbury (whose family name is Talbot) "and it is often to be found as a sign in places where they have, or have had, possessions." And yet still, according to QUAINT SIGNS OF OLDE INNS: "This name for a sign derived from the old name of a white sporting dog rather like an old-fashioned hound, only with black or blue spots over the whole body and legs, and in patches..." Lasted until it was pulled down in 1875.

Thomas à Becket - 320 Old Kent Road, Camberwell. Long (and now) known as the Thomas-á-Becket, but to medieval travelers it was known as "Thomas-à-Watering." A pub, also known for its boxing (it contains an unofficial museum, and a later gym above the pub.) Its present appearance dates from the very late 19th century.

Trip to Jerusalem, the - Nottingham (in northern England.) Founded in 1189, as a way station for crusaders journeying on to the Holy Land. Remains yet.

Welsh Harp, the - Brent, northwest London. Mid 18th century. Inn, originally called the Harp and Horn (name changed in 1803.) Became known as the Old Welsh Harp when later in the century another inn (the Upper Welsh Harp) glommed onto the name. Very poplar. Rebuilt in 1937. Now pulled down.

White Hart Inn - Piccadilly. (In author/courtesan Harriette Wilson's memoirs, she refers to it as "White Horse Cellar.") Near Hyde Park Corner (later became Albert Gate.) West corner of Old Bond Street, Piccadilly (stood where the Ritz Hotel is now.) Name note: Although a house across the way (Hatchett's, not to be confused with Hatchard's) has now managed to retain the White Horse Cellar name. Coaches to Brighton, Dorking, Tunbridge Wells, and Windsor.

White Hart Inn - Southwark. Existed by at least the time of the revolt of 1450. Retained its galleries (on the north and east sides) until 1889, when it was pulled down. Shakespeare wrote of it, and it was still there in Dickens' time. (Not to be confused with the "White Hart" under PUBS, below.)

White Horse Cellar - (See: White Hart Inn, Piccadilly, above.)

White Horse Inn - Longford, Hillingdon. Important 17th C. coaching inn, on the road to Bath. Still exists.

White Swan Inn - Chelsea. (AKA: Old White Swan Inn.) Site of where the race called Doggett's Coat and Badge Race ends. The inn existed from at least 1716 to 1873. This site now is home to Swan House, Cheyne Walk, Chelsea, built in 1875. (See: Doggett's Coat and Badge Race, under D in the Alpha section.)

Ye Olde Whyte Lyon - Locksbottom, near Orpington. A 1626 coaching inn, still standing. Now a pub.

PUBS (& Taverns):

Open from early hours until after midnight during the Regency. The morning closure on Sundays was not introduced until 1839. Pubs, short for public houses, were private businesses - that is, they were under the control of a specific brewery, and so sold only that brewery's products. A "free house," on the other hand, was not aligned with any particular brewery, and so could carry several varieties of brew. (Nowadays, even most pubs are free to sell more than one brand.)

Public houses were for drinking and socializing, whereas inns were about housing during travels.

Some pubs heated a griddle, for those (bachelors, or anyone who lacked a cooking space) who brought a steak or chop from the butcher's, to cook while they sampled the liquid wares.

SPECIAL NOTE: Into the 20th C., pubs were not for women. Eventually, as late as the 1950s, pubs provided separate entrances for women. Whereas, inns were frequented by women (all genders needed to travel,) albeit women would have a male or servant escort; only the common folk (who was female) might travel alone.

Anchor, the - 34 Park Street, on the Thames, Southwark. (AKA: Anchor Inn.) This pub yet remains. The door is described as being "cut in the angle of the wall, at its east end." Supposedly frequented by Shakespeare (as it was near his theatre, the Globe,) and certainly by the essayist/lexicographer Samuel Johnson. (See: Southwark/Anchor, under S in the Alpha section.)

Angel, the - 101 **Bermondsey** Wall East. Opened by monks in the 15th century. Became a pub in the 17th century. Place for thieves as well as locals (Samuel Pepys frequented here.) Was a seamen's tavern. It has a trap door (for use by smugglers) and a balcony off the back. Above the pub there is now a restaurant.

Angel, the - **Highgate**. Dates from the 15th century. (See: Highgate Hill/High Street/Angel, under H in the Alpha section.)

Archway Tavern - (See: Archway Road/Archway Tavern, under A in the Alpha section.)

Baynard's Castle - Tavern. (See: Baynard's Castle, under B in the Alpha section.)

Bear Inn - (AKA: The Bear.) Noak Hill, Havering. Pub. (See: Noak Hill/Bear Inn, under N in the Alpha section.)

Black Friars, the - (Also seen as: Blackfriars.) Built ca. 1875-97, by Fuller Clark. 174 Queen Victoria Street (not the Regency name for this street,) off Blackfriars Bridge. Has many interior mirrors, giving a bit of a funhouse effect.

Blue Boar - Cornmarket, Oxford. Jane Austen wrote of it in a letter dated April/1811.

Blue Posts, the - Rupert Street. Now a pub (possibly dating back 150 years or so.) Stands on the site of an 18th C. sedan chair pick up point.

Boar's Head - Eastcheap. Demolished in 1831.

Brown Bear - 139 Leman Street, Whitechapel, here by 1793. Featured the game blind-hookey, strong liquor, and flashcoves. Rebuilt in 1830.

Bucket of Blood, the - (See: Lamb and Flag, below.)

Bull, the - Highgate, 18th century. (See: Highgate Hill/Bull, under H in the Alpha section.)

Bull's Head - Strand-on-the-Green (350+ years.)

Camden Head - 2 Camden Walk. Founded in 1749. Described as "beautiful," with cut-glass windows.

Chalk Farm Tavern - Famous as a place where wounded 18-19th C. duelists were brought. Pulled down in 1853. (See: Chalk Farm, under C in the Alpha section.)

Chandos, the - Trafalgar Square. (Was Hog Lane during the Regency.) Licensed in 1647. Still there, still serving food.

Cheshire Cheese - (See: Ye Olde Cheshire Cheese, below.)

Cittie of Yorke Pub - 22-23 High Holborn, very near Gray's Inn. (See: High Holborn/Cittie of Yorke, under H in the Alpha section.) Was once where a medieval inn stood, dating from the 16th century. Then it was a 17-18th C. coffee house. Burned down in the 19th century. Present status dates from 1924. Described as "deceptively narrow," but with a "barn-like interior."

City Barge - Strand-on-the-Green (350+ years.)

Clarence - 18th C. pub, still there in Whitehall.

Coal Hole, the - 14-15 Fountain Court. Established in 1815. Took its name from coal haulers unloading cargo on the nearby Thames. (See under C, in the Alpha section.)

Cock, the - Blind-hookey (a card game,) and strong liquor, and flashcoves.

Colony Room Club, the - 41 Dean Street, the pub being at the top of a narrow set of stairs. Francis Bacon (16th C. statesman) spent much time here. Still exists.

Craven's Head - Blind-hookey, strong liquor, and flashcoves.

Crockers - 24 Aberdeen Place. By Frank Crocker. Opened in 1898 under the name "The Crown."

Crown, the - (See: Crockers, above.)

Crown and Anchor, the - Strand. In Charles Fox (Whig statesman's) day, this was the headquarters of the Westminster Reformists.

Dove, the - 19 Upper Mall, Hammersmith. Three hundred year old pub. Looks upon the Thames. Described as "authentic."

Dover Castle - Georgian. (See: Weymouth Mews/43, under W in the Alpha section.)

Eagle Tavern, the - A pleasure resort that became a pub. Mentioned in the children's rhyme *Pop Goes the Weasel.*

- See: City Road/Shepherd and Shepherdess, under C in the Alpha section.
- See: Finsbury/the Eagle, under F in the Alpha section.

Flask, the - Flask Walk, Highgate, Hampstead. (See: Hampstead/Flask Walk, under H in the Alpha section.)

Fortune of War Tavern - Cock Lane, off Pie Corner, Smithfield.

- See: Cock Lane/Fortune of War, under C in the Alpha section.
- See: Pie Corner/Fortune of War, under P in the Alpha section.

George and Vulture Tavern - 3 Castle Court, Cornhill, (just off Lombard Street.) Pub, dates from 1660. Is mentioned in Charles Dickens' *The Pickwick Papers.* (See: Hell-fire Club, under the CLUBS section.)

George Public House - (AKA: The George.) 213 The Strand. Named for George III (but also the first owner, a George.) The likes of Dr. Samuel Johnson (lexicographer) and Oliver Goldsmith (Irish author) tipped a glass or two here. Existed since 1723. Yet consists of one long-beamed room.

Grapes, the - Narrow Street, Stepney, Limehouse. Dates from no later than 1583. Described by Charles Dickens in *Le Jolly Fellowship Porters.* It served the local bargemen. (See: Limehouse/Narrow Street/Grapes.)

Grenadier, the - 18 Wilton Row, Mayfair. Close to Hyde Park Corner. Small pub, once Wellington's officers' mess, of the Guards' Barrack.

Guinea, the - Dates from the 15th century. (See: Burton Place/30, under B in the Alpha section.)

Hoop & Grapes, the - 47 Aldgate High Street. (See: Aldgate High Street/Hoop & Grapes, under A in the Alpha section.)

Horn Tavern - Knightrider Street. Had become the Horn Coffee House during Charles Dickens' time.

I Am the Only Running Footman - (See: Running Horse, below.)

Jack Straw's Castle - North End Way, Hampstead. Pub. The original building here was built ca. 1381 (the year the first poll tax was imposed.) Jack Straw was a priest who helped lead in the Wat Tyler rebellion. Is now flats. (See: Hampstead Heath/Jack Straw's Castle, under H in the Alpha section.)

Jerusalem, the - Pub. There was a pub of this name in the Clerkenwell area, nearby to where there is a modern pub of the same name, the latter of which has a coffee-house ambience. (See: Britton Street/55, under B in the Alpha section.)

King's Arms, the - 114 **Cheyne Walk**, Chelsea, here since 1856. Their prior address was: Davis Place, Cheyne Walk. Closed in the 1990s.

King's Arms, the - 81 New Gravel Lane, **Shadwell.** Pub, 1789-1841. In 1811 the landlord was murdered here, along with his wife and a maidservant. Is now pulled down.

King's Head and Eight Bells - 50 Cheyne Walk, Chelsea. Pub, dates from ca. 1580. Still has its 18th C. interior decor.

King's Head, the - **Harrow on the Hill**, 88 High Street. 1535, first built as a hunting lodge for Henry VIII. Became a pub. Believed to have been built in the late 18th century. Closed in the 20th century, converted into flats.

King's Head Tavern - In courtyard off Leadenhall Street. Old tavern, replaced in 1859 by the Peninsular and Oriental Steam Navigation Company.

King's Head and Eight Bells - 50 Cheyne Walk, Chelsea. 16th C. pub. Thomas More (martyred statesman) drank here with his noble one-time friend, Henry VIII. Redone in 1960, called "less Victorian, and more Victoriana." (See: Chelsea/Cheyne Walk/50, under C in the Alpha section.)

Lamb, the - 94 Lamb's Conduit Street, Bloomsbury. Built in the 1720s. The pub and the street were named for William Lamb (philanthropist,) who had built a water conduit nearby in 1577. Charles Dickens (author) drank here. Refurbished in the late Victorian era. Has "snob screens," etched glass partitions for skulking behind.

Lamb and Flag - 33 Rose Street, Covent Garden's oldest pub. To get there today you turn down Garrick Street (not a Regency era street,) then on to Rose Street. Cobbled courtyard. At the dead end is the pub, established in 1679. Parts of the pub do date back to 1623-27. John Dryden (poet) survived a mugging in the pub's alley in 1679. In the 19th C. it was better known as the "Bucket of Blood," due to prizefighters having matches here. Charles Dickens (author) frequented this pub.

Load of Hay Tavern - Haverstock Hill. 17th century. (See: Haverstock Hill/Load of Hay Tavern, under H in the Alpha section.)

Lord Raglan, the - (See: Aldersgate/61, under A in the Alpha section.)

Magpie and Stump - 18 Old Bailey. Old tavern, dates from the 15th century. Famous for providing "execution breakfasts" to those waiting to view the condemned, 1753-1868. (See: Old Bailey/18, under B in the Alpha section.)

Mason's Arm, the - Maddox Street, Mayfair. 1720. (See: Maddox Street, under M in the Alpha section.)

Mayflower, the - (See above, under INNS.)

Mermaid Tavern - **Cheapside**, on Bread Street. Shakespeare and Ben Jonson (playwrights) met here. Burned in the Great Fire of 1666, not rebuilt. (See: Cheapside/Mermaid Tavern, under C in the Alpha section.)

Mitre Tavern - Ely Place. (See: Ye Olde Mitre Tavern, below.)

Noah's Ark - Infamous, low pub/gin palace. (See: Holy Land/Noah's Ark, under H in the Alpha section.) Would not have been frequented by fine gentlemen unless they were looking to be robbed or have their throats cut.

Old Bell Tavern - **Fleet Street**. Wren, 1670. (See: Fleet Street/95, under F in the Alpha section.)

Old Bell Tavern - **Kilburn**. (See: Kilburn/Old Bell Tavern, under K in the Alpha section.)

Old Bull and Bush - North End Way, North End, Hampstead (right on the edge of Hampstead Heath.) Since 1721 beer has been sold here. Dickens (author,) Gainsborough (painter,) Hogarth (painter/social critic,) and Reynolds (painter) all drank here in their time.

Old Cock Tavern - Fleet Street. Still there. Dr. Samuel Johnson (lexicographer) used to have a special gout chair there.

Old Queen's Head - 44 Essex Road, Islington. Has 16th C. fireplaces. Was rebuilt in the early 19th century. Still exists.

Olde Wine Shades, the - Martin Lane. 1663. One of the few area pubs to not burn in the Great Fire of 1666. It's no longer useable, but can still see the cellar entrance here to a tunnel that smugglers used to get down to the river.

Palsgrave Head Tavern - The Strand. At least from the 17th century. It is unclear if it existed during the Regency, but possibly until ca. 1880. Now part of a bank.

Pied Bull - (AKA: the Old Pied Bull.) 100 Upper Street, Islington. Pub. Built in 1830. Now called just: the Bull.

Plume of Feathers - 19 Park Vista, Greenwich. Three hundred year old pub. Has a nice view of Greenwich Park.

Princess Louise, the - 208 High Holborn. Built in 1872; redone in 1891.

Prospect of Whitby - 57 Wapping Wall, High Street, Shadwell. Still in use; here since 1520; London's oldest surviving riverside inn. Originally called: the Devil's Tavern. Described as a rambling, helter-skelter building, but also described as being only two windows wide. A place frequented by smugglers and thieves as well as the local gentlemen. Has been "re-antiqued" over time. Yet exists.

Red House Tavern - Battersea. From at least the 18th century. Pulled down in 1848. (See: Battersea Fields/Red House Tavern, under B in the Alpha section.)

Red Lion Tavern - **Chick Lane** (called West Lane during the Regency,) West Smithfield. Frequented by thieves. Now there are dozens of Red Lion pubs in London, since pubs are often named for the brewery's product that they sell, but this one had an unsavory repute. (See: Chick Lane/Red Lion Tavern, under C in the Alpha section.)

Red Lion - **Crown Passage**, off Pall Mall. Dates from the 15th century. Described as small and charming. Possesses London's second oldest beer license. Black timbered frontage.

Red Lion Public House - 48 **Parliament Street**, Whitehall. From the 1480s. Charles Dickens, at the mere age of 11, stopped here once. The pub is known to be used by civil servants, MPs, and journalists.

Rising Sun, the - 38 Cloth Fair. 18th C. pub. Still there.

Roebuck, the - 130 Richmond Hill, Richmond. 1738 pub; still there at the top of Richmond Hill.

Rose and Crown Tavern - Lower Sloane Street, Chelsea. Built ca. mid 1700s. Rebuilt 1933.

Rose Tavern, the - Corner of Russell Street and Catherine Street. The Drury Lane Theatre is at this location, having first opened there in 1662. (See: Drury Lane Theatre, under the THEATRES section.) There was a duel here in 1712 between Lord Mohun (4th Baron Mohun/politician) and the 4th Duke of Hamilton (Scottish nobleman/Keeper of the Palace of Holyrood,) both of whom died as a result, 1712. The tavern was wiped away when Drury Lane was improved in 1766.

Running Horse, the - Charles Street, Mayfair. Name changed to (its present) *I Am the Only Running Footman* in the 1770s, for the 4th Duke of Queenbury's manservant, who could reportedly maintain an 8 miles/13 km per hour speed.

St. Stephen's Tavern - 10 Bridge Street, Westminster. View of the Thames. Built in 1873, refurbished in 2003 after a 15 year hiatus.

Salisbury, the - 90 St. Martin's Lane, Green Lanes. Built ca. 1899.

Seven Stars, the - 53-54 Carey Street, Holborn, London. The frontage has the date 1602, but the building likely dates from the 1680s, being at that time known as The Log and Seven Stars.

Survived the Great Fire of 1666. By the Regency era it was called the Seven Stars. "Seven Stars" could have been any one of several constellations ("The Bear" or "The Plough,") or it may have stood for the seven-starred celestial crown often worn by the Virgin Mary in paintings. Is a very small pub, "charming." Popular with lawyers.

Shakespearean, the - Public house. On the corner of Carnaby Street and Foubert's Place, in Paddington, since 1735; still stands.

Shepherd and Shepherdess - Ale house and tea garden; replaced by the Eagle Tavern in 1745.

- See: City Road/Shepherd and Shepherdess, under C in the Alpha section.
- See: Finsbury/the Eagle, under F in the Alpha section.

Shepherd's Tavern - 50 Hertford Street, Shepherd Market. (See: Mayfair/Shepherd Market/Shepherd's Tavern, under M in the Alpha section.)

Ship and Turtle Tavern - (See: Leadenhall/Ship and Turtle, under L in the Alpha section.)

Shoulder of Mutton, the - London Fields, Hackney. There since at least 1731. Busy; used by 18th through late 19th century architectural workers and drovers heading toward the City. Now the: Cat and Mutton; name change appears to have come along ca. 1849.

Silver Cross - Licensed in 1647 as a brothel and pub in 1647. The building dates all the way back to the 13th C., now possessing a Victorian facade. Wagon-vaulted ceiling, walls sheathed in lead in the ancient style. Served the members of the Old Admiralty (located next door) for the past 250+ years, and for journalists reporting on Whitehall.

Simpson's-in-the-Strand - (AKA: Simpson's. AKA: Simpson's Tavern.) Located at 100 Strand. Is a restaurant, not an inn or a pub. (See: Simpson's-in-the-Strand, under S in the Alpha section.)

Tabard Inn - (See: Talbot Inn, under the INNS section, above.)

Thatched House Tavern - 69 St. James's Street. There at least by 1711 (as a modest hostelry.) Served public dinners in a large room. The clientele would have been rather refined.

In 1774, 29 American colonials were present to sign a petition not to pass an Act closing the American port of Boston in the Crown's retaliation for the Boston Tea Party; the closing of the port went forward, as we well know, leading to American revolution.

Was "kept" (owned/managed) by William Almack (b.1741-d.1781, as in the manager of Almack's Assembly Rooms.)

But by the time of the Regency, this building was an ale-house; in the 18-19th centuries this tavern (so close to St. James's Palace) was the site of debates, speeches, and fencing duels.

The original tavern was demolished in 1814. Rebuilt (where the Conservative Club later was) and was there until 1843 (when it moved a few more doors down the street.) Today the Carlton Club stands here.

Three Pigeons, the - 87 Petersham Street, Richmond. A 1735 pub; still there.

Tiger Tavern - West of the Tower of London, on Tower Hill. Had a sign that read: "1500-1913. This house was honoured by Queen Elizabeth." The tavern closed in 1965 because of area development.

Tiger's Head - Lee Green, Lee. Public house. Built in 1766. Famous for its bowling green. Known haunt of smugglers. Still exists.

Tom Cribb, the - Panton Street (behind Haymarket.) Bought in 1811 by the Regency ex-prize-fighter Tom Cribb. Before then it was known as the Union Arms.

Town of Ramsgate - 62 Wapping High Street, Wapping. Riverside pub. Three hundred+ years old. Known for having kept prisoners in the cellar who were on their way to deportment in the Antipodes (or, less kindly, chained to the bank below the pub's garden, where the Thames' tide drowned them.)

Turf Tavern - 4 Bath Place (off Holywell Street,) Oxford. Its half-timbered facade probably dates from the early 17th C., but the pub may have been here since 1381. Described as small, and having oddly shaped rooms and passages. Still exists.

Two Chairmen, the - Dartmouth Street. It was adjacent to the Royal Cockpit, on Cockpit Steps; near Birdcage Walk. Possibly the oldest pub in Westminster. The sign from 1729 is of: two men carrying a sedan chair. Rebuilt in 1756. It is still there, although no longer a pub.

Union Arms, the - (See: Tom Cribb, above.)

White Hart - 191 Drury Lane, Covent Garden. Licensed in 1201; oldest Covent Garden pub. (Not to be confused with the "White Harts" under the INNS section, above.)

White Lion Pub - Paddington Green. Dates from 1524. (See: Paddington Green/White Lion, under P in the Alpha section.)

Ye Old Ship Tavern - Whitehall. 17th C. pub. Pulled down in 1930 to build the Art Décor style Whitehall Theatre.

Ye Olde Bell - 95 Fleet Street. Established in 1670; has existed for 300+ years. Was first called the Swan. It burned in the Great Fire of 1666. Rebuilt by Wren for the masons who were working at the nearby St. Bride's.

Ye Olde Cheshire Cheese - 145 Fleet Street (Wine Office Court, off of Fleet Street.) A pub and chop-house. Established in 1667. A vault underneath the pub dates from a very old monastery. Its name derived from the fact the pub specialized in serving Cheshire Cheese. Frequented by Dr. Johnson (essayist/lexicographer,) who knew it as "The Cheese." Has not changed its lay-out. Still puts sawdust on the floor; has low rafters and plastered ceilings.

- See: chophouse, under C in the Alpha section.
- See: Fleet Street/145, under F in the Alpha section.
- See: Ye Olde Cheshire Cheese, under Y in the Alpha section.

Ye Olde Cock Tavern - Originally known simply as Cock Tavern (Ale House.) Dates from 1549. Survived the Great Fire of 1666. Moved to 22 Fleet Street in 1883 to make way for a branch of the Bank of England Small. The gilded cock sign was carved by Grinling Gibbons. Alas, many original ornaments burned in a 1990s fire; restored by using photos as references. Long and narrow.

Ye Olde Dick Whittington - Cloth Fair. Probably London's oldest tavern, 15th century. Pulled down in 1916. (See: Highgate Hill/Statue of, under H in the Alpha section - For more on Dick Whittington.)

Ye Olde Leather Bottle - 1634 public house. (See: Picardy/Heron Hill/Ye Olde Leather Bottle, under P in the Alpha section.)

Ye Olde Mitre Tavern - 1 Ely Court, off Ely Place (narrow alley, between Ely Place and Hatton Garden.) Technically, Ely Place is (and always was, since the 14th century) in the residential area of the Bishop(s) of Ely, making it officially part of the bishops' dominion, (although it is in London proper.)

Built in 1546 as lodgings for the Bishop of Ely's servants, but by the 18th C. it was a tavern, from which period its design survives in part; there are Tudor beams, coal fires, and tiny rooms. There is a chunk of cherry tree trunk inside the pub, dating from 1576, and which Queen Elizabeth I is said to have danced the May Day around. Because of the jealously guarded territory (of the Beadles who guarded at Ely Place,) the City Police were not admitted, and they could not serve a writ or arrest a person in this tavern, so it was a refuge for those fleeing arrest.

Ye Olde Watling - Bow Lane. 1668. Huge, blackened ceiling beams, made from a ship's timbers, dismantled from sailing ships. Leaded windows. Used by Wren as an office while building St. Paul's, and reputedly built as a "watering spot" for his workmen. Restored in 1901, and in 1947.

Ye White Hart - The Terrace, Riverside (the latter being a 21st C. development.) The pub dates from 1662. Huge. Rebuilt in the 20th C. with an Edwardian style. Has Thames riverside balconies.

THEATRES:

GENERAL RULES -

There were three seating areas: the pit (was on the ground level close to the orchestra, parallel rows of backless wooden benches which were sometimes padded, were often crowded and invariably noisy.) The second level was rows of boxes, of which there might be several tiers. (In the London playhouses there was a separate box-lobby for upper class patrons.) The third area was the gallery, above the boxes, called "the heavens," this was where the common folk and servants would sit.

Tickets (as we know them) did not exist. Patrons could buy a token (oval or circular discs of bone, ivory, or even silver) for a season or more. On the disc, you might have engraved your name and box number, but the seats were not numbered. Printed cards were used only for actors' benefits or special performances. During the performance there was a second seating, at reduced prices.

The auditorium was lit by chandeliers and hanging candelabra, so "the lights" could not be dimmed. You could see other theatre-goers as well as the actors. The stage was illuminated by oil lamps hanging in the wings and by smaller lamps used as footlights.

Orange sellers sold the playbills as programs.

A double or triple bill was common; serious drama would almost always be followed by a light farce or pantomime. Following an Act of Parliament in 1737, it was reinforced that only theatres designated a Theatre Royal were allowed to do straight serious drama. (See: Haymarket Theatre/1730, below.) All others, if they chose to do drama, were required to insert five or more songs within the performance. The Theatre Act of 1843 broke the monopoly of the Theatres Royal, finally allowing other theatres to perform straight drama.

An opera concluded with a full ballet.

Oratorios had a season during Lent.

Most actors/actresses were responsible for providing their own wardrobe. Many a wardrobe was lost to theatre fires. Leading players were provided with a stipend to help defray the cost of costuming.

It was Charles II (b. 1630-d.1685,) having grown used to seeing females on stage during his exile in France, who insisted (upon granting theatre licenses) that actresses now be used in place of the ancient tradition of men playing women's parts.

The first theatre to have electric lights was: the Savoy Theatre, 1881. (See, below.)

A special note: "The Opera House," "The Royal Opera House," and the "Italian Opera House," etc. while having similar names, are all different buildings/theatres - and there have been more than one set of completely different theatre buildings with these identical names throughout London's history. Therefore, read with care.

Another note: I've used the British spelling theatre (as opposed to America's "theater,") because it is the actual place name.

ADELPHI, the - The Strand, near Bedford Street. (Not to be confused with the Adelphi on the Strand, a residence that became home to the Royal Society of Arts.)

1806: John Scott, who made a fortune from inventing a washing blue, built the "Sans-Pareil" (as this theatre was first called) for his stage-struck daughter. (She was usually in the starring role.) Opened with a Burletta license, which meant it must intersperse music within the drama.

1819: Scott sold the theatre to Jones and Rodwell, who gave it a facelift and renamed it the Adelphi. Lacking the Lord Chamberlain's license for "straight drama" meant they still had to put on Burlettas, which had the effect of meaning each scene must include no less than five musical (vocal) numbers, even works by Shakespeare.

1820s: Very popular.

1821: "Tom and Jerry; Or, Life in London," by William Moncrieff, ran for 100 consecutive performances (a record.)

1825: "The Pilot," adapted from James Fenimore Cooper. (At this time the theatre was being managed by Frederick Yates and Daniel Terry.)

1858: Closed. Reconstructed, and again in 1910, and again in 1930 to its present Art Deco style, in a larger building, on Maiden Lane on the north side of the Strand.

ASTLEY'S AMPHITHEATRE - (See: Astley's Amphitheatre, under A in the Alpha section.)

CITY OF LONDON THEATRE - Built 1837.

COLISEUM - (Full name: London Coliseum.) 1902.

COVENT GARDEN, THEATRE ROYAL - (AKA: Royal Opera House, Covent Garden.) Bow Street. Presently (meaning since 1858) referred to as the Royal Opera House (although it is still popularly referred to simply as "Covent Garden Theatre.")

Season: Mid September to June, and closed (as all theatres did) for a week at Easter. During Lent, Covent Garden presented oratorios.

Open every night. Opera was given every 2-3 nights.

Courtesans were known to pay the costly sum of £200 per season there, in order to display their charms.

1731-32: First built, opening as the "Theatre Royal, Covent Garden," by Edward Shepherd for John Rich, who held the Patent. At first was mainly plays, with a few scattered operas. When his son took over, there were many more operas held here. Referred to then as the "Opera House."

1774 (by): It was back to plays.

1792: Rebuilt by Henry Holland.

1803: Home to the actors John Philip Kemble and his sister Sarah Siddons (hired away from Richard Sheridan's Drury Lane.)

1804: A 13 year old tragedian, with the curious name of Master Betty, known as the young Roscius, caused a brief sensation.

1805 and on: Joe Grimaldi (famous clown) works from here.

Sep/20/1808: The building burned and Handel's organ with it. The company performed (during this time) at the Opera House in the summer, and at the Haymarket in the winter. Only 12 months later...

Sep/18/1809: ...another theatre stands, modeled on the Temple of Minerva/Acropolis (rebuilt to the designs of Sir Robert Smirke; London's first pure Doric style of the Greek Revival manner of architecture.) This theatre was rather larger than the one that stood a year earlier. Seat prices were raised for 61 nights, until actor-manager John Philip Kemble was forced by riotously protesting customers to lower the prices again two months later; (this fracas being known as the O.P. - old price - riots.) His sister, Sarah Siddons, last performed Lady Macbeth in 1812, to bid farewell to the stage.

Kemble retired (replace by younger brother Charles) in 1817. Charles did his best to bring historical accuracy to costumes, beginning in 1823 with *King John.*

The description from A PORTRAIT OF GEORGIAN LONDON reads: "There are three circles of boxes, with a row of side-boxes above them, on a level with the two-shilling gallery. Immediately behind them rise the slips, their fronts forming a perpendicular line with the back of the upper side-boxes. The one-shilling gallery in the center ranges with the fronts of the slips, the whole assuming the circular form, and upholding a range of arches, which support the circular ceiling... The covering of the seats is of a light blue. ...The Theatre is lighted by patent lamps and elegant chandeliers."

After the 1809 rebuild, the new gallery was so steeply pitched that it led to a riot, because theatregoers in this section could only see the feet and legs of the actors.

1812: Sarah Siddons retires.

1813: Redesigned by John Nash and Repton.

1815: Mrs. Jordan retires, and by then the lovely Miss Eliza O'Neill was the rage.

1817: John Kemble retires to Drury Lane, replaced here by brother Charles.

1820's: The German composer Weber is the musical director here at this time.

1847: The lease was bought by Giuseppe Persiani (Italian composer.) Was converted (by Benedict Albano) into the Royal Italian Opera House (when the opera company from the Her Majesty's moved here,) becoming then London's premiere opera house, also in part because the Her Majesty's burns in this year. Opened on April 6th. Its first season was a financial disaster, and Persiani fled England. Frederick Gye became the owner, and was successful.

1856: Burned again. The *Tragedy and Comedy* frieze under the portico survived this fire.

1858: Rebuilt and reopened by J. M. Barrie (of Peter Pan fame) as the "Royal Opera House" on May 16th, with its present design (with some 1950s alterations, and a 1982 West Wing.) Third theatre on the site. The portico frieze of tragedy and comedy survived the 1809 building (which burned in 1858.) Now home to the Royal Opera and the Royal Ballet.

1891: Pulled down, although it still exists on a new site (which was the site of the original 1732 Covent Garden Theatre. As to the old site (the 1891 pull-down site): it was replaced by the (present) Her Majesty's Theatre and the Carlton (hotel.)

1939: The name was amended to "Royal Opera House" (they dropped the "Italian" which had been added.)

1946: The Royal Opera Company makes their home here. (Still there.)

1950s: Alterations made here in the 1950s.

1956: The Royal Ballet Company makes their home here. (Still there.)

1982: A new west wing is added.

DRURY LANE, THEATRE ROYAL - Despite its name and its proximity to Drury Lane, the theatre actually resides in Catherine Street, Westminster. (See note, below, at "1812.") Between Bridges and Russell Streets. (See: Rose Tavern, under the INNS/PUBS section, which used to be at this location.)

Its name is usually shortened to just "Drury Lane," although you will see this particular theatre also referred to simply as "The Theatre Royal," (perhaps more so than you do for Covent Garden.)

The orchestra played under a cage, at least until 1794 (if not longer,) which provided protection for the orchestra from the boisterous crowds.

The supposed phantom of this theatre dates from approximately 1840 (and is supposedly of an unknown man whose remains were found years later behind a wall, with a knife protruding from his ribs.)

1662-63: It was the first purpose-built post-Elizabethan playhouse in Britain; 1 of 2 in Restoration London. Had no roof at this time. Built under the auspices of Charles II, who granted the company its Patent (royal charter.) The players and staff were therefore considered the King's Servants (part of the Royal Household) and were entitled to wear the scarlet and gold of the royal livery, which is still worn by the footmen there today; they are known as the King's Company.

At this time it was just called the Theatre Royal. ("Drury Lane" was added in 1674. See: 1672-74, below.) This was a small theatre.

1665 and 1666: The theatre closed during the Great Plague of 1665, and during the Great Fire of 1666.

1672: Gutted by fire.

1672-74: Rebuilt, designed by Wren. Renamed as: the Theatre Royal, Drury Lane. Three times as large (in capacity) as the former. At about this time it began to have a reputation for crime, disorder, and prostitution; this reputation stuck until the late 19th century.

1747: David Garrick became a part-owner. (He ran the theatre until 1776.)

1775: Redesigned frontage by Robert & James Adam, built on to Wren's design/theatre.

1776: Richard Brinsley Sheridan, the playwright, succeeded Garrick as manager. The theatre had the nickname: "Sheridan's Theatre."

1783: John Kemble (actor) had his debut here in 1783, as Hamlet. (He assumed the management in 1788.)

1791: Demolished after having been declared unsafe.

1794: Rebuilt after fire/demolition, designs by Henry Holland. The third theatre at this site. At this time, it was the first theatre in the world to be fitted with a safety curtain - although it still managed to burn down in 1809. (See, below.)

1800: King George III was shot at here one night, an attempted assassination.

1809: February 24th: Burned to the ground. When a friend met Richard Brinsley Sheridan (playwright/theatre manager) at the Piazza coffee house, surprised to see Sheridan calmly watching as his theatre burned, Sheridan is reported to have said: "A man may surely be allowed to take a glass of wine by his own fireside." Its company used the Haymarket theatre before finding a temporary home at the Lyceum, which they used until Drury Lane reopened in October, 1812. Open every night.

1812: Was completely rebuilt (and opened in October); designed and made larger (1809-1812) by Benjamin Wyatt, still facing on to Catherine Street. Fourth theatre on this site. Modeled after "the great theatre at Bordeaux;" has been called very expensive and too large for intimacy, but also "London's finest theatre" (and its largest.) It's the last standing Georgian theatre design in London. The money was raised by the brewer/reformer Samuel Whitbread. The re-opening address was written by Lord Byron (poet.) Described as having a striking hall and foyer. Lots of melodramas are presented.

1813: Taylor Coleridge (the poet's) play *Remorse* is run here.

1814: Remodeled; Lord Byron (poet) serves on its management committee. Edmund Kean (famous actor) makes his debut here, as "Shylock" in *The Merchant of Venice.* He performed here for five years.

1817: Gas lighting was introduced into the theatre.

1818: John Philip Kemble (actor) moves here (from Covent Garden) as the manager, replacing Sheridan. This year also saw a farewell benefit given for Joe Grimaldi, the clown (although a second source says his last performance here was in 1828.)

1820: The portico is added; designed by Spiller.

1831: The Colonnade, by Charles Beazley, was added. The columns for this colonnade cannot have been taken from the old Regent Street Quadrant (as is said) because the Quadrant's columns were not removed from their original site until 1848. Along Russell Street. Called "vibrant."

1922: The auditorium was remodeled, seating 3,000.

Other curious facts about Drury Lane:

- On one of the sweeping stairways, George III boxed the ears of the Prince Regent, humiliating his son, so that one set of stairs became known as the King's Side, the other as the Prince's Side (which they each used exclusively,) with these names still to be seen on the doors.
- Had an impressive rotunda, "magnificent" grand salon, and sweeping staircases (as noted, above,) all dating from the early 19th century.
- There probably was no center aisle, and the seats were probably not padded.
- Drury Lane is Britain's oldest continuously occupied theatre.
- ROMANTIC LONDON states: "...up to comparatively recent times, enjoyed the especial distinction of having two sentries mounting guard at its..." (Drury Lane's) "...door, while according to tradition 'Her Majesty's Servant,' as its company used to be described, had some curious privileges which they were entitled to claim. Eight of its members were said to have a right to a table at the Royal Palace, a right to wear Windsor uniform, a right of attending His or Her Majesty on State occasions, and a right to shoot on Crown land without a license! It would be curious to know whether such claims could be sustained at the present day, the last time anything of the sort occurred having apparently been at the end of the eighteenth century."

ENGLISH OPERA HOUSE - After 1816. (See: Lyceum, below.)

GREAT QUEEN STREET THEATRE - Great Queen Street, Bloomsbury. 1900. (Later known as the Kingsway Theatre.)

GLOBE THEATRE - Shaftesbury Avenue, South Bank. "Shakespeare's theatre" (not that he owned it, the Brend family did, but many of his plays were performed here.) Burned down completely in the early 17th century. Rebuilt, in charming imitation of the ancient one, in the 20th century; its rebuild is the first and only building in London, by law, since 1666's Great Fire to be allowed a thatched roof, for the sake of authenticity. (See: Globe Theatre, under G in the Alpha section.)

HAYMARKET, THE THEATRE ROYAL - (AKA: "The Little Theatre in the Haymarket," as it was called when it opened in 1720.) In the Haymarket, facing Charles Street. Primarily a summer theatre. Open from May through early autumn. Specialized in farce and lighter pieces.

1720: Built without license or patent, by a carpenter named John Potter, as the "Little Theatre."

1721: Opened just north of the current theatre.

1730: Defying the monopoly of "legitimate drama," Henry Fielding (dramatist) produced his satire on heroic drama in 1730 with his play *Tom Thumb.* These satires of the political parties and the Royal Family resulted in the Licensing Act of 1737 (reinforcing the monopoly of the Patent theatres, now under the control of the Lord Chamberlain.)

1766: The actor Samuel Foote was now managing the theatre, and when he lost half his leg following an accident from the Duke of York's unmanageable horse, the Duke compensated him by obtaining a license for the theatre to perform *drama* in the summer months when the other two theatres (Covent Garden, and Drury Lane) were closed.

1805: Tailors gathered and rioted there, protesting a revival of a satire "The Tailors." The riot was quelled by troops. The Little Theatre was closed for a while, because of the manager's imprisonment for debts. His brother-in-law left the old building and had the present one built a little to the south of it.

1821: John Nash designed the (new location) with graceful Corinthian portico so that it could be seen from St. James's Square. The theatre opened July 4, 1821. Opulent interior.

1867: It was destroyed, in under one hour, by fire. Rebuilt.

1907: Interior utterly rebuilt, but original Corinthian portico remains. Presently seats 906 people.

HER MAJESTY'S - In the Haymarket, St. James's, Westminster.

1705: This first version was designed by John Vanbrugh (playwright/architect.) At this time it was called Queen's Theatre.

1711-1739: Due to not being one of the two patent theatres (those being Covent Garden, and Drury Lane,) between these years more than 25 operas premiered here.

1714: George I ascended to the throne, so the theatre name changed to the King's Theatre.

1789: The 1704-5 theatre was destroyed by fire.

1791: Rebuilt, and then called the Opera House. Designed by M. Novosielski.

1813: Partly reconstructed by John Nash and G. S. Repton.

1820: The Roman Doric colonnade front was completed in 1820 to designs by Nash and Repton.

1837: Name changes to Her Majesty's.

1847: The theatre's opera company moved to the Theatre Royal, Covent Garden. The theatre burns.

1869: The 1813 theatre burned. It was presumably still known as the Opera House from 1791 to until it burned in 1869. A second source says it burned in 1847, (leaving the Covent Garden theatre to then become London's premiere opera house.) It was rebuilt, but never regained its popular standing.

1873: Renamed the "Her Majesty's."

1897: See "1899."

1899: The Carlton Hotel was built on the site of the old Her Majesty's, which was then rebuilt on its present site in 1897 on the corner of Charles Street, by Charles J. Phipps, on the site of what had been the Royal Opera House, and where it stands today and is still known as Her Majesty's.

1901-1952: Known as His Majesty's.

1952-Present: Known as Her Majesty's upon Queen Elizabeth II's ascension to the throne.

ITALIAN OPERA HOUSE - (See: Royal Italian Opera House, below.)

KING'S THEATRE, THE - As it was known in the Regency. (Now: the Italian Opera House, Haymarket.) Built in 1790.

1801: Renovated.

1813: The theatre closes, due to disputes among its proprietors. (One reason: they can no longer afford Madame Catalani, who was asking for too much money.)

1814, March: Opens anew.

1816: Madame Vestris sings. (Unmarried name: Lucia Elizabeth Bartolozzi.) Contralto. She married Armand Vestris in 1813; divorced in 1817.

1818: Renovated again. Five tiers of private boxes, 163 in all, each with 6 seats. Could be hired for the season for 300 guineas. Manager was William Taylor, a notorious debtor, who supervised from his lodgings in King's Bench Prison. Michael Kelly was the musical director. Their most famous (and expensive) prima donna was Madame Catalani (soprano with nearly a three octave range; first name was Angelica.) The ballet company was filled with French and Italian dancers, most notably Armand Vestris (the ballet master here from 1813-16,) and Fortunata Angiolini. Opera season lasted from late December until the first Saturday in August, with regular performances on Tuesdays and Saturdays.

KING'S THEATRE, PANTEHON - (See: Pantheon, under P in the Alpha section.)

LITTLE THEATRE IN THE HAYMARKET - (See: Haymarket, Theatre Royal, above.)

LONDON COLISEUM - (See: Coliseum, above.)

LYCEUM - Located on the Strand.

1794: Built as an opera house.

1809: Opened.

1809-12: Was the temporary home of the Drury Lane company (whose own building had burned.)

1813: Jane Austen went to performances here.

1816: After a refurbishment, S. J. Arnold manages it as the "English Opera House."

1834: Destroyed by fire.

(As late as the 1880s: The Lyceum's management was still resisting electric lighting (presumably preferring gas.)

NATIONAL THEATRE - Foundation stone laid in 1951.

NEW THEATRE, the - (See: Regency Theatre, below.)

OLD VIC - (See: Royal Coburg Theatre, below.)

OLYMPIC - (Also see: Wych Street/Olympic, under W in the Alpha section.)

1805: Built.

1806: Opened on Sept. 18th.

1813: Burletta license obtained.

1849: Destroyed by fire.

"OPERA HOUSE" - This is not the name (but rather a nickname) for several theatres known casually throughout London's history as "the Opera House." Examples: Her Majesty's, the King's Theatre, the Queen's Theatre. A handful of them switched back and forth from straight drama for a few years to operas for a while, not least because of having or not having the proper license and/or being able/unable to persuade an opera company to join their company.

- See: Her Majesty's, above.
- See: Lyceum, above.
- See: Royal Italian Opera House, below.

PALLADIUM, the - (AKA: the London Palladium.) 1910.

REGENCY THEATRE, the - Near Tottenham Court Road, off Charlotte Street. This was a theatre that took on many names over the centuries. Built in 1772, it was called: the New Rooms, for concerts. From 1780-86 it was called: the King's Concert Rooms. Throughout 1786-1802 it was: Rooms for Concerts of Ancient Music, and Hyde's Rooms. It became a private theatre club (1802-08) called: Cognoscenti Theatre. It was: the New Theatre from 1808-15. In 1815-20 it was the (unsuccessful): Regency Theatre. 1820-31: West London Theatre. 1831-65 (on and off): Queen's Theatre. 1833-35, and 1837-39: Fitzroy Theatre...and it has had even more incarnations since.

RICHMOND THEATRE - 1899. (See: Richmond/Richmond Theatre, under R in the Alpha section.)

ROYAL COBURG THEATRE **-** Waterloo Road. The building dates from 1816; Princess Charlotte's husband, Leopold of Saxe-Coburg laid the foundation stone. The Theatre opened on 5/11/1818, its opening melodrama being *Trial by Battle.* The "looking glass curtain" (covered with mirrors, and being 36 feet high and 32 feet wide) was installed in 1820, but proved too heavy and had to be removed in the same year. The mirrors were reused in the saloon and on the ceiling. In 1833 its name changed to the "Royal Victoria Theatre." Subsequently became known as the Old Vic. Purportedly the quality of performances declined after 1834, being dubbed "crude melodramas." It did not become as successful/popular as it is now until the early 20th century. (See: Lambeth/Royal Coburg Theatre.)

ROYAL COURT THEATRE - 1887-8. Sloane Square. (See: Sloane Square/Royal Court Theatre, under S in the Alpha section.)

ROYAL ENGLISH OPERA HOUSE - Shaftesbury Avenue. 1891, closed 1892, dubbed a flop. Is now the Palace Theatre of Varieties.

ROYAL ITALIAN OPERA HOUSE - In the Haymarket. Burned in 1808. Rebuilt. Opened in March, 1814. Did not burn again until 1856. Catalani, Bianchi, and Naldi sang here.

- See: King's Theatre, above.
- See: Opera House, above, (the note at.)

ROYAL NATIONAL THEATRE - 1967-77, by Sir Denys Lasdun, near the Thames, in the South Bank Arts Centre. Has three stages.

ROYAL OLYMPIC THEATRE - (See: Olympic, above.)

ROYAL OPERA HOUSE - (See: Covent Garden, above.)

ROYAL VICTORIA THEATRE - (See: Royal Coburg Theatre, above.)

SADLER'S WELLS - Rosebery Avenue, Finsbury. Built by Thomas Sadler in 1683, on the grounds of his pleasure garden. Because there were medicinal wells and springs there, hence was it called "Sadler's Wells." At the corner of Rosebery Avenue (not a Regency era street, Rosebery Avenue was not built until 1892,) and St. John Street (which did exist.) Thomas Roseman took over the theatre in 1746. Rebuilt by Roseman in 1765; he retired in 1772; Tom King (prior manager at Drury Lane) came in as manager, bringing with him a fashionable audience. Bought in 1802 by C. and T. Didbin, and it became the site of exhibitions and extravagances, as well as rope-walkers, strong men, etc. Joe Grimaldi, the famous clown, appeared here in the early 19th century. During the Regency, presentations tended to be aquatic in nature. In 1844 the theatre's repertoire shifted to dramatic works. Rebuilt 1927 or 1930-1. Now an opera and ballet house.

ST. JAMES'S THEATRE - Opened in December, 1835. King's Street, St. James's.

SAN PAREIL - 1806-1819. In 1819 became The Adelphi. (See: Adelphi, above.)

SAN SOUCI THEATRE - Leicester Place (next to Leicester Square.) Opened in 1796 "with major theatrical productions." In 1804 it changed ownership, being then used primarily by amateurs. Converted to a warehouse in 1830, then became part of a hotel. Demolished in 1898.

SAVOY THEATRE - Strand. 1881. First theatre to have electric lights.

STRAND THEATRE - (Later AKA: Royal Strand Theatre.) In 1832, built on the site of a prior panorama. Rebuilt in 1882, by Charles J. Phipps. Pulled down in 1905.

SURREY THEATRE - 1782, was a circus. By 1806 had a Burletta license. 1809, became the Surrey Theatre, made over by one Mr. Elliston. In 1814, when Elliston left, it again became a circus building, until 1827, when it was again the Surrey Theatre under Elliston. (See: Royal Circus, under R in the Alpha section.)

"THEATRE ROYAL" - That is, a theatre with a royal patent that (in theatre's early days) allowed it to put on serious (straight, non-musical) productions, which was illegal without the patent. (See: the "double or triple bill" note above, in the general notes about theatres.)

- See: Covent Garden, above.
- See: Drury Lane, above.
- See: Haymarket, above.
- See: Richmond/Richmond Theatre, under R in the Alpha section.

THEATRELAND - After-1888 nickname for Shaftesbury Avenue. (See under S in the Alpha section.)

BIBLIOGRAPHY:

These books are mentioned in the body of this work, being especially helpful. (Despite all the English addresses listed below, be assured that each of these titles was obtained in the United States):

AQUARIAN GUIDE TO LEGENDARY LONDON, THE - Eds. John Matthews and Chesca Potter. Thorsons Publishing Group, Wellingborough, Northamptonshire, NN8 2RQ, England. Printed in Great Britain by Mackays of Chatham, Kent. First published in 1990. ISBN: 085030881X.

BOOK OF LONDON, THE: THE EVOLUTION OF A GREAT CITY - Edited by Michael Leapman. New York: Weidenfeld & Nicolson, ca. 1989, 1st edition. ISBN: 1555843700.

BRITAIN DISCOVERED - General Consultant, Arthur Marwick. Artists House; 1982. Edited and designed by Mitchell Beazley International, Ltd., London. ISBN: 0861341228.

BRITISH BUILDING FIRSTS (THE FIRST CASTLE TO THE FIRST AIRPORT) - David Crawford, 1990. David & Charles Publishers plc. Printed in Great Britain by Butler & Tanner, Frome and London, for David & Charles Publishers plc, Brunel House, Newton Abbot, Devon. ISBN: 0715392719.

CASSELL'S COMPANION TO EIGHTEENTH CENTURY BRITAIN - Stephen Brumwell and W. A. Speck. U.K./Cassell & Co., 2001. ISBN: 0304347965.

CHAMBERS LONDON GAZETTEER - Russ Willey. 2006. ISBN: 9780550102591.

CONCISE GUIDE TO THE TOWN AND UNIVERSITY OF CAMBRIDGE, A - Originally written by John Willis Clark; tenth edition, revised; Bowes & Bowes, Cambridge; 1931. No known ISBN.

DISCOVERING AMERICAN HISTORY IN ENGLAND - Catherine Leitch. D. Giles Limited, London. 2007. ISBN No.: 9781904832386.

FACE OF LONDON, THE - Harold P. Clunn. Spring Books, Spring House, Spring Place, London N W 5 Printed in Czechoslovakia. (Estimated publishing date, ca. 1955-57.) No known ISBN.

GENTLEMEN'S CLUBS OF LONDON, THE - Anthony Lejeune. New York: Mayflower Books, 1979. ISBN: 0831738006.

GEORGE IV: PRINCE OF WALES 1762-1811 - by Christopher Hibbert. First U.S. edition; 1972; Harper & Row. ISBN: 0-06-011884-9.

GEORGIAN GRACE, A Social History of Design from 1660 to 1830 - John Gloag; from Adam and Charles Black, London; 1956. No known ISBN.

GEORGIAN LONDON (A New Illustrated and Revised Edition) - John Summerson. Pimlico, 20 Vauxhall Bridge Road, London, SW1V 2SA. This new edition first published by Barrie & Jenkins Ltd 1988; Pimlico edition 1991. ISBN: 0-7126-5036-9.

HIS MAJESTY'S TOWER OF LONDON - by Colonel E. H. Carkeet-James, 1951 reprint. Staples Press Incorporated, 70 East 45th St., New York. No known ISBN.

HISTORIC MAPS AND VIEWS OF LONDON - George Sinclair. Black Dog and Leventhal Publ., 2009. ISBN: 9781579127978.

HISTORY OF BRITISH TRADE UNIONISM, A - Henry Pelling, 1963. MacMillan & Co., Ltd., St. Martin's Street, London. No known ISBN.

HISTORY OF HORSE RACING - Roger Longrigg, 1972. Stein and Dey, New York. ISBN: 0812814886.

HOUSES OF HANOVER AND SAXE-COBURG-GOTHA, THE - Edited by Antonia Fraser, 2000. ISBN: 0520228014.

ILLUSTRATED ENCYCLOPEDIA OF ROYAL BRITAIN, THE - Charles Phillips. 2013. Metro Books, New York. ISBN: 9781435118355.

INTELLIGENT TRAVELER'S GUIDE TO HISTORIC LONDON, THE - Philipa Crowl, 1983. Published by Congdon & Weed, Inc., 298 Fifth Avenue, New York, NY 10001. ISBN: 0312923384.

JANE AUSTEN'S ENGLAND - Roy & Lesley Adkins, 2013. Penguin Group. First published in Great Britain as: "Eavesdropping on Jane Austen's England" by Little Brown. ISBN: 9780670785841.

JANE AUSTEN'S TOWN AND COUNTRY STYLE - Susan Watkins. First published in the USA in 1990 by Rizzoli International Publications, Inc., 300 Park Ave. S., New York, NY 10010; reprinted 1991. Published with corrections in 1996 as "Jane Austen in Style." ISBN: 0847812324.

JANE AUSTEN'S WORLD - Maggie Lane, 1996; Adams Media Corp., Holbrook, MA by arrangement with Carlton Books Limited. ISBN: 1558507485.

LONDON - Knopf Guides. A borzoi Book; published by Alfred A. Knopf, Inc.; 1993; New York. Fourth edition March 1996. ISBN: 0679749179.

LONDON - Martin Hürlimann; 1956; Produced by Thames and Hudson Ltd.; London, and Atlantis Verlag, Zurich; printed in Great Britain by Jarrold and Sons Ltd., Norwich. No known ISBN.

LONDON ACCESS - Richard Saul Wurman. Fourth edition, 1994, by Access Press. ISBN: 0062770519.

LONDON: EYEWITNESS TRAVEL GUIDES - Main contributor: Michael Leapman. Copyright: 1993, Dorling Kindersley Limited, London. First American version, 1993. Published in the USA by Dorling Kindersley, Inc., 232 Madison Avenue, New York, NY 10016. ISBN: 1564581837.

LONDON, FROM THE EARLIEST TIMES TO THE PRESENT DAY - John Hayes. Printed by Morrison and Gibb Ltd., London and Edinburgh. Print date unknown (estimated 1950.) No known ISBN.

LONDON REDISCOVERED - Louise Nicholson. Abbeville Press, New York, NY. 1998. ISBN: 0789204886.

LONDON STEP BY STEP - Christopher Turner; St. Martin's Press Inc., New York. First published by Pan Books Ltd., 1985; Revised version, Thomas Dunne Books, St. Martin's Press, 1995. ISBN: 0312136676.

LONDON THE AUTOBIOGRAPHY - Edited by Jon E. Lewis. 2010 reprint. ISBN: 9781845298753.

LOST TREASURES OF LONDON, THE - William Kent. Phoenix House Limited, 38 William IV Street, London; March 1947. No known ISBN.

NAIRN'S LONDON - Ian Nairn. 2002. (Orig. 1966.) By arrangement with Penguin Books Ltd. ISBN: 1585790443.

OLDE LONDON PUNISHMENTS - Alan Brooke and David Brandon. The History Press. ISBN: 9780752454566.

PARLIAMENT HOUSE - Maurice Hastings; The Architectural Press, London; Willmer Bros. & Co. Ltd., Birkenhead; 1950. No known ISBN.

PENGUIN LONDON MAPGUIDE, THE-The Essential Guide - Michael Middleditch; Penguin Books, 27 Wrights Lane, London, W8 5TZ, England; 375 Hudson Street, NY, NY 10014 USA; first published in 1983; updated edition 1996. No known ISBN.

PILGRIMS' LONDON, A Guide to London's Heritage of Faith - Robert H. Baylis. Lion Publishing plc., Oxford, England; first edition; 1990. ISBN: 0745916457.

PORTRAIT OF GEORGIAN LONDON, A - Fiona St. Aubyn. First published in Great Britain in 1985 by David Leader, Barford Court, Lampard Lane, Churt, Surrey GU1 2HU. ISBN: 095096980X.

REGENCY ENGLAND: THE GREAT AGE OF THE COLOURED PRINT - Reay Tannahill; London, The Folio Soceity; 1964. No known ISBN.

RISE & FALL OF A REGENCY DANDY, THE - The Life and Times of Scrope Berdmore Davies - T. A. J. Burnett; Little, Brown, and Co.; 1981. ISBN: 0316117099.

ROMANTIC LONDON - by Ralph Nevill. Cassell & Co. Ltd., printed in Great Britain; 1928. No known ISBN.

ROUGH GUIDE TO LONDON, THE - Written and researched by Rob Humphreys (with addt'l input) for Rough Guides, Ltd. Printed in the UK by Cox & Wyman Ltd (Reading,) and in the USA by Penguin Books USA Inc., 375 Hudson Street, New York, NY 10014. Published: 1995, first edition. ISBN: 1858281172.

ROYAL SHOPPING GUIDE, THE - Nina Grunfeld, copyright 1984. First US Edition. William Morrow and Company, Inc., 105 Madison Avenue, New York, NY 10016. ISBN: 0688040802.

SEA OF WORDS, A - A Lexicon and Companion for Patrick O'Brian's Seafaring Tales. By Dean King, with John B. Hattendorf and J. Worth Estes. 2nd Edition. 1997. ISBN: 0805051163.

SNUFF AND SNUFF-BOXES - Hugh McCausland; The Batchwork Press; 1951. No known ISBN.

STAPLE INN AND ITS HISTORY - T. Cato Worsfold; London; Samuel Bagster and Sons, Ltd., 15 Paternoster Row; third edition; 1913. No known ISBN.

TIMELINE HISTORY OF LONDON, PEOPLE, PLACES, PAGEANTRY, THE - Gill Davies, 2012, Worth Press, Cambridge, England. ISBN: 9781849310635.

TOWER OF LONDON, THE: PAST & PRESENT -- Geoffrey Parnell, 2009. The History Press, Stroud, Gloucestershire. ISBN: 9780752450360.

WORK OF ROBERT ADAM, THE - Geoffrey Beard. Edinburgh: J. Bartholomew, 1978. ISBN: 0702810878.

Other helpful/contributing works:

24 GREAT WALKS IN LONDON -- Frommer's, 2010. ISBN: 9780470228951.

AMAZING AND EXTRAORDINARY FACTS, GREAT BRITAIN - Stephen Halliday. ISBN: 9780715339077.

ANGEL OF THE PRISONS - by Cecil Northcott; Lutterworth Press, London; 1959. ISBN: 9781332514496.

BAEDEKER'S GREAT BRITAIN II, CENTRAL ENGLAND-WALES - George Allen & Unwin. 10th Edition. 1968. No known ISBN.

BIZARRE LONDON - by David Long, 2013. ISBN: 1628738254.

BLUE GUIDE

ENGLAND. ISBN: 9780713630282.

LONDON. ISBN: 9780393311907.

BOOK OF ROYAL LISTS, THE - Craig Brown & Lesley Cunliffe. No known ISBN.

BOSWELL'S LONDON JOURNAL, 1762-1763 - Edited by Frederick A. Pottle; 1950; Yale University. McGraw-Hill, New York. No known ISBN.

BRITAIN: THE QUEEN, CRICKET, SHERLOCK HOLMES, AND OTHER THINGS INDUBITABLY BRITISH - Norma Kolpas, Consulting Editor. ISBN: 9780894715348.

BRITONS: FORGING THE NATION 1707-1837 - Linda Colley. ISBN: 9780300152807.

CHIVALRY & COMMAND - Brian Harwood, 2006. ISBN: 9781846031090.

COMPLEAT GENTLEMAN, THE - Geoffrey Beard. ISBN: 9780847814688.

COMPLETE IDIOT'S GUIDE TO BRITISH ROYALTY, THE - Richard Buskin; Alpha Books. ISBN: 9780028623467.

COSTUME IN CONTEXT, THE REGENCY - Jennifer Ruby. ISBN: 0713459921.

COUNTRY HOUSE COMPANION, A - Mark Girouard. ISBN: 9780300040838.

COUNTY MAPS OF OLD ENGLAND, THE - Thomas Moule. ISBN: 1851704035.

CUSTOMS AND CEREMONIES OF BRITAIN, THE - Charles Kightly. ISBN: 9780500250969.

CUT OF MEN'S CLOTHES, THE: 1600-1900 - Nora Waugh. ISBN: 9780878300259.

DORE'S LONDON - Edited by Valerie Purton. 2012. ISBN: 9781848587113.

EVERYDAY ENGLAND - Monica Redlich, 1977. ISBN: 0715612328.

EXPERIENCE THE TOWER OF LONDON (Historic Royal Palaces - Tower of London) -- 2007. ISBN: 9781873993019.

FAMILY, SEX AND MARRIAGE, THE (IN ENGLAND, 1500-1800) - Lawrence Stone. ISBN: 0060141425.

FIELDING'S BRITAIN, 1995 - Fielding Travel Guides; Text by Joseph Raff; 1994. No known ISBN.

FODOR'S LONDON - ISBN: 0679013822.

FOOD CHRONOLOGY, THE - James Trager; 1995. ISBN: 0805033890.

FROM THE BALLROOM TO HELL (GRACE AND FOLLY IN NINETEENTH-CENTURY DANCE) - Elizabeth Aldrich. ISBN: 9780810109131.

GREAT BRITAIN SINCE 1688 - K. B. Smellie. No known ISBN.

GREAT CORINTHIAN, THE; A PORTRAIT OF THE PRINCE REGENT - Doris Leslie. ISBN: 9780854565979.

GREAT THEATRES OF LONDON, THE - Ronald Bergen. ISBN: 9780233000664.

HANDCOLOURED FASHION PLATES, 1770-1899 - Vyvyan Holland. ISBN: 0713460180.

HISTORIC HOTELS OF LONDON, THE - Wendy Arnold. ISBN: 9780030073038.

HISTORY OF LONDON IN MAPS, THE - F. Barker and P. Jackson. ISBN: 9780712636506.

HOUSE OF WINDSOR, THE - Andrew Roberts/edited by Antonia Fraser. ISBN: 9780520228030.

HOUSEHOLD CAVALRY, THE-On Ceremonial Occasions - Henry Legge-Bourke; 1952; MacDonald & Co., Great Britain. No known ISBN.

HOUSEKEEPING BOOK OF SUSANNA WHATMAN, THE - Published by Random Century, Inc., England and photos by Malcolm Lewis. ISBN: 071261755.

JANE AUSTEN COMPANION, THE - J. David Grey, et. al. ISBN: 9780025455405.

JANE AUSTEN'S CHRISTMAS: THE FESTIVE SEASON IN GEORGIAN ENGLAND - Maria Hubert. ISBN: 9780750913072.

JANE AUSTEN'S ENGLAND - Maggie Lane. ISBN: 9780670785841.

LANGUAGE OF LONDON, THE - Daniel Smith. ISBN: 9781843175742.

LAURA McKENZIE'S TRAVEL TIPS LONDON - Laura McKenzie. The Donning Company, Norfolk, Virginia; 1988. No known ISBN.

LEISURE & PLEASURE IN THE 19TH CENTURY - Stella Margetson. ISBN: 9781112689147.

LET'S GO-THE BUDGET GUIDE TO LONDON, 1995 - Let's Go, Inc., subsidiary of Harvard Student Agencies. No known ISBN.

LIFE IN GEORGIAN ENGLAND - E. N. Williams. 1962. No known ISBN.

LIFE IN REGENCY ENGLAND - R. J. White. 1964. No known ISBN.

LITERARY LONDON - Andrew Davies. 1944. No known ISBN.

LIVING THE PAST - by Val Horsler. 2003. ISBN: 0297843125.

LONDON & THE FAMOUS - Katy Carter. ISBN: 9780584950052.

LONDON, A LIFE IN MAPS - Peter Whitfield. ISBN: 9780712349192.

LONDON DAWN TO DUSK - Jenny Oulton. 2000. ISBN: 9781847739889.

LONDON FOR DUMMIES - Donald Olson. IDG Books Worldwide, Inc. 2001. No known ISBN.

LONDON QUIZ - Travis Elborough & Nick Rennison. ISBN: 9781892145871.

LONDON THROUGH THE AGES - Harold Bagust. ISBN: 0904110990.

LONDON UNDER - Peter Ackroyd. 2011. ISBN: 9780385531504.

LORD ELGIN AND THE MARBLES - William St. Clair. ISBN: 9780192880536.

MISCELLANY OF BRITAIN, A - Tom O'Mears. ISBN: 9781841936642.

MURDER GUIDE TO LONDON - Martin Fido. ISBN: 978029788065.

MYSTERY READER'S WALKING GUIDE: LONDON - by Alzina Stone Dale and Barbara Sloan Hendershott. ISBN: 97805935315130.

ORNAMENTAL ENGLISH GARDENS - Roddy Llewellyn. ISBN: 0847811581.

OUR TEMPESTUOUS DAY - Carolly Erickson. ISBN: 9780380813346.

OUR VILLAGE - Mary Russell Mitford. ISBN: 9781604507249.

PASSPORT'S ILLUSTRATED TRAVEL GUIDE TO LONDON - From Thomas Cook. No known ISBN.

PORT OF LONDON, THE - John Herbert. Part of the "London in Pictures" series. Jarrold and Sons, Ltd., Norwich. 1947. No known ISBN.

PRINCE OF PLEASURE, THE - J. B. Priestly. ISBN: 9780434603572.

PYNE'S BRITISH COSTUMES - William Pyne. ISBN: 9781853269264.

QUAINT SIGNS OF OLDE INNS - by G. J. Monson; first published in 1926; 1994 reprint by Senate. ISBN: 9781859580288.

REGENCY LONDON - Stella Margetson. 1964. No known ISBN.

REIGN OF BEAU BRUMMELL - Willard Connely. No known ISBN.

REMEMBER, REMEMBER - Judy Parkinson. ISBN: 9780385343640.

ROYAL CAVALCADE - Marylian Watney. ISBN: 0851314406.

ROYAL MEWS, THE - Mary Stewart-Wilson. ISBN: 9780370313450.

SAVILE ROW, AN ILLUSTRATED HISTORY - Richard Walker. ISBN: 9780847810208.

SECRET LONDON - Andrew Duncan. 2009. ISBN: 9781566566360.

SHOPPING IN STYLE - Alison Adburgham. ISBN: 9780500012055.

SHORT HISTORY OF ENGLISH EDUCATION, A: FROM 1760 TO 1944 - H. C. Barnard. 1947. No known ISBN.

SPLENDOUR AT COURT, DRESSING FOR ROYAL OCCASIONS SINCE 1700 - Nigel Arch and Joanna Marschner. ISBN: 9780713526615.

SQUARE MILE, THE - Warren Grynberg. 1995. ISBN: 0900075244.

STYLE CITY LONDON - Text by Phyllis Richardson. Harry N. Abrams, Inc., Publ. 2003. ISBN: 0810991071.

THIEVES' KITCHEN: THE REGENCY UNDERWORLD - Donald A. Low. ISBN: 9780460044387.

TIMETABLES OF HISTORY - Bernard Grun. ISBN: 9780671249885.

TOWER OF LONDON, THE - THE OFFICIAL GUIDE BOOK - Simon Thurley. 1996. ISBN is uncertain, although it does show an 8-digit number: 200003241.)

TOWER OF LONDON, THE - THE OFFICIAL ILLUSTRATED HISTORY - Edward Impey and Geoffrey Parnell. 2000. ISBN: 1858941067.

TRAVELLER'S HISTORY OF LONDON, A - Richard Tames. ISBN: 9781905214549.

VANISHING ENGLAND - P. H. Ditchfield and Fred Roe. ISBN: 9781858910482.

WHAT JANE AUSTEN ATE AND CHARLES DICKENS KNEW - Daniel Pool. ISBN: 9780671793371.

ABOUT THE AUTHOR

Teresa DesJardien lives in the Pacific Northwest with her husband, grown children, and growing grandkids. She's been a financial and a file clerk, a mommy, a page, a bookseller, a very young and hot grandma, and an author.

Website: teresadesjardien.com
Twitter: twitter.com/TDesJardien
Facebook: facebook.com/teresa.

www.ingramcontent.com/pod-product-compliance
Lightning Source LLC
Chambersburg PA
CBHW081142020426
42333CB00021B/2632

* 9 7 8 1 9 4 5 4 5 8 2 1 7 *